VALENCIA AND MURCIA
Pages 242–263

ARAGÓN
Pages 226–241

CATALONIA
Pages 206–225

Donostia (San Sebastián)

Iruña (Pamplona)

0 kilometres 100

0 miles 100

Zaragoza

Lleida

Barcelona

EASTERN SPAIN

BARCELONA
Pages136–195

THE BALEARIC ISLANDS

Cuenca

Palma de Mallorca

Valencia

Albacete

Alacant (Alicante)

Murcia

THE BALEARIC ISLANDS
Pages 506–527

THE CANARY ISLANDS
Pages 528–551

Almería

ANDALUSIA
Pages 458–501

THE CANARY ISLANDAS

Santa Cruz de Tenerife

Las Palmas de Gran Canaria

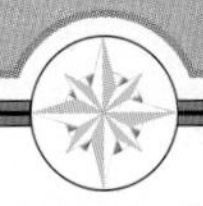

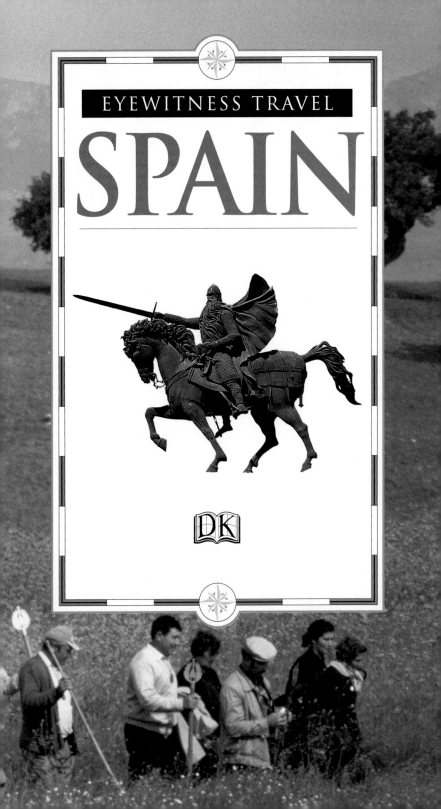

EYEWITNESS TRAVEL

SPAIN

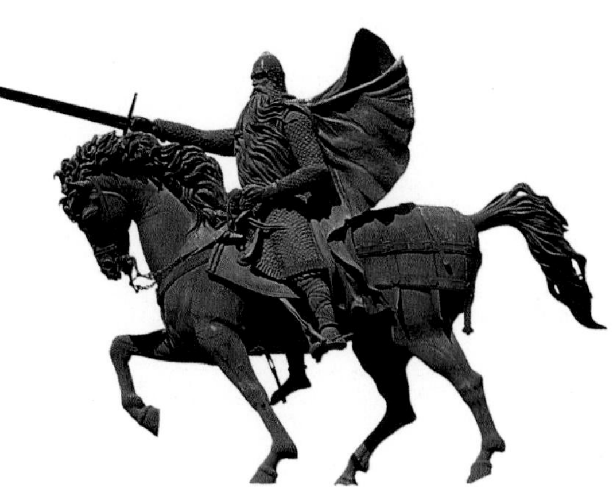

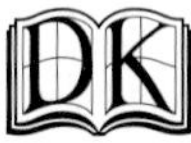

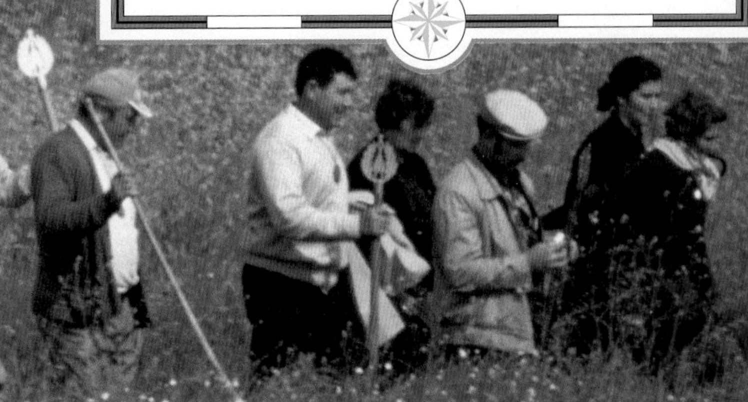

LONDON, NEW YORK,
MELBOURNE, MUNICH AND DELHI
www.dk.com

PROJECT EDITOR Nick Inman
ART EDITORS Jaki Grosvenor, Janis Utton
EDITORS Catherine Day, Lesley McCave, Seán O'Connell
DESIGNERS Susan Blackburn, Dawn Davies-Cook,
Joy Fitzsimmons, Helen Westwood

MAIN CONTRIBUTORS
John Ardagh, David Baird, Mary-Ann Gallagher, Vicky Hayward,
Adam Hopkins, Lindsay Hunt, Nick Inman, Paul Richardson,
Martin Symington, Nigel Tisdall, Roger Williams

PHOTOGRAPHERS
Max Alexander, Joe Cornish, Neil Lukas, Neil Mersh,
John Miller, Kim Sayer, Linda Whitwam, Peter Wilson

ILLUSTRATORS
Stephen Conlin, Gary Cross, Richard Draper, Isidoro González-Adalid
Cabezas (Acanto Arquitectura y Urbanismo S.L.), Claire Littlejohn,
Maltings Partnership, Chris Orr & Assocs, John Woodcock

Printed and bound by South China Printing Co. Ltd, China

First American Edition, 1996
Published in the United States by DK Publishing,
375 Hudson Street New York, New York 10014

13 14 15 16 10 9 8 7 6 5 4 3 2 1

Reprinted with revisions 1997, 1999, 2000, 2001, 2002, 2003, 2004, 2005, 2006, 2007, 2008, 2009, 2010, 2011, 2013

PUBLISHED IN GREAT BRITAIN BY DORLING KINDERSLEY LIMITED.

A CATALOG RECORD FOR THIS BOOK IS AVAILABLE FROM THE LIBRARY OF CONGRESS.

ISSN 1542-1554
ISBN 978-0-75669-493-7

FLOORS ARE REFERRED TO THROUGHOUT IN ACCORDANCE WITH EUROPEAN USAGE; IE THE "FIRST FLOOR" IS ONE FLOOR UP.

Front cover main image: Castle, Velez Blanco village, Almería, Southern Spain

The information in this DK Eyewitness Travel Guide is checked regularly.
Every effort has been made to ensure that this book is as up-to-date as possible at the time of going to press. Some details, however, such as telephone numbers, prices, opening hours, gallery hanging arrangements and travel information, are liable to change. The publishers cannot accept responsibility for any consequences arising from the use of this book, nor for any material on third-party websites, and cannot guarantee that any website address in this book will be a suitable source of travel information. We value the views and suggestions of our readers very highly. Please write to: Publisher, DK Eyewitness Travel Guides, 80 Strand, London WC2R 0RL, UK, or email: travelguides@dk.com.

CONTENTS

King Alfonso X the Learned

◁ **Previous pages: Pilgrimage of the Virgin of the Bridges, Belalcázar, near Córdoba in Andalusia**

Statue of Alfonso XII, Madrid

Wine grapes growing in La Mancha

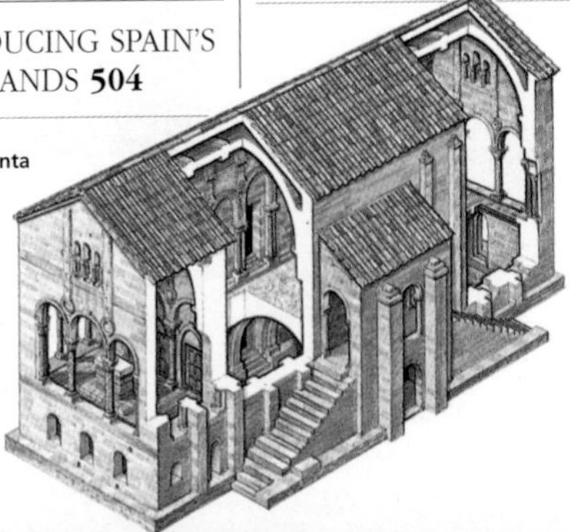

Iglesia de Santa María del Naranco in Asturias

HOW TO USE THIS GUIDE

This guide helps you to get the most from your visit to Spain. It provides detailed practical information and expert recommendations. Introducing Spain maps the country and sets it in its historical and cultural context. The five regional sections, plus Barcelona and Madrid, describe important sights, using maps, photographs and illustrations. Features cover topics from food and wine to fiestas and beaches. Restaurant and hotel recommendations can be found in Travellers' Needs. The Survival Guide has tips on everything from transport to using the telephone system.

BARCELONA, MADRID AND SEVILLE

These cities are divided into areas, each with its own chapter. A last chapter, *Further Afield*, covers peripheral sights. Madrid Province, surrounding the capital, has its own chapter. All sights are numbered and plotted on the chapter's area map. Information on each sight is easy to locate as it follows the numerical order on the map.

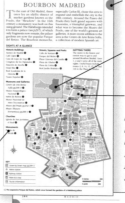

All pages relating to Madrid have green thumb tabs. Barcelona's are pink and Seville's are red.

A locator map shows where you are in relation to other areas of the city centre.

1 Area Map
For easy reference, sights are numbered and located on a map. City centre sights are also marked on Street Finders: Barcelona (pages 179–85); Madrid (pages 307–315); Seville (pages 447–53).

Sights at a Glance lists the chapter's sights by category: Churches and Cathedrals, Museums and Galleries, Streets and Squares, Historic Buildings, Parks and Gardens.

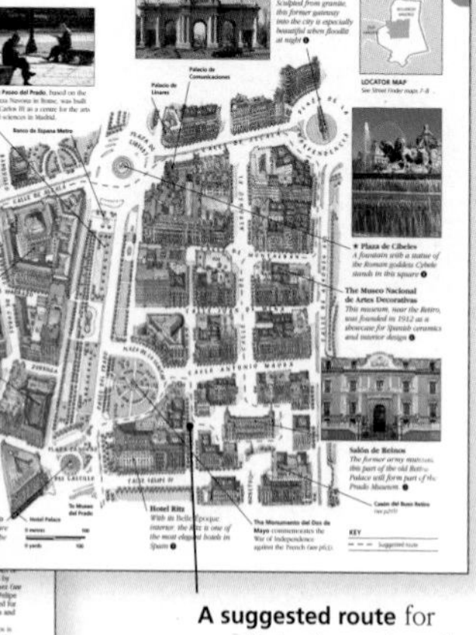

2 Street-by-Street Map
This gives a bird's-eye view of the key areas in each chapter.

Stars indicate the sights that no visitor should miss.

A suggested route for a walk is shown in red.

3 Detailed information
The sights in the three main cities are described individually. Addresses, telephone numbers, opening hours, admission charges, tours, photography and wheelchair access are also provided, as well as public transport links.

SPAIN AREA BY AREA

Apart from Barcelona, Madrid and Seville, the country has been divided into 12 regions, each of which has a separate chapter. The most interesting cities, towns and villages, and other places to visit are numbered on a *Regional Map.*

1 Introduction
The landscape, history and character of each region is outlined here, showing how the area has developed over the centuries and what it has to offer to the visitor today.

2 Regional Map
This shows the road network and gives an illustrated overview of the whole region. All interesting places to visit are numbered and there are also useful tips on getting to, and around, the region by car and public transport.

Fiesta boxes highlight the best traditional fiestas in the region.

Each area of Spain can be quickly identified by its colour coding, shown on the inside front cover.

3 Detailed information
All the important towns and other places to visit are described individually. They are listed in order, following the numbering on the Regional Map. *Within each town or city, there is detailed information on important buildings and other sights.*

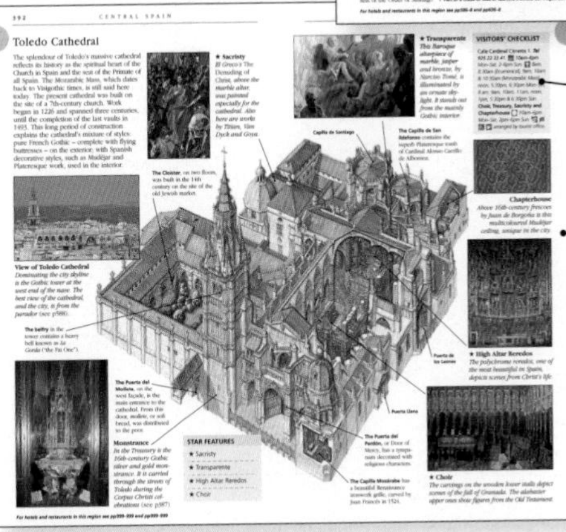

For all top sights, a Visitors' Checklist provides the practical information you will need to plan your visit.

4 Spain's top sights
These are given two or more full pages. Historic buildings are dissected to reveal their interiors. The most interesting towns or city centres are shown in a bird's-eye view, with sights picked out and described.

INTRODUCING SPAIN

DISCOVERING SPAIN

Few countries offer more choice to the visitor than Spain, with its lush forests and wild mountain peaks, its busy cities crammed with great art and architecture and the endless stretch of laid-back beach resorts. To find out what you want from a trip to Spain amid all this variety, you need to know where to look. These pages offer an at-a-glance guide on where to go, with the different characteristics of each region, city or island group explained and the main sights highlighted.

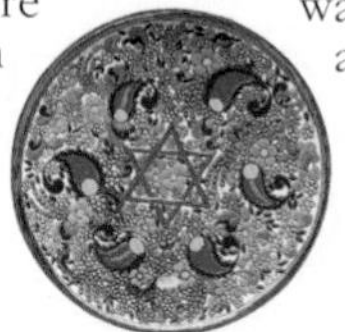
A decorative ceramic plate

Finisterre beach, Galicia

GALICIA

- **Verdant landscapes**
- **Santiago de Compostela**
- **Dramatic coastlines**
- **Rural idylls**

The northwest corner of Spain is the wettest and, because of this, also the greenest region of the country. The medieval city of **Santiago de Compostela** *(see pp90–93)* draws large numbers of visitors as it stands at the end of a legendary pilgrimage route and centres on an awe-inspiring cathedral. The other great attraction is the long, heavily indented coastline. One stretch of this, the **Rías Baixas** *(see p95)*, has just the right blend of beaches, low-key holiday resorts and scenery. Inland, Galicia has hills, meadows, forests, monasteries and handsome old towns where time seems slowed down and you can be sure to get away from the crowds.

CANTABRIA AND ASTURIAS

- **Picos de Europa mountains**
- **Enigmatic cave art**
- **Ancient churches of Oviedo**
- **Medieval towns**

These two regions form the central part of the green north coast. Both are composed of inland uplands descending to a gentle coastline punctuated by pretty bays and good beaches. The two regions share Spain's most approachable mountain range, the **Picos de Europa** *(see pp108–109)*, whose canyons and summits are a draw for hikers. Prehistory and history are other regional fortes. The most famous of many caves painted by early humans are those of **Altamira** *(see p112)*. The exquisite, pre-Romanesque churches of **Oviedo** *(see pp106–7)* and the town of **Santillana del Mar** *(see p112)*, seemingly frozen in the Middle Ages, are also worth a visit.

Parque Nacional de los Picos de Europa, Cantabria

The stunning titanium façade of Museo Guggenheim, Bilbao

THE BASQUE COUNTRY, NAVARRA AND LA RIOJA

- **Museo Guggenheim**
- **San Sebastián beaches**
- **Pamplona bullrunning**
- **Superb Riojan wines**

The futuristic **Museo Guggenheim** *(see pp120–21)* has put the city of Bilbao on the map and introduced the Basque Country to a wealth of new visitors, and its two neighbouring regions attract tourists in search of rural Spain. The pride of the Basque's short coast is **San Sebastián** *(see p122)*, a well-established resort on an

◁ *Rooftops, Fortna Lux, Mallorca* (1969) by Frederick Gore

almost perfectly rounded bay. Navarra is made up of picturesque green Pyrenean foothills and valleys in the north and charming little towns, castles and Romanesque churches in the south. Its capital, **Pamplona** *(see pp132–3)* – scene of the famous bullrunning festival in July – stands in the middle. For wine-lovers, La Rioja, the smallest region of Spain, is the place to visit.

BARCELONA

- **Gaudí and Modernisme**
- **Contemporary art**
- **Medieval streets**
- **Exhilarating nightlife**

For most people, Barcelona is synonymous with Modernisme, and in particular the enchanting buildings of Antoni Gaudí. It is also famed for its innovation and design, and leads Spain in contemporary art and architecture. At the heart of this city of cutting-edge creativity is the Gothic Quarter, with its well preserved medieval architecture. Barcelona's draw is also in its shops, bars, clubs and street life – any visit has to include a stroll down **Las Ramblas** *(see pp150–51)*.

Barcelona can easily be combined with a beach holiday in one of the resorts a short way north or south of the city.

CATALONIA

- **Cava wine region**
- **Beautiful beaches**
- **Poblet and Montserrat**
- **Dalí masterpieces**

This self-assured region with its own language stretches from the Pyrenees in the north to the rice fields of the Ebro delta in the south, taking in vineyards which produce the famous *cava* sparkling wine. The **Costa Brava** *(see p217)*, a rugged mix of cliffs and bays, is its most attractive strip of coast but the Costa Daurada,

The sculptured rooftop chimneys of Casa Milà ("La Pedrera"), Barcelona

around the Roman city of **Tarragona** *(see pp224–5)*, also has popular resorts. Catalonia also has two of Spain's greatest monasteries: **Poblet** *(see pp222–3)* and **Montserrat** *(see pp218–9)*.

The city of **Figueres** *(see p215)* is the birthplace of Surrealist artist Salvador Dalí, and many of his works can be viewed here.

ARAGÓN

- **Pyrenean grandeur**
- **Ordesa National Park**
- **San Juan de la Peña**
- **Mudéjar architecture**

Sculpture in Jaca cathedral, Aragón

Aragón is one of the least known regions of Spain, but rewarding to explore. Its sights are grouped to the north and south, with **Zaragoza** *(see pp236–7)*, the country's fifth largest city, in the centre. The Pyrenees and their foothills hold most appeal, particularly the awesome canyons and cliffs of the **Ordesa National Park** *(see pp232–3)*. Also worth seeking out is the secluded monastery of **San Juan de la Peña** *(see p234)*. The mountains are popular for walking, skiing and a range of other sports.

Teruel province in the south is known for its Mudéjar architecture, along with several historic towns, most notably **Albarracín** *(see p241)* and **Teruel** *(see pp240–41)*.

VALENCIA AND MURCIA

- **City of Arts and Sciences**
- **Costa Blanca beaches**
- **Baroque architecture**
- **Spectacular fiestas**

These two regions take up the middle of Spain's Mediterranean coast and enjoy a pleasant climate. Valencia city is drawing increasing numbers of visitors to its gleaming white **City of Arts and Sciences** *(see p253)*. The Costa Blanca, a popular coastline, has a range of resorts, from the brash **Benidorm** *(see p260)* to quieter places like **Xàbia** *(see p255)*. The region of Murcia is distinguished by its Baroque architecture and the coastal lagoon of **Mar Menor** *(see p262)*. Both regions have spectacular fiestas, such as the lively Fallas festival in **Valencia** *(see p255)*.

A stretch of golden beach in Calp, Costa Blanca

The imposing San Lorenzo de El Escorial palace, Madrid province

MADRID

- **World famous art museums**
- **Royal residences**
- **Historic squares and streets**
- **Vibrant nightlife**

Spain's capital has three of the world's greatest art museums within an easy stroll of each other: the **Museo del Prado** *(see pp292–5)*, the **Thyssen-Bornemisza** *(see pp288–9)* and the **Centro Reina Sofia** *(see pp298–9)*. Art can also be seen in Madrid's three magnificent royal palaces, two of them – the **Escorial** *(see pp330–31)* and **Aranjuez** *(see p333)* – involving pleasurable day trips into nearby countryside.

The medieval part of the city, meanwhile, is a dense tangle of streets around two squares dotted with many attractive bars and cafés. Madrid is known for its buzzing nightlife, and is also a great place to come for the finest in Spanish cuisine.

CASTILLA Y LEÓN

- **Historic cities**
- **Gothic cathedral of Burgos**
- **Defiant castles**

Distances between sights can be daunting in the country's largest region, but five historic cities reward the intrepid visitor: the harmonious Renaissance university city of **Salamanca** *(see pp358–61)*; **Segovia** *(see pp364–5)* with its towering Roman aqueduct and exquisite royal castle; **Burgos** *(see pp370–73)* built around a Gothic cathedral; **León** *(see pp353–5)*, its cathedral famous for its stained-glass windows; and **Ávila** *(see pp362–3)*, ringed by medieval walls. En route between these cities there are vast empty tracts of land but you are rarely out of sight of a castle, a distinguishing feature of this part of Spain.

Detail, Salamanca University

CASTILLA-LA MANCHA

- **Historic architecture**
- **Dramatically sited towns**
- **Don Quixote's windmills**

This region is not an obvious choice for many tourists but it does have one of Spain's most attractive cities – **Toledo** *(see pp388–91)*, crammed with interesting architecture from the Middle Ages. Two unusually sited towns also worth a visit are **Cuenca** *(see pp384–5)* perched on a ravine and **Alcalá del Júcar** *(see p395)*, where some of the houses have been extended into the soft rock of the chalky hills into which they are built.

Although daunting at first, the plains of **La Mancha** *(see pp379–99)*, well known for Spain's most famous fictional character, Don Quixote, has a certain charm in its quirky landscape of windmills and castles.

EXTREMADURA

- **Birds and wildflowers**
- **Roman theatre at Mérida**
- **Mansions of Cáceres**
- **Monastery of Guadalupe**

Although not a huge tourist destination, Extremadura has a lot to offer any visitor. With the lowest population density of any region, it has a corresponding richness in wildlife – in spring and summer the countryside is full of wildflowers and storks can be seen nesting on rooftops and church spires.

Extremadura also has a formidable collection of historic monuments, such as the Roman theatre at **Mérida** *(see pp410–11)*, which still hosts performances today, and the cluster of Renaissance mansions at **Cáceres** *(see pp408–9)*. The other place to see is **Guadalupe monastery** *(see pp406–7)*, though a long trek up winding mountain roads is required to get to it.

SEVILLE

- **Cathedral and La Giralda**
- **Moorish Real Alcázar**
- **Bars and bullfighting**
- **Semana Santa (Easter Week)**

This lively southern city on the Guadalquivir River combines the glories of Moorish and Christian Spain in its great cathedral and

The parade of the Virgin during Semana Santa, Seville

La Giralda, its bell tower *(see pp436–7)*, and in the lavishly decorated royal palace of the **Real Alcázar** *(see pp440–41)*.

Visitors also flock to Seville to relish the exciting atmosphere, particularly in the whitewashed streets of the Santa Cruz quarter and, when there's a fight on, in the **Plaza de Toros de la Maestranza** *(see p430)*, Spain's most famous bullring.

Seville is even more animated during the intense celebrations of *Semana Santa* (Holy Week) *(see p431)* and the passionate April Fair that follows, when the city hums to the sound of *Sevillanas*, its own brand of flamenco.

The Alhambra Palace, Granada

ANDALUSIA

- **Flamenco rhythms**
- **Sun and sea**
- **The Alhambra in Granada**
- **Doñana national park**

Stretching from the Atlantic to the Mediterranean across the south of the Iberian peninsula, this is Spain's second largest region and easily the most varied. It is the home to all things "typically Spanish": sherry *(see pp420–21)*, flamenco *(see pp424–5)*, guitars, tapas, gypsies, bullfighting, white towns and the Costa del Sol *(see pp472–3)*. Blazing Mediterranean sunshine makes it a good place for beach holidays, but it is not short of countryside or grandiose monuments either.

Coves d'Arta, Mallorca

The superb Moorish architecture of Granada's **Alhambra Palace** *(see pp490–91)* and the **Mezquita** in Cordoba *(see pp480–81)* continue to dazzle visitors. The region's landscapes vary enormously from the wildlife refuge of **Doñana** *(see pp464–5)* to Europe's only desert in **Almería** *(see p501)*.

THE BALEARIC ISLANDS

- **Beaches, cliffs and coves**
- **Pretty Ibizan villages**
- **Minorcan monuments**

This archipelago off Spain's eastern Mediterranean coast has long been regarded as a holiday playground for Europe. However, as well as beaches, there is plenty of interest to discover. **Mallorca** *(see pp514–21)*, the largest island, has impressive mountains and caves as well as a splendid Gothic cathedral in the capital, **Palma** *(see pp520–21)*.

Despite its reputation for a busy nightlife, **Ibiza** *(see pp510–12)* also has secluded coves, and quiet countryside dotted with pretty villlages. **Menorca** *(see pp522–3)* boasts prehistoric monuments, handsome small towns and a spectacular horse-riding fiesta *(see p523)*.

THE CANARY ISLANDS

- **Subtropical vegetation**
- **Volcanic landscapes**
- **Beaches and watersports**

Most visitors are drawn to the Canaries by their reliable subtropical warmth – despite many of the beaches being composed of black sand. The islands have a great contrast of scenery from luxuriant vegetation to spectacular volcanic formations.

La Gomera, **La Palma** and **El Hierro** *(see pp532–3)* are small but with wonderful scenery making for good hiking. **Lanzarote** *(see pp548–51)*, a choice place for beach holidays, is dry and still volcanically active. **Fuerteventura** *(see pp546–7)* also has beautiful beaches but with a windy climate. **Tenerife** *(see pp534–6)* and **Gran Canaria** *(see pp542–5)* offer the most variety, with northern coasts swathed in banana plantations and lively tourist spots in the hot and sunny south.

A cactus park in San Nicolás de Tolentino, Gran Canaria

Putting Spain on the Map

Spain, in southwestern Europe, covers the greater part of the Iberian Peninsula. The third largest country in Europe, it includes two island groups: the Canaries in the Atlantic and the Balearics in the Mediterranean, and two small territories in North Africa. Its southernmost point faces Morocco across a strait, making Spain a bridge between continents.

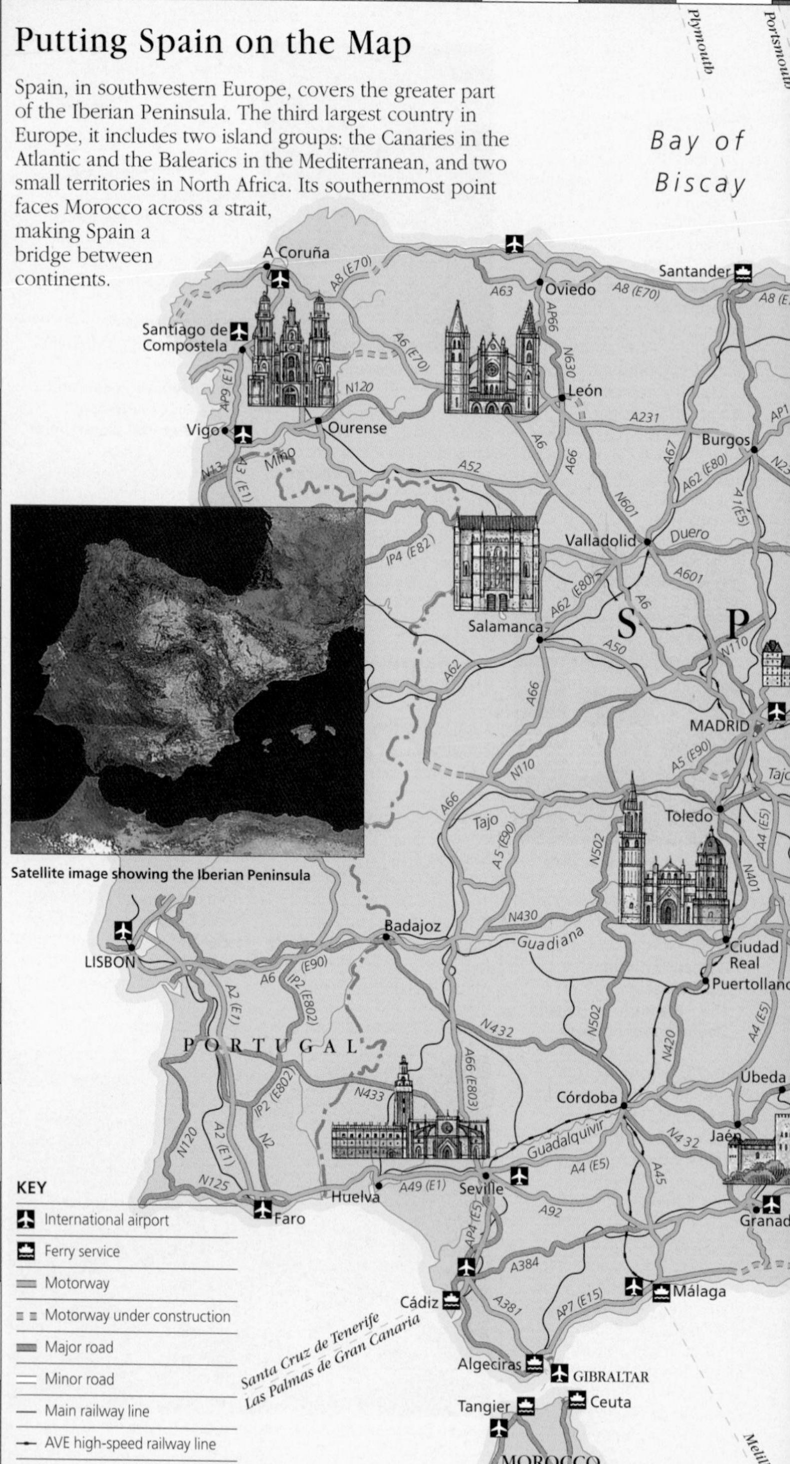

Satellite image showing the Iberian Peninsula

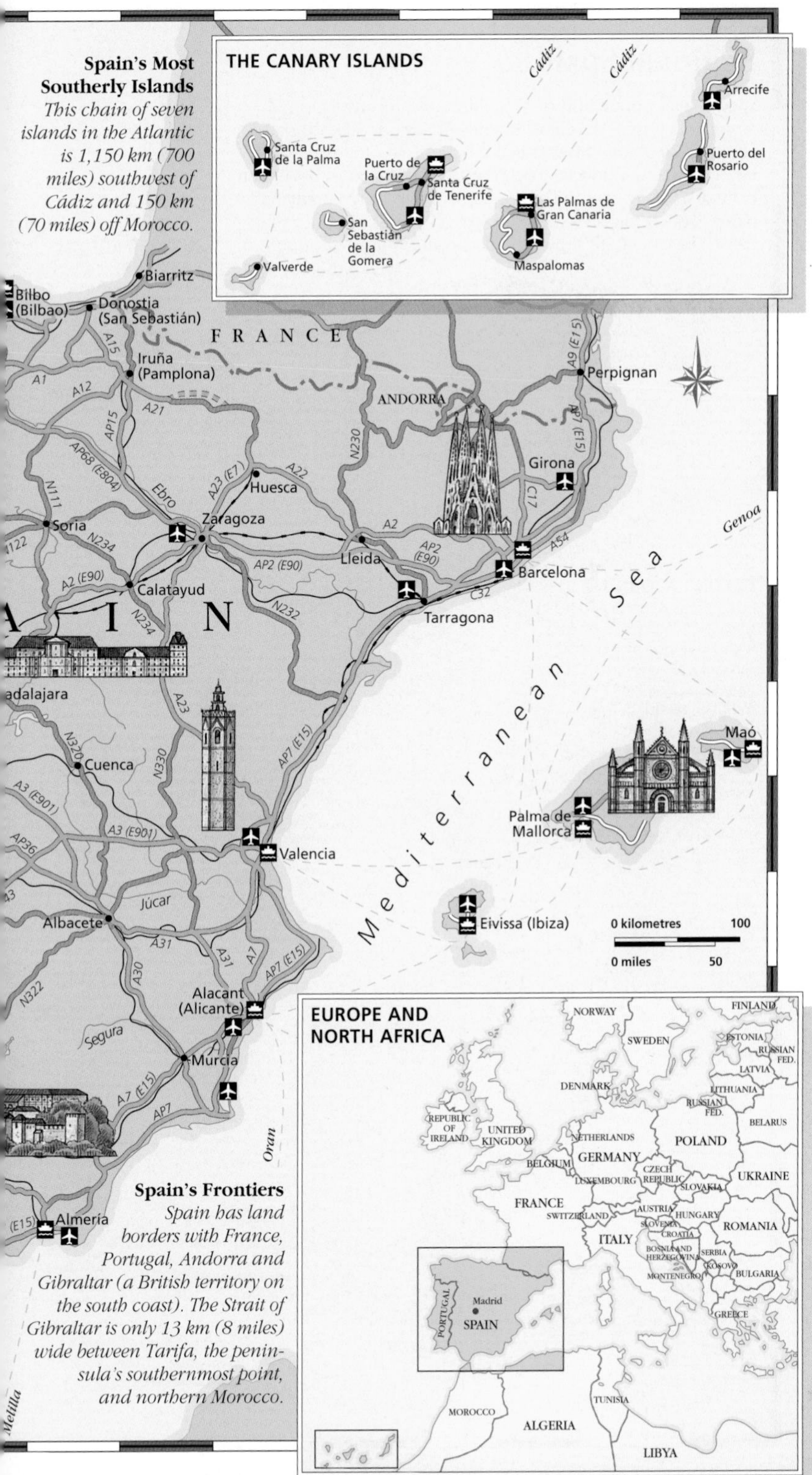

Spain's Most Southerly Islands
This chain of seven islands in the Atlantic is 1,150 km (700 miles) southwest of Cádiz and 150 km (70 miles) off Morocco.

Spain's Frontiers
Spain has land borders with France, Portugal, Andorra and Gibraltar (a British territory on the south coast). The Strait of Gibraltar is only 13 km (8 miles) wide between Tarifa, the peninsula's southernmost point, and northern Morocco.

Regional Spain

Spain has a population of 47 million and receives more than 40 million visitors a year. It covers an area of 504,780 sq km (194,900 sq miles). Madrid is the largest city, followed by Barcelona and Valencia. The country is dominated by a central plateau drained by the Duero, Tagus (Tajo) and Guadiana rivers. This book divides Spain into 15 areas, but officially it has 17 independent regions called *comunidades autónomas.*

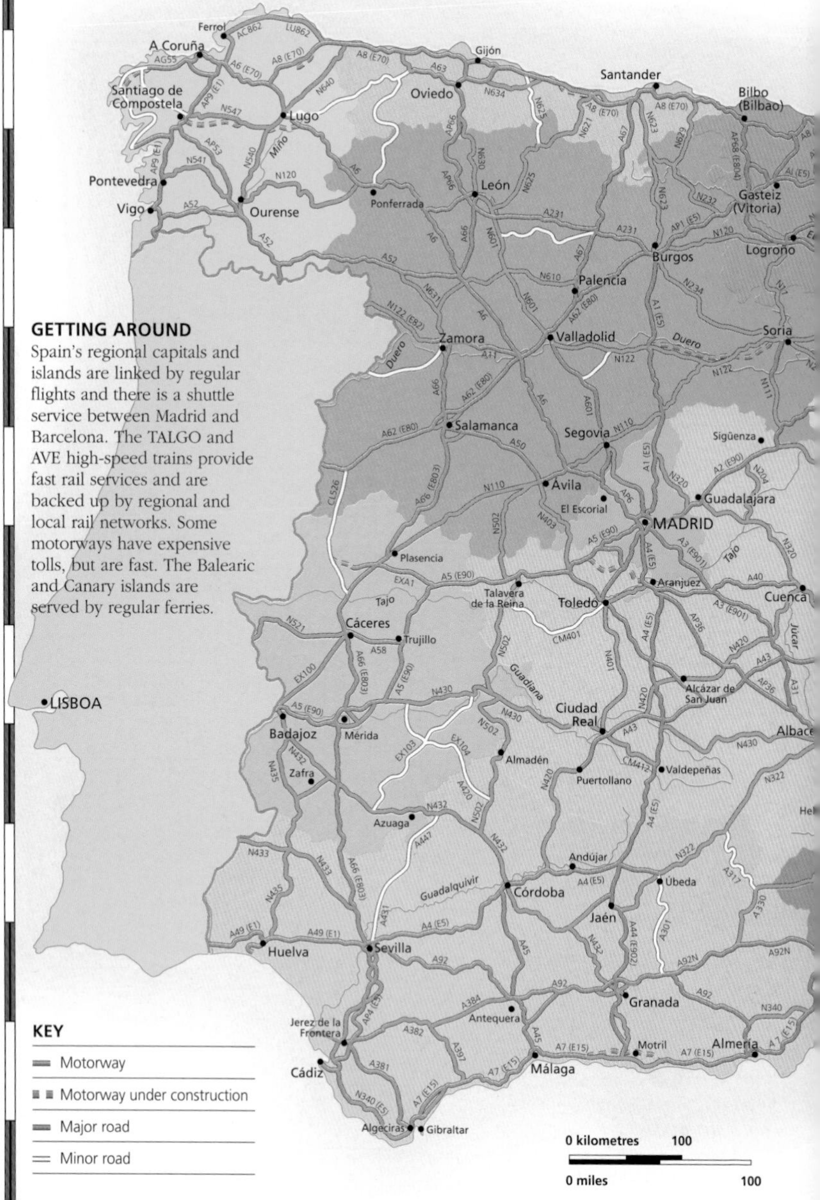

GETTING AROUND

Spain's regional capitals and islands are linked by regular flights and there is a shuttle service between Madrid and Barcelona. The TALGO and AVE high-speed trains provide fast rail services and are backed up by regional and local rail networks. Some motorways have expensive tolls, but are fast. The Balearic and Canary islands are served by regular ferries.

KEY

- Motorway
- Motorway under construction
- Major road
- Minor road

0 kilometres 100

0 miles 100

Eyewitness Spain Regions

Each of the chapters in this guide has a colour code. The chapters are grouped into five sections: Northern, Eastern, Central and Southern Spain and Spain's Islands; and two cities: Madrid and Barcelona.

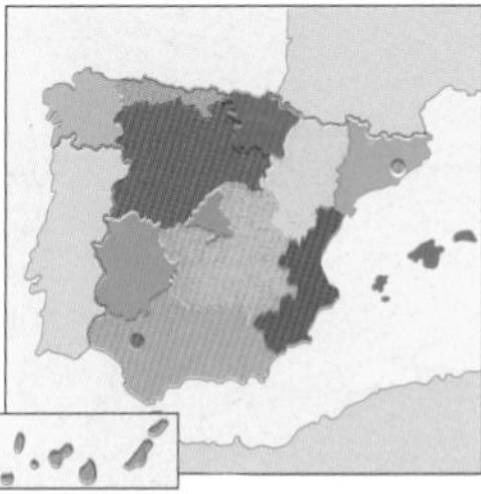

KEY TO COLOUR CODING

Northern Spain

- Galicia
- Asturias and Cantabria
- The Basque Country, Navarra and La Rioja

Eastern Spain

- Barcelona
- Catalonia
- Aragón
- Valencia and Murcia

Central Spain

- Madrid
- Castilla y León
- Castilla-La Mancha
- Extremadura

Southern Spain

- Seville
- Andalusia

Spain's Islands

- The Balearic Islands
- The Canary Islands

Iruña (Pamplona)
Huesca
Tudela
Zaragoza
Lleida
La Seu d'Urgell
Figueres
Girona
Vic
Manresa
Barcelona
Reus
Tarragona
Tortosa
Teruel
Castelló de la Plana
Sagunt
Valencia
Almansa
Alcoi
Benidorm
Alacant (Alicante)
Elx
Murcia
Cartagena
Ebro
Turia

THE BALEARIC ISLANDS

Ciutadella
Menorca
Maó
Mallorca
Palma de Mallorca
Manacor
Cabrera
Ibiza
Eivissa (Ibiza)
Formentera

THE CANARY ISLANDS

Lanzarote
Arrecife
La Palma
Santa Cruz de la Palma
Fuerteventura
Puerto del Rosario
Puerto de la Cruz
Santa Cruz de Tenerife
Tenerife
La Gomera
San Sebastián de la Gomera
Las Palmas de Gran Canaria
Gran Canaria
Maspalomas
El Hierro
Valverde

Spain's Atlantic Territories

The Canary Islands, in the Atlantic Ocean off the coast of Africa, are an integral part of Spain. They are one hour behind the rest of the country.

A PORTRAIT OF SPAIN

The familiar images of Spain – flamenco dancing, bullfighting, tapas bars and solemn Easter processions – do no more than hint at the diversity of the country. Spain has four official languages, two major cities of almost equal importance and a greater range of landscapes than any other European country. These remarkable contrasts make Spain an endlessly fascinating country to visit.

Separated from the rest of Europe by the Pyrenees, Spain reaches south to the coast of North Africa. It has both Atlantic and Mediterranean coastlines, and includes two archipelagos – the Balearics and the Canary Islands.

The climate and landscape vary from snow-capped peaks in the Pyrenees, through the green meadows of Galicia and the orange groves of Valencia, to the desert of Almería. Madrid is the highest capital in Europe, and Spain its most mountainous country after Switzerland and Austria. The innumerable sierras have always hindered communications. Until railways were built it was easier to move goods from Barcelona to South America than to Madrid.

Statue of Don Quixote and Sancho Panza, Madrid

In early times, Spain was a coveted prize for foreign conquerors including the Phoenicians and the Romans. During the Middle Ages, much of it was ruled by the Moors, who arrived from North Africa in the 8th century. It was reconquered by Christian forces, and unified at the end of the 15th century. A succession of rulers tried to impose a common culture, but Spain remains as culturally diverse as ever. Several regions have maintained a strong sense of their own independent identities. Many Basques and Catalans, in particular, do not consider themselves to

Landscape with a solitary cork tree near Albacete in Castilla-La Mancha

◁ The outlandishly dressed *Peliqueiros* who take to the streets during Carnival in Laza, Galicia

Peñafiel Castle in the Duero valley (Castilla y León), built between the 10th and 13th centuries

be Spanish. Madrid may be the nominal capital, but it is closely rivalled in commerce, the arts and sport by Barcelona, the capital city of Catalonia.

THE SPANISH WAY OF LIFE

The inhabitants of this very varied country have few things in common except for a natural sociability and a zest for living. Spaniards commonly put as much energy into enjoying life as they do into their work. The stereotypical "mañana" (leave everything until tomorrow) is a myth, but time is flexible in Spain and many people bend their work to fit the demands of their social life, rather than let themselves be ruled by the clock. The day is long in Spain and Spanish has a word, *madrugada*, for the time between midnight and dawn, when city streets are often still lively.

"Vinegar Face" in Pamplona's Los Sanfermines fiesta

Spaniards are highly gregarious. In many places people still go out in the evening for the *paseo*, when the streets are crowded with strollers. Eating is invariably communal and big groups often meet up for tapas or dinner. Not surprisingly, Spain has more bars and restaurants per head than any other country in Europe.

Tables outside a café in Madrid's Plaza Mayor

Underpinning Spanish society is the extended family. Traditionally, the state in Spain has been very inefficient at providing public services – although this has improved in the last 20 years. The Spanish have therefore always relied on their families and personal connections, rather than institutions, to find work or seek assistance in a crisis. This attitude has sometimes led to a disregard for general interests – such as the environment – when they have conflicted with private ones.

Most Spaniards place their family at the centre of their lives. Three generations may live together under one roof, or at least see each other often. Even lifelong city-dwellers refer fondly to their *pueblo* – the town or village where their family comes from and where they return whenever they can. Children are adored in Spain and, consequently, great importance is attached to education. The family in Spain, however, is under strain as couples increasingly opt for a higher income and better lifestyle rather than a large family. One of the most striking transformations in modern Spain has been in the birth rate, from one of the highest in Europe, at 2.72 children for every woman in 1975, to 1.38 children for every woman in 2010.

The windmills and castle above Consuegra, La Mancha

Virgin of Guadalupe in Extremadura

Catholicism is still a pervasive influence over Spanish society, although church attendance among those under 35 has been declining and now stands at below 10 per cent. The images of saints watch over some shops, bars and lorry drivers' cabs. Church feast days are marked by countless traditional fiestas, which are enthusiastically maintained in modern Spain.

SPORT AND THE ARTS

Spanish cultural life has been experiencing a rejuvenation. Spanish-made films – notably those of cult directors Pedro Almodóvar and Alejandro Amenábar – have been able to compete with Hollywood for audiences, and the actress Penélope Cruz won an Oscar in 2009. The overall level of reading has risen, and contemporary literature has steadily gained a wider readership. The performing arts have been restricted by a lack of facilities, but major investments have provided new venues, regional arts centres and new symphony

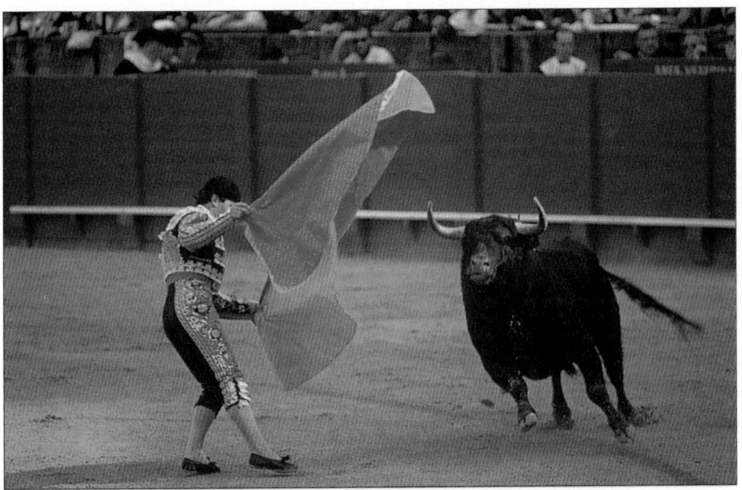
A matador plays a bull in the Plaza de Toros de la Maestranza, Seville

Poster for a Pedro Almodóvar film

orchestras. The country has produced many remarkable opera singers, including Montserrat Caballé, Plácido Domingo and José Carreras. Spain has also excelled in design, particularly evident in the interior furnishings shops of Barcelona.

Spaniards are the most avid TV-watchers in Europe after the British. There are two state-owned TV channels in Spain, as well as a growing number of private channels and regional TV stations thanks to digital platforms. Sports are one of the mainstays of TV programming. Spanish sportsmen and women have been very successful – for example, tennis player Rafael Nadal and Formula 1 driver Fernando Alonso. Such role models have encouraged participation in sport and more facilities have been provided to meet this demand. Most popular are basketball and, above all, soccer.

Bullfighting has enjoyed renewed popularity since the late 1980s. For aficionados, a *corrida* provides a link to Spain's roots, and the noise, colour and crowd are as much of an attraction as the bullfight itself. In Catalonia, however, bullfighting was banned in 2012.

SPAIN TODAY

Since the mid-20th century, Spain has undergone more social change than anywhere in western Europe. Until the 1950s, Spain was predominantly a poor, rural country, in which only 37 per cent of the population lived in towns of over 10,000 people. By the 1990s, the figure was 65 per cent. As people flooded into towns and cities many rural areas became depopulated. The 1960s saw the beginning of

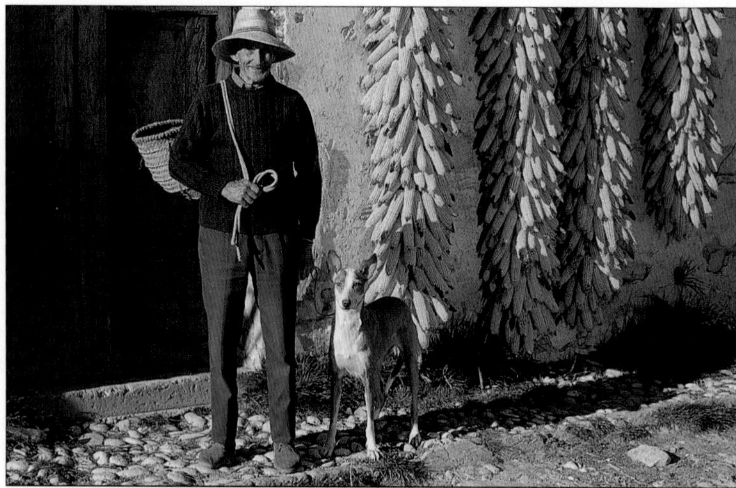

A farmer with his crop of maize hanging to dry on the outside of his house in the hills of Alicante

Beach near Tossa de Mar on the Costa Brava

spectacular economic growth, partly due to a burgeoning tourist industry. In that decade, car ownership increased from 1 in 100 to 1 in 10.

After the death of dictator General Franco in 1975 Spain became a constitutional monarchy under King Juan Carlos I. The post-Franco era, up until the mid-1990s, was dominated by the Socialist Prime Minister Felipe González. As well as presiding over major improvements in roads, education and health services, the Socialists increased Spain's international standing. The PSOE could not continue forever, however, and in 1996 revelations of a series of scandals lost the PSOE the election. Spain joined the European Community in 1986, triggering a spectacular increase in the country's prosperity. The country's fortunes seemed to peak in the extraordinary year of 1992, when Barcelona staged the Olympic Games and Seville hosted a world fair, Expo '92.

King Juan Carlos I and Queen Sofía

With the establishment of democracy, the 17 autonomous regions of Spain have acquired considerable powers. Several have their own languages, which are officially given equal importance to Spanish (strictly called Castilian). A significant number of Basques favour independence, and the Basque terrorist group ETA is a constant thorn in the side of Spanish democracy.

During the 1980s Spain enjoyed an economic boom as service industries and manufacturing expanded. Even so, GDP remains below the European Union average, and growth halted in 2009's economic downturn. Agriculture is an important industry but while it is highly developed in some regions, it is inefficient in others. Tourism provides approximately ten per cent of the country's earnings. Most tourists still come for beaches. But increasingly, foreign visitors are drawn by Spain's rich cultural heritage and spectacular countryside. Anyone who knows this country, however, will tell you that it is the Spanish people's capacity to enjoy life to the full that is Spain's biggest attraction.

Demonstration for Catalan independence

Architecture in Spain

Spain has always imported its styles of architecture: Moorish from North Africa, Romanesque and Gothic from France and Renaissance from Italy. Each style, however, was interpreted in a distinctively Spanish way, with sudden and strong contrasts between light and shady areas; façades alternating between austerity and extravagant decoration; and thick walls pierced by few windows to lessen the impact of heat and sunlight. Styles vary from region to region, reflecting the division of Spain before unification. The key design of a central patio surrounded by arcades has been a strong feature of civil buildings since Moorish times.

The 15th-century Casa de Conchas in Salamanca *(see p361)*

ROMANESQUE AND EARLIER (8TH–13TH CENTURIES)

Romanesque churches were mainly built in Catalonia and along the pilgrim route to Santiago *(see p83)*. Their distinctive features include round arches, massive walls and few windows. Earlier churches were built in Pre-Romanesque *(see p106)* or Mozarabic *(see p352)* style.

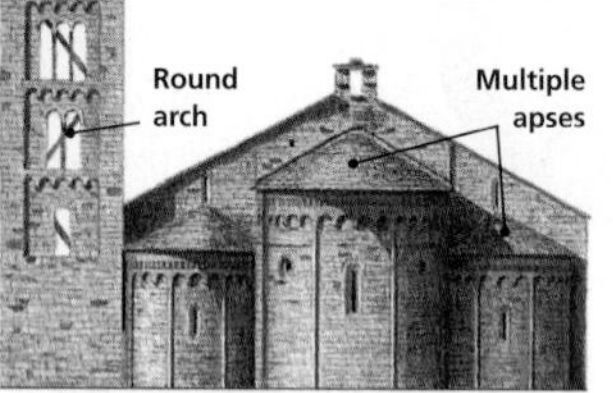

The Romanesque Sant Climent, Taüll *(p201)*

MOORISH (8TH–15TH CENTURIES)

The Moors *(see pp52–3)* reserved the most lavish decoration for the interior of buildings, where ornate designs based on geometry, calligraphy and plant motifs were created in *azulejos* (tiles) or stucco. They made extensive use of the horsehoe arch, a feature inherited from the Visigoths *(see pp50–1)*. The greatest surviving works of Moorish architecture *(see pp422–3)* are in Southern Spain.

The Salón de Embajadores *in the Alhambra (see p490) has exquisite Moorish decoration.*

GOTHIC (12TH–16TH CENTURIES)

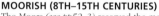

Gothic arched window

Gothic was imported from France in the late 12th century. The round arch was replaced by the pointed arch which, because of its greater strength, allowed for higher vaults and taller windows. External buttresses were added to prevent the walls of the nave from leaning outwards. Carved decoration was at its most opulent in the Flamboyant Gothic style of the 15th century. After the fall of Granada, Isabelline, a late Gothic style, developed. Meanwhile, Moorish craftsmen working in reconquered areas created the highly decorative hybrid Christian-Islamic style Mudéjar *(see p55)*.

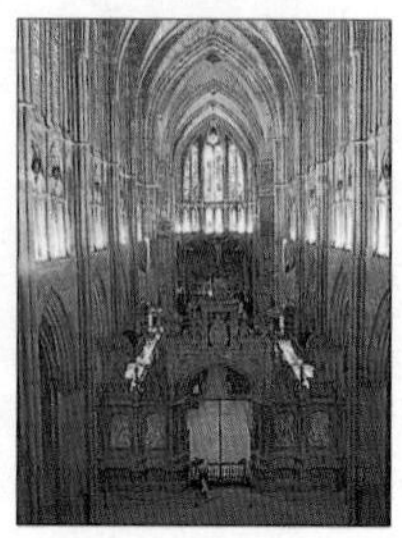

The nave *of León Cathedral (see pp354–5), built in the 13th century, is supported by rib vaulting and is illuminated by the finest display of stained glass in Spain.*

Sculptural decoration *above the doorways of León cathedral's south front depicted biblical stories for the benefit of the largely illiterate populace.*

RENAISSANCE (16TH CENTURY)

Around 1500 a new style was introduced to Spain by Italian craftsmen and Spanish artists who had studied in Italy. The Renaissance was a revival of the style of Ancient Rome. It is distinguished by its sense of symmetry and the use of the round arch, and Doric, Ionic and Corinthian columns. Early Spanish Renaissance architecture is known as Plateresque because its fine detail resembles ornate silverwork (*platero* means silversmith).

The Palacio de las Cadenas *in Úbeda (see p497) has a severely Classical façade.*

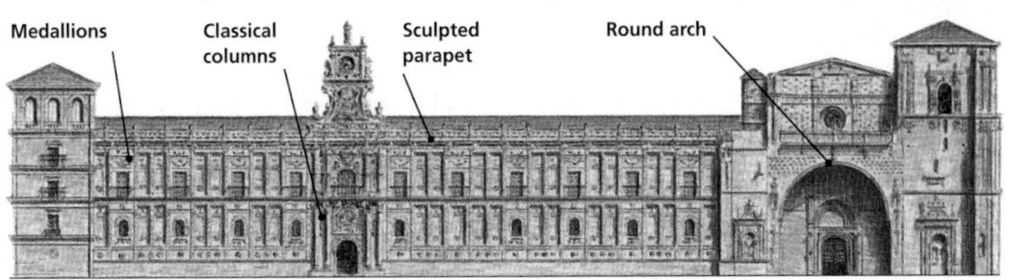

The Hostal de San Marcos in León *(see p353)*, one of Spain's finest Plateresque buildings

BAROQUE (17TH–18TH CENTURIES)

Baroque was driven by a desire for drama and movement. Decoration became extravagant, with exuberant sculpture and twisting columns. Although the excessive Baroque style of Churrigueresque is named after the Churriguera family of architects, it was their successors who were its main exponents.

The ornamentation *on the Baroque façade of Valladolid University (see p366) is concentrated above the doorway.*

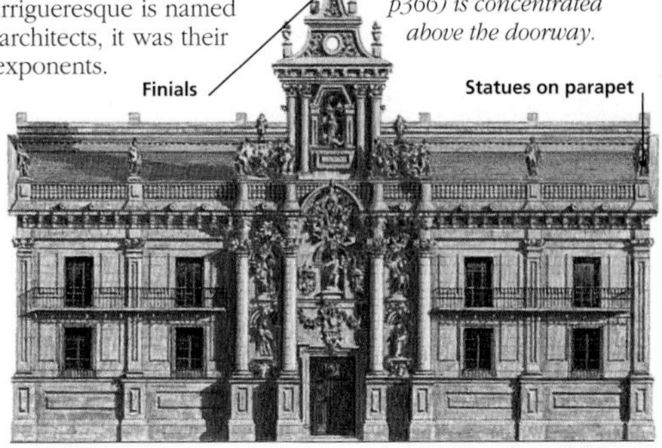

The façade of the Museo de Historia in Madrid *(pp304–5)*

MODERN (LATE 19TH CENTURY ONWARDS)

Modernisme *(see pp140–1)*, a Catalan interpretation of Art Nouveau, is seen at its best in Barcelona. Its architects experimented with a highly original language of ornament. In recent decades, Spain has seen an explosion of bold, functionalist architecture in which the form of a building reflects its use and decoration is used sparingly.

Torre de Picasso in Madrid

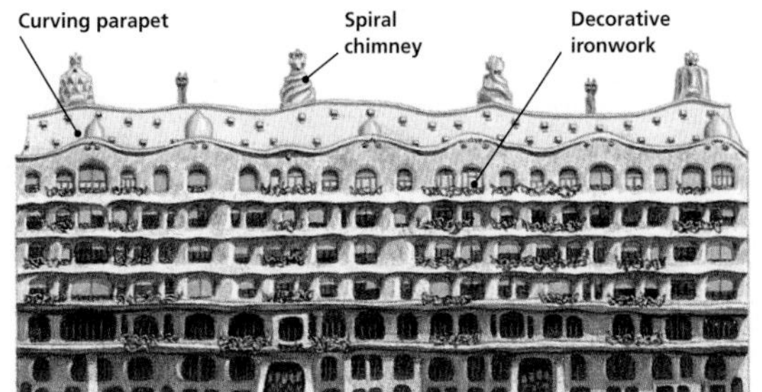

Casa Milà, *in Barcelona (see p165), was built in 1910 by Modernisme's most famous and best-loved architect, Antoni Gaudí, who drew much of his inspiration from nature.*

Vernacular Architecture

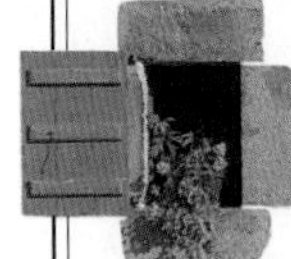
Window in Navarra

As well as its cathedrals and palaces, Spain has a great variety of charming vernacular buildings. These have been constructed by local craftsmen to meet the practical needs of rural communities and to take account of local climate conditions, with little reference to formal architectural styles. Due to the high expense involved in transporting raw materials, builders used whatever stone or timber lay closest to hand. The three houses illustrated below incorporate the most common characteristics of village architecture seen in different parts of Spain.

A cave church in Artenara ***(see p545)*****, on Gran Canaria**

STONE HOUSE

The climate is wet in the north and houses like this one in Carmona *(see p111)*, in Cantabria, are built with overhanging eaves to shed the rain. Wooden balconies catch the sun.

Detail of stonework

Family and farm *often share rural houses. The ground floor is used to stable animals, or store tools and firewood.*

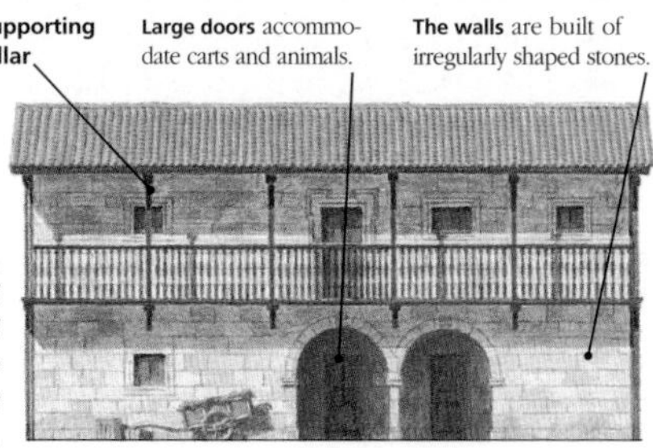
Supporting pillar
Large doors accommodate carts and animals.
The walls are built of irregularly shaped stones.

TIMBER-FRAMED HOUSE

Spain, in general, has few large trees and wood is in short supply. Castilla y León is one of the few regions where timber-framed houses, such as this one in Covarrubias *(see p370)*, can be found. These houses are quick and cheap to build. The timber frame is filled in with a coarse plaster mixed from lime and sand, or adobe (bricks dried in the sun).

Half-timbered wall

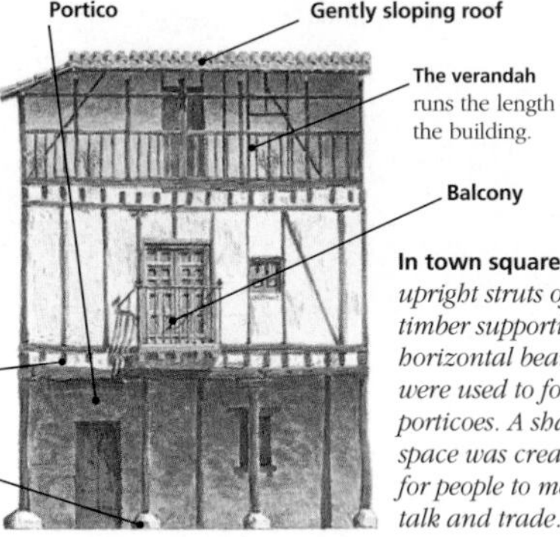
Portico
Gently sloping roof
The verandah runs the length of the building.
Balcony
The ends of the beams supporting the floorboards are visible.
Stone plinths below upright timbers provide protection from damp.

In town squares, *upright struts of timber supporting horizontal beams were used to form porticoes. A shady space was created for people to meet, talk and trade.*

WHITEWASHED HOUSE

Houses in the south of Spain – often built of baked clay – are regularly whitewashed to deflect the sun's intense rays. Andalusia's famous white towns *(see p468)* exemplify this attractive form of architecture.

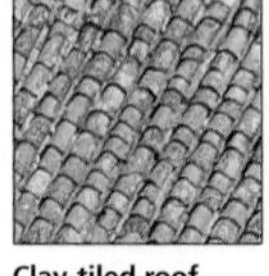
Clay-tiled roof

Windows *are small and few in number, and deeply recessed, in order to keep the interior cool.*

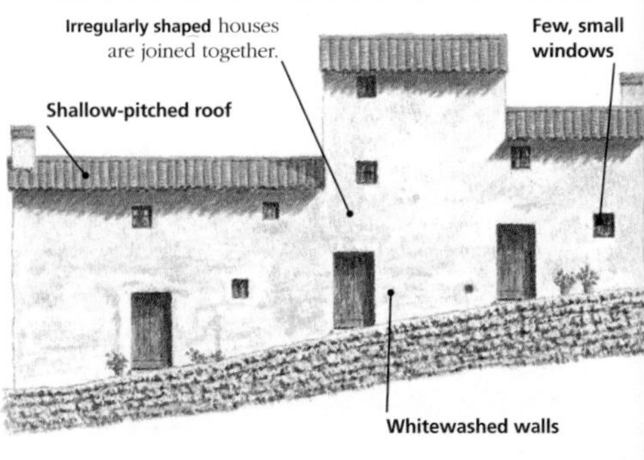
Irregularly shaped houses are joined together.
Few, small windows
Shallow-pitched roof
Whitewashed walls

THE PLAZA MAYOR

Almost every town in Spain centres on a main square, the plaza mayor, like this one in Pedraza de la Sierra *(see p365)*, near Segovia. More than a market square, it acts as a focus for local life. It is usually overlooked by the church, the town hall, shops and bars and the mansions of aristocratic families.

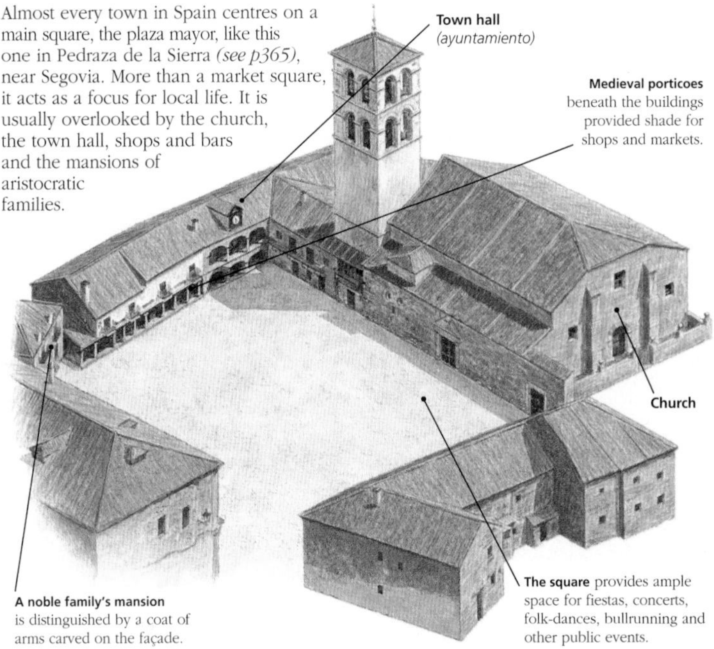

Town hall *(ayuntamiento)*

Medieval porticoes beneath the buildings provided shade for shops and markets.

Church

A noble family's mansion is distinguished by a coat of arms carved on the façade.

The square provides ample space for fiestas, concerts, folk-dances, bullrunning and other public events.

RURAL ARCHITECTURE

A variety of distinctive buildings dots the countryside.

Where the rock is soft and the climate hot, subterranean dwellings have been excavated. Insulated from extremes of temperature, they provide a comfortable place to live.

Hórreos, granaries raised on stone stilts to prevent rats climbing up into the grain, are a common sight in Galicia (where they are stone-built) and Asturias (where they are made of wood). In fields you will often see shelters for livestock or for storing crops, such as the *teitos* of Asturias.

Windmills provided power in parts of Spain where there was little running water but plentiful wind, like La Mancha and the Balearic Islands.

Almost everywhere in the Spanish countryside you will come across *ermitas*, isolated chapels or shrines dedicated to a local saint. An *ermita* may be opened only on the patron saint's feast day.

Cave houses in Guadix near Granada *(see p493)*

Teito* in Valle de Teverga in Asturias *(see p105)

***Hórreo*, a granary, on the Rías Baixas *(see p95)* in Galicia**

Windmill above Consuegra *(see p394)* in La Mancha

Farming in Spain

Spain's varied geography and climate have created a mosaic of farming patterns ranging from lush dairylands to stony hillsides where goats graze. Land can be broadly divided into *secano*, or dry cultivation (used for olives, wheat and vines), and much smaller areas of *regadío*, irrigated land (planted with citrus trees, rice and vegetables). Farming in many parts is a family affair relying on traditional, labour-intensive methods but it is becoming increasingly mechanized.

Donkey in Extremadura

Plains of cereals *make up much of the farmland of the central* meseta *of Spain. Wheat is grown in better-watered, more fertile western areas; barley is grown in the drier south.*

Cork oaks thrive in Extremadura and western Andalusia.

MADRID

SEVILLA

0 kilometres 200

0 miles 100

Sheep *grazed on the rough pastures of Central Spain are milked to make cheese, especially* manchego, *which is produced in La Mancha* (see p339).

THE AGRICULTURAL YEAR

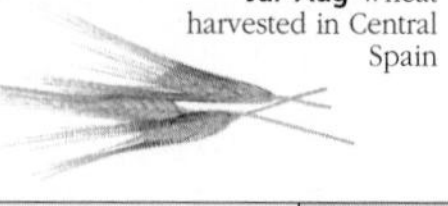

Jul–Aug Wheat harvested in Central Spain

Sep Rice harvest in Eastern Spain. Grape harvest at its height

Oct Maize harvested in Northern Spain

Oct–Nov Table olives picked

Dec–Mar Olives for making oil picked

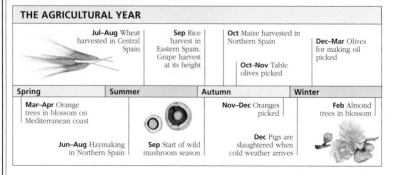

Spring	Summer	Autumn	Winter

Mar–Apr Orange trees in blossom on Mediterranean coast

Jun–Aug Haymaking in Northern Spain

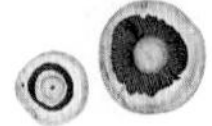

Sep Start of wild mushroom season

Nov–Dec Oranges picked

Dec Pigs are slaughtered when cold weather arrives

Feb Almond trees in blossom

The high rainfall *and mild summers of Northern Spain make it suitable for dairy farming. Farms are often small, especially in Galicia, one of the country's most underdeveloped regions. Crops such as maize and wheat are grown in small quantities.*

Wine is produced in many parts of Spain *(see pp606–7)*. The country's best sparkling wine grapes are grown in Catalonia.

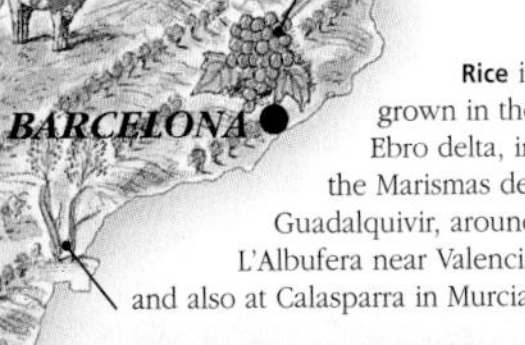

Rice is grown in the Ebro delta, in the Marismas del Guadalquivir, around L'Albufera near Valencia and also at Calasparra in Murcia.

Oranges, *lemons and clementines are grown on the irrigated coastal plains beside the Mediterranean. The region of Valencia is the prime producer of oranges.*

Olive trees *are planted in long, straight lines across large swaths of Andalusia, especially in the province of Jaén. Spain is the world's leading producer of olive oil.*

Cork oaks are stripped of their bark every ten years

CROPS FROM TREES

The almond, orange and olive create the three most characteristic landscapes of rural Spain but several other trees provide important crops. Wine corks are made from the bark of the cork oak. Tropical species, such as avocado and cherimoya, a delicious creamy fruit little known outside Spain, have been introduced to the so-called Costa Tropical of Andalusia *(see p483)*; and bananas are a major crop of the Canary Islands. Elsewhere, peaches and loquats are also grown commercially. Figs and carobs – whose fruit is used for fodder and as a substitute for chocolate – grow semi-wild.

Almonds *grow on dry hillsides in many parts of Spain. The spring blossom can be spectacular. The nut, enclosed by a fleshy green skin, is used in a variety of sweetmeats including the Christmas treat* turrón (see p201).

Olive trees *grow slowly and often live to a great age. The fruit is harvested in winter and either pickled in brine for eating as a to extract the oil which is widely used in Spanish cuisine.*

Sweet oranges *are grown in dense, well-irrigated groves near the frost-free coasts. The sweet smell of orange blossom in springtime is unmistakeable. Trees of the bitter orange are often planted for shade and decoration in parks and gardens.*

Spain's National Parks

Few other countries in western Europe have such unspoiled scenery as Spain, or can boast tracts of wilderness where brown bears live and wolves hunt. More than 200 nature reserves protect a broad range of ecosystems. The most important areas are the 13 national parks, the first of which was established in 1918. Natural parks *(parques naturales)* regulated by regional governments, are also vital to the task of conservation.

Giant orchid

Clear mountain river, Ordesa

Rough terrain in the Picos de Europa

MOUNTAINS

Much of Spain's finest scenery is found in the mountains. Rivers have carved gorges between the peaks of the Picos de Europa. Ordesa and Aigüestortes share some of the most dramatic landscapes of the Pyrenees, while the Sierra Nevada has an impressive range of indigenous wildlife.

Eagle owls *are Europe's largest owl, easily identified by their large ear tufts. At night they hunt small mammals and birds.*

Chamois *are well adapted to climbing across slopes covered in scree. They live in small groups, always alert to predators, and feed on grass and flowers.*

WETLANDS

Wetlands include coastal strips and freshwater marshes. Seasonal floods rejuvenate the water, providing nutrients for animal and plant growth. These areas are rich feeding grounds for birds. Spain's best-known wetland is Doñana. Catalonia's Delta de l'Ebre *(see p225)* and Tablas de Daimiel, in La Mancha, are much smaller.

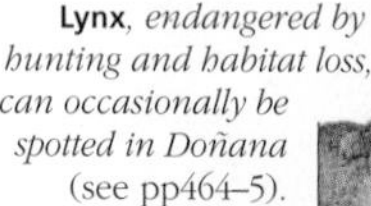
Lynx, *endangered by hunting and habitat loss, can occasionally be spotted in Doñana* (see pp464–5).

Black-winged stilts, *with their long, straight legs, are adept at stalking tiny freshwater crustaceans.*

Laguna del Acebuche, Parque Nacional de Doñana

ISLANDS

Cabrera archipelago, Balearic Islands

Cabrera, off Mallorca, is home to rare plants, reptiles and seabirds, such as Eleonara's falcon. The surrounding waters are important for their marine life.

Lizards *are often found in rocky terrain and on cliff faces.*

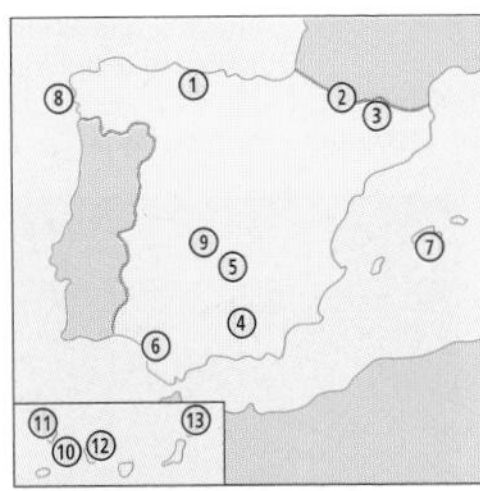

NATIONAL PARKS

① Mountains

⑤ Wetlands

⑦ Islands

⑨ Woods and Forests

⑪ Volcanic Landscapes

MOUNTAINS

① Picos de Europa *pp108–9*
② Ordesa y Monte Perdido *pp232–3*
③ Aigüestortes y Estany de Sant Maurici *p211*
④ Sierra Nevada *p485*

WETLANDS

⑤ Tablas de Daimiel *p399*
⑥ Doñana *pp464–5*

ISLANDS

⑦ Archipiélago de Cabrera *p517*
⑧ Islas Atlánticas de Galicia *p95*

WOODS AND FORESTS

⑨ Cabañeros *p387*
⑩ Garajonay *p533*

VOLCANIC LANDSCAPES

⑪ Caldera de Taburiente *p532*
⑫ Teide *pp538–9*
⑬ Timanfaya *pp548–9*

VISITORS' CHECKLIST

All but one of the national parks are managed by the Ministerio de Medio Ambiente. ***Tel*** *915 97 65 77. Parque Nacional d'Aigüestortes y Estany de Sant Maurici is administered jointly with Catalonia's Department of Environment.* ***Tel*** *973 69 61 89. Most of Spain's national parks have visitors' centres, often called Centros de Interpretació.*

WOODS AND FORESTS

Deciduous broad-leaved forests grow in the northwest of Spain, and stands of Aleppo and Scots pine cover many mountainous areas. On the central plateau there are stretches of open woodland of evergreen holm oak and cork oak in the Parque Nacional de Cabañeros. Dense, lush *laurasilva* woodland grows in the Parque Nacional de Garajonay, on La Gomera, one of the smaller Canary Islands.

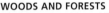

Black vultures *are the largest birds of prey in Europe, with an enormous wingspan of over 2.5 m (8 ft).*

Hedgehogs, *common in woodlands, root among fallen leaves and grass to find worms and slugs.*

Parque Nacional de Garajonay

VOLCANIC LANDSCAPES

Three very different parks protect parts of the Canary Islands' amazing volcanic scenery. Caldera de Taburiente on La Palma is a volcanic crater surrounded by woods. Mount Teide in Tenerife has unique alpine flora, and Lanzarote's Timanfaya is composed of barren but atmospheric lava fields.

Colonizing plant species, Mount Teide (Tenerife)

Rabbits *are highly opportunistic, quickly colonizing areas in which they can burrow. In the absence of predators, populations may increase, damaging fragile ecosystems.*

Canaries *belong to the finch family of songbirds. The popular canary has been bred from the wild serin, native to the Canaries.*

Spanish Art

Three Spanish painters stand out as milestones in the history of Western art. Diego de Velázquez was a 17th-century court portrait painter and his *Las Meninas* is a seminal work. Francisco de Goya depicted Spanish life during one of its most violent periods. The prolific 20th-century master, Pablo Picasso, is recognized as the founder of modern art. To these names must be added that of El Greco – who was born in Crete but who lived in Spain, where he painted religious scenes in an individualistic style. The work of these and Spain's many other great artists can be seen in world-renowned galleries, especially the Prado *(see pp292–5)*.

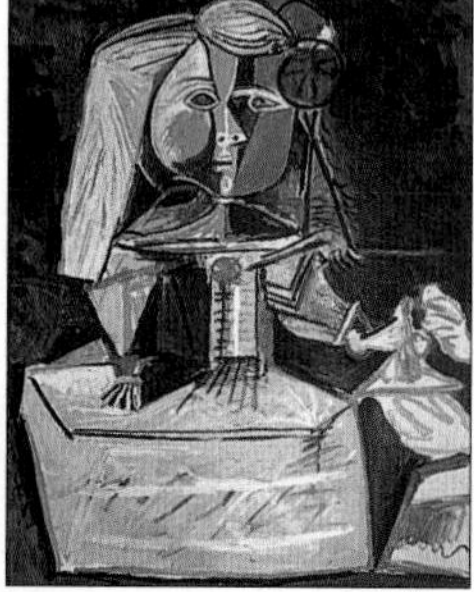

In his series Las Meninas *(1957), Picasso interprets the frozen gesture of the five-year-old Infanta Margarita. Altogether, Picasso produced 44 paintings based on Velázquez's canvas. Some of them are in Barcelona's Museu de Picasso* (see p153).

Self-portrait of Velázquez

The king and queen, reflected in a mirror behind the painter, may be posing for their portrait.

LAS MENINAS *(1656)*

In Velázquez's painting of the Infanta Margarita and her courtiers, in the Prado *(see pp292–5)*, the eye is drawn into the distance where the artist's patron, Felipe IV, is reflected in a mirror.

RELIGIOUS ART IN SPAIN

The influence of the Catholic Church on Spanish art through the ages is reflected in the predominance of religious imagery. Many churches and museums have Romanesque altarpieces or earlier icons. El Greco *(see p391)* painted from a highly personal religious vision. Baroque religious art of the 17th century, when the Inquisition *(see p274)* was at its height, often graphically depicts physical suffering and spiritual torment.

The Burial of the Count of Orgaz* by El Greco *(see p390)

TIMELINE OF GREAT SPANISH ARTISTS

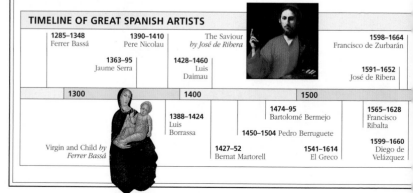

José Nieto, the queen's chamberlain, stands in the doorway in the background of the painting.

Court jester

MODERN ART

The early 20th-century artists Joan Miró *(see p172)*, Salvador Dalí *(see p215)* and Pablo Picasso *(see p152)* all belonged to the Paris School. More recent artists of note include Antonio Saura and Antoni Tàpies *(see p164)*. Among many great Spanish art collections, the Museo Reina Sofia in Madrid *(see pp298–9)* specializes in modern art. Contemporary artists are accorded great prestige in Spain. Their work is to be seen in town halls, banks and public squares, and many towns have a museum dedicated to a local painter.

Salvador Dalí's painting of the *Colossus of Rhodes* (1954)

***Collage* (1934) by Joan Miró**

The Family of King Charles IV *was painted in 1800 by Francisco de Goya* (see p239)*, nearly 150 years after* Las Meninas. *Its debt to Velázquez's painting is evident in its frontal composition, compact grouping of figures and in the inclusion of a self-portrait.*

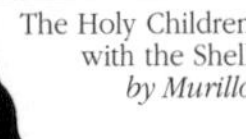

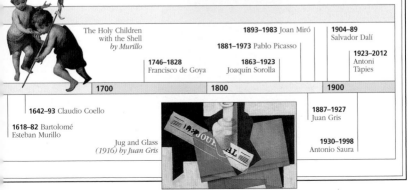

The Holy Children with the Shell *by Murillo*

1893–1983 Joan Miró

1904–89 Salvador Dalí

1881–1973 Pablo Picasso

1923–2012 Antoni Tàpies

1746–1828 Francisco de Goya

1863–1923 Joaquín Sorolla

1700 **1800** **1900**

1642–93 Claudio Coello

1618–82 Bartolomé Esteban Murillo

1887–1927 Juan Gris

Jug and Glass *(1916) by Juan Gris*

1930–1998 Antonio Saura

Literary Spain

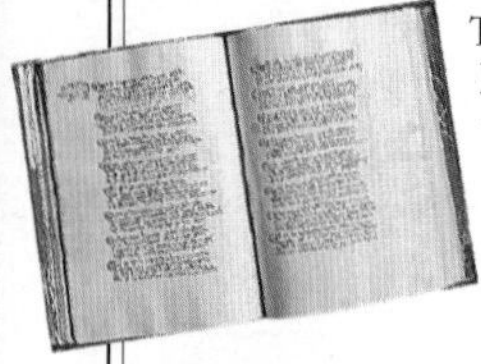

The 14th-century *El Libro de Buen Amor*

The best-known work of Spanish literature, *Don Quixote* is considered the first modern novel, but Spain has produced many major works over the last 2,000 years. The Roman writers Seneca, Lucan and Martial were born in Spain. Later, the Moors developed a flourishing, but now little-known, literary culture. Although Spanish (Castilian) is the national tongue, many enduring works have been written in the Galician and Catalan regional languages. Basque literature, hitherto an oral culture, is a more recent development. Many foreign writers, such as Alexandre Dumas, Ernest Hemingway and Karel Capek, have written accounts of their travels in Spain.

MIDDLE AGES

As the Roman empire fell, Latin evolved into several Romance languages. The earliest non-Latin literature in Spain derives from an oral tradition that arose before the 10th century. It is in the form of *jarchas*, snatches of love poetry written in Mozarab, the Romance language that was spoken by Christians living under the Moors.

In the 12th century, the first poems appeared in Castilian. During the next 300 years, two separate schools of poetry developed. The best-known example of troubadour verse is the anonymous epic, *El Cantar del Mío Cid,* which tells of the heroic exploits of El Cid *(see p370)* during the Reconquest. Works of clerical poetry – for example, Gonzalo de Berceo's *Milagros de Nuestra Señora*, relating the life of the Virgin – convey a moral message.

Spanish literature evolved in the 13th century after Alfonso X the Learned *(see p55)* replaced Latin with Castilian Romance (later called Spanish) as the official language. Under his supervision a team of Jews, Christians and Arabs wrote scholarly treatises. The king himself was a poet, writing in Galician Romance.

The first great prose works in Spanish appeared in the 14th and 15th centuries. *El Libro de Buen Amor,* by an ecclesiastic, Juan Ruiz, is a tale of the love affairs of a priest, interleaved with other stories. Fernando de Rojas uses skilful characterization in *La Celestina* to tell a tragic love story about two nobles and a scheming go-between. This was an age in which tales of chivalry were also popular.

Alfonso X the Learned (1221–84)

GOLDEN AGE

The prolific Golden Age dramatist, Félix Lope de Vega

The 16th century hailed the start of Spain's Golden Age of literature. But it was also a period of domestic strife. This found expression in the picaresque novel, a Spanish genre originating with the anonymous *El Lazarillo de Tormes*, a bitter reflection on the misfortunes of a blind man's guide.

Spiritual writers flourished under the austere climate of the Counter-Reformation. St John of the Cross's *Cántico Espiritual* was influenced by oriental erotic poetry and the Bible's *Song of Songs.*

The 17th century saw the emergence of more great talents. The life and work of Miguel de Cervantes *(see p333)* straddles the two centuries of the Golden Age. He published his masterpiece, *Don Quixote*, in 1615. Other important writers of the time include Francisco de Quevedo and Luis de Góngora.

Corrales (public theatres) appeared in the 17th century, opening the way for Lope de Vega *(see p290)*, Calderón de la Barca and other dramatists.

Don Quixote's adventures portrayed by José Moreno Carbonero

18TH AND 19TH CENTURIES

Influenced by the French Enlightenment, literature in the 18th century was seen as a way to educate the people. Such was the aim, for instance, of Leandro Fernández de Moratín's comedy *El Sí de las Niñas.* This period saw the development of journalism as well as the emergence of the essay as a literary form. Romanticism had a short and late life in Spain. *Don Juan Tenorio*, a tale of the legendary irrepressible Latin lover by José Zorrilla, is the best-known Romantic play.

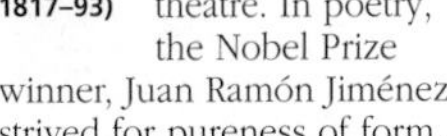

José Zorrilla (1817–93)

The satirical essayist Larra stands out from his contemporaries at the beginning of the 19th century. Towards the end of the century, the novel became a vehicle for realistic portrayals of Spanish society. Benito Pérez Galdós, regarded by many to be Spain's greatest novelist after Cervantes, studied the human condition in his *Episodios Nacionales*. The heroine in Clarín's *La Regenta* is undone by the reactionary prejudices of provincial town society.

20TH CENTURY

Writers at the turn of the century, including Pío Baroja *(see p64)*, Miguel de Unamuno and Antonio Machado, described Spain as falling behind the rest of Europe. Ramón María del Valle-Inclán wrote highly satirical plays that created the foundations of modern Spanish theatre. In poetry, the Nobel Prize winner, Juan Ramón Jiménez, strived for pureness of form.

The so-called "Generation of 27" combined European experimental art with Spain's traditional literary subjects. The best-known of them is the poet and playwright Federico García Lorca who was executed by a Fascist firing squad in 1936 *(see p67)*. He drew on the legends and stereotypes of his native Andalusia to make universal statements in his poems and plays, such as *Yerma*.

In the aftermath of the Civil War, many intellectuals who had backed the Republic were forced into exile. The Franco regime tried to create its own propagandist culture. Yet the finest literature of the period was written in spite of the political climate. Camilo José Cela's *La Colmena*, a description of everyday life in the hungry, postwar city of Madrid, set a mood of social realism that inspired other writers.

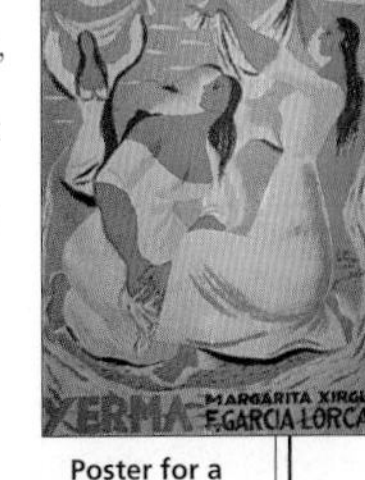

Poster for a Lorca play

Since the 1960s, the novel has become increasingly popular due to the emergence of writers like Joan Benet, Julio Llamazares, Antonio Muñoz Molina, José Manuel Caballero Bonald, Juan Marsé and the best-selling Carlos Ruiz Zafón.

The 20th century has also witnessed a surge of great Spanish literature from Latin America. Prominent authors include Jorge Luis Borges and Gabriel García Márquez.

Camilo José Cela, Nobel Prize-winning novelist, by Alvaro Delgado

The Art of Bullfighting

Poster for a bullfight

Bullfighting is a sacrificial ritual in which men (and also a few women) pit themselves against an animal bred for the ring. In this "authentic religious drama", as poet García Lorca described it, the spectator experiences vicariously the fear and exaltation felt by the matador. Although a growing number of Spaniards oppose it on grounds of cruelty, and it was banned in Catalonia in 2012, it is still popular. Many Spaniards see talk of banning bullfighting as striking at the essence of their being, for they regard the *toreo*, the art of bullfighting, as a noble part of their heritage. Bullfights today, however, are often debased by practices that weaken the bull, especially shaving its horns.

Plaza de Toros de la Maestranza, *Seville. This ring is regarded, with Las Ventas in Madrid, as one of the top venues for bullfighting in Spain.*

The matador wears a *traje de luces* (suit of lights), a colourful silk outfit embroidered with gold sequins.

The passes are made with a *muleta*, a scarlet cape stiffened along one side.

Well treated at the ranch, *the* toro bravo *(fighting bull) is specially bred for qualities of aggressiveness and courage. As aficionados of bullfighting point out in its defence, the young bull enjoys a full life while it is being prepared for its 15 minutes in the ring. Bulls must be at least four years old before they fight.*

THE BULLFIGHT

The *corrida* (bullfight) has three stages, called *tercios*. In the first one, the *tercio de varas*, the matador and *picadores* (horsemen with lances) are aided by *peones* (assistants). In the *tercio de banderillas*, *banderilleros* stick pairs of darts in the bull's back. In the *tercio de muleta* the matador makes a series of passes at the bull with a *muleta* (cape). He then executes the kill, the *estocada*, with a sword.

The matador *plays the bull with a* capa *(red cape) in the* tercio de varas. Peones *will then draw the bull towards the* picadores.

Horses are now padded.

Picadores *goad the bull with steel-pointed lances, testing its bravery. The lances weaken the animal's shoulder muscles.*

THE BULLRING

The *corrida* audience is seated in the *tendidos* (stalls) or in the *palcos* (balcony), where the *presidencia* (president's box) is situated. Opposite are the *puerta de cuadrillas,* through which the matador and team arrive, and the *arrastre de toros* (exit for bulls). Before entering the ring, the matadors wait in a corridor *(callejón)* behind *barreras* and *burladeros* (barriers). Horses are kept in the *patio de caballos* and the bulls in the *corrales*.

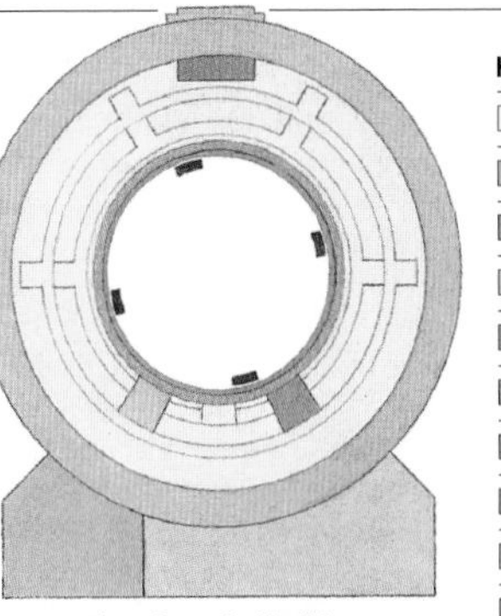

Plan of a typical bullring

KEY

- Tendidos
- Palcos
- Presidencia
- Puerta de cuadrillas
- Arrastre de toros
- Callejón
- Barreras
- Burladeros
- Patio de caballos
- Corrales

Banderillas, barbed darts, are thrust into the bull's already weakened back muscles.

Manolete *is regarded by most followers of bullfighting as one of the greatest matadors ever. He was eventually gored to death by the bull Islero at Linares, Jaén, in 1947.*

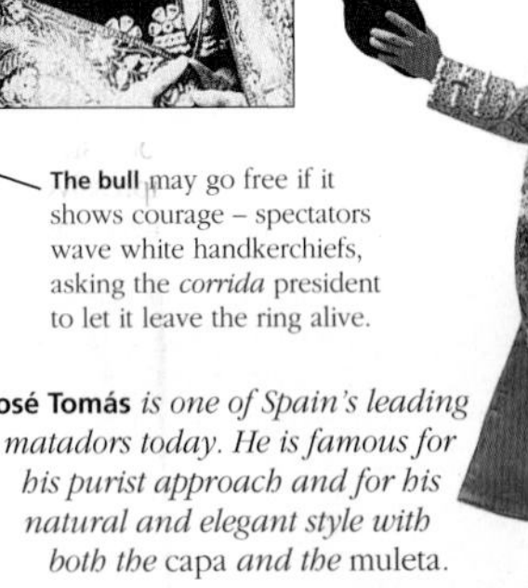

The bull may go free if it shows courage – spectators wave white handkerchiefs, asking the *corrida* president to let it leave the ring alive.

José Tomás *is one of Spain's leading matadors today. He is famous for his purist approach and for his natural and elegant style with both the* capa *and the* muleta.

Banderilleros *enter to provoke the wounded bull in the* tercio de banderillas, *sticking pairs of* banderillas *in its back.*

The bull weighs about 500 kg (1,100 lbs).

The matador *makes passes with the cape in the* tercio de muleta, *then lowers it and thrusts in the sword for the kill.*

The estocada recibiendo *is a difficult kill, rarely seen. The matador awaits the bull's charge rather than moving to meet it.*

The Fiestas of Spain

The Passion, Semana Santa

On any day of the year there is a fiesta happening somewhere in Spain – usually more than one. There isn't a village, town or city in the country which doesn't honour its patron saint, the Virgin or the changing seasons with processions, bullrunning, fireworks, re-enacted battles, some ancestral rite or a *romería* – a mass pilgrimage to a rural shrine. Whatever the pretext, a fiesta is a chance for everyone to take a break from normal life (most shops and offices close) and let off steam, with celebrations sometimes going on around the clock.

Many *romerías* wind through the countryside during the year

SPRING FIESTAS

The end of winter and the start of spring are marked by Valencia's great fire festival, Las Fallas *(see p255)*, in which huge papier-mâché sculptures are set alight in a symbolic act of burning the old in order to make way for the new.

Alcoi's noisy mock battles between costumed armies of Moors and Christians in April *(see p255)* are the most spectacular of the countless fiestas which commemorate the battles of the Reconquest. Seville's great April Fair *(see p431)*, is the biggest celebration held in Andalusia.

During Los Mayos, on 30 April and the following days, crosses are decorated with flowers in parts of Spain.

EASTER

Most communities observe Easter in some form with pomp and solemnity. It is heralded by the Palm Sunday processions. The most impressive of these is in Elx, where intricate sculptures are woven from blanched leaves cropped from the most extensive forest of palm trees in Europe *(see p261)*.

The best Semana Santa (Easter Week) processions are held in Seville *(see p431)*, Granada, Málaga, Murcia and Valladolid. Brotherhoods of robed men carry *pasos*, huge sculptures depicting the Virgin, Christ or scenes of the Passion, through the streets. They are accompanied by people dressed as biblical characters or penitents, in tall conical hats. In some towns passion plays are acted out. In others, people carry heavy crosses. Sometimes the centuries-old ritual of self-flagellation can be witnessed.

The Brotherhood of Candlemas, Semana Santa (Easter Week) in Seville

SUMMER FIESTAS

The first major fiesta of the summer is Pentecost (also known as Whitsun), in May or June, and its most famous celebration is at El Rocío *(see p463)*, where many thousands of people gather in a frenzy of religious devotion.

At Corpus Christi (in May or June) the consecrated host is carried in procession through many cities in an ornate silver monstrance. The route of the procession is often covered with a carpet of flowers. The main Corpus Christi celebrations take place in Valencia, Toledo and Granada.

On Midsummer's Eve, bonfires are lit all over Spain, especially in the areas along the Mediterranean coast, to herald the celebration of St John the Baptist on 24 June.

During Los Sanfermines *(see p128)* in Pamplona in July, young people run through the streets in front of six bulls.

The Virgin of Carmen, who is revered as the patron of fishermen, is honoured in many ports on 16 July.

The important Catholic holiday of Assumption Day, 15 August, is marked by a huge number and variety of fiestas.

The losers end up in the harbour in Denia's July fiesta *(see p255)*

AUTUMN FIESTAS

There are few fiestas in autumn, but in most wine regions the grape harvest is fêted. The annual pig slaughter has become a jubilant public event in some villages, especially in Extremadura. In Galicia it is traditional to roast chestnuts on street bonfires.

On All Saints' Day, 1 November, people remember the dead by visiting cemeteries to lay flowers, especially chrysanthemums, on graves.

CHRISTMAS AND NEW YEAR

Nochebuena (Christmas Eve) is the main Christmas celebration, when families gather for an evening meal before attending Midnight Mass, known as *misa del gallo* (Mass of the rooster). During the Christmas period, *belenes* (crib scenes) of painted figurines abound. You may also see a "living crib", peopled by costumed actors.

Spain's "April Fools' Day" is 28 December, when people play practical jokes on each other. Clown-like characters may make fun of passers-by.

To celebrate New Year's Eve *(Noche Vieja)*, crowds gather beneath the clock in Madrid's central square, the Puerta del Sol *(see p272)*. Traditionally people eat 12 grapes, one on each chime of midnight, to bring good luck for the year.

Epiphany, on 6 January, is celebrated with parades of the Three Kings through the streets of villages and towns the evening before.

WINTER FIESTAS

Animals hold centre stage in a variety of fiestas on 17 January, the Day of St Anthony, patron saint of animals, when pets and livestock are blessed by priests.

St Agatha, the patron saint of married women, is honoured on 5 February when women, for once, are the protagonists of many fiestas. In Zamarramala (Segovia), for example, women take over the mayor's privileges and powers for this particular day *(see p368)*.

St Anthony's Day in Villanueva de Alcolea (Castellón province)

CARNIVAL

Carnival, in February or early March (depending on the date of Easter), brings a chance for a street party as winter comes to an end and before Lent begins. The biggest celebrations are held in Santa Cruz de Tenerife *(see p536)* – comparable with those of Rio de Janeiro – and in Cádiz *(see p463)*. Carnival was prohibited by the Franco regime because of its licentiousness and frivolity. It ends on or after Ash Wednesday with the Burial of the Sardine, a "funeral" in which a mock sardine, representing winter, is ritually burned or buried.

A spectacularly costumed choir singing during Carnival in Cádiz

SPAIN THROUGH THE YEAR

Festivals, cultural events and sports competitions crowd the calendar in Spain. Even small villages have at least one traditional fiesta, lasting a week or more, when parades, bullfights and fireworks displays replace work *(see pp38–9)*. Many rural and coastal towns celebrate the harvest or fishing catch with a gastronomic fair at which you can sample local produce.

Matador with a cape playing a bull

Music, dance, drama and film festivals are held in Spain's major cities throughout the year. Meanwhile, the country's favourite outdoor sports – football, basketball, cycling, sailing, golf and tennis – culminate in several national and international championships. It is a good idea to confirm specific dates of events with the local tourist board as some vary from year to year.

SPRING

Life in Spain moves outdoors with the arrival of spring, and terrace-cafés begin to fill with people. The countryside is at its best as wild flowers bloom, and irrigation channels flow to bring water to the newly sown crops. The important Easter holiday is a time of solemn processions throughout the country.

Feria del Caballo (Festival of the Horses) in Jerez de la Frontera

MARCH

International Vintage Car Rally *(usually first Sun)*, from Barcelona to Sitges. More than 60 vintage cars make this annual 45-km (28-mile) journey.
Las Fallas *(15–19 Mar)*, Valencia *(see p255)*. This spectacular fiesta also marks the start of the bullfighting *(see pp36–7)* season.
Fiestas *(end Feb or mid-Mar)*, Castellón de la Plana. All in honour of Mary Magdalene.

APRIL

Spanish Motorcycle Grand Prix *(Apr)*, Jerez de la Frontera race track.
Religious Music Week *(Easter week, from Passion Sat)*, Cuenca.
Trofeo Conde de Godó *(mid-Apr)*, Barcelona. Spain's international tennis championship.
Moors and Christians *(21–24 Apr)*, Alcoi *(see p258)*. This colourful costumed event celebrates the Christian victory over the Moors in 1276.
April Fair *(two weeks after Easter)*, Seville. Exuberant Andalusian fiesta *(see p431)*.
Feria Nacional del Queso *(late Apr/early May)*, Trujillo (Cáceres). A festival celebrating Spanish cheese *(see p407)*.

MAY

Feria del Caballo *(first week)*, Jerez de la Frontera. Horse fair showing Andalusia at its most traditional, with fine horses and beautiful women in flamenco dresses.
Fiestas de San Isidro *(8–15 May)*, Madrid *(see p290)*. Bullfights at Las Ventas bullring are the highlights of the taurine year.
Spanish Formula One Grand Prix *(May/Jun)*, Montmeló circuit, Barcelona. International motor race.
Madrid Autumn Festival in Spring *(May/Jun)*. Drama, dance and music by national and foreign companies.

Onlookers lining the street during the Vuelta Ciclista a España

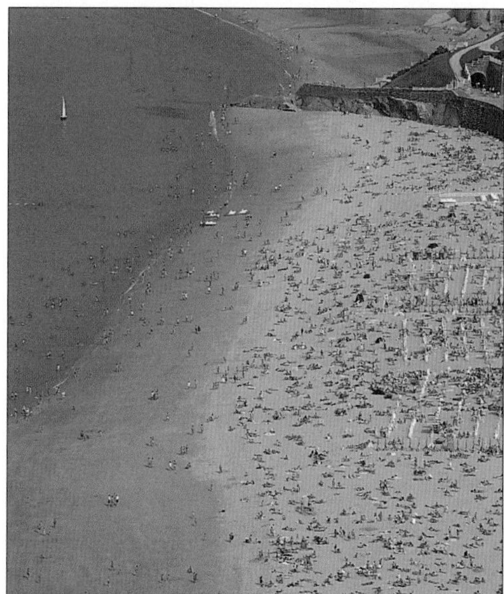

San Sebastián, one of the most popular resorts on the north coast

SUMMER

August is Spain's big holiday season. The cities empty as Spaniards flock to the coast or to their second homes in the hills. Their numbers are swelled by millions of foreign tourists, and beaches and camp sites are often full to bursting. As the heat starts in the centre and south, entertainment often takes place only in the evening, when the temperature has dropped. In late summer the harvest begins and there are gastronomic fiestas everywhere to celebrate food and drink, from the fishing catches of the north coast to the sausages of the Balearic Islands.

The pouring and tasting of cider in Asturias's Cider Festival

JUNE

International Festival of Music and Dance *(Jun–Jul)*, Granada. Classical music and ballet staged in the Alhambra and the Generalife.
Grec Arts Festival *(late Jun–Aug)*, Barcelona. Both Spanish and international theatre, music and dance.
A Rapa das Bestas *(Jun, Jul, Aug)*, Pontevedra, La Coruña and Lugo provinces (Galicia). Wild horses are rounded up so that their manes and tails can be cut *(see p99)*.
Classical Theatre Festival *(end Jun–Aug)*, Mérida. Staged in the Roman theatre and amphitheatre *(see p410)*.

JULY

Guitar Festival *(timing varies)*, Córdoba. From classical to flamenco *(see pp424–5)*.
International Classical Theatre Festival of Almagro *(1–25 Jul)*. Spanish and classical repertoire in one of the oldest theatres in Europe *(see p399)*.
Cider Festival *(second weekend)*, Nava (Asturias). Includes traditional cider-pouring competitions.
International Jazz Festivals in San Sebastián *(third week)*, Getxo *(first week)* and Vitoria *(mid-Jul)*.
Pyrenean Folklore Festival *(late Jul/early Aug, odd years)*, Jaca (Aragón). Folk costumes, music and dance.
Certamen Internacional de Habaneras y Polifonía *(late Jul–early Aug)*, Torrevieja (Alicante). Musical competition of 19th-century seafarers' songs.

AUGUST

International Festival of Santander *(Aug)*. Celebration of music, dance and theatre.
HM the King's International Cup *(first week)*, Palma de Mallorca. Sailing competition in which Juan Carlos I participates.
Descent of the Río Sella *(first Sat)*. Canoe race in Asturias from Arriondas to Ribadesella *(see p107)*.
Assumption Day *(15 Aug)* The Assumption is celebrated throughout the country.

Participants in the Descent of the Río Sella canoe race

Semanas Grandes *(mid-Aug)*, Bilbao and San Sebastián. "Great Weeks" of sporting and cultural events.
Misteri d'Elx *(14–15 Aug; also 29 Oct–1 Nov during Medieval Festival)*, Elx *(see p265)*. Unique liturgical drama featuring spectacular special effects.

Vines and the village of Larouco in the Valdeorras wine region of Galicia *(see p78)* in autumn

AUTUMN

Autumn usually brings rain after the heat of summer, and with the high tourist season over, a large number of resorts practically close down. Harvest festivities continue, however, and the most important celebrations are in honour of the grape. The first pressings are blessed and, in some places, wine is served for free.

Wild mushrooms

In woodland areas, freshly picked wild mushrooms start to appear in various dishes on local restaurant menus. The hunting season begins in the middle of October and runs until February. Autumn is also the start of the new drama and classical music seasons in the major cities of Spain.

SEPTEMBER

Vuelta Ciclista a España *(Sep)*. Annual bicycle race around Spain.
Grape Harvest *(mid-Sep)*, Jerez de la Frontera. Celebration of the new crop in the country's sherry capital.
San Sebastián Film Festival *(mid- to late Sep)*. Gathering of film-makers *(see p123)*.
Festival de la Mercé *(17–24 Sep)*, Barcelona. Free concerts and folkloric events.
Bienal de Arte Flamenco *(early Sep–early Oct, even years only)*, Seville. Top flamenco artists perform.

OCTOBER

Día de la Hispanidad *(12 Oct)*. Spain's national holiday marks Columbus's discovery of America in 1492. The biggest celebration in the country is the exuberant fiesta of Día del Pilar in Zaragoza *(see p239)*, which marks the end of the bullfighting year.
Moors and Christians *(mid-Oct)*, Callosa D'en Sarria (Alicante). Parades in honour of the local madonna.

Driving down the fairway at one of Spain's golfing championships

Saffron Festival *(last weekend)*, Consuegra (Toledo).

Lana Turner on centre-stage at the San Sebastián Film Festival

NOVEMBER

All Saints' Day *(1 Nov)*. This marks the start of the *matanza* (pig slaughter) in rural Spain.
Os Magostos *(11 Nov)*. Chestnut-harvest fairs abound in Galicia.
Latin American Film Festival *(mid-Nov for one week)*, Huelva *(see p462)*.
National Flamenco Competition *(mid-Nov for two weeks)*, Córdoba. Song, dance and guitar performances.

Assumption Day in La Alberca (Salamanca)

PUBLIC HOLIDAYS

Besides marking the national holidays below, each region *(comunidad autónoma)* celebrates its own holiday and every town and village has at least one other fiesta each year. If a holiday falls on a Tuesday or a Thursday, some people also choose to take holidays on the intervening Monday or Friday, making a long weekend called a *puente* ("bridge").

Año Nuevo *(New Year's Day)* (1 Jan)
Día de los Tres Reyes *(Epiphany)* (6 Jan)
Jueves Santo *(Maundy Thursday)* (Mar/Apr)
Viernes Santo *(Good Friday)* (Mar/Apr)
Día de Pascua *(Easter Sunday)* (Mar/Apr)
Día del Trabajo *(Labour Day)* (1 May)
Asunción *(Assumption Day)* (15 Aug)
Día de la Hispanidad *(National Day)* (12 Oct)
Todos los Santos *(All Saints' Day)* (1 Nov)
Día de la Constitución *(Constitution Day)* (6 Dec)
Inmaculada Concepción *(Immaculate Conception)* (8 Dec)
Navidad *(Christmas Day)* (25 Dec)

WINTER

Winter varies greatly from region to region. In the mountains, snowfalls bring skiers to the slopes; while in lower areas, olive and orange picking are in full swing. The higher parts of Central Spain can become very cold. Andalusia, the east coast and the Balearic Islands have cool nights but often sunny days. The winter warmth of the Canary Islands brings the high tourist season. Christmas is a special time of celebration – an occasion for families to reunite, share food and attend religious celebrations.

"El Gordo", the largest Spanish lottery prize, being drawn

Skiers in the Sierra de Guadarrama, north of Madrid *(see p329)*

DECEMBER

El Gordo *(22 Dec)*. Spain's largest lottery prize, "the Fat One", is drawn *(see p622)*.
Noche Buena *(24 Dec)* is a family Christmas Eve, followed by Midnight Mass.
Santos Inocentes *(28 Dec)*, Spain's version of April Fools' Day, when people play tricks.
Noche Vieja *(31 Dec)*. New Year's Eve is most celebrated in Madrid's Puerta del Sol.

JANUARY

Día de los Tres Reyes *(6 Jan)*. On the eve of the Epiphany, the Three Kings parade through town, throwing sweets to the children.
La Tamborrada *(19–20 Jan)*, San Sebastián. Drumming en masse in traditional costume.
Canary Islands International Music Festival *(Jan–Feb)*. Classical concerts are held on La Palma and Tenerife.

FEBRUARY

La Endiablada *(2–3 Feb)*, Almonacid del Marquesado (Cuenca). Townsfolk dress as devils in honour of San Blas.
ARCO *(mid-Feb)*, Madrid. International contemporary art fair.
Pasarela Cibeles (Fashion Week) *(mid-Feb)*, Madrid. Women's and men's fashion shows in the capital.
Carnival *(Feb/Mar)*. Final fiesta before Lent, with colourful costumes. Those in Santa Cruz de Tenerife and Cádiz are among the best.

The Climate of Spain

Spain's large landmass, with its extensive high plateaus and mountain ranges, and the influences of the Mediterranean and Atlantic produce a wide range of climatic variation, especially in winter. The north is wettest year round, the eastern and southern coasts and the islands have mild winters, while winter temperatures in the interior are often below freezing. Summers everywhere are hot, except in upland areas.

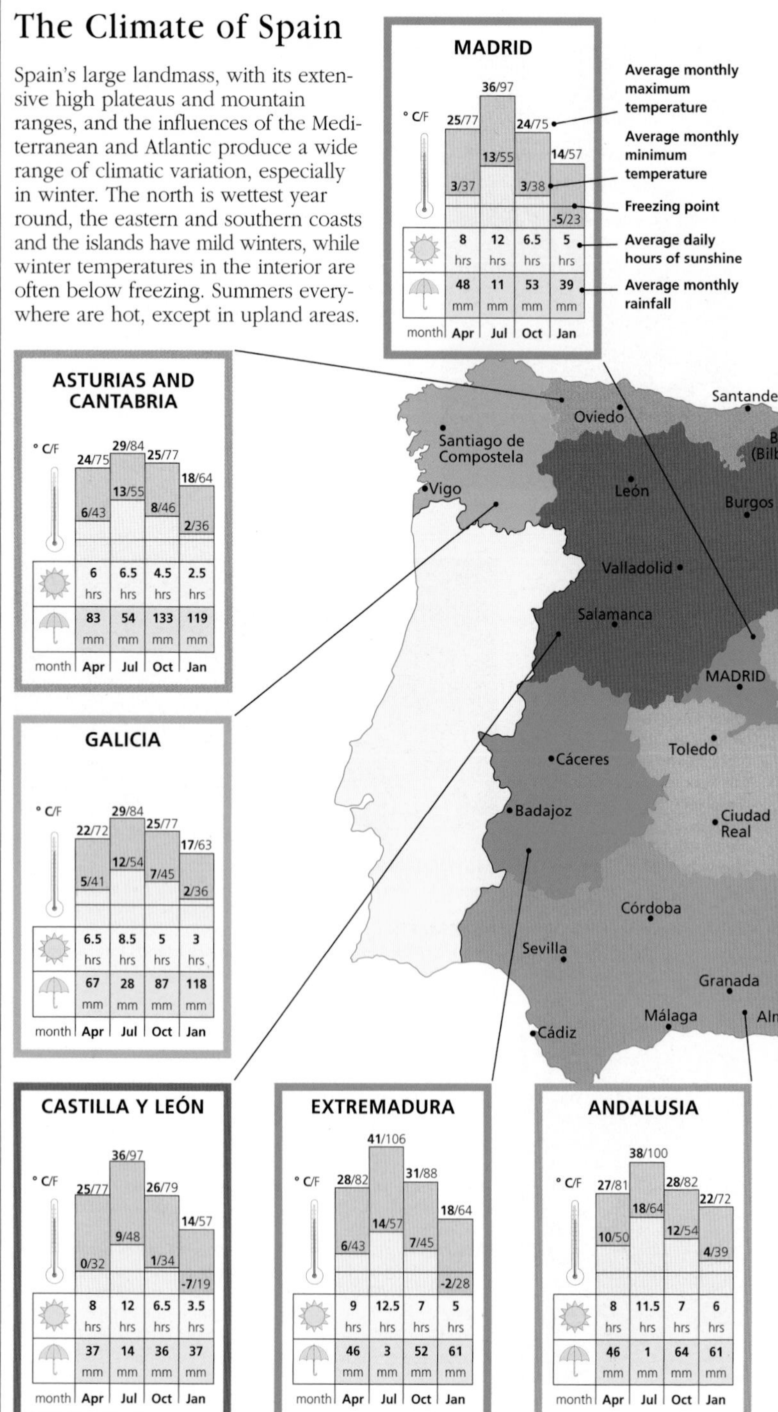

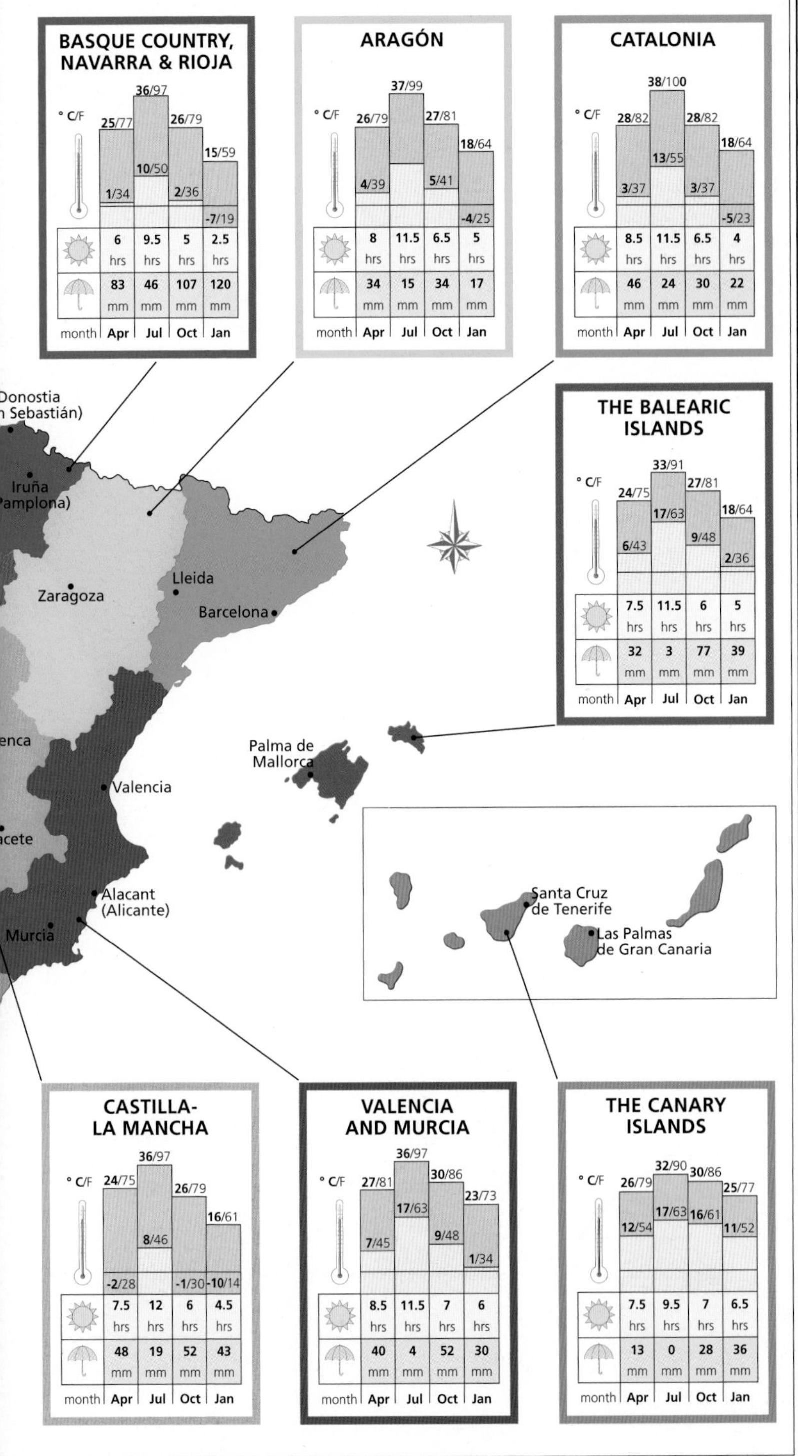
BASQUE COUNTRY, NAVARRA & RIOJA
° C/F
25/77 36/97 26/79 15/59
1/34 10/50 2/36 -7/19
6 hrs 9.5 hrs 5 hrs 2.5 hrs
83 mm 46 mm 107 mm 120 mm
month Apr Jul Oct Jan
ARAGÓN
° C/F
26/79 37/99 27/81 18/64
4/39 5/41 -4/25
8 hrs 11.5 hrs 6.5 hrs 5 hrs
34 mm 15 mm 34 mm 17 mm
month Apr Jul Oct Jan
CATALONIA
° C/F
28/82 38/100 28/82 18/64
3/37 13/55 3/37 -5/23
8.5 hrs 11.5 hrs 6.5 hrs 4 hrs
46 mm 24 mm 30 mm 22 mm
month Apr Jul Oct Jan
THE BALEARIC ISLANDS
° C/F
24/75 33/91 27/81 18/64
6/43 17/63 9/48 2/36
7.5 hrs 11.5 hrs 6 hrs 5 hrs
32 mm 3 mm 77 mm 39 mm
month Apr Jul Oct Jan
Donostia
n Sebastián)
Iruña
Pamplona)
Zaragoza
Lleida
Barcelona
enca
Palma de
Mallorca
Valencia
acete
Alacant
(Alicante)
Murcia
Santa Cruz
de Tenerife
Las Palmas
de Gran Canaria
CASTILLA-LA MANCHA
° C/F
24/75 36/97 26/79 16/61
-2/28 8/46 -1/30 -10/14
7.5 hrs 12 hrs 6 hrs 4.5 hrs
48 mm 19 mm 52 mm 43 mm
month Apr Jul Oct Jan
VALENCIA AND MURCIA
° C/F
27/81 36/97 30/86 23/73
7/45 17/63 9/48 1/34
8.5 hrs 11.5 hrs 7 hrs 6 hrs
40 mm 4 mm 52 mm 30 mm
month Apr Jul Oct Jan
THE CANARY ISLANDS
° C/F
26/79 32/90 30/86 25/77
12/54 17/63 16/61 11/52
7.5 hrs 9.5 hrs 7 hrs 6.5 hrs
13 mm 0 mm 28 mm 36 mm
month Apr Jul Oct Jan

THE HISTORY OF SPAIN

The Iberian Peninsula, first inhabited around 800,000 BC, has long been subject to foreign influences. From the 11th century BC it was colonized by sophisticated eastern Mediterranean civilizations, starting with the Phoenicians, then the Greeks and Carthaginians.

The Romans arrived in 218 BC to fight the Carthaginians, thus sparking off the Second Punic War. They harvested the peninsula's agricultural and mineral wealth and established cities with aqueducts, temples and theatres.

With the fall of the Roman Empire in the early 5th century AD, Visigothic invaders from the north assumed power. Their poor political organization, however, made them easy prey to the Moors from North Africa. In the 8th century, the peninsula came almost entirely under Moorish rule. Europe's only major Muslim territory, the civilization of Al Andalus excelled in mathematics, geography, astronomy and poetry. In the 9th and 10th centuries Córdoba was Europe's leading city.

From the 11th century, northern Christian kingdoms initiated a military reconquest of Al Andalus. The marriage, in 1469, of Fernando of Aragón and Isabel of Castile, the so-called Catholic Monarchs, led to Spanish unity. They took Granada, the last Moorish kingdom, in 1492. Columbus discovered the Americas in the same year, opening the way for the Spanish conquistadors, who plundered the civilizations of the New World.

Pre-Columbian gold statue

The succeeding Habsburg dynasty spent the riches from the New World in endless foreign wars. Spain's decline was exacerbated by high inflation and religious oppression. Although the Enlightenment in the late 18th century created a climate of learning, Spain's misfortunes continued into the next century with an invasion by Napoleon's troops and the loss of her American colonies. A new radicalism began to emerge, creating a strong Anarchist movement. The political instability of the late 19th and early 20th centuries led to dictatorship in the 1920s and a republic in the 1930s, which was destroyed by the Spanish Civil War. Victorious General Franco ruled by repression until his death in 1975. Since then Spain has been a constitutional monarchy.

Bullfighting in Madrid's Plaza Mayor in the 17th century

◁ **Moors paying homage to Fernando and Isabel, the 15th-century Catholic Monarchs**

Prehistoric Spain

Helmet of Celtiberian warrior

The Iberian Peninsula was first inhabited by hunter-gatherers around 800,000 BC. They were eclipsed by a Neolithic farming population from 5000 BC. First in a wave of settlers from over the Mediterranean, the Phoenicians landed in 1100 BC, to be followed by the Greeks and Carthaginians. Invading Celts mixed with native Iberian tribes (forming the Celtiberians). They proved a formidable force against the Romans, the next conquerors of Spain.

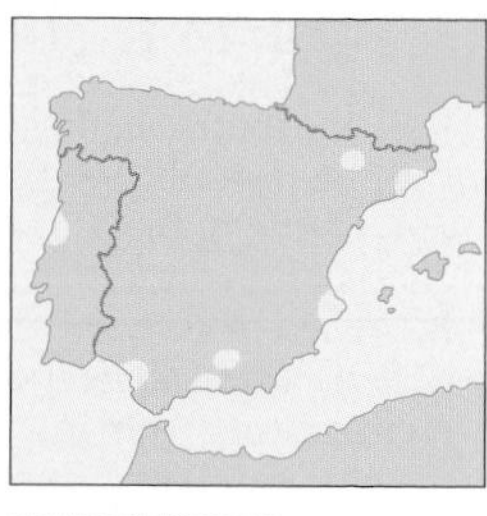
SPAIN IN 5000 BC

Neolithic farming settlements

Iron Dagger *(6th century BC)*
Weapons, like this dagger from Burgos, represent the later Iron Age, in contrast to earlier metal objects which were for domestic use.

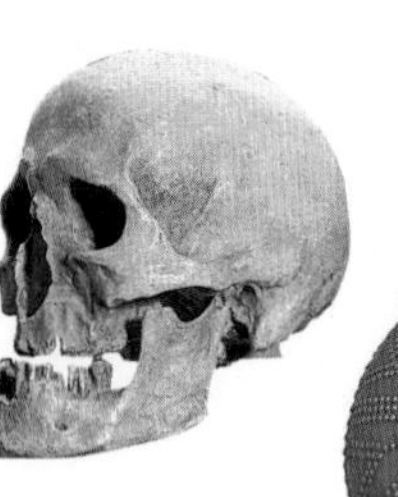
Stone Age Man
This skull belongs to a Palaeolithic man, who hunted deer and bison with tools made of wood and stone.

La Dama de Elche
Dating from the 4th century BC, this stone statue is a fine example of Iberian art. Her austere beauty reveals traces of Greek influence.

The 28 bracelets have perforations and moulded decorations.

Small silver bottle

Incised geometric pattern

THE VILLENA TREASURE

Discovered in 1963 during works in Villena, near Alicante, this Bronze Age find consists of 66 dazzling objects mostly of gold, including bowls, bottles and jewellery *(see p260)*. The treasure dates from around 1000 BC.

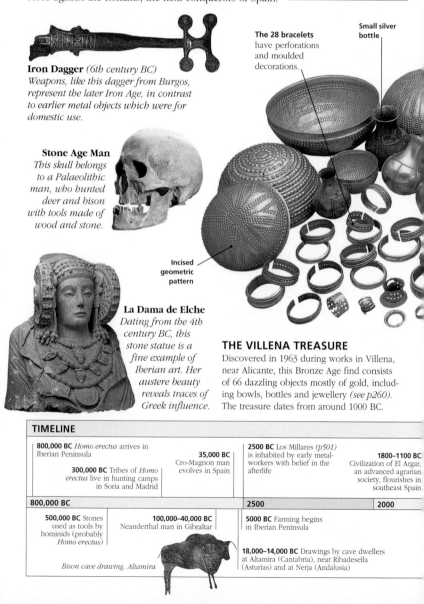

TIMELINE

800,000 BC *Homo erectus* arrives in Iberian Peninsula

300,000 BC Tribes of *Homo erectus* live in hunting camps in Soria and Madrid

35,000 BC Cro-Magnon man evolves in Spain

2500 BC Los Millares *(p501)* is inhabited by early metal-workers with belief in the afterlife

1800–1100 BC Civilization of El Argar, an advanced agrarian society, flourishes in southeast Spain

800,000 BC | **2500** | **2000**

500,000 BC Stones used as tools by hominids (probably *Homo erectus*)

100,000–40,000 BC Neanderthal man in Gibraltar

Bison cave drawing, Altamira

5000 BC Farming begins in Iberian Peninsula

18,000–14,000 BC Drawings by cave dwellers at Altamira (Cantabria), near Ribadesella (Asturias) and at Nerja (Andalusia)

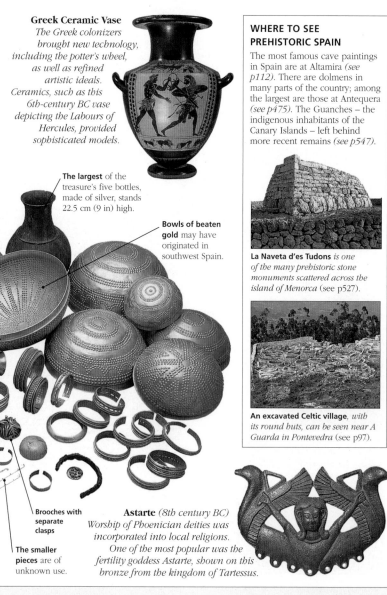

Greek Ceramic Vase
The Greek colonizers brought new technology, including the potter's wheel, as well as refined artistic ideals. Ceramics, such as this 6th-century BC vase depicting the Labours of Hercules, provided sophisticated models.

The largest of the treasure's five bottles, made of silver, stands 22.5 cm (9 in) high.

Bowls of beaten gold may have originated in southwest Spain.

Brooches with separate clasps

The smaller pieces are of unknown use.

Astarte *(8th century BC)*
Worship of Phoenician deities was incorporated into local religions. One of the most popular was the fertility goddess Astarte, shown on this bronze from the kingdom of Tartessus.

WHERE TO SEE PREHISTORIC SPAIN

The most famous cave paintings in Spain are at Altamira *(see p112)*. There are dolmens in many parts of the country; among the largest are those at Antequera *(see p475)*. The Guanches – the indigenous inhabitants of the Canary Islands – left behind more recent remains *(see p547)*.

La Naveta d'es Tudons *is one of the many prehistoric stone monuments scattered across the island of Menorca* (see p527).

An excavated Celtic village, *with its round huts, can be seen near A Guarda in Pontevedra* (see p97).

Phoenician gold ornament

1100 BC Phoenicians believed to have founded modern-day Cádiz

600 BC Greek colonists settle on northeast coast of Spain

228 BC Carthaginians occupy south-east Spain

1500 | 1000 | 500

1200 BC The "talaiotic" people of Menorca erect three unique types of stone building: *taulas, talaiots* and *navetas*

Taula *in Menorca*

775 BC Phoenicians establish colonies along the coast near Málaga

300 BC *La Dama de Elche* is carved *(p296)*

700 BC Semi-mythical kingdom of Tartessus thought to be at its height

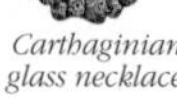

Carthaginian glass necklace

Romans and Visigoths

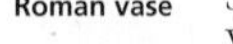

Roman vase

The Romans came to Spain to fight the Carthaginians and take possession of the region's huge mineral wealth. Later, Hispania's wheat and olive oil became mainstays of the empire. It took 200 years to subdue the peninsula, which was divided in three provinces: Tarraconensis, Lusitania and Baetica. In time, cities with Roman infrastructure developed. The fall of the empire in the 5th century left Spain in the hands of the Visigoths, invaders from the north. Politically disorganized, they fell victim to the Moors in 711.

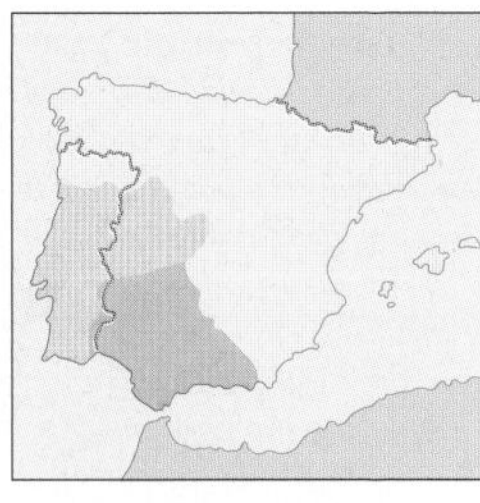

SPAIN (HISPANIA) IN 5 BC

- *Tarraconensis*
- *Lusitania*
- *Baetica*

Trajan *(AD 53–117)*
Trajan was the first Hispanic Roman emperor (AD 98–117). He improved public administration and expanded the empire.

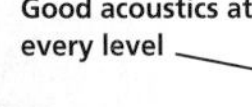

Seneca *(4 BC–AD 65)*
Born in Córdoba, the Stoic philosopher Seneca lived in Rome as Nero's adviser.

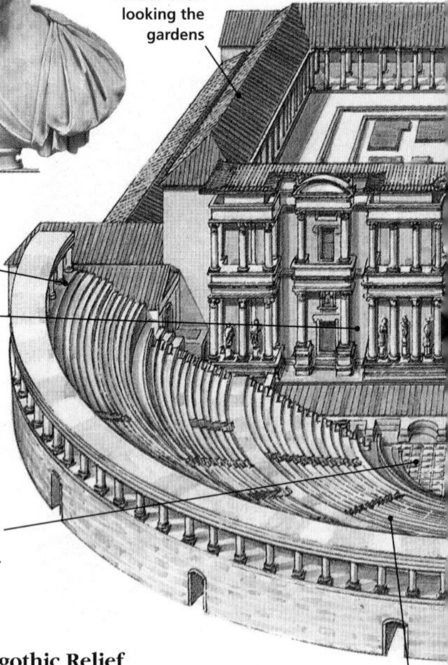

Portico overlooking the gardens

Good acoustics at every level

A Classical façade served as a backdrop for tragedies. Additional scenery was used for comedies.

The *orchestra*, a semicircular open space for the choir

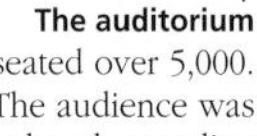

The auditorium seated over 5,000. The audience was placed according to social status.

Visigothic Relief
This crude Visigothic stone carving, based on a Roman relief, is in the 7th-century church of Quintanilla de las Viñas, near Burgos (p370).

TIMELINE

- **219 BC** Hannibal takes Saguntum *(p249)* for Carthaginians
- **218 BC** Scipio the Elder lands with a Roman army at Emporion *(p216)*. The Second Punic War begins
- **c.200 BC** Romans reach Gadir (modern Cádiz) after driving Carthaginians out of Hispania
- **155 BC** Lusitanian Wars begin. Romans invade Portugal
- **133 BC** Celt-Iberian Wars culminate in destruction of Numantia, Soria *(p377)*
- **82–72 BC** Roman Civil War. Pompey founds Pompaelo (Pamplona) in 75 BC
- **61 BC** Julius Caesar, governor of Hispania Ulterior, begins final conquest of northern Portugal and Galicia
- **26 BC** Emerita Augusta (Mérida) is founded and soon becomes capital of Lusitania
- **19 BC** Augustus takes Cantabria and Asturias, ending 200 years of war
- **AD 74** Emperor Vespasian grants Latin status to all towns in Hispania, completing process of Romanization

200 BC | 100 | AD 1 | AD 100

Hannibal

Gladiator Mosaic *Mosaics were used as decoration both indoors and out. Themes range from mythical episodes to portrayals of daily life. This 4th-century AD mosaic shows gladiators in action and has helpful labels to name the fighters and show who is dead or alive.*

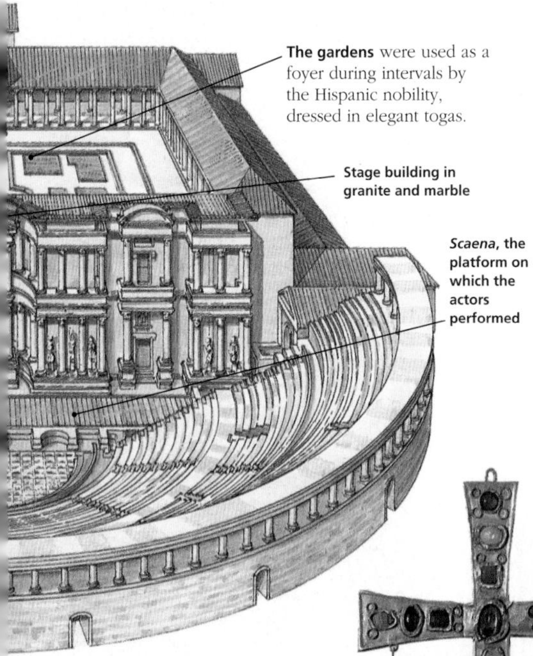

WHERE TO SEE ROMAN SPAIN

Like Mérida, Tarragona *(see p224)* has extensive Roman ruins and Itálica *(see p476)* is an excavated town. A magnificent Roman wall rings Lugo in Galicia *(see p99)*. Built in Trajan's rule, the bridge over the Tagus at Alcántara *(see p410)* has a temple on it.

Emporion *a Roman town, was built next to a former Greek colony in the 3rd century BC. The ruins include grand villas and a forum* (see p216).

Segovia's Roman aqueduct (see p365), *a huge monument with 163 arches, dates from the end of the 1st century AD.*

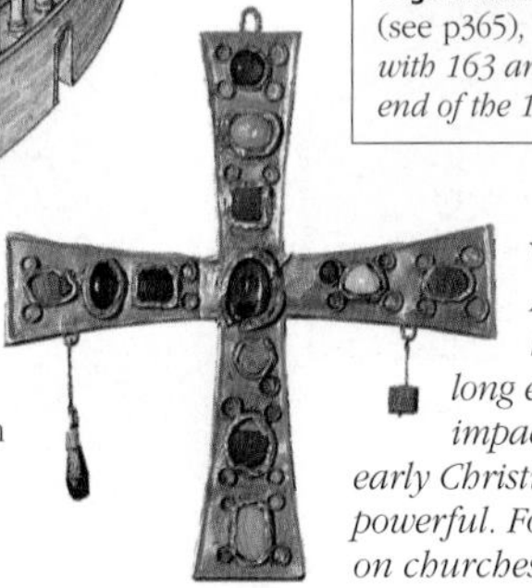

The gardens were used as a foyer during intervals by the Hispanic nobility, dressed in elegant togas.

Stage building in granite and marble

***Scaena*, the platform on which the actors performed**

ROMAN THEATRE, MÉRIDA

Theatre was an extremely popular form of entertainment in Hispania. This reconstruction shows the theatre at Mérida *(see p410)*, built in 16–15 BC.

Visigothic Cross *Although Visigothic kings seldom ruled long enough to make an impact on society, the early Christian Church grew powerful. Fortunes were spent on churches and religious art.*

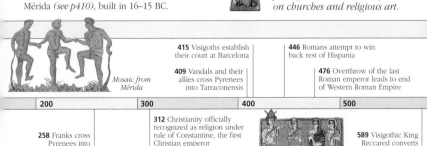

Mosaic from Mérida

415 Visigoths establish their court at Barcelona

409 Vandals and their allies cross Pyrenees into Tarraconensis

446 Romans attempt to win back rest of Hispania

476 Overthrow of the last Roman emperor leads to end of Western Roman Empire

200 | 300 | 400 | 500

258 Franks cross Pyrenees into Tarraconensis and sack Tarragona

312 Christianity officially recognized as religion under rule of Constantine, the first Christian emperor

The Codex Vigilianus, *a Christian manuscript*

589 Visigothic King Reccared converts from Arianism to Catholicism at Third Council of Toledo

Al Andalus: Muslim Spain

The arrival of Arab and Berber invaders from North Africa, and their defeat of the Visigoths, gave rise to the most brilliant civilization of early medieval Europe. These Muslim settlers, often known as the Moors, called Spain "Al Andalus". A rich and powerful caliphate was established in Córdoba and mathematics, science, architecture and the decorative arts flourished. The caliphate eventually broke up into small kingdoms or *taifas*. Meanwhile small Christian enclaves expanded in the north.

Alhambra Vase *(see p467)*

SPAIN IN AD 750

Extent of Moorish domination

Water Wheel
Moorish irrigation techniques, such as the water wheel, revolutionized agriculture. New crops, including oranges and rice, were introduced.

Astrolabe
Perfected by the Moors around AD 800, the astrolabe was used by navigators and astronomers.

Silver Casket of Hisham II
In the Caliphate of Córdoba, luxury objects of brilliant craftsmanship were worked in ivory, silver and bronze.

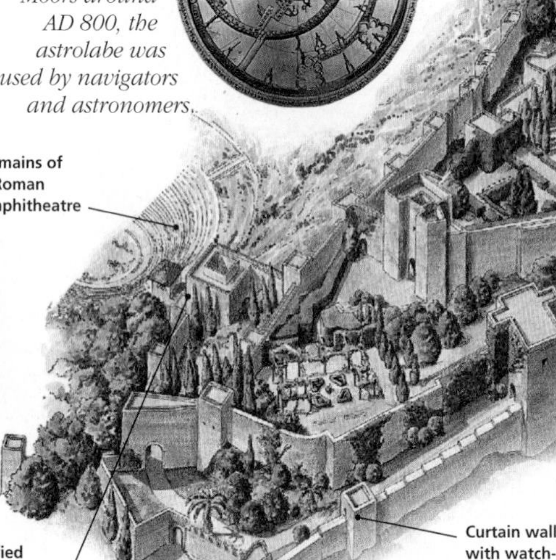

The palace, dating from the 11th century, was surrounded by patios, pools and gardens.

Remains of a Roman amphitheatre

Fortified entrance gate

Curtain walls with watchtowers

TIMELINE

711 Moors, led by Tariq, invade Spain and defeat Visigoths at battle of Guadalete

732 Moors' advance into France is halted by Charles Martel at Poitiers

778 Charlemagne's rearguard defeated by Basques at Roncesvalles *(p134)*

785 Building of great mosque at Córdoba begins

Charlemagne (742–814)

750 | 800 | 850

722 Led by Pelayo, Christians defeat Moors at Covadonga *(p109)*

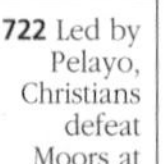

756 Abd al Rahman I proclaims independent emirate in Córdoba

744 Christians under Alfonso I of Asturias take León

Pelayo (718–37)

c.800 Tomb of St James (Santiago) is supposedly discovered at Santiago de Compostela

822 Abd al Rahman II begins 30-year rule marked by patronage of the arts and culture

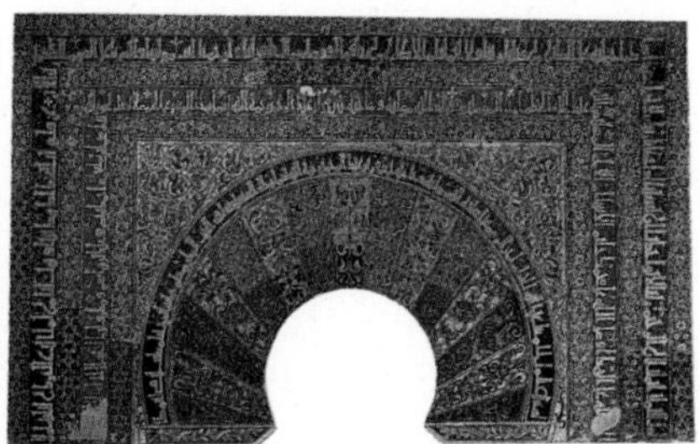

Puerta de Sabbath in Córdoba's Mezquita
Wealth and artistic brilliance were lavished on mosques, especially in Córdoba (see pp480–1). *Calligraphy was a major element in decoration.*

WHERE TO SEE MOORISH SPAIN

The finest Moorish buildings are in Andalusia, mainly in the cities of Córdoba *(see pp478–9)* and Granada *(see pp486–92)*. Almería *(see p501)* has a large, ruined *alcazaba* (castle). In Jaén *(see p493)* there are Moorish baths. Further north, in Zaragoza, is the castle-palace of La Aljafería *(see p237)*.

Medina Azahara (see p477), *sacked in the 11th century but partly restored, was the final residence of Córdoba's caliphs.*

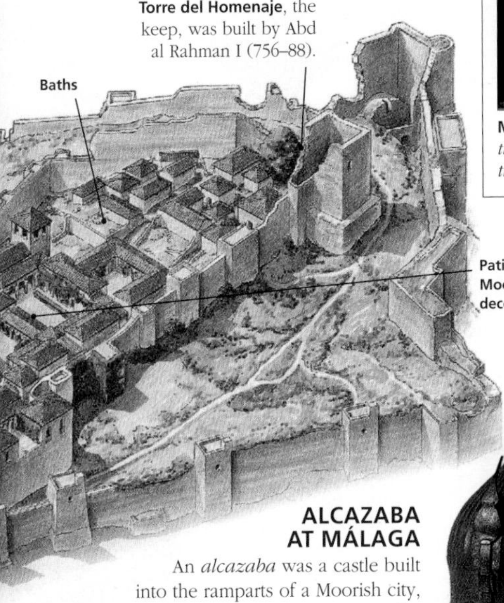

Torre del Homenaje, the keep, was built by Abd al Rahman I (756–88).

Moorish Sword
A fine example of late Moorish craftsmanship, this sword has a golden pommel. The blade is inscribed with Arabic writing.

Warrior Helmet
Practical as well as ornate, this Islamic nobleman's helmet, made of iron, gold and silver, incorporates inscriptions, a coat of arms and chain mail.

ALCAZABA AT MÁLAGA

An *alcazaba* was a castle built into the ramparts of a Moorish city, often protected by massive concentric walls. In Málaga *(see p474)* – the principal port of the Moorish kingdom of Granada – the vast Alcazaba was built in the 8–11th centuries on the site of a Roman fortress, and incorporated massive curtain walls and fortified gates.

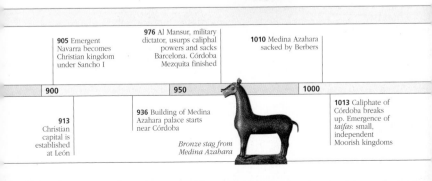

905 Emergent Navarra becomes Christian kingdom under Sancho I

913 Christian capital is established at León

936 Building of Medina Azahara palace starts near Córdoba

976 Al Mansur, military dictator, usurps caliphal powers and sacks Barcelona. Córdoba Mezquita finished

1010 Medina Azahara sacked by Berbers

1013 Caliphate of Córdoba breaks up. Emergence of *taifas*: small, independent Moorish kingdoms

900 | 950 | 1000

Bronze stag from Medina Azahara

The Reconquest

The infant Christian kingdoms in the north – León, Castile, Navarra, Aragón and Catalonia – advanced south gradually in the 11th century, fighting in the name of Christianity to regain land from the Moors. After the fall of Toledo in 1085, the struggle became increasingly a holy war. Militant North African Muslims – Almoravids and Almohads – rallied to the Moorish cause and ultimately took over Al Andalus in the 12th century. As the Christians pushed further south, soon only Granada remained under Moorish control.

Cross of the Knights of St James

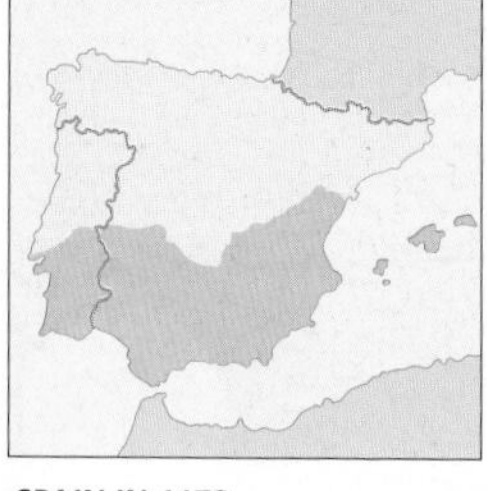

SPAIN IN 1173

Christian kingdoms

Al Andalus

Fernando I
Fernando formed the first Christian power bloc in 1037 by uniting Léon with Castile, which was emerging as a major military force.

Golden Goblet
The exquisite goblet (1063) of Doña Urraca, daughter of Alfonso VI, shows the quality of medieval Christian craftsmanship.

Alhambra, Palace of the Nasrids
Moorish art and architecture of singular beauty continued to be produced in the Nasrid kingdom of Granada. Its apogee is the exquisite Alhambra (see pp490–1).

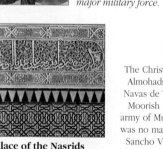

Armies of Castile, Aragón and Navarra

The Almohads fight until the bitter end, although many comrades lay slain.

LAS NAVAS DE TOLOSA

The Christian victory over the Almohads in the battle of Las Navas de Tolosa (1212) led to Moorish Spain's decline. The army of Muhammad II al Nasir was no match for the forces of Sancho VII of Navarra, Pedro II of Aragón and Alfonso VIII of Castile. A stained-glass window in Roncesvalles *(see p134)* depicts the battle.

TIMELINE

1037 León and Castile united for first time under Fernando I

1065 Death of Fernando I precipitates fratricidal civil war between his sons

1086 Almoravids respond to pleas for help from Moorish emirs by taking over *taifas* (splinter states)

Uniforms of military orders

1158 Establishment of the Order of Calatrava, the first military order of knights in Spain

1050 | 1100 | 1150 | 1200

El Cid

1085 Toledo falls to Christians under Alfonso VI of Castile

1094 The legendary El Cid *(see p370)* captures Valencia

1137 Ramón Berenguer IV of Catalonia marries Petronila of Aragón, uniting the two kingdoms under their son, Alfonso II

1143 Portugal becomes separate kingdom

1147 Almohads arrive in Al Andalus and make Seville their capital

1212 Combined Christian forces defeat Almohads at battle of Las Navas de Tolosa

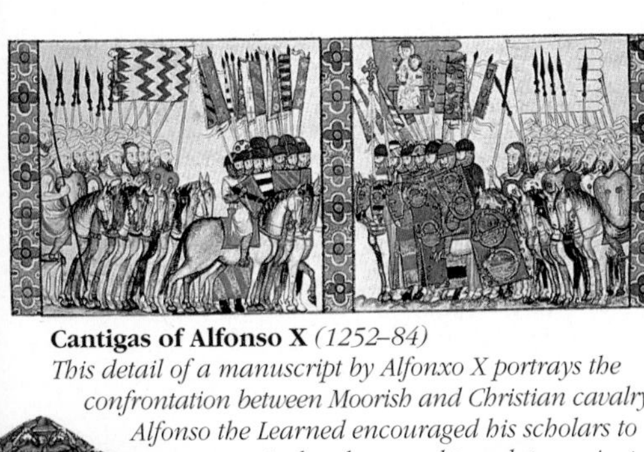

Cantigas of Alfonso X *(1252–84)*
This detail of a manuscript by Alfonxo X portrays the confrontation between Moorish and Christian cavalry. Alfonso the Learned encouraged his scholars to master Arab culture and translate ancient Greek manuscripts brought by the Moors.

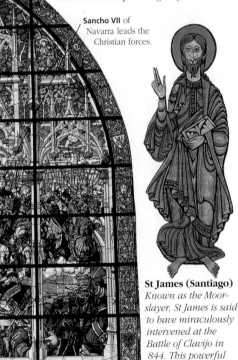

Sancho VII of Navarra leads the Christian forces.

St James (Santiago)
Known as the Moor-slayer, St James is said to have miraculously intervened at the Battle of Clavijo in 844. This powerful figurehead is the patron saint of Spain.

WHERE TO SEE MUDÉJAR SPAIN

The Mudéjares – Muslims who remained in territories under Christian occupation – created a distinctive architectural style distinguished by its ornamental work in brick, plaster and ceramics. Aragón, particularly Zaragoza *(see pp236–7)* and Teruel *(see pp240–41)*, boasts some of the finest Mudéjar buildings. Seville's Reales Alcázares is an exquisitely harmonious collection of patios and halls built under Pedro I *(see pp440–1)*.

The Mudéjar tower *of Teruel cathedral combines both brick and colourful ceramics to highly decorative effect.*

Santa María la Blanca (see p393), *a former synagogue and church, shows the fusion of cultures in medieval Toledo.*

1215 Foundation of Salamanca University

1230 Fernando III reunites Castile and León

Crest of Castile and León

1385 Portuguese defeat Castilians at Aljubarrota, crushing King Juan's aspirations to throne of Portugal

1388–9 Treaties end Spanish phase of Hundred Years War

1250 | 1300 | 1350 | 1400

1250 Toledo at its height as a centre of translation and learning, influenced by Alfonso X the Learned

1232 Granada becomes capital of future Nasrid kingdom. Building of the Alhambra begins

Alfonso X

1386 Invasion of Galicia by the English, ended by Bayonne Treaty

1401 Work starts in Seville on what was then the world's largest Gothic cathedral

The Catholic Monarchs

The foundation of the Spanish nation-state was laid by Isabel I of Castile and Fernando II of Aragón *(see p70)*. Uniting their lands in military, diplomatic and religious matters, the "Catholic Monarchs", as they are known, won back Granada, the last Moorish kingdom, from Boabdil. The Inquisition gave Spain a reputation for intolerance, yet in art and architecture brilliant progress was made and the voyages of Columbus opened up the New World.

Fernando of Aragón

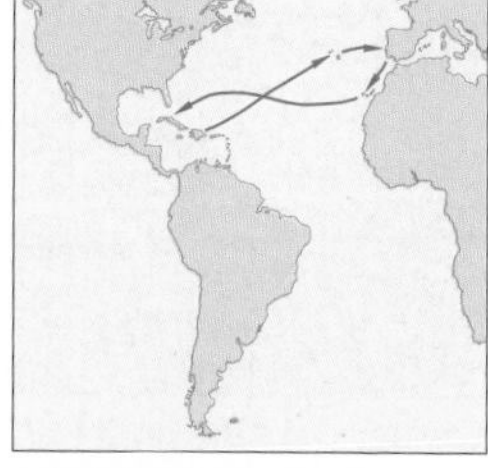

SPAIN'S EXPLORATION OF THE NEW WORLD

— *Route of Columbus's first voyage*

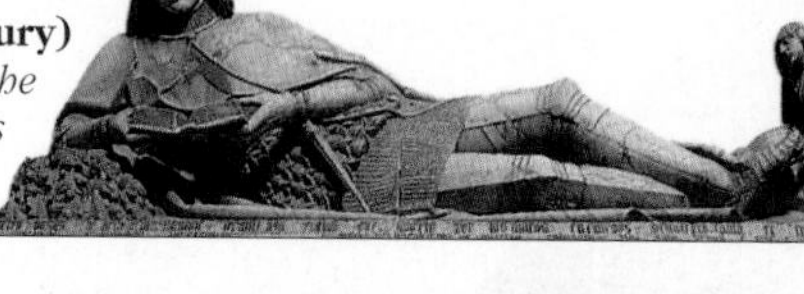

Tomb of El Doncel (15th century)
This effigy of a page who died in the fight for Granada combines ideals of military glory and learning (see p383).

The Inquisition
Active from 1478, the Inquisition (see p274) *persecuted those suspected of heresy with increasing vigour. This member of the Brotherhood of Death took victims to the stake.*

Boabdil, the grief-stricken king, moves forward to hand over the keys to Granada.

THE FALL OF GRANADA *(1492)*

This romantic interpretation by Francisco Pradilla (1846–1921) reflects the chivalry of Boabdil, ruler of Granada, as he surrenders the keys of the last Moorish kingdom to the Catholic Monarchs, Fernando and Isabel, following ten long years of war.

Baptizing Jews
After the Christian reconquest of Granada, Jews were forced to convert or leave Spain. The conversos (converted Jews) were often treated badly.

TIMELINE

1450

1451 Birth of Isabel of Castile

Fernando and Isabel on 15th-century gold coin

1454 Enrique IV, Isabel's half-brother, accedes to throne of Castile

1460

1465 Civil war erupts in Castile

1469 Marriage of Fernando and Isabel in Valladolid unites Castile and Aragón

1470

1474 Death of Enrique IV leads to civil war; Isabel triumphs over Juana la Beltraneja, Enrique's supposed daughter, to become queen

Torquemada

1478 Papal bull authorizes Castilian Inquisition with Tomás de Torquemada as Inquisitor General

1479 Fernando becomes Fernando II of Aragón

1480

Columbus Arriving in the Americas
The Catholic Monarchs financed Columbus's daring first voyage partly because they hoped for riches in return, but also because they expected him to convert infidels.

Boabdil
As the forlorn king left Granada, his mother reputedly said, "Don't cry as a child over what you could not defend as a man".

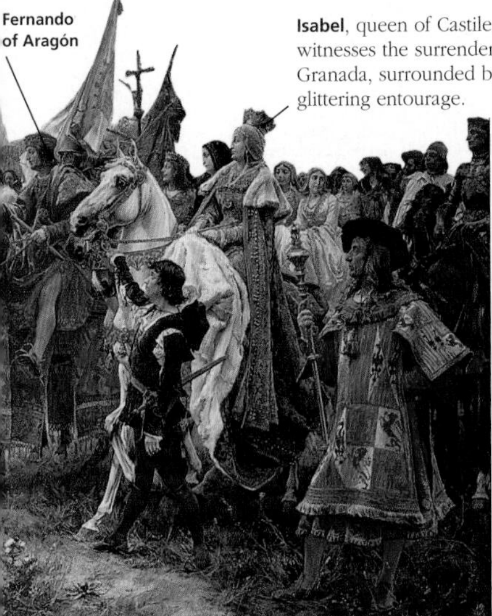

Fernando of Aragón

Isabel, queen of Castile, witnesses the surrender of Granada, surrounded by a glittering entourage.

Crown of Isabel
Worn at the surrender, Isabel's crown is now in her final resting place, the Capilla Real in Granada (see p486).

WHERE TO SEE GOTHIC ARCHITECTURE IN SPAIN

Spain has many great Gothic cathedrals, especially in Seville *(pp436–37)*, Burgos *(pp372–3)*, Barcelona *(pp148–9)*, Toledo *(pp392–3)* and Palma de Mallorca *(pp520–1)*. Secular buildings from this era include commodity exchanges like La Lonja in Valencia *(p251)* and castles *(pp344–5)*.

León cathedral (pp354–5) *has a west front covered in statuary. Here Christ is seen presiding over the Last Judgment.*

1494 Treaty of Tordesillas divides the New World territories between Portugal and Spain

1496 Foundation of Santo Domingo, on Hispaniola, first Spanish city in the Americas

1509 Cardinal Cisneros' troops attack Oran in Algeria and temporarily occupy it

Cardinal Cisneros

1490 | 1500 | 1510

1492 Fall of Granada after ten-year war. Columbus reaches America. Expulsion of Jews from Spain

Columbus's ship, the Santa María

1502 Unconverted Moors expelled from Spain

1504 Following death of Isabel, her daughter Juana la Loca becomes queen of Castile with Fernando as regent

1516 Death of Fernando

1512 Annexation of Navarra, leading to full unification of Spain

The Age of Discovery

Following Columbus's arrival in the Bahamas in 1492, the conquistadors went into Central and South America, conquering Mexico (1519), Peru (1532) and Chile (1541). In doing so, they destroyed Indian civilizations. In the 16th century, vast quantities of gold and silver flowed across the Atlantic to Spain. Carlos I and his son Felipe II spent some of it on battles to halt the spread of Protestantism in Europe, and in the Holy War against the Turks.

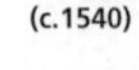

Aztec god (c.1540)

SPANISH EMPIRE IN 1580

Dominions of Felipe II

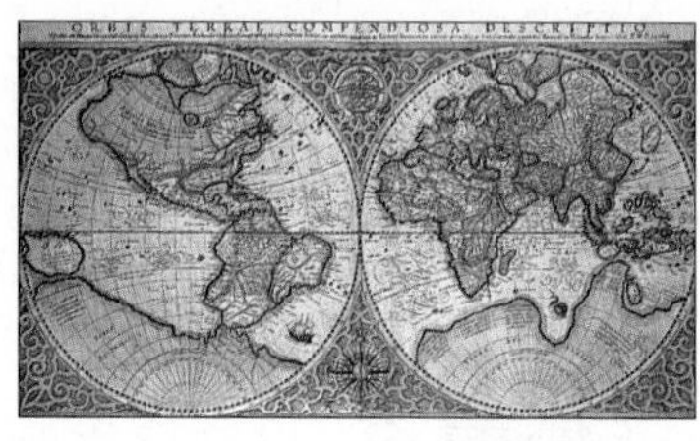

Mapping the World
This 16th-century German map reflects a new world, largely unknown to Europe before the era of conquistadors.

Aztec Mask
In their great greed and ignorance, the Spanish destroyed the empires and civilizations of the Aztecs in Mexico and the Incas in Peru.

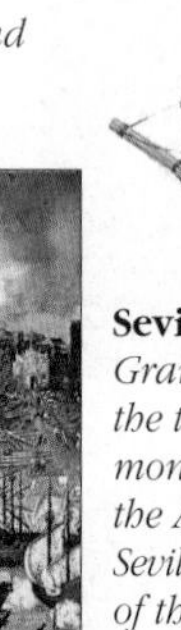

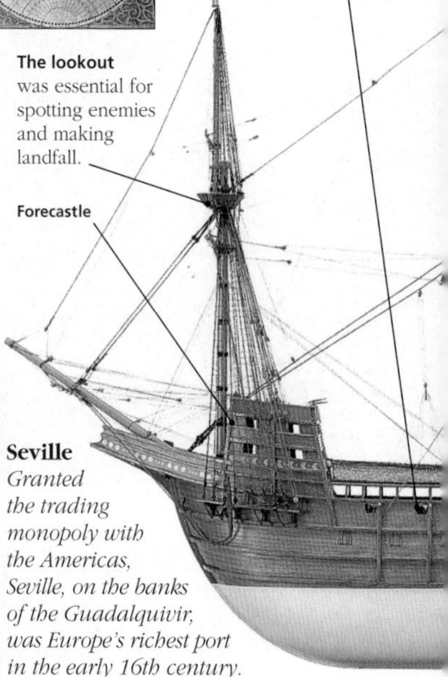

Galleons were armed with cannons as a defence against pirates and rival conquerors.

The lookout was essential for spotting enemies and making landfall.

Forecastle

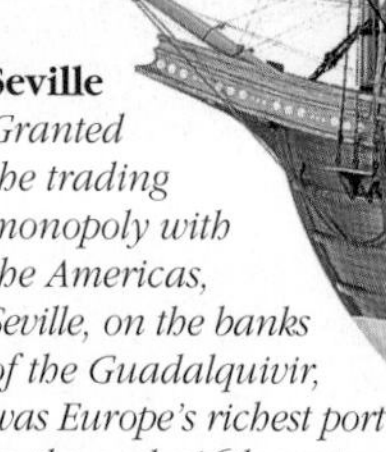

Seville
Granted the trading monopoly with the Americas, Seville, on the banks of the Guadalquivir, was Europe's richest port in the early 16th century.

TIMELINE

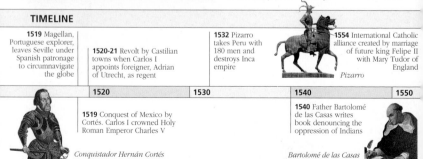

1519 Magellan, Portuguese explorer, leaves Seville under Spanish patronage to circumnavigate the globe

1520-21 Revolt by Castilian towns when Carlos I appoints foreigner, Adrian of Utrecht, as regent

1532 Pizarro takes Peru with 180 men and destroys Inca empire

Pizarro

1554 International Catholic alliance created by marriage of future king Felipe II with Mary Tudor of England

1520 | 1530 | 1540 | 1550

1519 Conquest of Mexico by Cortés. Carlos I crowned Holy Roman Emperor Charles V

Conquistador Hernán Cortés

1540 Father Bartolomé de las Casas writes book denouncing the oppression of Indians

Bartolomé de las Casas

Defeat of the Spanish Armada
Spain's self-esteem suffered a hard blow when its "invincible" 133-ship fleet was destroyed in an attempt to invade Protestant England in 1588.

NEW WORLD CROPS

Not only did Spain profit from the gold and silver brought across the ocean from the Americas, but also from an amazing range of new crops. Some, including potatoes and maize, were introduced for cultivation in Spain while others, such as tobacco and cacao, were mainly grown in native soil. Cocoa, from cacao beans, gained favour as a drink.

Cacao plant

Peruvian with exotic New World fruit

Armour of Felipe II
Felipe II (1556–98) was a cunning administrator, who claimed to rule the world with paper rather than military might.

Flag of Spain (until 1785)

Storage space for New World treasures

SPANISH GALLEON

Although sturdily built to carry New World treasure back to Spain, these ships were hard to manoeuvre except with the wind behind. They were often no match for smaller, swifter pirate vessels.

Carlos I *(1516–56)*
During his tumultuous 40-year reign, Carlos I (Holy Roman Emperor Charles V) often led his troops on the battlefield.

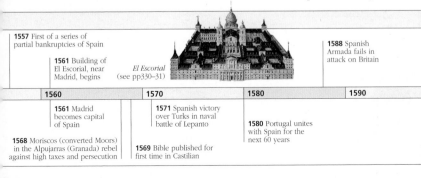

1557 First of a series of partial bankruptcies of Spain

1561 Building of El Escorial, near Madrid, begins

El Escorial (see pp330–31)

1588 Spanish Armada fails in attack on Britain

1560 | 1570 | 1580 | 1590

1561 Madrid becomes capital of Spain

1568 Moriscos (converted Moors) in the Alpujarras (Granada) rebel against high taxes and persecution

1569 Bible published for first time in Castilian

1571 Spanish victory over Turks in naval battle of Lepanto

1580 Portugal unites with Spain for the next 60 years

The Golden Age

Spain's Golden Age was a time of great artistic and literary achievement led by the painters – El Greco and Velázquez *(see pp32–3)* – and writers *(see pp34–35)*, especially Cervantes and the prolific dramatists, Lope de Vega and Calderón de la Barca. This brilliance occurred, however, against a background of economic deterioration and ruinous wars with the Low Countries and France. Spain was gradually losing its influence in Europe and the reigning house of Habsburg entered irreversible decline.

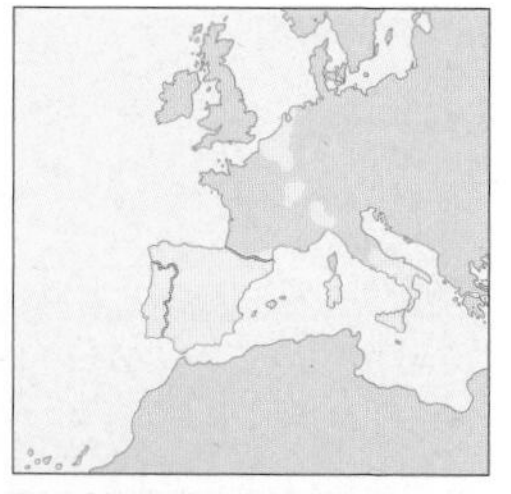

THE SPANISH EMPIRE IN EUROPE IN 1647

Spanish territories

Don Quixote and Sancho Panza
Cervantes' satire on chivalrous romance, Don Quixote, contrasts the fantasy of the main character with his servant's realism.

Duke of Lerma
This bronze statue depicts the Duke of Lerma (c.1550–1625), a favourite of King Felipe III.

A clock is a reminder of the inevitable passage of time.

The knight is dressed in mid-17th-century fashion.

Money represents worldly wealth.

THE KNIGHT'S DREAM *(1650)*

This painting, attributed to Antonio de Pereda, is on a familiar Golden Age theme: human vanity. A young gentleman sits asleep beside a table piled with objects symbolizing power, wealth and mortality. The pleasures of life, we are told, are no more real than a dream.

TIMELINE

Felipe III

1600 Capital temporarily moves to Valladolid

1605 Publication of first of two parts of Cervantes' Don Quixote

1609 Felipe III orders the expulsion of the Moriscos

1609 Lope de Vega publishes poem on the art of comic drama

1619 Construction of Plaza Mayor, Madrid

1621 Low Countries war resumes after 12-year truce

1622 Velázquez moves from Seville to Madrid to become court painter the following year

Lope de Vega (1562–1635)

1625 Capture of Breda, Netherlands, after one-year siege

1640 Secession of Portugal, amalgamated with Spain since 1580

1643 Fall of Count-Duke Olivares. Spain heavily defeated by France at battle of Rocroi

1600 | 1610 | 1620 | 1630 | 1640

Fiesta in the Plaza Mayor in Madrid
This famous square (see p273) *became the scene for pageants, royal celebrations, bullfights and executions, all overlooked from the balconies.*

An angel warns that death is near.

The banner says, "It [death] pierces perpetually, flies quickly and kills".

A mask symbolizes the Arts.

Weapons represent power.

The skull on the book shows death triumphant over learning.

SEVILLE SCHOOL OF ART

Seville's wealth, together with the patronage of the Church, made it a centre of the arts, second only to the royal court. Velázquez, who was born in Seville, trained under the painter Pacheco. Sculptor Juan Martínez Montañés and painters Zurbarán and Murillo created great works which are displayed in the Museo de Bellas Artes *(see p430)*.

San Diego de Alcalá Giving Food to the Poor **(c.1646) by Murillo**

Expulsion of the Moriscos
Although they had converted to Christianity, the last Moors were still expelled in 1609.

Surrender of Breda
Spain took the Dutch city of Breda on 5 June 1625 after a year-long siege. The event was later painted by Velázquez.

1652 Spanish troops regain Catalonia, following 12-year war with France

Calderón de la Barca

1669 Calderón de la Barca's last work, La Estátua de Prometeo, is published

1683–4 Louis XIV attacks Catalonia and Spanish Netherlands

1650 | 1660 | 1670 | 1680 | 1690 | 1700

1648 Holland achieves independence from Spain by Treaty of Westphalia, ending the Thirty Years War

1659 Peace of the Pyrenees signed with France. Louis XIV marries Felipe IV's daughter María Teresa, leading to Bourbon succession in Spain

Coin from the reign of Felipe IV

1700 Death of Carlos II brings Habsburg line to an end. Felipe V, the first Bourbon king, ascends the throne

Bourbons to First Republic

The War of the Spanish Succession ended in triumph for the Bourbons, who made Spain a centralized nation. Their power was at its height during the reign of the enlightened despot, Carlos III. But the 19th century was a troubled time. An invasion by revolutionary France led to the War of Independence (Peninsular War). Later came the Carlist Wars – caused by another dispute over the succession – liberal revolts and the short-lived First Republic.

Isabel II

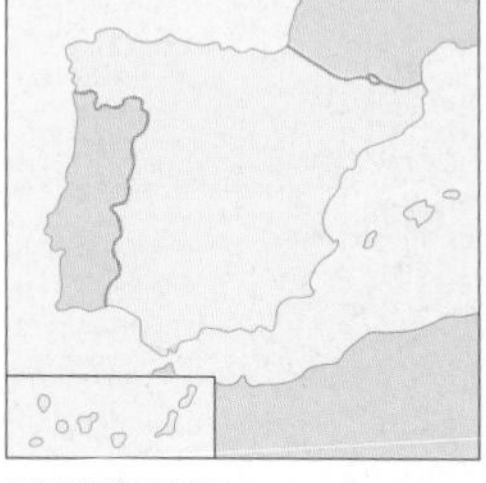

SPAIN IN 1714

Domain after Treaty of Utrecht

The Enlightenment
The Enlightenment brought new learning and novel projects. On 5 July 1784 this Montgolfier balloon rose above Madrid.

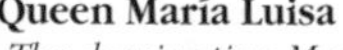

Queen María Luisa
The dominating María Luisa of Parma, portrayed by Goya, forced her husband Carlos IV to appoint her lover, Manuel Godoy, prime minister in 1792.

Spanish rebel faces death in a gesture of crucifixion.

A Franciscan friar is among the innocent victims.

Hundreds of lives were taken in the executions, which lasted several days.

Battle of Trafalgar
The defeat of the Franco-Spanish fleet by the British admiral, Lord Nelson, off Cape Trafalgar in 1805 was the end of Spanish sea power.

TIMELINE

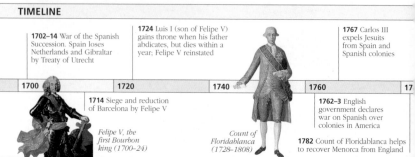

1702–14 War of the Spanish Succession. Spain loses Netherlands and Gibraltar by Treaty of Utrecht

1724 Luis I (son of Felipe V) gains throne when his father abdicates, but dies within a year; Felipe V reinstated

1767 Carlos III expels Jesuits from Spain and Spanish colonies

1700 | 1720 | 1740 | 1760 | 17

1714 Siege and reduction of Barcelona by Felipe V

Felipe V, the first Bourbon king (1700–24)

Count of Floridablanca (1728–1808)

1762–3 English government declares war on Spanish over colonies in America

1782 Count of Floridablanca helps to recover Menorca from England

Carlos III Leaving Naples
When Fernando VI died without an heir in 1759, his half-brother Carlos VII of Naples was put on the Spanish throne as Carlos III. His enlightened reign saw the foundation of academies of science and art and the beginning of free trade.

General Prim *(1814–70)*
General Prim was one of 19th-century Spain's most influential figures. He forced the abdication of Isabel II, and pursued liberal policies until assassinated in Madrid.

French soldiers, operating on orders from Marshal Murat, execute Spanish patriots.

French infantry helmet

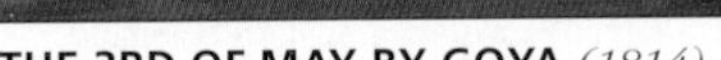

THE 3RD OF MAY BY GOYA *(1814)*

On 2 May 1808, in reaction to Napoleon's occupation of Spain, the people of Madrid rose in vain against the occupying French forces. The next day the French army took its revenge by executing hundreds of people, both rebels and bystanders. These events sparked off the War of Independence.

Baroque Magnificence
The sacristy of the Monasterio de la Cartuja in Granada is typical of Spanish Baroque, more sumptuous than anywhere else in Europe.

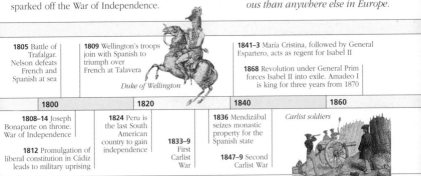

1805 Battle of Trafalgar. Nelson defeats French and Spanish at sea

1809 Wellington's troops join with Spanish to triumph over French at Talavera

Duke of Wellington

1841–3 María Cristina, followed by General Espartero, acts as regent for Isabel II

1868 Revolution under General Prim forces Isabel II into exile. Amadeo I is king for three years from 1870

1800 | 1820 | 1840 | 1860

1808–14 Joseph Bonaparte on throne. War of Independence

1812 Promulgation of liberal constitution in Cádiz leads to military uprising

1824 Peru is the last South American country to gain independence

1833–9 First Carlist War

1836 Mendizábal seizes monastic property for the Spanish state

1847–9 Second Carlist War

Carlist soldiers

Republicans and Anarchists

Spain's First Republic lasted only a year (1873) and consumed four presidents. The late 19th century was a time of national decline, with Anarchism developing in reaction to rampant political corruption. The loss of Cuba, in 1898, was a low point for Spain, although there was a flurry of literary and artistic activity in the following years. The country's increasing instability was briefly checked by the dictatorship of Primo de Rivera. Spanish politics, however, were becoming polarized. Alfonso XIII was forced to abdicate and the ill-fated Second Republic was declared in 1931.

Primo de Rivera

THE LEGACY OF SPANISH COLONIZATION IN 1900

Spanish-speaking territories

Anarchist Propaganda
Anarchism was idealistic, though often violent. This poster states, "Anarchist books are weapons against Fascism".

Workers unite, calling for radical social reform.

POWER TO THE PEOPLE

Political protest was rife under the Second Republic, as shown by this Communist demonstration in the Basque Country in 1932. Industrial workers banded together, forming trade unions to demand better pay and working conditions, and staging strikes. The Spanish Communist Party developed later than the Anarchists, but eventually gained more support.

Pío Baroja
Baroja (1872–1956) was one of the most gifted novelists of his day. He was too original to be grouped with the writers of the Generation of 1898, who tried to create a national renaissance after the loss of Spain's colonies.

TIMELINE

1873 Declaration of First Republic, lasting only one year

First Republic's last president, Emilio Castelar (1832–99)

1870–75 Third Carlist War

1875 Second Bourbon restoration puts Alfonso XII on throne

Alfonso XII and Queen María

1888 Universal Exhibition in Barcelona creates new buildings and parks, such as the Parc de la Ciutadella

1893 Anarchists bomb opera-goers in the Barcelona Liceu

1897 Prime Minister Cánovas del Castillo assassinated by an Italian Anarchist

1898 Cuba and Philippines gain independence from Spain following the Spanish-American War

1870 | 1880 | 1890 | 1900

Tragic Week

Led by Anarchists and Republicans, workers in Barcelona took to the streets in 1909 to resist a military call-up. The reprisals were brutal.

Universal Exhibitions

In 1929, Seville and Barcelona were transformed by exhibitions promoting art and industry. The fairs brought international recognition.

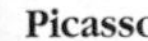

The banner appeals for working-class solidarity.

Picasso

Born in Málaga in 1881, the artist Pablo Picasso spent his formative years as a painter in the city of Barcelona (see p148) *before moving to Paris in the 1930s.*

Cuban War of Independence

Cuba began its fight for freedom in 1895, led by local patriots such as Antonio Maceo. In the disastrous campaign, Spain lost 50,000 soldiers and most of its navy.

The Garrotte

Convicted Anarchists were executed by the garrotte – an iron collar that brutally strangled the victim while crushing the neck.

1909 Semana Trágica (Tragic Week) in Barcelona. Workers' revolt against conscription for Moroccan Wars quashed by Government troops

1910

1912 Prime Minister José Canalejas murdered by Anarchists in Madrid

1920

1921 Crushing defeat of Spanish army at Anual, Morocco

1923 Primo de Rivera stages victorious coup to become military dictator under Alfonso XIII

Second Republic election poster

1930

1930 Primo de Rivera resigns after losing military support

1931 Republicans win local elections, causing Alfonso XIII to abdicate

1931 Proclamation of Second Republic with a two-year coalition between Socialists and Republicans

1933 General election returns right-wing government

1934 Revolution of Asturian miners suppressed by army under General Franco

Civil War and the Franco Era

Franco

Nationalist generals rose against the government in 1936, starting the Spanish Civil War. The Nationalists, under General Franco, were halted by the Republicans outside Madrid, but with support from Hitler and Mussolini they inched their way to victory in the north and east. Madrid finally fell in early 1939. After the war, thousands of Republicans were executed in reprisals. Spain was internationally isolated until the 1950s, when the United States brought her into the western military alliance.

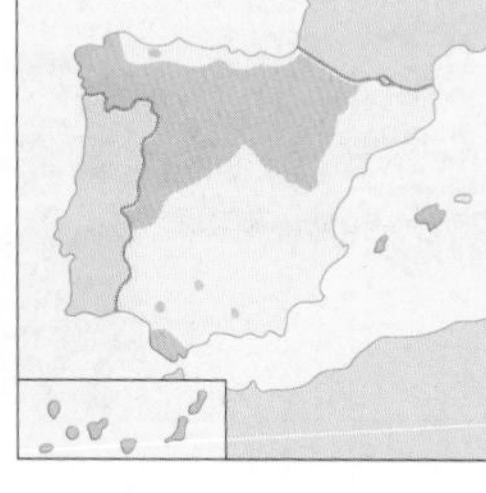

SPAIN ON 31 JULY 1936

- Republican-held areas
- Nationalist-held areas

Franco's Ideal World
Under Franco, Church and state were united. This poster shows the strong influence of religion on education.

Nationalist Poster
A Nationalist poster adorned with Fascist arrows reads "Fight for the Fatherland, Bread and Justice".

Anguished mother with dead child

Composition reflecting total chaos

GUERNICA *(1937)*
On behalf of advancing Nationalists, the Nazi Condor Legion bombed the Basque town of Gernika *(see p118)* on 26 April 1937 – a busy market day. This was Europe's first air raid on civilians, and it inspired Picasso's shocking *Guernica (see p299)*. Painted for a Republican Government exhibition in Paris, it is full of symbols of disaster.

TIMELINE

1936 Republican Popular Front wins the general election on 16 January. On 17 July, Nationalist generals rise against Republicans

1936 Nationalists declare Franco head of state on 29 September

1937 On 26 April, Nazi planes bomb Basque town of Guernika (Gernika-Lumo)

1938 On 8 January, Republicans lose battle for Teruel in bitter cold

1938 On 23 December, Nationalists bomb Barcelona

1939 In March, Madrid, Valencia and Alicante fall in quick succession to Franco's troops

1939 Franco declares end of war on 1 April and demands unconditional surrender from Republicans

1945 By end of World War II, Spain is diplomatically and politically isolated

1947 Spain declared monarchy with Franco as regent

1953 Deal with US permits American bases on Spanish soil in exchange for aid

1935 | 1940 | 1945 | 1950

Soldiers surrendering to Nationalist troops

Scene from his play *Blood Wedding*

GARCIA LORCA

Federico García Lorca (1898–1936) was Spain's most brilliant dramatist and lyric poet of the 1920s and 1930s. His homosexuality and association with the left, however, made him a target for Nationalist assassins. He was shot by an ad hoc firing squad near his home town of Granada.

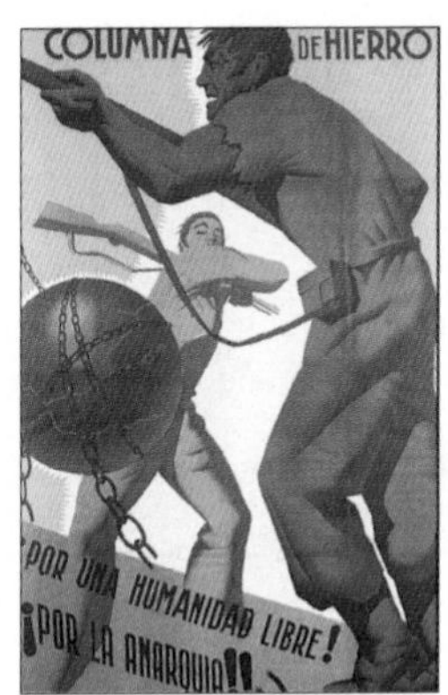

Anarchist Poster
Anarchists fought for the Republic, forming agricultural collectives behind the lines. Their influence waned when they were discredited by the Communist Party.

A wounded horse representing the Spanish people

Witnesses to the massacre stare in wonder and disbelief.

Crucifixion gesture

The flower is a symbol of hope in the midst of despair.

Spanish Refugees
As the Nationalists came closer to victory, thousands of artists, writers, intellectuals and other Republican supporters fled Spain into indefinite exile.

The Hungry Years
Ration cards illustrate the post-war period when Spain nearly starved. Shunned by other nations, she received aid from the US in 1953 in return for accepting military bases.

Sunbathers

1962 Tourism on the Mediterranean coast is boosted by official go-ahead

1969 Franco declares Prince Juan Carlos his successor

1973 ETA assassinates Admiral Carrero Blanco, Franco's hard-line prime minister

1955 | 1960 | 1965 | 1970 | 1975

1959 Founding of ETA, Basque separatist group

1955 Spain joins United Nations

Franco's funeral, 23 November 1975

1970 "Burgos trials" of the regime's opponents outrage world opinion

1975 Death of Franco results in third Bourbon restoration as Juan Carlos is proclaimed king

Modern Spain

Contemporary Spanish fashion

Franco's death left Spain's political future hanging in the balance. But few people wanted to preserve the old regime and the transition from dictatorship to democracy proved surprisingly swift and painless. The previously outlawed Socialist Workers' Party, under Felipe González, won the general election in 1982 and set about modernizing Spain. Considerable power has since been devolved to the regions. A major threat facing central government has been the persistent violence of ETA, the Basque separatist organization. Spain's international relations have been strengthened by her membership of NATO and the European Union.

SPAIN TODAY

- Spain
- Other European Union states

Coup d'Etat, 23 February 1981
Civil Guard colonel, Antonio Tejero, held parliament at gunpoint for several hours. Democracy survived because King Juan Carlos refused to support the rebels.

Anti-NATO Protest Rally
When Spain joined NATO in 1982, some saw it as a reversal of Socialist ideals. To others it represented an improvement in Spain's international standing.

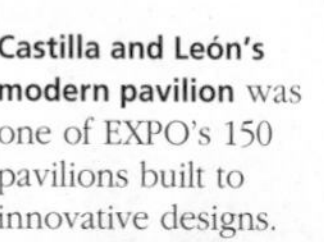

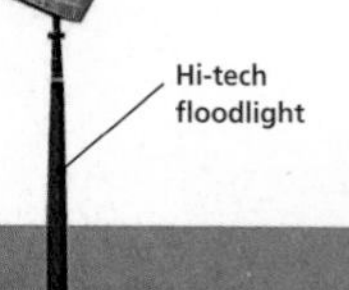

Castilla and León's modern pavilion was one of EXPO's 150 pavilions built to innovative designs.

Hi-tech floodlight

EXPO '92

Over 100 countries were represented at the Universal Exposition, which focused world attention on Seville in 1992. The many pavilions displayed scientific, technological and cultural exhibits.

TIMELINE

1977 First free elections return centrist government under Adolfo Suárez. Political parties, including Communists, are legalized

1980

1981 Military officers stage attempted coup d'etat to overthrow democracy

1982 Landslide electoral victory brings Socialist Workers' Party (PSOE), under Felipe González, to power. Football World Cup held in Spain

1983 Semi-autonomous regional governments are established to appease Basque Country and Catalonia

1985

1986 Spain joins EC (now EU) and NATO

1990

1992 Spain celebrates quincentenary of Columbus's voyage to America

1992 Barcelona Olym and Seville Expo '92 place Spain firmly wi community of mode European nations

1994/5 Corruption scandals rock the long-serving government

Spanish royal family

Felipe González Elected
In 1982 the Spanish Socialist Workers' Party (PSOE) leader was elected prime minister. González transformed Spain during his 13 years in power.

Tourism
From 1959–73 the number of annual visitors to Spain grew from 3 million to 34 million, transforming once-quiet coasts and islands.

Ana Belén
Spanish women enjoyed much greater freedom and opportunity upon the advent of democracy. In a 1980s opinion poll, they voted the singer and actress Ana Belén the woman they most admired.

Leaning blue tower rises above Andalusia's pavilion.

A monorail carried visitors around the site.

Barcelona Olympic Games
The opening ceremony of the Barcelona Olympics included stunning displays of music, dance and colourful costumes.

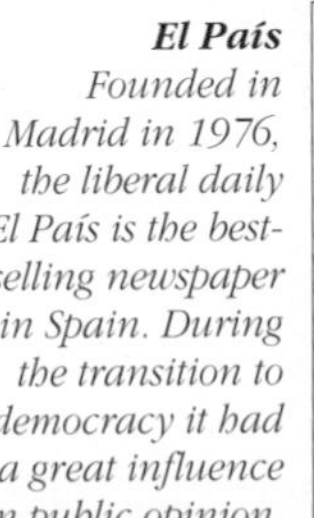

El País
Founded in Madrid in 1976, the liberal daily El País is the best-selling newspaper in Spain. During the transition to democracy it had a great influence on public opinion.

EL PAÍS

"Estoy en un polvorín. Casos como el de Mari Luz se pueden dar aquí"

Las exigencias del PP hacen invisible el Pacto de la Justicia

0,5€

Cobi, Barcelona Olympic Mascot

2000 Spain celebrates 25 years of democracy and reign of Juan Carlos I

2004 Madrid is hit by the worst terrorist attacks in Spain's modern history in March. Bombs detonated on the city's trains killed 191 people

2008 José Luis Rodríguez Zapatero of the Spanish Socialist Party is re-elected on 9 March

2011 ETA announces a permanent ceasefire

2000 | 2005 | 2010 | 2015

1998 ETA, the Basque separatist terrorist group, announces a ceasefire that lasts a year

6 In the general election on 3 March, nzález loses to a coalition led by Aznar

2004 José Luis Rodríguez Zapatero of the Spanish Socialist Party comes into power on 14 March

2011 Mariano Rajoy of the Popular Party comes into power on 20 November

Mariano Rajoy

Rulers of Spain

Spain became a nation-state under Isabel and Fernando, whose marriage eventually united Castile and Aragón. With their daughter Juana's marriage, the kingdom was delivered into Habsburg hands. Carlos I and Felipe II were both capable rulers, but in 1700 Carlos II died without leaving an heir. After the War of the Spanish Succession, Spain came under the French Bourbons, who have ruled ever since – apart from an interregnum, two republics and Franco's dictatorship. The current Bourbon king, Juan Carlos I, a constitutional monarch, is respected for his support of democracy.

1665–1700 Carlos II

1474–1504 Isabel, Queen of Castile

1479–1516 Fernando, King of Aragón

1516–56 Carlos I of Spain (Holy Roman Emperor Charles V)

1598–1621 Felipe III

1400	1450	1500	1550	1600	1650
INDEPENDENT KINGDOMS		HABSBURG DYNASTY			
1400	1450	1500	1550	1600	1650

1469 Marriage of Isabel and Fernando leads to unification of Spain

1504–16 Juana la Loca (with Fernando as regent)

1621–65 Felipe IV

Fernando and Isabel, the Catholic Monarchs

UNIFICATION OF SPAIN

In the late 15th century the two largest kingdoms in developing Christian Spain – Castile, with its military might, and Aragón (including Barcelona and a Mediterranean empire) – were united. The marriage of Isabel of Castile and Fernando of Aragón in 1469 joined these powerful kingdoms. Together the so-called Catholic Monarchs defeated the Nasrid Kingdom of Granada, the last stronghold of the Moors *(see pp56–7)*. With the addition of Navarra in 1512, Spain was finally unified.

1556–98 Felipe II

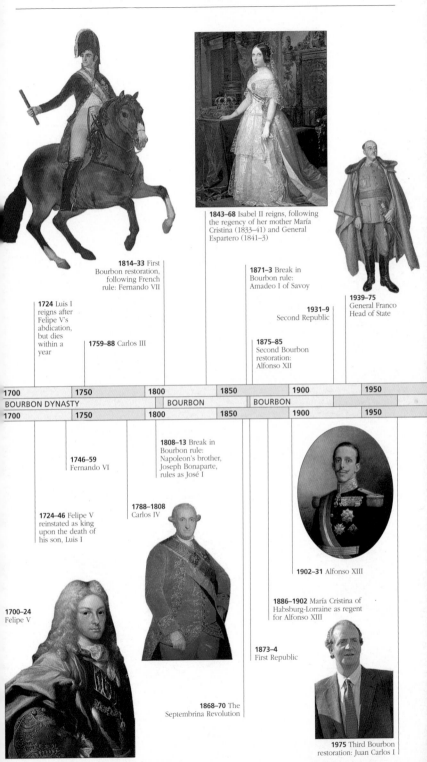

1843–68 Isabel II reigns, following the regency of her mother María Cristina (1833–41) and General Espartero (1841–3)

1814–33 First Bourbon restoration, following French rule: Fernando VII

1871–3 Break in Bourbon rule: Amadeo I of Savoy

1939–75 General Franco Head of State

1724 Luis I reigns after Felipe V's abdication, but dies within a year

1931–9 Second Republic

1759–88 Carlos III

1875–85 Second Bourbon restoration: Alfonso XII

1700	1750	1800	1850	1900	1950
BOURBON DYNASTY		BOURBON		BOURBON	
1700	1750	1800	1850	1900	1950

1808–13 Break in Bourbon rule: Napoleon's brother, Joseph Bonaparte, rules as José I

1746–59 Fernando VI

1788–1808 Carlos IV

1724–46 Felipe V reinstated as king upon the death of his son, Luis I

1902–31 Alfonso XIII

1886–1902 María Cristina of Habsburg-Lorraine as regent for Alfonso XIII

1700–24 Felipe V

1873–4 First Republic

1868–70 The Septembrina Revolution

1975 Third Bourbon restoration: Juan Carlos I

NORTHERN SPAIN

Introducing Northern Spain

Increasing numbers of visitors are discovering the quiet, sandy beaches and deep green landscapes of Northern Spain. The Atlantic coast, from the Pyrenees to the Portuguese border, is often scenic but at its most attractive in the cliffs and rías of Galicia. Inland, the mild, wet climate has created lush meadows and broad-leaved forests, making this area ideal for a peaceful, rural holiday. The famous medieval pilgrimage route to the city of Santiago de Compostela crosses Northern Spain, its way marked by magnificent examples of Romanesque architecture. Plentiful seafood and dairy produce, and the outstanding red wines of La Rioja, add to the pleasure of a tour through this part of Spain.

Oviedo (see p106) *has a number of Pre-Romanesque churches, most notably the graceful Santa María del Naranco, and a fine Gothic cathedral.*

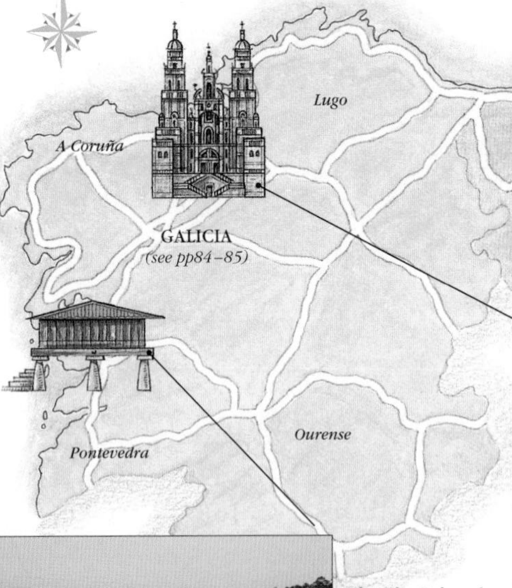

Santiago de Compostela (see pp90–3) *attracts thousands of pilgrims and tourists each year. Its majestic cathedral was one of the most important shrines in medieval Christendom.*

The Rías Baixas (see p95) *is one of Spain's prettiest coastlines. Scattered around its pretty towns and villages are many quaint* hórreos, *grain stores, raised on stone stilts.*

The Picos de Europa *mountain range* (see pp108–9) *dominates the landscape of Asturias and Cantabria. Rivers have carved deep gorges through the mountains and there are many footpaths through a variety of spectacular scenery.*

0 kilometres 50

0 miles 25

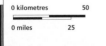

◁ **The coast of Galicia, south of Cabo Fisterra**

Santillana del Mar (see p112), *with its well-preserved medieval streets, is one of the most picturesque towns in Spain. The Convento de Regina Coeli houses a small museum containing a collection of painted wooden figures and other works of religious art.*

San Sebastián (see p122), *the most elegant holiday resort in the Basque Country, is sited around a beautiful horseshoe bay of golden sandy beaches. The city hosts international arts events, including Spain's premier film festival.*

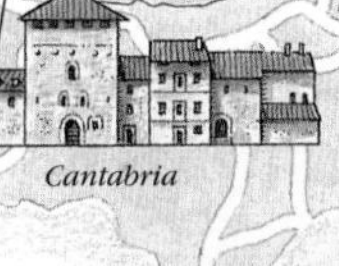

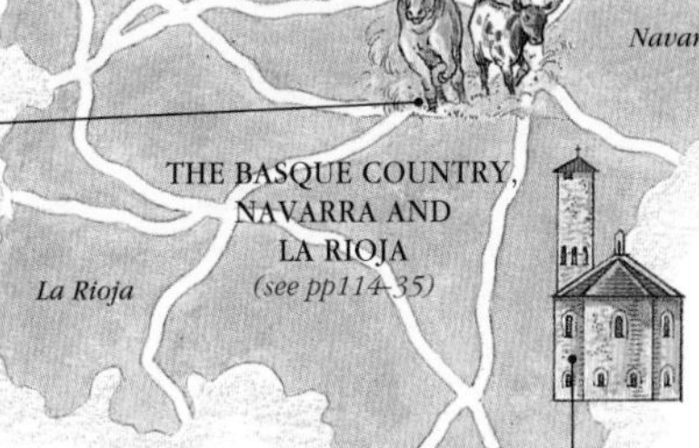

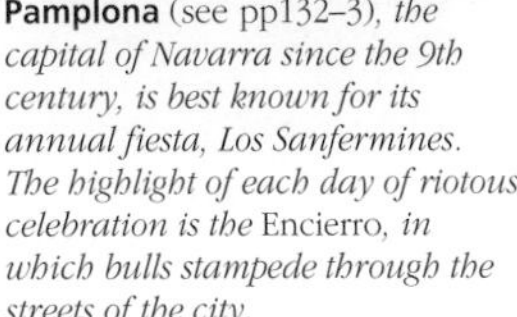

Pamplona (see pp132–3), *the capital of Navarra since the 9th century, is best known for its annual fiesta, Los Sanfermines. The highlight of each day of riotous celebration is the* Encierro, *in which bulls stampede through the streets of the city.*

The Monasterio de Leyre (see p135), *founded in the early 11th century, was built in a lonely but attractive landscape. The monastery was once the burial place of the kings of Navarra and its crypt is among the finest examples of early Romanesque art in Spain.*

The Flavours of Northern Spain

The wild, wet north of Spain is as famous for its rain as it is for its culinary excellence. The rain keeps the pastures lush and green – perfect dairy farming terrain – and the Atlantic provides an incredible variety of seafood. The Basques, in particular, are celebrated chefs, and the region boasts some of the finest restaurants in Europe, along with gastronomic societies (called *txokos*) in every village. Inland and in the remoter regions you'll find old-fashioned country cooking – roast lamb and tender young beef, slow-cooked stews – and traditionally made cheeses.

Idiazábal cheese

***Pulpo a la gallega*, Galicia's signature dish**

GALICIA

The westernmost tip of Spain, battered by the Atlantic into a series of plunging *rías*, is famous for its extraordinary wealth of seafood – from staples like cod to unusual delicacies like barnacles *(percebes)*, which look like tiny dinosaur feet. Every bar will serve up a plate of *pulpo a la gallega* or a dish of *pimientos del padrón* (one in every dozen has a spicy kick). Inland, you'll find tender veal, free-range chicken and delicate soft cheeses such as such as delicious *tetilla*.

ASTURIAS AND CANTABRIA

The bay-pocked coastline provides delicious fresh fish, often served simply grilled (try the fabulous sardines offered in almost every port) or slowly simmered in casseroles. Inland, the lush green pastures form Spain's dairy country – most Spanish milk, cream and some of its finest cheeses come from this region. Try Asturian Cabrales, a pungent blue cheese, best accompanied by a glass of local cider. The mountains provide succulent meat and game, often traditionally stewed with beans, as in the celebrated Asturian dish of *fabada*.

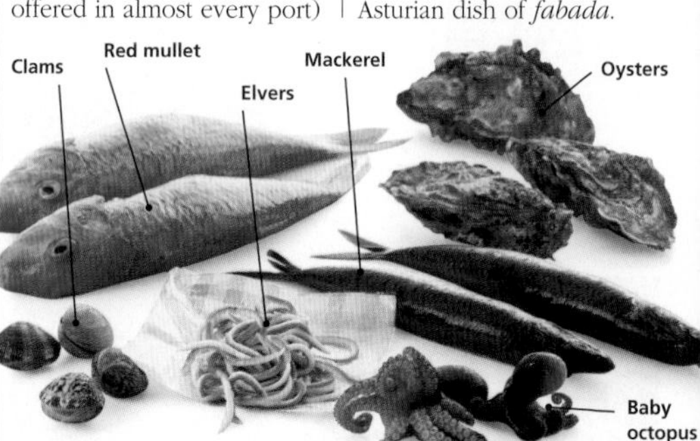

Fish and seafood from the waters of northern Spain

REGIONAL DISHES AND SPECIALITIES

Unsurprisingly, seafood rules supreme along the coastline, from the ubiquitous octopus in a piquant sauce served in Galicia, to the extraordinary spider crabs, which are a sought-after delicacy in the Basque Lands. The verdant pastures and rich farmland provide a wealth of fresh vegetables, including Navarra's justly famous asparagus, along with all kinds of wonderful cheeses. Slow-cooked stews, an Asturian speciality, are particularly good in the mountains, along with tender lamb and outstanding game in season. The renowned wines from La Rioja are excellent, but those of adjoining Navarra are less pricey and often equally interesting. The crisp whites of Galicia and the Basque Lands are the perfect accompaniment to the fresh seafood, and throughout the North you'll find powerful liqueurs flavoured with local herbs.

Cherries

Bacalao al Pil Pil *Salted cod is slowly cooked with olive oil, chilli and garlic to create this classic Basque dish.*

Array of *pinxos* laid out in a bar in the Basque Country

BASQUE COUNTRY

The Basque Country is a paradise for gourmets, renowned throughout Spain for the excellence of its natural produce and the creative brilliance of its chefs. Basque cuisine leans towards seafood, of which there is a dazzling variety: humble salted cod and hake (made extraordinary with delicious sauces) are most common, but sought-after delicacies include elvers (baby eels) and spider crab. Basque wines, drunk young and tart, are the perfect counterpoint. Bar counters groan with platters of *pintxos* (crusty bread with gourmet toppings), each one of them a miniature work of art, and the Basques also make wonderful cheeses, including delicate, smoky Idiazábal.

NAVARRA AND LA RIOJA

The fertile farmland of land-locked Navarra produces a spectacular array of fruit and vegetables such as asparagus, artichokes, cherries, chestnuts and peppers (often hung in pretty strings to dry and used to flavour *embutidos*, or cured meats). In the Navarrese mountains, lamb is the most popular meat and you will find *cordero al chilindrón* (lamb stew) featuring on almost every menu. In season, you'll also find richly flavoured game, including partridge, hare and pheasant.

Red peppers strung up to dry in the sun outside a house

Tiny La Rioja is Spain's most famous wine region, producing rich, oaky reds and whites *(see pp78–9)*. The cuisine of La Rioja borrows from the neighbouring Basque Country and Navarra, with lamb featuring heavily, along with seafood and top-quality local vegetables.

ON THE MENU

Angulas a la Bilbaína Baby eels cooked in olive oil with garlic – a Basque delicacy.

Cocido Montañés Cantabrian stew of pork, spicy sausage, vegetables – and a pig's ear.

Fabada Asturiana Asturian beans stewed with cured meats and pork.

Pimientos del padrón A Gallego dish of green peppers fried in olive oil with rock salt.

Pulpo a la Gallega Octopus, cooked until tender in a spicy paprika sauce.

Trucha a la Navarra Trout, stuffed with ham and quickly grilled or fried.

Empanada Gallega *The perfect picnic snack, these golden pastries are stuffed with all kinds of fillings.*

Chilindrón de Cordero *A rich, hearty stew from the mountains of Navarra, this is made with succulent lamb.*

Leche Frita *"Fried milk" is a scrumptious, custardy dessert from Cantabria. Simple but utterly delicious.*

Wines of Northern Spain

Spain's most prestigious wine region, La Rioja, is best known for its red wines, matured to a distinctive vanilla mellowness. Some of the most prestigious bodegas were founded by émigrés from Bordeaux, and Rioja reds are similar to claret. La Rioja also produces good white and rosé wines. Navarra reds and some whites have improved dramatically, thanks to a government research programme. The Basque region produces a tiny amount of the tart *txacoli (chacolí)*. Larger quantities of a similar wine are made further west in Galicia, whose best wines are full-bodied whites, particularly from the Albariño grape.

Repairing barrels in Haro, La Rioja

Viña Costeira
RIBEIRO

Ribeiro, *a popular wine of Galicia, is slightly fizzy. It is often served in white porcelain bowls* (cuencos).

A CORUÑA
SANTIAGO DE COMPOSTELA
Lugo
OVIEDO
Cambados
Barrantes
Pontevedra
Ribadavia
VIGO
OURENSE
O Barco
A Rúa
Larouco
Fornelos
Tui

0 kilometres 50
0 miles 25

KEY

- Rías Baixas
- Ribeiro
- Valdeorras
- Txacoli de Guetaria
- La Rioja
- Navarra

Lagar de Cervera *is from Rías Baixas, a region known for producing Spain's most fashionable white wines.*

WINE REGIONS

The wine regions of Northern Spain are widely dispersed. Cradled between the Pyrenees and the Atlantic are the important regions of Rioja and Navarra. Wines from La Rioja are divided into the DOs (denominations of origin) of Rioja Alavesa, Rioja Alta and Rioja Baja, divided by the Río Ebro. The river also cuts through the wine region of Navarra. To the north are some of the vineyards of the Basque country: the miniscule Txacoli de Guetaria region. In the far west lie the four wine regions of rugged, wet Galicia: Rías Baixas, Ribeiro, Valdeorras, and Ribeira Sacra.

Wine village of El Villar de Álava in Rioja Alta

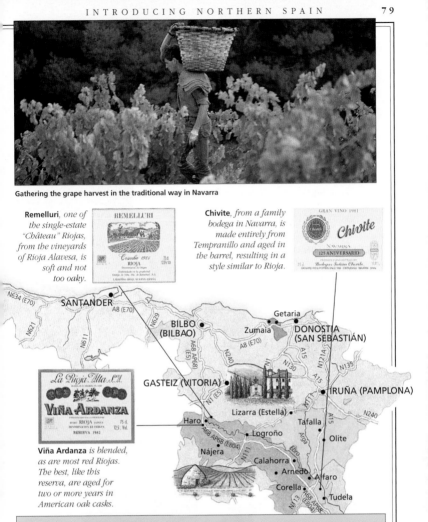

Gathering the grape harvest in the traditional way in Navarra

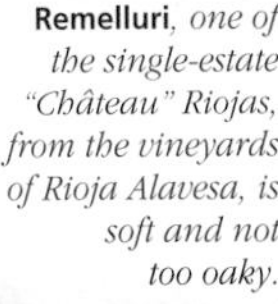

Remelluri, *one of the single-estate "Château" Riojas, from the vineyards of Rioja Alavesa, is soft and not too oaky.*

Chivite, *from a family bodega in Navarra, is made entirely from Tempranillo and aged in the barrel, resulting in a style similar to Rioja.*

SANTANDER
N634 (E70)
A8 (E70)
N621
N611
N629
BILBO (BILBAO)
A68 AP68 (E5)
N240
Getaria
Zumaia
A8 (E70)
DONOSTIA (SAN SEBASTIÁN)
A15
N121A
N1
N130
N135
A15
GASTEIZ (VITORIA)
N1 (E5)
IRUÑA (PAMPLONA)
N111
Lizarra (Estella)
N240
Haro
Tafalla
A15
A68 AP68 (E804)
Logroño
Arga
Olite
Nájera
N111
Ebro
Calahorra
Arnedo
Alfaro
Corella
N113
A68 AP68 (E804)
Tudela

Viña Ardanza *is blended, as are most red Riojas. The best, like this reserva, are aged for two or more years in American oak casks.*

KEY FACTS ABOUT WINES OF NORTHERN SPAIN

Location and Climate

La Rioja and Navarra are influenced by both Mediterranean and Atlantic weather systems. The hillier, northwestern parts receive some Atlantic rain while the hot Ebro plain has a Mediterranean climate. The Basque region and Galicia are both cool, Atlantic regions with high rainfall. Soils everywhere are stony and poor, except in the Ebro plain.

Grape Varieties

The great red grape of La Rioja and Navarra is Tempranillo. In Rioja it is blended with smaller quantities of Garnacha, Graciano and Mazuelo, while in Navarra Cabernet Sauvignon is permitted and blends well with Tempranillo. Garnacha, also important in Navarra, is used for the excellent *rosados* (rosés). Whites of Navarra and Rioja are made mainly from the Viura grape. Galicia has many local varieties, such as Albariño, Godello, Loureira and Treixadura.

Good Producers

Rías Baixas: Fillaboa, Palacio de Fefiñanes, Terras Gauda, Santiago Ruiz. ***Ribeiro:*** Viña Costeira. ***La Rioja:*** Baigorri, Bodegas Riojanas (Canchales, Monte Real), CVNE (Imperial, Viña Real Oro), Marqués de Cáceres, Marqués de Murrieta, Marqués de Riscal, Martínez Bujanda, Remelluri, La Rioja Alta (Barón de Oña). ***Navarra:*** Bodega de Sarría, Guelbenzu, Julián Chivite (Gran Feudo), Magaña, Ochoa, Príncipe de Viana.

Forests of the North

Purple emperor butterfly

Much of Spain was once blanketed by a mantle of trees. Today, just ten per cent of the original cover remains, mostly in the mountainous north, where rainfall is high and slopes too steep for cultivation. Large areas of mixed deciduous forest – mainly beech, Pyrenean oak and chestnut, with some ash and lime – dominate the landscape, particularly in Cantabria and the Basque Country. The undergrowth of shrubs and flowering plants provides habitats for many insects, mammals and birds. The forests are also the refuge of Spain's last brown bears *(see p104)*.

Forest in Northern Spain in autumn

REGENERATION OF THE FOREST

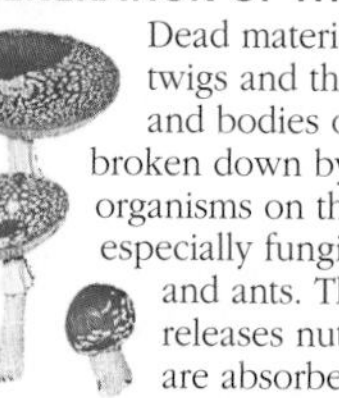
Fly agaric mushrooms

Dead materials – leaves, twigs and the excrement and bodies of animals – are broken down by various organisms on the forest floor, especially fungi, bacteria and ants. This process releases nutrients which are absorbed by trees and other plants, enabling them to grow.

Lichens *grow slowly and are sensitive to pollution. Their presence in a forest often indicates that it is in good health.*

The stag beetle *takes its name from the huge antler-like mandibles of the male. Despite their ferocious appearance, these beetles are harmless to humans.*

Millipede and fungus on a woodland floor

BEECH FOREST

Beech leaf and mast

Beech, the dominant species in the Cantabrian mountains and Pyrenees, grows on well-drained soils. Some trees retain their distinctive copper-red leaves through the winter. Beech mast (nuts) are collected to feed to pigs.

The thick crown shuts out light, inhibiting undergrowth.

Long, thin orange buds

Male golden orioles, *among the most colourful European birds, are hard to spot because they spend much of their time in the thick cover provided by old woodlands. Females and juveniles are a duller yellow-green with a brownish tail.*

Beech martens *are nocturnal. By day, they sleep in a hollow tree or another animal's abandoned nest. At night they feed on fruit, birds and small mammals.*

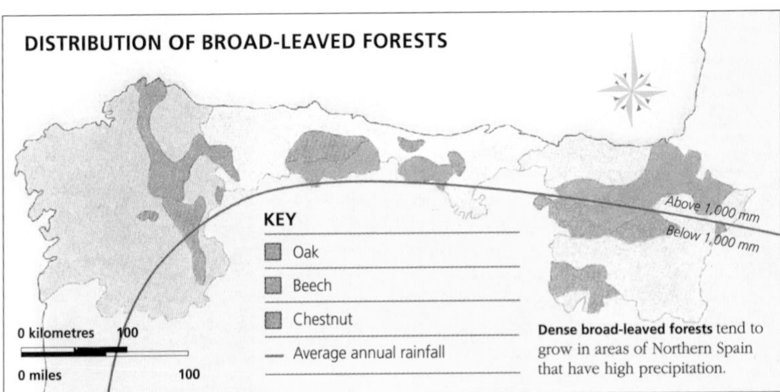

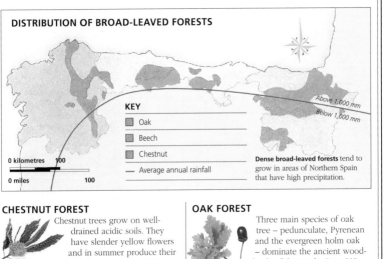

Dense broad-leaved forests tend to grow in areas of Northern Spain that have high precipitation.

CHESTNUT FOREST

Chestnut trees grow on well-drained acidic soils. They have slender yellow flowers and in summer produce their fruit, which is eaten by wild boar, dormice, squirrels and mice. The wood is hard and durable but splits easily.

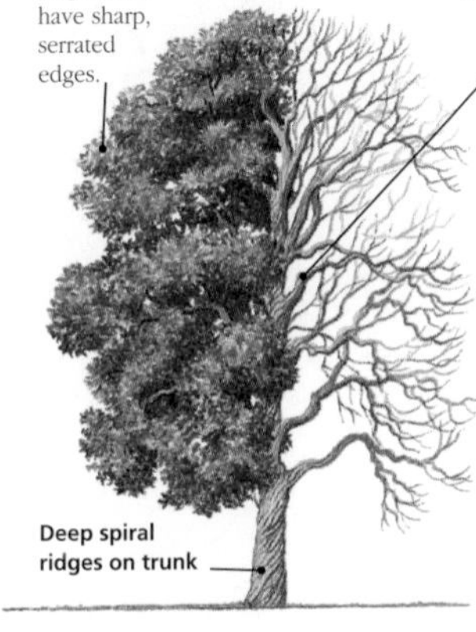

Leaf and chestnut

Large leaves have sharp, serrated edges.

Few massive, spreading branches

Deep spiral ridges on trunk

The pipistrelle bat *is a nocturnal species common in woodlands. It catches and eats small insects in flight. Larger insects are taken to a perch. The bat hibernates in winter in a hollow tree or cave.*

Blue tits *feed mainly in the tree canopy of broad-leaved woods and rarely come down to the ground. The male and female have similar, distinctive plumage. They may raise the back feathers of the crown if alarmed.*

OAK FOREST

Three main species of oak tree – pedunculate, Pyrenean and the evergreen holm oak – dominate the ancient woodlands of the north. Over 300 species of animal, such as wild boar, squirrels and nuthatches, feed off oaks.

Oak leaf and acorn

Grey twigs ending in numerous buds

The jay, *a member of the crow family, is a common but somewhat shy woodland bird with a distinctively raucous cry. It can be identified in flight by its white rump, black tail and above all by its bright blue wing patch.*

Red squirrels *bury large numbers of acorns during autumn to last through winter, since these diurnal creatures do not hibernate. Many of the acorns are left to sprout into seedlings.*

The Road to Santiago

St James on horseback

According to legend the body of Christ's apostle James was brought to Galicia. In AD 813 the relics were supposedly discovered at Santiago de Compostela, where a cathedral was built in his honour *(see pp92–3)*. In the Middle Ages half a million pilgrims a year flocked there from all over Europe, crossing the Pyrenees at Roncesvalles *(see p134)* or via the Somport Pass *(see p230)*. They often donned the traditional garb of cape, long staff and curling felt hat adorned with scallop shells, the symbol of the saint. The various routes, marked by the cathedrals, churches and hospitals built along them, are still used by travellers today.

19th-century painting of the Pórtico da Gloria of Santiago Cathedral

Astorga (see p352), *once a Roman city, was an important halt on the pilgrim route in the Middle Ages. The museum within its cathedral has a collection of gold and silver plate including a 13th-century gold filigree cross.*

A certificate *is given to pilgrims covering 100 km (62 miles) of the route on foot, or 200 km (125 miles) on horseback.*

León *was one of the main pilgrim stops. Its cathedral* (see pp354–5) *contains one of Spain's finest collections of stained glass.*

O Cebreiro *(see p99)* has a 9th-century church and some of the ancient *pallozas* the pilgrims often used for shelter.

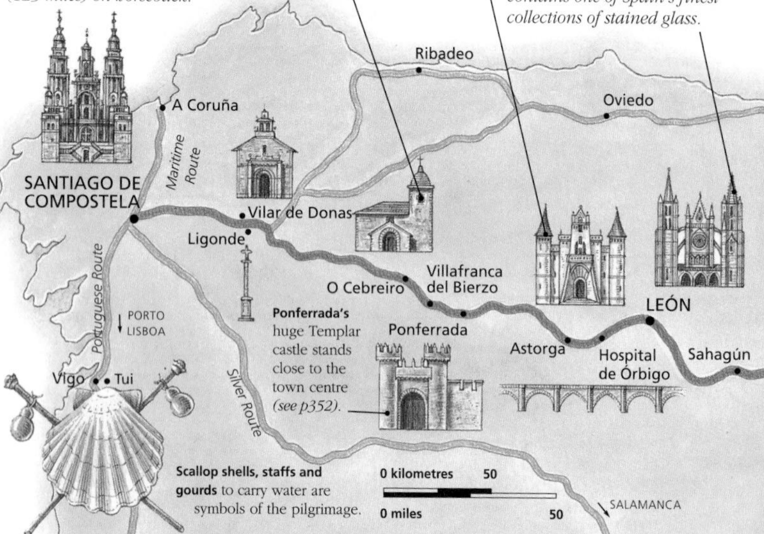

Ponferrada's huge Templar castle stands close to the town centre *(see p352)*.

Scallop shells, staffs and gourds to carry water are symbols of the pilgrimage.

ROMANESQUE CHURCH ARCHITECTURE

Carved capital

The Romanesque style of architecture *(see p24)* was brought to Spain from France during the 10th and 11th centuries. As the pilgrimage to Santiago became more popular, many glorious religious buildings were constructed along its main routes. Massive walls, few windows, round heavy arches and barrel vaulting are typical features of Romanesque architecture.

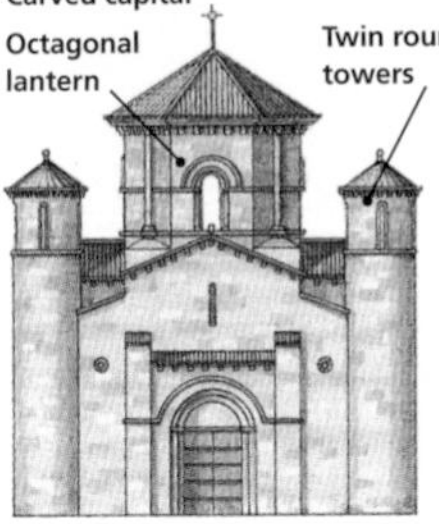

Octagonal lantern

Twin round towers

Façade

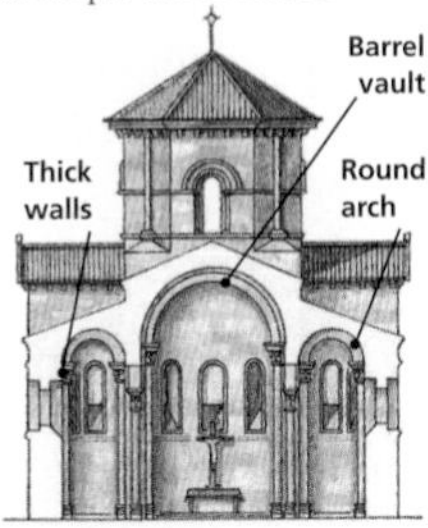

Thick walls

Barrel vault

Round arch

Cross-section

San Martín de Frómista (see p368), *built in the 11th century, is the only complete example of the "pilgrimage" style of Romanesque. The nave and aisles are almost the same height and there are three parallel apses.*

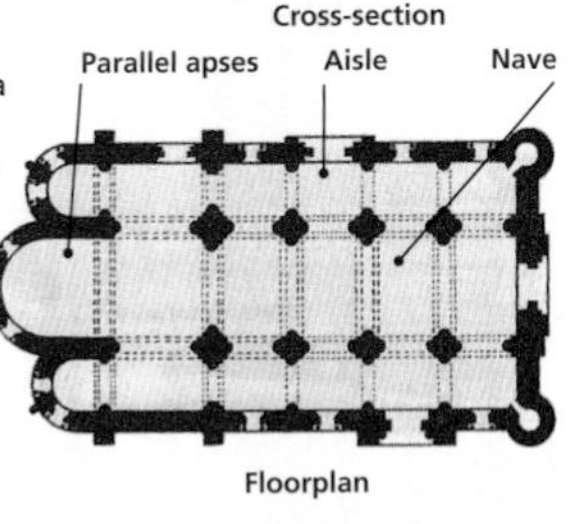

Floorplan

Pamplona's (see p132) *Gothic cathedral was one of the pilgrims' first stops after crossing the Pyrenees at Roncesvalles.*

Puente la Reina (see p131) *takes its name from the 11th-century humpbacked bridge* (puente), *built for pilgrims and still used by pedestrians.*

Santo Domingo de la Calzada's *(see p128)* pilgrim hospital is now a parador.

Santander

Donostia (San Sebastián)

PARIS

Northern Route

Bilbo (Bilbao)

LE PUY VEZELAY

Valcarlos

Orreaga (Roncesvalles)

ARLES

Frómista preserves one of the finest Romanesque churches on the French route.

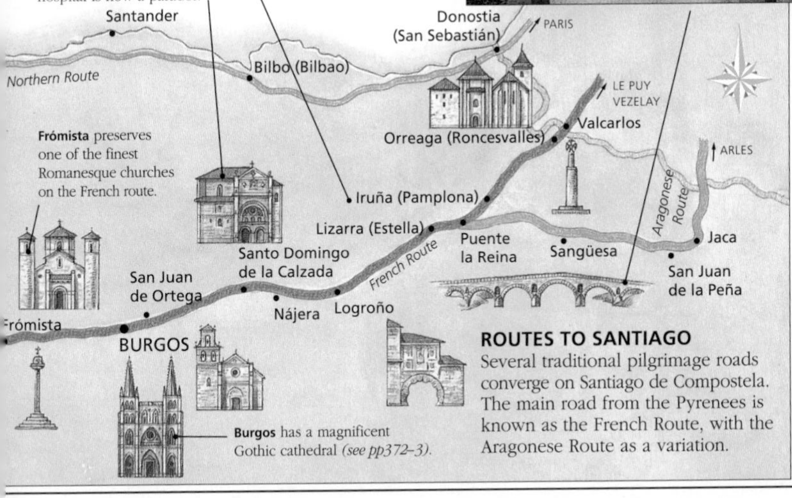

Iruña (Pamplona)

Aragonese Route

Lizarra (Estella)

Puente la Reina

Sangüesa

Jaca

Santo Domingo de la Calzada

French Route

San Juan de la Peña

San Juan de Ortega

Nájera

Logroño

Frómista

BURGOS

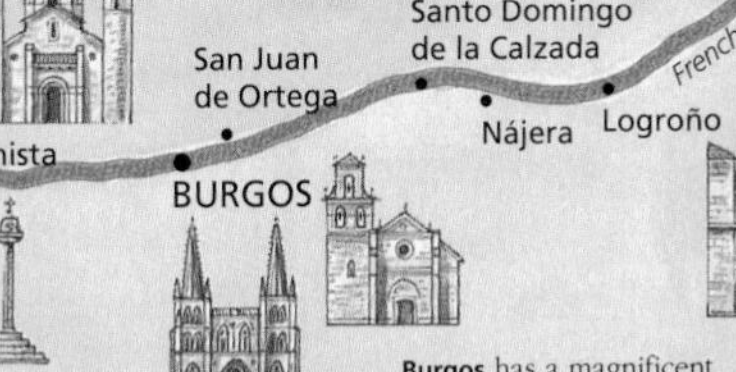

Burgos has a magnificent Gothic cathedral *(see pp372–3).*

ROUTES TO SANTIAGO

Several traditional pilgrimage roads converge on Santiago de Compostela. The main road from the Pyrenees is known as the French Route, with the Aragonese Route as a variation.

GALICIA

LUGO · A CORUNA · PONTEVEDRA · OURENSE

Remote in the northwest corner of the peninsula, Galicia is the country's greenest region. In its hilly interior, smallholdings are farmed by traditional methods. Galicia is Spain's main seafaring region – three of its four provinces have an Atlantic coastline, and its cuisine is based on superb seafood. The Galicians, whose origins are Celtic, are fiercely proud of their culture and language.

Much of Galicia still has a medieval quality. Some inland farms are divided into plots too tiny or steep for tractors to work, so oxen and horses are used for ploughing. Grain is stored in quaint, pillared granaries called *hórreos*. The misty, emerald countryside abounds with old granite villages and is dotted with *pazos* – traditional stone manor houses.

The discovery of the supposed tomb of St James the Apostle, in the 9th century, confirmed medieval Santiago de Compostela as Europe's most important religious shrine after St Peter's in Rome. Pilgrims and tourists still follow this ancient route of pilgrimage across Northern Spain.

The Galician coast is incised by many fjord-like rías; the loveliest of these are the Rías Baixas in the west. Elsewhere it juts defiantly into the Atlantic in rocky headlands, such as Cabo Fisterra, Spain's most westerly point. Many people still make a living from the sea. Vigo in Pontevedra is the most important fishing port in Spain.

Galicia's official language, used on most signs, is *gallego*. It has similarities to the language of Portugal, which borders Galicia to the south. The Celtic character of this haunting land is still evident in the Galicians' favourite traditional instrument, the bagpipes.

Staple crops – maize, cabbages and potatoes – growing on the harsh land around Cabo Fisterra

◁ The west façade of Santiago de Compostela's cathedral, overlooking the Praza do Obradoiro

Exploring Galicia

Santiago de Compostela is Galicia's major tourist attraction. This beautiful city is the centrepiece of a region with many fine old towns, especially Betanzos, Mondoñedo, Lugo and Pontevedra. The resorts along the coastline of the wild Rías Altas, with their backdrop of forest-covered hills, offer good bathing. The Rías Baixas, the southern part of Galicia's west coast, has sheltered coves and sandy beaches, and excellent seafood in abundance. Travelling through the interior, where life seems to have changed little in centuries, is an ideal way to spend a peaceful, rural holiday.

Musicians dressed in traditional costumes playing in Pontevedra

SIGHTS AT A GLANCE

Baiona 11
Betanzos 3
O Cebreiro 21
Celanova 14
A Coruña 4
Costa da Morte 5
A Guarda 12
Lugo 20
Monasterio de Oseira 18
Monasterio de Ribas de Sil 17
Mondoñedo 2
Ourense 16
Padrón 7
Pontevedra 9
Rías Altas 1
Santiago de Compostela pp90–91 6
A Toxa 8
Tui 13
Verín 15
Vigo 10
Vilar de Donas 19

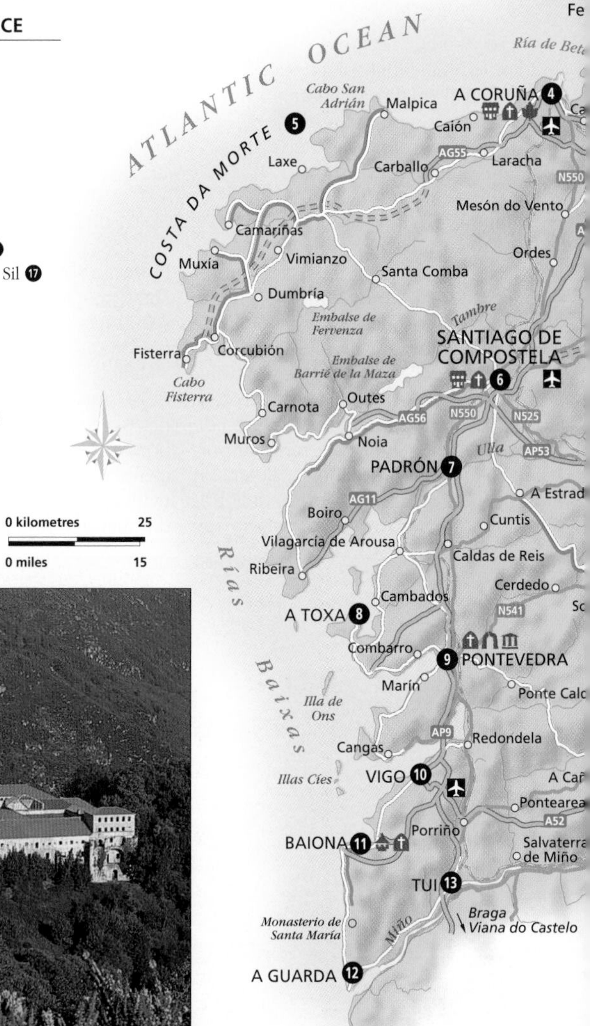

The isolated monastery at Ribas de Sil

SEE ALSO

- ***Where to Stay*** pp560–62
- ***Where to Eat*** pp608–10

GETTING AROUND

The region's main airports are at A Coruña, Santiago de Compostela and Vigo. A network of motorways connects Verín, Vigo, A Coruña and O Cebreiro, but traffic along the coast can be heavy. Rail lines link Galicia's major cities, and towns along the north coast are served by the FEVE line *(see p677)*. Coach services run between the major cities.

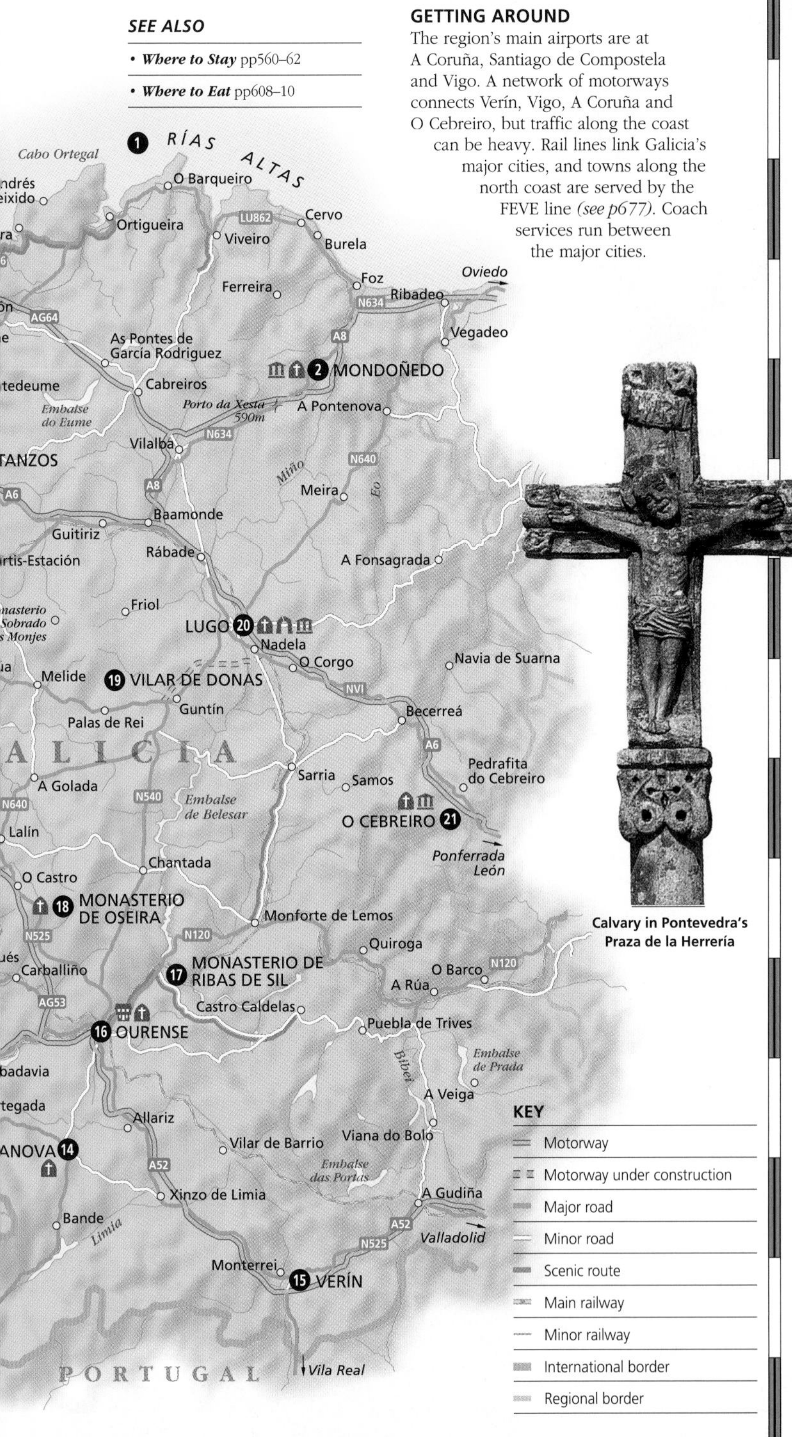

Calvary in Pontevedra's Praza de la Herrería

Carved coat of arms on a house-front in Mondoñedo

Rías Altas ❶

Lugo & A Coruña. 10,000. Ribadeo. Viveiro. Foz, 982 13 24 26. Tue.

Deep rías are interspersed with coves and headlands along the beautiful north coast from Ribadeo to A Coruña. Inland are hills covered with forests of pine and eucalyptus. Many of the small resorts and fishing villages are charming.

The lovely, winding **Ría de Ribadeo** forms the border with Asturias. To the west of it is the small fishing port of **Foz**, which has two good beaches. Nearby, the 10th-century Iglesia de San Martín de Mondoñedo, standing alone on a hill, contains carvings of biblical scenes on its transept capitals – note the story of Lazarus. **Viveiro**, a summer holiday resort 35 km (22 miles) away, is a handsome old town surrounded by Renaissance walls and gateways, typically Galician glassed-in balconies or *galerías*, and a Romanesque church. Near the pretty fishing village of O Barqueiro is the headland of Estaca de Bares, with its lighthouse and wind turbines.

Westward along the coast, the lovely **Ría de Ortigueira** leads to the fishing port of the same name, characterized by neat white houses. Around this area there are also many wild and unspoiled beaches.

High cliffs rise out of the sea near the village of **San Andrés de Teixido**, whose church is the focal point for pilgrims on 8 September. According to legend, those who fail to visit the church in their lifetime will come back to it as an animal in the afterlife. The village of **Cedeira**, which sits on a quiet bay, is a rich summer resort with neat lawns, modern houses with *galerías*, and a long, curving beach.

Mondoñedo ❷

Lugo. 4,300. Plaza de la Catedral 34, 982 50 71 77. Thu. As Quendas (1 May), Nuestra Señora de los Remedios (2nd Sun in Sep), San Lucas (18 Oct).

This delightful town is set in a fertile inland valley. Stately houses with carved coats of arms and *galerías* are in the main square. This is dominated by the **cathedral**, a building of golden stone with a Romanesque portal, a 16th-century stained-glass rose window, 17th-century cloisters and 18th-century Baroque towers. A statue in a chapel in the cathedral, Nuestra Señora la Inglesa, was rescued from St Paul's Cathedral in London. The **Museo Diocesano**, entered through the cathedral, contains works by Zurbarán and El Greco.

Museo Diocesano
Plaza de la Catedral. ***Tel*** *982 52 10 06. 11am–1:30pm, 4:30–7:30pm daily.*

Betanzos ❸

A Coruña. 13,500. Plaza de Galicia 1, 981 77 66 66. Tue, Thu & Sat. San Roque (14–25 Aug).

The handsome town of Betanzos lies in a fertile valley slightly inland. Its broad main square has a replica of the Fountain of Diana at Versailles. In its steep narrow streets are fine old houses and Gothic churches. The **Iglesia de Santiago**, built in the 15th century by the tailors' guild, has a statue of St James on horseback above the door. The **Iglesia de San Francisco**, dated 1387, has statues of wild boars and a heraldic emblem of Knight Fernán Pérez de Andrade, whose 14th-century tomb is inside the church. For centuries his family were the overlords of the region.

Environs: 20 km (12 miles) north is the large, though pretty, fishing village of **Pontedeume**, with its narrow, hilly streets. Its medieval bridge still carries the main road to the large industrial town of **Ferrol**, to the north. Originally a medieval port, Ferrol became an important naval base and dockyard town in the 18th century, and its Neo-Classical buildings survive from that time. General Franco *(see pp66–7)* was born in Ferrol in 1892.

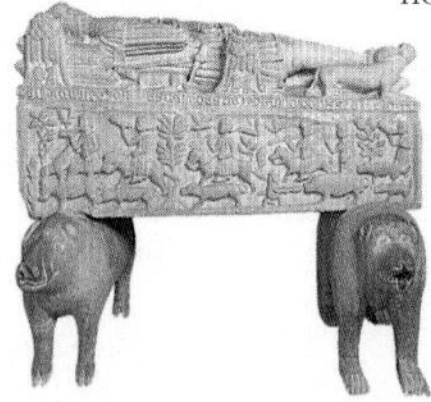

Ornate tomb in the Iglesia de San Francisco in Betanzos

Pavement cafés in Betanzos' Plaza de García Hermanos

Stone cross standing above the perilous waters of the Costa da Morte

A Coruña ❹

A Coruña. 246,000. Plaza de María Pita, 981 92 30 93. Fiestas de María Pita (Aug). www.turismocoruna.com

This proud city and busy port has played a sizeable role in Spanish maritime history. Felipe II's doomed Armada sailed from here to England in 1588 *(see p59)*. Today, the sprawling industrial suburbs contrast with the elegant town centre, which is laid out on an isthmus leading to a headland. The **Torre de Hércules**, Europe's oldest working lighthouse, is a famous local landmark. Built by the Romans and rebuilt in the 18th century, it still flashes across the deep. Climb its 242 steps for a wide ocean view.

On the large, arcaded Plaza de María Pita, the city's main square, is the handsome town hall. The sea promenade of **La Marina** is lined with tiers of glass-enclosed balconies or *galerías*. Built as protection against the strong winds, they explain why A Coruña is often referred to as the City of Glass. The peaceful, tiny Plazuela da las Bárbaras is enchanting.

A Coruña has several fine Romanesque churches, such as the **Iglesia de Santiago**, with a carving of its saint on horseback situated beneath the tympanum, and the **Iglesia de Santa María**. This church, featuring a tympanum carved with the Adoration of the Magi, is one of the best-preserved 12th-century buildings in Galicia.

The quiet Jardín de San Carlos contains the tomb of the Scottish general Sir John Moore who was killed in 1809 as the British army evacuated the port during Spain's War of Independence from France *(see p62)*.

The lofty Torre de Hércules lighthouse at A Coruña

Costa da Morte ❺

A Coruña. A Coruña, Malpica. Plaza de María Pita, A Coruña, 981 92 30 93. Fiesta de la Virgen del Carmen (16 Jul). www.turismocostadamorte.com

From Malpica to Fisterra the coast is wild and remote. It is called the "Coast of Death" because of the many ships lost in storms or smashed on the rocks by gales over the centuries. The headlands are majestic. There are no coastal towns, only simple villages, where fishermen gather gastronomic *percebes* (barnacles), destined for the region's restaurants.

One of the most northerly points of the Costa da Morte, **Malpica**, has a seabird sanctuary. Laxe has good beaches and safe bathing. **Camariñas**, one of the most appealing places on this coast, is a fishing village where women make bobbin-lace in the streets. Beside the lighthouse on nearby Cabo Vilán, a group of futuristic wind turbines, tall and slender, swirl in graceful unison – a haunting sight.

To the south is Corcubión, exuding a faded elegance, and lastly, **Cabo Fisterra** "where the land ends". This cape, with its lighthouse, is a good place to watch the sun go down over the Atlantic.

Street-by-Street: Santiago de Compostela ❻

Vegetable stall in Santiago market

In the Middle Ages Santiago de Compostela was Christendom's third most important place of pilgrimage *(see pp82–3)*, after Jerusalem and Rome. Around the Praza do Obradoiro is an ensemble of historic buildings that has few equals in Europe. The local granite gives a harmonious unity to the mixture of architectural styles. With its narrow streets and old squares, the city centre is compact enough to explore on foot. Two other monuments worth seeing are the Convento de Santo Domingo de Bonaval, to the east of the centre and the Colegiata Santa Maria la Real del Sar, a 12th-century Romanesque church, located to the east of the city.

★ Monasterio de San Martiño Pinario
The Baroque church of this monastery has a huge double altar and an ornate Plateresque façade with carved figures of saints and bishops.

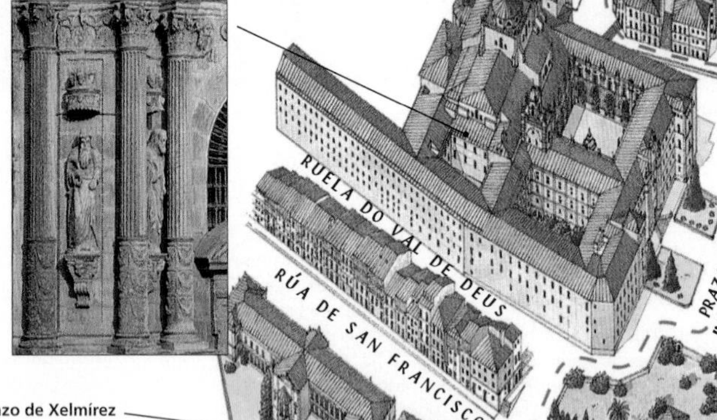

Pazo de Xelmírez

★ Hostal de los Reyes Católicos
Built by the Catholic Monarchs as an inn and hospital for sick pilgrims, and now a parador (see p562), *this magnificent building has an elaborate Plateresque doorway.*

Praza do Obradoiro
This majestic square is one of the world's finest and the focal point for pilgrims arriving in the city. The cathedral's Baroque façade dominates the square.

The Pazo de Raxoi with its Classical façade, was built i 1772 and houses the town hall.

Convento de San Paio de Antealtares
This is one of the oldest monasteries in Santiago. It was founded in the 9th century to house the tomb of St James, now in the cathedral.

VISITORS' CHECKLIST

A Coruña. 95,000. *12 km (6 miles) north. Calle Hórreo s/n, 902 32 03 20. Calle San Caetano s/n, 981 54 24 16. Calle Rúa do Vilar 63, 902 33 20 10. Wed (animal), Thu. Semana Santa (Easter Week), Santiago Day (24–25 Jul).*
www.santiagoturismo.com

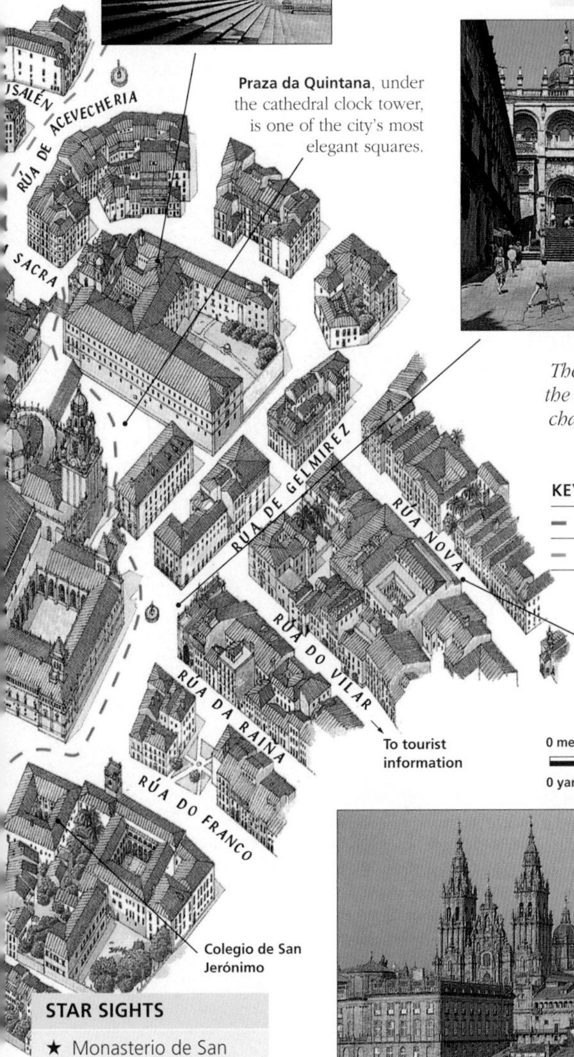

Praza da Quintana, under the cathedral clock tower, is one of the city's most elegant squares.

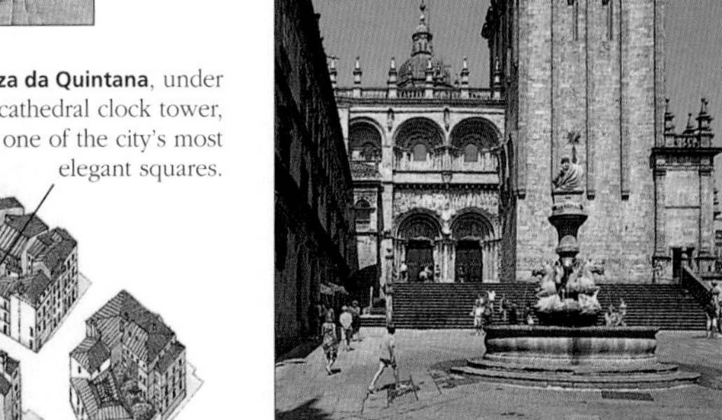

Praza das Praterias
The Silversmiths' Doorway of the cathedral opens on to this charming square with a stone fountain in the centre.

KEY

Suggested route

Pilgrims' route

Rúa Nova is a handsome arcaded old street leading from the cathedral to the newer part of the city.

To tourist information

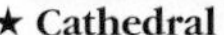

Colegio de San Jerónimo

★ Cathedral
This grand towering spectacle has welcomed pilgrims to Santiago for centuries. Though the exterior has been remodelled over the years, the core of the building has remained virtually unchanged since the 11th century.

STAR SIGHTS

- ★ Monasterio de San Martiño Pinario
- ★ Hostal de los Reyes Católicos
- ★ Cathedral

Santiago Cathedral

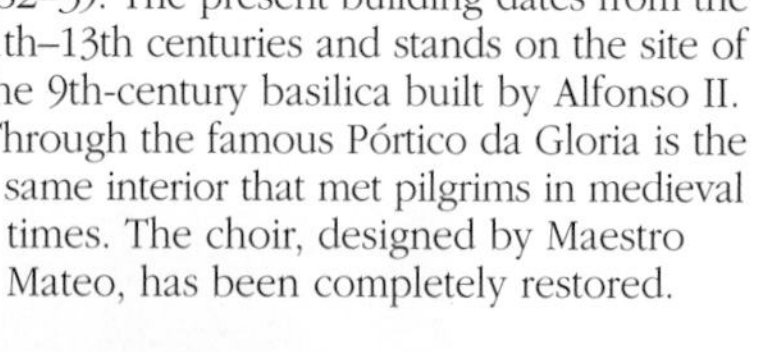

With its twin Baroque towers soaring high over the Praza do Obradoiro, this monument to St James is a majestic sight, as befits one of the great shrines of Christendom *(see pp82–3)*. The present building dates from the 11th–13th centuries and stands on the site of the 9th-century basilica built by Alfonso II. Through the famous Pórtico da Gloria is the same interior that met pilgrims in medieval times. The choir, designed by Maestro Mateo, has been completely restored.

The gigantic *botafumeiro*

"Passport" – proof of a pilgrim's journey

★ West Façade
The richly sculpted Baroque Obradoiro façade was added in the 18th century.

The twin towers are the cathedral's highest structures at 74 m (243 ft).

Statue of St James

Pazo de Xelmírez

The Santo dos Croques (Saint of Bumps) has greeted pilgrims since the 12th century. Touching this statue with the forehead is said to impart luck and wisdom.

★ Pórtico da Gloria
The sculpted Doorway of Glory, with its statues of apostles and prophets, is 12th century.

Cathedral Museum
Visitors can view items such as this version of Goya's The Swing (right), *as well as the cathedral's cloister, chapterhouse, library, reliquary chapel and crypt.*

STAR FEATURES

- ★ West Façade
- ★ Pórtico da Gloria
- ★ Porta das Praterias

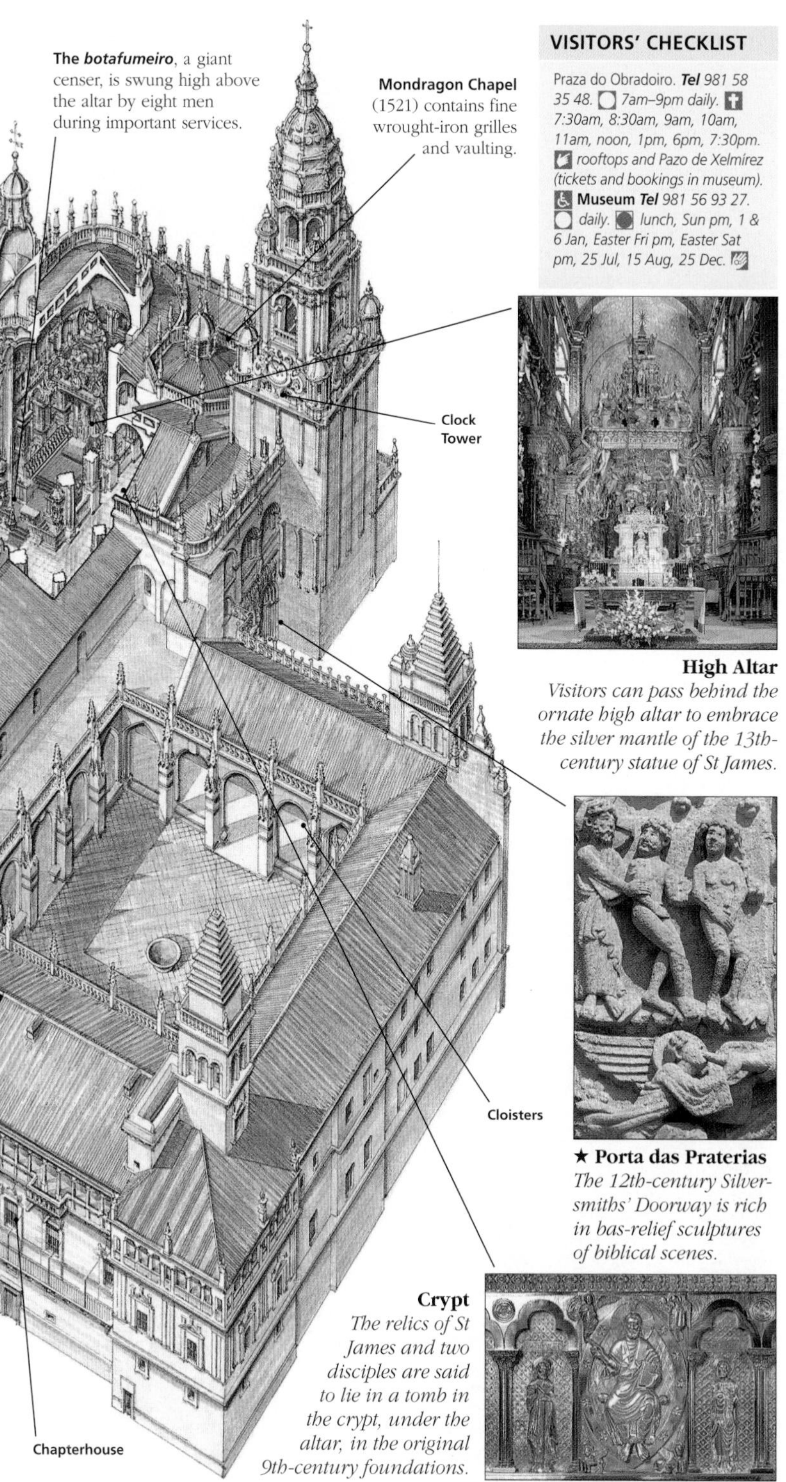

The *botafumeiro*, a giant censer, is swung high above the altar by eight men during important services.

Mondragon Chapel (1521) contains fine wrought-iron grilles and vaulting.

VISITORS' CHECKLIST

Praza do Obradoiro. ***Tel*** *981 58 35 48.* 7am–9pm daily. 7:30am, 8:30am, 9am, 10am, 11am, noon, 1pm, 6pm, 7:30pm. rooftops and Pazo de Xelmírez (tickets and bookings in museum). **Museum *Tel*** 981 56 93 27. daily. lunch, Sun pm, 1 & 6 Jan, Easter Fri pm, Easter Sat pm, 25 Jul, 15 Aug, 25 Dec.

High Altar
Visitors can pass behind the ornate high altar to embrace the silver mantle of the 13th-century statue of St James.

★ Porta das Praterias
The 12th-century Silversmiths' Doorway is rich in bas-relief sculptures of biblical scenes.

Crypt
The relics of St James and two disciples are said to lie in a tomb in the crypt, under the altar, in the original 9th-century foundations.

Padrón 7

A Coruña. 9,000. *Avenida Compostela, 627 21 07 77.* *Sun.* *Santiago (24–25 Jul).*

This quiet town on the Río Ulla, known for its piquant green peppers, was a major seaport until it silted up. Legend has it the boat carrying the body of St James to Galicia *(see p82)* arrived here. The supposed mooring stone, or *padrón*, lies below the altar of the church by the bridge.

The leafy avenue beside the church features in the poems of one of Galicia's greatest writers, Rosalia de Castro (1837–85). Her home, where she spent her final years, has been converted into a museum.

Environs

The estuary town of Noia (Noya) lies on the coast 20 km (12 miles) west. Its Gothic church has a finely carved portal. East of Padron is Pazo de Oca, a manor house, with a crenellated tower, idyllic gardens and a lake.

Museo Rosalia de Castro
La Matanza. ***Tel*** *981 81 12 04.* *Tue–Sun.*

The picturesque gardens and lake of Pazo de Oca

A Toxa 8

Near O Grove. *Praza do Corgo, O Grove, 986 73 14 15.* *Fri.*

A tiny pine-covered island joined to the mainland by a bridge, A Toxa (La Toja) is one of the most stylish resorts in Galicia. The *belle époque* palace-hotel *(see p561)* and luxury villas add to the island's elegant atmosphere. A Toxa's best-known landmark is the small church covered with scallop shells. Across the bridge is O Grove (El Grove), a thriving family resort and fishing port on a peninsula, with holiday hotels and flats alongside glorious beaches.

Scallop-covered roof of the church on A Toxa island

Pontevedra 9

Pontevedra. *82,000.* *Calle Marqués de Riestra 30, 986 85 08 14.* *1st, 8th, 15th & 23rd of each month.* *Fiestas de la Peregrina (second week in Aug).*

Pontevedra lies inland, at the head of a long ría backed by green hills. The delightful old town is typically Galician and has a network of cobbled alleys and tiny squares with granite calvaries, flower-filled balconies and excellent tapas bars. On the south side of the old town are the Gothic **Ruinas de San Domingos**, now part of the Museo de Pontevedra, with Roman steles and Galician coats of arms and tombs. To the west, the 16th-century **Iglesia de Santa María la Mayor** contains a magnificent Plateresque *(see p25)* façade.

On the **Praza de la Leña**, two 18th-century mansions, along with two other buildings in the adjacent streets, form the **Museo de Pontevedra**, one of the best museums in Galicia. The Bronze Age treasures are superb. Among the paintings are 15th-century Spanish primitives, canvases by Zurbarán and Goya, and on the top floor a collection by Alfonso Castelao, a Galician artist and nationalist who forcefully depicted the misery endured by his people during the Spanish Civil War.

Museo de Pontevedra
Calle Pasanteria 2–12. ***Tel*** *986 85 14 55.* *10am–9pm Tue–Sat, 11am–2pm Sun. Ruinas de San Domingos close at 2pm in winter and on Sun.*
www.museo.depo.es

Rías Baixas

This southern part of Galicia's west coast consists of four large rías or inlets between pine-covered hills. The beaches are good, the scenery is lovely, the bathing safe and the climate much milder than on the wilder coast to the north. Though areas such as Vilagarcía de Arousa and Panxón have become popular holiday resorts, much of the Rías Baixas (Rías Bajas) coastline is unspoiled, such as the quiet stretch from Muros to Noia. This part of the coastline provides some of Spain's most fertile fishing grounds. Mussel-breeding platforms are positioned in neat rows along the rías, looking like half-submerged submarines; and in late summer, the women harvest clams.

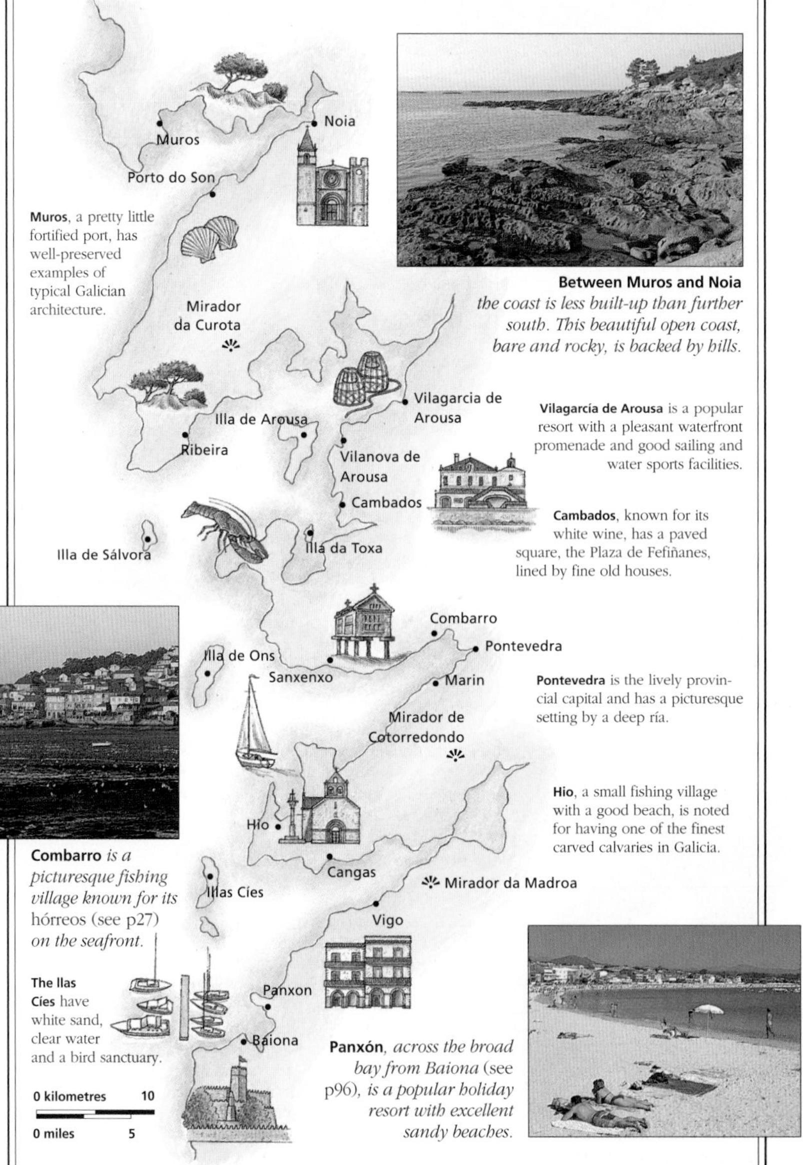

Muros, a pretty little fortified port, has well-preserved examples of typical Galician architecture.

Between Muros and Noia *the coast is less built-up than further south. This beautiful open coast, bare and rocky, is backed by hills.*

Vilagarcía de Arousa is a popular resort with a pleasant waterfront promenade and good sailing and water sports facilities.

Cambados, known for its white wine, has a paved square, the Plaza de Fefiñanes, lined by fine old houses.

Pontevedra is the lively provincial capital and has a picturesque setting by a deep ría.

Combarro *is a picturesque fishing village known for its* hórreos (see p27) *on the seafront.*

Hio, a small fishing village with a good beach, is noted for having one of the finest carved calvaries in Galicia.

The Ilas Cíes have white sand, clear water and a bird sanctuary.

Panxón, *across the broad bay from Baiona* (see p96), *is a popular holiday resort with excellent sandy beaches.*

Cannons on the battlements of Monterreal fortress, Baiona

Vigo ⑩

Pontevedra. 300,000. Cánovas del Castillo 3, 986 22 47 57. Wed, Sun. Cristo de los Afligidos (3rd weekend in Jul), Cristo de la Victoria (1st week in Aug). **www**.turismodevigo.es

Galicia's largest town is also the biggest fishing port in Spain. It is situated in an attractive setting near the mouth of a deep ría spanned by a high suspension bridge, and is surrounded by wooded hills. Vigo is not noted for its old buildings but does have striking modern sculptures such as Juan José Oliveira's horses statue in the Praza de España. The oldest part of the town, Barrio del Berbes, is near the port and used to be the sailors' quarter. Its cobbled alleys are full of bars and cafés where you can find some of the finest tapas. The Mercado de la Piedra, near the port, sells reasonably priced fish and shellfish.

Bronze sculpture by Oliveira in Vigo's Praza de España

Baiona ⑪

Pontevedra. 12,000. Paseo Ribeira, 986 68 70 67. Mon in Sabaris (nearby). Santa Liberata (20 Jul), Virgen de la Anunciada (2nd Sun in Aug). **www**.baiona.org

The Pinta, one of the caravels from the fleet of Christopher Columbus, arrived at this small port on 1 March 1493, bringing the first news of the discovery of the New World. Today Baiona (Bayona), which is sited on a broad bay, is a popular summer resort, its harbour a mix of pleasure and fishing boats. The 12th- to 17th-century **Iglesia Antigua Colegiata de Santa María** is Romanesque with Cistercian influences. Symbols on the arches indicate the local guilds that helped build the church.

A royal fortress once stood on Monterreal promontory, to the north of town. Sections of its defensive walls remain, but the interior has been converted into a smart parador *(see p560)*. A walk around the battlements offers superb views of the coast.

On the coast a short distance to the south is a huge granite and porcelain statue of the **Virgen de la Roca** sculpted by Antonio Palacios in 1930. It is possible for visitors to climb up inside the statue.

A Guarda ⑫

Pontevedra. 10,500. Plaza del Reloj 1, 986 61 45 46. Sat. Virgen del Carmen (16 Jul), Monte de Santa Tecla (2nd week Aug). **www**.aguarda.es

The little fishing port of A Guarda (La Guardia) is famous for seafood and is particularly well known for its lobsters.

On the slopes of Monte de Santa Tecla are the remains of a Celtic settlement of some 100 round stone dwellings dated around 600–200 BC. The **Museo de Monte de Santa Tecla** sits on a nearby hilltop.

Environs

About 10 km (6 miles) north, the tiny Baroque **Monasterio de Santa María** stands by the beach at Oia. Semi-wild horses roam the surrounding hills and, in May and June, are rounded up for branding in a series of day-long fiestas *(see p98)*.

Museo de Monte de Santa Tecla
A Guarda. ***Tel*** *986 61 45 46.*
Tue–Sun. for hilltop access (free Mon).

Circular foundations of Celtic dwellings at A Guarda

Tui ⑬

Pontevedra. 17,000. Calle Colon 2, 986 60 17 89. Thu. San Telmo (first weekend after Easter).

Spain's main frontier town with Portugal, Tui (Tuy) stands on a hillside above the Río Miño. Its graceful old streets curve up to an old quarter and the 12th-century hilltop **cathedral**. The two countries were often at war during the Middle Ages, and

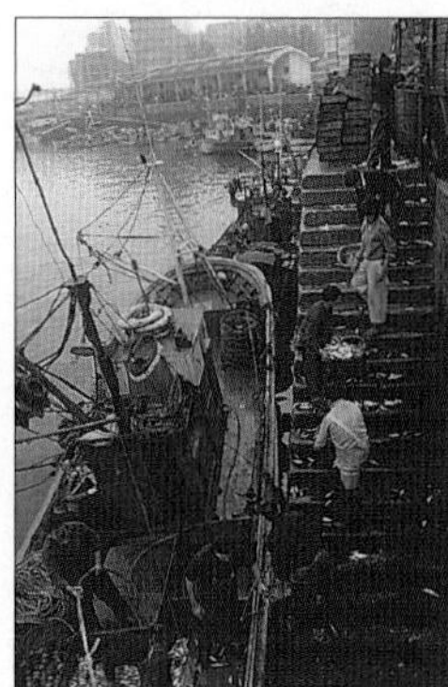
Unloading the catch in Spain's largest fishing port, Vigo

FISHING IN SPAIN

The Spanish eat more seafood per head than any other European nation except Portugal. Almost half of this is caught by Galician fishing fleets. Over 40,000 fishermen and 8,000 boats land over a million tonnes of fish and shellfish a year. Much of this is caught offshore, where octopus, mackerel, clams and lobster are plentiful. The stocks in the seas around Spain have become depleted by overfishing and an oil spill in 2002, forcing deep-sea trawlers to travel as far as Canada and Iceland.

as a result, the church is built in the style of a fortress, with towers and battlements. It has a cloister and choir stalls and a richly decorated west porch.

Nearby is the **Iglesia de San Telmo**, dedicated to the patron saint of fishermen, whose Baroque ornamentation shows a Portuguese influence. Near the cathedral is an iron bridge, the **Puente Internacional**, built by Gustave Eiffel in 1884 to stretch across the river to Valença do Minho in Portugal.

The Romanesque **Iglesia de Santo Domingo**, beside the Parque de la Alameda, has ivy-covered cloisters and tombs with carved effigies. The church overlooks the river, which is used in August for the Descent of the Río Miño, a festive canoe race.

Celanova ⓮

Ourense. 6,000. Plaza Mayor 1, 988 43 22 01. Thu. San Roque (15 Aug).

On the main square of this little town is the massive **Monasterio de San Salvador**, also known as the Monasterio de San Rosendo, after its founder. Founded during the 10th century and later rebuilt, it is mainly Baroque, though one of its two lovely cloisters is Renaissance. The enormous church of this Benedictine monastery has an ornate altarpiece and Gothic choir stalls. In the garden is the 10th-century Mozarabic **Iglesia de San Miguel**.

Ceramic tiled floor of the Iglesia de San Miguel

Environs

At **Santa Comba de Bande**, 26 km (16 miles) to the south, is an even older little church. The features of this 7th-century Visigothic *(see pp50–51)* church include a lantern turret and a horseshoe arch that has carved marble pillars.

Verín ⓯

Ourense. 14,600. Avda San Lazaro 26–28, 988 41 16 14. 3rd, 11th & 23rd of month. Carnival (Feb), Santa María (15 Aug).

Though it stands amid vineyards, Verín produces more than wine. Its mineral springs have given it a thriving bottled water industry. The town has many old houses with arcades and glass balconies (*galerías*).

The **Castillo de Monterrei**, built during the wars with Portugal, is 3 km (2 miles) to the west. Inside its three rings of walls are two 15th-century keeps, an arcaded courtyard, and a 13th-century church with a carved portal. The castle once housed a monastery and hospital, and is now open to visitors Wed–Sun.

The Castillo de Monterrei, standing high above the town of Verín

GALICIA'S FIESTAS

Os Peliqueiros *(Carnival, Feb/Mar)*, Laza (Ourense). Dressed up in grinning masks and outlandish costumes, with cowbells tied to their belts and brandishing sticks, Os Peliqueiros take to the streets on Carnival Sunday. They are licensed to lash out at onlookers, who are forbidden to retaliate. On Carnival Monday morning a battle takes place, with flour, water and live ants used as ammunition. Laza's carnival comes to an end on the Tuesday with a reading of the satirical "Donkey's Will" and the burning of an effigy.

The outrageous costumes of *Os Peliqueiros* in Laza

Flower pavements *(Corpus Christi, May/Jun)*, Ponteareas (Pontevedra). The streets of the town along which the Corpus Christi procession passes are carpeted with intricate designs made from brightly coloured flower petals.
A Rapa das Bestas *(Jun–Aug)*, Oia (Pontevedra). Semi-wild horses are rounded up by local farmers for their manes and tails to be cut. What was once a chore is now a popular fiesta.
St James's Day *(25 Jul)*, Santiago de Compostela. On the night before, there is a firework display in the Praza do Obradoiro. The celebrations are especially wild in a holy year (when 25 July falls on a Sunday).

Ourense ⓰

Ourense. *108,000.* *Isabel la Católica 2, 988 36 60 64.* *7th, 17th & 26th of each month.* *Os Maios (1–3 May), Fiestas de Ourense (end Jun).*

The old quarter of Ourense was built around the city's well-known thermal springs, Fonte das Burgas. Even today, these spout water at a temperature of 65°C (150°F) from three fountains.

This old part of the town is the most interesting, particularly the small area around the arcaded Plaza Mayor. Here the **cathedral**, founded in 572 and rebuilt in the 12th–13th centuries, has a vast gilded reredos by Cornelis de Holanda. On the triple-arched doorway are carved figures reminiscent of the Pórtico da Gloria at Santiago *(see p92)*. Nearby is the elegant 14th-century cloister, the **Claustro de San Francisco**.

One of the city's landmarks is the 13th-century **Puente Romano**, a seven-arched bridge which crosses the Río Miño, north of the town. It is built on Roman foundations and is still used by traffic.

Environs

Allariz, 25 km (16 miles) south, and Ribadavia, to the west, have old Jewish quarters with narrow streets and Romanesque churches. Ribadavia is also noted for its Ribeiro wines – a dry white and a port-like red *(see p78)* – and has a wine museum.

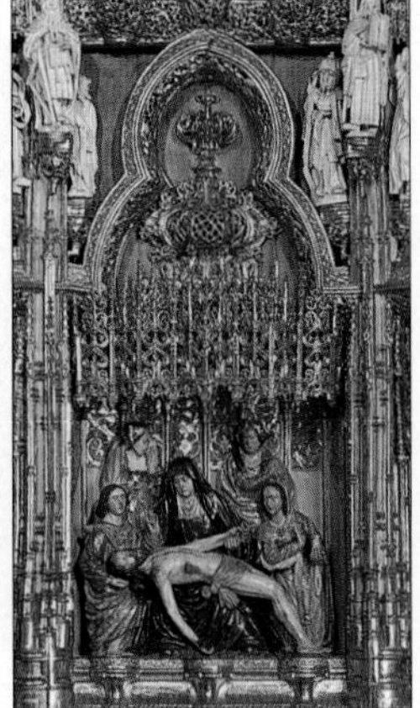

Ornate Gothic reredos in the cathedral at Ourense

Monasterio de Ribas de Sil ⓱

Ribas de Sil. ***Tel*** *988 01 01 10.* *daily.*

Near its confluence with the Miño, 28 km (17 miles) from Ourense, the Río Sil carves a deep curving gorge in which dams form two reservoirs of dark green water. A hairpin road winds to the top of the gorge, where the Romanesque-Gothic Monasterio de Ribas de Sil is situated high on a crag above the chasm. Restored and converted into a parador *(see p558)*, it has an enormous glass wall in one of the three cloisters and fine views.

The Río Sil winding its way through the gorge

The grandiose Monasterio de Oseira surrounded by the forests of the Valle de Arenteiro

Monasterio de Oseira ⓲

Oseira. ***Tel*** *988 28 20 04.* *10am–noon Mon–Sat, 3:30–6:30pm daily (guided visits only).* *compulsory.* **www**.mosteirodeoseira.org

This monastery stands on its own in a wooded valley near the hamlet of Oseira, named after the bears *(osos)* that once lived in this region. It is a grey building with a Baroque façade dating from 1709. On the doorway is a statue of the Virgin as nurse, with St Bernard kneeling at her feet. The interior of the 12th–13th-century church is typically Cistercian in its simplicity.

Fresco of a *dona* in the monastery at Vilar de Donas

Vilar de Donas ⓳

Lugo. *80.* *Palas de Rey, Avda de Compostela 47, 982 38 07 40.* **Church** *Easter–Oct: 11am–2pm, 3:30–6:30pm Tue–Sun; rest of the year: ask for key.* *San Antonio (13 Jun), San Salvador (6 Aug).*

This hamlet on the Road to Santiago *(see pp82–3)* has a small church, San Salvador, just off the main road. Inside are tombs of some of the Knights of the Order of Santiago. Also inside are frescoes painted by the nuns who lived here until the 15th century.

The Cistercian **Monasterio Sobrado de los Monjes**, to the northwest, has a medieval kitchen and chapterhouse, and a church with unusual domes.

Lugo ⓴

Lugo. *98,000.* *Plaza del Campo 11, 982 25 16 58.* *Tue & Fri.* *San Froilán (4–12 Oct).* **www**.lugoturismo.com

Capital of Galicia's largest province, Lugo was also an important centre under the Romans. Attracted to the town by its thermal springs, they constructed what is now the finest surviving **Roman wall** in Spain. The wall, which encircles the city, is about 6 m (20 ft) thick and 10 m (33 ft) high with ten gateways. Six of these give access to the top of the wall, from where there is a good view of the city.

Inside the wall, the old town is lively, with pretty squares. In the **Praza de Santo Domingo** is a black statue of a Roman eagle, built to commemorate Augustus' capture of Lugo from the Celts in the 1st century BC. The large, Romanesque **cathedral** is modelled on that of Santiago. It features an elegant Baroque cloister, and a chapel containing the alabaster statue of Nuestra Señora de los Ojos Grandes (Virgin of the Big Eyes). The **Museo Provincial** exhibits local Celtic and Roman finds, a life-size model of a farm kitchen, modern Galician paintings and a statue of a peasant woman holding a miniature priest.

Environs

The stone hamlet of **Santa Eulalia**, situated in lovely open country to the west, conceals a curious building, discovered in 1924: a tiny temple, with lively, bright frescoes of birds and leaves. Though its exact purpose is unknown, it is thought to be an early Christian church and has been dated at around the 3rd century AD.

Museo Provincial
Praza da Soedade. ***Tel*** *982 24 21 12.* *Jul & Aug: Mon–Sat (am only Sat); Sep–Jun: daily (am only Sun).* **www**.museolugo.org

O Cebreiro ㉑

Lugo. *16.* *982 36 70 25.* *Santa María Real (8 Sep), Santo Milagro (9 Sep).*

Up in the hills in the east of Galicia, close to the border with León, is one of the most unusual villages on the Road to Santiago. Its 9th-century church was supposedly the scene of a miracle in 1300 when the wine was turned into blood and the bread into flesh. Near the church there are several *pallozas*, round thatched stone huts of a Celtic design. Some have been restored, and are now part of a folk museum.

Painted gourd in O Cebreiro's museum

Museo Etnográfico
O Cebreiro.
Tel *982 36 90 25.*
Tue–Sun.

ASTURIAS AND CANTABRIA

ASTURIAS · CANTABRIA

The spectacular Picos de Europa massif sits astride the border between Asturias and Cantabria. In this rural region cottage crafts are kept alive in villages in remote mountain valleys and forested foothills. There are many ancient towns and churches, and pretty fishing ports on the coasts. Cave paintings, such as those at Altamira, were made by people living here about 18,000 years ago.

Asturias is proud that it resisted invasion by the Moors. The Reconquest of Spain is held to have begun in 718 when a Moorish force was defeated by Christians at Covadonga in the Picos de Europa.

The Christian kingdom of Asturias was founded in the 8th century, and in the brilliant, brief artistic period that followed many churches were built around the capital, Oviedo. Some of these Pre-Romanesque churches still stand. Today, Asturias is a province and a principality under the patronage of the heir to the Spanish throne. In the charming, unspoiled Asturian countryside cider is produced and a quaint dialect, *bable,* is spoken.

Cantabria centres on Santander, its capital, a port and an elegant resort. It is a mountainous province with a legacy of Romanesque churches in isolated spots. It also has well-preserved towns and villages such as Santillana del Mar, Carmona and Bárcena Mayor.

Mountains cover more than half of both provinces, so mountain sports are a major attraction. Expanses of deciduous forests remain in many parts, some sheltering Spain's last wild bears. Along the coasts are pretty fishing ports and resorts, such as Castro Urdiales, Ribadesella and Comillas, and sandy coves for bathing. Both the coastal plains and uplands are ideal for quiet rural holidays.

Peaceful meadow around Lago de la Ercina in the Picos de Europa massif

◁ **One of the pretty cobbled streets of Santillana del Mar, Cantabria**

Exploring Asturias and Cantabria

The most obvious attraction in this area is the group of mountains that straddles the two provinces – the Picos de Europa. These jagged peaks offer excellent rock climbing and rough hiking, and in certain parts can be explored by car or bicycle. These and several other nature reserves in the area are home to rare species of flora and fauna, including the capercaillie and brown bear. The coast offers many sandy coves for bathing. Santander and Oviedo are lively university cities with a rich cultural life. There are innumerable unspoiled villages to explore, especially the ancient town of Santillana del Mar. Some of the earliest examples of art exist in Cantabria, most notably at Altamira, where the cave drawings and engravings are among the oldest to be found in Europe.

Typical flower-covered balcony in the village of Bárcena Mayor

A view along the crowded beach of Playa del Camello, Santander

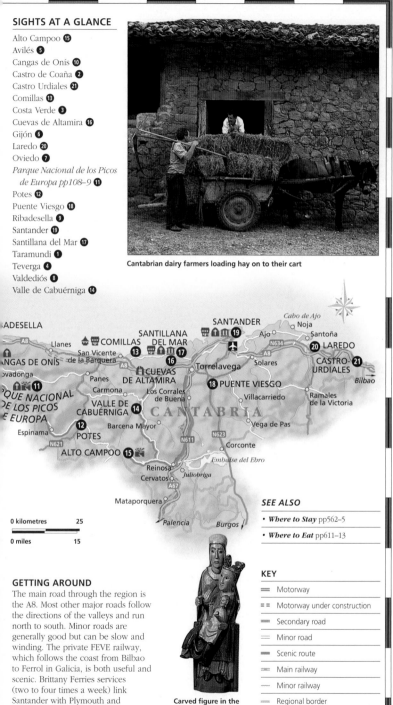

SIGHTS AT A GLANCE

Alto Campoo 15
Avilés 5
Cangas de Onís 10
Castro de Coaña 2
Castro Urdiales 21
Comillas 13
Costa Verde 3
Cuevas de Altamira 16
Gijón 6
Laredo 20
Oviedo 7
Parque Nacional de los Picos de Europa pp108–9 11
Potes 12
Puente Viesgo 18
Ribadesella 9
Santander 19
Santillana del Mar 17
Taramundi 1
Teverga 4
Valdediós 8
Valle de Cabuérniga 14

Cantabrian dairy farmers loading hay on to their cart

SEE ALSO

- ***Where to Stay*** pp562–5
- ***Where to Eat*** pp611–13

GETTING AROUND

The main road through the region is the A8. Most other major roads follow the directions of the valleys and run north to south. Minor roads are generally good but can be slow and winding. The private FEVE railway, which follows the coast from Bilbao to Ferrol in Galicia, is both useful and scenic. Brittany Ferries services (two to four times a week) link Santander with Plymouth and Portsmouth. Asturias has a small international airport near Avilés.

Carved figure in the Convento de Regina Coeli, Santillana del Mar

KEY

- Motorway
- Motorway under construction
- Secondary road
- Minor road
- Scenic route
- Main railway
- Minor railway
- Regional border
- Summit

Craftsman making knife blades in a forge at Taramundi

Taramundi ❶

Asturias. 750. *Calle Solleiro 14, 985 64 68 77.* *San José (19 Mar).* **www**.taramundi.net

Situated in the remote Los Oscos region, this small village houses a rural tourism centre which organizes forest tours in four-wheel drive vehicles and has several hotels and holiday cottages to rent. Taramundi has a tradition of wrought-iron craftsmanship. Iron ore was first mined in the area by the Romans. There are approximately 13 forges in and around the village, where craftsmen can still be seen making traditional knives with decorated wooden handles.

Environs

About 20 km (12 miles) to the east, at **San Martín de Oscos**, there is an 18th-century palace. At **Grandas de Salime**, 10 km (6 miles) further southeast, the Museo Etnográfico has displays showing local crafts, traditional life and farming.

Museo Etnográfico
Esquios. ***Tel*** *985 97 96 40.* *daily.*

Castro de Coaña ❷

Asturias. *5 km (3 miles) from Navia.* ***Tel*** *985 97 84 01.* *Wed–Sun.*

One of the best-preserved prehistoric sites of the Cantabrian area, Castro de Coaña was later occupied by the Romans. Set on a hillside in the Navia valley are the remains of its fortifications and the stone foundations of oval and rectangular dwellings, some of which stand head high. Inside can be found hollowed-out stones which are thought to have been used for crushing corn.

The museum on the site displays many of the finds that have been unearthed at Castro de Coaña. Among the interesting remains on display are pottery, tools and Roman coins.

Circular stone foundations of dwellings at Castro de Coaña

Costa Verde ❸

Asturias. *Avilés.* *Oviedo, Gijón.* *Avilés, Calle Ruiz Gomez 21, 985 54 43 25.*

The aptly named "green coast" is a succession of attractive sandy coves and dramatic cliffs, punctuated by deep estuaries and numerous fishing villages. Inland, there are lush meadows, and pine and eucalyptus forests, backed by mountains. This stretch of coastline has been less spoiled than most in Spain; the resorts tend to be modest in size, like the hotels.

Two pretty fishing ports, **Castropol** and **Figueras**, stand by the eastern shore of the Ría de Ribadeo, forming the border with Galicia. To the east are other picturesque villages such as Tapia de Casariego and Ortiguera, in a small rocky cove. Following the coast, **Luarca** lies beside a church and a quiet cemetery on a headland, and has a neat little harbour packed with red, blue and white boats. The village of **Cudillero** is even more delightful – outdoor cafés and excellent seafood restaurants crowd the tiny plaza beside the port, all of which are squeezed into a narrow cove. Behind, white cottages are scattered over the steep hillsides.

Further along the coast is the rocky headland of Cabo de Peñas where, in the fishing village of **Candas**, bullfights are held on the sand at low tide on 14 September. East of Gijón, **Lastres** is impressively located below a cliff, and **Isla** has a broad open beach. Beyond Ribadesella is the

THE BROWN BEAR

The population of Spain's brown bears *(Ursus arctos)* has dwindled from about 1,000 at the beginning of the 20th century to about 80 today. Hunting by man and the destruction of the bear's natural forest habitat have caused the decline. But now, protected by nature reserves such as Somiedo, where most of the bears in Asturias are found, together with new conservation laws, this magnificent omnivore is increasing in numbers again.

One of the remaining bears in the forests of Asturias

For hotels and restaurants in this region see pp562–5 and pp611–13

Church and cemetery overlooking the sea from the headland at Luarca

lively town of **Llanes**. Among the attractions of this old fortified seaport, with its dramatic mountain backdrop, are ruined ramparts and good beaches.

Teverga ❹

Asturias. 1,900. La Plaza. Dr García Miranda s/n, San Martin de Teverga, 985 76 42 93. 15 Jun–15 Sep: Tue–Sun; rest of year: Sat & Sun only. **www**.infoteverga.com

This area is rich in scenery, wildlife and ancient churches. Near the southern end of the Teverga gorge is **La Plaza**. Its church, Iglesia de San Pedro de Teverga, is a fine example of Romanesque architecture. West of La Plaza is **Villanueva**, with its Romanesque Iglesia de Santa María. The 20 km (12 mile) Senda del Oso path skirts the edge of a bear enclosure.

Environs

The large **Parque Natural de Somiedo** straddles the mountains bordering León. Its high meadows and forests are a sanctuary for wolves, brown bears and capercaillies, as well as a number of rare species of wild flowers.

The park has 4 glacial lakes, and is peppered with herdsmen's traditional thatched huts, known as *teitos (see p27)*.

Avilés ❺

Asturias. 84,000. Calle Ruîz Gómez 21, 985 54 43 25. Mon. San Agustín (last week Aug).

Avilés became the capital of Asturias' steel industry in the 1800s and is still ringed by big factories. Even though it is sometimes criticized for having little to offer the visitor, the town hides a medieval heart of some character, especially around the Plaza de España. The **Iglesia de San Nicolás Bari** is decorated with frescoes and has a Renaissance cloister. The **Iglesia de Padres Franciscanos** contains a fine 14th-century chapel and holds the tomb of the first Governor of the US state of Florida. All around are arcaded streets. The international airport outside Avilés serves all Asturias.

Gijón ❻

Asturias. 278,000. Puerto Deportivo, Espigón Central de Fomento, 985 34 17 71. Sun. Semana Negra (mid-Jul), La Virgen de Begoña (15 Aug). **www**.gijon.info

The province's largest city, this industrial port has been much rebuilt since the Civil War when it was bombarded by the Nationalist navy. The city's most famous son is Gaspar Melchor de Jovellanos, an eminent 18th-century author, reformer and diplomat.

Gijon's old town is on a small isthmus and headland. It centres on the arcaded Plaza Mayor and the 18th-century **Palacio de Revillagigedo**, a Neo-Renaissance folly now housing a cultural centre. The beach is popular in summer.

Palacio de Revillagigedo/ Centro Cultural Cajastur

Plaza del Marqués 2. ***Tel*** *985 34 69 21.* *daily for temporary exhibitions.*

The pretty 12th-century Iglesia de San Pedro at La Plaza

Oviedo 7

225,000. Plaza de la Constitución 4, 984 08 60 60. Thu, Sat & Sun. San Mateo (14–21 Sep).

Oviedo, a university city and the cultural and commercial capital of Asturias, stands on a raised site on a fertile plain. The nearby coal mines have made it an important industrial centre since the 19th century. It retains some of the atmosphere of that time, as described by Leopoldo Alas ("Clarín") in his great novel *La Regenta (see p35)*.

In and around Oviedo are many Pre-Romanesque buildings. This style flourished in the 8th–10th centuries and was confined to a small area of the kingdom of Asturias, one of the few enclaves of Spain not invaded by the Moors.

The nucleus of the medieval city is the stately Plaza Alfonso II, bordered by a number of handsome old palaces. On this square is situated the Flamboyant Gothic **cathedral** *(see p24)* with its high tower and asymmetrical west façade. Inside are tombs of Asturian kings and a majestic 16th-century gilded reredos. The cathedral's supreme treasure is the Cámara Santa, a restored 9th-century chapel containing statues of Christ and the apostles. The chapel also houses many works of 9th-century Asturian art including two crosses and a reliquary – all made of gold, silver and precious stones.

Cross of Angels in the treasury of Oviedo cathedral

Also situated in the Plaza Alfonso II is the **Iglesia de San Tirso**. This church was originally constructed in the 9th century, but subsequent restorations have left the east window as the only surviving Pre-Romanesque feature.

Sited behind the cathedral is the **Museo Arqueológico**, housed in the old Benedictine monastery of San Vicente, with its fine cloisters. It contains local prehistoric, Romanesque and Pre-Romanesque treasures.

The **Museo de Bellas Artes**, in Velarde Palace, has a good range of Asturian and Spanish paintings, such as Carreño's portrait of Carlos II *(see p70)* and others by Greco, Goya, Dalí, Miró and Picasso.

Two of the most magnificent Pre-Romanesque churches are

SANTA MARÍA DEL NARANCO

This church, on Mount Naranco, was originally built as a summer palace for Ramiro I in the 9th century. It is one of the finest examples of Pre-Romanesque or Asturian architecture, a style characterized by the slender proportions of its buildings and their original and graceful ornamentation.

The Hall has an unusually high ceiling.

Arcaded galleries at both ends of the building were designed to let in an enormous amount of light and were an architectural innovation.

Columns carved with *soqueado* or rope effect, were typical of the Pre-Romanesque style.

Vaultings of this size were a technical achievement and not adopted throughout Europe until the 11th century.

For hotels and restaurants in this region see pp562–5 and pp611–13

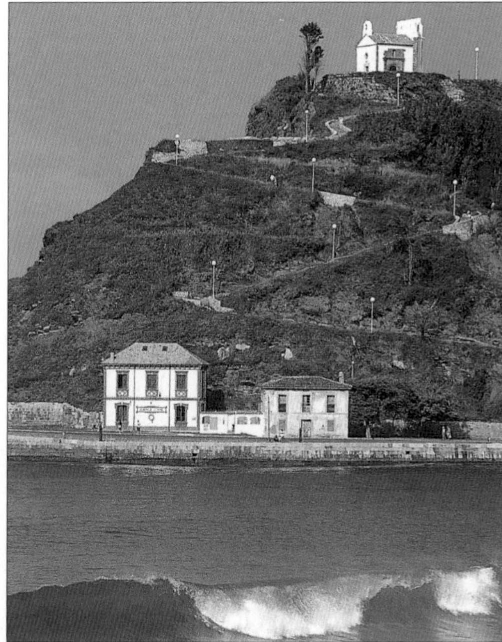

Church overlooking the sea at Ribadesella

on Mount Naranco, to the north. **Santa María del Naranco** has a large barrel-vaulted hall on the main floor and arcaded galleries at either end. Some of the intricate reliefs on the door jambs of the nearby **San Miguel de Lillo** show acrobats and animal tamers in a circus.

The early 9th-century church of **San Julián de los Prados** stands on the road leading northeast out of Oviedo. The largest of Spain's surviving Pre-Romanesque churches, it is noted for the frescoes which cover all of its interior.

Museo Arqueológico
Calle San Vicente 3. ***Tel*** *985 20 89 77.* *Wed–Sun.*

Museo de Bellas Artes
Calle Santa Ana 1. ***Tel*** *985 21 30 61.* *Tue–Sun.*

Valdediós 8

Asturias. *150.* *Monasterio de Sta María, 985 89 23 24.* **Monastery** *11am–1:30pm, 4:30–7pm Tue–Sun (11am–1pm Nov–Apr).*

Set alone in a field near this hamlet, the tiny 9th-century **Iglesia de San Salvador** is a jewel of Pre-Romanesque art. Its ceiling has vivid Asturian frescoes, and by the portal are recesses where pilgrims slept. The church in the **Monasterio de Santa María** next door is 13th-century Cistercian, with cloisters from the 16th century.

Environs

To the north, the resort town of **Villaviciosa** lies amid apple orchards. In nearby **Amandi**, the hilltop Iglesia de San Juan has a 13th-century portal and delicate carvings and friezes.

Iglesia de San Salvador de Valdediós in its idyllic setting

Ribadesella 9

Asturias. *6,000.* *Paseo Princesa Letizia, 985 86 00 38.* *Wed.* *Descent of the Río Sella (first Sat of Aug).* **www**.ribadesella.es

This enchanting little seaside town bestrides a broad estuary. On one side is the lively old seaport full of tapas bars below a clifftop church. Across the estuary is a holiday resort. A multicoloured flotilla of kayaks arrives here from Arriondas (upstream) in an international regatta that is held every year on the first Saturday in August.

On the edge of town is the **Cueva de Tito Bustillo**. This cave is rich in stalactites but is best known for its many prehistoric drawings, which were discovered in 1968, some dating from around 18,000 BC. These include red and black pictures of stags and horses. To protect the paintings, only 360 visitors are allowed in per day; tickets are given out from 10am every day and should be booked in advance. There is a museum on the site.

Cueva de Tito Bustillo
Ribadesella. ***Tel*** *985 86 12 55.* *Apr–Oct: Wed–Sun.* *(free Wed).*

Cangas de Onís 10

Asturias. *6,500.* *Plaza del Ayuntamiento 1, 985 84 80 05.* *Sun.* *San Antonio (13 Jun), Cheese Festival (12 Oct).* **www**.cangasdeonis.com

Cangas de Onís, one of the gateways to the Picos de Europa *(see pp108–9)*, is where Pelayo, the 8th-century Visigothic nobleman and hero of the Reconquest, set up his court. The town has a Romanesque bridge and the 8th-century chapel of Santa Cruz.

Environs

About 3 km (2 miles) east in Cardes is the **Cueva del Buxu**, which has engravings and rock-drawings over 10,000 years old. Only 25 visitors are allowed daily, and no visitors under 7.

Cueva del Buxu
Tel *608 17 54 67 (mobile).* *Wed–Sun.* *reservations essential; call 3–5pm Wed–Sun (free Wed).*

Parque Nacional de los Picos de Europa ⓫

Lefebvre's Ringlet

These beautiful mountains were reputedly christened the "Peaks of Europe" by returning sailors for whom this was often the first sight of their homeland. The range straddles three regions – Asturias, Cantabria and Castilla y León – and has diverse terrain. In some parts, deep winding gorges cut through craggy rocks while elsewhere verdant valleys support orchards and dairy farming. The celebrated creamy blue cheese, Cabrales *(see p77)*, is made here. The Picos offer rock climbing and upland hiking as well as a profusion of flora and fauna. Tourism in the park is well organized.

Covadonga
The Neo-Romanesque basilica, built between 1886 and 1901, stands on the site of Pelayo's historic victory.

Lago de la Ercina
Together with the nearby Lago Enol, this lake lies on a wild limestone plateau above Covadonga and below the peak of Peña Santa.

RIBADESELLA
Cangas de Onís
AS114
N625
DESFILADERO DE LOS BEYOS
Covadonga
LAGO ENOL
LAGO DE LA ERCINA
Sella
N625
Posada de Valdeón
GARGANTA DEL
Cares
LE244
Oseja de Sajambre
Puerto de Panderruedas
Puerto del Pontón
RIAÑO

Desfiladero de los Beyos
This deep, narrow gorge with its high limestone cliffs winds spectacularly for 10 km (6 miles) through the mountains. Tracing the route of the Río Sella below, it carries the main road from Cangas de Onís to Riaño.

KEY

- Major road
- Minor road
- Footpath
- National park boundary
- Cable car
- Tourist information
- Parador
- Viewpoint

Desfiladero del Río Cares
The River Cares forms a deep gorge in the heart of the Picos. A dramatic footpath follows the gorge, passing through tunnels and across high bridges up to 1,000 m (3,280 ft) above the river.

dramatic view of the mountains of the Picos de Europa

VISITORS' CHECKLIST

Casa Dago, Cangas de Onís, 985 84 86 14. Oviedo to Cangas de Onís. **Fuente Dé cable car** ***Tel*** *942 73 66 10.* *Jul–Sep: 9am–8pm daily, Oct–Jun: 10am–6pm daily.* **www**.picosdeeuropa.com

PELAYO THE WARRIOR

A statue of this Visigothic nobleman who became king of Asturias guards the basilica at Covadonga. It was close to this site, in 722, that Pelayo and a band of men – though vastly outnumbered – are said to have defeated a Moorish army. The victory inspired Christians in the north of Spain to reconquer the peninsula *(see pp53–5)*. The tomb of the warrior is in a cave which has become a shrine, also containing a painted image of the Virgin.

Pelayo's statue

ulnes, one of the remotest villages in Spain, enjoys ne views of Naranjo de Bulnes and can now be ccessed by an underground funicular railway from 'uente Poncebos as well as by foot.

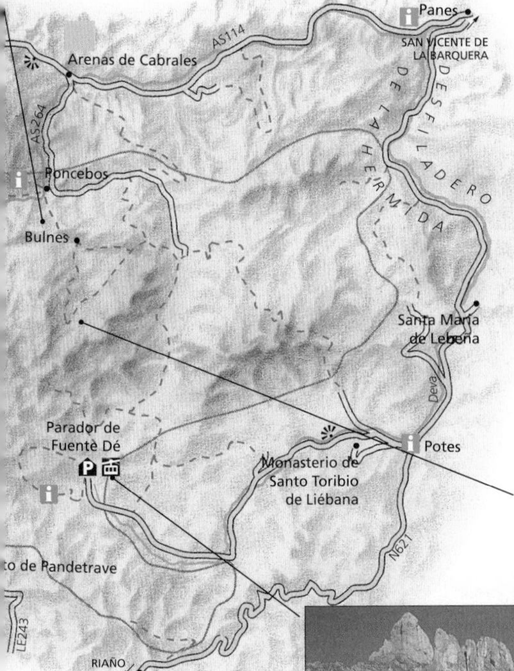

Naranjo de Bulnes, with its tooth-like crest, is in the heart of the massif. At 2,519 m (8,264 ft) it is one of the highest summits in the Picos de Europa.

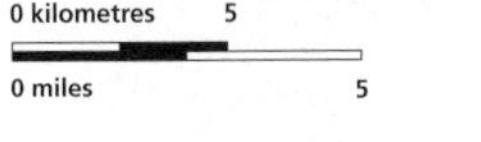

Fuente Dé Cable Car
The 900-m (2950-ft) ascent from Fuente Dé takes visitors up to a wild rocky plateau pitted with craters. From here there is a spectacular panorama of the Picos' peaks and valleys.

Statue of the Virgin, San Vicente de la Barquera

ASTURIAS AND CANTABRIA'S FIESTAS

La Folía *(second Sun after Easter)*, San Vicente de la Barquera (Cantabria). The statue of the Virgen de la Barquera is said to have arrived at San Vicente in a boat with no sails, oars or crew. Once a year, it is put in a fishing boat decorated with flags and flowers, which sails at the head of a procession to bless the sea. Groups of young girls, called *picayos,* stand on the shore singing traditional songs of the region in honour of the Virgin. La Folía usually takes place on the second Sunday after Easter, depending on local tides.
Fiesta del Pastor *(25 Jul)*, near Cangas de Onís (Asturias). Regional dances are performed at this festival beside the shores of Lake Enol in the Picos de Europa National Park.
Battle of the Flowers *(last Fri of Aug)*, Laredo (Cantabria). Floats adorned with flowers are paraded through this small resort. A flower-throwing free-for-all follows the procession.
Nuestra Señora de Covadonga *(8 Sep)*, Picos de Europa (Asturias). Huge crowds converge on the shrine of Covadonga *(see p108)* to pay homage to the patron saint of Asturias.

Potes ⓬

Cantabria. *1,500.* *Calle Independencia 12, 942 73 07 87.* *Mon.* *Ntra. Sra. de Valmayor (15 Aug), Santísima Cruz (14 Sep).*

A small ancient town, with old balconied houses lining the river, Potes is the main centre of the eastern Picos de Europa. It is situated in the broad Valle de Liébana, whose fertile soil yields prime crops of walnuts, cherries and grapes. A potent spirit called *orujo* is made in the town. The **Torre del Infantado**, in the main square, is a defensive tower built in the 15th century.

Environs
Between Potes and the coast runs a gorge, the **Desfiladero de la Hermida**. Halfway up it is **Santa María de Lebeña**, a 10th-century Mozarabic *(see p335)* church.

West of Potes is the monastery church of **Santo Toribio de Liébana**, one of the most revered spots in the Picos de Europa. Founded in the 7th century, it became known throughout Spain a century later when it received reputedly the largest fragment of the True Cross. An 8th century monk, St Beatus of Liébana, wrote the *Commentary on the Apocalypse*. The restored Romanesque monastic buildings were rebuilt in the 1200s, and are now occupied by Franciscan monks.

Comillas ⓭

Cantabria. *2,400.* *Plaza Joaquín del Piélago 1, 942 72 25 91.* *Fri.* *El Cristo (16 Jul).*
Palacio Sobrellano *Mar–Oct: 9:30am–2:30pm, 3:30–6:30pm daily (to 7:30pm mid-Jun–mid-Sep); Nov–Feb: 9:30am–3:30pm daily.*

This pretty resort is known for its buildings by Catalan Modernista architects *(see pp140–41)*. Antonio López y López, the first Marquis of Comillas, hired Joan Martorell to design the Neo-Gothic

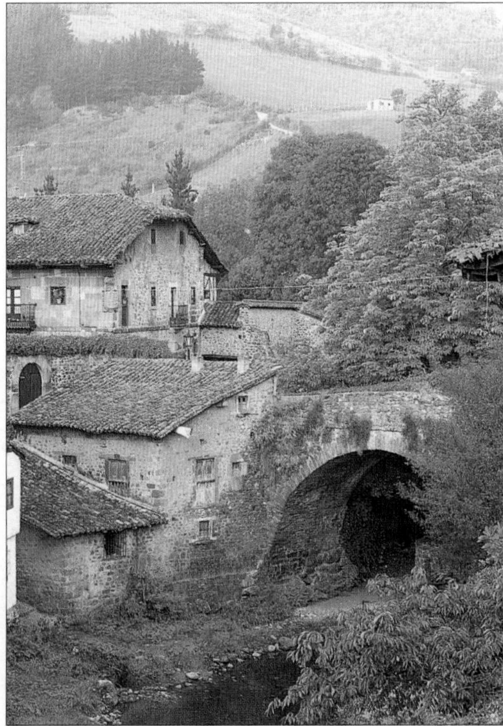
Stone bridge and houses in the ancient town of Potes

Surviving Classical columns among the ruins of the Roman town of Juliobriga, near Reinosa

Palacio Sobrellano (1881), now a museum. Comilla's best-known monument is Gaudí's *(see p164)* **El Capricho**, now a restaurant *(see p611)*. It was designed from 1883–9 and is a Mudéjar-inspired fantasy with a minaret-like tower covered in green and yellow tiles. Another Modernista building is the **Universidad Pontificia**, on a hilltop overlooking the sea. It was designed by Joan Martorell to plans by Domènech i Montaner *(see p140)*.

Wall tile on the façade of El Capricho

Environs

The fishing port of **San Vicente de la Barquera** has arcaded streets, ramparts and the Gothic Romanesque church of Nuestra Señora de los Ángeles.

Valle de Cabuérniga ⓮

Cantabria. Bárcena Mayor.
Ayuntamiento de Cabuerniga, 942 70 60 01.

Two exceptionally picturesque towns, notable for their superb examples of rural architecture, draw visitors to the Cabuérniga Valley. A good road takes you to the once-remote **Bárcena Mayor**. Its cobbled streets are furnished with old lamps and filled with boutiques, and restaurants serving regional dishes. The pretty houses have flower-covered balconies and cattle byres.

Carmona is an old, unspoiled village approximately 20 km (12 miles) to the northwest of Bárcena Mayor. Its solid stone houses, with pantiled roofs and wooden balconies, are typically Cantabrian *(see p26)*. Woodcarving, the traditional craft of the region, is still practised in this village, where men work outside their houses on a variety of artifacts including bowls, fiddles, *albarcas* (clogs) and chairs. The 13th-century Palacio de los Mier, a manor house in the centre of the village, has been restored and is now a hotel.

The extensive, wild beech woods near **Saja** have been designated a nature reserve.

Traditional balconied houses in Bárcena Mayor

Alto Campoo ⓯

Cantabria. 1,900. Reinosa.
Estación de Montaña, 942 77 92 23 (am only); Reinosa, 942 75 52 15.
San Sebastián (20 Jan, Reinosa).

Sited high in the Cantabrian mountains, this winter resort lies below the Pico de Tres Mares (2,175 m/7,000 ft), the "Peak of the Three Seas", so called because the rivers rising near it flow into the Mediterranean, the Atlantic and the Bay of Biscay. The Río Ebro, one of Spain's longest rivers, rises in this area and its source, at Fontibre, is a beauty spot. A road and a chair lift reach the summit of Tres Mares for a breathtaking panorama of the Picos de Europa and other mountain chains. The resort is small, with 23 pistes totalling 27 km (17 miles) in length, and has few facilities for après-ski.

Environs

Reinosa, some 26 km (16 miles) to the east of Alto Campoo, is a handsome market town with old stone houses. Further southeast is Retortillo, a hamlet where the remains of **Juliobriga**, a town built by the Romans as a bastion against the wild tribes of Cantabria, can be seen.

The main road south out of Reinosa leads to **Cervatos**, where the former collegiate church has erotic carvings on its façade. This novel device was meant to deter the villagers from pleasures of the flesh.

At **Arroyuelo** and **Cadalso**, to the southeast, are two churches built into rock faces in the 8th and 9th centuries.

One of the many paintings of bison at Altamira

Cuevas de Altamira ⓰

Cantabria. ***Tel** 942 81 80 05.* *Santillana del Mar.* **Caves** *to the public.* **Museum** *9:30am–6pm Tue–Sat (to 8pm May–Oct), 9:30am–3pm Sun.* *1 & 6 Jan, 1 May, 28 Jun, 24, 25 & 31 Dec.* *(advance booking advisable, 902 24 24 24).* **http**://museodealtamira.mcu.es

These caves contain some of the world's finest examples of prehistoric art. The earliest engravings and drawings, discovered in 1879, date back to around 16,000 BC *(see p48)*. Public entry to the caves is no longer permitted, but the on-site museum contains a replica of the caves. Similar sites that remain open to the public can be found at nearby Puente Viesgo, Ribadesella *(see p107)* in Asturias and at Nerja *(see p483)* in Andalusia.

Santillana del Mar ⓱

Cantabria. *4,000.* *Calle Jesus Otero 20, 942 81 88 12.* *Santa Juliana (28 Jun), San Roque (16 Aug).* **www.**santillanadelmarturismo.com

Set just inland, belying its name, this town is one of the prettiest in Spain. Its ensemble of 15th- to 18th-century stone houses survives largely intact.

The town grew up around a monastery, which was an important pilgrimage centre, the Romanesque **La Colegiata**. The church houses the tomb of the local early medieval martyr St Juliana, and contains a 17th-century painted reredos and a carved south door. In its lovely cloisters, vivid biblical scenes have been sculpted on the capitals. On the town's two main cobbled streets there are houses built by local noblemen. These have either fine wooden galleries or iron balconies, and coats of arms inlaid into their stone façades. In the past, farmers used the open ground floors as byres for stabling their cattle.

Carved figure of Christ in the Convento de Regina Coeli

In the enchanting **Plaza Mayor**, in the centre of town, is a mansion-turned-parador *(see p564)*. The **Museo Diocesano** is housed in the restored Convento de Regina Coeli, east of the town centre, and has a collection of painted carvings of religious figures.

Museo Diocesano
El Cruce. ***Tel** 942 84 03 17.*
Tue–Sun (daily Jul & Aug).

Puente Viesgo ⓲

Cantabria. *2,800.* *Calle Manuel Pérez Mazo 2, 942 59 81 05 (town hall).* *La Perolá (20 Jan), San Miguel (28–29 Sep).*

This spa village is best known for **El Monte Castillo**, a complex of caves dotted around the limestone hills above the town. Decorated by prehistoric man, it is thought the late Palaeolithic cave dwellers used the deep interior as a sanctuary. They left drawings of horses, bison and other animals, and some 50 hand prints. The colours used to create the images were made from minerals in the cave.

Environs

The lush Pas valley, to the southeast, is home to transhumant dairy farmers, the Pasiegos. In the main town of **Vega de Pas**, you can buy two Pasiego specialities – *sobaos*, or sponge cakes *(see p77)*, and *quesadas*, a sweet which is made from milk, butter and eggs. In **Villacarriedo** there is a handsome 18th-century mansion, with two Baroque façades of carved stone hiding a medieval tower.

El Monte Castillo
Puente Viesgo. ***Tel** 942 59 84 25.*
Wed–Sun (mid-Jun–mid-Sep: Tue–Sun; Nov–Feb: am only).

Main façade of La Colegiata in Santillana del Mar

The Palacio de la Magdalena in El Sardinero

Santander 19

Cantabria. 180,000. Jardines de Pereda s/n, 942 20 30 00. Mon–Thu. Santiago (25 Jul). **www**.turismodecantabria.com

Cantabria's capital, a busy port, enjoys a splendid site near the mouth of a deep bay. The town centre is modern – after being ravaged by fire in 1941 it was reconstructed. The **cathedral** was rebuilt in Gothic style, but retains its 12th-century crypt. The **Museo de Bellas Artes** houses work by Goya as well as other artists of the 19th and 20th centuries. The town's **Museo de Prehistoria y Arqueología** displays finds from caves at Altamira and Puente Viesgo *(see p112)*, such as Neolithic axe heads, and Roman coins, pottery and figurines. The **Museo Marítimo** has rare whale skeletons and 350 species of local fish.

The town extends along the coast around the Península de la Magdalena, a headland on which there is a park, a small zoo and the **Palacio de la Magdalena** – a summer palace built for Alfonso XIII in 1912, reflecting the resort's popularity at the time with the Royal Family.

The seaside suburb of **El Sardinero**, north of the headland, is a smart resort with a long graceful beach, backed by gardens, elegant cafés and a majestic white casino. In July and August El Sardinero plays host to a major theatre and music festival.

Museo de Bellas Artes
Calle Rubio 6. ***Tel*** *942 20 31 20.* *Mon–Sat.*

Museo de Prehistoria y Arqueología
Calle Casimiro Sainz 4. ***Tel*** *942 20 71 09.* *Tue–Sun.*

Museo Marítimo
C/ San Martin de Bajamar. ***Tel*** *942 27 49 62.* *Tue–Sun (May–Sep: daily).*

Laredo 20

Cantabria. *13,000. Alameda Miramar, 942 61 10 96. Batalla de Flores (last Fri of Aug), Carlos V's last landing (3rd week in Sep)*

Its long, sandy beach has made Laredo one of Cantabria's most popular bathing resorts. The attractive old town has narrow streets with balconied houses leading up to the 13th-century **Iglesia de Santa María de la Asunción**, with its Flemish altar and bronze lecterns. One of the highlights of the year in Laredo is the colourful Battle of the Flowers *(see p110)*.

Castro Urdiales 21

Cantabria. *32,000. Calle de Belén 1, 942 87 15 12. Thu. San Pelayo (26 Jun), Coso Blanco (1st Fri of Jul), San Andrés (30 Nov).* **Iglesia** *daily.*

Castro Urdiales, a busy fishing town and popular holiday resort, is built around a picturesque harbour. Above the port, on a high promontory, stands the pinkish Gothic **Iglesia de Santa María**, as big as a cathedral. Beside it the restored castle, said to have been built by the Knights Templar, has been converted into a lighthouse. Handsome glass-fronted houses, or *galerías*, line the promenade. The small town beach often becomes crowded but there are bigger ones to the west, such as the Playa de Ostende.

Environs
Near the village of **Ramales de la Victoria**, 40 km (25 miles) south, are prehistoric caves containing etchings and engravings, reached by a very steep mountain road.

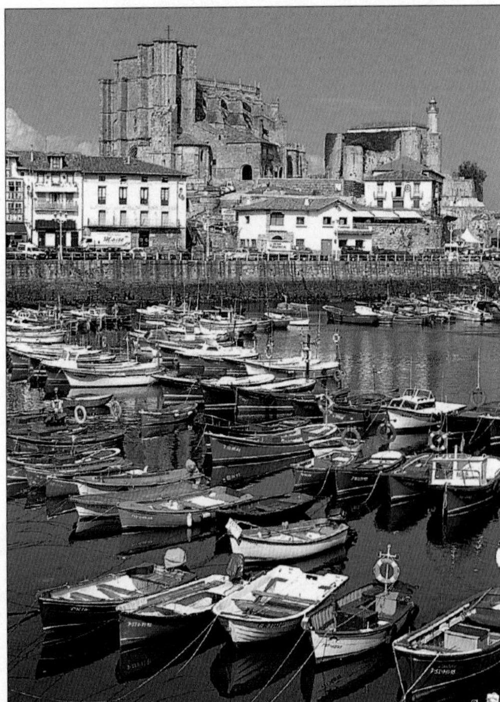

Small boats moored in the harbour at Castro Urdiales

THE BASQUE COUNTRY, NAVARRA AND LA RIOJA

VIZCAYA · GUIPUZCOA · ÁLAVA · LA RIOJA · NAVARRA

Green hills meet Atlantic beaches in the Basque Country, land of an ancient people of mysterious origin. Navarra, also partly Basque, was a powerful medieval kingdom. The beautiful western Pyrenees form part of its charming countryside. The vineyards of La Rioja, to the south, produce many of Spain's finest wines.

The Basques are a race apart – they will not let you forget that theirs is a culture different from any in Spain. Although the Basque regional government enjoys considerable autonomy, there is a strong separatist movement seeking to sever links with the government in Madrid.

The Basque Country (Euskadi is the Basque name) is an important industrial region. The Basques are great deep-sea fishermen and fish has a major role in their imaginative cuisine, regarded by many as the best in Spain.

Unrelated to any other tongue, the Basque language, *Euskera*, is widely used on signs and most towns have two names; the fashionable resort of San Sebastián, for example, is known to locals as Donostia. *Euskera* is also spoken in parts of Navarra, which is counted as part of the wider (unofficial) Basque Country. Many of its finest sights – the towns of Olite and Estella, and the monastery of Leyre – date from the Middle Ages when Navarra was a kingdom straddling the Pyrenees. Pamplona, its capital, is best known for its daredevil bullrunning fiesta, which is held in July.

As well as its vineyards and bodegas, La Rioja is a region of market gardens. Among its many historic sights are the cathedral of Santo Domingo de la Calzada and the monasteries of San Millán de la Cogolla and Yuso.

Basque farmhouse near Gernika-Lumo in the Basque Country

◁ **A street in the village of Roncal, in the foothills of the Navarrese Pyrenees**

Exploring the Basque Country, Navarra and La Rioja

These green, hilly regions have diverse attractions. The Pyrenees in Navarra offer skiing in winter and climbing, caving and canoeing the rest of the year. The cliffs of the Basque Country are broken by rocky coves, rías, and wide bays with beaches of fine yellow sand, interspersed with fishing villages. Inland, minor roads wind through wooded hills, valleys and gorges, past lonely castles and isolated homesteads. In La Rioja, to the south, they cross vineyards, passing villages and towns clustered round venerable churches and monasteries.

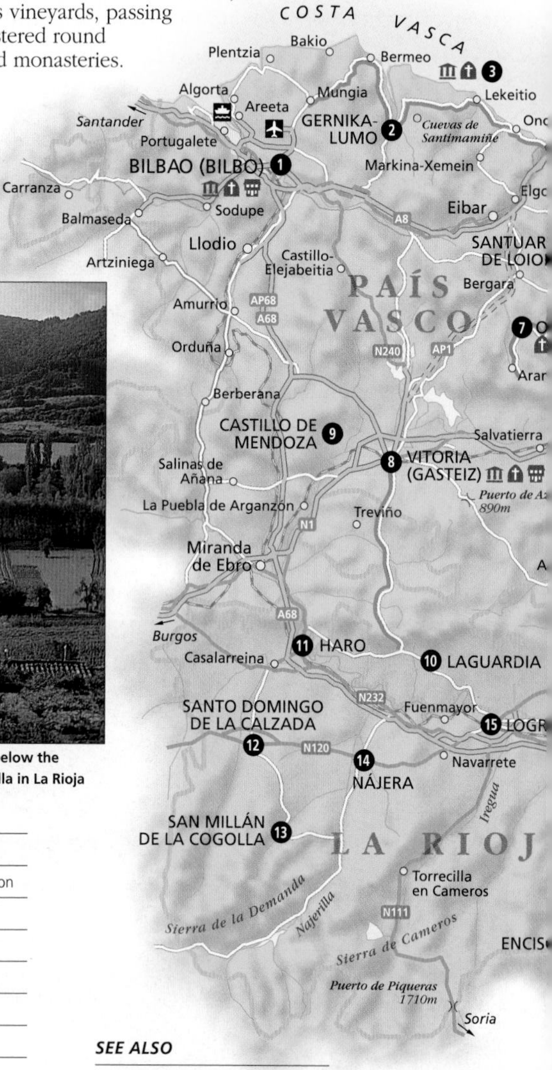

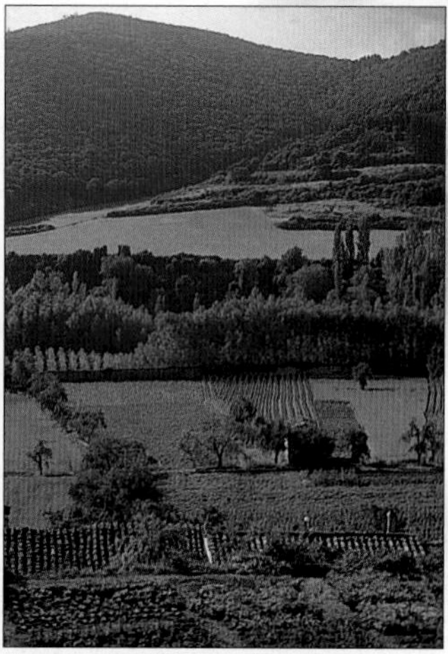

The scenic Río Cárdenas valley below the village of San Millán de la Cogolla in La Rioja

KEY

- Motorway
- Motorway under construction
- Major road
- Minor road
- Scenic route
- Main railway
- Minor railway
- International border
- Regional border

SEE ALSO

- ***Where to Stay*** pp565–8
- ***What to Eat*** pp613–17

0 kilometres 25

0 miles 15

For additional map symbols *see back flap*

SIGHTS AT A GLANCE

Bilbao (Bilbo) 1
Castillo de Javier 29
Las Cinco Villas del Valle de Bidasoa 24
Costa Vasca 3
Elizondo 25
Enciso 16
Estella (Lizarra) 22
Gernika-Lumo 2
Haro 11
Hondarribia (Fuenterrabía) 5
Laguardia 10
Logroño 15
Monasterio de Leyre 28
Monasterio de La Oliva 18
Nájera 14
Olite 20
Oñati 7
Pamplona (Iruña) 23
Puente la Reina 21
Roncesvalles (Orreaga) 26
Sangüesa 30
San Millán de la Cogolla 13
San Sebastián (Donostia) 4
Santo Domingo de la Calzada 12
Santuario de Loiola 6
Torre Palacio de los Varona 9
Tudela 17
Ujué 19
Valle de Roncal 27
Vitoria (Gasteiz) 8

GETTING AROUND

The main road in the north is the A8 (E5). The A68 AP68 (E804) runs southwards from Bilbao via Haro and follows the Ebro Valley. Motorway spurs extend to Vitoria and Pamplona. The rail network connects the cities and the larger towns, and most towns are served by coach. Bilbao has an international airport. In the Basque Country, signs are in both Basque and Castilian.

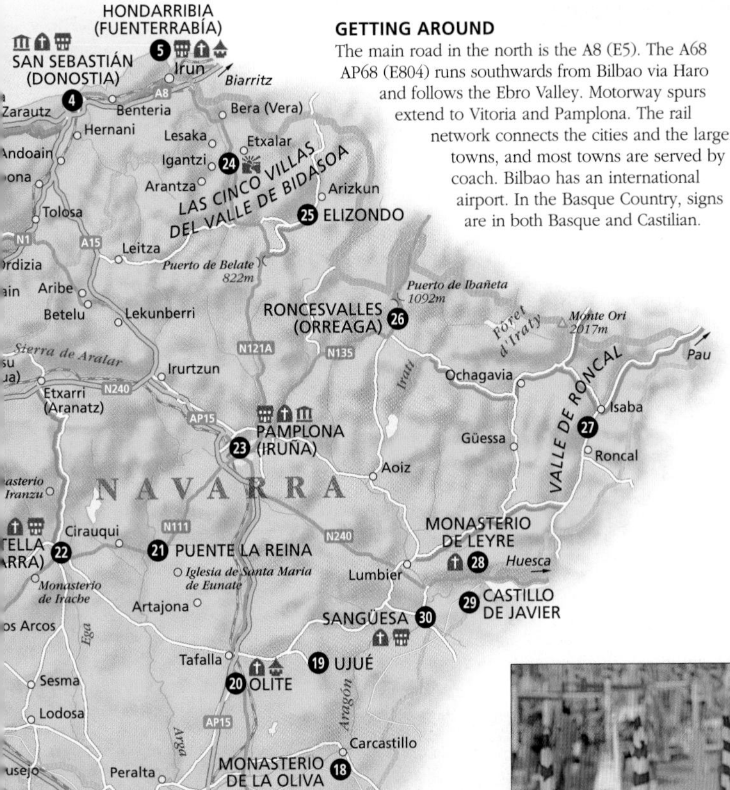

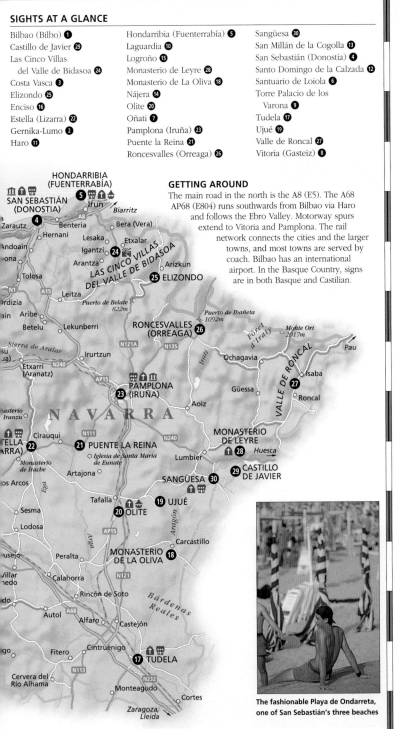

The fashionable Playa de Ondarreta, one of San Sebastián's three beaches

Buildings overlooking the Río Nervión in Bilbao

Bilbao ❶

Vizcaya. 354,000.
Pl. Ensanche 11, 944 79 57 60. *Santiago (25 Jul), La Asunción (15 Aug), Semana Grande (late Aug).* **www**.bilbao.net/bilbaoturismo

Bilbao (Bilbo) is the centre of Basque industry, an important port and the largest Basque city. It is surrounded by high, bare hills. Its suburbs spread 16 km (10 miles) along the Río Nervión (Nerbioi) to its estuary. The river between Las Arenas and the fishing port of Portugalete is crossed via the **Puente Colgante** (a UNESCO World Heritage site). This iron transporter bridge, built in 1888, has a suspended cabin for cars and passengers. On the east bank of the estuary is Santurtzi (Santurce), from where ferries sail to the UK *(see p675)*.

Bilbao has flourished as an industrial city since the mid-19th century, when iron ore began to be extracted from deposits northwest of the city. Soon, steelworks and chemical factories became a major part of the local landscape.

The city is not beautiful, but it is prosperous and its once heavy pollution is now much reduced. An urban development scheme has introduced pieces of fascinating modernist architecture to break up the monotone industrial sprawl.

By the river, however, is the city's medieval heart, the *casco viejo*, built in the 14th century. Here, amid alleys lively with tapas bars, is the arcaded Plazuela de Santiago and the **Catedral Basílica de Santiago**. The **Museo Vasco** displays Basque art, folk artifacts and photographs of Basque life. In the cloister is the Idol of Mikeldi, an animal-like carving dating from the 3rd–2nd century BC.

In the newer town is the large **Museo de Bellas Artes** (Museum of Fine Art), one of Spain's best art museums. It displays art ranging from 12th-century Basque and Catalan pieces to works by modern artists of international fame, including Vasarely, Kokoschka, Bacon, Delaunay and Léger. There are also paintings by Basque artists.

The jewel in the area's cultural crown is the **Museo Guggenheim Bilbao** *(see pp120–21)*, which opened in 1997. The museum is part of a redevelopment of the city which includes the expansion of its port and the metro system, designed in a futuristic style by Norman Foster. Another striking building is the **Palacio de la Música y Congresos Euskalduna**. Designed to resemble a ship, it has a number of auditoriums, one seating 2,200 people and is the home of the Bilbao Symphony Orchestra.

West of the city, a funicular railway ascends to the village of La Reineta and a panorama across the dockyards.

Museo Vasco
Plaza Miguel Unamuno 4. ***Tel*** *94 415 54 23.* *Tue–Sun.* *public hols.* *(except Thu).*

Museo de Bellas Artes
Plaza del Museo 2. ***Tel*** *94 439 60 60.* *Tue–Sun.* *(except Wed).*

Palacio de la Música y Congresos Euskalduna
Avenida Abandoibarra 4. ***Tel*** *94 403 50 00.* *for concerts.*

Zuloaga's *Condesa Mathieu de Noailles* (1913), Bilbao Museum of Fine Art

Gernika-Lumo ❷

Vizcaya. *16,000.* *Artekalea 8, 94 625 58 92.* *Mon (Jun–Dec: also Sat).* *Aniversario del Bombardeo de Guernica (26 Apr), San Roke (14–18 Aug).*

This little town is of great symbolic significance to the Basques. For centuries, Basque leaders met in democratic assembly under an oak on a hillside here. On 26 April 1937 Gernika-Lumo (Guernica) was the target of the world's first saturation bombing raid, carried out by Nazi aircraft at the request of General Franco. Picasso's powerful painting *(see pp66–7)* of this outrage can be seen in Madrid *(see p299)*.

The town has since been rebuilt and is rather dull. But in a garden, inside a pavilion and closely guarded, is the 300-year-old petrified trunk of the oak tree, the *Gernikako Arbola*, or Oak of Gernika, symbol of the ancient roots of the Basque people. Younger oaks, nurtured from its acorns, have been planted beside it. The Basque people make visits to this ancient tree as if

Basque fishermen depicted in the stained-glass ceiling of the Casa de Juntas in Gernika-Lumo

on a pilgrimage. The **Casa de Juntas**, nearby, is a former chapel where the parliament of the province of Vizcaya reconvened in 1979, when the Basque provinces regained their autonomy. In one room a stained-glass ceiling depicts the Oak of Gernika with Basque citizens debating their rights.

The Europa Park, next door, has peace sculptures by Henry Moore and Eduardo Chillida.

Environs

Five km (3 miles) northeast of Gernika, near Kortézubi (Cortézubi), are the **Cuevas de Santimamiñe**. On the walls of a small chamber are charcoal drawings of animals made by cave dwellers around 11,000 BC. Discovered in 1917, the drawings cannot be seen, but replicas are projected on the walls at the entrance. For conservation reasons the caves are closed to the public, but a 3D simulation in the nearby hermitage offers an impressive virtual reproduction. Guided visits last 90 minutes and must be booked in advance.

Casa de Juntas
C/ Allende Salazar. ***Tel*** *94 625 11 38.* *daily.* *1 & 6 Jan, 16 Aug, 24, 25 & 31 Dec.* *book ahead.*

Cuevas de Santimamiñe
Kortézubi. ***Tel*** *944 65 16 57.*
Tue–Sun. *book ahead.*

Costa Vasca 3

Vizcaya & Guipúzcoa. *Bilbao.* *Bilbao.* *Getxo, 94 491 08 00.*

The Basque country's 176 km (110 miles) of coastline is heavily indented: rugged cliffs alternate with inlets and coves, the whole backed by wooded hills. Some of the fishing villages are over-developed, but the scenery inland is attractive.

There are good beaches north of Algorta (near Bilbao). **Plentzia** is a pleasant estuary town with a marina. Eastwards on the coast is **Bakio**, a large fishing village also known for its beaches. Beyond it the BI3101, a dramatic corniche road, winds high above the sea past the tiny island hermitage, San Juan de Gaztelugatxe, and Matxitxaco, a headland lighthouse. It passes Bermeo, a port with a fishery museum, the **Museo del Pescador**, and Mundaka, a small surfing resort. On the serene Ría de Guernica there are two sandy beaches, **Laida** and **Laga**.

Anglers on the quayside at Lekeitio, a port on the Costa Vasca

At the fishing port of **Lekeitio**, old Basque houses line the seafront below the 15th-century church of Santa María. One long beach, good for swimming, sweeps round the village of **Saturrarán** and the old port of **Ondarroa**. The Lekeitio–Ondarroa road is lined with pines.

Zumaia is a beach resort with an old quarter. In the **Museo de Ignacio Zuloaga**, the former home of the well-known Basque painter who lived from 1870–1945, colourful studies of Basque rural and maritime life are on display. **Getaria**, along the coast, is a trawler port with lively cafés. and the 14th-century Iglesia de San Salvador. **Zarautz**, once a fashionable resort, has sizeable beaches and elegant mansions.

Museo del Pescador
Plaza Torrontero 1. ***Tel*** *94 688 11 71.* *Tue–Sun.* *public hols.* *(free last Thu of the month).*

Museo de Ignacio Zuloaga
Santiago Etxea 4, Zumaia. ***Tel*** *943 86 23 41.* *Apr–Sep: 4–8pm Wed–Sun; other times by appt.*

Bilbao: Museo Guggenheim

The Museo Guggenheim Bilbao is the jewel in the city's cultural crown. The building itself is a star attraction: a mind-boggling array of silvery curves by the American architect Frank Gehry, which are alleged to resemble a ship or a flower. The Guggenheim's collection represents an intriguingly broad spectrum of modern and contemporary art, and includes works by Abstract Impressionists such as Willem de Kooning and Mark Rothko. Most of the art shown here is displayed as part of an ongoing series of temporary exhibitions and shows from the permanent collections of the Guggenheim museums in New York, Venice and Berlin.

Roofscape
The Guggenheim's prow-like points and metallic material make it comparable to a ship.

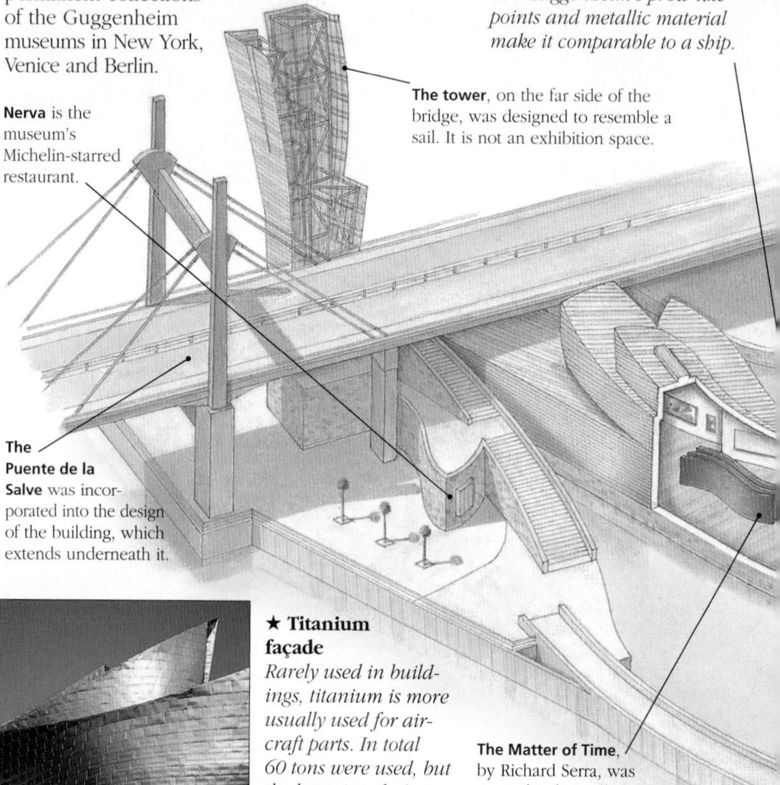

The tower, on the far side of the bridge, was designed to resemble a sail. It is not an exhibition space.

Nerva is the museum's Michelin-starred restaurant.

The Puente de la Salve was incorporated into the design of the building, which extends underneath it.

★ Titanium façade
Rarely used in buildings, titanium is more usually used for aircraft parts. In total 60 tons were used, but the layer is only 3 mm (0.1 inches) thick.

The Matter of Time, by Richard Serra, was created in hot-rolled steel. It is over 30 m (100 ft) long.

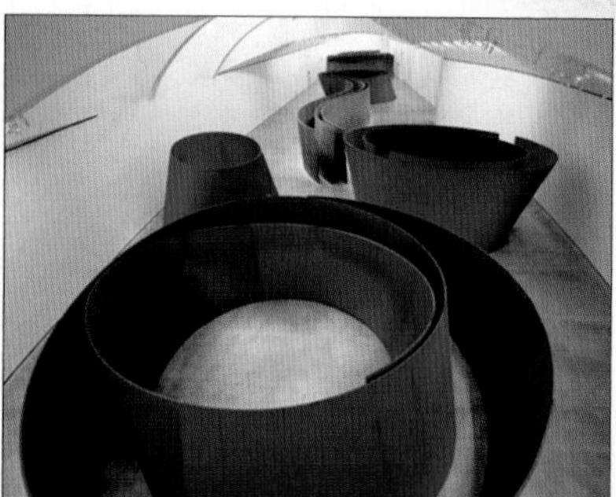

Arcelor Gallery
Dominated by Richard Serra's The Matter of Time, *this gallery is the museum's largest. The fish motif, seen in the flowing shape, is one of architect Frank Gehry's favourites.*

★ Atrium
The space in which visitors to the museum first find themselves is the extraordinary 60-m- (165-ft-) high atrium. It serves as an orientation point and its height makes it a dramatic setting for exhibiting large pieces.

VISITORS' CHECKLIST

Avenida Abandoibarra 2. **Tel** *944 35 90 00. Moyua. 1, 10, 11, 13, 18, 27, 38, 48, 71. 10am–8pm Tue–Sun (daily Jul & Aug).*
www.guggenheim-bilbao.es

Puppy, by American artist Jeff Koons, is a 13-m (43-ft) West Highland terrier with a coat of flowers watered by an internal irrigation system. It has become a favourite icon of the city.

Second-floor balcony

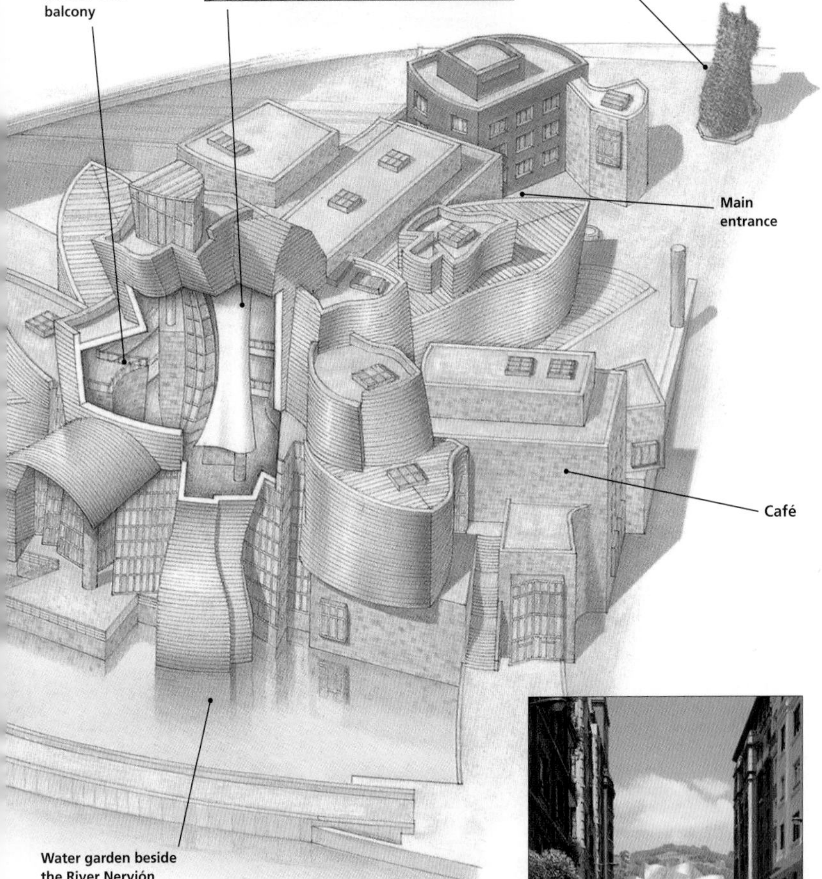

Main entrance

Café

Water garden beside the River Nervión

View from the City
Approaching along the Calle de Iparraguirre, the Guggenheim stands out amid traditional buildings.

STAR FEATURES

★ Titanium façade

★ Atrium

San Sebastián's Playa de Ondarreta, with its view across the bay

San Sebastián ❹

Guipúzcoa. *186,000.* *Hondarribia (20 km).* *Alameda del Bulevard 8, 943 48 11 66.* *Sun.* *San Sebastián (20 Jan); Semana Grande (week of 15 Aug).* **www**.sansebastianturismo.com

Gloriously situated on a neat, shell-shaped bay, San Sebastián (Donostia) is the most elegant and fashionable Spanish seaside resort. At either end of the bay is a tower-topped hill – Monte Urgull in the east and Monte Igueldo in the west. Between the two, in the mouth of the bay, lies a small island, the Isla de Santa Clara.

San Sebastián became a smart resort in the late 19th century. It still has many luxury shops and one of Spain's grandest hotels, the María Cristina *(see p567)*, but San Sebastián is now primarily a family resort.

The city is renowned for its great summer arts festivals. The theatre festival is held in May, jazz festivals are held in July, a classical music festival in August, and the San Sebastián International Film Festival in September. The Semana Grande in August is the city's principal fiesta.

Cuisine plays a huge part in local life: many Basque men here belong to gastronomic clubs where they gather to cook, eat, drink and talk. Women are invited to such meetings, but they don't take part in the food preparation.

The Old Town

San Sebastián's fascinating old town, called the Parte Vieja, is wedged between the bay and the Río Urumea. The alleys of the old town, packed with restaurants and tapas bars, are intensely animated at night. In the large local fish market, stalls piled high with delicacies testify to the key role of fish in the life of the town.

The heart of the old town is the **Plaza de la Constitución**, a handsome, arcaded square with coloured shutters. The numbers on the balconies date from when the square was used as a bullring – organizers sold a ticket for each numbered place. Nearby is the 16th-century church of **Iglesia de San Vicente**.

Monte Urgull rises behind the old town. On the summit are a statue of Christ and the ruined **Castillo de Santa Cruz de la Mota**, with old cannons.

Beaches

San Sebastián's two principal beaches follow the bay round to **Monte Igueldo**. The **Playa de Ondarreta** is the more fashionable of the two, while the **Playa de la Concha** is the larger. Between them is the **Palacio Miramar**, built in 1889 by the Basque architect, José Goicoa, to designs by Selden Wornum, a British architect. The palace, built for Queen María Cristina, established San Sebastián as an aristocratic resort. The gardens are open to the public.

At the water's edge near the Playa de Ondarreta is a striking group of modern iron sculptures, *The Comb of the Winds* by Eduardo Chillida. A road and a funicular railway, built in 1912, lead to the top of Monte Igueldo, where there is a small amusement park.

To the east of the Playa de la Concha is the surfer's favourite beach, **Playa de la Zurriola**, which is overlooked by the hill, **Monte Ulía**.

Aquarium

Plaza Carlos Blasco de Imaz 1.
Tel *943 44 00 99.* *Easter–Jun & Sep: 10am–8pm daily (to 9pm Sat & Sun); Jul–Aug: 10am–9pm daily; Oct–Easter: 10am–7pm (to 8pm Sat & Sun).* *1 Jan, 25 Dec.*

This remodelled aquarium boasts a 360° underwater tunnel, where visitors can view over 5,000 fish, including four species of shark. Tickets allow entry to a Naval Museum with exhibits of Basque naval history.

The Comb of the Winds **by Eduardo Chillida**

Josep Maria Sert's murals of Basque life in the Museo de San Telmo

Kursaal

Avenida de Zurriola 1. ***Tel*** *943 00 30 00.* **www**.kursaal.org

These giant cubes stand out as the most prominent feature on Zurriola beach, especially when lit up at night. Designed by Rafael Moneo, the cubes contain large auditoriums, for most of the year home to conferences and concerts.

Museo de San Telmo

Plaza Zuloaga. ***Tel*** *943 48 15 80.* *10am–8pm Tue–Sun.* *1 & 20 Jan, 25 Dec.* *(free Tue).*

This is a large museum in a 16th-century monastery below Monte Urgull. In the cloister is a collection of Basque funerary columns dating from the 15th–17th centuries.

The museum also contains displays of furniture, tools and other artifacts, and paintings by local Basque artists: 19th-century works by Antonio Ortiz Echagüe, modern paintings by Ignacio Zuloaga, portraits by Vicente López and masterpieces by El Greco. The chapel holds 11 murals by the Catalan artist Josep Maria Sert, depicting Basque legends, culture and the region's seafaring life.

Environs

5 km (3 miles) east of San Sebastián is **Pasai Donibane**, a picturesque fishing village consisting of a jumble of houses built along one cobbled main street, which has some good fish restaurants.

Around 8 km (5 miles) south of San Sebastián is the interesting medieval town of **Hernani**, which has been awarded the status of Cultural Interest Site. The forests surrounding the town are dotted with prehistoric remains, including dolmen, megalithic monuments and burial mounds.

The waterfront of the tiny fishing village of Pasaia Donibane

SAN SEBASTIÁN FILM FESTIVAL

This festival, founded in 1953, is one of the five leading European annual film festivals. It is held in late September, drawing more than 200,000 spectators. The special Donostia Prize is awarded as a tribute to the career of a star or director: winners have included Meryl Streep, Ian McKellen and Woody Allen. Visiting celebrities have included Quentin Tarantino, Ethan Coen and Bertrand Tavernier. Prizes also go to individual new films. An early winner was Hitchcock's *Vertigo*. The festival's website is www.sansebastianfestival.com

Lauren Bacall receiving an award

Old balconied houses in the upper town, Hondarribia

Hondarribia 5

Guipúzcoa. *16,500.* *Arma Plaza 9, 943 64 36 77.* *La Kutxa Entrega (25 Jul), Alarde (6–8 Sep).* **www**.bidasoaturismo.com

Hondarribia (Fuenterrabía), the historic town at the mouth of the Río Bidasoa, was attacked by the French over many centuries. The upper town is protected by 15th-century walls and entered via their original gateway, the handsome **Puerta de Santa María**. They enclose alleys of old houses with carved eaves, balconies and coats of arms.

The streets cluster round the church of **Nuestra Señora de la Asunción y del Manzano**, with its massive buttresses, tall Baroque tower, and, inside, a gold reredos. At the town's highest point is the 10th century **castle**, now a parador *(see p566)*.

Hondarribia has seafront cafés in La Marina, its lively fishermen's quarter. It is also a seaside resort, with beaches stretching to the north.

Environs

A hill road climbs westwards to the shrine of the Virgin of Guadalupe. Further along this road are panoramic views of the coast and the mountains. From the **Ermita de San Marcial**, which stands on a hill 9 km (6 miles) to the south, there are views of the Bidasoa plain straddling the border – the French towns are neatly white, the Spanish ones are greyer.

The Renaissance façade of the former Basque university in Oñati

Santuario de Loiola 6

Loiola (Guipúzcoa). ***Tel*** *943 02 50 00.* *10am–12:30pm, 3–6:15pm Tue–Sun (am only Sun).* **www**.santuariodeloyola.org

Saint Ignatius of Loiola (San Ignacio de Loyola), founder of the Jesuits, was born in the 1490s in the Santa Casa (holy house), a stone manor near Azpeitia. In the 1600s it was enclosed by the Basílica de San Ignacio, and the rooms in which the aristocratic Loiola family lived were converted into chapels. The Chapel of the Conversion is where Ignatius, as a young soldier, recovered from a war injury and had a profound religious experience.

A diorama depicts episodes in the saint's life: dedicating his life to Christ at the Monastery of Montserrat *(see pp218–19)*; writing his *Spiritual Exercises* in a cave at Manresa; his imprisonment by the Inquisition; and his pilgrimage to the Holy Land. The basilica, built from 1681–1738, has a Churrigueresque dome and a circular nave with rich carvings.

Oñati 7

Guipúzcoa. *11,000.* *C/ San Juan 14, 943 78 34 53.* *Sat.* *Corpus Christi (May/Jun), San Miguel (29 Sep–1 Oct).* **www**.oinati.org

This historic town in the Udana Valley has a distinguished past. In the First Carlist War, 1833–9 *(see p63)*, it was a seat of the court of Don Carlos, brother of King Fernando VII and pretender to the throne. Its former **university**, built in about 1540, was for centuries the only one in the Basque Country. It has a Renaissance façade, decorated with statues of saints, and an elegant patio.

In the Plaza de los Fueros is the **Iglesia de San Miguel**, a Gothic church with a stone cloister in Gothic-Flemish style. It contains the tomb of Bishop Zuázola of Ávila, the founder of the university. Opposite is the Baroque **town hall** *(ayuntamiento)*.

Environs

A mountain road ascends 9 km (6 miles) to the **Santuario de Arantzazu**, below the peak of Aitzgorri. In 1469 it is believed a shepherd visualized the Virgin here. Over the door of the church, built in the 1950s, are sculptures of the apostles by Jorge Oteiza.

Universidad de Sancti Spiritus
Avenida de la Universidad Vasca. ***Tel*** *943 78 34 53.* *Mon–Sun for guided tours (phone Oñati tourist information in advance).*

The imposing Santuario de Loiola, with its Churrigueresque cupola

THE FOUNDING OF THE JESUIT ORDER

The Society of Jesus was founded in Rome in 1539 by Saint Ignatius and a group of priests who were dedicated to helping the poor. Pope Paul III soon approved the order's establishment, with Ignatius as Superior General. The order, which grew wealthy, vowed military obedience to the Pope and became his most powerful weapon against the Reformation. Today, there are approximately 20,000 Jesuits working, mainly in education, in 112 countries.

Saint Ignatius of Loiola

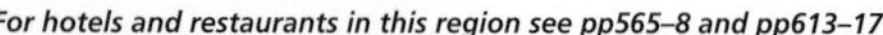

Basque Culture

The Basques may be Europe's oldest race. Anthropologists think they could be descended from Cro-Magnon people, who lived in the Pyrenees 40,000 years ago. The dolmens and carved stones of their ancestors are evidence of the Basques' pagan roots.

Long isolated in their mountain valleys, the Basques preserved their unique language, myths and art for millennia, almost untouched by other influences.

Basque policeman

Many families still live in the isolated, chalet-style stone *caseríos*, or farmhouses, built by their forebears. Their music and high-bounding dances are unlike those of any other culture, and their cuisine is varied and imaginative.

The *fueros* or ancient Basque laws and rights were suppressed under General Franco, but since the arrival of democracy in 1975 the Basques have had their own parliament and police force, having won great autonomy over their own affairs.

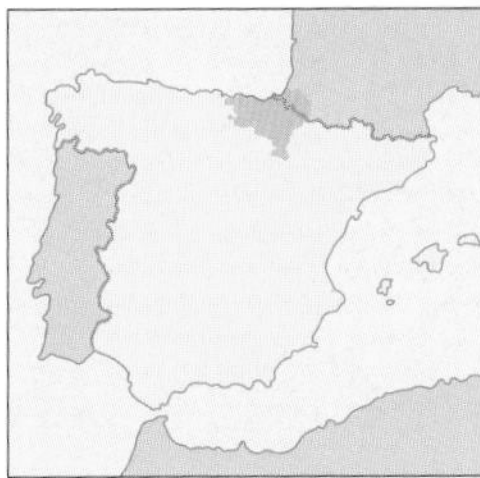

THE BASQUE REGION

▢ *Areas of Basque culture*

The national identity *is symbolized by the region's flag:* La Ikurriña. *The white cross symbolizes Christianity. The green St Andrew's Cross commemorates a battle won on his feast day.*

Bertsolaris *are bards. They improvise witty, sometimes humorous songs, whose verses relate current events or legends.* Bertsolaris *sing, unaccompanied, to gatherings in public places, such as bars and squares, often in competition. This oral tradition has preserved Basque folklore, legends and history. No texts were written in* Euskera *(Basque) until the 16th century.*

The Basque economy *has always relied on fishing and associated industries, such as shipbuilding and agriculture. In recent history, heavy industries have made this region prosperous.*

Traditional sports *are highly respected in Basque culture. In pelota* (frontón), *teams hit a ball at a wall then catch it with a wicker scoop or their hands. Sports involving strength, such as log-splitting and weightlifting, are the most popular.*

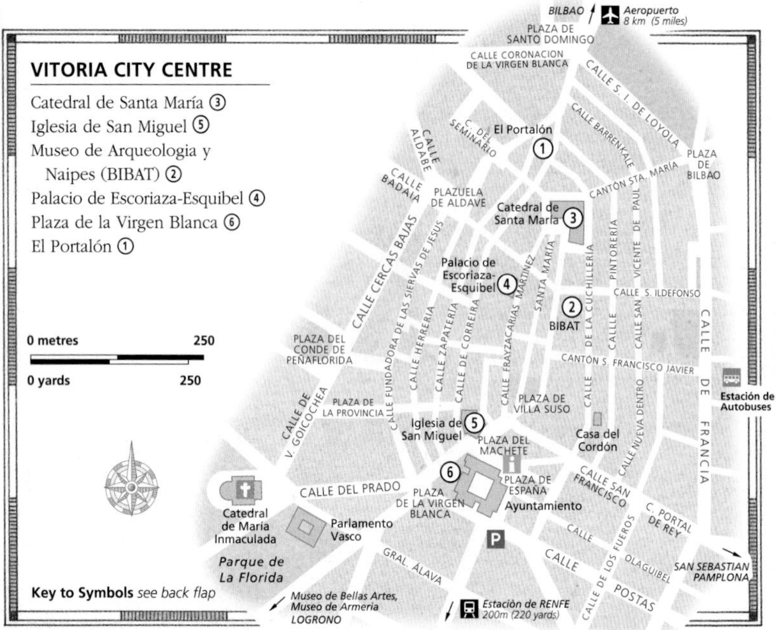

VITORIA CITY CENTRE

Catedral de Santa María ③
Iglesia de San Miguel ⑤
Museo de Arqueologia y Naipes (BIBAT) ②
Palacio de Escoriaza-Esquibel ④
Plaza de la Virgen Blanca ⑥
El Portalón ①

0 metres 250
0 yards 250

Key to Symbols *see back flap*

Vitoria ❽

Álava. 240,000. *Plaza de España 1, 945 16 15 98.* *Thu.* *Romería de San Prudencio (27–28 Apr), Fiestas de la Virgen Blanca (4–9 Aug).* **www**.vitoria-gasteiz.org/turismo

Vitoria (Gasteiz), the seat of the Basque government, was founded on a hill – the province's highest point and the site of an ancient Basque town, Gasteiz. Vitoria's oldest part, El Campillo, was rebuilt in 1200 after a fire. The city later grew rich on the iron and wool trades.

The old town focuses on the **Plaza de la Virgen Blanca**, with its monument to a battle fought nearby in 1813, when the British Duke of Wellington defeated the French. Around the plaza are old houses with miradores (glazed balconies).

On the hillside above the plaza is the Gothic **Iglesia de San Miguel**. An outside niche contains a statue of the Virgen Blanca (White Virgin), Vitoria's patron saint. A big festival *(see p132)* starts before her feast day, which is on 5 August. On the wall of San Miguel facing the **Plaza del Machete** there is a recess with a replica of the machete on which the city's rulers swore to uphold the laws or be slain.

The old town has several Renaissance palaces, including the 16th-century **Palacio de Escoriaza-Esquibel**, with its Plateresque *(see p25)* patio. Around it is a charming area of alleys linked by steep steps.

The city has two cathedrals. The oldest, currently under restoration, is the Gothic **Catedral de Santa María**, with a sculpted west porch. Close by, in Calle Correría, a street of old houses, is **El Portalón**, a merchant's house and hostel from the 15th century. The building, which is full of Basque country furniture and art, is now a restaurant.

Among the city's later architectural gems are an arcaded street, **Los Arquillos**, and the adjoining **Plaza de España**, also arcaded. They were built in the late 18th century to link the old town with the new quarter then being built. South of the old town is the Neo-Gothic **Catedral Nueva de María Inmaculada**, begun in 1907 and finished in 1973.

The quiet Plaza de España in the centre of Vitoria

Museo de Arqueología y Naipes (BIBAT)

Palacio de Bendaña, C/ Cuchillería 54. ***Tel*** *945 20 37 07.* *Tue–Sun.*
Vitoria's archaeology museum is set in a stunning purpose-built edifice and features 1,500 pieces, including prehistory artifacts and Roman sculptures found at Álava.

For hotels and restaurants in this region see pp565–68 and pp613–17

The Gothic west door of Vitoria's Catedral de Santa María

Visitors can experience multimedia projections and sound effects.

The grandson of Heraclio Fournier, who founded a playing cards factory in Vitoria in 1868, also displays his collection of more than 6,000 items in this museum. The oldest exhibits are late 14th-century Italian cards. Among the many sets of tarot cards are some designed by Salvador Dalí in the 1980s.

Museo de Armería

Paseo Fray Francisco 3. ***Tel*** *945 18 19 25.* *Tue–Sun.* *phone 945 18 19 18 for guided tours.*

The weapons here range from prehistoric axes to 20th-century pistols. Medieval armour and an exhibit on the 1813 Battle of Vitoria are also on display.

Museo de Arte Sacro

Catedral Nueva de María Inmaculada, Calle Monseñor Cadena y Eleta s/n. ***Tel*** *945 15 06 31.* *10am–2pm, 4–6:30pm Tue–Fri, 10am–2pm Sat, 11am–2pm Sun & public hols.* *call ahead.*

The design of this museum is considerate to the surrounding cathedral. Exhibits of religious art are displayed in sections related to their medium.

Torre Palacio de los Varona 9

Villanañe (Álava). ***Tel*** *945 35 30 40.* *11am–2pm, 4–7pm Tue–Sat, 11am–2pm Sun (winter: Sat & Sun only).*

The small town of Villanañe hosts a beautiful example of medieval civil architecture, the best preserved 14th-century fortified military building in the region – now a museum displaying original furniture. The upper rooms are decorated with colourful 17th-century wallpaper, while some of the floors are made with traditional Manisse porcelain tiles.

Environs

On the A2622 Pobes–Tuesta road are the **Salinas de Añana**, a group of saltpans fed by mineral springs. The nearby village of **Tuesta** boasts a Romanesque church. Inside are capitals carved with historical scenes, and a medieval wood sculpture of St Sebastian.

Laguardia 10

Álava. *1,500.* *Calle Mayor 52, 945 60 08 45.* *Tue.* *San Juan and San Pedro (23–29 Jun).*

This little wine town is the capital of La Rioja Alavesa, a part of southern Álava province where Rioja wines *(see pp78–9)* have been produced for centuries. It is a fertile, vine-clad plain, sheltered by high hills to the north. There are fine panoramic views from the road that climbs up to the Herrera pass.

Virgin and child statue in Laguardia

Laguardia is a medieval hill town, its encircling ramparts, towers and fortified gateways visible from afar. Along its steep, narrow cobbled streets there are many **bodegas** (wine cellars), offering wine tastings and tours throughout the year. It is usually necessary to make a booking in advance.

The Gothic **Iglesia de Santa María de los Reyes** has an austere façade and a richly embellished inner portal that has retained its original colouring.

Vineyards near Laguardia, capital of La Rioja Alavesa, a wine-producing region since the Middle Ages

Haro ⓫

La Rioja. 11,800. *Plaza Monseñor Florentino Rodriguez, 941 30 33 66.* *Tue & Sat.* *Wine Battle (29 Jun), San Juan, San Felices, San Pedro (24–29 Jun), Virgen de la Vega (8 Sep).* **www**.haro.org

A graceful town on the Río Ebro, Haro has a lively old quarter with wine taverns and mansions. It is crowned by the hilltop **Iglesia de Santo Tomás**, a Gothic church with a Plateresque *(see p25)* portal.

Haro is the centre for the vineyards and bodegas of the Rioja Alta wine region, which is higher and cooler than the Rioja Baja *(see pp78–9)*. The clay soil and the climate – Haro is sheltered by a sierra to the north – create the conditions in which the famous regional wines are produced. Many bodegas run tours and tastings. To join one, you may need to book ahead at the bodega. There may be a small charge. The cafés in the old town offer local wines and tapas at low prices and a convivial atmosphere.

A wine-throwing orgy is the climax of the area's fiesta *(see p132)* held every June.

Rows of Rioja vines on the rolling hills near Haro

Tomb of St Dominic in the cathedral of Santo Domingo de la Calzada

Santo Domingo de la Calzada ⓬

La Rioja. 6,700. *Calle Mayor 33, 902 11 26 60.* *Sat.* *Fiestas del Santo (25 Apr–15 May), Día del Patron (12 May).*

This town on the Road to Santiago de Compostela *(see pp82–3)* is named after the 11th-century saint who built bridges and roads *(calzadas)* to help pilgrims. Santo Domingo also founded a hospital, which now serves as a parador *(see p567)*.

Miracles performed by the saint are recorded in carvings on his tomb in the town's part-Romanesque, part-Gothic **cathedral**, and in paintings on the wall of the choir. The most obvious and bizarre record is a sumptuously decorated cage set in a wall in which, for centuries, a live cock and hen have been kept. The cathedral has a carved walnut reredos at the high altar, the last work, in 1541, of the artist Damià Forment. The restored 14th-century **ramparts** of the town are also worth seeing.

THE COCK AND HEN OF ST DOMINIC

A live cock and hen are kept in the cathedral of Santo Domingo de la Calzada as a tribute to the saint's miraculous life-giving powers. Centuries ago, it is said, a German pilgrim refused the advances of a local girl, who denounced him as a thief. He was hanged as a consequence, but later his parents found him alive on the gallows. They rushed to a judge, who said, dismissively, "Nonsense, he's no more alive than this roast chicken on my plate". Whereupon, the chicken stood up on the plate and crowed.

The cock and hen in their decorated cage

San Millán de la Cogolla ⓭

La Rioja. 300. *from Logroño.* *Monasterio de Yuso (open Tue–Sun; also Mon in Aug), Portería de Yuso, piso de abajo, 941 37 30 49; Monasterio de Suso, 941 37 30 82 (book ahead).* *compulsory.* *Traslación de las Reliquias (26 Sep), San Millán (12 Nov).* **www**.monasteriodeyuso.org

This village grew up around two monasteries. On a hillside above the village is the **Monasterio de San Millán de Suso**. It was built in the 10th century on the site of a community founded by St Emilian, a shepherd hermit, in 537. The church, hollowed out of pink sandstone, has Romanesque and Mozarabic features. It contains the carved alabaster tomb of St Emiliano.

Below it is the **Monasterio de San Millán de Yuso**, built between the 16th and 18th centuries. The part-Renaissance church has Baroque golden doors and a rococo sacristy with 17th-century paintings.

In the treasury there is a collection of ivory plaques. They were once part of two 11th-century jewelled reliquaries, which were plundered by French troops in 1813.

Medieval manuscripts are also displayed in the treasury. Among them is a facsimile of one of the earliest known texts in Castilian Romance *(see p34)*. It is a commentary by a 10th-century Suso monk on a work by San Cesáreo de Arles, the *Glosas Emilianenses*.

The Monasterio de San Millán de Yuso in the Cárdenas valley

Cloister of the Monasterio de Santa María la Real, Nájera

Nájera ⓮

La Rioja. 8,500. *Plaza de San Miguel 10, 941 36 00 41.* *Thu.* *San Prudencio (28 Apr), Santa María la Real (16–19 Sep).*

The old town of Nájera, west of Logroño, was the capital of La Rioja and Navarra until 1076, when La Rioja was incorporated into Castile. The royal families of Navarra, León and Castile are buried in the **Monasterio de Santa María la Real**. It was founded in the 11th century beside a sandstone cliff where a statue of the Virgin was found in a cave. A 13th-century Madonna can be seen in the cave, beneath the carved choir stalls of the 15th-century church.

The 12th-century carved tomb of Blanca of Navarra, the wife of Sancho III, is the finest of many royal sarcophagi.

Monasterio de Santa María la Real
Plaza Santa María 1, Nájera.
Tel *941 36 10 83.* *Tue–Sun.*

Logroño ⓯

La Rioja. 152,000. *Paseo del Espolón, 941 29 12 60.* *San Bernabé (11 Jun), San Mateo (21 Sep).* **www**.lariojaturismo.com

The capital of La Rioja is a tidy, modern city of wide boulevards and smart shops. It is the commercial centre of a fertile plain where quality vegetables are produced, in addition to Rioja wines.

In Logroño's pleasant old quarter on the Río Ebro is the Gothic **cathedral**, with twin towers. Above the south portal of the nearby **Iglesia de Santiago el Real**, which houses an image of the patron saint Our Lady of Hope, is an equestrian statue of St James as Moorslayer *(see p55)*.

Environs
About 50 km (30 miles) south of Logroño, the N111 winds through the dramatic **Iregua Valley**, through tunnels, to the Sierra de Cameros.

The ornate Baroque west door of Logroño Cathedral

Enciso ⓰

La Rioja. 160. *from Logroño.* *Plaza Mayor, 941 39 60 05.* *San Roque (16 Aug).*

Near this remote hill village west of Calahorra is Spain's "Jurassic Park". Signposts point to the *huellas de dinosaurios* (dinosaur footprints). Embedded in rocks overhanging a stream are the prints of many giant, three-toed feet, up to 30 cm (1 ft) long. They were made around 150 million years ago, when dinosaurs moved between the marshes of the Ebro valley, at that time a sea, and these hills. Prints can also be seen at other locations in the area.

Environs
Arnedillo, 10 km (6 miles) to the north, is a spa with thermal baths once used by Fernando VI. In **Autol**, to the east, there are two unusual limestone peaks.

The intricately carved portal of Tudela Cathedral

Tudela ⓱

Navarra. 35,500.
Plaza Fueros 5, 948 84 80 58.
Sat. Santa Ana (26–30 Jul).

Navarra's second city is the great commercial centre of the vast agricultural lands of the Ebro valley in Navarra, the Ribera. Much of Tudela consists of modern developments, but its origins are ancient. Spanning the Ebro is a 13th-century bridge with 17 irregular arches. The old town has two well-preserved Jewish districts.

The **Plaza de los Fueros** is old Tudela's main square. It is surrounded by houses with wrought-iron balconies. On some of their façades are paintings of bullfights, a reminder that the plaza was formerly used as a bullring.

The **cathedral**, begun in 1194, exemplifies the religious toleration under which Tudela was governed after the Reconquest. It is Early Gothic, with a carved portal depicting the Last Judgement. There is a Romanesque cloister, and beside the cathedral sits a 9th-century chapel that is thought to have once been a synagogue.

Environs

To the north is the **Bárdenas Reales**, an arid area of limestone cliffs and crags. About 20 km (12 miles) west of Tudela is the spa town of **Fitero**, with the 12th-century Monasterio de Santa María.

Monasterio de La Oliva ⓲

Carcastillo (Navarra). ***Tel*** *948 72 50 06.* *from Pamplona.* *daily.* **www**.monasteriodelaoliva.eu

French Cistercian monks built this small monastery on a remote plain in the 1100s. The church is simple but adorned with rose windows.

One of the cloisters in the Monasterio de La Oliva

The serene cloister, dating from the 14th and 15th centuries, adjoins a 12th-century chapter-house. The church also has a 17th-century tower. Today, the monks survive by selling local honey and cheese, their own wine, and by accepting paying guests *(see p556)*.

Ujué ⓳

Navarra. 225. Plaza Municipal, 948 73 90 46. Virgen de Ujué (Sun after 25 April).

An unspoiled hill village, Ujué commands a high spur at the end of a winding road. It has quaint façades, cobbled alleys and steep steps. The **Iglesia de Santa María** (closed for renovations) is in Gothic style, with a Romanesque chancel and an exterior lookout gallery. The ruined fortifications around the church offer views of the Pyrenees.

On the Sunday after 25 April, pilgrims in black capes visit the Virgin of Ujué, whose Romanesque image is displayed in the church.

Olite ⓴

Navarra. 3,700. Pl. de Teobaldos 10, 948 74 17 03. Wed. Medieval Markets (late Aug), Exaltación de la Santa Cruz (13–19 Sep). **www**.olite.es

The historic town of Olite was founded by the Romans and later chosen as a royal residence by the kings of Navarra. Parts of the town's old walls

THE KINGDOM OF NAVARRA

Navarra emerged as an independent Christian kingdom in the 10th century, after Sancho I Garcés became king of Pamplona. Sancho III the Great expanded the kingdom, and at his death, in 1035, Navarra stretched all the way from Ribagorza in Aragón to Valladolid. Sancho VI the Wise, who reigned 1150–94, recognized the independent rights *(fueros)* of many towns. In 1234, Navarra passed by marriage to a line of French rulers. One, Carlos III, the Noble, built Olite Castle. His grandson, Carlos de Viana, wrote the *Chronicle of the Kings of Navarra* in 1455. In 1512 Navarra was annexed by Fernando II of Castile, as part of united Spain, but it kept its own laws and currency until the 1800s.

Prince Carlos de Viana, Carlos III's grandson

can be seen. They enclose a delightful jumble of steep, narrow streets and little squares, churches and the **Monasterio de Santa Clara**, begun in the 13th century. The houses along the Rúa Cerco de Fuera and the Rúa Mayor were built between the 16th and 18th centuries.

The castle, the **Palacio Real de Olite**, was built in the early 15th century by Carlos III, and has earned Olite its nickname "the Gothic town". It was heavily fortified, but was brilliantly decorated inside by Mudéjar artists with *azulejos* (ceramic tiles) and marquetry ceilings. The walkways were planted with vines and orange trees, and there was an aviary and a lions' den.

During the War of Independence *(see pp62–3)* the castle was burned to prevent it falling into French hands. Since 1937, however, it has been restored to a semblance of its former glory. Part of it houses a parador *(see p567)*.

Today, the castle is a complex of courtyards, passages, large halls, royal chambers, battlements and turrets. From the "windy tower", monarchs could watch tournaments.

Adjoining the castle is a 13th-century former royal chapel, the **Iglesia de Santa María**, with its richly carved Gothic portal.

Olite is in the Navarra wine region *(see pp78–9)* and the town has several bodegas.

Palacio Real de Olite
Plaza de Carlos III. ***Tel*** *948 74 00 35.* *daily.*

The battlements and towers of the Palacio Real de Olite

The five-arched, medieval pilgrims' bridge at Puente la Reina

Puente la Reina 21

Navarra. *2,900.* *C/ Mayor 105, 948 34 13 01 (closed Jan & Feb).* *Sat.* *Santiago (24–30 Jul).*

Few towns along the Road to Santiago de Compostela *(see pp82–3)* evoke the past as vividly as Puente la Reina. The town takes its name from the graceful, humpbacked pedestrian bridge over the Río Arga. The bridge was built for pilgrims during the 11th century by royal command.

On Puente la Reina's narrow main street is the **Iglesia de Santiago**, which has a gilded statue by the west door showing the saint as a pilgrim. On the edge of town is the **Iglesia del Crucifijo**, another pilgrim church which was built in the 12th century by the Knights Templar. Contained within the church is a Y-shaped wooden crucifix of a sorrowful Christ with arms upraised, which is said to have been a gift from a German pilgrim in the 14th century.

Distinctive crucifix in Puente la Reina

Environs

Isolated in the fields about 5 km (3 miles) to the east is the 12th-century **Iglesia de Santa María de Eunate**. This octagonal Romanesque church may once have been a cemetery church for pilgrims, as human bones have been unearthed here. Pilgrims would shelter beneath the church's external arcade. West of Puente la Reina is the showpiece hill village of **Cirauqui**. It is also charming, if rather over-restored. Chic little balconied houses line tortuously twisting alleys linked by steps. The Iglesia de San Román, built in the 13th century on top of the hill, has a sculpted west door.

BASQUE COUNTRY, NAVARRA AND LA RIOJA'S FIESTAS

Los Sanfermines *(6–14 Jul)*, Pamplona (Navarra). In the famous *encierro* (bullrunning) six bulls are released at 8am each morning to run from their corral through the narrow, cobbled streets of the old town. On the last night of this week-long, non-stop party, crowds with candles sing Basque songs in the main square. The event gained worldwide fame after Ernest Hemingway described it in his novel, published in 1926, *The Sun Also Rises*.

Bulls scattering the runners in Pamplona

Wine Battle *(29 Jun)*, Haro (La Rioja). People dressed in white clothes squirt each other with wine from leather drinking bottles in the capital of the Rioja Alta wine region.
Danza de los Zancos *(22 Jul and last Sat of Sep)*, Anguiano (La Rioja). Dancers on stilts, wearing ornate waistcoats and yellow skirts, hurtle down the stepped alley from the church to the main square.
La Virgen Blanca *(4 Aug)*, Vitoria (Álava). A dummy holding an umbrella (the *celedón*) is lowered from San Miguel church to a house below – from which a man in similar dress emerges. The mayor fires a rocket and the crowds in the square light cigars.

Pilgrims drinking from the wine tap near the monastery at Irache

Estella 22

Navarra. *14,000.* *Calle de San Nicolás 3, 948 55 63 01.* *Thu.* *San Andrés (first week in Aug).* **www**.estella-lizarra.com

In the Middle Ages Estella (Lizarra) was the centre of the royal court of Navarra and a major stopping point on the pilgrims' Road to Santiago de Compostela *(see pp82–3)*. The town was a stronghold of the Carlists *(see p63)* in the 19th century. A memorial rally is held here on the first Sunday of May every year.

The most important monuments in Estella are sited on the edge of town, across the bridge over the Río Ega. Steps climb steeply from the arcaded Plaza de San Martín to the remarkable **Iglesia de San Pedro de la Rúa**, built on top of a cliff from the 12th to 14th century. It features a Cistercian Mudéjar-influenced, sculpted doorway. The carved capitals are all that now remain of the Romanesque cloister, which was destroyed when a castle overlooking the church was blown up in 1592. The **Palacio de los Reyes de Navarra** (now a museum), on the other side of the Plaza de San Martín, is a rare example of civil Romanesque architecture.

In the town centre, on Plaza de los Fueros, **Iglesia de San Juan Bautista** has a Romanesque porch. The north portal of the **Iglesia de San Miguel** has Romanesque carvings of St Michael slaying a dragon.

Environs

The **Monasterio de Nuestra Señora de Irache**, 3 km (2 miles) southwest of Estella, was a Benedictine monastery which sheltered pilgrims on their way to Santiago. The church is mainly Transitional Gothic in style, but it has Romanesque apses and a cloister in Plateresque style. It is capped by a remarkable dome.

A bodega next to the monastery provides pilgrims with wine from a tap in a wall.

A small road branches off the NA120 north of Estella and leads to the **Monasterio de Iranzu**, built in the 12th–14th century. The graceful austerity of its church and cloisters are typically Cistercian features.

The Lizarraga Pass, further up the NA120, offers views of attractive beech woods.

Pamplona 23

Navarra. *198,000.* *Avda Roncesvalles 4, 848 420 420.* *Sanfermines (6–14 Jul), San Saturnino (29 Nov).* **www**.pamplona.net

The old fortress city of Pamplona (Iruña) is said to have been founded by the Roman general, Pompey. In the 9th century it became the capital of Navarra. This fairly busy city explodes into even more life in July during the fiesta of Los Sanfermines, with its daredevil bullrunning.

From the old **city walls** *(murallas)* you can get a good overview of Pamplona. The nearby **cathedral**, which

Sumptuous interior of the Palacio de Navarra, Pamplona

Stone tracery in the elegant cloister of Pamplona cathedral

is built in ochre-coloured stone, looks down on a loop in the Río Arga. It was built on the foundations of its 12th-century predecessor, and is mainly Gothic in style, with twin towers and an 18th-century façade. Inside there are lovely choir stalls and the alabaster tomb of Carlos III and Queen Leonor.

The southern entrance to the cloister is the beautifully carved, medieval Puerta de la Preciosa. The cathedral priests would gather here to sing an antiphon (hymn) to La Preciosa (Precious Virgin) before the night service.

The Museo Diocesano in the cathedral's 14th-century kitchen and refectory displays Gothic altarpieces, polychrome wood statues from all over Navarra, and a French 13th-century reliquary of the Holy Sepulchre.

West of the cathedral is the old town, cut through with many alleys. The Neo-Classical **Palacio del Gobierno de Navarra** lies in the Plaza del Castillo and is the seat of the Navarrese government. Outside, a statue of 1903 shows a symbolic woman upholding the *fueros* (historic laws) of Navarra *(see p130)*.

North of the palace is the medieval **Iglesia de San Saturnino**, built on the site where St Saturninus is said to have baptized some 40,000 pagan townspeople, and the Baroque **town hall** *(ayuntamiento)*.

Beneath the old town wall, in a 16th-century hospital with a Plateresque doorway, is the **Museo de Navarra**. This is a museum of regional archaeology, history and art. Exhibits include Roman mosaics and an 11th-century, Islam-inspired ivory casket. There are murals painted during the 14th–16th centuries, a portrait by Goya, and a collection of paintings by Basque artists.

To the southeast is the city's massive 16th-century **citadel**, erected in Felipe II's reign. It is designed with five bastions in a star shape. Beyond it are the spacious boulevards of the new town, and also the university's green campus.

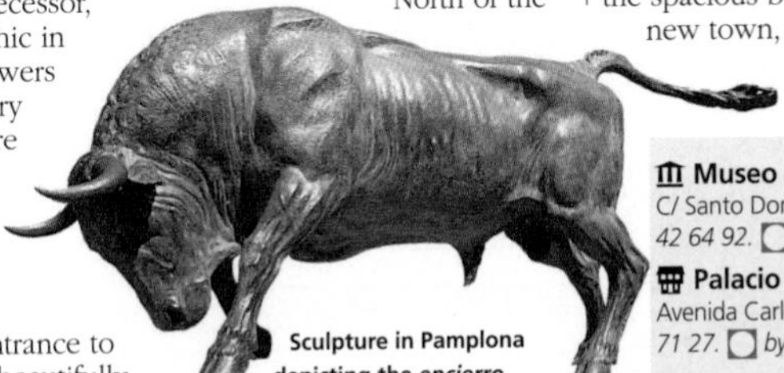

Sculpture in Pamplona depicting the *encierro*

Museo de Navarra
C/ Santo Domingo 47. ***Tel*** *848 42 64 92.* *Tue–Sun.*

Palacio de Navarra
Avenida Carlos III 2. ***Tel*** *848 42 71 27.* *by appointment.*

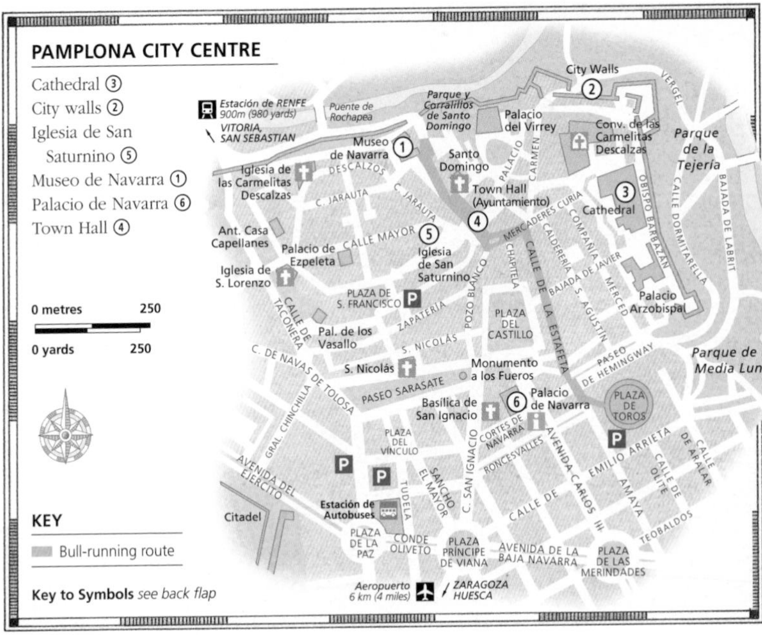

PAMPLONA CITY CENTRE

Cathedral ③
City walls ②
Iglesia de San Saturnino ⑤
Museo de Navarra ①
Palacio de Navarra ⑥
Town Hall ④

0 metres 250
0 yards 250

KEY
Bull-running route

Key to Symbols *see back flap*

Basque houses in the picturesque town of Etxalar, Valle de Bidasoa

Las Cinco Villas del Valle de Bidasoa ㉔

Navarra. Pamplona, San Sebastián. 948 63 12 22 (Easter week & summer; 948 59 23 86 rest of year). **www**.turismo.navarra.es

Five attractive Basque towns lie in or near this valley, the most northerly being **Bera** (Vera). The houses in **Lesaka** have wooden balconies under deep eaves. The road south passes hills dotted with white farmsteads to reach **Igantzi**, (Yanci), with its red-and-white houses. **Arantza** is the most remote town. Since the 12th century, pigeons have been caught in huge nets strung across a pass above **Etxalar** (Echalar). At the summit of La Rhune on the French border is a great view of the Pyrenees.

Elizondo ㉕

Navarra. 3,000. Palacio de Arizkunenea, 948 58 15 17. Thu. Santiago (25 Jul).

This is the biggest of a string of typical Basque villages in the very beautiful valley of Baztán. By the river are noble houses bearing coats of arms.

Arizkun, further up the valley, has old fortified houses and a 17th-century convent. The **Cueva de Brujas**, in Zugarramurdi, was once a meeting place for witches.

The forested countryside around Roncesvalles

Canopy over the Virgin and Child in the Colegiata Real

Roncesvalles ㉖

Navarra. 24. Antiguo Molino s/n, 948 76 03 01. Día de la Virgen de Roncesvalles (8 Sep).

Roncesvalles (Orreaga), on the Spanish side of a pass through the Pyrenees, is a major halt on the Road to Santiago *(see pp82–3)*. Before it became associated with the pilgrim's way, Roncesvalles was the site of a major battle in 778, in which the Basques of Navarra slaughtered the rearguard of Charlemagne's army as it marched homeward. This event is described in the 12th-century French epic poem, *The Song of Roland*.

The 13th-century **Colegiata Real**, which has served travellers down the centuries, has a silver-plated Virgin and Child below a high canopy. In the graceful chapterhouse, off the cloister, is the white tomb of Sancho VII the Strong (1154–1234), looked down upon by a stained-glass window of his great victory, the Battle of Las Navas de Tolosa *(see pp54–5)*. Exhibits in the church museum include "Charlemagne's chessboard", an enamelled reliquary which is so-called because of its chequered design.

Valle de Roncal ㉗

Navarra. from Pamplona. Paseo Julian Gayarre s/n, Roncal, 948 47 52 56; Isaba, 948 89 32 51. **www**.vallederoncal.es

Running perpendicular to the Pyrenees, this valley is still largely reliant on sheep, and the village of **Roncal** is known for its cheeses. Because of the valley's relative isolation, the inhabitants have preserved their own identity, and local costumes are worn during fiestas. The ski resort of **Isaba**, further up the valley, has a museum of local history and life. A spectacular road winds from Isaba to the tree-lined village of Ochagavia in the parallel **Valle de Salazar**. To the north, the **Selva de Irati**, one of Europe's largest woodlands, spreads over the Pyrenees into France, below snowy Monte Ori at 2,017 m (6,617 ft).

Colourful balconies of houses in the village of Roncal

Monasterio de Leyre ㉘

Yesa (Navarra). ***Tel*** *948 88 41 50.* *Yesa. daily. Chants: 7:30am, 9am and 7pm daily. 1 Jan, 25 Dec.* **www**.monasteriodeleyre.com

The monastery of San Salvador de Leyre is situated high above a reservoir, alone amid grand scenery, backed by limestone cliffs. The abbey has been here since the 11th century when it was a great spiritual and political centre. Sancho III and his successors made it the royal pantheon of Navarra. The monastery began to decline in the 12th century. It was abandoned from 1836 until 1954, when it was restored by the Benedictines, who turned part of it into a hotel *(see p568)*. To see the monastery, you must join one of the tours run every morning and afternoon.

The big 11th century church has a Gothic vault and three lofty apses. On its west portal are weatherworn carvings of strange beasts, as well as biblical figures. The Romanesque crypt has unusually short columns with chunky capitals. The monks' Gregorian chant *(see p376)* during services is wonderful to hear.

The roughly carved columns in the crypt of the Monasterio de Leyre

Castillo de Javier ㉙

Javier (Navarra). ***Tel*** *948 88 40 24.* *from Pamplona. daily.*

St Francis Xavier, the patron saint of Navarra, a missionary and a co-founder of the Jesuit order *(see p124)*, was born in this 13th-century castle in 1506. It has since been restored and is now a Jesuit spiritual centre. Of interest are the saint's bedroom and a museum in the keep devoted to his life. In the oratory is a 13th-century polychrome Christ on the cross and a macabre 15th-century mural of grinning skeletons entitled *The Dance of Death*.

Crucifix in the oratory of the Castillo de Javier

Sangüesa ㉚

Navarra. *5,000. C/ Mayor 2, 948 87 14 11 (closed Mon in winter). Fri. San Sebastián (11 Sep).* **www**.sanguesa.es

Since medieval times this small town beside a bridge over the Río Aragón has been a stop on the Aragonese pilgrimage route to Santiago *(see pp82–3)*.

The richly sculpted south portal of the **Iglesia de Santa María la Real** is a 12th- and 13th-century treasure of Romanesque art *(see p24)*. It has many figures and details depicting the Last Judgement and society in the 13th century.

The Gothic **Iglesia de Santiago** and the 12th- to 13th-century Gothic **Iglesia de San Francisco** are also worth seeing. On the main street the 16th-century **town hall** *(ayuntamiento)* and the square beside it stand on sites that were once part of the medieval palace of the Prince of Viana and a residence of the kings of Navarra. The library beside the square is housed in what remains of the palace and is open to the public.

Environs

To the north of Sangüesa there are two deep, narrow gorges. The most impressive is the **Hoz de Arbayún**, whose limestone cliffs are inhabited by colonies of vultures. It is best seen from the NA178 north of Domeño. The **Hoz de Lumbier** can be seen from a point on the A-21.

BARCELONA

Introducing Barcelona

Barcelona, one of the Mediterranean's busiest ports, is more than the capital of Catalonia. In culture, commerce and sport it not only rivals Madrid, but also considers itself on a par with the greatest European cities. The success of the 1992 Olympic Games, staged in the Parc de Montjuïc, confirmed this to the world. Although there are plenty of historical monuments in the Old Town (Ciutat Vella), Barcelona is best known for the scores of buildings in the Eixample left by the artistic explosion of Modernisme *(see pp140–41)* in the decades around 1900. Always open to outside influences because of its location on the coast, not too far from the French border, Barcelona continues to sizzle with creativity: its bars and the public parks speak more of bold contemporary design than of tradition.

Casa Milà (see p165), *also known as La Pedrera, is the most avant-garde of all the works of Antoni Gaudí* (see p164). *Barcelona has more Art Nouveau buildings than any other city in the world.*

Palau Nacional (see p172), *on the hill of Montjuïc, dominates the fountain-filled avenue built for the 1929 International Exhibition. It now houses the Museu Nacional d'Art de Catalunya, which covers a thousand years of Catalan art and includes a splendid Romanesque section.*

MONTJUÏC
(see pp168–73)

Montjuïc Castle (see p173) *is a massive fortification dating from the 17th century. Sited on the crest of the hill of Montjuïc, it offers panoramic views of the city and port, and forms a sharp contrast to the ultra-modern sports halls built nearby for the 1992 Olympic Games.*

Christopher Columbus *surveys the waterfront from the top of a 60-m (200-ft) column* (see p156) *in the heart of the Port Vell (Old Port). From the top, visitors can look out over the promenades and quays that revitalized the area.*

0 kilometres 1

0 miles 0.5

◁ **The Ramblas and the Old Town stretching out behind Barcelona's monument to Columbus**

The Sagrada Família (see pp166–7), *Gaudí's unfinished masterpiece, begun in 1882, rises above the streets of the Eixample. Its polychromatic ceramic mosaics and sculptural forms inspired by nature are typical of his work.*

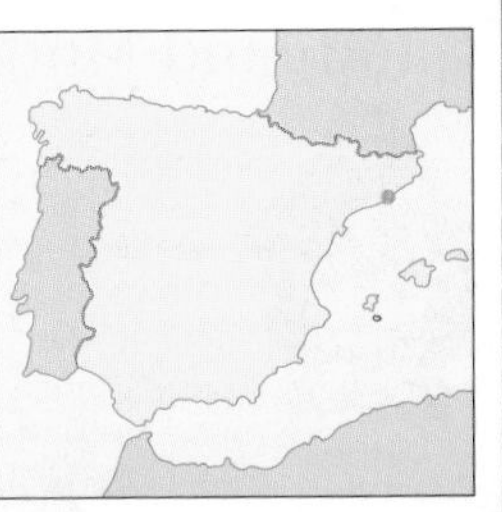

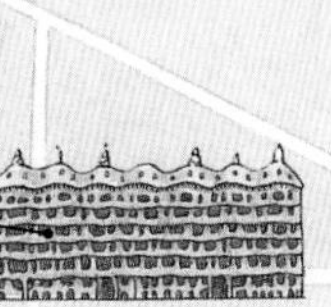

EIXAMPLE
(see pp158–67)

Barcelona Cathedral (see pp148–9) *is a magnificent 14th-century building in the heart of the Barri Gòtic (Gothic Quarter). It has 28 side chapels, which encircle the nave and contain some splendid Baroque altarpieces. The keeping of white geese in the cloisters is a centuries-old tradition.*

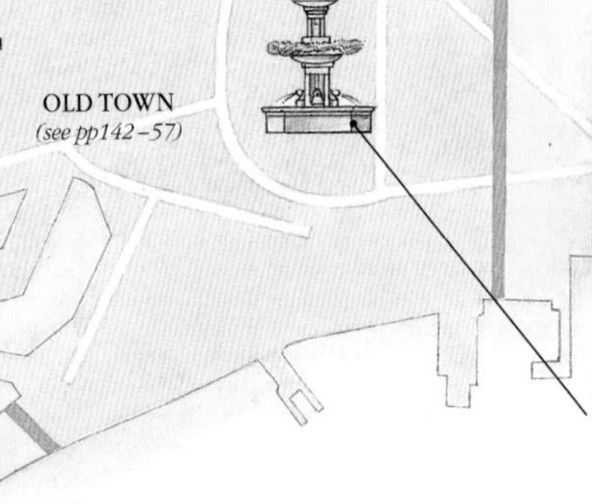

OLD TOWN
(see pp142–57)

Parc de la Ciutadella (see p154), *between the Old Town and the Vila Olímpica, has something for everyone. The gardens full of statuary offer relaxation, the boating lake and the zoo are fun, while the museum within its gates covers natural history.*

Las Ramblas (see pp150–51) *is the most famous street in Spain, alive at all hours of the day and night. A stroll down its length to the seafront, taking in its palatial buildings, shops, cafés and street vendors, makes a perfect introduction to Barcelona life.*

Gaudí and Modernisme

Chimney, Casa Vicens

Towards the end of the 19th century a new style of art and architecture, Modernisme, a variant of Art Nouveau, was born in Barcelona. It became a means of expression for Catalan nationalism and counted Josep Puig i Cadafalch, Lluís Domènech i Montaner and, above all, Antoni Gaudí i Cornet *(see p164)* among its major exponents. Barcelona's Eixample district *(see pp158–67)* is full of the highly original buildings that they created for their wealthy clients.

All aspects of decoration *in a Modernista buildin[g], even interior design[s] were planned by th[e] architect. This door and its tiled surround are in Gaudí's 1906 Casa Batlló* (see p164).

A dramatic cupola *covers the central salon, which rises through three floors. It is pierced by small round holes, inspired by Islamic architecture, giving the illusion of stars.*

Upper galleries are richly decorated with carved wood and cofferwork.

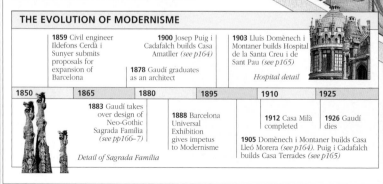

The spiral carriage ramp *is an early sign of Gaudí's predilection for curved lines. He would later exploit this to the full in the wavy façade of his masterpiece, the Casa Milà (La Pedrera)* (see p165).

THE EVOLUTION OF MODERNISME

1859 Civil engineer Ildefons Cerdà i Sunyer submits proposals for expansion of Barcelona

1878 Gaudí graduates as an architect

1900 Josep Puig i Cadafalch builds Casa Amatller *(see p164)*

1903 Lluís Domènech i Montaner builds Hospital de la Santa Creu i de Sant Pau *(see p165)*

Hospital detail

1850 | 1865 | 1880 | 1895 | 1910 | 1925

1883 Gaudí takes over design of Neo-Gothic Sagrada Família *(see pp166–7)*

Detail of Sagrada Família

1888 Barcelona Universal Exhibition gives impetus to Modernisme

1905 Domènech i Montaner builds Casa Lleó Morera *(see p164)*. Puig i Cadafalch builds Casa Terrades *(see p165)*

1912 Casa Milà completed

1926 Gaudí dies

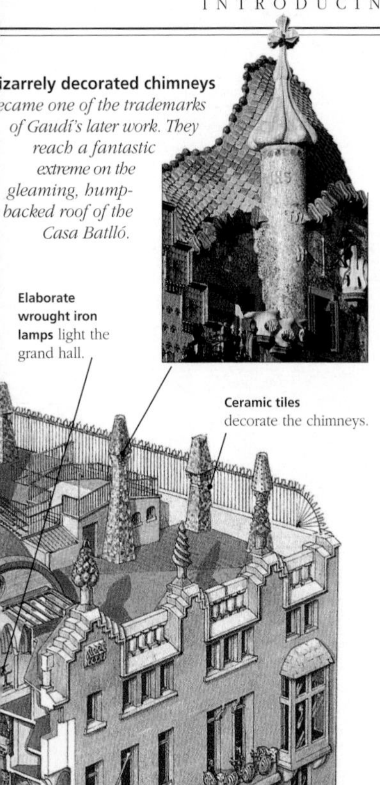

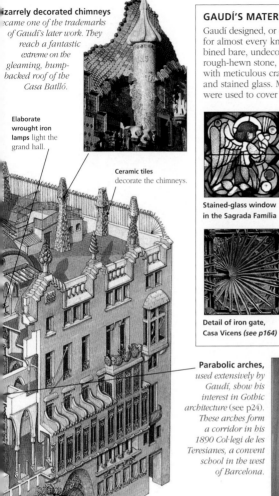

izarrely decorated chimneys *ecame one of the trademarks of Gaudí's later work. They reach a fantastic extreme on the gleaming, hump-backed roof of the Casa Batlló.*

Elaborate wrought iron lamps light the grand hall.

Ceramic tiles decorate the chimneys.

GAUDÍ'S MATERIALS

Gaudí designed, or collaborated on designs, for almost every known media. He combined bare, undecorated materials – wood, rough-hewn stone, rubble and brickwork – with meticulous craftwork in wrought iron and stained glass. Mosaics of ceramic tiles were used to cover his fluid, uneven forms.

Stained-glass window in the Sagrada Família

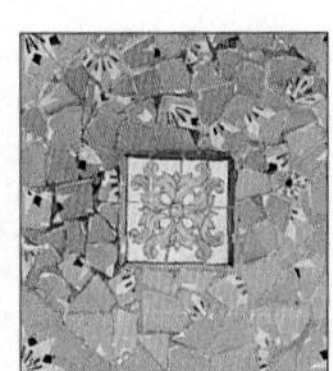

Mosaic of ceramic tiles, Park Güell *(see p178)*

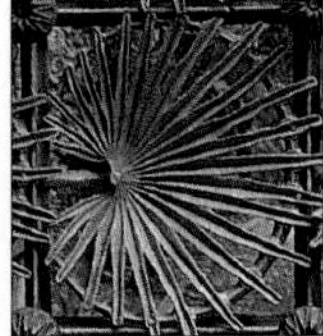

Detail of iron gate, Casa Vicens *(see p164)*

Ceramic tiles on El Capricho *(see p111)*

Parabolic arches, *used extensively by Gaudí, show his interest in Gothic architecture* (see p24). *These arches form a corridor in his 1890 Col·legi de les Teresianes, a convent school in the west of Barcelona.*

Escutcheon alludes to the Catalan coat of arms.

Organic forms *inspired the wrought iron around the gates to the palace. Gaudí's later work teems with wildlife, such as this dragon, covered with brightly coloured tiles, which guards the steps in the Park Güell.*

PALAU GÜELL *(1889)*

Gaudí's first major building in the centre of the city *(see p151)* established his international reputation for outstandingly original architecture. Built for his life-long patron, the industrialist Eusebi Güell, the mansion stands on a small plot of land in a narrow street, making the façade difficult to view. Inside, Gaudí creates a sense of space by using carved screens, galleries and recesses. His unique furniture is also on display.

OLD TOWN

The Old Town, traversed by the city's most famous avenue, Las Ramblas, is one of the most extensive medieval city centres in Europe. The Barri Gòtic contains the cathedral and a maze of streets and squares. Across from the Via Laietana, the El Born neighbourhood is dominated by the Santa Maria del Mar church and is replete with 14th-century mansions. This area is bounded by the leafy Parc de la Ciutadella, home to the city's zoo. The revitalized seafront is a stimulating mix of old and new. Trendy shops and restaurants make up the fashionable marina, contrasted with the old maritime neighbourhood of Barceloneta and the modern Olympic port.

SIGHTS AT A GLANCE

Museums and Galleries

Castell dels Tres Dragons 21
Museu d'Art Contemporani 9
Museu Frederic Marès 2
Museu d'Idees i Invents de Barcelona (MIBA) 4
Museu Marítim and Drassanes 29
Museu Martorell 22
Museu Picasso 14
Museu de la Xocolata 18

Streets and Districts

Barceloneta 25
El Born 13
Carrer Montcada 16
Las Ramblas 10
El Raval 8

Harbour Sights

Golondrinas 28
Port Olímpic 24
Port Vell 26

Churches

Basílica de Santa Maria del Mar 15
Cathedral (pp148–9) 7

Historic Buildings

Ajuntament 5
Casa de l'Ardiaca 1
Conjunt Monumental de la Plaça del Rei 3
La Llotja 12
Mercat del Born 17
Palau de la Generalitat 6
Palau de la Música Catalana 11

Monuments

Arc del Triomf 19
Monument a Colom 27

Parks and Gardens

Parc de la Ciutadella 20
Parc Zoològic 23

GETTING THERE

The area is well served by metro lines 1, 3 and 4; Jaume I station is in the heart of the Barri Gòtic. Many buses pass the Plaça de Catalunya, the centre of the modern city.

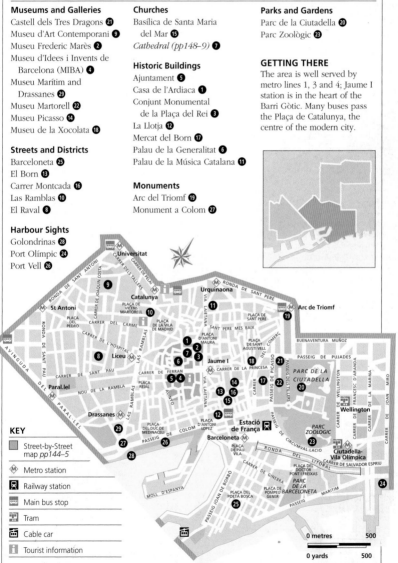

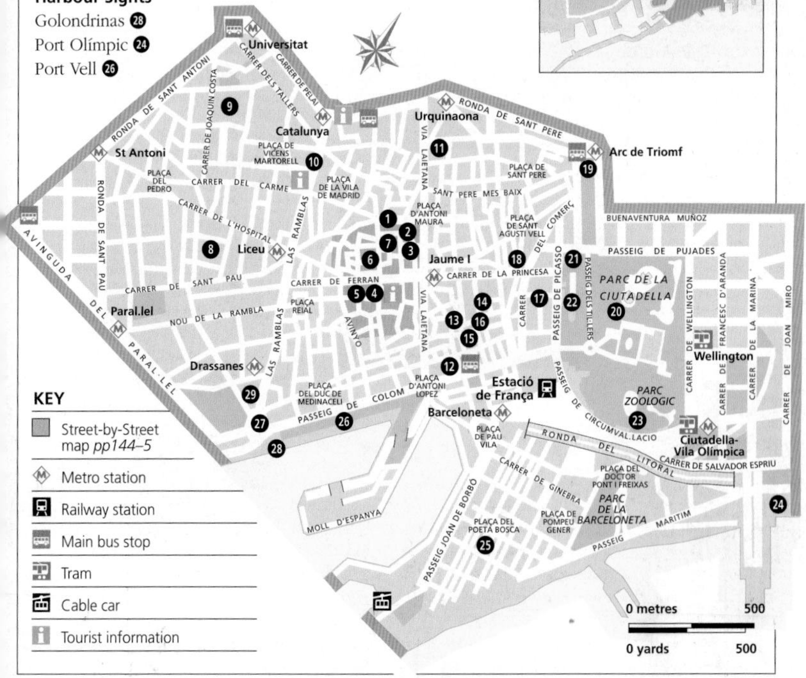

KEY

- Street-by-Street map *pp144–5*
- Metro station
- Railway station
- Main bus stop
- Tram
- Cable car
- Tourist information

0 metres 500
0 yards 500

◁ **Stunning floral mosaic pillars in the Palau de la Música Catalana**

Street-by-Street: Barri Gòtic

The Barri Gòtic (Gothic Quarter) is the true heart of Barcelona. The oldest part of the city, it was the site chosen by the Romans in the reign of Augustus (27 BC–AD 14) on which to found a new *colonia* (town), and has been the location of the city's administrative buildings ever since. The Roman forum was on the Plaça de Sant Jaume, where now stand the medieval Palau de la Generalitat, Catalonia's parliament, and the Casa de la Ciutat, Barcelona's town hall. Close by are the Gothic cathedral and royal palace, where Columbus was received by Fernando and Isabel on his return from his voyage to the New World in 1492 *(see p57).*

Wax candle, Cereria Subirà

Casa de l'Ardiaca
Built on the Roman city wall, the Gothic-Renaissance archdeacon's residence now houses Barcelona's historical archives ❶

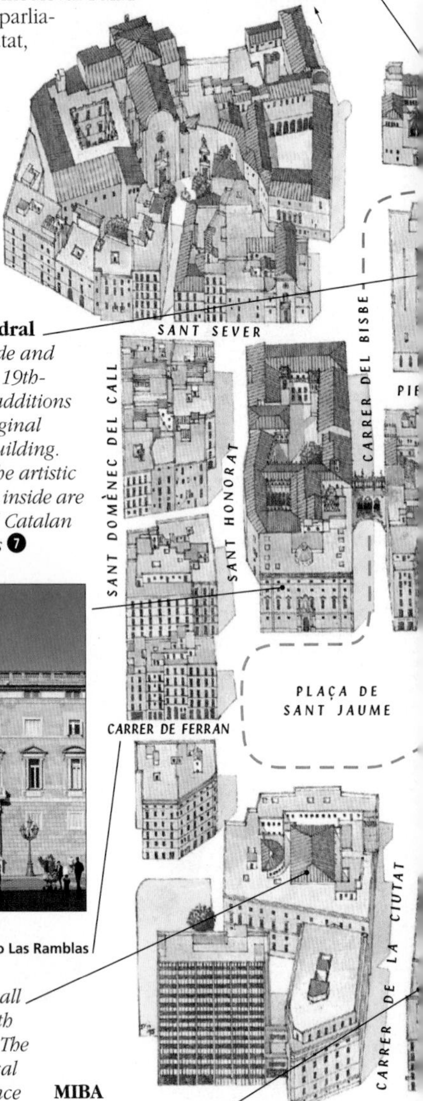

To Plaça de Catalunya

★ Cathedral
The façade and spire are 19th-century additions to the original Gothic building. Among the artistic treasures inside are medieval Catalan paintings ❼

SANT SEVER

SANT DOMÈNEC DEL CALL

SANT HONORAT

CARRER DEL BISBE

PLAÇA DE SANT JAUME

CARRER DE FERRAN

CARRER DE LA CIUTAT

Palau de la Generalitat
The seat of Catalonia's governor has superb Gothic features, which include the chapel and a stone staircase rising to an open-air, arcaded gallery ❻

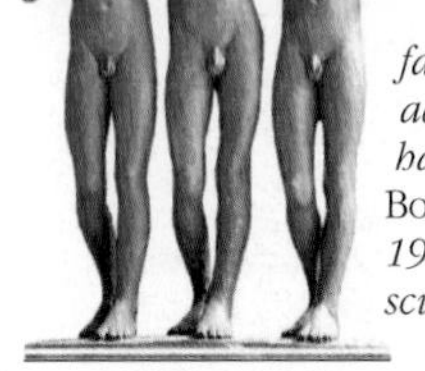

To Las Ramblas

Ajuntament
Barcelona's town hall was built in the 14th and 15th centuries. The façade is a Neo-Classical addition. In the entrance hall stands Three Gypsy Boys *by Joan Rebull (1899–1981), a 1976 copy of a sculpture he originally created in 1946* ❺

MIBA
The Museu d'Idees i Invents de Barcelona (MIBA) is a collection of fascinating inventions ❹

0 metres 100

0 yards 100

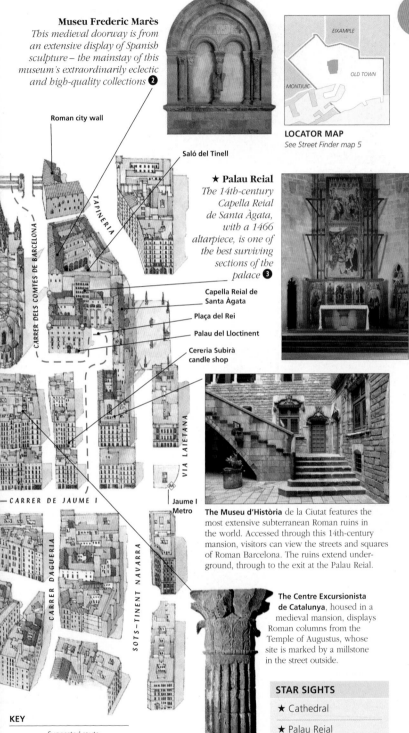

Museu Frederic Marès
This medieval doorway is from an extensive display of Spanish sculpture – the mainstay of this museum's extraordinarily eclectic and high-quality collections ❷

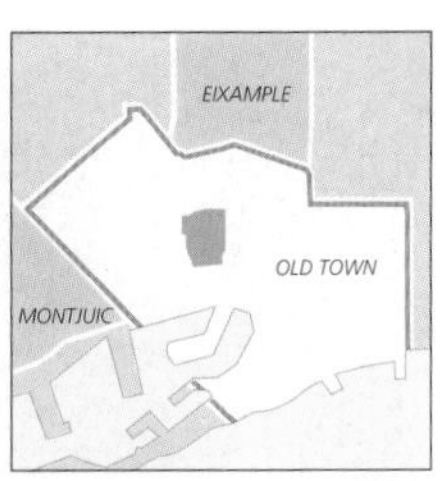

LOCATOR MAP
See Street Finder map 5

★ Palau Reial
The 14th-century Capella Reial de Santa Àgata, with a 1466 altarpiece, is one of the best surviving sections of the palace ❸

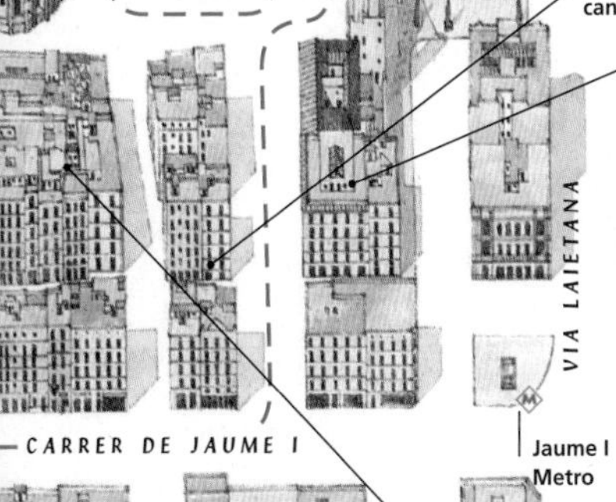

The Museu d'Història de la Ciutat features the most extensive subterranean Roman ruins in the world. Accessed through this 14th-century mansion, visitors can view the streets and squares of Roman Barcelona. The ruins extend underground, through to the exit at the Palau Reial.

The Centre Excursionista de Catalunya, housed in a medieval mansion, displays Roman columns from the Temple of Augustus, whose site is marked by a millstone in the street outside.

KEY

– – – Suggested route

STAR SIGHTS

★ Cathedral

★ Palau Reial

Decorated marble letterbox, Casa de l'Ardiaca

Casa de l'Ardiaca ❶

Carrer de Santa Llúcia 1. **Map** *5 B2.* ***Tel*** *93 318 11 95.* Ⓜ *Jaume I.* *9am–8:45pm Mon–Fri, 9am–1pm Sat.* *Sat in Jul & Aug, public hols.* **www**.bcn.cat/arxiu/arxiuhistoric

Standing beside what was originally the Bishop's Gate in the Roman wall is the Archdeacon's House. It was built in the 12th century, but its present appearance dates from around 1500 when it was remodelled and a colonnade added. In 1870 this was extended to form the Flamboyant Gothic *(see p24)* patio around a fountain. The Modernista architect Domènech i Montaner (1850–1923) added the fanciful marble letterbox, carved with three swallows and a tortoise, beside the Renaissance portal. Upstairs is the Arxiu Històric de la Ciutat (City Archives).

Museu Frederic Marès ❷

Plaça de Sant Iu 5. **Map** 5 B2. ***Tel*** *93 256 35 00.* Ⓜ *Jaume I.* *10am–7pm Tue–Sat, 10am–3pm Sun.* *(free first Sun of each month & Wed pm).* *by appt.* **www**.museumares.bcn.cat

The sculptor Frederic Marès i Deulovol (1893–1991) was also a traveller and collector, and this extraordinary museum is a monument to his eclectic taste. The building is part of the Royal Palace complex and was occupied by 13th-century bishops, 14th-century counts of Barcelona, 15th-century judges, and 18th-century nuns, who lived here until they were expelled in 1936. Marès, who had a small apartment in the building, opened this museum in 1948. It is one of the most fascinating in the city and has an outstanding collection of Romanesque and Gothic religious art. On the ground and first floors there are stone sculptures and two complete Romanesque portals. Exhibits on the three floors above range through clocks, crucifixes, costumes, antique cameras, pipes, tobacco jars and postcards to an amusement room full of toys.

Virgin, Museu Frederic Marès

Conjunt Monumental de la Plaça del Rei ❸

Plaça del Rei. **Map** 5 B2. ***Tel*** *93 256 21 00.* Ⓜ *Jaume I.* *Apr–Sep: 10am–8pm Tue–Sun; Oct–Mar: 10am–2pm, 4–8pm Tue–Sat, 10am–8pm Sun.* *1 Jan, 1 May, 24 Jun, 25 Dec.* *(free pm of 1st Sat of each month.)* *by appointment.*

The Conjunt Monumental de la Plaça del Rei refers to the ensemble of buildings on the square, including the Palau Reial (Royal Palace), which was the residence of the count-kings of Barcelona from its foundation in the 13th century, and the royal chapel. It can be visited as part of the Museu d'Història de Barcelona. The complex also includes the 14th-century Gothic Saló del Tinell, a vast room with arches spanning 17 m (56 ft). This is where Isabel and Fernando *(see p70)* received Columbus on his return from America. It is also where the Holy Inquisition sat.

On the right, built into the Roman city wall, is the royal chapel, the Capella de Santa Àgata, with an altarpiece (1466) by Jaume Huguet. Its bell tower is formed by part of a watchtower on the Roman wall. Stairs on the right of the altar lead to the 16th-century tower of Martí the Humanist

BARCELONA'S EARLY JEWISH COMMUNITY

Hebrew tablet

From the 11th to the 13th centuries, Jews dominated Barcelona's commerce and culture, providing doctors and founding the first seat of learning. But in 1243, 354 years after they were first documented in the city, violent anti-Semitism led to the Jews being consigned to a ghetto, El Call. Ostensibly to provide protection, the ghetto had only one entrance, which led into the Plaça de Sant Jaume. Jews were heavily taxed by the monarch, who viewed them as "royal serfs"; but in return they also received privileges, as they handled most of Catalonia's lucrative trade with North Africa. However, official and popular persecution finally led to the disappearance of the ghetto in 1401, 91 years before Judaism was fully outlawed in Spain *(see p57)*.

Originally there were three synagogues. The main one, Sinagoga Mayor at No. 5 Carrer de Marlet, is said to be the oldest in Europe and can be visited. A 14th-century Hebrew tablet that reads, "Holy Foundation of Rabbi Samuel Hassardi, His soul will rest in Heaven" is embedded in the wall.

(who reigned 1396–1410), the last of Barcelona's count-kings.

The main attraction of the Museu d'Història lies underground. Entire streets of old Barcino are accessible via a lift and walkways suspended over the ruins of Roman Barcelona. The site was found when the Casa Clariana-Padellàs, the Gothic building from which you enter, was moved here stone by stone in 1931. The water and drainage systems, baths, homes with mosaic floors and even the old forum are among some of the most extensive and complete subterranean Roman ruins in the world.

Museu d'Idees i Invents Barcelona (MIBA) ❹

Calle Ciutat 7. **Map** 5 A2. ***Tel*** *93 332 79 30. Jaume I, Liceu. 10am–7pm Mon–Fri, 10am–8pm Sat, 10am–2pm Sun & public hols.* **www**.mibamuseum.com

This small museum contains a diverse collection of brilliant inventions, ranging from the useful (water purifiers) to the bizarre (a mop which doubles as a microphone). A swirling slide links the galleries, and there's a great hands-on invention area for children.

Ajuntament ❺

Plaça de Sant Jaume 1. **Map** 5 A2. ***Tel*** *934 02 73 00. Jaume I, Liceu. 10am–1:30pm Sun & public hols; 10am–8pm 12 Feb, 10am–6:30pm 23 Apr, or by appointment (93 402 73 64).* **www**.bcn.cat

The magnificent 14th-century city hall faces the Palau de la Generalitat. Flanking the entrance of the Ajuntament are statues of Jaime (Jaume) I, who granted the city rights to elect councillors in 1249, and Joan Fiveller, who levied taxes on court members in the 1500s.

Inside is the huge council chamber, the 14th-century Saló de Cent, built for the city's 100 councillors. The Saló de les Cròniques, on the first floor, was commissioned for the 1929 International Exhibition and decorated by Josep-Marià Sert with murals of momentous events in Catalan history.

Palau de la Generalitat ❻

Plaça de Sant Jaume 4. **Map** 5 A2. ***Tel*** *93 402 46 00. Jaume I. 10am–1:30pm 2nd & 4th Sun of every month. phone to book.* **www**.gencat.cat

Since 1403, the Generalitat has been the seat of the Catalonian Governor. Above the entrance, in its Renaissance façade, is a statue of Sant Jordi (St George) – the patron saint of Catalonia – and the Dragon. The late Catalan-Gothic courtyard is by Marc Safont (1416).

The Italianate façade of the Palau de la Generalitat

Among the fine interiors are the Gothic chapel of Sant Jordi, also by Safont, and Pere Blai's Italianate Saló de Sant Jordi. At the back, one floor above street level, lies the *Pati dels Tarongers*, the Orange Tree Patio, by Pau Mateu, which has a bell tower built by Pere Ferrer in 1568.

The Catalan president has offices here as well as in the Casa dels Canonges. The two buildings are connected by a bridge across Carrer del Bisbe, built in 1928 and modelled on the famous Bridge of Sighs in Venice.

The magnificent council chamber, the Saló de Cent, in the Ajuntament

Barcelona Cathedral ❼

This compact Gothic cathedral, with a Romanesque chapel (Capella de Santa Llúcia) and beautiful cloister, was begun in 1298 under Jaime (Jaume) II, on the foundations of a site dating back to Visigothic times. It was not finished until the late 19th century, when the main façade was completed. A white marble choir screen, sculpted in the 16th century, depicts the martyrdom of St Eulàlia, the city's patron. Next to the font, a plaque records the baptism of six Caribbean Indians, whom Columbus brought back from the Americas in 1493.

Statue of St Eulalia

The twin octagonal bell towers date from 1386–93. The bells were installed in this tower in 1545.

The main façade was not completed until 1889, and the central spire until 1913. It was based on the original 1408 plans of the French architect Charles Galters.

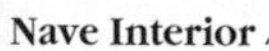

Nave Interior
The Catalan-style Gothic interior has a single wide nave with 28 side chapels. These are set between the columns supporting the vaulted ceiling, which rises to 26 m (85 ft).

★ Choir Stalls
The top tier of the beautifully carved 15th-century stalls contains the coats of arms (1518) of the 12 knights of the Order of Toisón del Oro.

Capella del Santíssim Sagrament
This small chapel houses the 16th-century Christ of Lepanto crucifix.

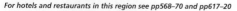

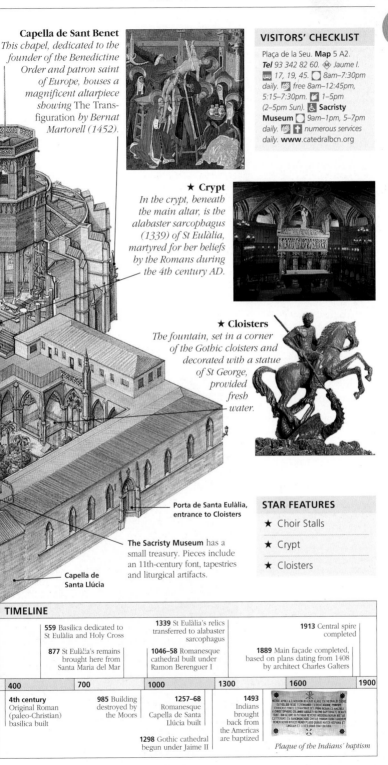

Capella de Sant Benet
This chapel, dedicated to the founder of the Benedictine Order and patron saint of Europe, houses a magnificent altarpiece showing The Transfiguration *by Bernat Martorell (1452).*

VISITORS' CHECKLIST

Plaça de la Seu. **Map** 5 A2. ***Tel*** *93 342 82 60.* *Jaume I.* *17, 19, 45.* *8am–7:30pm daily.* *free 8am–12:45pm, 5:15–7:30pm.* *1–5pm (2–5pm Sun).* **Sacristy Museum** *9am–1pm, 5–7pm daily.* *numerous services daily.* **www**.catedralbcn.org

★ Crypt
In the crypt, beneath the main altar, is the alabaster sarcophagus (1339) of St Eulàlia, martyred for her beliefs by the Romans during the 4th century AD.

★ Cloisters
The fountain, set in a corner of the Gothic cloisters and decorated with a statue of St George, provided fresh water.

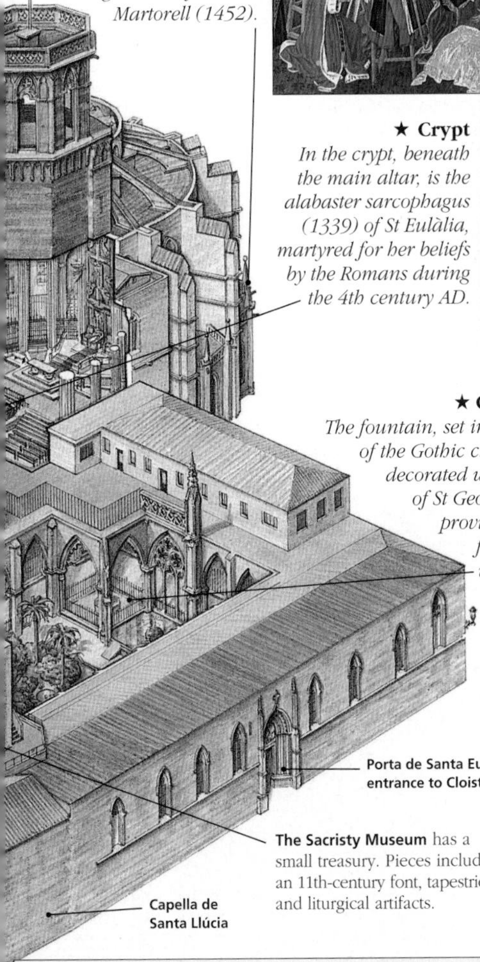

Porta de Santa Eulàlia, entrance to Cloisters

The Sacristy Museum has a small treasury. Pieces include an 11th-century font, tapestries and liturgical artifacts.

Capella de Santa Llúcia

STAR FEATURES

- ★ Choir Stalls
- ★ Crypt
- ★ Cloisters

TIMELINE

- **4th century** Original Roman (paleo-Christian) basilica built
- **559** Basilica dedicated to St Eulàlia and Holy Cross
- **877** St Eulàlia's remains brought here from Santa Maria del Mar
- **985** Building destroyed by the Moors
- **1046–58** Romanesque cathedral built under Ramon Berenguer I
- **1257–68** Romanesque Capella de Santa Llúcia built
- **1298** Gothic cathedral begun under Jaime II
- **1339** St Eulàlia's relics transferred to alabaster sarcophagus
- **1493** Indians brought back from the Americas are baptized
- **1889** Main façade completed, based on plans dating from 1408 by architect Charles Galters
- **1913** Central spire completed

400 | 700 | 1000 | 1300 | 1600 | 1900

Plaque of the Indians' baptism

El Raval 8

Map 2 F3. Ⓜ *Catalunya, Liceu.*

The district of El Raval lies to the west of Las Ramblas and includes the old red-light area near the port, which was once known as the Barri Xinès (Chinese quarter).

From the 14th century, the city hospital was in Carrer de l'Hospital, which still has some herbal and medicinal shops. Gaudí *(see p160)* was brought here after being fatally hit by a tram in 1926. The buildings now house the Biblioteca de Catalunya (Catalonian Library), but the elegant former dissecting room has been fully restored.

Towards the port in Carrer Nou de la Rambla is Gaudí's Palau Güell *(see p141)*. At the end of Sant Pau is the city's most complete Romanesque church, the 12th-century Sant Pau del Camp, with a charming cloister featuring exquisitely carved capitals.

Museu d'Art Contemporani 9

Plaça dels Àngels 1. **Map** 2 F2. ***Tel*** *93 412 08 10.* Ⓜ *Universitat, Catalunya.* *11am–7:30pm Mon–Fri, 10am–8pm Sat, 10am–3pm Sun.* *1 Jan, 25 Dec.* *guided tour times change according to the exhibits; check calendar on website.* **www**.macba.cat **Centre de Cultura Contemporània** Montalegre 5. ***Tel*** *93 306 41 00.* **www**.cccb.org

This dramatic, glass-fronted building was designed by the American architect Richard Meier. Its light, airy galleries act as the city's contemporary art mecca. The permanent collection of predominantly Spanish painting, sculpture and installation from the 1950s onwards is complemented by temporary exhibitions by foreign artists like US painter Susana Solano and South African photojournalist David Goldblatt.

Next to the MACBA, a remodelled 18th-century hospice houses the **Centre de Cultura Contemporània**, a lively arts centre that hosts major arts festivals and regular shows.

Las Ramblas 10

The historic avenue of Las Ramblas (Les Rambles in Catalan) is busy around the clock, especially in the evenings and at weekends. Newsstands, caged bird and flower stalls, tarot readers, musicians and mime artists throng the wide, tree-shaded central walkway. Among its famous buildings are the Liceu Opera House, the huge Boqueria food market and some grand mansions.

Exploring Las Ramblas

The name of this long avenue, also known as Les Rambles, comes from the Arabic *ramla*, meaning the dried-up bed of a seasonal river. The 13th-century city wall followed the left bank of such a river that flowed from the Collserola hills to the sea. Convents, monasteries and the university were built on the other bank in the 16th century. As time passed, the riverbed was filled in and those buildings demolished, but they are remembered in the names of the five consecutive Rambles that make up the great avenue between the Port Vell and Plaça de Catalunya.

Palau Güell C/ Nou de la Rambla 3–5. **Map** 2 F3. ***Tel*** *93 472 57 75.* Ⓜ *Liceu.* *Apr–Sep: 10am–8pm Tue–Sun (last adm 7pm); Oct–Mar: 10am–5:30pm Tue–Sun (last adm 4:30pm).* *ground floor only.* **www**.palauguell.cat **Museu de Cera** Pg de la Banca 7. **Map** 2 F4. ***Tel*** *93 317 26 49.* Ⓜ *Drassanes.* *10am–1:30pm, 4–7:30pm Mon–Fri, 11am–2pm, 4:30–8:30pm Sat, Sun & public hols.*

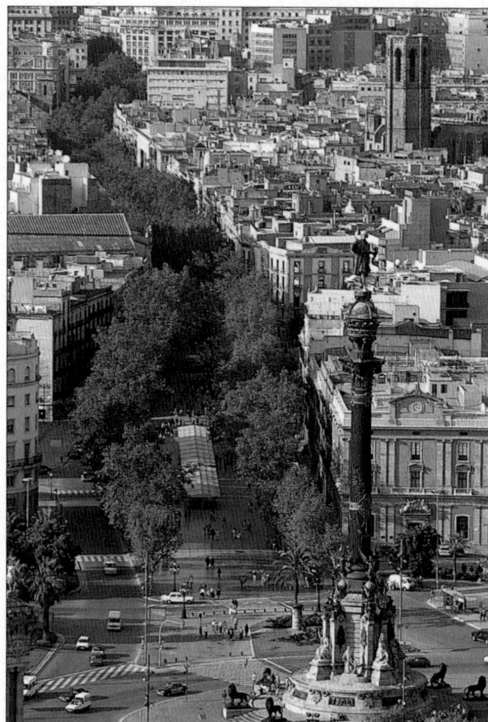

The monument to Columbus at the bottom of the tree-lined Ramblas

Font de Canaletes ①
Saying that someone "drinks the waters of Canaletes" – from this 19th-century fountain – indicates he or she is from Barcelona.

Reial Acadèmia de Ciències i Arts ②
Converted to a theatre in 1910, this building has Barcelona's first official public clock.

Palau de la Virreina ④
The first occupant of this great palace, in 1777, was the *virreina* (viceroy's wife) of Spain in Peru.

Mercat de Sant Josep ⑤
Popularly known as "La Boquería", this is Barcelona's most colourful food market.

Palau Moja ③
The Baroque first-floor salon of this Classical building of 1790 is used for exhibitions.

Gran Teatre del Liceu ⑦
The opera house has had to be restored twice after fires – in 1861 and 1994.

Plaça de la Boquería ⑥
This square features a mosaic pavement by Miró (1976) and an Art Deco dragon designed for a former umbrella shop.

Palau Güell ⑨
This Neo-Gothic palace is considered to be one of Gaudí's most important works *(see p141)*.

Plaça Reial ⑧
Barcelona's most lively square was built in the 1850s. The Neo-Classical lampposts were designed by Gaudí.

Museu de Cera ⑩
This waxwork museum, in an atmospheric, 19th-century building, contains about 300 exhibits.

Glorious stained-glass dome, Palau de la Música Catalana

Palau de la Música Catalana ⓫

Carrer de Sant Francesc de Paula 2. **Map** 5 B1. ***Tel*** *902 47 54 85.* *Urquinaona.* *10am–3:30pm daily (10am–6pm Easter & Aug); and for concerts.* *limited.* *in English on the hour, 10am–3pm.* **www**.palaumusica.org

This is a real palace of music, a Modernista celebration of tilework, sculpture and glorious stained glass. It is the only concert hall in Europe lit by natural light. Designed by Lluís Domènech i Montaner, it was completed in 1908. Although a few extensions have been added, the building still retains its original appearance. The elaborate red-brick façade is hard to appreciate fully in the confines of the narrow street. It is lined with mosaic-covered pillars topped by busts of the great composers Palestrina, Beethoven and Bach. The large stone sculpture of St George and other figures at the corner of the building portrays an allegory from Catalan folksong by Miquel Blay.

But it is the interior of the building that is truly inspiring. The auditorium is lit by a huge inverted dome of stained glass depicting angelic choristers. The sculptures of composers Wagner and Clavé on the proscenium arch that frames the stage area were designed by Domènech but finished by Pau Gargallo. The stunning "Muses of the Palau", the group of 18 highly stylized, instrument-playing maidens, are the stage's back-drop. Made of terracotta and trencadís (pieces of ceramic), the muses have become the building's most admired feature.

The work of Josep Anselm Clavé (1824–74) in promoting Catalan song led to the creation of the Orfeó Català choral society in 1891, a focus of Catalan nationalism and the inspiration behind the Palau. Although the Orfeó is now based at the more state-of-the-art L'Auditori in Plaça de les Glòries *(see p191)*, there is a concert at the Palau nearly every night; it is the main venue for the city's jazz and guitar festivals, and world music, flamenco and symphony orchestras regularly grace its flamboyant stage.

The Palau's new era began with the completion of the work carried out by the top local architect Oscar Tusquets. An underground concert hall and an outdoor square for summer concerts were added, consolidating the Palau's reputation as Barcelona's most loved music venue.

La Llotja ⓬

Carrer del Consolat de Mar 2. **Map** 5 B3. ***Tel*** *933 19 24 12.* *Barceloneta, Jaume I.* *to the public (except twice a year, days vary).*

La Llotja (meaning commodity exchange) was built in the 1380s as the headquarters of the Consolat de Mar. It was remodelled in Neo-Classical style in 1771 and housed the city's stock exchange until 1994, the original Gothic hall acting as the main trading room. It can still be seen through the windows.

The upper floors housed the Barcelona School of Fine Arts from 1849 to 1970, attended by Pablo Picasso and Joan Miró. It is now occupied by the local chamber of commerce.

Statue of Poseidon in the courtyard of La Llotja

El Born ⓭

Map 5 B3. Ⓜ *Jaume I.*

Named after the jousting sessions that once took place in its central boulevard, El Born is a tiny pocket of the La Ribera district. The village-like atmosphere of the neighbourhood makes it popular with local residents and young urbanites. Trendy bars, fashion and design shops are juxtaposed with medieval architecture. The 14th-century mansions of Carrer Montcada have remained intact and now house high-calibre galleries and museums, whilst the tiny, pedestrianised streets and squares fanning out from the Mercat del Born are the centre of the city's café culture. The numerous bars and restaurants are a magnet for revellers, much to the annoyance of the full-time residents who voice their complaints visually through the banners hanging from El Born's balconies.

Museu Picasso ⓮

Carrer Montcada 15–23. **Map** 5 B2. ***Tel*** *932 56 30 00.* Ⓜ *Jaume I.* *10am–8pm Tue–Sun.* *(free under age 16, 1st Sun of month & every Sun after 3pm).* *11am Sun in English, book in advance.* **www**.museupicasso.bcn.cat

One of Barcelona's most popular attractions, the Picasso Museum is housed in five adjoining medieval palaces on Carrer Montcada: Berenguer d'Aguilar, Baró de Castellet, Meca, Mauri and Finestres.

The museum opened in 1963 showing works donated by Jaime Sabartes, a friend of Picasso. Following Sabartes' death in 1968, Picasso himself donated paintings, including early examples. These were complemented by graphic works, left in his will, and 141 ceramic pieces given by his widow, Jacqueline.

The strength of the 3,000-piece collection is Picasso's early works. These show how, even at the ages of 15 and 16, he was painting major works such as *The First Communion* (1896) and *Science and Charity* (1897). There are only a few pictures from his Blue and Rose periods. The most famous work is his series of 44 paintings, *Las Meninas*, inspired by Velázquez's masterpiece.

Basílica de Santa Maria del Mar ⓯

Plaça Sta Maria 1. **Map** 5 B3. ***Tel*** *93 310 23 90.* Ⓜ *Jaume I.* *9am–1:30pm, 4:30–8pm daily (Sun from 10:50am).*

The city's favourite church, with superb acoustics for concerts, is the only example of a church entirely in the Catalan Gothic style. It took just 55 years to build, with money donated by merchants and shipbuilders. The speed – unrivalled in the Middle Ages – gave it a unity of style both inside and out. The west front has a 15th-century rose window of the Coronation of the Virgin. More stained glass, from the 15th–18th centuries, lights the nave and aisles.

The choir and furnishings were burned in the Civil War *(see p67)*, adding to the sense of space and simplicity.

A wedding service in the Gothic interior of Santa Maria del Mar

Pablo Picasso, *Self-Portrait* in charcoal (1899–1900)

PABLO PICASSO IN BARCELONA

Picasso (1881–1973) was born in Málaga and was almost 14 when he came to Barcelona, where his father had found a job in the city's art academy. Picasso enrolled, and was a precocious talent among his contemporaries. He was a regular visitor to Els Quatre Gats, an artists' café still in existence in Carrer Montsió, where he held his first exhibition. He also exhibited in Sala Parks, a gallery still functioning in Carrer Petritxol. The family lived in Carrer Mercé and Picasso had a studio in Carrer Nou de la Rambla. It was among the prostitutes of Carrer d'Avinyò that he found inspiration for the work that many art historians see as the wellspring of modern art, *Les Demoiselles d'Avignon* (1906–7). Picasso left Barcelona for Paris in his early twenties and initially returned several times. After the Civil War his opposition to Franco kept him in France, but he designed a frieze for Barcelona's College of Architects in 1962 and was persuaded to allow the city to open a museum of his work, which it did the following year.

Renaissance-style 17th-century façades lining Carrer Montcada

Carrer Montcada ⓰

Map 5 B3. *Jaume I.* **Disseny Hub Barcelona (DHUB)** *at No. 12.* ***Tel*** *93 256 23 00.* *11am–7pm Tue–Sat, 11am–8pm Sun & public hols.* *1 Jan, 1 May, 24 Jun, 25 & 26 Dec.* *(free 1st Sun of each month).*

The most authentic medieval street in the city is a narrow lane, overshadowed by gargoyles and roofs that almost touch overhead. The Gothic palaces that line it date back to Catalonia's expansion in the 13th century. Almost all of the buildings were modified over the years, particularly during the 17th century. Only Casa Cervelló-Guidice at No. 25 retains its original façade.

The **Disseny Hub Barcelona** in Palau del Marqués de Lliò has temporary exhibitions on product design, architecture, visual communication and fashion. At No. 22 is the city's best-known champagne and *cava* bar, El Xampanyet.

The entrance to the Disseny Hub Barcelona

Mercat del Born ⓱

Map 5 C3. *Jaume I, Barceloneta.*

This covered market, with its ornate iron work and crystal roof, was inspired by the original Les Halles in Paris and it was Barcelona's principal wholesale market until the early 1970s when it outgrew its location. The street names in the vicinity reflect what went on in Barcelona's former mercantile hub: L'Argenteria was lined with silversmiths, Flassaders was where you went for a weaved blanket and Vidrieria was once lit up with glass blowers' torches. A few of these establishments remain, but they are now outnumbered by chic fashion and interiors boutiques.

The market itself has been the focus of a fierce debate. When work started in 2002 to convert the space into a library, extensive remains dating from the 1700s were discovered. The architectural importance of the subterranean streets and homes were questioned, but the historical significance of the dig sealed the market's fate as a future cultural centre. In 1714 Barcelona fell to French-Spanish forces in the War of Succession *(see p62)*, with particularly heavy losses in El Born, and became an occupied city. This key event in Catalonia's history is remembered each year on September 11th in flag-waving celebrations centred near the market.

Museu de la Xocolata ⓲

Comerç 36. **Map** 5 C2. *Jaume I, Arc de Triomf.* ***Tel*** *93 268 78 78.* *10am–7pm Mon–Sat, 10am–3pm Sun & pub hols.* *1 Jan, 1 May, 25 & 26 Dec.* *(free 1st Mon of the month).* *by appointment.* **http**://pastisseria.com/en/portadamuseu

Founded by Barcelona's chocolate- and pastry-makers union, this museum celebrates the history of one of the most universally loved foodstuffs: from the discovery of cocoa in South America to the invention of the first chocolate machine in Barcelona. This is executed through old posters, photographs and footage. The real thing is displayed in a homage to the art of the *mona*. This was a traditional Easter cake that over the centuries evolved into an edible sculpture. Every year, pâtissiers compete for the most imaginative piece, decorating their chocolate versions of well-known buildings or folk figures with jewels, feathers and other materials. The museum shop sells chocolate goods.

The pink brick façade of the late 19th-century Arc del Triomf

Arc del Triomf ⓳

Passeig Lluís Companys. **Map** 5 C1. *Arc de Triomf.*

The main gateway to the 1888 Universal Exhibition, which filled the Parc de la Ciutadella, was designed by Josep Vilaseca i Casanovas. It is built of brick in Mudéjar *(see p55)* style, with sculpted allegories of crafts, industry and business. The frieze by Josep Reynés on the main façade represents the city welcoming foreign visitors.

Parc de la Ciutadella ⓴

Avda del Marquès de l'Argentera. **Map** 6 D2. *Barceloneta, Ciutadella-Vila Olímpica, Arc de Triomf.* *8am–dusk daily.*

This popular park has a boating lake, orange groves and parrots living in the palm trees. It was once the site of a massive star-shaped citadel, built for Felipe V between 1715 and 1720 following a 13-month siege of the city. The fortress was intended to house soldiers to keep law and order, but was never used for this purpose. Converted into a prison, the citadel became notorious during the Napoleonic occupation *(see p63)* and, during the 19th-century liberal repressions, it was hated as a symbol of centralized power. In 1878, under General Prim, whose statue stands in the middle of the park, the citadel was pulled down and the park given to the city, to become, in 1888, the venue of the Universal Exhibition *(see p64)*. Three buildings survived: the Governor's Palace, now a school; the chapel; and the arsenal, occupied by the Catalan parliament.

The park offers more cultural and leisure activities than any other in the city and is particularly popular on Sunday afternoons when people gather to play instruments, dance and relax, or visit the museums and zoo. A variety of works by Catalan sculptors such as Marès, Arnau, Carbonell, Clarà, Llimona, Gargallo, Dunyach and Fuxà, can be seen in the park, alongside work by modern artists such as Tàpies and Botero.

The gardens in the Plaça de Armes were laid out by the French landscape gardener Jean Forestier and centre on a cascade based around a triumphal arch. It was designed by architect Josep Fontseré, with the help of Antoni Gaudí, then still a young student.

Modernist exterior of the Castell dels Tres Dragons

Castell dels Tres Dragons ㉑

Passeig de Picasso. **Map** 5 C2.
Arc de Triomf, Jaume I.
closed to the public.

At the entrance to the Parc de la Ciutadella is the Castell dels Tres Dragons (Castle of the Three Dragons), named after a play by Frederic Soler. A fine example of Modernista architecture *(see pp140–41)*, the combination of visible iron supports and exposed red brickwork were radical innovations at the time.

It was built by Lluís Domènech i Montaner for the 1888 Universal Exhibition and was later used as a workshop for Modernista design. Once part of the Museu de Ciències Naturals, the Castell now houses a laboratory for the museum and is open only to researchers.

Museu Martorell ㉒

Parc de la Ciutadella. **Map** 5 C3. ***Tel*** *93 319 69 12. Arc de Triomf, Jaume I. closed for renovations; phone ahead before visiting.*

Part of the Museu de Ciències Naturals, the Museu Martorell is Barcelona's oldest museum. It opened in 1882 and was the first building in the city to be constructed expressly for the purpose of housing a museum. Beside it is the Hivernacle, a glass-house by Josep Amargós, and the Umbracle, a conservatory by the park's architect, Josep Fontseré. Both date from 1884 and were designed for the 1888 Universal Exhibition.

Parc Zoològic ㉓

Parc de la Ciutadella. **Map** 6 D3. ***Tel*** *93 225 67 80. Ciutadella-Vila Olímpica. 10am–5pm (Mar–May & Oct: to 6pm, Jun–Sep: to 7pm).* **www**.zoobarcelona.com

The animals in this zoo, laid out in the 1940s, are separated by moats instead of bars. Dolphin and whale shows are held in one of the aquariums. All the aquatic creatures here will eventually move to a designated marine zoo, but plans are currently on hold due to budget cuts. The zoo has pony rides, electric cars and a train. Roig i Soler's 1885 sculpture by the entrance, *The Lady with the Umbrella*, has become a symbol of the city.

Ornamental cascade in the Parc de la Ciutadella designed by Josep Fontseré and Antoni Gaudí

Smart boats and the twin skyscrapers at the Port Olímpic

Port Olímpic 24

Map 6 F4. Ⓜ *Ciutadella-Vila Olímpica.*

The most dramatic rebuilding for the 1992 Olympics was the demolition of the old industrial waterfront and the laying out of 4 km (2 miles) of promenade and pristine sandy beaches. Suddenly Barcelona seemed like a seaside resort. At the heart of the project was a 65-ha (160-acre) new estate of 2,000 apartments and parks called Nova Icària. The area is still popularly known as the Vila Olímpica because the buildings originally housed the Olympic athletes.

On the sea front there are twin 44-floor blocks, two of Barcelona's tallest skyscrapers, one occupied by offices and the other by the Arts hotel *(see p569)*. They stand beside a bustling marina, which was also built for 1992. The marina is the setting for several restaurants and bars.

Barceloneta 25

Map 5 B5. Ⓜ *Barceloneta.*

Barcelona's fishing "village", which lies on a triangular tongue of land jutting into the sea just below the city centre, is renowned for its fish restaurants and port-side cafés.

Barceloneta was built by the architect and military engineer Juan Martín de Cermeño in 1753 to rehouse people made homeless by the construction of a large fortress, La Ciutadella *(see p154)*. Since then it has housed largely workers and fishermen. Laid out on a grid system with narrow houses of two or three floors, the area has a friendly air.

In the small Plaça de la Barceloneta, at the centre of the district, is the Baroque church of Sant Miquel del Port, also by Cermeño. Nearby is the striking contemporary covered market.

Today, the remnants of Barceloneta's fishing fleet are based in the nearby industrial docks by a small clock tower. On the opposite side of this harbour is the Torre de Sant Sebastià, terminus of the cable car that runs across the port, via the World Trade Centre, to Montjuïc. Ricardo Bofill's sail-shaped Hotel W is a landmark on Barceloneta beach.

Port Vell 26

Map 5 A4. Ⓜ *Barceloneta, Drassanes.* **Aquàrium** ***Tel*** *93 221 74 74.* ◯ *Jun & Sep: 9:30am–9:30pm daily; Jul–Aug: 9:30am–11pm daily; Oct–May: 9:30am–9pm Mon–Fri, 9:30am–9:30pm Sat, Sun & public hols.* **www**.aquariumbcn.com

The city's leisure port is at the foot of Las Ramblas, just beyond the old customs house. This was built in 1902 at the Portal de la Pau, the former maritime entrance to the city, where steps lead into the water. To the south, the Moll de Barcelona, with a World Trade Centre, serves as the passenger pier for visiting cruise ships. In front of the customs house, Las Ramblas is linked to the yacht clubs on the Moll d'Espanya by a swing bridge and pedestrian jetty. The Moll d'Espanya (*moll* meaning quay, wharf or pier) has a shopping and restaurant complex, the Maremagnum, plus an IMAX cinema and the largest aquarium in Europe.

The Moll de la Fusta (Timber Wharf), with terrace cafés, has red structures inspired by Van Gogh's painting of the bridge at Arles. At the end of the wharf stands *El Cap de Barcelona (Barcelona Head)*, a 20-m (66-ft) sculpture by Pop artist Roy Lichtenstein.

Monument a Colom 27

Plaça del Portal de la Pau. **Map** 2 F4. ***Tel*** *93 302 52 24.* Ⓜ *Drassanes.* ◯ *9am–8:30pm daily.*

The Columbus Monument in the Portal de la Pau (the "Gate of Peace") was designed by Gaietà Buigas for the 1888 Universal Exhibition.

The 60-m (200-ft) cast iron monument marks the spot where Columbus stepped ashore in 1493 after discovering America, bringing with him six Caribbean Indians. He was accorded a state welcome by the Catholic Monarchs in the Saló del Tinell *(see p146)*. The Indians' conversion to Christianity is commemorated in the cathedral *(see pp148–9)*.

A lift provides visitors with access to a small viewing platform at the top of the monument, where a 7-m (24-ft) bronze statue of Columbus points out to sea.

Fishing boat moored at the quayside of Barceloneta

A *golondrina* departing from the Plaça del Portal de la Pau

Golondrinas 28

Plaça del Portal de la Pau. **Map** 2 F5. ***Tel*** *93 442 31 06. Drassanes.* *times vary – phone ahead.* **www**.lasgolondrinas.com

Sightseeing trips around the harbour can be made on small double-decker boats called *golondrinas* ("swallows"). They moor beside the steps of the Plaça del Portal de la Pau in front of the Columbus Monument. Tours last around half an hour. The boats go out beneath the steep, castle-topped hill of Montjuïc towards the industrial port.

An alternative one-and-a-half-hour trip in modern catamarans takes in Barcelona Harbour, the commercial port and beaches.

Museu Marítim and Drassanes 29

Avinguda de les Drassanes. **Map** 2 F4. ***Tel*** *93 342 99 20. Drassanes.* *10am–8pm daily (collection only partially open due to refurbishment).* *1 & 6 Jan, 25 & 26 Dec.* **www**.mmb.cat

The great galleys that made Barcelona a major seafaring power were built in the sheds of the Drassanes (shipyards), which now house the maritime museum. These royal dry docks are the largest and most complete surviving medieval complex of their kind in the world. They were founded in the mid-13th century, when dynastic marriages uniting the kingdoms of Sicily and Aragón meant that better maritime communications between the two became a priority. Three of the yards' four original corner towers survive.

Among the vessels to slip from the Drassanes' vaulted halls was the *Real*, flagship of Don Juan of Austria, Charles V's illegitimate son, who led the Christian fleet to victory against the Turks at Lepanto in 1571 *(see p59)*. The museum's showpiece is a full-scale replica decorated in red and gold. A restored century-old schooner, the *Santa Eulàlia*, is moored in the Port Vell and can be visited.

The *Llibre del Consulat de Mar*, a book of nautical codes and practice, is a reminder that Catalonia was once the arbiter of Mediterranean maritime law. The expertise of its sailors is also evident in the collection of Pre-Columbian charts and maps, including one of 1439 that was used by Amerigo Vespucci.

Stained-glass window in the Museu Marítim

BARCELONA'S FIESTAS

La Mercè *(24 Sep)*. The patroness of Barcelona, Nostra Senyora de la Mercè (Our Lady of Mercy), whose church is near the port, is honoured for a week around 24 September with masses, concerts and dances. The biggest events are the *correfoc* – a wild procession of people dressed as devils and monsters, dancing with fireworks – and the *piro musical* – an impressive firework display with music held at the Font Màgica in Montjuïc.

Firework display during the fiesta of La Mercè

Els Tres Tombs *(17 Jan)*. Horsemen, dressed in top hats and tails, ride three times through the streets in honour of St Anthony, the patron saint of animals.

Dia de Sant Ponç *(11 May)*. Stalls along Carrer Hospital sell herbs, honey and candied fruit on the day of the patron saint of beekeepers and herbalists.

La Diada *(11 Sep)*. Catalonia's "national" day is an occasion for singing the Catalan anthem and separatist demonstrations.

Festa Major *(varies)*. Each district hosts its own *festa* in which streets compete to outdo each other in the inventiveness and beauty of their decorations. The most spectacular take place in the neighbourhood of Gràcia.

EIXAMPLE

Barcelona claims to have the greatest collection of Art Nouveau buildings of any city in Europe. The style, known in Catalonia as Modernisme, flourished after 1854, when it was decided to pull down the medieval walls to allow the city to develop into what had previously been a construction-free military zone.

The designs of the civil engineer Ildefons Cerdà i Sunyer (1815–76) were chosen for the new expansion *(eixample)* inland. These plans called for a rigid grid system of streets, but at each intersection the corners were chamfered to allow the buildings there to overlook the junctions or squares. The few exceptions to this grid system include the Diagonal, a main avenue running from the wealthy area of Pedralbes down to the sea, and the Hospital de la Santa Creu i de Sant Pau by Modernista architect Domènech i Montaner (1850–1923). He hated the grid system and deliberately angled the hospital to look down the diagonal Avinguda de Gaudí towards Antoni Gaudí's church of the Sagrada Família, the city's most spectacular Modernista building *(see pp166–7)*. The wealth of Barcelona's commercial elite, and their passion for all things new, allowed them to give free rein to the age's most innovative architects in designing their residences as well as public buildings.

***Jesus of the Column*, Sagrada Família**

SIGHTS AT A GLANCE

Museums and Galleries
Fundació Antoni Tàpies ❷

Churches
Sagrada Família pp166–7 ❻

Modernista Buildings
Casa Milà, "La Pedrera" ❸
Casa Terrades, "Casa de les Punxes" ❹
Hospital de la Santa Creu i de Sant Pau ❺
Illa de la Discòrdia ❶

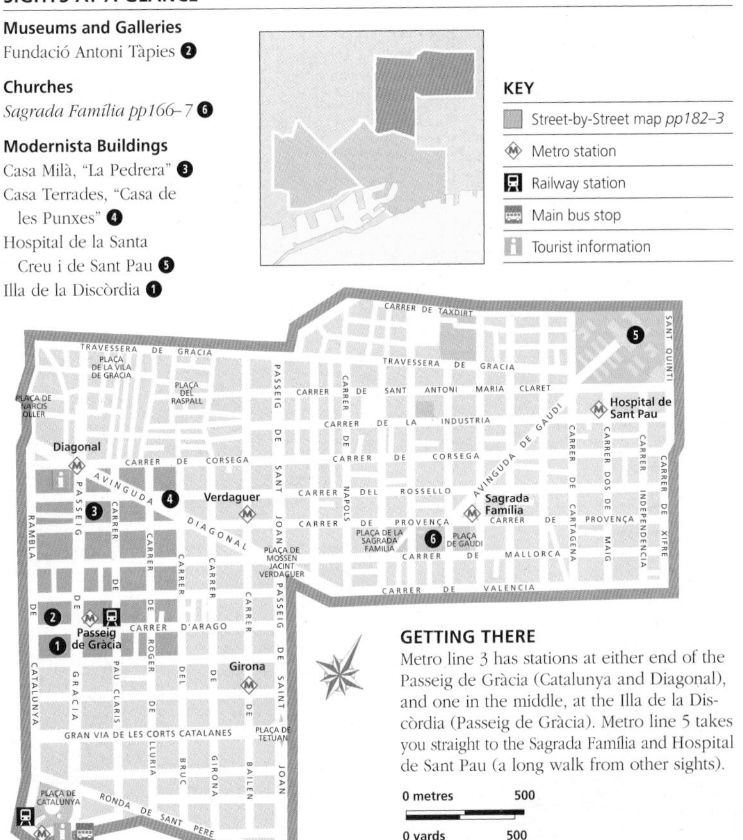

GETTING THERE

Metro line 3 has stations at either end of the Passeig de Gràcia (Catalunya and Diagonal), and one in the middle, at the Illa de la Discòrdia (Passeig de Gràcia). Metro line 5 takes you straight to the Sagrada Família and Hospital de Sant Pau (a long walk from other sights).

◁ **Nativity façade of the Sagrada Família – the only façade to be more or less completed in Gaudí's lifetime**

Street-by-Street: Quadrat d'O

The hundred or so city blocks centring on the Passeig de Gràcia are known as the Quadrat d'Or, "Golden Square", because they contain so many of Barcelona's best Modernista buildings *(see pp140–41)*. This was the area within the Eixample favoured by the wealthy bourgeoisie, who embraced the new artistic and architectural style with enthusiasm, not only for their residences, but also for commercial buildings. Most remarkable is the Illa de la Discòrdia, a single block containing houses by Modernisme's most illustrious exponents. Many interiors can be visited by the public, revealing a feast of stained glass, ceramics and ornamental ironwork.

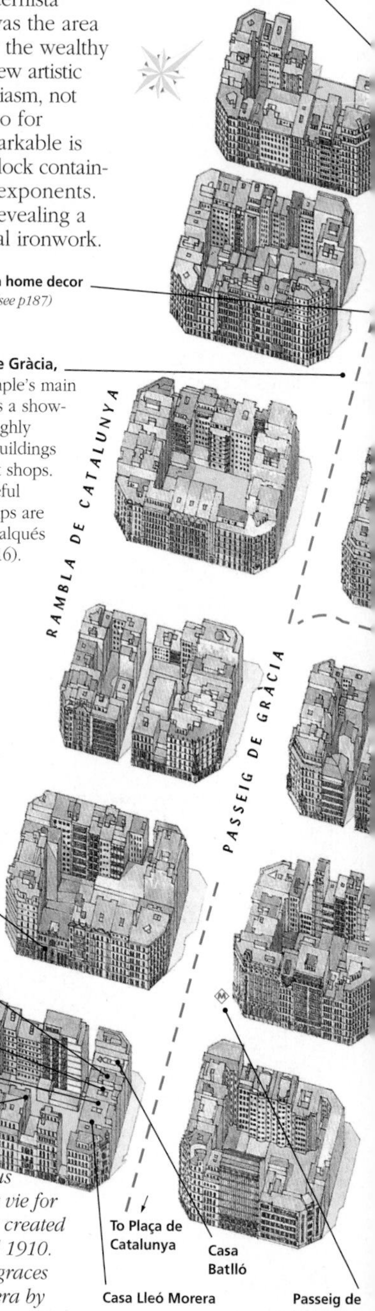

Perfume bottle, Museu del Perfum

Diagonal Metro

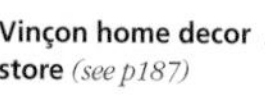

Vinçon home decor store *(see p187)*

Passeig de Gràcia, the Eixample's main avenue, is a showcase of highly original buildings and smart shops. The graceful street lamps are by Pere Falqués (1850–1916).

RAMBLA DE CATALUNYA

PASSEIG DE GRÀCIA

Fundació Tàpies
Topped by Antoni Tàpies' wire sculpture Cloud and Chair, this 1879 building by Domènech i Montaner houses a wide variety of Tàpies' paintings, graphics and sculptures ❷

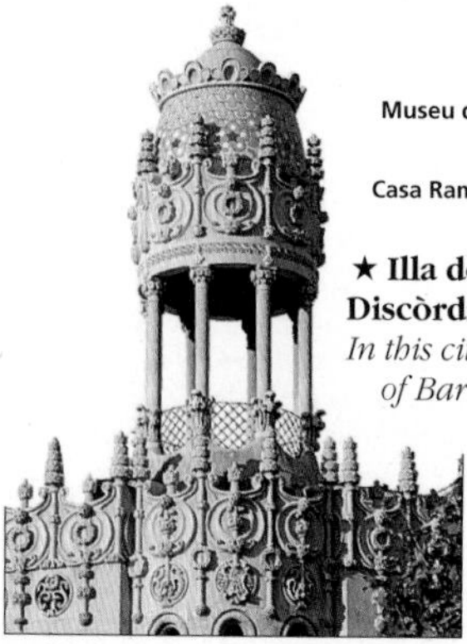

Casa Amatller

Museu del Perfum

Casa Ramon Mulleras

★ Illa de la Discòrdia
In this city block, three of Barcelona's most famous Modernista houses vie for attention. All were created between 1900 and 1910. This ornate tower graces the Casa Lleó Morera by Domènech i Montaner ❶

To Plaça de Catalunya

Casa Batlló

Casa Lleó Morera

Passeig de Gràcia Metro

The Palau Baró de Quadras was designed by Puig i Cadafalch in 1904. The façade, in neo-Gothic style, is highly ornate and covered with distinctive sculptures. This carving adorns the doorway.

LOCATOR MAP
See Street Finder map 3

Casa Terrades "Les Punxes"
Built in red brick with carved stone ornamentation, this 1905 house by Puig i Cadafalch echoes the Gothic buildings of northern Europe ❹

★ Casa Milà "La Pedrera"
Gaudí put all his architectural daring into this, his most famous house. The result is a remarkable wave-like façade and a roofscape of chimneys and vents resembling abstract sculptures ❸

KEY

– – – Suggested route

STAR SIGHTS

★ Illa de la Discòrdia

★ Casa Milà "La Pedrera"

Sumptuous interior of the Casa Lleó Morera, Illa de la Discòrdia

Illa de la Discòrdia ❶

Passeig de Gràcia, between Carrer d'Aragó and Carrer del Consell de Cent. **Map** 3 A4. *Passeig de Gràcia.* **Casa Amatller** ***Tel*** *93 216 01 75.* *10am–8pm Mon–Sat, 10am–3pm Sun.* **Casa Batlló** ***Tel*** *93 488 06 66.* *9am–8pm daily.* **www**.casabatllo.cat

The most famous group of Modernista *(see pp140–41)* buildings in Barcelona amply illustrates the range of styles involved in the movement. The city block in which they stand has been dubbed the Illa de la Discòrdia, "Block of Discord", owing to the startling visual argument between them.

The three most famous houses, on Passeig de Gràcia, were remodelled in Modernista style from existing houses early in the 20th century, but named after their original owners.

No. 35 is **Casa Lleó Morera** (1902–6), the first residential work of Lluís Domènech i Montaner. The ground floor was gutted to create a shop in 1943, but the Modernista interiors upstairs still exist.

At No. 41 is **Casa Amatller**, designed by Puig i Cadafalch in 1898. Its façade is a harmonious blend of styles, featuring Moorish and Gothic windows. The stepped gable roof is dotted with tiles. Inside the wrought-iron main doors is a fine stone staircase beneath a stained-glass roof. The Amatller family apartments are being restored and should reopen to visitors in 2015. The rest of the building is occupied by the **Institut Amatller d'Art Hispanic**.

The third house is Antoni Gaudí's **Casa Batlló** (1904–6). Its façade has heavily tiled walls and curving iron balconies pierced with holes to look like masks or skulls. The hump-backed, scaly-looking roof is thought to represent a dragon, with St George (the patron saint of Catalonia) as a chimney.

Fundació Antoni Tàpies ❷

Carrer d'Aragó 255. **Map** 3 A4. ***Tel*** *93 487 03 15.* *Passeig de Gràcia.* *10am–8pm Tue–Sun & public hols.* *1 & 6 Jan, 25 & 26 Dec.* *by appointment (932 07 58 62).* **www**.fundaciotapies.org

Antoni Tàpies (1923–2012) was one of Spain's foremost contemporary artists. Inspired by Surrealism, his abstract work was executed in a variety of materials, including concrete and metal *(see p160)*. Only a small part of the collection can be shown at one time, and exhibits rotate regularly. There are also excellent temporary exhibitions. All are housed in the first domestic building in Barcelona to be built with iron (1880), designed by Domènech i Montaner.

ANTONI GAUDÍ (1852–1926)

Born in Reus (Tarragona) into a family of artisans, Gaudí was the leading exponent of Catalan Modernisme. Following a stint as a blacksmith's apprentice, he studied at Barcelona's School of Architecture. Inspired by a nationalistic search for a romantic medieval past, his work was supremely original. His first major achievement was the Casa Vicens (1888) at No. 24 Carrer de les Carolines. But his most celebrated building is the extravagant church of the Sagrada Família *(see pp166–7)*, to which he devoted his life from 1914. He gave all his money to the project and often went from house to house begging for more, until his death a few days after being run over by a tram.

Decorated chimney pot, Casa Vicens

◁ Extraordinary sculptured and ceramic-encrusted chimneys of Gaudí's Casa Milà

The rippled façade of Gaudí's apartment building, Casa Milà

Casa Milà "La Pedrera" ❸

Passeig de Gràcia 92. **Map** 3 B3. ***Tel*** *93 483 59 00.* *Diagonal.* *9am–8pm daily (Nov–Feb: to 6:30pm).* *pub holidays.* *(temporary exhibitions free.)* **www**.fundaciocaixacatalunya.org

Usually called "La Pedrera" ("the stone quarry"), the Casa Milà is Gaudí's greatest contribution to Barcelona's civic architecture, and his last work before he devoted himself entirely to the Sagrada Família *(see pp166–7).*

Built 1906–10, "La Pedrera" completely departed from the established construction principles of the time and, as a result, was strongly attacked by Barcelona's intellectuals.

Gaudí designed this corner apartment block, eight storeys high, around two circular courtyards. The intricate iron-work balconies, by Josep Maria Jujol, are like seaweed against the wave-like walls of white undressed stone. There are no straight walls in the building.

The Milà family had an apartment on the first floor. The top floor now houses the Gaudí Museum. Regular guided tours take in the extraordinary roof, where the multitude of sculpted air ducts and chimneys are so sinister they have been dubbed the *espanta-bruixes*, the witch-scarers.

Casa Terrades ❹

Avinguda Diagonal 416. **Map** 3 B3. *Diagonal.* *to public.*

This free-standing, six-sided apartment block by Modernista architect Puig i Cadafalch gets its nickname, "Casa de les Punxes" (House of the Points), from the spires on its six corner turrets, which are shaped like witches' hats. It was built between 1903 and 1905 by converting three existing houses on the site and was Puig's largest work. It is an eclectic mixture of medieval and Renaissance styles. The towers and gables are influenced in particular by north European Gothic architecture. However, the deeply carved, floral stone ornament of the exterior, in combination with red brick as the principal building material, are typically Modernista.

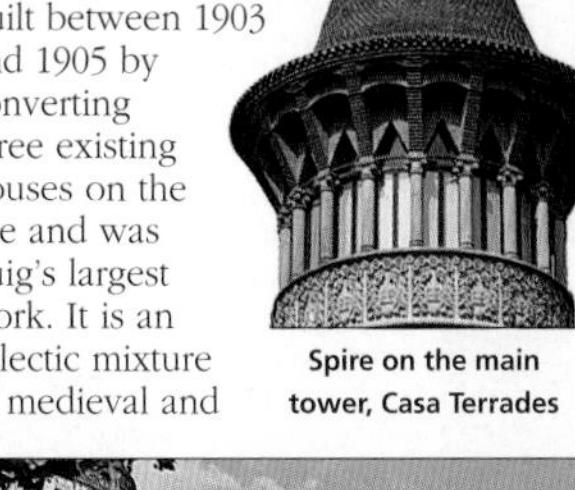

Spire on the main tower, Casa Terrades

Hospital de la Santa Creu i de Sant Pau ❺

Carrer de Sant Antoni Maria Claret 167. **Map** 4 F1. ***Tel*** *93 317 76 52.* *Hospital de Sant Pau.* **Grounds** *10am–2pm daily.* *tours in English at 10am, 11am, noon & 1pm.* **www**.santpau.es

Lluis Domènech i Montaner began designing a new city hospital in 1902. Totally innovative in concept, his scheme consisted of 26 Mudéjar-style pavilions set in large gardens, as he disliked huge wards and believed that patients would recover better amid fresh air and trees. All the connecting corridors and service areas were hidden underground.

Also believing art and colour to be therapeutic, he decorated the pavilions profusely. The turreted roofs were tiled with ceramics, and the reception pavilion embellished with sculptures by Pau Gargallo and mosaic murals. During refurbishment some parts of the tour may be inaccessible.

Statue of the Virgin, Hospital de la Santa Creu i de Sant Pau

Sagrada Família ❻

A carved whelk

Europe's most unconventional church, the Temple Expiatori de la Sagrada Família, is an emblem of a city that likes to think of itself as individualistic. Crammed with symbolism inspired by nature and striving for originality, it is Gaudí's *(see pp140–41)* greatest work. In 1883, a year after work had begun on a Neo-Gothic church on the site, the task of completing it was given to Gaudí who changed everything, extemporizing as he went along. It became his life's work and he lived like a recluse on the site for 14 years. He is buried in the crypt. At his death only one tower on the Nativity façade had been completed, but work resumed after the Civil War and several more have since been finished to his original plans. Work continues today, financed by public subscription.

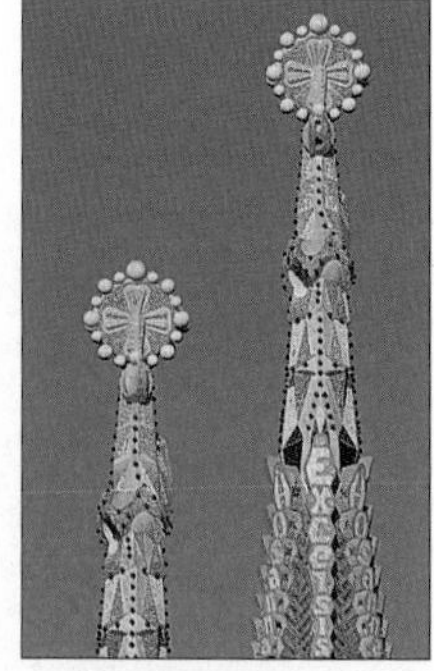

Bell Towers
Eight of the 12 spires, one for each apostle, have been built. Each is topped by Venetian mosaics.

THE FINISHED CHURCH

Gaudí's initial ambitions have been kept over the years, using various new technologies to achieve his vision. Still to come is the central tower, which is to be encircled by four large towers representing the Evangelists. Four towers on the Glory (south) façade will match the existing four on the Passion (west) and Nativity (east) façades. An ambulatory – like an inside-out cloister – will run round the outside of the building.

★ Passion Façade
This bleak façade was completed from 1986 to 2000 by artist Josep Maria Subirachs. A controversial work, its sculpted figures are angular and often sinister.

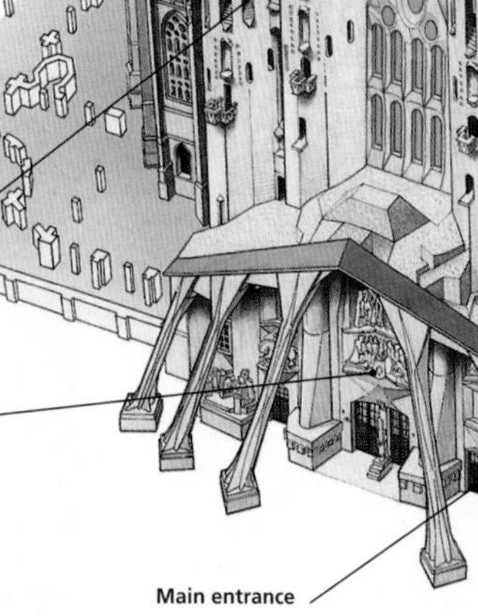

Tower with lift

The apse was the first part of the church Gaudí completed. Stairs lead down from here to the crypt below.

The altar canopy, designed by Gaudí, is still waiting for the altar.

Main entrance

Spiral Staircases
Steep stone steps – 400 in each – allow access to the towers and upper galleries. Majestic views reward those who climb or take the lift.

VISITORS' CHECKLIST

C/ Sardenya. **Map** 4 E3. **Tel** 93 208 04 14. *Sagrada Família.* *19, 43, 51.* *daily. Apr–Sep: 9am–8pm; Oct–Mar: 9am–6pm (to 2pm some public hols). in English 11am & 1pm daily (also 3pm & 5pm in summer). numerous services are held daily. ground floor.* **www**.sagradafamilia.org

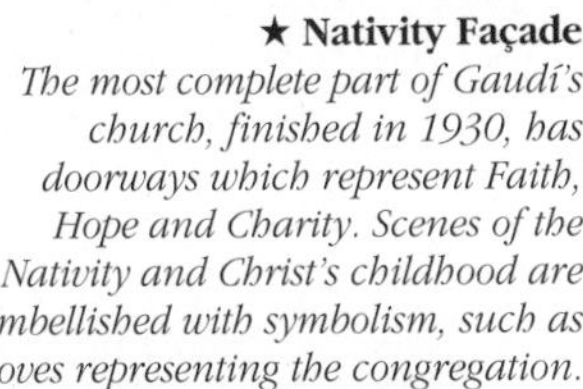

★ Nativity Façade
The most complete part of Gaudí's church, finished in 1930, has doorways which represent Faith, Hope and Charity. Scenes of the Nativity and Christ's childhood are embellished with symbolism, such as doves representing the congregation.

★ Crypt
The crypt, where Gaudí is buried, was begun by the original architect, Francesc de Paula Villar i Lozano, in 1882. This is where services are held. On the lower floor a museum traces the careers of both architects and the church's history.

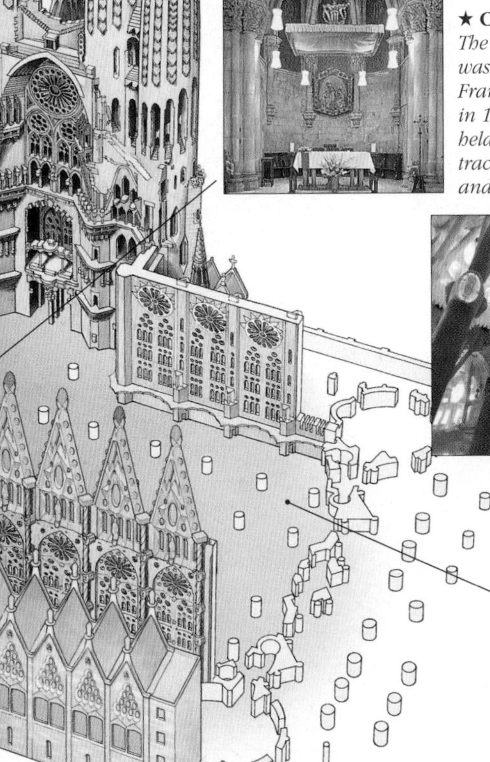

Nave
In the nave, a forest of fluted pillars support four galleries above the side aisles; a large number of skylights let in both natural and artificial light.

STAR FEATURES

- ★ Passion Façade
- ★ Nativity Façade
- ★ Crypt

FIB ENTRADA VISITANTES PROFESIONALES

MONTJUÏC

The hill of Montjuïc, rising to 213 m (699 ft) above the commercial port on the south side of the city, is Barcelona's biggest recreation area. Its museums, art galleries, gardens and nightclubs make it a popular place in the evenings as well as during the day.

There was probably a Celtiberian settlement here before the Romans built a temple to Jupiter on their Mons Jovis, which may have given Montjuïc its name – though another theory suggests that a Jewish cemetery on the hill inspired the name Mount of the Jews.

The absence of a water supply meant that there were few buildings on Montjuïc until the castle was erected on the top in 1640.

Statue, gardens of the Palau Nacional

The hill finally came into its own as the site of the 1929 International Fair. With great energy and flair, buildings were erected all over the north side, with the grand Avinguda de la Reina Maria Cristina, lined with huge exhibition halls, leading into it from the Plaça d'Espanya. In the middle of the avenue is the Font Màgica (Magic Fountain), which is regularly illuminated in colour. Above it is the Palau Nacional, home of the city's historic art collections. The Poble Espanyol is a crafts centre housed in copies of buildings from all over Spain. The last great surge of building on Montjuïc was for the 1992 Olympic Games, which left Barcelona with international-class sports facilities.

SIGHTS AT A GLANCE

Historic Buildings
Castell de Montjuïc 7

Modern Architecture
Estadi Olímpic de Montjuïc 8
Pavelló Mies van der Rohe 4

Museums and Galleries
Fundació Joan Miró 1
Museu Arqueològic 2
Museu Nacional d'Art de Catalunya 3

Squares
Plaça d'Espanya 6

Theme Parks
Poble Espanyol 5

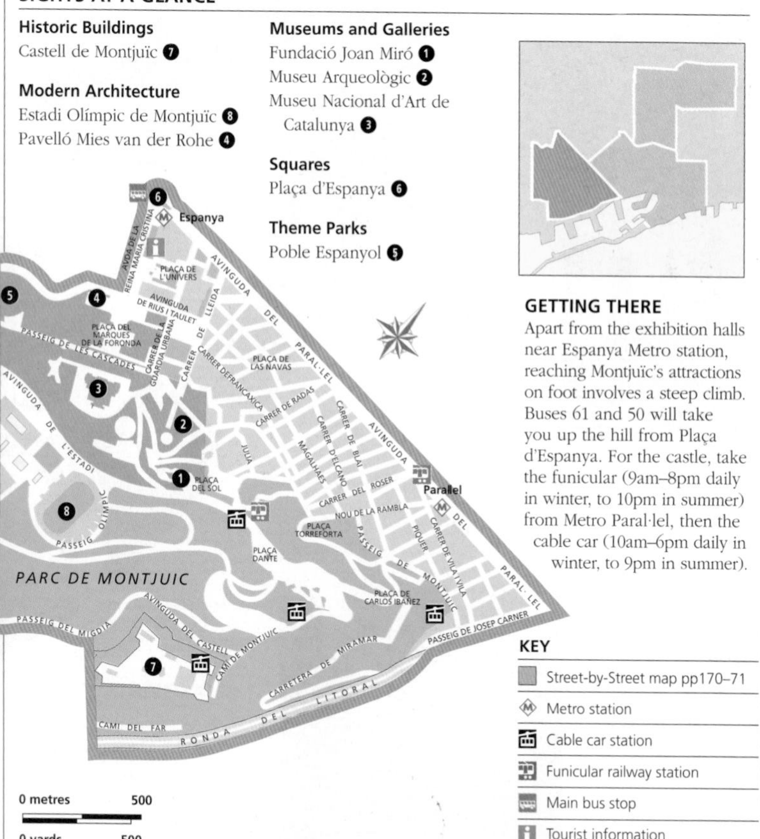

GETTING THERE

Apart from the exhibition halls near Espanya Metro station, reaching Montjuïc's attractions on foot involves a steep climb. Buses 61 and 50 will take you up the hill from Plaça d'Espanya. For the castle, take the funicular (9am–8pm daily in winter, to 10pm in summer) from Metro Paral·lel, then the cable car (10am–6pm daily in winter, to 9pm in summer).

KEY

- Street-by-Street map pp170–71
- Metro station
- Cable car station
- Funicular railway station
- Main bus stop
- Tourist information

◁ **Changing colours of the Font Màgica (Magic Fountain) on the grand avenue leading up to Montjuïc**

Street-by-Street: Montjuïc

Montjuïc is a spectacular vantage point from which to view the city. It has a wealth of art galleries and museums, an amusement park and an open-air theatre. The most interesting buildings lie around the Palau Nacional, where Europe's greatest Romanesque art collection is housed. Montjuïc is approached from the Plaça d'Espanya between brick pillars based on the campanile of St Mark's in Venice, which give a foretaste of the eclecticism of building styles. The Poble Espanyol illustrates the traditional architecture of Spain's regions, while the Fundació Joan Miró is boldly modern.

Pavelló Mies van der Rohe
This statue by Geo *Kolbe* (see p173) *stands serenely in the steel, glass, ston and onyx pavilion built in the Bauha style as the Germa contribution to the 1929 Internationa Exhibition* ❹

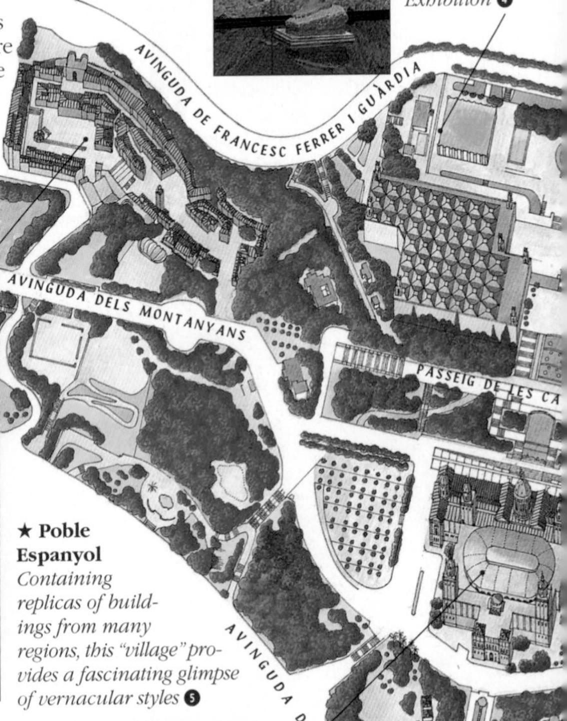

★ Poble Espanyol
Containing replicas of buildings from many regions, this "village" provides a fascinating glimpse of vernacular styles ❺

★ Museu Nacional d'Art de Catalunya
Displayed in the National Palace, the main building of the 1929 International Exhibition is Europe's finest collection of early medieval frescoes. These were a great source of inspiration for Joan Miró (see p172) ❸

To Montjuïc castle and Olympic stadium

STAR SIGHTS

- ★ Poble Espanyol
- ★ Museu Nacional d'Art de Catalunya
- ★ Fundació Joan Miró

Fountains and cascades descend in terraces from the Palau Nacional. Below them is the Font Màgica (Magic Fountain). In the evening, from Thursday to Sunday, its jets are programmed to a multi-coloured music and light shc . This marvel of water-and-electrical engineering was originally built by Carles Buigas (1898–1979) for the 1929 International Exhibition.

LOCATOR MAP
See Street Finder map 1

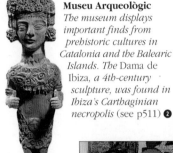

Museu Arqueològic
The museum displays important finds from prehistoric cultures in Catalonia and the Balearic Islands. The Dama de Ibiza, *a 4th-century sculpture, was found in Ibiza's Carthaginian necropolis* (see p511) ❷

laça d'Espanya

IUS I TAULET
CARRER DE LA GUARDIA URBANA
CARRER DE LLEIDA
PASSEIG DE LA SANTA MADRONA
PASSEIG DE LA SANTA MADRONA
PASSEIG DE LA SANTA MADRONA
AVINGUDA DE MIRAMAR

Museu Etnològic displays artifacts from Oceania, Africa, Asia and Latin America.

Mercat de les Flors theatre *(see p191)*

Teatre Grec is an open-air theatre set among gardens.

★ Fundació Joan Miró
This tapestry by Joan Miró hangs in the centre he created for the study of modern art. In addition to Miró's works in various media, the modern building by Josep Lluís Sert is of architectural interest ❶

To Montjuïc castle and cable car

KEY

— — — Suggested route

0 metres **100**

0 yards **100**

Flame in Space and Naked Woman (1932) by Joan Miró

Fundació Joan Miró ❶

Parc de Montjuïc. **Map** 1 B3. ***Tel*** *93 443 94 70. Espanya, then bus 50, 55 or Paral.lel, then Montjuïc funicular. 10am–7pm Tue, Wed, Fri & Sat (Jul–Sep: to 8pm), 10am–9:30pm Thu, 10am–2:30pm Sun & public hols. 1 Jan, 25 & 26 Dec.* **www**.fundaciomiro-bcn.org

Joan Miró (1893–1983) studied at the fine art school at La Llotja *(see p152)*. From 1919, he spent much of his time in Paris. Though opposed to Franco, he returned to Spain in 1940 and lived mainly in Mallorca, where he died.

An admirer of primitive Catalan art and Gaudí's Modernisme *(see p140)*, Miró always remained a Catalan painter but developed a Surrealistic style, with vivid colours and fantastical forms suggesting dream-like situations.

In 1975, after the return of democracy to Spain *(see p68)*, his friend, the architect Josep Lluís Sert, designed the stark, white building to house a permanent collection of paintings, sculptures and tapestries lit by natural light. Miró himself donated the works and some of the best pieces on display include his *Barcelona Series* (1939–44), a set of 50 black-and-white lithographs. Periodic exhibitions of other artists' work are also held.

Museu Arqueològic ❷

Passeig Santa Madrona 39–41. **Map** 1 B3. ***Tel*** *93 423 21 49. Espanya, Poble Sec. 9:30am–7pm Tue–Sat, 10am–2:30pm Sun & public hols. 1 Jan, 25 & 26 Dec. (free last Sun of month, 23 Apr, 18 May, 11 & 24 Sep).* **www**.mac.cat

Housed in the Renaissance-inspired 1929 Palace of Graphic Arts, the museum shows artifacts from prehistory to the Visigothic period (AD 415–711). Highlights are finds from the Greco-Roman town of Empúries *(see p216)* and Iberian silver treasure. There is also a splendid collection of Visigothic jewellery.

Museu Nacional d'Art de Catalunya ❸

Parc de Montjuïc, Palau Nacional. **Map** 1 A2. ***Tel*** *93 622 03 76. Espanya. PM, 55. 10am–7pm Tue–Sat, 10am–2:30pm Sun & pub hols. 1 Jan, 1 May, 25 Dec. by appt (93 622 03 75), free 1st Sun of month.* **www**.mnac.cat

The austere Palau Nacional was built for the 1929 International Exhibition, but in 1934 it was used to house an art collection that has since become the most important in the city.

The museum has probably the world's greatest display of Romanesque *(see pp24–5)* items, centered around a series of magnificent 12th-century frescoes taken from Catalan Pyrenean churches. The most remarkable are the wall paintings from Sant Climent de Taüll *(see p24)* and from Santa Maria de Taüll *(see p211)*.

There is also an expanding Gothic collection, covering the whole of Spain but particularly good on Catalonia, and a collection of notable Baroque and Renaissance works from all over Europe.

A fine collection of modern art includes Modernista furniture by Gaudí *(see p140)*, and paintings by Picasso, Ramon Casas and Salvador Dalí.

As a whole, the museum offers a rare opportunity to view more than a millennium of Catalan artistic activity in a single location.

12th-century *Christ in Majesty*, Museu Nacional d'Art de Catalunya

Morning by Georg Kolbe (1877–1945), Pavelló Mies van der Rohe

Pavelló Mies van der Rohe ❹

Avinguda del Marqués de Comillas. **Map** 1 B2. ***Tel*** *93 215 10 11.* *Espanya.* *50.* *10am–8pm daily.* *1 Jan, 25 Dec.* *under-18s free.* **www**.miesbcn.com

If the simple lines of the glass and polished stone German Pavilion look modern today, they must have shocked visitors to the International Exhibition in 1929. Designed by Ludwig Mies van der Rohe (1886–1969), director of the avant-garde Bauhaus school, it includes his famous *Barcelona Chair*, designed for the king and queen's visit and now an icon of Modernism. The building was demolished after the exhibition, but a replica was built on the centenary of his birth.

Poble Espanyol ❺

Avinguda del Marqués de Comillas. **Map** 1 A2. ***Tel*** *93 508 63 00.* *Espanya.* *9am–8pm Mon, 9am–2am Tue–Thu, 9am–3am Fri (to 4am Sat), 9am–midnight Sun.* **www**.poble-espanyol.com

The idea behind the Poble Espanyol (Spanish Village) was to display Spanish architectural styles and crafts. It was laid out for the 1929 International Exhibition, but has proved enduringly popular.

Building styles from all over Spain are illustrated by 116 houses. These are arranged on streets radiating from a main square and were created by many well-known architects and artists of the time. The village was refurbished at the end of the 1980s and is now a favorite place to visit for both tourists and native Barcelonins.

Resident artisans produce a wide range of crafts including hand-blown glass, ceramics, sculpture, Toledo damascene *(see p390)* and Catalan canvas sandals. There are also numerous bars and restaurants dotted around, plus nightclubs and a flamenco *tablao* *(see p192)*.

View from Palau Nacional downhill towards the Plaça d'Espanya

Plaça d'Espanya ❻

Avinguda de la Gran Via de les Corts Catalanes. **Map** 1 B1. *Espanya.* **Magic Fountain Music and Light Show:** *May–Sep: 9–10:30pm Thu–Sun; Oct–Apr: 7–8:30pm Fri & Sat.*

The fountain in the middle of this road junction, the site of public gallows until 1715, is by Josep Maria Jujol, one of Gaudí's followers. The 1899 bullring to one side is by Font i Carreras. Catalans have never taken to bullfighting, and the arena has been converted into Las Arenas, a shopping and entertainment centre by the British architect Richard Rogers.

On the Montjuïc side of the roundabout is the Avinguda de la Reina Maria Cristina. This is flanked by two 47-m- (154-ft-) high brick campaniles by Ramon Raventós, modelled on the bell towers of St Mark's in Venice. The avenue, lined with exhibition buildings, leads up to Carles Buigas's illuminated *Font Màgica* (Magic Fountain) in front of the Palau Nacional.

Castell de Montjuïc ❼

Parc de Montjuïc. **Map** 1 B5. ***Tel*** *93 329 86 13.* *Paral·lel, then funicular & cable car.* *PM from Plaça Espanya.* *10am–8pm Tue–Sun.*

The summit of Montjuïc is occupied by an 18th-century castle, first built in 1640 but destroyed by Felipe V in 1705. The present fortress was built for the Bourbon family. During the War of Independence the castle was captured by the French, and after the Civil War it became a prison, where the Catalan leader Lluís Companys was executed in 1940. The castle is currently being converted into a Centre for Peace, but visitors can climb the battlements.

Estadi Olímpic de Montjuïc ❽

Passeig Olímpic 17–19. **Map** 1 A3. ***Tel*** *93 426 20 89.* *Espanya, Poble Sec.* *50, 55, 61, 125.* *for events.* **Museum** *10am–6pm Tue–Sat, 10am–2:30pm Sun (Apr–Sep: to 8pm Tue–Sat).*

The Neo-Classical façade has been preserved from the stadium, built by Pere Domènech i Roura for the 1936 Olympics, cancelled at the onset of the Civil War. The arena was refitted for the 1992 Olympics.

Nearby are the steel-and-glass **Palau Sant Jordi** indoor stadium, by Japanese architect Arata Isozaki, swimming pools by Ricardo Bofill and the **Museu Olímpic i de l'Esport**, which has interactive exhibits on all aspects of sport.

Entrance to the refurbished 1992 Olympic Stadium

FURTHER AFIELD

The radical redevelopment of Barcelona's outskirts in the late 1980s and early 1990s gave it a wealth of new buildings, parks and squares. The city's main station, Sants, was rebuilt and the neighbouring Parc de l'Espanya Industrial and Parc de Joan Miró were created, containing lakes, modern sculpture and futuristic architecture. The Plaça de Glòries is being remodelled to contain the design museum and a park. In the west of the city, where the streets start to climb steeply, are the historic royal palace and monastery of Pedralbes, and Gaudí's famous Park Güell, dating from 1910. Beyond is the Serra de Collserola, the city's closest rural area. Two funiculars provide an exciting way of reaching its heights, which offer superb views of the city. Tibidabo, the highest point, with a funfair, the Neo-Gothic church of the Sagrat Cor and a modern steel-and-glass communications tower, is a favourite place among Barcelonins for a day out.

Park Güell gateway signs

SIGHTS AT A GLANCE

Museums and Galleries
Camp Nou (FC Barcelona Museum) 3
Cosmocaixa – Museu de la Ciència 8

Historic Buildings
Monestir de Pedralbes 5
Palau Reial de Pedralbes 4

Modern Buildings
Torre de Collserola 6

Parks and Gardens
Parc de l'Espanya Industrial 2
Parc de Joan Miró 1
Park Güell 9

Theme Parks
Tibidabo 7

KEY
- Barcelona city centre
- Built-up area
- Railway station
- Funicular railway station
- Motorway
- Major road
- Minor road

0 metres 500
0 yards 500

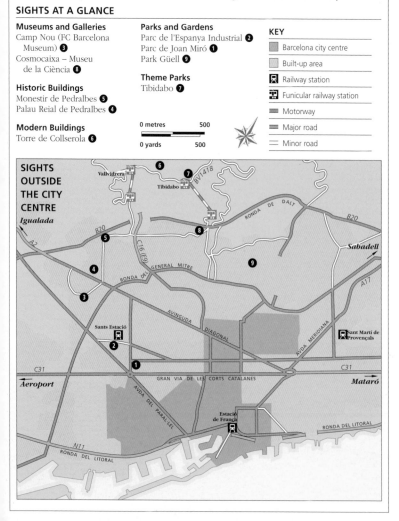

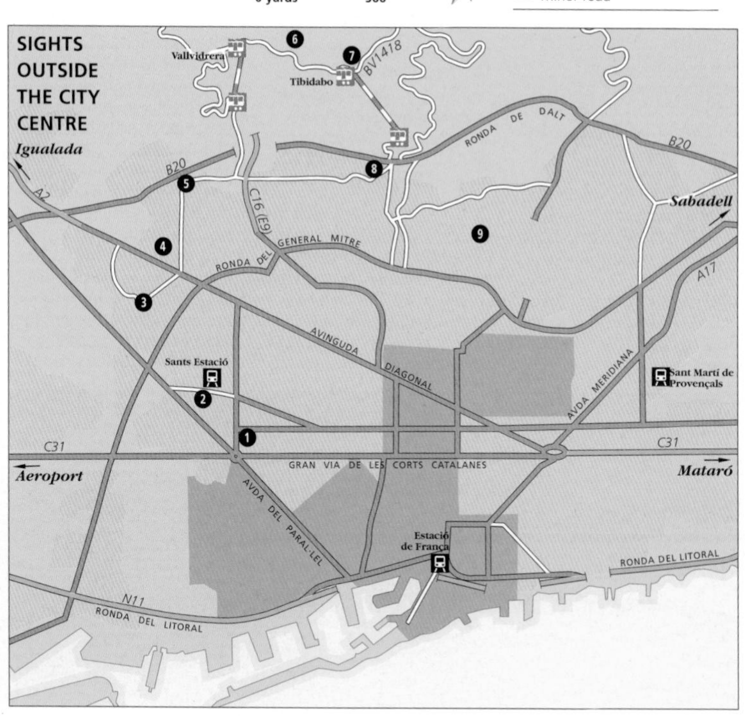

◁ The Neo-Gothic Temple Expiatori del Sagrat Cor, dominating Barcelona from the summit of Tibidabo

Dona i Ocell (1983) by Joan Miró in the Parc de Joan Miró

Parc de Joan Miró ❶

Carrer d'Aragó 1. Ⓜ *Tarragona.*

Barcelona's 19th-century slaughterhouse *(escorxador)* was transformed in the 1980s into this unusual park, hence its alternative name, Parc de l'Escorxador.

It is constructed on two levels, the lower of which is devoted to football pitches interspersed with landscaped areas of palms, pines and eucalyptus trees. The upper level is paved and dominated by a 1983 sculpture by Joan Miró *(see p172)* entitled *Dona i Ocell* (Woman and Bird). Standing 22 m (72 ft) high in the middle of a pool, its surface is coated with colourful pieces of glazed tile. There are also several play areas for kids.

Parc de l'Espanya Industrial ❷

Plaça de Joan Peiró. Ⓜ *Sants-Estació.*

This modern park, designed by the Basque architect Luis Peña Ganchegui, owes its name to the textile mill that used to stand on the 5-hectare (12-acre) site.

Laid out in 1986 as part of Barcelona's policy to provide more open spaces within the city, the park has canals and a rowing lake – with a Classical statue of Neptune at its centre. Tiers of steps rise around the lake like an amphitheatre and on one side a row of ten futuristic watchtowers dominates the entire area. Their only function is to serve as public viewing platforms and lamp standards.

Six contemporary sculptors are represented in the park, among them Andrés Nagel, whose huge metal dragon incorporates a children's slide.

Camp Nou (FC Barcelona Museum) ❸

Avda de Aristides Maillol. ***Tel*** *90 218 99 00.* Ⓜ *Maria Cristina, Collblanc.* *10am–6:30pm Mon–Sat (to 8pm early Apr–early Oct), 10am–2:30pm Sun & public hols.* *1 & 6 Jan, 25 Dec.* *of the stadium.* **www**.fcbarcelona.com

Camp Nou, Europe's largest football stadium, is home to the city's famous football club, Barcelona FC (Barça, as it is known locally). Founded in 1899, it is one of the world's richest soccer clubs, and has more than 100,000 members. The stadium is a magnificent, sweeping structure, built in 1957 to a design by Francesc Mitjans. An extension was added in 1982 and it can now comfortably seat 100,000 fans.

Line of watchtowers in the Parc de l'Espanya Industrial

The club's popular museum is a glossy interactive experience, with touch-screen panels detailing the club's history and their many victories. There are also paintings and sculptures of famous club footballers commissioned for an exhibition held in celebration of the club in 1985 and 1987. *Blaugrana* (blue-burgundy) are the colours of Barça's strip. The club's flags were used as an expression of local nationalist feelings during the Franco dictatorship, when the Catalan flag was banned.

As well as hosting its own high-profile matches (mainly at weekends), Camp Nou also accommodates affiliated local soccer clubs and promotes a number of other sports.

View across Camp Nou stadium, prestigious home of the Futbol Club Barcelona

Palau Reial de Pedralbes ❹

Avinguda Diagonal 686. *Palau Reial.* *to the public.* **Museu de Ceràmica, Museu de les Arts Decoratives & Museu Textil i d'Indumentària** ***Tel*** *93 256 34 65.* *10am–6pm Tue–Sun.* *1 Jan, 1 May, 24 Jun, 25 & 26 Dec.* *(free first Sun of each month and 3–6pm every Sun).* *by appt.*

The Palace of Pedralbes was once the main house on the estate of Count Eusebi Güell. In 1919 he offered it to the Spanish royal family. The first visit was from Alfonso XIII in 1926, before which the interior was refurbished.

Three fascinating museums and the gardens are open to the public. The Museu de Arts Decoratives, opened in 1937, displays period furniture and fine household items from the Middle Ages to the present. A genealogical tree traces the 500-year dynasty of the count-kings of Barcelona.

The Museu de Ceràmica has displays of historic Catalan and Moorish pottery and modern ceramics, including works by Miró and Picasso *(see p152)* The Textil Museum contains beautiful fabrics and costumes from the 16th century onwards.

The gardens are well laid out with small ponds and paths. Just behind them, in Avinguda de Pedralbes, is the entrance to the original Güell estate. It is guarded by a black wrought-iron gate, its top forged into a dragon, and two gate houses, all by Gaudí *(see pp140–41)*.

***Madonna of Humility*, Monestir de Santa Maria de Pedralbes**

Monestir de Santa Maria de Pedralbes ❺

Baixada del Monestir 9. ***Tel*** *93 256 34 34.* *Reina Elisenda or bus 22, 63, 64, 78.* *10am–2pm Tue–Sat (5pm Apr–Sep), 10am–8pm Sun.* *by appt.* *1 Jan, Good Friday, 1 May, 24 Jun, 25 Dec.* *(free after 3pm Sun and for under age 16s. Also allows admission to the Museu d'Història, see p146).* *ground floor only.*

Approached through an arch in its walls, the monastery of Pedralbes still has the air of a living enclosed community. This is heightened by its furnished cells, kitchens, infirmary and refectory. But the nuns of the Order of St Clare moved to an adjoining building in 1983. The monastery was founded in 1326 by Elisenda de Montcada de Piños, fourth wife of Jaime II of Catalonia and Aragón. Her tomb lies between the church and the cloister. On the church side her effigy is dressed in royal robes; on the other as a nun.

The monastery is built around a three-storey cloister. The main rooms encircling the cloister include a dormitory, a refectory, a chapter-house, an abbey and day cells. Artworks and liturgical ornaments, pottery, furniture, altar cloths and gold and silver work, are on display.

The most important room in the monastery is the Capella (chapel) de Sant Miquel, with murals of the *Passion* and the *Life of the Virgin*, both painted by Ferrer Bassa in 1346, when Elisenda's niece, Francesca Saportella, was abbess.

Torre de Collserola ❻

Carretera de Vallvidrera al Tibidabo. ***Tel*** *93 211 79 42.* *Peu de Funicular, then Funicular de Vallvidrera & bus 111.* *timetables change regularly so check website for latest information.* *1 & 6 Jan, 25, 26 & 31 Dec.* **www.** torredecollserola.com

In a city that enjoys thrills, the ultimate ride is offered by the communications tower near Tibidabo mountain *(see p178)*. A glass-sided lift swiftly reaches the top of this 288-m (944-ft) tall structure standing on the summit of a 445-m (1,460-ft) hill.

The tower was designed by English architect Norman Foster for the 1992 Olympic Games. Needle-like in form, it is a tubular steel mast on a concrete pillar. There are 13 levels. The top one has an observatory with a powerful telescope, and a public viewing platform with a 360° view encompassing Barcelona, the sea and the mountains.

BARCELONA V REAL MADRID

FC Barcelona

Més que un club is the motto of Barcelona FC: "More than a club". More than anything else it has been a symbol of the struggle of Catalan nationalism against the central government in Madrid. To fail to win the league is one thing. To come in behind Real Madrid is a complete disaster. Each season the big question is which of the two teams will win the title. Under the Franco regime in a memorable episode in 1941, Barça won 3–0 at home. At the return match in Madrid, the crowd was so hostile that the police and referee "advised" Barça to prevent trouble. Demoralized by the intimidation, they lost 11–1. Loyalty is paramount: one Barça player who left to join Real Madrid received death threats.

Real Madrid

Merry-go-round, Tibidabo

Tibidabo 7

Plaça del Tibidabo 3–4. ***Tel*** *93 211 79 42. Avda Tibidabo, then Tramvia Blau & Funicular. 111.* **Amusement Park** *variable – phone ahead for times. Oct–Apr: Mon–Fri.* **Temple del Sagrat Cor** ***Tel*** *93 417 56 86. 10am–8pm daily.* **www**.tibidabo.cat

The heights of Tibidabo are reached by the Tramvia Blau (Blue Tram) and a funicular railway. The name, inspired by Tibidabo's views of the city, comes from the Latin *tibi dabo* (I shall give you) – a reference to the Temptation of Christ when Satan took him up a mountain and offered him the world spread at his feet.

The hugely popular Parc d'Atraccions first opened in 1908. While the old rides retain their charm, new ones have been added over the years, including the thrilling 80 km/h (50 mph) Dragon Khan rollercoaster. The hilltop location at 517 m (1,696 ft) adds to the thrill. Also in the park is the Museu d'Automates, displaying automated toys, juke boxes and gaming machines.

Tibidabo is crowned by the Temple Expiatori del Sagrat Cor (Church of the Sacred Heart), built with religious zeal but little taste by Enric Sagnier between 1902 and 1911. A lift takes you up to the feet of an enormous figure of Christ.

Just a short bus ride away is another viewpoint worth visiting – the Torre de Collserola *(see p177)*.

Cosmocaixa - Museu de la Ciència 8

Calle Isaac Newton 196. ***Tel*** *93 212 60 50. Avinguda del Tibidabo, then Tramvia Blau. 17, 22, 58, 196. 10am–8pm Tue–Sun. 1 & 6 Jan, 25 Dec. (free 5–8pm Tue–Fri, 6–8pm Sat, Sun & public hols, first Sun of every month).*

This excellent science museum is located in a striking Modernista building. Exhibits include the Flooded Forest, which allows visitors to experience the Amazonian rainforest both above and below the waterline. A science lab is one of several great areas for children.

Park Güell 9

Carrer d'Olot. ***Tel*** *010 (from Barcelona). Lesseps. 24. summer 10am–9pm daily; winter 10am–6pm daily.* **Casa-Museu Gaudí** ***Tel*** *93 219 38 11. Apr–Sep: 10am–8pm daily; Oct–Mar: 10am–6pm daily. 1 Jan. (combined ticket with Sagrada Família available).*

A UNESCO World Heritage Site, the Park Güell is Antoni Gaudí's *(see pp140–41)* most colourful creation. He was commissioned in the 1890s by Count Eusebi Güell to design a garden city on 20 hectares (50 acres) of the family estate. Little of the grand design for decorative public buildings and 60 houses among landscaped gardens became reality. What we see today was completed between 1910 and 1914, and the park opened in 1922.

The Room of a Hundred Columns is a cavernous hall of 84 crooked pillars that is brightened by glass and ceramic mosaics; it was intended as the marketplace for the estate. Above it is the Gran Plaça Circular, an open space with a snaking balcony of coloured mosaics that offers stunning views of the city and is said to have the world's longest bench.

Two pavilions at the entry are by Gaudí, but the Casa-Museu Gaudí, a gingerbread-style house where Gaudí lived from 1906 to 1926, was built by Francesc Berenguer.

Mosaic-encrusted chimney by Gaudí at the entrance of the Park Güell

BARCELONA STREET FINDER

The map references given with the sights, shops and entertainment venues described in the Barcelona section of the guide refer to the street maps on the following pages. Map references are also given for Barcelona hotels *(see pp568–70)*, and for bars and restaurants *(see pp617–20)*. The schematic map below shows the area of Barcelona covered by the *Street Finder*. The symbols used for sights and other features and services are listed in the key at the foot of the page.

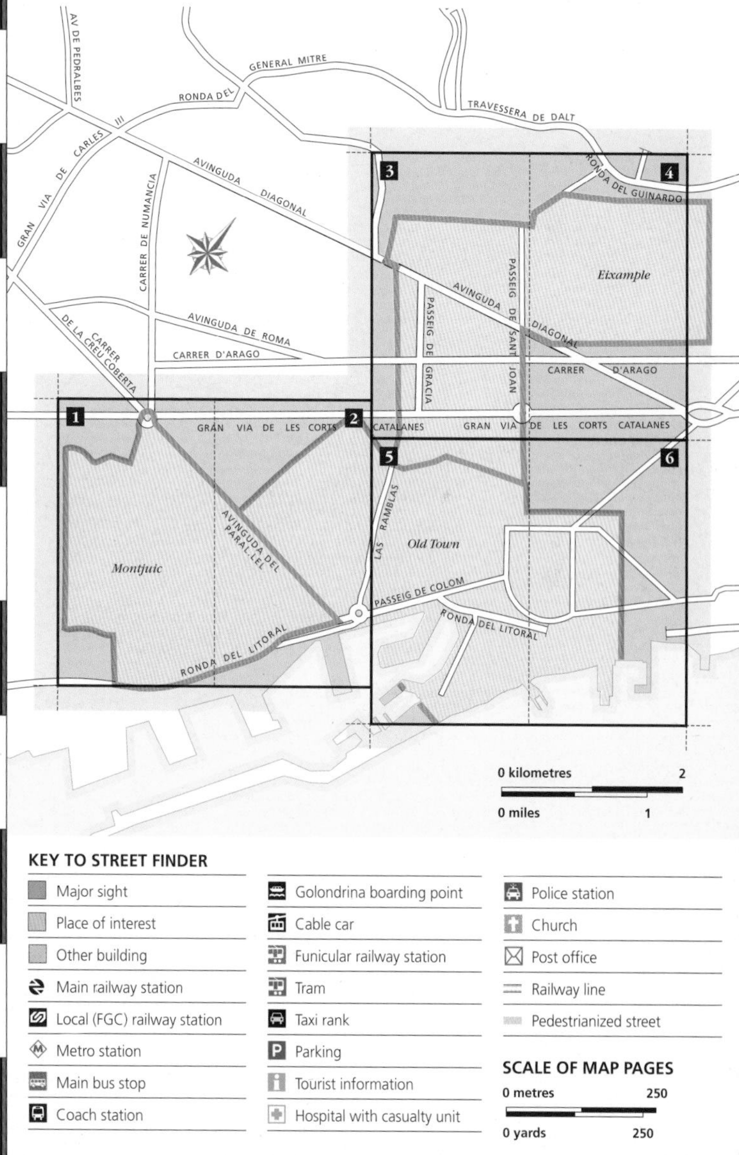

KEY TO STREET FINDER

- Major sight
- Place of interest
- Other building
- Main railway station
- Local (FGC) railway station
- Metro station
- Main bus stop
- Coach station
- Golondrina boarding point
- Cable car
- Funicular railway station
- Tram
- Taxi rank
- Parking
- Tourist information
- Hospital with casualty unit
- Police station
- Church
- Post office
- Railway line
- Pedestrianized street

SCALE OF MAP PAGES

0 metres 250

0 yards 250

1
A
B
C
Les Arenas Building
Espanya
PLAÇA D'ESPANYA
GRAN VIA DE LES
Fira de Barcelona
Poble Espanyol
Pavelló Mies van der Robe
AVINGUDA DE RIUS I TAULET
AVINGUDA DEL PARAL·LEL
Palau Nacional (Museu Nacional d'Art de Catalunya)
Mercat de les Flors
Museu Arqueològic
Teatre Lliure
Teatre Grec
Piscines Bernat Piconell
Palau Saint Jordi
JARDINS JOAN MARAGALL
Fundació Joan Miró
Estadi Olímpic de Montjuïc
AVINGUDA DE MIRAMAR
Avinguda de Miramar
MONTJUÏC
PARC DE MONTJUÏC
PASSEIG DEL MIGDIA
CAMI DEL MOLI
AVINGUDA DEL CASTELL
Castell de Montjuïc
CAMI DE MONTJUIC
CAMI DEL FAR
2
3
4
5

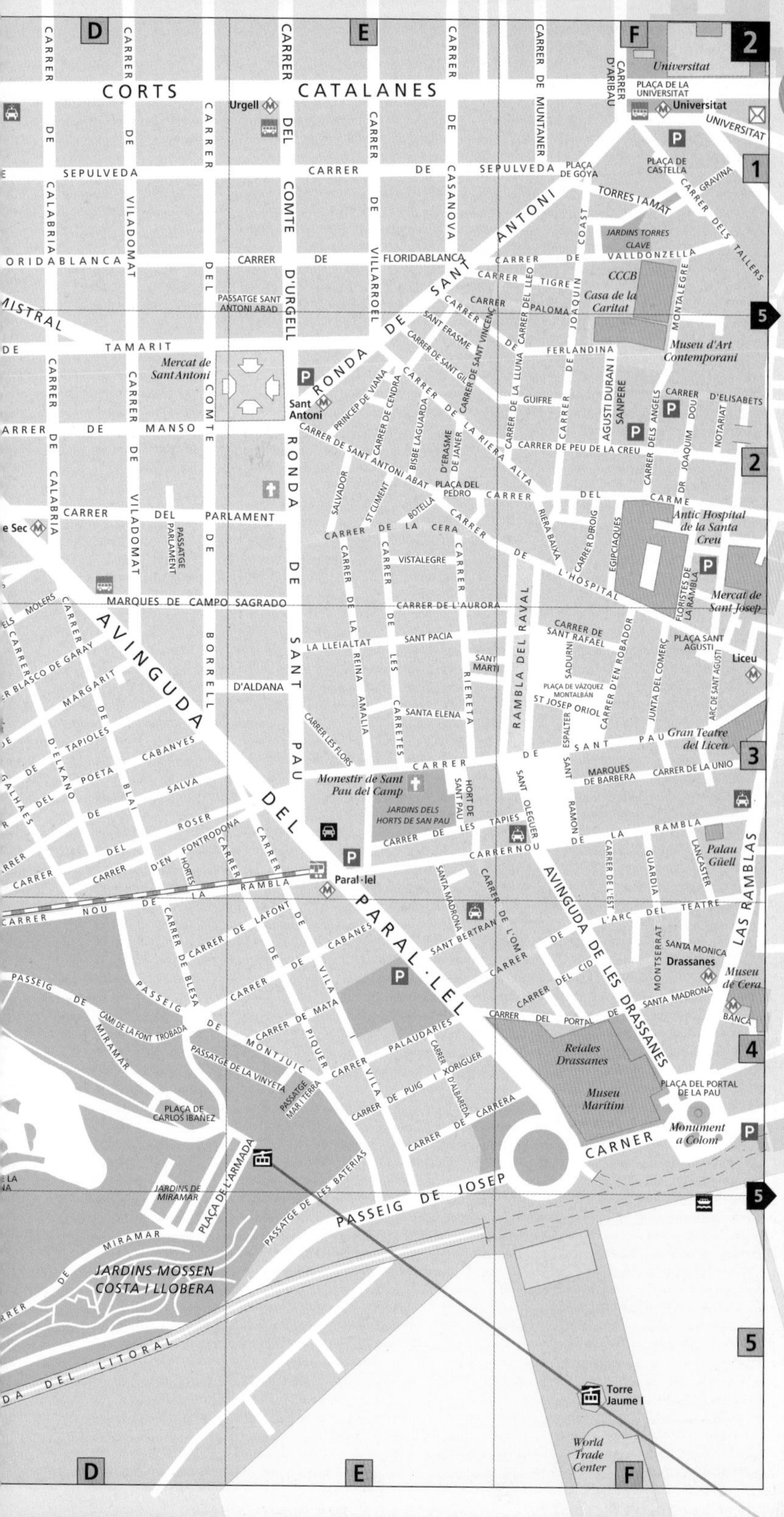

D
E
F
2
Universitat
CORTS CATALANES
Urgell
PLAÇA DE LA UNIVERSITAT
Universitat
UNIVERSITAT
CARRER DE SEPULVEDA
PLAÇA DE GOYA
PLAÇA DE CASTELLA
TORRES I AMAT
JARDINS TORRES CLAVE
CCCB
Casa de la Caritat
Museu d'Art Contemporani
RONDA DE SANT ANTONI
Mercat de Sant Antoni
Sant Antoni
CARRER DE FLORIDABLANCA
CARRER DE MANSO
CARRER DEL PARLAMENT
RONDA DE SANT PAU
CARRER DE SANT ANTONI ABAT
PLAÇA DEL PEDRO
CARRER DE LA RIERA ALTA
CARRER DE PEU DE LA CREU
CARRER DEL CARME
Antic Hospital de la Santa Creu
CARRER DE L'HOSPITAL
Mercat de Sant Josep
RAMBLA DEL RAVAL
CARRER DE L'AURORA
MARQUES DE CAMPO SAGRADO
Liceu
Gran Teatre del Liceu
CARRER DE SANT PAU
Monestir de Sant Pau del Camp
JARDINS DELS HORTS DE SAN PAU
AVINGUDA DEL PARAL·LEL
Paral·lel
Palau Güell
LAS RAMBLAS
AVINGUDA DE LES DRASSANES
Drassanes
Museu de Cera
Reiales Drassanes
Museu Marítim
PLAÇA DEL PORTAL DE LA PAU
Monument a Colom
PASSEIG DE JOSEP CARNER
PLAÇA DE CARLOS IBAÑEZ
JARDINS DE MIRAMAR
PLAÇA DE L'ARMADA
JARDINS MOSSEN COSTA I LLOBERA
RONDA DEL LITORAL
Torre Jaume I
World Trade Center
Sec
1
3
4
5

3
A
B
C
1
2
3
4
5
CARRER DE SARAGOSSA
AVINGUDA DEL PRINCEP D'ASTURIES
AULESTIA I PIJOAN
BRETON DE LOS HERROS
ST MAGDALENA
SANTA ROSA
CARRER DE BADIA
CARRER DE MADROZO
CARRER DE LINCOLN
CARRER DE BALMES
RAMBLA DEL PRAT
CARRER DE LAFORJA
CARRER DE SANT MARC
CARRER DE MARIA CUBI
CARRER DE REGAS
VIA AUGUSTA
BENET MERCADE
BERGA
CARRER D'ORENETA
CIGNE
Gràcia
PLAÇA DE LA LLIBERTAT
CARRER DE MILTON
STA EUGENIA
PLAÇA DE GALLA PLACIDIA
ST GABRIEL
ST CRISTOBAL
TRAVESSERA DE GRACIA
JULIAN ROMEA
NEPTU
RIERA
CARRER DE VIC
GRANADA DEL PENEDES
LUIS ANTUNEZ
CARRER DE GOYA
BOSCH
C. DEL COMTE DE SALVATIERRA
PLAÇA DE NARCIS OLLER
DOCTOR RIZAL
CARRER DE SENECA
CARRER DE MINERVA
SANT MIQUEL
AVINGUDA DIAGONAL
CARRER GRAN DE GRACIA
PASSEIG DE GRACIA
CARRER DE CORSEGA
Diagonal
Palau Baró de Quadras
CARRER DEL ROSSELLO
Casa Milá "La Pedrera"
Casa Terrades "Casa de les Punxes"
RAMBLA DE CATALUNYA
PASSATGE DE LA CONCEPCIO
Provença
CARRER DE PROVENÇA
PTGE MERCADER
CARRER DE MALLORCA
PTGE DE DOMINGO
PASSATGE DELS CAMPS ELISIS
CARRER DE VALENCIA
Fundació Antoni Tàpies
Passeig de Gràcia
CARRER D'ARAGO
Casa Batlló
Illa de la Discòrdia
Casa Amatller
Casa Lleó Morera
PTGE DE MENDEZ VIGO
CARRER DEL CONSELL DE CENT
PTGE DE PERMANYER
CARRER DE LA DIPUTACIO
GRAN VIA DE
UNIVERSITAT
CARRER DE CASP
CARRER DE PAU CLARIS
CARRER DE ROGER DE LLURIA
CARRER DEL BRUC
CARRER DE GIRONA
CARRER DE BAILEN
PASSEIG DE SANT JOAN
PTGE DEL RECTOR OLIVERAS
PTGE DE LES ESCOLES
PTGE DEL MERCAT
Mercat Concepció
Girona
Verdaguer
PLAÇA MOSSEN VERDA
PASSATGE CAPUTXINS
CARRER DE ANGEL
TRAVESSIA ST ANTONI
CARRER DE JAEN
CARRER DE MONTSENY
CARRER DE ROS DE OLANO
CARRER DEL PERE SERAFI
CARRER DE ST JOAQUIM
SOL
LA VIRTUT
PLANETA
PLAÇA DEL SOL
MASPONS
ESCUDER
XIQUETS DE VALLS
CANO
CARRER DE MATEU
CARRER DE ASTURIES
CARRER DEL TORRENT DE L'OLLA
CARRER DE TOPAZI
GUILLERIES
CARRER DE VERDI
VERNTALLAT
CARRER DE L'OR
CARRER DE LA PERLA
CARRER DE VALLFOGONA
CARRER DE TEROL
PLAÇA REVOLUCIO DE SETEMBRE DE 1858
CARRER DE LOS TORRIJOS
LA CIUDAD REAL
CARRER DEL TORRENT DEN VIDALET
CARRER DE RAMON
CARRER DE MONTMANY
CARRER DE JOAN
CARRER VIADA
D'ALZINA
ROBI
TRES SENYORES
MASSENS
BLANQUES
CARRER DE CONGOST
ESGLESIA
CARRER DE ST DOMENEC
PERE MARTIR
PLAÇA DE LA VILA DE GRACIA
CARRER DEL PENEDES
DESAMPARATS
CARRER DE PUIGMARTI
CARRER RAMIS
CARRER DE QUEVEDO
MILA FONTANALS
CARRER DEL DILUVI
MARIA
SANT
CARRER DE JESUS
CARRER DE MOZART
CARRER DE FRANCISCO GINER
CARRER DE MARTINEZ DE LA ROSA
CARRER DE SIRACUSA
PLAÇA DEL RASPALL
CARRER ALBA
CARRER DE TORDERA
CARRER DEL PROGRES
LA FRATERNITAT
CARRER DE BANYOLES
CARRER D'IGUALADA
CARRER DE TORRES
GRACIA
DOMENECH
FERRER DE BLANES
CARRER DE LA LLIBERTAT
CARRER DE MONISTROL
CARRER DE BONAVISTA
CARRER DEL PERILL
CARRER SANTA EULALIA
CARRER DE CAMPRODON
D'ABDO TERRADAS
VENUS
SANTA TERESA
SANTA TECLA
ST AGUSTI

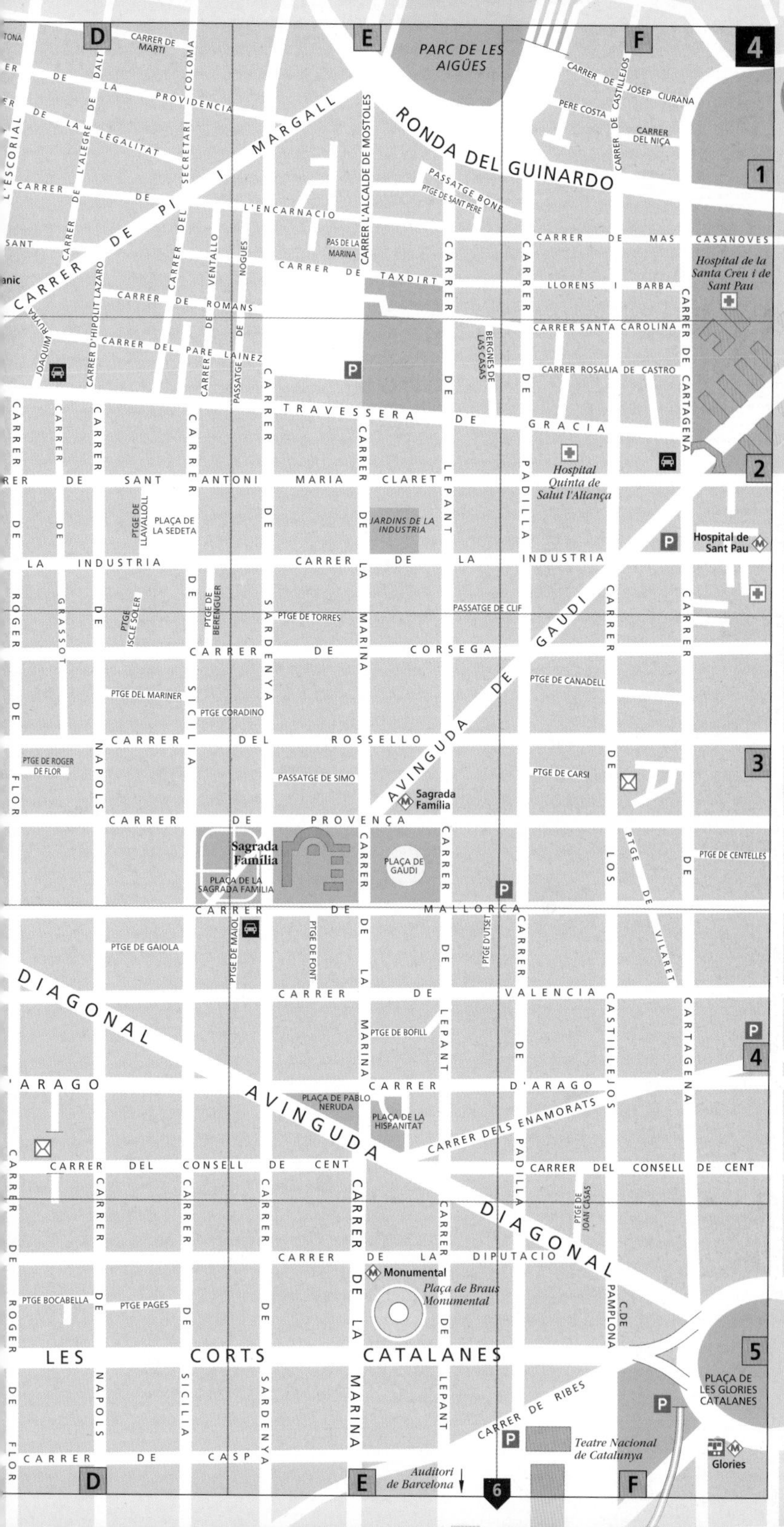

D
E
F
4
PARC DE LES AIGÜES
RONDA DEL GUINARDO
CARRER DE PI I MARGALL
CARRER DE MARTI
CARRER DE LA PROVIDENCIA
CARRER DE LA LEGALITAT
CARRER DE L'ESCORIAL
CARRER DE L'ALEGRE DE DALT
CARRER DE SECRETARI COLOMA
CARRER DE L'ENCARNACIO
CARRER DE JOSEP CIURANA
CARRER DE CASTILLEJOS
PERE COSTA
CARRER DEL NIÇA
PASSATGE BONET
PTGE DE SANT PERE
CARRER L'ALCALDE DE MOSTOLES
PAS DE LA MARINA
CARRER DE TAXDIRT
CARRER DE MAS CASANOVES
CARRER LLORENS I BARBA
Hospital de la Santa Creu i de Sant Pau
CARRER SANTA CAROLINA
CARRER ROSALIA DE CASTRO
BERGNES DE LAS CASAS
CARRER DE CARTAGENA
CARRER DE ROMANS
CARRER DEL PARE LAINEZ
CARRER D'HIPOLIT LAZARO
JOAQUIM RUYRA
CARRER DEL VENTALLO
CARRER DE NOGUES
PASSATGE DE
TRAVESSERA DE GRACIA
CARRER DE SANT ANTONI MARIA CLARET
Hospital Quinta de Salut l'Aliança
CARRER DE LEPANT
CARRER DE PADILLA
1
2
PTGE DE LLAVALLOLL
PLAÇA DE LA SEDETA
JARDINS DE LA INDUSTRIA
Hospital de Sant Pau
CARRER DE LA INDUSTRIA
AVINGUDA DE GAUDI
PASSATGE DE CLIF
PTGE DE TORRES
PTGE DE BERENGUER
PTGE ISCLE SOLER
CARRER DE CORSEGA
CARRER DE ROGER DE FLOR
GRASSOT
CARRER DE SICILIA
CARRER DE SARDENYA
CARRER DE LA MARINA
PTGE DE CANADELL
PTGE DEL MARINER
PTGE CORADINO
CARRER DEL ROSSELLO
PTGE DE ROGER DE FLOR
PASSATGE DE SIMO
Sagrada Família
PTGE DE CARSI
3
CARRER DE PROVENÇA
Sagrada Família
PLAÇA DE LA SAGRADA FAMILIA
PLAÇA DE GAUDI
CARRER DE LOS CASTILLEJOS
PTGE DE VILARET
PTGE DE CENTELLES
CARRER DE MALLORCA
PTGE DE GAIOLA
PTGE DE MAIOL
PTGE DE FONT
PTGE D'UTSET
CARRER DE VALENCIA
AVINGUDA DIAGONAL
PTGE DE BOFILL
4
CARRER D'ARAGO
PLAÇA DE PABLO NERUDA
PLAÇA DE LA HISPANITAT
CARRER DELS ENAMORATS
CARRER DEL CONSELL DE CENT
PTGE DE JOAN CASAS
CARRER DE LA DIPUTACIO
Monumental
Plaça de Braus Monumental
PTGE BOCABELLA
PTGE PAGES
CARRER DE NAPOLS
C.DE PAMPLONA
LES CORTS CATALANES
5
PLAÇA DE LES GLORIES CATALANES
CARRER DE RIBES
Teatre Nacional de Catalunya
Glories
CARRER DE CASP
Auditori de Barcelona
6

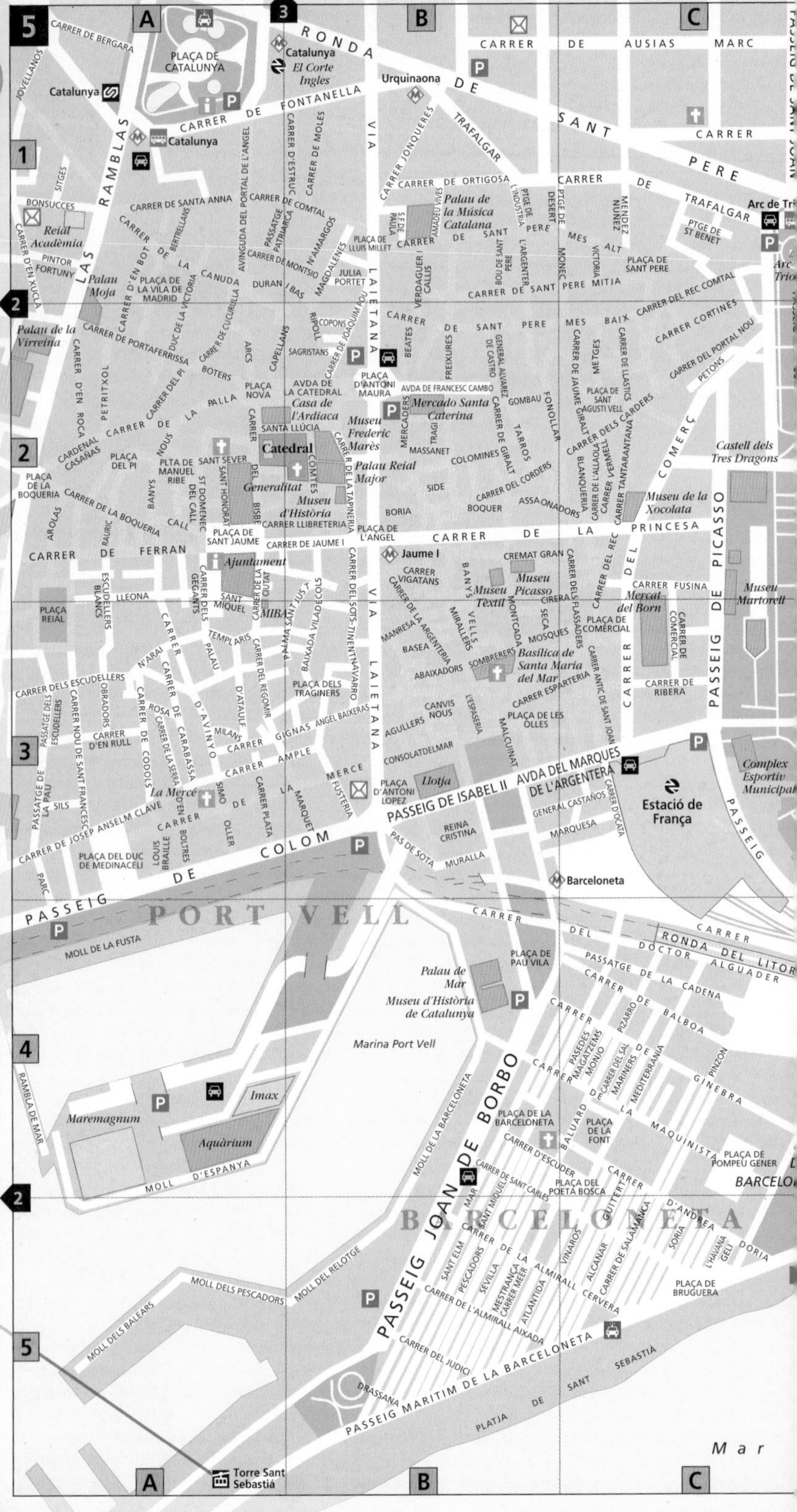

5
A
B
C
3
1
2
3
4
5
PLAÇA DE CATALUNYA
Catalunya
El Corte Ingles
Urquinaona
RONDA DE SANT PERE
CARRER DE AUSIAS MARC
CARRER DE FONTANELLA
LAS RAMBLAS
Palau de la Música Catalana
Arc de Triomf
Reial Acadèmia
Palau Moja
Palau de la Virreina
VIA LAIETANA
Mercado Santa Caterina
Casa de l'Ardiaca
Catedral
Museu Frederic Marès
Palau Reial Major
Generalitat
Museu d'Història
Ajuntament
PLAÇA DE SANT JAUME
CARRER DE FERRAN
PLAÇA REIAL
MIBA
Jaume I
CARRER DE LA PRINCESA
Museu Picasso
Museu Tèxtil
Museu de la Xocolata
Castell dels Tres Dragons
Mercat del Born
Museu Martorell
PASSEIG DE PICASSO
Basílica de Santa Maria del Mar
Llotja
PASSEIG DE ISABEL II
AVDA DEL MARQUES DE L'ARGENTERA
Estació de França
Complex Esportiu Municipal
La Mercè
PASSEIG DE COLOM
PORT VELL
Barceloneta
MOLL DE LA FUSTA
Palau de Mar
Museu d'Història de Catalunya
Marina Port Vell
Maremagnum
Imax
Aquàrium
MOLL D'ESPANYA
PASSEIG JOAN DE BORBO
BARCELONETA
MOLL DELS PESCADORS
MOLL DEL RELOTGE
MOLL DELS BALEARS
PASSEIG MARITIM DE LA BARCELONETA
PLATJA DE SANT SEBASTIÀ
Mar
Torre Sant Sebastià

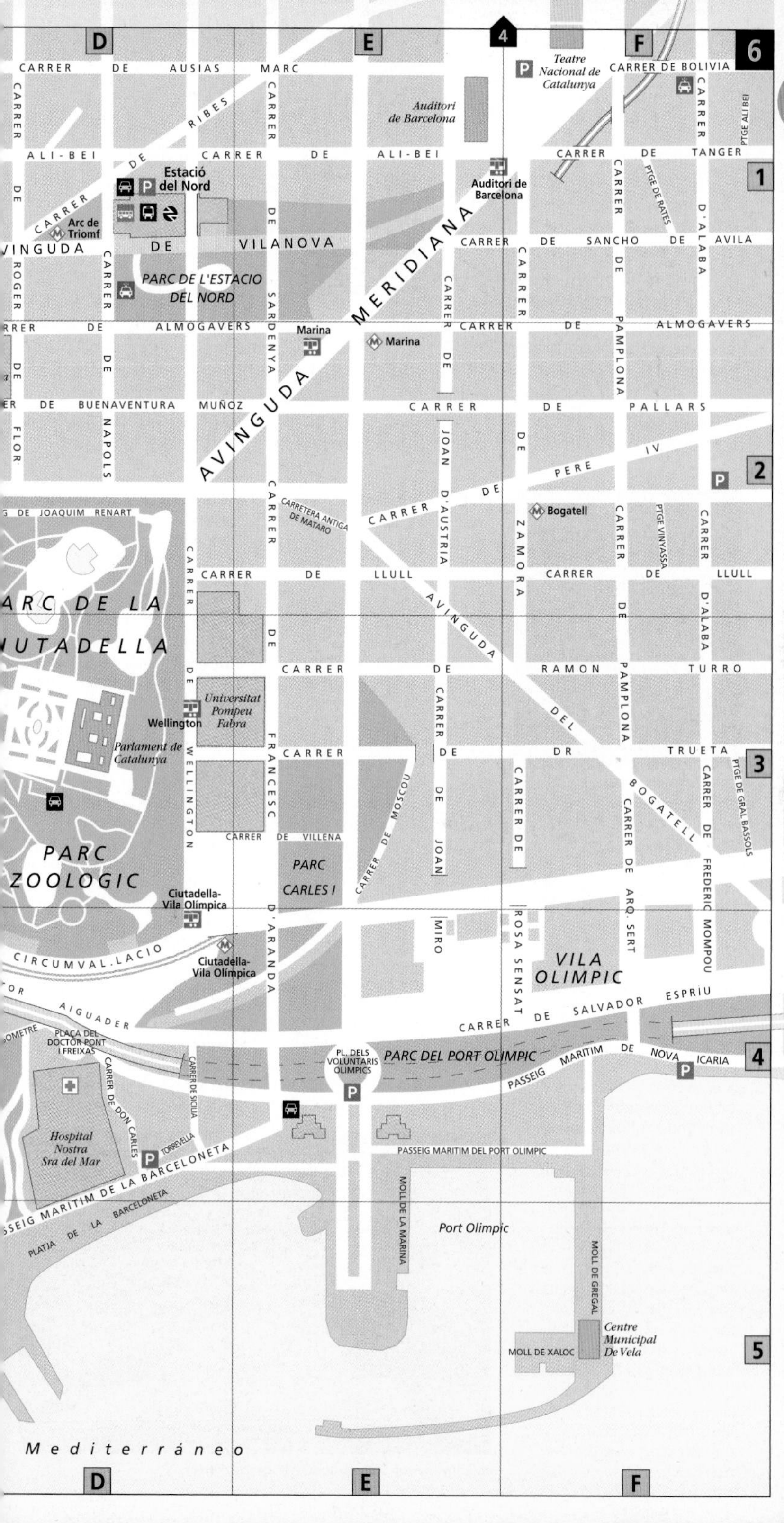

D
E
F
6
4
1
2
3
4
5
Teatre Nacional de Catalunya
Auditori de Barcelona
Estació del Nord
Arc de Triomf
PARC DE L'ESTACIO DEL NORD
Marina
Bogatell
PARC DE LA CIUTADELLA
Universitat Pompeu Fabra
Wellington
Parlament de Catalunya
PARC ZOOLOGIC
PARC CARLES I
Ciutadella-Vila Olímpica
VILA OLIMPIC
PARC DEL PORT OLIMPIC
PL. DELS VOLUNTARIS OLIMPICS
Hospital Nostra Sra del Mar
PLAÇA DEL DOCTOR PONT I FREIXAS
Port Olimpic
Centre Municipal De Vela
MOLL DE LA MARINA
MOLL DE GREGAL
MOLL DE XALOC
Mediterráneo
CARRER DE AUSIAS MARC
CARRER DE BOLIVIA
CARRER DE ALI-BEI
CARRER DE TANGER
CARRER DE RIBES
AVINGUDA DE VILANOVA
AVINGUDA MERIDIANA
CARRER DE SANCHO DE AVILA
CARRER DE ALMOGAVERS
CARRER DE BUENAVENTURA MUÑOZ
CARRER DE PALLARS
CARRER DE PERE IV
CARRETERA ANTIGA DE MATARO
CARRER DE LLULL
CARRER DE RAMON TURRO
CARRER DE DR TRUETA
CARRER DE VILLENA
AVINGUDA DEL BOGATELL
CARRER DE SARDENYA
CARRER DE NAPOLS
CARRER DE ROGER DE FLOR
CARRER DE JOAN D'AUSTRIA
CARRER DE ZAMORA
CARRER DE PAMPLONA
CARRER D'ALABA
CARRER DE WELLINGTON
CARRER DE FRANCESC D'ARANDA
CARRER DE MOSCOU
CARRER DE JOAN MIRO
CARRER DE ROSA SENSAT
CARRER DE ARQ. SERT
CARRER DE FREDERIC MOMPOU
PTGE ALI BEI
PTGE DE RATES
PTGE VINYASSA
PTGE DE GRAL BASSOLS
CARRER DE JOAQUIM RENART
CIRCUMVAL.LACIO
AIGUADER
CARRER DE SALVADOR ESPRIU
PASSEIG MARITIM DE NOVA ICARIA
PASSEIG MARITIM DEL PORT OLIMPIC
CARRER DE SICILIA
CARRER DE DON CARLES
TORREVELLA
PASSEIG MARITIM DE LA BARCELONETA
PLATJA DE LA BARCELONETA

SHOPPING IN BARCELONA

Barcelona is known for its style and sophistication, and can be neatly divided into distinctive shopping districts – Passeig de Gràcia for designer stores and old shops with beautiful Modernista frontages, Barri Gòtic for eclectic antiques and boutiques, El Born for serious fashion divas, and El Raval for markets, quirky designs and museum shops. These categories are not fixed, but do provide a useful rule of thumb, and help define the city when time is limited. There are many food markets as well – 44 in all – and a scattering of flea markets such as the Parisian-style Els Encants and the charming Sant Cugat antiques fair. There is something for everyone in Barcelona – from high-street fashion and unique boutiques to local shops selling traditional crafts. All shops close on Sundays, except Maremagnum.

Wall tile outside La Manual Alpargatera

Some of the beautifully displayed confectionery at Escribà

MARKETS

Barcelona has an impressive range of markets selling a wide variety of things. Everyone should explore **La Boqueria** on Las Ramblas, one of the the most spectacular food markets in Europe. The small and lively Plaça del Pi is also home to a food market selling cheese, honey and sweets. It is held on the 1st and 3rd Friday, Saturday and Sunday of each month.

On Sunday mornings, coin and stamp stalls are set up in the Plaça Reial, while antiques are sold in Plaça Nova on Thursdays. The city's main flea market, **Encants Vells**, takes place on Monday, Wednesday, Friday and Saturday. It offers a variety of goods including jewellery and clothing.

In December, a Christmas street market is held near the cathedral, where Christmas trees, figurines and other decorative items are sold.

FOOD AND DRINK

Barcelonians are proud of their culinary heritage, and rightly so. The land produces superlative vegetables and fruits, flavourful meats and a huge array of cheeses. The bountiful sea offers fresh fish and other seafood, and the wine-growing regions of the Penedès and the Priorat make some of the best vintages in the world. As if all this wasn't enough, chocolate shops, candy makers and patisseries also do their best to complete the feast.

La Boqueria food market is the obvious place to start a gastronomical journey, but Barcelona's numerous specialist food shops are not to be ignored either.

Olive in El Born stocks a superb selection of olive oils from around the Mediterranean, all beautifully arranged in a traditional delicatessen-style setting. Around the corner, **La Botifarrería de Santa María** stocks wonderful artisan charcuterie and a lip-smacking selection of home-made sausages. These include inventive combinations such as pork and cuttlefish, beef and beetroot, and lamb and wild mushroom. **Casa Gispert** is the stop for top-grade dried fruit and nuts, as well as coffee toasted in-house. The fabulous **Formatgeria La Seu** is a walk-in dairy where you can choose from a great seasonal collection of cheeses made by small producers.

Xocoa is the trendiest of the many chocolate-makers in the city, with its retro packaging and fun shapes, including chocolate CDs and giant keys. **Escribà Pastisseries** is more extravagant, with magnificently sculpted cakes and life-size chocolate models of famous personalities. **Cacao Sampaka** is an innovative sweet shop that stocks amazing off-the-wall fillings such as anchovy, black olive and blue cheese,

Mouthwatering fruit stalls in La Boqueria market

as well as more familiar herb, spice and floral flavours.

Antiga Casa Mauri is ideal for those who want to sample traditional Spanish sweets such as *turrón* (nougat made with almonds). **Caelum**, where all the sweetmeats are made by nuns, sells lovely *yemas* (a sweet made with egg yolks) and *mazapans* (marzipan treats) and other tasty confections. **Papabubble**, a gorgeous wood-panelled shop, adds modern touches to old-fashioned sweets. You can watch the sweet chefs preparing these handmade concoctions.

For some of the best bread in town, visit **Bopan** near Rambla de Catalunya. This smart café has its own versions of many different types of bread, from Continental favourites to African specialities.

In El Born, **Vila Viniteca** sells a formidable range of Spanish and Catalan wines. Among more than 7,500 labels here you can find cheap and cheerful table wines, as well as decadently expensive Priorats and Riojas. Also remember that leaving Barcelona without a bottle of the nation's beloved Catalan champagne, *cava*, would be verging on the sacrilegious. The delightfully old-fashioned grocery store **Colmado Quilez** sells a wonderful range of conserves, wines, oils and other deli items, including its own excellent *cava*.

DEPARTMENT STORES AND GALERÍAS

The Plaça Catalunya branch of **El Corte Inglés**, the largest department store chain in Spain, is a Barcelona landmark. It is a handy place with everything under one roof, including plug adaptors and services such as photographic development. There are other branches around the city.

The *galerías* (fashion malls), built mostly during the 1980s, are hugely popular. **Bulevard Rosa** on the Passeig de Gràcia has hundreds of stores selling clothes and accessories. On the Avinguda Diagonal is **L'Illa**, a large, lively shopping mall containing chain stores as well as specialist retailers. The **Maremagnum** shopping centre has all the usual Spanish chains and is open daily, including Sundays and holidays.

Menswear department in Adolfo Domínguez

HIGH STREET AND SPORTS FASHION

Ubiquitous Spanish fashion houses Zara and Mango have stores all over the city, with both flagships on the Passeig de Gràcia. They are great for good value basics, workwear and fashionable party dresses. Both also offer a decent menswear range.

Those looking for more upmarket buys can rely on **Massimo Dutti** and **Adolfo Domínguez**. Both labels offer classically styled, elegant and fairly affordable clothing for men and women.

For more individualized fashion, try one of the smaller, independent shops in El Born and the Barri Gòtic. Carrer Flassaders and the lanes that lead off it in El Born are a particularly good hunting ground for cutting-edge fashion boutiques.

Custo Barcelona is one of the city's most famous design labels. Several branches of this store are in the Old Town, and are piled high with the trademark bright prints and daringly mismatched coats and skirts.

For outlets, head to Calle Girona, where several of them are clustered.

Finally, football fans can head for FC Barcelona's official store, the **Botiga del Barça**. It stocks every conceivable item of merchandise related to the team, including stripes, scarves, boots, balls and keychains.

SPANISH AND INTERNATIONAL DESIGNER LABELS

Independent design house **Giménez & Zuazo** offers truly unique clothing for women, and is well worth seeking out if reasonably priced couture is what you are looking for.

The Barri Gòtic has several stores that stock a range of top designer labels, and this is where you'll find seasonal collections from Vivienne Westwood, Dolce & Gabbana and many others.

Host to big designer labels such as Gucci, Chanel and Caroline Herrera, Avenida Diagonal and the Passeig de Gràcia are where fashionistas like to go shopping. Passeig de Gràcia is home to **Loewe**, which stocks sleek luxury luggage, and is also a reputed name in fashion.

The stylishly sparse display of furniture at Vinçon ***(see p188)***

SECOND-HAND AND VINTAGE FASHION

The diminutive Carrer Riera Baixa in El Raval is home to many interesting second-hand stores. Once a theatre, the vintage shop **Lailo** sells whimsical collectibles such as costumes from the Liceu opera house and 1950s bathing suits. Across the road is **Mies & Felj**, which specializes in fashions from the 1960s and 70s, vintage sportswear, Chinese dresses and brightly patterned curtains.

JEWELLERY, BAGS AND ACCESSORIES

Barcelona has plenty of tiny, Aladdin's Cave-type shops to help put together the perfect outfit. **Joid'Art** has top-quality silver pieces at good prices, both imported and by local designers. Visit **Minu Madhu** for embroidered jackets, patchwork scarves, appliqué handbags and hand-painted silk kerchiefs in sumptuous textures and colours.

Take a bit of the city's street-life home – literally – with a Demano handbag. Recycled polyester PVC from banners and placards is transformed into bags in this endeavour by three designers and the city hall. The innovative and eco-friendly range is available from stockists all over town.

With around 650 designers on its books, **Hipótesis** stores many unique pieces. It stocks jewellery as well as scarves and bags. Materials as diverse as white gold, wood, platinum, buttons and beads have been used to create a number of interesting designs.

HATS AND SHOES

Patterned leather shoes and decorative soles from the cult Mallorcan shoemaker, **Camper**, can be purchased at numerous branches around the city. **Vialis** is a home-grown Barcelona outfit selling beautifully stylish leather women's shoes and cool unisex trainers. **La Manual Alpargatera** is another cult classic, beloved by Sardana dancers *(see p225)* and celebrities alike for its exquisite, individually fitted espadrilles and straw hats. **Le Shoe** is the place for the discerning buyer willing to spend lavishly for superbly classy stilettos. The store has a collection of gorgeous Miu Mius, Jimmy Choos and Manolo Blahniks.

For the best in designer sports shoes, head to **Czar** in the Born. Their hip selection includes Puma, Paul Smith, Rizzo, Fluxa and Le Coq Sportif.

For trendily old-fashioned hats, go to **Sombrerería Obach** where you will find classics ranging from Basque berets to stetsons and hand-woven Montecristi Panamas.

BOOKS AND MUSIC

Arguably the finest specialist travel bookshop in Spain, **Altaïr** stocks a stupendous range of maps, travel guides and coffee-table books for anyone who loves to live on the move. If you are simply looking for some holiday reading, try **Casa del Llibre**, the city's biggest bookstore for books and magazines in English.

Barcelona has also become a hot spot for music collectors, largely due to Sonár, the city's annual electronica festival. **Wah Wah Discos** and **Discos Revolver** are good for stocking up on the latest club tunes and old vinyl, while **FNAC** has a wide variety of books, CDs and DVDs.

UNUSUAL GIFTS AND KNICK-KNACKS

Barcelona is a wonderful city for unearthing intriguing knick-knacks and one-of-a-kind gifts. **Sabater Hnos. Fábrica de Jabones** sells home-made soaps, which come in all shapes and smells, from traditional lavender to delicious chocolate.

Cereria Subirà is the city's oldest shop, and sells a phenomenal array of decorative and votive candles in a variety of beautiful designs.

Arlequí Màscares specializes in hand-painted, papier-mâché folk masks such as Italian Commedia dell'Arte masks, glossy French party masks, Japanese Noh masks and many others.

ARTS AND ANTIQUES

Antiques aficionados will be delighted by what Barcelona has to offer. Equivalent to an antiques shopping mall, the Bulevard dels Antiquaris, in Passeig de Gràcia, is home to over 70 shops filled with vintage relics and every sort of antique imaginable. These range from ancient coins to tin drums and 19th-century candelabras.

Carrer del Call in the Barri Gòtic is another such hub with plush shops, including **L'Arca de l'Àvia**, which sells antique lace, dolls and fine furniture. **Heritage** is a purveyor of semi-precious stone jewellery and antique silks. Also check out the several **Artur Ramon** shops on Carrer de la Palla for 18th- and 19th-century ceramics, and 14th-century paintings.

Sala Parés, the city's oldest and most prestigious gallery, exhibits Catalan artists, both past and present. For pictures that won't break the bank, try the **Boutique Galería Picasso** for prints, lithographs and posters of works by the great Spanish masters, Picasso, Dalí and Miró.

INTERIORS

L'Appartement is an eclectic gallery and shop that exhibits and sells furniture ranging from funky lamps to stylish folding armchairs. **Zara Home** has four basic styles in its collection: classic, ethnic, contemporary and white, all at very reasonable prices. **Dom**, on the other hand, is more trendy and quirky, with its metallic bead curtains and inflatable sofas in shocking neon shades.

Vinçon is the star among Barcelona's design stores, and a favourite with fans of gizmos and gadgets. Housed in a 1900s apartment, it is filled with everything from French Le Creuset cookware to straight-edged tumblers and Coderch lighting.

DIRECTORY

MARKETS

La Boqueria
Las Ramblas 101.
Map 5 A2.

Encants Vells
Plaça de les Glòries.
Map 4 F5.

FOOD AND DRINK

Antiga Casa Mauri
C/ Flassaders 32.
Map 5 C2.
Tel *933 10 04 58.*

Bopan
Rambla de Catalunya 119.
Map 3 A3.
Tel *932 38 73 93.*

Cacao Sampaka
C/ Consell de Cent 292.
Map 3 A4.
Tel *932 72 08 33.*

Caelum
C/ Palla 8. **Map** 5 A2.
Tel *933 01 69 93.*

Casa Gispert
C/ Sombrerers 23.
Map 5 B3.
Tel *933 19 75 35.*

Colmado Quilez
Rambla Catalunya 63.
Map 3 A4.
Tel *932 15 23 26.*

Escribà Pastisseries
Las Ramblas 83.
Map 5 A1.
Tel *933 01 60 27.*

Formatgeria La Seu
C/ Dagueria 16.
Map 5 B3.
Tel *934 12 65 48.*

La Botifarrería de Santa María
Carrer Santa María 4.
Map 5 B3.
Tel *933 19 97 84.*

Olive
Plaça de les Olles 2.
Map 5 B3.
Tel *933 10 58 83.*

Papabubble
C/ Ample 28.
Map 5 A3.
Tel *932 68 86 25.*

Vila Viniteca
C/ Agullers 7.
Map 5 B3.
Tel *902 32 77 77.*

Xocoa
C/ Vidrería 4. **Map** 5 B2.
Tel *933 19 63 71.*

DEPARTMENT STORES AND GALERÍAS

Bulevard Rosa
Passeig de Gràcia 55. **Map** 3 A4. ***Tel*** *932 15 83 31.*

El Corte Inglés
Plaça de Catalunya 14.
Map 5 B1.
Tel *933 06 38 00.*

L'Illa
Avinguda Diagonal 557.
Tel *934 44 00 00.*

Maremagnum
Moll d'Espanya 5. **Map** 5 A4. ***Tel*** *932 25 81 00.*

HIGH STREET AND SPORTS FASHION

Adolfo Domínguez
Passeig de Gràcia 89.
Map 3 A2–A5.
Tel *934 87 98 01.*

Botiga del Barça
Ronda Universitat 37.
Map 5 A1.
Tel *933 18 64 77.*

Custo Barcelona
Plaça de les Olles 7.
Map 5 B3.
Tel *932 68 78 93.*

Massimo Dutti
Portal de L'Angel 16.
Map 5 A1.
Tel *933 01 89 11.*

SPANISH AND INTERNATIONAL DESIGNER LABELS

Giménez & Zuazo
C/ Elisabets 20. **Map** 2 F2. ***Tel*** *934 12 33 81.*

Loewe
Passeig de Gràcia 35.
Map 3 A2–A5.
Tel *932 16 04 00.*

SECOND-HAND AND VINTAGE FASHION

Lailo
C/ Riera Baixa 20. **Map** 2 F2. ***Tel*** *934 41 37 49.*

Mies & Felj
C/ Riera Baixa 4. **Map** 2 F2. ***Tel*** *934 42 07 55.*

JEWELLERY, BAGS AND ACCESSORIES

Hipótesis
Rambla de Catalunya 105.
Map 3 A3.
Tel *932 15 02 98.*

Joid'Art
Plaça Sta. María 7.
Map 5 B3.
Tel *933 10 10 87.*

Minu Madhu
C/ Sta. María 18.
Map 5 B3.
Tel *933 10 27 85.*

HATS AND SHOES

Camper
C/ Elizabets 9.
Map 2 F2.
Tel *933 42 41 41.*

Czar
Passeig del Born 20.
Map 5 C3.
Tel *933 10 72 22.*

La Manual Alpargatera
C/ Avinyó 7.
Map 5 A3.
Tel *933 01 01 72.*

Le Shoe
C/ Tenor Viñas 4.
Map 3 A2–A5.
Tel *932 00 54 20.*

Sombrereria Obach
Carrer del Call 2.
Map 5 A2.
Tel *933 18 40 94.*

Vialis
C/ Vidrieria 15. **Map** 5 B3. ***Tel*** *933 19 94 91.*

BOOKS AND MUSIC

Altaïr
Gran Via 616. **Map** 3 A4.
Tel *933 42 71 71.*

Casa del Llibre
Passeig de Gràcia 62.
Map 3 A2–A5.
Tel *932 72 34 80.*

Discos Revolver
Tallers 11. **Map** 5 A1.
Tel *933 01 61 78.*

FNAC
Plaça de Catalunya 4.
Map 3 A4.
Tel *933 44 18 00.*

Wah Wah Discos
Riera Baixa 14.
Map 2 F2.
Tel *934 42 37 03.*

UNUSUAL GIFTS AND KNICK-KNACKS

Arlequí Màscares
C/ Princesa 7. **Map** 5 B2.
Tel *932 68 27 52.*

Cereria Subirà
Baixada Llibreteria 7.
Map 5 A2.
Tel *933 15 26 06.*

Sabater Hnos. Fábrica de Jabones
Pl Sant Felip Neri 1, Barri Gòtic. **Map** 5 B2.
Tel *933 01 98 32.*

ARTS AND ANTIQUES

Artur Ramón
C/ Palla 23. **Map** 5 A2.
Tel *933 02 59 70.*

Boutique Galería Picasso
C/ Tapinería 10. **Map** 5 B2. ***Tel*** *933 10 49 57.*

Heritage
C/ Banys Nous 14.
Map 5 A2.
Tel *933 17 85 15.*

L'Arca de l'Àvia
C/ Banys Nous 20.
Map 5 A2.
Tel *933 02 15 98.*

Sala Parés
C/ Petritxol 5. **Map** 5 A2.
Tel *933 18 70 08.*

INTERIORS

L'Appartement
C/ Enric Granados 44.
Map 3 A4.
Tel *934 52 29 04.*

Dom
Consell de Cent 248, Eixample. **Map** 3 A4.
Tel *934 52 17 68.*

Vinçon
Passeig de Gràcia 96.
Map 3 A2–A5.
Tel *932 15 60 50.*

Zara Home
Rambla de Catalunya 71.
Map 3 A4.
Tel *934 87 49 72.*

ENTERTAINMENT IN BARCELONA

Barcelona has one of the most colourful and alternative live arts scenes in Europe, offering a variety of entertainment, from the spectacular Modernista masterpiece the Palau de la Música and the gilded Liceu opera house, to small independent theatres hosting obscure Catalan comedies and dark Spanish dramas. But there's also much to see simply by walking around the city. Street peformances you may stumble upon range from the human statues on Las Ramblas to excellent classical, ragtime and jazz buskers in the squares. In addition, there are a series of weekend-long musical and arts fiestas that run throughout the year, many of which now attract international performers from all over Europe and beyond.

Busker in the Barri Gòtic

The magnificent interior of the Palau de la Música Catalana

ENTERTAINMENT GUIDES

The most complete guide to what's going on each week in Barcelona is the Catalan-language *Time Out*, out every Thursday. This guide also includes cinema listings. The Friday *La Vanguardia* features the entertainment supplement *Què Fem?* Barcelona's free English-language magazine, *Metropolitan*, also offers details of cultural events going on in town.

SEASONS AND TICKETS

Theatre and concert seasons for the main venues run from September to June, with limited programmes at other times. The city's varied menu of entertainment reflects its rich, multi-cultural artistic heritage. In summer, the city hosts the **Barcelona Festival del Grec**, a showcase of international music, theatre and dance, held at open-air venues. There is also a wide variety of concerts to choose from during the **Festa de la Mercè**, held in September. The **Festival del Sónar**, which takes place in June, has become Europe's biggest electronic music festival, drawing musicians from around the world. The **Clàssics als Parcs**, held in June and July, presents classical music in serene surroundings.

The simplest way to get theatre and concert tickets is to buy them at the box office, although tickets for many theatres can also be bought from branches of Caixa de Catalunya and the Caixa savings banks, or from ServiCaixa machines. Tickets for the Grec festival are sold at tourist offices and at the Palau de la Virreina.

THEATRE AND DANCE

Most theatre in Barcelona is performed in Catalan and English-language productions are still in short supply. However, many Catalan and Spanish shows are well worth seeing, regardless of language constraints. There are some good independent theatre groups, such as Els Comediants and La Cubana, that perform at the **Llantiol Teatre** in El Raval. They offer a thrilling mélange of theatre, music, mime and elements from traditional Mediterranean fiestas. Also staged at the tiny Llantiol is a weekly repertoire of alternative shows, comedy, magic and other off-the-cuff performances designed to attract a mixed crowd, from the city's growing expatriate community to local arts lovers. Similarly, the **L'Antic Teatre** in La Ribera is a laid-back cultural centre and bar with a scruffy, but pleasant, summer roof-terrace and a small restaurant. It hosts a number of alternative production companies and also shows films outside on the terrace throughout the summer.

Las Ramblas and Paral.lel are the main hubs of the city's bigger and more mainstream

Outrageous stage show at one of Barcelona's many clubs

The façade of the modern Teatre Nacional de Catalunya

theatres. The **Teatre Tívoli** is a gargantuan theatre where high-quality productions, dance and musical recitals by Catalan, Spanish and international stars are held. The **Teatre Poliorama** on Las Ramblas, meanwhile, is known more for musicals, occasional operas and contemporary flamenco performances. The **Teatre Apolo** is good for big-bang musicals such as Queen's "We Will Rock You" and ABBA's "Mamma Mia!"

For serious theatre-lovers, the **Teatre Nacional de Catalunya (TNC)** is an imposing, columned affair designed by the Catalan architect Ricard Bofill, with state-of-the-art facilities and a weighty line-up of Spanish and Catalan directors. Good for avant-garde performances and music is the **Mercat de les Flors**, a converted flower market in the Montjuïc area that is known as Barcelona's "City of Theatre". This is the same part of town that contains Barcelona's drama school and the **Teatre Lliure**, home to the most prestigious Catalan-language theatre company.

Modern dance has always been popular in Barcelona and performances can often be caught at the city's main theatres. The **Teatre Victòria** on Avinguda del Paral.lel is good for ballet and more classical dance productions, as is the **Liceu** opera house.

OPERA AND CLASSICAL MUSIC

Opera and classical music are loved by Catalans who lap it up with near-religious reverence. Indeed, many of the great artists of the 20th century were locals, including the celebrated cellist Pau Casals and opera singers José Carreras and Montserrat Caballé.

The city of Barcelona is also home to some of the most spectacular venues in the world, including the glamorous, gilded **Gran Teatre del Liceu**, which first opened its doors in 1847. The opera house has been a continuing beacon of Catalan arts for more than 150 years, with a rich and dramatic history of fire and bomb attacks. It burned down for the third time in 1994, but careful renovations have restored it to its former glory. Despite its misfortunes, it has sustained a stellar line-up of the greatest composers in the world. Among them are Puccini and Tchaikovsky, as well as Catalan composers such as Felip Pedrell, Vives and Enric Granados. Sergei Diaghilev's Russian ballets were also staged here.

The whimsical fancy of the **Palau de la Música Catalana** is another of Barcelona's architectural triumphs (*see p152*). A jewel-bright vision by the Modernista master Lluís Domènech i Montaner, this sublime concert hall has a dedicated audience, and performers who vie to play here. This is also the main venue for the city's jazz and guitar festivals, as well as national and international symphony orchestras.

Both venues, the Gran Teatre del Liceu and Palau de la Música Catalana, can be visited on daytime guided tours, but booking tickets for a production is the best way to experience the ambience.

Modern, but no less important as a shrine to the Catalan arts scene, **L'Auditori de Barcelona** was built to accommodate growing demands for better facilities and to attract ever greater numbers of world-class musicians. It began primarily as a place for classical concerts and orchestral recitals, but has since begun to embrace giants of jazz, pop and rock.

It is also worth keeping abreast of regular choral music that is performed at the city's churches and cathedrals. Most notable among these are the **Església Santa Maria del Pi**, the main cathedral on Plaça del Pi, and the **Basílica Santa Maria del Mar**, particularly around Christmas and Easter.

Packed house at the gigantic Nou Camp stadium

SPORTS

The undoubted kings of sport in Catalonia are **FC Barcelona**, known locally as Barça. They have the largest football stadium in Europe, Camp Nou *(see p176)*, and a fanatical following.

Tickets for Barça home matches in the national league (*La Liga*), the King's Cup (*Copa del Rey*) and Champions League can be purchased at the FC Barcelona ticket offices (in person or by telephone), at ServiCaixa machines, or perhaps most conveniently, they can be bought online. Barcelona also has a high-ranking basketball team.

AMUSEMENT PARK

In summer, Barcelona's giant amusement park on the summit of **Tibidabo** (*see p178*) is extremely busy and is usually open till the early hours on weekends. Getting there by tram, funicular or cable car is even more fun.

FILM

Directors such as Alejandro Amenábar (*The Sea Inside* and *Agora*), Catalan writer and director Isabel Coixet (*My Life Without You* and *Elegy*) and, of course, Spain's bad boy of film, Pedro Almodóvar (*All About My Mother* and *The Skin I Live In*) have revitalized Spanish cinema. Woody Allen's *Vicky, Cristina, Barcelona* (2008) brought the city to an even wider audience. Today, Barcelona has become the venue for many independent film festivals. The biggest event of the year is the International Film Festival in Sitges, which is held in October.

Most cinemas dub films in Spanish or Catalan, but there are an increasing number of VO (original version) venues that screen Hollywood block-busters as well as independent art-house movies.

The **Icària Yelmo Cineplex** is the town's biggest multiscreen VO complex, built around a US-style mall, with a variety of fast-food eateries and shops. The **Renoir Floridablanca**, on the edge of El Raval and the Eixample, screens a range of European and international movies, usually with Spanish or Catalan subtitles. In Gràcia, **Verdi** and **Verdi Park** feature good independent movies, with an interesting selection of foreign films. In summer, both the Castell de Montjuïc and the Piscina Bernat Picornell, the Olympic swimming pool in Montjuïc, host a number of open-air cinema screenings.

The two-screen **Méliès** is a gem showcasing art-house movies, Hollywood classics, B&W horrors and anything by Fellini or Alfred Hitchcock. For children, there is the **IMAX Port Vell**, which shows the usual 3-D roller coaster knuckle-biters, Everest expeditions and squid-entangled journeys to the bottom of the sea.

It's worth knowing that the prices for movie tickets are lower for weekend matinées. Some cinemas offer midnight and early-hour screenings.

LIVE MUSIC: ROCK, JAZZ AND BLUES

In terms of popular music, Barcelona may not compare to London, whose endless clubs, pubs, stadiums and music emporiums make it one of the best places for live music. However, it doesn't do too badly, given its size. The city attracts a star-studded cast that ranges from pop stars such as Kylie Minogue and Madonna to contemporary jazz musicians such as the Brad Mehldau Quartet, hip-hoppers, rappers and world groove mixers, country singers and good old-fashioned rock and rollers.

Barcelona has a clutch of tiny, intimate venues, including the cellar-like **Jamboree**, attracting a number of jazz heavyweights as well as more experimental outfits. Later on it becomes a club.

Another good bet is the **Jazz Sí Club**, a more obscure destination but much beloved by aficionados of the genre. It doubles up as a jam session space for students from the nearby music school. The narrow, crowded and smoky **Harlem Jazz Club** is one of the city's longest surviving clubs for alternative and lesser-known jazz troupes.

One of the two major venues for pop and rock maestros is **Bikini**, Barcelona's very own Studio 54. It opened in 1953, preceding the New York icon by a year. This veteran of the scene, which is open from midnight onwards, is still going strong with a robust line-up of big-name bands and a cocktail of different club nights. The other, **Razzmatazz**, arguably the city's most important live music venue, has played host to big-name pop bands such as the Arctic Monkeys, Noel Gallagher's High Flying Birds and James Morrison. Club sessions go on until dawn in some clubs, including Razz Club and The Loft, next door. This trendy venue also holds rock and jazz concerts several nights a week.

Barcelona boasts an architectural masterpiece to host visiting bands: Arata Isozaki's flying saucer, **Palau Sant Jordi**, on Montjuïc, houses extravaganzas like Disney on Ice, the Rolling Stones and Madonna.

One of the city's most popular smaller venues is **Sala BeCool**, which puts on live bands and club nights focused on electronic music.

For a touch of unbeatable glam, **Luz de Gas** is a glitzy ballroom that oozes old-fashioned atmosphere with its lamp-lit tables and chandeliers and features lists of bands and shows that enjoyed their heyday here in the 1970s and '80s. It's not quite cabaret, but gets close, though not as close as the infamous **El Cangrejo**. This club features outrageous drag cabaret, with shockingly attired queens in full make-up and sequins miming along to numbers by Sara Montiel (the Spanish sex symbol) and back-chatting with the crowd.

FLAMENCO

One of the best places to catch a flamenco show is **El Tablao de Carmen**, a stylish restaurant serving both Catalan and Andalusian dishes. The venue is named after Carmen Amaya, a famous dancer who performed for King Alfonso XIII in 1929, in the very spot where it now stands. Various dinner and show packages are available.

For a less formal ambience, **Los Tarantos** (above Jamboree) is an atmospheric nightspot with live flamenco and Latin music every night of the week.

Those who would like to try their hand at flamenco can visit **Flamenco Barcelona**, a shop and cultural activity centre that specialises in the passionate dance. They offer flamenco and guitar lessons, as well as live shows at weekends.

DIRECTORY

FESTIVALS

Barcelona Festival del Grec
Tel *010.*
Contact any tourist office.

Classics als Parcs
Tel *010.*
www.bcn.es/parcsijardins

Festa de la Mercè
see p157.

Festival del Sónar
Palau de la Virreina.
www.sonar.es

TICKETS

Palau de la Virreina
Las Ramblas 99.
Map 5 A1.
Tel *933 16 10 00.*

ServiCaixa
Tel *902 33 22 11.*
www.servicaixa.com

TelEntrada
Tel *902 10 12 12.*
www.telentrada.com

Tourist Office
Plaça de Catalunya.
Map 5 A1.
Tel *932 85 38 34.*
www.barcelonaturisme.com

THEATRE AND DANCE

L'Antic Teatre
C/ Verdaguer i Callís 12.
Map 5 A1.
Tel *933 15 23 54.*

Llantiol Teatre
C/ Riereta 7.
Map 2 E2.
Tel *933 29 90 09.*

Mercat de les Flors
C/ de Lleida 59.
Map 1 B2.
Tel *934 26 18 75.*
www.mercatflors.cat

Teatre Apolo
Av del Paral.lel 57.
Map 1 B1.
Tel *934 41 90 07.*
www.teatreapolo.com

Teatre Lliure
Plaça Margarida Xirgu 1.
Tel *932 89 27 70.*
www.teatrelliure.com

Teatre Nacional de Catalunya (TNC)
Plaça de les Arts 1.
Tel *933 06 57 00.*
www.tnc.cat

Teatre Poliorama
Las Ramblas 115.
Map 5 A1.
Tel *933 17 75 99.*
www.teatrepoliorama.com

Teatre Tívoli
C/ Casp 8–10.
Map 3 B5.
Tel *934 12 20 63.*
www.grupbalana.com

Teatre Victòria
Av del Paral.lel 67–9.
Map 1 B1.
Tel *933 29 91 89.*
www.teatrevictoria.com

OPERA AND CLASSICAL MUSIC

Basílica Santa Maria del Mar
Plaça de Santa Maria.
Map 5 B3.
Tel *933 10 23 90.*

Església Santa Maria del Pi
Plaça del Pi.
Map 5 A2.
Tel *933 18 47 43.*

Gran Teatre del Liceu
Las Ramblas 51–9.
Map 2 F3.
Tel *934 85 99 00.*
www.liceubarcelona.cat

L'Auditori de Barcelona
C/ de Lepant 150.
Map 4 E1.
Tel *932 47 93 00.*
www.auditori.catt

Palau de la Música Catalana
C/ Palau de la Música 4–6.
Map 5 B1.
Tel *902 44 28 82.*
www.palaumusica.org

SPORTS

FC Barcelona
Camp Nou,
Avda Aristides Maillol.
Tel *934 96 36 00.*
www.fcbarcelona.com

AMUSEMENT PARK

Tibidabo
Plaça del Tibidabo, 3.
Tel *932 11 79 42.*
www.tibidabo.cat

FILM

Icària Yelmo Cineplex
C/ Salvador Espriu 61.
Map 6 E4.
Tel *932 21 42 02.*
www.yelmocines.es

IMAX Port Vell
Moll d'Espanya.
Map 5 A4.
Tel *932 25 11 11.*
www.imaxportvell.com

Méliès
C/ Villarroel 102.
Map 2 E1.
Tel *934 51 00 51.*
www.cinesmelies.net

Renoir Floridablanca
C/ Floridablanca 135.
Map 1 C1.
Tel *934 26 33 37.*
www.cinesrenoir.com

Verdi
C/ Verdi 32.
Map 3 B1.
Tel *932 38 78 00.*
www.cines-verdi.com

Verdi Park
C/ Torrijos 49.
Map 3 C2.
Tel *932 38 78 00.*
www.cines-verdi.com

LIVE MUSIC: ROCK, JAZZ AND BLUES

Bikini
Deu i Mata 105.
Tel *933 22 08 00.*
www.bikinibcn.com

El Cangrejo
C/ Montserrat 9.
Map 2 F4.
Tel *933 01 29 78.*

Harlem Jazz Club
C/ Comtessa de Sobradiel 8.
Tel *933 10 07 55.*
www.harlemjazzclub.es

Jamboree
Plaça Reial 17.
Map 5 A3.
Tel *933 04 12 10.*
www.masimas.com

Jazz Sí Club
C/ Requesens 2.
Tel *933 29 00 20.*
www.tallerdemusics.com

Luz de Gas
C/ Muntaner 246.
Map 2 F1.
Tel *932 09 77 11.*
www.luzdegas.com

Palau Sant Jordi
Passeig Olímpic 5–7.
Map 1 B4.
Tel *934 26 20 89.*

Razzmatazz
C/ Pamplona 88.
Map 4 F5.
Tel *933 20 81 67.*
www.salarazzmatazz.com

Sala BeCool
Plaça Joan Llongueras 5.
Tel *933 62 04 13.*
www.salabebecool.com

FLAMENCO

El Tablao de Carmen
Avda Marqués de Comillas s/n.
Map 1 B1.
Tel *933 25 68 95.*
www.tablaodecarmen.com

Flamenco Barcelona
Marqués de Barberá 6.
Map 2 F3.
Tel *934 41 88 52.*
www.barcelonaflamenco.es

Los Tarantos
Plaça Reial 17.
Map 5 A3.
Tel *933 19 17 89.*
www.masimas.com/en/tarantos

Nightlife

Barcelona has one of the most varied nightlife scenes, with something for everybody. Old-fashioned dance halls rub shoulders with underground drum and bass clubs and trashy techno discos, and club-goers are either glammed-up or grunged-out. Each *barrio* (neighbourhood) offers a different flavour, while clubs and bars with outdoor terraces enliven the beachfront during the summer months.

NIGHTLIFE

In the summer the beaches become party havens when the *xiringuitos* (beach bars) spring back into life. Wander from Platja de Sant Sebastià in Barceloneta, all the way to Bogatell (a few kilometres beyond the Hotel Arts) and you'll find people dancing barefoot on the sand to the tune of Barcelona's innumerable DJs. Way uptown (above the Diagonal), the city's most glamorous terraces morph into social hubs while the Barri Gòtic – lively at the best of times – becomes one massive street party throughout the summer. If you want to hang with the locals, the demolition of some of El Raval's less salubrious streets has meant that the neighbourhood has become much safer and easier to move about. The underground vibe, however, remains steadfastly intact with tiny hole-in-the-wall-style bars where folks drink and boogie till the early hours. Similarly Gràcia has a bohemian, studenty ambience. If it's an alternative scene you seek Poble Sec has a handful of "ring-to-enter" joints and the city's only serious drum and bass club, **Plataforma**. The city also has a thriving and friendly gay scene, most notably within the Eixample Esquerra, also known as the Gay Eixample, boasting numerous late-night drinking holes, discothèques, saunas and cabarets.

BARRI GÒTIC

The Plaça Reial is overrun with tourists banging on tin drums and whooping it up, but if you're looking for more grown-up fun, check out **Fantástico Club**. Pop and electro music combine with candy-coloured decor to make this club a hit. The tiny but ultra-hip **Macarena** is one of the city's most prestigious clubs. It majors in electronica and features the city's best DJs, renowned international artists and new talent. Jazz lovers shouldn't miss the daily concerts at **Jamboree**, one of Spain's mythical jazz clubs. Later, the venue becomes one of the most popular funk and hip-hop discos in town. The nightclub **New York** is inclined towards more commercially gratifying tunes. The vibe on the dancefloor is more disco, but the venue also hosts live music nights that bring in a wide range of local and international bands.

EL RAVAL

Designer clubs proliferate in Barcelona these days. With slinky red, black and white decor and a specially designed underlit bar, **Zentraus** is one of the best-looking clubs in the neighbourhood. A restaurant until midnight or so, the tables are cleared away once the DJ sessions get under way. **Moog** is more extreme, with blaring, heart-pumping techno for aficionados of the genre. The stark industrial interior gives it the character of a New York nightclub in the mid-1990s. Likewise, the state-of-the-art sound system ensures a thumping, ear-bleedingly good night out. Going back in time, check out the old-school ambience of **El Cangrejo**, where in 1924 the famous copla singer Carmen Amaya made her debut. On Friday and Saturday nights you can see drag shows here (the best ones are by Carmen de Mairena) followed by pop revival DJ sessions. Other nights feature a '70s and '80s music theme.

PORT VELL AND PORT OLÌMPIC

Beach parties aside, this area continues to be a hub for creatures of the night. The Port Olìmpic itself is nothing but bars and boats, while **Maremagnum** has a clutch of music bars and cocktail bars. **Catwalk** is one of the few clubs in Barcelona offering hip hop and R&B. **C.D.L.C.** in front of the Hotel ArtsV still draws celebrities staying nearby, while neighbouring **Shôko**, with an Oriental theme, gets the crowd overflow.

EIXAMPLE

One of the city's best loved discos, **City Hall**, is a multiple space and terrace, where you can pick and choose your groove according to your mood. It has different themes every night from Saturday night-fever discos to Sunday chill-outs. **Ommsessions Club**, in the Hotel Omm, is one of Barcelona's most glamorous addresses, beloved by models and fashionistas. Salsa fans should head to **Antilla**, where live music is combined with salsa classes and exotic cocktails. **Dow Jones** is Barcelona's "drinks stock exchange" where the prices of drinks rise and fall throughout the evening according to demand.

POBLE SEC

The most alternative nightlife has come to roost in the "dry village", though in name only. The bars are wet and the music is happening. **Apolo** is another old-fashioned music hall, though it attracts a more independent breed of DJ and performer. Expect anything from soulful gypsy folk singers from Marseille, to the legendary purveyor of deep funk, Keb Darge. Further into the village, **Mau Mau** is an alternative club and cultural centre with a firm eye on what's new and happening. This could mean local DJs, Japanese musicians such as the cultish Cinema Dub Monks, alternative cinema, and multimedia art installations. If it's of the here and now, chances are Mau Mau's on it. At the other end of the spectrum, head to tiny **Tinta Roja** for low lights, romance and tango shows (from Thursday to Sunday nights) in a bar which recalls the Buenos Aires of the 1940s.

GRÀCIA AND TIBIDABO

Friendly **Eldorado**, on the lively Plaça del Sol, manages to combine café, bar, club and games room (with table football, pool and pinball). Spanish music and 1980s pop dominate in what is just one of many relaxed "music bars" in laid-back Gràcia. And high up above the rest, **Elephant** offers the best in mansion-house clubbing experiences, with chill-out lounges, two dance floors, a VIP area, sprawling terraces and prices to suit the altitude.

OUT OF TOWN

Barcelona's mega-clubs are located away from the city centre and from anyone trying to sleep. Most of them are only open on Friday and Saturday nights. The big boys are based in Poble Espanyol where folks can party until the sunrise. **La Terrrazza** is a summer club that hosts rave-like parties under the stars. It takes its name from the giant terrace it occupies. Nearby on Plaça Espanya, the Ibiza-style **Privilege** is very popular. Don't even think about getting in without an appropriately glamorous outfit, and remember: less is most definitely more.

Further out of town you will find the world's most famous nightclub, **Pacha**. Although born in Barcelona, you'll have to travel out to Sitges to enjoy this trademark sensational night out. Alternatively, **Liquid** is the only summer club in the city with a swimming pool (though the pool is only open from June to September). The only drawback is that should you wish to leave before the party's over, finding a taxi can be a big problem.

DIRECTORY

BARRI GÒTIC

Fantástico Club
Passatge Escudellers 3, Barri Gòtic. **Map** 5 A3.
Tel *93 317 54 11.*
www.fantasticoclub.com

Jamboree
Plaça Reial 17, Barri Gòtic. **Map** 5 A3.
Tel *93 319 17 89.*
www.masimas.com

Macarena
C/ Nou de la Rambla 3. **Map** 5 A3.
Tel *93 317 90 32.*

New York
C/ Escudellers 5, Barri Gòtic. **Map** 5 A3.
Tel *93 318 87 30.*

EL RAVAL

El Cangrejo
C/ Montserrat 9. **Map** 2 F4. ***Tel*** *93 301 29 78.*

Moog
C/ Arc del Teatre 3, El Raval. **Map** 2 F4.
Tel *93 301 49 91.*
www.masimas.com

Zentraus
Rambla de Raval 41, El Raval. **Map** 2 F3.
Tel *93 448 80 78.*
www.zentraus.cat

PORT VELL AND PORT OLÌMPIC

Catwalk
C/ Ramon Trias Fargas 2–4, Port Olìmpic. **Map** 6 E4.
Tel *93 224 07 40.*
www.clubcatwalk.net

C.D.L.C.
Passeig Marítim 32, Port Olìmpic. **Map** 6 E4.
Tel *93 224 04 70.*
www.cdlcbarcelona.com

Shôko
Passeig Marítim 36, Port Olìmpic. **Map** 6 E4.
Tel *93 225 92 00.*
www.shoko.biz

EIXAMPLE

Antilla
Carrer d'Aragó 141–3.
Tel *93 451 45 64.*
www.antillasalsa.com

City Hall
Rambla Catalunya 2–4, Eixample. **Map** 3 A3.
Tel *93 238 07 22.*
www.ottozutz.es

Dow Jones
C/ Bruc 97. **Map** 3 B4.
Tel *93 476 38 31.*

Ommsessions Club
Hotel Omm, C/ Rosselló 265. **Map** 3 B3.
Tel *93 445 40 00.*
www.hotelomm.es

POBLE SEC

Apolo
C/ Nou de la Rambla 113, Poble Sec. **Map** 2 D4.
Tel *93 441 40 01.*
www.sala-apolo.com

Mau Mau
C/ Fontrodona 33, Poble Sec. **Map** 2 D3.
Tel *93 441 80 15.*
www.maumaunderground.com

Tinta Roja
C/ Creu dels Molers 17, Poble Sec. **Map** 2 D3.
Tel *93 443 32 43.*

GRÀCIA AND TIBIDABO

Eldorado
Plaça del Sol 4, Gràcia. **Map** 3 B1.

Elephant
Passeig des Til.lers 1, Tibidabo.
Tel *93 334 02 58.*
www.elephantbcn.com

OUT OF TOWN

La Terrrazza
Poble Espanyol, Avda Marquès de Comillas. **Map** 1 B1.
Tel *93 272 49 80.*
www.laterrrazza.com

Liquid
Complex Esportiu Hospitalet Nord, C/ Manuel Azaña.

Pacha
Urb. Vallpineda, C/ San Didac, Sitges.
Tel *93 894 38 12.*
www.pachasitges.com

Privilege
C/ Tarragona 141.
Tel *93 426 47 86.*
www.privilegebarcelona.com

EASTERN SPAIN

Introducing Eastern Spain

Eastern Spain covers an extraordinary range of climates and landscapes, from the snowbound peaks of the Pyrenees in Aragón to the beaches of the Costa Blanca and Costa Cálida, popular for their winter warmth and sunshine. The region has a wealth of historical sights including ancient monasteries near Barcelona, magnificent Roman ruins in Tarragona, Mudéjar churches and towers in Aragón and the great cathedrals of Valencia and Murcia. Away from the busy coasts, the countryside is often attractive but little visited.

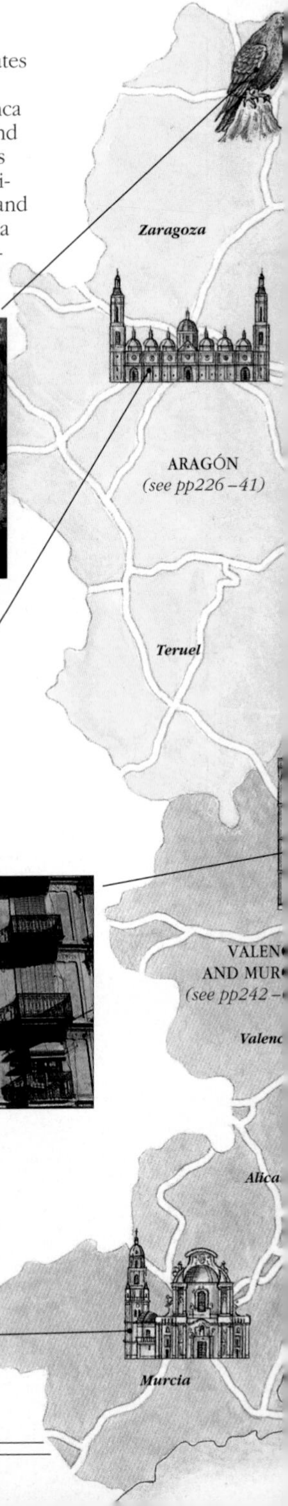

Ordesa National Park (see pp232–3) *in the Pyrenees has some of the most dramatic mountain scenery in Spain. It makes excellent walking country.*

Zaragoza (see pp236–7) *has many striking churches, especially the cathedral, the Basílica de Nuestra Señora del Pilar, and the Mudéjar-style Iglesia de la Magdalena.*

Valencia (see pp250–53) *is Spain's third largest city. It has an old centre of narrow streets overlooked by venerable houses and monuments, such as El Miguelete, the cathedral's conspicuous bell tower. The city hosts a spectacular festival, Las Fallas, in March.*

Murcia Cathedral (see p262), *built in the 14th century, has a Baroque façade and belfry, and two ornate side chapels – one in late-Gothic style and the other Renaissance. The cathedral museum houses Gothic altarpieces and other fascinating exhibits.*

0 kilometres 50

0 miles 50

◁ **The 12th-century monastery at Gerri de la Sal in Catalonia**

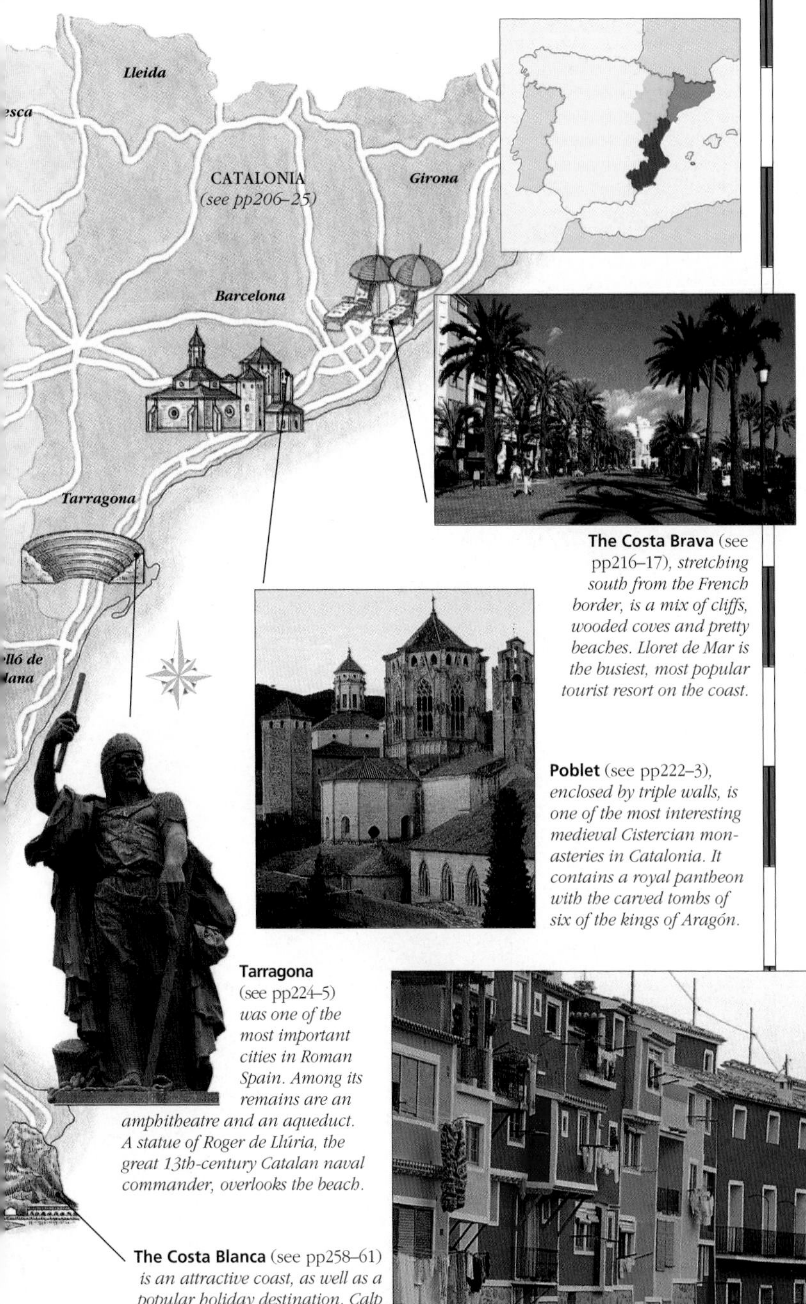

The Costa Brava (see pp216–17), *stretching south from the French border, is a mix of cliffs, wooded coves and pretty beaches. Lloret de Mar is the busiest, most popular tourist resort on the coast.*

Poblet (see pp222–3), *enclosed by triple walls, is one of the most interesting medieval Cistercian monasteries in Catalonia. It contains a royal pantheon with the carved tombs of six of the kings of Aragón.*

Tarragona (see pp224–5) *was one of the most important cities in Roman Spain. Among its remains are an amphitheatre and an aqueduct. A statue of Roger de Llúria, the great 13th-century Catalan naval commander, overlooks the beach.*

The Costa Blanca (see pp258–61) *is an attractive coast, as well as a popular holiday destination. Calp is overshadowed by a huge rock, the Penyal d'Ifach. In La Vila Joiosa, a line of houses has been painted in striking colours to make them visible to sailors at sea.*

The Flavours of Eastern Spain

The current stars of Spain's culinary firmament are Catalans like Ferran Adriá or Carme Ruscalleda, whose creativity and innovation have brought them international acclaim. Fashionable new eateries and traditional country inns alike still place the emphasis firmly on fresh local ingredients. Along with adjoining Murcia and Catalonia, Valencia produces a huge array of fruit, vegetables, seafood, meat and game, all heaped colourfully in local markets. Rice is the key ingredient in paella and its many local variations. In land-locked Aragón, country cooking includes dishes that recall the Arabic occupation more than a thousand years ago.

Valencian rice

Fresh octopus lie on the ice of a fish-seller's stall

CATALONIA

The incredible variety of fresh produce in Catalonia is a reflection of the varied landscape – the Mediterranean provides all manner of fish and shellfish, the inland plains offer a wealth of vegetables and fields of golden rice, and the mountains contribute meat, game and wild mushrooms (a Catalan obsession). Spain's finest chefs create culinary fireworks in their celebrated restaurants, but Catalan cuisine, even at its most experimental, is essentially simple and relies on the wonderful freshness of its produce.

ARAGÓN

In land-locked, mountainous Aragón, the emphasis is firmly on meat – particularly lamb, but also beef, rabbit and free-range chicken, often served simply grilled or slowly simmered in earthenware pots. There is also much excellent charcuterie, including hams and cured sausages, some flavoured with spices, which are often used to flavour the hearty stews popular in the mountainous north. River trout and eels are regularly found on local menus and,

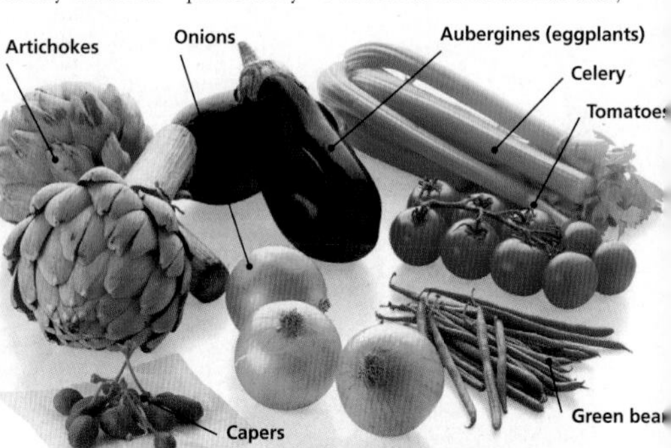

A range of fresh vegetables grown in eastern Spain

REGIONAL DISHES AND SPECIALITIES

The lush Mediterranean coastline, backed by fertile plains and cool mountains, offers an extraordinary abundance of fresh produce here. From the sturdy stews of land-locked Aragón and the traditional cured meats of inland Murcia, to the celebrated seafood paellas and other rice dishes of Valencia, this is a region that dazzles with the variety of its cuisine. Spring and summer bring tiny broad beans, asparagus, and all manner of other vegetables and fruits. In autumn and winter, the annual pig slaughter is followed by the preparation of hams and cured meats, mushrooms proliferate on shady hills, and gamey stews keep out the winter cold. Seafood remains a constant, whether in *zarzuela de mariscos* (a rich shellfish stew), or the Murcian favourite of sea bream baked in a salty crust.

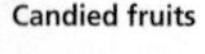

Candied fruits

Suquet de peix *A Catalan stew of fresh, firm-fleshed fish, flavoured with tomatoes, garlic and toasted almonds.*

Spectacular harvest of wild autumn mushrooms in a local market

perhaps unusually so far north, the ancient Arabic heritage can still be tasted in exquisite local sweets and desserts, from candied fruits to heavenly *guirlache*, made from almonds and sugar.

VALENCIA

Valencia, the "Orchard of Spain", is magnificently lush and fertile. Most famous for its oranges, it also produces countless other fruits and vegetables, partnered in local recipes with Mediterranean seafood and mountain lamb, rabbit and pork. In spring, hillsides blaze with cherry and almond blossom and, in autumn, the golden rice fields are spectacular. Spain's signature dish, paella, is a Valencian invention – the local plump *bomba* rice is perfect for soaking up juices.

MURCIA

Tiny, arid Murcia is almost a desert in parts but, thanks to irrigation methods introduced by the Arabs more than a thousand years ago, it has become one of the largest fruit- and vegetable-growing regions in Europe. The mountainous hinterland is famous for its flavoursome *embutidos* (cured meats), especially *morcilla* (black pudding/blood sausage) and *chorizo* (spicy, paprika-flavoured cured sausage), along with excellent rice which has earned its own DO *(denominación de origen)*. Along the coast, you can enjoy a wide range of fresh Mediterranean seafood, including sea bream baked in a salt crust, or lobster stew from the Mar Menor. The Arabic heritage lingers particularly in the desserts, flavoured with saffron, pine nuts and delicate spices.

An *embutidos* (cured meats) producer shows off his wares

ON THE MENU

Arroz Negro A Valencian rice dish; squid ink gives the distinctive dark colour.

Caldero Murciano Fishermen's stew, flavoured with saffron and plenty of garlic.

Dorada a la Sal Sea bream baked in a salty crust to keep the fish moist and succulent.

Fideuá A paella made with shellfish and tiny noodles instead of rice.

Guirlache An Aragonese sweet, made of toasted whole almonds and buttery caramel.

Migas con Tropezones Crusty breadcrumbs fried with garlic, pork and spicy cured sausage.

Paella *In Spain's best-known dish, ingredients include saffron, round* bomba *rice, and meat, fish and shellfish.*

Lentejas al estilo del Alto Aragón *Lentils are slowly cooked with garlic, chunks of ham and black sausage.*

Crema Catalana *This hugely popular dessert is an eggy custard topped with a flambéed sugar crust.*

Wines of Eastern Spain

Spain's eastern seaboard offers a wide spread of wines of different styles. Catalonia deserves pride of place, and here the most important region is Penedès, home of *cava* (traditional-method sparkling wine) and some high-quality still wine. In Aragón, Cariñena reds can be good, and Somontano, in the Pyrenees, has fine, international-style varietals. Valencia and Murcia provide large quantities of easy-drinking reds, whites and *rosados* (rosés). Most notable among these are the rosés of Utiel-Requena, the Valencian Moscatels and the strong, full-bodied reds made in Jumilla.

Cabernet Sauvignon vines

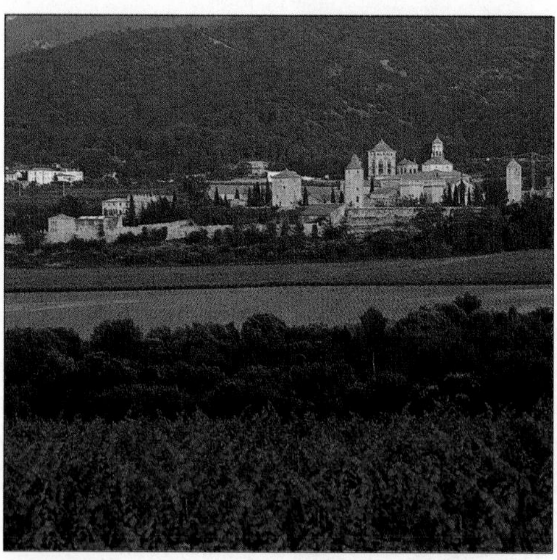

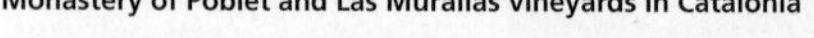

Monastery of Poblet and Las Murallas vineyards in Catalonia

Somontano *has had remarkable success due to the cultivation of international grape varieties such as Chardonnay and Pinot Noir.*

0 kilometres 100

0 miles 50

KEY FACTS ABOUT WINES OF EASTERN SPAIN

Location and Climate

The climate of Eastern Spain varies mainly with altitude – low-lying parts are hot and dry; it also gets hotter the further south you go. The wine regions of Catalonia have a Mediterranean climate along the coast, which becomes drier futher inland. The middle Penedès is a favoured location with a range of climates which suits many grape varieties. Somontano has a cooler, altitude-tempered climate. Valencia and Murcia can be, in contrast, unrelentingly hot.

Grape Varieties

The most common native red grape varieties planted in much of Eastern Spain are Garnacha, Tempranillo – which is called Ull de Llebre in Catalonia – Monastrell and Cariñena. Bobal makes both reds and, to a greater extent, rosés in Utiel-Requena. For whites, Catalonia has Parellada, Macabeo and Xarel·lo (the trio most commonly used for *cava*), while in Valencia, Merseguera and Moscatel predominate. In the regions furthest to the southeast, Airén and Pedro Ximénez are sometimes found. French grape varieties, such as Chardonnay, Merlot, Cabernet Sauvignon and Sauvignon Blanc, flourish in the regions of Penedès, Costers del Segre and Somontano.

Good Producers

Somontano: Viñas del Vero, Viñedos del Altoaragón. ***Alella:*** Marqués de Alella, Parxet. ***Penedès:*** Codorníu, Conde de Caralt, Freixenet, Juvé y Camps, Masía Bach, Mont-Marçal, René Barbier, Miguel Torres. ***Costers del Segre:*** Castell del Remei, Raimat. ***Priorato:*** Cellers Scala Dei, Masía Barril. ***Valencia:*** Vicente Gandía. ***Utiel-Requena:*** C. Augusto Egli. ***Alicante:*** Gutiérrez de la Vega. ***Jumilla:*** Asensio Carcelén (Sol y Luna), Bodegas Vitivino.

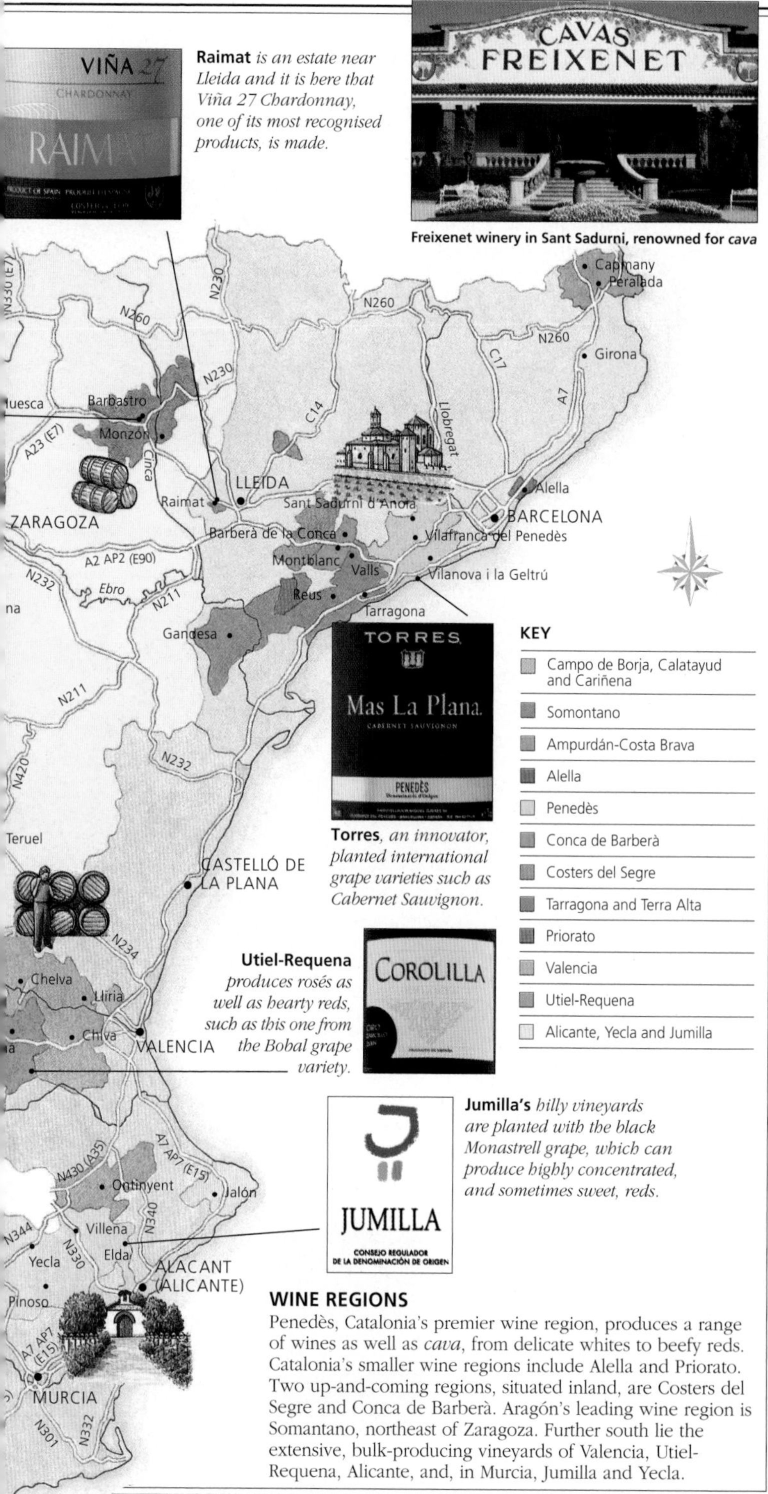

Raimat *is an estate near Lleida and it is here that Viña 27 Chardonnay, one of its most recognised products, is made.*

Freixenet winery in Sant Sadurni, renowned for *cava*

Torres, *an innovator, planted international grape varieties such as Cabernet Sauvignon.*

Utiel-Requena *produces rosés as well as hearty reds, such as this one from the Bobal grape variety.*

Jumilla's *hilly vineyards are planted with the black Monastrell grape, which can produce highly concentrated, and sometimes sweet, reds.*

KEY

- Campo de Borja, Calatayud and Cariñena
- Somontano
- Ampurdán-Costa Brava
- Alella
- Penedès
- Conca de Barberà
- Costers del Segre
- Tarragona and Terra Alta
- Priorato
- Valencia
- Utiel-Requena
- Alicante, Yecla and Jumilla

WINE REGIONS

Penedès, Catalonia's premier wine region, produces a range of wines as well as *cava*, from delicate whites to beefy reds. Catalonia's smaller wine regions include Alella and Priorato. Two up-and-coming regions, situated inland, are Costers del Segre and Conca de Barberà. Aragón's leading wine region is Somantano, northeast of Zaragoza. Further south lie the extensive, bulk-producing vineyards of Valencia, Utiel-Requena, Alicante, and, in Murcia, Jumilla and Yecla.

Flowers of the Matorral

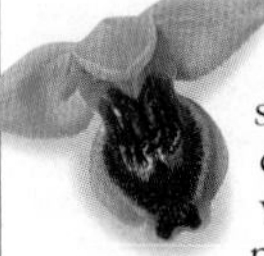
Yellow bee orchid

The Matorral, a scrubland rich in wild flowers, is the distinctive landscape of Spain's eastern Mediterranean coast. It is the result of centuries of woodland clearance, during which the native holm oak was felled for timber and to provide land for grazing and cultivation. Many colourful plants have adapted to the extremes of climate here. Most flower in spring, when hillsides are daubed with pink and white cistuses and yellow broom, and the air is perfumed by aromatic herbs such as rosemary, lavender and thyme. Buzzing insects feed on the abundance of nectar and pollen.

Spanish broom *is a small bush with yellow flowers on slender branches. The black seed pods split when dry, scattering the seeds on the ground.*

Jerusalem sage, *an attractive shrub which is often grown in gardens, has tall stems surrounded by bunches of showy yellow flowers. Its leaves are greyish-white and woolly.*

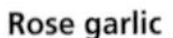

The century plant's flower stalk can reach 10 m (32 ft).

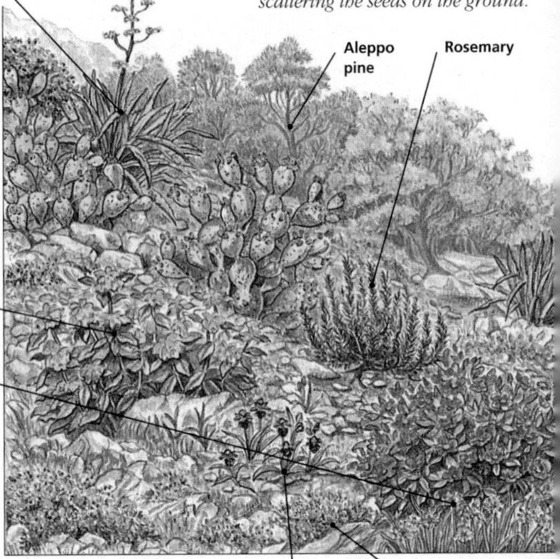

Rose garlic *has round clusters of violet or pink flowers at the end of a single stalk. It survives the summer as the bulb familiar to all cooks.*

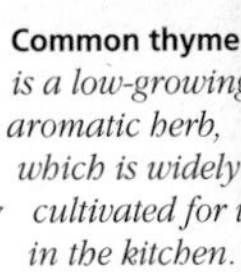
Common thyme *is a low-growin aromatic herb, which is widely cultivated for in the kitchen.*

The mirror orchid, *a small plant that grows on grassy sites, is easily distinguished from other orchids by the brilliant metallic blue patch inside the lip, fringed by brown hairs.*

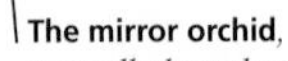

FOREIGN INVADERS

Prickly pear in fruit

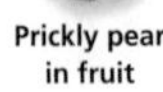

Several plants from the New World have managed to colonize the bare ground of the *matorral*. The prickly pear, thought to have been brought back by Christopher Columbus, produces a delicious fruit which can be picked only with thickly gloved hands. The rapidly growing century plant, a native of Mexico which has tough spiny leaves, sends up a tall flower shoot only when it is 10–15 years old, after which it dies.

Flowering shoots of the century plant

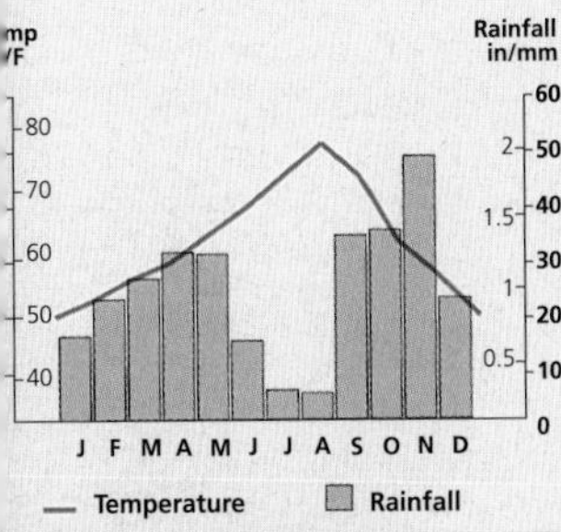

CLIMATE CHART

Most plants found in the *matorral* come into bloom in the warm, moist spring. The plants protect themselves from losing water during the dry summer heat with thick leaves or waxy secretions, or by storing moisture in bulbs or tubers.

Holm oaks *are very common in Eastern Spain. The leaves are tough and rubbery to prevent water loss.*

The strawberry tree *is an evergreen shrub with glossy serrated leaves. Its edible, strawberry-like fruit turns red when ripe.*

Tree heather

Grey-leaved cistus, *growing on sunny sites, has crumpled petals and bright yellow anthers.*

Narrow-leaved cistus *exudes a sticky aromatic gum used in perfumes.*

Star clover *is a low-growing annual whose fruit develops into a star-shaped seed head. Its flowers are often pale pink.*

WILDLIFE OF THE MATORRAL

The animals that live in the *matorral* are most often seen early in the morning, before the temperature is high. Countless insects fly from flower to flower, providing a source of food for birds. Smaller mammals, such as mice and voles, are active only at night when it is cooler and there are few predators around.

Ladder snakes *feed on small mammals, birds and insects. The young are identified by a black pattern like the rungs of a ladder, but adults are marked with two simple stripes.*

Scorpions *hide under rocks or wood by day. When disturbed, the tail is curled quickly over the body in a threatening gesture. The sting, lethal to small animals, can cause some irritation to humans.*

The Dartford warbler, *a skulking bird that has dark plumage and a cocked tail, sings melodiously during its mating display. Males are more vividly coloured than females.*

The swallow-tail butterfly *is one of the most conspicuous of the great many insects living in the* matorral. *Bees, ants and grasshoppers are also extremely common.*

CATALONIA

LLEIDA · ANDORRA · GIRONA BARCELONA PROVINCE · TARRAGONA

Catalonia is a proud nation-within-a-nation, which was once, under the count-kings of Barcelona-Aragón, one of the Mediterranean's great sea powers. It has its own semi-autonomous regional government and its own language, Catalan, which is used in place names, menus and on road signs throughout the region.

The Romans first set foot on the Iberian Peninsula at Empúries on Catalonia's Costa Brava ("wild coast"). They left behind them great monuments, especially in and around Tarragona, the capital of their vast province of Tarraconensis. Later, Barcelona emerged as the region's capital, economically and culturally important enough to rival Madrid.

In the 1960s the Costa Brava became one of Europe's first mass package-holiday destinations. Although resorts such as Lloret de Mar continue to draw the crowds, former fishing villages such as Cadaqués remain relatively unspoiled on this naturally attractive coast.

Inland, there is a rich artistic heritage to be explored. Catalonia has several spectacular monasteries, especially Montserrat, its spiritual heart, and Poblet. There are also many medieval towns, such as Montblanc, Besalú and Girona – which contain a wealth of monuments and museums.

In the countryside there is a lot to seek out, from the wetland wildlife of the Río Ebro delta to the vineyards of Penedès (where most of Spain's sparkling wine is made). In the high Pyrenees rare butterflies brighten remote mountain valleys, and little hidden villages encircle exquisite Romanesque churches.

Aigüestortes i Estany Sant Maurici National Park in the central Pyrenees, in the province of Lleida

◁ **A fisherman inspects his nets in Cadaqués on the Costa Brava**

Exploring Catalonia

Catalonia includes a long stretch of the Spanish Pyrenees, whose green, flower-filled valleys hide picturesque villages with Romanesque churches. The Parc Nacional d'Aigüestortes and Vall d'Aran are paradises for naturalists, while Baqueira-Beret offers skiers reliable snow. Sun-lovers can choose between the rugged Costa Brava or the long sandy stretches of the Costa Daurada. Tarragona is rich in Roman monuments. Inland are the monasteries of Poblet and Santes Creus and the well-known vineyards of Penedès.

Isolated houses in the countryside around La Seu d'Urgell

KEY

- Motorway (highway)
- Other highway
- Main road
- Minor road
- Scenic route
- Main railway
- Minor railway
- International border
- Regional border
- △ Summit

GETTING AROUND

A tunnel near Puigcerdà has made the central Catalan Pyrenees easily accessible. Buses, more frequent in summer, connect most towns. The main north-south railway hugs the coast from Blanes southwards. Other lines run from Barcelona through Vic, Lleida and Tortosa.

SEE ALSO

- *Where to Stay* pp571–4
- *Where to Eat* pp620–24

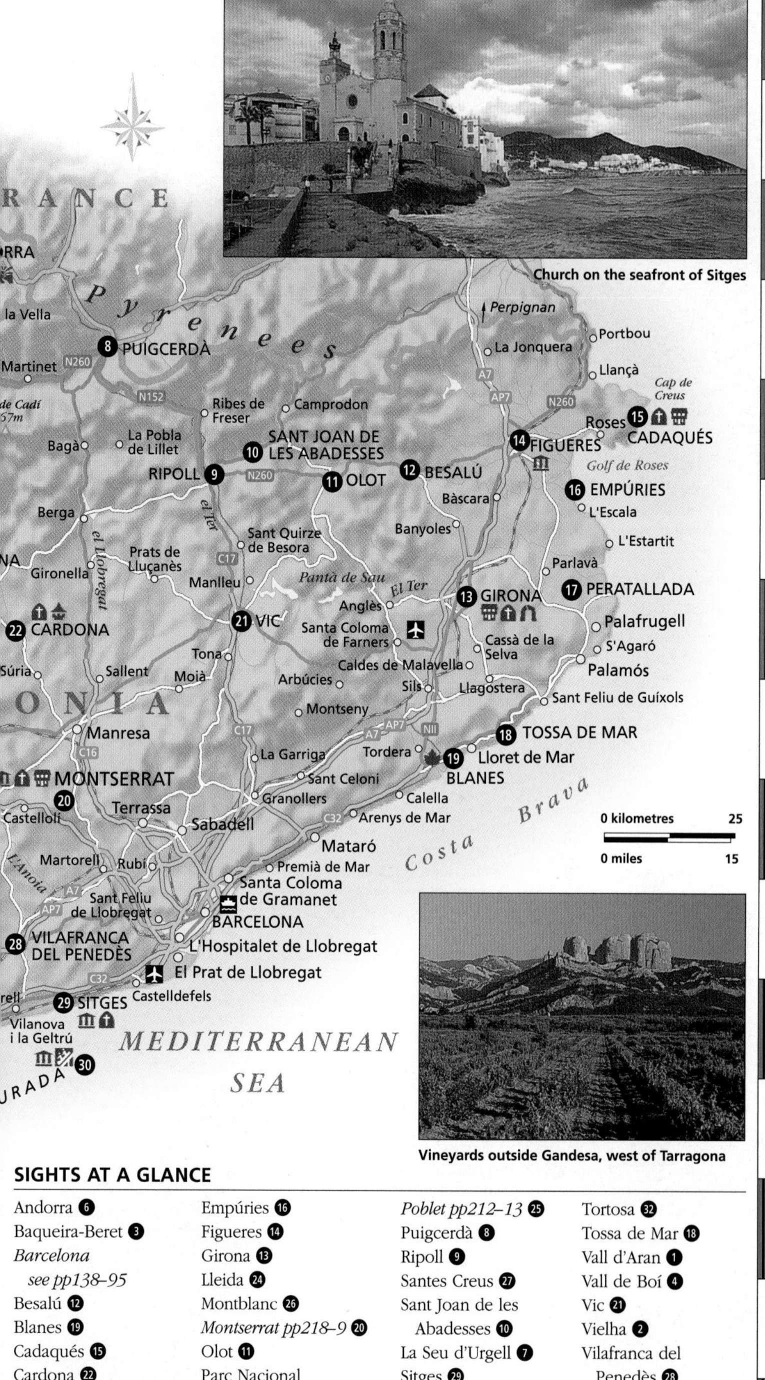

Church on the seafront of Sitges

Vineyards outside Gandesa, west of Tarragona

SIGHTS AT A GLANCE

Andorra 6
Baqueira-Beret 3
Barcelona see pp138–95
Besalú 12
Blanes 19
Cadaqués 15
Cardona 22
Costa Daurada 30
Delta de l'Ebre 33
Empúries 16
Figueres 14
Girona 13
Lleida 24
Montblanc 26
Montserrat pp218–9 20
Olot 11
Parc Nacional d'Aigüestortes 5
Peratallada 17
Poblet pp212–13 25
Puigcerdà 8
Ripoll 9
Santes Creus 27
Sant Joan de les Abadesses 10
La Seu d'Urgell 7
Sitges 29
Solsona 23
Tarragona 31
Tortosa 32
Tossa de Mar 18
Vall d'Aran 1
Vall de Boí 4
Vic 21
Vielha 2
Vilafranca del Penedès 28

The Vall d'Aran, surrounded by the snow-capped mountains of the Pyrenees

BUTTERFLIES OF THE VALL D'ARAN

A huge variety of butterflies and moths is found high in the mountains and valleys of the Pyrenees. In particular, the isolated Vall d'Aran is the home of several unique and rare subspecies. The best time of year to see the butterflies is between May and July.

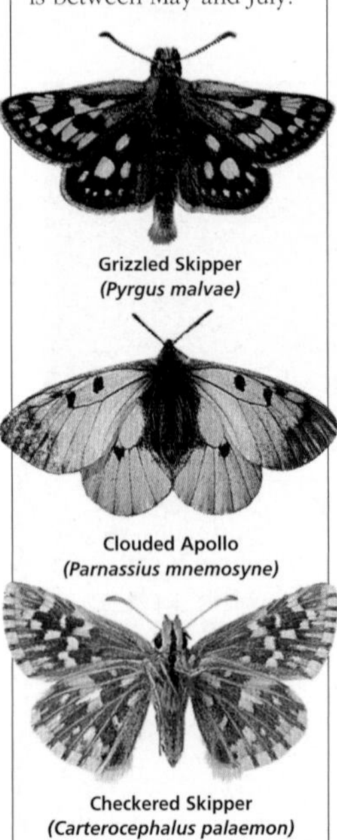

Grizzled Skipper *(Pyrgus malvae)*

Clouded Apollo *(Parnassius mnemosyne)*

Checkered Skipper *(Carterocephalus palaemon)*

Vall d'Aran ❶

Lleida N230. *Vielha.* *Vielha, 973 64 06 88.* **www**.visitvaldaran.com

This Valley of Valleys – *aran* means valley – is a beautiful 600-sq-km (230-sq-mile) haven of forests and flower-filled meadows, surrounded by towering mountain peaks.

The Vall d'Aran was formed by the Riu Garona, which rises in the area and flows out to France as the Garonne. With no proper link to the outside world until 1924, when a road was built over the Bonaigua Pass, the valley was cut off from the rest of Spain for most of the winter. Snow still blocks the narrow pass from November to April, but today access is easy through the Túnel de Vielha from El Pont de Suert.

The fact that the Vall d'Aran faces north means that it has a climate similar to that found on the Atlantic coast. Many rare wild flowers and butterflies flourish in the perfect conditions created by the damp breezes and shady slopes. It is also a noted habitat for many species of narcissus.

Tiny villages have grown up beside the Riu Garona, often around Romanesque churches, notably at **Bossòst**, **Salardú**, **Escunhau** and **Arties**. The valley is also ideal for outdoor sports such as skiing and is popular with walkers.

Vielha ❷

Lleida. *2,000.* *Carrer Sarriulera 10, 973 64 01 10.* *Thu.* *Fiesta de Vielha (8 Sep), Feria de Vielha (8 Oct).*

Now a modern ski resort, the capital of the Vall d'Aran preserves relics of its medieval past. The Romanesque church of **Sant Miquel** has an octagonal bell tower, a tall, pointed roof and a superb wooden 12th-century crucifix, the *Mig Aran Christ*. It once formed part of a larger carving, since lost, which represented the Descent from the Cross. The **Museu de la Vall d'Aran** is a museum devoted to Aranese history and folklore.

Museu de la Vall d'Aran

Carrer Major 26. ***Tel*** 973 64 18 15. Tue–Sun. public hols.

Mig Aran Christ **(12th-century), Sant Miquel church, Vielha**

For hotels and restaurants in this region see pp571–4 and pp620–24

Baqueira-Beret ❸

Lleida. 100. Baqueira-Beret, 973 63 90 10. *Romería de Nuestra Señora de Montgarri (2 Jul).* **www**.baqueira.es

This extensive ski resort, one of the best in Spain, is popular with both the public and the Spanish royal family. There is reliable winter snow cover and a choice of over 40 pistes at altitudes from 1,520 m to 2,470 m (4,987 ft to 8,104 ft).

Baqueira and Beret were separate mountain villages before skiing became popular, but now form a single resort. The Romans took full advantage of the thermal springs located here; nowadays they are appreciated by tired skiers.

Vall de Boí ❹

Lleida N230. *La Pobla de Segur. Pont de Suert. Barruera, 973 69 40 00.* **www**.vallboi.com

This small valley on the edge of the Parc Nacional d'Aigüestortes is dotted with tiny villages, many of which are built around magnificent Catalan Romanesque churches.

Dating from the 11th and 12th centuries, these churches are distinguished by their tall belfries, such as the **Església de Santa Eulàlia** at Erill-la-Vall, which has six floors.

The two churches at Taüll, **Sant Climent** *(see p24)* and **Santa Maria**, have superb frescoes. Between 1919 and 1923 the originals were taken for safekeeping to the Museu Nacional d'Art de Catalunya in Barcelona *(see p172)* and replicas now stand in their place. You can climb the towers of Sant Climent for superb views of the surrounding countryside.

Other churches in the area worth visiting include those at **Coll**, for its fine ironwork, **Barruera**, and **Durro**, which has another massive bell tower.

At the head of the valley is the hamlet of **Caldes de Boí**, popular for its thermal springs and ski facilities. It is also a good base for exploring the Parc Nacional d'Aigüestortes, the entrance to which is only 5 km (3 miles) from here.

The tall belfry of Sant Climent church at Taüll in the Vall de Boí

Parc Nacional d'Aigüestortes ❺

Lleida. *La Pobla de Segur. Pont de Suert, La Pobla de Segur. Boí, 973 69 61 89; Espot, 973 62 40 36.*

The pristine mountain scenery of Catalonia's only national park *(see pp30–31)* is among the most spectacular to be seen in the Pyrenees.

Established in 1955, the park covers an area of 102 sq km (40 sq miles). Its full title is Parc Nacional d'Aigüestortes i Estany de Sant Maurici, named after the lake *(estany)* of Sant Maurici in the east and the Aigüestortes (literally, twisted waters) area in the west. The main access towns are Espot, to the east, and Boi, to the west. Dotted around the park are waterfalls and the sparkling, clear waters of around 150 lakes and tarns which, in an earlier era, were scoured by glaciers to depths of up to 50 m (164 ft).

The finest scenery is around Sant Maurici lake, which lies beneath the twin shards of the Serra dels Encantats, (Mountains of the Enchanted). From here, there is a variety of walks, particularly along the string of lakes that lead north to the towering peaks of Agulles d'Amitges. To the south is the dramatic vista of Estany Negre, the highest and deepest tarn in the park.

Early summer in the lower valleys is marked by a mass of pink and red rhododendrons, while later in the year wild lilies bloom in the forests of fir, beech and silver birch.

The park is also home to a variety of wildlife. Chamois (also known as izards) live on the mountain screes and in the meadows, while beavers and otters can be spotted by the lakes. Golden eagles nest on mountain ledges, and grouse and capercaillie are found in the woods.

During the summer the park is popular with walkers, while in winter, the snow-covered mountains are ideal for cross-country skiing.

A crystal-clear stream, Parc Nacional d'Aigüestortes

THE CATALAN LANGUAGE

Catalan has now fully recovered from the ban it suffered under Franco's dictatorship and has supplanted Castilian (Spanish) as the language in everyday use all over Catalonia. Spoken by more than 9.5 million people, it is a Romance language akin to the Provençal of France. Previously it was suppressed by Felipe V in 1717 and only officially resurfaced in the 19th century, when the Jocs Florals (medieval poetry contests) were revived during the rebirth of Catalan literature. A leading figure of the movement was the poet Jacint Verdaguer (1845–1902).

Catalonia's national emblem

Andorra ❻

Principality of Andorra. *77,000.* *Andorra la Vella.* *Plaça de la Rotonda, Andorra la Vella, 00 376 87 31 03.* **www**.andorra.ad

Andorra occupies 464 sq km (179 sq miles) of the Pyrenees between France and Spain. In 1993, it became fully independent and held its first ever democratic elections. Since 1278, it had been an autonomous feudal state under the jurisdiction of the Spanish bishop of La Seu d'Urgell and the French Count of Foix (a title adopted by the President of France). These are still the ceremonial joint heads of state.

Andorra's official language is Catalan, though French and Castilian are also spoken. The currency changed from the peseta to the euro in 2002.

For many years Andorra has been a tax-free paradise for shoppers, reflected in the crowded shops of the capital **Andorra la Vella**. Les Escaldes (near the capital), as well as Sant Julià de Lòria and El Pas de la Casa (near the Spanish and French borders), have also become shopping centres.

Most visitors never see Andorra's rural charms, which match those of other parts of the Pyrenees. The region is excellent for walkers. One of the main routes leads to the **Cercle de Pessons**, a bowl of lakes in the east, and past Romanesque chapels such as **Sant Martí** at La Cortinada. In the north is the picturesque Sorteny valley where traditional farmhouses have been converted into snug restaurants.

La Seu d'Urgell ❼

Lleida. *13,000.* *Avda Valles de Andorra 33, 973 35 15 11.* *Tue & Sat.* *Festa Major (Aug).*

This ancient Pyrenean town was made a bishopric by the Visigoths in the 6th century. Feuds between the bishops of Urgell and the Counts of Foix over land ownership led to the emergence of Andorra in the 13th century.

The 12th-century **cathedral** has a much venerated Romanesque statue of Santa Maria d'Urgell. The **Museu Diocesà** contains medieval works of art and manuscripts, including a 10th-century copy of St Beatus of Liébana's *Commentary on the Apocalypse (see p110).*

Museu Diocesà
Plaça del Deganat. ***Tel*** *973 35 32 42.* *daily.* *public hols.*

Carving, La Seu d'Urgell cathedral

Puigcerdà ❽

Girona. *9,000.* *Carrer Querol 1, 972 88 05 42.* *Sun.* *Festa de l'Estany (third Sun of Aug).* **www**.puigcerda.com

Puig is Catalan for hill. Although Puigcerdà sits on a relatively small hill compared with the encircling mountains, which rise to 2,900 m (9,500 ft), it nevertheless has a fine view right down the beautiful Cerdanya valley, watered by the trout-filled Riu Segre. Puigcerdà, very close to the French border, was founded in 1177 by Alfonso II as the capital of Cerdanya, which shares a past and its culture with the French Cerdagne. The Spanish enclave of **Llívia**, an attractive little town with a medieval pharmacy, lies 6 km (4 miles) inside France.

Cerdanya is the largest valley in the Pyrenees. At its edge is the nature reserve of **Cadí-Moixeró**, which has a population of alpine choughs.

Portal of Monestir de Santa Maria

Ripoll ❾

Girona. *11,000.* *Plaça Abat Oliba, 972 70 23 51.* *Sat.* *Festa Major (11–12 May).* **www**.ripoll.cat/turisme

Once a tiny mountain base from which raids against the Moors were made, Ripoll is now best known for the **Monestir de Santa Maria**, built in AD 888. The town has been called "the cradle of Catalonia" as the monastery was both the power base and cultural centre of Guifré el Pélos (Wilfred the Hairy), founder of the 500-year dynasty of the House of Barcelona. He is buried in the monastery.

In the later 12th century, the huge west portal gained a series of intricate carvings, which are perhaps the finest Romanesque carvings in Spain. They depict historical and biblical scenes. The two-storey cloister is the only other part of the original monastery to have survived wars and anticlerical purges. The rest is a 19th-century reconstruction.

The medieval town of Besalú on the banks of the Riu Fluvià

Sant Joan de les Abadesses ⓾

Girona. 3,600. Plaza de Abadía 9, 972 72 05 99. Sun. Festa Major (second Sun of Sep). **www**.santjoandelesabadesses.cat

A fine, 12th-century Gothic bridge arches over the Riu Ter to this unassuming market town, whose main attraction is its **monastery**.

Founded in AD 885, it was a gift from Guifré, first count of Barcelona, to his daughter, the first abbess. The church is unadorned except for a superb wooden calvary, *The Descent from the Cross*. Made in 1150, it looks modern; part of it, a thief, was burnt in the Civil War and replaced with such skill that it is hard to tell which is new. The monastery's museum has Baroque and Renaissance altarpieces.

12th-century calvary, Sant Joan de les Abadesses monastery

Environs

To the north is **Camprodon**, a small town full of grand houses, and shops selling local produce. The region is especially noted for its *embutits* (charcuterie).

Olot ⓫

Girona. 32,000. Hospici 8, 972 26 01 41. Mon. Corpus Christi (Jun), Festa del Tura (8 Sep). **www**.turismeolot.com

This small market town is at the centre of a landscape pockmarked with the conical hills of extinct volcanoes. But it was an earthquake in 1474 which last disturbed the town, destroying its medieval past.

During the 18th century the town's textile industry spawned the "Olot School" of art: finished cotton fabrics were printed with drawings, and in 1783 the Public School of Drawing was founded.

Much of the school's work, which includes sculpted saints and paintings such as Joaquim Vayreda's *Les Falgueres*, is in the **Museu Comarcal de la Garrotxa**, housed in an 18th-century hospice. There are also pieces by Modernista sculptor Miquel Blay, whose damsels support the balcony at No. 38 Passeig Miquel Blay.

Museu Comarcal de la Garrotxa
C/ Hospici 8. ***Tel*** *972 27 11 66.*
Tue–Sun. 1 Jan, 25 Dec.

Besalú ⓬

Girona. 2,300. Plaça de la Llibertat 1, 972 59 12 40. Tue. Sant Vicenç (22 Jan), Festa Major (last weekend of Sep). **www**.besalu.cat

A magnificent medieval town, with a striking approach across a fortified bridge over the Riu Fluvià, Besalú has two fine churches. These are the Romanesque **Sant Vicenç** and **Sant Pere**, the sole remnant of Besalú's Benedictine monastery. It was founded in AD 948, but pulled down in 1835.

In 1964 a **mikvah**, a ritual Jewish bath, was discovered. It was built in 1264 and is one of only three of that period to survive in Europe. The tourist office organizes guided visits to all the town's attractions.

To the south, the sky-blue lake of **Banyoles**, where the 1992 Olympic rowing contests were held, is ideal for picnics.

Sausage shop in the mountain town of Camprodon

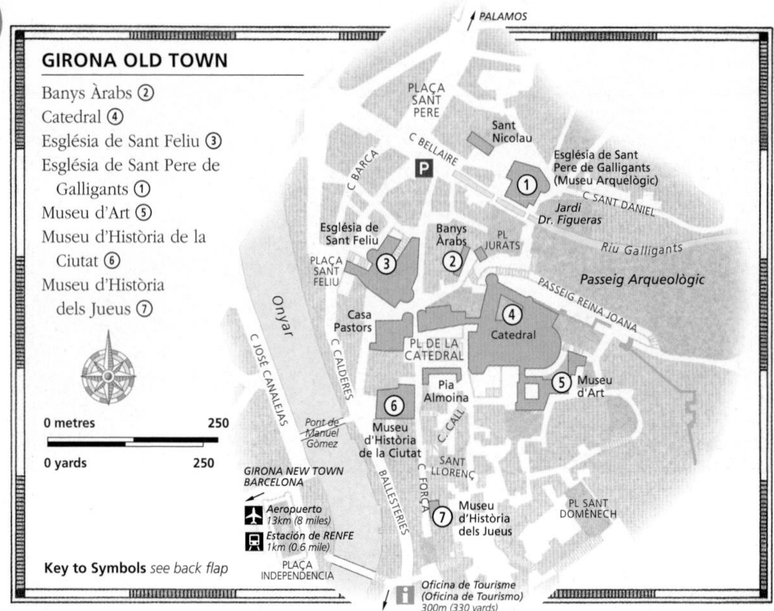

Girona ⑬

Girona. 97,000. *Rambla de la Llibertat 1, 972 22 65 75.* *Tue, Sat.* *Sant Narcís (late Oct).* **www**.girona.cat/turisme

This handsome town puts on its best face beside the Riu Onyar, where tall, pastel-coloured buildings rise above the water. Behind them, in the old town, the Rambla de la Llibertat is lined with busy shops and street cafés.

The houses were built in the 19th century to replace sections of the city wall damaged during a seven-month siege by French troops in 1809. Most of the rest of the ramparts, first raised by the Romans, are still intact and have been turned into the **Passeig Arqueològic** (Archaeological Walk), which runs right around the city.

The starting point of the walk is on the north side of the town, near the **Església de Sant Pere de Galligants** (St Peter of the Cock Crows). The church now houses the city's archaeological collection.

From here a narrow street into the old part of town passes through the north gate, where huge Roman foundation stones are still visible. They mark the route of the Via Augusta, the road that originally ran from Tarragona to Rome. The most popular place of devotion for the people of Girona is the **Església de Sant Feliu**. The church, begun in the 14th century, was built over the tombs of St Felix and St Narcissus, both patrons of the city. Next to the high altar are eight Roman sarcophagi embedded in the apse wall.

Despite their name, the nearby **Banys Àrabs** (Arab Baths), lit by a fine octagonal lantern, were built in the late 12th century, about 300 years after the Moors had left.

Painted houses crowded along the bank of the Riu Onyar in Girona

Museu d'Història dels Jueus

Carrer de la Força 8. ***Tel*** *972 21 67 61.* *daily.* *public hols.* **www**.girona.cat/call

Amid the maze of alleyways and steps in the old town is the former, partially restored, Jewish quarter of El Call. The Museu d'Història dels Jueus gives a history of Girona's Jews, who were expelled in the late 15th century.

Cathedral

Apr–Oct: 10am–8pm daily; Nov–Mar: 10am–7pm daily. **www**.catedraldegirona.org

The style of Girona Cathedral's solid west face is pure Catalan Baroque, but the rest of the building is Gothic. The single nave, built in 1416 by Guillem Bofill, is the widest Gothic span in Christendom. Behind

For hotels and restaurants in this region see pp571–4 and pp620–24

the altar is a marble throne known as "Charlemagne's Chair" after the Frankish king whose troops took Girona in 785. In the chancel is a 14th-century jewel-encrusted silver and enamel altarpiece. Among the Romanesque paintings and statues in the cathedral's museum are a 10th-century illuminated copy of St Beatus of Liébana's *Commentary on the Apocalypse*, and a 14th-century statue of the Catalan king, Pere the Ceremonious.

The collection's most famous item is a large, well-preserved 11th- to 12th-century tapestry, called *The Creation*.

Tapestry of *The Creation*

Museu d'Art

Pujada de la Catedral 12. **Tel** *972 20 38 34. Tue–Sun. 1 & 6 Jan, 25 & 26 Dec.* **www**.museuart.com

This former episcopal palace is one of Catalonia's best art galleries, with works ranging from the Romanesque period to the 20th century. Items from churches destroyed through war or neglect give an idea of church interiors long ago. Highlights are 10th-century carvings, a silver-clad altar from the church at Sant Pere de Rodes and a 12th-century beam from Cruïlles.

Museu d'Història de la Ciutat

Carrer de la Força 27. **Tel** *972 22 22 29. 10am–2pm, 5–7pm Tue–Sat, 10am–2pm Sun.*

The city's history museum is housed in an 18th-century former convent. Parts of the cemetery are preserved, including the recesses where the bodies of members of the Capuchin Order were placed while decomposing. The collection includes old *sardana* *(see p225)* instruments.

Figueres 14

Girona. *45,000. Plaça del Sol, 972 50 31 55. Thu. Santa Cruz (3 May), San Pedro (29 Jun).* **www**.figueres.cat

Figueres is in the north of the Empordà (Ampurdán) region, the fertile plain that sweeps inland from the Gulf of Roses. Every Thursday, the market here fills with fruit and vegetables from the area.

The **Museu del Joguet** (Toy Museum) is housed on the top floor of the old Hotel de Paris, on the Rambla, Figueres' main street. Inside are exhibits from all over Catalonia. At the lower end of the Rambla is a statue of Narcís Monturiol i Estarriol (1819–85), claimed to be the inventor of the submarine.

A much better known son of the town is Salvador Dalí, who founded the **Teatre-Museu Dalí** in 1974. The most visited museum in Spain after the Prado, the galleries occupy Figueras's old main theatre. Its roof has an eye-catching glass dome. Not all the work shown is by Dalí, and none of his best-known works are here.

***Rainy Taxi*, a monument in the garden of the Teatre-Museu Dalí**

But the displays, including *Rainy Taxi* – a black Cadillac being sprayed by a fountain – are a monument to the man who, fittingly, is buried here.

Museu del Joguet

Carrer Sant Pere 1. **Tel** *972 50 45 85. daily.*

Teatre-Museu Dalí

Plaça Gala-Salvador Dalí. **Tel** *972 67 75 00. Jul–Sep: daily; Oct–Jun: Tue–Sun. Mon in winter, 1 Jan, 25 Dec.*
www.salvador-dali.org

THE ART OF DALI

Salvador Dalí i Domènech was born in Figueres in 1904 and mounted his first exhibition at the age of 15. After studying at the Escuela de Bellas Artes in Madrid, and dabbling with Cubism, Futurism and Metaphysical painting, the young artist embraced Surrealism in 1929, becoming the movement's best-known painter. Never far from controversy, the self-publicist Dalí became famous for his hallucinatory images – such as *Woman-Animal Symbiosis* – which he described as "hand-painted dream photographs". Dalí's career also included writing and film-making, and established him as one of the 20th century's greatest artists. He died in his home town in 1989.

Ceiling fresco in the Wind Palace Room, Teatre-Museu Dalí

Cadaqués 15

Girona. 3,000. Carrer Cotxe 1, 972 25 83 15. Mon. Festa Major de Verano (first week of Sep), Santa Esperança (18 Dec).

This pretty resort is overlooked by the Baroque **Església de Santa Maria**. In the 1960s it was dubbed the "St Tropez of Spain", due to the young crowd that sought out Salvador Dalí in nearby Port Lligat. The house where he lived from 1930 until his death in 1989 is known as the **Casa-Museu Salvador Dalí**. Visitors can see the painter's workshop, the library, private bedrooms and the garden area and swimming pool. Book in advance as group visits are permitted only in small numbers. In summer, a "bus-train" takes visitors there from (but not back to) Cadaqués.

Casa-Museu Salvador Dalí
Port Lligat. ***Tel*** *972 25 10 15. Reservations required, email pllgrups@fundaciodali.org 1 Jan, 7 Jan–10 Feb, 25 Dec.*
www.salvador-dali.org

Empúries 16

Girona. L'Escala. ***Tel*** *972 77 02 08. varies with season; check website before visiting. ruins. noon on last Sun of month; book ahead.* **www**.mac.cat

The ruins of this Greco-Roman town *(see p51)* are beside the sea. Three settlements were built between the 7th and 3rd centuries BC: the old town (Palaiapolis); the new town (Neapolis); and the Roman

An excavated Roman pillar in the ruins of Empúries

Looking south along the Costa Brava from Tossa de Mar

town. The **old town** was founded by the Greeks in 600 BC as a trading port. It was built on what was a small island, and is now the site of the hamlet of Sant Martí de Empúries. In 550 BC this was replaced by a town on the shore which the Greeks named Emporion, meaning "trading place". In 218 BC, the Romans landed at Empúries and built a city next to the new town.

A nearby museum exhibits some of the site's finds, but the best are in Barcelona's Museu Arqueològic *(see p172)*.

Peratallada 17

Girona. 400. C/ Unió 2, Ajuntament de Forallac, Vullpellac (972 64 55 22). Fira Peratallada (last weekend in Apr or first in May), Festa Major (6 & 7 Aug), Medieval Market (first weekend in Oct). **www**.forallac.cat

This tiny village is stunning and only a short inland trip from the Costa Brava. With Pals and Palau Sator it forms part of the "Golden Triangle" of medieval villages. Its mountain-top position gives some dramatic views of the area. A labyrinth of cobbled streets wind up to the well-conserved castle and lookout tower, whose written records date from the 11th century. Both counts and kings made doubly sure of fending off any attackers by constructing a sturdy wall enclosing the entire village that even today limits the nucleus from further expansion, ensuring it retains its medieval character.

Tossa de Mar 18

Girona. 6,000. Avinguda Pelegrí 25, 972 34 01 08. Thu. Festa Major d'Hivern (22 Jan), Festa Major d'Estin (29 Jun–2 Jul). **www**.infotossa.com

At the end of a corniche, the Roman town of Turissa is one of the prettiest along the Costa Brava. Above the new town is the **Vila Vella** (old town), a protected national monument. In the old town, the **Museu Municipal** has a collection of local archaeological finds and modern art including *The Flying Violinist*, by the artist Marc Chagall.

Museu Municipal
Plaça Roig i Soler 1.
Tel *972 34 07 09. Tue–Sun.*

Blanes 19

Girona. 40,000. Passeig de Catalunya 21, 972 33 03 48. Mon. El Bilar (6 Apr), Sta Ana (late Jul). **www**.blanes.cat

The working port of Blanes has one of the longest beaches on the Costa Brava, but the highlight of the town is the **Jardí Botànic Mar i Murtra**. These fine gardens, designed by Karl Faust in 1928, are spectacularly sited above cliffs. There are 7,000 species of Mediterranean and tropical plants.

Jardí Botànic Mar i Murtra
Passeig Karl Faust 9. ***Tel*** *972 33 08 26. daily. 1 & 6 Jan, 24 & 25 Dec.*
www.marimurtra.cat

The Costa Brava

The Costa Brava ("wild coast") runs for some 200 km (125 miles) from Blanes northwards to the region of Empordà (Ampurdán), which borders France. It is a mix of pine-backed sandy coves, golden beaches and crowded, modern resorts. The busiest resorts – Lloret de Mar, Tossa de Mar and La Platja d'Aro – are to the south. Sant Feliu de Guíxols and Palamós are still working towns behind the summer rush. Just inland there are medieval villages to explore, such as Peralada, Peratallada and Pals. Wine, olives and fishing were the mainstays of the area before the tourists came in the 1960s.

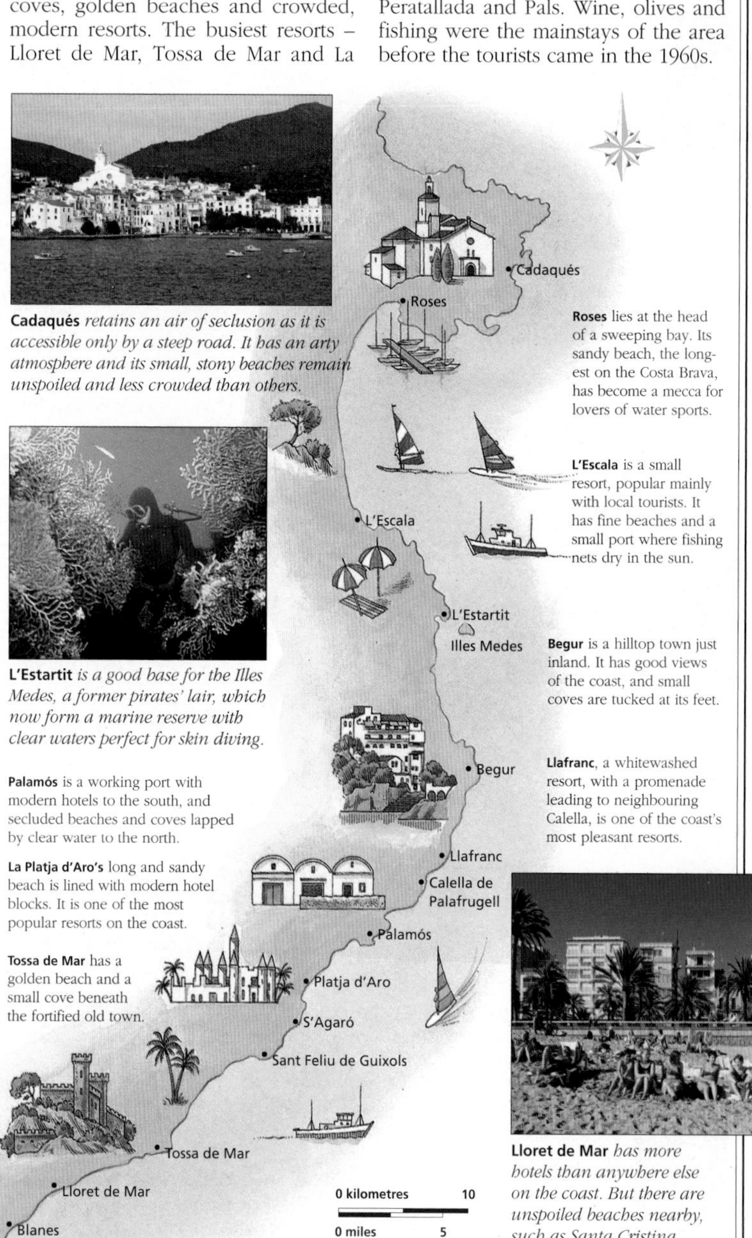

Cadaqués *retains an air of seclusion as it is accessible only by a steep road. It has an arty atmosphere and its small, stony beaches remain unspoiled and less crowded than others.*

Roses lies at the head of a sweeping bay. Its sandy beach, the longest on the Costa Brava, has become a mecca for lovers of water sports.

L'Escala is a small resort, popular mainly with local tourists. It has fine beaches and a small port where fishing nets dry in the sun.

L'Estartit *is a good base for the Illes Medes, a former pirates' lair, which now form a marine reserve with clear waters perfect for skin diving.*

Begur is a hilltop town just inland. It has good views of the coast, and small coves are tucked at its feet.

Palamós is a working port with modern hotels to the south, and secluded beaches and coves lapped by clear water to the north.

Llafranc, a whitewashed resort, with a promenade leading to neighbouring Calella, is one of the coast's most pleasant resorts.

La Platja d'Aro's long and sandy beach is lined with modern hotel blocks. It is one of the most popular resorts on the coast.

Tossa de Mar has a golden beach and a small cove beneath the fortified old town.

Lloret de Mar *has more hotels than anywhere else on the coast. But there are unspoiled beaches nearby, such as Santa Cristina.*

Monestir de Montserrat ⓴

The "Serrated Mountain" *(mont serrat)*, its highest peak rising to 1,236 m (4,055 ft), is a magnificent setting for Catalonia's holiest place, the Monastery of Montserrat, which is surrounded by chapels and hermits' caves. A chapel was first mentioned in the 9th century, the monastery was founded in the 11th century and in 1811, when the French attacked Catalonia in the War of Independence *(see p63)*, it was destroyed and the monks killed. Rebuilt and repopulated in 1844, it was a beacon of Catalan culture during the Franco years. Today Benedictine monks live here. Visitors can hear the Escolania singing the *Salve Regina i Virolai* (the Montserrat hymn) in the basilica at 1pm and 7pm Monday to Friday, 6:45pm Monday to Thursday and noon and 6:45pm on Sundays, except in the summer and during the Christmas period.

A Benedictine monk

Plaça de Santa Maria
The focal points of the square are two wings of the Gothic cloister built in 1477. The modern monastery façade is by Françesc Folguera.

Gothic cloister

Funicular to the holy site of Santa Cova

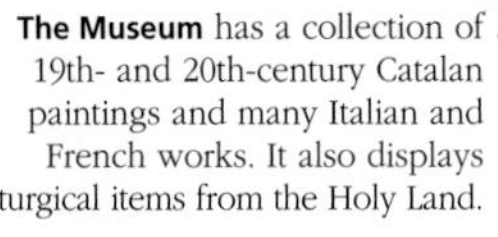

The Museum has a collection of 19th- and 20th-century Catalan paintings and many Italian and French works. It also displays liturgical items from the Holy Land.

The Way of the Cross
This path passes 14 statues representing the stations of the Cross. It begins near the Plaça de l'Abat Oliba.

STAR FEATURES

★ Basilica Façade

★ Black Virgin

View of Montserrat
The complex includes cafés and a hotel. A second funicular transports visitors to nature trails above the monastery.

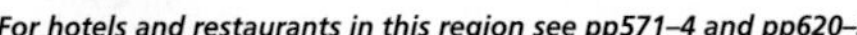

★ Basilica Façade
Agapit and Venanci Vallmitjana sculpted Christ and the apostles on the basilica's Neo-Renaissance façade. It was built in 1900 to replace the Renaissance façade of the original church, consecrated in 1592.

VISITORS' CHECKLIST

Montserrat (Barcelona province). ***Tel*** *93 877 77 01.* *Aeri de Montserrat, then cable car; Monistrol-Enllaç, then La Cremallera rack railway.* *from Barcelona.* **Basilica** *7:30am–8pm daily.* *from 7:30am daily.* **Museum** *10am–5:45pm daily.* **www**.montserratvisita.com

★ Black Virgin
La Moreneta looks down from behind the altar. Protected behind glass, her wooden orb protrudes for pilgrims to touch.

Basilica Interior
The sanctuary in the domed basilica is adorned by a richly enamelled altar and paintings by Catalan artists.

The rack railway (La Cremallera) follows the course of a historic rail line built in 1880.

Cable car to Aeri de Montserrat station

THE VIRGIN OF MONTSERRAT

The small wooden statue of La Moreneta (the dark one) is the soul of Montserrat. It is said to have been made by St Luke and brought here by St Peter in AD 50. Centuries later, the statue is believed to have been hidden from the Moors in the nearby Santa Cova (Holy Cave). Carbon dating suggests, however, that the statue was carved around the 12th century. In 1881 Montserrat's Black Virgin became patroness of Catalonia.

The blackened Virgin of Montserrat

Inner Courtyard
On one side of the courtyard is the baptistry (1902), with sculptures by Carles Collet. Pilgrims may approach the Virgin through a door to the right.

Vic 21

Barcelona. 40,900.
Carrer Ciutat 4, 93 886 20 91.
Tue & Sat. Mercat del Ram (Sat before Easter), Sant Miquel (5–15 Jul), Música Viva (Sep), Mercat Medieval (6–10 Dec). www.victurisme.cat

Market days – Tuesdays and Saturdays – are the best time to go to this small country town. This is when the renowned local sausages *(embotits)* are piled high in the large Gothic Plaça Major, along with other produce from the surrounding plains.

In the 3rd century BC Vic was the capital of an ancient Iberian tribe, the Ausetans. The town was then colonized by the Romans – the remains of a Roman temple survive today. Since the 6th century the town has been a bishop's see. In the 11th century, Abbot Oliva commissioned the El Cloquer tower, around which the cathedral was built in the 18th century. The interior of the cathedral is covered with vast murals by Josep Maria Sert (1876–1945). They are painted in reds and golds, and represent scenes from the Bible.

Adjacent to the cathedral is the **Museu Episcopal de Vic**, which has one of the best collections of Romanesque artifacts in Catalonia. Its large display of mainly religious art and relics includes bright, simple murals and wooden sculptures from rural churches. Also on display are 11th- and 12th-century frescoes.

Cardona dominating the surrounding area from its hilltop site

Museu Episcopal
Plaça Bisbe Oliba. ***Tel*** *93 886 93 60.* *Tue–Sun.* *1 & 6 Jan, Easter Sun, 25 & 26 Dec.*

Cardona 22

Barcelona. 5,100.
Avinguda Rastrillo, 93 869 27 98.
Sun. Festa Major (2nd last Sun of Sep). www.cardona.cat

The 13th-century castle of the dukes of Cardona, constables to the crown of Aragón, is set on the top of a hill. The castle was rebuilt in the 18th century and is now a parador *(see p558)*. Beside the castle is an early 11th-century church, the **Església de Sant Vicenç**, where the dukes are buried.

The castle gives views of the town below and of the Montanya de Sal (Salt Mountain), a huge salt deposit beside the Riu Cardener which has been mined since Roman times.

12th-century altar frontal, Museu Episcopal de Vic

Solsona 23

Lleida. 9,200. Carretera de Bassella 1, 973 48 23 10. Tue & Fri. Carnival (Feb); Corpus Christi (May/Jun), Festa Major (8–11 Sep). www.solsonaturisme.com

Nine towers and three gateways remain of Solsona's fortifications. Inside the walls is an ancient town of noble mansions. The cathedral has a black stone Virgin. The **Museu Diocesà i Comarcal** contains Romanesque paintings and archaeological finds.

Museu Diocesà i Comarcal
Plaça Palau 1. ***Tel*** *973 48 21 01.*
Tue–Sun. *1 Jan, 25 & 26 Dec.*

Lleida 24

Lleida. 138,400.
Plaça Ramón Berenguer IV s/n, 902 10 11 10. Thu & Sat.
Sant Anastasi (11 May), Sant Miquel (29 Sep). www.lleidatur.es

Dominating Lleida (Lérida), the capital of Catalonia's only landlocked province, is **La Suda**, a large, ruined fort taken from the Moors in 1149. The old cathedral, **La Seu Vella**, founded in 1203, is situated within the walls of the fort, high above the town. It was transformed into barracks by Felipe V in 1707 but today, sadly, is desolate. It remains imposing, however, with Gothic windows in the cloister.

A lift descends from the Seu Vella to the Plaça de Sant Joan in the town below. This square is at the mid-point of a busy street sweeping round the foot of the hill. The new cathedral is here, as are manorial buildings such as the rebuilt 13th-century town hall, the **Paeria**.

Poblet 25

See pp222–3.

Montblanc 26

Tarragona. *7,300.* *Antiga Església de Sant Francesc, 977 86 17 33.* *Tue, Fri.* *Setmana Medieval (2 weeks in Apr), Festa Major (8–9 Sep).* **www**.montblanc medieval.org

The medieval grandeur of Montblanc lives on within its walls, said to be Catalonia's finest piece of military architecture. At the **Sant Jordi** gate, St George allegedly slew the dragon. The **Museu Comarcal de la Conca de Barberà** has displays on local crafts.

Museu Comarcal de la Conca de Barberà
Carrer Josa 6. ***Tel*** *977 86 03 49.* *Tue–Sun & public hols.*

Santes Creus 27

Tarragona. *150.* *Plaça de Sant Bernat 1, 977 63 81 41.* *Sat & Sun.* *Sta Llúcia (13 Dec).*

Home to the the prettiest of the "Cistercian triangle" monasteries is the tiny village of Santes Creus. The other two, Vallbona de les Monges and Poblet *(see pp222–3)*, are nearby. The **Monestir de Santes Creus** was founded in 1150 by Ramon Berenguer IV *(see p54)* during his reconquest of Catalonia. The Gothic cloisters are decorated with figurative sculptures, a style first permitted by Jaime II, who ruled from 1291 to 1327. His finely carved tomb, along with that of other nobles, is in the 12th-century church, which has a beautiful rose window.

Monestir de Santes Creus
Tel *977 63 83 29.* *Tue–Sun.* *(free Tue).* *by appt.*

Vilafranca del Penedès 28

Barcelona. *38,700.* *Carrer Cort 14, 93 818 12 54.* *Sat.* *Festa Major (29 Aug–2 Sep).* **www**.vilafranca.cat

This busy market town is set in the heart of Catalonia's main wine-producing region *(see pp202–3)*. The **Vinseum** (Wine Museum), in a 14th-century palace, documents the history of the area's wine trade. Local bodegas can be visited for wine tasting.

Eight km (5 miles) to the north is **Sant Sadurní**, the capital of Spain's sparkling wine, *cava (see pp606–7)*.

Vinseum
Plaça Jaume I. ***Tel*** *93 890 05 82.* *Tue–Sun & public hols.*

Monestir de Santes Creus, surrounded by poplar and hazel trees

Anxaneta* climbing to the top of a tower of *castellers

CATALONIA'S FIESTAS

Human Towers *(various dates and locations)*. The province of Tarragona is famous for its *castellers* festivals, where teams of men stand on each others' shoulders in an effort to build the highest human tower. Each tower, which can be up to seven people high, is topped by a small child called the *anxaneta*. *Castellers* can be seen in action in many towns, especially Vilafranca del Penedès and Valls.

Dance of Death *(Maundy Thu)*, Verges (Girona). Men dressed as skeletons perform a macabre dance.

St George's Day *(23 Apr)*. Lovers give each other a rose and a book on the day of Catalonia's patron saint. The book is in memory of Cervantes, who died on this day in 1616.

La Patum *(Corpus Christi, May/Jun)*, Berga (Barcelona province). Giants, devils and bizarre monsters parade through the town.

Midsummer's Eve *(23 Jun)*. Celebrated all over Catalonia with bonfires and fireworks.

Monestir de Poblet ㉕

The Monastery of Santa Maria de Poblet is a haven of tranquillity and a resting place of kings. It was the first and most important of three Cistercian monasteries, known as the "Cistercian triangle" *(see p221)*, that helped to consolidate power in Catalonia after it had been recaptured from the Moors by Ramon Berenguer IV. The monastery was abandoned and fell into disrepair as a result of the Ecclesiastical Confiscations Act of 1835. Restoration, now largely complete, began in 1930 and monks returned in 1940.

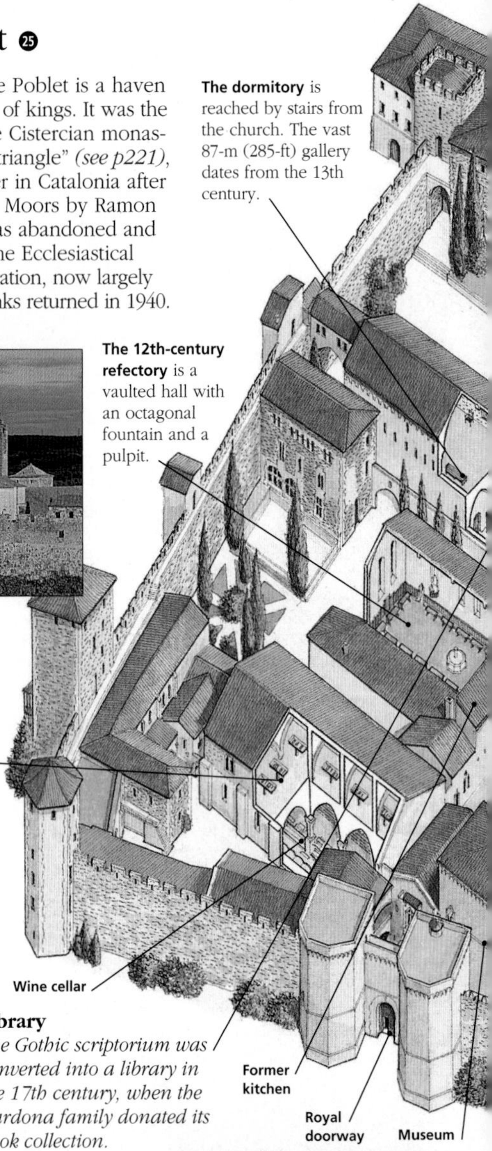

The dormitory is reached by stairs from the church. The vast 87-m (285-ft) gallery dates from the 13th century.

The 12th-century refectory is a vaulted hall with an octagonal fountain and a pulpit.

View of Poblet
The abbey, its buildings enclosed by fortified walls that have hardly changed since the Middle Ages, is in an isolated valley near the Riu Francolí's source.

Museum

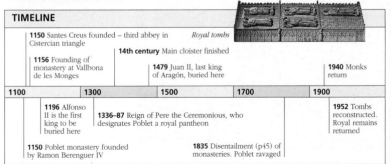

Wine cellar

Library
The Gothic scriptorium was converted into a library in the 17th century, when the Cardona family donated its book collection.

Former kitchen

Royal doorway

Museum

TIMELINE

Royal tombs

- **1150** Poblet monastery founded by Ramon Berenguer IV
- **1150** Santes Creus founded – third abbey in Cistercian triangle
- **1156** Founding of monastery at Vallbona de les Monges
- **1196** Alfonso II is the first king to be buried here
- **14th century** Main cloister finished
- **1336–87** Reign of Pere the Ceremonious, who designates Poblet a royal pantheon
- **1479** Juan II, last king of Aragón, buried here
- **1835** Disentailment (p45) of monasteries. Poblet ravaged
- **1940** Monks return
- **1952** Tombs reconstructed. Royal remains returned

1100 | 1300 | 1500 | 1700 | 1900

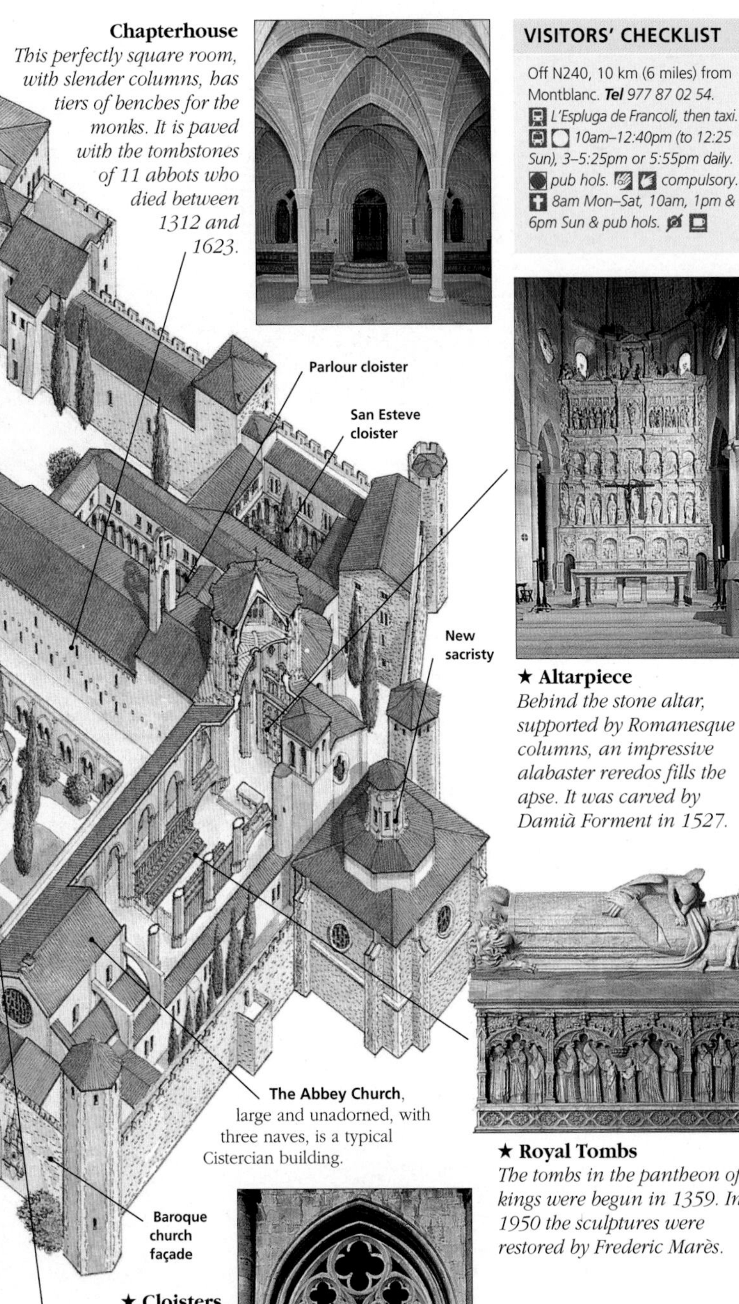

Chapterhouse
This perfectly square room, with slender columns, has tiers of benches for the monks. It is paved with the tombstones of 11 abbots who died between 1312 and 1623.

The Abbey Church, large and unadorned, with three naves, is a typical Cistercian building.

★ Cloisters
The evocative, vaulted cloisters were built in the 12th and 13th centuries and were the centre of monastic life. The capitals are beautifully decorated with carved scrollwork.

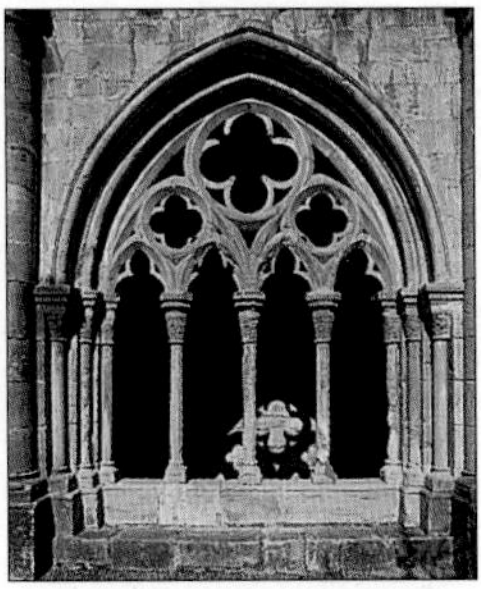

VISITORS' CHECKLIST

Off N240, 10 km (6 miles) from Montblanc. ***Tel*** *977 87 02 54.* *L'Espluga de Francolí, then taxi.* *10am–12:40pm (to 12:25 Sun), 3–5:25pm or 5:55pm daily.* *pub hols.* *compulsory.* *8am Mon–Sat, 10am, 1pm & 6pm Sun & pub hols.*

★ Altarpiece
Behind the stone altar, supported by Romanesque columns, an impressive alabaster reredos fills the apse. It was carved by Damià Forment in 1527.

★ Royal Tombs
The tombs in the pantheon of kings were begun in 1359. In 1950 the sculptures were restored by Frederic Marès.

STAR FEATURES

★ Altarpiece

★ Royal Tombs

★ Cloisters

Palm trees lining the waterfront at Sitges

Sitges ㉙

Barcelona. *28,600.* *C/ Sínia Morera 1 (93 810 93 40).* *Thu.* *Carnival (Feb–Mar), Festa Major (22–27 Aug).* **www**.sitgestour.com

There are no less than nine beaches to choose from at this seaside town. It has a reputation as a gay resort but is just as popular with all. Lively bars and restaurants line its main boulevard, the Passeig Marítim, and there are many examples of *modernista* architecture among the 1970s apartment blocks. Modernista artist Santiago Rusiñol (1861–1931) spent much time here and bequeathed his quirky collection of ceramics, sculptures, painting and ornate iron-work to the **Museu Cau Ferrat**. It lies next to Sitges's landmark, the 17th century church of **Sant Bartomeu i Santa Tecla**.

Museu Cau Ferrat
Carrer Fonollar. ***Tel*** *93 894 03 64.* *closed for restoration; phone before visiting.*

Costa Daurada ㉚

Tarragona. *Calafell, Sant Vicenç de Calders, Salou.* *Tarragona (977 23 34 15).* **www**.costadaurada.info

The long, sandy beaches of the Costa Daurada (Golden Coast) run along the shores of Tarragona province. **El Vendrell** is one of the area's active ports. The **Museu Pau Casals** in Sant Salvador (El Vendrell) is dedicated to the famous cellist. **Port Aventura**, south of Tarragona, is one of Europe's largest theme parks and has many exotically themed attractions, such as Polynesia and Wild West. **Cambrils and Salou** to the south are the liveliest resorts – the others are low-key, family holiday spots.

Museu Pau Casals
Avinguda Palfuriana 67. ***Tel*** *977 68 42 76.* *Tue–Sun.*

Port Aventura
Autovia Salou–Vila-seca. ***Tel*** *902 20 22 20.* *mid-Mar–6 Jan.*

Tarragona ㉛

Tarragona. *140,100.* *Carrer Major 39 (977 25 07 95).* *Tue, Thu & Sun.* *Sant Magí (19 Aug), Santa Tecla (23 Sep).* **www**.tarragonaturisme.cat

Tarragona is now a major industrial port, but it has preserved many remnants of its Roman past. As the capital of Tarraconensis, the Romans used it as a base for the conquest of the peninsula in the 3rd century BC *(see pp50–51)*.

The avenue of Rambla Nova ends abruptly on the clifftop Balcó de Europa, in sight of the ruins of the **Amfiteatre Romà** and the ruined 12th-century church of **Santa Maria del Miracle**.

Nearby is the Praetorium, a Roman tower that was converted into a palace in medieval times. It now houses the **Pretori i Circ Romans**. This displays Roman and medieval finds, and gives access to the cavernous passageways of the excavated Roman circus, built in the 1st century AD. Next to the Praetorium is the **Museu Nacional Arqueològic**, containing the most important collection of Roman artifacts in Catalonia. It has an extensive collection of bronze

The remains of the Roman amphitheatre, Tarragona

tools and beautiful mosaics, including a *Head of Medusa*. Among the most impressive remains are the huge Pre-Roman stones on which the Roman wall is built. An archaeological walk stretches 1 km (half a mile) along the wall.

Behind the wall lies the 12th-century **cathedral**, built on the site of a Roman temple. This evolved over many centuries, as seen from the blend of styles of the exterior. Inside is an alabaster altarpiece of St Tecla, carved by Pere Joan in 1434. The 13th-century cloister has Gothic vaulting, but the doorway is Romanesque.

In the west of town is a 3rd- to 6th-century Christian cemetery (ask about opening times in the archaeological museum).

Ruins of the Palaeo-Christian Necropolis

Environs

The **Aqüeducte de les Ferreres** lies just outside the city, next to the A7 motorway. This 2nd-century aqueduct was built to bring water to the city from the Riu Gaià, 30 km (19 miles) to the north. The **Arc de Berà**, a 1st-century triumphal arch on the Via Augusta, is 20 km (12 miles) northeast on the N340.

The bustling, provincial town of **Reus** lies inland from Tarragona. Although its airport serves the Costa Daurada, it is often overlooked by holiday-makers. However there is some fine *modernista* architecture to be seen here, notably some early work by Antoni Gaudí who was born in Reus. The Pere Mata Psychiatric Institute was designed by Domènech i Montaner before his master-piece, the Hospital de la Santa Creu i de Sant Pau *(see p165)*.

Museu Nacional Arqueològic de Tarragona
Plaça del Rei 5. ***Tel*** *977 23 62 09.*
Tue–Sun. *(senior citizens and under 18s free).* **www**.mnat.es

Pretori i Circ Romans
Plaça del Rei. ***Tel*** *977 24 19 52.*
Tue–Sun.

Tortosa 32

Tarragona. *34,500.* *Plaça Carrilet 1, 977 44 96 48.* *Mon.* *Nostra Senyora de la Cinta (late Aug & early Sep).*
www.tortosaturisme.cat

A ruined castle and medieval walls are clues to Tortosa's historical importance. Sited at the lowest crossing point on the Riu Ebre (Río Ebro), it has been strategically significant since Iberian times. The Moors held the city from the 8th century until 1148. The old Moorish castle, known as La Zuda, is all that remains of their defences. It has been renovated as a parador *(see p573)*. The Moors also built a mosque in 914. Its foundations were used for the cathedral, on which work began in 1347. Although not completed for 200 years, the style is Gothic.

Tortosa was badly damaged in 1938–9 during one of the fiercest battles of the Civil War *(see pp64–7)*, when the Ebre formed the front line between the opposing forces.

Delta de L'Ebre 33

Tarragona. *Aldea.* *Deltebre, Aldea.* *Deltebre 977 48 96 79.*
www.turismedeltebre.com

The delta of the Riu Ebre is a prosperous rice-growing region and wildlife haven. Some 70 sq km (27 sq miles) have been turned into a nature reserve, the **Parc Natural del Delta de L'Ebre**. In Deltebre there is an information centre and an interesting **Eco-Museu**, with an aquarium containing species found in the delta.

The main towns in the area are **Amposta** and **Sant Carles de la Ràpita**, both of which serve as good bases for exploring the reserve.

The best sites for seeing wildlife are along the shore, from the Punta del Fangar in the north to the Punta de la Banya in the south. Everywhere is accessible by car except Illa de Buda. Flamingoes breed on this island and other water birds, such as avocets, can be seen from tourist boats that leave from Riumar and Deltebre.

Eco-Museu
Carrer Martí Buera 22. ***Tel*** *977 48 96 79.* *Tue–Sun.* *1 & 6 Jan, 25 & 26 Dec.*

THE SARDANA

Catalonia's national dance is more complicated than it appears. The success of the Sardana depends on all of the dancers accurately counting the complicated short- and long-step skips and jumps, which accounts for their serious faces. Music is provided by a *cobla*, an 11-person band consisting of a leader playing a three-holed flute *(flabiol)* and a little drum *(tabal)*, five woodwind players and five brass players. When the music starts, dancers join hands and form circles. The Sardana is performed during most local fiestas *(see p221)* and at special day-long gatherings called *aplecs*.

A group of Sardana dancers captured in stone

ARAGÓN

HUESCA · ZARAGOZA · TERUEL

Stretching almost half the length of Spain, and bisected by the Ebro, one of the country's longest rivers, Aragón takes in a wide variety of scenery, from the snow-capped summits of Ordesa National Park in the Pyrenees to the dry plains of the Spanish interior. This largely unsung and undervisited region contains magnificent Mudéjar architecture and many unspoiled medieval towns.

From the 12th–15th centuries Aragón was a powerful kingdom, or, more accurately, a federation of states, including Catalonia. In its heyday, in the 13th century, its dominions stretched across the Mediterranean as far as Sicily. By his marriage to Isabel of Castile and León in 1469, Fernando II of Aragón paved the way for the unification of Spain.

After the Reconquest, Muslim architects and craftsmen were treated more tolerantly here than elsewhere, and they continued their work in the distinctive Mudéjar style, building with elaborate brickwork and patterned ceramic decoration. Their work can be seen in churches all over Aragón and there are outstanding examples in the cities of Teruel and the capital, Zaragoza, Spain's fifth largest city, which stands on the banks of the Ebro.

The highest peaks of the Pyrenees lie in Huesca province. Some of the region's finest sights are in the Pyrenean foothills, which are crossed by the Aragonese variation of the pilgrims' route to Santiago de Compostela. Probably the most spectacular of them is the monastery of San Juan de la Peña – half-concealed beneath a rock overhang – which was founded in the 9th century.

The climate of the region varies as much as the landscape: winters can be long and harsh and summers hot.

A view of the rooftops and medieval walls of Daroca

◁ Torla village church, on the edge of Ordesa National Park

Exploring Aragón

Stone carving, San Juan de la Peña

The landscapes of Aragón range from the high Pyrenees, north of Huesca, through the desiccated terrain around Zaragoza to the forested hills of Teruel province. The cities of Teruel and Zaragoza have some of the most striking Mudéjar monuments in Spain. There are many small, picturesque preserved towns in the region. Ordesa National Park contains stunning mountain scenery, but it can only be visited fully after the snow melts in spring, and even then much of it has to be explored on foot. Pretty Los Valles offers less dramatic but equally enjoyable landscapes and is a popular tourist destination. Other attractive places include the impressively sited Castillo de Loarre and Monasterio de San Juan de la Peña, and the waterfalls of Monasterio de Piedra.

The Puerto de Somport, near Panticosa

SOS DEL REY CATÓLICO 1
N240
Uncastillo
Sádaba
Valareña
Ejea de los Caballeros
Burgos
TARAZONA 15
Parque Natural de Moncayo
16 MONASTERIO DE VERUELA
N122
A68
N232
Gallur
Tauste
Alagón
Tierga
Épila
Torrelapaja
La Almunia de Doña Godina
A2
A23
CALATAYUD 18
Ariza
Ateca
Jalón
Madrid
Cariñena
N234
N330
19 MONASTERIO DE PIEDRA
DAROCA 20
Jiloca
Calamocha
Caminreal
N211
Monreal del Campo
N330
A23
Orihuela del Tremedal
Cella
ALBARRACÍN 27
Montes Universales
TERUEL 26
N330
28

SIGHTS AT A GLANCE

- Agüero 9
- Ainsa 6
- Albarracín 27
- Alcañiz 22
- Alquézar 12
- Benasque 5
- Calatayud 18
- Castillo de Loarre 10
- Daroca 20
- Fuendetodos 21
- Graus 14
- Huesca 11
- Jaca 7
- Monasterio de Piedra 19
- Monasterio de San Juan de la Peña 8
- Monasterio de Veruela 16
- Mora de Rubielos 25
- *Parque Nacional de Ordesa pp232–3* 4
- Puerto de Somport 3
- Rincón de Ademuz 28
- Santuario de Torreciudad 13
- Sierra de Gúdar 24
- Sos del Rey Católico 1
- Tarazona 15
- Teruel 26
- Valderrobres 23
- Los Valles 2
- Zaragoza 17

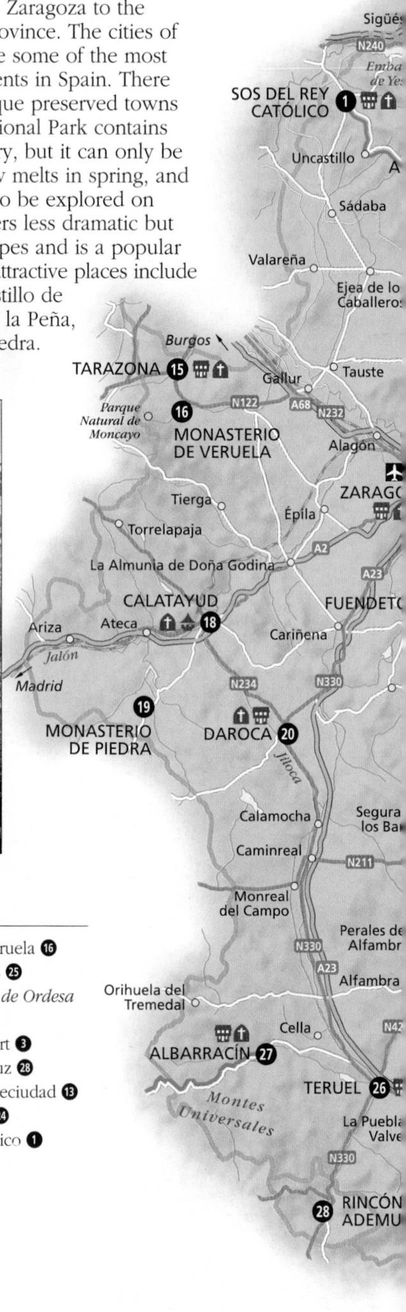

For additional map symbols *see back flap*

GETTING AROUND

Zaragoza is linked by motorway to the Basque Country, Navarra, Madrid and Barcelona. Major roads link the region's main cities with each other, and Teruel with Valencia. Many minor roads have been improved and may be fast and uncongested in the flatter, central areas. The principal railway lines run from Zaragoza to Madrid and Barcelona, both of which are linked by high-speed AVE trains, and to Valencia. Coaches are in-frequent, except between the main population centres. Zaragoza has a small international airport.

KEY

- Motorway
- Motorway under construction
- Major road
- Minor road
- Scenic route
- Main railway
- Minor railway
- International border
- Regional border
- △ Summit

0 kilometres 20

0 miles 20

SEE ALSO

• **Where to Stay** pp574–6

• **Where to Eat** pp624–6

Mudéjar tower of Iglesia de Santa Magdalena, Tarazona

The town hall, Sos del Rey Católico

Sos del Rey Católico ❶

Zaragoza. 660. Palacio de Sada, Madrigal de las Altas Torres s/n, 948 88 85 24 (closed Mon & Tue in winter). Fri. Fiesta Mayor (third week of Aug).

Fernando of Aragón – the so-called "Catholic King" who married Isabel of Castile, thereby uniting Spain *(see pp56–7)* – was born in this small town in 1452, hence its distinguished royal name.

The **Palacio de Sada**, the king's reputed birthplace, with a beautiful inner courtyard, is among the town's grandest stone mansions. It stands in a small square amid a maze of narrow cobbled streets. At the top of the town are the remnants of a castle and the **Iglesia de San Esteban**. The church's font and carved capitals are noteworthy, as are the 13th-century frescoes in two of the crypt's apses. From here there are fine views over the surrounding hills.

The Gothic-arched **Lonja** (commodities exchange) and the 16th-century **town hall** *(ayuntamiento)* are located on the adjacent main square.

Environs

The "Cinco Villas" are five towns recognized by Felipe V for their loyalty during the War of the Spanish Succession *(see p62)*. **Sos del Rey Católico** is the most appealing of these. The others are Ejea de los Caballeros, Tauste, Sádaba and **Uncastillo**. This last town, 20 km (12 miles) to the southeast, has a fortress and a Romanesque church, the Iglesia de Santa María.

Los Valles ❷

Huesca. Jaca. from Jaca to Hecho. Plaza Conde Xiquena 1, Hecho (ayuntamiento) 974 37 50 02.

The delightful valleys of Ansó and Hecho, formed by the Veral and Aragón Subordán rivers respectively, were once isolated due to poor road links. Their villages have retained traditional customs and a local dialect called *cheso*, passed down the generations. Now the area's crafts and costumes have made it popular with tourists. The Pyrenean foothills and forests above the valleys are good for walking, fishing and cross-country skiing.

Ansó lies in the prettiest valley, which becomes a shadowy gorge where the Río Veral and the road next to it squeeze between vertical crags and through rock tunnels. Many of its buildings have stone façades and steep, tiled roofs. The Gothic church (16th century) has a museum dedicated to local costume. Pieces of modern sculpture lie scattered beside the tourist information office of **Hecho**, from an open-air festival previously held in the village. The bucolic village of **Siresa**, which contains the 11th-century church of San Pedro, lies to the north of Hecho.

Puerto de Somport ❸

Huesca. Somport, Astun or Jaca. Pl Ayuntamiento 1, Canfranc, 974 37 30 29 (closed Sun & Mon).

Just inside the border with France, the Somport Pass was for centuries a strategic crossing point for the Romans and Moors, and for medieval pilgrims en route to Santiago de Compostela *(see pp82–3)*. Today the austere scenery is specked with holiday apartments built for skiing. **Astún** is modern and well organized, while **El Formigal**, to the east, is a stylish, purpose-built resort. Non-skiers can enjoy the scenery around the Panticosa gorge. **Sallent de Gállego** is popular for rock-climbing and fishing.

Steep, tiled roofs of Hecho, with a typical pepperpot chimney

Rough and craggy landscape around Benasque

Parque Nacional de Ordesa ❹

See pp232–3.

Benasque ❺

Huesca. 2,200. Calle de San Sebastián 5, 974 55 10 01. Tue. San Pedro (29 Jun), San Marcial (30 Jun). **www**.turismobenasque.com

Tucked away in the northeast corner of Aragón, at the head of the Esera valley, the village of Benasque presides over a ruggedly beautiful stretch of Pyrenean scenery. Although the village has expanded greatly to meet the holiday trade, a sympathetic use of wood and stone has resulted in buildings which complement the existing older houses. A stroll through the old centre filled with aristocratic mansions is a delight.

The most striking buildings in Benasque are the 13th-century **Iglesia de Santa María Mayor**, and the **Palacio de los Condes de Ribagorza**. The latter has a Renaissance façade.

Above the village rises the Maladeta massif. There are magnificent views from its ski slopes and hiking trails. Several local mountain peaks, including **Posets** and **Aneto**, exceed 3,000 m (9,800 ft).

Environs

For walkers, skiers and climbers, the area around Benasque has a great deal to offer. The neighbouring resort of **Cerler** was developed with care from a rustic village into a popular base for skiing and other winter sports.

At Castejón de Sos, 14 km (9 miles) south of Benasque, the road passes through the **Congosto de Ventamillo**, a scenic rocky gorge.

Aínsa ❻

Huesca. 2,000. Cruce de Carreteras, Avda Pirinaica 1, 974 50 07 67. Tue. San Sebastián (20 Jan), Fiesta Mayor (14 Sep).

The capital of the kingdom of Sobrarbe in medieval times, Ainsa has retained its charm. The Plaza Mayor, a broad cobbled square, is surrounded by neat terraced arcades of brown stone. On one side stands the belfry of the **Iglesia de Santa María** – consecrated in 1181 – and on the other the restored castle.

Jaca ❼

Huesca. 13,400. Plaza de San Pedro 11, 974 36 00 98. Fri. La Victoria (first Fri of May), Santa Orosia y San Pedro (25–29 Jun). **www**.jaca.es

Jaca dates back as far as the 2nd century AD. In the 8th century the town bravely repulsed the Moors – an act which is commemorated in the festival of La Victoria – and in 1035 became the first capital of the kingdom of Aragón. Jaca's 11th-century **cathedral**, one of Spain's oldest, is much altered inside. Traces of its original splendour can be seen on the restored south porch and doorway, where carvings depict biblical scenes. The dim nave and chapels are decorated with ornate vaulting and sculpture. A museum of sacred art, in the cloisters, contains a collection of Romanesque and Gothic frescoes and sculptures from local churches. The streets that surround the cathedral form an attractive quarter.

Sculpture in Jaca cathedral

Jaca's only other significant tourist sight is its 16th-century **citadel**, a fort decorated with corner turrets, on the edge of town. Today the town serves as a principal base for the Aragonese Pyrenees.

The arcaded main square of Ainsa with the Iglesia de Santa María

Parque Nacional de Ordesa ❹

Signpost in Ordesa National Park

Within its borders the Parque Nacional de Ordesa y Monte Perdido combines all the most dramatic elements of Spain's Pyrenean scenery. At the heart of the park are four glacial canyons – the Ordesa, Añisclo, Pineta and Escuain valleys – which carve the great upland limestone massifs into spectacular cliffs and chasms. Most of the park is accessible only on foot: even then, snow during autumn and winter makes it inaccessible to all except those with specialist climbing equipment. In high summer, however, the crowds testify to the park's well-earned reputation as a paradise for walkers and nature lovers alike.

Valle de Ordesa
The Río Arazas cuts through foreste limestone escarpments, providing some of Ordesa's most popular walk.

Torla
This village, at the gateway to the park, huddles beneath the forbidding slopes of Mondarruego. With its core of cobbled streets and slate-roofed houses around the church, Torla is a popular base for visitors to Ordesa.

0 kilometres 2

0 miles 2

KEY

- Major road
- Minor road
- Footpath
- Spanish/French border
- National park boundary
- Tourist information
- Viewpoint

PYRENEAN WILDLIFE

Ordesa is a spectacle of flora and fauna, with many of its species unique to the region. Trout streams rush along the valley floor, where slopes provide a mantle of various woodland harbouring creatures such as otters, marmots and capercaillies (large grouse). On the slopes, flowers burst out before the snow melts, with gentians and orchids sheltering in crevices and edelweiss braving the most hostile crags. Higher up, the Pyrenean chamois is still fairly common; but the Ordesa ibex, or mountain goat, became extinct in 2000. Attempts to resurrect it by cloning have had little success so far. The rocky pinnacles above the valley are the domain of birds of prey, among them the huge bearded vulture.

Spring gentian *(Gentiana verna)*

For hotels and restaurants in this region see pp574–6 and pp624–6

View from Parador de Bielsa
The parador (see p574), *at the foot of Monte Perdido, looks out at stunning sheer rock faces streaked by waterfalls.*

VISITORS' CHECKLIST

Visitors' centre (open all year), Torla, 974 48 64 72. change at Sabiñánigo for Torla. Sabiñánigo. **www**.ordesa.net

Cola de Caballo
The 70-m (230-ft) "Horse's Tail" waterfall makes a scenic stopping point near the northern end of the long hike around the Circo Soaso. It provides a taste of the spectacular scenery found along the route.

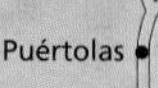

Cañon or Garganta de Añisclo
A wide path leads along this beautiful, steep-sided gorge, following the wooded course of the turbulent Río Vellos through dramatic limestone scenery.

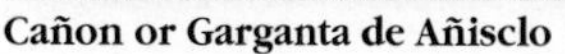

Hikers in Ordesa National Park

TIPS FOR WALKERS

Several well-marked trails follow the valleys and can be easily tackled by anyone reasonably fit, though walking boots are a must. The mountain routes may require climbing gear so check first with the visitors' centre and get a detailed map. Pyrenean weather changes rapidly – beware of ice and snow early and late in the season. Overnight camping is permitted, but only for a single night above certain altitudes.

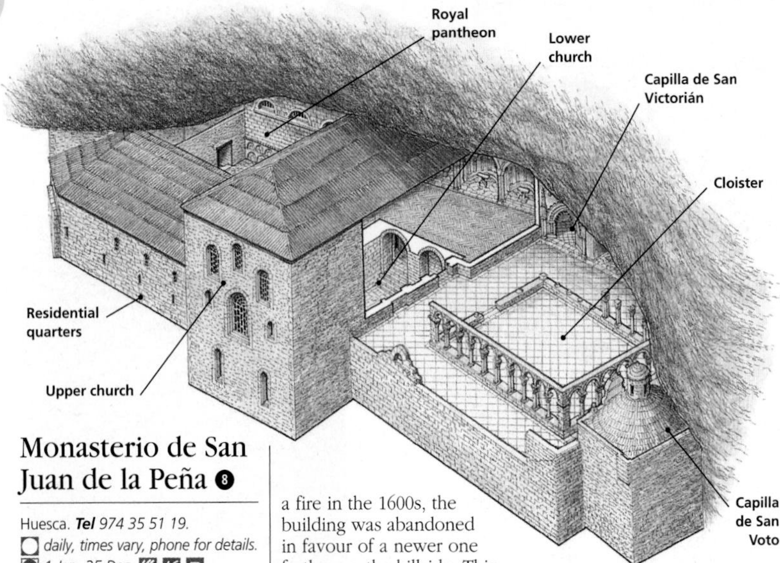

Monasterio de San Juan de la Peña ❽

Huesca. ***Tel*** *974 35 51 19.*
daily, times vary, phone for details.
1 Jan, 25 Dec.
www.monasteriosanjuan.com

Set under a bulging rock, this monastery was an early guardian of the Holy Grail *(see p250)*. In the 11th century it underwent reformation in Cluniac style, and was the first monastery to introduce the Latin Mass in Spain. After a fire in the 1600s, the building was abandoned in favour of a newer one further up the hillside. This was later sacked by Napoleon's troops. It has been restored to house a four-star hotel and interpretation centre.

The church of the old monastery is on two floors. The lower one is a primitive rock-hewn crypt built in the early 10th century. The upper floor contains an 11th-century church with a simple triple apse hollowed out of the side of the cliff. The well-preserved Romanesque pantheon contains the stacked tombs of the early Aragonese kings. The exterior cloister is San Juan de la Peña's *pièce de résistance*, the capitals of its columns carved with biblical scenes.

Agüero ❾

Huesca. *160.* *San Jaime 1, 974 38 04 89.* *San Blas (3 Feb), San Roque (16 Aug).* **www**.aytoaguero.es

The picturesque setting of this attractive village, clustered against a dramatic crag of eroded pudding stone, amply rewards a brief detour from the main road. The most important reason for visiting Agüero, however, is to see the 12th-century **Iglesia de Santiago**. This Romanesque church is reached by a long stony track leading uphill just before the village.

The capitals of the columns in this unusual triple-naved building are carved with fantastical beasts as well as scenes from the life of Jesus and the Virgin Mary. The beautiful carvings on the doorway display biblical events, including scenes from the Epiphany and Salome dancing ecstatically. The lively, large-eyed figures are attributed to the mason responsible for the superb carvings in the monastery at San Juan de la Peña.

Village of Agüero, situated under a rocky crag

Castillo de Loarre ❿

Loarre (Huesca). ***Tel*** *974 34 21 61.*
Ayerbe. *from Huesca.*
daily. *1 Jan, 25 Dec.*
www.castillodeloarre.es

The ramparts of this fortress stand majestically above the road from Ayerbe. The fortress is so closely moulded around the contours of a rock that in poor visibility it could be easily mistaken for a natural outcrop. It was used as a set for Ridley Scott's film *Kingdom of Heaven* (2005). On a clear day, the hilltop setting is stupendous, with clear views of the surrounding orchards and reservoirs of the Ebro plain. Inside the curtain walls lies a complex founded in the 11th century on the site of what had originally been a Roman settlement. It was later remodelled under Sancho I (Sancho Ramírez) of Aragón, who established a religious community here, placing the complex under the rule of the Order of St Augustine.

Within the castle walls is a Romanesque church with carved capitals, a chequered frieze and alabaster windows.

Sentry paths, iron ladders and flights of steps ramble precariously around the castle's towers, dungeons and keep.

The formidable Castillo de Loarre looming above the surrounding area

Huesca ⓫

Huesca. 52,000. *Plaza López Allué, 974 29 21 70.* *Tue, Thu & Sat.* *San Vicente (22 Jan); San Lorenzo (9–15 Aug).*

Altarpiece by Damià Forment, in Huesca cathedral

Founded in the 1st century BC, the independent state of Osca (present-day Huesca) had a senate and an advanced education system. From the 8th century, the area grew into a Moorish stronghold. In 1096 it was captured by Peter of Aragón and was the region's capital until 1118, when the title passed to Zaragoza.

Huesca is now the provincial capital. The pleasant old town has a Gothic **cathedral**. The eroded west front is surmounted by an unusual wooden gallery in Mudéjar style. Above the nave is slender-ribbed star vaulting studded with golden bosses. The cathedral's best feature is an alabaster altarpiece by the master sculptor, Damià Forment. On the altarpiece, a series of energetic Crucifixion scenes in relief are highlighted by illumination.

Opposite the cathedral is the Renaissance **town hall** *(ayuntamiento)*. Inside hangs *La Campana de Huesca*, a gory 19th-century painting depicting the town's most memorable event: the beheading of a group of troublesome nobles in the 12th century by order of King Ramiro II. The massacre occurred in the former Palacio de los Reyes de Aragón, later the university and now the superb **Museo Arqueológico Provincial**, containing archaeological finds and a collection of art.

Museo Arqueológico Provincial
Plaza de la Universidad 1. ***Tel*** *974 22 05 86.* *10am–2pm, 5–8pm Tue–Sat, 10am–2pm Sun & pub hols.* *1 & 6 Jan, 24, 25 & 31 Dec.*

Alquézar ⓬

Huesca. *300.* *Calle Nueva 14, 974 31 89 40.* *San Sebastián (20 Jan), San Ipolito (12 Aug).*

This Moorish village attracts much attention because of its spectacular setting. Its main monument, the stately 16th-century **collegiate church**, dominates a hill jutting above the strange rock formations of the canyon of the Río Vero. Inside, the church's cloisters have capitals carved with biblical scenes. Next to it is the chapel built after Sancho I recaptured Alquézar from the Moors. Nearby are the ruined walls of the original *alcazar*, which gives the village its name.

Santuario de Torreciudad ⓭

Huesca. ***Tel*** *974 30 40 25.* *to El Grado from Barbastro.* *daily.* **www**.torreciudad.org

This shrine was built to honour the devotion of the founder of the Catholic lay order of Opus Dei – San Jose María Escrivá de Balaguer – to the Virgin. It occupies a promontory with picturesque views over the waters of the **Embalse de El Grado** at Torreciudad. The huge church is made of angular red brick in a stark, modern design.

Inside, the elaborate modern altarpiece of alabaster, sheltering a glittering Romanesque Virgin, is in contrast to the bleak, functional nave.

Environs

The town of **Barbastro**, 30 km (18 miles) to the south, has an arcaded *plaza mayor* and a 16th-century cathedral with an altar by Damià Forment.

The ruins of Alquézar Castle, rising above the village

Houses with frescoed façades on the Plaza de España, Graus

Graus ⓮

Huesca. 4,000. Plaza de la Compañià 1, 974 54 00 01. Mon. San Antonio (19 Jan), Santa Agneda (5 Feb), San Miguel (29 Sep–1 Oct). **www**.turismograus.com

In the heart of Graus's old town is the unusual **Plaza de España**, surrounded by stone arcades and columns. It has brightly frescoed half-timbered houses and a 16th-century city hall. The home of the infamous Tomás de Torquemada *(see p56)* is in the narrow streets of the old quarter. At fiesta time, Graus is a good spot to see Aragonese dancing.

Environs
About 20 km (12 miles) north-east, the hill village of **Roda de Isábena** is the smallest village in Spain to boast a cathedral. Dating from 1067, this striking building has a 12th-century cloister off which is a chapel with 13th-century frescoes. North of the village is the picturesque Isábena valley.

Tarazona ⓯

Zaragoza. 10,700. Plaza San Francisco 1, 976 64 00 74. every other Thu. San Atilano (27 Aug–1 Sep). **www**.tarazona.es

Mudejar towers stand high above the earth-coloured, mottled pantiles of this ancient bishopric. On the outskirts of the old town is the **cathedral**, all turreted finials and pierced brickwork with Moorish cloister tracery and Gothic tombs. In the upper town on the other side of the river, more churches, in typical Mudéjar style, can be found amid the maze of narrow hilly streets. More unusual perhaps are the former bullring, now a circular plaza enclosed by houses, and the splendid Renaissance **town hall** *(ayuntamiento)*. The town hall, built of golden stone, has a façade carved with mythical giants and a frieze showing Carlos V's homage to Tarazona.

Monasterio de Veruela ⓰

Vera de Moncayo (Zaragoza). ***Tel*** *976 64 90 25. Vera de Moncayo. Wed–Mon. by appt.*

This isolated Cistercian retreat, set in the green Huecha valley near the Sierra de Moncayo, is one of the greatest monasteries in Aragón. Founded in the 12th century by French monks, the huge abbey church has a mixture of Romanesque and Gothic features. Worn green and blue Aragonese tiles line the floor of its handsomely vaulted triple nave. The well-preserved cloisters sprout exuberantly decorated beasts, heads of human beings and foliage in the Gothic style *(see p24)*. The plain, dignified chambers make a suitable venue for art exhibitions in the summer.

Environs
In the hills to the west the small **Parque Natural de Moncayo** rises to a height of 2,315 m (7,600 ft). Streams race through the woodland of this nature reserve, which throngs with bird life. A tortuous potholed road leads to a chapel at 1,600 m (5,250 ft).

Zaragoza ⓱

Zaragoza. 666,000. Plaza del Pilar, 902 14 20 08. Wed & Sun. San Valero (29 Jan), Cincomarzada (5 Mar), San Jorge (23 Apr), Virgen del Pilar (12 Oct). **www**.zaragoza.es/turismo

A Celtiberian settlement called Salduba existed on the site of the present city; but it is from the Roman settlement of Cesaraugusta that Zaragoza takes its name. Its location on the fertile banks of the Río Ebro ensured its ascendancy, now Spain's fifth largest city and the capital of Aragón.

Badly damaged during the War of Independence *(see p62)*, the city was largely rebuilt but the old centre retains some interesting buildings. Most of the main sights are grouped around Plaza del Pilar. The most impressive of

Entrance and tower of the Monasterio de Veruela

them is the **Basílica de Nuestra Señora del Pilar**, with its huge church sporting 11 brightly tiled cupolas. Inside, the Santa Capilla (Lady Chapel) by Ventura Rodríguez contains a small statue of the Virgin on a pillar amid a blaze of silver and flowers. Her skirt-like *manta* is changed every day, and pilgrims pass behind the chapel to kiss an exposed part of the pillar. The basílica also has frescoes by Goya.

Nearby, on the square, stand the **town hall** *(ayuntamiento)*, the 16th-century Renaissance **Lonja** (commodities exchange) and the **Palacio Arzobispal**.

Occupying the east end of the square is Zaragoza's cathedral, **La Seo**, displaying a great mix of styles. Part of the exterior is faced with typical Mudéjar brick and ceramic decoration, and inside are a fine Gothic reredos and splendid Flemish tapestries.

Close by is the flamboyant Mudéjar bell tower of the **Iglesia de la Magdalena**, and remains of the Roman forum. Parts of the **Roman walls** can also be seen at the opposite side of the Plaza del Pilar, near the **Mercado de Lanuza**, a market with sinuous ironwork in Art Nouveau style.

Some of the cupolas of the Basílica de Nuestra Señora del Pilar

The **Museo Camón Aznar** in the Pardo's Palace exhibits the eclectic collection of a wealthy local art historian, whose special interest was Goya. The top floor contains a collection of his etchings. Minor works by artists of other periods can be seen, as well as good contemporary art. The **Museo de Zaragoza** has a Goya room and archaeological artifacts.

The **Museo Pablo Gargallo** is a showroom for the Aragonese sculptor after whom it is named, who was active at the beginning of the 20th century. One of the most important monuments in Zaragoza lies on the busy road to Bilbao. The **Aljafería** is an enormous Moorish palace built in the 11th century. A courtyard of lacy arches surrounds a sunken garden and a small mosque.

Museo Camón Aznar
Calle Espoz y Mina 23. ***Tel*** *976 39 73 28.* *Tue–Sun.*

Museo de Zaragoza
Plaza de los Sitios 6. ***Tel*** *976 22 58 62.* *Tue–Sun.*

Museo Pablo Gargallo
Plaza de San Felipe 3. ***Tel*** *976 72 49 22.* *Tue–Sun.*

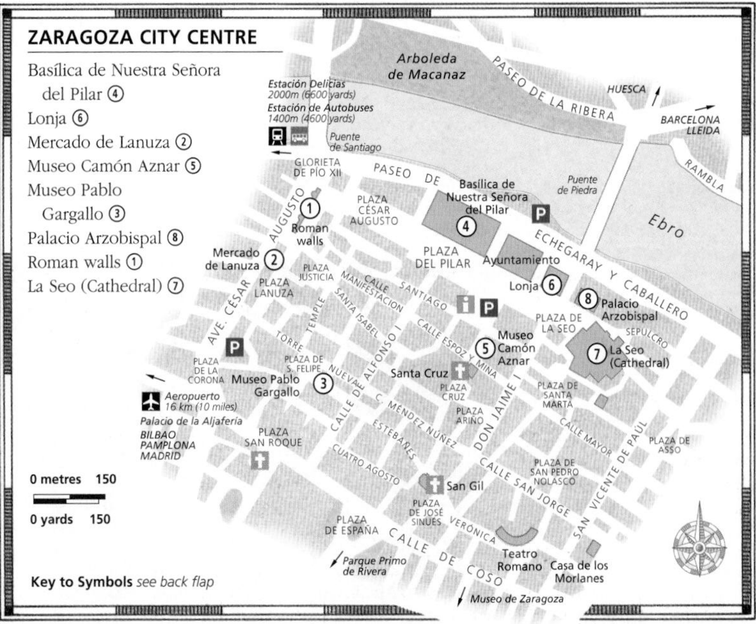

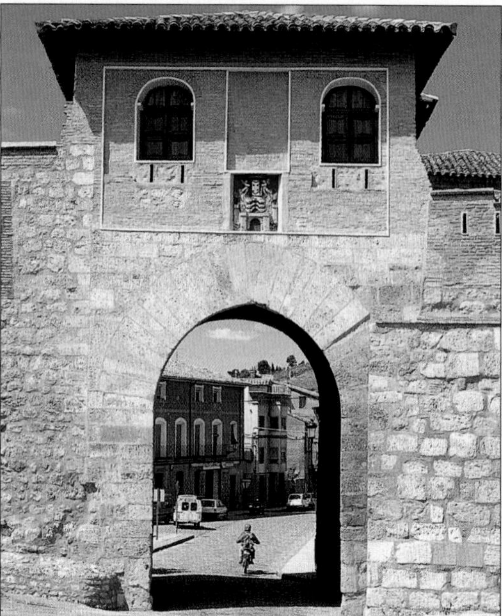
Gateway through the medieval walls of Daroca

Calatayud 18

Zaragoza. 21,900.
Plaza del Fuerte, 976 88 63 22.
Tue. San Roque (14–17 Aug), Virgen de la Peña (6–10 Sep).

The huge Moorish fortress and minaret-like church towers are visible from miles around. Only ruins are left of the 8th-century Arab castle of the ruler, Ayub, which gave the town its name. The church of **Santa María la Mayor** has a Mudéjar tower and an elaborate façade in the Plateresque style. The 17th-century Baroque-style church of **San Juan Real** holds paintings by Goya.

The ruins of the Roman settlement of Bílbilis are east of Calatayud, near Huérmeda.

Monasterio de Piedra 19

3 km (2 miles) south of Nuévalos.
Tel 976 84 90 11. Calatayud.
from Zaragoza. daily.
www.monasteriopiedra.com

Built on the site of a Moorish castle conquered by Alfonso II of Aragón and given to Cistercian monks in the 12th century, this monastery was damaged in the 19th century and subsequently rebuilt. Some of the 12th-century buildings remain, including the chapter-house, refectory and hostel.

In the damp cellars, the monks once distilled strong potions of herbal liqueur. This was allegedly the first place in Europe where drinking chocolate, from Mexico, was made *(see p59)*, and there is now a chocolate exhibition.

The park in which the monastery stands is a nature reserve full of grottoes and waterfalls. A hotel is now located in the old monastery buildings.

Daroca 20

Zaragoza. 2,300. Plaza de España 4, 976 80 01 29. Thu.
Santo Tomás (7 Mar).

An impressive array of battlemented medieval walls stretches approximately 4 km (2 miles) around this old Moorish stronghold. Although parts of the walls have decayed, some of the 114 towers and gateways are still a remarkable sight, particularly from the main road to Zaragoza.

The **Colegial de Santa María**, a church in the Plaza España, houses the Holy Cloths from the Reconquest *(see pp54–5)*. After a surprise attack by the Moors in 1239, priests celebrating Mass bundled the consecrated bread into the linen sheets used for the altar. Upon being unwrapped, the cloths were miraculously stained with blood.

Environs

The agricultural town of **Monreal del Campo**, 42 km (26 miles) south of Daroca, has a saffron museum. Towards Molina de Aragón, 20 km (12 miles) from Daroca, is the **Laguna de Gallocanta**, a lake and wildlife refuge.

Fuendetodos 21

Zaragoza. 180. Calle Cortes de Aragón 7, 976 14 38 67. San Roque (last Sat of May), San Bartolomé (24 Aug). **www**.fuendetodos.org

This small village was the birthplace of one of Spain's best-known artists of the late

Interior of Goya's cottage in Fuendetodos

Castle-parador above Alcañiz

18th and early 19th centuries, Francisco de Goya. The **Casa-Museo de Goya** is a neat cottage said to have been the painter's home. It has been restored and furnished in a style appropriate for the period.

Environs

Lying 14 km (9 miles) east of Fuendetodos is **Belchite**, the site of one of the most horrific battles of the Spanish Civil War *(see pp66–7)*, for control of the strategic Ebro valley. Remains of the old, shell-torn town have been left tottering as a monument to the horrors of war.

In **Cariñena**, 25 km (16 miles) west of Fuendetodos, bodegas offer the opportunity to sample and buy the excellent, full-bodied red wine for which the region is justly renowned *(see pp202–3)*.

Casa-Museo de Goya
Calle Zuloaga 3. ***Tel*** *976 14 38 30.*
11am–2pm, 4–7pm Tue–Sun.

Alcañiz 22

Teruel. *16,300.* *Calle Mayor 1, 978 83 12 13.* *Tue.*
Fiestas Patronales (8–13 Sep).
www.alcaniz.es

Two buildings rise above the town of Alcañiz. One is the **castle**, once the headquarters of the Order of Calatrava. This historic building has been converted into a parador *(see p574)*. The keep, the Torre del Homenaje, has a collection of 14th-century frescoes depicting the conquest of Valencia by Jaime I.

The other building is the **Iglesia de Santa María**. This church, on the sloping Plaza de España, has a Gothic tower and a Baroque façade.

On the same square are the elegantly galleried **Lonja** (commodities exchange), with its lacy Gothic arches, and the **town hall** *(ayuntamiento)*, with one Mudéjar and one Renaissance façade.

FRANCISCO DE GOYA

Self-portrait by Goya

Born in Fuendetodos in 1746, Francisco de Goya specialized in designing cartoons for the tapestry industry *(see p306)* in his early life, and in decorating churches such as Zaragoza's Basílica del Pilar with vivacious frescoes. In 1799 he became painter to Carlos IV, and depicted the king and his wife María Luisa with unflattering accuracy *(see p33)*. The invasion of Madrid by Napoleon's troops in 1808 *(see pp62–3)* and its attendant horrors had a profound and lasting effect on Goya's temperament, and his later works are imbued with cynical despair and isolation. He died in Bordeaux in 1828.

ARAGÓN'S FIESTAS

Las Tamboradas *(Maundy Thursday and Good Friday)*, Teruel province. During Easter Week, brotherhoods of men wearing long black robes beat drums in mourning for Christ. Las Tamboradas begins with "the breaking of the hour" at midnight on Thursday in Híjar. The Tamborada in Calanda begins the following day at midday. The solemn drum rolls continue for several hours. Aching arms and bleeding hands are considered to be signs of religious devotion.

Young drummer in Las Tamboradas, Alcorija

Carnival *(Feb/Mar)*, Bielsa (Huesca). The protagonists of this fiesta, known as *Trangas*, have rams' horns on their heads, blackened faces and teeth made of potatoes. They are said to represent fertility.

Romería de Santa Orosia *(25 Jun)*, Yebra de Basa (Huesca). Pilgrims in folk costume carry St Orosia's skull to her shrine.

Día del Pilar *(12 Oct)*, Zaragoza. Aragón's distinctive folk dance, the *jota*, is performed everywhere during the city's festivities in honour of its patroness, the Virgin of the Pillar *(see p237)*. On the Día del Pilar there is a procession with cardboard giants, and a spectacular display of flowers dedicated to the Virgin.

Alcalá de la Selva Castle, overlooking the town

Valderrobres ㉓

Teruel. 2,200. *Avda Cortes de Aragón 7, 978 89 08 86. Sat. San Roque (mid-Aug).* **www**.valderrobres.es

Just inside Aragón's border with Catalonia, the town of Valderrobres overlooks the trout-filled Río Matarraña. Dominating the town is the **castle**, formerly a palace for Aragonese royalty. Below it stands the imposing Gothic **Iglesia de Santa María la Mayor**, with a huge rose window in Catalan Gothic style. The arcaded plaza has a pleasing late 16th-century town hall *(ayuntamiento)*.

Environs

Near Valderrobres is the mountain peak of **La Caixa**. At 14 km (9 miles) are the mountain passes of Beceite.

Castillo de Valderrobres
Tel *679 63 44 38. Tue–Sun (Oct–Jun: Fri–Sun & public hols).*

Sierra de Gúdar ㉔

Teruel. *Mora de Rubielos. Alcalá de la Selva. C/ Diputación 2, Mora de Rubielos, 978 80 05 29.* **www**.sierradegudar.com

This range of hills, northeast of Teruel, is a region of pine woods, jagged limestone outcrops and scrub-covered slopes. At 2,028 m (6,653 ft), **Peñarroya** is the highest point. Nearby Valdelinares, Spain's highest village, is a ski station. From the access roads there are panoramic views of the hills. Especially noteworthy are the views from the towns of **Linares de Mora** and **Alcalá de la Selva**, which has a castle set against a backdrop of rock faces. Its Gothic-Renaissance church, with shell motifs and twisted columns, shelters the shrine of the Virgen de la Vega.

Mora de Rubielos ㉕

Teruel. *1,650. C/ Diputación 2, 978 80 05 29. Mon & Fri. San Miguel (28 Sep–1 Oct).*

Dominated by one of the best-preserved castles in Aragón, Mora de Rubielos displays the remains of the old walled city with its bridges and a medieval old town. There is a fine 17th-century town hall as well as the **collegiate church** of Santa María.

Environs

Rubielos de Mora, lying 14 km (9 miles) to the southeast, is worth exploring simply for its well-preserved stone and timber buildings. Among the balconied houses is an Augustinian convent with a Gothic reredos.

Teruel ㉖

Teruel. *34,200. Calle San Francisco 1, 978 64 14 61. Thu. Día del Sermón de las Tortillas (Tue of Easter week), La Vaquilla del Ángel (mid-Jul), Feria del Jamón (mid-Sep).* **www**.teruel.es

This industrial town has been the scene of much desperate fighting throughout the centuries. It began with the Romans, the first to capture and civilize Celtiberian Turba.

During the Reconquest the town became a strategic frontier prize. In 1171 Alfonso II recaptured Teruel for Christian Spain, but many Muslims continued to live peacefully in the city, which they embellished with beautiful Mudéjar towers. The last mosque was closed only at the height of the Inquisition *(see p274)*, in 1502. More recently, during the terrible, freezing winter of 1937, the bitterest battle of the Civil War *(see pp66–7)* was fought here. There were many thousands of casualties.

The old quarter is home to the wedge-shaped Plaza del Torico, with a monument of a

Tiled towers and rooftops of Teruel Cathedral

Balconied café above Albarracín's main square

small bull, the city's emblem. Within walking distance lie the five remaining Mudéjar towers. Most striking are those of **San Salvador** and **San Martín**, both dating back to the 12th century. The latter has multi-patterned brickwork studded with blue and green ceramics.

Beside the **Iglesia de San Pedro** are the tombs of the famous Lovers of Teruel. The **cathedral** has more colourful Mudéjar work, including a lantern dome of glazed tiles, and a tower completed in the 17th century. The dazzling coffered ceiling is painted with lively scenes of medieval life.

The **Museo Provincial**, one of Aragón's best museums, is housed in an elegant mansion. It has a large collection of ceramics, testifying to an industry for which Teruel has long been known. North of the centre is the **Acueducto de los Arcos**, a 16th-century aqueduct.

Museo Provincial
Pl Fray Anselmo Polanco 3. ***Tel*** *978 60 01 50.* *Tue–Sun.*

Albarracín 27

Teruel. *1,100.* *C/ San Antonio 2, 978 71 02 62.* *Wed.* *Los Mayos (30 Apr–1 May), Fiestas Patronales (8–17 Sep).* **www**.albarracin.org

It is easy to see why this picturesque town earned an international award for historical preservation. A dramatic cliff above the Río Guadalaviar is the perfect setting for this attractive cluster of mellow pink buildings. Standing on a ridge behind the town are the defensive walls and towers which date from Muslim times.

There is a good view of the town from below the **Palacio Episcopal** (Bishop's Palace). Inside the neighbouring 16th-century **cathedral**, which is topped by a belfry, there is a Renaissance carved wooden altarpiece depicting scenes from the life of St Peter. The treasury museum contains 16th-century Brussels tapestries and enamelled chalices.

Some of Albarracín's sturdy beamed and galleried houses have an unusual two-tier structure. The ground floor is limestone, and the overhanging upper storey is covered in rough coral-pink plasterwork. Many have been restored to their medieval form. Just outside the town are the caves of Navazo and Callejón, with their prehistoric rock paintings. Reproductions can be seen in Teruel's Museo Provincial.

Environs

In the surrounding **Montes Universales**, which rise to 1,935 m (6,348 ft), is the source of the Tagus, one of Spain's longest rivers. From fertile cereal plains to crumbling rocks, this area is a colourful mixture of poplars, junipers and thick pine woods, with poppies in spring. At **Cella**, northeast of Albarracín, the Río Jiloca has its source.

Rincón de Ademuz 28

Valencia. *1,200.* *Ademuz.* *Plaza del Ayuntamiento 1, Ademuz, 978 78 20 00.* *Wed.* *Fiestas de Agosto (15 Aug), Fiestas de la Virgen del Rosario (early Oct).*

This remote enclave south of Teruel belongs to the Comunidad Valenciana *(see p243)*; but is effectively an island of territory, stranded between the borders of Aragón and Castilla-La Mancha. The area has not prospered in modern times, but still has an austere charm and some peaceful tracts of country scattered with red rocks.

THE LOVERS OF TERUEL

According to legend, in 13th-century Teruel two young people, Diego de Marcilla and Isabel de Segura, fell in love and wished to marry. However, her wealthy family forbade the match because he was poor. Diego was given five years in which to make his fortune. When he returned to Teruel, laden with wealth, he found Isabel already married. Diego died of a broken heart and Isabel, full of despair, died the following day. The Bodas de Isabel de Segura, a festival held in mid-February, includes a re-enactment of the events.

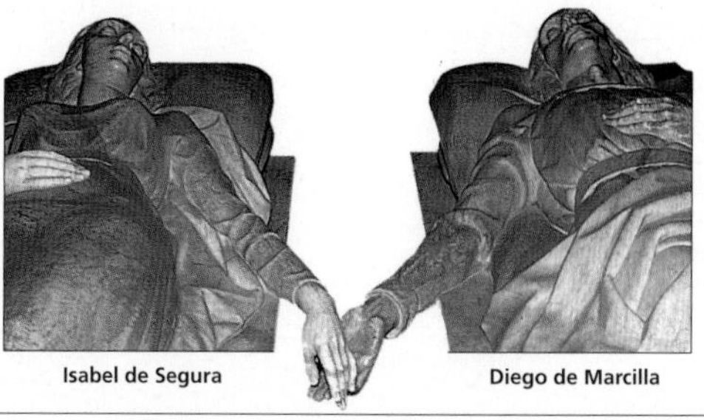

Isabel de Segura — Diego de Marcilla

VALENCIA AND MURCIA

CASTELLÓN · VALENCIA · ALICANTE · MURCIA

Today, the central region of Spain's eastern Mediterranean coast is an important holiday destination – the beaches of the Costa Blanca, the Costa del Azahar and the Costa Cálida draw millions of tourists annually. Centuries ago, Muslim settlers made these regions bloom, and the fertile fields and citrus groves of the coastal plains are still Spain's citrus orchard and market garden.

These productive lands have been occupied for more than 50,000 years. The Greeks, Phoenicians, Carthaginians and Romans all settled here before the Moors arrived, trading the products of land and sea.

The provinces of Castellón, Valencia and Alicante (which make up the Comunidad Valenciana) were reconquered from the Moors by a Catalan army. The language these troops left behind them developed into a dialect, *valenciano*, which is widely spoken and increasingly seen on signposts. Murcia, to the south, is one of Spain's smallest autonomous regions.

The population is concentrated on the coast where the historic towns and cities of Valencia, Alicante and Cartagena have been joined by modern package holiday resorts, such as Benidorm and La Manga del Mar Menor. Inland, where tourism has barely reached, the landscape rises into the chains of mountains that stand between the coast and the plateau of Central Spain. The scenery inland ranges from picturesque valleys and hills in the Maestrat, in the north of Castellón, to the semi-desert terrain around Lorca in southern Murcia.

The warm climate encourages outdoor life and exuberant fiestas. Most famous of these are Las Fallas of Valencia; the mock battles between Moors and Christians staged in Alcoi; and the lavish, costumed Easter processions in Murcia and Lorca.

Hill terraces of olive and almond trees ascending the hillsides near Alcoi

◁ The Penyal d'Ifach, rising directly out of the sea to tower above the Costa Blanca near Calp

Exploring Valencia and Murcia

The coasts of Valencia and Murcia are popular for seaside holidays and ideal for water sports almost all year round. Principal resorts include Benidorm, Benicassim, La Manga del Mar Menor and Oropesa. Some coastal towns such as Peñíscola, Gandía, Denia, Alicante and Cartagena have charming old quarters, castles and other sites well worth visiting. Close to the sea are several scenic nature reserves: the freshwater lagoon of L'Albufera, and, on the Costa Blanca, the saltpans of Santa Pola and the striking limestone crag of the Penyal d'Ifach.

Inland, the region offers excursions to such undiscovered beauty spots as El Maestrat and the mountains around Alcoi, as well as the undervisited historic towns of Xàtiva and Lorca. The two regional capitals, Valencia and Murcia, are both lively university cities with fine cathedrals and numerous museums.

Fishing nets strung out in the lagoon of L'Albufera

GETTING AROUND

The region's principal roads are the A7/AP7/E15 motorway and the N332 along the coast. Other motorways connect Valencia with Madrid, A3 (E901), and Alicante with Madrid, N330 A31. There are main rail lines from Alicante, Valencia and Murcia to Madrid and Barcelona, but the rest of the rail network is rather fragmented and buses are often quicker than trains. A scenic narrow-gauge railway line along the Costa Blanca connects Denia to Alicante via Benidorm. The region's international airports are at Alicante and Valencia.

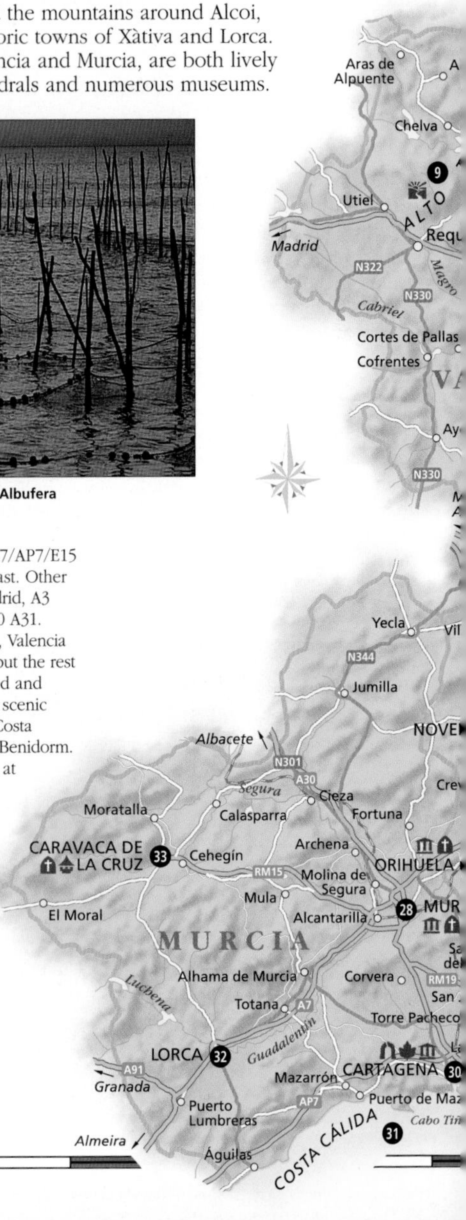

KEY

- Motorway
- Major road
- Secondary road
- Scenic route
- Main railway
- Minor railway
- Regional border
- △ Summit

For additional map symbols *see back flap*

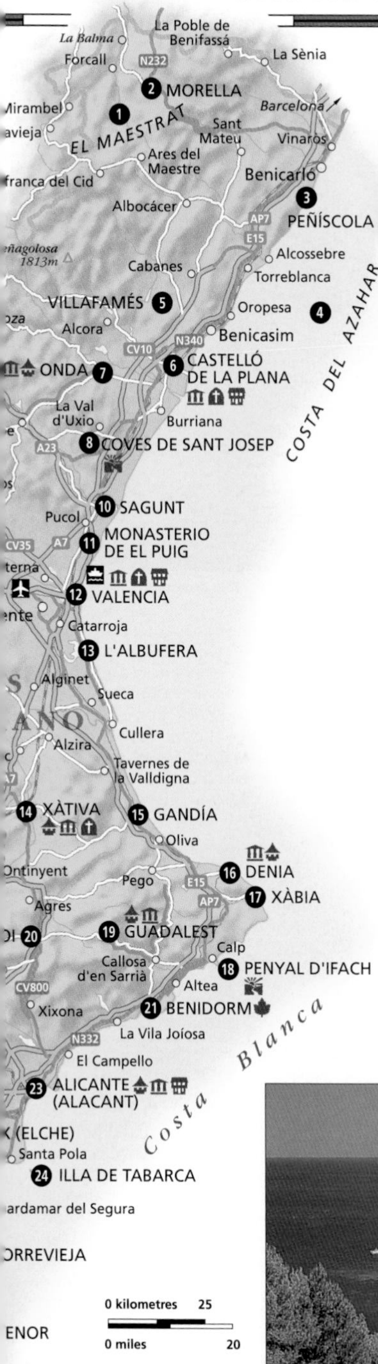

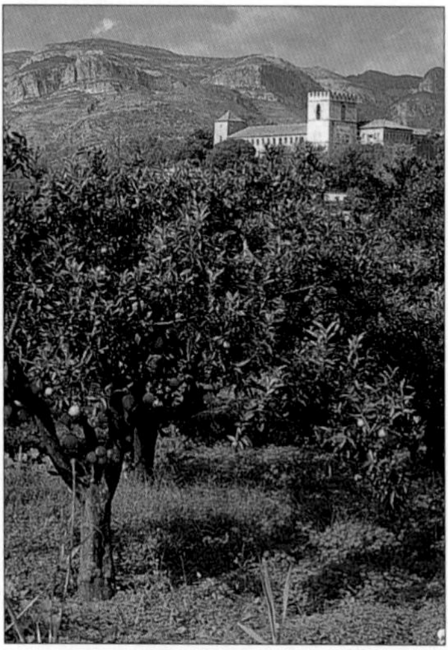

Lemon groves outside Denia

SIGHTS AT A GLANCE

Alicante (Alacant) 23
L'Albufera 13
Alcoi 20
Alto Turia 9
Benidorm 21
Caravaca de la Cruz 33
Cartagena 30
Castelló de la Plana 6
Costa del Azahar 4
Costa Cálida 31
Coves de Sant Josep 8
Denia 16
Elx (Elche) 25
Gandía 15
Guadalest 19
Illa de Tabarca 24
Lorca 32
El Maestrat 1
Mar Menor 29
Monasterio de El Puig 11
Morella 2
Murcia 28
Novelda 22
Onda 7
Orihuela 26
Peñíscola 3
Penyal d'Ifac 18
Sagunt 10
Torrevieja 27
Valencia pp250–53 12
Vilafamés 5
Xàbia 17
Xàtiva 14

SEE ALSO

• ***Where to Stay*** pp576–9

• ***Where to Eat*** pp626–9

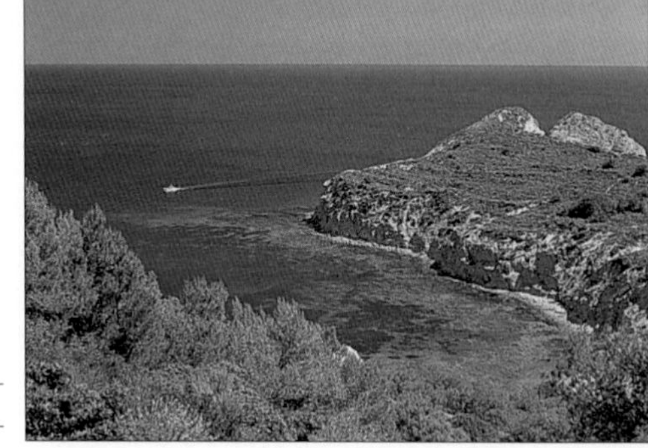

One of the many coves on Xàbia's rugged coast

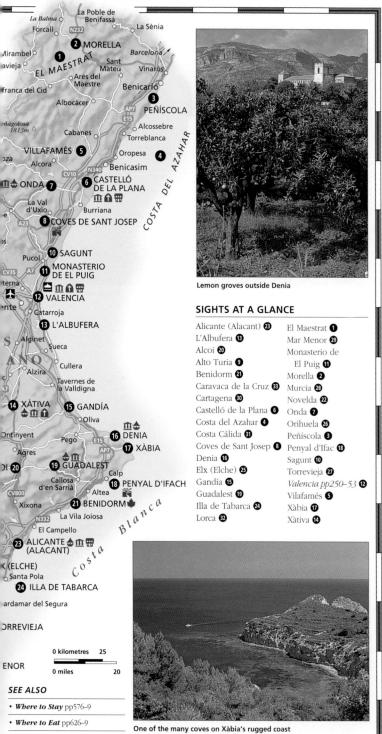

The unbroken medieval wall surrounding the historic hilltop town of Morella in El Maestrat

El Maestrat ❶

Castellón & Teruel. Morella. *Plaza de San Miguel, Morella, 964 17 30 32.* **www**.turismomaestrazgo.com

Crusading warlords of the Knights Templar and the Knights of Montesa – known as *maestres* (masters) – gave their name to this lonely upland region. To rule over this frontier land, which straddles the border between Valencia and Aragón, they built fortified settlements in dramatic defensive positions, often on rocky crags. The best preserved of them is **Morella**, the principal town. **Forcall**, not far from Morella, has two 16th-century mansions on its porticoed square. To the south, the village of **Ares del Maestre** is spectacularly sited beneath a 1,318-m- (4,300-ft-) high rock.

Cantavieja is the main town in the Aragonese part of El Maestrat (where it is known as El Maestrazgo). It has a pretty arcaded square. The walled village of **Mirambel**, nearby, has been restored to its medieval condition.

There are several spooky but fascinating shrines to the Virgin in El Maestrat, notably the cave of La Balma at **Zorita**, which is reached via a rocky ledge.

The scenery in most parts is striking: fertile valleys alternate with breathtaking cliffs and bare, flat-topped mountains overflown by eagles and vultures. Tourism is developing very slowly here: there are few places to stay and the roads can be windy and slow.

The Torre de la Sacristía, in the restored village of Mirambel

Morella ❷

Castellón. *2,800.* *Plaza de San Miguel, 964 17 30 32.* *Sun.* *Fiestas Patronales (mid–late Aug).*

Built on a high, isolated outcrop and crowned by a ruined castle, Morella cuts a dramatic profile. Its unbroken medieval walls retain six gateways, which lead into a fan-shaped maze of streets and steep, tapering alleys, many of which are shaded by the eaves of ancient houses. The main street is lined with shady porticoes. In the upper part of town is the **Basílica de Santa María la Mayor**. Its unique raised choirloft is reached by a finely carved spiral staircase.

NESTA CASA OBRO SAN VICENTE FERRER EL PRODIGIOSO
LAGRO DE LA RESURRECCIÓN DE UN NIÑO QUE SU MADRE
AJENADA HABIA DESCUARTIZADO Y GUISADO E
BSEQUIO AL SANTO (1414)

MORELLA'S MIRACLE

A plaque on the wall of Morella's Calle de la Virgen marks the house in which St Vincent Ferrer is said to have performed a bizarre miracle in the early 15th century. A housewife, distraught at having no meat to offer the saint, cut up her son and put him in the cooking pot. When St Vincent discovered this, he reconstituted the boy – except for one of his little fingers, which his mother had eaten to see if the dish was sufficiently salted.

For hotels and restaurants in this region see pp276–9 and pp626–9

Peñíscola ❸

Castellón. 7,000. Paseo Marítimo, 964 48 02 08. Mon. Fiestas Patronales (2nd week Sep). www.peniscola.es

The fortified old town of Peñíscola clusters around the base of a castle built on a rocky promontory, surrounded on three sides by the sea. This labyrinth of narrow winding streets and white houses is enclosed by massive ramparts. These are entered by either the Fosch Gate – reached by a ramp from the Plaza del Caudillo – or through the San Pedro Gate, from the harbour. Some visitors are drawn to the town because the 1961 Hollywood blockbuster *El Cid* was filmed there.

The **Castell del Papa Luna** was built on the foundations of an Arab fortress in the late 13th century by the Knights Templar. Their cross is carved above the door. It later became the residence of the papal pretender Pedro de Luna, cardinal of Aragón. He was elected Pope Benedict XIII during the Great Schism that split the Catholic Church at the end of the 14th century. Although he was deposed by the Council of Constance in 1414, he continued to proclaim his right to the papacy until his death as a nonagenarian in 1423.

Castell del Papa Luna
Calle Castillo. ***Tel*** *964 48 00 21.* *daily.* *1 & 6 Jan, 9 Sep, 9 Oct, 25 Dec.*

Sunset view of the beach and old town of Peñíscola

Costa del Azahar ❹

Castellón. Castelló de la Plana. Castelló de la Plana. Castelló de la Plana, 964 35 86 88. http://turismodecastellon.com

The "Orange Blossom Coast" of Castellón province is named after the dense citrus groves of the coastal plain. The three principal resorts are Oropesa, Peñíscola and Benicassim, where handsome old villas stand beside modern hotels and other tourist amenities. Alcossebre also has a popular beach. Vinaròs – the most northerly point – and Benicarló are key fishing ports supplying prawns and date mussels to local restaurants.

Sculpture in the Casa del Batlle

Vilafamés ❺

Castellón. 2,000. Plaza del Ayuntamiento 2, 964 32 99 70. Fri. San Miguel (late Mar), Patronales (mid-Aug).

This medieval town climbs from a flat plain along a rocky ridge to the restored round keep of its castle. The older, upper part of the town is a warren of sloping streets.

A 15th-century mansion houses the **Museo de Arte Contemporáneo de Vilafamés**. The artworks on display date from 1959 to the present.

Museo de Arte Contemporáneo de Vilafamés
Casa del Batlle, Calle Diputación 20. ***Tel*** *964 32 91 52.* *Tue–Sun.*

Castelló de la Plana's planetarium, close to the beach

Castelló de la Plana ❻

Castellón. 167,500. Plaza María Agustina 5, 964 35 86 88. Mon. Fiesta de la Magdalena (3rd Sun of Lent). www.castellonturismo.com

Originally founded on high ground inland, the capital of Castellón province was relocated nearer to the coast in the 13th century.

The city centre, the Plaza Mayor, is bordered by the market, the cathedral, the town hall and **El Fadri**, a 58-m- (190-ft-) high octagonal bell tower begun in 1590 and finished in 1604.

The **Museo de Bellas Artes** contains a collection of artifacts dating from the middle Palaeolithic era, paintings from the 14th to the 19th centuries and modern ceramics from the region. Most of the older works come from the nearby convents, because the government seized many church possessions in the 19th century. An important collection of paintings attributed to Francisco de Zurbarán is also on display here.

In **El Planetario** there are demonstrations of the night sky, the solar system and the nearest stars. Two rooms hold temporary exhibits.

Museo de Bellas Artes
Avda Hermanos Bou 28. ***Tel*** *964 72 75 00.* *10am–8pm Tue–Sat, 10am–2pm Sun.* *by appt.*

El Planetario
Paseo Marítimo 1, El Grao. ***Tel*** *964 28 29 68.* *11am–2pm Tue–Sat (also 4:30–8pm Jul & Aug), 11am–2pm Sun.* *Sep.* *(planetarium).*

Onda ❼

Castellón. 25,700. Calle la Cossa, 964 60 28 55. Thu. Feria del Santísimo Salvador (6 Aug). **www**.onda.es

Onda, home to a thriving ceramics industry, is overlooked by a ruined **castle**, which was known to its Moorish founders as the "Castle of the Three Hundred Towers". The castle houses a museum of local history.

However, the main reason to visit Onda is to take a look at the **Museo de Ciencias Naturales El Carmen**, a natural history museum belonging to a Carmelite monastery.

The collection was begun in 1952 by the monks for their own private scientific study. It was only opened to the public a decade later. The clever use of subdued lighting lends dramatic effect to the 10,000 plant and animal specimens which are exhibited over three floors. Objects include large stuffed animals placed in naturalistic settings, butterflies and other insects, shells, fossils, minerals and grisly, preserved anatomical specimens.

Museo de Ciencias Naturales El Carmen
Carretera de Tales. ***Tel*** *964 60 07 30.* *Tue–Sun.* *20 Dec–6 Jan.*

Two butterfly exhibits in the Museo El Carmen

Boat ride through the winding Coves de Sant Josep

Coves de Sant Josep ❽

Vall d'Uixó (Castellón). ***Tel*** *964 69 05 76.* *Vall d'Uixó.* *daily.* *1 & 6 Jan, 25 Dec.* **www**.riosubterraneo.com

The caves of St Joseph were first explored in 1902. The subterranean river that formed them and that still flows through them, has been charted for almost 3 km (2 miles). However, only part of this distance can be explored on a visit.

Boats take visitors along the serpentine course of the river. You may have to duck to avoid projections of rock on the way. Sometimes the narrow caves open out into large chambers such as the *Sala de los Murciélagos* (Hall of the Bats – the bats left when the floodlights were installed). The water is at its deepest – 12 m (39 ft) – in the *Lago Azul* (Blue Lake). You can explore a further 250 m (820 ft) along the *Galería Seca* (Dry Gallery) on foot. The caves are often closed after heavy rain.

Alto Turia ❾

Valencia. *Chelva.* *CV35 Valencia–Ademúz km 73, 96 163 50 84.*

The attractive wooded hills of the upper reaches of the Río Turia in Valencia (Alto Turia) are popular with hikers and day-trippers. **Chelva**, the main town, has an unusual clock on its church, which shows not only the hour but the day and month as well. The town is overlooked by the **Pico del Remedio** (1,054 m/3,458 ft), from the summit of which there is a fine panoramic view of the region. In a valley near Chelva, at the end of an unsurfaced but drivable track, are the remains of a Roman aqueduct, **Peña Cortada**.

The most attractive and interesting village in Alto Turia is **Alpuente**, situated above a dry gorge. Between 1031 and 1089, when it was captured by El Cid *(see p370)*, Alpuente was the capital of a small *taifa*, a Moorish kingdom. In the 14th century it was still important enough for the kingdom of Valencia's parliament to meet here. The town hall is confined to a small tower over a 14th-century gateway, which was later extended in the 16th century by the addition of a rectangular council chamber.

Requena, to the south is Valencia's main wine town. Further south, Valencia's other principal river, the Xúquer (Júcar), carves tremendous gorges near Cortes de Pallas on its way past the **Muela de Cortes**. This massive, wild plateau and nature reserve is crossed by one small road and a lonely dirt track.

LA TOMATINA

The highpoint of the annual fiesta in Buñol (Valencia) is a sticky food fight on the last Wednesday of August, which attracts thousands of visitors dressed in their worst clothes. Lorry loads of ripe tomatoes are provided by the town council at 11am for participants to hurl at each other. No one in range of the combatants is spared: foreigners and photographers are prized targets.

The battle originated in 1944. Some say it began with a fight between friends. Others say irreverent locals pelted civic dignitaries with tomatoes during a procession. Increasing national and international press coverage means that more people attend, and more tomatoes are thrown, every year.

Sagunt's ruined fortifications, added to by successive rulers of the town

Sagunt ⑩

Valencia. 66,000. Pl Cronista Chabret, 96 265 58 59. Wed. Fallas (15–19 Mar), Fiestas (end Jul–Aug). **www**.aytosagunto.es

Sited near the junction of two Roman roads, Sagunt (Sagunto) played a crucial role in Spain's ancient history.

In 219 BC Hannibal, the Carthaginian commander in southern Spain, stormed and sacked Rome's ally Saguntum. All the inhabitants of the town were said to have died in the assault, the last throwing themselves on to bonfires rather than fall into the hands of Hannibal's troops. The incident sparked off the Second Punic War, a disaster for the Carthaginians, which ended with Rome's occupation of the peninsula *(see pp50–51)*.

The town still contains several reminders of the Roman occupation, including the 1st-century AD **Roman theatre**. Built out of limestone in a natural depression on the hillside above the town, it has been controversially restored using modern materials. The theatre is now used as a venue for music, plays and Sagunt's annual theatre festival.

The ruins of the **castle**, sprawling along the crest of the hill above the modern-day town, mark the original site of Saguntum. Superimposed on each other are the excavated remains of various civilizations, including the Iberians, the Carthaginians, the Romans and the Moors. The ruins of the castle are divided into seven divisions, the highest being La Ciudadella, and the most important Armas.

Castillo de Sagunt
Tue–Sun.

Monasterio de El Puig ⑪

El Puig (Valencia). ***Tel*** *96 147 02 00.* *El Puig.* *Tue–Sat.* *only, 10am, 11am, noon, 4pm, 5pm.* **www**.monasteriodelpuig.es.tl

This Mercedarian monastery was founded by King Jaime I of Aragón, who conquered Valencia from the Moors in the 13th century. The monastery is now home to a collection of paintings from between the 16th and 18th centuries and the Museo de la Imprenta y de la Obra Gráfica (Museum of Printing and Graphic Art). The museum commemorates the printing of the first book in Spain – thought to have been in Valencia in 1474 – and illustrates the development of the printing press. Exhibits include printers' blocks and a copy of the smallest printed book in the world.

Messy participants throwing tomatoes at each other in the annual fiesta of La Tomatina

Valencia ⓬

Spain's third largest city is sited in the middle of the *huerta*: a fertile plain of orange groves and market gardens, which is one of Europe's most intensively farmed regions. With its warm coastal climate, Valencia is known for its exuberant outdoor living and nightlife. In March the city stages one of Spain's most spectacular fiestas, Las Fallas *(see p255)*, in which giant papier-mâché sculptures are burned in the streets. Modern Valencia is a centre for trade and manufacturing, notably ceramics. A ferry service connects the city with the Balearic Islands.

Flowers in honour of Valencia's patroness, Virgen de los Desamparados

Exploring Valencia

Valencia stands on the course of the Río Turia. The city centre and the crumbling old quarter of El Carmen are on the right bank. Most of the monuments are within walking distance of the Plaza del Ayuntamiento, the triangular main square, which is presided over by the town hall.

The city was founded by the Romans in 138 BC and later conquered by the Moors. It was captured by El Cid *(see p370)* in 1096, retaken by the Moors, and finally recaptured by Jaime I, the Conqueror, in 1238, to become absorbed into the kingdom of Aragón.

The three finest buildings in Valencia were built during its economic and cultural heyday in the 14th and 15th centuries: the Torres de Serranos, a gateway that survived the demolition of the medieval walls in the 19th century, La Lonja and the cathedral.

Palau de la Generalitat

Plaza de Manises. ***Tel*** *96 386 34 61.*
Mon–Thu and by prior appt only.

This palace, which is now used by the Valencian regional government, was built in Gothic style between 1482 and 1579 but added to in the 17th and 20th centuries. It surrounds an enclosed stone patio from which two staircases ascend to splendidly decorated rooms.

The larger of the two Salas Doradas (Golden Chambers), on the mezzanine level, has a multicoloured coffered ceiling and tiled floor. The walls of the parliament chamber are decorated with frescoes.

Basílica de la Virgen de los Desamparados

Pl de la Virgen. ***Tel*** *96 391 92 14.*
7am–2pm, 4:30–9pm daily.

The ornately dressed statue of Valencia's patroness, the Virgin of the Helpless, stands above an altar in this 17th-century church, lavishly adorned with flowers and candles. She is honoured during Las Fallas by La Ofrenda ("the Offering"), a display of flowers in the square outside the church.

Cathedral

Plaza de la Reina. ***Tel*** *96 391 81 27.*
20 Mar–31 Oct: 10am–6:30pm Mon–Fri, 10am–5:30pm Sat, 2–5:30pm Sun & public hols; Nov–19 Mar: 10am–5:30pm Mon–Sat. *includes entry to the museum.* **Museo** *as above.* **Miguelete** *daily.*

Built originally in 1262, the cathedral has been added to over the ages, and its three doorways are all in different styles. The oldest is the Romanesque Puerta del Palau but the main entrance is the 18th-century Baroque portal, the Puerta de los Hierros.

A unique court meets on Thursdays at noon in front of the Gothic Puerta de los Apóstoles. For about 1,000 years, the Water Tribunal has settled disputes between farmers over irrigation in the *huerta*.

The Miguelete, the cathedral's bell tower on Plaza de la Reina

Inside the cathedral, a chapel holds an agate cup, claimed to be the Holy Grail and formerly kept in the San Juan de la Peña monastery *(see p234)*. Behind the main altar are some 15th-century frescoes.

The cathedral's bell tower, the **Miguelete**, is Valencia's main landmark. The cathedral also houses a museum.

La Lonja

Plaza del Mercado. ***Tel*** *96 352 54 78 ext. 4153.* *Tue–Sun (daily in summer).*

An exquisite Late Gothic hall, built between 1482 and 1498 as a commodities exchange, La Lonja now hosts cultural events. The outside walls are decorated with gargoyles and other grotesque figures. The ceiling of the transactions hall features star-patterned vaulting, supported by spiral columns.

Mercado Central

Plaza del Mercado 6. ***Tel*** *96 382 91 00.* *7:30am–3pm Mon–Sat.*

This huge iron, glass and tile Art Nouveau building, with its parrot and swordfish weathervanes, opened in 1928 and is one of the largest and most attractive markets in Europe. Every morning its 350 or so stalls are filled with a bewildering variety of food.

Ornate toilet sign outside Valencia's Mercado Central

Museo Nacional de Cerámica Gonzalez Martí

Poeta Querol 2. ***Tel*** *96 351 63 92.* *Tue–Sun.* *1 Jan, 1 May, 24, 25 & 31 Dec.* *(free Sat pm & Sun).*

Spain's Ceramics Museum is housed in the mansion of the Marqués de Dos Aguas, an 18th-century fantasy of coloured plasterwork. The doorway is edged by a carving by Ignacio Vergara. The 5,000 exhibits include prehistoric, Greek and Roman ceramics and pieces by Picasso.

VISITORS' CHECKLIST

Valencia. 798,000. 8 km (5 miles) SW. C/ Játiva 24, 902 24 02 02. Avda Menéndez Pidal 13, 96 346 62 66. 96 393 95 00. Plaza de la Reina 19, 963 15 39 31. Mon–Sat. Las Fallas (15–19 Mar). **www**.turisvalencia.es

Colegio del Patriarca

Calle Nave 1. ***Tel*** *96 351 41 76.* *11am–1:30pm daily.* *Aug.*

This seminary was built in 1584. The walls and ceiling of the church are covered with frescoes by Bartolomé Matarana. During Friday morning Mass, the painting above the altar, *The Last Supper* by Francisco Ribalta, is lowered to reveal a sculpture of the crucifixion by an anonymous 15th-century German artist.

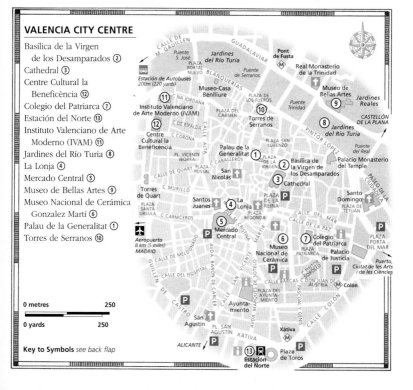

VALENCIA CITY CENTRE

- Basílica de la Virgen de los Desamparados ②
- Cathedral ③
- Centre Cultural la Beneficència ⑫
- Colegio del Patriarca ⑦
- Estación del Norte ⑬
- Instituto Valenciano de Arte Moderno (IVAM) ⑪
- Jardines del Río Turia ⑧
- La Lonja ④
- Mercado Central ⑤
- Museo de Bellas Artes ⑨
- Museo Nacional de Cerámica Gonzalez Martí ⑥
- Palau de la Generalitat ①
- Torres de Serranos ⑩

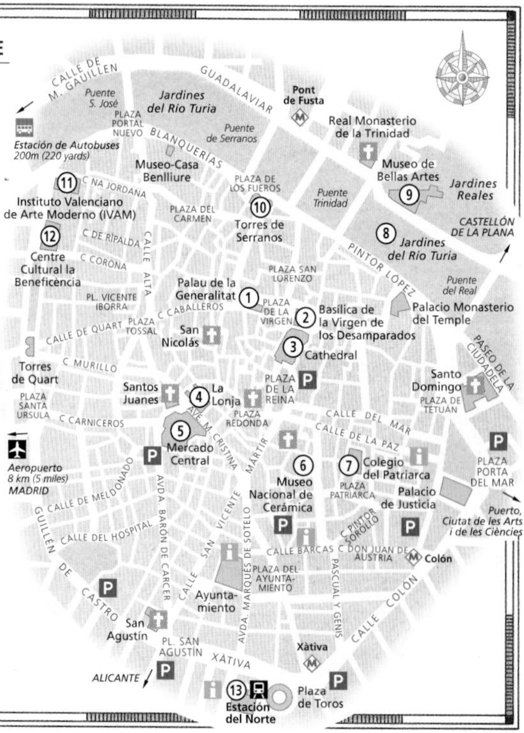

0 metres 250

0 yards 250

Key to Symbols *see back flap*

The Palau de la Música, Valencia's prestigious concert hall

Beyond the Centre

The centre of the city is bordered by the Gran Vía Marqués del Túria and the Gran Vía Ramón y Cajal. Beyond these lie the 19th-century suburbs laid out on a grid plan.

The best way to get around beyond the centre is by the metro, one line of which is a tramway to the beaches of El Cabañal and La Malvarrosa. The port area, redeveloped for the 2007 America's Cup, is full of bars and restaurants.

Jardines del Río Túria

Where once there was a river there is now a 10-km- (6-mile-) long strip of gardens, sports fields and playgrounds crossed by 19 bridges. In a prominent position above the riverbed stands the Palau de la Música, a concert hall built in the 1980s. The centrepiece of the nearby children's playground is the giant figure of Gulliver pinned to the ground and covered with steps and slides. Jardín de Cabecera aims to recreate the Túria River's original landscape, with a lake, beach, waterwheel, waterfall and riverside wood.

The best of Valencia's other public gardens stand near the banks of the river. The largest of them, the Jardines del Real – known locally as Los Viveros – occupy the site of a royal palace which was torn down in the Peninsular War. The Jardín Botánico, created in 1802, is planted with 7,000 species of shrubs and trees.

Ecce Homo by Juan de Juanes in the Museo de Bellas Artes

Museo De Bellas Artes

Museo San Pio V, Calle San Pio V 9. ***Tel*** *96 387 03 00. 11am–5pm Mon, 10am–7pm Tue–Sun. 1 Jan, Good Fri, 25 Dec. by appt.*

An important collection of 2,000 paintings and statues dating from the 14th to the 19th centuries is housed in this former seminary, which was built between 1683 and 1744.

Valencian art dating from the 14th and 15th centuries is represented by a series of golden altarpieces by Alcanyis, Pere Nicolau and Maestro de Bonastre. Velázquez's self-portrait and works by Bosch, El Greco, Murillo, Ribalta, Van Dyck and the local Renaissance painter Juan de Juanes hang on the first floor. On the top floor there are six paintings by Goya and others by important 19th- and 20th-century Valencian artists: Ignacio Pinazo, Joaquín Sorolla and Antonio Muñoz Degrain. A large collection of the latter's hallucinatory coloured paintings are gathered together in one room, among them the disturbing *Amor de Madre*.

Torres de Serranos

Plaza de los Fueros. ***Tel*** *96 391 90 70. Tue–Sun (daily Jul–Nov). (free Sun).*

Erected in 1391 as a triumphal arch in the city's walls, this gateway combines defensive and decorative features. Its two towers combine battlements and delicate Gothic tracery.

Instituto Valenciano de Arte Moderno (IVAM)

Calle Guillem de Castro 118. ***Tel*** *96 386 30 00. 10am–5pm Mon & Tue, 10am–8pm Wed–Sun. (free Sun). by appointment.* **www**.ivam.es

The Valencian Institute of Modern Art is one of Spain's most highly respected spaces for displaying contemporary art. The core of its permanent collection is formed of work by Julio Gonzalez, one of the most important 20th-century sculptors. All art forms are represented in its temporary exhibitions, with emphasis on photography and photomontage. One of the eight galleries, Sala Muralles, incorporates a stretch of the old city walls.

Art Nouveau-style column in the Estación del Norte

Estación del Norte

Calle Xátiva 24. ***Tel*** *902 24 02 02 (RENFE). daily.*

Valencia's mainline railway station was built from 1906–17 in a style inspired by Austrian Art Nouveau. The exterior is decorated with orange and orange blossom flower motifs whilst inside, ceramic murals and stained glass in the foyer and cafeteria depict the life and crops of the *huerta* and L'Albufera *(see p254)*.

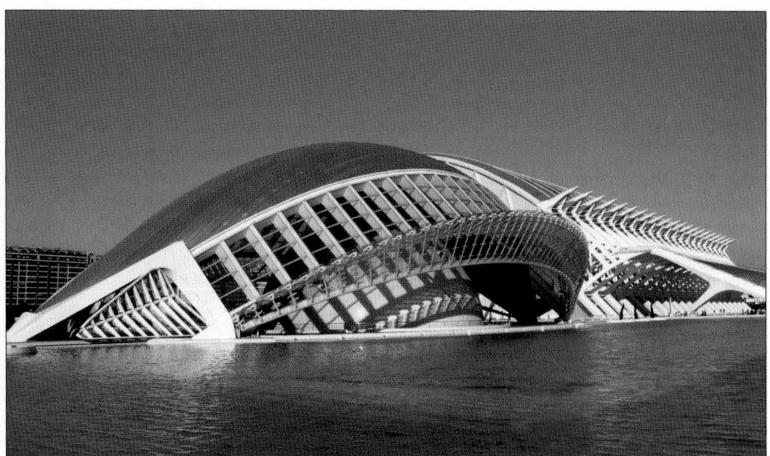

The hemispherical IMAX cinema at the Ciutat de les Arts i de les Ciències

Ciutat de les Arts i de les Ciències

Avenida Autovia del Saler 1–7. **Tel** *902 10 00 31.* **Museum** *10am–7pm daily (to 9pm 1 Jul–15 Sep).* www.cac.es

The futuristic complex of the City of Arts and Sciences stands at the seaward end of the Río Túria gardens. It is made up of five stunning buildings, four of them designed by Valencian architect Santiago Calatrava.

The Palau de les Arts, the final building to be added to the complex, has a concert hall with four performance spaces including an open-air theatre. On the other side of the Puente de Monteolivete is L'Hermisfèric, an architectural pun by Calatrava on the theme of vision, consisting of a blinking eye. The "eyeball" is an auditorium equipped as an IMAX cinema and planetarium. Next to this is the Museu de les Ciències Príncipe Felipe, a science museum contained within a structure of glass and gleaming white steel arches. The displays inside are mainly geared towards visiting school parties. Opposite the museum is L'Umbracle, a giant pergola of parabolic arches covering the complex's car park.

The last part of the "city" is an aquarium, the Oceanografic, designed by architect Felix Candela as a series of lagoons and pavillions linked up by bridges and tunnels.

Museo de Historia de Valencia

Calle Valencia 42, Mislata. **Tel** *963 701 105.* *Tue–Sun.* *(free Sat & Sun).*

Valencia's history museum is housed in the 19th-century cistern that used to supply the city with water, now an atmospheric labyrinth of pillars and arches. The displays tell the story of the city's development, from its foundations by the Romans to the present day. In each section there is a "time machine", a full-sized screen on which a typical scene of daily life is reproduced in the language of the visitor's choice.

El Cabañal and La Malvarrosa Beaches

To the east of the city, the beaches of El Cabañal and La Malvarrosa are bordered by a broad and lively esplanade about 2 km (1 mile) long. Although these two former fishermen's districts were carelessly developed in the 1960s and 1970s, they retain some quaint, traditional houses tiled on the outside to keep them cool in summer. The light of La Malvarrosa inspired the Impressionist painter Joaquín Sorolla *(see p305)*. The Paseo de Neptuno, near the port, is lined with restaurants, many of which specialize in paella. The revamped port district and marina also feature many modern hotels.

Environs

The intensively farmed plain of the *huerta* is a maze of fields planted with artichokes and *chufas*, the raw ingredient of *horchata*.

Manises, near the airport, is famous for its ceramics, which are sold in shops and factories. There is also a ceramics museum.

VALENCIA'S SUMMER SPECIALITY

In summer, the bars and cafés of Valencia offer a thirst-quenching drink unique to the area. *Horchata*, a sweet, milky drink produced mainly in the nearby town of Alboraia, is made from *chufas* (earth almonds). It is served semi-frozen or in liquid form and usually eaten with *fartons* – soft, sweet bread sticks – or *rosquilletas* – crunchy biscuit sticks. The oldest *horchatería* in the city centre is Santa Catalina, off the Plaza de la Virgen.

Painted tiles showing woman serving *horchata*

Fishing boats on the shore of the freshwater lake, L'Albufera

L'Albufera ⓭

Valencia. 🚌 ℹ *Carretera del Palmar, Racó de l'Olla, 96 162 73 45.*

A freshwater lake situated on the coast just south of Valencia, L'Albufera is one of the prime wetland habitats for birds in Eastern Spain.

It is cut off from the sea by a wooded sandbar, the Dehesa, and fringed by a network of paddy fields, which produce a third of Spain's rice.

L'Albufera is fed by the Río Turia and connected to the sea by three channels, which are fitted with sluice gates to control the water level. The lake reaches a maximum depth of 2.5 m (8 ft), and is gradually shrinking because of natural silting and the reclamation of land. In the Middle Ages the lake encompassed an area over ten times its present size.

Over 250 species of birds – including large numbers of egrets and herons – have been recorded in the lake's reed beds and marshy islands, the *matas*. L'Albufera was declared a nature reserve in 1986 to protect its birdlife. Many birds can be seen with binoculars from the shores of the lake.

A visitors' centre at Racó de l'Olla provides information on the ecology of lake, the paddy fields and the Dehesa.

Xàtiva ⓮

Valencia. *29,000.* 🚉 🚌 ℹ *Alameda de Jaime I 50, 96 227 33 46.* *Tue & Fri.* *Las Fallas (16–19 Mar); Fira de Agosto (14–20 Aug).*

Along the narrow ridge of Mount Vernissa, above Xàtiva, run the ruins of a once-grand **castle** of 30 towers. It was largely destroyed by Felipe V in the War of the Spanish Succession *(see p62)*. Felipe also set fire to the town, which continues to wreak its revenge in an extraordinary way – by hanging Felipe's full-length portrait upside down in the **Museo Municipal**.

Until the attack, Xàtiva was the second town of the kingdom of Valencia. It is thought to have been founded by the Iberians. Under the Moors it became prosperous, and in the 12th century it was the first European city to make paper.

Among the sights in the streets and squares of the old town are a former hospital with a Gothic-Renaissance façade, and a Gothic fountain in the Plaça de la Trinidad.

The oldest church in Xàtiva is the **Ermita de San Feliú** (Chapel of St Felix) on the road up to the fortress. It dates from around 1262 and is hung with a number of 14th- to 16th-century icons.

Felipe V's full-length portrait hanging upside down in Xàtiva

Castillo de Xàtiva
Subida del Castillo. ***Tel*** *96 227 42 74.* *Tue–Sun.*

Museo Municipal
Carrer de la Corretgeria 46. ***Tel*** *96 227 65 97.* *Tue–Sun.*

Gandía ⓯

Valencia. *78,000.* 🚉 🚌 ℹ *Avda Marqués de Campo, 96 287 77 88.* *Thu, Sat.* *Las Fallas (16–19 Mar).* **www**.gandiaturismo.com

In 1485, Rodrigo Borja (who became Pope Alexander VI) was granted the title of Duchy of Gandía. He founded the Borgia clan and, together with his children, was later implicated in murder and debauchery.

For hotels and restaurants in this region see pp576–9 and pp626–9

Rodrigo's great-grandson later redeemed the family name by joining the Jesuit order. He was canonized as St Francis Borja by Pope Clement X in 1671.

The house in which he was born and lived, the **Palau Ducal** (Duke's Palace), is now owned by the Jesuits. Its simple Gothic courtyard belies the richly decorated chambers within, especially the Baroque Golden Gallery. The small patio has a tiled floor depicting the four elements of earth, air, fire and water.

Palau Ducal
C/ Duc Alfons el Vell 1. ***Tel*** *96 287 14 65.* *daily.*

The ornate and gilded interior of the Palau Ducal, Gandía

Dénia 16

Alicante. *44,500.* *C/ Dr Manuel Lettur, 96 642 23 67.* *Mon & Fri.* *Fiestas Patronales (early Jul).* **www**.denia.net

This town was founded as a Greek colony. It takes its name from the Roman goddess Diana – a temple in her honour was excavated here. In the 11th century it became the capital of a short-lived Muslim kingdom, whose dominion extended from Andalusia to the Balearic Islands.

It is now a fishing port and holiday resort. The town centre spreads around the base of a low hill. A large **castle**, once an Arab fortress, on its summit overlooks the harbour. The entrance gate, the Portal de la Vila, survives, but it was altered in the 17th century. The Palacio del Gobernador (Governor's House), within the castle, contains an archaeological museum, which shows the development of Denia from 200 BC to the 18th century.

North of the harbour is the sandy beach of Las Marinas. To the south is the rocky and less developed Las Rotas beach, which is good for snorkelling.

Castillo de Dénia
C/ San Francisco. ***Tel*** *96 642 06 56.* *daily.* *1 Jan, 25 Dec.*

Xàbia 17

Alicante. *31,000.* *Plaza de la Iglesia 6, 96 579 43 56.* *Thu.* *San Juan (24 Jun), Moros Y Cristianos (third weekend of Jul), Bous a la Mar (first week of Sep).* **www**.xabia.org

Pirates and smugglers once took advantage of the hiding places afforded by the cliffs, caves, inlets and two rocky islands along the coastline of Xàbia (also known as Jávea).

The town centre is perched on a hill on the site of an Iberian settlement. Many buildings here are made from the local Tosca sandstone. The 16th-century **Iglesia de San Bartolomé** was fortified to serve as a refuge in times of invasion. Missiles could be dropped on to attackers via openings over the door.

The seafront at Cabo de San Antonio is overlooked by ruined 17th- and 18th-century windmills. The bay is filled with modern developments, but the beaches are free of high-rise apartment blocks.

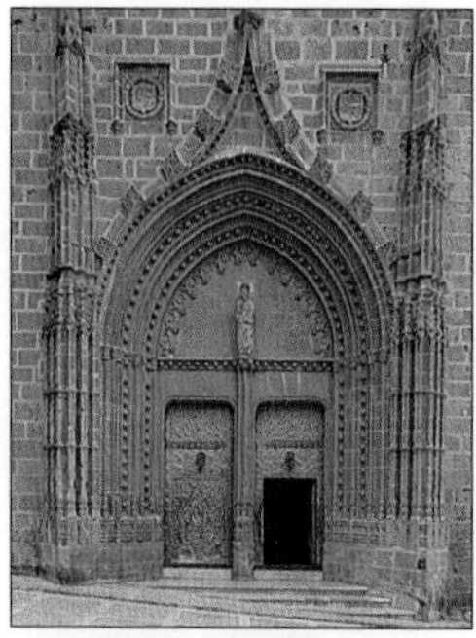

Entrance to the Gothic Iglesia de San Bartolomé in Xàbia

The ceremonial burning of Las Fallas on St Joseph's Day

VALENCIA AND MURCIA'S FIESTAS

Las Fallas *(15–19 Mar).* Huge papier-mâché monuments *(fallas)* are erected in the crossroads and squares of Valencia around 15 March and ceremonially set alight on the night of the 19th, St Joseph's Day. Costing thousands of euros each, the *fallas* depict satirical scenes. During the fiesta, the city echoes to the sound of fire crackers.

Good Friday, Lorca (Murcia). The "blue" and "white" brotherhoods compete to outdo each other in pomp and finery during a grand procession of biblical characters.

Moors and Christians *(21–24 Apr)*, Alcoi (Alicante). Two costumed armies march into the city, where they perform ceremonies and fight mock battles in commemoration of the Reconquest.

Bous a la Mar *(early Jul)*, Denia (Alicante). People dodge bulls on the quay until one or the other falls into the sea *(see p39)*.

Misteri d'Elx *(11–15 Aug)*, Elx (Alicante). This choral play, in the Iglesia de Santa María, has spectacular special effects.

La Tomatina *(last Wed of Aug)*, Buñol (Valencia). Thousands of participants pelt each other with ripe tomatoes *(see pp248–9)*.

The Costa Blanca

Less hectic than the Costa del Sol *(see pp472–3)* and with warmer winters than the Costa Brava *(see p217)*, the Costa Blanca occupies a prime stretch of Spain's Mediterranean coastline. Alicante, with its airport and mainline railway station, is the arrival and departure point for most tourists. Between Alicante and Altea there are long stretches of sandy beach, which have been heavily built up with apartment blocks and hotels. North of Altea there are more fine beaches, but they are broken by cliffs and coves. South from Alicante, as far as the resort of Torrevieja, the scenery is drier and more barren, relieved only by the wooded sand dunes of Guardamar del Segura.

Gandía marks the southern end of the Costa de Valencia, whose extensive beaches of fine sand and shallow water are popular with the Spanish.

Dénia's Las Marinas beach is a flat, sandy strip lined by hotels. The rocky Les Rotes beach is good for snorkelling.

Xàbia's busiest beach is El Arenal. Most of the resort's coastline is punctuated by cliffs and coves.

Altea is a resort with an unspoiled, whitewashed old town on a hilltop. Beneath it is a long, shingle beach.

Santa Pola *is still a working fishing port, but its long, sandy beaches are very popular.*

Benidorm's liveliest beach, Levante, has been voted one of the ten best beaches in the world. Poniente is further from the town centre.

Platja de Sant Joan has a long strip of seamless sand bordered by a road and a narrow-gauge railway, which gives easy access to the beach.

The Illa de Tabarca attracts day-trippers for its natural beauty and clear waters, good for snorkelling.

Guardamar del Segura has one of the coast's least busy beaches. It is bordered by windswept sand dunes covered with aromatic pine woods.

Torrevieja is a very popular package holiday resort with sweeping, sandy beaches to the south. It has been highly developed in recent years.

Alicante's *city centre is served by the popular Postiguet beach. Nearby are vast, sandy beaches, such as La Albufereta and Sant Joan.*

◁ **Entrance of the Moorish army, part of a festival to commemorate the Reconquest, Ontinyent, Valencia**

Penyal d'Ifac ⑱

Alicante, Calp. Calp. Calp. C/ Illa de Formentera s/n, Calp, 96 583 75 96.

When viewed from afar, the rocky outcrop of the Penyal d'Ifac seems to rise vertically out of the sea. One of the Costa Blanca's most dramatic sights, this 332-m-(1,089-ft-) tall block of limestone looks virtually unclimbable. However, a short tunnel, built in 1918, allows walkers access to the gentler slopes on its seaward side.

Allow about two hours for the round trip, which starts at the visitors' centre above Calp harbour. It takes you up gentle slopes covered with juniper and fan palm, with the waves crashing below. As you climb, and at the exposed summit, there are spectacular views of a large stretch of the Costa Blanca. On a clear day you can see the hills of Ibiza *(see p510)*.

The Penyal d'Ifac is also home to 300 types of wild plant, including several rare species. Migrating birds use it as a landmark, and the salt flats below it are an important habitat for them. The rock was privately owned until 1987, when the regional government acquired it and turned it into a nature reserve.

Situated below the rock is the Iberian town of Calp, renowned for its beaches.

The magnificent limestone rock Penyal d'Ifac

Guadalest ⑲

Alicante. 240. Avenida de Alicante, 96 588 52 98. Fiestas de San Gregorio (1st week of Jun), Virgen de la Asunción (14–17 Aug).

Despite drawing coach loads of day-trippers from Benidorm, the pretty mountain village of Castell de Guadalest remains relatively unspoiled. This is largely because its older part is accessible only on foot by a single entrance: a sloping tunnel cut into the rock on which the castle ruins and the church's distinctive belfry are precariously perched.

Guadalest was founded by the Moors, who carved the surrounding hillsides into terraces and planted them with crops. These are still irrigated by the original ditches constructed by the Moors.

From the **castle** there are fine views of the surrounding mountains. Access to the castle is through the Casa Orduña.

The **Museo de Micro-Miniaturas**, displays a microscopic version of Goya's *Fusilamiento 3 de Mayo* painted on a grain of rice; his *The Naked Maja (see p293)*, painted on the wing of a fly; and a sculpture of a camel passing through the eye of a needle.

Museo de Micro-Miniaturas
Calle de la Iglesia 5. ***Tel*** *96 588 50 62.* *10am–8pm daily (summer); 10am–6pm Tue–Sun (winter).*

The belfry of Guadalest, perched on top of a rock

Alcoi ⑳

Alicante. 61,000. Sant Llorenç 2, 965 53 71 55. Wed & Sat. Mercado Medieval (mid- to late Mar), Moors and Christians (23 Apr). **www**.alcoiturisme.com

Sited at the confluence of three rivers and surrounded by high mountains, Alcoi is an industrial city. But it is best known for its mock battles between Moors and Christians *(see p255)* and its *peladillas* – almonds coated in sugar.

On the slopes above it is **Font Roja**, a nature reserve offering pleasant walks, and a shrine marked by a towering statue of the Virgin Mary.

Environs

To the north of Alcoi is the **Sierra de Mariola**, a mountain range famed for its herbs. The best point of access is the village of **Agres**. A scenic route runs from here to the summit of Mont Cabrer at 1,390 m (4,560 ft). It passes two ruined *neveras* – pits once used to store ice for preserving fish and meat.

The bullring of **Bocairent**, 10 km (6 miles) west of Agres, was carved out of rock in 1813. A nearby cliff is pockmarked with **Les Covetes dels Moros** ("the Moors' Caves"), but their origin remains a mystery.

Benidorm 21

Alicante. 71,000. Plaza Canalejas, El Torrejó, 96 585 13 11. Wed & Sun. Las Fallas (16–19 Mar), Virgen del Carmen (16 Jul), Moros y Cristianos (late Sep, early Oct), Fiestas Patronales (second weekend in Nov). **www**.visitbenidorm.es

With forests of skyscrapers overshadowing its two long beaches, Benidorm is more reminiscent of Manhattan than the obscure fishing village it once was in the early 1950s.

Benidorm boasts more accommodation than any other resort on the Mediterranean, but its clientele has changed since the 1980s when its name was synonymous with "lager louts". A huge public park and open-air auditorium used for cultural events, the **Parque de l'Aigüera**, is emblematic of the facelift Benidorm has gone through. The town now attracts more elderly holidaymakers from the north of Spain than English youths. Even so, beyond the splendid sandy beaches, the top attractions are still said to be sex, sun, nightclubs and "English" pubs.

A park on a promontory between the Levante and Poniente beaches, the **Balcón del Mediterráneo**, ends in a giant waterspout – a single-jet fountain. From here there is a panoramic view of the town. A short way out to sea is the Illa de Benidorm, a wedge-shaped island served by ferries from the harbour. The island is being converted into a nature reserve for sea birds.

Main staircase with floral lamp in the Casa Modernista, Novelda

Environs

La Vila Joiosa (Villajoyosa), to the south, is much older than Benidorm. Its principal sight is a line of brightly painted houses that overhang the riverbed. They were painted in such vivid colours, it is said, so that their fishermen owners would be able to identify their homes when they were out at sea.

The older part of **Altea**, to the north of Benidorm, stands on a hill above modern beach-front developments. It is a delightful jumble of white houses, narrow streets and long flights of steps around a blue-domed church.

The old town of Altea, dominated by its domed church

Novelda 22

Alicante. 27,000. Calle Mayor 6, 96 560 92 28. Wed & Sat. Santa María Magdalena (19–25 Jul). **www**.novelda.es

The industrial town of Novelda is dominated by its many marble factories. But it is the exquisitely preserved Art Nouveau house, the **Casa Modernista**, that is of special interest. It was built in 1903 and and rescued from demolition in 1970. The building's three floors are furnished in period style. There are few straight lines or functional shapes and almost every inch of wall space has some floral or playful motif.

Environs: Villena's town hall has a collection of Bronze Age gold objects, the **Tesoro de Villena** *(see pp48–9)*.

Casa Modernista
Calle Mayor 24. ***Tel*** *965 60 02 37. 10am–2pm Mon–Fri. by appt.*

Tesoro de Villena
Plaza de Santiago 1. ***Tel*** *965 80 11 50. Tue–Sun am.*

Alicante 23

Alicante. 320,000. Explanada de España 1, 965 14 70 38. Thu & Sat. Hogueras (20–24 Jun). **www**.alicanteturismo.com

A port and seaside resort built around a natural harbour, Alicante (Alacant) is the principal city of the Costa Blanca. Both the Greeks and Romans established settlements here. In the 8th century the Moors refounded the city under the shadow of Mount Benacantil. The summit of this hill is now occupied by the **Castillo de Santa Bárbara**, which dates mainly from the 16th century. From its top battlements there is a view over the whole city.

The focus of the city is the **Explanada de España**, a palm-lined promenade along the waterfront. The 18th-century **town hall** *(ayuntamiento)*, is worth seeing for the Salón Azul (Blue Room). A metal disc on the marble staircase is used as a reference point in measuring the sea level all

For hotels and restaurants in this region see pp576–9 and pp626–9

Yachts moored in Alicante harbour, beside the Explanada de España

around Spain. A fine collection of 20th-century art can be seen at the **Museo de Arte Contemporáneo (MACA)**. Local artist Eusebio Sempere (1924–85) assembled works by Dalí, Miró, Picasso *(see pp32–3)* and others.

Castillo de Santa Bárbara
Playa del Postiguet. ***Tel*** *965 15 29 69.* *daily.* *(for elevator only).*

Ayuntamiento
Plaza del Ayuntamiento 1. ***Tel*** *96 514 91 00.* *9am–2pm Mon–Fri.*

Museo de Arte Contemporáneo (MACA)
Plaza de Santa María 3. ***Tel*** *96 521 31 56.* *10am–8pm Tue–Sat, 10am–2pm Sun.* *1 & 6 Jan, 25 Dec & local hols.*

Illa de Tabarca ㉔

Alicante. *from Santa Pola/Alicante.* *Santa Pola, 902 51 05 90.*

The best point of departure for the Illa de Tabarca is Santa Pola. This small, flat island is divided into two parts: a stony, treeless area of level ground known as *el campo* (the countryside), and a walled settlement, which is entered through three gateways. The settlement was laid out on a grid plan in the 18th century, on the orders of Carlos III, to deter pirates.

Tabarca is a popular place to swim or snorkel and it can get crowded in the summer.

Fish and salt have long been important to the economy of Santa Pola. A Roman fish salting works has been excavated here, and outside the town are some modern saltpans.

Elx ㉕

Alicante. *230,000.* *Parque Municipal, 96 665 81 95.* *Mon & Sat.* *Misteri d'Elx (11–15 Aug).* **www**.visitelche.com

The forest of over 300,000 palm trees that surrounds Elx (Elche) on three sides is said to have been planted by the Phoenicians around 300 BC. Part of it has been enclosed as a private garden called the **Huerto del Cura**. Some of the palms – one with a trunk which has divided into eight branches – are dedicated to notable people, like the Empress Elizabeth of Austria, who visited here in 1894.

The first settlement in the area, around 5000 BC, was at La Alcudia, where a 5th-century BC Iberian stone bust of a priestess, *La Dama de Elche (see p48)*, was discovered in 1897. The original is in Madrid, but there are several replicas scattered around Elx.

The blue-domed Baroque church, the **Basílica de Santa María**, was built in the 17th century to house the **Misteri d'Elx** *(see p41)*. Next to it is **La Calahorra**, a Gothic tower, which is a surviving part of the city's defences.

A clock on the roof next to the town hall has two 16th-century mechanical figures, which strike the hours on bells.

Huerto del Cura
Porta de la Morera 49. ***Tel*** *96 545 19 36.* *daily.*
www.huertodelcura.com

La Calahorra
Calle Uberna. *to the public.*

Orihuela ㉖

Alicante. *86,000.* *Calle Francisco Die 25, 96 530 46 45.* *Tue.* *Moros y Cristianos (10–17 Jul).* **www**.orihuelaturistica.es

In the 15th century Orihuela was prosperous enough for Fernando and Isabel to stop and collect men and money on their way to do battle against the Moors at Granada. The Gothic **cathedral** houses Velázquez's *The Temptation of St Thomas Aquinas* in its museum. Among the exhibits in the **Museo San Juan de Dios** archaeological museum is a processional float bearing a 17th-century statue of a she-devil, *La Diablesa*.

Museo San Juan de Dios
Calle del Hospital. ***Tel*** *96 674 31 54.* *Tue–Sun.*

***La Diablesa*, Orihuela**

Torrevieja ㉗

Alicante. *101,800.* *Plaza Ruiz Capdepont, 96 570 34 33.* *Fri.* *Habaneras (22–30 Jul).*

During the 1980s, Torrevieja grew at a prodigious rate as thousands of Europeans purchased homes here. Before tourism, the town's source of income was sea salt. The salt works are the most productive in Europe and the second most important in the world.

Torrevieja stages a festival of *habaneras*, melodic songs originating in Cuba, brought back to Spain by salt exporters.

Capilla del Junterón, Murcia

Murcia ㉘

Murcia. *425,000.*
Plaza Cardenal Belluga, Ayuntamiento Building, 968 35 87 49. *Thu.* *Semana Santa (Easter Week).* www.turismodemurcia.es

A regional capital and university city on the River Segura, Murcia was founded in 825 by the Moors, following successful irrigation of the surrounding fertile plain.

The pedestrianized Calle de la Trapería, linking the cathedral and the former marketplace (now the Plaza Santo Domingo), is the city's main street.

On it stands the **Casino**, a gentlemen's club founded in 1847. It is entered through an Arab-style patio, fashioned on the royal chambers of the Alhambra. The huge ballroom has a polished parquet floor and is illuminated by five crystal chandeliers. Visitors can take a tour of the interior and splash out on a meal in the top-class restaurant.

Work on the **cathedral** began in 1394 over the foundations of Murcia's central mosque, and it was finally consecrated in 1467. The large tower was added much later and constructed in stages from the 16th to the 18th centuries. The architect Jaime Bort built the main, Baroque façade between 1739 and 1754.

The cathedral's finest features are two exquisitely ornate side chapels. The first, the Capilla de los Vélez, is in Late Gothic style and was built between 1490 and 1507. The second, the Renaissance Capilla del Junterón, dates from the early 16th century.

The **cathedral museum** displays grand Gothic altarpieces, a frieze from a Roman sarcophagus and the third-largest monstrance in Spain.

Francisco Salzillo (1707–83), one of Spain's greatest sculptors, was born in Murcia, and a museum in the **Iglesia de Jesús** (Church of Jesus) exhibits nine of his *pasos* – sculptures on platforms. These are carried through the streets on Good Friday morning. The figures are so lifelike that a fellow sculptor is said to have told the men carrying a *paso*: "Put it down, it will walk by itself".

Arab-style patio, Murcia Casino

The **Museo Etnológico de la Huerta de Murcia**, 7 km (4.5 miles) out of Murcia, stands beside a large water wheel – a 1955 copy in iron of the original 15th-century wooden wheel. The three galleries display agricultural and domestic items, some of them 300 years old. A traditional, thatched Murcian farmhouse *(barraca)* forms part of the museum.

Casino
Calle Trapería 18. ***Tel*** *968 21 53 99.* *10:30am–7:30pm daily.*

Museo Etnológico de la Huerta de Murcia
Avda Principe, Alcantarilla. ***Tel*** *968 89 25 86.* *Tue–Sun.* *public hols.*

Mar Menor ㉙

Murcia. *San Javier.* *to Cartagena, then bus.* *La Manga.* *La Manga, 968 14 61 36.* www.marmenor.es

The elongated, high-rise holiday resort of La Manga, built on a long, thin, sandy strip, separates the Mediterranean and the Mar Menor, literally "the Smaller Sea".

Really a large lagoon, the sheltered Mar Menor can be 5°C (9°F) warmer than the Mediterranean in summer. Its high mineral concentrations first drew rest-cure tourists in the early 20th century. They stayed at the older resorts of Santiago de la Ribera and Los Alcázares, which still have pretty wooden jetties.

From either La Manga or Santiago de la Ribera you can make a ferry trip to the Isla Perdiguera, one of the five islands in the Mar Menor.

The region is very built-up, but to escape the crowds head to the Parque Regional de Calblanque. Its dunes and beaches are wild and unspoilt.

The resort of Los Alcázares on the edge of the Mar Menor

For hotels and restaurants in this region see pp576–9 and pp626–9

View of the domes and spires of Cartagena's town hall from the seafront

Cartagena 30

Murcia. 218,200. San Javier. Plaza Almirante Bastarreche, 968 50 64 83. Wed. Semana Santa (Easter Wk), Carthaginians and Romans (last two weeks Sep). **www**.cartagenaturismo.es

The first settlement founded in the natural harbour of Cartagena was constructed in 223 BC by the Carthaginians, who called it *Quart Hadas* (New City). After conquering the city in 209 BC, the Romans renamed it *Carthago Nova* (New Carthage). Although the city declined in importance in the Middle Ages, its prestige increased in the 18th century when it became a naval base.

You can get an overview of the city from the park, which surrounds the ruins of the **Castillo de la Concepción**, Cartagena's castle. It has views over the impressive Roman theatre. The city hall marks the end of the Calle Mayor, a street overlooked by balconies and lined with handsome buildings. Excavations in the city include a Roman street and the **Muralla Bizantina** (Byzantine Wall), built between 589 and 590.

The **Museo Nacional de Arqueología Marítima** has a collection of treasures from Greek and Roman wrecks.

Muralla Bizantina
Calle Doctor Tapia Martínez. ***Tel*** *968 50 79 66. Tue–Sat.*

Museo Nacional de Arqueología Marítima
Paseo Alfonso XII. ***Tel*** *968 12 11 66. Tue–Sat. some public hols.*

Costa Cálida 31

Murcia. Murcia. Murcia. C/ Antonio Cortijos, Águilas, 968 49 31 73. **www**.murciaturistica.es

The most popular resorts of Murcia's "Warm Coast" are around the Mar Menor. Between Cabo de Palos and Cabo Tinoso the few small beaches are dwarfed by cliffs. The resorts of the southern part of the coast are relatively quiet. There are several fine beaches at Puerto de Mazarrón; and at nearby Bolnuevo the wind has eroded soft rocks into strange shapes. The growing resort of Águilas marks the southern limit of the coast, at the border with Andalusia.

Lorca 32

Murcia. 98,800. Calle Lope Gisbert, 968 44 19 14. Thu. Semana Santa (Easter Week), Feria (3rd week of Sep), Día de San Clemente (23 Nov). **www**.lorca.es, **www**.lorcaturismo.es

The farmland around Lorca, Murcia's third most important town, is a fertile oasis in one of Europe's most arid areas. Lorca was an important staging post on the Via Heraclea, as witnessed by the Roman milepost standing in a corner of the Plaza San Vicente. During the wars between Moors and Christians in the 13th to 15th centuries, Lorca became a frontier town between Al Andalus and the Castilian territory of Murcia. Its castle dates from this era, although only two of its original 35 towers remain. In 2011, the city was hit by Spain's worst earthquake for more than 50 years. The castle was badly damaged and repair work is ongoing. After Granada fell the town lost its importance and, except for one surviving gateway, its walls were demolished.

The central Plaza de España is lined with handsome stone buildings. One side is occupied by the **Colegiata de San Patricio** (Church of St Patrick), built between 1533 and 1704, the only church in Spain dedicated to the Irish saint.

Roman milepost topped by a statue of St Vincent, Lorca

Caravaca de la Cruz 33

Murcia. 26,400. Calle de las Monjas 17, 968 70 24 24. Mon, 3rd Sun of month (crafts). Vera Cruz (1–5 May). **www**.caravaca.org

A town of ancient churches, Caravaca de la Cruz's fame lies in its castle which houses the **Santuario de la Vera Cruz** (Sanctuary of the True Cross). This is where a double-armed cross is said to have appeared miraculously in 1231 – twelve years before the town was seized by Christians. The highlight of the Vera Cruz fiesta is the Race of the Wine Horses, which commemorates the lifting of a Moorish siege of the castle and the appearance of the cross. The cross was dipped in wine, which the thirsty defenders then drank and recovered their fighting strength.

Environs

Just to the north, among the foothills on Murcia's western border, is the village of **Moratalla**, a jumble of steep streets and stone houses lying beneath a 15th-century castle. **Cehegín**, east of Caravaca, is a partially preserved 16th- and 17th-century town.

MADRID

Introducing Madrid

Spain's capital, a city of over three million people, is situated close to the geographical centre of the country, at the hub of both road and rail networks. Because of its distance from the sea and its altitude – 660 m (2,150 ft) – the city endures cold winters and hot summers, making spring and autumn the best times to visit. Madrid's attractions include three internationally famous art galleries, a royal palace, grand public squares and many museums filled with the treasures of Spain's history. The city is surrounded by its own small province, the Comunidad de Madrid, which takes in the Sierra de Guadarrama and one of Spain's most famous monuments, the palace of El Escorial.

The Palacio Real (see pp276–7), *the royal palace built by Spain's first Bourbon kings, dominates the western part of Old Madrid. Its lavishly decorated chambers include the throne room.*

The Plaza Mayor (see p273), *Old Madrid's great 17th-century square, has been a focal point of the city since the days when it was used as a public arena for bullfights, trials by the Inquisition and executions* (see p274). *An equestrian statue of Felipe III stands in the middle of the square.*

OLD MADRID
(see pp268–81)

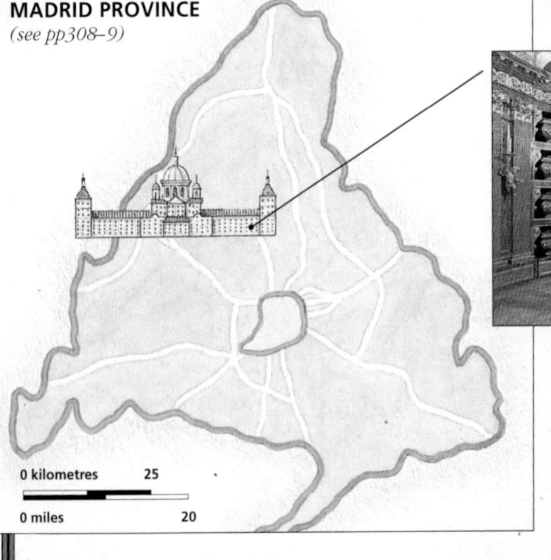

El Escorial (see pp330–31), *the massive, architecturally austere monastery-palace built by Felipe II, has some sumptuous apartments decorated with great works of art. Marble sarcophagi in the octagonal Royal Pantheon contain the mortal remains of most Spanish monarchs.*

◁ **Sculpted fountain of the Goddess Cybele in the Plaza de Cibeles, with the City Hall and main post office behind**

The Museo Thyssen-Bornemisza (see pp288–9), *one of the most important privately assembled art collections in the world, was sold to Spain in 1993. The 18th-century palace houses major works by Titian, Rubens, Goya, Van Gogh and Picasso.*

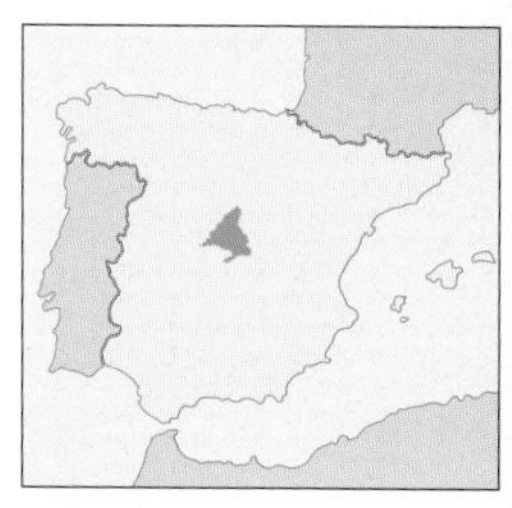

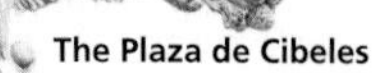

The Plaza de Cibeles (see p286), *one of the city's most impressive squares, is ringed by distinctive buildings, including the 19th-century Banco de España and Madrid's main post office, with sculptures on its white façade.*

BOURBON MADRID
(see pp282–99)

The Parque del Retiro (see p297) *has leafy paths and avenues, and a boating lake overlooked by a majestic colonnade. It is an ideal place in which to relax between visits to the great art galleries and museums of Bourbon Madrid.*

The Museo del Prado (see pp292–5) *is one of the world's greatest art galleries. It has important collections of paintings by Velázquez and Goya, whose statues stand outside the main entrances.*

0 metres 500

0 yards 500

The Museo Reina Sofía (see pp298–9), *an outstanding museum of 20th-century art, is entered by highly original exterior glass lifts. Inside, the star exhibit is* Guernica, *Picasso's famous painting of the horrors of the Civil War.*

HOTEL

OLD MADRID

When Felipe II chose Madrid as his capital in 1561, it was a small Castilian town of little real significance. In the following years, it was to grow into the nerve centre of a mighty empire.

According to tradition, it was the Moorish chieftain Muhammad ben Abd al Rahman who established a fortress above the Río Manzanares. Magerit, as it was called in Arabic, fell to Alfonso VI of Castile between 1083 and 1086. Narrow streets with houses and medieval churches began to grow up on the higher ground behind the old Arab *alcazar* (fortress), which was replaced by a Gothic palace in the 15th century. When this burned down in 1734, it was replaced by the present Bourbon palace, the Palacio Real.

Drawer designed for storing herbs, Palacio Real

The population had scarcely reached 20,000 when Madrid was chosen as capital, but by the end of the century it had more than trebled. The 16th-century city is known as the "Madrid de los Austrias", after the reigning Habsburg dynasty. During this period royal monasteries were endowed and churches and private palaces were built. In the 17th century, the Plaza Mayor was added and the Puerta del Sol, the "Gate of the Sun", became the spiritual and geographical heart not only of Madrid but of all Spain.

SIGHTS AT A GLANCE

Historic Buildings
Palacio Real pp276–7 9

Museums and Galleries
Real Academia de Bellas Artes 14

Churches and Convents
Catedral de la Almudena 7
Colegiata de San Isidro 2
Iglesia de San Nicolás 5
Monasterio de las Descalzas Reales 13
Monasterio de la Encarnación 10

Streets, Squares and Parks
Campo del Moro 8
Gran Vía 12
Plaza de España 11
Plaza Mayor 4
Plaza de Oriente 6
Plaza de la Villa 3
Puerta del Sol 1

GETTING THERE

The metro is the fastest and easiest way to get to Old Madrid. Take line 1 to Gran Vía or Sol; alternatively, lines 2, 3, 5 and 10 are good for getting to the main sights. Buses 15, 51, 52 and 150 to the Puerta del Sol are useful.

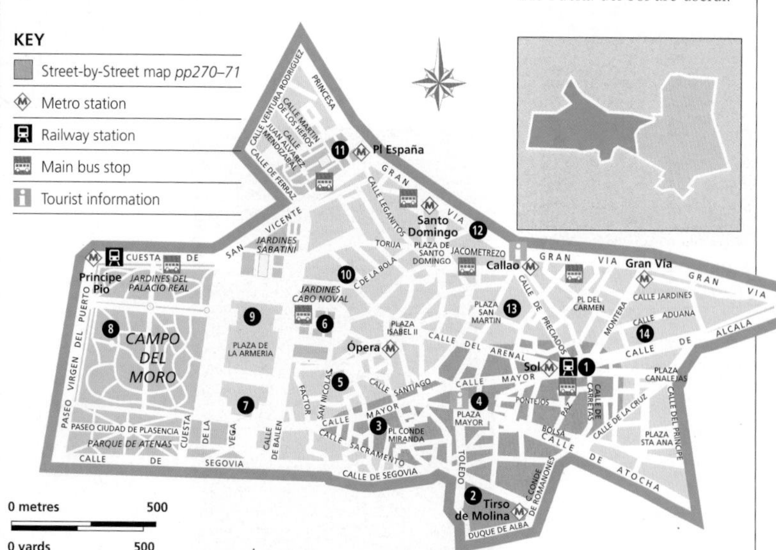

◁ **Monument to Cervantes by Lorenzo Coullaut-Valera in the Plaza de España**

Street-by-Street: Old Madrid

Stretching from the charming Plaza de la Villa to the busy Puerta del Sol, the compact heart of Old Madrid is steeped in history and full of interesting sights. Trials by the Inquisition *(see p274)* and executions were once held in the Plaza Mayor. This porticoed square is Old Madrid's finest piece of architecture, a legacy of the Habsburgs *(see pp58–61)*. Other buildings of note are the Colegiata de San Isidro and the Palacio de Santa Cruz. For a more relaxing way of enjoying Old Madrid, sit in one of the area's numerous cafés or browse among the stalls of the Mercado de San Miguel.

★ Plaza Mayor
This beautiful 17 century square competes with th Puerta del Sol as the focus of Old Madrid. The arcades at the ba of the three-store buildings are fill with cafés and craft shops ❹

The Mercado de San Miguel is housed in a 19th-century building with wrought-iron columns. The market has several excellent delicatessens and a restaurant.

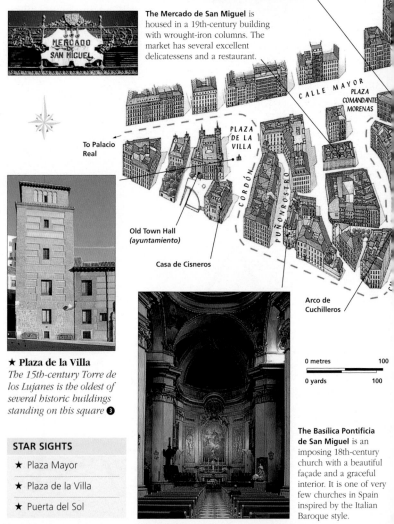

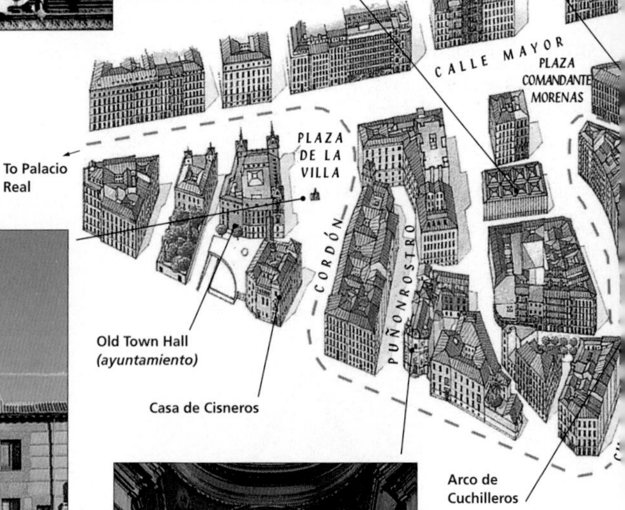

CALLE MAYOR

PLAZA COMANDANTE MORENAS

PLAZA DE LA VILLA

CORDÓN

PUÑONROSTRO

To Palacio Real

Old Town Hall *(ayuntamiento)*

Casa de Cisneros

Arco de Cuchilleros

★ Plaza de la Villa
The 15th-century Torre de los Lujanes is the oldest of several historic buildings standing on this square ❸

0 metres 100

0 yards 100

The Basílica Pontificia de San Miguel is an imposing 18th-century church with a beautiful façade and a graceful interior. It is one of very few churches in Spain inspired by the Italian Baroque style.

STAR SIGHTS

- ★ Plaza Mayor
- ★ Plaza de la Villa
- ★ Puerta del Sol

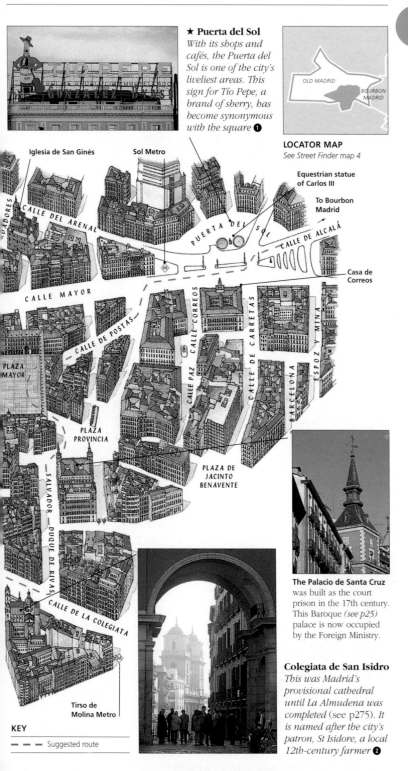

★ Puerta del Sol
With its shops and cafés, the Puerta del Sol is one of the city's liveliest areas. This sign for Tío Pepe, a brand of sherry, has become synonymous with the square ❶

LOCATOR MAP
See Street Finder map 4

Iglesia de San Ginés

Sol Metro

Equestrian statue of Carlos III

To Bourbon Madrid

CALLE DEL ARENAL

PUERTA DEL SOL

CALLE DE ALCALÁ

Casa de Correos

CALLE MAYOR

CALLE DE POSTAS

CALLE CORREOS

CALLE DE CARRETAS

ESPOZ Y MINA

PLAZA MAYOR

CALLE PAZ

BARCELONA

PLAZA PROVINCIA

PLAZA DE JACINTO BENAVENTE

SALVADOR

DUQUE DE RIVAS

CALLE DE LA COLEGIATA

Tirso de Molina Metro

KEY

– – – Suggested route

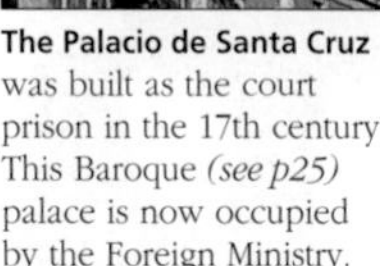
The Palacio de Santa Cruz was built as the court prison in the 17th century. This Baroque *(see p25)* palace is now occupied by the Foreign Ministry.

Colegiata de San Isidro
This was Madrid's provisional cathedral until La Almudena was completed (see p275). *It is named after the city's patron, St Isidore, a local 12th-century farmer* ❷

Kilometre Zero, the centre of Spain's road network, Puerta del Sol

Puerta del Sol ❶

Map 4 F2. Ⓜ *Sol.*

Crowded and noisy with chatter and policemen's whistles, the Puerta del Sol makes a fitting centre for Madrid. This is one of the city's most popular meeting places, and huge crowds converge here on their way to the shops and sights in the old part of the city.

The square marks the site of the original eastern entrance to the city, once occupied by a gatehouse and castle. These disappeared long ago and in their place came a succession of churches. In the late 19th century the area was turned into a square and became the centre of café society.

Today the "square" is shaped like a half moon. A recent addition is the modern glass train station in front of the statue of Carlos III. The southern side of the square is edged by an austere red-brick building, originally the city's post office, built in the 1760s under Carlos III. In 1847 it became the headquarters of the Ministry of the Interior. The clocktower, which gives the building much of its identity, was added in 1866. During the Franco regime *(see pp66–7)*, the police cells beneath the building were the site of many human rights abuses. In 1963, Julián Grimau, a member of the underground Communist party, allegedly fell from an upstairs window and miraculously survived, only to be executed soon afterwards.

The bronze bear and strawberry tree of Madrid, Puerta del Sol

The building is now home to the regional government and is the focus of many festive events. At midnight on New Year's Eve crowds fill the square to eat a grape on each stroke of the clock, a tradition supposed to bring good luck for the year. Outside a symbol on the ground marks Kilometre Zero, considered the centre of Spain's huge road network.

The buildings opposite are arranged in a semicircle and contain modern shops and cafés. On the corner of Calle del Carmen is a bronze statue of the symbol of Madrid – a bear reaching for the fruit of a *madroño* (strawberry tree).

The Puerta del Sol has witnessed many important historical events. On 2 May 1808 the uprising against the occupying French forces began here, but the crowd, pitted against the well-armed French troops, was crushed *(see p63)*. In 1912 the liberal prime minister José Canalejas was assassinated in the square and, in 1931, the Second Republic *(see p65)* was proclaimed from the balcony of the Ministry of the Interior.

Colegiata de San Isidro ❷

Calle Toledo 37. **Map** 4 E3.
Tel *91 369 20 37.* Ⓜ *La Latina.*
8am–1pm, 6–8pm Mon–Sat, 9am–2:30pm, 6–8pm Sun.

Built in the Baroque style *(see p25)* for the Jesuits in the mid-17th century, this twin-towered church served as Madrid's cathedral until La Almudena *(see p275)* was completed in 1993.

After Carlos III expelled the Jesuits from Spain in 1767 *(see p62)*, Ventura Rodríguez was commissioned to redesign the interior of the church. It was then rededicated to Madrid's patron saint, St Isidore, and two years later the saint's remains were moved here from the Iglesia de San Andrés. San Isidro was returned to the Jesuits during the reign of Fernando VII (1814–33).

Altar in the Colegiata de San Isidro

Plaza de la Villa ❸

Map 4 D3. Ⓜ *Ópera, Sol.*

The much restored and frequently remodelled Plaza de la Villa is one of the most atmospheric spots in Madrid. Some of the city's most historic secular buildings are situated around this square.

The oldest building is the early 15th-century Torre de los Lujanes, with its Gothic portal and Mudéjar-style horseshoe arches. François I of France was allegedly imprisoned in it following his defeat at the Battle of Pavia in 1525. The Casa de Cisneros was built in 1537 for the nephew

Portal of the Torre de los Lujanes

of Cardinal Cisneros, founder of the historic University of Alcalá *(see pp332–3)*. The main façade, on the Calle de Sacramento, is an excellent example of the Plateresque style *(see p25)*.

Linked to this building, by an enclosed bridge, is the town hall *(ayuntamiento)*. Designed in the 1640s by Juan Gómez de Mora, architect of the Plaza Mayor, it exhibits the same combination of steep roofs with dormer windows, steeple-like towers at the corners and an austere façade of brick and stone. Before construction was finished – more than 30 years later – the building had acquired handsome Baroque doorways. A balcony was later added by Juan de Villanueva, the architect of the Prado *(see pp292–5)*, so that the royal family could watch Corpus Christi processions passing by.

Plaza Mayor ❹

Map 4 E3. Ⓜ *Sol.*

The Plaza Mayor forms a splendid rectangular square, all balconies and pinnacles, dormer windows and steep slate roofs. The square, with its theatrical atmosphere, is very Castilian in character. Much was expected to happen here and a great deal did – bullfights, executions, pageants and trials by the Inquisition *(see p274)* – all watched by crowds, often in the presence of the reigning king and queen. The first great public scene was the beatification of Madrid's patron, St Isidore, in 1621. In the same year, the execution of Rodrigo Calderón, secretary to Felipe III, was held here. Although hated by the Madrid populace, Calderón bore himself with such dignity on the day of his death that the phrase "proud as Rodrigo on the scaffold" survives to this day. Perhaps the greatest occasion of all, however, was the arrival here – from Italy – of Carlos III in 1760.

The square was started in 1617 and built in just two years, replacing slum houses. Its architect, Juan Gómez de Mora, was successor to Juan de Herrera, designer of Felipe II's austere monastery-palace, El Escorial *(see pp330–31)*. Gómez de Mora echoed the style of his master, softening it slightly. The square was later reformed by Juan de Villanueva. The fanciest part of the arcaded construction is the Casa de la Panadería (bakery). Its façade, now crudely reinvented, is decorated with allegorical paintings. Madrid's main tourist office is sited here.

The equestrian statue in the centre is of Felipe III, who ordered the square's construction. Started by the Italian Giovanni de Bologna and finished by his pupil Pietro Tacca in 1616, the statue was moved here in 1848 from the Casa de Campo *(see p302)*. Today the square is lined with cafés, and is the venue for a collectors' market on Sundays *(see p317)*. The square's southern exit leads into Calle de Toledo towards the streets where the Rastro, Madrid's flea-market *(see p302)*, is held. A flight of steps in the south-west corner takes you under the Arco de Cuchilleros to the Calle de Cuchilleros, and some *mesones*, traditional restaurants.

Allegorical paintings on the Casa de la Panadería, Plaza Mayor

The Spanish Inquisition

The Spanish Inquisition was set up by Fernando and Isabel in 1480 to create a single, monolithic Catholic ideology in Spain. Protestant heretics and alleged "false converts" to Catholicism from the Jewish and Muslim faiths were tried, to ensure the religious unity of the country. Beginning with a papal bull, the Inquisition was run like a court, presided over by the Inquisitor-General. However, the defendants were denied counsel, not told the charges facing them and tortured to obtain confessions. Punishment ranged from imprisonment to beheading, hanging or burning at the stake. A formidable system of control, it gave Spain's Protestant enemies a major propaganda weapon by contributing to the *Leyenda Negra* (Black Legend) which lasted, along with the Inquisition, into the 18th century.

Inquisition banner

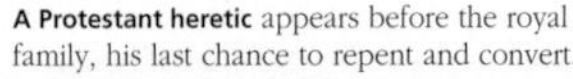

A Protestant heretic appears before the royal family, his last chance to repent and convert.

A convicted defendant, forced to wear a red *sanbenito* robe, is led away to prison.

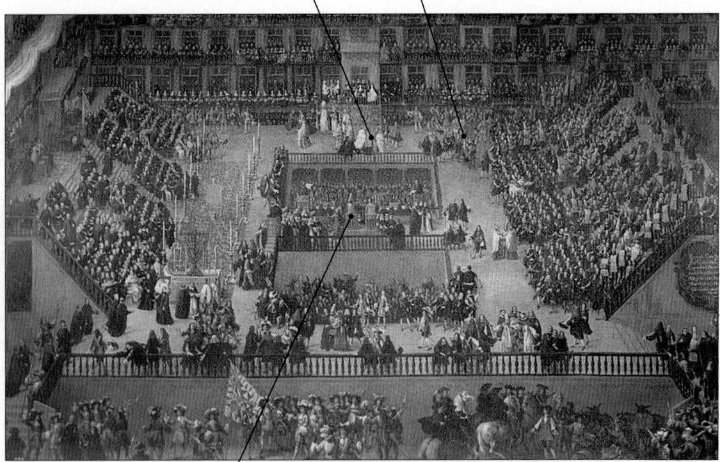

Those who have refused to confess are sentenced in public by day, and then executed before nightfall.

AUTO-DE-FE IN THE PLAZA MAYOR

This painting by Francisco de Ricci (1683) depicts a trial, or *auto-de-fe* – literally, show of faith – held in Madrid's main square on 30 June 1680. Unlike papal inquisitions elsewhere in Europe, it was presided over by the reigning monarch, Carlos II, accompanied by his queen.

Torture *was widely used by the Inquisitors and their assistants to extract confessions from their victims. This early 19th-century German engraving shows a man being roasted on a wheel.*

The Procession of the Flagellants *(c.1812) by Goya shows the abiding influence of the Inquisition on the popular imagination. The penitents in the picture are wearing the tall conical hats of heretics tried by the Inquisition. These hats can still be seen in Easter Week processions* (see p38) *throughout Spain.*

Iglesia de San Nicolás de Bari ❺

Plaza de San Nicolás 1. **Map** 3 C2. ***Tel*** *91 559 40 64.* Ⓜ *Ópera.* ◯ *8:30am–1:30pm Mon, 6:30–8:30pm Tue–Sat, 10am–1:30pm Sun.*

The first mention of the church of San Nicolás is in a document of 1202. Its brick tower, with horseshoe arches, is the oldest surviving ecclesiastical structure in Madrid. It is thought to be 12th-century Mudéjar in style, and may have originally been the minaret of a Moorish mosque.

Plaza de Oriente ❻

Map 3 C2. Ⓜ *Ópera.*

During his days as king of Spain, Joseph Bonaparte *(see p63)* carved out this stirrup-shaped space from the jumble of buildings to the east of the Palacio Real *(see pp276–7)*, providing the view of the palace enjoyed today.

The square was once an important meeting place for state occasions; kings, queens and dictators all made public appearances on the palace balcony. The many statues of early kings that stand here were originally intended for the palace roof, but proved too heavy. The equestrian statue of Felipe IV in the centre of the square is by Italian sculptor Pietro Tacca, and is based on drawings by Velázquez. Across the square is the imposing Teatro Real, or Teatro de la Ópera, inaugurated in 1850 by Isabel II.

Equestrian statue of Felipe IV, by Pietro Tacca, Plaza de Oriente

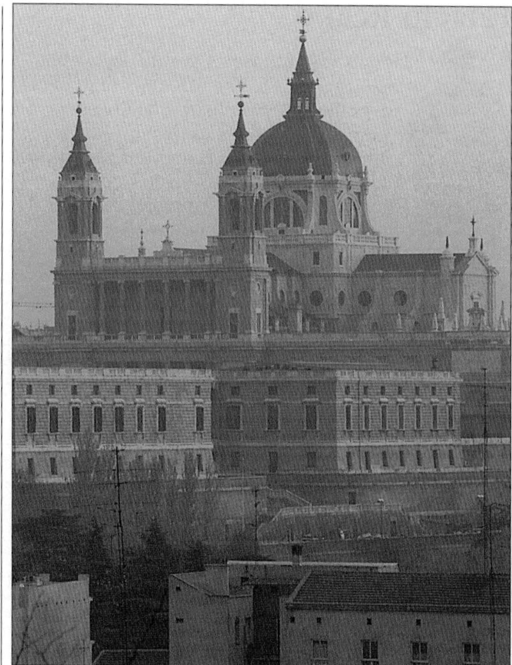

View of the Catedral de la Almudena and the Royal Palace

Catedral de la Almudena ❼

Calle Bailén 8–10. **Map** 3 B2. ***Tel*** *91 542 22 00.* Ⓜ *Ópera.* ◯ *9am–8:30pm daily (10am–9pm Jul & Aug); Museum & Dome 10am–2:30pm Mon–Sat.*

Dedicated to the city's patron, the cathedral was begun in 1879 and completed over a century later. The cathedral's Neo-Gothic grey and white façade is similar to that of the Palacio Real, which stands opposite. The crypt houses a 16th-century image of the Virgen de la Almudena.

Further along the Calle Mayor is the site of archaeological excavations of the remains of Madrid's Moorish and medieval city walls.

The first royal wedding took place in the cathedral between Prince Felipe and Letizia Ortiz in May 2004.

Campo del Moro ❽

Map 3 A2. Ⓜ *Príncipe Pío.* ◯ *Oct–Mar: 10am–6pm daily; Apr–Sep: 10am–8pm daily.* ● *1 & 6 Jan, 1 & 15 May, 12 Oct, 9 Nov, 24, 25 & 31 Dec and for official functions.* **www**.patrimonionacional.es

The Campo del Moro (the "Field of the Moor") is a pleasing park, rising steeply from the Río Manzanares to offer one of the finest views of the Palacio Real *(see pp276–7)*.

The park has a varied history. In 1109 a Moorish army, led by Ali ben Yusuf bivouacked here, hence the name. The park went on to become a jousting ground for Christian knights. In the late 19th century it was used as a lavish playground for royal children. Around the same time it was landscaped in what is described as English style, with winding paths, grass and woodland, fountains and statues. It was reopened to the public in 1931 under the Second Republic *(see p65)*, closed again under Franco, and not reopened until 1978.

Palacio Real ❾

Statue of Carlos III

Madrid's vast and lavish Royal Palace was built to impress. The site, on a high bluff over the Río Manzanares, had been occupied for centuries by a royal fortress, but after a fire in 1734, Felipe V commissioned a truly palatial replacement. Construction lasted 17 years, spanning the reign of two Bourbon monarchs, and much of the exuberant decor reflects the tastes of Carlos III and Carlos IV *(see p71)*. The palace was used by the royal family until the abdication of Alfonso XIII in 1931. The present king, Juan Carlos I, lives in the more modest Zarzuela Palace outside Madrid, but the Royal Palace is still used for state occasions.

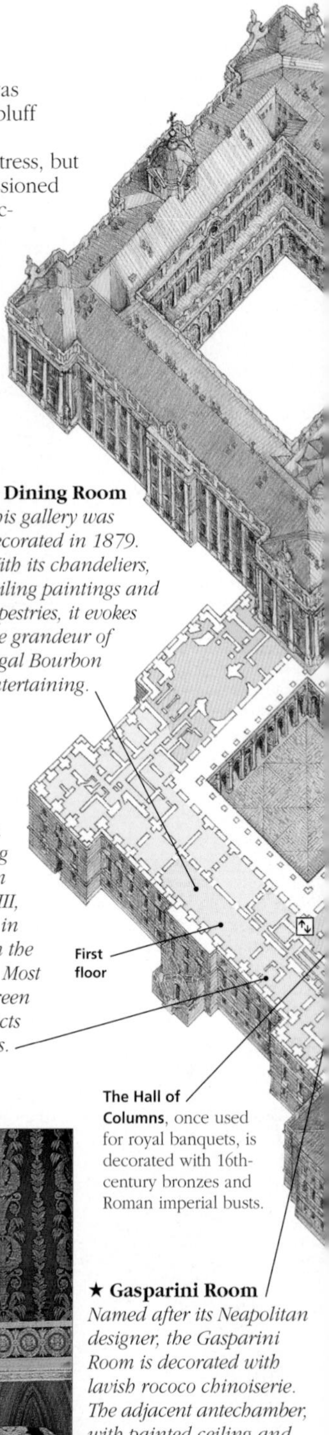

★ Dining Room
This gallery was decorated in 1879. With its chandeliers, ceiling paintings and tapestries, it evokes the grandeur of regal Bourbon entertaining.

★ Porcelain Room
The walls and ceiling of this room, built on the orders of Carlos III, are entirely covered in royal porcelain from the Buen Retiro factory. Most of the porcelain is green and white, and depicts cherubs and wreaths.

First floor

The Hall of Columns, once used for royal banquets, is decorated with 16th-century bronzes and Roman imperial busts.

★ Gasparini Room
Named after its Neapolitan designer, the Gasparini Room is decorated with lavish rococo chinoiserie. The adjacent antechamber, with painted ceiling and ornate chandelier, houses Goya's portrait of Carlos IV.

STAR FEATURES

- ★ Gasparini Room
- ★ Porcelain Room
- ★ Dining Room
- ★ Throne Room

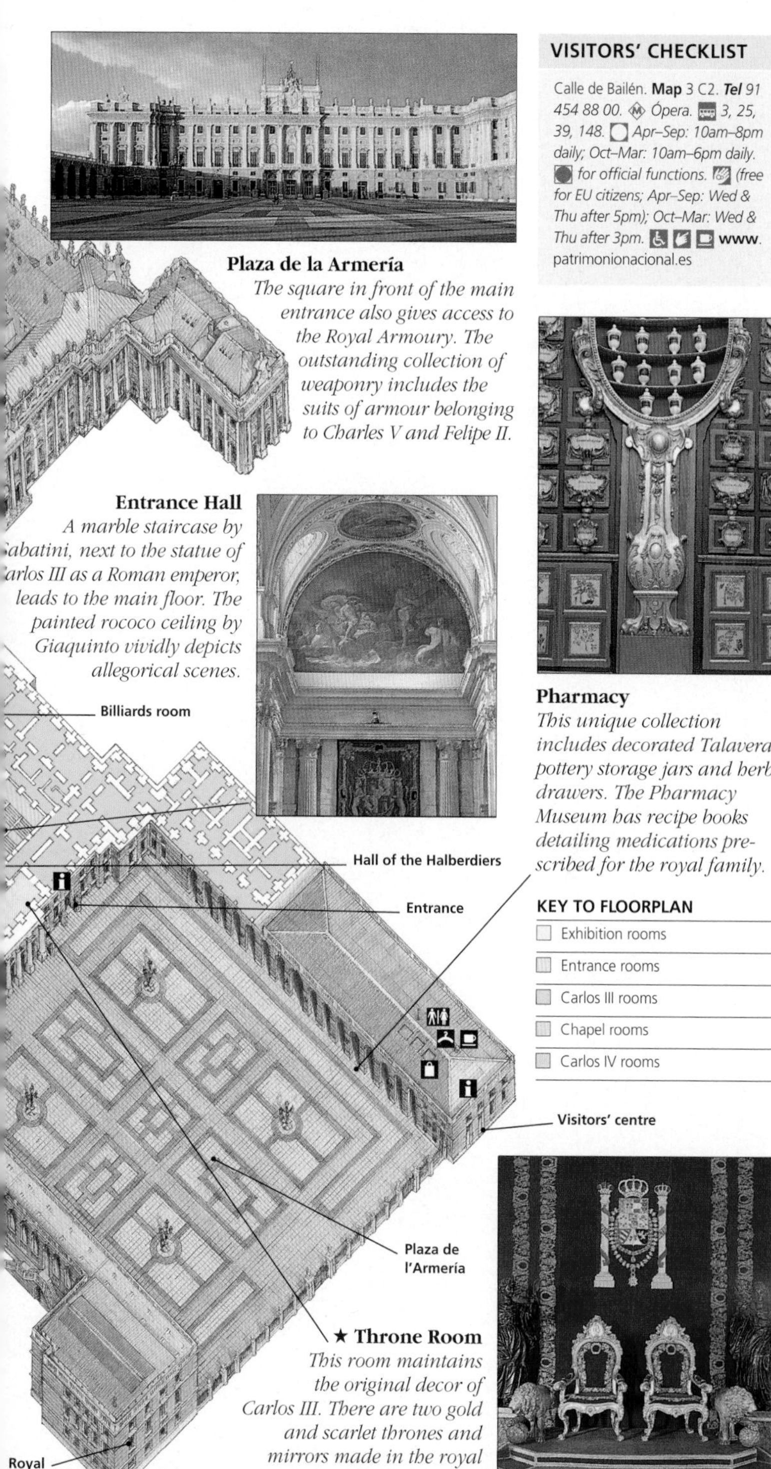

Plaza de la Armería
The square in front of the main entrance also gives access to the Royal Armoury. The outstanding collection of weaponry includes the suits of armour belonging to Charles V and Felipe II.

Entrance Hall
A marble staircase by Sabatini, next to the statue of Carlos III as a Roman emperor, leads to the main floor. The painted rococo ceiling by Giaquinto vividly depicts allegorical scenes.

★ Throne Room
This room maintains the original decor of Carlos III. There are two gold and scarlet thrones and mirrors made in the royal glass factory of La Granja.

VISITORS' CHECKLIST

Calle de Bailén. **Map** 3 C2. ***Tel*** *91 454 88 00.* Ópera. 3, 25, 39, 148. *Apr–Sep: 10am–8pm daily; Oct–Mar: 10am–6pm daily.* *for official functions.* *(free for EU citizens; Apr–Sep: Wed & Thu after 5pm); Oct–Mar: Wed & Thu after 3pm.* **www.** patrimonionacional.es

Pharmacy
This unique collection includes decorated Talavera pottery storage jars and herb drawers. The Pharmacy Museum has recipe books detailing medications prescribed for the royal family.

KEY TO FLOORPLAN

- Exhibition rooms
- Entrance rooms
- Carlos III rooms
- Chapel rooms
- Carlos IV rooms

HOTEL WASHINGTON
H. MAGERIT
COLISEVM
COLISEVM
CINE
Metro

VP
EUROPA
MADRID
CALDERON

Entrance to the Convento de la Encarnación

Monasterio de la Encarnación ❿

Plaza de la Encarnación 1. **Map** 4 D1. ***Tel*** *91 454 88 00. Ⓜ Ópera, Santo Domingo. 10am–2pm, 4–6:30pm Tue–Sat, 10am–3:30pm Sun & public hols. 1 & 6 Jan, Easter, 1 & 15 May, 27 Jul, 9 Nov, 24, 25 & 31 Dec. (free Wed and Thu afternoons for EU residents).* **www.** patrimonionacional.es

Standing in a delightful tree-shaded square, this tranquil Augustinian convent was founded in 1611 for Margaret of Austria, wife of Felipe III. The architect, Juan Gómez de Mora, also built the Plaza Mayor *(see p273)* and the façade clearly reveals his work.

Still inhabited by nuns, the convent has the atmosphere of old Castile, with its blue and white Talavera tiles, wooden doors, exposed beams and portraits of royal benefactors. Inside is a collection of 17th-century art, with paintings by José de Ribera and Vincente Carducho lining the walls. Polychromatic wooden statues include *Cristo Yacente* (*Lying Christ*), by Gregorio Fernández.

The convent's main attraction is the reliquary chamber with a ceiling painted by Carducho. It is used to store the skulls and bones of saints. There is also a phial containing the dried blood of St Pantaleon. According to a popular myth, the blood liquefies each year on 27 July, the anniversary of the saint's death. Should the blood fail to liquefy, it is said that disaster will befall Madrid. The church was rebuilt by Ventura Rodríguez after a fire in 1767.

Plaza de España ⓫

Map 1 C5. *Ⓜ Plaza de España.*

One of Madrid's busiest traffic intersections and most popular meeting places is the Plaza de España, which slopes down towards the Palacio Real *(see pp276–7)* and the Sabatini Gardens. In the 18th and 19th centuries the square was occupied by military barracks, built here because of the square's close proximity to the palace. However, further expansion of Madrid resulted in its becoming a public space.

The square acquired its present appearance during the Franco period *(see pp66–7)*, with the construction, on the northern side, of the massive Edificio España between 1947 and 1953. Across the square is the Torre de Madrid (1957), known as *La Jirafa* (the Giraffe), which, for a while, was the tallest concrete structure in the world. The most attractive part of the square is its centre, occupied by a massive stone obelisk built in 1928. In front of it is a statue of the author Cervantes *(see p333)*. Below him, Don Quixote *(see pp394–5)* rides his horse Rocinante while the plump Sancho Panza trots alongside on his donkey. On the left-hand side is Dulcinea, Don Quixote's sweetheart.

Gran Vía ⓬

Map 2 D5. *Ⓜ Plaza de España, Santo Domingo, Callao, Gran Vía.*

A main traffic artery of the modern city, the Gran Vía was inaugurated in 1910. Its construction spanned several decades and required the demolition of large numbers of run-down buildings and small lanes between the Calle de Alcalá and the Plaza de España. This somewhat haphazard road-building scheme soon became the subject of a

Stone obelisk with statue of Miguel de Cervantes, Plaza de España

◁ Night-time traffic on the Gran Vía, seen from the Plaza de España

One of the many 1930s buildings lining the Gran Vía

zarzuela – a comic opera – that most *Madrileño* of art forms *(see p320)*. Nowadays, the Gran Vía is at the centre of city life and, following a much-needed restoration programme, has become an architectural showpiece.

The most interesting buildings are clustered at the Alcalá end, starting with the Corinthian columns, high-level statuary and tiled dome of the Edificio Metrópolis *(see p284)*.

A temple with Art Nouveau mosaics on its upper levels crowns No. 1 Gran Vía. One striking feature of buildings at this end of the street is colonnaded galleries on the upper floors, imitating medieval Aragonese and Catalan architecture. Another is the fine wrought-iron balconies and carved stone details, such as the gargoyle-like caryatids at No. 12. This part of the Gran Vía has a number of old-world Spanish shops.

On the Red de San Luis, an intersection of four major roads, is the Telefónica building. The first skyscraper to be erected in the capital, built between 1926 and 1929, it caused a sensation. Beyond here, the Gran Vía becomes much more American in character, with cinemas, tourist shops and many cafés.

Opposite Callao metro station, on the corner of the Calle Jacometrezo, is another well-known building, the Art Deco Capitol cinema and bingo hall, built in the 1930s.

Monasterio de las Descalzas Reales ⓭

Plaza de las Descalzas 3. **Map** 4 E2. ***Tel*** *91 454 88 00. Sol, Callao. 10am–2pm, 4–6:30pm Tue–Sat, 10am–3pm Sun & public hols. 1 & 6 Jan, Easter, 1 & 15 May, 9 Nov, 24, 25 & 31 Dec. (free Wed for EU residents).*
www.patrimonionacional.es

Madrid's most notable religious building has a fine exterior in red brick and granite. This is one of the few surviving examples of 16th-century architecture in the city.

Around 1560, Felipe II's sister, Doña Juana, decided to convert the original medieval palace which stood here into a convent for nuns and women of the royal household. Her high rank, and that of her fellow nuns, accounts for the massive store of art and wealth of the Descalzas Reales (Royal Barefoot Sisters).

The stairway has a fresco of Felipe IV's family looking down, as if from a balcony, and a fine ceiling by Claudio Coello and his pupils. It leads up to a small first-floor cloister, which is ringed with chapels containing works of art relating to the lives of the former nuns. The main chapel houses Doña Juana's tomb. The Sala de Tapices contains a series of tapestries, one woven in 1627 for Felipe II's daughter, Isabel Clara Eugenia. Another, *The Triumph of the Eucharist,* is based on cartoons by Rubens. Major paintings on show include works by Brueghel the Elder, Titian and Zurbarán.

Decorated chapel, Monasterio de las Descalzas Reales

Fray Pedro Machado **by Zurbarán**

Real Academia de Bellas Artes ⓮

Calle Alcalá 13. **Map** 7 A2. ***Tel*** *91 524 08 64. Sevilla, Sol. 9am–3pm Tue–Sat, 9am–2:30pm Sun. some public hols. (free Wed). by appt.* **http**://rabasf.insde.es

Famous former students of this arts academy, housed in an 18th-century building by Churriguera *(see p25)*, include Dalí and Picasso. Its art gallery's collection includes works such as drawings by Raphael and Titian. Among the old masters are paintings by Rubens and Van Dyck. Spanish artists from the 16th to the 19th centuries are well represented, with magnificent works by Ribera, Murillo, El Greco and Velázquez. One of the highlights is Zurbarán's *Fray Pedro Machado*, typical of the artist's paintings of monks.

An entire room is devoted to Goya, a former director of the academy. On show here are his painting of a relaxed Manuel Godoy *(see p62)*, the *Burial of the Sardine (see p39)*, the grim *Madhouse*, and a self-portrait painted in 1815.

BOURBON MADRID

To the east of Old Madrid, there once lay an idyllic district of market gardens known as the Prado, the "Meadow". In the 16th century a monastery was built and later the Habsburgs extended it to form a palace *(see p297)*, of which only fragments now remain; the palace gardens are now the popular Parque del Retiro. The Bourbon monarchs chose this area to expand and embellish the city in the 18th century. They built grand squares with fountains, a triumphal gateway, and what was to become the Museo del Prado, one of the world's greatest art galleries. A more recent addition to the area is the Museo Nacional Centro de Arte Reina Sofía, a collection of modern Spanish and international art.

SIGHTS AT A GLANCE

Historic Buildings

Ateneo de Madrid ⓭
Café Gijón ⓯
Congreso de los Diputados ⓮
Estación de Atocha ㉑
Hotel Ritz ❶
Real Academia de la Historia ⓫
Teatro Español ⓬

Museums and Galleries

Casa-Museo de Lope de Vega ❿
Museo Arqueológico Nacional ⓲
Museo Nacional de Artes Decorativas ❻
Museo Nacional Centro de Arte Reina Sofía pp298–9 ㉒
Museo del Prado pp292–5 ❾
Museo Thyssen-Bornemisza pp288–9 ❸
Salón de Reinos ❼

Monuments

Puerta de Alcalá ❺

Churches

Iglesia de San Jerónimo el Real ❽

Streets, Squares and Parks

Calle de Serrano ⓱
Parque del Retiro ⓳
Plaza Cánovas del Castillo ❷
Plaza de Cibeles ❹
Plaza de Colón ⓰
Real Jardín Botánico ⑳

GETTING THERE

The metro is the fastest and easiest way to get to and around Bourbon Madrid. Lines 1, 2 and 4 serve all of the main sights. Useful buses include routes 2, 14, 15, 21, 27, 34, 74, and 146 to the Plaza de Cibeles.

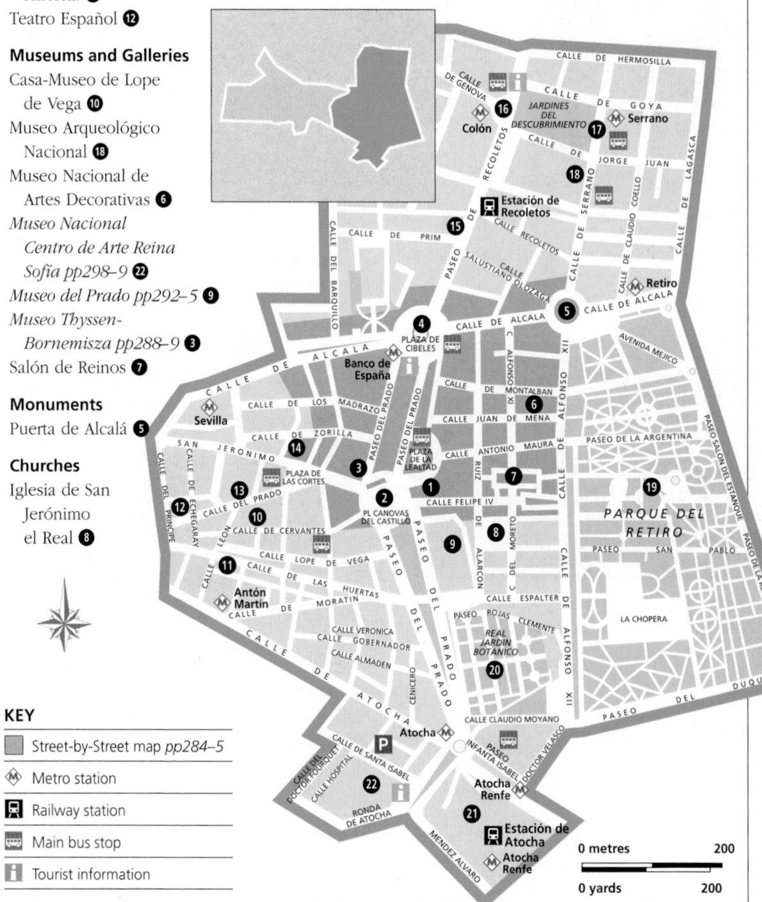

◁ **The expansive Parque del Retiro, which once formed the gardens of a Habsburg palace**

Street-by-Street: Paseo del Prado

Façade of Banco de España

In the late 18th century, before the museums and lavish hotels of Bourbon Madrid took shape, the Paseo del Prado was laid out and soon became a fashionable spot for strolling. Today the Paseo's main attraction lies in its museums and art galleries. Most notable are the Museo del Prado (just south of the Plaza Cánovas del Castillo) and the Museo Thyssen-Bornemisza, both displaying world-famous collections. Among the grand monuments built under Carlos III are the Puerta de Alcalá, the Fuente de Neptuno and the Fuente de Cibeles, which stand in the middle of busy roundabouts.

The Paseo del Prado, based on the Piazza Navona in Rome, was built by Carlos III as a centre for the arts and sciences in Madrid.

The Edificio Metrópolis *(see p281)*, on the corner of Gran Vía and Calle de Alcalá, was built in 1910. Its façade is distinctively Parisian.

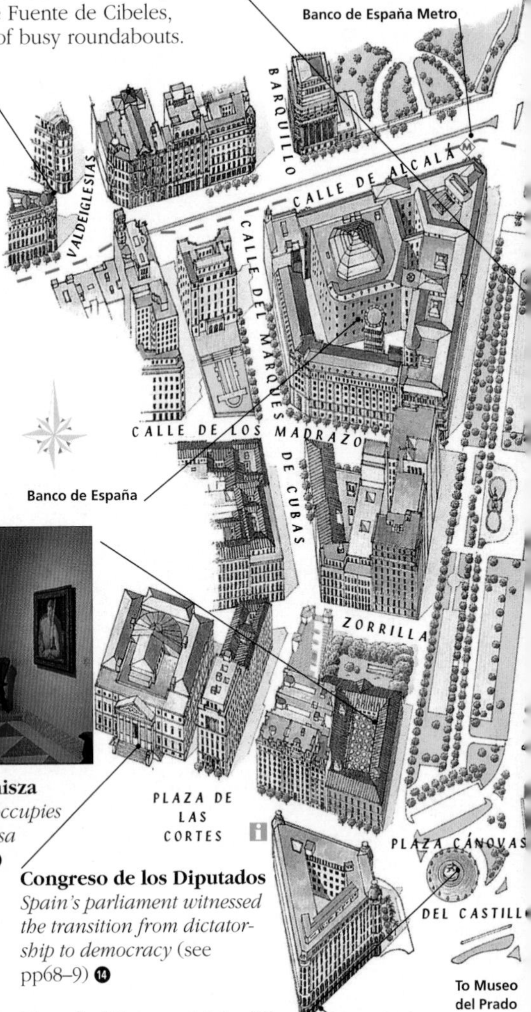

Banco de España Metro

Banco de España

Hotel Palace

To Museo del Prado

★ Museo Thyssen-Bornemisza
This excellent art collection occupies the Neo-Classical Villahermosa Palace, completed in 1806 ❸

Congreso de los Diputados
Spain's parliament witnessed the transition from dictatorship to democracy (see pp68–9) ⓮

Plaza de Cánovas del Castillo
In the middle of this large square stands a sculpted fountain of the god Neptune in his chariot ❷

STAR SIGHTS

- ★ Museo Thyssen-Bornemisza
- ★ Puerta de Alcalá
- ★ Plaza de Cibeles

★ Puerta de Alcalá
Sculpted from granite, this former gateway into the city is especially beautiful when floodlit at night ❺

LOCATOR MAP
See Street Finder maps 7–8

Palacio de Comunicaciones and City Hall

Palacio de Linares

★ Plaza de Cibeles
A fountain with a statue of the Roman goddess Cybele stands in this square ❹

The Museo Nacional de Artes Decorativas
This museum, near the Retiro, was founded in 1912 as a showcase for Spanish ceramics and interior design ❻

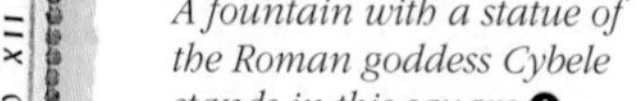

Salón de Reinos
The former army museum, this section of the Palacio del Buen Retiro will form part of the Prado Museum ❼

Casón del Buen Retiro
(see p295)

Hotel Ritz
With its Belle Époque *interior, the Ritz is one of the most elegant hotels in Spain* ❶

The Monumento del Dos de Mayo commemorates the War of Independence against the French *(see p63).*

KEY

– – – Suggested route

Hotel Ritz ❶

Plaza de la Lealtad 5. **Map** 7 C2. ***Tel*** *91 701 67 67.* Ⓜ *Banco de España.* **www**.ritz.es

A few minutes' walk from the Prado, this hotel is said to be Spain's most extravagant. It was part of the new breed of hotels constructed as luxury accommodation for the wedding guests of Alfonso XIII in 1906.

The opulence of the Ritz *(see p581)* is reflected in its prices. Each of the 158 rooms is beautifully decorated in a different style, with carpets made by hand at the Real Fábrica de Tapices *(see p306)*.

At the start of the Civil War *(see pp66–7)* the hotel was converted into a hospital, and it was here that the Anarchist leader Buenaventura Durruti died of his wounds in 1936.

The Fuente de Neptuno

Plaza Cánovas del Castillo ❷

Map 7 C3. Ⓜ *Banco de España.*

This busy roundabout is named after Antonio Cánovas del Castillo, one of the leading statesman of 19th-century Spain *(see p64)*, who was assassinated in 1897.

Dominating the plaza is the Fuente de Neptuno – a fountain with a statue depicting Neptune in his chariot, being pulled by two horses. The statue was designed in 1780 by Ventura Rodríguez as part of Carlos III's scheme to beautify eastern Madrid.

Visitors admiring the works of art in the Museo Thyssen-Bornemisza

Museo Thyssen-Bornemisza ❸

See pp288–9.

Plaza de Cibeles ❹

Map 7 C1. Ⓜ *Banco de España.* **Casa de América exhibition room** ***Tel*** *91 595 48 00.* *11am–8pm Mon–Sat, 11am–3pm Sun.* *Aug & public hols.* *11am, noon, 1pm Sat & Sun.* **www**.casamerica.es

As well as being one of Madrid's best-known landmarks, the Plaza de Cibeles is also one of the most beautiful.

The Fuente de Cibeles stands in the middle of the busy traffic island at the junction of the Paseo del Prado and the Calle de Alcalá. This fine sculpted fountain is named after Cybele, the Graeco-Roman goddess of nature, and shows her sitting in her lion-drawn chariot. Designed in the late 18th century by José Hermosilla and Ventura Rodríguez, it is considered a symbol of Madrid. Around the square rise four important buildings. The most impressive are the town hall, where the mayor has his office, and the main post office, the Palacio de Comunicaciones. Its appearance – white, with high pinnacles – is often likened to a wedding cake. It was built between 1905 and 1917 on the site of former gardens.

On the northeast side of the square is the stone façade of the Palacio de Linares, built by the Marquis of Linares at the time of the second Bourbon restoration of 1875 *(see p64)*. Once threatened with demolition, the palace was reprieved and converted into the Casa de América, and now hosts art exhibitions by Latin American artists as well as theatrical performances and lectures.

In the northwest corner of the Plaza de Cibeles, surrounded by attractive gardens, is the heavily guarded Army Headquarters, which is housed in the buildings of the former Palacio de Buenavista. The palace was commissioned by the Duchess of Alba in 1777, though its construction was twice delayed by fires.

On the opposite corner is the Banco de España, constructed between 1884 and 1891. Its design was inspired by the Venetian Renaissance style, with delicate ironwork adorning the roof and windows. Much-needed renovation work has returned the bank to its late 19th-century magnificence.

The Fuente de Cibeles, with the Palacio de Linares in the background

View through the central arch of the Puerta de Alcalá

Puerta de Alcalá ❺

Map 8 D1. Ⓜ *Retiro.*

This ceremonial gateway is the grandest of the monuments erected by Carlos III in his attempt to improve the looks of eastern Madrid. It was designed by Francesco Sabatini to replace a smaller Baroque gateway, which had been built by Felipe III for the entry into Madrid of his wife, Margarita de Austria.

Construction of the gate began in 1769 and lasted nine years. It was built from granite in Neo-Classical style, with a lofty pediment and sculpted angels. It has five arches – three central and two outer rectangular ones.

Until the mid-19th century the gateway marked the city's easternmost boundary. It now stands in the busy Plaza de la Independencia, and is best seen when floodlit at night.

Museo Nacional de Artes Decorativas ❻

Calle Montalbán 12. **Map** 8 D2. ***Tel*** *91 532 64 99.* Ⓜ *Retiro, Banco de España.* *9:30am–3pm Tue–Sat (& 5–8pm Thu), 10am–3pm Sun.* *public hols.* *(free Thu pm & Sun).* *Sun.* **http**://mnartes decorativas.mcu.es

Housed in a 19th-century palace near the Parque del Retiro, the National Museum of Decorative Arts contains an interesting collection of furniture and *objets d'art*. The exhibits are mainly from Spain and date back as far as Phoenician times.

There are also some excellent ceramic pieces from Talavera de la Reina *(see p386)*, and ornaments from the Far East.

Refurbishment and reorganization work may affect some rooms.

Salón de Reinos ❼

Calle Méndez Núñez 1. **Map** 8 D2. Ⓜ *Retiro, Banco de España* *closed for refurbishment until 2015.*

The Salón de Reinos (Hall of Kingdoms) is one of the two remaining parts of the 17th-century Palacio del Buen Retiro and gets its name from the shields of the 24 kingdoms of the Spanish monarchy, part of the decor supervised by court painter Velázquez *(see p32)*. In the time of Felipe IV, the Salón was used for diplomatic receptions and official ceremonies.

The Salón de Reinos is currently undergoing an extensive refurbishment to restore the interiors to their former glory. It will ultimately become part of the Prado *(see pp292–5)*. Among the exhibits to be housed in the new gallery will be five equestrian portraits by Velázquez, and Zurbarán's series of ten paintings on the life of Hercules, along with other 17th-century royal paintings. It is hoped that the building will be open by 2015. Despite this closure, the Palacio del Buen Retiro is worth visiting to admire its impressive façade. The original Palacio was built for King Felipe IV in 1637 on a large stretch of land situated next to the Monastery of San Jerónimo.

Impressive façade of the Salón de Reinos

Museo Thyssen-Bornemisza ❸

This magnificent museum is based on the collection assembled by Baron Heinrich Thyssen-Bornemisza and his son, Hans Heinrich, the preceding baron. In 1992 it was installed in Madrid's 18th-century Villahermosa Palace, and was sold to the nation the following year. From its beginnings in the 1920s, the collection was intended to illustrate the history of Western art, from Italian and Flemish primitives, through to 20th-century Expressionism and Pop Art. The museum's collection, consisting of more than 1,000 paintings, includes masterpieces by Titian, Goya, Van Gogh and Picasso. Carmen Thyssen's collection of mainly Impressionist art opened to the public in 2004. It is regarded by many critics as the most important private art collection in the world.

★ Harlequin with a Mirror
The figure of the harlequin was a frequent subject of Picasso's. The careful composition in this 1923 canvas, which is thought by some to represent the artist himself, is typical of Picasso's "Classical" period.

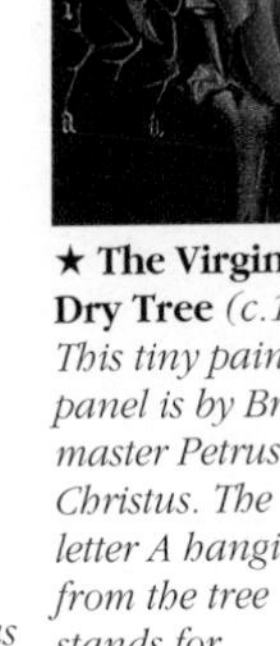

★ The Virgin of the Dry Tree *(c.1450)*
This tiny painted panel is by Bruges master Petrus Christus. The letter A hanging from the tree stands for "Ave Maria".

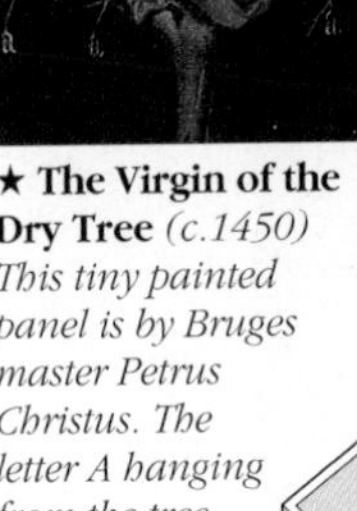

GALLERY GUIDE
The galleries are arranged around a covered central courtyard, which rises the full height of the building. The top floor starts with early Italian art and goes through to the 17th-century. The first floor continues the story with 17th-century Dutch works and ends with German Expressionism. The ground floor is dedicated to 20th-century paintings.

STAR PAINTINGS

- ★ Harlequin with a Mirror by Picasso
- ★ The Virgin of the Dry Tree by Christus
- ★ Venus and Cupid by Rubens

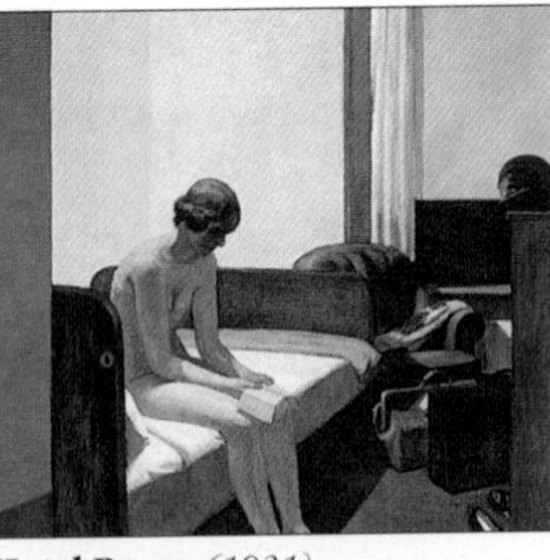

Hotel Room *(1931)*
Edward Hopper's painting is a study of urban isolation. The solitude is made less static by the suitcases and the train timetable on the woman's knee.

Portrait of Baron Thyssen-Bornemisza
This informal portra of the previous baror against the background of a Watteau painting, was painte by Lucian Freud.

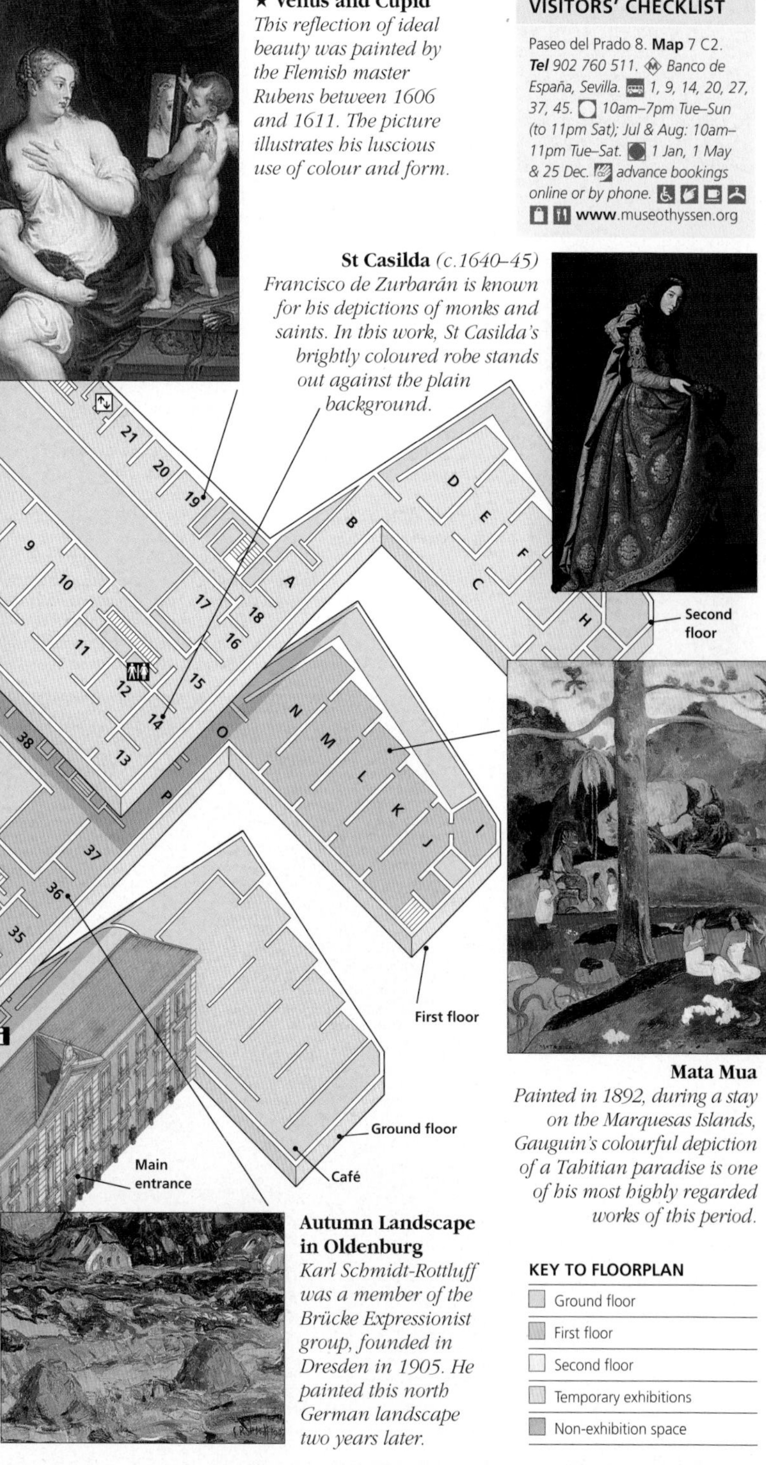

★ Venus and Cupid
This reflection of ideal beauty was painted by the Flemish master Rubens between 1606 and 1611. The picture illustrates his luscious use of colour and form.

St Casilda *(c.1640–45)*
Francisco de Zurbarán is known for his depictions of monks and saints. In this work, St Casilda's brightly coloured robe stands out against the plain background.

Mata Mua
Painted in 1892, during a stay on the Marquesas Islands, Gauguin's colourful depiction of a Tahitian paradise is one of his most highly regarded works of this period.

Autumn Landscape in Oldenburg
Karl Schmidt-Rottluff was a member of the Brücke Expressionist group, founded in Dresden in 1905. He painted this north German landscape two years later.

VISITORS' CHECKLIST

Paseo del Prado 8. **Map** 7 C2. ***Tel*** *902 760 511.* *Banco de España, Sevilla.* *1, 9, 14, 20, 27, 37, 45.* *10am–7pm Tue–Sun (to 11pm Sat); Jul & Aug: 10am–11pm Tue–Sat.* *1 Jan, 1 May & 25 Dec.* *advance bookings online or by phone.* **www**.museothyssen.org

KEY TO FLOORPLAN

- Ground floor
- First floor
- Second floor
- Temporary exhibitions
- Non-exhibition space

Iglesia de San Jerónimo el Real ❽

Calle del Moreto 4. **Map** 8 D3. ***Tel*** *91 420 35 78. Banco de España. Oct–Jun: 10am–1pm, 5–8:30pm Mon–Sat, 9:30am–2:30pm, 5:30–8:30pm Sun (6–8:30pm Jul–Sep).*

Built in the 16th century for Queen Isabel, but since remodelled, San Jerónimo is Madrid's royal church. From the 17th century it became virtually a part of the Retiro palace which once stood here *(see p297)*. The church was originally attached to the Hieronymite monastery. The cloister and part of the atrium now form part of a building at the Prado Museum.

The marriage of Alfonso XIII and Victoria Eugenia of Battenberg took place here in 1906, as did King Juan Carlos I's coronation in 1975.

Museo del Prado ❾

See pp292–5.

Casa-Museo de Lope de Vega ❿

Calle Cervantes 11. **Map** 7 B3. ***Tel*** *91 429 92 16. Antón Martín. 10am–3pm Tue–Sun by appointment only. public hols. available in English.*

Félix Lope de Vega, a leading Golden Age writer *(see p34)*, moved into this sombre house in 1610. Here he wrote over two-thirds of his plays, thought to total almost 1,500. Meticulously restored in 1935 using some of Lope de Vega's own furniture, the house gives a great feeling of Castilian life in the early 17th century. A dark chapel with no external windows occupies the centre, separated from the writer's bedroom by only a barred window. The small garden at the rear is planted with the flowers and fruit trees mentioned by the writer in his works. He died here in 1635.

Félix Lope de Vega

***Castizos* during San Isidro**

MADRID'S FIESTAS

San Isidro *(15 May)*. Madrid's great party around 15 May is in honour of St Isidore, the humble 12th-century farmworker who became the city's patron. With a *corrida* every day, this is Spain's biggest bullfighting event. Throughout the city there are also art exhibitions, open-air concerts and fireworks. Many people dress in *castizo (see p302)* folk costume for the occasion.

The Passion *(Easter Saturday)*, Chinchón. A passion play is performed in the town's atmospheric arcaded Plaza Mayor.

Dos de Mayo *(2 May)*. This holiday marks the city's uprising against Napoleon's troops in 1808 *(see p63)*.

New Year's Eve. The nation focuses on the Puerta del Sol *(see p272)* at midnight as crowds gather to swallow a grape on each chime of the clock.

Statue of Goya in front of the Prado

Sunlit balcony of the magnificent Teatro Español

Real Academia de la Historia ⓫

Calle León 21. **Map** 7 A3. ***Tel*** *91 429 06 11. Antón Martín. to the public.* **www**.rah.es

The Royal Academy of History is an austere brick building built by Juan de Villanueva in 1788. Its location, in the so-called Barrio de las Letras (Writers' Quarter), is apt.

In 1898, the great intellectual and bibliophile, Marcelino Menéndez Pelayo, became director of the academy, living here until his death in 1912. The library holds more than 200,000 books.

The building is closed to the public and can only be viewed from the outside.

Teatro Español ⓬

Calle del Príncipe 25. **Map** 7 A3. ***Tel*** *91 360 14 80. Sol, Sevilla. for performances from 7pm Tue–Sun.*

Dominating the Plaza Santa Ana is the Teatro Español, one of Madrid's oldest and most beautiful theatres. From 1583 many of Spain's finest plays, by leading dramatists of the time such as Lope de Rueda, were first performed in the Corral del Príncipe, which originally stood on this site. In 1802 this was replaced by the Teatro Español. The Neo-Classical façade, with pilasters and medallions, is by Juan de Villanueva. Engraved on it are the names of great Spanish dramatists, including that of celebrated writer Federico García Lorca *(see p35)*.

Ateneo de Madrid ⓭

Calle del Prado 21. **Map** 7 B3. ***Tel*** *91 429 17 50. Antón Martín, Sevilla. by appt 10am–1pm Mon–Fri.* **Library** *9am–12:45am Mon–Sat, 9am–9:45pm Sun.* **www**.ateneodemadrid.com

Formally founded in 1835, this learned association is similar to a gentlemen's club in atmosphere, with a grand stairway and panelled hall hung with the portraits of famous fellows. Closed down during past periods of repression and dictatorship, it is a mainstay of liberal thought in Spain. Many leading Socialists are members, along with writers and other Spanish intellectuals.

Carving on the façade of the Ateneo de Madrid

Congreso de los Diputados ⓮

Plaza de las Cortes. **Map** 7 B2. ***Tel*** *91 390 65 25. Sevilla. 10:30am–12:30pm Sat, by appt Mon–Fri. Aug & public hols.* **www**.congreso.es

This imposing yet attractive building is home to the Spanish parliament, the Cortes. Built in the mid-19th century, it is characterized by Classical columns, heavy pediments and guardian bronze lions. It was here, in 1981, that Colonel Tejero of the Civil Guard held the deputies at gunpoint on national television, as he tried to spark off a military coup *(see p68)*. His failure was seen as an indication that democracy was now firmly established in Spain.

Bronze lion guarding the Cortes

Café Gijón ⓯

Paseo de Recoletos 21. **Map** 5 C5. ***Tel*** *91 521 54 25. Banco de España. 7:30am–1:30am Mon–Fri, 8am–2am Sat & public hols, 8am–1:30am Sun.*

Madrid's café life *(see pp320–25)* was one of the most attractive features of the city from the turn of the 20th century, right up to the outbreak of the Civil War. Of the many intellectuals' cafés which once thrived, only the Gijón survives. Today the café continues to attract a lively crowd of *literati*. With its cream-painted wrought-iron columns and black and white table tops, it is perhaps better known for its atmosphere than for its appearance.

Museo del Prado ❾

The Prado Museum contains the world's greatest assembly of Spanish painting – especially works by Velázquez and Goya – ranging from the 12th to 19th centuries. It also houses impressive foreign collections, particularly of Italian and Flemish works. The Neo-Classical building was designed in 1785 by Juan de Villanueva on the orders of Carlos III, and it opened as a museum in 1819. The Spanish architect Rafael Moneo has constructed a new building, over the adjacent church's cloister, where the temporary exhibitions are located. The Casón del Buen Retiro, now an art school, can be visited occasionally, on Sundays.

★ Velázquez Collection
The Triumph of Bacchus *(1629), Velázquez's first portrayal of a mythological subject, shows the god of wine (Bacchus) with a group of drunkards.*

The Adoration of the Shepherds
(1612–14)
This dramatic work shows the elongated figures and swirling garments typical of El Greco's style. It was painted during his late Mannerist period for his own funerary chapel.

The Garden of Delights *(c.1505) Hieronymus Bosch (El Bosco in Spanish), one of Felipe II's favourite artists, is especially well represented in the Prado. This enigmatic painting depicts paradise and hell.*

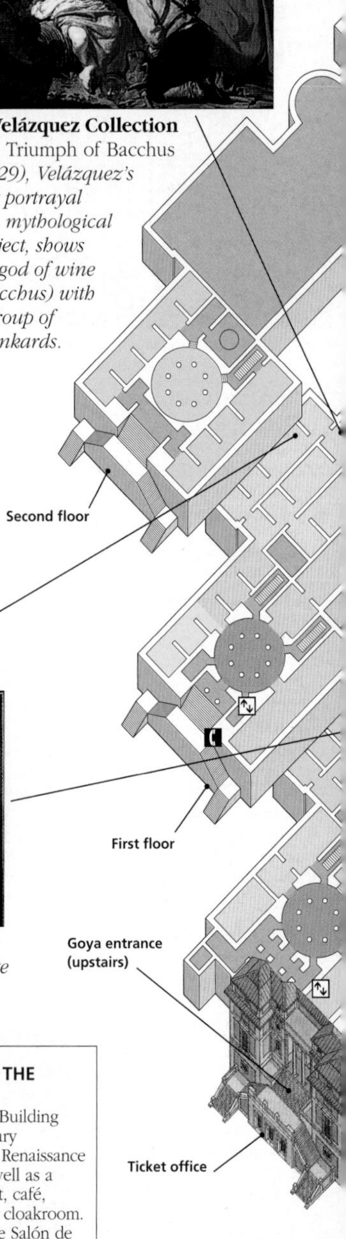

Second floor

First floor

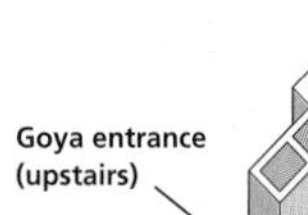

Ticket office

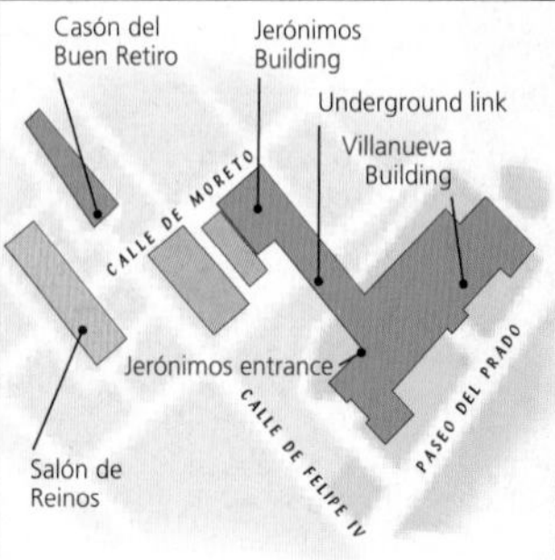

CHANGES AT THE PRADO

The Jerónimos Building houses temporary exhibitions and Renaissance sculptures, as well as a shop, restaurant, café, auditorium and cloakroom. In the future the Salón de Reinos *(see p287)* will also become part of the Prado.

Museum buildings

Due to open in 2015

STAR EXHIBITS

★ Velázquez Collection

★ Goya Collection

GALLERY GUIDE

The museum's permanent collection is arranged chronologically over three main floors. Classical sculpture is on the ground floor, Velázquez on the first floor, and the extensive Goya collection across the Murillo side of all three floors. The permanent collection is accessed via the Velázquez and Goya entrances. Visitors to the temporary exhibitions should use the Jerónimos entrance.

VISITORS' CHECKLIST

Paseo del Prado. **Map** 7 C3. ***Tel*** *902 107 077.* Atocha, Banco de España. *10, 14, 19, 27, 34, 37, 45.* *10am–8pm Mon–Sat, 10am–7pm Sun & public hols.* *1 Jan, Good Fri, 1 May, 25 Dec.* *(€1 discount for tickets bought in advance).* **www**.museoprado.es

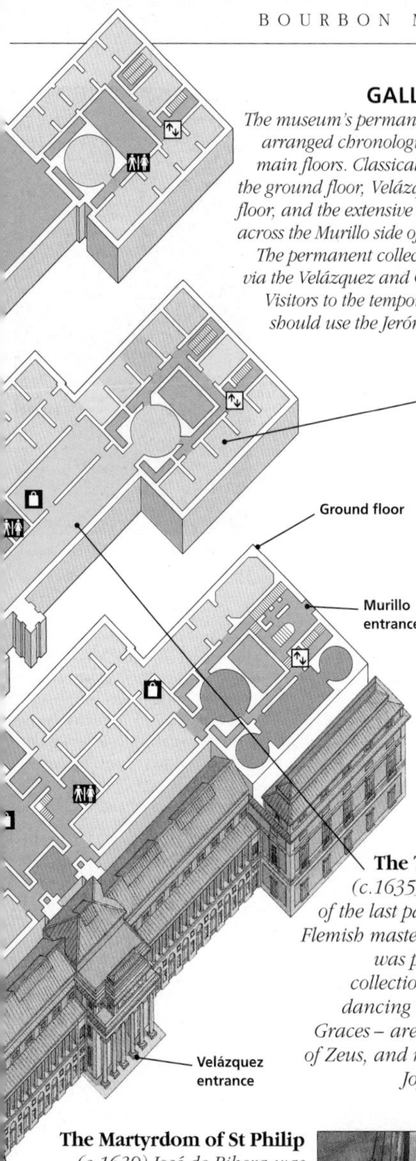

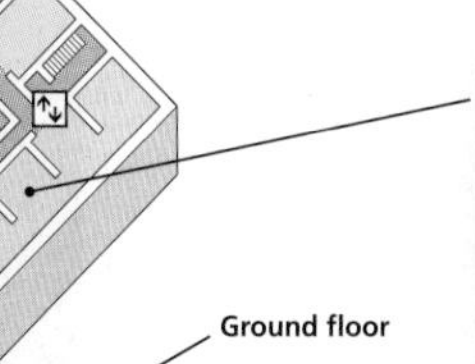

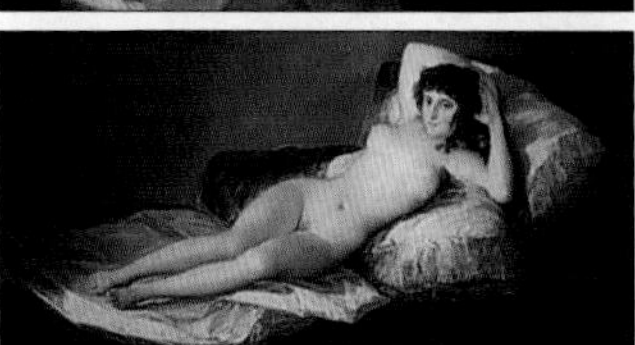

★ Goya Collection
In The Clothed Maja *and* The Naked Maja *(both c.1800), Goya tackled the taboo subject of nudity, for which he was later accused of obscenity.*

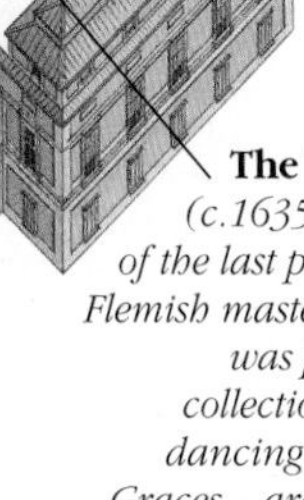

The Three Graces
(c.1635) This was one of the last paintings by the Flemish master Rubens, and was part of his own collection. The women dancing in a ring – the Graces – are the daughters of Zeus, and represent Love, Joy and Revelry.

The Martyrdom of St Philip
(c.1639) José de Ribera was influenced by Caravaggio's dramatic use of light and shadow, known as chiaroscuro, *as seen in this work.*

The Annunciation
Fra Angelico's work of c.1425–8 is a high point of Italy's Early Renaissance, as illustrated by the detailed architectural setting.

KEY TO FLOORPLAN

- Spanish painting
- Flemish and Dutch painting
- Italian painting
- French painting
- German painting
- British painting
- Sculpture
- Non-exhibition space

Exploring the Prado's Collection

The importance of the Prado is founded on its royal collections. The wealth of foreign art, including many of Europe's finest works, reflects the historical power of the Spanish crown. The Low Countries and parts of Italy were under Spanish domination for centuries. The 18th century was an era of French influence, following the Bourbon accession to the Spanish throne. The Prado is worthy of repeated visits, but if you go only once, see the Spanish works of the 17th century.

St Dominic of Silos Enthroned as Abbot (1474–7) by Bermejo

SPANISH PAINTING

Right up to the 19th century, Spanish painting focused on religious and royal themes. Although the limited subject matter was in some ways a restriction, it also offered a sharp focus that seems to have suited Spanish painters.

Spain's early medieval art is represented somewhat sketchily in the Prado, but there are some examples, such as the anonymous mural paintings from the Holy Cross hermitage in Maderuelo, which show a Romanesque heaviness of line and forceful characterization.

Spanish Gothic art can be seen in the Prado in the works of Bartolomé Bermejo and Fernando Gallego. The sense of realism in their paintings was borrowed from Flemish masters of the time.

Renaissance features began to emerge in the works of painters such as Pedro de Berruguete, whose *Auto-de-fé* is both chilling and lively. *St Catherine*, by Fernando Yáñez de la Almedina, shows the influence of Leonardo da Vinci, for whom Yáñez probably worked while training in Italy.

What is often considered as a truly Spanish style – with its highly-wrought emotion and deepening sombreness – first started to emerge in the 16th century in the paintings of the Mannerists. This is evident in Pedro Machuca's fierce *Descent from the Cross* and in the Madonnas of Luis de Morales, "the Divine". The elongation of the human figure in Morales' work is carried to a greater extreme by Domenikos Theotocopoulos, who is better known as El Greco *(see p391)*. Although many of his master pieces remain in his adopted town of Toledo, the Prado has an impressive collection, including *The Nobleman with his Hand on his Chest*.

Saturn Devouring One of his Sons (1820–23) by Francisco de Goya

The Golden Age of the 17th century was a productive time for Spanish art. José de Ribera, who lived in (Spanish) Naples, followed Caravaggio in combining realism of character with the techniques of *chiaroscuro* (use of light and dark) and tenebrism (large areas of dark colours, with a shaft of light). Another master who used this method was Francisco Ribalta, whose *Christ Embracing St Bernard* is here. Zurbarán, known for still lifes and portraits of saints and monks, is also represented in the Prado.

This period, however, is best represented by the work of Diego de Velázquez. As Spain's leading court painter from his late twenties until his death, he produced scenes of heightened realism, royal portraits, and religious and mythological paintings. Examples of his art are displayed in the Prado. His greatest work is perhaps *Las Meninas (see p32)*, in Room 12.

Another great Spanish painter, Goya, revived Spanish art in the 18th century. He first specialized in cartoons for tapestries, then became a court painter. His work went on to embrace the horrors of war, as seen in *The 3rd of May in Madrid (see p63)*, and culminated in a sombre series known as *The Black Paintings*.

Still Life with Four Vessels (c.1658–64) by Francisco de Zurbarán

FLEMISH AND DUTCH PAINTING

Spain's long connection with the Low Countries naturally resulted in an intense admiration for the so-called Flemish primitives. Many exceptional examples of Flemish and Dutch art now hang in the Prado. *St Barbara*, by Robert Campin, has a quirky intimacy, while Rogier van der Weyden's *The Descent from the Cross* is an unquestioned masterpiece. Most notable of all, however, are Hieronymus Bosch's weird and eloquent inventions. The Prado has some of his major paintings, including the *Temptation of St Anthony* and *The Haywain*. Works from the 16th century include the *Triumph of Death* by Brueghel the Elder. There are nearly 100 canvases by the 17th-century Flemish painter Peter Paul Rubens, including *The Adoration of the Magi*. The most notable Dutch painting on display is Rembrandt's *Artemisia*, a portrait of the artist's wife. Other Flemish and Dutch artists featured at the Prado are Antonis Moor, Anton Van Dyck and Jacob Jordaens, considered one of the finest portrait painters of the 17th century.

***David Victorious over Goliath* (c.1600) by Caravaggio**

ITALIAN PAINTING

The Prado is the envy of many museums, not least for its vast collection of Italian paintings. Botticelli's dramatic wooden panels telling *The Story of Nastagio degli Onesti*, a vision of a knight forever condemned to hunt down and kill his own beloved, were commissioned by two rich Florentine families and are a sinister high point.

Raphael contributes the superb *Christ Falls on the Way to Calvary* and the sentimental *The Holy Family of the Lamb*. *Christ Washing the Disciples' Feet*, an early work by Tintoretto, is a profound masterpiece and reveals the painter's brilliant handling of perspective.

Caravaggio had a profound impact on Spanish artists, who admired his characteristic handling of light, as seen in *David Victorious over Goliath*. Venetian masters Veronese and Titian are also very well represented. Titian served as court painter to Charles V, and few works express the drama of Habsburg rule so deeply as his sombre painting *The Emperor Charles V at Mühlberg*. Also on display are works by Giordano and Tiepolo, the master of Italian Rococo, who painted *The Immaculate Conception* as part of a series intended for a church in Aranjuez.

***The Descent from the Cross* (c.1430) by Rogier van der Weyden**

FRENCH PAINTING

Marriages between French and Spanish royalty in the 17th century, culminating in the Bourbon accession to the throne in the 18th century, brought French art to Spain. The Prado has eight works attributed to Poussin, among them his serene *St Cecilia* and *Landscape with St Jerome*. The magnificent *Landscape with the Embarkation of St Paula Romana at Ostia* is the best work here by Claude Lorrain. Among the 18th-century artists featured are Antoine Watteau and Jean Ranc. *Felipe V* is the work of the royal portraitist Louis-Michel van Loo.

***St Cecilia* (c.1635) by the French artist Nicolas Poussin**

GERMAN PAINTING

Although German art is not especially well represented in the Prado, there are a number of paintings by Albrecht Dürer, including his classical depictions of Adam and Eve. His lively *Self-Portrait* of 1498, painted at the age of 26, is undoubtedly the highlight of the small but valuable German collection in the museum. Lucas Cranach is also featured and works by the late 18th-century painter Anton Raffael Mengs include some magnificent portraits of Carlos III.

Roman mosaic at the Museo Arqueológico Nacional

Plaza de Colón 16

Map 6 D5. *Serrano, Colón.*
Teatro Fernán Gómez Centro de Arte www.teatrofernangomez.com

This large square, one of Madrid's undisputed focal points, is dedicated to the 15th-century explorer Christopher Columbus (Colón in Spanish).

It is overlooked by huge tower blocks, built in the 1970s to replace the 19th-century mansions which stood here.

On the south side of the square is a palace housing the National Library and Archaeological Museum. The Post-Modernist sky-scraper of the Heron Corporation towers over the Plaza de Colón from the far side of the Paseo de la Castellana.

The real feature of the square, however, is the pair of monuments dedicated to the discoverer of the Americas. The prettiest, and oldest, is a Neo-Gothic spire erected in 1885, with Columbus at its top, pointing west. Carved reliefs on the plinth give highlights of his discoveries. Across the square is the second, more modern monument – a cluster of four large concrete shapes inscribed with quotations about Columbus's journey to America *(see p57)*.

Constantly busy with traffic, the plaza may seem an unlikely venue for cultural events. Beneath it, however, is an extensive complex, the Teatro Fernán Gómez Centro de Arte. Formerly known as the Centro Cultural de la Villa, this centre is now named after the Spanish cinema and theatre actor, director and writer Fernando Fernán Gómez, who died in Madrid in 2007.

Exhibitions are held in its prestigious halls. The complex also includes lecture rooms, a theatre and a café.

Calle de Serrano 17

Map 8 D1. *Serrano.*

Named after the 19th-century politician Francisco Serrano y Dominguez, Madrid's smartest shopping street runs north from the Plaza de la Independencia, in the district of Salamanca, to the Plaza del Ecuador, in the district of El Viso. Calle de Serrano is lined with attractive shops *(p316)* – many specializing in expensive luxury items – housed in old-fashioned mansion-blocks.

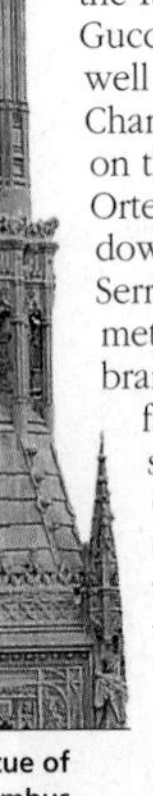

Statue of Columbus, Plaza de Colón

Several of the country's top designers, including Adolfo Domínguez and Purificación García, have boutiques towards the north, near the ABC Serrano *(see p317)* and the Museo Lázaro Galdiano *(see p305)*. Branches of the Italian shops Versace, Gucci and Armani, as well as the French Chanel, can be found on the Calle de José Ortega y Gasset. Lower down the Calle de Serrano, towards Serrano metro station, are two branches of Spain's famous department store El Corte Inglés. On the Calle de Claudio Coello, which runs parallel with Serrano, there are several lavish antique shops, in keeping with the area's upmarket atmosphere.

Museo Arqueológico Nacional 18

Calle Serrano 13. **Map** 6 D5. ***Tel*** *91 577 79 12. Serrano.* *5, 14, 21, 27, 45. 9:30am–8pm Tue–Sat, 9:30am–3pm Sun. public hols (free during refurbishment).*
http://man.mcu.es

Madrid's archaeological museum is being extensively refurbished and during the renovations some sections are likely to be closed; check the museum website or call before visiting.

Founded by Isabel II in 1867, the museum's collection consists mainly of material uncovered during excavations all over Spain, as well as important pieces from Egypt, Ancient Greece and the Etruscan civilization.

Highlights of the earliest finds include an exhibition on the ancient civilization of El Argar in Andalusia *(see p48)*, and a display of jewellery uncovered at the Roman settlement of Numantia, near Soria *(see p377)*.

Another area is devoted to the period between Roman and Mudéjar Spain. Iberian culture is also represented, with two notable funerary sculptures – *La Dama de Elche (see p48)* and *La Dama de Baza*. The Roman period is illustrated with some impressive mosaics, including one from the 3rd century. The underside shows a combat between two gladiators, Simmachius and Maternus; the upper register displays Simmachius' victory.

Outstanding pieces from the Visigothic period include several splendid 7th-century gold votive crowns from Toledo province.

On show from the Islamic era is pottery uncovered from Medina Azahara in Andalusia *(see p477)*, and metal objects.

Romanesque exhibits include an ivory crucifix carved in 1063 for Fernando I of Castilla-León, and the *Madonna and Child* from Sahagún, considered a masterpiece of Spanish art.

Parque del Retiro ⓳

Map 8 E3. ***Tel*** *91 409 23 36.* *Retiro, Ibiza, Atocha.* *6am–10pm (Apr–Oct: 6am–midnight).*

The Retiro Park, in Madrid's smart Jerónimos district, takes its name from Felipe IV's royal palace complex, which once stood here. Today, all that is left of the palace is the **Casón del Buen Retiro** *(see p295)* and the **Salón de Reinos** *(see p287)*.

Used privately by the royal family from 1632, the park became the scene of elaborate pageants, bullfights and mock naval battles. In the 18th century it was partially opened to the public, provided visitors were formally dressed, and in 1869 it was fully opened. Today, the Retiro remains one of the most popular places for relaxing in Madrid.

A short stroll from the park's northern entrance down the tree-lined avenue leads to the pleasure lake, where rowing boats can be hired. On one side of the lake is a half-moon colonnade in front of which an equestrian statue of Alfonso XII rides high on a column. Opposite, portrait painters and fortune-tellers ply their trade.

To the south of the lake are two palaces. The Neo-Classical **Palacio de Velázquez** and the **Palacio de Cristal** (Crystal Palace) were built by Velázquez Bosco in 1883 and 1887 respectively as venues for exhibitions held in that year.

Statue of Bourbon King Carlos III in the Real Jardín Botánico

Real Jardín Botánico ⓴

Plaza de Murillo 2. **Map** 8 D4. ***Tel*** *91 420 30 17.* *Atocha, Banco de España.* *10am–dusk daily.* *1 Jan, 25 Dec.* **www**.rjb.csic.es

South of the Prado *(see pp292–5)*, and a suitable place for resting after visiting the gallery, are the Royal Botanical Gardens. Inspired by Carlos III, they were designed in 1781 by Gómez Ortega, Francesco Sabatini and Juan de Villanueva, architect of the Prado.

Interest in the plants of South America and the Philippines took hold during the Spanish Enlightenment *(see p62)*, and the neatly laid out beds offer a huge variety of flora, ranging from trees to herbs.

Estación de Atocha ㉑

Plaza del Emperador Carlos V. **Map** 8 D5. **Tel** *902 240 202.* *Atocha RENFE.* *6am–1am daily.*

Madrid's first railway service, from Atocha to Aranjuez, was inaugurated in 1851. Forty years later Atocha station was replaced by a new building, which was extended in the 1980s. The older part of the station, built of glass and wrought iron, now houses an indoor palm garden. Next to it is the terminus for high-speed AVE trains to Seville, Toledo, Córdoba, Zaragoza, Lleida, Barcelona, Málaga, Valencia, Valledollid and France *(see p676)*.

The Ministerio de Agricultura, opposite, is a splendid late 19th-century building.

Entrance of Madrid's Estación de Atocha, busy with travellers

Monument of Alfonso XII (1901), facing the Retiro's boating lake

Museo Nacional Centro de Arte Reina Sofía ㉒

The highlight of this museum of 20th-century art is Picasso's *Guernica*. There are, however, other major works by influential artists, including Miró and Dalí. The collection is housed in Madrid's former General Hospital, built in the late 18th century. Major extensions, designed by Jean Nouvel, were inaugurated in 2005, allowing a new arrangement for the permanent collection. The Nouvel Building includes the Collection 3: From Revolt to Postmodernity (1962–1982), a library, a bookshop and a café-restaurant.

Portrait II *(193*
Joan Miró's huge
work shows elem
of Surrealism, bu
was painted mor
than ten years af
his true Surrealis
period ended.

Nouvel building

★ Woman in Blue *(1901)*
Picasso disowned this work after it won only an honourable mention in a national competition. Decades later it was located and acquired by the Spanish state.

Landscape at Cadaqués
Salvador Dalí was born in Figueres in Catalonia. He became a frequent visitor to the town of Cadaqués, on the Costa Brava (see p217), *where he painted this landscape in the summer of 1923.*

Accident
Alfonso Ponce de León's disturbing work, painted in 1936, prefigured his death in a car crash later that same year.

STAR EXHIBITS

- ★ Woman in Blue by Picasso
- ★ The Gathering at Pombo Café by Solana
- ★ Guernica by Picasso

★ The Gathering at Pombo Café *(1920)*
José Gutiérrez Solana depicts a gathering of intellectuals (tertulia) *in a famous café in Madrid, which no longer exists.*

Toki-Egin
(Homenaje a San Juan de la Cruz) *(1990)*
In his abstract sculptures, Eduardo Chillida used a variety of materials, such as wood, iron and steel, to convey strength.

VISITORS' CHECKLIST

Calle Santa Isabel 52. **Map** 7 C5. ***Tel*** *91 774 10 00. Atocha. 6, 14, 19, 27, 45, 55, 86. 10am–9pm Mon, Wed–Sat, 10am–2:30pm Sun. 1 & 6 Jan, 1 & 15 May, 9 Nov, 24, 25 & 31 Dec, some pub hols. (free Sat pm & Sun).* **www**.museoreinasofia.es

GALLERY GUIDE

The permanent collection is in the Sabatini Building. Collection 1 on the second floor displays works dating from 1900 to 1945, and includes rooms dedicated to important movements such as Cubism and Surrealism; Collection 2 on the fourth floor has works dating from 1945 to 1968, including representatives of Pop Art, Minimalism and more recent tendencies. Collection 3: From Revolt to Postmodernity (1962–1982) is located in the Nouvel Building.

KEY TO FLOORPLAN

- Exhibition space
- Non-exhibition space

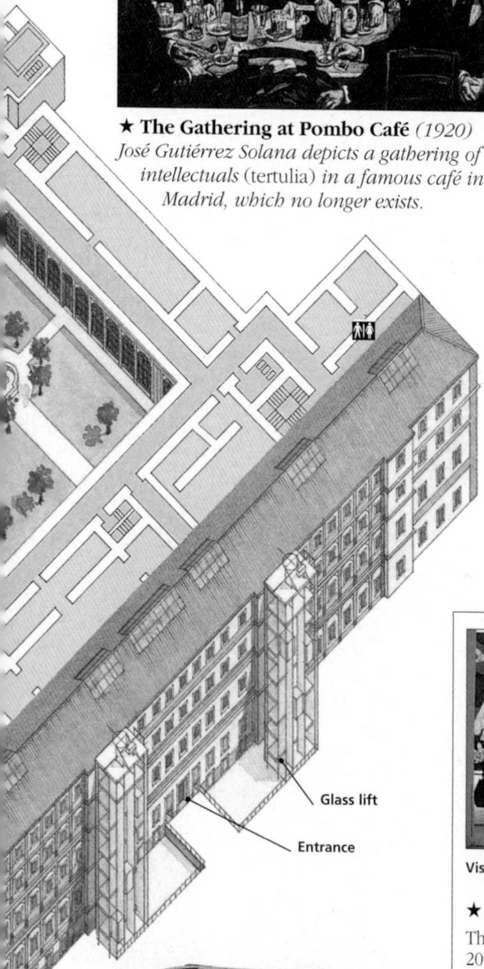

Visitors admiring *Guernica*

★ PICASSO'S *GUERNICA*

The most famous single work of the 20th century, this Civil War protest painting *(see pp66–7)* was commissioned by the Spanish Republican government in 1937 for a Paris exhibition. The artist found his inspiration in the mass air attack of the same year on the Basque town of Gernika-Lumo *(see p118)*, by German pilots flying for the Nationalist air force. The painting hung in a New York gallery until 1981, reflecting the artist's wish that it should not return to Spain until democracy was re-established. It was moved here from the Prado in 1992.

FURTHER AFIELD

Several of Madrid's best sights, including some interesting but little-known museums, lie outside the city centre. The axis of modern Madrid is the Paseo de la Castellana, a long, wide avenue lined by skyscraper offices and busy with traffic. A journey along it gives a glimpse of Madrid as Spain's commercial and administrative capital. La Castellana skirts the Barrio de Salamanca, an upmarket district of stylish boutiques, named after the 19th-century aristocrat who built it, the Marquis de Salamanca.

Statue in Plaza de Cascorro

The districts around Old Madrid, especially Malasaña and La Latina, offer a more typically authentic *Madrileño* atmosphere. On Sundays, some of the old streets are crowded with bargain-hunters at the sprawling second-hand market, El Rastro. If you need to escape from the bustle of the city for a while, west of Old Madrid, across the Río Manzanares, is Madrid's vast, green recreation ground, the Casa de Campo, with its pleasant pine woods, boating lake, amusement park and zoo.

SIGHTS AT A GLANCE

Historic Buildings
Palacio de Liria 9
Real Fábrica de Tapices 16
Templo de Debod 6

Churches and Convents
Ermita de San Antonio de la Florida 5

Museums and Galleries
Museo de América 7
Museo Cerralbo 8
Museo de Historia 11
Museo Lázaro Galdiano 13
Museo Sorolla 12

Streets, Squares and Parks
Casa de Campo 4
La Latina 2
Malasaña 10
Paseo de la Castellana 14
Plaza de la Paja 3
Plaza de Toros de Las Ventas 15
El Rastro 1

0 kilometres 2
0 miles 1

KEY
Main sightseeing area
Parks and open spaces
Railway station
Motorway
Major road
Minor road

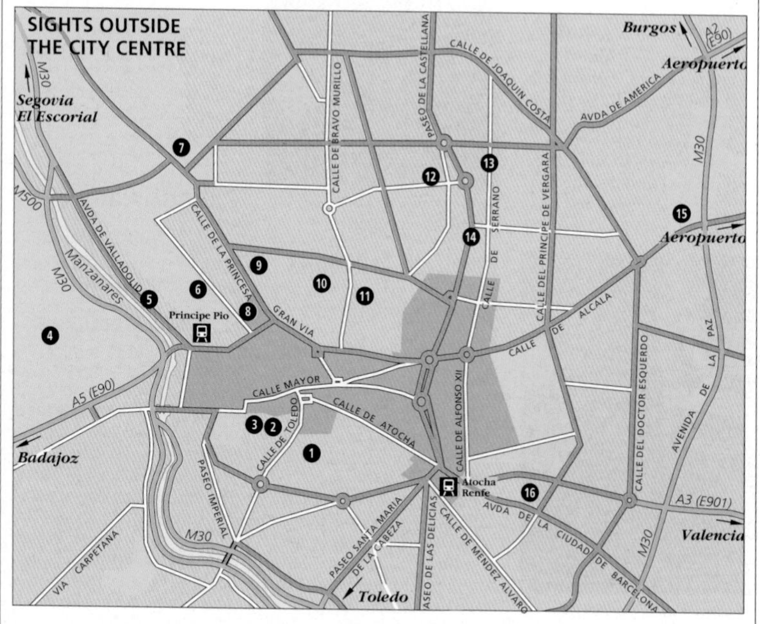

◁ **Mudéjar arches and tilework on the exterior of the Plaza de Toros de Las Ventas**

El Rastro ❶

Calle Ribera de Curtidores. **Map** 4 E4. Ⓜ *La Latina, Tirso de Molina.* ◯ *10am–3pm Sun & public hols.*

Madrid's celebrated flea market *(see p317)*, established in the Middle Ages, has its hub in the Plaza de Cascorro and sprawls downhill towards the Río Manzanares. The main street is the Calle Ribera de Curtidores, or "Tanners' Riverbank", once the centre of the slaughterhouse and tanning industry.

Although some people claim that the Rastro has changed a great deal since its heyday during the 19th century, there are still plenty of *Madrileños*, as well as tourists, who shop here. They come in search of a bargain from the stalls which sell a huge range of wares – anything from new furniture to second-hand clothes. The wide range of goods and the lively crowds in the Rastro make it an ideal way to spend a Sunday morning.

The Calle de Embajadores is the market's other main street. It runs down past the dusty Baroque façade of the Iglesia de San Cayetano, designed by José Churriguera and Pedro de Ribera. Its interior has been restored since fire destroyed it during the Civil War.

Further along the street is the former Real Fábrica de Tabacos (the Royal Tobacco Factory), begun as a state enterprise in 1809. Its female workers had a reputation for taking a hard-line stance in industrial disputes.

Shoppers browsing around the Rastro flea market

La Latina ❷

Map 4 D4. Ⓜ *La Latina.*

The district of La Latina, together with the adjacent Lavapiés, is considered to be the heart of *castizo* Madrid. This term is used to describe the culture of the traditional working classes of Madrid – that of the true *Madrileño.*

La Latina runs along the city's southern hillside from the Plaza Puerta de Moros, southwards through the streets where the Rastro is held. To the east it merges with Lavapiés. La Latina's steep streets are lined with tall, narrow houses, renovated to form an attractive neighbourhood. There are old-fashioned bars around the Plaza del Humilladero, although the streets to the east of La Latina, in the Lavapiés district, have sadly become notorious for petty crime.

Bottles of wine for sale in an old-style bar in Lavapiés

Plaza de la Paja ❸

Map 4 D3. Ⓜ *La Latina.*

Once the focus of medieval Madrid, the area around the Plaza de la Paja – literally Straw Square – is extremely atmospheric and many interesting buildings are located on the square.

Climbing upwards from the Calle de Segovia, a glimpse left along the Calle Príncipe Anglona yields a view of the Mudéjar-style brick tower of the Iglesia de San Pedro, dating from the 14th century.

Interior of San Francisco el Grande

Up past the fountain, the Plaza de la Paja ends with the harsh stone walls of the Capilla del Obispo, or Bishop's Chapel, belonging originally to the adjoining Palacio Vargas. The superb Plateresque altarpiece is by Francisco Giralte. Up to the left, the Baroque, cherub-covered dome of the Iglesia de San Andrés stands out.

Nearby is a small cluster of interlinked squares, ending in the Plaza Puerta de Moros, a reminder of the Muslim community which once occupied the area. From here, a right turn leads to the domed bulk of San Francisco el Grande, an impressive landmark. Inside the church is a painting by Goya and his brother-in-law Francisco Bayeu. The choir-stalls were moved here from the monastery of El Paular *(see pp328–9).*

Casa de Campo ❹

Avenida de Portugal. ***Tel*** *91 463 63 34.* Ⓜ *Batán, Lago, Príncipe Pío, Casa de Campo.* ◼ *partially to cars.*

This former royal hunting ground, with pines and scrubland stretching over 1,740 ha (4,300 acres), lies in south-western Madrid. Its wide range of amenities make it a popular daytime recreation area. Attractions include a boating lake, a zoo, and an amusement park – the Parque de Atracciones *(see p321).* Sports enthusiasts can make use of the swimming pool and jogging track. In the summer the park is also used as a venue for rock concerts.

Egyptian temple of Debod, with two of its original gateways

Ermita de San Antonio de la Florida 5

Glorieta San Antonio de la Florida 5. **Tel** *91 542 07 22.* *Príncipe Pío.* *9:30am–8pm Tue–Fri, 10am–2pm Sat & Sun.* *public hols.* **www**.munimadrid.es

Goya enthusiasts should not miss a visit to the Neo-Classical Ermita de San Antonio de la Florida, built during the reign of Carlos IV. The present church stands on the site of two previous ones, and is dedicated to St Anthony. It is named after the pastureland of la Florida, on which the original church was built.

Goya took four months, in 1798, to paint the cupola. It depicts the resurrection of a murdered man who rises in order to prove the innocence of the falsely accused father of St Anthony. The characters in it are everyday people of the late 18th century: lurking, low-life types and lively *majas* *(see p293)* – shrewd but elegant women. The fresco is considered by many art critics to be among Goya's finest works.

The tomb of the artist is housed in the chapel. His remains were brought here from Bordeaux, where he died in exile in 1828 *(see p239)*.

Templo de Debod 6

Paseo de Pintor Rosales. **Map** 1 B5. **Tel** *91 366 74 15.* *Ventura Rodríguez, Plaza de España.* *10am–2pm Sat & Sun; Apr–Sep: 10am–2pm, 6–8pm Tue–Fri; Oct–Mar: 9:45am–1:45pm, 4:15–6:15pm Tue–Fri.* *public hols.* **www**.munimadrid.es

The Egyptian temple of Debod, built in the 2nd century BC, was rescued from the area flooded by the Aswan Dam and given to Spain as a tribute to Spanish engineers involved in the project. The temple is carved with shallow reliefs, and stands in a line with two of its original three gateways. They are situated on high ground above the Río Manzanares, in the gardens of the Parque del Oeste. From the park there are sweeping views over the Casa de Campo to the Guadarrama mountains.

The park is the site of the former Montaña barracks, which were stormed by the populace at the start of the Civil War in 1936. Further west, below the brow of the hill, is an attractive rose garden.

Museo de América 7

Avenida de los Reyes Católicos 6. **Tel** *91 549 26 41.* *Moncloa.* *9:30am–6:30pm Tue–Sat, 10am–3pm Sun.* *some public hols.* *(free Sun & some public hols).* **http**://museodeamerica.mcu.es

This handsome museum houses artifacts related to Spain's colonization of parts of the Americas. Many of the exhibits, which range from prehistoric times to the present, were brought back to Europe by early explorers of the New World *(see pp58–9)*.

The collection is arranged on the first and second floors, and individual rooms are given a cultural theme such as society, communication and religion. There is documentation of the Atlantic voyages by the first explorers, and examples of the objects which they found. The highlight of the museum is perhaps the rare Mayan *Códice Trocortesiano* (AD 1250–1500) from Mexico, a type of parchment illustrated with hieroglyphics of scenes from everyday life. Also worth seeing are the solid gold funereal ornaments from Colombia, the Treasure of the Quimbayas (AD 500–1000), and the collection of contemporary folk art from some of Spain's former American colonies.

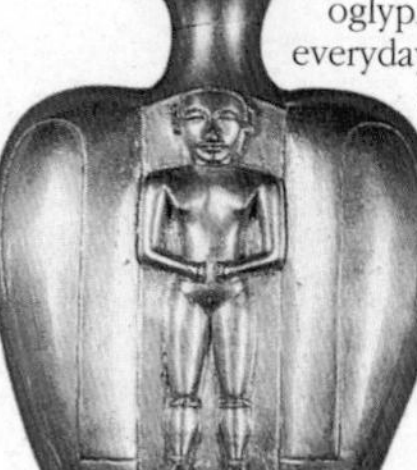

Piece of the Treasure of the Quimbayas

Museo Cerralbo 8

C/ Ventura Rodríguez 17. **Map** 1 C5. ***Tel*** *91 547 36 46.* *Plaza de España, Ventura Rodríguez.* *9:30am–3pm Tue–Sat (also 5–8pm Thu), 10am–3pm Sun.* *some public hols.* *(free after 5pm Thu, after 2pm Sat & all day Sun).*

This 19th-century mansion near the Plaza de España is a monument to Enrique de Aguilera y Gamboa, the 17th Marquis of Cerralbo. A compulsive collector of art and artifacts, he bequeathed his lifetime's collection to the nation in 1922, stipulating that the exhibits be arranged exactly as he left them. They range from Iberian pottery to 18th-century marble busts.

One of the star exhibits is El Greco's magnificent *The Ecstasy of Saint Francis of Assisi*. There are also paintings by Ribera, Zurbarán, Alonso Cano and Goya.

The focal point of the main floor is the ballroom, lavishly decorated with mirrors. A large collection of weaponry is on display on this floor.

Palacio de Liria 9

Calle la Princesa 20. ***Tel*** *91 547 53 02.* *Ventura Rodríguez.* *write a year in advance for permission.* *obligatory.*

The lavish but much restored Palacio de Liria was completed by Ventura Rodríguez in 1780. Once the residence of the Alba family, and still owned by the Duchess, it can be visited by appointment only.

The palace houses the Albas' outstanding collection of art, and Flemish tapestries. There are paintings by Titian, Rubens and Rembrandt. Spanish art is particularly well represented, with major works by Goya, such as his 1795 portrait of the Duchess of Alba, as well as examples of work by El Greco, Zurbarán and Velázquez.

Behind the palace is the **Cuartel del Conde-Duque**, the former barracks of the Count-Duke Olivares, Felipe IV's minister. They were built in 1720 by Pedro de Ribera, who adorned them with a Baroque façade. The barracks now house a cultural centre.

Main staircase of the exuberant Museo Cerralbo

Rooftops in the Malasaña district

Malasaña 10

Map 2 F5. *Tribunal, Bilbao.*

A feeling of the authentic old Madrid pervades this district of narrow, sloping streets and tall houses. For some years it was the centre of the *movida*, the frenzied nightlife which began after the death of Franco.

A walk along the Calle San Andrés leads to the Plaza del Dos de Mayo. In the centre is a monument to artillery officers Daoíz and Velarde, who defended the barracks which stood here at the time of the uprising against the French in 1808 *(see p63)*.

On Calle de la Puebla is the Iglesia de San Antonio de los Alemanes. The church was founded by Felipe III in the 17th century as a hospital for Portuguese immigrants, and was later given over for use by German émigrés. Inside, the walls are decorated with 18th-century frescoes by Giordano.

Museo de Historia 11

Calle de Fuencarral 78.
Map 5 A4. ***Tel*** *91 701 18 63.*
Tribunal. *for restoration until further notice.* *by appt.*
www.munimadrid.es

The History Museum is worth visiting just for its Baroque doorway *(see p25)* by Pedro de Ribera, arguably the finest in Madrid. Housed in the former hospice of St Ferdinand, the museum was inaugurated in 1929.

Upstairs is a series of bird's-eye views and maps of Madrid. Among them is Pedro Teixeira's map of 1656, thought to be the oldest of the city. There is also a model of Madrid, made in 1830 by León Gil de Palacio.

Modern exhibits include a reconstruction of the collage-filled study of Ramón Gómez de la Serna, a key figure of the literary gatherings in the Café de Pombo *(see p299)*. The museum is currently undergoing refurbishment, so parts or all of the collection may be closed.

Baroque façade of the Museo de Historia, by Pedro de Ribera

Museo Sorolla ⓬

Paseo del General Martínez Campos 37. ***Tel*** *91 310 15 84.* Ⓜ *Rubén Darío, Iglesia, Gregorio Marañón.* ◯ *9:30am–8pm Tue–Sat, 10am–3pm Sun.* ⬤ *public hols.* *(free Sun).*

The former studio-mansion of Valencian Impressionist painter Joaquín Sorolla has been left virtually as it was when he died in 1923.

Although Sorolla is perhaps best known for his brilliantly lit Mediterranean beach scenes, the changing styles of his paintings are well represented in the museum, with examples of his gentle portraiture and a series of works representing people from different parts of Spain. Also on display are various objects amassed during the artist's lifetime, including Spanish tiles and ceramics. The house, constructed in 1910, has an Andalusian-style garden designed by Sorolla himself.

Sorolla's former studio in the Museo Sorolla

Museo Lázaro Galdiano ⓭

Calle Serrano 122. ***Tel*** *91 561 60 84.* Ⓜ *Rubén Darío, Gregorio Marañón.* ◯ *10am–4:30pm Mon & Wed–Sat, 10am–3pm Sun.* ⬤ *public hols.* *(free for last hour).* *by appt.* **www**.flg.es

This art museum is housed in the former mansion-home of the editor and financier José Lázaro Galdiano, and consists of his private collection of fine and applied art, bequeathed to the nation in 1947. The collection ranges from the 6th to the 20th century and contains items of exceptional quality, ranging from less familiar Goya portraits to a mass of fob watches, including a cross-shaped pocket-watch worn by Charles V. Among the most beautiful objects are a series of Limoges enamels, miniature sculptures, and *The Saviour*, a portrait attributed to a student of Leonardo da Vinci. The Museo features paintings by English artists Constable, Turner, Gainsborough and Reynolds, as well as 17th-century paintings by the likes of Spanish painters Madrazo, Zurbarán, Ribera, Murillo and El Greco.

Charles V's fob watch

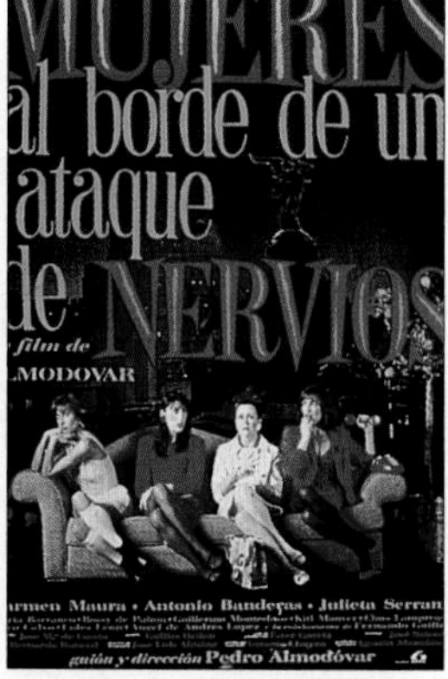

Poster for Almodóvar's *Women on the Verge of a Nervous Breakdown*

LA MOVIDA

With Franco's death in 1975 came a new period of personal and artistic liberty. For the young, this was translated into the freedom to stay out late, drinking and sometimes sampling drugs. The phenomenon was known as *la movida*, "the action", and it was at its most intense in Madrid. Analysts at the time saw it as having serious intellectual content, and *la movida* has had a few lasting cultural results, like the emergence of satirical film director Pedro Almodóvar.

Torre de Picasso towering over the Paseo de la Castellana

Paseo de la Castellana ⓮

Ⓜ Santiago Bernabéu, Cuzco, Plaza de Castilla, Gregorio Marañón, Colón.

The busy traffic artery which cuts through eastern Madrid comprises several parts. Its southernmost portion – the Paseo del Prado *(see pp284–5)* – starts just north of the Estación de Atocha *(see p297)*. The oldest section of the road, it dates from the reign of Carlos III, who built it as part of his embellishment of eastern Madrid *(see p297)*. At the Plaza de Cibeles, the avenue becomes the handsome Paseo de Recoletos, which boasts fashionable cafés, including the Café Gijón *(see p291)*.

The Plaza de Colón marks the start of the Paseo de la Castellana, whose pavement cafés have become a focal point for young Madrid's social life. This northernmost section has several notable examples of modern architecture, including the huge grey Nuevos Ministerios building, completed under Franco. Further on, before reaching the Plaza de Lima, is the Torre de Picasso *(see p25)*, one of Spain's tallest buildings. East of the square is the Estadio Bernabéu, home of Real Madrid Football Club *(see p177)*. The building that dominates the Paseo, however, is the Puerta de Europa, locally known as "Torres Kio": twin glass blocks on either side of the road, built at an angle as if leaning toward each other.

Plaza de Toros de Las Ventas ⓯

Calle Alcalá 237. ***Tel*** *91 356 22 00.* Ⓜ *Ventas.* ☐ *for bullfights & concerts.* ☐ *every half hour from 10:30am to 1:30pm Tue–Sun (91 556 92 37).* **Museo Taurino** ***Tel*** *91 725 18 57.* ☐ *Mar–Oct: 9:30am–2:30pm Tue–Fri, 10am–1pm Sun; Nov–Feb: 9:30am–2:30pm Mon–Fri.* ♿

Whatever your opinion of bullfighting, Las Ventas is undoubtedly one of the most beautiful bullrings in Spain. Built in 1929 in Neo-Mudéjar style, it replaced the city's original bullring which stood near the Puerta de Alcalá. With its horsehoe arches around the outer galleries and the elaborate tilework decoration, it makes an attractive venue for the *corridas* held during the bullfighting season, from May to October. The statues outside the bullring are monuments to two renowned Spanish bullfighters: Antonio Bienvenida and José Cubero.

Adjoining the bullring is the Museo Taurino. Memorabilia includes portraits and sculptures of famous matadors, as well as the heads of several bulls killed during fights at Las Ventas. Visitors can view close up the tools of the bullfighter's trade: capes and *banderillas* – sharp darts used to wound the bull *(see pp36–7)*. For some people, the gory highlight of the exhibition is the blood-drenched *traje de luces* worn by the legendary Manolete during his fateful bullfight at Linares in Andalusia in 1947. Also on display is a costume which belonged to Juanita Cruz, a female bullfighter of the 1930s who was forced, in the face of prejudice, to leave Spain. In September and October, the bullring hosts rock concerts.

Real Fábrica de Tapices ⓰

Calle Fuenterrabía 2. ***Tel*** *91 434 05 51.* Ⓜ *Menéndez Pelayo.* ☐ *10am–2pm Mon–Fri.* ● *public hols & Aug.* **www**.realfabricadetapices.com

Founded by Felipe V in 1721, the Royal Tapestry Factory is the sole survivor of several factories which were opened by the Bourbons *(see pp62–3)* during the 18th century. In 1889 the factory was relocated to this building just south of the Parque del Retiro.

Visitors can see the making of the carpets and tapestries by hand, a process which has changed little. Goya and his brother-in-law Francisco Bayeu created drawings, or cartoons, which were the inspiration for tapestries made for the royal family. Some of the cartoons are on display here; others can be seen in the Museo del Prado *(see pp292–5)*. Some of the tapestries can be seen at El Pardo *(see p332)* and at El Escorial *(see pp330–31)*. Nowadays one of the factory's main tasks is making and repairing the beautiful carpets decorating the Hotel Ritz *(see p286)*.

Plaza de Toros de Las Ventas, Madrid's beautiful bullring

MADRID STREET FINDER

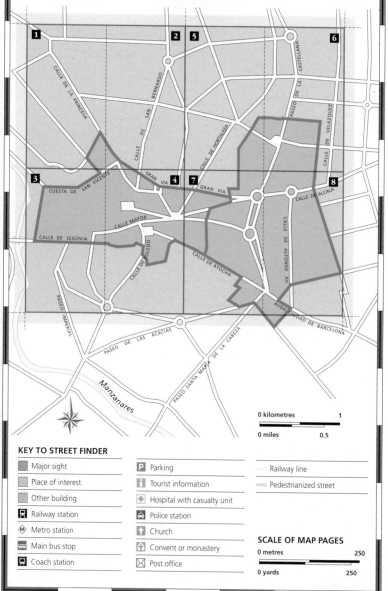

The map references given with the sights, shops and entertainment venues described in the Madrid section of the guide refer to the street maps on the following pages. Map references are also given for Madrid hotels *(see pp579–82)*, and for bars and restaurants *(pp629–32)*. The schematic map below shows the area of Madrid covered by the *Street Finder*. The symbols used for sights and other features are listed in the key at the foot of the page.

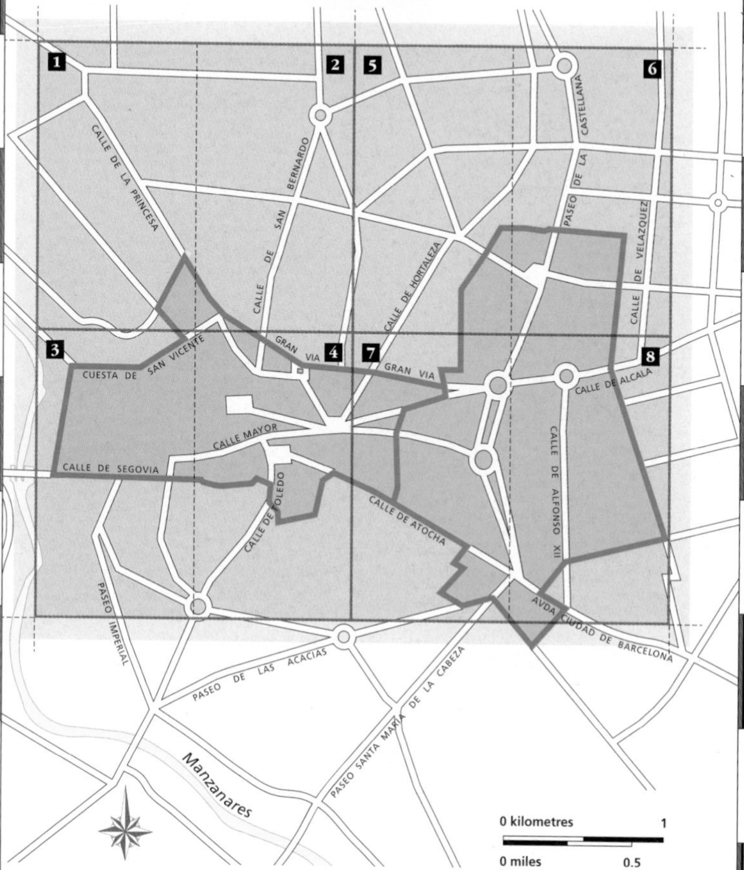

0 kilometres 1

0 miles 0.5

KEY TO STREET FINDER

- Major sight
- Place of interest
- Other building
- Railway station
- Metro station
- Main bus stop
- Coach station
- Parking
- Tourist information
- Hospital with casualty unit
- Police station
- Church
- Convent or monastery
- Post office
- Railway line
- Pedestrianized street

SCALE OF MAP PAGES

0 metres 250

0 yards 250

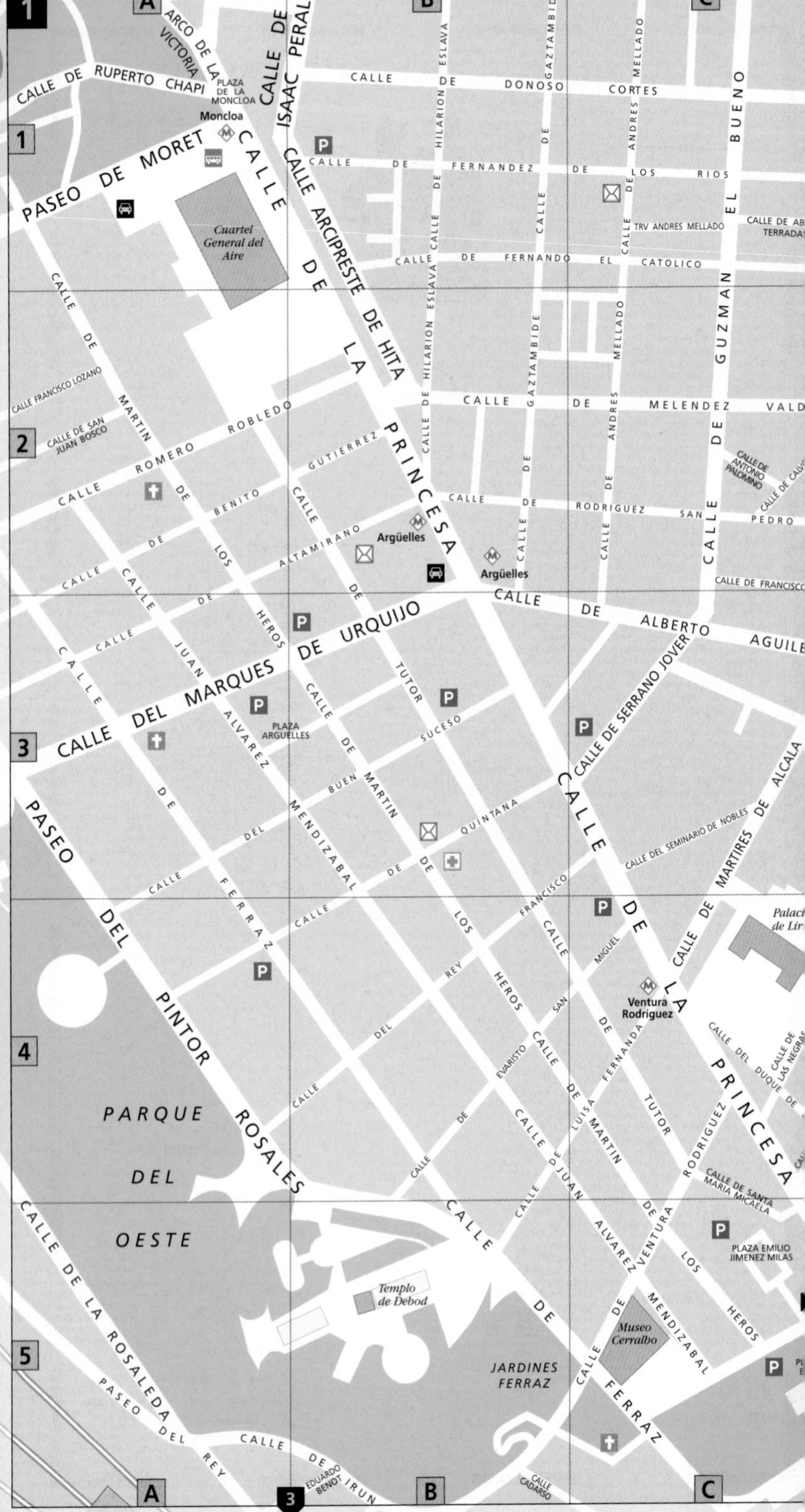

1
A
B
C
1
2
3
4
5
3
ARCO DE LA VICTORIA
CALLE DE RUPERTO CHAPI
PLAZA DE LA MONCLOA
Moncloa
PASEO DE MORET
CALLE DE ISAAC PERAL
CALLE DE LA PRINCESA
CALLE ARCIPRESTE DE HITA
Cuartel General del Aire
CALLE DE DONOSO CORTES
CALLE DE FERNANDEZ DE LOS RIOS
CALLE DE HILARION ESLAVA
CALLE DE GAZTAMBIDE
CALLE DE ANDRES MELLADO
CALLE DE GUZMAN EL BUENO
TRV ANDRES MELLADO
CALLE DE FERNANDO EL CATOLICO
CALLE DE MELENDEZ VALD
CALLE DE RODRIGUEZ SAN PEDRO
CALLE DE ANTONIO PALOMINO
CALLE DE FRANCISCO
CALLE DE MARTIN DE LOS HEROS
CALLE FRANCISCO LOZANO
CALLE DE SAN JUAN BOSCO
CALLE ROMERO ROBLEDO
CALLE GUTIERREZ
CALLE DE BENITO
CALLE DE ALTAMIRANO
Argüelles
Argüelles
CALLE DE JUAN
CALLE DE ALBERTO AGUILE
CALLE DEL MARQUES DE URQUIJO
CALLE TUTOR
CALLE DE SERRANO JOVER
CALLE DE ALVAREZ MENDIZABAL
PLAZA ARGUELLES
CALLE DEL BUEN SUCESO
CALLE DE MARTIN
CALLE DE QUINTANA
PASEO DEL PINTOR ROSALES
CALLE DE FERRAZ
CALLE DEL SEMINARIO DE NOBLES
CALLE DE MARTIRES DE ALCALA
Palaci de Lir
CALLE FRANCISCO
CALLE DE SAN MIGUEL
Ventura Rodriguez
CALLE DEL REY
CALLE DE EVARISTO
CALLE DE FERNANDA
CALLE DEL DUQUE DE
CALLE DE LAS NEGRAS
CALLE DE LUISA
CALLE DE RODRIGUEZ
CALLE DE SANTA MARIA MICAELA
PARQUE DEL OESTE
CALLE DE JUAN ALVAREZ MENDIZABAL
CALLE DE VENTURA
CALLE DE LOS HEROS
PLAZA EMILIO JIMENEZ MILAS
CALLE DE LA ROSALEDA
Templo de Debod
Museo Cerralbo
JARDINES FERRAZ
CALLE DE FERRAZ
PASEO DEL REY
CALLE DE IRUN
EDUARDO BENOT
CALLE CADARSO

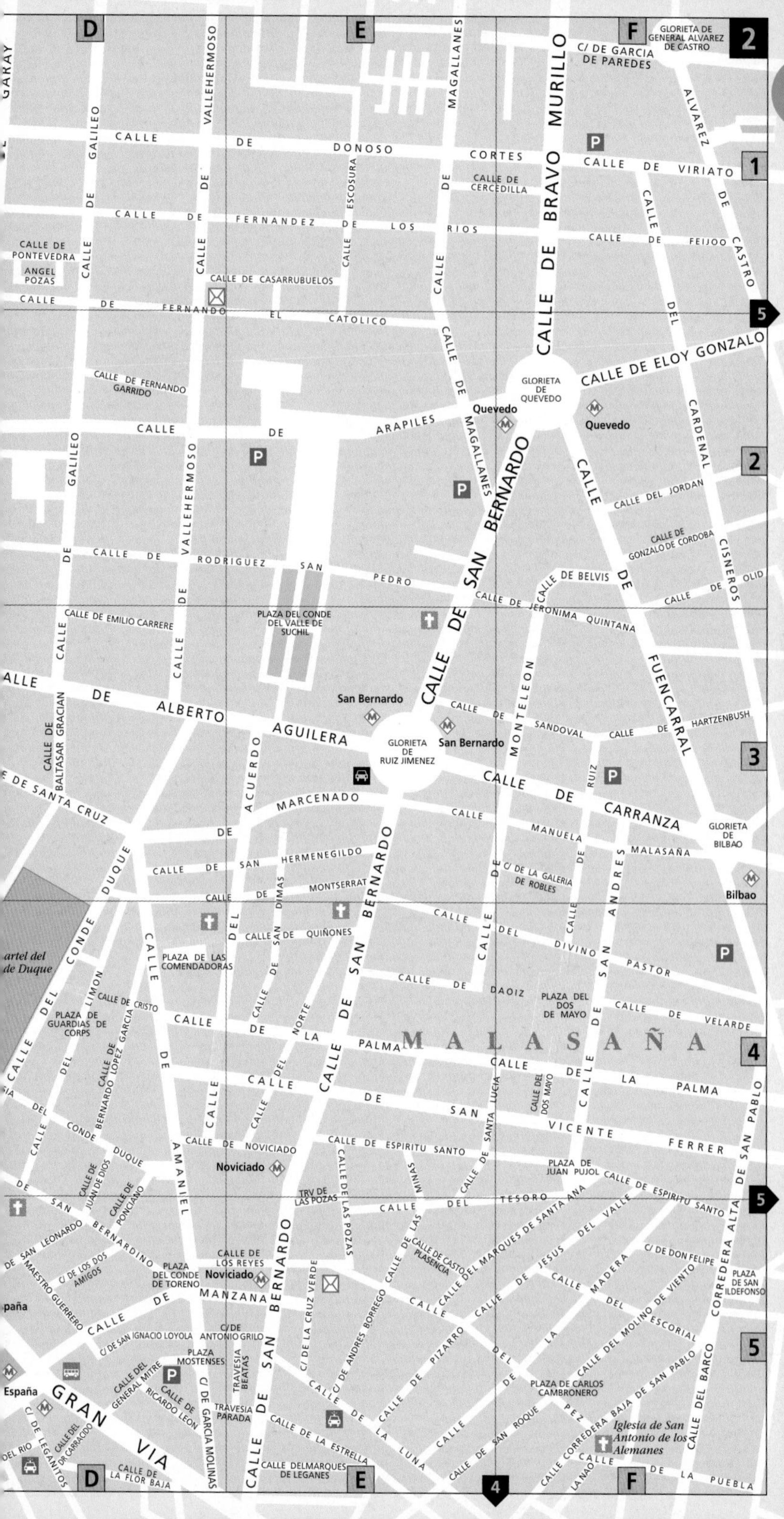
D
E
F
2
1
2
3
4
5
5
5
4
GLORIETA DE GENERAL ALVAREZ DE CASTRO
C/ DE GARCIA DE PAREDES
CALLE DE BRAVO MURILLO
CALLE DE DONOSO CORTES
CALLE DE VIRIATO
CALLE DE CERCEDILLA
CALLE DE FERNANDEZ DE LOS RIOS
CALLE DE FEIJOO
ALVAREZ DE CASTRO
CALLE DE PONTEVEDRA
ANGEL POZAS
CALLE DE CASARRUBUELOS
CALLE DE FERNANDO EL CATOLICO
CALLE DE GALILEO
CALLE DE VALLEHERMOSO
CALLE ESCOSURA
CALLE DE MAGALLANES
CALLE DEL CARDENAL CISNEROS
CALLE DE ELOY GONZALO
GLORIETA DE QUEVEDO
Quevedo
CALLE DE FERNANDO GARRIDO
CALLE DE ARAPILES
CALLE DE SAN BERNARDO
CALLE DEL JORDAN
CALLE DE GONZALO DE CORDOBA
CALLE DE FUENCARRAL
CALLE DE OLID
CALLE DE RODRIGUEZ SAN PEDRO
CALLE DE BELVIS
CALLE DE JERONIMA QUINTANA
CALLE DE EMILIO CARRERE
PLAZA DEL CONDE DEL VALLE DE SUCHIL
CALLE DE ALBERTO AGUILERA
San Bernardo
GLORIETA DE RUIZ JIMENEZ
CALLE DE SANDOVAL
CALLE DE MONTELEON
CALLE DE HARTZENBUSH
CALLE DE BALTASAR GRACIAN
CALLE DE CARRANZA
CALLE DE SANTA CRUZ DE MARCENADO
CALLE DEL ACUERDO
CALLE MANUELA MALASAÑA
GLORIETA DE BILBAO
Bilbao
CALLE DE SAN HERMENEGILDO
C/ DE LA GALERIA DE ROBLES
CALLE RUIZ
CALLE DE SAN ANDRES
CALLE DE MONTSERRAT
CALLE DEL CONDE DUQUE
Cuartel del Conde Duque
CALLE DE SAN DIMAS
CALLE DE QUIÑONES
CALLE DEL DIVINO PASTOR
PLAZA DE LAS COMENDADORAS
CALLE DE AMANIEL
CALLE DE LIMON
CALLE DE CRISTO
CALLE DE DAOIZ
PLAZA DEL DOS DE MAYO
CALLE DE VELARDE
PLAZA DE GUARDIAS DE CORPS
CALLE DE BERNARDO LOPEZ GARCIA
CALLE DE LA PALMA
CALLE DEL NORTE
MALASAÑA
CALLE DEL DOS DE MAYO
CALLE DE SAN VICENTE FERRER
CALLE DE SANTA LUCIA
CALLE DE SAN PABLO
CALLE DE NOVICIADO
Noviciado
CALLE DE ESPIRITU SANTO
CALLE DE LAS POZAS
CALLE DE LAS MINAS
PLAZA DE JUAN PUJOL
CALLE DE JUAN DE DIOS
CALLE DE PONCIANO
TRV DE LAS POZAS
CALLE DEL TESORO
CALLE DE SAN BERNARDINO
CALLE DE SAN LEONARDO
CALLE DE LAS CALLE DE CASTO PLASENCIA
CALLE DEL MARQUES DE SANTA ANA
CALLE DE JESUS DEL VALLE
C/ DE DON FELIPE
PLAZA DE SAN ILDEFONSO
CORREDERA ALTA DE SAN PABLO
MAESTRO GUERRERO
C/ DE LOS DOS AMIGOS
PLAZA DEL CONDE DE TORENO
CALLE DE LOS REYES
CALLE DE LA CRUZ VERDE
CALLE DE LA MADERA
CALLE DEL ESCORIAL
CALLE DEL MOLINO DE VIENTO
España
CALLE DE MANZANA
C/ DE ANDRES BORREGO
CALLE DE PIZARRO
C/ DE SAN IGNACIO LOYOLA
C/ DE ANTONIO GRILO
PLAZA MOSTENSES
TRAVESIA BEATAS
CALLE DE LA LUNA
PLAZA DE CARLOS CAMBRONERO
CALLE DEL BARCO
GRAN VIA
CALLE DEL GENERAL MITRE
CALLE DE RICARDO LEON
C/ DE GARCIA MOLINAS
TRAVESIA PARADA
CALLE DE LA ESTRELLA
CALLE DE SAN ROQUE
CALLE DEL PEZ
CALLE CORREDERA BAJA DE SAN PABLO
Iglesia de San Antonio de los Alemanes
C/ DE LEGANITOS
CALLE DEL DR CARRACIDO
DEL RIO
CALLE DE LA FLOR BAJA
CALLE DELMARQUES DE LEGANES
CALLE DE LA NAO
CALLE DE LA PUEBLA

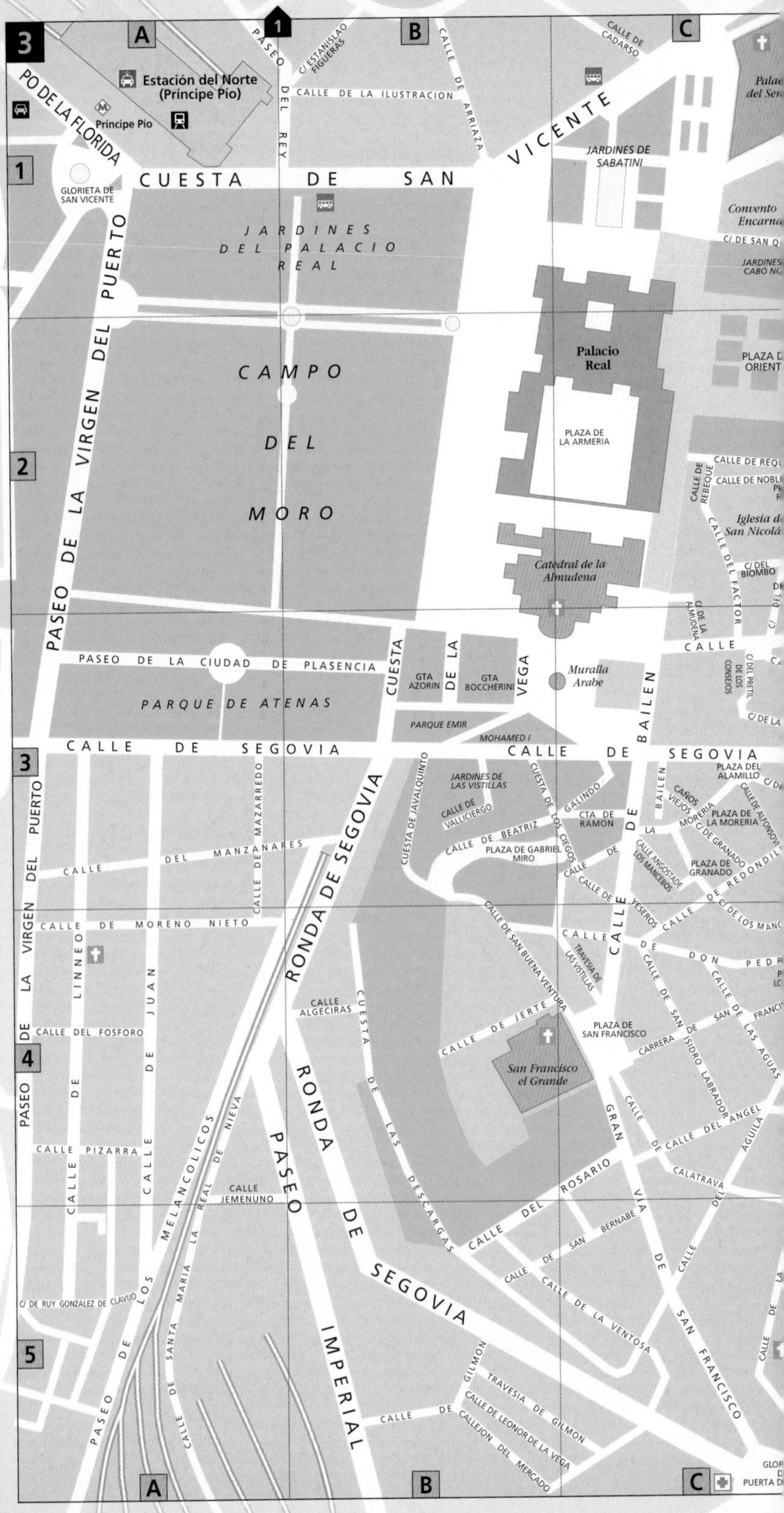
3
A
B
C
1
2
3
4
5
Estación del Norte (Príncipe Pío)
Príncipe Pío
PO DE LA FLORIDA
GLORIETA DE SAN VICENTE
PASEO DEL REY
C/ ESTANISLAO FIGUERAS
CALLE DE LA ILUSTRACION
CALLE DE ARRIAZA
CALLE DE CADARSO
CUESTA DE SAN VICENTE
JARDINES DE SABATINI
Palacio del Senado
Convento Encarnación
C/ DE SAN Q
JARDINES CABO NO
JARDINES DEL PALACIO REAL
CAMPO DEL MORO
Palacio Real
PLAZA DE LA ARMERIA
PLAZA DE ORIENTE
PASEO DE LA VIRGEN DEL PUERTO
CALLE DE REQU
CALLE DE NOBL
CALLE DE REBEQUE
Iglesia de San Nicolás
CALLE DEL FACTOR
C/ DEL BIOMBO
Catedral de la Almudena
C/ DE LA ALMUDENA
CALLE
C/ DEL PRETIL DE LOS CONSEJOS
PASEO DE LA CIUDAD DE PLASENCIA
PARQUE DE ATENAS
CUESTA DE LA VEGA
GTA AZORIN
GTA BOCCHERINI
Muralla Arabe
CALLE DE BAILEN
PARQUE EMIR MOHAMED I
C/ DE LA
CALLE DE SEGOVIA
PLAZA DEL ALAMILLO
JARDINES DE LAS VISTILLAS
CUESTA DE JAVALQUINTO
CUESTA DE LOS CIEGOS
CALLE DE VALLICIERGO
CALLE DE BEATRIZ GALINDO
CTA DE RAMON
PLAZA DE GABRIEL MIRO
CAÑOS VIEJOS
MORERIA
PLAZA DE LA MORERIA
C/ DE GRANADO
CALLE DE ALFONSO VI
PLAZA DE GRANADO
CALLE ANGOSTA DE LOS MANCEBOS
CALLE DE MAZARREDO
CALLE DEL MANZANARES
RONDA DE SEGOVIA
CALLE DE YESEROS
CALLE DE REDONDILLA
C/ DE LOS MANC
CALLE DE MORENO NIETO
CALLE DE LINNEO
CALLE DE SAN BUENA VENTURA
TRAVESIA DE LAS VISTILLAS
CALLE DE DON PEDRO
CALLE DE JUAN
CALLE ALGECIRAS
CUESTA DE LAS DESCARGAS
CALLE DE JERTE
PLAZA DE SAN FRANCISCO
CARRERA DE SAN FRANCISCO
CALLE DE SAN ISIDRO LABRADOR
CALLE DE LAS AGUAS
CALLE DEL FOSFORO
San Francisco el Grande
CALLE DEL ANGEL
CALLE DE CALATRAVA
CALLE DEL AGUILA
CALLE PIZARRA
PASEO DE LOS MELANCOLICOS
CALLE DE SANTA MARIA LA REAL DE NIEVA
CALLE JEMENUNO
PASEO IMPERIAL
CALLE DEL ROSARIO
GRAN VIA DE SAN FRANCISCO
CALLE DE SAN BERNABE
CALLE DE LA VENTOSA
C/ DE RUY GONZALEZ DE CLAVIJO
CALLE DE GILMON
TRAVESIA DE GILMON
CALLE DE LEONOR DE LA VEGA
CALLEJON DEL MERCADO
GLORIETA DE PUERTA DE

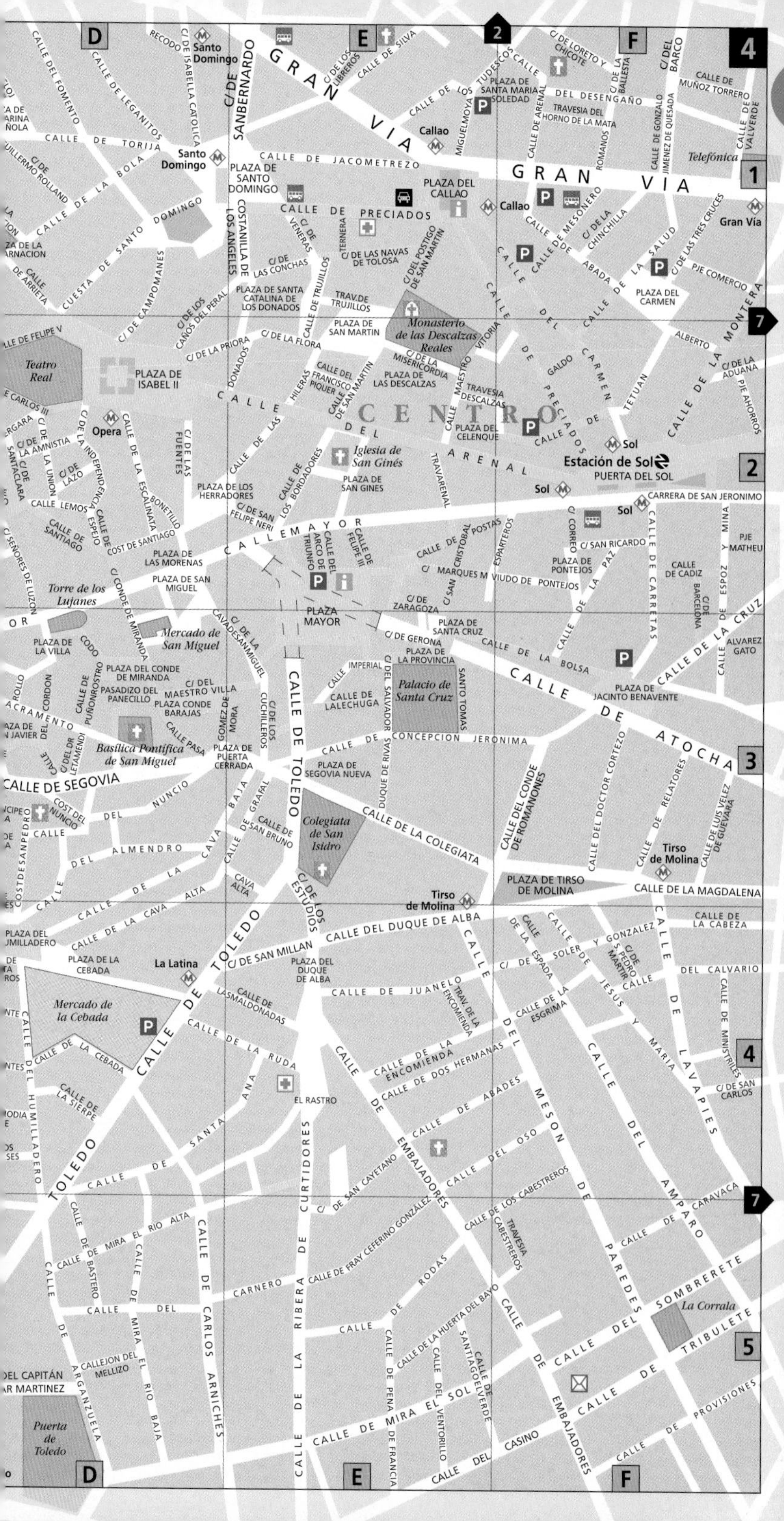
D
E
F
4
2
7
1
2
3
4
5
GRAN VIA
CENTRO
Santo Domingo
Callao
Telefónica
Gran Vía
PLAZA DEL CALLAO
PLAZA DE SANTO DOMINGO
CALLE DE PRECIADOS
Monasterio de las Descalzas Reales
PLAZA DE LAS DESCALZAS
Teatro Real
PLAZA DE ISABEL II
Opera
Iglesia de San Ginés
Estación de Sol
PUERTA DEL SOL
Sol
CALLE MAYOR
PLAZA MAYOR
Torre de los Lujanes
Mercado de San Miguel
PLAZA DE LA VILLA
Palacio de Santa Cruz
CALLE DE ATOCHA
CALLE DE TOLEDO
CALLE DE SEGOVIA
Basílica Pontífica de San Miguel
Colegiata de San Isidro
CALLE DE LA COLEGIATA
PLAZA DE TIRSO DE MOLINA
Tirso de Molina
CALLE DE LA MAGDALENA
CALLE DEL DUQUE DE ALBA
La Latina
Mercado de la Cebada
PLAZA DE LA CEBADA
EL RASTRO
CALLE DE EMBAJADORES
CALLE DE LAVAPIES
CALLE DEL AMPARO
CALLE DE MESON DE PAREDES
La Corrala
CALLE DE TRIBULETE
CALLE DEL SOMBRERETE
CALLE DE LA RIBERA DE CURTIDORES
CALLE DE CARLOS ARNICHES
CALLE DE MIRA EL SOL
CALLE DEL CASINO
Puerta de Toledo
CALLE DE ARGANZUELA
CALLE DEL HUMILLADERO
TOLEDO

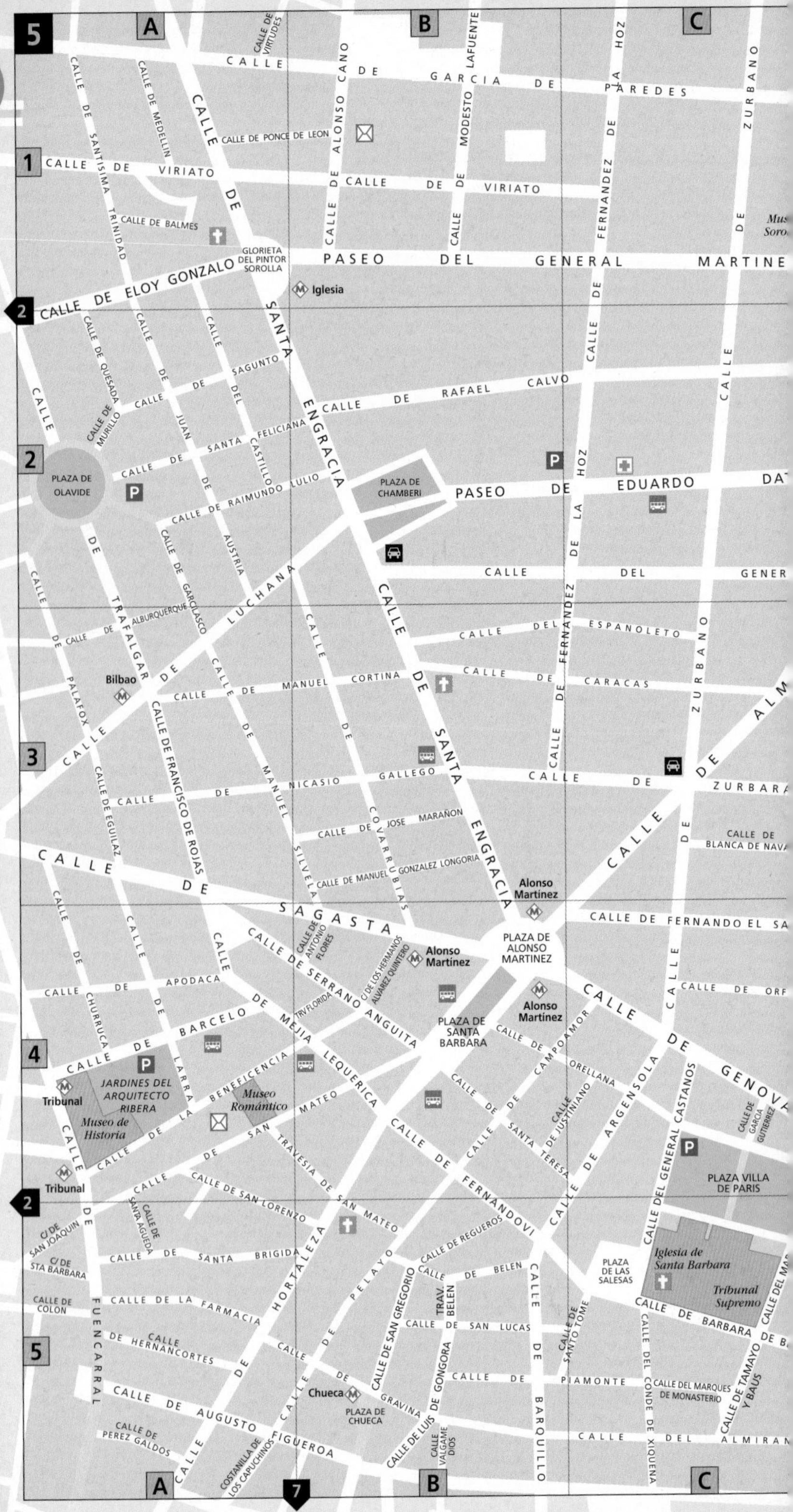
5
A
B
C
1
2
3
4
5
CALLE DE GARCIA DE PAREDES
CALLE DE VIRIATO
CALLE DE SANTA ENGRACIA
CALLE DE PONCE DE LEON
CALLE DE ALONSO CANO
CALLE DE MODESTO LAFUENTE
CALLE DE FERNANDEZ DE LA HOZ
CALLE DE ZURBANO
CALLE DE SANTISIMA TRINIDAD
CALLE DE MEDELLIN
CALLE DE BALMES
GLORIETA DEL PINTOR SOROLLA
PASEO DEL GENERAL MARTINE
CALLE DE ELOY GONZALO
Iglesia
CALLE DE QUESADA
CALLE DE JUAN DE AUSTRIA
CALLE DEL CASTILLO
CALLE DE SAGUNTO
CALLE DE RAFAEL CALVO
CALLE DE MURILLO
CALLE DE SANTA FELICIANA
PLAZA DE OLAVIDE
CALLE DE RAIMUNDO LULIO
PLAZA DE CHAMBERI
PASEO DE EDUARDO DAT
CALLE DE GARCILASO
CALLE DE TRAFALGAR
CALLE DE LUCHANA
CALLE DEL GENER
CALLE DE ALBURQUERQUE
CALLE DE PALAFOX
CALLE DEL ESPANOLETO
Bilbao
CALLE DE MANUEL CORTINA
CALLE DE CARACAS
CALLE DE FRANCISCO DE ROJAS
CALLE DE MANUEL SILVELA
CALLE DE COVARRUBIAS
CALLE DE NICASIO GALLEGO
CALLE DE ZURBARA
CALLE DE ALM
CALLE DE EGUILAZ
CALLE DE JOSE MARAÑON
CALLE DE BLANCA DE NAVA
CALLE DE MANUEL GONZALEZ LONGORIA
CALLE DE SAGASTA
Alonso Martínez
CALLE DE FERNANDO EL SA
PLAZA DE ALONSO MARTINEZ
CALLE DE ANTONIO FLORES
C/ DE LOS HERMANOS ALVAREZ QUINTERO
CALLE DE SERRANO ANGUITA
TRV. FLORIDA
CALLE DE APODACA
CALLE DE CHURRUCA
CALLE DE LARRA
CALLE DE BARCELO
CALLE DE MEJIA LEQUERICA
PLAZA DE SANTA BARBARA
CALLE DE CAMPOAMOR
CALLE DE ORELLANA
CALLE DE ORF
CALLE DE GENOV
CALLE DE ARGENSOLA
CALLE DEL GENERAL CASTAÑOS
Tribunal
JARDINES DEL ARQUITECTO RIBERA
Museo de Historia
Museo Romántico
CALLE DE LA BENEFICENCIA
CALLE DE SAN MATEO
CALLE DE SANTA TERESA
CALLE DE JUSTINIANO
CALLE DE GARCIA GUTIERREZ
PLAZA VILLA DE PARIS
CALLE DE FERNANDO VI
TRAVESIA DE SAN MATEO
CALLE DE SAN LORENZO
CALLE DE SANTA AGUEDA
C/ DE SAN JOAQUIN
C/ DE STA BARBARA
CALLE DE SANTA BRIGIDA
CALLE DE HORTALEZA
CALLE DE REGUEROS
CALLE DE BELEN
PLAZA DE LAS SALESAS
Iglesia de Santa Barbara
Tribunal Supremo
CALLE DE BARBARA DE B
CALLE DE COLON
CALLE DE LA FARMACIA
CALLE DE FUENCARRAL
CALLE DE PELAYO
CALLE DE SAN GREGORIO
TRAV. BELEN
CALLE DE SAN LUCAS
CALLE DE SANTO TOME
CALLE DE BARQUILLO
CALLE DEL CONDE DE XIQUENA
CALLE DE HERNAN CORTES
CALLE DE GRAVINA
CALLE DE PIAMONTE
CALLE DEL MARQUES DE MONASTERIO
CALLE DE TAMAYO Y BAUS
Chueca
PLAZA DE CHUECA
CALLE DE LUIS DE GONGORA
CALLE DE AUGUSTO FIGUEROA
CALLE DE PEREZ GALDOS
COSTANILLA DE LOS CAPUCHINOS
CALLE VALGAME DIOS
CALLE DEL ALMIRAN
7

6
D
E
F
1
2
3
4
5
8
Museo Lázaro Galdiano
Glorieta de Emilio Castelar
Paseo de la Castellana
Calle de Lopez de Hoyos
Calle del Pinar
Calle de Hermanos Becquer
Calle del General Oraa
Calle de Serrano
Calle de Claudio Coello
Calle de Lagasca
Calle de Velazquez
Calle de Diego de Leon
Calle de Maldonado
Calle de Juan Bravo
Calle de Padilla
Calle de Jose Ortega y Gasset
Calle de Don Ramon de la Cruz
Calle de Ayala
Calle de Hermosilla
Calle de Goya
Calle de Jorge Juan
Calle de Villanueva
Calle de Nuñez de Balboa
Calle de Miguel Angel
Campos
Calle de Fortuny
Calle de Rafael Calvo
Paseo de Eduardo Dato
Calle de Jenner
Calle de Marques de Villamejor
Calle del Marques del Riscal
Calle del Marques de Villamagna
Museo de Escultura al Aire Libre
Rubén Darío
Núñez de Balboa
SALAMANCA
Pje Paz
Mercado de la Paz
C/ de Amador de los Rios
Alcalagaliano
Marques de Zurgena
Colón
Plaza de Colon
Jardines del Descubrimiento
Serrano
Velázquez
Paseo de Recoletos
Biblioteca Nacional
Museo Arqueológico Nacional
Calle del Cid
Calle Gil de Santivanes
Estación de Recoletos
Calle de Recoletos
C/ de Puigcerda
Calle de Jorge Juan
Calle de Gurtubay
C/ de Maria de Molina

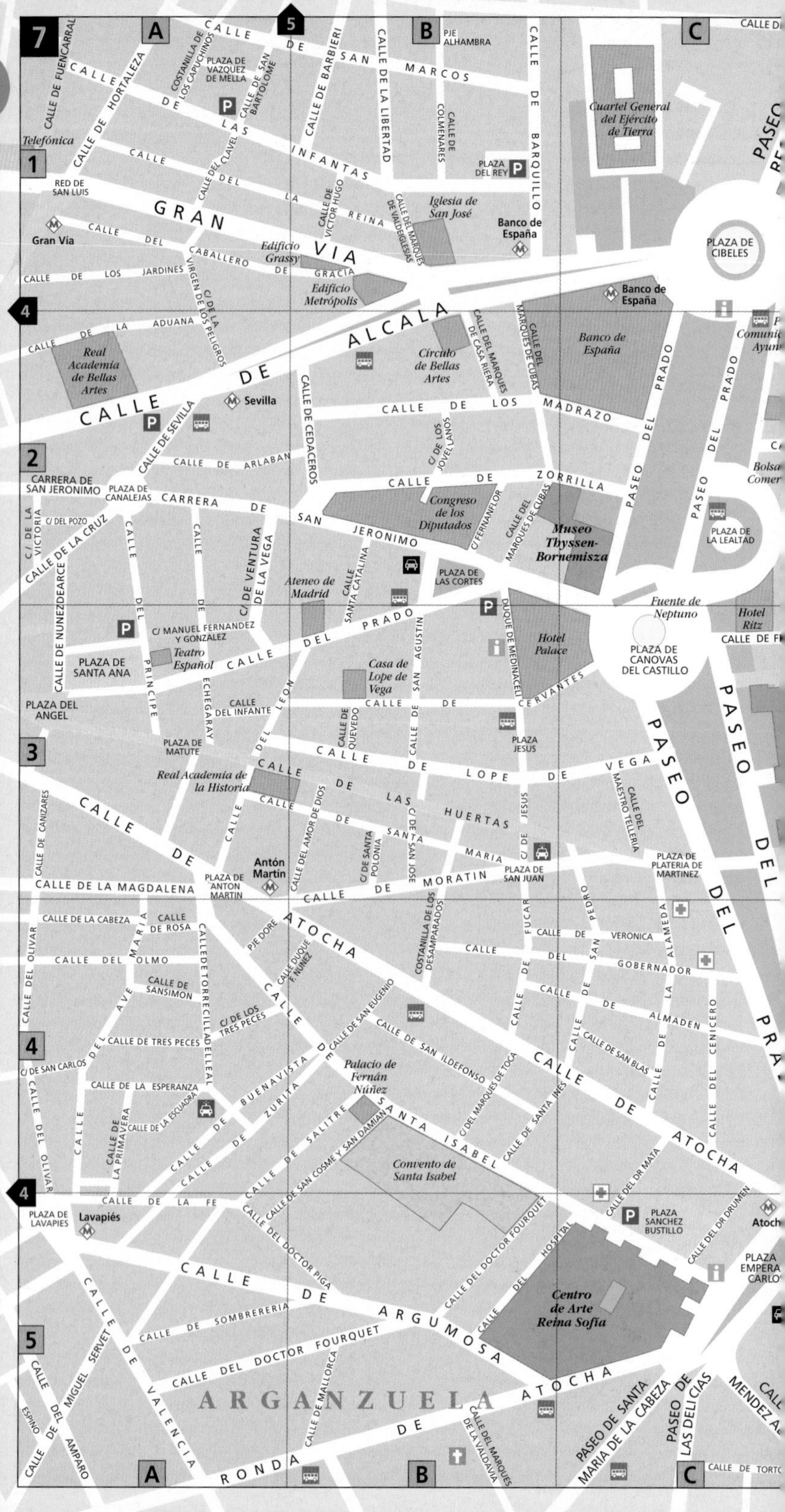
7
A
B
C
5
4
1
2
3
4
5
CALLE DE FUENCARRAL
CALLE DE HORTALEZA
COSTANILLA DE LOS CAPUCHINOS
PLAZA DE VAZQUEZ DE MELLA
CALLE DE SAN BARTOLOME
CALLE DE SAN MARCOS
CALLE DE BARBIERI
CALLE DE LA LIBERTAD
PJE ALHAMBRA
CALLE DE COLMENARES
CALLE DE BARQUILLO
CALLE DE LAS INFANTAS
Cuartel General del Ejército de Tierra
PASEO
Telefónica
CALLE DEL CLAVEL
PLAZA DEL REY
RED DE SAN LUIS
GRAN VIA
CALLE DE LA REINA
CALLE DE VICTOR HUGO
CALLE DEL MARQUES DE VALDEIGLESIAS
Iglesia de San José
Banco de España
PLAZA DE CIBELES
Gran Vía
CALLE DEL CABALLERO DE GRACIA
Edificio Grassy
Edificio Metrópolis
CALLE DE LOS JARDINES
VIRGEN DE LOS PELIGROS
C/ DE LA
CALLE DE LA ADUANA
Real Academia de Bellas Artes
CALLE DE ALCALA
CALLE DEL MARQUES DE CASA RIERA
CALLE DEL MARQUES DE CUBAS
Banco de España
Círculo de Bellas Artes
Sevilla
CALLE DE SEVILLA
CALLE DE CEDACEROS
CALLE DE LOS MADRAZO
PASEO DEL PRADO
C/ DE LOS JOVELLANOS
CALLE DE ARLABAN
CARRERA DE SAN JERONIMO
PLAZA DE CANALEJAS
CALLE DE ZORRILLA
Bolsa de Comercio
C/ DE LA VICTORIA
C/ DEL POZO
CALLE DE LA CRUZ
CARRERA DE SAN JERONIMO
Congreso de los Diputados
C/ FERNANFLOR
CALLE DEL MARQUES DE CUBAS
Museo Thyssen-Bornemisza
PLAZA DE LA LEALTAD
CALLE DEL PRINCIPE
C/ DE VENTURA DE LA VEGA
Ateneo de Madrid
CALLE SANTA CATALINA
PLAZA DE LAS CORTES
CALLE DE NUÑEZ DE ARCE
C/ MANUEL FERNANDEZ Y GONZALEZ
CALLE DEL PRADO
DUQUE DE MEDINACELI
Hotel Palace
Fuente de Neptuno
Hotel Ritz
CALLE DE FELIPE IV
PLAZA DE SANTA ANA
Teatro Español
CALLE DE SAN AGUSTIN
Casa de Lope de Vega
PLAZA DE CANOVAS DEL CASTILLO
PLAZA DEL ANGEL
CALLE DEL INFANTE
CALLE DEL LEON
CALLE DE ECHEGARAY
CALLE DE CERVANTES
CALLE DE QUEVEDO
PLAZA JESUS
PLAZA DE MATUTE
CALLE DE LOPE DE VEGA
PASEO DEL PRADO
Real Academia de la Historia
CALLE DE LAS HUERTAS
CALLE DEL MAESTRO TELLERIA
CALLE DE CANIZARES
CALLE DEL AMOR DE DIOS
CALLE DE JESUS
CALLE DE ATOCHA
CALLE DE SANTA MARIA
C/ DE SANTA POLONIA
C/ DE SAN JOSE
Antón Martín
PLAZA DE ANTON MARTIN
CALLE DE MORATIN
PLAZA DE SAN JUAN
PLAZA DE PLATERIA DE MARTINEZ
CALLE DE LA MAGDALENA
CALLE DE LA CABEZA
CALLE DE ROSA
CALLE DE TORRECILLA DEL LEAL
PIE DORE
COSTANILLA DE LOS DESAMPARADOS
CALLE DE FUCAR
CALLE DE SAN PEDRO
CALLE DE VERONICA
CALLE DE LA ALAMEDA
CALLE DEL OLIVAR
CALLE DEL OLMO
CALLE DE MARIA
CALLE DUQUE F. NUÑEZ
CALLE DEL GOBERNADOR
CALLE DE SANSIMON
C/ DE LOS TRES PECES
CALLE DE SAN EUGENIO
CALLE DE ALMADEN
CALLE DE TRES PECES
CALLE DE SAN ILDEFONSO
CALLE DE SAN BLAS
CALLE DEL CENICERO
C/ DE SAN CARLOS
CALLE DE LA ESPERANZA
CALLE DE BUENAVISTA
Palacio de Fernán Núñez
C/ DEL MARQUES DE TOCA
CALLE DE SANTA INES
CALLE DE LA ESCUADRA
CALLE DE LA PRIMAVERA
CALLE DE ZURITA
CALLE DE SANTA ISABEL
CALLE DE SAN COSME Y SAN DAMIAN
Convento de Santa Isabel
CALLE DE SALITRE
CALLE DE LA FE
CALLE DEL DR MATA
CALLE DEL DR DRUMEN
PLAZA DE LAVAPIES
Lavapiés
CALLE DEL DOCTOR PIGA
CALLE DEL DOCTOR FOURQUET
CALLE DEL HOSPITAL
PLAZA SANCHEZ BUSTILLO
Atocha
PLAZA EMPERADOR CARLOS V
CALLE DE ARGUMOSA
CALLE DE SOMBRERERIA
Centro de Arte Reina Sofía
CALLE DE VALENCIA
CALLE DE MIGUEL SERVET
CALLE DEL AMPARO
CALLE DEL DOCTOR FOURQUET
ESPINO
ARGANZUELA
CALLE DE MALLORCA
RONDA DE ATOCHA
CALLE DEL MARQUES DE LA VALDAVIA
PASEO DE SANTA MARIA DE LA CABEZA
PASEO DE LAS DELICIAS
CALLE DE TORTOSA

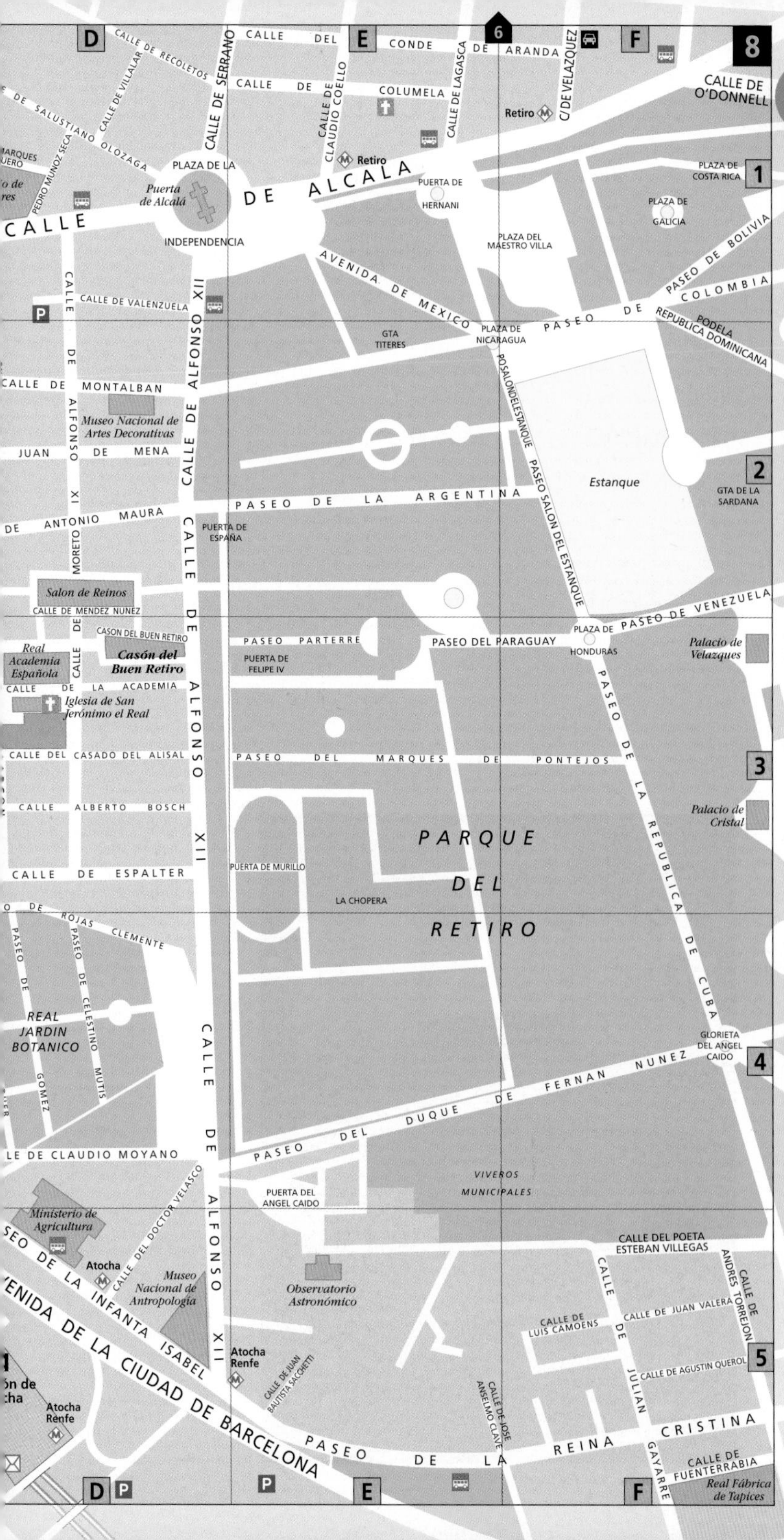
D
E
F
6
CALLE DEL CONDE DE ARANDA
CALLE DE RECOLETOS
CALLE DE SERRANO
CALLE DE COLUMELA
CALLE DE CLAUDIO COELLO
CALLE DE LAGASCA
C/ DE VELAZQUEZ
Retiro
CALLE DE O'DONNELL
CALLE DE SALUSTIANO OLOZAGA
CALLE DE VILLALAR
PEDRO MUNOZ SECA
PLAZA DE LA INDEPENDENCIA
Puerta de Alcalá
CALLE DE ALCALA
PUERTA DE HERNANI
PLAZA DE COSTA RICA
PLAZA DE GALICIA
PLAZA DEL MAESTRO VILLA
AVENIDA DE MEXICO
PASEO DE BOLIVIA
COLOMBIA
PASEO DE REPUBLICA DOMINICANA
PODELA
PLAZA DE NICARAGUA
GTA TITERES
CALLE DE VALENZUELA
CALLE DE MONTALBAN
Museo Nacional de Artes Decorativas
JUAN DE MENA
CALLE DE ALFONSO XII
CALLE DE ALFONSO XI
PASEO SALON DEL ESTANQUE
Estanque
GTA DE LA SARDANA
PASEO DE LA ARGENTINA
DE ANTONIO MAURA
PUERTA DE ESPAÑA
MORETO
Salon de Reinos
CALLE DE MENDEZ NUNEZ
CASON DEL BUEN RETIRO
Casón del Buen Retiro
Real Academia Española
PASEO PARTERRE
PUERTA DE FELIPE IV
PASEO DEL PARAGUAY
PLAZA DE HONDURAS
PASEO DE VENEZUELA
Palacio de Velazques
CALLE DE LA ACADEMIA
Iglesia de San Jerónimo el Real
CALLE DEL CASADO DEL ALISAL
PASEO DEL MARQUES DE PONTEJOS
PASEO DE LA REPUBLICA DE CUBA
CALLE ALBERTO BOSCH
Palacio de Cristal
PARQUE DEL RETIRO
CALLE DE ESPALTER
PUERTA DE MURILLO
LA CHOPERA
DE ROJAS CLEMENTE
PASEO DE GOMEZ
PASEO DE CELESTINO MUTIS
REAL JARDIN BOTANICO
GLORIETA DEL ANGEL CAIDO
PASEO DEL DUQUE DE FERNAN NUNEZ
CALLE DE CLAUDIO MOYANO
VIVEROS MUNICIPALES
PUERTA DEL ANGEL CAIDO
Ministerio de Agricultura
CALLE DEL DOCTOR VELASCO
Atocha
Museo Nacional de Antropología
Observatorio Astronómico
CALLE DEL POETA ESTEBAN VILLEGAS
CALLE DE ANDRES TORREJON
CALLE DE LUIS CAMOENS
CALLE DE JUAN VALERA
CALLE DE JULIAN GAYARRE
CALLE DE AGUSTIN QUEROL
PASEO DE LA INFANTA ISABEL
AVENIDA DE LA CIUDAD DE BARCELONA
Atocha Renfe
CALLE DE JUAN BAUTISTA SACCHETTI
CALLE DE JOSE ANSELMO CLAVE
PASEO DE LA REINA CRISTINA
CALLE DE FUENTERRABIA
Real Fábrica de Tapices
1
2
3
4
5

SHOPPING IN MADRID

Selection of cakes

Madrid is a shoppers' paradise, where designer stores compete for attention with small, quirky shops. Madrid still has more independent and family-run shops than most European capitals, so it should not be hard to pick up some truly original gifts. There are two main shopping hearts in the city – the crowded and popular streets around the pedestrianized Preciados and the Plaza del Sol, and Calle de la Princesa and adjacent streets. The Salamanca district is host to designer brands as well as up-market antiques, while for the latest streetware visit the Chueca district. The colourful food markets dotted around the city are well worth a visit.

OPENING HOURS

Most shops in Madrid are open from 10am to 2pm and 5 to 8:30pm, though larger stores tend to stay open during lunch and close at 10pm. Small shops often close on Saturday afternoon. Shopping centres, department stores and big shops are permitted to open on Sundays, and the downtown shops open on the first Sunday of the month. Many small shops close for a month (usually August) in the summer.

FOOD AND DRINK

Madrid is a paradise for gourmet food shopping. Strongly scented saffron, matured ewe's cheese or a fruity extra-virgin olive oil all make ideal gifts. Spain has a deep-rooted tradition of pork products, ranging from whole hams to sausages of every shape and size. The best and most expensive ham is Ibérico, from the small, black-hoofed Iberian pig. In Old Madrid, branches of Museo del Jamón have an enormous range of Spanish hams, cheeses and cured sausages. The department store **El Corte Inglés** has its own department dedicated to gourmet delicacies, as well as a supermarket for more general groceries. There are smaller delicatessens in nearly every district. In the Salamanca area visit **Mantequerías Bravo**, famous for its excellent cheeses, preserves and sweets.

If you are looking for good wine, head to **Reserva y Cata**, an outlet with a long history of selling Spanish and Portuguese wines. It also organizes tasting sessions. **Lavinia**, in the Salamanca district, is said to be Europe's biggest wine shop, with more than 1,500 brands available. For a truly authentic Madrileño souvenir, try **La Violeta**, famous for its fragrant violet sweets.

The enticing frontage of the Museo del Jamón

MARKETS

A favourite local activity is shopping at the street, or flea, markets, where you can spend a pleasant few hours browsing for antiques, second-hand clothes, pottery, handicrafts and furniture. Some markets are focused on only one item, such as the Sunday morning stamp, postcard and coin market under the arches of Plaza Mayor, or the Cuesta de Moyano at the Atocha end of Paseo de Prado, where stalls selling second-hand books are set up daily. The legendary El Rastro Sunday flea market *(see p302)*. is a must for any visitor to Madrid, not only for the variety of goods to be found, from

Inside one of the many antique shops in the streets around El Rastro

antiques to trendy garments, but also for its lively atmosphere. It gets really crowded from 12 noon onwards, with bargain-hunters rubbing shoulders with those out to enjoy a pre-lunch apéritif at the numerous bars of the La Latina area. Be careful, however, as pick-pockets frequent the market.

Visit the handicrafts market in Plaza Comendadoras on Saturdays from 11am to 9pm for diverse pieces by Madrid's artists. The best place for paintings is the street market near Sol on Sunday mornings, organized by the art association, Taller Abierto.

It is worth visiting the colourful Mercado de San Miguel in Plaza San Miguel. Set up in a refurbished early 20th-century building, the market stalls offer an array of produce and delicious delicatessen items, including traditional cured meats and Spanish cheeses. Mercado de San Antón in Chueca is another excellent market.

ANNUAL FAIRS

The contemporary art fair, ARCO, takes place in February. Whether you want to buy or simply browse, it provides a great opportunity to catch up on the latest trends in the art world.

In the week prior to Madrid's Fiesta de San Isidro (*see p40*) which begins on 15th May, you can buy earthern cookware and wine jugs at the Feria de la Cerámica held in the Plaza de las Comendadoras in the colourful district of Malasaña. The Feria del Libro, held in June, is an impressive outdoor bookfair. Hundreds of stalls are set up in the Parque del Retiro, and publishers and bookshop owners exhibit their wares for two weeks, with book signings taking place as well.

On the Paseo de Recoletos, the Feria de Artesanos takes place every December, selling all kinds of crafts, making it ideal for Christmas shopping. Throughout December, the Plaza Mayor is the venue for a traditional Christmas fair – the Mercado de Artículos Navideños, where Christmas bric-à-brac can be picked up.

ANTIQUES AND ARTS

The commercial galleries and antiques shops of Madrid are all conveniently located around the Calle Barquillo in the Alonso Martinez district, along the streets of Serrano, Velázquez, Jorge Juán and Claudio Coello. For cutting-edge Spanish art, head to the **Juana de Aizpuru** gallery, considered to be one of Madrid's top galleries for contemporary art.

Antique shops can also be found in El Rastro flea market, mainly along Calle de la Ribera de Curtidores. **Hidalgo** is a classic that sells unusual collectors' items, such as keys, metal boxes and corkscrews.

For specialist antique outlets, ranging from 18th-century lacquered furniture, to Spanish paintings from the 16th to 18th centuries, visit **María Gracia Cavestany** and **Theotokopoulos**. On Calle Lagasca an antique centre, **Centro de Anticuarios**, hosts some of Madrid's top dealers under one roof. There are also opportunities for pricier antique shopping along the streets of the Prado, Santa Catalina and in the Mercado Puerta de Toledo. In Madrid, art and antiques auctions are held by both Spanish and international firms, including Sotheby's and Christie's.

SHOPPING CENTRES AND DEPARTMENT STORES

Among the best shopping centres, or *centros comerciales*, are the tempting and expensive malls of the elegant Salamanca neighbourhood. **El Jardín de Serrano** is a high-quality *galleria*, housed in two restored 19th-century palaces that stocks fashion, jewellery, gifts and accessories. **ABC Serrano** has a range of shops that includes home furniture as well as designer fashions and gifts.

If you want more variety at a cheaper price, visit the huge **La Vaguada** on the north side of Madrid, or **El Corte Inglés**, a national institution with branches throughout the city. The latter also has a travel agency and offers services such as photo development and shoe repairs. Also good value for money are the shops in the new **Príncipe Pío** shopping centre, located in the former Northern Railway Station. Shops, restaurants and cinemas sit under the original glass and iron roof.

Sunday morning in the busy Rastro flea market

FASHION

The Spanish chain stores **Zara** and **Mango** have now become international phenomena, offering easy-to-wear clothes for women at very good prices. Zara also caters to men and children. Both stores have branches all over the city. For up-market fashion there are many well-known Spanish designers, such as **Amaya Arzuaga**, who have their own shops in Madrid, mainly in the elegant Salamanca district.

Those in favour of a more unusual or original look should try **Ágatha Ruiz de la Prada**'s creations (for children and adults), while the minimalist **Antonio Pernas**' shop specializes in more classic styles.

For high-quality designer menswear check out **Roberto Verino**, **Custo Barcelona**, **Adolfo Domínguez** or **Caramelo**. These shops also offer women's clothes. Another popular, reasonably-priced Spanish chain store for men is **Springfield**. At the top end of the market is the **Loewe** store for men, where a silk tie with a Spanish art motif makes a stylish gift.

The Chueca district is the best place for the latest in streetwear, with offbeat local designers and second-hand shops on almost every corner. Many outlets also sell international brands at reduced prices.

SHOES AND LEATHER GOODS

Madrid is a haven for those with a shoe fetish. You will find every type of shoe here, from the traditional espadrille sold at **Antigua Casa Crespo** to the popular Majorcan **Camper** shoes. Try **Pretty Ballerinas** for beautiful ballerina shoes and pumps, while for sophistication, opt for the elegant **Farrutx**. If you are after trendy flip-flops head to Jocomomola in Callejón de Jorge Juan. Visit **Bravo** for some of the best national and international labels. Chic shoes, sandals and handbags with an innovative touch are available at **Cristina Castañer**. For trainers or other budget buys, visit the shops along Calle de Fuencarral, or go to **Los Guerrilleros** in Calle Montera, near Puerta del Sol.

Spain undoubtedly produces some of the best quality leather in the world. The ultimate in bags and leather goes under the prestigious label of **Loewe**, whose products are sold all over the world. Another impressive (and perhaps more budget friendly) national brand is **Salvador Bachiller**, where you will find quality leather and exclusively designed bags, suitcases, wallets and other accessories. If you are looking for a touch of the more traditional Andalusian style, take a look at the range of the handbags and belts for sale at **El Caballo**.

JEWELLERY

In Calle Serrano and Gran Vía you will find both small shops, stacked with trays of gold studs, chains and bracelets, and grand, more exclusive jewellers. Man-made "Majorica" pearls, as well as the cultivated variety, can be found all over Madrid, including at the department store El Corte Inglés.

The innovative Catalan **Tous** is popular among the young for its ubiquitous teddy-bear logo. If you are interested in original, simple designs, visit the acclaimed jeweller **Joaquín Berao**. His shop resembles an art gallery devoted to tastefully designed pieces. Museum shops are also a good place to shop for designer jewellery. Look out for original pieces from Verili, sold at the main museums in the city.

CRAFTS AND DESIGN

Traditional crafts such as woven baskets or embroidered linen are hard to find in Madrid and those that are available often tend to be Asian imports. However, lovely and inexpensive ceramics are widely available, though sometimes the more colourful pieces are from Morocco. A wide choice of ceramics can be found at **Cántaro**, near the Plaza de España. Well stocked in regional styles, the shop also carries so-called "extinct" ceramics – traditional styles of pottery no longer regularly produced. Many shops around Puerta del Sol stock embroidered tablecloths and shawls, but be aware that the authentic pieces can be quite expensive.

In the Plaza Mayor, adjoining the Arco de Cuchilleros, is **El Arco Artesasinas**, which sells handmade modern Spanish crafts, such as pottery, glassware and ironwork.

For contemporary design, head to **Víctimas del Celuloide**, an original shop with a great variety of unusual goods, from Chinese chopsticks to kits to make-your-own silicone lamps. It is the perfect place to find something a little different.

BOOKS AND MUSIC

The giant French-owned **FNAC** book and video store has an extensive selection of books and magazines in English and other languages, as does **Casa del Libro**. **Booksellers**, a little further afield, stocks English classics, though only a limited selection of new books. The second-hand bookstalls of the Mercado del Libro near the Parque del Retiro are good for cheap paperbacks and, sometimes, rare volumes. Art books can be found at one of the best specialist art bookshops, **Gaudí**, near Chueca.

For all types of music, go to the FNAC or one of the El Corte Inglés branches, either in Calle de Preciados or Paseo de la Castellana.

For flamenco buffs, the specialist **El Flamenco Vive** stocks the widest selection of books, guitars and CDs in the world.

DIRECTORY

FOOD AND DRINK

Lavinia
C/ de José Ortega y Gasset 16.
Map 6 F3.
Tel *914 26 06 04.*

La Violeta
Plaza Canalejas 6.
Map 7 A2.
Tel *915 22 55 22.*

Mantequerías Bravo
C/ de Ayala 24.
Map 6 E4.
Tel *915 75 80 72.*

Museo del Jamón
Carrera de San Jerónimo 1. **Map** 7 A2.
Tel *915 21 03 46.*

Reserva y Cata
C/ del Conde de Xiquena 13.
Map 5 C5.
Tel *913 19 04 01.*

ANTIQUES AND ARTS

Centro de Anticuarios
C/ de Lagasca 75.
Tel *915 77 37 52.*
Map 6 E5.

Hidalgo
Galerías Piquer, shop 23. C/ la Ribera de Curtidores 29.
Map 4 E5.
Tel *915 30 56 53.*

Juana de Aizpuru
C/ Barquillo 44.
Map 5 B5.
Tel *913 10 55 61.*

María Gracia Cavestany
C/ Ayala 14.
Map 6 E4.
Tel *915 77 76 32.*

Theotokopoulos
C/ Alcalá 97. **Map** 8 F1.
Tel *915 75 84 66.*

SHOPPING CENTRES AND MALLS

ABC Serrano
C/ Serrano 61.
Map 6 E2.
Tel *915 77 50 31.*
www.abcserrano.com

El Corte Inglés
C/ Preciados 1–3.
Map 4 F2.
Tel *913 79 80 00.*
www.elcorteingles.es
One of several branches.

El Jardín de Serrano
C/ Goya 6–8.
Map 6 E4.
Tel *915 77 00 12.*
www.jardindeserrano.es

La Vaguada
Av Monforte de Lemos 36.
Tel *917 30 10 00.*
www.enlavaguada.com

Príncipe Pío
Estación del Norte.
Map 3 A1.
Tel *917 58 00 40.*
www.ccprincipepio.com

FASHION

Adolfo Domínguez
C/ Serrano 18.
Map 6 E5.
Tel *915 77 82 80.*

Ágatha Ruiz de la Prada
C/ Serrano 27.
Map 6 E4.
Tel *913 19 05 01.*

Amaya Arzuaga
C/ Lagasca 50.
Map 6 F4.
Tel *914 26 28 15.*

Antonio Pernas
C/ Claudio Coello 46.
Map 6 E4.
Tel *915 78 16 76.*

Caramelo
C/ Serrano 19.
Map 6 E4.
Tel *914 35 01 77.*

Custo Barcelona
Gran Vía 26. **Map** 7 A1.
Tel *915 21 48 95.*
www.custo-barcelona.com

Mango
C/ de la Princesa 75.
Map 1 B2.
Tel *915 43 92 67.*
One of several branches.

Roberto Verino
C/ Serrano 61.
Map 6 E2.
Tel *917 81 25 13.*

Springfield
C/ Fuencarral 107.
Map 2 F3.
Tel *914 47 59 94.*
One of several branches.

Zara
Gran Vía 34.
Map 4 F1.
Tel *915 21 12 83.*

SHOES AND LEATHER GOODS

Antigua Casa Crespo
C/ del Divino Pastor 9.
Map 2 F4.
Tel *915 21 56 54.*

Bravo
C/ Serrano 42.
Map 6 E4.
Tel *914 35 49 30.*
One of several branches.

Camper
C/ de la Princesa 75.
Map 1 B2.
Tel *902 36 45 98.*
www.camper.es

Cristina Castañer
C/ del Almirante 24.
Map 5 C5.
Tel *915 23 72 11.*
www.castaner.com

El Caballo
C/ Lagasca 55.
Map 6 E5.
Tel *915 76 40 37.*

Farrutx
C/ Serrano 7.
Map 8 D1.
Tel *915 76 94 93.*

Loewe
C/ Serrano 26.
Map 6 E4.
Tel *915 77 60 56.*

Los Guerrilleros
C/ Montera 25.
Map 4 F2.
Tel *915 21 59 29.*

Pretty Ballerinas
C/ de Lagasca 30.
Map 6 F4.
Tel *914 31 95 09.*
www.prettyballerinas.com

Salvador Bachiller
Gran Vía 65.
Map 2 D5.
Tel *915 59 83 21.*

JEWELLERY

Joaquín Berao
C/ Claudio Coello 35.
Map 6 E5.
Tel *915 77 28 28.*

Tous
C/ Serrano 86.
Map 6 E3.
Tel *915 77 48 37.*

CRAFTS AND DESIGN

Cántaro
Calle de la Flor Baja 8.
Map 2 D5.
Tel *915 47 95 14.*

El Arco Artesasinas
Plaza Mayor 9. **Map** 4 E3.
Tel *913 65 26 80.*
www.elarcoartesania.com

Víctimas del Celuloide
C/ Santiago 8.
Map 4 D2.
Tel *915 47 61 35.*

BOOKS AND MUSIC

Booksellers
C/ Fernández de la Hoz 40.
Tel *914 42 81 04.*

Casa del Libro
Gran Vía 29.
Map 4 F1.
Tel *902 02 64 02.*
www.casadellibro.com

El Flamenco Vive
C/ del Conde de Lemos 7.
Map 4 D2.
Tel *915 47 39 17.*

FNAC
C/ Preciados 28.
Map 4 E1.
Tel *915 95 62 00.*
www.fnac.es

Gaudí
C/ Argensola 13.
Map 5 C4.
Tel *913 08 18 29.*

ENTERTAINMENT IN MADRID

As a major European capital, Madrid takes its arts and entertainment very seriously, hosting the finest and most diverse dance, music and theatre productions from around the world. Vibrant art, music and film festivals are held around the year, supplemented by a pulsating nightlife, raucous street parties and lively cafés.

Flamenco guitarist in Parque del Retiro

Even traditional art forms, such as flamenco, bullfighting and Madrid's version of the operetta, *zarzuela*, are characterized by flamboyance and spectacle. Football is also a major draw, and Real Madrid is a hugely celebrated team. Between fiestas, flamenco, football and much more, the revelry never stops in Madrid.

Madrid's Teatro Real (*see p322*)

ENTERTAINMENT GUIDES

Madrid's entertainment guides are mostly in Spanish. *Guía del Ocio*, a handy weekly guide to what's on in the city, comes out every Friday and can be bought from kiosks. Three daily newspapers have entertainment supplements on Friday as well: *El Mundo, ABC* and *El País*.

The English-language monthly, *InMadrid*, publishes cultural listings and reviews of the latest bars and clubs. It is available in bookshops, record stores and **Barajas Airport** information office.

Information on forthcoming events can also be obtained from one of the tourist information offices in the city, where English will be spoken. The tourist board also publishes *Es Madrid,* a free, bilingual brochure.

SEASONS AND TICKETS

There is always something going on in Madrid's theatres and stadiums, but the cultural season is at its peak from September to June. May's Fiesta de San Isidro, Madrid's patron saint festival, and the Festival de Otoño, a music, theatre and dance festival held from October to November, attract many big Spanish and international names. Tickets can be bought in advance from **Entradas.com** or Telentrada.com.

In July and August, Madrid hosts Veranos de la Villa (book through tourist offices), a special programme that includes art exhibitions, jazz, opera, flamenco, cinema and drama at various venues.

Tickets for a number of events can be bought at **FNAC** and **El Corte Inglés** stores and websites. Many other reliable internet sites also sell tickets. Check the websites of venues too, since many of them offer online booking services.

CAFES, BARS AND TERRACES

Madrid's social life revolves around an endless array of cafés, bars and summer terraces. These venues are perfect places to relax and people-watch. Especially popular areas for *terraceo* (doing the rounds of various terraces) are Plaza de Santa Ana, Paja, Chueca and Dos de Mayo. The glamorous crowd often spend evenings strolling down avenues, such as Paseo de la Castellana and Rosales, stopping now and then to nip into a terrace bar or café.

Madrid has retained many of its old grand cafés. **Café Comercial**, a city landmark, is an excellent meeting place with its wonderful early 20th-century ambience. **Café del Círculo de Bellas Artes** is housed in a cultural foundation, and is an institution in itself. It is ideal for coffee or lunch after spending a day pursuing cultural interests. Of the literary cafés, the famous **Café Gijón** *(see p291)* should not be missed.

In the evening, it is almost essential to head to a *taberna*, where you can order a *ración*, the more substantial version

Dancing the night away at the Joy Madrid Discoteque (*see p324*)

Exterior of the historic Café Gijón

of tapas, and accompany it with a good local wine. Go for a *taberna* crawl and visit the the older and most interesting establishments such as **Taberna Antonio Sánchez**, which is well known for its history and the quality of its tapas. **Bodega La Ardosa** is popular with both tourists and locals, and **Taberna Maceiras** is favoured for its Galician wines and other specialities.

BULLFIGHTING

Although bullfighting *(see pp36–7)* is not as popular as it used to be in many other parts of Spain, it continues to thrive in Madrid. The **Plaza de Toros de las Ventas** is the most important ring in the world, holding *corridas* every Sunday from March to October. In May, during the Fiesta de San Isidro, there are *corridas* every day, with some of the biggest names participating in the spectacle.

The Las Ventas box office is open on Fridays from 10am to 2pm and from 5pm to 8pm. You can also purchase tickets from abroad through the **Taquilla Toros** website, and collect them at the box office up to two hours before the fight.

FOOTBALL

Madrid is very proud of its team, **Real Madrid** *(see p177)*, and the players are celebrities in Spain. With a capacity of 80,000, their home stadium Santiago Bernabéu is one of the greatest theatres of the game. Tickets can be bought on the phone, or through the stadium's Internet site.

For those wishing to visit the stadium, guided tours are conducted on Mondays and Saturdays between 10am and 7pm (10:30am to 6:30pm on Sundays and holidays); on days when there are matches times may vary. Tickets can be bought at the box office with no need to book in advance.

Real Madrid's rivals, **Atlético de Madrid**, are based at the Vicente Calderón stadium.

DANCE

Madrid's dance scene has come a long way over recent years, with international companies and local talent performing regularly around the city. Madrid is the home of Spain's prestigious Ballet Nacional de España and the more contemporary Compañía Nacional de Danza, directed by the world famous dancer and choreographer Nacho Duato. Víctor Ullate's Ballet de la Comunidad de Madrid presents a more avant-garde mix of classical and contemporary dance.

A good time to experience Madrid's rich dance tradition is around April, when the annual En Danza festival takes place. Both Spanish and international dancers perform at this time in various theatres and other venues in and around Madrid.

Two major venues hosting dance are the **Teatro Madrid** and the **Teatro Real** where opera is usually performed. Smaller venues such as **Cuarta Pared** occasionally present alternative dance performances.

Details can usually be found in the entertainment listings or on the individual venue's website.

FLAMENCO

Although flamenco originated in Andalusia *(see pp424–5)*, Madrid is often seen as its spiritual home and some of the best flamenco dancers and musicians regularly perform here. The scene is sparklingly vibrant, and interpretations of the art range from the traditional to the daringly innovative, inspired by dancers such as Joaquín Cortés.

Most *tablaos* (flamenco venues) offer drinks and dinner with the show. Do note, however, that the show may sometimes feature only singing and not the familar rhythmic dancing.

Café de Chinitas and **Corral de la Moreria** are among the older and better *tablaos* in town, but are somewhat touristy. Also well worth a visit are **Arco de Cuchilleros** and **Casa Patas**.

Flamenco bars such as **Cardamomo** are full of boisterous young people, but are a fun way of experiencing the sound and feel of flamenco. Two bars that feature regular, spontaneous performances are the atmospheric **Candela** and **Las Tablas**. Note that as these places are frequented by local flamenco aficionados, visitors should be respectful of the art.

Take into account that although bars are fun and a good introduction to the art of flamenco, some of the best dance troupes, singers and players usually perform at the city's theatres.

Las Ventas bullring on the day of a bullfight

CLASSICAL MUSIC, OPERA AND ZARZUELA

Madrid's **Auditorio Nacional de Música** is home to Spain's national orchestra, Orquesta Nacional, as well as its national choir, Coro Nacional de España. With two concert halls, the auditorium also hosts many high-profile performances.

The illustrious and recently renovated **Teatro Real** is best known as the home of the city's opera company. It also houses Orquesta Sinfónica de Madrid, Spain's oldest orchestra with a rich history dating back to more than a century. The magnificent Real is the best place to watch top-class international and national opera performances. Tickets for a show can be bought at a maximum of two weeks in advance by phone or from the website and can be collected at the box office up to half an hour before the show begins.

The **Teatro Monumental** is the main venue for the excellent Orquesta Sinfónica y Coro de RTVE, the orchestra and choir of Spain's state television and radio company. The **Centro Cultural Conde Duque** hosts classical concerts among many other art events.

Those who want to experience a Spanish, especially a *Madrileño*, take on the operetta, should definitely make time to see a *zarzuela* being performed. The origins of this lively form of musical drama-cum-social satire can be traced back to early 17th-century Madrid, and the tradition is still going strong. With both spoken and sung parts as well as dancing, the *zarzuela* can be comic, ribald and even romantic. It is always enjoyable to watch.

The best productions are usually staged at the **Teatro de la Zarzuela**. Other theatres also host *zarzuela* performances occasionally. Check listings for details.

Look our for details on free, outdoor concerts in the papers. The Teatro Real always opens the opera season with a live transmission of the first show on massive video screens in Plaza de Oriente.

ROCK, JAZZ AND WORLD MUSIC

Madrid's music scene is eclectic and energetic, mixing top international pop stars with independent local bands performing at a variety of venues. Madrid's increasingly multicultural mix has ensured an explosion of Latin American and African sounds recently, as well as intersting fusions of both with more familiar Spanish sounds. In the 1980s, the heady days of *la movida* *(see p305)* gave birth to Spanish pop and the momentum continues to this day with Madrid remaining the centre of the country's music scene.

For rock music, **Sala la Riviera**, located next to the Manzanares river, has an excellent and well-deserved reputation. It has hosted major international stars such as Bob Dylan, the Cranberries and guitarist Joe Satriani among countless others. **Honky Tonk**, in the Chamberí district, often has performances from local bands, so keep an eye out for posters advertising events, some of which are free.

Siroco has devoted itself to discovering new alternative and indie bands, and also doubles as a club with live music performances.

One of Europe's best jazz clubs, **Café Central**, with its Art Deco elegance, is one place that should not be missed. Also popular is the lively **Populart** jazz and blues venue.

Musicians from all over the world representing a range of musical genres can be heard at **El Sol**. One of the most important clubs of the *Movida Madrileña (see p305)*, El Sol is the only one that continues to promote the underground style of music of the 1980s.

There are plenty of other well-reputed venues in the city that feature live music daily. The best way to keep abreast of the latest events is to check out weekly listings and to keep an eye out for adverts on the street.

THEATRE

Madrid has a theatrical tradition that stretches back to the Golden Age of the 17th century, with writers such as Lope de Vega and Calderón de la Barca creating a canon of work that is still performed today.

One of the most prestigious theatres in the city, the **Teatro de la Comedia** is traditionally home to the Compañía Nacional de Teatro Clásico, which stages classic works by Spanish playwrights. However, since the Comedia is under renovation, the company is now performing at the **Teatro Pavón** (until the year 2009).

Another one of the most highly regarded theatres is the **Teatro María Guerrero**, which presents Spanish modern drama, as well as foreign plays.

For contemporary and alternative theatre, Madrid has a thriving network of fringe venues such as **Cuarta Pared** and **Círculo de Bellas Artes**.

For musicals, try **Teatro Nuevo Apolo** or **Teatro Häagen-Dazs** Other venues such as **La Latina** and **Teatro Muñoz Seca** specialize in comedy productions.

A wide range of Spanish and international theatrical talent take part in the annual Festival de Otoño in October and November.

CINEMA

Spanish cinema *(see p192)* has earned great international acclaim in recent years. For those with a grasp of the language, Spanish film is a rewarding experience, especially enjoyed at one of the grand film theatres along Gran Vía, such as **Capitol**, which has screened films since the early 1900s.

Non-Spanish movies can be seen in their original-language versions at **Verdi**, **Ideal**, **Golem** and **Renoir**. Screenings will be found listed in newspapers and listings magazines. Note that tickets cost less on the *día del espectador*, which is usually on Monday or Wednesday.

DIRECTORY

TOURIST OFFICES

Comunidad de Madrid Tourist Office
C/ Duque de Medinacelli 2. **Map** 7 B3. ***Tel*** *902 10 00 07.*

Municipal Tourist Office
Pl Mayor 27. **Map** 4 E3. ***Tel*** *915 88 16 36.*

TICKETS

El Corte Inglés
Tel *902 40 02 22.* **www**.elcorteingles.com

Entradas.com
Tel *902 48 84 88.*

FNAC
Tel *902 10 06 32.* **www**.fnac.es

Tel Entrada
Tel *902 10 12 12.* **www**.telentrada.com

CAFES, BARS AND TERRACES

Bodega La Ardosa
C/ Colón 13. **Map** 5 A5. ***Tel*** *915 21 49 79.*

Café Comercial
Glorieta de Bilbao 7. **Map** 4 F2. ***Tel*** *915 21 56 55.*

Café del Círculo de Bellas Artes
C/ Alcalá 42. **Map** 4 E3. ***Tel*** *913 60 54 00.*

Café Gijón
Paseo de Recoletos 21. **Map** 7 C1. ***Tel*** *915 21 54 25.*

Taberna Antonio Sánchez
C/ de Mesón de Paredes 13. **Map** 4 F5. ***Tel*** *915 39 78 26.*

Taberna Maceiras
C/ de Jesús 7. **Map** 7 B3. ***Tel*** *914 29 58 18.*

BULLFIGHTING

Las Ventas
C/ Alcalá 237. ***Tel*** *913 56 22 00.* **www**.las-ventas.com

Taquilla Toros
www.taquillatoros.com

FOOTBALL

Atlético de Madrid
Estadio Vicente Calderón, Paseo de la Virgen del Puerto 67. ***Tel*** *902 26 04 03.* **www**.clubatleticodemadrid.com

Real Madrid
Estadio Santiago Bernabéu, C/ Concha Espina 1. ***Tel*** *913 98 43 00.* **www**.realmadrid.es

DANCE

Cuarta Pared
C/ del Ercilla 17. ***Tel*** *915 17 23 17.* **www**.cuartapared.es

Teatro Madrid
Avda de la Ilustración s/n. **Map** 3 B1. ***Tel*** *917 40 52 74.*

FLAMENCO

Arco de Cuchilleros
C/ de los Cuchilleros 7. **Map** 4 E3. ***Tel*** *913 64 02 63.*

Café de Chinitas
C/ Torija 7. **Map** 4 D1. ***Tel*** *915 47 15 02.*

Candela
C/ Olmo 2. **Map** 7 A4. ***Tel*** *914 67 33 82.*

Cardamomo
C/ Echegaray 15. **Map** 7 A2. ***Tel*** *913 69 07 57.*

Casa Patas
C/ Cañizares 10. **Map** 7 A3. ***Tel*** *913 69 04 96.*

Corral de la Morería
C/ de la Morería 17. **Map** 3 C3. ***Tel*** *913 65 84 46.*

Las Tablas
Plaza España 9. **Map** 1 C5. ***Tel*** *915 42 05 20.*

CLASSICAL MUSIC OPERA AND ZARZUELA

Auditorio Nacional de Música
C/ del Príncipe de Vergara 146. ***Tel*** *913 37 01 40.* **www**.auditorionacional.mcu.es

Centro Cultural Conde Duque
C/ del Conde Duque 11. **Map** 2 D4. ***Tel*** *915 88 58 34.*

Teatro Häagen-Dazs
C/ Atocha 28. **Map** 4 F3. ***Tel*** *902 00 66 17.*

Teatro Monumental
C/ Atocha 65. **Map** 7 A3. ***Tel*** *914 29 12 81.*

Teatro Real
Pl de Oriente. **Map** 4 D2. ***Tel*** *915 16 06 00.* **www**.teatro-real.com

Teatro de la Zarzuela
C/ de los Jovellanos 4. **Map** 7 B2. ***Tel*** *915 24 54 00.* **http**://teatrodelazarzuela.mcu.es

ROCK, JAZZ AND WORLD MUSIC

Café Central
Pl del Ángel 10. **Map** 7 A3. ***Tel*** *913 69 41 43.* **www**.cafecentralmadrid.com

El Sol
C/ Jardínes 3. **Map** 7 A1. ***Tel*** *915 32 64 90.* **www**.elsolmad.com

Honky Tonk
C/ de Covarrubias 24. **Map** 5 B3. ***Tel*** *914 45 68 86.*

Populart
Huertas 22. **Map** 7 A3. ***Tel*** *914 29 84 07.* **www**.populart.es

Sala La Riviera
Paseo Virgen del Puerto s/n. ***Tel*** *913 65 24 15.*

Siroco
C/ de San Dimas 3. **Map** 2 E4. ***Tel*** *915 93 30 70.* **www**.siroco.es

THEATRE

Bellas Artes
Marqués de Casa Riera 2. **Map** 7 B2. ***Tel*** *915 32 44 37.*

La Latina
Pl de la Cebada 2. **Map** 4 D4. ***Tel*** *913 65 28 35.*

Lope de Vega
Gran Vía 57. **Map** 4 E1. ***Tel*** *915 47 20 11.*

Teatro de la Comedia
C/ del Príncipe 14. **Map** 7 A2. ***Tel*** *915 21 49 31.*

Teatro María Guerrero
C/ de Tamayo y Baus 4. **Map** 5 C5. ***Tel*** *913 10 29 49.*

Teatro Muñoz Seca
Pl del Carmen 1. **Map** 4 F1. ***Tel*** *915 23 21 28.*

Teatro Nuevo Apolo
Pl Tirso de Molina 1. **Map** 4 F3. ***Tel*** *913 69 06 37.*

Teatro Pavón
C/ de Embajadores 9. **Map** 4 E4. ***Tel*** *915 28 28 19.*

CINEMA

Capitol
Gran Vía 41. **Map** 4 E1. ***Tel*** *902 33 32 31*

Golem
C/ de Martín de los Heros 14. **Map** 1 A1. ***Tel*** *915 59 38 36.*

Ideal
C/ del Doctor Cortezo 6. **Map** 4 F3. ***Tel*** *913 69 10 53.*

Renoir
C/ de Martín de los Heros 12. **Map** 1 C5. ***Tel*** *915 41 41 00.*

Verdi
C/ Bravo Murillo 28. ***Tel*** *914 47 39 30.*

Nightlife

Madrid's reputation as the city that never sleeps persists, despite recent political measures for earlier closing times. In fact, partygoers in Madrid are known as *gatos* (cats) around Spain because of their nocturnal habits. The best nightlife is concentrated around specific districts, each with its own unique atmosphere and a wealth of places for people to get down to one of Madrid's best talents: *la marcha* (partying). Things hot up first in the Huertas area, moving on to Malasaña, Bilbao, Lavapiés and Chueca into the early hours of the morning. You don't need to go to a club for dancing as *Madrileños* also dance to DJs and live music in smaller clubs, called *pubs* – all sorts of musical tastes are catered to more than amply *(see p322)*. Expect to find places crowded from Thursday to Sunday. Also prepare for late nights because things don't get going for *gatos* until midnight.

SANTA ANA AND HUERTAS

With many tapas bars, cafés and terraces, the Huertas area is the perfect place to begin preparing for the wild night ahead. The atmosphere is made by the crowd, which is a heady amalgam of ages, looks and origins. If you want to stay in one area, this is a good choice.

There are several little bars overlooking the lively Plaza de Santa Ana. Pop into any one of them to begin the night. **Viva Madrid** attracts a vivacious crowd of locals and foreigners. **Cardamomo**, a famous club, is a mandatory stop for any bar crawl. There is live flamenco at least once a week.

For late-night dancing, try the house DJs at **Joy Madrid Discoteque** or the extravagant 19th-century **Palacio Gaviria** near Sol, resplendent in its Baroque decor. Near Atocha, you will find the spectacular seven-floor **Kapital**, which features every kind of music, and a rooftop bar that allows drinkers to gaze at the starlit sky. **Populart**, also a hugely popular club, features live jazz and occasional shows by Latin and world music bands. Weekends can get crowded.

It is a local tradition to end the night with hot chocolate and *churros* (dough sticks) in one of the cafés around Plaza del Sol. The **Chocolatería San Ginés** is open all night.

ALONSO MARTÍNEZ AND BILBAO

This is one of the city's most animated areas. You will find hundreds of great haunts that play music ranging from R&B to Spanish pop.

To begin with, try some of the local bars around Plaza de Santa Bárbara, such as the **Cervecería Santa Bárbara**, the perfect place to start the night with a *caña* (beer). Later on (if you can get past the queues), try the glamorous club **Alegoría**, with its eclectic decor and pop music, where you can dance until late with the beautiful people. Alternatively, you can head for **Pachá**, one of Madrid's most famous discotheques. There are also plenty of live-music venues around, such as **Clamores**, one of Madrid's many temples of jazz music. However, note that areas such as Huertas are more active during weekdays.

ARGÜELLES AND MONCLOA

This area is a favourite haunt of students, thanks to its proximity to the halls of residence of one of Madrid's major universities. The celebrated "basements of Argüelles" are huge double-storeyed patios with several bars and discotheques. The atmosphere is fresh and young.

Another popular district is Moncloa, which has a more mature crowd, as well as several places where you can listen to local Spanish pop and dance tunes, such as **La Sal**, which is also a venue for concerts.

CHUECA

The Chueca district dominates Madrid's gay scene. As well as having a large resident gay community, there are plenty of trendy late-night bars and clubs where gays and non-gays party together. In fact, what sets Chueca apart from other gay neighbourhoods in the world is the *mezcla*, the tolerant gay/straight mix.

The heart of the area is the Plaza de Chueca, packed with crowds visiting the terraces in the summer. Close by are mixed bars such as **Liqüid** and **Acuarela**, with its camp, religious-artifact decor. The Gay Pride Week in late June, focuses around this area, though there are also plenty of well-established gay bars elsewhere in the city.

MALASAÑA

Malasaña was the centre of *la movida* in the Madrid of the 1980s (*see p305*), and still has an alternative flavour that attracts many young bohemian types. The hub of this cosmopolitan district is the Dos de Mayo square. However, the characteristic atmosphere of the area is changing rapidly into a more design driven space. An example is the **La Ida** bar which has cultivated a revolutionary, arty atmosphere. **Bar & Co** is a typical Malasaña venue, where local bands play weekly. You can relax there after 3am if you don't feel like clubbing.

Tupperware, a fusion of past and present, is a rock bar with an ultra pop decor, where you can also listen to garage, indie and pop music.

LAVAPIÉS

Once the Jewish quarter of Madrid, the narrow streets of Lavapiés are rich with an eclectic mix of races and cultures. One of the most fascinating and diverse districts in town, the locals' old habit of sitting outside their doors on summer nights continues as does the multiracial crowd on the terraces of Calle de Argumosa. A vibrant fusion of artists, immigrants, hipsters and squatters results in some of the most brilliant music, art, food, alternative theatre and nightlife in the city.

La Escalera de Jacob holds concerts, theatre performances and intercultural workshops. The endearingly eccentric bar, **La Colonia de San Lorenzo**, hosts Verbena de San Lorenzo, a street party with live bands, dancing, stalls and freely flowing drink.

LA LATINA

Still the best district in town for cosy little hideaways and tapas bars, La Latina is an especially good place to go on Sundays after wandering around the Rastro flea market. For an excellent cocktail, head to **Delic**, and for a cultural experience try **Anti Café**, where you can listen to unique DJs, poetry, drama and jazz on Sundays. For a taste of the best delicatessen tapas, visit **Corazón Loco**, where top quality wines are available at reasonable prices. Another worthwhile bar is **Taberna del Tempranillo**, which also serves a variety of Spanish wines, cheeses and ham. In the exquisite **María Pandora** bar, you can try a selection of champagnes and *cavas,* surrounded by books and antiques. Afterwards, you can dance until late at **Berlín Cabaret**, a modern nightclub that runs a 1930s cabaret every night.

AZCA

With a skyline punctuated by the highest buildings, this is one of the most modern areas in town. Near the Paseo de la Castellana and the Santiago Bernabéu stadium, this financial district has a multitude of clubs and bars doing brisk business in basements.

If visitors feel the urge to dance to the sensuous rhythms of salsa, Calle Orense is definitely the best place to head to. Avenida de Brasil is also full of large clubs, however, these tend to be a little overcrowded.

Around the Chamartín train station nearby, you will find the centre of the hardcore clubbing scene, which vibrantly unfolds late at night. Of the many clubs in the area, **Macumba** is generally considered to have the most cutting-edge sound and lighting equipment in Europe. It is particularly famous for its "Space of Sound" sessions from 10am to 12pm one Sunday a month.

DIRECTORY

BARS, CLUBS AND CAFES

Acuarela
C/ Gravina 10.
Map 5 B5.
Tel *915 22 21 43.*

Alegoría
C/ Villanueva 2.
Map 6 D5.
Tel *915 57 27 85.*

Anti Café
C/ Unión 2.
Map 4 E2.
Tel *915 41 76 57.*

Bar & Co
C/ Barco 34.
Map 2 F5.
Tel *915 21 24 47.*

Berlín Cabaret
Costanilla de San Pedro 11.
Tel *913 66 20 34.*

Cardamomo
C/ De Echegaray 15.
Map 7 A3.
Tel *913 69 07 57.*

Cervecería Santa Bárbara
Pl Santa Bárbara 8.
Tel *913 19 04 49.*

Chocolatería San Ginés
Pasadizo de San Ginés, C/ Arenal 11.
Map 4 E2.
Tel *913 65 65 46.*

Clamores
C/ Alburquerque 14.
Map 5 A3.
Tel *914 45 79 38.*

Corazón Loco
C/ de Almendro 22.
Map 4 D3.
Tel *913 66 57 83.*

Delic
Pl De La Paja s/n.
Map 4 D3.
Tel *913 64 54 50.*

Joy Madrid Discoteque
C/ Arenal 11.
Map 4 E2.
Tel *913 66 37 33.*

Kapital
C/ Atocha 125.
Map 7 C4.
Tel *914 20 29 06.*

La Colonia de San Lorenzo
C/ Salitre 38.
Map 7 A5.

La Escalera de Jacob
C/ de Lavapíes 11.
Map 4 F4.
Tel *915 39 10 44.*

La Ida
C/ Colón 11.
Map 5 A5.
Tel *915 22 91 07.*

La Sal
C/ Guzmán el Bueno 98.
Tel *686 41 09 90.*

Liqüid
C/ Barbieri 7.
Map 7 B1.
Tel *915 32 89 21.*

Macumba
Agustín de Foxá s/n, Estación de Charmartín.
Tel *902 49 99 94.*

María Pandora
Pl Gabriel Miró 1.
Map 3 B3.
Tel *913 64 00 39.*

Pachá
C/ de Barceló 11.
Map 5 A4.
Tel *914 47 01 28.*

Palacio Gaviria
C/ de Arenal 9.
Map 4 E2.
Tel *915 26 60 69.*

Populart
Huertas 22.
Map 7 A3.
Tel *914 29 84 07.*

Taberna del Tempranillo
C/ de la Cava Baja 38.
Tel *913 64 15 32.*

Tupperware
C/ Corredera Alta de San Pablo 26.
Tel *914 46 42 04.*

Viva Madrid
C/ Manuel Fernández González 7.
Tel *914 29 36 40.*

MADRID PROVINCE

Madrid province (the Comunidad de Madrid) sits high on Spain's central plateau. There is plenty of superb scenery and good walking country in the sierras to the north, which are a refuge for city dwellers who go there to ski in winter or cool down during the torrid summers. In the western foothills of these mountains stands El Escorial, the royal palace-cum-monastery built by Felipe II, from which he ruled his empire. Close by is the Valle de los Caídos, the war monument erected by Franco. The smaller royal palace of El Pardo is on the outskirts of Madrid, and south of the city is the 18th-century summer palace of Aranjuez, set in lush parkland. Historic towns include Alcalá de Henares, which has a Renaissance university building, and Chinchón, where taverns cluster around a picturesque arcaded market square.

SIGHTS AT A GLANCE

Towns and Cities
Alcalá de Henares 9
Buitrago del Lozoya 2
Chinchón 10
Manzanares el Real 7

Historic Buildings
El Escorial pp330–31 6
Monasterio de Santa María de El Paular 3
Palacio de El Pardo 8
Palacio Real de Aranjuez 11
Santa Cruz del Valle de los Caídos 5

Mountain Ranges
Sierra Centro de Guadarrama 4
Sierra Norte 1

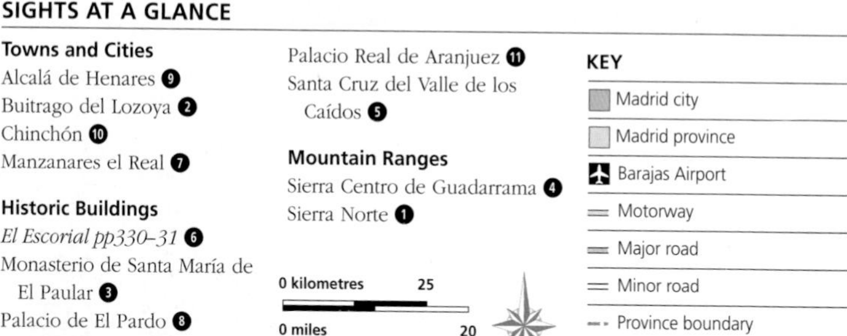

KEY
Madrid city
Madrid province
Barajas Airport
Motorway
Major road
Minor road
Province boundary

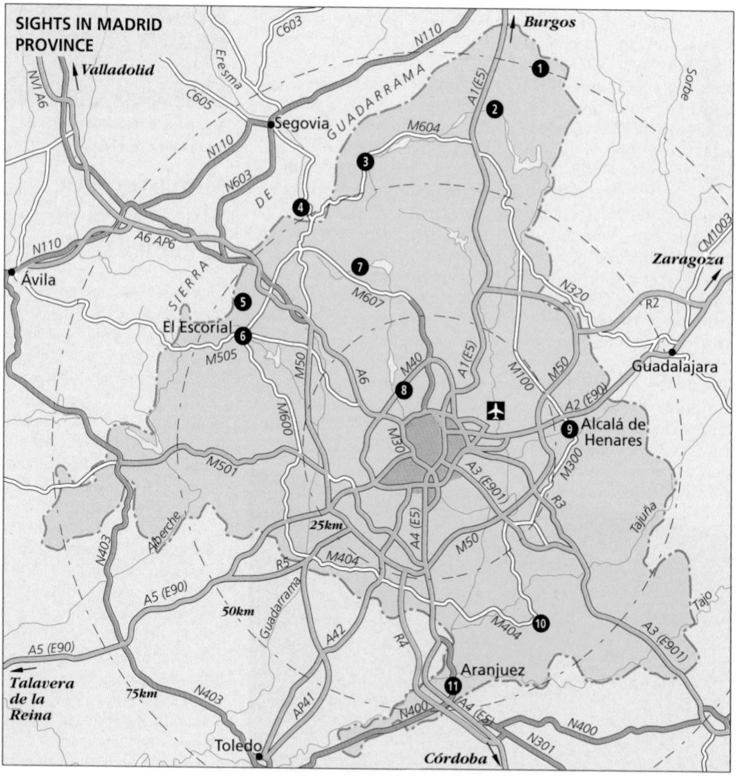

SIGHTS IN MADRID PROVINCE

◁ Celebration of Mass in the church of the Monasterio de Santa María de El Paular

The village of Montejo de la Sierra in the Sierra Norte

Sierra Norte ❶

Madrid. *Montejo.* *Calle Real 64, Montejo, 91 869 70 58.*

The black slate hamlets of the Sierra Norte, which were once known as the Sierra Pobre (Poor Sierra), are located in the most attractively rural part of Madrid province.

At **Montejo de la Sierra**, the largest village in the area, an information centre organizes riding, the rental of traditional houses *(see p555)*, and visits to the nearby nature reserve of the **Hayedo de Montejo de la Sierra**. This is one of the most southern beech woods *(see p80)* in Europe, and a relic of a previous era, when climatic conditions here were more suitable for the beech. From Montejo, you can drive on to picturesque hamlets such as **La Hiruela** or **Puebla de la Sierra**, both of which are set in lovely walking country.

The drier southern hills slope down to the **Embalse de Puentes Viejas**, a reservoir where summer chalets cluster around artificial beaches. On the eastern edge of the sierra is the village of **Patones**, which is thought to have escaped invasion by the Moors and Napoleon's troops because of its isolated location.

Buitrago del Lozoya ❷

Madrid. *2,000.* *Calle Tahona 11, 91 868 16 15.* *Sat.* *La Asunción and San Roque (15–16 Aug), Cristo de los Esclavos (14–15 Sep).*

Picturesquely sited above a meander in the Río Lozoya is the walled town of Buitrago del Lozoya. Founded by the Romans, it was fortified by the Arabs, and became an important market town in medieval times. The 14th-century Gothic-Mudéjar castle is in ruins, although the gatehouse, arches and stretches of the original Arab wall have survived. Today, the castle is used as a venue for bullfights and hosts a festival of ancient theatre and music in the summer.

The old quarter, within the walls, retains its charming atmosphere. The church of **Santa María del Castillo**, dating from the 14–15th century, has a Mudéjar tower and ceilings which were moved here from the old hospital. The **town hall** *(ayuntamiento)*, in the newer part of Buitrago, preserves a 16th-century processional cross. In the basement is the **Museo Picasso**. The prints, drawings and ceramics were collected by the artist's friend, Eugenio Arias.

Buitrago del Lozoya, standing next to the river

Museo Picasso
Plaza de Picasso 1. ***Tel*** *91 868 00 56 15.* *Mon, Wed pm & Sun pm.*

Altarpiece in the Monasterio de Santa María de El Paular

Monasterio de Santa María de El Paular ❸

Southwest of Rascafría on M604. ***Tel*** *91 869 14 25.* *Rascafria.* *noon, 1pm, 5pm Mon–Wed & Fri; noon, 1pm, 4pm, 5pm Sat; 1pm, 4pm, 5pm Sun.* *obligatory.* *Jan.*

Founded in 1390 as Castile's first Carthusian monastery, Santa María de El Paular stands on the site of a medieval royal hunting lodge. Although it is mainly Gothic in style, Plateresque and Renaissance features were added later. The monastery was abandoned in 1836 when government minister Mendizábal ordered the sale of church goods *(see p63)*. It fell into disrepair until its restoration in the 1950s. Today the complex comprises a working Benedictine monastery, church and private hotel *(see p582)*.

The church's delicate alabaster altarpiece, attributed to Flemish craftsmen, dates from the 15th century. Its panels depict scenes from the life of Jesus. The lavish Baroque *camarín* (chamber), behind the altar, was designed by Francisco de Hurtado in 1718.

Every Sunday, the monks sing an hour-long Gregorian chant in the church. If they are not busy, they will show you the cloister's Mudéjar brick vaulting and double sun-clock.

The monastery is a good starting point for exploring the towns of **Rascafría** and **Lozoya**. To the southwest is the nature reserve **Lagunas de Peñalara**.

Sierra Centro de Guadarrama ❹

Madrid. *Puerto de Navacerrada, Cercedilla.* *Navacerrada, Cercedilla.* *Navacerrada, 91 856 03 08.*

The central section of the Sierra de Guadarrama was little visited until the 1920s, when the area was first linked by train to Madrid. Today, the granite slopes are planted with pines and specked by holiday chalets. Villages such as **Navacerrada** and **Cercedilla** have grown into popular resorts for skiing, mountain-biking, rock-climbing and horse riding. Walkers wanting to enjoy the pure mountain air can follow marked routes from Navacerrada.

The **Valle de Fuenfría**, a nature reserve of wild forests, is best reached via Cercedilla. It has a well-preserved stretch of the original Roman road, as well as several picnic spots and marked walking routes.

The gigantic cross at Valle de los Caídos

Navacerrada pass in the Sierra de Guadarrama

Santa Cruz del Valle de los Caídos ❺

North of El Escorial on M600. ***Tel** 91 890 56 11.* *from El Escorial.* *for restoration; call or check website for details.* **www**.valledeloscaidos.es

General Franco had the Holy Cross of the Valley of the Fallen built as a memorial to those who died in the Civil War *(see pp66–7)*. The vast cross is located some 13 km (8 miles) north of El Escorial *(see pp330–31)*, and dominates the surrounding countryside. Some Spanish people find it too chilling a symbol of the dictatorship to be enjoyable, while for others its sheer size is rewarding.

The cross is 150 m (490 ft) high and rises above a basilica carved 250 m (820 ft) deep into the rock by prisoners. A number of them died during the 20-year-plus project. A funicular connects the basilica with the base of the cross.

Next to the basilica's high altar is the plain white tombstone of Franco, and, opposite, that of José Antonio Primo de Rivera, founder of the Falange Española party. A further 40,000 coffins of soldiers from both sides in the Civil War lie here out of sight, including those of two unidentified victims.

El Escorial ❻

Fresco by Luca Giordano

Felipe II's imposing grey palace of San Lorenzo de El Escorial stands out against the foothills of the Sierra de Guadarrama to the northwest of Madrid. It was built between 1563 and 1584 in honour of St Lawrence, and its unornamented severity set a new architectural style which became one of the most influential in Spain. The interior was conceived as a mausoleum and contemplative retreat rather than a splendid residence. Its artistic wealth, which includes some of the most important works of art of the royal Habsburg collections, is concentrated in the museums, chapterhouses, church, royal pantheon and library. In contrast, the royal apartments are remarkably humble.

★ Royal Pantheon
The funerary urns of Spanish monarchs line the marble mausoleum.

Basílica
The highlight of this huge decorated church, is the lavish altarpiece. The chapel houses a superb marble sculpture of the crucifiction by Cellini.

The Alfonso XII College was founded by monks in 1875 as a boarding school.

★ Library
This impressive array of 40,000 books incorporates Felipe II's personal collection. On display are precious manuscripts, including a poem by Alfonso X the Learned. The 16th-century ceiling frescoes are by Tibaldi.

STAR FEATURES

- ★ Library
- ★ Royal Pantheon
- ★ Museum of Art

For hotels and restaurants in this region see p582 and pp632–3

The royal apartments, on the second floor of the palace, consist of Felipe II's modestly decorated living quarters. His bedroom opens directly on to the high altar of the basilica.

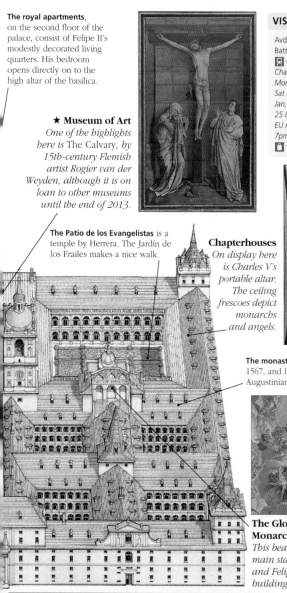

★ Museum of Art
One of the highlights here is The Calvary, *by 15th-century Flemish artist Rogier van der Weyden, although it is on loan to other museums until the end of 2013.*

VISITORS' CHECKLIST

Avda de Juan de Borbón y Battemberg. ***Tel*** *91 890 59 04.* *C3 or C8 from Atocha, Chamartín.* *661, 664 from Moncloa.* *10am–8pm Tue–Sat (Oct–Mar to 6pm).* *1 & 6 Jan, 1 May, 10 Aug, 13 Sep, 24, 25 & 31 Dec.* *(free Wed for EU residents).* *9:30am daily; 7pm, 8pm Sat & Sun.* **www**.patrimonionacional.es

The Patio de los Evangelistas is a temple by Herrera. The Jardín de los Frailes makes a nice walk.

Chapterhouses
On display here is Charles V's portable altar. The ceiling frescoes depict monarchs and angels.

The monastery was founded in 1567, and has been run by Augustinian monks since 1885.

The Glory of the Spanish Monarchy by Luca Giordano
This beautiful fresco, above the main staircase, depicts Charles V and Felipe II, and scenes of the building of the monastery.

The Building of El Escorial
When chief architect Juan Bautista de Toledo died in 1567 he was replaced by Juan de Herrera, royal inspector of monuments. The plain architectural style of El Escorial is called desornamentado, *literally, "unadorned".*

Climber resting on a rock face of La Pedriza, near Manzanares el Real

Manzanares el Real ❼

Madrid. 7,200. Plaza Puebla 1, 639 17 96 02 (Sat– Sun). Tue & Fri. Fiesta de Verano (early Aug), Cristo de la Nave (14 Sep).

The skyline of Manzanares el Real is dominated by its restored 15th-century castle. Although the castle has some traditionally military features, such as double machicolations and turrets, it was used mainly as a residence by the Dukes of Infantado. Below the castle is a 16th-century church, a Renaissance portico and fine capitals. Behind the town, bordering the foothills of the Sierra de Guadarrama, is **La Pedriza**, a mass of granite screes and ravines, very popular with climbers. It now forms part of an attractive nature reserve.

Environs

Colmenar Viejo, 12 km (7.5 miles) to the southeast of Manzanares, has a superb Gothic-Mudéjar church.

Palacio de El Pardo ❽

El Pardo, northwest of Madrid off the A6. ***Tel*** *91 376 15 00.* *601 from Moncloa.* *daily.* *during royal visits & on public hols.* *(free from 3pm Wed & Thu for EU residents; from 8pm Apr–Sep).* **www**.patrimonionacional.es

This royal hunting lodge and palace, set in parkland just outside Madrid's city limits, boasts General Franco among its former residents. A guided tour takes visitors round the moated palace's Habsburg wing and the identical 18th-century extension, designed by Francesco Sabatini.

The Bourbon interior is heavy with frescoes, gilt mouldings and tapestries, many made to designs by Goya *(see p306)*. Today the palace hosts visiting heads of state and royal guests. Surrounding the palace and the 18th-century village of El Pardo is a vast forest of holm oak. The area is popular for picnicking, and game animals still run free.

Façade of Colegio de San Ildefonso in Alcalá de Henares

Alcalá de Henares ❾

Madrid. 205,000. Callejón Santa María, 91 889 26 94. Mon, Wed. Feria de Alcalá (late Aug). weekend city tours.

At the heart of a modern industrial town is one of Spain's most renowned university quarters. Founded in 1499 by Cardinal Cisneros, Alcalá's

Lavish 18th-century tapestry inside the Palacio de El Pardo

university became one of the foremost places of learning in 16th-century Europe. The most historic college, **San Ildefonso**, survives. Former students include Golden Age playwright Lope de Vega *(see p290)*. In 1517 the university produced Europe's first polyglot bible, with text in Latin, Greek, Hebrew and Chaldean.

Alcalá's other sights are the cathedral and the **Casa-Museo de Cervantes**, birthplace of the Golden Age author. The restored 19th-century neo-Moorish palace, **Palacio de Laredo** has splendid decorations.

Casa-Museo de Cervantes
Calle Mayor 48. ***Tel*** *91 889 96 54.*
Tue–Sun. *public hols.*

Chinchón ⑩

Madrid. *5,300.* *Plaza Mayor 6, 91 893 53 23.* *Sat.* *Semana Santa (Easter Week), San Roque (12–18 Aug).* **www**.ciudadchinchon.com

Chinchón is arguably Madrid province's most picturesque town. The 15–16th-century, typically Castilian, porticoed **Plaza Mayor** has a splendidly theatrical air. It comes alive for the Easter passion play, acted out by the townspeople *(see p290)*, and during the August bullfights. The 16th-century church, perched above the square, has an altar painting by Goya, whose brother was a priest here. Just off the square is the 18th-century Augustinian monastery, which has been converted into a **parador** with a peaceful patio garden *(see p582)*. A ruined 15th-century castle is on a hill to the west of town. Although it is closed to the public, there are views of Chinchón and the countryside from outside it.

Chinchón's unique porticoed Plaza Mayor

Chinchón is a popular weekend destination for *Madrileños*, who come here to sample the excellent chorizo and locally produced *anís (see p607)* in the town's many taverns.

Palacio Real de Aranjuez ⑪

Plaza de Parejas, Aranjuez.
Tel *91 891 07 40.*
Tue–Sun. *some public hols.*
(free from 3pm Wed & Thu for EU residents; from 8pm Apr–Sep).
www.patrimonionacional.es

The Royal Summer Palace and Gardens of Aranjuez grew up around a medieval hunting lodge standing beside a natural weir, the meeting point of the Tagus and Jarama rivers.

Today's palace of brick and white stone was built in the 18th century and later redecorated by the Bourbons. A guided tour takes you through numerous Baroque rooms, among them the Chinese Porcelain Room, the Hall of Mirrors and the Smoking Room, modelled on the Alhambra in Granada. It is worth visiting Aranjuez to walk in the 300 hectares (740 acres) of shady royal gardens which inspired Joaquín Rodrigo's *Concierto de Aranjuez*. The Parterre Garden and the Island Garden survive from the original 16th-century palace.

Between the palace and the River Tagus is the 18th-century Prince's Garden, decorated with sculptures, fountains and lofty trees from the Americas. In the garden is the Casa de Marinos (Sailors' House), a museum housing the launches once used by the royal family for trips along the river. At the far end of the garden is the Casa del Labrador (Labourer's Cottage), a decorative royal pavilion built by Carlos IV.

The town's restaurants are popular for the exceptional quality of their asparagus and strawberries. In summer, a 19th-century steam train, built to carry strawberries, runs between here and the capital.

MIGUEL DE CERVANTES

Miguel de Cervantes Saavedra, Spain's greatest literary figure *(see p34)*, was born in Alcalá de Henares in 1547. After fighting in the naval Battle of Lepanto (1571), he was held captive by the Turks for more than five years.

In 1605, when he was almost 60 years old, the first of two parts of his comic masterpiece *Don Quixote (see p395)* was published to popular acclaim. He continued writing novels and plays until his death in Madrid on 23 April 1616, the same day that Shakespeare died.

Gardens surrounding the Royal Palace at Aranjuez

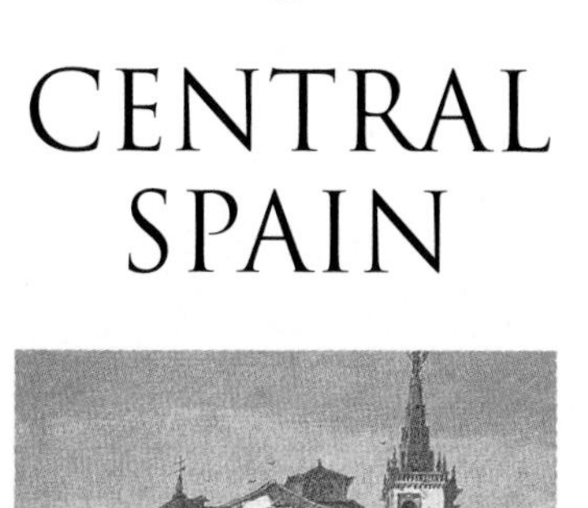

CENTRAL SPAIN

Introducing Central Spain

Much of Spain's vast central plateau, the *meseta*, is covered with wheat fields or dry, dusty plains, but there are many attractive places to explore. Central Spain's mountains, gorges, forests and lakes are filled with wildlife. A deep sense of history permeates the towns and cities of the tableland, reflected in some stunning architecture: the Roman ruins of Mérida, the medieval mansions of Cáceres, the Gothic cathedrals of Burgos, León and Toledo, the Renaissance grandeur of Salamanca, and castles almost everywhere.

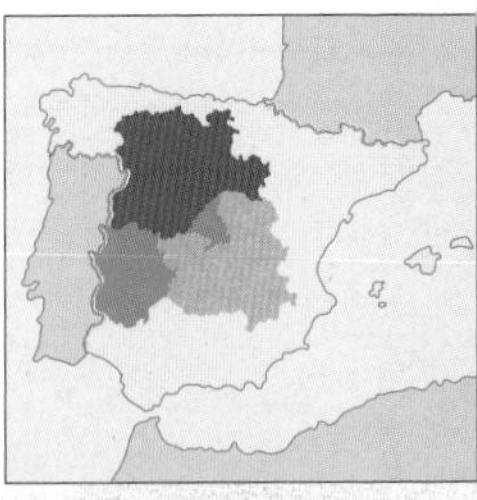

León Cathedral (see p354–5), *an outstanding Gothic building, was completed during the 14th century. As well as many glorious windows of medieval glass, it has superb carved choir stalls depicting biblical scenes and everyday life.*

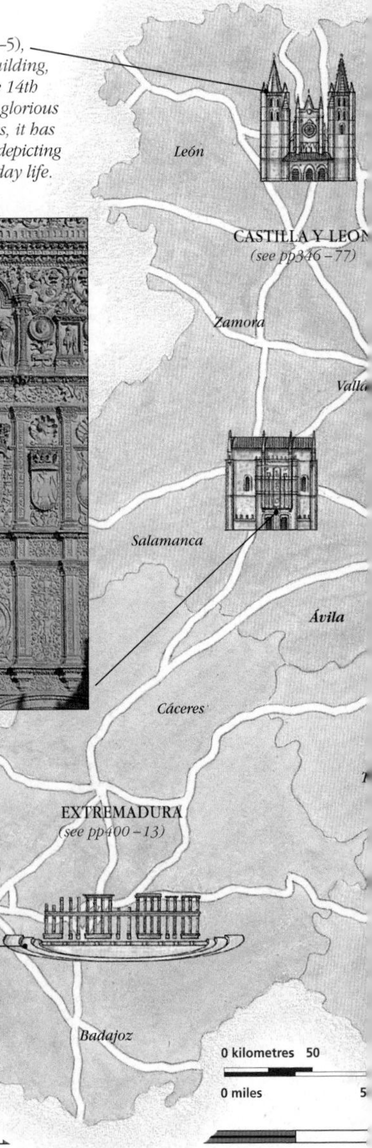

Salamanca (see pp358–61) *is the site of some of the finest Renaissance and Plateresque architecture in Spain. Among the city's most notable buildings are the university, its façade a mass of carved detail; the old and new cathedrals (built side by side); and the handsome Plaza Mayor, built in warm golden sandstone.*

The Museo Nacional de Arte Romano *in Mérida* (see p410) *houses Roman treasures. The city has a well-preserved Roman theatre.*

León

CASTILLA Y LEON

(see pp346–77)

Zamora

Salamanca

Ávila

Cáceres

EXTREMADURA

(see pp400–13)

Badajoz

0 kilometres 50

0 miles

◁ **Roofs and walls in the old part of Toledo**

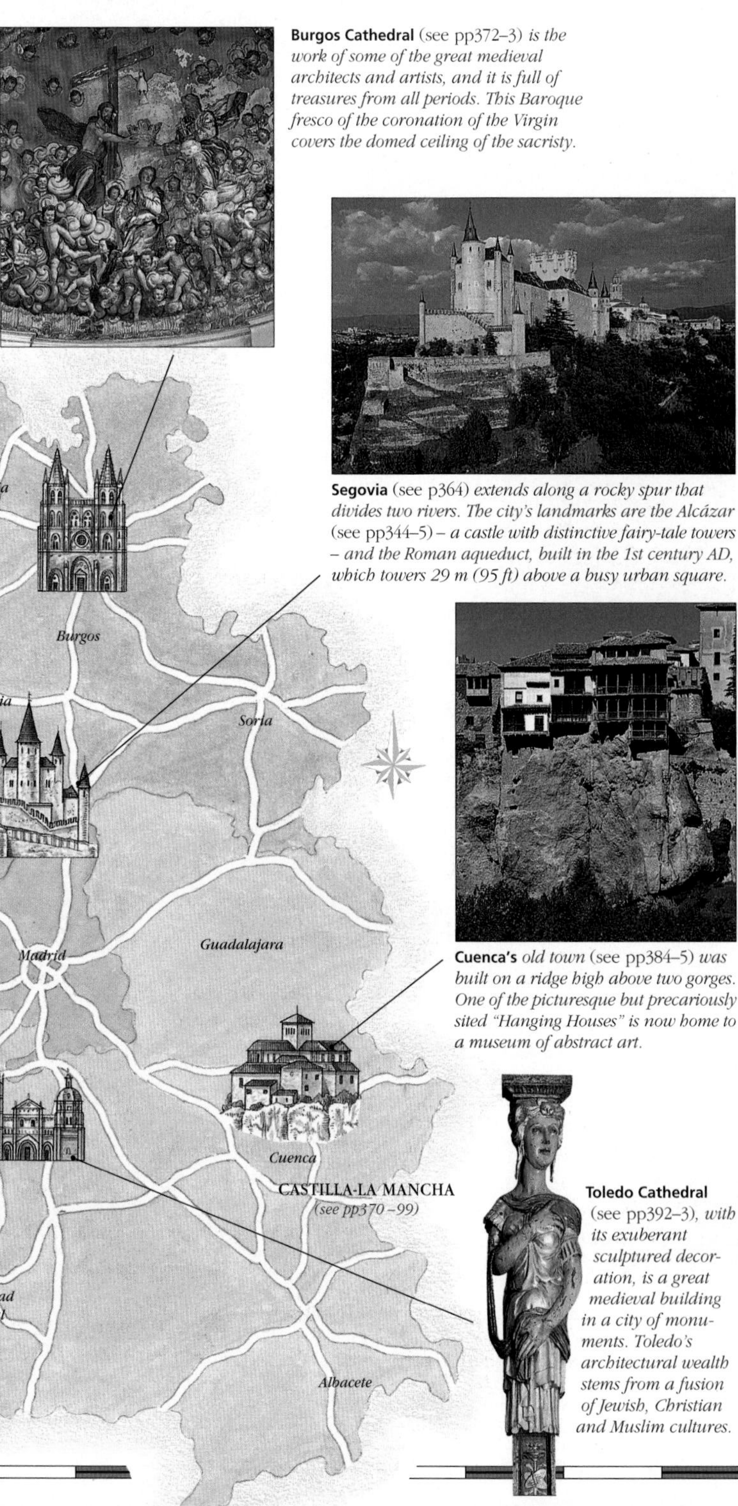

Burgos Cathedral (see pp372–3) *is the work of some of the great medieval architects and artists, and it is full of treasures from all periods. This Baroque fresco of the coronation of the Virgin covers the domed ceiling of the sacristy.*

Segovia (see p364) *extends along a rocky spur that divides two rivers. The city's landmarks are the Alcázar* (see pp344–5) *– a castle with distinctive fairy-tale towers – and the Roman aqueduct, built in the 1st century AD, which towers 29 m (95 ft) above a busy urban square.*

Cuenca's *old town* (see pp384–5) *was built on a ridge high above two gorges. One of the picturesque but precariously sited "Hanging Houses" is now home to a museum of abstract art.*

Toledo Cathedral (see pp392–3), *with its exuberant sculptured decoration, is a great medieval building in a city of monuments. Toledo's architectural wealth stems from a fusion of Jewish, Christian and Muslim cultures.*

The Flavours of Central Spain

Madrid is famous for its extremes of temperature – a climate that has given rise to the rueful local saying "nine months of winter and three months of hell". The surrounding regions suffer the same extremes, and their traditional cuisines reflect both the wintry cold and the dusty, scorched terrain. Meat predominates as roasts and stews and in warming soups, thickened with beans and pulses, which thrive despite the weather. Cured hams, spicy sausages and pungent cheeses are excellent accompaniments to the strong local wine. The finest ham is from Extremadura, where black-footed *(pata negra)* pigs forage freely among the oaks.

Manchego cheese

A chef preparing *gambas al ajillo*, a popular tapas dish

MADRID

Restaurants in Madrid, as befits the Spanish capital, offer cuisine from every corner of the country. Curiously, considering its distance from the ocean, the capital is famed for its seafood, flown in freshly every day. Madrileños appreciate every part of an animal, particularly when it comes to pork, and Madrid menus regularly feature brains, ears, pigs' trotters, and *callos a la Madrileña* (tripe) is a classic local dish. Sturdy stews, such as the celebrated *cocido Madrileño*, keep out the bitter winter cold. The *tapeo* – a bar crawl between tapas bars – is an institution in the city, and each bar has its own speciality dish.

CASTILLA Y LEON

Spread out high on a plain, searingly hot in summer, and bitingly cold in winter, Castilla y León is famous for its roasted meats, served in *asadores* (grillhouses). The most celebrated local dish is *cochinillo* (suckling pig), but pork, chicken, game in season and lamb are also popular. These are often combined with local pulses and lentils in hearty soups

Beans and pulses, key ingredients in the cooking of central Spain

REGIONAL DISHES AND SPECIALITIES

The cuisine of Spain's often wild and remote interior is characterized by warming soups and stews; traditionally made hams, cured meats and cheeses; plenty of filling beans and pulses; and flavourful fruit and vegetables. On the high plains of Castilla y León, locals keep out the winter cold with succulent roasted meats, and Extremaduran ham is the best you'll taste. In Don Quijote country, a glass of robust local wine and a chunk of Manchegan cheese is sheer delight. Fancy restaurants with fashionable food are few and far between, but welcoming, old-fashioned inns offer simple and tasty home-cooking. Madrid, of course, is the exception: here you'll find every possible cuisine, along with excellent seafood, which is harder to find anywhere else in this landlocked region.

Fresh figs

Cocido Madrileño *This rich stew is traditionally eaten in two stages: first the broth, and then the meat and vegetables.*

Plucking the stamens from crocus flowers to make saffron

and stews, which are given extra flavour with local *embutidos* (cured meats). The region also produces delicious cheeses such as soft Burgos, often served with honey, *membrillo* (quince jelly) or nuts for dessert. Local wines are robust and simple, a good accompaniment to the strong flavours of the regional cuisine of Castilla y León.

CASTILLA LA MANCHA

This is Don Quijote country: empty, flat, dusty and scattered with windmills. Local inns and taverns serve traditional country cooking, with plenty of hearty soups, substantial casseroles and simply grilled local meat, poultry and seasonal game. Manchegan *gazpacho*, unlike its cold, vegetable soup, Andaluz namesake, is a hefty stew made with whatever meat is available. A common accompaniment to it is *pisto*, a ratatouille-like dish made with a range of tasty, fresh local vegetables. The Arabs brought with them saffron, which is still grown around Consuegra, and their influence also lingers on in Toledo's famous marzipan sweets and the fragrant Alajú almond soup from Cuenca.

Cured hams hanging in an *embutidos* shop

EXTREMADURA

Wild, beautiful Extremadura sees few visitors and, in many places, life continues virtually untouched by the 21st century. Endless rolling fields dotted with holm oak shelter the acorn-fed, black-footed pigs that make Spain's most highly prized hams *(jamón Ibérico)*. Thanks to the deeply rooted hunting tradition, partridge, hare and wild boar regularly feature on local menus along with river fish such as tench and trout. There are some delicious cheeses, as well as perfumed local honey and wonderful fruit, particularly cherries, peaches and figs.

ON THE MENU

Chocolate con Churros The typical Spanish breakfast – thick hot chocolate with sugary strips of fried batter for dipping, originated in Madrid.

Cochinillo The speciality of Segovia: 21-day-old suckling pig, roasted until so tender it can be cut with a plate.

Gazpacho Manchego Sometimes called a galiano, this is a rich stew traditionally made with hare and partridge.

Macarraca Extremaduran salad of chopped ripe tomatoes with peppers, onion and garlic.

Tortilla de Patata A simple potato omelette, now a staple in restaurants all over Spain.

Albóndigas *Meatballs – sturdy country fare from the high plain of Castilla y León.*

Migas Extremeñas *Chunks of country bread are fried up with peppers, pork and chorizo or cured sausage.*

Yemas *A delicious treat from Ávila, these lemony, custardy cakes are made with egg yolks and sugar.*

Wines of Central Spain

The wines of Central Spain originate in either the small, high-quality regions of northwest Castilla y León or in the vast wine-producing plains of La Mancha and Valdepeñas. Ribera del Duero has become Spain's most fashionable red wine region, with its aromatic, rich yet fine reds made from Tinto Fino grapes (the local name for Tempranillo) and, more recently, lighter, fruity wines. Rueda makes a good white wine, made from the Verdejo grape. La Mancha and Valdepeñas both produce lots of simple white wine, and reds which can be mellow and fruity.

Harvesting Viura grapes at Rueda

Artesian well for irrigating vines in La Mancha

Toro *makes the most powerful and fiery of all red wines from the ubiquitous Tempranillo grape.*

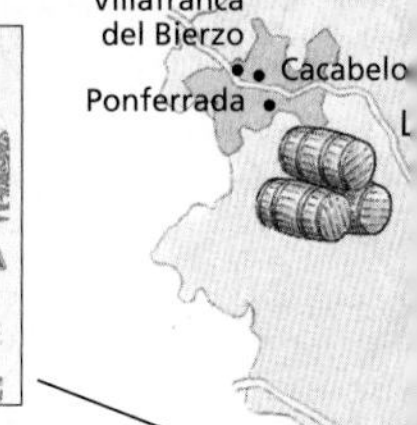

KEY FACTS ABOUT WINES OF CENTRAL SPAIN

Location and Climate
Ribera del Duero, Rueda and Toro are all high-lying areas with extreme climates – very hot summer days combined with cool nights, and cold winters. The marked difference of temperature between day and night helps to preserve the acidity in the grapes. Both La Mancha and Valdepeñas are extremely hot and dry areas. In recent years, droughts have caused a severe shortage of grapes.

Grape Varieties
The Tempranillo grape – also known as Tinto Fino, Tinto del Toro and Cencibel – produces nearly all the best red wines of Central Spain. Cabernet Sauvignon is permitted in some regions; it is used in some Ribera del Duero wines and occasionally surfaces as a single varietal, as at the estate of the Marquis of Griñón in Méntrida. Verdejo, Viura and Sauvignon Blanc are used for white Rueda. The white Airén grape predominates in the vineyards of Valdepeñas and La Mancha.

Good Producers
Toro: Fariña (Gran Colegiata). ***Rueda:*** Álvarez y Diez, Los Curros, Marqués de Riscal, Sanz. ***Ribera del Duero:*** Alejandro Fernández (Pesquera), Boada, Hermanos Pérez Pascuas (Viña Pedrosa), Ismael Arroyo (Valsotillo), Vega Sicilia, Victor Balbás. ***Méntrida:*** Marqués de Griñón. ***La Mancha:*** Fermín Ayuso Roig (Estola), Vinícola de Castilla (Castillo de Alhambra). ***Valdepeñas:*** Casa de la Viña, Félix Solís, Luis Megía (Marqués de Gastañaga), Los Llanos.

Traditional earthenware *tinaja*, st used for fermenting wine

0 kilometres 100

0 miles 100

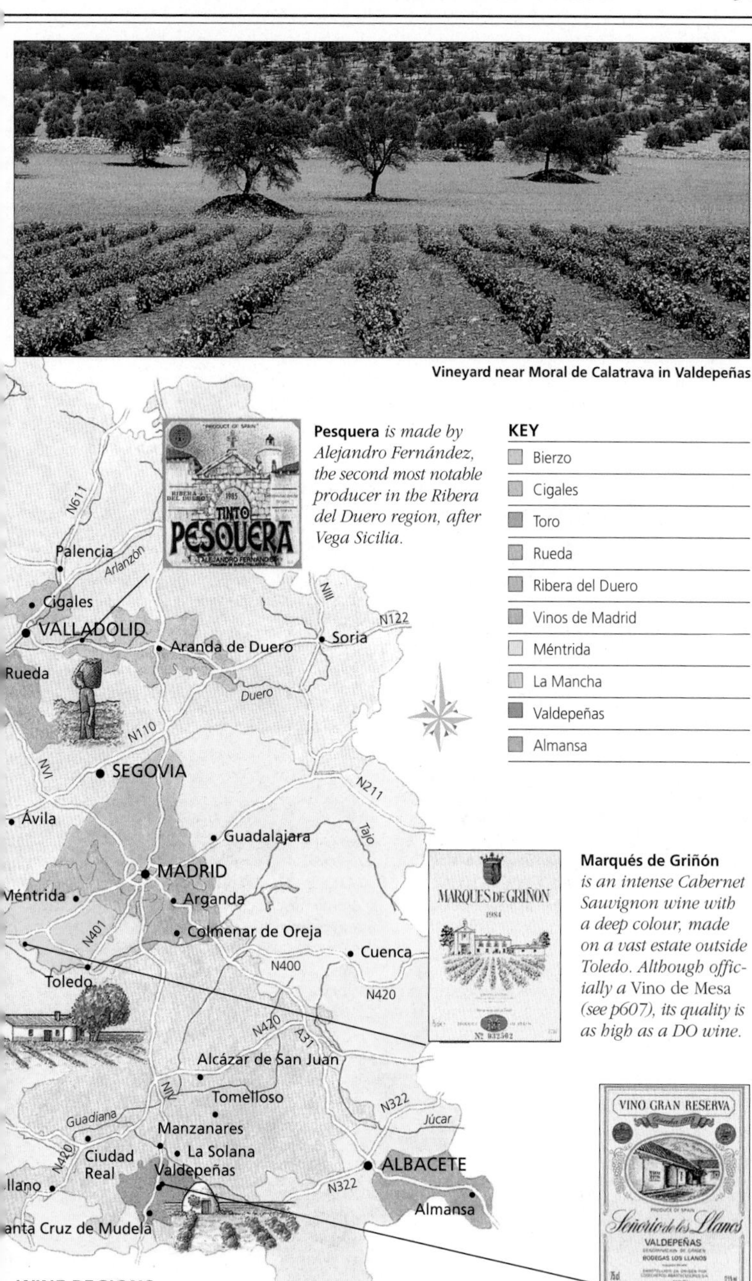

Vineyard near Moral de Calatrava in Valdepeñas

Pesquera *is made by Alejandro Fernández, the second most notable producer in the Ribera del Duero region, after Vega Sicilia.*

Marqués de Griñón *is an intense Cabernet Sauvignon wine with a deep colour, made on a vast estate outside Toledo. Although officially a* Vino de Mesa *(see p607), its quality is as high as a DO wine.*

WINE REGIONS

The wine regions of Ribera del Duero, Toro and Rueda, are situated on remote, high plateaus, straddling the Río Duero. To the northwest lies the isolated region of Bierzo, whose wines have more in common with neighbouring Valdeorras in Galicia. Some wine is produced around Madrid, and southwest of the capital is the largely undistinguished region of Méntrida. Most of Central Spain's wine is produced in La Mancha – the world's largest single wine region – and in the smaller enclave of Valdepeñas, which produces a great deal of "vino de mesa".

Señorío de los Llanos *is produced in Valdepeñas. Its fine reds – made from Cencibel (Tempranillo) and aged in oak – are of excellent value.*

Birds of Central Spain

The vast and varied wild habitats of Central Spain are home to the richest avifauna in the peninsula. White storks' nests are a common sight on the church towers and chimneypots of towns. Grebes, herons and shovelers can be seen in the marshlands; the distinctive hoopoe is often spotted in woods; and grasslands are the nesting grounds of bustards and cranes. The mountains and high plains are the domain of birds of prey such as the imperial eagle, peregrine falcon and vultures. Deforestation, changing agricultural practices and hunting have all taken their toll in recent decades. Today, almost 160 bird species are the subject of conservation initiatives.

Bee-eater

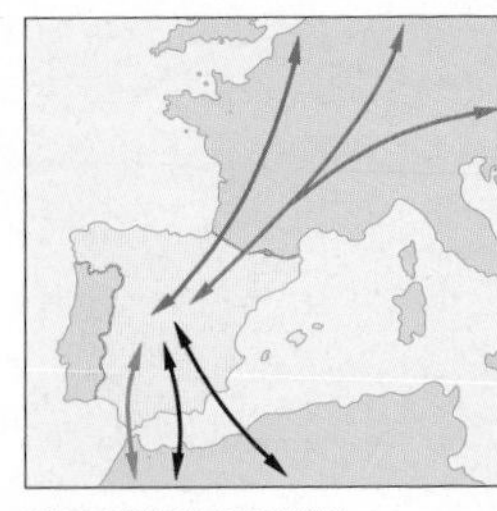

MIGRATION ROUTES

- Cranes
- Storks
- Raptors
- Wildfowl

MARSHLAND AND WET MEADOW

Wetlands, such as Lagunas de Ruidera *(see p397)*, on the edge of the plains of La Mancha, are vital feeding grounds for a wide range of waterfowl, some of which may remain in Spain throughout the year. Other migratory species use such sites as stopover points to feed, rest and build up enough energy to enable them to complete their journeys.

Little egrets *are recognized by their snow white plumage and graceful slow flight. They feed largely on frogs, snails and small fish.*

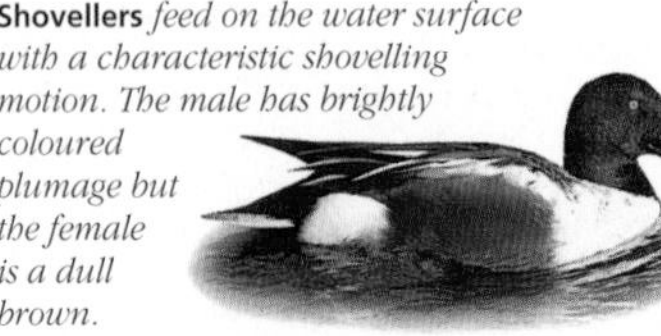

Shovellers *feed on the water surface with a characteristic shovelling motion. The male has brightly coloured plumage but the female is a dull brown.*

WOODLAND AND SCRUB

Habitats in areas of woodland, such as the Parque Nacional de Cabañeros *(see p387)*, and scrub support many species, such as rollers and woodpeckers, throughout the year. Food is plentiful and there are many places to roost and nest. Early in the morning is the best time for spotting some of the rarer species, such as the bluethroat.

Rollers *are commonly found in woodland, often nesting in tree stumps or holes left by woodpeckers. Their food includes grasshoppers, crickets and beetles.*

Hoopoes *can be easily identified by their striking plumage and by the crest which can be raised if the bird is alarmed. They feed on ground insects.*

STORKS

Both the white and the (much rarer) black stork breed in Spain. They can be recognized in flight by their slow, steady wingbeats and may occasionally be seen soaring on thermals, usually during migrations. During the breeding season they put on elaborate courtship displays, which involve "dancing", wing-beating and bill-clapping. Their large nests, made of branches and twigs and lined with grasses, are constructed on roofs, towers, spires and chimneypots, where they are easy to watch. They feed on insects, fish and amphibians. Stork populations are threatened by wetland reclamation and the use of pesticides.

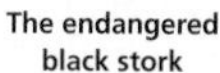

The endangered black stork

Nesting on a monastery roof

GRASSLAND AND FIELD

Many of Spain's natural grasslands have been ploughed over to plant cereals and other crops. Remaining vestiges are rich in wild grasses and flowers and are vital habitats for species such as bustards and larks.

Cranes *perform elegant courtship dances and are also stately birds in flight, their long necks extended to the limit. They are omnivores, feeding on amphibians, crustaceans, plants and insects.*

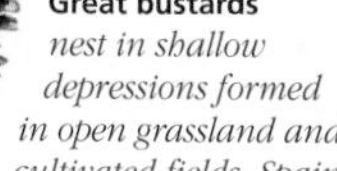

Great bustards *nest in shallow depressions formed in open grassland and cultivated fields. Spain is home to half of the world's population.*

MOUNTAIN AND HIGH PLAIN

Some of Spain's most spectacular birds of prey live in mountain ranges, such as the Sierra de Gredos *(see p362)*, and the high plains of Central Spain. The broad wingspans of eagles and vultures allow them to soar on currents of warm air as they scan the ground below for prey and carrion.

Imperial eagles, *with their vast wingspan of 2.25 m (7 ft), are extremely rare – only around 100 pairs are left in the whole of Spain.*

Griffon vultures, *a gregarious species, nest in trees and on rocky crags, often using the same place from year to year. Their broad wingspans can exceed 2 m (6 ft).*

The Castles of Castile

13th-century fresco of the siege of a castle

The greatest concentration of Spain's 2,000 castles is in Castilla y León (now part of Castile), which derived its name from the word *castillo*, or castle. In the 10th and 11th centuries this region was the battleground between Moors and Christians. Villages and towns were fortified as protection against one side or the other. Most of the surviving castles in Castile, however, were built as noble residences after the area had been reconquered and there was no longer a military purpose for them. Fernando and Isabel *(see pp56–7)* banned the building of new castles at the end of the 15th century; many existing ones were converted to domestic use.

Coca Castle ***(see p365)*****, a classic Mudéjar design in brick**

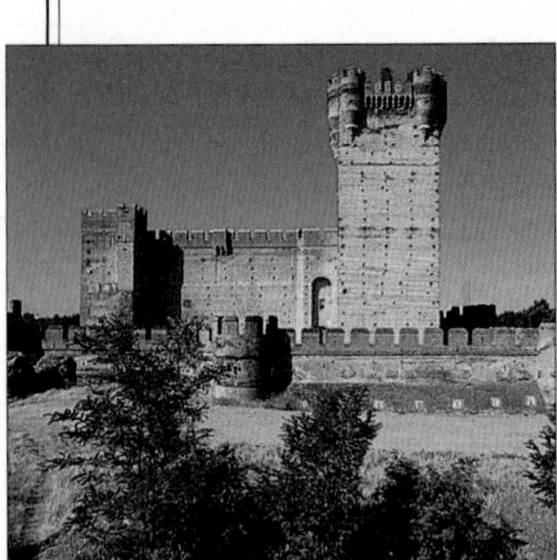

La Mota Castle (see p366), *at Medina del Campo, near Valladolid, was originally a Moorish castle but was rebuilt after 1440 and later became the property of Fernando and Isabel. The square-shaped Torre del Homenaje has twin bartizan turrets at its corners and machicolations beneath its battlements. Great curtain walls surround the castle.*

Patio de armas (courtyard)
Bartizan turrets
The Torre de Juan II contained the dungeons.
The barbican, with the coat of arms of the Catholic Monarchs carved over the gate, contains the portcullis and guards' watchrooms.

Belmonte Castle (see p394) *was built in the 15th century as the stronghold of the quarrelsome Marquis of Villena, Juan Pacheco. Late-Gothic in style, it has a sophisticated, hexagonal ground plan, with a triangular bailey.*

THE ALCAZAR, SEGOVIA

The plan of the royal castle of Segovia *(see p364)* is determined by the contours of the rocky outcrop on which it stands. Although first records date from the 12th century, it was mostly built between 1410 and 1455 and had to be largely rebuilt following a fire in 1862. The fortress's walls conceal several sumptuous apartments.

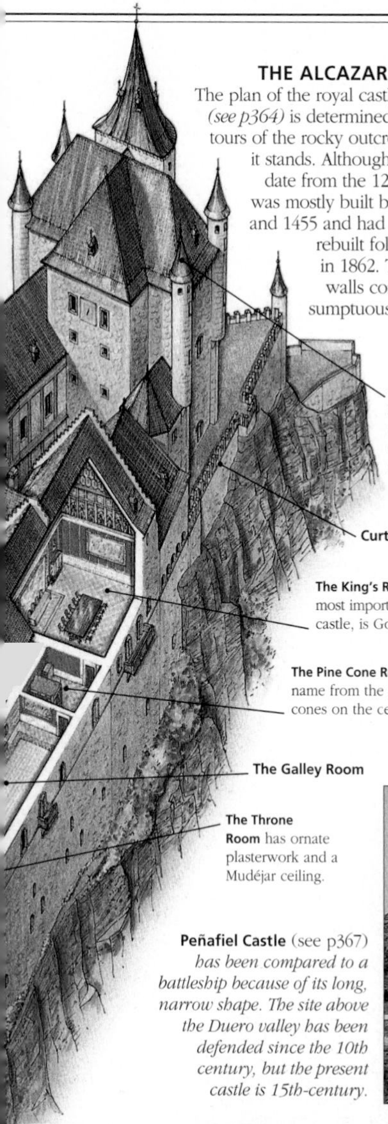

Torre del Homenaje has pointed turrets, atypical of Spanish castles.

Curtain wall

The King's Room, the most important room in the castle, is Gothic in style.

The Pine Cone Room gets its name from the golden pine cones on the ceiling.

The Galley Room

The Throne Room has ornate plasterwork and a Mudéjar ceiling.

TERMS USED IN THIS GUIDE

Alcazar: Castle or palace used as a royal residence.

Bartizan: A small turret which projects from the battlements of a tower above attackers.

Cross and orb loophole: Narrow slit, shaped to allow archers to shoot at various angles.

Curtain wall: Outer, windowless wall, often low enough for archers to fire over it from the keep and other towers.

Machicolation: A projection overhanging the wall beneath a battlement to allow boiling oil, missiles or human waste to be dropped on to the enemy.

Torre del Homenaje: The fortified tower or keep at the heart of a castle, often built to a square plan, in which the nobleman's family lived.

Peñafiel Castle (see p367) *has been compared to a battleship because of its long, narrow shape. The site above the Duero valley has been defended since the 10th century, but the present castle is 15th-century.*

THE CASTLES OF CASTILLA Y LEÓN

Some of Central Spain's finest surviving castles can be visited today. A few, such as Ciudad Rodrigo *(see p357)*, have been turned into luxurious paradors *(see pp558–9)*.

CASTILLA Y LEÓN

LEÓN · ZAMORA · SALAMANCA · ÁVILA · SEGOVIA
VALLADOLID · PALENCIA · BURGOS · SORIA

Awesome expanses of ochre plains stretch to hills crowned with the castles that cover this vast region. Through Spain's history, these central provinces have had a major influence on its language, religion and culture. Their many historic cities preserve some of the country's most magnificent architectural sights.

The territories of the two rival medieval kingdoms of Castile and León, occupying the northern half of the great plateau in the centre of Spain, now form the country's largest region, or *comunidad autónoma.*

Castile and León were first brought together under one crown in 1037 by Fernando I; but the union was not consolidated until the early 13th century. The kingdom of Castile and León was one of the driving forces of the Reconquest. El Cid, the legendary hero, was born near Burgos.

Wealth pouring in from the wool trade and the New World, reaching a peak in the 16th century, financed the many great artistic and architectural treasures that can be seen today in the cities of Castilla y León. Burgos has an exuberantly decorated Gothic cathedral. León Cathedral is famous for its wonderful stained glass. At the heart of the monumental city of Salamanca is the oldest university in the peninsula. Segovia's aqueduct is the largest Roman structure in Spain and its Alcázar is the country's most photographed castle. Ávila is surrounded by an unbroken wall, built by Christian forces against the Moors. In Valladolid, the regional capital, a superb collection of multicoloured sculpture is displayed in a magnificent 15th-century building.

Beyond the cities, in Castilla y León's varied countryside, there are many attractive small towns which preserve outstanding examples of the region's vernacular architecture.

Cereal fields and vineyards covering the fertile Tierra de Campos in Palencia province

◁ The battle-scarred castle of Calatañazor (Soria), site of a Christian victory against the Moors in 1002

Exploring Castilla y León

Covering the northern part of Central Spain's vast tableland, Castilla y León has a huge variety of sights. Many – the University of Salamanca, the Alcázar and aqueduct of Segovia, the medieval walls of Ávila, the monastery at Santo Domingo de Silos, and the great cathedrals of Burgos and León – are well known. Other historic towns and villages worthy of a detour include Ciudad Rodrigo, Covarrubias, Pedraza de la Sierra and Zamora. This region also has beautiful mountainous countryside in the Sierra de Francia, Sierra de Bejar and Sierra de Gredos.

SIGHTS AT A GLANCE

Aguilar de Campoo 25
Astorga 5
Ávila 13
El Bierzo 1
Briviesca 26
El Burgo de Osma 32
Burgos pp370–1 28
Castillo de Coca 18
Ciudad Rodrigo 9
Covarrubias 27
Cueva de Valporquero 6
Frómista 24
La Granja de San Ildefonso 14
León pp353–5 7
Lerma 29
Medinaceli 34
Medina del Campo 19
Medina de Rioseco 22
Palencia 23
Pedraza de la Sierra 16
Peñaranda de Duero 31
Ponferrada 3
Puebla de Sanabria 4
Salamanca pp358–61 11
Santo Domingo de Silos 30
Segovia 15
Sepúlveda 17
Sierra de Gredos 12
Soria 33
Tordesillas 20
Valladolid 21
Villafranca del Bierzo 2
Zamora 8

Tour

Sierra de Francia and Sierra de Bejar 10

SEE ALSO

• ***Where to Stay*** pp582–5

• ***Where to Eat*** pp633–6

GETTING AROUND

Madrid makes a convenient springboard for touring in Castilla y León. The major cities of the region are connected by rail, but the coach is often a quicker alternative. If you intend on exploring rural areas or small towns, it is advisable to hire a car.

Sunflowers growing in Burgos province

KEY

- Motorway
- Motorway under construction
- Major road
- Secondary road
- Scenic route
- Main railway
- Minor railway
- International border
- Regional border
- Summit

Peñaranda de Duero castle

El Bierzo ❶

León. Ponferrada. Ponferrada. *Ponferrada, 987 42 42 36.* **www**.ccbierzo.com

This northwestern region of León province was at one time the bed of an ancient lake. Sheltered by hills from the worst extremes of Central Spain's climate, its sun-soaked, alluvial soils make for fertile orchards and vineyards. Over the centuries, the area has also yielded rich mineral pickings including coal, iron and gold. Many hiking routes and picnic spots are within reach of the main towns of Ponferrada and Villafranca del Bierzo.

In the eastern section, you can trace the course of the old Road to Santiago *(see pp82–3)* through the **Montes de León**, past the pilgrim church and medieval bridge of Molinaseca. Turning off the road at the remote village of El Acebo, you pass through a deep valley where there are signs pointing to the **Herrería de Compludo**, a water-powered 7th-century ironworks. The equipment still works and is demonstrated regularly, although the site is currently closed for restoration.

The **Lago de Carucedo**, to the southwest of Ponferrada, is an ancient artificial lake. It acted as a reservoir in Roman times, a by-product of a vast gold-mining operation. Using slave labour, millions of tonnes of

A *palloza* in the Sierra de Ancares

alluvium were washed from the hills of Las Médulas by a complex system of canals and sluice gates. The ore was then panned, and the gold dust collected on sheep's wool. It is estimated that more than 500 tonnes of precious metal were extracted between the 1st and 4th centuries AD. These ancient workings lie within a memorable landscape of wind-eroded crags, and hills pierced by tunnels and colonized by gnarled chestnut trees. You can best appreciate the area from a viewpoint at Orellán, which is reached via a rough, steep track. **Las Médulas**, a village south of Carucedo, is another place to go for a fine view.

To the north of the A6 highway lies the Sierra de Ancares, a wild region of rounded, slate mountains marking the borders of Galicia and Asturias. Part of it now forms the **Reserva Nacional de los Ancares Leoneses**, an attractive nature reserve. The heathland is home to deer, wolves, brown bears and capercaillies.

Several isolated villages high in the hills contain *pallozas* – primitive, pre-Roman stone dwellings. One of the most striking collections of these huts can be found in isolated **Campo del Agua**, in the west.

Herrería de Compludo
Compludo. *for restoration.*

Las Médulas
Tel *987 42 07 08. daily. 20 Dec– 6 Jan.*

Villafranca del Bierzo ❷

León. *3,500. Avenida Díez Ovelar 10, 987 54 00 28. Tue. Santo Tirso (28 Jan), Spring Fiesta (1 May), Fiesta del Cristo (14 Sep).* **www**.villafrancadelbierzo.org

Emblazoned mansions line the ancient streets of this delightful town. The solid, early 16th-century, drum-towered castle is still inhabited. Near the Plaza Mayor a number of imposing churches and convents compete for attention. Particularly worth seeing are the fine sculptures adorning the north portal of the simple, Romanesque **Iglesia de Santiago**. At the church's

Craggy, tree-clad hills around the ancient gold workings near the village of Las Médulas

Puerta del Perdón (Door of Mercy), pilgrims who were too weak to make the final gruelling hike across the hills of Galicia could obtain dispensation. Be sure to sample the local speciality, cherries in *aguardiente*, a spirit.

Environs
One of the finest views over El Bierzo is from **Corullón,** to the south. This pretty village with grey stone houses is set in a sunny location above the broad, fertile basin of the Río Burbia where the vines of the Bierzo wine region flourish (*see pp78–9*). Two churches, the late 11th-century San Miguel and the restored, Romanesque San Esteban, are worth a visit. Down in the valley, the Benedictine monastery at **Carracedo del Monasterio** stands in splendour. Founded in 990, it was once the most powerful religious community in El Bierzo.

Puerta del Perdón of Villafranca's Iglesia de Santiago

Ponferrada ❸

León. 68,700. *C/ Gil y Carrasco 4, 987 42 42 36. Wed & Sat. Virgen de la Encina (8 Sep).* **www**.ponferrada.org

A medieval bridge reinforced with iron *(pons ferrata)*, erected for the benefit of pilgrims on their way to Santiago de Compostela, gave this town its name. Today, prosperous from both iron and coal deposits, Ponferrada has expanded into a sizeable town.

Most of its attractions are confined to the small old quarter. Ponferrada's majestic **castle**

The imposing Templar castle of Ponferrada

was constructed between the 12th and 14th centuries by the Knights Templar to protect pilgrims. During the Middle Ages it was one of the largest fortresses in northwest Spain.

Standing on the main square is the Baroque **town hall** *(ayuntamiento)*. One entrance to the square is straddled by a tall clock tower which sits above one of the gateways of the medieval wall. Nearby is the Renaissance **Basílica de la Virgen de la Encina**. The older **Iglesia de Santo Tomás de las Ollas** is hidden away in the town's village-like northern suburbs. Mozarabic, Romanesque and Baroque elements combine in the architecture of this simple church. The 10th-century apse has beautiful horseshoe arches. Ask at the nearest house for the key.

Environs
A drive through the idyllic **Valle de Silencio** (Valley of Silence), south of Ponferrada, follows a poplar-lined stream past several bucolic villages. The last and most beautiful of these is **Peñalba de Santiago**. The 10th-century Mozarabic church of Santiago de Peñalba has horseshoe arches above its double portal.

Puebla de Sanabria ❹

Zamora. *1,600. Muralla del Mariquillo s/n, 980 62 07 34. Fri. Candelas (first Sun in Feb), Las Victorias (8 & 9 Sep).*

This attractive old village lies beyond the undulating broom and oak scrub of the Sierra de la Culebra. A steep cobbled street leads past stone and slate houses with huge, overhanging eaves and walls bearing coats of arms, to a hilltop church and castle.

The village has become the centre of a popular inland holiday resort based around the largest glacial lake in Spain, the **Lago de Sanabria**, now a nature park. Among the many activities available are fishing, walking and water sports.

Most routes beckon visitors to Ribadelago, but the road to the quaint hill village of **San Martín de Castañeda** gives better views. There's a small visitors' centre for the nature reserve in San Martín's restored monastery. The village is very traditional – you may see cattle yoked to carts, and women dressed completely in black.

The 12th-century church and 15th-century castle of Puebla de Sanabria

The nave of Astorga Cathedral

Astorga ❺

León. 11,900. Plaza Eduardo de Castro 5. ***Tel*** *987 61 82 22.* *Tue.* *Roman Festival (end Jun), Santa Marta (late Aug).*
www.ayuntamientodeastorga.com

The Roman town of Asturica Augusta was a strategic halt on the Vía de la Plata (Silver Road), a Roman road linking Andalusia and northwest Spain. Later it came to form a stage on the pilgrimage route to Santiago *(see pp82–3)*.

Soaring above the ramparts in the upper town are Astorga's two principal monuments, the cathedral and the Palacio Episcopal. The **cathedral** was built between the 15th and the 18th centuries and displays a variety of architectural styles ranging from its Gothic apse to the effusive Baroque of its two towers, which are carved with various biblical scenes. The gilt altarpiece by Gaspar Becerra is a masterpiece of the Spanish Renaissance. Among the many fine exhibits in the cathedral's museum are the 10th-century carved casket of Alfonso III the Great, the jewelled Reliquary of the True Cross and a lavish silver monstrance studded with enormous emeralds.

Opposite the cathedral is a fairy-tale building of multiple turrets and quasi-Gothic windows. The unconventional **Palacio Episcopal** (Bishop's Palace) was designed at the end of the 19th century by Antoni Gaudí, the highly original Modernista architect *(see p164)*, for the incumbent bishop, a fellow Catalan, after a fire in 1887 had destroyed the previous building. Its bizarre appearance as well as its phenomenal cost so horrified the diocese that no subsequent bishops ever lived in it. Today it houses an assembly of medieval religious art devoted to the history of Astorga and the pilgrimage to Santiago. Roman relics, including coins unearthed in the Plaza Romana, are evidence of Astorga's importance as a Roman settlement. The palace's interior is decorated with Gaudí's ceramic tiles and stained glass.

Reliquary of the True Cross

Palacio Episcopal

Plaza Eduardo de Castro. ***Tel*** *987 61 68 82.* *Tue–Sun.* *Mon, Sun pm, public hols.*

Cueva de Valporquero ❻

Valporquero. ***Tel*** *987 57 64 08.* *from León.* *Oct–Dec & Mar–Apr: 10am–5pm Thu–Sun, public hols; May–Sep: 10am–6pm daily.*
www.turisleon.com

This complex of limestone caves – technically a single cave with three separate entrances – is directly beneath the village of Valporquero de Torío. The caves were formed in the Miocene period between 5 and 25 million years ago.

Severe weather conditions in the surrounding mountains make the caverns inaccessible between December and Easter. Less than half of the huge system, which stretches 3,100 m (10,200 ft) under the ground, is open to the public. Guided tours take parties through an impressive series of galleries in which lighting picks out the beautiful limestone concretions. Iron and sulphur oxides have tinted the rocks many subtle shades of red, grey and black. The vast Gran Rotonda, covering an area of 5,600 sq m (18,350 sq ft) and reaching a height of 20 m (65 ft), is the most stunning.

As the interior is cold, and the surface often slippery, it is advisable to wear warm clothes and sturdy shoes.

Illuminated stalactites hanging from the roof of one of the chambers in the Cueva de Valporquero

León 7

León. 132,700. Plaza de Regla 2, 987 23 70 82. Wed & Sat. San Juan and San Pedro (21–29 Jun), San Froilán (5 Oct). www.leon.es

Founded as a camp for the Romans' Seventh Legion, León became the capital of a kingdom in the Middle Ages. As such it played a central role in the early years of the Reconquest *(see pp52–3)*.

The city's most important building – apart from its great **cathedral** *(see pp354–5)* – is the **Colegiata de San Isidoro**, built into the Roman walls which encircle the city. A separate entrance leads through to the Romanesque **Panteón Real** (Royal Pantheon), the last resting place of more than 20 monarchs. It is superbly decorated with carved capitals and 12th-century frescoes illustrating a variety of biblical and mythical subjects, as well as scenes of medieval life.

Frescoes in Basílica de San Isidoro showing medieval seasonal tasks

The alleyways in the picturesque old quarter around the Plaza Mayor are interspersed with bars and cafés, decrepit mansions and churches. Two well-preserved palaces stand near to the Plaza de Santo Domingo: the **Palacio de los Guzmanes**, with its elegantly arcaded Renaissance patio, and Antoni Gaudí's unusually restrained **Casa de Botines**.

The **Hostal de San Marcos** is a fine example of Spanish Renaissance architecture *(see p25)*. Founded during the 12th century as a monastery lodging pilgrims going to Santiago, the present building was begun in 1513 as the headquarters of the Knights of Santiago. The main hall has a fine 16th-century coffered ceiling. A parador *(see p558)* now occupies the main part of the Hostal. The **Museo de León** has many treasures including a haunting little ivory crucifix, the *Cristo de Carrizo*. The **MUSAC**, Museo de Arte Contemporáneo de Castilla y León, has a radical, interactive approach to exhibiting contemporary art.

Environs

Around 30 km (20 miles) east of León is the **Iglesia de San Miguel de Escalada**. Dating from the 10th century, it is one of the finest surviving churches built by the Mozarabs – Christians influenced by the Moors. It has Visigothic panels and stately horseshoe arches resting on carved capitals. At **Sahagún**, 70 km (40 miles) southeast of León, are the Mudéjar churches of San Tirso and San Lorenzo, with triple apses and belfries. A colossal ruined castle overlooks the Río Esla beside **Valencia de Don Juan**, 40 km (25 miles) south of León.

Museo de León
Plaza Santo Domingo 8.
Tel *987 23 64 05. Tue–Sun. Mon, Sun pm. (free Sat & Sun).*

MUSAC
Avenida de los Reyes Leoneses 24.
Tel *987 09 00 00. Tue–Sun.*
http://musac.es

THE MARAGATOS

Astorga is the principal town of the Maragatos, an ethnic group of unknown origin, thought to be descended from 8th-century Berber invaders. By marrying only among themselves, they managed to preserve their customs through the centuries and keep themselves apart from the rest of society. Although the demise of their traditional trade of mule-driving has changed their way of life, the Maragatos still keep to their communities. Their costumes can be seen during fiestas.

Maragatos dressed in traditional costume

León Cathedral

Carved detail from the choir

The master builders of this Spanish Gothic cathedral *par excellence (see p24)* were inspired by French techniques of vaulting and buttressing. The present structure of golden sandstone, built on the site of King Ordoño II's 10th-century palace, was begun in the mid-13th century and completed less than 100 years later. It combines a slender but very high nave with the huge panels of stained glass which are its most magnificent feature. Although the cathedral has survived for 700 years, today there is concern about air pollution attacking the soft stone.

West Rose Window
This largely 14th-century window depicts the Virgin and Child, surrounded by twelve trumpet-blowing angels.

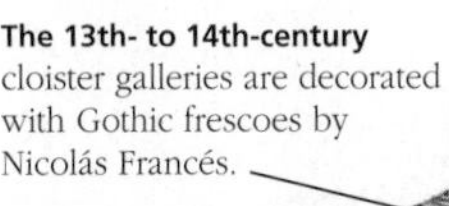

The 13th- to 14th-century cloister galleries are decorated with Gothic frescoes by Nicolás Francés.

The silver reliquary is an ornate chest dating from the 16th century.

Cathedral Museum
Pedro de Campaña's panel, The Adoration of the Magi, *is one of the many magnificent treasures displayed in the museum.*

★ 13th-Century Carvings
Among the Gothic carvings on the front of León's cathedral, above the Puerta de la Virgen Blanca, is one depicting a scene from the Last Judgment.

Inside the Cathedral
The plan of the building is a Latin cross. The tall nave is slender but long, measuring 90 m (295 ft) by 40 m (130 ft) at its widest. To appreciate the dazzling colours of the stained glass it is best to visit on a sunny day.

VISITORS' CHECKLIST

Plaza de Regla. ***Tel*** *987 87 57 70.* *8:30am–1:30pm & 4–7pm Mon–Sat, 8:30am–2:30pm, 5–7pm Sun.* *9am, noon, 1pm & 6pm daily, plus 11am & 2pm Sun.* **Museum** *9:30am–1:30pm, 4–7pm Mon–Fri; 9:30am–1:30pm Sat (Jul–Sep: 9:30am–2pm, 4–7:30am Mon–Sat).*

The altarpiece includes five original panels created by Gothic master Nicolás Francés.

The Virgen Blanca
is a Gothic sculpture of a smiling Virgin. The original is kept in this chapel. A copy stands by the west door.

The choir has two tiers of 15th-century stalls. Behind it is the carved and gilded retrochoir, in the shape of a triumphal arch.

★ Stained Glass
The windows, covering an area of 1,800 sq metres (19,350 sq ft), are the outstanding feature of the cathedral.

LEÓN'S STAINED GLASS

León Cathedral's great glory is its magnificent glasswork. The 125 large windows and 57 smaller, round ones date from every century from the 13th to the 20th. They cover an enormous range of subjects. Some reveal fascinating details about medieval life: *La Cacería*, in the north wall, depicts a typical hunting scene, while the rose window in the Capilla del Nacimiento shows pilgrims worshipping at the tomb of St James in Santiago de Compostela in Galicia *(see pp92–3)*. Some of the windows may be covered due to ongoing restoration work.

Window with plant motif

A large window in the south wall

STAR FEATURES

- ★ 13th-Century Carvings
- ★ Stained Glass

Zamora ❽

Zamora. 65,500. Avenida Príncipe de Asturias 1, 980 53 18 45. Tue. Semana Santa (Easter Week), San Pedro (23–29 Jun). **www**.turismocastillayleon.com

Little remains of Zamora's past as an important strategic frontier town. In Roman times, it was on the Vía de la Plata *(see p352)*, and during the Reconquest was fought over fiercely. The city has now expanded far beyond its original boundaries, but the old quarter contains a wealth of Romanesque churches.

The ruins of the **city walls**, built by Alfonso III in 893, are pierced by the Portillo de la Traición (Traitor's Gate), through which the murderer of Sancho II passed in 1072. The 16th-century **parador** *(see p585)* is in an old palace with a Renaissance courtyard adorned with coats of arms.

Two other palaces, the **Palacio de los Momos** and the **Palacio del Cordón**, have ornately carved façades and windows. Zamora's most important monument is its unique **cathedral**, a 12th-century structure built in Romanesque style but with a number of later Gothic additions. The building's most eyecatching feature is its striking, scaly, hemispherical dome. Inside, there are superb iron grilles and Mudéjar pulpits surround Juan de Bruselas' 15th-century choir stalls. The allegorical carvings of nuns and monks on the misericords and armrests were once considered risqué. The museum, off the cloisters, has a collection of 15th- and 16th-century Flemish tapestries. These illustrate biblical passages and classical and military scenes.

Peaceful gardens of the Colegiata de Santa María in Toro

Nearby, several churches exhibit features characteristic of Zamora's architectural style, notably multi-lobed arches and heavily carved portals. The best are the 12th-century **Iglesia de San Ildefonso** and the **Iglesia de la Magdalena**.

Another reason for visiting Zamora is for its lively Easter Week celebrations, when elaborate *pasos* (sculpted floats) are paraded in the streets. Otherwise they can be admired in the **Museo de Semana Santa**.

Environs

The 7th-century Visigothic church of **San Pedro de la Nave**, 23 km (14 miles) northwest of Zamora, is Spain's

Sierra de Francia and Sierra de Béjar ❿

These attractive schist hills buttress the western edges of the Sierra de Gredos *(see p362)*. Narrow roads wind their way through picturesque chestnut, olive and almond groves, and quaint rural villages of wood and stone. The highest point of the range is La Peña de Francia, which, at 1,732 m (5,700 ft), is easily recognizable from miles around. The views from the peak, and from the roads leading up to it, offer a breathtaking panorama of the surrounding empty plains and rolling hills.

La Peña de Francia ①
Crowning the peak is a windswept Dominican monastery sheltering a blackened statue of the Virgin and Child dating from 1890.

La Alberca ②
This pretty and much-visited village sells local honey, hams and handicrafts. On 15 August each year it celebrates the Assumption with a traditional mystery play performed in costume.

The unmistakable peak of La Peña de Francia

0 kilometres 5

0 miles 5

KEY

Tour route

Other roads

Viewpoint

Las Batuecas ③
The road from La Alberca careers dow into a green valley, the monastery wher Luis Buñuel made h film *Tierra sin Pan (Land without Brea*

Fish-scale tiling on dome of Zamora Cathedral

oldest church. Carvings adorn its capitals and friezes. **Toro**, 30 km (18 miles) east of Zamora, is at the heart of a wine region *(see pp 340–1)*. The highlights of its **Colegiata de Santa María** are the Gothic west portal and a fine 16th-century Hispano-Flemish painting, *La Virgen de la Mosca*. In 1476, the forces of Isabel I *(see pp56–7)* secured a victory over the Portuguese at Toro, confirming her succession to the Castile throne.

Ciudad Rodrigo ❾

Salamanca. 14,000. *Plaza de Amayuelas 5, 923 46 05 61. Tue, Sat. San Sebastián (20 Jan), Carnaval del Toro (before Lent), Easter week.* **www**.turismociudadrodrigo.com

Despite its lonely setting – stranded on the country's western marches miles from anywhere – this lovely old town is well worth a detour. Its frontier location inevitably gave rise to fortification, and its robust 14th-century castle is now an atmospheric **parador** *(see p583)*. The prosperous 15th and 16th centuries were Ciudad Rodrigo's heyday. During the War of Independence *(see pp62–3)*, the city, then occupied by the French, was besieged for two years before falling to the Duke of Wellington's forces.

The golden stone buildings within the ramparts are delightful. The main monument is the **cathedral** (closed Mon), whose belfry still bears the marks of shellfire from the siege. The exterior has a shapely curved balustrade and accomplished portal carvings. Inside, it is worth seeing the cloisters and the choir stalls, carved with lively scenes by Rodrigo Alemán. The main attraction of the adjacent 16th-century **Capilla de Cerralbo** (Cerralbo Chapel) is a 17th century altarpiece. Off the chapel's south side is the arcaded Plaza del Buen Alcalde.

Miranda del Castañar ④
The narrow streets of this pretty, fortified village are lined with ancient houses with wide eaves.

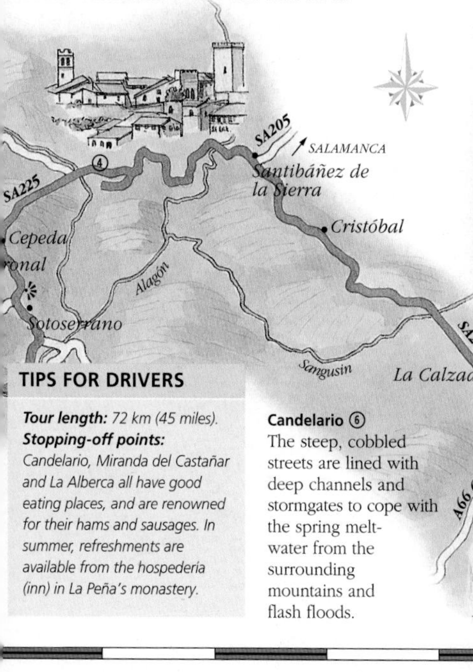

SA205
SALAMANCA
Santibáñez de la Sierra
SA225
Cepeda
Cristóbal
Alagón
Sotoserrano
SA220
Sangusín
La Calzada
A66 (E803)
SALAMANCA

Béjar ⑤
This textile town is strung out along a ridge at the foot of the Sierra de Béjar. From the approach road, 19th-century factories and mills can be seen.

TIPS FOR DRIVERS

Tour length: *72 km (45 miles).*
Stopping-off points:
Candelario, Miranda del Castañar and La Alberca all have good eating places, and are renowned for their hams and sausages. In summer, refreshments are available from the hospedería (inn) in La Peña's monastery.

Candelario ⑥
The steep, cobbled streets are lined with deep channels and stormgates to cope with the spring melt-water from the surrounding mountains and flash floods.

Street-by-Street: Salamanca ⓫

Shell detail, façade of the Casa de las Conchas

The great university city of Salamanca is Spain's finest showcase of Renaissance and Plateresque architecture. Founded as an Iberian settlement in pre-Roman times, the city fell to Hannibal in 217 BC. Pre-eminent among its artists and master crafts-men of later years were the Churriguera brothers *(see p25)*. Their work can be seen in many of Salamanca's golden stone buildings, notably in the Plaza Mayor. Other major sights are the two cathedrals and the 13th-century university, one of Europe's oldest and most distinguished.

The Casa de las Conchas is easily identifiable fron stone scallop shells that its walls. It is now a lib

The Palacio de Monterrey is a Renaissance mansion.

Convento de las Ursulas

Casa de Muertes

CALLE DE LA COMPAÑÍA

CALLE DE SERRANOS

CALLE DE LOS LIBREROS

CALLE VERACRUZ

PASEO

★ Universidad

In the centre of the university's elaborate façade is this medallion, carved in relief, which depicts the Catholic Monarchs.

★ Catedral Vieja and Catedral Nueva

Despite being in different architectural styles, the adjoining old and new cathedrals blend well together. This richly coloured altarpiece painted in 1445 is in the old cathedral.

Puente Romano

The Roman bridge across the Río Tormes, built in the 1st century AD, retains 15 of its original 26 arches. It provides an excellent view of the city.

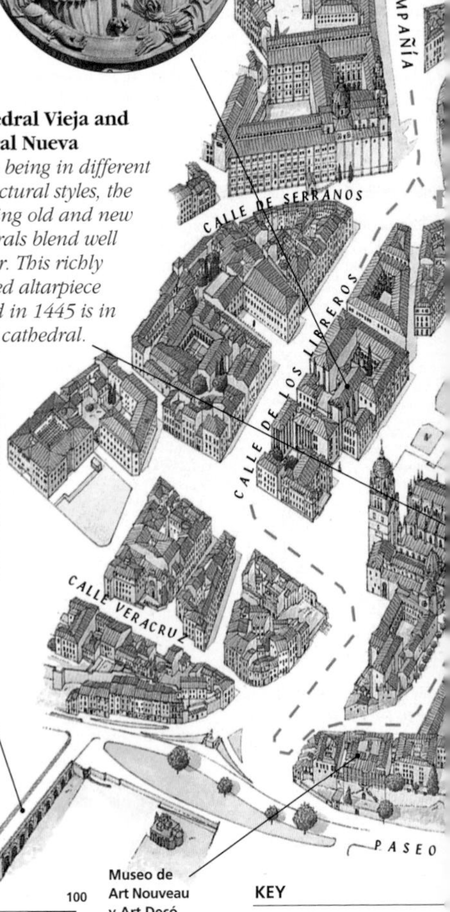

STAR SIGHTS

★ Universidad

★ Catedral Vieja and Catedral Nueva

★ Plaza Mayor

0 metres 100

0 yards 100

Museo de Art Nouveau y Art Decó

KEY

– – – Suggested route

★ Plaza Mayor
This 18th-century square is one of Spain's largest and grandest. On the east side is the Royal Pavilion, decorated with a bust of Felipe V, who built the square.

VISITORS' CHECKLIST

Salamanca. 153,500. 15 km (9 miles) east. *Paseo de la Estación, 902 32 03 20.* *Avda de Filiberto Villalobos 71, 923 23 67 17.* *Plaza Mayor 32, 923 21 83 42; Casa de las Conchas, 923 26 85 71.* *Sun.* *San Juan de Sahagún (10–12 Jun), Virgen de la Vega (8 Sep).*
www.turismocastillayleon.com

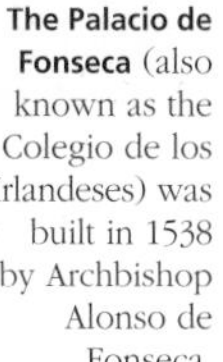

The Palacio de Fonseca (also known as the Colegio de los Irlandeses) was built in 1538 by Archbishop Alonso de Fonseca.

Torre del Clavero
This 15th-century tower still has its original turrets. They are adorned with the coats of arms of its founders, and Mudéjar trelliswork.

Iglesia-Convento de San Esteban
The Plateresque façade of the church is carved with delicate relief. Above the door is a frieze decorated with medallions and coats of arms.

Convento de las Dueñas
Sculptures on the capitals of the beautiful two-storey cloister show demons, skulls and tormented faces, which contrast with serene carvings of the Virgin.

Exploring Salamanca

The majority of Salamanca's monuments are located inside the city centre, which is compact enough to explore on foot. The university, the Plaza Mayor, and the old and new cathedrals are all unmissable.

Catedral Vieja and Catedral Nueva

Unusually, the new cathedral (built during the 16th–18th centuries) did not replace the old, but was constructed beside it. It combines a mix of architectural styles, being mainly Gothic, with Renaissance and Baroque additions. The west front has elaborate Late Gothic stonework.

The 12th- to 13th-century Romanesque old cathedral is entered through the new one. The highlight is a wonderful altarpiece of 53 panels, painted in lustrous colours by Nicolás Florentino. It frames a statue of Salamanca's patron saint, the 12th-century Virgen de la Vega, which was crafted in Limoges enamel. In the vault above it is a fresco depicting scenes from the Last Judgment, which is also by Florentino.

The 15th-century Capilla de Anaya (Anaya Chapel) contains the superb 15th-century alabaster tomb of Diego de Anaya, an archbishop of Salamanca.

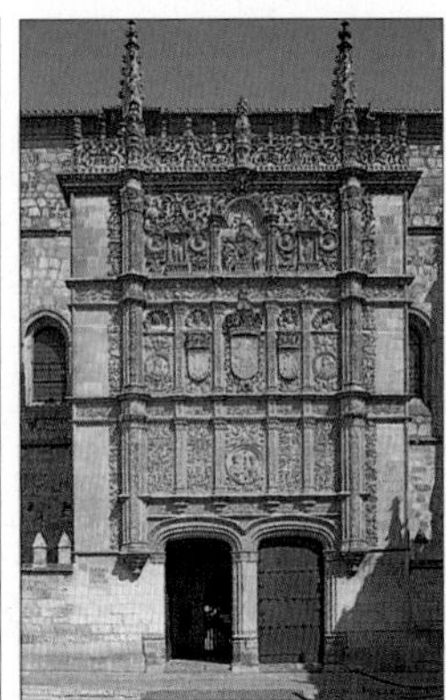
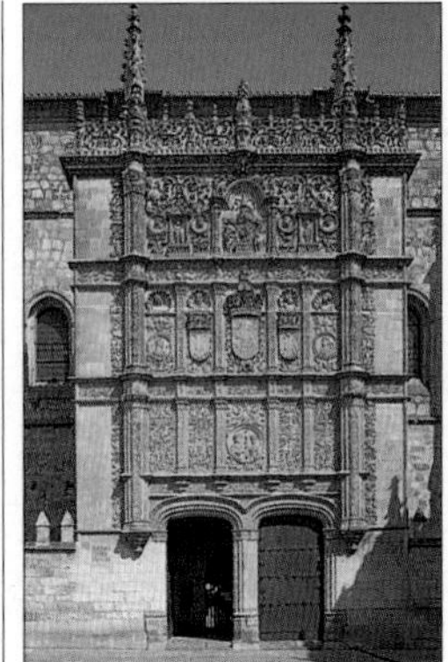

Façade of Salamanca University, on the Patio de las Escuelas

Universidad

Calle Libreros. ***Tel*** *923 29 44 00.* *daily.* *1 & 6 Jan, 25 Dec and for official functions.* *(free Mon am).* **www**.usal.es

The university was founded by Alfonso IX of León in 1218, making it the oldest in Spain. The 16th-century façade of the Patio de las Escuelas (Schools Square) is a perfect example of the Plateresque style *(see p25)*. Opposite is a statue of Fray Luis de León, who taught theology here. His former lecture room is preserved in its original style. The Escuelas Menores building houses a huge zodiac fresco, *The Salamanca Sky*.

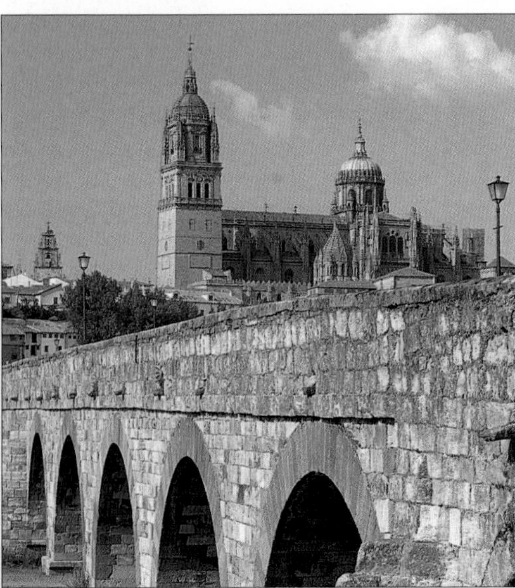

Salamanca's double cathedral, towering over the city

Plaza Mayor

This magnificent square was built by Felipe V to thank the city for its support during the War of the Spanish Succession *(see p62)*. Designed by the Churriguera brothers *(see p25)* in 1729 and completed in 1755, it was once used for bullfights, but nowadays is a delightful place to stroll or shop. Within the harmonious blend of arcaded buildings and cafés are the Baroque town hall and, opposite, the Royal Pavilion, from where the royal family used to watch events in the square. The Plaza Mayor is built of warm golden sandstone, and is especially resplendent at dusk.

Royal Pavilion in Salamanca's beautiful Plaza Mayor

Iglesia-Convento de San Esteban

The 16th-century church of this Dominican monastery is particularly interesting for its superb ornamented façade. The relief on the central panel, completed by Juan Antonio Ceroni in 1610, depicts the stoning of St Stephen, to whom the monastery is dedicated. Above this is a frieze, delicately carved with figures of children and horses.

The interior of the large single-nave church is equally stunning. The ornate altarpiece, of twisted gilt columns decorated with vines, is the work of José Churriguera and dates from 1693. Below it is one of Claudio Coello's last paintings, another representation of the martyrdom of St Stephen.

The double-galleried Claustro de los Reyes, completed in Plateresque style in 1591, has capitals which are carved with the heads of the prophets.

Sculpted shells on the walls of the Casa de las Conchas

Casa de las Conchas

Calle de la Compañía 2. **Tel** *923 26 93 17.* *daily.* **Library** *9am–9pm Mon–Fri, 9am–2pm Sat.*

This mansion's name – House of the Shells – derives from the stone scallop shells that cover its walls. They are a symbol of the Order of Santiago, one of whose knights, Rodrigo Arias Maldonado, built the mansion in the early 1500s. He also adorned it with his family's coat of arms. The building houses a public library and a tourist office.

Convento de las Dueñas

Pl del Concilio de Trento. **Tel** *923 21 54 42.* *Mon–Sat.* *pub hols.*

The main feature of this Dominican convent, beside San Esteban, is its Renaissance double cloister, whose tranquil gardens seem strangely at odds with the grotesques carved on the capitals. The cloister also preserves tiled Moorish arches.

Casa Lis Museo Art Nouveau y Art Deco

Calle Gibraltar 14. **Tel** *923 12 14 25.* *Tue–Sun.* *(free Thu am).*

This important art collection, housed in a 19th-century building, includes paintings, jewellery and furniture from all over Europe. Individual rooms are devoted to porcelain and Limoges enamel, and stained-glass work by Lalique.

Colegio de los Irlandeses

Calle de Fonseca 4. **Tel** *923 29 45 70.* *daily.* *(free Mon).*

The Archbishop of Toledo, Alfonso de Fonseca, built this Renaissance palace in 1521, and the coat of arms of the Fonseca family appears over the main entrance. Its name arises from the fact that it became a seminary for Irish priests at the end of the 19th century. The interior Italianate courtyard has a first-floor gallery and a chapel. Today the building is used as a restaurant and university offices.

Convento de las Úrsulas

C/ de las Úrsulas 2. **Tel** *923 21 98 77.* *Tue–Sun.* *last Sun of mth.*

In the church of this convent is the superbly carved tomb of its founder, Alonso de Fonseca, the powerful 16th-century Archbishop of Santiago. The museum includes fine paintings by Luis de Morales.

Casa de las Muertes

Calle Bordadores. *to the public.*

The House of the Dead takes its name from the small skulls that embellish its façade. Grotesques and other figures also feature, and there is a cornice decorated with cherubs. The façade is a wonderfully accomplished example of the early Plateresque style.

The adjacent house is where author and philosopher Miguel de Unamuno died in 1936. The Casa-Museo de Unamuno, next door to the university, contains information about his life.

Skull carving on the façade of the Casa de las Muertes

Torre del Clavero

Plaza de Colón.

The tower is the last vestige of a palace that once stood here. It was built around 1480 and is named after a former resident, the key warden *(clavero)* of the Order of Alcántara.

Tower opposite Casa de las Muertes

Environs

Northwest of the city, the Río Tormes leads through the fortified old town of **Ledesma**, across lonely countryside to the Arribes del Duero, a series of massive reservoirs near to the Portuguese border.

Dominating the town of **Alba de Tormes**, 20 km (12 miles) east of Salamanca, is the Torre de la Armería, the only remaining part of the castle of the Dukes of Alba. The Iglesia de San Juan was built in the 12th century in Romanesque style. The Iglesia-Convento de las Madres Carmelitas was founded by St Teresa of Ávila in 1571, and is where her remains are now kept.

The castle of **Buen Amor**, 24 km (15 miles) to the north, was founded in 1227. Later, it was converted into a palace and used by the Catholic Monarchs while fighting Juana la Beltraneja *(see p56)*.

Sierra de Gredos 12

Ávila. *Navarrendonda.* *Navarrendonda C/ Del Río s/n, 920 34 80 01 or 920 34 52 52 (Jul–Sep).*

This great mountain range, west of Madrid, has abundant wildlife, especially ibex and birds of prey. Some parts have been developed to cater for weekenders who come skiing, fishing, hunting or hiking. Tourism here isn't a recent phenomenon – Spain's first parador opened in Gredos in 1928 *(see p584)*. Despite this, there are many traditional villages off the beaten track.

The slopes on the south side of the range, extending into Extremadura, are fertile and sheltered, with pinewoods, and apple and olive trees. The northern slopes, in contrast, have a covering of scrub and a scattering of granite boulders.

A single main road, the N502, crosses the centre of the range via the Puerto del Pico, a pass at 1,352 m (4,435 ft), leading to Arenas de San Pedro, the largest town of the Sierra de Gredos. On this road is the castle of **Mombeltrán**, built at the end of the 14th century.

Near Ramacastañas, south of the town of Arenas de San Pedro, are the limestone caverns of the **Cuevas del Águila**.

The sierra's highest summit, the Pico Almanzor (2,592 m, 8,500 ft) dominates the west. Around it lies the **Reserva Nacional de Gredos**, protecting the mountain's wildlife.

The Toros de Guisando near El Tiemblo in the Sierra de Gredos

Near El Tiemblo, in the east, stand the **Toros de Guisando**, four stone statues resembling bulls, believed to be of Celtiberian origin *(see pp48–9)*.

Ávila 13

Ávila. *59,000.* *Calle San Segundo 17, 920 21 13 87.* **Walls** *Tue–Sun.* *Fri.* *San Segundo (2 May); Sta Teresa (15 Oct).* **www**.avilaturismo.com

At 1,131 m (3,710 ft) above sea level, Ávila de los Caballeros ("of the Knights") is the highest provincial capital in Spain. In winter access roads can be blocked with snow. The centre of the city is encircled by the finest-preserved **medieval walls** in Europe. The walls are open to visitors (except Monday and from November to February). One of the best views of the walls is from Los Cuatro Postes (Four Posts) on the road to Salamanca. Built in the 12th century, the walls are over 2 km (1 mile) long. They are punctuated by 88 sturdy turrets, on which storks can be seen nesting in season. The ground falls away very steeply from the walls on three sides, making the city practically impregnable. The east side, however, is relatively flat, and therefore had to be fortified more heavily. The oldest sections of the wall are here. They are guarded by the most impressive of the city's nine gateways, the **Puerta de San Vicente**. The apse of the **cathedral** also forms part of the walls. The cathedral's warlike (and unfinished) exterior, decorated with beasts and scaly wild men, is an unusual design. The interior is a mixture of Romanesque and Gothic styles

***Tuna* in Ávila**

The superbly preserved 11th-century walls, punctuated with 88 cylindrical towers, which encircle Ávila

using an unusual mottled red and white stone. Finer points to note are the carvings on the retrochoir and, in the apse, the tomb of a 15th-century bishop known as El Tostado, "the Tanned One", because of his dark complexion.

Many churches and convents in Ávila are linked to St Teresa, who was born in the city. The **Convento de Santa Teresa** was built on the site of her home within the walls and she also lived for more than 20 years in the **Monasterio de la Encarnación** outside the walls. There is even a local sweetmeat, *yemas de Santa Teresa*, named after the saint.

The **Basílica de San Vicente**, also located just outside the eastern walls, is Ávila's most important Romanesque church, distinguished by its ornamented belfry. It was begun in the 11th century but has some Gothic features which were added later. The west doorway is often compared to the Pórtico da Gloria of Santiago cathedral *(see p92)*. Inside, the carved tomb of St Vincent and his sisters depicts their hideous martyrdom in detail. Another Romanesque-Gothic church worth seeing is the **Iglesia de San Pedro**.

Cloisters of the Real Monasterio de Santo Tomás in Ávila

Some way from the centre is the **Real Monasterio de Santo Tomás**, with three cloisters. The middle one, carved with the yoke and arrow emblem of the Catholic Monarchs, is the most beautiful. The last cloister leads to a museum displaying chalices and processional crosses. The church contains the tomb of Prince Juan, the only son of Fernando and Isabel. In the sacristy lies another historic figure: Tomás de Torquemada, head of the Inquisition *(see p56)*.

In Ávila, you may see groups of *tunas* – students dressed in traditional costume walking the town's streets while singing songs and playing guitars.

ST TERESA OF JESUS

Teresa de Cepeda y Ahumada (1515–82) was one of the Catholic Church's greatest mystics and reformers. When aged just seven, she ran away from home in the hope of achieving martyrdom at the hands of the Moors, only to be recaptured by her uncle on the outskirts of the city. She became a nun at 19 but rebelled against her order. From 1562, when she founded her first convent, she travelled around Spain with her disciple, St John of the Cross, founding more convents for the followers of her order, the Barefoot Carmelites. Her remains are in Alba de Tormes near Salamanca *(see p361)*.

Statue of St Teresa in the cathedral museum

Beautiful gardens and palace of La Granja de San Ildefonso

La Granja de San Ildefonso ⓮

Segovia. ***Tel*** *921 47 00 19. [bus] from Madrid or Segovia. [open] 10am–8pm Tue–Sun (to 6pm Oct–Mar); gardens open until dusk. [closed] 1, 6 & 23 Jan, 1 May, 25 Aug, 24, 25 & 31 Dec. [charge] (free Wed pm & Thu pm for EU residents). [restricted access]* **www**.patrimonionacional.es

This sumptuous royal pleasure palace is set against the backdrop of the Sierra de Guadarrama mountains, standing on the site of the old Convento de Jerónimos.

In 1720, Felipe V embarked on a project to create a fine palace. A succession of different artists and architects contributed to the rich furnishings inside and the splendid gardens without.

A guided tour meanders through countless impressive salons decorated with ornate *objets d'art* and Classical frescoes against settings of marble, gilt and velvet. Huge glittering chandeliers, produced locally, hang from the ceiling. In the private apartments there are superb tapestries. The church is adorned in lavish high Baroque style, and the Royal Mausoleum contains the tomb of Felipe V and his queen.

In the gardens, stately chestnut trees, clipped hedges and statues frame a complex series of pools. On 30 May, 25 July and 25 August each year all of the spectacular fountains are set in motion. Four fountains run every Wednesday, Saturday and Sunday at 5:30pm.

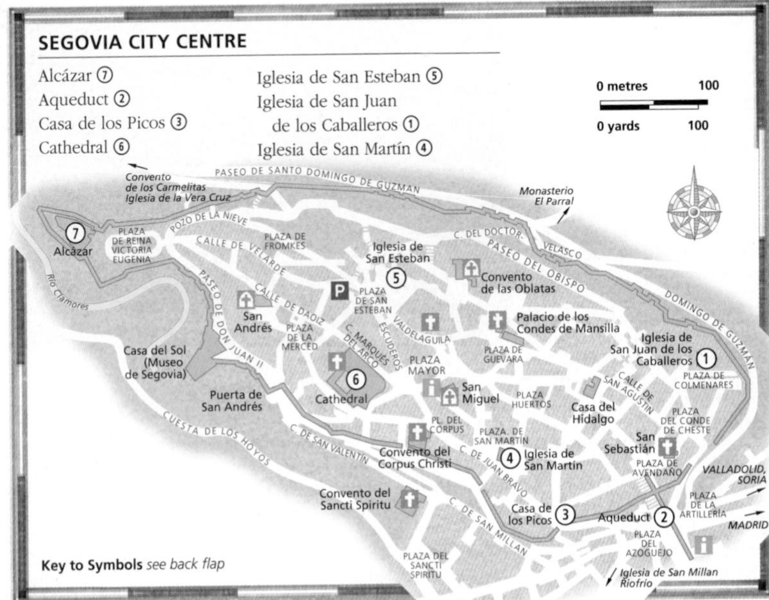

Segovia ⓯

Segovia. 55,200. *Plaza del Azoguejo 1, 921 46 67 20.* *Thu & Sat.* *San Pedro (29 Jun), San Frutos (25 Oct).* **www**.turismodesegovia.com

Segovia is the most spectacularly sited city in Spain. The old town is set high on a rocky spur and surrounded by the Río Eresma and Río Clamores. It is often compared to a ship – the Alcázar on its sharp crag forming the prow, the pinnacles of the cathedral rising like masts, and the aqueduct trailing behind like a rudder. The view of it from the valley below at sunset is magical.

The **aqueduct**, in use until the late 19th century, was built at the end of the 1st century AD by the Romans, who turned the ancient town into an important military base.

The **cathedral**, dating from 1525 and consecrated in 1678, is the last great Gothic church in Spain. It was built to replace the old cathedral, which was destroyed in 1520 during the revolt of the Castilian towns *(see p58)*. The cloister, however, survived and was rebuilt on the new site. The pinnacles, flying buttresses, tower and dome form an impressive silhouette, while the interior is light and elegantly vaulted. Graceful ironwork grilles enclose the side chapels. The chapterhouse museum, with a coffered ceiling, houses 17th-century Brussels tapestries.

At the city's western end is the **Alcázar** *(see pp344–5)*. Rising sheer above crags with a multitude of gabled roofs, turrets and crenellations, it appears like the archetypal fairy-tale castle. The present building is mostly a fanciful reconstruction following a fire in 1862. It contains a museum of weaponry and a series of elaborately decorated rooms. Climb the keep for great views.

Notable churches include the Romanesque **San Juan de los Caballeros**, which has an outstanding sculptured portico, **San Martín** with its beautiful arcades and capitals, and **San Miguel**, where Isabel the Catholic was crowned Queen of Castille. Just inside the city walls, **Casa de los Picos** has a unique façade adorned with diamond-shaped stones.

Environs

The vast palace of **Riofrío**, 11 km (7 miles) to the southwest,

The imposing Gothic cathedral of Segovia

SEGOVIA'S AQUEDUCT

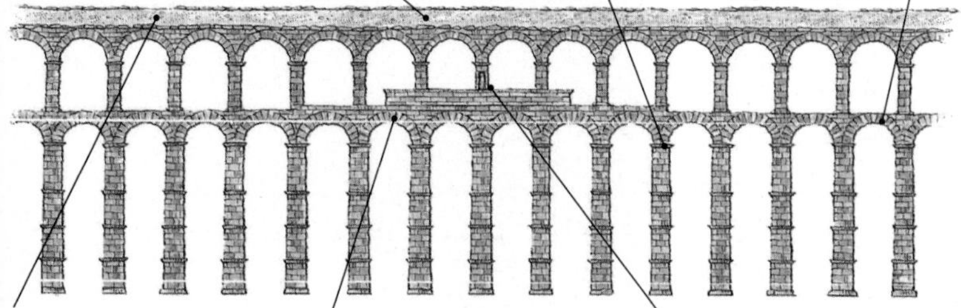
Water channel
Slots used to support blocks of ashlar
Arches reach a maximum height of 29 m (95 ft).
Water from the Río Frío flowed into the city, filtered through a series of tanks along the way.
Two tiers of arches – a total of 728 m (2,400 ft) in length – were needed to cope with the ground's gradient.
In this niche a statue of the Virgin Mary replaces an earlier inscription relating to the founding of the aqueduct.

Segovia's distinctive Alcázar, towering over the city

is set in a deer park. It was built as a hunting lodge in 1752, and has richly decorated rooms.

Alcázar de Segovia
Plaza de la Reina Victoria Eugenia. ***Tel*** *921 46 07 59.* *daily.* *1 & 6 Jan, 25 Dec.* *(free for EU residents 3rd Tue of each month).*

Palacio de Riofrío
Tel *921 47 00 19.* *Tue–Sun.* *(free for EU res Wed pm & Thu pm).*

Pedraza de la Sierra ⓰

Segovia. *500.* *C/ Real 3, 921 50 86 66 (closed Mon).* *Nuestra Señora la Virgen del Carrascal (8 Sep).* **www**.pedraza.info

The aristocratic little town of Pedraza de la Sierra is perched high over rolling countryside. Within its medieval walls, old streets lead to the porticoed **Plaza Mayor** *(see p27)*. The huge **castle**, standing on a rocky outcrop, was owned by Basque artist Ignacio Zuloaga (1870–1945). The castle museum shows some of his works. On the first and second Saturdays of July, concerts are held in Plaza Mayor.

Environs
The main sight at **Turégano**, 30 km (19 miles) west, is a large hilltop castle with the 15th-century Iglesia de San Miguel.

Sepúlveda ⓱

Segovia. *1,200.* *Museo de los Fueros, 921 54 04 25 (closed Mon Jul–Sep; Mon, Tue Oct–Jun).* *Wed.* *Los Toros (last week of Aug).*

Spectacularly sited on a slope above the Río Duratón, this picturesque town offers views of the Sierra de Guadarrama. Parts of its medieval walls and castle survive. Of its several Romanesque churches, the **Iglesia del Salvador**, behind the main square, is notable for possessing one of the oldest atria in Spain (1093).

Environs
Winding through a canyon haunted by griffon vultures is the Río Duratón, 7 km (4 miles) west of Sepúlveda. This area of striking beauty has been designated a natural park, the **Parque Natural de las Hoces del Duratón**.

Ayllón, 45 km (28 miles) northeast of Sepúlveda, has an arcaded main square and the Plateresque *(see p25)* Palacio de Juan de Contreras of 1497.

The Iberian and Roman ruins at **Tiermes**, 28 km (17 miles) further southeast, have been partially excavated, and finds can be seen in Soria's Museo Numantino *(see p377)*.

Castillo de Coca ⓲

Coca (Segovia). ***Tel*** *617 57 35 54.* *daily.* *15 days in Jan, 1st Tue of month.*

Built in the late 15th century for the influential Fonseca family, Coca castle *(see p344)* is one of Castilla y León's most memorable fortresses. It was used more as a residential palace than a defensive castle, although its turrets and battlements are a fine example of Mudéjar military architecture. The complex moated structure comprises three concentric walls around a massive keep. It is now a forestry school, with a display of Romanesque woodcarvings.

Environs
The 14th-century castle of **Arévalo** in Avila, 26 km (16 miles) southwest, is where Isabel I spent her childhood. The porticoed Plaza de la Villa is surrounded by some attractive half-timbered houses.

Massive keep of the 15th-century Castillo de Coca

Medina del Campo ⓳

Valladolid. 21,000. Plaza Mayor 48, 983 81 13 57. Sun. San Antolín (1–8 Sep). www.medinadelcampo.es

Medina became wealthy in medieval times on the proceeds of huge sheep fairs and is still an important agricultural centre today. The vast brick Gothic-Mudejár **Castillo de la Mota** *(see p344)*, on its outskirts, began as a Moorish castle but was rebuilt in 1440. The town transferred the castle's ownership to the Crown in 1475. Isabel I and her daughter Juana "la Loca" ("the Mad") both stayed here. Later, it served as a prison – Cesare Borja was incarcerated here from 1506–08. In a corner of the Plaza Mayor stands the modest house where Isabel died in 1504.

Environs

Towering over the plains, some 25 km (16 miles) to the south of Medina del Campo, are the walls of **Madrigal de las Altas Torres**, which owes its name to the hundreds of bastions that marked the old wall; only 23 remain. In 1451 Isabel was born here in a palace that later became the Monasterio de las Agustinas in 1527.

Castillo de la Mota
Tel 983 81 00 63. daily for guided tours only. Sun pm, pub hols. in Eng if booked ahead.

Castillo de la Mota at Medina del Campo

Tordesillas ⓴

Valladolid. 9,000. Casas del Tratado, 983 77 10 67 (closed Mon). Tue. Fiestas de la Peña (mid-Sep). www.tordesillas.net

This pleasant town is where the historic treaty between Spain and Portugal was signed in 1494, dividing the lands of the New World *(see p57)*. A fateful oversight by the Spanish map makers left the immense prize of Brazil to Portugal.

The town's main place to visit is the **Monasterio de Santa Clara**. It was constructed by Alfonso XI around 1340 and then converted by his son Pedro the Cruel into a stunning residence for his mistress, María de Padilla. Pining for her native Andalusia, she had the convent decorated with fine Moorish arches, baths and tiles. Most impressive are the beautiful patio and the main chapel. There is a fantastic display of royal musical instruments, including the portable organ of Juana "la Loca".

In the old quarter, the **Iglesia de San Antolín** now houses a fascinating religious art museum, which displays paintings as well as a collection of liturgical objects.

Monasterio de Santa Clara
Tel 983 77 00 71. Tue–Sun. (free Wed pm & Thu pm for EU citizens).

Iglesia de San Antolín
Calle Postigo. *Tel* 983 77 09 80. Tue–Sun.

Moorish patio in the Monasterio de Santa Clara, Tordesillas

Valladolid ㉑

Valladolid. 313,500. Glass Pavilion, Acera de Recoletos, 983 21 93 10. Wed, Sat, Sun. Easter week, San Pedro Regalado (13 May), Virgen de San Lorenzo (8 Sep). www.info.valladolid.es

The Arabic city of Belad-Walid (meaning "Land of the Governor") is located at the confluence of the Río Esgueva and Río Pisuerga. Although it has become sprawling and industrialized, Valladolid has some of Spain's best Renaissance art and architecture.

Fernando and Isabel *(see pp56–7)* were married in the Palacio Vivero in 1469 and, following the completion of the Reconquest in 1492, they made Valladolid their capital. Less spectacularly, Columbus died here, alone and forgotten, in 1506. In 1527 Felipe II was born in the Palacio de los Pimentel. José Zorrilla, who popularized the legendary Don Juan in his 1844 play *(see p35)*, was also born in the city.

The Baroque façade *(see p25)* of the city's 15th-century **university** was begun in 1715 by Narciso Tomé. He later created the Transparente of Toledo Cathedral *(see p393)*.

The **Iglesia de San Pablo** has a spectacular façade, embellished with angels and coats of arms in Plateresque style. Among the other noteworthy churches are **Santa María la Antigua**, with its Romanesque

For hotels and restaurants in this region see pp582–5 and pp633–6

belfry, and the **Iglesia de Las Angustias**, where Juan de Juni's fine sculpture of the Virgen de los Cuchillos (Virgin of the Knives) is on display.

Casa de Cervantes

C/ Rastro 2. *Tel 983 30 88 10.* *Tue–Sun.* *pub hols.* *(free Sun am).* **www**.museocasacervantes.mcu.es

The author of *Don Quixote* *(see p35)* lived in this simple house with white-washed walls from 1603 to 1606. The rooms contain some of Cervantes' original furnishings.

Cathedral

Calle Arribas 1. *Tel 983 30 43 62.* *Mon.* *(free Thu).* *by appt.*

Work started on the unfinished cathedral in 1580 by Felipe II's favourite architect, Juan de Herrera, but gradually lost momentum over the centuries. Churrigueresque *(see p25)* flourishes on the façade are in contrast to the sombre, square-pillared interior, whose only redeeming flamboyance is a Juan de Juni altarpiece. The Museo Diocesano inside, however, contains some fine pieces of religious art and sculpture.

Museo Nacional de Escultura

Cadenas de S Gregorio 1, 2, 3. *Tel 983 25 03 75.* *Tue–Sun.* *Sun pm, public hols.* *(free Sat pm & Sun).* **http**://museoescultura.mcu.es

This permanent art collection in the 15th-century Colegio de San Gregorio consists mainly of wooden religious sculptures from the 13th–18th centuries. They include Juan de Juni's

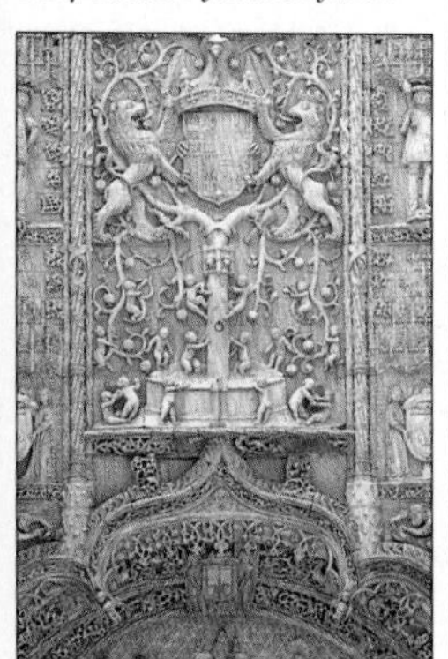

Façade of Colegio de San Gregorio, Valladolid

Berruguete's *Natividad*, in Museo Nacional de Escultura, Valladolid

emotive depiction of the burial of Christ and *Recumbent Christ* by Gregorio Fernández. An Alonso Berruguete altarpiece, and walnut choir stalls by Diego de Siloé and other artists, are among the other fine works to be found here.

The building itself is worthy of attention, particularly the Plateresque staircase, the chapel by Juan Güas, and the patio of twisted columns and delicate basket arches. The façade is a fine example of Isabelline *(see p24)* sculpture, portraying a mêlée of naked children scrambling about in thorn trees and strange beasts.

The nearby 16th-century Palacio de Villena displays the valuable Belén Napolitano (Naples Christmas crib).

Patio Herreriano Museo de Arte Contemporáneo Español

Calle Jorge Guillén 6. *Tel 983 36 27 71.* *Tue–Sun.* *Sun pm.* **www**.museopatioherreriano.org

This private collection of contemporary Spanish art opened in 2002, housed in the former Monastery of San Benito with its fine cloisters. More than 800 works by 200 Spanish artists are displayed, including work by Joan Miró, Eduardo Chillida, Antoni Tàpies and Miquel Barceló.

Environs

The moated grey castle that dominates the village of **Simancas**, 11 km (7 miles) southwest of Valladolid, was converted by Charles V into Spain's national archive. The Visigothic church in the village of Wamba, 15 km (9 miles) to the west, contains the tomb of King Recceswinth.

An unusual long, narrow 15th-century castle on a ridge overlooks the wine town of Peñafiel, 60 km (40 miles) east of Valladolid *(see p345).*

Medina de Rioseco ㉒

Valladolid. *5,000.* *Paseo de San Francisco, 983 72 03 19 (closed Mon).* *Wed.* *Easter week; San Juan (24 Jun); Virgen del Castillviejo (8 Sep).* **www**.medinaderioseco.com

During the Middle Ages this town grew wealthy from the profitable wool trade, enabling it to commission leading artists, mainly of the Valladolid school, to decorate its churches. The dazzling star vaulting and superb woodwork of the **Iglesia de Santa María de Mediavilla**, in the centre of town, are evidence of this. Inside, the Los Benavente Chapel is a *tour de force*, with a colourful stucco ceiling by Jerónimo del Corral (1554), and an altarpiece by Juan de Juni.

The interior of the **Iglesia de Santiago** is stunning, with a triple altarpiece designed by the Churriguera brothers of Salamanca *(see p25).*

The ancient buildings on Medina de Rioseco's main street, the Calle de la Rúa, are supported on wooden pillars, forming shady porticoes.

Altarpiece by Juan de Juni, Iglesia de Santa María de Mediavilla

CASTILLA Y LEON'S FIESTAS

El Colacho *(Sun after Corpus Christi, May/ Jun),* Castrillo de Murcia (Burgos). Babies born during the previous 12 months are dressed in their best Sunday clothes and laid on mattresses in the streets. Crowds of people, including the anxious parents, watch as *El Colacho* – a man dressed in a bright red and yellow costume – jumps over the babies in order to free them from illnesses, especially hernias. He is said to represent the devil fleeing from the sight of the Eucharist. This ritual is thought to have originated in 1621.

El Colacho jumping over babies in Castrillo de Murcia

St Agatha's Day *(Sun closest to 5 Feb),* Zamarramala (Segovia). Every year two women are elected as mayoresses to run the village on the day of St Agatha, patron saint of married women. They ceremonially burn a stuffed figure representing a man.
Good Friday, Valladolid. The procession of 28 multi-coloured sculptures, which depict various scenes of the Passion, is one of the most spectacular in Spain.
Fire-walking *(23 Jun),* San Pedro Manrique (Soria). Men, some carrying people on their backs, walk barefoot over burning embers. It is said that only local people can do this without being burned.

The beautiful carved retrochoir of Palencia Cathedral

Palencia ㉓

Palencia. *81,500.* *Calle Mayor 105, 979 74 00 68.* *Tue, Wed.* *Virgen de la Calle (2 Feb).* **www**.turismocastillayleon.com

In medieval times, Palencia was a royal residence and the site of Spain's first university, founded in 1208. The city gradually diminished in importance following its involvement in the failed revolt of the Castilian towns of 1520 *(see p58).*

Although Palencia has since expanded considerably on profits from coal and wheat, its centre, by the old stone bridge over the Río Carrión, remains almost village-like.

The city's main sight is the **cathedral**, known as *La Bella Desconocida* (the Unknown Beauty). It is especially worth a visit for its superb works of art, many the result of Bishop Fonseca's generous patronage. The retrochoir, exquisitely sculpted by Gil de Siloé and Simon of Cologne, and the two altarpieces, are also noteworthy. The altarpiece above the high altar was carved by Philippe de Bigarny early in the 16th century. The inset panels are by Juan de Flandes, Isabel I's court painter. Behind the high altar is the Chapel of the Holy Sacrament, with an altarpiece dating from 1529 by Valmaseda. In this chapel, high on a ledge to the left, is the colourful tomb of Doña Urraca of Navarra. Below the retrochoir, a Plateresque *(see p25)* staircase leads down to the fine Visigothic crypt.

Environs

Baños de Cerrato, 12 km (7 miles) to the south, boasts the tiny Visigothic Iglesia de San Juan Bautista, founded in 661. It is alleged to be the oldest intact church in Spain. Carved capitals and horseshoe arches decorate the interior.

Frómista ㉔

Palencia. *820.* *C/ Arquitecto Aníbal 2, 979 81 01 80.* *Fri.* *San Telmo (week after Easter).* **www**.fromista.com

This town on the Road to Santiago de Compostela *(see pp82–3)* is the site of one of Spain's purest Romanesque churches. The **Iglesia de San Martín** is the highlight of the town, partly due to a restoration in 1904, leaving the church, dating from 1066, entirely Romanesque in style. The presence of Pagan and Roman motifs suggest it may have pre-Christian origins.

Environs

Carrión de los Condes, 20 km (12 miles) to the northwest, is also on the Road to Santiago. The frieze on the door of the Iglesia de Santiago depicts not religious figures but local artisans. There are carvings of bulls on the façade of the 12th-century Iglesia de Santa María del Camino. The Monasterio de San Zoilo has a Gothic cloister and now operates as a hotel.

Located at **Gañinas**, 20 km (12 miles) to the northwest (just south of Saldaña), is the well-preserved Roman villa,

Interior of the Iglesia de San Juan Bautista at Baños de Cerrato

Posada of the Monasterio de Santa María la Real, Aguilar de Campoo

La Olmeda. It has a number of impressive mosaics, including a hunting scene with lions and tigers. Finds from the villa are displayed in the archaeological museum located in the Iglesia de San Pedro in Saldaña.

Villa Romana La Olmeda
Pedrosa de la Vega. ***Tel*** *979 11 99 97.* *Tue–Sun.* *23 Dec–31 Jan.* *includes archaeological museum.*

Aguilar de Campoo ㉕

Palencia. 7,300. Plaza España 30, 979 12 36 41 (closed Mon). Tue. San Juan y San Pedro (23–29 Jun), Virgen del Llano (1st Sun in Sep).
www.palenciaturismo.es

Situated between the parched plains of Central Spain and the lush green foothills of the Cantabrian Mountains is the old fortified town of Aguilar de Campoo. In the centre of its ancient porticoed main square is the impressive bell tower of the **Colegiata de San Miguel**. In this church is a mausoleum containing the tomb of the Marquises of Aguilar.

Among the other places of interest are the **Ermita de Santa Cecilia**, and the restored Romanesque-Gothic **Monasterio de Santa María la Real**, which has a small, friendly *posada* (inn).

Environs

Six km (4 miles) south, at **Olleros de Pisuerga**, is a church built in a cave. From the parador at **Cervera de Pisuerga**, 25 km (15 miles) northwest of Aguilar, there are stunning views, and tours of the **Reserva Nacional de Fuentes Carrionas**. This is a rugged region overlooked by Curavacas, a 2,540-m (8,333-ft) peak.

Briviesca ㉖

Burgos. 7,700. Calle Santa María Encimera 1, 947 59 39 39. first Sat of month. Feria de San José (19 Mar), Santa Casilda (9 May).

This little walled town, in the northeast of Burgos province, has an arcaded main square and several dignified mansions. The best known of its churches is the **Convento de Santa Clara**, with its 16th-century walnut reredos carved with religious scenes. In 1387 Juan I of Aragón created the title Príncipe de Asturias for his son, Enrique, in the town. The **Santuario de Santa Casilda**, situated outside Briviesca, has a collection of votive objects.

Environs

Oña, 25 km (15 miles) north, is an attractive town. A Benedictine monastery was founded here in 1011.

Overlooking a fertile valley, 20 km (12 miles) further north-east, is the little hilltop town of **Frías**. Its castle overlooks cobbled streets and pretty old houses. Crossing the Río Ebro is a fortified medieval bridge, still with its central gate tower.

At **Medina de Pomar**, 30 km (20 miles) north of Oña, there is a 15th-century castle, once the seat of the Velasco family. Inside are the ruins of a palace with fine Mudéjar stucco decoration and Arabic inscriptions.

The medieval bridge over the Río Ebro at Frías, with its central gate tower

Flemish triptych inside the collegiate church in Covarrubias

Covarrubias ㉗

Burgos. 630. C/ Monseñor Vargas, 947 40 64 61 (closed Sun pm, Mon; Mon–Wed in winter). Tue. San Cosme and San Damián (26–27 Sep). **www**.covarrubias.es

Named after the reddish caves on its outskirts, Covarrubias stands on the banks of the Río Arlanza. Medieval walls surround the charming old centre with its arcaded half-timbered houses *(see p26)*. The distinguished **collegiate church** (closed Tue) shows the historical importance of Covarrubias: here is the tomb of Fernán González, first independent Count of Castile, and one of the great figures in Castilian history. By uniting several fiefs against the Moors in the 10th century, he started the rise in Castilian power that ensured the resulting kingdom of Castile would play a leading role in the unification of Spain. The church museum contains a Flemish triptych of the Adoration of the Magi, attributed to the school of Gil de Siloé, and a 17th-century organ.

Environs

A short distance east along the Río Arlanza lies the ruins of the 11th-century Romanesque monastery of San Pedro de Arlanza. At Quintanilla de las Viñas, 24 km (15 miles) north of Covarrubias, is a ruined 7th-century Visigothic church. The reliefs on the columns of the triumphal arch are remarkable, depicting sun and moon symbols that may be pagan.

Burgos ㉘

Burgos. 179,000. Plaza de Alonso Martínez 7, 947 20 31 25. Tue, Wed, Sun. San Lesmes (30 Jan); Pedro and San Pablo (29 Jun). **www**.turismoburgos.org

Founded in 884, Burgos has played a significant political and military role in Spanish history. It was the capital of the united kingdoms of Castile and León from 1073 until losing that honour to Valladolid after the fall of Granada in 1492 *(see pp56–7)*. During the 15th and 16th centuries Burgos grew rich from the wool trade and used its riches to finance most of the great art and architecture which can be seen in the city today. Less auspiciously, Franco chose Burgos as his headquarters during the Civil War *(see pp66–7)*.

The city's strategic location on the main Madrid–France highway and on the route to Santiago *(see pp82–3)* ensure many visitors; but even without this Burgos would justify a long detour. Despite its size and extremes of climate, it is one of most agreeable provincial capitals in Castilla y León.

Approach via the bridge of Santa María, which leads into the old quarter through the **Arco de Santa María**, a gateway carved with statues of various local worthies. The main bridge into the city, however, is the Puente de San Pablo, where a statue commemorates the city's hero, El Cid. Not far from the bridge stands the **Casa del Cordón**, a 15th-century palace (now a bank) which has a Franciscan cord motif carved over the portal. A plaque declares that this is the spot where the Catholic Monarchs welcomed Columbus on his return, in 1497, from the second of his famous voyages to the Americas.

The lacy, steel-grey spires of the **cathedral** *(see pp372–3)* are a prominent landmark from almost anywhere in the city. On the rising ground behind it stands the restored **Iglesia de San Nicolás**, whose main feature is a superb altarpiece by Simon of Cologne (1505). Other churches worth visiting are the **Iglesia de San Lorenzo**, with its superb Baroque ceiling, and the **Iglesia de San Esteban**, which opens to the public during summer and on Saturdays in winter. The **Iglesia de Santa Águeda** is the place where El Cid made King Alfonso VI swear that he played no part in the murder

The Arco de Santa María in Burgos, adorned with statues and turrets

EL CID (1043–99)

Rodrigo Díaz de Vivar was born into a noble family in Vivar del Cid, north of Burgos, in 1043. He served Fernando I, but was banished from Castile after becoming embroiled in the fratricidal squabbles of the king's sons, Sancho II and Alfonso VI. He switched allegiance to fight for the Moors, then changed side again, capturing Valencia for the Christians in 1094, ruling the city until his death. For his heroism he was named El Cid, from the Arabic *Sidi* (Lord). He was a charismatic man of great courage, but it was an anonymous poem, *El Cantar del Mío Cid*, in 1180, that immortalized him as a romantic hero of the Reconquest *(see pp54–5)*. The tombs of El Cid and his wife, Jimena, are in Burgos cathedral.

Statue of El Cid in Vivar del Cid

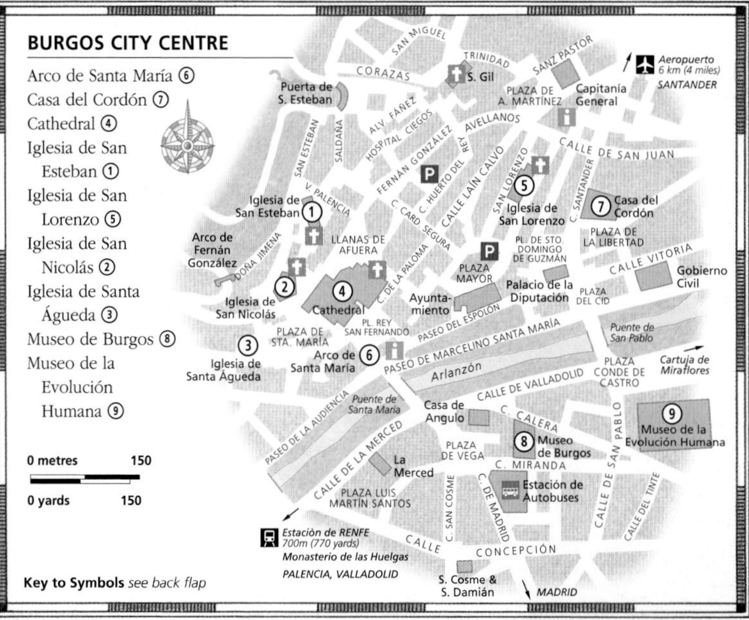

of his elder brother, King Sancho II *(see p356)*.

Across the river, the palace of the Casa de Miranda houses the archaeological section of the **Museo de Burgos**, with finds from the Roman city of Clunia. Nearby, the **Casa de Angulo** contains the Fine Arts section, whose prize exhibits are Juan de Padilla's tomb by Gil de Siloé, and a Moorish casket in enamelled ivory. Also nearby is the **Museo de la Evolución Humana**, which exhibits fossils from the site of the Sierra de Atapuerca, dating from some 780,000 years ago.

Sculpted tomb of Juan de Padilla by Gil de Siloé, in Museo de Burgos

A combined entrance ticket includes the museum, the **Yacimientos de Atapuerca**, the site of Europe's earliest settlement (on the outskirts of Burgos), and a bus to the site.

Two religious houses, on the outskirts of Burgos, are worth visiting. Just west of the city is the **Real Monasterio de Huelgas**, a late 12th-century Cistercian convent founded by Alfonso VIII. One of the most interesting parts is the **Museo de Ricas Telas**, a textile museum of ancient fabrics from the convent's royal tombs. In the Capilla de Santiago is a curious wooden figure of St James holding a sword, with which, according to tradition, royal princes were dubbed Knights of Santiago.

To the east of Burgos is the **Cartuja de Miraflores**, a Carthusian monastery founded during the 15th century. The church includes two of Spain's most notable tombs, attributed to Gil de Siloé. One holds the bodies of Juan II and Isabel of Portugal; the other contains that of their son, Prince Alfonso. The altarpiece by Gil de Siloé, allegedly gilded with the first consignment of gold brought back to Spain from the New World, is spectacular.

Polychrome altarpiece by Gil de Siloé, in Cartuja de Miraflores

Museo de Burgos
Calle Calera 25. ***Tel** 947 26 58 75.*
Tue–Sun. *(free Sat & Sun).*

Museo de la Evolución Humana
Paseo Sierra de Atapuerca. ***Tel** 902 02 42 46.* *Tue–Sun.* *(ticket offers combined entry to Yacimientos de Atapuerca and transport).* **www.** museoevolucionhumana.com

Real Monasterio de Huelgas
Calle de los Compases. ***Tel** 947 20 16 30.* *Tue–Sun.* *Sun pm.* *(free Wed pm & Thu pm).*

Cartuja de Miraflores
Ctra Burgos-Cardeña, km 3. ***Tel** 947 26 34 25.* *daily.*

Burgos Cathedral

Spain's third-largest cathedral was founded in 1221 by Bishop Don Mauricio under Fernando III. The groundplan – a Latin cross – measures 84 m (92 yds) by 59 m (65 yds). Its construction was carried out in stages over three centuries and involved many of the greatest artists and architects in Europe. The style is almost entirely Gothic, and shows influences from Germany, France, and the Low Countries. First to be built were the nave and cloisters, while the intricate, crocketed spires and the richly decorated side chapels are mostly later work. The architects cleverly adapted the cathedral to its sloping site, incorporating stairways inside and out.

Christ at the Column, by Diego de Siloé

West Front
The lacy, steel-grey spires soar above a sculpted balustrade depicting Castile's early kings.

★ Golden Staircase
This elegant Renaissance staircase by Diego de Siloé (1519–22) links the nave with a tall door (kept locked) at street level.

Lantern

Tomb of El Cid

STAR FEATURES

- ★ Golden Staircase
- ★ The Crossing
- ★ Constable's Chapel

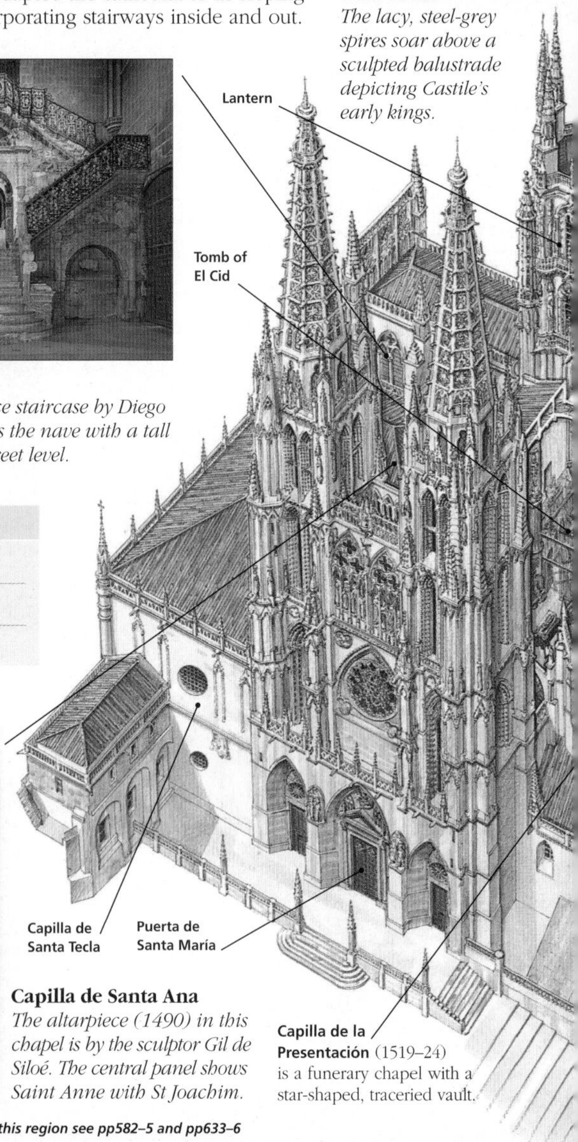

Capilla de Santa Ana
The altarpiece (1490) in this chapel is by the sculptor Gil de Siloé. The central panel shows Saint Anne with St Joachim.

Capilla de Santa Tecla

Puerta de Santa María

Capilla de la Presentación (1519–24) is a funerary chapel with a star-shaped, traceried vault.

For hotels and restaurants in this region see pp582–5 and pp633–6

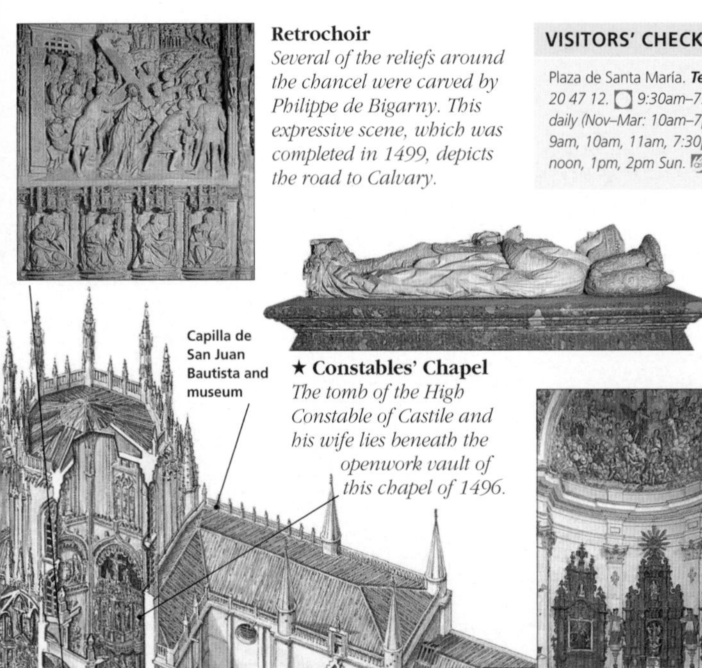

Retrochoir
Several of the reliefs around the chancel were carved by Philippe de Bigarny. This expressive scene, which was completed in 1499, depicts the road to Calvary.

VISITORS' CHECKLIST

Plaza de Santa María. ***Tel*** *947 20 47 12.* *9:30am–7:30pm daily (Nov–Mar: 10am–7pm).* *9am, 10am, 11am, 7:30pm daily; noon, 1pm, 2pm Sun.*

★ Constables' Chapel
The tomb of the High Constable of Castile and his wife lies beneath the openwork vault of this chapel of 1496.

Sacristy *(1765)*
The sacristy was rebuilt in Baroque style, with an exuberant plasterwork vault and Rococo altars.

Puerta del Sarmental
The tympanum of this portal of 1240 shows Christ flanked by the Evangelists. This is the main entrance for tourists.

★ The Crossing
The magnificent star-ribbed central dome, begun in 1539, rises on four huge pillars. It is decorated with effigies of prophets and saints. Beneath it is the tomb of El Cid and his wife.

Lerma ㉙

Burgos. 2,800. *Calle Audiencia 6, 947 17 70 02 (closed Mon, except Aug). Wed. Nuestra Señora de la Natividad (8 Sep).* **www**.citlerma.com

The grandiose appearance of this town is largely due to the ambition of the notorious first Duke of Lerma *(see p60)*, Felipe III's corrupt favourite and minister from 1598–1618. He misused vast quantities of Spain's new-found wealth on new buildings in his home town – all strictly Classical in style, in accordance with prevailing fashion. At the top of the town, the **Palacio Ducal**, built in 1605 as his residence, has been transformed into a parador.

There are good views over the Río Arlanza from the archways near to the **Convento de Santa Clara** and also from the **Colegiata de San Pedro** church, which has a bronze statue of the Duke's uncle.

The narrow, sloping streets of the old town of Lerma

Cloisters of the Monasterio de Santo Domingo de Silos

Monasterio de Santo Domingo de Silos ㉚

Santo Domingo de Silos (Burgos). ***Tel** 947 39 00 49. from Burgos. Tue–Sat, Sun pm. pub hols. 9am, 7pm Mon–Sat, noon Sun.* **www**.abadiadesilos.es

St Dominic gave his name to the monastery he built in 1041 over the ruins of an abbey destroyed by the Moors. It is a place of spiritual and artistic pilgrimage – its tranquil setting has inspired countless poets.

Others come to admire the beautiful Romanesque cloisters, whose capitals are sculpted in a great variety of designs, both symbolistic and realistic. The carvings on the corner piers depict various scenes from the Bible and the ceilings are coffered in Moorish style. The body of St Dominic rests in a silver urn, supported by three Romanesque lions, in a chapel in the north gallery. The old pharmacy, just off the cloister, has a display of jars from Talavera de la Reina *(see p386)*.

The Benedictine community holds regular services in Gregorian chant in the Neo-Classical church by Ventura Rodríguez. The monastery offers accommodation for male guests.

Environs

To the southwest lies the **Garganta de la Yecla** (Yecla Gorge), where a path leads to a narrow fissure cut by the river. To the northeast, the peaks and wildlife reserve of the **Sierra de la Demanda** extend over into La Rioja.

GREGORIAN PLAINCHANT

At regular intervals throughout the day, the monks of Santo Domingo de Silos sing services in plainchant, an unaccompanied singing of Latin texts in unison. The origins of chant date back to the beginnings of Christianity, but it was Pope Gregory I (590–604) who codified this manner of worship. It is an ancient and austere form of music which has found a new appeal with modern audiences. In 1994 a recording of the monks became a surprise hit all over the world.

Manuscript for an 11th-century Gregorian chant

The 15th-century castle of Peñaranda de Duero

Peñaranda de Duero ㉛

Burgos. 580. *C/ Trinquete 7, **Tel** 947 55 20 63 (closed Mon; also Wed in winter). Fri. Santiago (25 Jul); Santa Ana (26 Jul); Virgen de los Remedios (8 Sep).* **www**.penarandadeduero.com

The castle of Peñaranda was built during the Reconquest *(see pp54–5)* by the Castilians, who had driven the Moors back south of the Río Duero. From its hilltop site, there are views down to one of the most charming villages in old Castile, where pantiled houses cluster around a huge church. The main square is lined with porticoed, timber-framed buildings and the superb Renaissance **Palacio de Avellaneda**. Framing its main doorway are various

◁ **View from the castle over the church and town of Peñaranda, on the Río Duero**

Curtain walls and drum towers of Berlanga de Duero castle

heraldic devices, and inside is a patio with fine decorated ceilings. On Calle de la Botica is a 17th-century **pharmacy**.

Environs

In **Aranda de Duero**, 18 km (10 miles) to the west, the **Iglesia de Santa María**, has an Isabelline façade *(see p24)*.

Palacio de Avellaneda
Plaza Condes de Miranda 1. ***Tel*** *947 55 20 13. phone to check. only (every half hour).*

El Burgo de Osma ㉜

Soria. *5,250.* *Plaza Mayor 9, 975 36 01 16.* *Sat.* *Santa Cristina (24 Jul), Virgen del Espino and San Roque (14–19 Aug).*

The most interesting sight in this attractive village is the **cathedral**. Although it is mostly Gothic (dating from 1232), with Renaissance additions, the tall tower is Baroque (1739). Its treasures include a Juan de Juni altarpiece and the tomb of the founder, San Pedro de Osma. The museum has a valuable collection of illuminated manuscripts and codices.

Porticoed buildings line the streets and the Plaza Mayor, and storks nest on the Baroque Hospital de San Agustín.

Environs

Overlooking the Río Duero at **Gormaz**, 12 km (7 miles) south, is a massive castle with 28 towers. There are also medieval fortresses at **Berlanga de Duero**, 20 km (12 miles) further southeast, and at **Calatañazor**, 25 km (16 miles) northeast of El Burgo de Osma, near to where the Moorish leader al Mansur was killed in 1002 *(see p53)*.

Soria ㉝

Soria. *40,000.* *C/ Medinaceli 2, 975 21 20 52.* *Thu.* *San Juan (24 Jun).* **www**.dipsoria.org

Castilla y León's smallest provincial capital stands on the banks of the Río Duero. Soria's stylish, modern parador *(see p557)* is named after the poet Antonio Machado (1875–1939, *see p35*), who wrote in praise of the town and the surrounding plains. Many of the older buildings are gone, but notable among those remaining are the imposing russet **Palacio de los Condes de Gómara**, and the handsome **Concatedral de San Pedro**, both built in the 16th century.

The **Museo Numantino**, opposite the municipal gardens, displays a variety of finds from the nearby Roman ruins of Numantia and Tiermes *(see p365)*. Across the Duero is the ruined monastery of **San Juan de Duero**, with a 13th-century cloister of interlacing arches.

Environs

North of Soria are the ruins of **Numantia**, whose inhabitants endured a year-long Roman siege in 133 BC before defiantly burning the town and themselves *(see p50)*. To the northwest is the Sierra de Urbión, a range of pine-clad hills with a lake, the **Laguna Negra de Urbión**.

Museo Numantino
Paseo del Espolón. ***Tel*** *975 22 14 28. Tue–Sun. (free Sat & Sun).*

Medinaceli ㉞

Soria. *820.* *C/ San Nicolás, 975 32 63 47.* *Beato Julián de San Agustín (28 Aug); Cuerpos Santos (13 Nov).* **www**.medinaceli.es

Only a triumphal arch remains of Roman Ocilis, perched on a high ridge over the Río Jalón. Built in the 1st century AD, it is the only one in Spain with three arches. It has been adopted as the symbol for ancient monuments on Spanish road signs.

Environs

Lying just to the east are the red cliffs of the Jalón gorges. On the Madrid–Zaragoza road is the Cistercian monastery of **Santa María de Huerta**, founded in the 12th century. Its glories include a 13th-century Gothic cloister and the superb, crypt-like Monks' Refectory.

Monasterio de Santa María de Huerta
Tel *975 32 70 02. daily.*

Decorative arches in the cloister of the monastery of San Juan de Duero

CASTILLA–LA MANCHA

GUADALAJARA · CUENCA · TOLEDO · ALBACETE · CIUDAD REAL

La Mancha's empty beauty, its windmills and medieval castles, silhouetted above the sienna plains, was immortalized by Cervantes in Don Quixote's epic adventures. Its brilliantly sunlit, wide horizons are one of the classic images of Spain. This scarcely visited region has great, scenic mountain ranges, dramatic gorges and the two monument-filled cities of Toledo and Cuenca.

You will always find a castle nearby in this region – as the name Castilla suggests. Most were built in the 9th–12th centuries, when the region was a battleground between Christians and Moors. Others mark the 14th- and 15th-century frontiers between the kingdoms of Aragón and Castile. Sigüenza, Belmonte, Alarcón Molina de Aragón and Calatrava La Nueva are among the most impressive.

Toledo, which was the capital of Visigothic Spain, is an outstanding museum city. Its rich architectural and artistic heritage derives from a coalescence of Muslim, Christian and Jewish cultures with medieval and Renaissance ideas and influences.

Cuenca is another attractive city. Its old town is perched above converging gorges; on two sides it spills down steep hillsides. Villanueva de los Infantes, Chinchilla, Alcaraz and Almagro are towns of character built between the 16th and 18th centuries. Ocaña and Tembleque each has a splendid *plaza mayor* (main square).

La Mancha's plains are brightened by natural features of great beauty in its two national parks – the Tablas de Daimiel, and Cabañeros, within the Montes de Toledo. Rimming the plains are beautiful upland areas: the olive groves of the Alcarria; Cuenca's limestone mountains; and the peaks of the Sierra de Alcaraz. The wine region of La Mancha is the world's largest expanse of vineyards. Around Consuegra and Albacete fields turn mauve in autumn as the valuable saffron crocus blooms.

Windmills above Campo de Criptana on the plains of La Mancha

◁ **Old houses in Cuenca, a city dramatically located over two gorges**

Exploring Castilla-La Mancha

The historic city of Toledo is Castilla-La Mancha's major tourist destination. Less crowded towns with historical charm include Almagro, Oropesa, Alcaraz and Guadalajara. At Sigüenza, Calatrava, Belmonte and Alarcón there are medieval castles, reminders of the region's eventful past. Some towns on the plains of La Mancha, such as El Toboso and Campo de Criptana, are associated with the adventures of Don Quixote *(see p395)*. The wooded uplands of the Serranía de Cuenca, the Alcarria and the Sierra de Alcaraz provide picturesque scenic routes. A haven for bird lovers is the wetland nature reserve of the Tablas de Daimiel.

The village of Alcalá del Júcar

SIGHTS AT A GLANCE

Alarcón 20
Albacete 22
Alcalá del Júcar 21
Alcaraz 24
La Alcarria 4
Almagro 30
Atienza 1
Belmonte 19
Calatrava la Nueva 29
Campo de Criptana 17
Consuegra 16
Cuenca pp384–5 7
Guadalajara 5
Illescas 10
Lagunas de Ruidera 25
Molina de Aragón 3
Montes de Toledo 13
Oropesa 12
Segóbriga 8
Serranía de Cuenca 6
Sigüenza 2
Tablas de Daimiel 31
Talavera de la Reina 11
Tembleque 15
El Toboso 18
Toledo pp388–93 14
Uclés 9
Valdepeñas 27
Valle de Alcudia 32
Villanueva de los Infantes 26
Viso del Marqués 28

Tours

Sierra de Alcaraz 23

SEE ALSO

- ***Where to Stay*** pp586–8
- ***Where to Eat*** pp636–8

Cattle grazing on the isolated plains of La Mancha

GETTING AROUND

Castilla-La Mancha is best explored by car as it is well-endowed with a network of motorways radiating outwards from Madrid. The region is also served by high-speed AVE trains which run between Madrid, Seville, Toledo and Albacete (via Cuenca). Otherwise, public transport is infrequent and slow.

The tranquil Montes de Toledo

Atienza ❶

Guadalajara. 470. Cervantes 22, 949 39 92 93 (closed Mon–Fri). Fri. La Caballada (Pentecost Sun).

Rising high above the valley it once protected, Atienza contains vestiges of its medieval past. Crowning the hill are a ruined 12th-century castle. The arcaded Plaza Mayor and the Plaza del Trigo are joined by an original gateway. The **Museo de San Gil**, a religious art museum, is in the church of the same name. The **Iglesia de Santa María del Rey**, at the foot of the hill, displays a Baroque altarpiece.

Environs
Campisábalos, to the west, has an outstanding 12th-century Romanesque church. The **Hayedo de Tejera Negra**, further west, is a nature reserve of beech woods.

Museo de San Gil
C/ San Gil. ***Tel*** *949 39 90 41.*
Sep–Jun: Sat & Sun; Jul–Aug: daily; by appt weekdays.

Sigüenza ❷

Guadalajara. 5,000. Calle Serrano Sanz 9, 949 34 70 07. Sat. San Vicente (22 Jan), San Juan (24 Jun), Fiestas Patronales (mid-Aug). **www**.siguenza.es

Dominating the hillside town of Sigüenza is its impressive castle-parador *(see p587)*. The **cathedral** is Romanesque, with later additions such as the Gothic-Plateresque cloisters. In one of the chapels is the Tomb of El Doncel, built for Martín

Semi-recumbent figure of El Doncel on his tomb in Sigüenza Cathedral

Vázquez de Arce, Isabel of Castile's page *(see p56)*. He was killed in battle against the Moors in 1486. The sacristy has a ceiling carved with flowers and cherubs.

Molina de Aragón ❸

Guadalajara. 3,700. Calle de las Tiendas, 949 83 20 98. Thu. Día del Carmen (16 Jul), Ferias (30 Aug–5 Sep). **www**.molina-aragon.com

Molina's attractive medieval quarter is at the foot of a hill next to the Río Gallo. The town was disputed during the Reconquest and captured from the Moors by Alfonso I of Aragón in 1129. Many monuments were destroyed during the War of Independence *(see p63)*, but the 11th-century hilltop castle preserves seven original towers. It is possible to visit the Romanesque-Gothic **Iglesia de Santa Clara**.

Environs
West of Molina is the **Virgen de la Hoz** chapel, set in a rust-red ravine. Further south-west is a nature reserve, the **Parque Natural del Alto Tajo**.

Arab ramparts above Molina de Aragón's old town

La Alcarria ❹

Guadalajara. Guadalajara. Palacio Ducal, Plaza de la Hora, Pastrana, 949 37 06 72. **www**.pastrana.org

This vast stretch of undulating olive groves and fields east of Guadalajara is still evocative of Camilo José Cela's *(see p35)* classic book *Journey to the Alcarria*. Driving through the rolling hills, it seems that little has changed since this account of the hardship of Spanish rural life was written in the 1940s.

Towards the centre of the Alcarria are three immense, adjoining reservoirs called the **Mar de Castilla** (Sea of

Olive groves in La Alcarria in the province of Guadalajara

Castile). The first reservoir was built in 1946, and holiday homes have subsequently sprung up close to the shores and on the outskirts of villages.

Historic **Pastrana**, 45 km (28 miles) southeast of Guadalajara, is one of the prettiest towns in the Alcarria. The town developed alongside the **Palacio Mendoza**, and by the 17th century was larger and more affluent than Guadalajara. The **Iglesia de la Asunción** contains four 15th-century Flemish tapestries and paintings from El Greco's school.

Brihuega, 30 km (19 miles) northeast of Guadalajara, has a pleasant old centre.

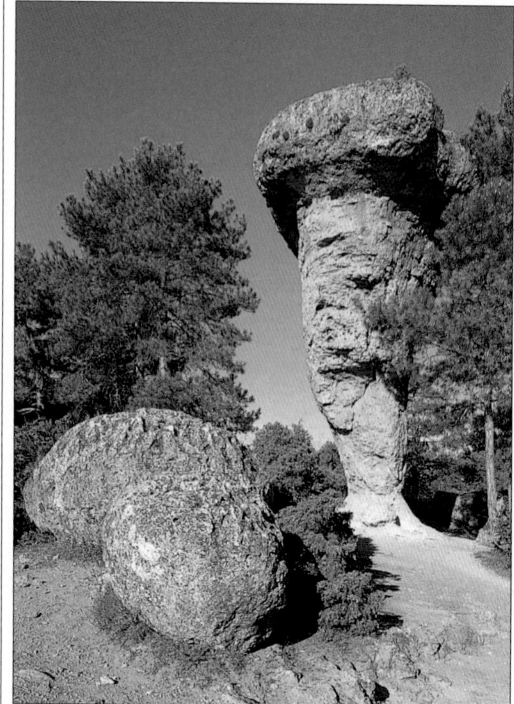

Sculpted rock figures in Ciudad Encantada

Guadalajara ❺

Guadalajara. 84,500. Plaza de los Caídos 6, 949 21 16 26. Tue, Sat. Virgen de la Antigua (Sep). **www**.guadalajara.es

Guadalajara's history is largely lost within the modern city, although traces of its Renaissance splendour survive. The **Palacio de los Duques del Infantado**, built between the 14th and 17th centuries by the powerful Mendoza dynasty, is an outstanding example of Gothic-Mudéjar architecture *(see p24)*. The main façade and patio are adorned with carving. The restored palace now houses the Museo Provincial. Among the churches in the town is the **Iglesia de Santiago**, with a Gothic-Plateresque chapel by Alonso de Covarrubias. The 15th-century **Iglesia de San Francisco** is home to the mausoleum of the Mendoza family; it cannot, however, be visited. The cathedral is built on the site of a mosque.

Detail of the façade of the Palacio de los Duques del Infantado

Environs

At **Lupiana**, 11 km (7 miles) east of Guadalajara, is the two-storey Monasterio de San Bartolomé, which was founded in the 14th century.

Palacio de los Duques del Infantado
Avenida del Ejército. ***Tel*** *949 21 33 01.* **Palace** *daily;* **Museum** *Tue–Sun.*

Serranía de Cuenca ❻

Cuenca. Cuenca. Cuenca, 969 24 10 51. **www**.serraniaaltadecuenca.es

To the north and east of Cuenca stretches the vast *serranía*, a mountainous area of forests and pastures dissected by deep gorges. Its two most popular beauty spots are the **Ciudad Encantada** (Enchanted City), where the limestone has been eroded into spectacular shapes, and the moss-clad waterfalls and rock pools of the **Nacimiento del Río Cuervo** (Source of the River Cuervo).

The main river flowing through the area, the Júcar, carves a gorge near Villalba de la Sierra. The viewpoint of the **Ventano del Diablo** gives the best view of the gorge.

Between Beteta and Priego, to the north, is another spectacular river canyon, the **Hoz de Beteta**, where the Río Guadiela has cut its way through the surrounding cliffs. There are good views from the convent of **San Miguel de las Victorias**. A small road leads to the 18th-century royal spa of **Solán de Cabras**.

In the emptier eastern and southern tracts is **Cañete**, a pretty, fortified old town with a parish church displaying 16th-century paintings. To the southeast of Cañete are the eerie ridgetop ruins of the abandoned town of **Moya**.

Street-by-Street: Cuenca ❼

Cuenca's picturesque old town sits astride a steeply sided spur which drops precipitously on either side to the deep gorges of the Júcar and Huécar rivers. Around the Moorish town's narrow, winding streets grew the Gothic and Renaissance city, its monuments built with with the profits of the wool and textile trade. The main sight is the cathedral, one of the most original works of Spanish Gothic, with Anglo-Norman influences. One of the picturesque Hanging Houses, which jut out over the Huécar ravine, has been converted into the excellent Museum of Abstract Art.

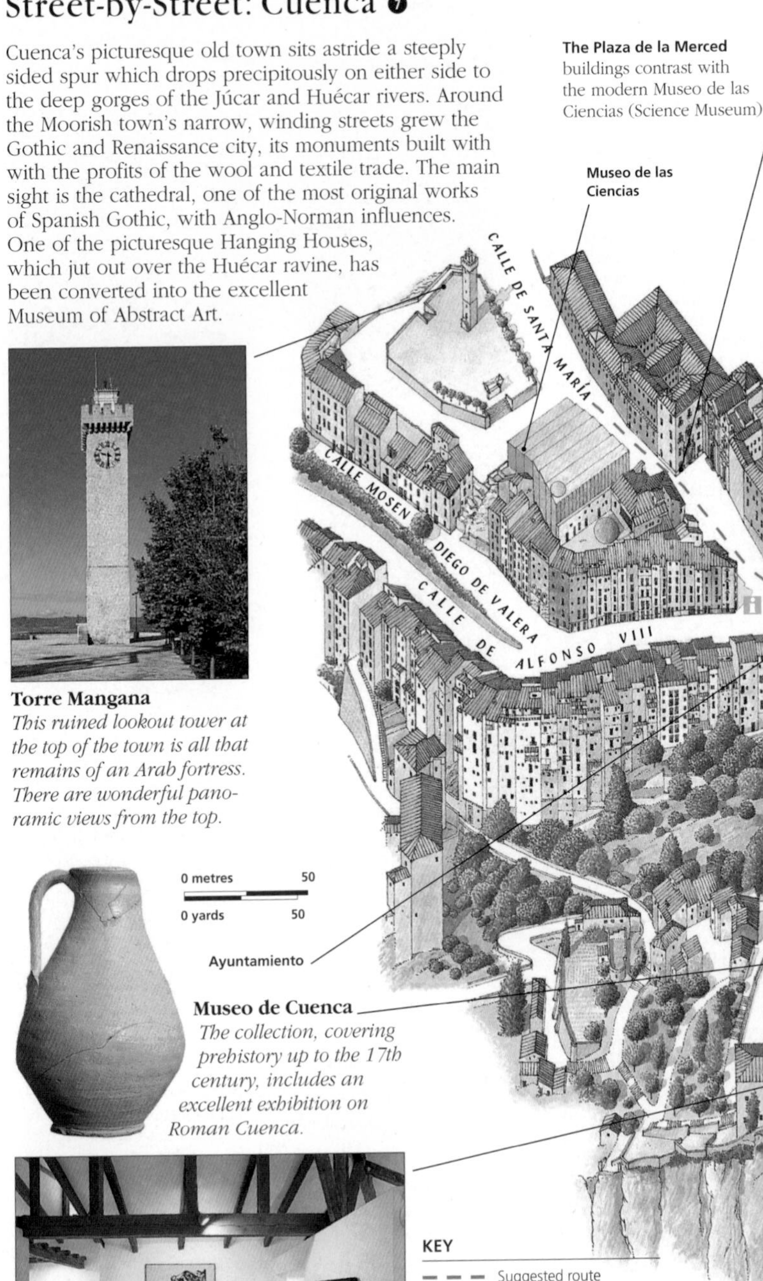

The Plaza de la Merced buildings contrast with the modern Museo de las Ciencias (Science Museum).

Museo de las Ciencias

Torre Mangana
This ruined lookout tower at the top of the town is all that remains of an Arab fortress. There are wonderful panoramic views from the top.

Ayuntamiento

Museo de Cuenca
The collection, covering prehistory up to the 17th century, includes an excellent exhibition on Roman Cuenca.

KEY

— — — Suggested route

★ Museo de Arte Abstracto
Spain's abstract art museum is inside one of the Hanging Houses. It contains works by the movement's leading artists, including Antoni Tàpies and Eduardo Chillida.

Plaza Mayor
This café-lined, arcaded square is in the heart of the old town. The 18th-century Baroque town hall (ayuntamiento), *built with arches, stands at the south end.*

VISITORS' CHECKLIST

Cuenca. 55,900. *Calle Mariano Catalina, 902 32 03 20.* *Calle Fermín Caballero 20, 969 22 70 87.* *Plaza Mayor 1, 969 24 10 51.* *Tue.* **Museo Diocesano** *Tue–Sun.* **Museo de Arte Abstracto** *Tue–Sun.* **Museo de las Ciencias** *Tue–Sun.* **Museo de Cuenca** *Tue–Sat, Sun am.* **www**.cuenca.es

The Iglesia de San Miguel, perched over the Júcar gorge, was built in the Romanic style.

Museo Diocesano
The cathedral's treasures, which are housed in the Palacio Episcopal, include paintings by El Greco.

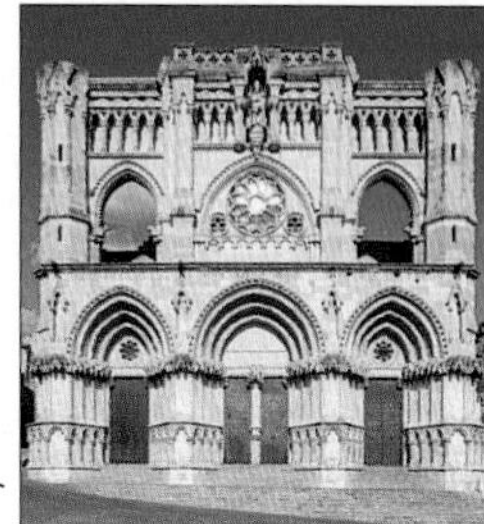

★ Cathedral
Highlights of the 12th- to 18th-century building are the decorated altar, chapter-house and the side chapels.

★ Hanging Houses
The 14th-century beamed Casas Colgadas were once used as a summer residence for the royal family.

STAR SIGHTS

- ★ Museo de Arte Abstracto
- ★ Hanging Houses
- ★ Cathedral

Remains of a Roman building in Segóbriga

Segóbriga ❽

Saelices (Cuenca). ***Tel*** *629 75 22 57.* *Tue–Sun.* **Museum** *1 Jan, last Sat May & 24, 25 & 31 Dec.*

The small ruined Roman city of Segóbriga, near the town of Saelices, is located in open, unspoiled countryside close to the Madrid–Valencia motorway. The Romans who lived here exploited the surrounding area, growing cereals, felling timber and mining minerals.

Many parts of the city can be explored. The 1st-century theatre – which has a capacity of 2,000 people – is sometimes used for dramatic performances today. Segóbriga also had a necropolis, an amphitheatre, a temple to Diana and public baths. The quarries which supplied the stone to build the city can also be seen.

Nearby, there is a small museum containing some of the site's finds, although the best statues are in Cuenca's Museo Arqueológico *(see p384)*.

Monasterio de Uclés ❾

Uclés (Cuenca). ***Tel*** *969 13 50 58.* *10am–6pm daily (till 8pm Jul & Aug).* *1 & 6 Jan, 25 Dec.*

The small village of Uclés, to the south of the Alcarria, is dominated by its impressive castle-monastery, nicknamed "El Escorial de La Mancha" for the similarity of its church's profile to that of El Escorial *(see pp330–31)*. Originally an impregnable medieval fortress, Uclés became the monastery seat of the Order of Santiago from 1174, because of its central location. The austere building you see today, used as a seminary school, is mainly Renaissance, but overlaid with ornamental Baroque detail. It has a magnificent carved wooden ceiling and staircase.

Illescas ❿

Toledo. *23,500.* *Plaza Mercado 14, 925 51 10 51.* *Thu.* *Fiesta de Milagro (11 May), Virgen de la Caridad (31 Aug).* **www**.illescas.es

Just off the Madrid–Toledo motorway, Illescas was the summer location for Felipe II's court. While there is little to see of its old town, the 16th-century **Hospital de la Caridad**, near the Iglesia de Santa María (12th–13th century and renovated in the 15th), has an important art collection, including five late El Grecos *(see p373)*. The subjects of three of these are the Nativity, the Annunciation and the Coronation of the Virgin.

Hospital de la Caridad
Calle Cardenal Cisneros 2. ***Tel*** *925 54 00 35.* *daily.*

Talavera de la Reina ⓫

Toledo. *89,000.* *C/ Palenque 2, 925 82 63 22.* *Wed & 1st Sat of month.* *Las Mondas (Sat after Easter), Feria de San Isidro (15–18 May), Virgen del Prado (8 Sep), Feria de San Mateo (20–23 Sep).*

A ruined 15th-century bridge across the Tagus marks the entrance to the old part of this busy market town. From the bridge you can walk past the surviving part of the Moorish and medieval wall to the 12th-century **collegiate church**. It has a small but beautiful Gothic cloister, and the belfry is from the 18th century.

Talavera's ceramic workshops still produce the blue and yellow *azulejos* (tiles) which have been a trademark of the town since the 16th century; but nowadays they also make domestic and decorative objects.

Ceramics in Talavera workshop

A good selection of *azulejos* can be seen in the large **Ermita de la Virgen del Prado** by the river. Many of the interior walls have superb 16th- to 20th-century tile friezes of religious scenes.

Part of a frieze of tiles in Talavera's Ermita del Virgen del Prado

Traditional embroidery work in Lagartera, near Oropesa

Oropesa ⓬

Toledo. *2,900.* *Calle Hospital 9, 925 43 02 01.* *Mon & Thu.* *Virgen de Peñitas (8–10 Sep), Beato Alonso de Orozco (19 Sep).*

Oropesa's medieval and Renaissance splendour as one of Toledo's satellite communities has left a charming old quarter at the centre of today's small farming town. A circular Ruta Monumental starts from the massive, mainly 15th-century **castle** on the top of the hill. A Renaissance extension – thought to be the work of Juan de Herrera, co-architect of El Escorial *(see pp330–31)* – was added to the castle in the 16th century by the wealthy and influential Álvarez family. A large part of the castle has been converted into a parador *(see p587)*.

The Ruta Monumental continues around the town, taking in a number of churches, convents, a small ceramics museum and the town hall which presides over the main square.

Environs

The area around Oropesa is excellent for buying handicrafts. **Lagartera**, just to the west of the town, is famous for the embroidery and lacework by the women in the village and **El Puente del Arzobispo**, 12 km (7 miles) south of Oropesa, is a good source of painted ceramics and esparto (grass-weaving) work. **Ciudad de Vascos**, further southeast, is a ruined 10th-century Arab city in splendid countryside around Azután.

Montes de Toledo ⓭

Toledo. *Pueblo Nuevo del Bullaque.* *Parque Nacional de Cabañeros, 926 78 32 97.*

To the southwest of Toledo a range of low mountains sweeps towards Extremadura. In medieval times the Montes de Toledo were owned by bishops and the kings. They cover an area of approximately 1,000 sq km (386 sq miles).

The attractive nature reserve of the **Parque Nacional de Cabañeros** *(see pp30–31)* encloses a sizeable area of woodland and pastures used for grazing sheep. The easiest access to the park is from **Pueblo Nuevo del Bullaque**. From here it is possible to make four-hour guided trips in Land Rovers, during which you may spot wild boar, deer and imperial eagles. In the pasturelands stand *chozos*, conical refuges for shepherds.

In the eastern foothills of the Montes de Toledo is **Orgaz**, with a parish church which contains works by El Greco. Nearby villages, such as **Los Yébenes** and **Ventas con Peña Aguilera**, are known for their leather goods and restaurants serving game.

On the plains stands the small church of **Santa María de Melque**, believed to date back to the 8th century. Close by is the Templar castle of **Montalbán**, a vast but ruined 12th-century fortress. Nearer to Toledo, at **Guadamur**, there is another handsome castle.

A *chozo* (shepherd's cabin) in the Parque Nacional de Cabañeros

CASTILLA-LA MANCHA'S FIESTAS

La Endiablada *(2–3 Feb)* Almonacid del Marquesado (Cuenca). At the start of the two-day-long "Fiesta of the Bewitched", men and boys, gaudily dressed as "devils", with cowbells strapped to their backs, gather in the house of their leader, the *Diablo Mayor*. They accompany the images of the Virgen de la Candelaria (Virgin of Candlemas) and St Blaise in procession. As the devils dance alongside the floats bearing the saints' images, they ring their bells loudly and incessantly.

One of the so-called "devils" in La Endiablada fiesta

Romería del Cristo del Sahúco *(Pentecost, May/Jun)*, Peñas de San Pedro (Albacete). A cross-shaped coffin bearing a figure of Christ is carried 15 km (9 miles) here from its shrine by men dressed in white.

La Caballada *(early Jun)*, Atienza (Guadalajara). Horsemen follow the route across country taken by the 12th-century muleteers of Atienza, who are said to have saved the boy King Alfonso VIII of Castile from his uncle, Fernando II.

Corpus Christi *(May/Jun)*, Toledo. One of Spain's most dramatic Corpus Christi *(see p38)* processions. The cathedral monstrance *(see p392)* is paraded in the streets.

Street-by-Street: Toledo ⓮

Damascene work, typical of Toledo

Picturesquely sited on a hill above the River Tagus is the historic centre of Toledo. Behind the old walls lies much evidence of the city's rich history. The Romans built a fortress on the site of the present-day Alcázar. The Visigoths made Toledo their capital in the 6th century AD, and left behind several churches. In the Middle Ages, Toledo was a melting pot of Christian, Muslim and Jewish cultures, and it was during this period that the city's most outstanding monument – its cathedral – was built. In the 16th century the painter El Greco came to live in Toledo, and today the city is home to many of his works.

The Iglesia de San Román, of Visigothic origin, now contains a museum relating the city's past under the Visigoths.

Puerta Cristo de la Cruz

0 metres 100

0 yards 100

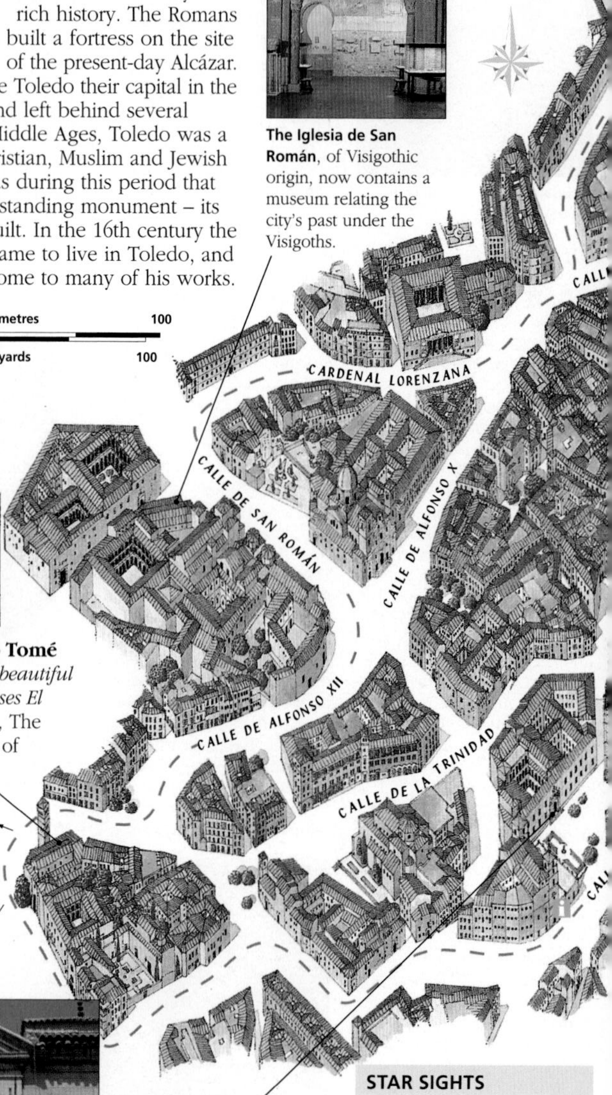

★ Iglesia de Santo Tomé

This church, with a beautiful Mudéjar tower, houses El Greco's masterpiece, The Burial of the Count of Orgaz (see p32).

To Sinagoga de Santa María la Blanca and Monasterio de San Juan de los Reyes

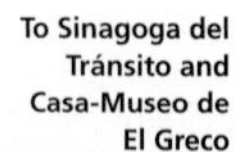

To Sinagoga del Tránsito and Casa-Museo de El Greco

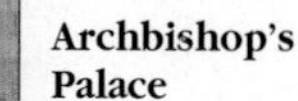

Archbishop's Palace

Spread over a large block, with façades on three streets, this 16th-century palace features an austere Renaissance design.

STAR SIGHTS

- ★ Iglesia de Santo Tomé
- ★ Cathedral
- ★ Museo de Santa Cruz

Puerta de Sol has a double ...rish arch and ... two towers.

Mezquita del Cristo de la Luz
This mosque, one of the city's two remaining Muslim buildings, dates from around AD 1000.

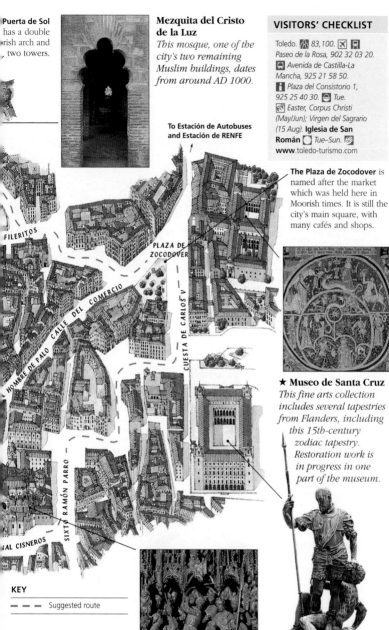

VISITORS' CHECKLIST

Toledo. 83,100. *Paseo de la Rosa, 902 32 03 20.* *Avenida de Castilla-La Mancha, 925 21 58 50.* *Plaza del Consistorio 1, 925 25 40 30.* *Tue.* *Easter, Corpus Christi (May/Jun); Virgen del Sagrario (15 Aug).* **Iglesia de San Román** *Tue–Sun.* **www**.toledo-turismo.com

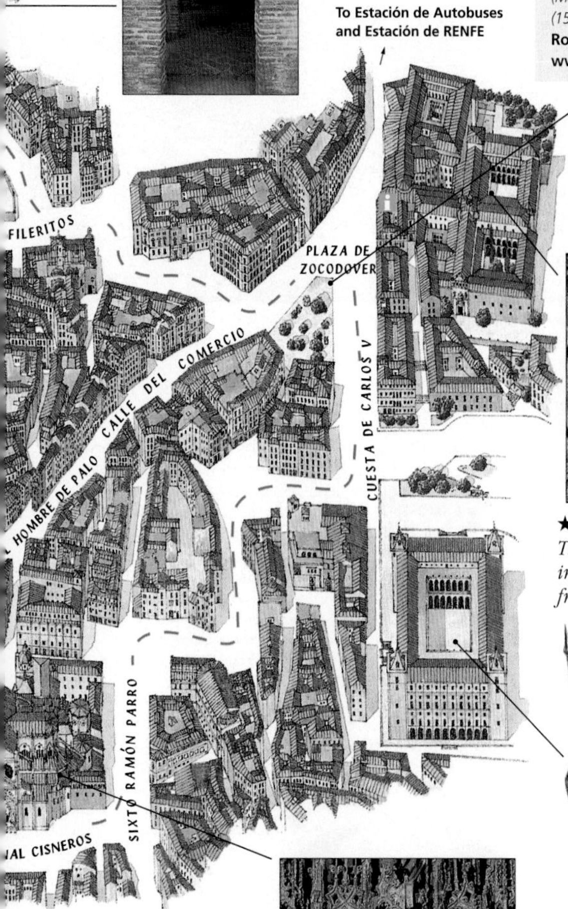

To Estación de Autobuses and Estación de RENFE

FILERITOS

PLAZA DE ZOCODOVER

CALLE DEL COMERCIO

HOMBRE DE PALO

CUESTA DE CARLOS V

SIXTO RAMÓN PARRO

...AL CISNEROS

The Plaza de Zocodover is named after the market which was held here in Moorish times. It is still the city's main square, with many cafés and shops.

★ Museo de Santa Cruz
This fine arts collection includes several tapestries from Flanders, including this 15th-century zodiac tapestry. Restoration work is in progress in one part of the museum.

Alcázar
The National Army Museum is housed here. In the central patio is a replica of the statue Carlos V y el Furor.

KEY

— — — Suggested route

★ Cathedral
Built on the site of a Visigothic cathedral and a mosque, this impressive structure is one of the largest cathedrals in Christendom (see pp392–3)*. The Flamboyant Gothic high altar reredos (1504) is the work of several artists.*

Toledo Cathedral rising above the rooftops of the medieval part of the city

Exploring Toledo

Toledo is easily reached from Madrid by rail, bus or car, and is then best explored on foot. To visit all the main sights you need at least two days, but it is possible to walk around the medieval and Jewish quarters in a long morning. To avoid the heavy crowds, go midweek and stay for a night, when the city is at its most atmospheric.

Alcázar

Cuesta de Carlos V. **Tel** *925 23 88 00.* *Thu–Sun am.* *(free Sun).*

Charles V's fortified palace stands on the site of former Roman, Visigothic and Muslim fortresses. Its severe square profile suffered damage by fire three times before being almost completely destroyed in 1936 when the Nationalists survived a 70-day siege by the Republicans. Restoration followed the original plans and the siege headquarters have been preserved as a monument to Nationalist heroism. The former National Museo del Ejército was transferred from Madrid to this building, making the Alcázar the main army museum in Spain.

The Borbón-Lorenzana Library (open to the public) contains 100,000 books and manuscripts from the 16th to 19th centuries.

Museo de Santa Cruz

Calle Miguel de Cervantes 3. **Tel** *925 22 10 36.* *daily (am only on Sun).* **www**.patrimoniohistoricoclm.es

This museum is housed in a 16th-century hospital founded by Cardinal Mendoza. The building has some outstanding Renaissance architectural features, including the main doorway, staircase and cloister. The four main wings, laid out in the shape of a Greek cross, are dedicated to the fine arts. The collection is especially strong in medieval and Renaissance tapestries, paintings and sculptures. There are also works by El Greco, including one of his last paintings, *The Assumption* (1613), still in its original altarpiece. Decorative arts on display include two typically Toledan crafts: armour and damascened swords, made by inlaying blackened steel with gold wire. Damascene work, such as plates and jewellery (as well as swords), is still produced in the city.

The Assumption **by El Greco (1613) in the Museo de Santa Cruz**

Iglesia de Santo Tomé

Plaza del Conde 4. **Tel** *925 25 60 98.* *daily.* **www**.santotome.org

Visitors come to Santo Tomé mainly to admire El Greco's masterpiece, *The Burial of the Count of Orgaz* *(see p32)*. The Count paid for much of the 14th-century building that stands today. The painting, commissioned in his memory by a parish priest, depicts the miraculous appearance of St Augustine and St Stephen at his burial, to raise his body to heaven. It has never been moved from the setting for which it was painted, nor restored. Nevertheless, it is remarkable for its contrast of glowing and sombre colours. In the foreground, allegedly, are the artist and his son (both looking out) as well as Cervates. The church is thought to date back to the 11th century, and its tower is a fine example of Mudéjar architecture.

Nearby is the **Pastelería Santo Tomé**, a good place to buy locally made marzipan.

Sinagoga de Santa María la Blanca

Calle de los Reyes Católicos 4. **Tel** *925 22 72 57.* *daily.* *1 Jan, 25 Dec.*

The oldest and largest of the city's original synagogues, this monument dates back to the 12–13th century. In 1405 it was taken over as a church by San Vincente Ferrer after the expulsion of the Jews. Restoration has returned it to its original beauty – carved stone capitals and wall panels stand out against white horse-shoe arches and plaster-work. In the main chapel is a Plater-esque altarpiece. In 1391 a massacre of Jews took place on this site, a turning point after years of religious tolerance in the city.

Mudéjar arches in the Sinagoga de Santa María la Blanca

Sinagoga del Tránsito, Museo Sefardí

C/ Samuel Leví. **Tel** *925 22 36 65.* *Tue–Sun (Sun am only).* *public hols.* *(free Sat pm & Sun).* **www**.museosefardi.net

The most elaborate Mudéjar interior in the city is hidden behind the deceptively humble façade of this former synagogue, built in the 14th century by Samuel Ha-Leví, the Jewish treasurer to Pedro the Cruel. The interlaced frieze of the lofty prayer hall harmoniously fuses Islamic, Gothic and Hebrew geometric motifs below a wonderful coffered ceiling.

The synagogue houses a museum of Sephardi (Spanish Jewish) culture. The items on display date from both before and after the Jews' expulsion from Spain in the late 15th century *(see p57)*.

Ornate ceiling in the Monasterio de San Juan de los Reyes

Monasterio de San Juan de los Reyes

Calle de los Reyes Católicos 17. **Tel** *925 22 38 02.* *daily.* *(ground floor only).* **www**. sanjuandelosreyes.org

A wonderful mixture of architectural styles, this monastery was commissioned by the Catholic Monarchs in honour of their victory at the battle of Toro in 1476 *(see p357)*. It was originally intended to be their burial place, but they were actually laid to rest in Granada *(see p486)*. Largely the work of Juan Guas, the church's main Isabelline structure was completed in 1496. Although it was badly damaged by Napoleon's troops in 1808 *(see p63)*, it has been restored to its original splendour with features such as a Gothic cloister (1510) which has a multicoloured Mudéjar ceiling. Near to the church is a stretch of the Jewish quarter's original wall.

Museo del Greco

Paseo del Tránsito. **Tel** *925 22 36 65.* *Tue–Sun.* *Mon, Sun pm.* *(free Sat pm, Sun).* **http**://museodelgreco.mcu.es

It is not clear whether El Greco actually lived in or simply near to this house in the heart of the Jewish quarter, now a museum housing a collection of his works. Canvases on display include *View of Toledo*, a detailed depiction of the city at the time, and the superb series *Christ and the Apostles*. Underneath the museum, on the ground floor, is a domestic chapel with a fine Mudéjar ceiling and a collection of art by painters of the Toledan School.

Iglesia de Santiago del Arrabal

Calle Real del Arrabal. *closed to the public.*

This is one of Toledo's most beautiful Mudéjar monuments. It can be easily identified by its tower, which dates from the 12th-century Reconquest *(see pp54–5)*. The church, which was built slightly later, has a beautiful woodwork ceiling and an ornate Mudéjar pulpit, but only the exterior of the building can be visited.

Puerta Antigua de Bisagra

When Alfonso VI conquered Toledo in 1085, he entered it through this gateway, alongside El Cid. It is the only gateway in the city to have kept its original 10th-century military architecture. The huge towers are topped by a 12th-century Arab gatehouse.

EL GRECO

Born in Crete in 1541, El Greco ("the Greek") came to Toledo in 1577 to paint the altarpiece in the convent of Santo Domingo el Antiguo. Enchanted by the city, he stayed here, painting religious portraits and altarpieces for other churches. Although El Greco was trained in Italy and influenced by masters such as Tintoretto, his works are closely identified with the city where he settled. He died in Toledo in 1614.

Domenikos Theotocopoulos, better known as El Greco

Toledo Cathedral

The splendour of Toledo's massive cathedral reflects its history as the spiritual heart of the Church in Spain and the seat of the Primate of all Spain. The Mozarabic Mass, which dates back to Visigothic times, is still said here today. The present cathedral was built on the site of a 7th-century church. Work began in 1226 and spanned three centuries, until the completion of the last vaults in 1493. This long period of construction explains the cathedral's mixture of styles: pure French Gothic – complete with flying buttresses – on the exterior; with Spanish decorative styles, such as Mudéjar and Plateresque work, used in the interior.

★ Sacristy
El Greco's The Denuding of Christ, *above the marble altar, was painted especially for the cathedral. Also here are works by Titian, Van Dyck and Goya.*

View of Toledo Cathedral
Dominating the city skyline is the Gothic tower at the west end of the nave. The best view of the cathedral, and the city, is from the parador (see p588).

The Cloister, on two floors, was built in the 14th century on the site of the old Jewish market.

The belfry in the tower contains a heavy bell known as *La Gorda* ("the Fat One").

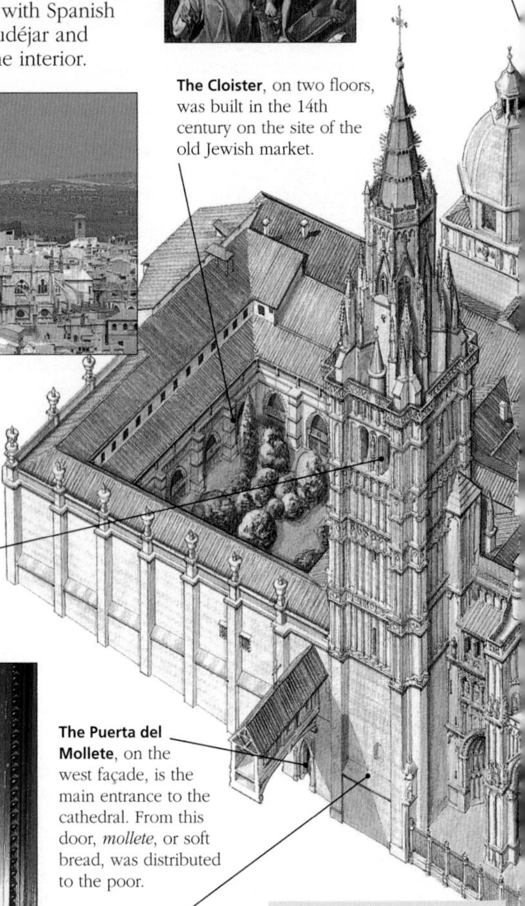

The Puerta del Mollete, on the west façade, is the main entrance to the cathedral. From this door, *mollete*, or soft bread, was distributed to the poor.

Monstrance
In the Treasury is the 16th-century Gothic silver and gold monstrance. It is carried through the streets of Toledo during the Corpus Christi celebrations (see p387).

STAR FEATURES

- ★ Sacristy
- ★ Choir
- ★ High Altar Reredos
- ★ Transparente

★ Transparente
This Baroque altarpiece of marble, jasper and bronze, by Narciso Tomé, is illuminated by an ornate sky-light. It stands out from the mainly Gothic interior.

VISITORS' CHECKLIST

Calle Cardenal Cisneros 1.
Tel *925 22 22 41.* *10am–6:30pm daily (from 2pm Sun).* *8am, 10am, 10:30am, 5:30pm, 6:30pm Mon–Sat; 8am, 9am, 11am, noon, 1pm, 5:30pm, 6:30pm Sun (Catholic); 9am Mon–Sat, 9:45am Sun (Monzarabic).*
Choir, Treasury, Sacristy and Chapterhouse *as above.*
arranged by tourist office. **www**.visitclm.com

Capilla de Santiago

The Capilla de San Ildefonso contains the superb Plateresque tomb of Cardinal Alonso Carrillo de Albornoz.

Puerta de los Leones

Entrance via Puerta Llana

The Puerta del Perdón, or Door of Mercy, has a tympanum decorated with religious characters.

The Capilla Mozárabe has a beautiful Renaissance ironwork grille, carved by Juan Francés in 1524.

Chapterhouse
Above 16th-century frescoes by Juan de Borgoña is this multicoloured Mudéjar ceiling, unique in the city.

★ High Altar Reredos
The polychrome reredos, one of the most beautiful in Spain, depicts scenes from Christ's life.

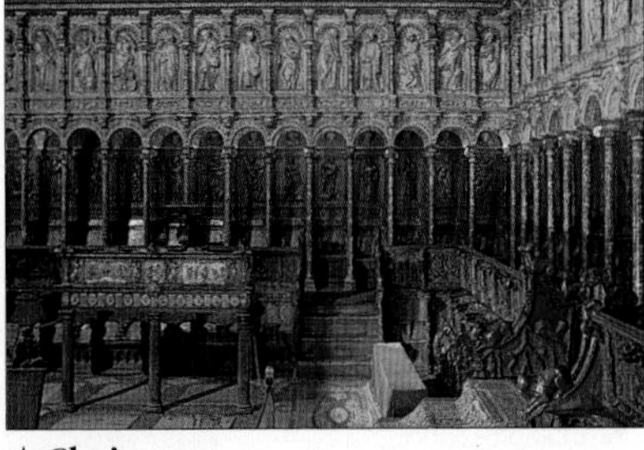

★ Choir
The carvings on the wooden lower stalls depict scenes of the fall of Granada. The alabaster upper ones show figures from the Old Testament.

Windmills on the ridge above Consuegra, overlooking the plains of La Mancha

Tembleque ⓯

Toledo. 2,300. Plaza Mayor 1, 925 14 55 53. Wed. Jesús de Nazareno (23–27 Aug).

The well-preserved stone Plaza Mayor *(see p27)* at Tembleque dates from the 17th century. It is decorated with the red cross of the Knights Hospitallers, the military order which once ruled the town.

Environs

Ocaña, 30 km (20 miles) north of Tembleque, centres on the huge yet elegant, late 18th-century *plaza mayor*, the third largest town square in Spain, after Madrid and Salamanca.

Consuegra ⓰

Toledo. 11,000. Molino Bolero s/n, Cerro Calderico, 925 47 57 31. Sat. Consuegra Medieval (mid-Aug), La Rosa de Azafrán (last weekend Oct).

Consuegra's 11 windmills *(see p27)* and restored castle stand on a ridge, overlooking the plains of La Mancha. One windmill is set in motion every year during the town's festival to celebrate the autumn harvest of saffron *(see p338)*. During the fiesta, pickers compete to see who can strip petals from the saffron crocus the fastest.

Environs

About 4 km (2 miles) from Consuegra, on the road to **Urda**, is a Roman dam. An old restaurant *(see p638)* at **Puerto Lápice**, off the A4 20 km (13 miles) south of Consuegra, claims to be the inn in which Don Quixote was "knighted" by the landlord.

Campo de Criptana ⓱

Ciudad Real. 15,000. C/ Barbero 1, 926 56 22 31 (closed Mon). Tue. Virgen de Criptana (Easter Mon), Cristos de Villejos (first Thu in Aug), Ferias (23–28 Aug).

The remaining ten windmills of what was once La Mancha's largest group – 32 – stand on a hillcrest in the town. Three are 16th-century and have their original machinery intact. One is the tourist information office, and three others are museums.

Environs

More windmills stand above **Alcázar de San Juan** and **Mota del Cuervo**, a good place to buy *queso Manchego*, local sheep's cheese *(see p339)*.

El Toboso ⓲

Toledo. 2,200. C/ Antonio Machado, 925 56 82 26 (closed Mon). Wed. Carnival (17–20 Jan), Cervantes Days (23 Apr), San Agustín (27–30 Aug). **www**.eltoboso.org

Of all the villages of La Mancha claiming links to Don Quixote, El Toboso has the clearest ties. It was chosen by Cervantes as the birthplace of Dulcinea, Don Quixote's sweetheart. The **Casa de Dulcinea**, the home of Doña Ana Martínez Zarco, on whom Dulcinea was allegedly based, has been refurbished in its original 16th-century style.

The French army allegedly refused to attack the village during the War of Independence *(see pp62–3)*.

Casa de Dulcinea
Tel *925 19 72 88. Tue–Sun. (free Sun am).*

Belmonte ⓳

Cuenca. 2,200. Avenida Luis Pinedo, 967 17 07 41. Mon. San Bartolomé (24 Aug); Virgen de Gracia (second weekend of Sep).

Belmonte's magnificent 15th-century **castle** *(see p344)* is one of the best preserved in the region. It was built by Juan Pacheco, Marquis of Villena, after Enrique IV gave him the town in 1456. Inside it has decorative carved coffered ceilings, and Mudéjar plasterwork. The **collegiate church** is especially remarkable for its

Belmonte's splendid 15th-century castle

richly decorated chapels and Gothic choir stalls, which were brought here from Cuenca cathedral *(see p385)*. There is also outstanding ironwork, a Renaissance reredos and the font at which the Golden Age poet Fray Luis de León (1527–91), was baptized.

Environs

Two villages near Belmonte also flourished under the Marquis of Villena. The church at **Villaescusa de Haro**, 6 km (4 miles) to the northeast, has an outstanding 16th-century reredos. **San Clemente**, some 40 km (25 miles) further southeast, clusters around two near-perfect Renaissance squares. There is a Gothic alabaster cross in the Iglesia de Santiago Apóstol.

Castillo de Belmonte
Tel *690 203 076. Tue–Sun.*

The castle of Alarcón, which has been converted into a parador

Alarcón ⑳

Cuenca. 200. Calle Posadas 6, 969 33 03 01. San Sebastián (20 Jan), Fiesta del Emigrante (2nd w/end in Aug), Cristo de la Fe (14 Sep).

Perfectly preserved, the fortified village of Alarcón guards a narrow loop of the Río Júcar from on top of a rock. As you drive through its defences, you may have the impression of entering a film set for a medieval epic.

The village dates back to the 8th century. It became a key military base for the Reconquest *(see pp54–5)* and was recaptured from the Moors by Alfonso VIII in 1184 following a nine-month siege. It was later acquired by the Marquis of Villena. Alarcón has dramatic walls and three defensive precincts. The small, triangular **castle**, high above the river, has been turned into a parador *(see p586)*, preserving much of its medieval atmosphere.

The **Iglesia de Santa María** is a Renaissance church with a fine portico and an altarpiece attributed to the Berruguete school. The nearby **Iglesia de Santísima Trinidad** is in Gothic-Plateresque style *(see p25)*.

The chalk cliffs of Alcalá del Júcar, honeycombed with tunnels

Alcalá del Júcar ㉑

Albacete. 1,350. Av de los Robles 1, 967 47 30 90 (winter: Sat & Sun only). Sun. San Lorenzo (7–15 Aug). **www**.alcaladeljucar.net

Where the Rio Júcar runs through the chalk hills to the northeast of Albacete, it cuts a deep, winding gorge, the Hoz de Júcar, along which you can drive for a stretch of 40 km (25 miles). Alcalá del Júcar is dramatically sited on the side of a spur of rock jutting out into the gorge. The town is a warren of steep alleys and flights of steps. At the top of the town, below the castle, houses have been extended by digging caves into the soft rock. Some of these have been transformed into tunnels cut from one side of the spur to the other.

Environs: To the west, the gorge runs past fertile orchards to the Baroque **Ermita de San Lorenzo**. Further on is the picturesque village of **Jorquera**, which was an independent state for a brief period during the Middle Ages, refusing to be ruled by the crown. It retains its Arab walls. A collection of shields is on display in the Casa del Corregidor.

DON QUIXOTE'S LA MANCHA

Cervantes *(see p333)* doesn't specify where his hero was born but several places are mentioned in the novel. Don Quixote is knighted in an inn in Puerto Lápice, believing it to be a castle. His sweetheart, Dulcinea, lives in El Toboso. The windmills he tilts at, imagining them to be giants, are thought to be those at Campo de Criptana. Another adventure takes place in the Cueva de Montesinos *(see p397)*.

Illustration from a 19th-century edition of *Don Quixote*

Albacete 22

Albacete. 171,500. Calle Tinte 2, 967 58 05 22. Tue. Virgen de los Llanos (8 Sep).

Although labelled as one of Spain's least interesting cities, this provincial capital is not without its attractions. The excellent **Museo de Albacete** is located in a pleasant park and has exhibits ranging from Iberian sculptures and unique Roman amber and ivory dolls to 20th-century paintings. The **cathedral**, begun in 1515 and devoted to San Juan Bautista, has Renaissance altarpieces.

Albacete, also known for its daggers and jackknives, crafted here since Muslim times, holds an agricultural fair, every year.

Museo de Albacete
Parque Abelardo Sánchez. **Tel** *967 22 83 07. Tue–Sun (Jul–mid-Sep: am only). (free Sat & Sun).*

The castle of Chinchilla de Monte Aragón, overlooking the town

Environs
Chinchilla de Monte Aragón, 12 km (7 miles) to the south-east, has a well-preserved old quarter. Above the town is the shell of its 15th-century castle (closed to the public).

Almansa, 70 km (43 miles) further east, is dominated by another imposing castle, which is of Moorish origin.

Alcaraz 24

Albacete. 1,600. Plaza Mayor 1, 967 38 08 27 (winter: closed Mon). Wed. Canto de Los Mayos (30 Apr–1 May), La Romería de la Virgen (26 Aug, 8 Sep), Feria (4–9 Sep).

An important Arab and Christian stronghold, Alcaraz's military power waned after the Reconquest but its economy flourished around its (now defunct) carpet-making industry.

Standing in the attractive Renaissance Plaza Mayor are the "twin towers" of **Tardón**

Sierra de Alcaraz 23

Where the Sierras of Segura and Alcaraz push northwards into the southeastern plains of La Mancha, they form spectacular mountains, broken up by dramatic gorges and fertile valleys. The source of the Río Mundo is a favourite beauty spot. Nearby Riópar, perched on the side of the mountain, has a 15th-century parish church. Among the less-explored villages, Letur, Ayna, Yeste and Liétor are especially picturesque. Their narrow, winding streets and craft traditions clearly reflect their Muslim origins.

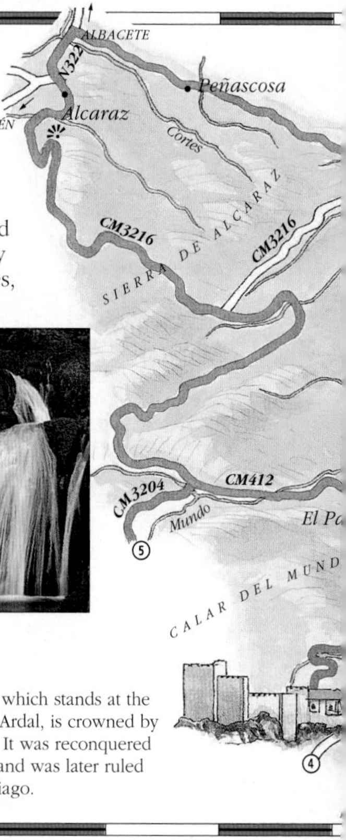

Source of the Río Mundo ⑤
The river begins as a waterfall, inside the Cueva de Los Chorros, and tumbles down a dramatic cliff face into a bubbling spring at the bottom.

Yeste ④
The village of Yeste, which stands at the foot of the Sierra de Ardal, is crowned by a hilltop Arab castle. It was reconquered under Fernando III, and was later ruled by the Order of Santiago.

0 kilometres 5

0 miles 5

KEY

- Tour route
- Other roads
- Viewpoint

and **Trinidad**, and an 18th-century commodity exchange, the **Lonja del Corregidor**, with Plateresque decoration. The square is surrounded by lively, narrow streets. On the outskirts of the town are the castle ruins and surviving arch of a Gothic aqueduct. Alcaraz makes a good base for touring the sierras of Alcaraz and Segura.

The "twin towers" of Tardón and Trinidad on Alcaraz's main square

Lagunas de Ruidera ㉕

Ciudad Real. Ruidera.
Ruidera (Sep–Jun: Wed–Sun, Jul–Aug: daily), 926 52 81 16.
www.lagunasderuidera.es

Once nicknamed "The Mirrors of La Mancha", the 15 interconnected lakes which make up the Parque Natural de las Lagunas de Ruidera stretch for 39 km (24 miles) through a valley. They allegedly take their name from a story in *Don Quixote* *(see p395)* in which a certain Mistress Ruidera, her daughters and her nieces are said to have been turned into lakes by a magician.

Although La Mancha's falling water table has led to a decline in the amount of water in the lakes, they are still worth visiting for their wealth of wildlife, which includes great and little bustards, herons and many types of duck. The wildlife has increasingly come under threat

One of the lakes in the Parque Natural de las Lagunas de Ruidera

due to the number of tourists, and the development of holiday chalets on the lakes' shores. Near one of the lakes, the Laguna de San Pedro, is the **Cueva de Montesinos**, a deep, explorable cave which was also used as the setting for an episode in *Don Quixote*.

To the northwest, the lakes link up with the Embalse de Peñarroya reservoir.

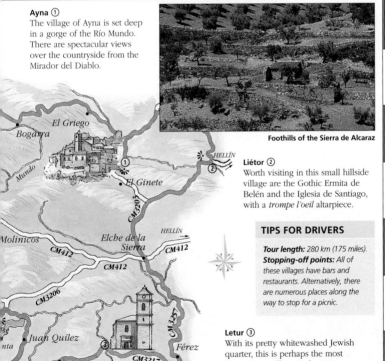

Ayna ①
The village of Ayna is set deep in a gorge of the Río Mundo. There are spectacular views over the countryside from the Mirador del Diablo.

Foothills of the Sierra de Alcaraz

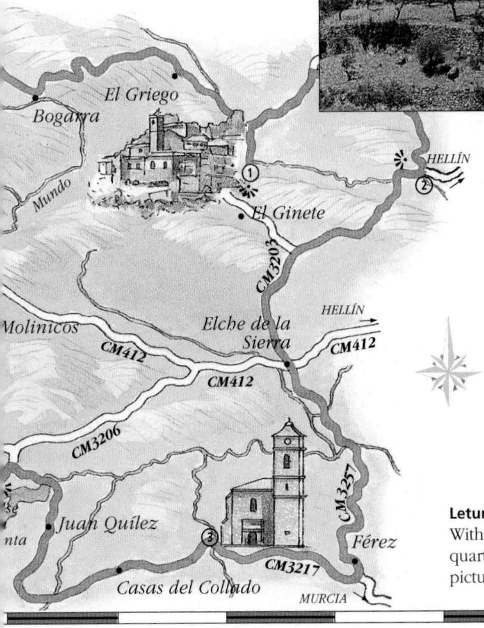

Liétor ②
Worth visiting in this small hillside village are the Gothic Ermita de Belén and the Iglesia de Santiago, with a *trompe l'oeil* altarpiece.

TIPS FOR DRIVERS

Tour length: *280 km (175 miles).*
Stopping-off points: *All of these villages have bars and restaurants. Alternatively, there are numerous places along the way to stop for a picnic.*

Letur ③
With its pretty whitewashed Jewish quarter, this is perhaps the most picturesque village in the area.

Villanueva de los Infantes ㉖

Ciudad Real. 5,800. Plaza Mayor 3, 926 36 13 21. Fri. Cruz de Mayo (2–3 May), Ferias (late Aug), Virgen de Antigua (8 Sep), Santo Tomás (18 Sep). **www**.infantes.org

Villanueva's old town, which centres on the graceful Neo-Classical Plaza Mayor, is one of the most attractive in La Mancha. Many buildings on the square have wooden balconies and arcades. Also on the square is the **Iglesia de San Andrés**, which has a Renaissance façade. Inside are a Baroque altarpiece and organ, as well as the now empty tomb of the Golden Age author Francisco de Quevedo. He lived and died in the **Convento de los Domínicos**.

Environs

The village of **San Carlos del Valle**, 25 km (15 miles) to the northwest, has an 18th-century square and galleried houses of rust-red stone.

Valdepeñas ㉗

Ciudad Real. 31,000. Plaza de España, 926 31 25 52. Thu. Grape Harvest (1–8 Sep). **www**.valdepenas.es

Valdepeñas is the capital of La Mancha's vast wine region, the world's largest expanse of vineyards, producing vast quantities of red wine *(see pp202–3)*. This largely modern town comes alive for its wine festival in September. In the network of older streets around the café-lined Plaza de España are the **Iglesia de la Asunción** and the municipal museum.

Valdepeñas has over 30 bodegas that can be visited. One of them has been converted into the **Museo del Vino**, illustrating the various stages of wine production.

Museo del Vino
Calle Princesa 39. ***Tel*** *926 32 11 11.* *Tue–Sat & Sun am.*

Courtyard of the Palacio del Viso in Viso del Marqués

Viso del Marqués ㉘

Ciudad Real. 2,750. Calle Real 39, 926 33 68 15 (closed Sun & Mon). Tue. San Andrés (second Sun of May), Feria (24–28 Jul). **www**.visodelmarques.es

The small village of Viso del Marqués in La Mancha is the unlikely setting of the **Palacio del Viso**, a grand Renaissance mansion commissioned in 1564 by the Marquis of Santa Cruz, the admiral of the fleet that defeated the Turks at Lepanto in 1571 *(see p59)*. One of the main features of the house is a Classical patio. Inside, the main rooms are decorated with Italian frescoes.

Environs

About 25 km (16 miles) to the northeast of Viso del Marqués is Spain's oldest bullring at **Las Virtudes**. Square and galleried, it was built in 1641 next to a 14th-century church, which has a Churrigueresque altarpiece.

Palacio del Viso
Plaza del Pradillo 12. ***Tel*** *926 33 75 18.* *Tue–Sun.* *Sun pm.*

Calatrava la Nueva ㉙

Ciudad Real. Aldea de Rey. ***Tel*** *926 69 31 19.* *Tue–Sun.* **www**.visitclm.com

Magnificent in its isolated hilltop setting, the ruined castle-monastery of Calatrava la Nueva is reached by a stretch of original medieval road.

It was founded in 1217 by the Knights of Calatrava, Spain's first military-religious order *(see p54)*, to be their headquarters. The complex is of huge proportions, with a double patio and a church with a triple nave. The church has been restored and is illuminated by a beautiful rose window above the entrance.

Expanse of vineyards near Valdepeñas

Calatrava la Nueva castle-monastery, dominating the plains of La Mancha

After the Reconquest, the building continued to be used as a monastery until it was abandoned in 1802 following fire damage.

Opposite the castle are the ruins of a Muslim frontier fortress, **Salvatierra**, which was captured from the Moors by the Order of Calatrava in the 12th century.

Almagro ㉚

Ciudad Real. *9,000.* *Plaza Mayor 1, 926 86 07 17.* *Wed.* *Virgen de las Nieves (5 Aug), San Bartolomé (23–24 Aug).* **www**.ciudad-almagro.com

Almagro was disputed during the Reconquest, until the Order of Calatrava captured it and built the castle of Calatrava la Nueva to the southwest of the town. The rich architectural heritage of the atmospheric old town is partly the legacy of the Fugger brothers, the Habsburgs' bankers who settled in nearby Almadén during the 16th century.

The town's main attraction is its colonnaded stone plaza, with characteristic enclosed, green balconies. On one side is a 17th-century courtyard-theatre – the **Corral de Comedias** – where a drama festival is held for the Festival de Teatro Clásico every summer.

Other monuments worth seeing include the Fuggers' Renaissance warehouse and former university, and also the parador *(see p586)*.

Environs

To the northwest is **Ciudad Real**, founded by Alfonso X the Learned in 1255. Its sights include the Iglesia de San Pedro and the Mudéjar gateway, the Puerta de Toledo.

Raised walkway in the Parque Nacional de Las Tablas de Daimiel

Tablas de Daimiel ㉛

Ciudad Real. *Daimiel.* *Daimiel, Calle Santa Teresa s/n, 926 26 06 39 (closed Mon).* *book in advance.* **www**.lastablasdedaimiel.com

The marshy wetlands of the Tablas de Daimiel, northeast of Ciudad Real, are the feeding and nesting grounds of a huge range of aquatic and migratory birds. Despite being national parkland since 1973, they have become an ecological *cause célèbre* due to the growing threat from the area's lowering water table.

One corner of the park is open to the public, with walking routes to islets and observation towers. Breeding birds here include great crested grebes and mallards. Otters and red foxes are among the mammals found in the park.

Valle de Alcudia ㉜

Ciudad Real. *Fuencaliente.* *Almadén, 926 71 04 38.*

Alcudia's lush lowlands, which border the Sierra Morena foothills to the south, are among central Spain's most unspoiled countryside. The area is used largely as pasture land. In late autumn it is filled with sheep, whose milk makes the farmhouse cheese for which the valley is known.

The mountain village of **Fuencaliente** has thermal baths that open in the summer. Further north, **Almadén** is the site of a large mercury mine with a museum. **Chillón**, to the northwest, has a late Gothic church.

Small isolated farmhouse in the fertile Valle de Alcudia

Exploring Extremadura

Extremadura is ideal for nature lovers and those who want to get off the beaten track to discover the old Spain. It offers beautiful driving and walking country in its northern sierras and valleys, and exceptional wildlife in Monfragüe Natural Park. Some of the best Roman ruins in Spain can be found throughout Extremadura, especially in the regional capital, Mérida. The walled old town of Cáceres, with its well-preserved Jewish quarter, and the monasteries of Guadalupe and Yuste, are other historic sights not to be missed. To the south, the Templar towns in the Sierra Morena, such as Jerez de los Caballeros, have fine old buildings, while the small, historic towns of Coria, Zafra and Llerena all make charming bases for excursions.

SIGHTS AT A GLANCE

Alcántara 12
Arroyo de la Luz 11
Badajoz 15
Cáceres pp408–9 10
Cancho Roano 17
Coria 4
Guadalupe 8
Hervás 3
Las Hurdes 1
Jerez de los Caballeros 19
Llerena 20
Mérida 14
Monasterio de Yuste 6
Olivenza 16
Parque Natural de Monfragüe 7
Plasencia 5
Sierra de Gata 2
Tentudía 21
Trujillo 9
Valencia de Alcántara 13
Zafra 18

Orchards near Hervás in the Valle del Ambroz

SEE ALSO

- ***Where to Stay*** pp588–90
- ***Where to Eat*** pp638–40

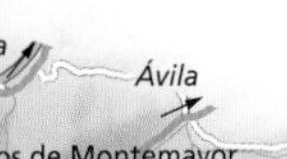

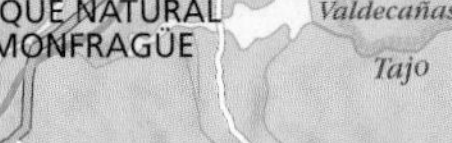
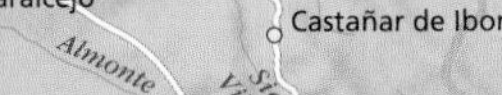

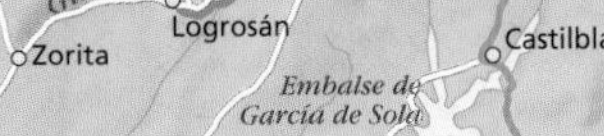
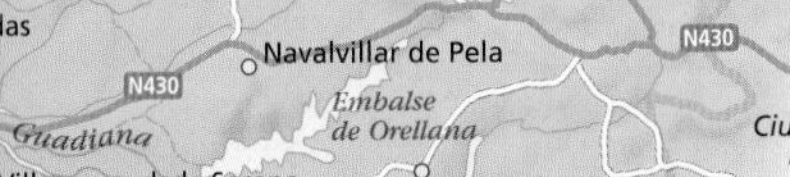

Cattle grazing in the fields near Cáceres

KEY

- Motorway
- Motorway under construction
- Major road
- Secondary road
- Scenic route
- Main railway
- Minor railway
- International border
- Regional border
- Summit

GETTING AROUND

Extremadura is not very well connected by air or rail services. Badajoz has the only (domestic) airport in the region, while the main rail link is the line from Madrid to Cáceres, Mérida and Badajoz. Coach services are infrequent, and in many areas, such as the northern sierras, they are non-existent. It is generally much more convenient to travel by car.

Roman bridge crossing the Río Guadiana at Mérida

Beehives, a common sight in Las Hurdes

Las Hurdes ❶

Cáceres. Pinofranqueado, Caminomorisco, Nuñomoral. Caminomorisco, 927 43 53 29. **www**.todohurdes.com

Las Hurdes' slate mountains, goats and beehives were memorably caught in the 1932 Luis Buñuel film, *Tierra sin Pan (Land without Bread)*. The area's legendary poverty disappeared with the arrival of roads in the 1950s, but the black slopes, riverbeds and hill terraces remain.

From Pinofranqueado or Vegas de Coria, roads climb past picturesque "black" villages like Batuequilla, Fragosa, and El Gasco, which sits under an extinct volcano. The more developed **Lower Hurdes** area, crossed by the Río Hurdano and the main access route (C512), is dotted with camp sites and restaurants.

Sierra de Gata ❷

Cáceres. Cáceres. San Martín, 927 51 45 85. **www**.sierradegata.es

There are 40 hamlets in the Sierra de Gata, scattered between olive groves, orchards and fields. The area has retained its old-fashioned rural charm by conserving hunters' paths for woodland walking, and its local crafts, most notably lace-making. In the lowland towns of **Valverde de Fresno** and **Acebo**, the local dialect, *chapurriau,* is still spoken. On the higher slopes, **Eljas**, **Gata** and **Villamiel** have remains of medieval fortresses. The old granite houses have carved family crests on the front and distinctive outside staircases.

Coat of arms on a house front in Acebo

Hervás ❸

Cáceres. 4,200. C/ Braulio Navas 6, 927 47 36 18. Sat. Las Ferias Cristo de la Salud (15–16 Sep). **www**.hervas.es

Sitting at the top of the wide Valle del Ambroz, Hervás is known for its medieval Jewish quarter, with its whitewashed houses. The tiny streets, dotted with taverns and craft workshops, slope down towards the Río Ambroz. Just off the main plaza is the **Museo Pérez Comendador-Leroux**, named after the town's noted 20th-century sculptor and his wife, whose work is exhibited here.

The next town up towards the Béjar pass is **Baños de Montemayor**, whose name comes from its sulphurous baths, which date back to Roman times. These were revived in the early 1900s and are open to the public. At **Cáparra**, south-west of Hervás, four triumphal arches stand on the Roman road, the Vía de la Plata *(see p352)*.

Museo Pérez Comendador-Leroux
C/ Asensio Neila 5. ***Tel*** *927 48 16 55.*
pm Tue; Wed–Fri; am Sat, Sun.

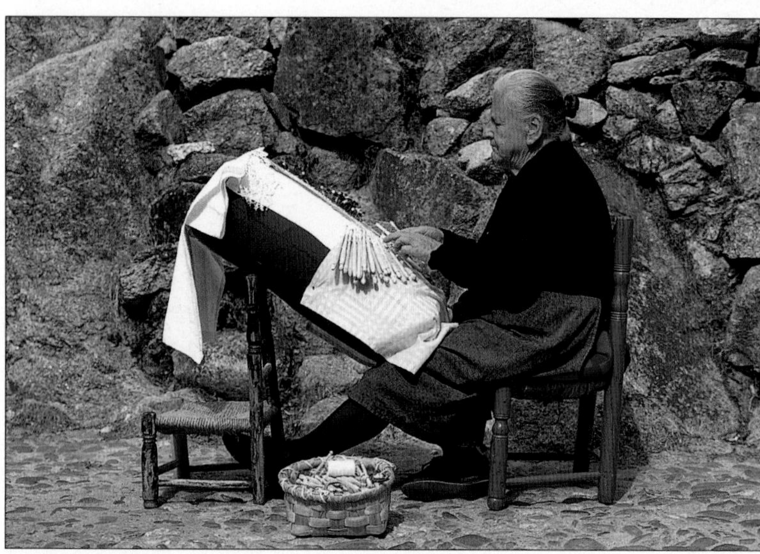
Traditional lace-making in one of the villages of the Sierra de Gata

Ancient wall and olive groves in the Valle del Ambroz

Coria ❹

Cáceres. 13,000. Avenida de Extremadura 39, 927 50 13 51. Thu. Día de la Virgen (2nd Mon in May), San Juan (23–29 Jun).
www.turismo.coria.org

Coria's walled old town, perched above the Río Alagón, boasts a Gothic-Renaissance **cathedral** with rich Plateresque carving, and the 16th-century **Convento de la Madre de Dios**, which has a fine Renaissance cloister.

Forming part of the town walls, which are a Muslim and medieval patchwork, are an imposing castle tower, and four gates, two of which date back to Roman times. The gates are closed for the fiesta of San Juan in June for night-time bullrunning. Situated below the old town is the **Puente Seco**, or Puente Viejo, a Roman bridge.

Plasencia ❺

Cáceres. 41,000. Santa Clara 2, 927 42 38 43. Tue. Ferias (6–8 Jun).
http://plasenciaweb.com/turismo

Plasencia's golden-grey walls, rising above a curve in the banks of the Río Jerte, tell of the town's past as a military bastion. Nowadays Plasencia is best known for its Tuesday market, dating back to the 12th century.

A short walk away are the town's two cathedrals, which are built back-to-back. The 15th–16th-century **Catedral Nueva** has a Baroque organ and carved wooden choir stalls. The Romanesque **Catedral Vieja**, next to it, has a museum with works by Ribera, and a late 14th-century Bible.

The **Museo Etnográfico y Textil Pérez Enciso**, housed in a 14th-century hospital, has displays of crafts and costumes.

The rest of the Jerte valley has pockets of outstanding beauty, such as the **Garganta de los Infiernos**, a nature reserve with dramatic, rushing waterfalls.

Museo Etnográfico y Textil Pérez Enciso
Plaza del Marqués de la Puebla.
Tel *927 42 18 43. Wed–Sun.*

Monasterio de Yuste ❻

Cuacos de Yuste (Cáceres). ***Tel*** *927 17 21 97. Tue–Sun.*

The Hieronymite monastery of Yuste, where Charles V *(see p59)* retired from public life in 1556 and died two years later, is remarkable for its simplicity and its lovely setting in the wooded valley of La Vera.

The church's Gothic and Plateresque cloisters and the austere palace are open to visitors. Just below it is **Cuacos de Yuste**, the most unspoiled of La Vera's old villages, where peppers, for making paprika, hang outside the houses.

Paprika peppers hanging up around a door in Cuacos de Yuste

A *Carantoña*, during the fiesta of St Sebastian, Acehuche

EXTREMADURA'S FIESTAS

Carantoñas *(20–21 Jan)*, Acehúche (Cáceres). During the fiesta of St Sebastian, the *Carantoñas* take to the streets of the town dressed up in animal skins, with their faces covered by grotesque masks designed to make them look terrifying. They represent the wild beasts which are said to have left the saint unharmed.

Pero Palo *(Carnival Feb/Mar)*, Villanueva de la Vera (Cáceres). In this ancient ritual a wooden figure dressed in a suit and representing the devil is paraded around the streets and then destroyed – except for the head, which is reused the year after.

Los Empalaos *(Maundy Thursday)*, Valverde de la Vera (Cáceres). Men do penance by walking in procession through the town with their arms outstretched and bound to small tree trunks.

La Encamisá *(7–8 Dec)*, Torrejoncillo (Cáceres). Riders on horseback parade around town, where bonfires are set alight for the occasion.

Los Escobazos *(7 Dec)*, Jarandilla de la Vera (Cáceres). At night, the town is illuminated by bonfires in the streets, and torches are made from burning brooms.

Parque Natural de Monfragüe ❼

Cáceres. [bus] *Villarreal de San Carlos.* [i] *Villarreal de San Carlos, 927 19 91 34.* **www**.turismoextremadura.com

To the south of Plasencia, rolling hills drop from scrubby peaks through wild olive, cork and holm oak woods to the dammed Tagus and Tiétar river valleys. In 1979, some 500 sq km (200 sq miles) of these hills were granted natural park status in order to safeguard the area's outstandingly varied wildlife species, which includes a large proportion of Spain's protected bird species *(see pp342–3).*

The many species of bird which breed here include the black-winged kite, black vulture and, most notably, the black stork, as well as more common aquatic species on and near the water. Mammals living here include the lynx, red deer and wild boar. At **Villarreal de San Carlos**, a hamlet founded in the 18th century, there is parking and an information centre. An ideal time to visit the park is September, when many migrating birds stop off here.

Birdwatchers in the Parque Natural de Monfragüe

Guadalupe ❽

Cáceres. [population] *2,100.* [bus] [i] *Pl Mayor, 927 15 41 28.* **Monasterio *Tel*** *927 36 70 00.* [open] *daily.* [ ] [ ] *only.* [closed] *Wed.* [festivals] *Cruz de Mayo (3 May), La Virgen y Día de la Comunidad (8 Sep).* **www**.monasterioguadalupe.com

This village grew around the magnificent Hieronymite **Monasterio de Guadalupe**, founded in 1340. In the main square there are shops that sell handmade ceramics and beaten copper cauldrons, both traditional monastic crafts, now made as souvenirs.

The turreted towers of the monastery, which is set in a deep wooded valley, help give it a fairy-tale air. According to legend, a shepherd found a wooden image of the Virgin Mary here in the early 14th century. The monastery grew to splendour under royal patronage, acquiring schools of grammar and medicine, three hospitals, an important pharmacy and one of the largest libraries in Spain.

The 16th-century *hospedería* where royalty once stayed was destroyed by fire; the 20th-century reconstruction is now a hotel run by the monks *(see p589).* The old hospital has been converted into a parador. In the car park is a plaque commemorating Spain's first human dissection, which took place here in 1402.

By the time the New World was discovered, the monastery was very important and in 1496 was the site of the baptism of some of the first native Caribbeans brought to Europe by Columbus *(see pp56–7).*

The monastery was sacked by Napoleon in 1808 but was refounded by Franciscans a century later. It is a major centre of Catholicism, visited by thousands of pilgrims.

Guided tours (in Spanish only) begin in the museums of illuminated manuscripts, embroidered vestments and fine art. They continue to the choir and the magnificent Baroque sacristy, nicknamed "the Spanish Sistine Chapel", because of Zurbarán's portraits of monks hanging on the highly decorated walls. For many, the chance to touch or kiss the tiny Virgin's dress in the *camarín* (chamber) behind the altar is the highlight of the tour. The 16th-century Gothic cloister has two tiers of horseshoe arches around an ornate central pavilion. The church, with a magnificent 16th-century iron grille partly forged from the chains of freed slaves, may be visited separately.

Monasterio de Guadalupe, overlooking the town

Environs

The surrounding **Sierra de las Villuercas** and **Los Ibores** sierras, where herbs were once picked for the monastery pharmacy, have good woodland walks. The road south also gives access to the pasture lands of **La Serena**, a vital breeding ground for birds of the steppe *(see pp342–3)*, and the huge reservoir of **Cíjara**, surrounded by a game reserve.

Trujillo ❾

Cáceres. *9,600.* *Plaza Mayor, 927 32 26 77.* *Thu.* *Chíviri (Easter Sun), Feria del Queso (weekend of 1 May).* **www.**turismotrujillo.com

When the Plaza Mayor of the medieval hilltop town of Trujillo is floodlit at night, it is one of the most beautiful squares in Spain. By day, there is much to visit, including the **Iglesia de Santa María la Mayor**, on one of the town's winding streets, which contains various sarcophagi.

At the top of the hill there is an Islamic fortress, which defended the town against the Christian advance during the Reconquest *(see pp54–5)*; but in 1232 it was retaken by the forces of Fernando III.

Statue of Francisco Pizarro in Trujillo's main square

Trujillo was the birthplace of several conquistadors, most notably Francisco Pizarro, who conquered Peru *(see p58)*, of whom there is a statue in the main square. His brother, Hernando Pizarro, founded the **Palacio del Marqués de la Conquista**, one of several palaces and convents built with New World wealth. It has an elaborate corner window with carved stone heads of the Pizarro brothers and their Inca wives. The beautiful 16th-century **Palacio de Juan Pizarro de Orellana** was built by descendants of Francisco de Orellana, the explorer of Ecuador and the Amazon.

In late April or early May, gourmets flock here for the four-day cheese fair.

Palacio del Marqués de la Conquista
Plaza Mayor. *to the public.*

Palacio de Juan Pizarro de Orellana
Plaza de Don Juan Tena. ***Tel*** *927 32 11 58.* *10am–dusk daily.*

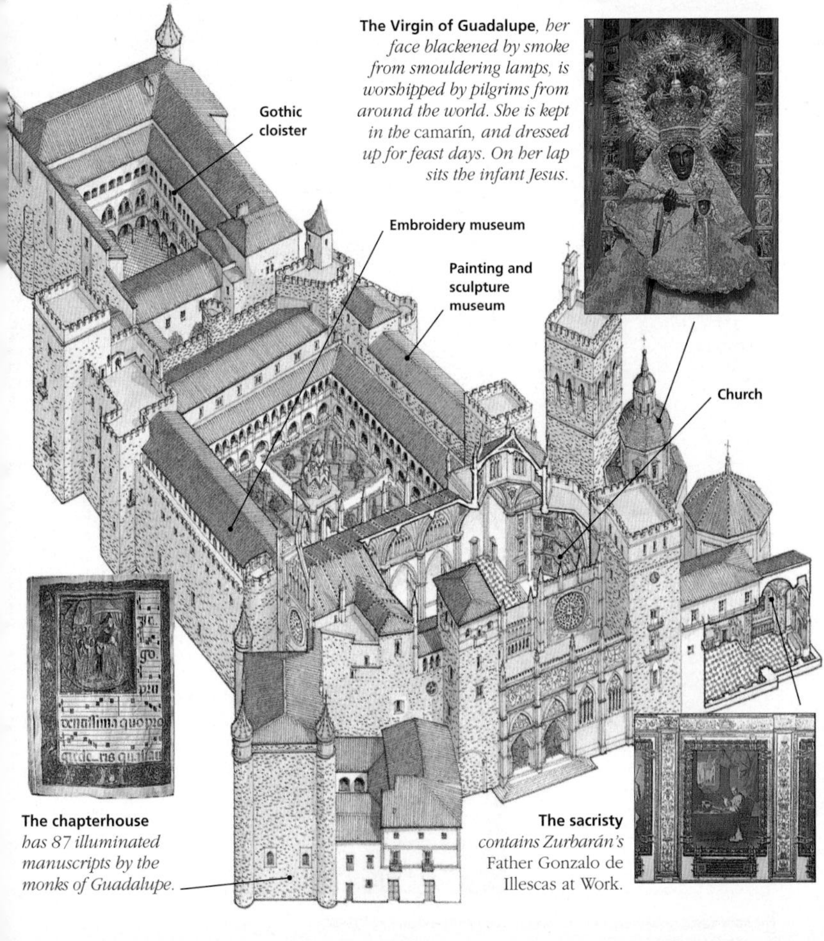

The Virgin of Guadalupe, *her face blackened by smoke from smouldering lamps, is worshipped by pilgrims from around the world. She is kept in the* camarín*, and dressed up for feast days. On her lap sits the infant Jesus.*

Gothic cloister

Embroidery museum

Painting and sculpture museum

Church

The chapterhouse *has 87 illuminated manuscripts by the monks of Guadalupe.*

The sacristy *contains Zurbarán's* Father Gonzalo de Illescas at Work.

Street-by-Street: Cáceres ⑩

After Alfonso IX of Leon conquered Cáceres in 1227, its growing prosperity as a free trade town attracted merchants, and later aristocracy, to settle here. They rivalled each other with stately homes and palaces fortified by watchtowers, most of which Isabel and Fernando, the reigning monarchs *(see pp56–7)*, ordered to be demolished in 1476 to halt the continual jostling for power. Today's serene Renaissance town dates from the late 15th and 16th centuries, after which economic decline set in. Untouched by the wars of the 19th and 20th centuries, Cáceres became Spain's first listed heritage city in 1949.

★ Casa de los Golfines de Abajo
The ornamental façade of this 16th-century mansion displays the shield of one of the town's leading families, the Golfines.

Casa y Torre de Carvajal
This typical Renaissance mansion has a 13th-century round Arab tower and a peaceful garden with a patio.

CALLE DE LA AMARGURA
CUESTA DEL MARQUÉS
PÍAS DE ROCO
CALLE OBRAS
PLAZA DE SANTA MARÍA
PLAZA MAYOR

★ Iglesia de Santa María
Facing the Palacio Episcopal, this Gothic-Renaissance church has a beautiful cedarwood reredos and a 15th-century crucifix – the Cristo Negro *(Black Christ).*

The Torre de Bujaco is a 12th-century tower that visitors can climb for good views of Plaza Mayor.

Arco de la Estrella
This low-arched gateway was built by Manuel Churriguera in 1726. It leads through the city walls from the Plaza Mayor into the old town and is flanked by a 15th-century watchtower.

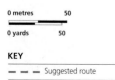

0 metres 50

0 yards 50

KEY

— — — Suggested route

Barrio de San Antonio
This quaint old Jewish quarter, with narrow streets of whitewashed houses restored to their original condition, takes its name from the nearby hermitage of St Anthony.

VISITORS' CHECKLIST

Cáceres. 95,000. *Juan Pablo II, 6, 902 32 03 20.* *C/ de Túnez 1, 927 23 25 50.* *Plaza Mayor 3, 927 01 08 34.* *Wed.* *San Jorge (23 Apr), San Fernando (30 May).* **Museo de Cáceres** ***Tel*** *927 01 08 77.* *Tue–Sun.*

★ Museo de Cáceres
Housed in the Casa de las Veletas, this museum has contemporary art and archaeology from the region.

The Convento de San Pablo sells delicious *yemas* (candied egg yolks) made by the nuns.

Casa y Torre de las Cigüeñas
The slender, battlemented tower of the House of the Storks was allowed to remain after 1476 because of the owner's loyalty to Isabel. It is now owned by the army and not open to the public.

The Iglesia de San Mateo, built between the 14th and 17th centuries, is one of Cáceres' earliest churches.

Casa del Sol (Casa de los Solis)
he façade of this elegant Renaissance uilding, once home of the Solis family, is emblazoned with a sun (sol) *motif.*

STAR SIGHTS

- ★ Casa de los Golfines de Abajo
- ★ Iglesia de Santa María
- ★ Museo de Cáceres

Arroyo de la Luz ⓫

Cáceres. 6,400. Plaza de la Constitución 21, 927 27 04 37. Thu. Día de la Luz (Easter Mon), Fiestas (15 Aug).

The small town of Arroyo de la Luz is home to one of the artistic masterpieces of Extremadura. Its **Iglesia de la Asunción**, completed in 1565, contains a spectacular altarpiece which incorporates 20 paintings by the mystical religious painter Luis de Morales.

Environs
The area has a large population of white storks *(see p343)*. Nearby **Malpartida** is home to the largest colony, whose nests adorn the church roof. There are some good picnic spots in the surrounding countryside.

Alterpiece in the Iglesia de la Asunción, Arroyo de la Luz

Alcántara ⓬

Cáceres. 1,700. Avenida de Mérida 21, 927 39 08 63. Tue. Classic Drama Festival (first 2 wks in Aug), San Pedro (18–19 Oct).

Alcantara has two important sights. One is the drystone **Roman bridge**, above the Tagus River, with its honorary arch and a temple. The other the restored **Convento de San Benito**. This was built as the headquarters of the Knights of the Order of Alcántara during the 16th century and was sacked by Napoleon. Its surviving treasures are in the **Iglesia de Santa María de Almocovar**.

Walls of the 16th-century Convento de San Benito, Alcántara

Valencia de Alcántara ⓭

Cáceres. 6,000. Calle de Hernán Cortés, 927 58 21 84. Mon. San Isidro (15 May), San Bartolomé (24 Aug).

The Gothic quarter of this hilltop frontier town is given an elegant air by its fountains and orange trees. The **Castillo de Piedra Buena** was built near the town by the Knights of the Order of Alcántara and on the outskirts of the town there are more than 40 dolmens, or megalithic burial sites.

Environs
Alburquerque, to the southeast, is sited on a rocky outcrop with a panoramic view from the ramparts and keep of its castle. Below is the old town and the 15th-century Iglesia de Santa María del Mercado.

Mérida ⓮

Badajoz. 57,800. C/ José Álvarez Sáenz de Buruaga, 924 33 07 22. Tue. Easter Week, Classic Drama Festival (Jul–Aug), Feria (1–5 Sep). **www**.merida.es

Founded by Augustus in 25 BC, Augusta Emerita grew into the cultural and economic capital of Rome's westernmost province, Lusitania, but lost its eminence under the Moors. Though a small city, Mérida, the capital of Extremadura, has many fine Roman monuments.

The best approach is from the west of town, via the modern suspension bridge over the Río Guadiana, bringing you to the original entrance of the Roman city and Arab fortress.

The city's centrepiece is the **Roman theatre** *(see pp50–51)*. One of the best-preserved Roman theatres anywhere, it is still used in summer for the city's drama festival and is part of a larger site with an **amphitheatre** *(anfiteatro)* and gardens. Nearby are the remains of a Roman house, the **Casa del Anfiteatro**, where there are underground galleries and large areas of well-preserved mosaics.

Opposite stands Rafael Moneo's stunning red-brick **Museo Nacional de Arte Romano**. The semicircular arches of its main hall are built to the same height as the city's Los Milagros aqueduct. Off this hall, which features sculptures from the Roman theatre, there are three galleries exhibiting ceramics, mosaics, coins and statuary. There is also an

Megalithic tomb on the outskirts of Valencia de Alcántara

Mérida's well-preserved Roman theatre, still used as a venue for classical drama

excavated Roman street. Near the museum are several other monuments, namely two villas with fine mosaics, and a racecourse.

A chapel in front of the 3rd-century **Iglesia de Santa Eulalia** is dedicated to the child saint who was martyred on this site in Roman times. Towards the centre of the town are the **Templo de Diana** (1st century AD), with tall, fluted columns, and the **Arco de Trajano**. The **Museo de Arte Visigodo** (Museum of Visigothic Art) is in the Convento de Santa Clara, which is situated off the main square. From the huge **Puente Romano** there is a good view of the massive walls of the **Alcazaba**, one of Spain's oldest Moorish buildings (AD 835), whose precinct includes towers, a cistern and Roman ruins. To the east stands the **Casa del Mithraeo**, with its Pompeiian-style frescoes and fine mosaics.

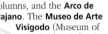

Sculpture of Emperor Augustus

The magnificent, ruined Los Milagros aqueduct, with its granite and brick arches, is off the N630 towards Cáceres.

Museo de Arte Visigodo
C/ Sta Julia. ***Tel** 924 30 01 06.*
Tue–Sun am. public hols.

Museo Nacional de Arte Romano
C/ José Ramón Mélida. ***Tel** 924 31 16 90. Tue–Sun am. (free Sat pm & Sun am).* **www**.mnar.es

MÉRIDA TOWN CENTRE

Alcazaba ⑦
Amphitheatre ④
Arco de Trajano ⑩
Casa del Anfiteatro ③
Casa del Mithraeo ⑥
Iglesia de Santa Eulalia ①
Museo de Arte Visigodo ⑨
Museo Nacional de Arte Romano ②
Puente Romano ⑧
Roman Theatre ⑤
Templo de Diana ⑪

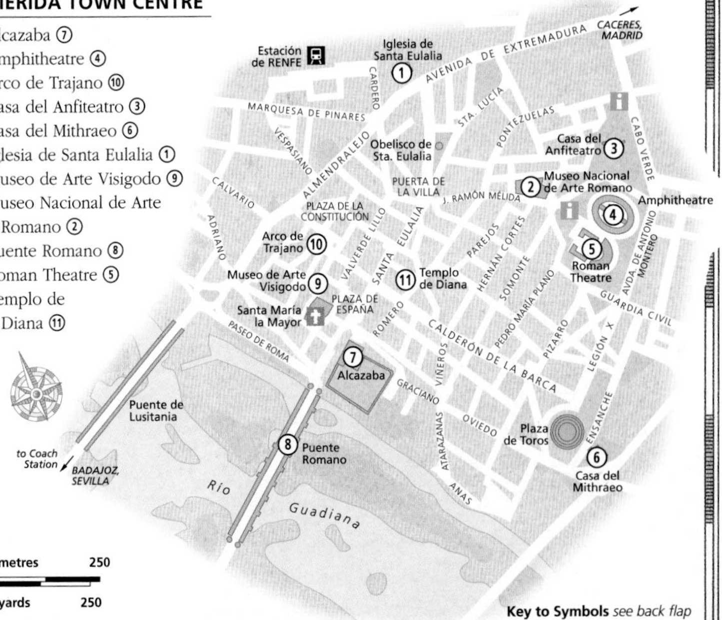

0 metres 250
0 yards 250

Key to Symbols *see back flap*

Badajoz ⓯

Badajoz. *151,500.*
Pasaje de San Juan, 924 22 49 81.
Tue & Sun. *Feria (24 Jun).*
www.turismobadajoz.es

Badajoz is a plain, modern city, though it retains traces of its former importance. It was a major city under the Moors but centuries of conflict robbed Badajoz of its former glories.

The Alcazaba now houses the **Museo Arqueológico**, which has over 15,000 pieces from around the province, as far back as Paleolithic times. Nearby is the cathedral, dating from the 13th–18th centuries, with a stunning tiled cloister. A museum of contemporary art is situated on Calle Museo and is open every day except Sunday evening and Monday.

Museo Arqueológico
Pl José Álvarez Saez de Buruaga.
Tel *924 00 19 08.* *Tue–Sun.*

Olivenza ⓰

Badajoz. *12,000.* *Plaza España, 924 49 01 51.* *Sat.*
Muñecas de San Juan (23 Jun).

A Portuguese enclave until 1801, Olivenza has a colourful character. Within the walled town are the medieval castle, housing the **Museo Etnográfico González Santana**, a museum of rural life, and three churches. **Santa María del Castillo** has a naive family tree of the Virgin Mary. **Santa María Magdalena**, is a fine example of the 16th-century Portuguese

Interior of Santa María Magdalena church, Olivenza

Manueline style. The 16th-century **Santa Casa de Misericordia** has blue and white tiled friezes. In one, God is shown offering Adam and Eve 18th-century coats to cover their nakedness.

Off the main square is the **Pasteleria Fuentes**, which sells *Pécula Mécula* cake.

Museo Etnográfico González Santana
Plaza de Santa María. ***Tel*** *924 49 02 22.* *Tue–Sun am.*

Cancho Roano ⓱

Zalamea de la Serena, BA632 (Carretera Zalamea-Quintana) km 3.
Tel *629 23 52 79.* *daily (except Sun pm).*

This sanctuary-palace, which is thought to have been built under the civilization of Tartessus *(see p49)*, was discovered in 1978. Excavations on this small site have revealed a moated temple that was rebuilt three times – many of the walls and slate floors are still intact. Each temple was constructed on a grander scale than the previous one and then burned in the face of invasion during the 6th century BC.

Most of the artifacts unearthed from the site are on display in the archaeological museum at Badajoz.

Environs

A Roman funereal monument stands next to the church in nearby **Zalamea de la Serena**. The town comes alive during the August fiestas, when the townsfolk act out the classic 17th-century play, *The Mayor of Zalamea*, by Calderón de la Barca *(see p34)*, which was supposedly based on a local character. Shops in the town also sell *torta de la Serena*, a cheese made of sheep's milk.

Remains of the Tartessan sanctuary at Cancho Roano

Zafra ⓲

Badajoz. *16,500.*
Plaza de España 8B, 924 55 10 36.
Sun. *San Miguel (end Sep–early Oct).*

At the heart of this graceful town, nicknamed "little Seville" because of its similarity to the capital of Andalusia, are two arcaded squares. The **Plaza Grande**, the larger of the two, near the **Iglesia de la Candelaria**, was built in the 15th century. The older square is **Plaza Chica**, which used to be the marketplace. On Calle Sevilla is the

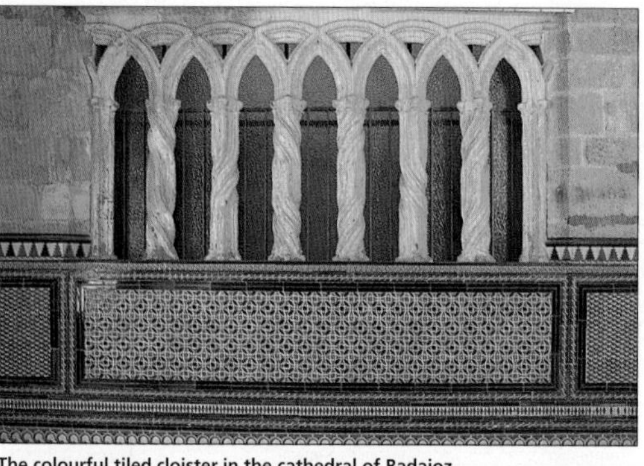
The colourful tiled cloister in the cathedral of Badajoz

Altarpiece by Zurbarán in the Iglesia de la Candelaria at Zafra

15th-century Convento de Santa Clara. Nearby is the **Alcázar de los Duques de Feria**, now a parador *(see p590)* with a patio of Herriano style.

Environs
Some 25 km (16 miles) to the south, in **Fuente de Cantos**, is the house in which the painter Francisco de Zurbarán was born in 1598.

Jerez de los Caballeros ⓳

Badajoz. 10,000. Plaza Constitucíon 4, 924 73 03 72. Wed. Easter week, Feria del Jamón (early May). www.jerezdeloscaballeros.es

The hillside profile of Jerez, broken by three Baroque church towers, is one of Extremadura's most picturesque. This small town is also historically important – Vasco Núñez de Balboa, who discovered the Pacific, was born here. In the **castle**, now laid out as gardens, knights of the Order of Knights Templar were beheaded in the Torre Sangrienta (Bloody Tower) in 1312. The old quarters of the town grew up around three churches: **San Bartolomé**, its façade studded with glazed ceramics; **San Miguel**, whose brick tower dominates the Plaza de España; and **Santa María de la Encarnación**.

Environs
Fregenal de la Sierra, 25 km (16 miles) to the south, is an attractive old town with a bullring and a castle.

Llerena ⓴

Badajoz. 6,000. Calle Aurora 2, 924 87 05 51. Thu. Nuestra Señora de la Granada (1–15 Aug). www.llerena.org

Extremadura's southeastern gateway to Andalusia, the town of Llerena, is a mixture of Mudéjar and Baroque buildings. In the pretty square, lined with palm trees, stands the arcaded, whitewash-and-stone church of **Nuestra Señora de la Granada**, its sumptuous interior reflecting its former importance as a seat of the Inquisition *(see p274)*. At one end of the square is a fountain designed by Zurbarán, who lived here for 15 years. Also worth seeing is the 16th-century **Convento de Santa Clara**, on a street leading out of the main square.

Environs
At **Azuaga**, 30 km (20 miles) to the east, is the Iglesia de la Consolación, containing Renaissance and Mudéjar tiles.

Tentudía ㉑

Badajoz. *Calera de León.*
Calera de León, 924 584 084.
Monasterio *Tue–Sun.*
www.turismoextremadura.com

Where the Sierra Morena runs into Andalusia, fortified towns and churches founded by the medieval military orders stand among the wooded hills of Tentudía. Here, on a hilltop, stands the tiny **Monasterio de Tentudía**. Founded in the 13th century by the Order of Santiago, the monastery contains a superb Mudéjar cloister, and reredos with Seville *azulejos* (tiles).

Calera de León, just 6 km (4 miles) north of Tentudía, has a Renaissance convent, also founded by the Order of Santiago, with a Gothic church and a cloister on two floors.

Bullring at Fregenal de la Sierra

SOUTHERN SPAIN

Southern Spain at a Glance

One large region – Andalusia – extends across the south of Spain. Its landscape varies from the deserts of Almería in the east, to the wetlands of Doñana National Park in the west; and from the snow-capped peaks of the Sierra Nevada to the beaches of the Costa del Sol. Three inland cities between them share the greatest of Spain's Moorish monuments: Granada, Córdoba and Seville, the capital, which stands on the banks of the Río Guadalquivir. Andalusia has many other historic towns as well as attractive, whitewashed villages, important nature reserves and the sherry-producing vineyards around Jerez de la Frontera.

Córdoba's Mezquita *(see pp480–81) has a remarkable forest of arches in its interior and an exquisitely decorated mihrab (prayer niche) facing Mecca.*

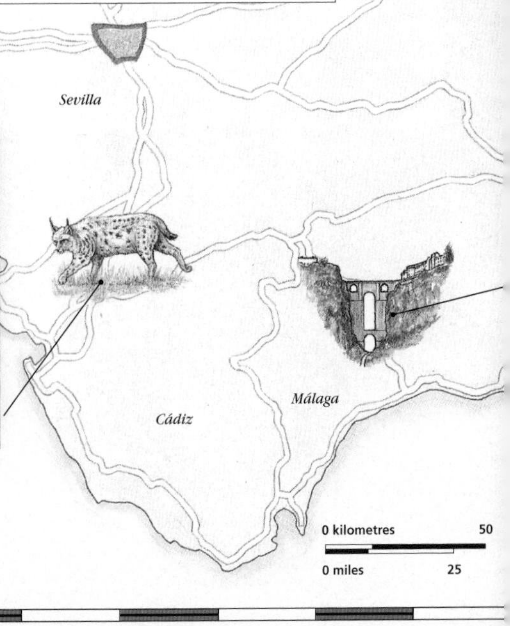

SEVILLE

EL ARENAL
(see pp426–31)

SANTA CRUZ
(see pp432–41)

La Giralda (see pp436–37), *the Moorish bell tower of Seville Cathedral, was built as a minaret in 1198, but extended to include a belfry in the 16th century.*

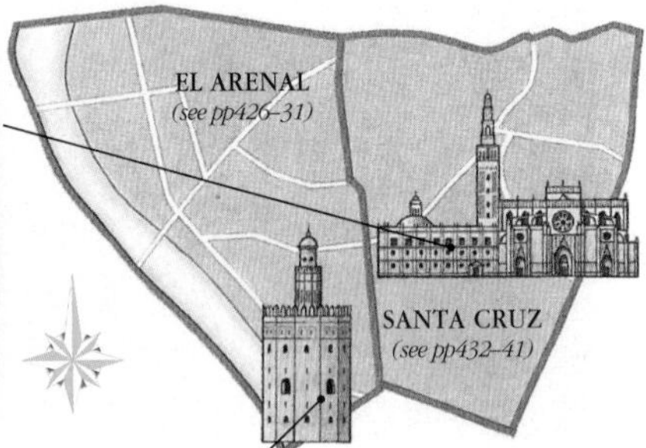

The Torre del Oro (see p431), *a 13th-century Moorish tower, stands beside the Río Guadalquivir.*

0 metres 500
0 yards 500

Córdoba

ANDALUSIA
(see pp458–50

Huelva

Sevilla

Málaga

Cádiz

The Parque Nacional de Doñana *(see pp464–5), a large wetland protected area, is home to a vast array of wildlife including lynxes, flamingoes, eagles, deer and wild cattle.*

0 kilometres 50
0 miles 25

◁ **Whitewashed houses with red-tiled roofs in Montefrío, near Granada**

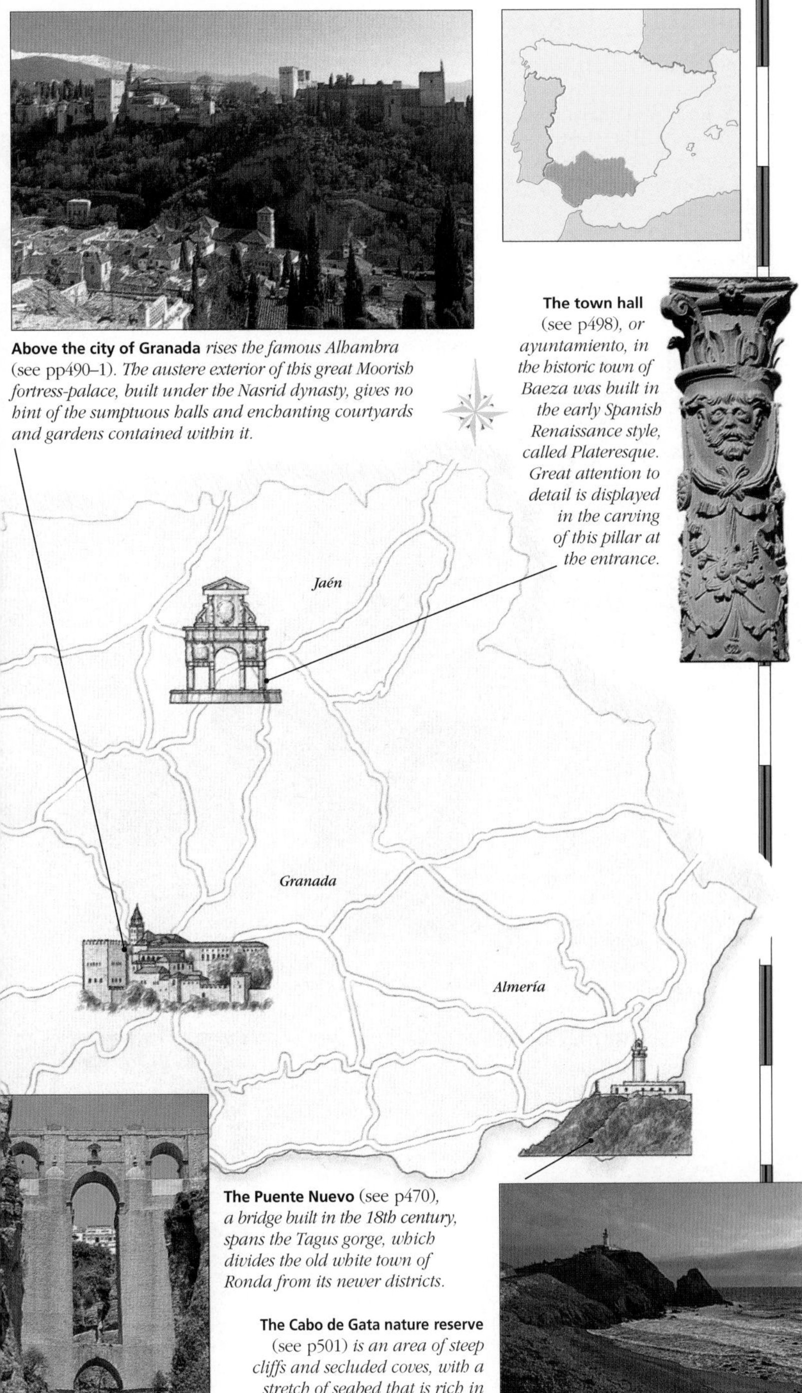

Above the city of Granada *rises the famous Alhambra* (see pp490–1). *The austere exterior of this great Moorish fortress-palace, built under the Nasrid dynasty, gives no hint of the sumptuous halls and enchanting courtyards and gardens contained within it.*

The town hall (see p498), *or ayuntamiento, in the historic town of Baeza was built in the early Spanish Renaissance style, called Plateresque. Great attention to detail is displayed in the carving of this pillar at the entrance.*

The Puente Nuevo (see p470), *a bridge built in the 18th century, spans the Tagus gorge, which divides the old white town of Ronda from its newer districts.*

The Cabo de Gata nature reserve (see p501) *is an area of steep cliffs and secluded coves, with a stretch of seabed that is rich in marine flora and fauna.*

The Flavours of Southern Spain

Andalusia is vast, bordered on one side by the Mediterranean and on the other by the Atlantic. Inland are lofty mountains and undulating hills, endless olive groves and bright fields of sunflowers. The cuisine is as varied as the terrain, with a huge array of seafood, superb meat and game, and a harvest of sun-ripened fruit and vegetables. The *tapeo* (tapas-bar-hopping) is a regional institution and, around Granada, these little morsels are still served free with drinks. Along the coast, especially the Costa del Sol, the influx of foreigners has brought glamorous international restaurants but, inland, traditional recipes are still the norm at old-fashioned inns.

Olives and olive oil

Diners choosing from a selection at a tapas bar

TAPAS

The *tapeo*, or tapas crawl, is an intrinsic part of daily life in Andalusia. Each bar is usually known for a particular speciality: one might be well known for its home-made *croquetas* (potato croquettes, usually filled with ham or cod), while another will serve exceptional hams, and yet another might make the best *albóndigas* (meatballs) in the neighbourhood. Tapas are often accompanied by a glass of chilled, refreshing sherry, or perhaps a cold draught beer *(una caña)*. Tapas were once free, but that tradition has largely died out.

SEAFOOD

It's not surprising, given its extensive coastline, that southern Spain offers every imaginable variety of seafood, including cod, hake, prawns, crayfish, clams, razor clams, octopus, cuttlefish, sole and tuna. Almost every seaside resort will offer *pescaíto frito* (fried fish) originally a Malaga dish, made with the freshest catch of the day. In Cádiz, they are served appealingly in a paper cone, and in nearby Sanlúcar do not miss the sweet and juicy *langostinos* (king prawns).

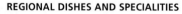

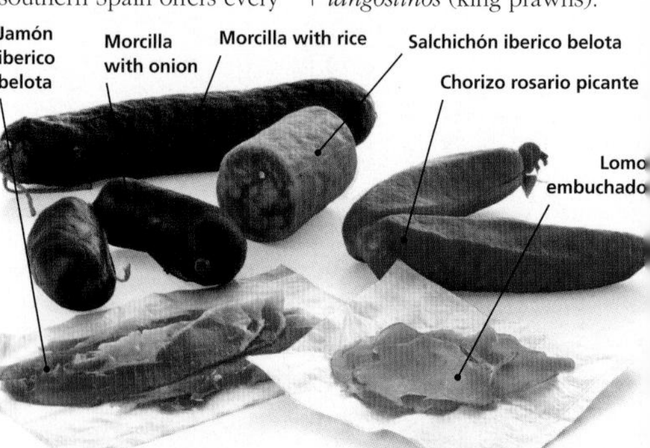

Selection of delicious Spanish *embutidos* (cured meats)

REGIONAL DISHES AND SPECIALITIES

Andalusia embodies many of the images most closely associated with Spain – the heady rhythms of flamenco, striking white villages and bullfighting. And tapas – in Andalusia, you can easily make a meal of these delectable treats, and every bar has an excellent range. Don't miss the mouthwatering hams from Jabugo and Trevélez which are famed throughout Spain, or the platters of freshly fried fish liberally doused with lemon juice. An ice-cold sherry (the word comes from Jérez, where most sherry is produced) is deliciously refreshing in the searing summer heat and is the most popular tipple at southern fiestas. While pork remains the most appreciated local meat, duck, beef and lamb are also favourites, subtly flavoured with aromatic bay leaves.

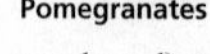

Pomegranates

Gazpacho *This famous chilled soup is made with plump, ripe tomatoes, garlic and red peppers.*

Andalusian vegetable seller displaying fresh local produce

MEAT AND GAME

Pork and beef are the most popular meats in Andalusia. Glossy black bulls (some raised for bull-fighting but most for meat) are a common sight, and one of the most popular local dishes is *rabo de toro* (bull's tail). The famous hams of Jabugo (in the southwest) and Trevélez (near Granada) are among the finest produced in Spain, and are made with free-range, black-footed pigs fed on a diet of acorns. All kinds of cured meats are made here, often to traditional recipes which have remained unchanged for centuries. In the wild inland Sierras, you will find an abundance of game in season, along with the traditional country staples of lamb and rabbit.

Prawns and sardines on display at the fishmarket

FRUIT AND VEGETABLES

The undulating Andalusian fields and hillsides are densely covered with beautiful olive groves, and the best oils are graded as carefully as fine wines. Olive oil is liberally used in Andaluz cuisine, and the typical southern breakfast is toasted country bread topped with thin slices of tomato and drizzled with olive oil – utterly delicious. The hot climate is perfect for fruit and vegetables, including luscious peaches, papayas, persimmons, and mangoes, as well as tomatoes, asparagus, aubergines (eggplants) and artichokes. The chilled tomato soup, *gazpacho*, is a classic, but *salmorejo*, which is thicker and topped with a sprinkling of chopped boiled eggs and ham, is even tastier.

ON THE MENU

Chocos con habas Cuttlefish is cooked with beans, white wine and plenty of bay leaves.

Pato a la Sevillana Succulent duck, cooked slowly with onion, leeks, carrots, bayleaf and a dash of sherry, this is a speciality of Seville.

Rabo de Toro An Andaluz classic, made with chunks of bull's tail, slowly braised with vegetables, bay leaf and a dash of sherry until tender.

Salmorejo Cordobés A creamy tomato dip thickened with breadcrumbs.

Torta de Camarones Delicious fritters filled with tiny, whole shrimp.

Tortilla del Sacromonte A speciality of Granada: omelette with brains, kidney or other offal, peppers and peas.

Huevos a la Flamenca *Eggs are baked in a terracotta dish with vegetables, ham and chorizo sausage.*

Pescaíto Frito *A seaside favourite, this is a platter of small fish tossed in batter and fried in olive oil.*

Tocino de Cielo *This simple but delicious dessert consists of creamy egg custard with a caramel syrup topping.*

Wines of Southern Spain

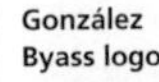

González Byass logo

Andalusia is a land of fortified wines, and the best of these is *Jerez* (sherry). Andalusians drink the light, dry fino and manzanilla styles of sherry as wines (they only have 15.5 per cent alcohol) – always chilled, and often as an accompaniment to tapas *(see pp606–7)*. The longer-aged, richer, yet still dry styles of amontillado and oloroso sherry go well with the cured *jamón serrano (see p604)*. Other wines include fino, which may or may not be fortified, and Madeira-like Málaga.

Working the soil in Jerez

Tío Pepe *is one of the finos of Jerez, which are noted for their bouquet of flor (yeast), pale colour and appetizing finish.*

WINE REGIONS

The Jerez wine region covers the chalky downs between the towns of Jerez, Sanlúcar and El Puerto de Santa María. South of the Montilla-Moriles region are Málaga's vineyards, which have been reduced by urban development.

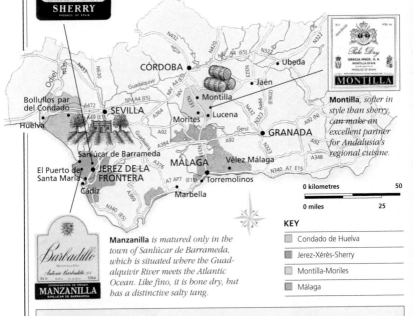

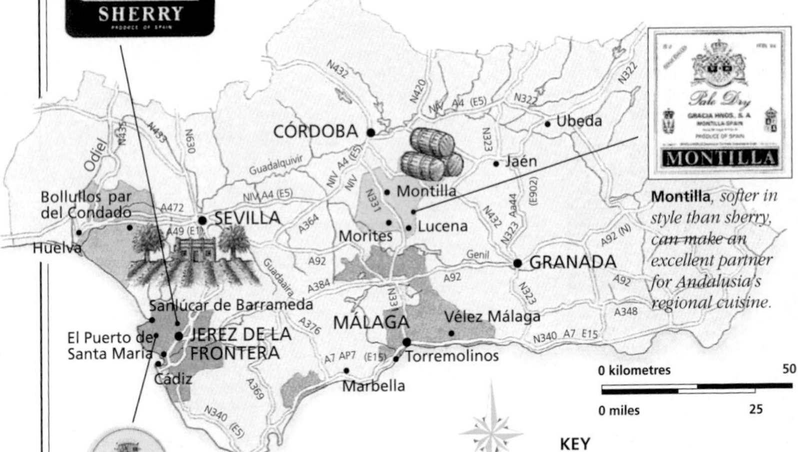

Montilla, *softer in style than sherry, can make an excellent partner for Andalusia's regional cuisine.*

Manzanilla *is matured only in the town of Sanlúcar de Barrameda, which is situated where the Guadalquivir River meets the Atlantic Ocean. Like fino, it is bone dry, but has a distinctive salty tang.*

0 kilometres 50

0 miles 25

KEY

- Condado de Huelva
- Jerez-Xérès-Sherry
- Montilla-Moriles
- Málaga

KEY FACTS ABOUT WINES OF SOUTHERN SPAIN

Location and Climate

The Jerez region has one of the sunniest climates in Europe – summer heat tempered by ocean breezes. The best type of soil is white, chalky *albariza*. In Montilla it is more clayey.

Grape Varieties

The best dry sherry is produced from the Palomino grape. Pedro Ximénez is used for the sweeter styles and is the main grape in Montilla and Málaga. Moscatel is also grown in Málaga.

Good Producers

Condado de Huelva: Manuel Sauci Salas (Riodiel), A.Villarán (Pedro Ximénez Villarán). ***Jerez:*** Barbadillo (Solear), Blázquez (Carta Blanca), Caballero (Puerto), Garvey (San Patricio), González Byass (Alfonso, Tío Pepe), Hidalgo (La Gitana, Napoleón), Lustau, Osborne (Quinta), Pedro Domecq (La Ina), Sandeman. ***Montilla-Moriles:*** Alvear (C.B., Festival), Gracia Hermanos, Pérez Barquero, Tomás García. ***Málaga:*** Scholtz Hermanos, López Hermanos.

HOW SHERRY IS MADE

Sherry is mixed from two principal grape varieties: Palomino, which makes a drier, more delicate sherry; and Pedro Ximénez, which is made into a fuller, sweeter type of sherry.

Grape-picking *takes place during the first three weeks in September. Palomino grapes are taken to the presses quickly to ensure freshness.*

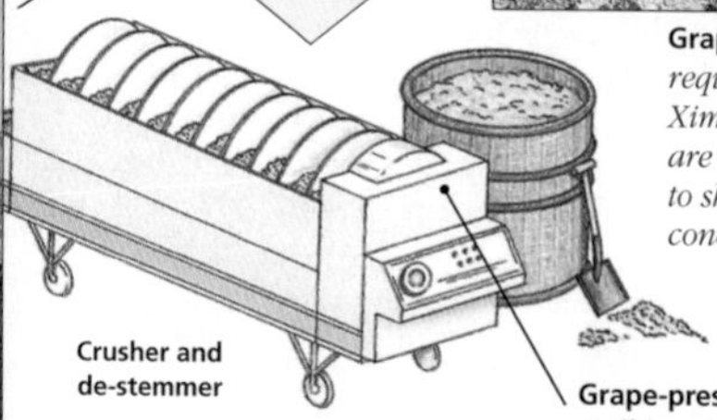

Grape-drying *is only required for Pedro Ximénez grapes. They are laid on esparto mats to shrivel in the sun, concentrating the sugar.*

Crusher and de-stemmer

Grape-pressing *and de-stalking, in cylindrical stainless steel vats, is usually done at night to avoid the searing Andalusian heat.*

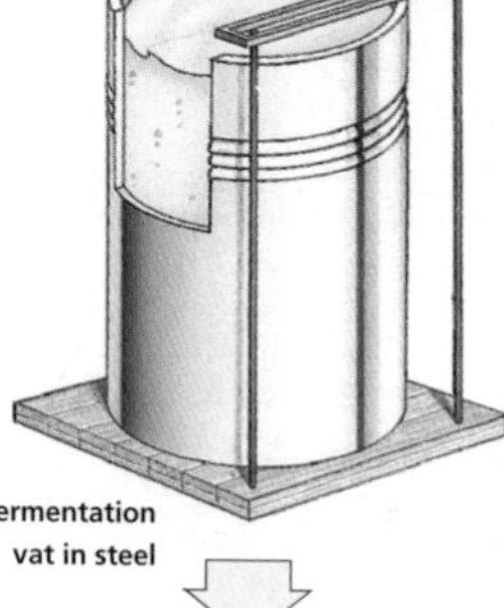

Fermentation vat in steel

Flor, *a yeast, may form on the exposed surface of young wine in the fermentation vat, preventing oxidization and adding a delicate taste. If* flor *develops, the wine is a fino.*

Fortification *is the addition of pure grape spirit, raising the level of alcohol from around 11 per cent by volume to around 18 per cent for olorosos, and 15.5 per cent for finos.*

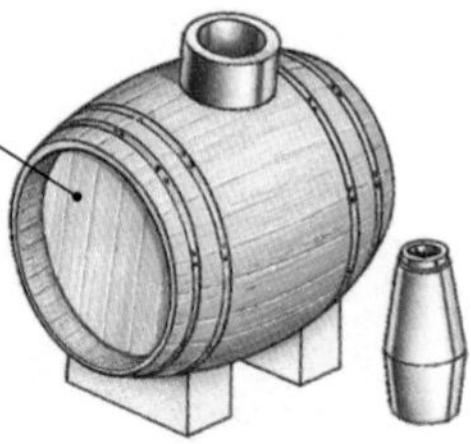

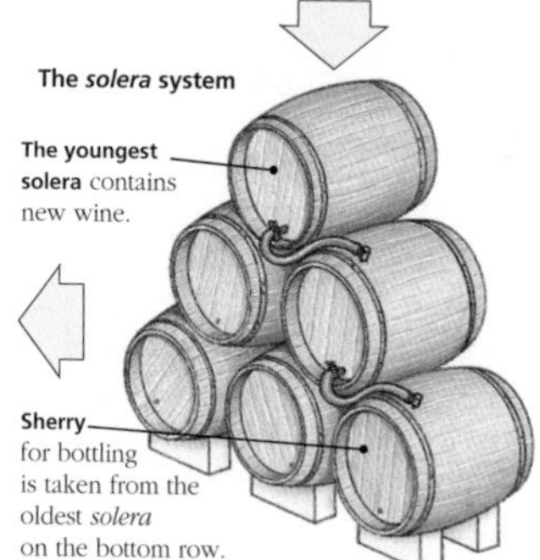

The *solera* system

The youngest solera contains new wine.

Sherry for bottling is taken from the oldest *solera* on the bottom row.

The finished product

The *solera* system *assures that the qualities of a sherry remain constant. The wine from the youngest* solera *is mixed with the older in the barrels below and as a result takes on its character.*

Moorish Architecture

The first significant period of Moorish architecture arrived with the Cordoban Caliphate. The Mezquita was extended lavishly during this period and possesses all the enduring features of the Moorish style: arches, stucco work and ornamental use of calligraphy. Later, the Almohads imported a purer Islamic style, as can be seen in La Giralda *(see pp436–7)*. The Nasrids built the superbly crafted Alhambra *(see pp490–91)* and the Mudéjares *(see p55)* used their skill to create beautiful Moorish-style buildings such as the Palacio Pedro I in Seville's Real Alcázar *(see pp440–41)*.

Reflections *in water, combined with an overall play of light, were central to Moorish architecture.*

Moorish domes *were frequently unadorned on the outside. Inside, an intricate lattice of stone ribs supported the dome's weight. Like this one in the Mezquita* (see pp480–81)*, they were inlaid with multicoloured mosaics featuring stylized flowers.*

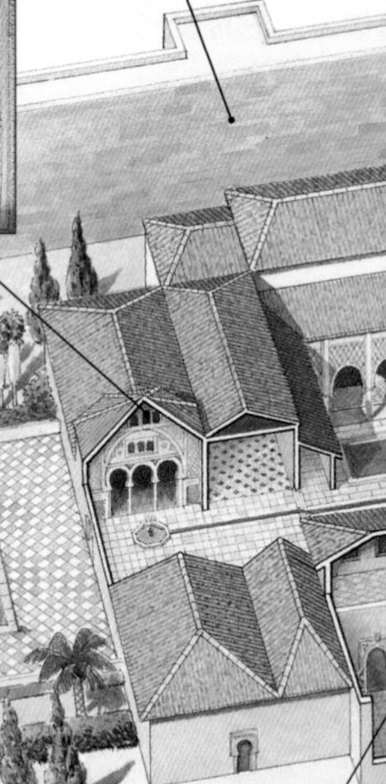

Moorish gardens were often arranged around gently rippling pools and channels.

DEVELOPMENT OF MOORISH ARCHITECTURE

Pre-Caliphal era	710–929
Caliphal era	929–1031
Almoravid and Almohad era	1091–1248
Nasrid era	c.1238–1492
Mudéjar era	after c.1215

700	800	900	1000	1100	1200	1300	1400

- **785** Mezquita in Córdoba begun
- **936** Medina Azahara near Córdoba begun
- **1031–91** *Taifa* period *(see p54)*
- **1184** La Giralda in Seville begun
- **c.1350** Alhambra palace
- **c.1350** Palacio Pedro I

Azulejos (see p438)*, glaze[d] tiles, often adorned walls [with] geometric patterns, as her[e] in the Real Alcázar* (p440)

MOORISH ARCHES

The Moorish arch was developed from the horseshoe arch that the Visigoths used in the construction of churches. The Moors modified it and used it as the basis of great architectural endeavours, such as the Mezquita. Subsequent arches show more sophisticated ornamentation and the slow demise of the basic horseshoe shape.

Caliphal arch, Medina Azahara ***(see p477)***

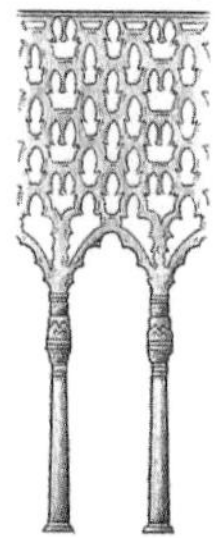

Almohad arch, Real Alcázar ***(see p440)***

Mudéjar arch, Real Alcázar ***(see p440)***

Nasrid arch, the Alhambra ***(see p490)***

MOORISH PALACE

The palaces of the Moors were designed with gracious living, culture and learning in mind. The imaginary palace here shows how space, light, water and ornamentation were combined to harmonious effect.

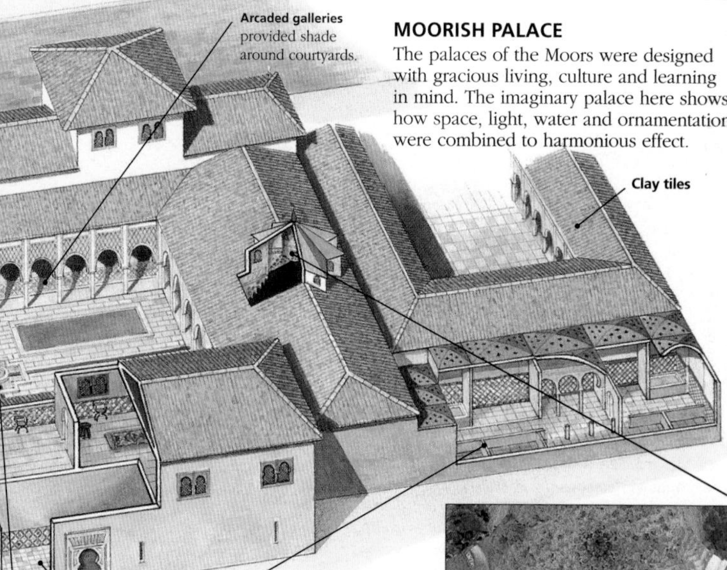
Arcaded galleries provided shade around courtyards.
Clay tiles
Entrance halls were complex to confuse unwanted visitors.
Moorish baths made use of steam and hot water. Like Roman baths, they often had underfloor heating.

Water *cooled the Moors' elegant courtyards and served a contemplative purpose, as here in the Patio de los Leones in the Alhambra* (see p491).

Elaborate stucco work *typifies the Nasrid style of architecture. The Sala de los Abencerrajes in the Alhambra* (see p491) *was built using only the simplest materials, but it is nevertheless widely regarded as one of the most outstanding monuments of the period of the Moorish occupation.*

Flamenco, the Soul of Andalusia

Seville feria poster 1953

More than just a dance, flamenco is a forceful artistic expression of the sorrows and joys of life. Although it has interpreters all over Spain and even the world, it is a uniquely Andalusian art form, traditionally performed by gypsies. There are many styles of *cante* (song) from different parts of Andalusia, but no strict choreography – dancers improvise from basic movements, following the rhythm of the guitar and their feelings. Flamenco was neglected in the 1960s and 1970s, but recent years have seen a revival of serious interest in traditional styles and the development of exciting new forms.

Sevillanas, *a folk dance strongly influenced by flamenco, is danced by Andalusians in their bars and homes.*

The origins of flamenco *are hard to trace. Gypsies may have been the main creators of the art, mixing their own Indian-influenced culture with existing Moorish and Andalusian folklore, and with Jewish and Christian music. There were gypsies in Andalusia by the early Middle Ages, but only in the 18th century did flamenco begin to develop into its present form.*

At a *tablao* (flamenco club) there will be at least four people on stage, including the hand clapper.

THE SPANISH GUITAR

The guitar has a major role in flamenco, traditionally accompanying the singer. The flamenco guitar developed from the modern classical guitar, which evolved in Spain in the 19th century. Flamenco guitars have a lighter, shallower construction and a thickened plate below the soundhole, used to tap rhythms. Today, flamenco guitarists often perform solo. One of the greatest, Paco de Lucía, began by accompanying singers and dancers, before making his debut as a soloist in 1968. His inventive style, which combines traditional playing with Latin, jazz and rock elements, has influenced many musicians outside the realm of flamenco, such as the group Ketama, who play flamenco-blues.

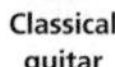
Classical guitar

Expert guitarist Paco de Lucía

Singing *is an integral part of flamenco and the singer often performs solo. Camarón de la Isla (1950–92), a gypsy born near Cádiz, was among the most famous contemporary* cantaores *(flamenco singers). He began as a singer of expressive* cante jondo *(literally, "deep song"), from which he developed his own distinctive style. He has inspired many singers.*

WHERE TO ENJOY FLAMENCO

Madrid has several good *tablaos,* flamenco venues, *(see p321).* In Granada, Sacromonte's caves *(p489)* are an exciting location. In Seville, the Barrio de Santa Cruz *(pp432–41)* has good *tablaos.*

The bailaora *(female dancer) is renowned for amazing footwork as well as intensive dance moments. Eva Yerbabuena and Sara Baras are both famous for their personal styles. Both lead their own acclaimed flamenco companies. Another flamenco star is Juana Amaya.*

The proud yet graceful posture of the *bailaora* is suggestive of a restrained passion.

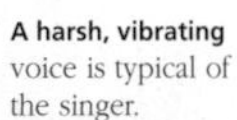

A harsh, vibrating voice is typical of the singer.

Traditional polka-dot dress

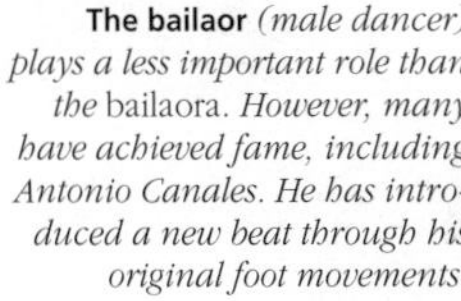

The bailaor *(male dancer) plays a less important role than the* bailaora. *However, many have achieved fame, including Antonio Canales. He has introduced a new beat through his original foot movements.*

THE FLAMENCO TABLAO

These days it is rare to come across spontaneous dancing at a *tablao*, but if dancers and singers are inspired, an impressive show usually results. Artists performing with *duende* ("magic spirit") will hear appreciative *olés* from the audience.

FLAMENCO RHYTHM

The unmistakable rhythm of flamenco is created by the guitar. Just as important, however, is the beat created by hand-clapping and by the dancer's feet in high-heeled shoes. The *bailaoras* may also beat a rhythm with castanets; Lucero Tena (born in 1939) became famous for her solos on castanets. Graceful hand movements are used to express the dancer's feelings of the moment – whether pain, sorrow, or happiness. Like the movements of the rest of the body, they are not choreographed, and the styles used vary from person to person.

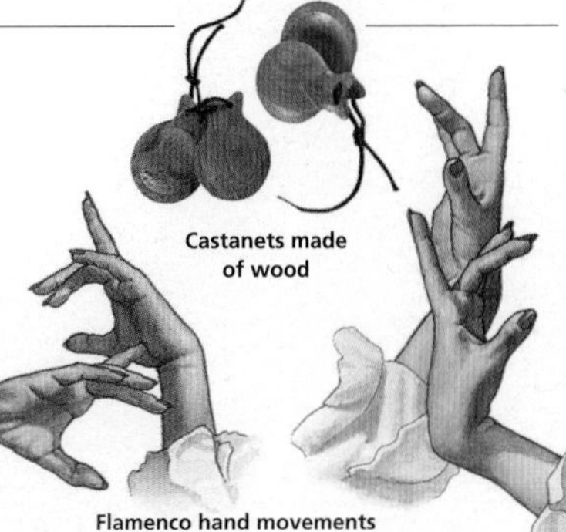

Castanets made of wood

Flamenco hand movements

Plaza de Toros de
SEVILLA
PROPIEDAD DE LA REAL MAESTRANZA DE CABALLERIA · Empresa PAGES
ESCACENA
(FUERA DE ABONO)
18
SEPTIEMBRE 1994
GRANDIOSA NOVILLADA CON PICADORES
6 ESCOGIDOS NOVILLOS 6
JANDILLA
PARA LOS NOVILLEROS
ADOLFO DE LOS REYES
LUIS REINOSO
"EL CARTUJANO"
GREGORIO BRAVO
LA NOVILLADA DARA COMIENZO A LAS 7 DE LA TARDE
GIN RIVES
GIN RIVES

EL ARENAL

Bounded by the Río Guadalquivir and guarded by the 13th-century Torre del Oro, El Arenal used to be a district of munitions stores and shipyards. Today this quarter is dominated by the dazzling white bullring, the Plaza de Toros de la Maestranza, where the Sevillians have been staging corridas for more than two centuries. The many bars and bodegas in the neighbouring streets are especially busy during the summer bullfighting season.

Torre del Oro shown on 20th-century tiles

Once central to the city's life, the influence of the Guadalquivir declined as it silted up during the 17th century. By then El Arenal had become a notorious underworld haunt clinging to the city walls. The river was converted into a canal in the early 20th century but restored to its former navigable glory in time for Expo '92. The east bank was transformed into a tree-lined promenade with excellent views of Triana and La Isla de la Cartuja across the water *(see p446)*.

The Hospital de la Caridad testifies to the city's continuing love affair with the Baroque. Its church is filled with famous paintings by Murillo, and the story of the Seville School is told in the immaculately restored Museo de Bellas Artes further north. The city's stunning collection of art includes great works by Zurbarán, Murillo and Valdés Leal.

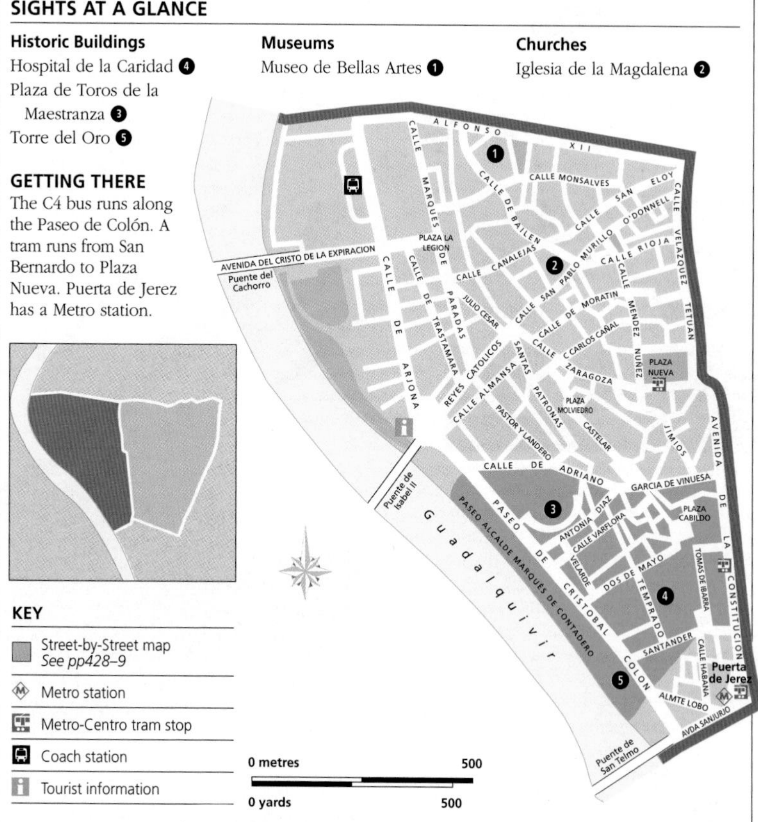

SIGHTS AT A GLANCE

Historic Buildings

Hospital de la Caridad ❹
Plaza de Toros de la Maestranza ❸
Torre del Oro ❺

Museums

Museo de Bellas Artes ❶

Churches

Iglesia de la Magdalena ❷

GETTING THERE

The C4 bus runs along the Paseo de Colón. A tram runs from San Bernardo to Plaza Nueva. Puerta de Jerez has a Metro station.

KEY

Street-by-Street map *See pp428–9*

Metro station

Metro-Centro tram stop

Coach station

Tourist information

◁ **Pasting up an advertisement for a bullfight on the walls of the Plaza de Toros de la Maestranza**

Street-by-Street: El Arenal

Once home to the port of Seville, El Arenal also housed the ammunition works and the artillery headquarters. Now its atmosphere is set by the city's bullring, the majestic Plaza de Toros de la Maestranza. During the bullfighting season *(see p430)* the area's bars and restaurants are packed, but for the rest of the year El Arenal's backstreets remain quiet. The riverfront is dominated by one of Seville's best-known monuments, the Moorish Torre del Oro, while the long, tree-lined promenade beside the Paseo de Cristóbal Colón is perfect for a slow, romantic walk along the Guadalquivir.

Statue of Carmen

★ Plaza de Toros de la Maestran
Seville's 18th-century bullring, one Spain's oldest, has a Baroque façac in white and ochre ❸

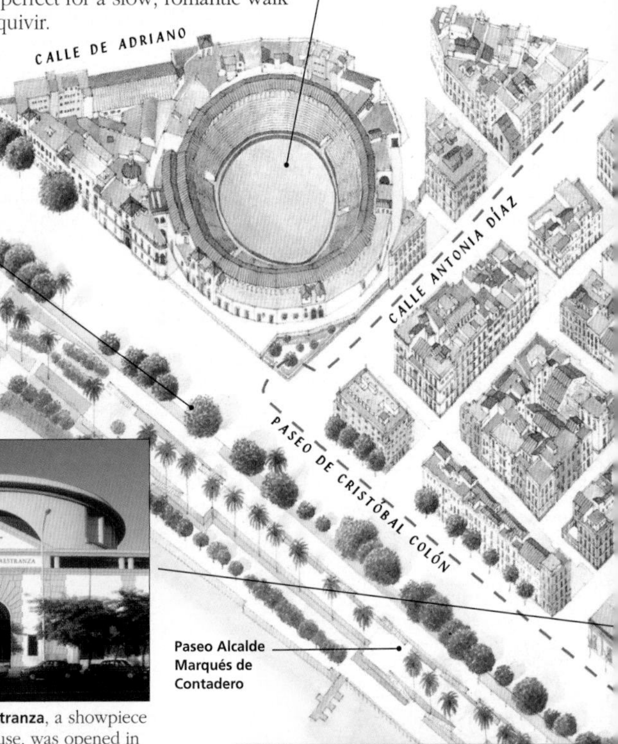

CALLE DE ADRIANO

Carmen *(see p445)*, sculpted in bronze, stands opposite the bullring.

CALLE ANTONIA DÍAZ

PASEO DE CRISTÓBAL COLÓN

The Teatro de la Maestranza, a showpiece theatre and opera house, was opened in 1991. Home of the Orquesta Sinfónica de Sevilla, the theatre also features international opera and dance companies.

Paseo Alcalde Marqués de Contadero

The Guadalquivir used to cause catastrophic inundations. Following floods in 1947 a barrage was constructed. Today, tourists enjoy peaceful boat trips, starting from the Torre del Oro.

STAR SIGHTS

- ★ Plaza de Toros de la Maestranza
- ★ Hospital de la Caridad
- ★ Torre del Oro

El Buzo ("The Diver") is one of many traditional tapas bars and *freidurías* on or just off Calle Arfe. Nearby is Meson Cinco Jotas, a bar where *jamón ibérico* *(see p462)* is served.

LOCATOR MAP

See Street Finder map 3

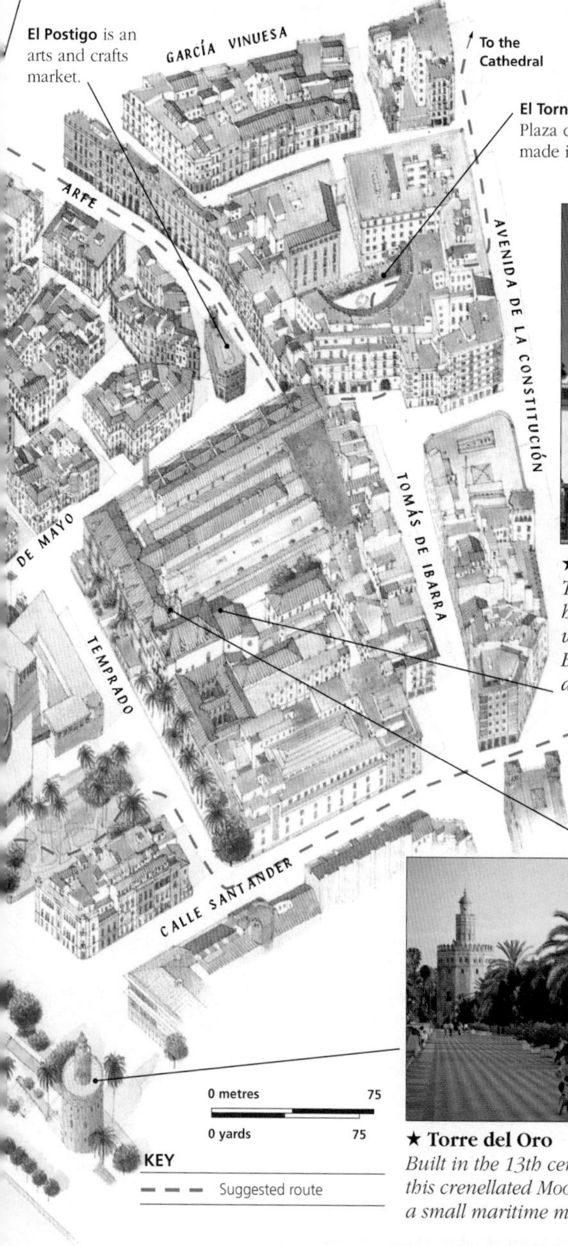

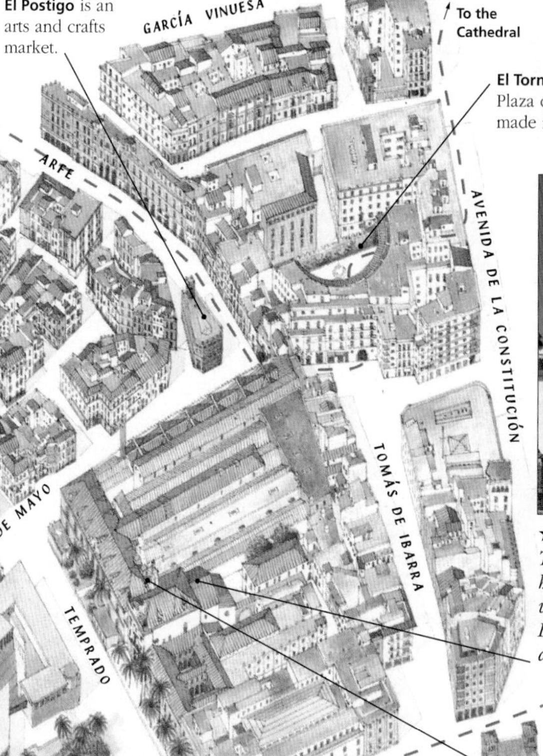

El Postigo is an arts and crafts market.

To the Cathedral

El Torno, in the secluded Plaza de Cabildo, sells sweets made in a convent.

★ Hospital de la Caridad

The walls of this Baroque hospital church are hung with fine paintings by Bartolomé Esteban Murillo and Juan de Valdés Leal ❹

To Real Alcázar

Maestranza de Artillería

0 metres 75

0 yards 75

KEY

Suggested route

★ Torre del Oro

Built in the 13th century to protect the port, this crenellated Moorish tower now houses a small maritime museum ❺

Madonna and Child in the Baroque Iglesia de la Magdalena

Museo de Bellas Artes ❶

Plaza del Museo 9. **Map** 1 B5. ***Tel*** *95 478 65 00. C2, C4, C5, 6, 13, 14, 43. 9am–8:30pm Tue–Sat, 9am–2:30pm Sun, public hols. Groups of 20: by appt. (free for EU citizens)* **www**.juntadeandalucia.es/cultura/museos

The Convento de la Merced Calzada houses one of the best art museums in Spain. Completed in 1612 by Juan de Oviedo, the building is designed around three patios. The Patio Mayor is the largest of these, remodelled by the architect Leonardo de Figueroa in 1724. The convent church is notable for its Baroque domed ceiling, painted by Domingo Martínez.

The museum's collection of Spanish art and sculpture, from the medieval to the modern, focuses on the work of Seville School artists. Among the star attractions is *La Servilleta*, a Virgin and Child (1665–8), which is said to be painted on a napkin *(servilleta)*. One of Murillo's most popular works, it may be seen in the restored convent church.

The boisterous *La Inmaculada* (1672) by Juan de Valdés Leal is in a gallery devoted to the artist's forceful religious paintings. Several fine works by Zurbarán include *San Hugo en el Refectorio* (1655), painted for the monastery at La Cartuja *(see p446)*.

San Jerónimo Penitente in the Museo de Bellas Artes

Iglesia de la Magdalena ❷

Calle San Pablo 10. **Map** 3 B1. ***Tel*** *95 422 96 03. Plaza Nueva. 43. 8–11am, 6:30–9pm Mon–Sat, 9am–1:30pm, 6:30–9pm Sun.*

This immense Baroque church by Leonardo de Figueroa, completed in 1709, is gradually being restored to its former glory. In its southwest corner stands the Capilla de la Quinta Angustia, a Mudéjar chapel with three cupolas. This chapel survived from an earlier church where the great Seville School painter Bartolomé Murillo was baptized in 1618. The font that was used for his baptism is now in the baptistry of the present building. The church's west front is topped by a belfry which is painted in vivid colours.

Among the religious works in the church are a painting by Francisco de Zurbarán, St *Dominic in Soria*, housed in the Capilla Sacramental (to the right of the south door), and frescoes by Lucas Valdés over the sanctuary. On the wall of the north transept there is a cautionary fresco of a medieval *auto-da-fe (see p274)*.

Plaza de Toros de la Maestranza ❸

Paseo de Cristóbal Colón 12. **Map** 3 B2. ***Tel*** *95 422 45 77. Puerta Jerez. Archivo de Indias. 9:30am–7pm daily (May–Oct: to 8pm). Good Friday, 25 Dec.* **www**.realmaestranza.com

Seville's famous bullring was built between 1761 and 1881.

The arcaded arena holds up to 14,000 spectators. Guided tours of this immense building start from the main entrance on Paseo de Cristóbal Colón. On the west side is the Puerta del Príncipe (Prince's Gate), through which the triumphant matadors are carried aloft by admirers from the crowd.

Just beyond the *enfermería* (emergency hospital) is a museum of portraits, posters and costumes, including a purple cape painted by Pablo Picasso. The tour continues on to the chapel where matadors pray for success, and then to the stables where the horses of the *picadores* (lance-carrying horsemen) are kept.

The bullfighting season starts on Easter Sunday and continues intermittently until October. Most *corridas* take place on Sunday evenings. Tickets can be bought from the *taquilla* (booking office) at the bullring.

A few doors down from the Plaza de Toros is the Teatro de la Maestranza. Seville's opera house and theatre, designed by Luis Marín de Terán and Aurelio de Pozo, opened in 1991. Fragments of ironwork from the 19th-century ammunition works that first occupied the site adorn the river façade.

Arcaded arena of the Plaza de Toros de la Maestranza, begun in 1761

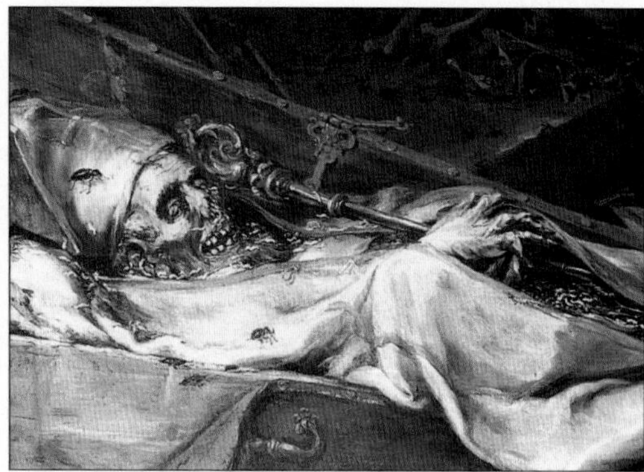

Finis Gloriae Mundi **by Juan de Valdés Leal in the Hospital de la Caridad**

Hospital de la Caridad ❹

Calle Temprado 3. **Map** *3 B2.* ***Tel*** *95 422 32 32. Puerta Jerez. C4. 9am–1:30pm, 3:30–6:30pm Mon–Sat, 9am–1pm Sun & public hols.*

This charity hospital was founded in 1674 and it is still used today as a sanctuary for elderly and infirm people. In the gardens stands a statue of its benefactor, Miguel de Mañara, whose dissolute life before he joined a brotherhood is said to have inspired the story of Don Juan. The façade of the hospital church, with its whitewashed walls, reddish stonework and framed *azulejos*, provides a glorious example of Sevillian Baroque.

Inside are two square patios decorated with plants, 18th-century Dutch tiles, and fine fountains with Italian statues depicting Charity and Mercy. At their northern end a passage to the right leads to another patio, containing a 13th-century arch which survives from the city's shipyards.

Inside the church there are a number of original canvases by some of the leading painters of the 17th century, despite the fact that some of its greatest artworks were looted by Marshal Soult during the Napoleonic occupation of 1808–14 *(see p62)*. Directly above the entrance is the ghoulish *Finis Gloriae Mundi* (The End of the World's Glory) by Juan de Valdés Leal, and opposite hangs his morbid *In Ictu Oculi* (In the Blink of an Eye). Many of the other works that can be seen are by Murillo, including *St John of God Carrying a Sick Man* and portraits of the Child Jesus and *St John the Baptist as a Boy*.

Torre del Oro ❺

Paseo de Cristóbal Colón. **Map** *3 B2.* ***Tel*** *95 422 24 19. Puerta Jerez. C3, C4. 10am–2pm Tue–Fri, 11am–2pm Sat & Sun. Aug & Mon. (free Tue & for EU citizens).*

In Moorish Seville the Tower of Gold formed part of the walled defences, linking up with the Real Alcázar *(see pp440–41)*. It was built as a defensive lookout in 1220, with a companion tower on the opposite bank. A metal chain stretched between them to prevent hostile ships from sailing upriver. The turret was added in 1760. The gold in its name may be the gilded *azulejos* that once clad its walls, or treasures from the Americas unloaded here. The tower has had many uses, such as a chapel and a prison. Now, as the Museo Marítimo, it exhibits maritime maps and antiques.

The Torre del Oro, built by the Almohads

SEVILLE'S FIESTAS

April Fair *(two weeks after Easter).* Life in the city moves over the river to the fairground for a week. Here, members of clubs, trade unions and neighbourhood groups meet in *casetas* (entertainment booths) to drink and dance all night to the infectious rhythm of sevillanas. (Access to booths may be limited to private parties.) Every day, from around 1pm, elegant, traditionally dressed riders on horseback and mantilla-crowned women in open carriages show off their finest flamenco attire in parades. During the afternoons, bullfights are often staged in the Maestranza bullring.

Float in Holy Week procession

Holy Week *(Mar/Apr).* Over 100 gilded *pasos* (floats bearing religious images) are borne through the streets between Palm Sunday and Easter Day. Singers in the crowds often spontaneously burst into *saetas*, fragments of song in praise of Christ or the Virgin. Emotions are high in the early hours of Good Friday as the images of the Virgen de la Macarena and the Virgen de la Esperanza of Triana emerge from their churches.

Corpus Christi *(May/Jun).* The *Seises*, boys dressed in Baroque costume, dance before the main altar of the cathedral *(see p437)*.

Street-by-Street: Santa Cruz

Window grille, Santa Cruz

The maze of narrow streets to the east of Seville Cathedral and the Real Alcázar represents Seville at its most romantic and compact. As well as the expected souvenir shops, tapas bars and strolling guitarists, there are plenty of picturesque alleys, hidden plazas and flower-decked patios to reward the casual wanderer. Once a Jewish ghetto, its restored buildings, with characteristic window grilles, are now a harmonious mix of upmarket residences and tourist accommodation. Good bars and restaurants make the area well worth an evening visit.

Plaza Virgen de los Reyes is often lined by horse-drawn carriages. In the centre of the square is an early 20th-century fountain by José Lafita.

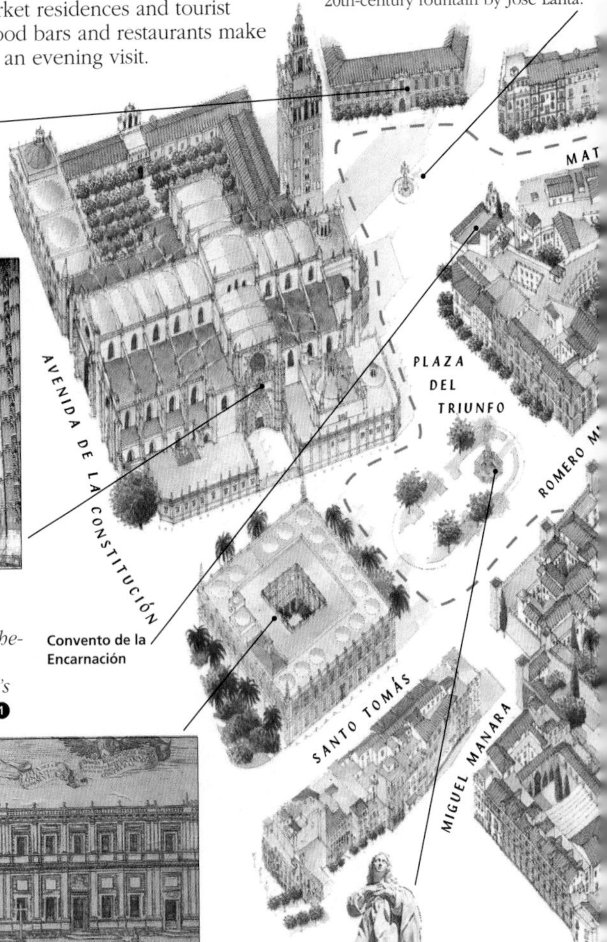

Palacio Arzobispal, the 18th-century Archbishop's Palace, is still used by Seville's clergy.

AVENIDA DE LA CONSTITUCIÓN

PLAZA DEL TRIUNFO

ROMERO M

MAT

SANTO TOMÁS

MIGUEL MANARA

★ Cathedral and La Giralda

This huge Gothic cathedral and its Moorish bell tower are Seville's most popular sights ❶

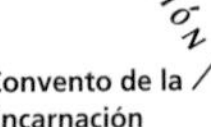

Convento de la Encarnación

Archivo de Indias

Built in the 16th century as a merchants' exchange, the Archive of the Indies now houses documents relating to the Spanish colonization of the Americas ❻

Plaza del Triunfo has a Baroque column celebrating the city's survival of the great earthquake of 1755. I the centre is a mode statue of the Virgin Mary (Immaculate Conception).

For hotels and restaurants in this region see pp590–91 and pp640–42

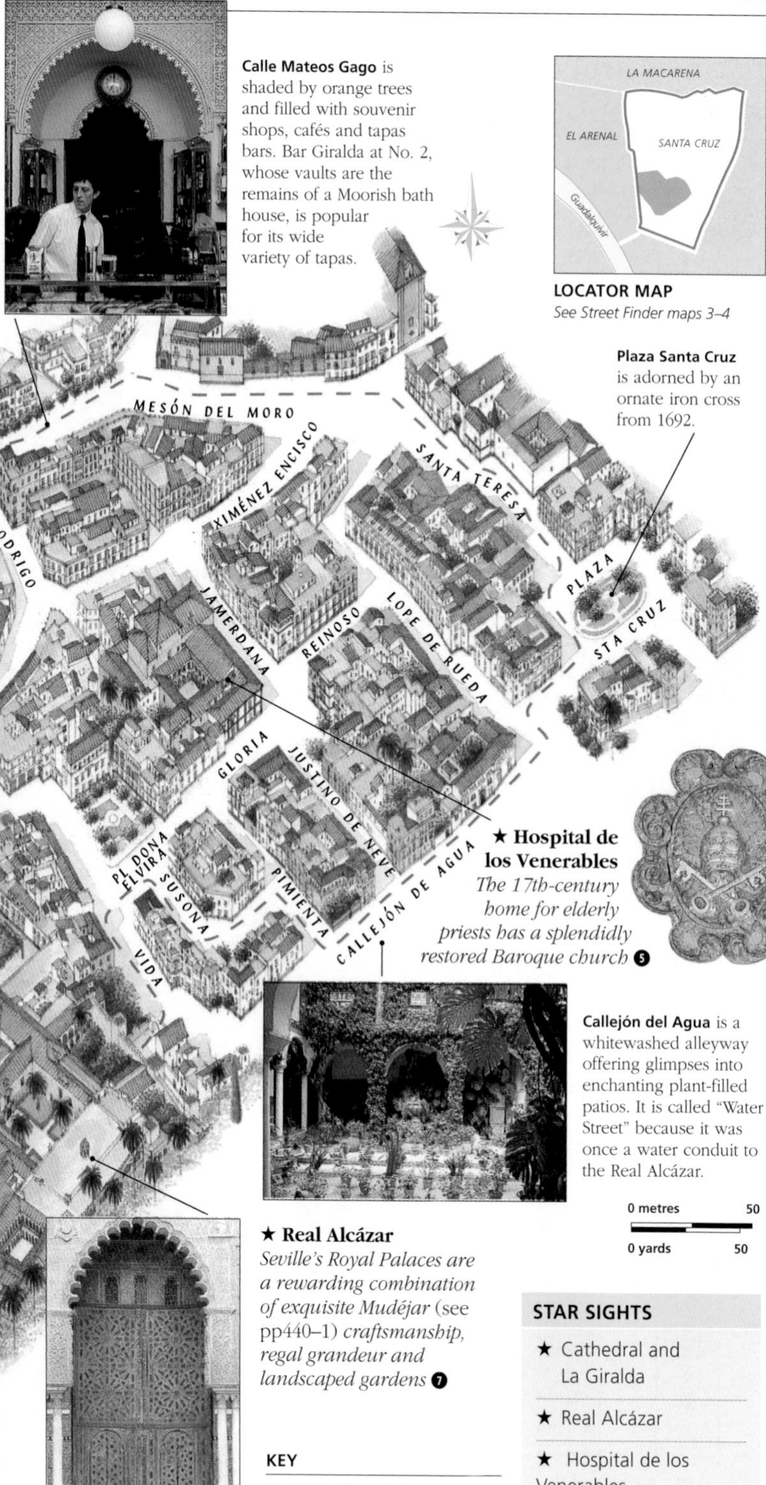

Calle Mateos Gago is shaded by orange trees and filled with souvenir shops, cafés and tapas bars. Bar Giralda at No. 2, whose vaults are the remains of a Moorish bath house, is popular for its wide variety of tapas.

LOCATOR MAP

See Street Finder maps 3–4

Plaza Santa Cruz is adorned by an ornate iron cross from 1692.

★ Hospital de los Venerables

The 17th-century home for elderly priests has a splendidly restored Baroque church 5

Callejón del Agua is a whitewashed alleyway offering glimpses into enchanting plant-filled patios. It is called "Water Street" because it was once a water conduit to the Real Alcázar.

★ Real Alcázar

Seville's Royal Palaces are a rewarding combination of exquisite Mudéjar (see pp440–1) *craftsmanship, regal grandeur and landscaped gardens* 7

KEY

– – – Suggested route

STAR SIGHTS

★ Cathedral and La Giralda

★ Real Alcázar

★ Hospital de los Venerables

Seville Cathedral and La Giralda ❶

16th-century stained glass

Seville's cathedral occupies the site of a great mosque built by the Almohads (see p54) in the late 12th century. La Giralda, its bell tower, and the Patio de los Naranjos are a legacy of this Moorish structure. Work on the Christian cathedral, the largest in Europe, began in 1401 and took just over a century to complete. As well as enjoying its Gothic immensity and the works of art in its chapels and sacristy, visitors can climb La Giralda or visit the cathedral roof for stunning city views.

★ La Giralda
The bell tower is crowned by a bronze weathervane (giraldillo) *portraying Faith, from which it takes its name. A replica has replaced the original vane.*

★ Patio de los Naranjos
In Moorish times worshippers would wash their hands and feet in the fountain under the orange trees before praying.

Group Entrance

Puerta del Perdón (Exit)

Roman pillars brought from Itálica (see p476) surround the cathedral steps.

THE RISE OF LA GIRALDA

The tower was built as a minaret in 1198. In the 14th century the bronze spheres at its top were replaced by Christian symbols. A new belfry was planned in 1557, but built to a more ornate design by Hernán Ruiz in 1568.

1198

1400

1557 (plan)

1568

Retablo Mayor
Santa María de la Sede, the cathedral's patron saint, sits at the high altar below a waterfall of gold. The 44 gilded relief panels of the reredos were carved by Spanish and Flemish sculptors between 1482 and 1564.

VISITORS' CHECKLIST

Avenida de la Constitución. **Map** 3 C2. ***Tel*** *954 21 49 71.* *Puerta Jerez.* *Archivo de Indias.* *C3, C4, C5, 5, 41, 42.* **Cathedral & La Giralda** *Sep–Jun: 11am–5:30pm Mon–Sat; 2:30–6:30pm Sun; Jul–Aug: 9:30am–4:30pm Mon–Sat, 2:30–6:30pm Sun.* *8:30am, 9am, 10am, 12:30pm, 5pm Mon–Sat (Sat also 8pm); 8:30am, 10am, 11am, noon, 1pm, 5pm, 6pm Sun.* **www**.catedraldesevilla.es

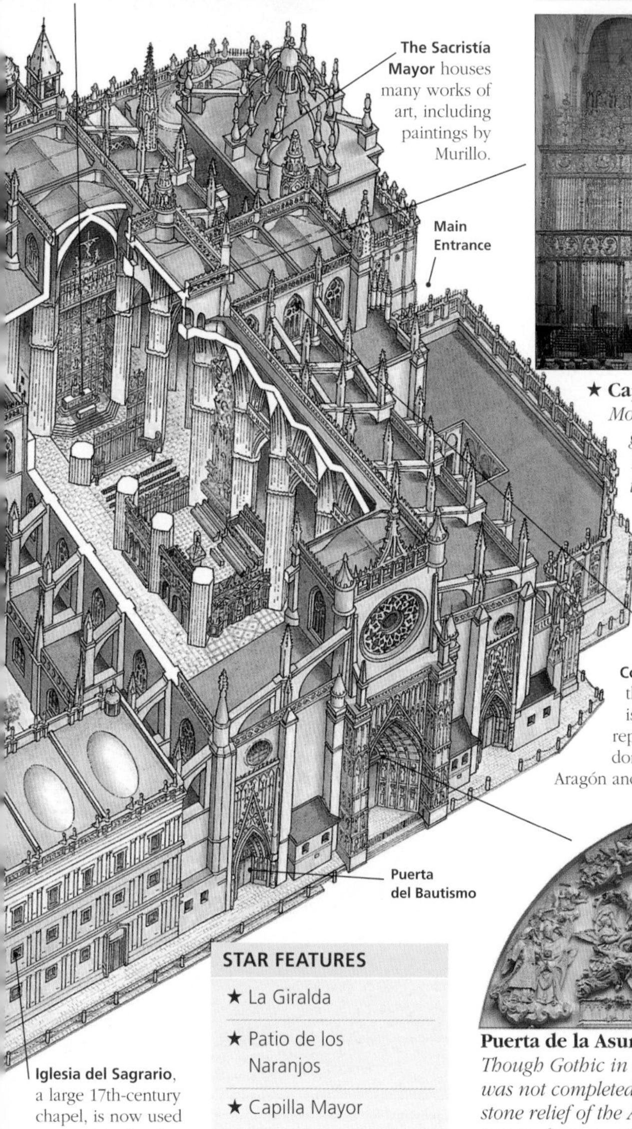

The Sacristía Mayor houses many works of art, including paintings by Murillo.

Main Entrance

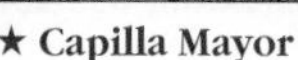

★ Capilla Mayor
Monumental iron grilles forged in 1518–32 enclose the main chapel, which is dominated by the overwhelming Retablo Mayor.

The Tomb of Columbus dates from the 1890s. His coffin is carried by bearers representing the kingdoms of Castile, León, Aragón and Navarra *(see p54)*.

Puerta del Bautismo

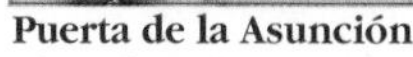

Puerta de la Asunción
Though Gothic in style, this portal was not completed until 1833. A stone relief of the Assumption of the Virgin decorates the tympanum.

Iglesia del Sagrario, a large 17th-century chapel, is now used as a parish church.

STAR FEATURES

- ★ La Giralda
- ★ Patio de los Naranjos
- ★ Capilla Mayor

Genoese fountain in the Mudéjar Patio Principal of the Casa de Pilatos

Ayuntamiento ❷

Plaza Nueva 1. **Map** 3 C1. ***Tel*** *95 459 01 01.* *Plaza Nueva.* *tours at 5:30pm & 6pm Tue, Wed & Thu.* *Jul & Aug.* **www**.sevilla.org

Seville's City Hall stands between the Plaza de San Francisco, where *autos-da-fe* (public trials of heretics) were held, and the Plaza Nueva.

Building was completed between 1527 and 1534. The side bordering the Plaza de San Francisco is a fine example of ornate Plateresque style *(see p25)* favoured by the architect Diego de Riaño. The west front is Neo-Classical, built in 1891. Sculpted ceilings survive in the vestibule and the lower Casa Consistorial (Council Meeting Room), containing Velázquez's *Imposition of the Chasuble on St Ildefonso*. The upper Casa Consistorial has a dazzling coffered ceiling and paintings by Zurbarán and Valdés Leal.

Calle de las Sierpes ❸

Map 3 C1. *10, 11, 12, 15, 20, 21, 24, 27, 30, 32.* **Casa de la Condesa Lebrija** ***Tel*** *95 422 78 02.* *Plaza Nueva.* *10:30am–7:30pm Mon–Fri, 10am–2pm, 4–6pm Sat, 10am–2pm Sun; earlier closing Jul & Aug.* *Sun in Jul & Aug.* **www**.palaciodelebrija.com

Seville's main shopping promenade, the "Street of the Snakes", runs north from Plaza de San Francisco. Long-established stores selling hats, fans and traditional *mantillas* (lace headdresses) stand alongside clothes and souvenir shops. The parallel streets of Cuna and Tetuán also offer some enjoyable window-shopping. Halfway up the road walking north, Calle Jovellanos to the left leads to the 17th-century Capillita de San José. Further on at the junction with Calle Pedro Caravaca is the Real Círculo de Labradores, a men's club founded in 1856.

Opposite – with its entrance in Calle Cuna – is a 15th-century private mansion, the **Casa de la Condesa Lebrija**. Treasures on display include a Roman mosaic from the ruins of nearby Itálica *(see p476)* and a collection of *azulejos*.

Right at the end of the street is La Campana, Seville's best-known *pastelería*.

Casa de Pilatos ❹

Plaza de Pilatos 1. **Map** 4 D1. ***Tel*** *95 422 52 98.* *C3, C4.* *9am–6pm daily (until 7pm Apr–Sep).* *first floor.* *ground floor.*

Enraptured by by the architectural and decorative wonders of High Renaissance Italy and the Holy Land, the first Marquis of Tarifa built the Casa de Pilatos. So called because it was thought to resemble Pontius Pilate's home in Jerusalem, today it is the residence of the Dukes of Medinaceli and is one of the finest palaces in Seville.

Visitors enter through a marble portal, commissioned by the Marquis in 1529 from Genoese craftsmen. Across the arcaded Apeadero (carriage yard) is the Patio Principal. This courtyard is essentially Mudéjar *(see p55)* in style and decorated with *azulejos* and intricate plasterwork. In its corners are three Roman statues, depicting Minerva, a dancing muse and Ceres, and a Greek statue of Athena, dating from the 5th century BC.

In its centre is a fountain which was imported from Genoa. To the right, through the Salón del Pretorio with its coffered ceiling and marquetry, is the Corredor de Zaquizamí.

AZULEJOS

Colourful *azulejos*, glazed ceramic tiles, are a striking feature of Seville. The craft was introduced to Spain by the Moors, who created fantastic mosaics in sophisticated geometric patterns for palace walls – the word *azulejo* derives from the Arabic for "little stone". New techniques were introduced in the 16th century and later mass production extended their use to decorative signs, shop façades and advertising hoardings.

Azulejo billboard for Studebaker Motor Cars (1924), Calle Tetuán

Fresco by Juan de Valdés Leal in the Hospital de los Venerables

The antiquities on display in adjacent rooms include a bas-relief of *Leda and the Swan* and two Roman reliefs commemorating the Battle of Actium of 31 BC.

Coming back to the Patio Principal, you turn right into the Salón de Descanso de los Jueces. Beyond is a rib-vaulted Gothic chapel, with Mudéjar plasterwork walls and ceiling. On the altar is a copy of a 4th-century sculpture in the Vatican, *The Good Shepherd*. Left through the Gabinete de Pilatos, with its small central fountain, is the Jardín Grande.

Returning once more to the main patio, behind the statue of Ceres, a tiled staircase leads to the upper floor. It is roofed with a wonderful *media naranja* (half orange) cupola built in 1537. There are Mudéjar ceilings in some rooms, full of family portraits and antiques.

Hospital de los Venerables ❺

Plaza de los Venerables 8. **Map** 3 C2. ***Tel*** *95 456 26 96.* *Archivo de Indias.* *10am–1:30pm, 4–7:30pm daily.* *1 Jan, Good Friday, 25 Dec.*

Set in the heart of the Barrio de Santa Cruz, this home for elderly priests was begun in 1675 and completed around 20 years later by Leonardo de Figueroa. It has now been restored as a cultural centre by FOCUS (Fundación Fondo de Cultura de Sevilla).

Stairs from the central, rose-coloured, sunken patio lead to the upper floors, which, along with the infirmary and cellar, are used as exhibition galleries.

The Hospital church, a showcase of Baroque splendours, has frescoes by both Juan de Valdés Leal and his son Lucas Valdés. Other highlights of the church include sculptures of St Peter and St Ferdinand by Pedro Roldán, flanking the east door; and *The Apotheosis of St Ferdinand* by Lucas Valdés, top centre in the reredos of the main altar. Its frieze (inscribed in Greek) advises to "Fear God and Honour the Priest".

In the sacristy, the ceiling has an effective *trompe l'oeil* depicting *The Triumph of the Cross* by Juan de Valdés Leal.

Archivo de Indias ❻

Avda de la Constitución. **Map** 3 C2. ***Tel*** *95 450 05 28.* *Puerta Jerez.* *Archivo de Indias.* *9am–4pm Mon–Sat, 10am–2pm Sun.*

The Archive of the Indies illustrates Seville's pre-eminent role in the colonization and exploitation of the New World. Built between 1584–98 to designs by Juan de Herrera, co-architect of El Escorial *(see pp330–31)*, it was originally a lonja (exchange), where merchants traded. In 1785, Carlos III had all Spanish documents relating to the "Indies" collected under one roof. Among the archive's 86 million handwritten pages and 8,000 maps and drawings are letters from Columbus, Cortés, and Cervantes and the extensive correspondence of Felipe II.

Upstairs, the library rooms contain regularly changing displays of drawings, maps and facsimile documents.

Façade of the Archivo de Indias by Juan de Herrera

Real Alcázar 7

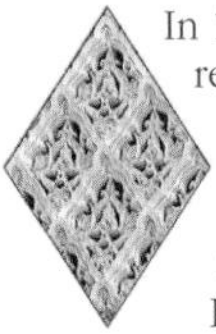

In 1364 Pedro I ordered the construction of a royal residence within the palaces which had been built by the city's Almohad *(see p54)* rulers. Within two years, craftsmen from Granada and Toledo had created a jewel box of Mudéjar patios and halls, the Palacio Pedro I, now at the heart of Seville's Real Alcázar. Later monarchs added their own distinguishing marks: Isabel I *(see p56)* dispatched navigators to explore the New World from her Casa de la Contratación, while Carlos I (the Holy Roman Emperor Charles V – *see p58*) had grandiose, richly decorated apartments built.

Mudéjar stucco

Gardens of the Alcázar
Laid out with terraces, fountains and pavilions, these gardens provide a delightful refuge from the heat and bustle of Seville.

Jardín de Troya

★ Charles V Rooms
Vast tapestries and lively 16th-century azulejos *decorate the vaulted halls of the apartments and chapel of Charles V.*

Patio del Crucero lies above the old baths.

PLAN OF THE REAL ALCÁZAR

The complex has been the home of Spanish kings for almost seven centuries. The palace's upper floor is used by the royal family today.

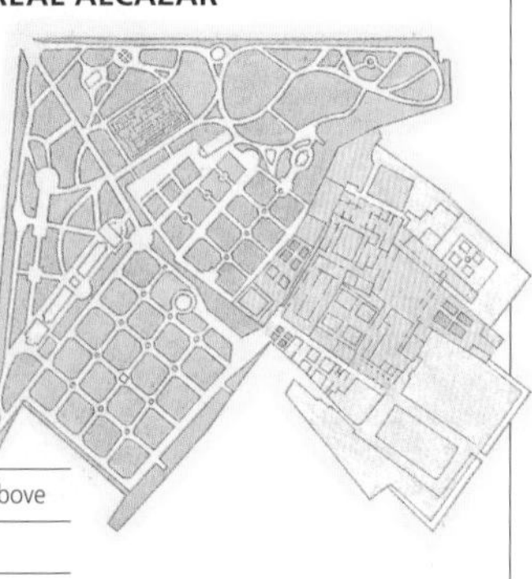

KEY

Area illustrated above

Gardens

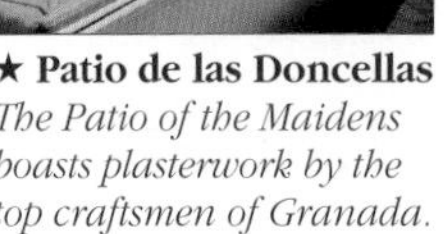

★ Patio de las Doncellas
The Patio of the Maidens boasts plasterwork by the top craftsmen of Granada.

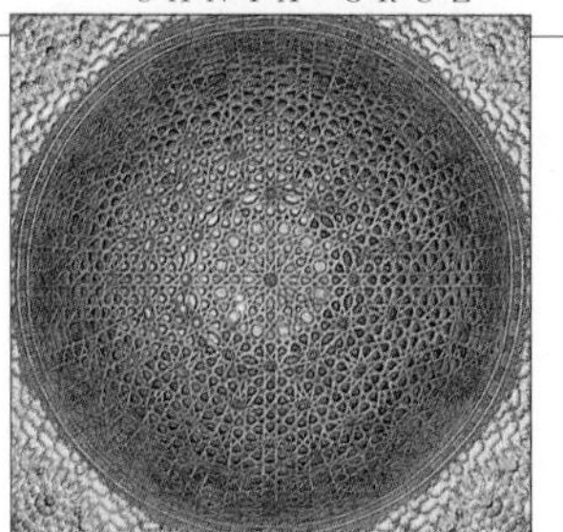

★ Salón de Embajadores
Built in 1427, the dazzling dome of the Ambassadors' Hall is of carved and gilded, interlaced wood.

VISITORS' CHECKLIST

Patio de Banderas. **Map** 3 C2. ***Tel*** *95 450 23 24.* Ⓜ *Puerta Jerez.* *Archivo de Indias.* *9:30am–7pm daily (to 5pm Oct–Mar).* **www**.patronato-alcazarsevilla.es

Horseshoe Arches
Azulejos and complex plasterwork decorate the Ambassadors' Hall, which has three symmetrically arranged, ornate archways, each with three horseshoe arches.

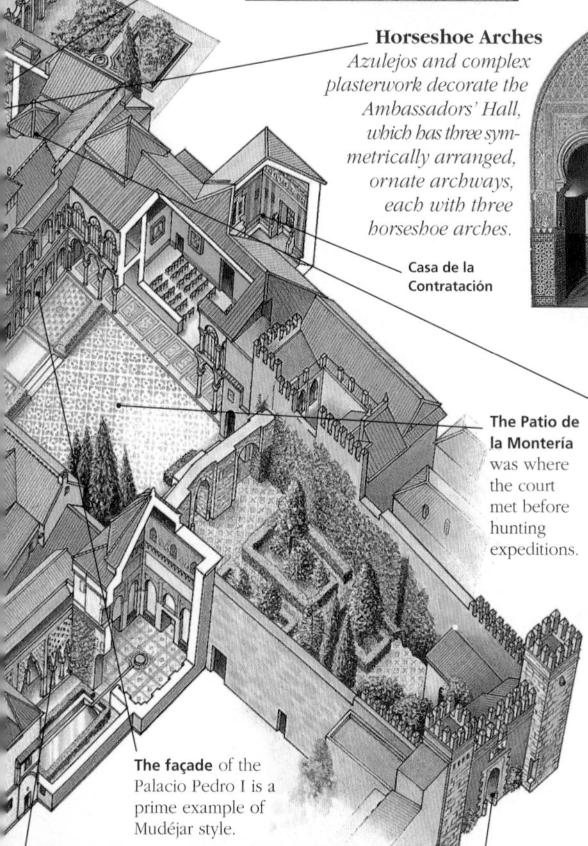

Casa de la Contratación

The Patio de la Montería was where the court met before hunting expeditions.

Patio de las Muñecas
The Patio of the Dolls and its surrounding bedrooms formed the domestic heart of the palace. It derives its name from two tiny faces on one of its arches.

The façade of the Palacio Pedro I is a prime example of Mudéjar style.

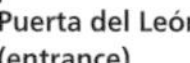

Puerta del León (entrance)

Patio del Yeso
The Patio of Plaster, a garden with flower beds and a water channel, retains features of the earlier, 12th-century Almohad Alcázar.

STAR FEATURES

- ★ Charles V Rooms
- ★ Patio de las Doncellas
- ★ Salón de Embajadores

FURTHER AFIELD

The north of Seville, La Macarena, is a characterful mix of decaying Baroque and Mudéjar churches, and old-style tapas bars. The place to visit here is the Basílica de la Macarena, a shrine to Seville's much-venerated Virgen de la Esperanza Macarena. Among the many convents and churches in the area, the Convento de Santa Paula offers a rare opportunity to peep behind the walls of an enclosed community.

Roman column, Alameda de Hércules

The area south of the city is dominated by the extensive, leafy Parque María Luisa. A large part of the park originally formed the grounds of the Baroque Palacio de San Telmo. Many of the historic buildings in the park were erected for the Ibero-American Exposition of 1929. The grand five-star Hotel Alfonso XIII and the crescent-shaped Plaza de España are the most striking legacies of this upsurge of Andalusian pride. Nearby is the Royal Tobacco Factory, forever associated with the fictional gypsy heroine Carmen, who toiled in its sultry halls. Today, it is part of the Universidad, Seville's university.

There is more to see across the river from the city centre. With its cobbled streets and shops selling ceramics, the Triana quarter retains the feel of old Seville. In the 15th century a Carthusian monastery, the Monasterio de Santa María de las Cuevas, was built north of Triana. Columbus resided there and the area around it, the Isla de la Cartuja, was chosen as the site for Expo '92. Today the site is home mainly to offices but the Isla Mágica amusement park and Teatro Central are also located here.

SIGHTS AT A GLANCE

Historic Buildings

Camera Oscura, Torre de Los Perdigones ⑩
Palacio de San Telmo ⑤
Universidad ⑥

Churches and Convents

Basílica de la Macarena ①
Convento de Santa Paula ②
Iglesia de San Pedro ③

Historic Areas

Isla de la Cartuja ⑨
Metropol Parasol ④
Parque María Luisa ⑦
Triana ⑧

0 kilometres 1
0 miles 0.5

KEY

City centre
Parks and open spaces
Coach station
Railway station
Major road
Minor road

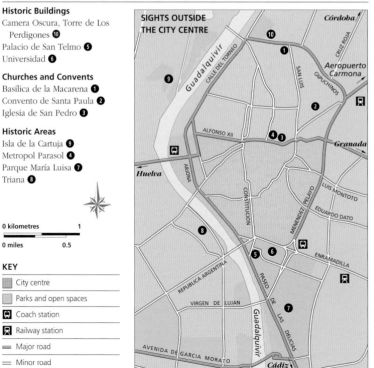

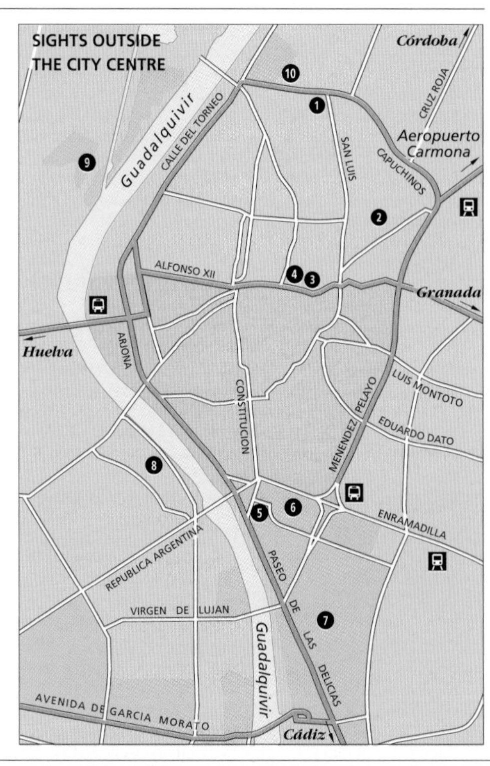

◁ **Pabellón de Andalucía, built on the Isla de la Cartuja for Expo '92**

St John the Baptist **by Montañés in the Convento de Santa Paula**

Basílica de la Macarena ❶

Calle Bécquer 1. **Map** 2 D3. ***Tel*** *95 437 01 95.* C1, C2, C3, C4, 2, 10, 13, 14. *9am–2pm, 5–9pm daily (from 9:30am Sun & public hols). Easter Fri. for museum.*

The Basílica de la Macarena was built in 1949 in the Neo-Baroque style by Gómez Millán as a new home for the much-loved Virgen de la Esperanza Macarena. It butts on to the 13th-century Iglesia de San Gil, where the image was housed until a fire in 1936.

The image of the Virgin, standing above the main altar amid waterfalls of gold and silver, has been attributed to Luisa Roldán (1656–1703), the most talented female artist of the Seville School. The wall-paintings, by Rafael Rodríguez Hernández, date from 1982.

The Virgin's magnificent processional gowns and jewels are held in the Treasury museum.

Convento de Santa Paula ❷

C/ Santa Paula 11. **Map** 2 E5. ***Tel*** *95 453 63 30.* C1, C2, C3, C4, C5, 10, 11. *10am–1pm Tue–Sun.*

Founded in 1475, Santa Paula is a working convent and home to 40 nuns. The museum consists of two galleries filled with religious artifacts and paintings. The nave of the convent church has an elaborate wooden roof, dating from 1623. Among the statues in the church are St John the Evangelist and St John the Baptist, both the work of Juan Martínez Montañés.

Iglesia de San Pedro ❸

Plaza San Pedro. **Map** 2 D5. ***Tel*** *954 21 68 58.* 10, 11, 12, 15, 16, 20, 24, 27, 32, C5. *8:30am–1pm, 7–8pm Mon–Sat; 9:30am–1pm, 7–8pm Sun.*

Diego Velázquez, the Golden Age painter *(see p32)*, was baptized in this church in 1599. It is built in a typically Sevillian mix of architectural styles. Mudéjar elements survive in the lobed brickwork of its tower, which is surmounted by a Baroque *(see p25)* belfry. The principal portal – facing the Plaza de San Pedro – is also Baroque, and was added by Diego de Quesada in 1613.

The poorly lit interior has a Mudéjar wooden ceiling. The vault of one of its chapels is decorated with exquisite geometric patterns of bricks.

Behind the church, in Calle Doña María Coronel, cakes are sold from a revolving drum in the wall of the 14th-century Convento de Santa Inés.

Metropol Parasol ❹

Plaza de la Encarnación. **Map** 2 D5. ***Tel*** *902 45 99 54.* C5, 10, 11, 12, 15, 16, 20, 24, 27, 32. **Observation deck & walkways** *10:30am–10:30pm Tue–Sun, 10:30am–12:30am Fri & Sat.* **Museum** *10am–8pm Tue–Sat, 10am–2pm Sun.*

Referred to as *"Las Setas"* ("The Mushrooms") by locals, this ultra-modern structure, designed by architect Jürgen Mayer H, opened in 2011. Its stunning latticed timber canopy spans the Plaza de la Encarnación on giant pillars. The complex includes an archaeological museum, a market and several bars and restaurants. An observation deck offers fabulous city views.

Palacio de San Telmo ❺

Avenida de Roma. **Map** 3 C3. ***Tel*** *955 00 10 10.* *Puerta de Jerez.* *C3, C4, C5, 5, 41.* *for guided visits by appointment at: 4pm & 8pm Thu; 10am, 11:30am, 1:30pm, 4pm, 5:30pm & 7:30pm Sat.*

This imposing palace, named after the patron saint of navigators, was built in 1682 as a university to train ships' pilots, navigators and high-ranking officers. In 1849 it became the residence of the Dukes of Monpensier and until 1893 its grounds included what is now Parque María Luisa. Today it is the presidential headquarters of the Junta de Andalucía (the regional government).

Parque María Luisa ❼

Map 4 D4. *Prado de San Sebastián.* **Museo Arqueológico** ***Tel*** *95 478 64 74.* *9am–8:30pm Tue–Sat, 9am–2:30pm Sun.* *1 & 6 Jan, 1 May, 24, 25 & 31 Dec.* *(free for EU citizens).* **Museo de Artes y Costumbres Populares** ***Tel*** *95 471 23 91.* *as above.*

Princess Maria Luisa donated part of the grounds of the Palacio de San Telmo to the city

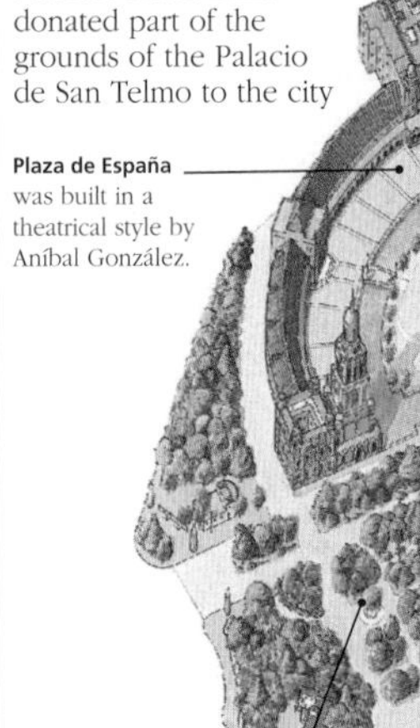

Plaza de España was built in a theatrical style by Aníbal González.

The Glorieta de Bécquer is an arbour with sculpted figures depicting the phases of love – a tribute to poet Gustavo Adolfo Bécquer.

The most striking feature of the Palacio de San Telmo is the exuberant Churrigueresque portal designed by Leonardo de Figueroa, and completed in 1734. Surrounding the Ionic columns are allegorical figures representing the Sciences and Arts. St Telmo, holding a ship and charts, is flanked by the sword-bearing St Ferdinand and St Hermenegildo, with a cross. On the north façade is ranged a row of sculptures of Sevillian celebrities, added by Susillo in 1895. Among them are artists such as Montañés, Murillo and Velázquez.

Opposite is Seville's most famous hotel, the Alfonso XIII, dating from the 1920s. Non-residents are welcome to visit the bar and the restaurant.

Universidad ❻

Calle San Fernando 4. **Map** 3 C3. ***Tel*** *95 455 10 00.* *Puerta de Jerez.* *Puerta de Jerez or Prado de San Sebastian.* *C3, C4, 5, 25.* *8am–8:30pm Mon–Fri.* *public hols.* **www**.us.es

The former Real Fábrica de Tabacos (Royal Tobacco Factory) is now part of Seville University. In the 19th century, three-quarters of Europe's cigars were manufactured here, rolled by 10,000 *cigarreras* (female cigar-makers) – the inspiration for French author Mérimée's *Carmen*.

Built in 1728–71, the factory complex is the largest building in Spain after El Escorial *(see pp330–31)* near Madrid.

Baroque fountain in one of the patios in the Universidad

The moat and watchtowers are evidence of the importance given to protecting the king's lucrative tobacco monopoly.

for this park in 1893. Landscaped by Jean Forestier, director of the Bois de Boulogne in Paris, the park was the leafy setting for the 1929 Ibero-American Exposition. The legacies of this extravaganza are the Plaza de España, decorated with regional scenes on ceramic tiles, and the Plaza de América, both the work of Aníbal González. On the latter, in the Pabellón Mudéjar, the Museo de Artes y Costumbres Populares displays traditional Andalusian folk arts. The Neo-Renaissance Pabellón de las Bellas Artes houses the provincial Museo Arqueológico. Exhibits include statues and fragments found at Itálica *(see p476)*.

Museo Arqueológico

Fuente de los Leones

Plaza de América

Pabellón Real

The Isleta de los Patos sits in a lake graced by ducks and swans.

Museo de Artes y Costumbres Populares

Decorative tiles at Cerámica Santa Ana, a popular ceramics shop in Triana

Triana ❽

Map 3 A2. *Plaza de Cuba, Parque de los Príncipes.*

This close-knit area, named after the Roman Emperor Trajan, was once Seville's gypsy quarter. Triana remains a traditional working-class district, with compact, flower-filled streets. For centuries it has been famous for its potteries. The best-known of its ceramics shops today is Cerámica Santa Ana at No. 31 Calle San Jorge.

A good way to approach Triana is across the Puente de Isabel II, leading to the Plaza del Altozano. The **Museo de la Inquisición**, in Castillo de San Jorge, avoids sensational images and concludes with a presentation on human rights today. Nearby is one of the characteristic streets of the area, the Calle Rodrigo de Triana, named after the Andalusian sailor who was the first to sight the shores of the New World on Columbus's voyage of 1492.

The Iglesia de Santa Ana, founded in the 13th century, is Triana's most popular church. In the baptistry is the Gypsy Font, believed to pass on the gift of flamenco song to the children of the faithful.

Isla de la Cartuja ❾

Map 1 B3. **www**.caac.es *C1, C2.* **Monasterio de Santa María de las Cuevas** *Tue–Sun.* **Centro Andaluz de Arte Contemporáneo** ***Tel*** *95 503 70 70.* *as above.* *(free Tue for EU citizens).* **Isla Mágica** ***Tel*** *902 16 17 16.* *Apr: Sat & Sun; May: Wed–Sun; Jun, Jul: Tue–Sun; Aug & 1–10 Sep: daily; mid-Sep–Dec & 1st week Jan: Sat, Sun.* *1 Jan, last 3 weeks of Jan–Mar, 24, 25 & 31 Dec.* **www**.islamagica.es

The site of Expo '92 *(see pp68–9)*, this area has since been transformed into a complex of exhibition halls, museums and leisure spaces.

The 15th-century Carthusian Monasterio de Santa María de las Cuevas was inhabited by monks until 1836. Columbus stayed and worked here, and it houses the Centro Andaluz de Arte Contemporáneo, which contains works by Andalusian artists, as well as Spanish and international art.

The centrepiece of Expo, the Lago de España, is part of the Isla Mágica theme park. This re-creates the journeys and exploits of the explorers who left Seville in the 16th century for the New World.

Cámara Oscura ❿

Torre de los Perdigones, C/ Resolana. **Map** 2 D3. *C1, C2, C3, C4, 2, 13, 14.* ***Tel*** *679 09 10 73.* *daily.*

This huge camera obscura uses mirrors and magnifying lenses to display an image of the surrounding area. The Tower of Perdigones also offers scenic views of the city.

Main entrance of the Carthusian Monasterio de Santa María de las Cuevas, founded in 1400

SEVILLE STREET FINDER

The map references given with the sights described in the Seville section of the guide refer to the maps on the following pages. Map references are also given for Seville hotels *(see pp590–91)* and restaurants *(pp640–42)*. The schematic map below shows the area of Seville covered by the *Street Finder*. The symbols used for the sights and other features are listed in the key at the foot of the page.

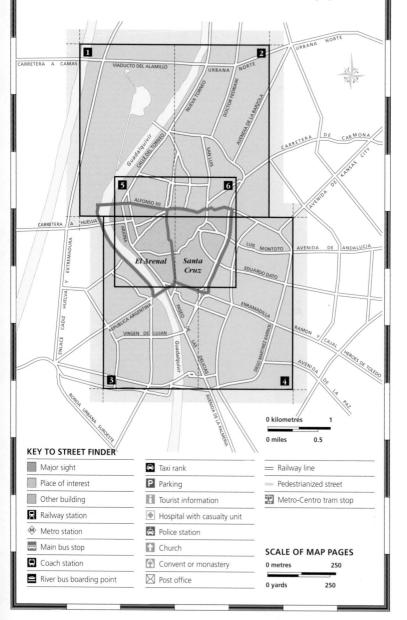

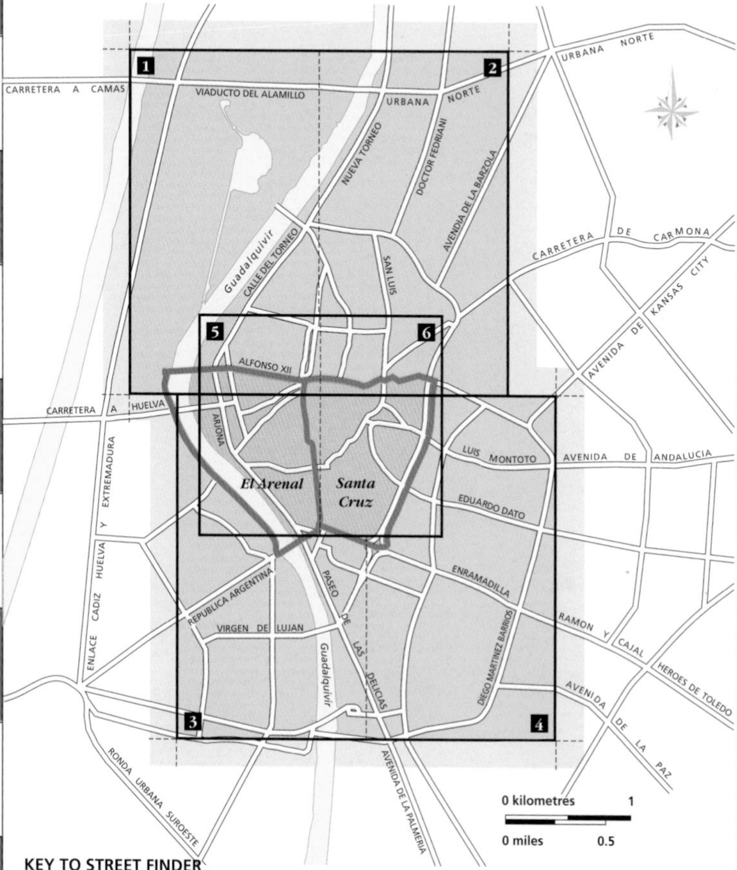

1
2
3
4
5
6
CARRETERA A CAMAS
VIADUCTO DEL ALAMILLO
URBANA NORTE
NUEVA TORNEO
DOCTOR FEDRIANI
AVENIDA DE LA BARZOLA
Guadalquivir
CALLE DEL TORNEO
SAN LUIS
CARRETERA DE CARMONA
AVENIDA DE KANSAS CITY
ALFONSO XII
CARRETERA A HUELVA
ARJONA
El Arenal
Santa Cruz
LUIS MONTOTO
AVENIDA DE ANDALUCIA
EDUARDO DATO
ENLACE CADIZ HUELVA Y EXTREMADURA
ENRAMADILLA
REPUBLICA ARGENTINA
VIRGEN DE LUJAN
PASEO DE LAS DELICIAS
DIEGO MARTINEZ BARRIOS
RAMON Y CAJAL
HEROES DE TOLEDO
AVENIDA DE LA PAZ
RONDA URBANA SUROESTE
AVENIDA DE LA PALMERIA

0 kilometres 1
0 miles 0.5

KEY TO STREET FINDER

- Major sight
- Place of interest
- Other building
- Railway station
- Metro station
- Main bus stop
- Coach station
- River bus boarding point
- Taxi rank
- Parking
- Tourist information
- Hospital with casualty unit
- Police station
- Church
- Convent or monastery
- Post office
- Railway line
- Pedestrianized street
- Metro-Centro tram stop

SCALE OF MAP PAGES

0 metres 250
0 yards 250

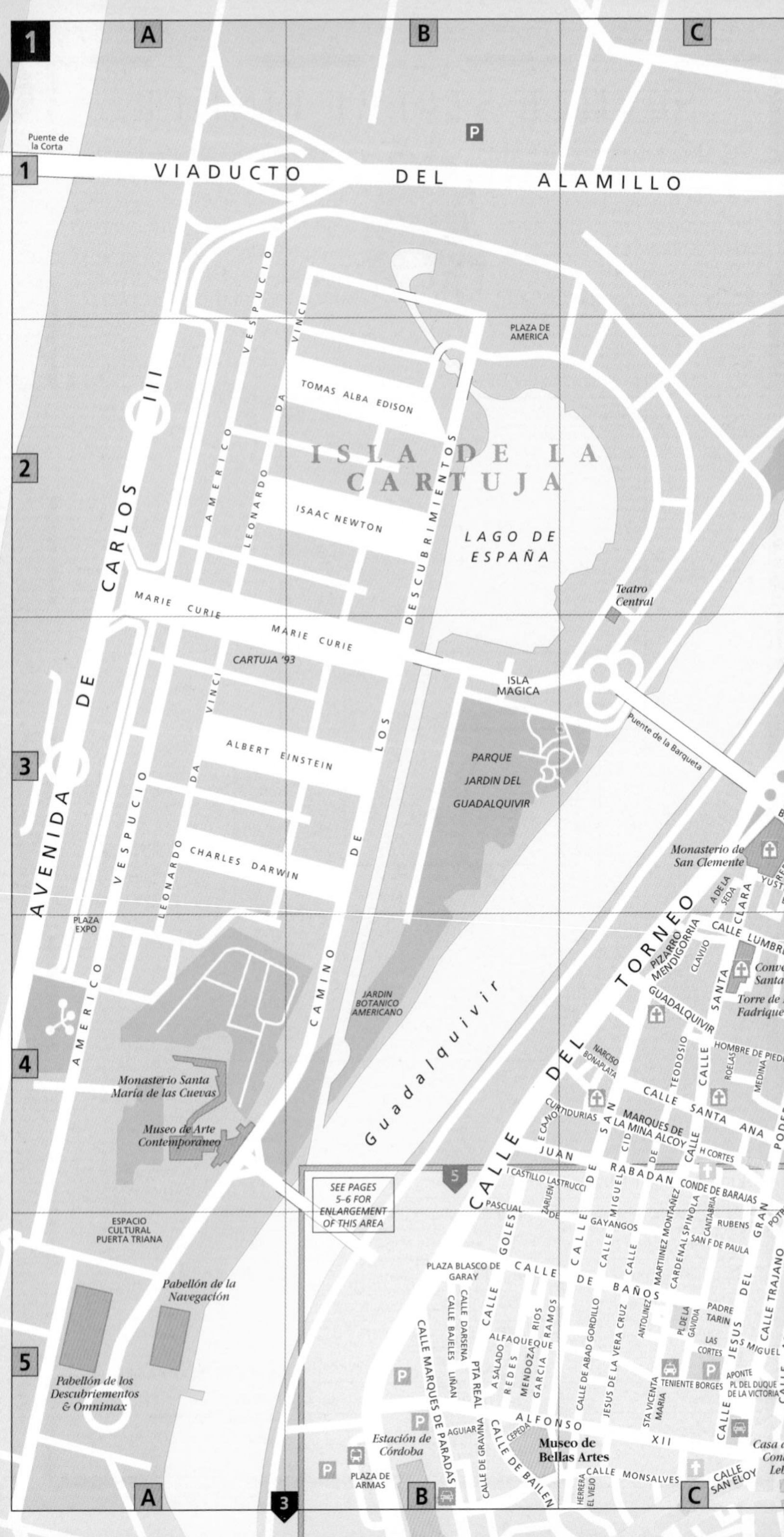

1
A
B
C
Puente de la Corta
VIADUCTO DEL ALAMILLO
PLAZA DE AMERICA
ISLA DE LA CARTUJA
LAGO DE ESPAÑA
Teatro Central
AVENIDA DE CARLOS III
AMERICO VESPUCIO
LEONARDO DA VINCI
TOMAS ALBA EDISON
ISAAC NEWTON
MARIE CURIE
CARTUJA '93
ISLA MAGICA
Puente de la Barqueta
ALBERT EINSTEIN
CHARLES DARWIN
CAMINO DE LOS DESCUBRIMIENTOS
PARQUE JARDIN DEL GUADALQUIVIR
JARDIN BOTANICO AMERICANO
Guadalquivir
PLAZA EXPO
Monasterio Santa María de las Cuevas
Museo de Arte Contemporaneo
Monasterio de San Clemente
CALLE DEL TORNEO
PIZARRO
MENDIGORRIA
CLAVIJO
SANTA CLARA
CALLE LUMBRERAS
Torre de D. Fadrique
GUADALQUIVIR
TEODOSIO
CALLE
HOMBRE DE PIEDRA
ROELAS
MEDINA
CALLE SANTA ANA
NARCISO BONAPLATA
CURTIDURIAS
E CANO
MARQUES DE LA MINA
ALCOY
JUAN RABADAN
CALLE SAN MIGUEL
CID
H CORTES
CONDE DE BARAJAS
I CASTILLO LASTRUCCI
PASCUAL
ZARUEN
GOLES
GAYANGOS
MARTIINEZ MONTAÑEZ
CARDENAL SPINOLA
CANTABRIA
SAN F DE PAULA
RUBENS
POTRO
GRAN PODER
SEE PAGES 5–6 FOR ENLARGEMENT OF THIS AREA
5
ESPACIO CULTURAL PUERTA TRIANA
Pabellón de la Navegación
Pabellón de los Descubriementos & Omnimax
PLAZA BLASCO DE GARAY
CALLE DE BAÑOS
CALLE DARSENA
CALLE BAJELES
CALLE MARQUES DE PARADAS
LIÑAN
PTA REAL
A SALADO
REDES
ALFAQUEQUE
MENDOZA RIOS
GARCIA RAMOS
CALLE DE ABAD GORDILLO
JESUS DE LA VERA CRUZ
ANTOLINEZ
STA VICENTA MARIA
PL DE LA GAVIDIA
PADRE TARIN
LAS CORTES
JESUS DEL GRAN PODER
CALLE SAN MIGUEL
CALLE TRAJANO
TENIENTE BORGES
APONTE
PL DEL DUQUE DE LA VICTORIA
ALFONSO XII
Estación de Córdoba
PLAZA DE ARMAS
AGUIAR
CALLE DE GRAVINA
CEPEDA
CALLE DE BAILEN
Museo de Bellas Artes
HERRERA EL VIEJO
CALLE MONSALVES
CALLE SAN ELOY
Casa de Cond. Lebr.
2
3
4
5
P

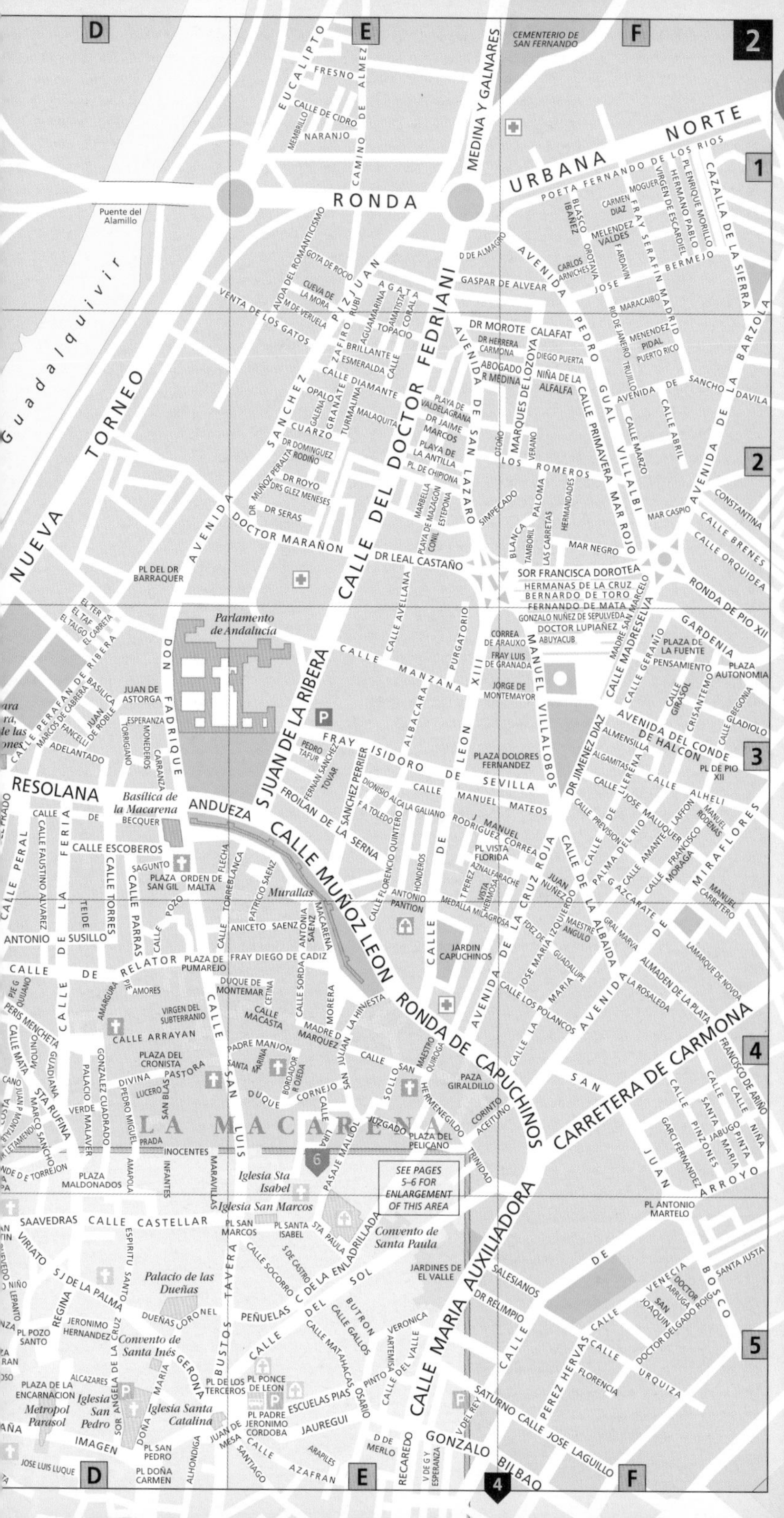

D
E
F
2
1
2
3
4
5
CEMENTERIO DE SAN FERNANDO
EUCALIPTO
FRESNO
CALLE DE CIDRO
MEMBRILLO
NARANJO
CAMINO DE ALMEZ
MEDINA Y GALNARES
RONDA
URBANA NORTE
POETA FERNANDO DE LOS RIOS
Puente del Alamillo
Guadalquivir
NUEVA TORNEO
AVDA DEL ROMANTICISMO
GOTA DE ROCIO
CUEVA DE LA MORA
M DE VERUELA
VENTA DE LOS GATOS
PIZJUAN
RUBI
AGATA
AGUAMARINA
AMATISTA
CORAL
TOPACIO
ZAFIRO
BRILLANTE
ESMERALDA
CALLE DIAMANTE
OPALO
GALENA
GRANATE
TURMALINA
MALAQUITA
CUARZO
SANCHEZ
DR DOMINGUEZ RODIÑO
DR MUÑOZ PERALTA
DR ROYO
DRS GLEZ MENESES
DR SERAS
AVENIDA DOCTOR MARAÑON
PL DEL DR BARRAQUER
CALLE DEL DOCTOR FEDRIANI
DR LEAL CASTAÑO
AVENIDA DE SAN LAZARO
D DE ALMAGRO
GASPAR DE ALVEAR
DR MOROTE
CALAFAT
DR HERRERA CARMONA
DIEGO PUERTA
ABOGADO R MEDINA
MARQUES DE LOZOYA
NIÑA DE LA ALFALFA
PLAYA DE VALDELAGRANA
DR JAIME MARCOS
PLAYA DE LA ANTILLA
PL. DE CHIPIONA
MARBELLA
PLAYA DE MAZAGON
CONIL
ESTEPONA
OTOÑO
VERANO
LOS ROMEROS
SIMPECADO
BLANCA
TAMBORIL
PALOMA
LAS CARRETAS
HERMANDADES
MAR NEGRO
AVENIDA PEDRO GUAL VILLALBI
CALLE PRIMAVERA
MAR ROJO
CARLOS ARNICHES
BLASCO IBAÑEZ
CARMEN DIAZ
MELENDEZ VALDES
OROTAVA
FARDAJIN
FRAY SERAFIN MADRID
MOGUER
VIRGEN DE ESCARDIEL
HERMANO PABLO
PL ENRIQUE MORILLO
JOSE BERMEJO
CAZALLA DE LA SIERRA
MARACAIBO
RIO DE JANEIRO
TRUJILLO
MENENDEZ PIDAL
PUERTO RICO
AVENIDA DE SANCHO DAVILA
CALLE MARZO
CALLE ABRIL
AVENIDA DE LA BARZOLA
MAR CASPIO
CONSTANTINA
CALLE BRENES
CALLE ORQUIDEA
RONDA DE PIO XII
SOR FRANCISCA DOROTEA
HERMANAS DE LA CRUZ
BERNARDO DE TORO
FERNANDO DE MATA
GONZALO NUÑEZ DE SEPULVEDA
DOCTOR LUPIAÑEZ
ABUYACUB
CORREA DE ARAUXO
FRAY LUIS DE GRANADA
JORGE DE MONTEMAYOR
MADRE SAN MARCELO
CALLE MADRESELVA
GARDENIA
PLAZA DE LA FUENTE
PENSAMIENTO
PLAZA AUTONOMIA
CALLE GERANIO
CALLE GIRASOL
CRISANTEMO
CALLE BEGONIA
GLADIOLO
AVENIDA DEL CONDE DE HALCON
PL DE PIO XII
ALMENSILLA
ALGAMITAS
CALLE DE LLERENA
CALLE ALHELI
EL TER
EL TAF
EL TALGO
EL CARRETA
Parlamento de Andalucía
DON FADRIQUE
CALLE PERAFAN DE RIBERA
BASILICA
MARCOS DE CABRERA
JUAN DE ROBLE
FANCELLI
JUAN DE ASTORGA
ESPERANZA
TORRIGIANO
MONEDEROS
CARRANZA
ADELANTADO
RESOLANA
S JUAN DE LA RIBERA
CALLE MANZANA
CALLE AVELLANA
PURGATORIO
ALBACARA
XIII
CALLE DE LEON
MANUEL VILLALOBOS
FRAY ISIDORO DE SEVILLA
PEDRO TAFUR
FERNAN SANCHEZ TOVAR
SANCHEZ PERRIER
DIONISIO ALCALA GALIANO
F A TOLEDO
FROILAN DE LA SERNA
PLAZA DOLORES FERNANDEZ
CALLE MANUEL MATEOS
J MANUEL RODRIGUEZ CORREA
PL VISTA FLORIDA
AZNALFARACHE
VISTA HERMOSA
T PEREZ
MEDALLA MILAGROSA
DR JIMENEZ DIAZ
JUAN NUÑEZ
CALLE DE LA CRUZ ROJA
CALLE JOSE MALUQUER
CALLE PREVISION
PALMA DEL RIO
CALLE AMANTE LAFFON
FRANCISCO MORAGA
MANUEL RODENAS
MIRAFLORES
MANUEL CARRETERO
CALLE DE LA ALBAIDA
G AZCARATE
LAMARQUE DE NOVOA
ALMADEN DE LA PLATA
LA ROSALEDA
GRAL MARVA
MAESTRE ANGULO
JOSE MARIA IZQUIERDO
FDEZ DE GUADALUPE
MARIA
CALLE LOS POLANCOS
AVENIDA
CARRETERA DE CARMONA
FRANCISCO DE ARIÑO
CALLE SANTA MARIA
CALLE NIÑA
PINTA
JABUGO
CALLE PINZONES
GARCI FERNANDEZ
JUAN ARROYO
SAN
Basílica de la Macarena
BECQUER
ANDUEZA
CALLE MUÑOZ LEON
RONDA DE CAPUCHINOS
CALLE PERAL
CALLE FAUSTINO ALVAREZ
CALLE DE LA FERIA
CALLE ESCOBEROS
TEIDE
CALLE TORRES
CALLE PARRAS
SAGUNTO
PLAZA SAN GIL
ORDEN DE MALTA
FLECHA
TORREBLANCA
PATRICIO SAENZ
Murallas
ANTONIA SAENZ
MACARENA
CALLE FLORENCIO QUINTERO
HONDEROS
ANTONIO PANTION
JARDIN CAPUCHINOS
ANTONIO SUSILLO
POZO
ANICETO SAENZ
CALLE DE RELATOR
PLAZA DE PUMAREJO
FRAY DIEGO DE CADIZ
DUQUE DE MONTEMAR
CETINA
CALLE MACASTA
CALLE SORDA
MORERA
LA HINIESTA
MADRE D MARQUEZ
SAN JULIAN
MAESTRO QUIROGA
CALLE SAN
AMORES
VIRGEN DEL SUBTERRANIO
CALLE ARRAYAN
PLAZA DEL CRONISTA
PADRE MANJON
SANTA MARINA
BORDADOR R OJEDA
DIVINA PASTORA
LUCERO
SAN BLAS
DUQUE CORNEJO
CALLE LIRA
SOLLO
HERMENEGILDO
PAZA GIRALDILLO
CORINTO
ACEITUNO
JUZGADO
PLAZA DEL PELICANO
TRINIDAD
PIE G QUIJANO
PERIS MENCHETA
CALLE MATA
MONTOYA
GUADIANA
STA RUFINA
VERDE
GONZALEZ CUADRADO
PALACIO MALAVER
PEDRO MIGUEL
LA MACARENA
PRADA
INOCENTES
CALLE SAN LUIS
PASAJE MALLOL
6
SEE PAGES 5–6 FOR ENLARGEMENT OF THIS AREA
PLAZA MALDONADOS
AMAPOLA
INFANTES
MARAVILLAS
Iglesia Sta Isabel
Iglesia San Marcos
Convento de Santa Paula
STA PAULA
PL SAN MARCOS
PL SANTA ISABEL
SAAVEDRAS
CALLE CASTELLAR
VIRIATO
ESPIRITU SANTO
CALLE SOCORRO
S DE CASTRO
C DE LA ENLADRILLADA
SOL
JARDINES DE EL VALLE
CALLE MARIA AUXILIADORA
SALESIANOS
DR RELIMPIO
S J DE LA PALMA
Palacio de las Dueñas
DUEÑAS
CORONEL
BUSTOS TAVERA
PEÑUELAS
DEL
BUTRON
CALLE GALLOS
VERONICA
ARTEMISA
CALLE MATAHACAS
CALLE DEL VALLE
PINTO
OSARIO
REGINA
JERONIMO HERNANDEZ
PL POZO SANTO
Convento de Santa Inés
GERONA
SOR ANGELA DE LA CRUZ
DOÑA MARIA
ALCAZARES
PLAZA DE LA ENCARNACION
Metropol Parasol
Iglesia San Pedro
Iglesia Santa Catalina
PL DE LOS TERCEROS
PL PONCE DE LEON
ESCUELAS PIAS
PL PADRE JERONIMO CORDOBA
JAUREGUI
JUAN DE MESA
IMAGEN
PL SAN PEDRO
PL DOÑA CARMEN
ALHONDIGA
SANTIAGO
AZAFRAN
ARAPILES
D DE MERLO
RECAREDO
V DE G Y ESPERANZA
GONZALO BILBAO
V DEL REY
SATURNO
CALLE JOSE LAGUILLO
PEREZ HERVAS
CALLE FLORENCIA
CALLE URQUIZA
DOCTOR DELGADO ROIG
SAN JOAQUIN
DOCTOR ARRUGA
VENECIA
BOSCO
SANTA JUSTA
PL ANTONIO MARTELO
JOSE LUIS LUQUE
4

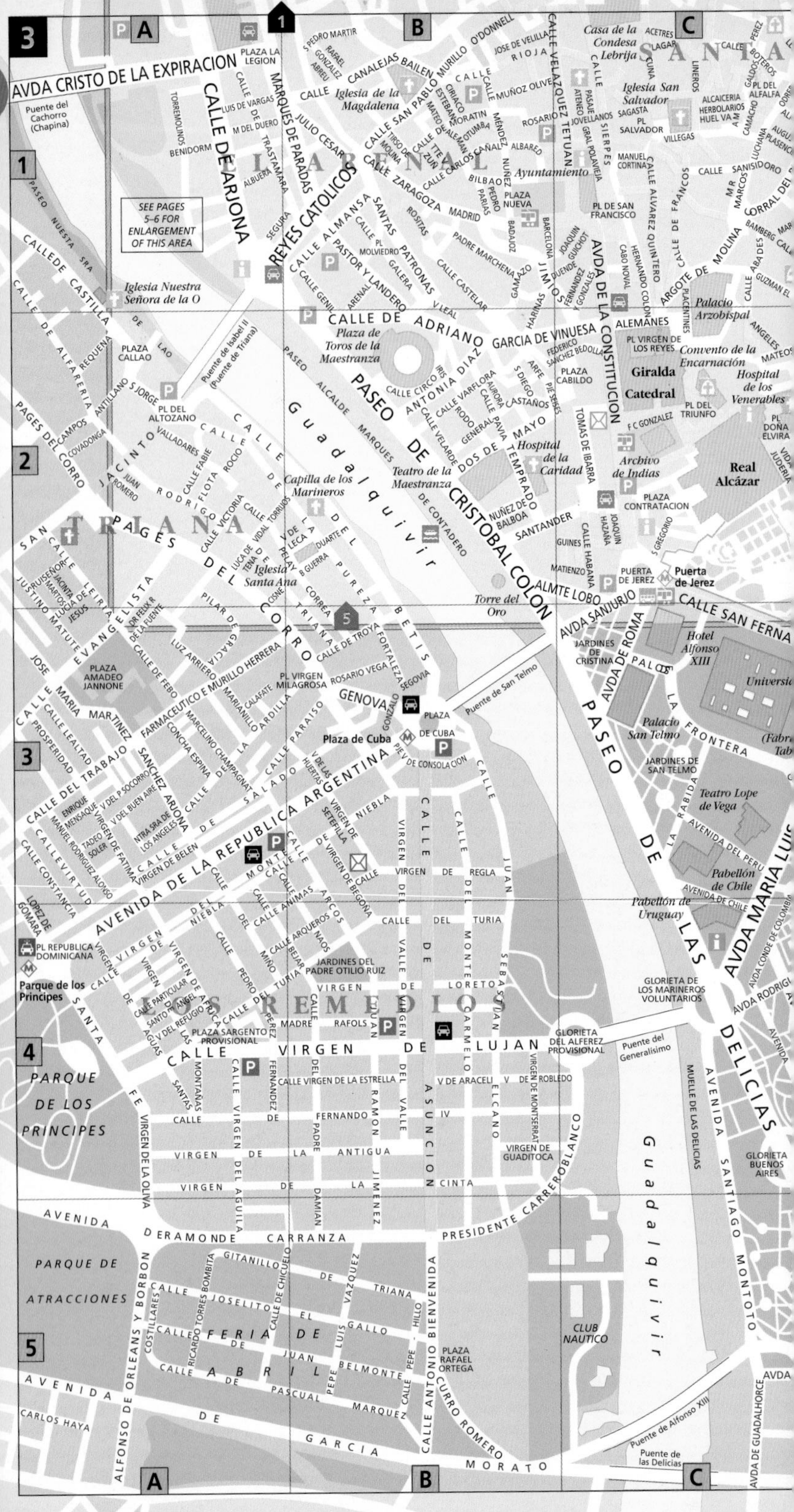

3
A
B
C
1
2
3
4
5
AVDA CRISTO DE LA EXPIRACION
Puente del Cachorro (Chapina)
CALLE DE ARJONA
REYES CATOLICOS
MARQUES DE PARADAS
PLAZA LA LEGION
Iglesia de la Magdalena
EL ARENAL
SEE PAGES 5–6 FOR ENLARGEMENT OF THIS AREA
Iglesia Nuestra Señora de la O
Casa de la Condesa Lebrija
Iglesia San Salvador
PL SALVADOR
Ayuntamiento
PLAZA NUEVA
PL DE SAN FRANCISCO
AVDA DE LA CONSTITUCION
CALLE VELAZQUEZ TETUAN
ARGOTE DE MOLINA
Palacio Arzobispal
Convento de la Encarnación
Hospital de los Venerables
Giralda
Catedral
PL VIRGEN DE LOS REYES
PL DEL TRIUNFO
Archivo de Indias
Real Alcázar
PLAZA CONTRATACION
CALLE DE ADRIANO
Plaza de Toros de la Maestranza
GARCIA DE VINUESA
PLAZA CABILDO
Hospital de la Caridad
Teatro de la Maestranza
PASEO DE CRISTOBAL COLON
PASEO ALCALDE MARQUES DE CONTADERO
Guadalquivir
Puente de Isabel II (Puente de Triana)
PLAZA CALLAO
PL DEL ALTOZANO
Capilla de los Marineros
TRIANA
PAGES DEL CORRO
Iglesia Santa Ana
Torre del Oro
ALMTE LOBO
PUERTA DE JEREZ
Puerta de Jerez
CALLE SAN FERNANDO
AVDA SANJURJO
JARDINES DE CRISTINA
AVDA DE ROMA
Hotel Alfonso XIII
Universidad
Palacio San Telmo
JARDINES DE SAN TELMO
Teatro Lope de Vega
Pabellón de Chile
Pabellón de Uruguay
AVDA MARIA LUISA
PASEO DE LAS DELICIAS
PLAZA AMADEO JANNONE
PL VIRGEN MILAGROSA
Puente de San Telmo
Plaza de Cuba
PLAZA DE CUBA
AVENIDA DE LA REPUBLICA ARGENTINA
CALLE ASUNCION
JARDINES DEL PADRE OTILIO RUIZ
LOS REMEDIOS
PL REPUBLICA DOMINICANA
Parque de los Principes
PARQUE DE LOS PRINCIPES
PLAZA SARGENTO PROVISIONAL
CALLE VIRGEN DE LUJAN
GLORIETA DEL ALFEREZ PROVISIONAL
Puente del Generalísimo
GLORIETA DE LOS MARINEROS VOLUNTARIOS
MUELLE DE LAS DELICIAS
PRESIDENTE CARRERO BLANCO
AVENIDA DE RAMON DE CARRANZA
PARQUE DE ATRACCIONES
FERIA DE ABRIL
PLAZA RAFAEL ORTEGA
CLUB NAUTICO
GLORIETA BUENOS AIRES
AVENIDA SANTIAGO MONTOTO
AVENIDA DE CARLOS HAYA
AVENIDA DE GARCIA MORATO
ALFONSO DE ORLEANS Y BORBON
CALLE ANTONIO BIENVENIDA
CURRO ROMERO
Puente de Alfonso XIII
Puente de las Delicias
AVDA DE GUADALHORCE

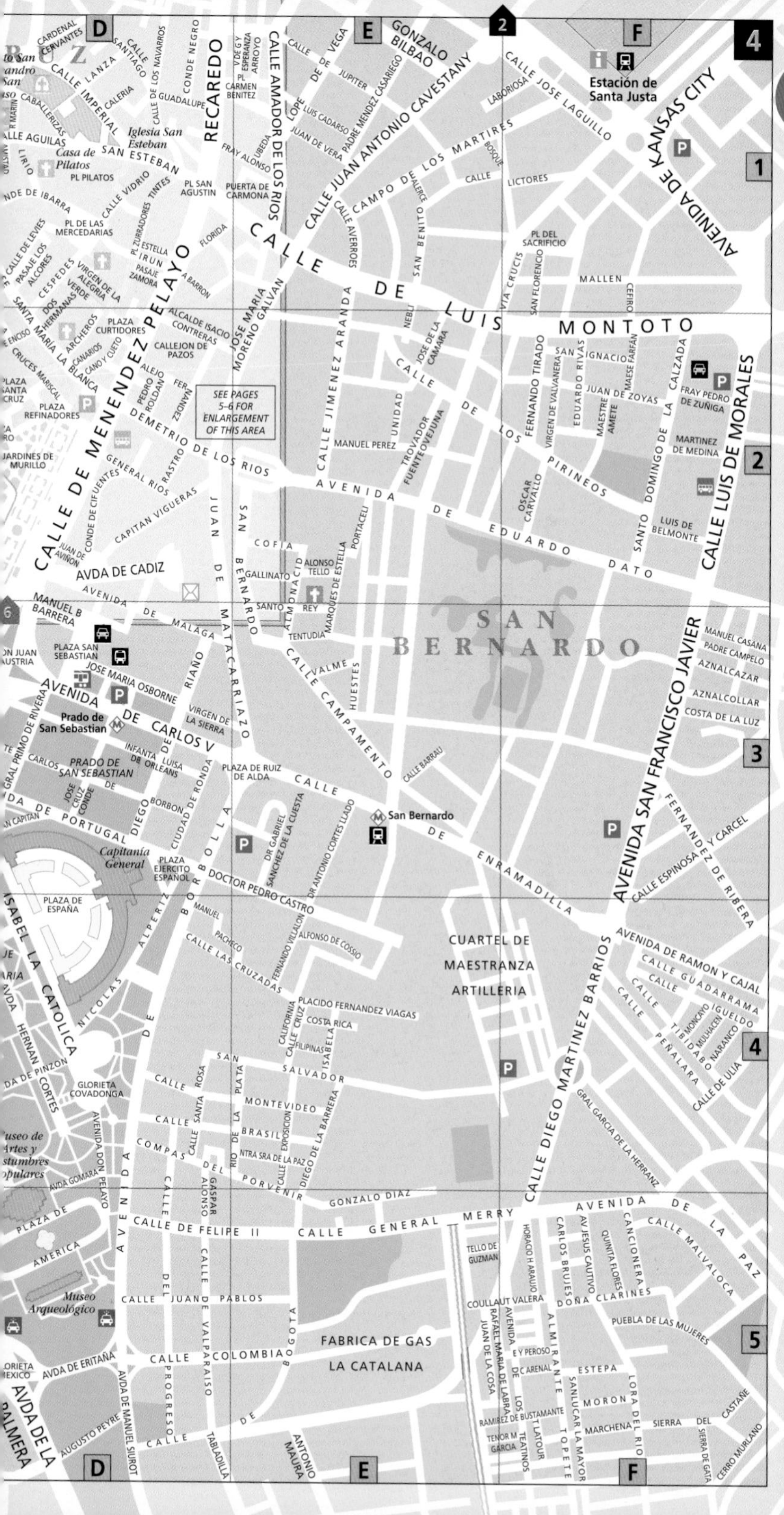

D
E
F
2
4
1
2
3
4
5
6
Estación de Santa Justa
AVENIDA DE KANSAS CITY
CALLE JOSE LAGUILLO
LABORIOSA
GONZALO BILBAO
CALLE DE VEGA
JUPITER
LOPE
LUIS CADARSO
PADRE MENDEZ CASARIEGO
JUAN DE VERA
CALLE JUAN ANTONIO CAVESTANY
CAMPO DE LOS MARTIRES
BOSQUE
CALLE LICTORES
CALLE AMADOR DE LOS RIOS
RECAREDO
CONDE NEGRO
CALLE DE LOS NAVARROS
VIDRIO
PL CARMEN BENITEZ
ESPERANZA
ARROYO
GUADALUPE
CARDENAL CERVANTES
CALLE SANTIAGO
CALLE LANZA
CALLE IMPERIAL
CALERIA
CABALLERIZAS
CALLE AGUILAS
LIRIO
Iglesia San Esteban
Casa de Pilatos
SAN ESTEBAN
PL PILATOS
FRAY ALONSO
UBEDA
PL SAN AGUSTIN
PUERTA DE CARMONA
CALLE VIDRIO
TINTES
DE IBARRA
PL DE LAS MERCEDARIAS
PL ZURRADORES
ESTELLA
IRUN
PASAJE ZAMORA
A BARRON
FLORIDA
CALLE DE LUIS MONTOTO
CALLE AVERROES
SAN BENITO
ALERCE
PL DEL SACRIFICIO
VIA CRUCIS
SAN FLORENCIO
MALLEN
CEFIRO
CALLE DE LEVIES
PASAJE LOS ALCORES
CESPEDES
VIRGEN DE LA ALEGRIA
VERDE
DOS HERMANAS
SANTA MARIA LA BLANCA
ARCHEROS
PLAZA CURTIDORES
ALCALDE ISACIO CONTRERAS
CALLEJON DE PAZOS
CALLE DE MENENDEZ PELAYO
JOSE MARIA MORENO GALVAN
CALLE JIMENEZ ARANDA
NEBLI
JOSE DE LA CAMARA
CALLE DE LOS PIRINEOS
FERNANDO TIRADO
SAN IGNACIO
MAESE FARFAN
EDUARDO RIVAS
VIRGEN DE VALVANERA
JUAN DE ZOYAS
MAESTRE AMETE
CALZADA
FRAY PEDRO DE ZUÑIGA
CALLE LUIS DE MORALES
ENCISO
CRUCES
MARISCAL
CANARIOS
CANO Y CUETO
PLAZA SANTA CRUZ
PLAZA REFINADORES
ALEJO
PEDRO ROLDAN
FERNANDEZ
SEE PAGES 5–6 FOR ENLARGEMENT OF THIS AREA
DEMETRIO DE LOS RIOS
JARDINES DE MURILLO
GENERAL RIOS
RASTRO
CONDE DE CIFUENTES
CAPITAN VIGUERAS
JUAN DE AVIÑON
AVDA DE CADIZ
UNIDAD
TROVADOR
FUENTEOVEJUNA
MANUEL PEREZ
AVENIDA DE EDUARDO DATO
OSCAR CARVALLO
DOMINGO DE LA
SANTO
MARTINEZ DE MEDINA
LUIS DE BELMONTE
JUAN DE MATACARRIAZO
SAN BERNARDO
COFIA
GALLINATO
ALMONACID
ALONSO TELLO
MARQUES DE ESTELLA
PORTACELI
SANTO REY
TENTUDIA
SAN BERNARDO
AVENIDA DE MALAGA
MANUEL B BARRERA
DON JUAN DE AUSTRIA
PLAZA SAN SEBASTIAN
JOSE MARIA OSBORNE
RIAÑO
AVENIDA DE CARLOS V
VIRGEN DE LA SIERRA
Prado de San Sebastian
CALLE CAMPAMENTO
VALME
HUESTES
MANUEL CASANA
PADRE CAMPELO
AZNALCAZAR
AZNALCOLLAR
COSTA DE LA LUZ
AVENIDA SAN FRANCISCO JAVIER
GRAL PRIMO DE RIVERA
CARLOS
PRADO DE SAN SEBASTIAN
INFANTA LUISA DE ORLEANS
JOSE CRUZ CONDE
CIUDAD DE RONDA
PLAZA DE RUIZ DE ALDA
CALLE DE ENRAMADILLA
CALLE BARRAU
San Bernardo
BORBON
AVDA DE PORTUGAL
JUAN CAPITAN
DIEGO
Capitanía General
PLAZA EJERCITO ESPAÑOL
BORBOLLA
DR GABRIEL SANCHEZ DE LA CUESTA
DR ANTONIO CORTES LLADO
DOCTOR PEDRO CASTRO
FERNANDEZ DE RIBERA
CALLE ESPINOSA Y CARCEL
PLAZA DE ESPAÑA
ISABEL LA CATOLICA
ALPERIZ
MANUEL PACHECO
CALLE LAS CRUZADAS
FERNANDO VILLALON
ALFONSO DE COSSIO
CUARTEL DE MAESTRANZA ARTILLERIA
AVENIDA DE RAMON Y CAJAL
CALLE GUADARRAMA
CALLE DIEGO MARTINEZ BARRIOS
CALLE
CALLE PEÑALARA
MONCAYO
IGUELDO
MULHACEN
TIBIDABO
NARANCO
CALLE DE ULIA
NICOLAS
PLACIDO FERNANDEZ VIAGAS
CALIFORNIA
CALLE CRUZ
COSTA RICA
FILIPINAS
ISABELA
SAN SALVADOR
CALLE ROSA
PLATA
AVDA HERNAN CORTES
DE PINZON
GLORIETA COVADONGA
CALLE SANTA
MONTEVIDEO
CALLE BRASIL
EXPOSICION
RIO DE LA PLATA
NTRA SRA DE LA PAZ
DIEGO DE LA BARRERA
GRAL GARCIA DE LA HERRANZ
Museo de Artes y Costumbres Populares
AVENIDA DON PELAYO
AVDA GOMARA
COMPAS DEL PORVENIR
GASPAR ALONSO
GONZALO DIAZ
PLAZA DE AMERICA
CALLE DE FELIPE II
CALLE GENERAL MERRY
AVENIDA DE LA PAZ
CALLE MALVALOCA
TELLO DE GUZMAN
HORACIO H ARAUJO
CARLOS BRUJES
AV JESUS CAUTIVO
QUINTA FLORES
CANCIONERA
AVENIDA
Museo Arqueológico
CALLE JUAN PABLOS
CALLE DEL
CALLE DE VALPARAISO
BOGOTA
COULLAUT VALERA
DOÑA CLARINES
PUEBLA DE LAS MUJERES
RAFAEL MARIA DE LABRA
JUAN DE LA COSA
ALMIRANTE
FABRICA DE GAS LA CATALANA
CALLE COLOMBIA
GLORIETA MEXICO
AVDA DE ERITAÑA
CALLE PROGRESO
E Y PEROSO
C ARENAL
ESTEPA
MORON
LORA DEL RIO
SANLUCAR LA MAYOR
RAMIREZ DE BUSTAMANTE
MARCHENA
SIERRA DEL
CASTAÑE
TENOR M GARCIA
LOS TEATINOS
TOPETE
SIERRA DE GATA
CERRO MURIANO
AVDA DE LA PALMERA
AUGUSTO PEYRE
AVDA DE MANUEL SIUROT
CALLE DE
TABLADILLA
ANTONIO MAURA

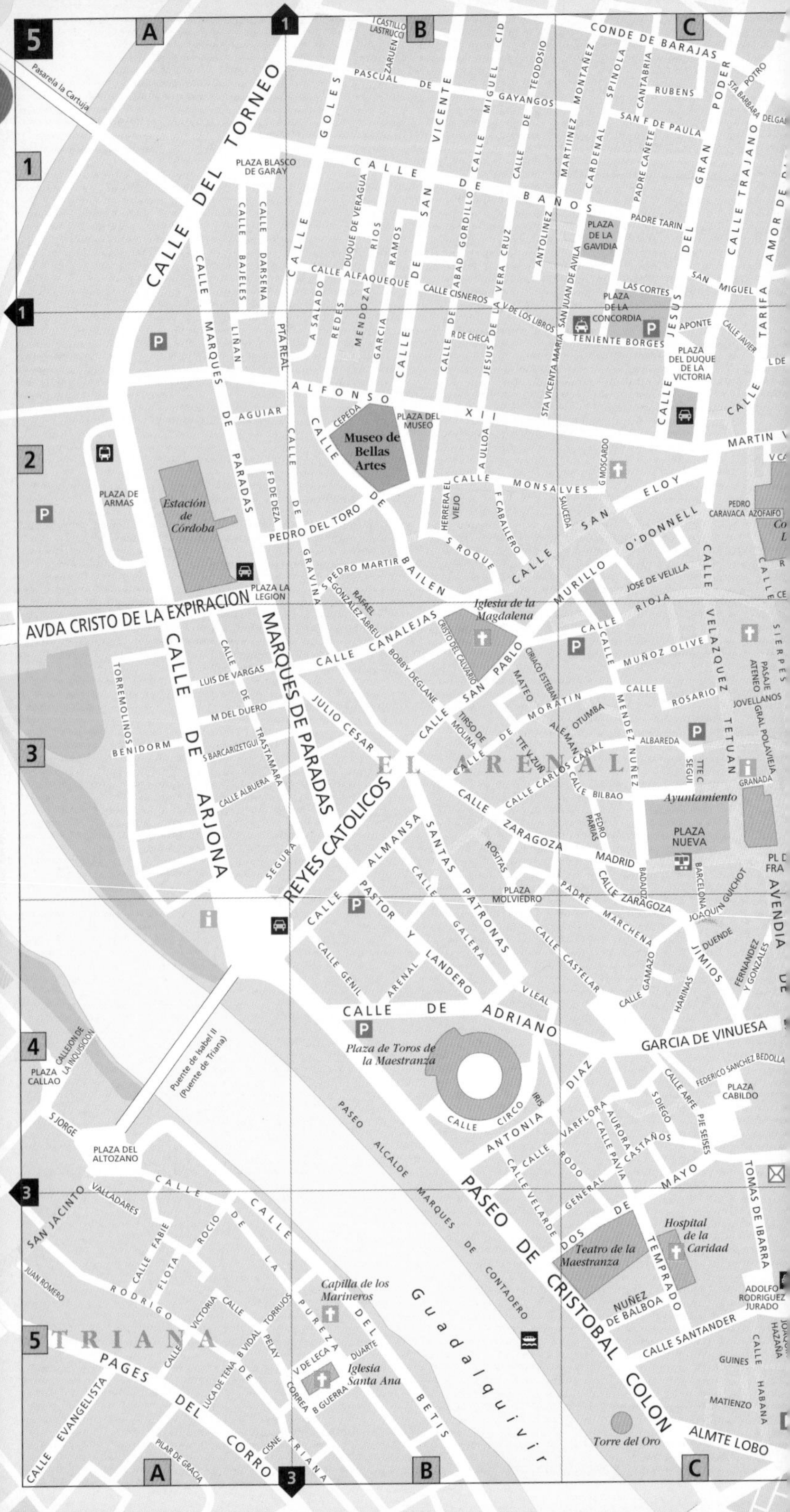

5
A
B
C
1
2
3
4
5
CALLE DEL TORNEO
CONDE DE BARAJAS
PLAZA BLASCO DE GARAY
CALLE DE BAÑOS
PLAZA DE LA GAVIDIA
PLAZA DE LA CONCORDIA
PLAZA DEL DUQUE DE LA VICTORIA
ALFONSO XII
Museo de Bellas Artes
PLAZA DEL MUSEO
PLAZA DE ARMAS
Estación de Córdoba
PLAZA LA LEGION
AVDA CRISTO DE LA EXPIRACION
CALLE DE ARJONA
MARQUES DE PARADAS
Iglesia de la Magdalena
EL ARENAL
REYES CATOLICOS
Ayuntamiento
PLAZA NUEVA
PLAZA MOLVIEDRO
CALLE DE ADRIANO
Plaza de Toros de la Maestranza
GARCIA DE VINUESA
PLAZA CABILDO
Puente de Isabel II (Puente de Triana)
PLAZA CALLAO
PLAZA DEL ALTOZANO
PASEO ALCALDE MARQUES DE CONTADERO
PASEO DE CRISTOBAL COLON
Teatro de la Maestranza
Hospital de la Caridad
Capilla de los Marineros
Iglesia Santa Ana
Guadalquivir
TRIANA
Torre del Oro
ALMTE LOBO
CALLE SANTANDER
PAGES DEL CORRO
CALLE BETIS
Pasarela la Cartuja

D
E
F
6
2
1
2
3
4
5
4
Iglesia Sta Isabel
Convento de Santa Paula
Iglesia San Marcos
PLAZA SAN MARCOS
PL SANTA ISABEL
PLAZA MALDONADOS
CONDE DE TORREJON
ALBERTO LISTA
PL SAN MARTIN
SAAVEDRAS
CALLE CASTELLAR
MENJIBAR
FERIA
VIRIATO
QUEVEDO
APOSENTADORES
S J DE LA PALMA
ESPIRITU SANTO
AMAPOLA
INFANTES
MARAVILLAS
HINIESTA
LAUREL
PIE MALLOL
STA PAULA
CALLE ENLADRILLADA
CALLE MARTELES
SOL
CALLE DE LA SOL
JARDINES DE EL VALLE
CALLE SOCORRO
S DE CASTRO
PLAZA S ROMAN
CALLE DEL
BUTRON
CALLE GALLOS
CALLE MATAHACAS
CALLE MARIA AUXILIADORA
VERONICA
ARTEMISA
VALLE
PINTO
SATURNO
VARA DEL REY
PUÑONROSTRO
OSARIO
G BILBAO
D DE MERLO
A TENORIO
JUPITER
ARROYO
V DE G Y ESPERANZA
CALLE DE RECAREDO
CALLE AMADOR DE LOS RIOS
PL CARMEN BENITEZ
CALLE JUAN DE VERA
CALLE UBEDA
FRAY ALONSO
PUERTA DE CARMONA
LUIS MONTOTO
PL SAN AGUSTIN
PEDRO
NIÑO
LEPANTO
AMPARO
REGINA
Palacio de las Dueñas
DUEÑAS
CORONEL
PEÑUELAS
TAVERA
BUSTOS
HERNANDEZ
JERONIMO
ATIENZA
PL POZO SANTO
CALLE GERONA
PLAZA URBARAN
MISERICORDIA
PLAZA DE LA ENCARNACION
Metropol Parasol
GESTOSO
ARGUIJO
LARAÑA
ALCAZARES
Convento de Santa Ines
SOR ANGELA DE LA CRUZ
Iglesia San Pedro
DOÑA MARIA
PLAZA DE LOS TERCEROS
PLAZA PONCE DE LEON
Iglesia Santa Catalina
ESCUELAS PIAS
PLAZA PADRE JERONIMO CORDOBA
JAUREGUI
JUAN DE MESA
CALLE AZAFRAN
ARAPILES
LEONCILLOS
CENICERO
IMAGEN
PLAZA SAN PEDRO
ESCARPIN
PL BUEN SUCESO
M DE VELILLA
JOSE LUIS LUQUE
CALLE GOYENETA
COMPAÑIA
PUENTE Y PELLON
BUIZA Y MENSAQUE
CETRES
DE LAGAR
CEDACEROS
ORTIZ DE ZUÑIGA
PL CRISTO DE BURGOS
PL DOÑA CARMEN
MORERIA
DON ALONSO EL SABIO
GALDOS
DESCALZOS
CALLE DE ALHONDIGA
FRANCISCO MEJIAS
CARDENAL CERVANTES
AVE MARIA
LOPEZ PINTADO
ENSENADA
SANTIAGO
NAVARROS
CONDE NEGRO
SANTA CRUZ
LINEROS
REVUELTAS
SIETE
GOLFO
PEREZ
LLOP
SALES Y FERRE
ZAMUDIO
CALLE
Convento San Leandro
LANZA
CALLE IMPERIAL
CABALLERIZAS
Casa de Pilatos
CALERIA
GUADALUPE
V DE LA LUZ
DE LOS
CONCEPCION
CALLE
CÓRDOBA
ALCAICERIA
HERBOLARIOS
HUELVA
Iglesia San Salvador
SAN JUAN
PL DEL ALFALFA
ODREROS
BOTEROS
ALFALFA
A M CAMACHO
CABEZA DEL REY DON PEDRO
Iglesia San Ildefonso
R MARIN
CALLE AGUILAS
Iglesia San Esteban
SAN ESTEBAN
VILLEGAS
BLANCO DE LOS RIOS
GALINDO
ROSARIO
AUGUSTO PLASENCIA
LUCHANA
AMISTAD
LIRIO
PLAZA PILATOS
CALLE SAN ISIDORO
FRANCOS
CALLE DE
M R MARCOS
CORRAL DEL REY
DIAMELA
CELINDA
VIRGENES
VIDRIO
TINTES
CALLE PAJARITOS
GANDESA
MUÑOZ Y PAVON
CONDE DE IBARRA
CALLE ARMENTA
PL DE LAS MERCEDARIAS
MARMOLES
BAMBERG
CALLE AIRE
FEDERICO RUBIO
SAN JOSE
CALLE DE LEVIES
PASAJE LOS ALCORES
GARCI-PEREZ
ESTELLA
IRUN
PLAZA ZURRADORES
LA FLORIDA
PASAJE ZAMORA
ATANASIO BARRON
ARGOTE DE MOLINA
ABADES
M DE DIOS
CESPEDES
VIRGEN DE LA ALEGRIA
SAN CLEMENTE
VERDE
PLACENTINES
Palacio Arzobispal
CALLE
GUZMAN EL BUENO
GAGO
FABIOLA
FARNESIO
DOS HERMANAS
SANTA MARIA LA BLANCA
NARDO
G DE LEON
PLAZA CURTIDORES
ALCALDE ISACIO CONTRERAS
GALVAN
MORENO
PL VIRGEN DE LOS REYES
ANGELES
CALLE
MATEOS
CARLOS ALONSO
DE ENCISO
CRUCES
ARCHEROS
CANARIOS
CANO Y CUETO
MESON DEL MORO
XIMENEZ DE SANTA
ralda
dral
Convento de la Encarnación
PIE VILLA JAMERDANA
PIE ANDREU
Hospital de los Venerables
LOPE DE RUEDA
TERESA
PLAZA SANTA CRUZ
PLAZA REFINADORES
MARISCAL
CALLE DE MENENDEZ PELAYO
J CASTILLO
PEDRO ROLDAN
ALEJO
FERNANDEZ
DEMETRIO
JOSE MARIA
PLAZA DEL TRIUNFO
GLORIA
J DE NEVE
PL DOÑA ELVIRA
PIMIENTA
VIDA
JUDERIA
AGUA
PLAZA ALFARO
JARDINES DE MURILLO
Real Alcázar
MAÑARA
PLAZA CONTRATACION
GENERAL RIOS
RASTRO
DE LOS RIOS
JUAN DE MATACARRIAZO
CIFUENTES
CONDE DE
CAPITAN VIGUERAS
SAN BERNARDO
COFIA
GALLINATO
SANTO REY
JARDINES DEL REAL ALCÁZAR
MARIANA DE PINEDA
JUAN DE AVIÑON
AVENIDA DE CADIZ
AVENIDA DE MALAGA
SAN FERNANDO
Hotel Alfonso XIII

SHOPPING IN SEVILLE

The shopping experience in Seville is influenced by its culture – bustling with energy until the moment the siesta arrives, then relaxing over lunch before the frenzy begins again. Seville has a good mix of well-known chain stores and independently owned shops, and the stores in this vibrant city are as colourful and diverse as the people themselves. The main shopping district winds through Calle Tetuán and Calle Sierpes, and flows on towards Plaza Nueva and over to Plaza Alfalfa, where you will find a fantastic range of goods – anything from the latest fashions to unique Spanish arts and crafts. Yet more diverse items can be found while strolling along Amor de Dios towards Alameda de Hercules, where there are many wonderful Moroccan, Indian and African import shops to explore.

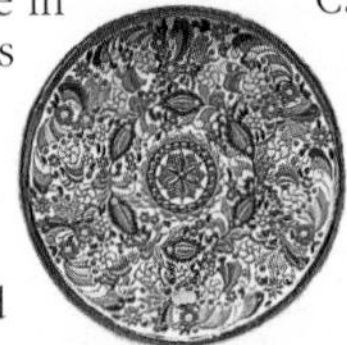

One of several styles of plate made in Seville

SPECIALIST SHOPS

The streets of Calle Cuna, Calle Francos and Calle Lineros are lined with shops that capture the flamenco spirit. **Lina Boutique** has impeccably styled, unique dresses as well as accessories. **Calzados Mayo** sells flamenco dance shoes, while beautiful handmade shawls and intricate lace *mantillas* (veils) can be found at **Juan Foronda**. Handmade *sombreros* (hats), in addition to tasteful men's accessories, are available at **Maquedano**. For a fabulous range of leather goods and fashions, **El Caballo** is the place to shop.

To relive the spirit of Semana Santa (Easter Week), religious items can be bought at **Casa Rodríguez**. If you are enraptured by the aroma of orange blossom, visit **Agua de Sevilla**, known for its scintillating range of perfumes that capture the scents of the region.

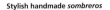

Stylish handmade *sombreros*

An array of fans at Díaz, Calle Sierpes, Seville

DEPARTMENT STORES AND GALERIAS

El Corte Inglés, Spain's national department store, has two main locations in the centre – Plaza Duque de la Victoria and Plaza Magdalena. The larger building at Plaza Duque offers clothes, shoes, sporting goods, cosmetics, a gourmet shop and a supermarket; the smaller building stocks music, books and art supplies. The outlet in Plaza Magdalena sells fine china, kitchenware and appliances. It also houses a supermarket. El Corte Inglés is open Monday to Saturday until 10pm.

Plaza de Armas is the only shopping centre in the heart of town, with shops, bars, restaurants, a nightclub, cinema and a supermarket. Nervion Plaza, the largest shopping hub close to the city centre (and accessible by metro), is lined with shops, restaurants, bars, a cinema and a mall. Shopping centres are open from 10am to 8:30pm Monday to Saturday.

OPEN-AIR MARKETS

The lively and colourful open-air markets feature a dazzling display of unique wares and are a great way to spend a leisurely morning. Distinctive accessories and clothing can be found in the markets of Plaza Duque de la Victoria and Plaza Magdalena, open all day (weather permitting) Thursday to Saturday.

The markets at Plaza Encarnación, El Arenal, Plaza del Altozano, in Triana, and Calle Fería (open Monday to Saturday) offer local produce, fish, meat and cheese, while the Thursday market at Calle Fería specializes in bric-a-brac. On Sundays, stamps, coins and other collectibles are traded in Plaza del Cabildo, and the painters' market in Plaza del Museo has displays of local art.

ANTIQUES AND CRAFTS

Antique shops are scattered throughout the city centre, mainly in Barrio Santa Cruz and Alfalfa. **Antigüedades el Museo** has classic Spanish and European furnishings and art, while handmade goods can be found at **El Postigo**, an arts and crafts centre. **Sevillarte** boasts unique ceramics and functional artwork with Andalusian influences. Seville's great ceramic tradition is visible in the Triana district, which still has several operating ceramic workshops. Ceramic shops can also be found along Calle Sierpes and Calle Tetuán.

FOOD AND WINE

To bring home some of Seville's gastronomic specialities or to prepare a nice picnic, visit **Baco**. The gourmet shop in El Corte Inglés has exquisite luxuries for the discerning palate, as well as an ample wine cellar. For general groceries try the supermarket downstairs. Every area has several small convenience stores. For out-of-hours shopping **Open Cor** is open 8am–2am daily.

FASHION

The shops of Calle Tetuán and Calle Sierpes bustle with an exciting range of the latest fashions. **Luchi Cabrera** has exclusive women's clothes and accessories in a range of styles – from flamenco to formal and bridal wear. **Loewe** offers classic lines of clothing, luggage and accessories for both men and women, while **Zara** stocks all the latest high-street trends. **Adolfo Domínguez** offers high fashion for men, women and children. For unique and exotic accessories, head to the Alfalfa district, where several shops offer distinctive jewellery, handbags and other goods. **Esmeralda** has the biggest selection. For stylish baby clothes with Sevillian flair, head to **Larrana**.

The well-heeled of Seville shop at the vast array of shoe stores in the area as well as at the well-stocked "shoe street" of Calle Córdoba.

BOOKS, MUSIC AND SOUVENIRS

Small bookshops are tucked into numerous corners of the city, but for the biggest selection of books in multiple languages, go to **Casa del Libro**. Music aficionados can find regional sounds of flamenco, Rock Andaluz and Semana Santa music, as well as international artists at **FNAC** with its impressive collection of CDs, DVDs and books. Also, a large selection of musical instruments and equipment can be found at **Sevilla Musical.**

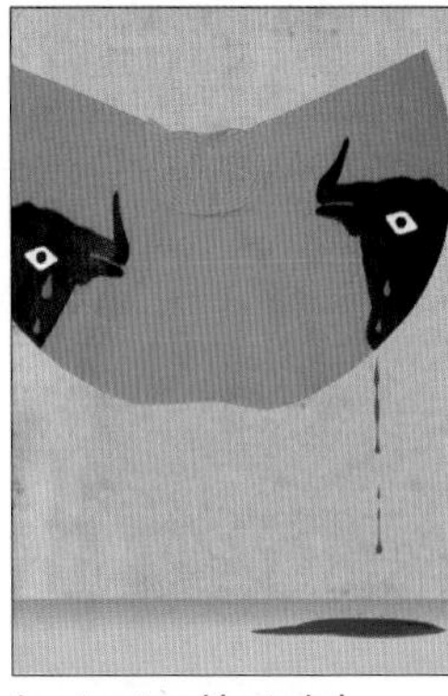

An art poster with a typical Sevillian flavour

Typical souvenir shops are abundant along Avenida de la Constitución, Calle Mateos de Gago and all throughout Barrio Santa Cruz.

DIRECTORY

SPECIALIST SHOPS

Agua de Sevilla
San Fernando 3. **Map** 3 C3, 6 D5. ***Tel*** *954 50 15 38.*

Calzados Mayo
Pl Alfalfa 2. **Map** 3 C1, 6 D3. ***Tel*** *954 22 55 55.*

Casa Rodríguez
C/ Alcaiceria 10. **Map** 3 C1. ***Tel*** *954 21 24 27.*

El Caballo
C/ Antonio Diaz 7. **Map** 5 B4. ***Tel*** *954 21 81 27.*

Juan Foronda
C/ Tetuan 28. **Map** 3 C1, 5 C3. ***Tel*** *954 22 60 60.*

Lina Boutique
C/ Lineros 17. **Map** 3 C1, 5 D3. ***Tel*** *954 21 24 23.*

Maquedano
C/ Sierpes 40. **Map** 3 C1, 5 C3. ***Tel*** *954 56 47 71.*

DEPARTMENT STORES AND GALERIAS

El Corte Inglés
Pl Duque de la Victoria 8, 13B. **Map** 1 C5, 5 C2. ***Tel*** *954 59 70 00.*
One of several branches.

ANTIQUES AND CRAFTS

Antigüedades el Museo
Plaza del Museo 4. **Map** 1 C5, 5 B2. ***Tel*** *954 56 01 28.*

El Postigo
C/ Arfe s/n. **Map** 3 B2, 5 B4. ***Tel*** *954 56 00 13.*

Sevillarte
C/ Sierpes 66. **Map** 3 C1. ***Tel*** *954 21 28 36.*

FOOD AND WINE

Baco
C/ Cuna 4. **Map** 3 C1, 6 D2. ***Tel*** *954 21 66 73.*

Open Cor
Av Sanjurio. **Map** 3 C3, 5 C5.

FASHION

Adolfo Domínguez
C/ Cuna 30 & Cerra Jeria 2 (corner). **Map** 6 D2. ***Tel*** *954 21 30 67.*

Esmeralda
C/ Alcaiceria de la Loza 26. **Map** 3 C1, 6 D3. ***Tel*** *954 22 55 11.*

Larrana
C/ Blanca de los Rios 4. **Map** 3 C1, 6 D3. ***Tel*** *954 21 52 80.*

Loewe
Pl Nueva 12. **Map** 3 B1, 5 C3. ***Tel*** *954 22 52 53.*

Luchi Cabrera
Pl El Salvador s/n. **Map** 6 D3. ***Tel*** *954 22 39 76.*

Zara
C/ Rioja 10. **Map** 3 B1, 5 C3. ***Tel*** *954 21 10 58.*
One of several branches.

BOOKS, MUSIC AND SOUVENIRS

Casa del Libro
C/ Velázquez 8. **Map** 3 C1, 5 C3. ***Tel*** *902 02 64 10.*

FNAC
Avda de la Constitución 8. **Map** 3 C1, 5 C4. ***Tel*** *902 10 06 32.*

Sevilla Musical
C/ Cardinal Spinola 3. **Map** 1 C5. ***Tel*** *954 91 57 55.*

ENTERTAINMENT IN SEVILLE

Seville is universally famed as being a city of celebration and vitality, and this is reflected in its two spring festivals, Semana Santa and Feria de Abril *(see p431)*. In fact, the city has a year-round programme of interesting cultural events. The modern Teatro de la Maestranza and Teatro Lope de Vega, along with a number of independent venues, host a range of dance, music, theatre and arts festivals, while the world's most important flamenco festival, the Bienal de Flamenco, takes place in the city. Seville also has an enviable selection of night spots, from the quiet, more relaxed area surrounding the cathedral to the buzzing bars of Calle Betis and the Alfalfa district. For sports fans, a local derby between Real Betis and Sevilla FC is an absolute must-see.

Flamenco dancer in traditional dress

Decorative tile commemorating Seville's Real Betis football club

SEASONS AND TICKETS

In Seville, the arts season usually starts in September, lasting until June–July. From April to the end of the summer, the streets and open-air stages also host shows.

Two of the city's biggest events – the Bienal de Flamenco and the Bienal de Arte Contemporáneo – are biannual and take place in the autumn in even-numbered years.

Tickets for major sports events, opera, concerts and festivals should be booked in advance – details can be provided by the city's tourist information offices. Football matches are very popular, so buy these in advance too.

ENTERTAINMENT GUIDES

A monthly events guide, *El Giraldillo* (www.giraldillo.es) covers film, music, theatre, clubs, art, sport, books, gay life, travel and much more. *La Teatral*, a bimonthly publication, is specifically focused on theatre and dance.

FLAMENCO

Flamenco embraces a broad spectrum of dancing, singing and musical styles. One venue with high-quality performances is **Los Gallos**. For something really authentic, venture out to **La Anselma** in the Triana quarter – the traditional home of the gypsy community. **La Carbonería** is an informal bar where free flamenco shows are often performed by amateur artists.

Promoting semi-professional local artists, **Casa de la Memoria** in the Santa Cruz district presents varied shows daily. As the venue is quite small, it is recommended you buy tickets in advance, and show up early to get a seat. In Calle Betis, there are bars where the public can watch and join in with *Sevillanas*, a popular Andalusian folk dance.

The **Museo de Baile Flamenco** is a good place to learn about the origins of the dance and current developments, as well as see performances.

MUSIC AND DANCE

The setting of Bizet's *Carmen*, Rossini's *The Barber of Seville* and Mozart's *Don Giovanni* and *Figaro*, Seville is a city of opera lovers. Prestigious international opera companies perform at the elegant **Teatro de la Maestranza**, starting in December and lasting until May. This theatre is home to the Real Orquesta Sinfónica de Sevilla, whose performances are highly regarded. The annual programme of the theatre also includes chamber and classical music seasons. **Teatro Lope de Vega** and

A live performance of flamenco at Los Gallos

Rosario Flores, the famous Andalusian singing star, performing at one of her concerts

Conservatorio Superior de Música Manuel Castillo are two other remarkable venues for classical music.

The Maestranza and **Teatro Central** are the main venues hosting a wide range of national and international classical and contemporary dance performances. **Sala Endanza** is the ideal venue for smaller productions.

ROCK, JAZZ AND BLUES

Few international rock stars make it to Seville, as Barcelona and Madrid tend to attract all the big names. However, large concerts are sometimes held at **Estadio Olímpico**. Some of Spain's most popular groups and singers in the flamenco pop genre, such as Niña Pastori and Rosario Flores, are from Andalusia. **Café Naima** and **Sala Malandar**, have live music from local bands, including jazz, folk and rock, but the highlight of the jazz calendar in Seville has to be the International Jazz Festival, held in November at the Teatro Central.

NIGHTLIFE

The nightlife of Seville offers an endless array of possibilities. Calle Betis, along the Triana side of the river, has many bars, restaurants and clubs. Alameda de Hércules is one of the liveliest areas, with **Café Habanilla** and **Café Central** as main bohemian hotspots. **Las Columnas** is the most popular tapas bar in Barrio de Santa Cruz district and **Bar Garlochi** is recommended for the first drink of the night. **La Terraza** at Eme Catedral Hotel is *the* place to see and be seen at (booking essential). The streets around Plaza de la Alfalfa overflow with youthful revellers. Frequented by Spanish celebrities, **Antique** in Isla de la Cartuja is the place to dance till dawn. In summer, their outdoor terrace boasts two pools and fashion shows.

BULLFIGHTING

The Maestranza Bullring *(see p430)* is mythical among fans of bullfighting. Some of the most important bullfights in Spain are held here during the Feria de Abril. The season runs from April to October. It is advisable to book in advance if the matadors are famous, and also if you want a seat in the *sombra* (shade). Tickets are sold at the *taquilla* (box office) at the bullring.

AMUSEMENT PARKS

Isla Mágica re-creates the exploits of 16th-century New World explorers. The eight zones which visitors experience are Sevilla – Puerto de Indias, Mundo Maya, Puerta de América, Amazonia, La Guarida de los Piratas, La Fuente de Juventud, ElDorado and La Metrópolis de España. Fun for children of all ages.

DIRECTORY

FLAMENCO

Casa de la Memoria
C/ Ximenez de Enciso 28. **Map** 4 D2, 6 E4. ***Tel*** *954 56 06 70.*

La Anselma
C/ Pages del Corro 49. **Map** 3 A2.

La Carbonería
C/ Levíes 18. **Map** 4 D1, 6 E3. ***Tel*** *954 21 44 60.*

Los Gallos
Pl de Santa Cruz 11. **Map** 4 D2, 6 E4. ***Tel*** *954 21 69 81.* **www**.tablaolosgallos.com

Museo de Baile Flamenco
C/ Manuel Rojas Marcos 3. **Map** 6 D3. ***Tel*** *954 34 03 11.*

MUSIC AND DANCE

Conservatorio Superior de Música Manuel Castillo
C/ Baños 48. **Map** 1 C5, 5 B1. ***Tel*** *954 91 56 30.*

Sala Endanza
Cas C/ Torneo 18. **Map** 1 C3. ***Tel*** *954 90 40 34.*

Teatro Central
Av José Gálvez s/n, Isla de la Cartuja. **Map** 1 C2. ***Tel*** *955 03 72 00.*

Teatro Lope de Vega
Av María Luisa s/n. **Map** 3 C3. ***Tel*** *955 47 28 22.*

Teatro de la Maestranza
Paseo de Colón 22. **Map** 5 C5, 3 B2. ***Tel*** *954 22 33 44.*

ROCK, JAZZ AND BLUES

Café Naima
C/ Trajano 47. **Map** 1 C5, 5 C1. ***Tel*** *954 38 24 85.*

Estadio Olímpico
Isla de la Cartuja, s/n. **Map** 1 B1. ***Tel*** *954 48 94 00.* **www**.eosevilla.com

Sala Malandar
Avda Torneo 43. **Map** 1 B4. ***Tel*** *954 37 01 88.*

NIGHTLIFE

Antique
Matemáticos Rey Pastor y Castro s/n. **Map** 1 B3. ***Tel*** *954 46 22 07.*

Bar Garlochi
C/ Boteros 26. **Map** 3 C1, 6 E3.

Café Central
Pl Alameda de Hércules 64. **Map** 1 D4. ***Tel*** *954 38 73 12.*

Café Habanilla
Pl Alameda de Hércules 63. **Map** 1 D4. ***Tel*** *954 90 27 18.*

La Terraza
Eme Catedral Hotel, C/ Alemanes 27. **Map** 3 C2, 6 D4. ***Tel*** *954 56 00 00.*

Las Columnas
C/ Rodrigo Caro 1. **Map** 3 C2, 5 E4.

AMUSEMENT PARKS

Isla Mágica
Pabellón de España, Isla de la Cartuja. **Map** 1 B2. ***Tel*** *902 16 17 16.* **www**.islamagica.es

ANDALUSIA

HUELVA · CÁDIZ · MÁLAGA · GIBRALTAR · SEVILLA CÓRDOBA · GRANADA · JAÉN · ALMERÍA

Andalusia is where all Spain's stereotypes meet. Bullfighters, beaches, flamenco, white villages, cave houses, gaudy fiestas, religious processions, tapas and sherry are all here in abundance. But each is part of a larger whole, which includes great art and architecture, nature reserves and an easy-going way of life.

The eight provinces of Andalusia stretch across Southern Spain from the deserts of Almería to the Portuguese border. One of Spain's longest rivers, the Guadalquivir, bisects the region. Andalusia is linked to the central tableland by a pass, the Desfiladero de Despeñaperros. The highest peaks on the Spanish mainland are in Andalusia's Sierra Nevada.

Successive invaders left their mark on Andalusia. The Romans built cities in this southern province, which they called Baetica, among them Córdoba, its capital, and the well-preserved Itálica near Seville. It was in Andalusia that the Moors lingered longest and left their greatest buildings – Córdoba's Mezquita and the splendid palace of the Alhambra in Granada.

Inevitably, perhaps, the most visited places are the great cities and the busy Costa del Sol, with Gibraltar, a geographical and historical oddity, at its western end. But there are many attractions tucked into other corners of the region. Many of the sights of Huelva province, bordering Portugal, are associated with Christopher Columbus, who set sail from here in 1492. Film directors have put to good use the atmospheric landscapes of Almería's arid interior, which are reminiscent of the Wild West or Arabia. Discreetly concealed among the countless olive groves that cover Jaén province, but not to be missed, are Andalusia's two lovely Renaissance towns, Úbeda and Baeza.

The city of Jaén surrounded by olive groves, seen from the Castillo de Santa Catalina

◁ Doorway into the *mihrab* (prayer niche) in the Mezquita at Córdoba

Exploring Andalusia

Andalusia is Spain's most varied region. It offers dramatic desert scenery at Tabernas, water sports on the Costa del Sol, skiing in the Sierra Nevada and sherry tasting in Jerez. Of the many nature reserves, the vast, watery Doñana teems with birdlife, while Cazorla is a rugged limestone massif. Granada and Córdoba are unmissable for their Moorish heritage; Úbeda and Baeza are Renaissance gems; and Ronda is one of dozens of superb white towns.

KEY

- Motorway
- Major road
- Secondary road
- Scenic route
- Main railway
- Minor railway
- International border
- Regional border
- Summit

0 kilometres 25

0 miles 25

The smart marina at Sotogrande

GETTING AROUND

Andalusia has a modern motorway network, with the principal NIV A4 (E5) from Madrid following the Guadalquivir valley to Córdoba, Seville and Cádiz. The fast AVE train links Málaga, Seville and Córdoba with Madrid. Coaches cover most of the region. The main airports are Málaga, Seville, Jerez and Gibraltar.

For additional map symbols *see back flap*

SEE ALSO

- ***Where to Stay*** pp591–7
- ***Where to Eat*** pp642–8

Singers in festive spirit at a village christening

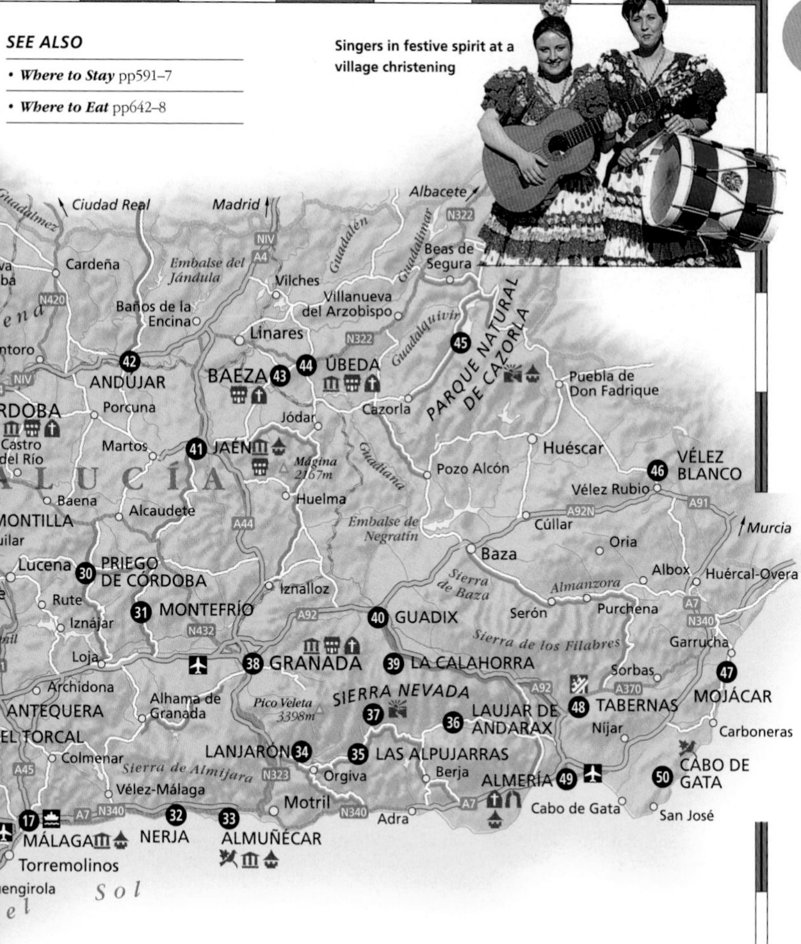

SIGHTS AT A GLANCE

Algeciras 14
Almería 49
Almuñécar 33
Andújar 42
Antequera 20
Arcos de la Frontera 11
Baeza pp498–9 43
Cádiz 9
Carmona 22
Córdoba pp478–81 28
Costa de la Luz 10
Écija 26
Garganta del Chorro 18
Gibraltar 15
Granada pp486–92 38
Guadix 40
Huelva 2
Itálica 23
Jaén 41
Jerez de la Frontera 8
La Calahorra 39
Lanjarón 34
Laujar de Andarax 36
Málaga 17
Marbella 16
Medina Azahara 27
Mojácar 47
Monasterio de la Rábida 3
Montefrío 31
Montilla 29
Nerja 32
Osuna 21
Palma del Río 25
Palos de la Frontera 4
Parque Nacional de Doñana pp464–5 6
Parque Natural de Cabo de Gata 50
Parque Natural de Cazorla 45
Priego de Córdoba 30
El Rocío 5
Ronda pp470–71 13
Sanlúcar de Barrameda 7
Seville *see pp426–57*
Sierra de Aracena 1
Sierra Morena 24
Sierra Nevada 37
Tabernas 48
El Torcal 19
Úbeda 44
Vélez Blanco 46

Tours

Las Alpujarras 35
Pueblos Blancos 12

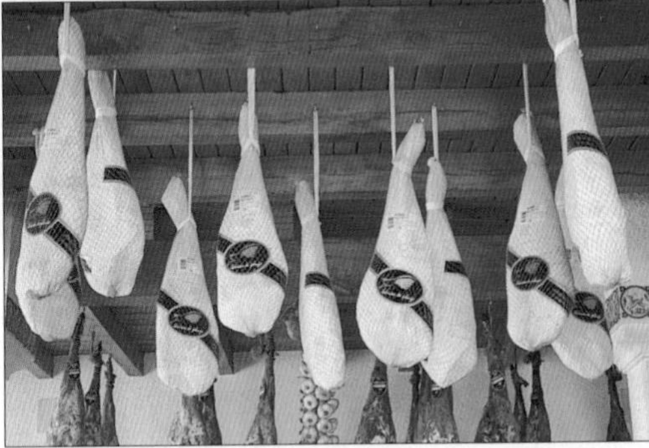

The famed *jamón ibérico* hanging in a bar in Jabugo, Sierra de Aracena

Sierra de Aracena ❶

Huelva. *El Repilado.* *Aracena.* *C/ Pozo de la Nieve s/n, Aracena, 663 93 78 77.* *Sat.*

This wild mountain range is one of the most remote and least visited corners of Andalusia. On the hillside are the ruins of a Moorish fort. The hill is pitted with caverns and in one, the **Gruta de las Maravillas**, is a lake in a chamber hung with many stalactites.

The village of **Jabugo** is famed for its ham, *jamón ibérico,* or *pata negra (see p419).*

Off the A–471 are the giant opencast mines at Minas de Riotinto, where iron, copper and silver have been exploited since Phoenician times. The **Museo Minero** traces the history of the Rio Tinto Company.

Gruta de las Maravillas
Pozo de la Nieve. ***Tel*** *663 93 78 77 (for info about availability).* *10am–1:30pm, 3–6pm.*

Museo Minero
Plaza del Museo. ***Tel*** *959 59 00 25.* *daily.* *1 & 6 Jan, 25 Dec.*

Huelva ❷

Huelva. *130,000.* *Pl Alcalde Coto Mora 2, 959 65 02 00.* *Fri.* *Las Columbinas (3 Aug).*

Founded as Onuba by the Phoenicians, Huelva had its grandest days as a Roman port. It was almost wiped out in the great Lisbon earthquake of 1755. It is an industrial city today, sprawling around the quayside on the Río Odiel.

Columbus's departure for the New World *(see p56)* from Palos de la Frontera, across the Río Odiel estuary, is celebrated in the excellent **Museo Provincial**, which also charts the history of the Rio Tinto mines. To the east of the centre, the Barrio Reina Victoria is a bizarre example of English mock-Tudor suburban bungalows built by the Rio Tinto Company for its workers in the early 20th century.

Bronze jug, Museo Provincial, Huelva

South of the town, at Punta del Sebo, the Monumento a Colón, a rather bleak statue of Columbus created by Gertrude Vanderbilt Whitney in 1929, dominates the Odiel estuary.

Environs
There are three resorts with sandy beaches near Huelva: **Punta Umbria**, on a promontory next to the bird-rich wetlands of the Marismas del Odiel; **Isla Cristina**, an important fishing port with excellent seafood restaurants; and **Mazagón** with miles of windswept dunes.

The hilly region east of Huelva known as **El Condado** produces many of Andalusia's finest wines, and Bollullos del Condado has the largest wine cooperative in the region. **Niebla**, nearby, has a Roman bridge. The town walls and 12th-century **Castillo de los Guzmanes** are both Moorish.

Museo Provincial
Alameda Sundheim 13. ***Tel*** *959 65 04 24.* *Tue –Sun.*

Castillo de los Guzmanes
C/ Campo Castillo, Niebla. ***Tel*** *959 36 22 70.* *daily.*

Monasterio de la Rábida ❸

Huelva. *from Huelva.* ***Tel*** *959 35 04 11.* *Tue–Sun.*

Four kilometres (2 miles) to the north of Palos de la Frontera is the Franciscan **Monasterio de la Rábida**, founded in the 15th century.

In 1491, a dejected Columbus sought refuge here after his plans to sail west to find the East Indies had been rejected by the Catholic Monarchs. Its prior, Juan Pérez, fatefully used his considerable influence as Queen Isabella's confessor to reverse the royal decision.

Inside, frescoes painted by Daniel Vásquez Díaz in 1930 glorify the explorer's life and discoveries. Also worth seeing are the Mudéjar cloisters, the flower-filled gardens and the beamed chapterhouse.

Frescoes depicting the life of Columbus at the Monasterio de la Rábida

Palos de la Frontera ❹

Huelva. 12,000. *Parque Botánico José Celestino Mutis Paraje de la Rábida, 959 53 05 35.* *Sat.* *Santa María de la Rábida (3 &16 Aug).*

Columbus put to sea on 3 August 1492 from Palos, the home town of his two captains, the brothers Martín and Vicente Pinzón. Martín's former home, the **Casa Museo de Martín Alonso Pinzón**, is now a small museum of exploration, and his statue stands in the main square.

The 15th-century **Iglesia de San Jorge** has a fine portal, through which Columbus left after hearing Mass before boarding the *Santa María*. The pier is now silted up.

Environs

In the beautiful white town of **Moguer** are treasures such as the 16th-century hermitage of Nuestra Señora de Montemayor, and the Neo-Classical town hall. The **Convento de Santa Clara** houses the Museo Diocesano de Arte Sacro and has a pretty cloister.

Casa Museo de Martín Alonso Pinzón
Calle Colón 24. ***Tel** 959 35 08 51 (for guided tours).* *Mon–Fri.*

Convento de Santa Clara
Plaza de las Monjas. ***Tel** 959 37 01 07.* *Tue–Sat.* *public hols.*

El Rocío ❺

Huelva. *2,500.* *Avda de la Canaliega, 955 77 79 56.* *Romeria (May/Jun).*

Bordering the Parque Nacional de Doñana *(see pp464–5)*, El Rocío is famous for its annual *romería*, which sees almost a million people converge on the village. Many of the pilgrims travel from distant parts of Spain, some on gaudily decorated ox-carts, to visit the **Iglesia de Nuestra Señora del Rocío**. A statue of the Virgin in the church is believed to have performed miraculous healings since 1280. Early on the Monday morning of the festival, men from Almonte fight to carry the statue in procession, and the crowd clambers on to the float to touch the image.

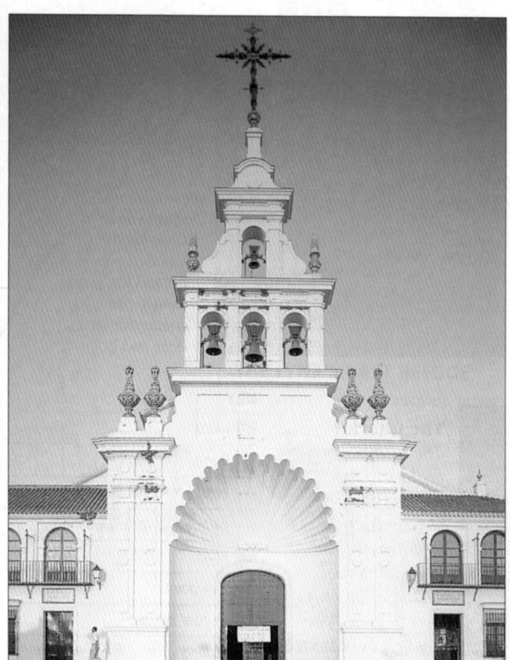

Iglesia de Nuestra Señora del Rocío, El Rocío

ANDALUSIA'S FIESTAS

Crowds following the image of the Virgin at El Rocío

Carnival *(Feb/Mar)*, Cádiz. The whole city puts on fancy dress for one of Europe's largest and most colourful carnivals. Groups of singers practise for many months to perform ditties satirizing current fashions, celebrities and politicians.

Romería de la Virgen de la Cabeza *(last Sun in Apr)*, Andújar (Jaén). A mass pilgrimage to a lonely sanctuary in the Sierra Morena.

Día de la Cruz *(first week in May)*, Granada and Córdoba. Neighbourhood groups compete to create the most colourful crosses adorned with flowers on squares and street corners.

Córdoba Patio Fiesta *(mid-May)*. Flower-decked patios in old Córdoba are opened to the public with displays of flamenco.

El Rocío *(May/Jun)*. More than 70 brotherhoods of pilgrims arrive at the village of El Rocío to pay homage to the Virgen del Rocío.

Columbus Festival *(late Jul/early Aug)*, Huelva. This celebration of Columbus's voyage is dedicated to the native music and dance of a different Latin American country every year.

Exaltación al Río Guadalquivir *(mid-Aug)*, Sanlúcar de Barrameda (Cádiz). Horses are raced on the beach at the mouth of the Río Guadalquivir.

Sanlúcar de Barrameda ❼

Cádiz. 63,000. Calzada del Ejército, 956 36 61 10. Wed. Exaltación al Río Guadalquivir and horse races (mid-Aug).

A fishing port at the mouth of the Río Guadalquivir, Sanlúcar is overlooked by a Moorish **castle**. This was the departure point for Columbus's third voyage in 1498 and also for Magellan's 1519 expedition to circumnavigate the globe.

Sanlúcar is best known for its light, dry manzanilla sherry made by, among other producers, **Bodegas Barbadillo**. Boats from the quay take visitors across the river to the Parque Nacional de Doñana *(see pp464–5)*.

Environs

Chipiona, along the coast, is a lively little resort town with an excellent beach. The walled town of **Lebrija**, inland, enjoys views over vineyards. Its Iglesia de Santa María de la Oliva is a reconsecrated 12th-century Almohad mosque.

Bodegas Barbadillo
C/ Luis de Eguilaz 11. ***Tel*** *956 38 55 21. Tue–Sat.*

Entrance to the Barbadillo bodega in Sanlúcar de Barrameda

Jerez de la Frontera ❽

Cádiz. 190,000. Alameda Cristina 7, 956 34 17 11. Mon. Grape Harvest (Sep).

Jerez is the capital of sherry production *(see pp420–21)* and many bodegas can be visited. Among the well-known names are **González Byass** and **Pedro Domecq**.

The city is also famous for its **Real Escuela Andaluza de Arte Ecuestre**, a school of equestrian skills. There are public dressage displays on Thursdays. If you visit on another day you may be able to watch the horses being trained. The **Palacio del Tiempo**, nearby, has one of the largest clock collections in Europe. On the Plaza de San Juan, the 18th-century **Palacio de Penmartín** houses the Centro Andaluz de Flamenco, where exhibitions give a good introduction to this music and dance tradition *(see pp424–5)*. The partially restored, 11th-century **Alcázar** encompasses a well-preserved mosque, now a church. Just to the north is the **cathedral**.

Environs

Not far from Jerez, the **Monasterio de la Cartuja Santa María de la Defensión** is considered one of the most beautiful in Spain. The port of **El Puerto de Santa María** has several bodegas that can be visited, including **Osborne** and **Terry**. The town also has a 13th-century castle and a large bullring.

Real Escuela Andaluza de Arte Ecuestre
Duque de Abrantes. ***Tel*** *956 31 96 35 (by appt). Mon–Fri.*
www.realescuela.org

Palacio del Tiempo
Calle Cervantes 3. ***Tel*** *956 18 21 00. Tue–Sun.*

Palacio de Penmartín
Plaza de San Juan 1. ***Tel*** *856 81 41 32. Mon–Fri. public hols.*

Alcázar
Alameda Vieja. ***Tel*** *956 14 99 55. daily. 1 & 6 Jan, 25 Dec.*

Sherry Bodegas
phone for tour times.
González Byass, C/ Manuel María González 12, Jerez. ***Tel*** *902 44 00 77.* **Pedro Domecq,** C/ San Ildefonso 3, Jerez. ***Tel*** *956 15 15 00.* **Sandeman,** C/ Pizarro 10, Jerez. ***Tel*** *956 31 29 95.* **Osborne,** C/ de los Moros, Puerto de Santa María. ***Tel*** *956 86 91 00.* **Terry,** C/ Tonelero, Puerto de Santa María. ***Tel*** *956 15 15 00.*

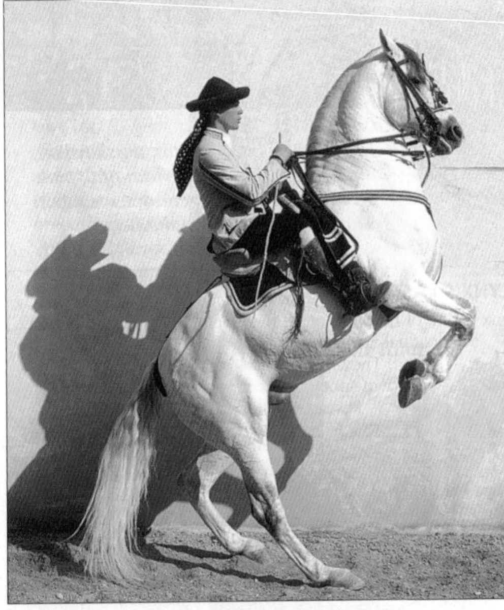
Real Escuela Andaluza de Arte Ecuestre, Jerez de la Frontera

Cádiz ❾

Egyptian mask, Museo de Cádiz

Jutting out of the Bay of Cádiz, and almost entirely surrounded by water, Cádiz lays claim to being Europe's oldest city. Legend names Hercules as its founder, although history credits the Phoenicians with establishing the town of Gadir in 1100 BC. Occupied by the Carthaginians, Romans and Moors in turn, the city also prospered after the Reconquest *(see pp54–5)* on wealth taken from the New World. In 1587 Sir Francis Drake sacked the city in the first of many British attacks in the war for world trade. In 1812 Cádiz briefly became Spain's capital when the nation's first constitution was declared here *(see p63)*.

Exploring Cádiz

The joy of visiting Cádiz is to wander along the waterfront with its well-tended gardens and open squares before exploring the old town, which is full of narrow alleys busy with market and street life.

The pride of the city is its Carnival *(see p463)* – a riotous explosion of festivities, fancy dress, singing and drinking.

Catedral

Known as the Catedral Nueva (New Cathedral) and built on the site of an older one, this Baroque and Neo-Classical church, with its dome of golden-yellow tiles, is one of Spain's largest. In the crypt is the tomb of composer Manuel de Falla (1876–1946), native of Cádiz. The cathedral's treasures are stored in the Casa de la Contaduria, behind the cathedral.

Museo de Cádiz

Plaza de Mina. ***Tel*** *956 20 33 68.* *2:30–8:30pm Tue; 9am–8:30pm Wed–Sat; 9am–2:30pm Sun & hols.*

The museum has archaeological exhibits charting the history of Cádiz and the largest art gallery in Andalusia, with works by Rubens, Zurbarán and Murillo. On the third floor is a collection of puppets made for village fiestas.

Torre Tavira

Calle Marqués del Real Tesoro 10. ***Tel*** *956 21 29 10.* *daily.*

The city's official watchtower in the 18th century has now been converted into a camera obscura, and offers great views.

Oratorio de San Felipe Neri

This 18th-century church has been a shrine to liberalism since 1812. In that year, as Napoleon tightened his grip on Spain during the War of Independence *(see pp62–3)*, a provisional government assembled here to try to lay the foundations of Spain's first constitutional monarchy. The liberal constitution it declared was bold but ineffectual.

VISITORS' CHECKLIST

Cádiz. 155,000. Plaza de Sevilla, 902 24 02 02. Plaza de la Hispanidad, 902 19 92 08. Paseo de Canalejas s/n, 956 24 10 01. Mon. Carnival (Feb/ Mar).
www.cadizturismo.com

Zurbarán's *Saint Bruno in Ecstasy*, in the Museo de Cádiz

CÁDIZ CATHEDRAL

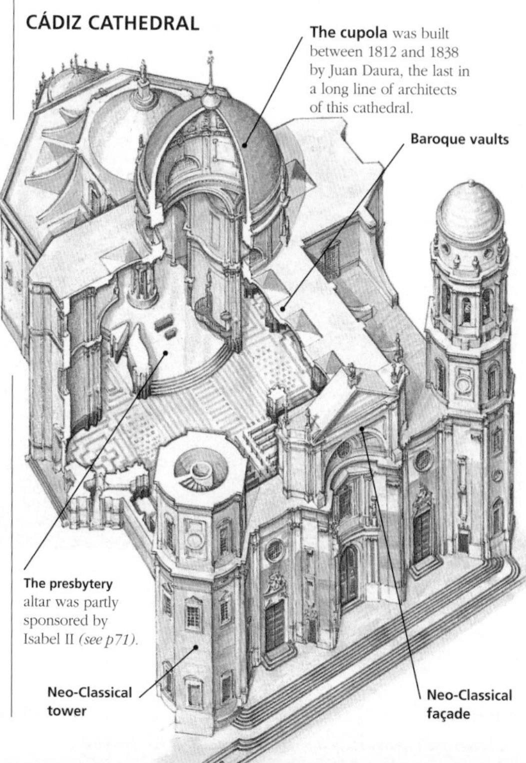
The cupola was built between 1812 and 1838 by Juan Daura, the last in a long line of architects of this cathedral.

Baroque vaults

The presbytery altar was partly sponsored by Isabel II *(see p71)*.

Neo-Classical tower

Neo-Classical façade

Fishing boats at the resort of Zahara de los Atunes on the Costa de la Luz

Costa de la Luz ⑩

Cádiz. *Cádiz.* *Cádiz, Tarifa.* *Paseo de la Alameda s/n, Tarifa, 956 68 09 93.*

The Costa de la Luz (Coast of Light) between Cádiz and Tarifa, at Spain's southernmost tip, is an unspoiled, windswept stretch of coast characterized by strong, pure light – the source of its name. From the Sierra del Cabrito, to the west of Algeciras, it is often possible to see the outline of Tangier and the parched Moroccan landscape below the purple-tinged Rif mountains across the narrow Strait of Gibraltar.

Tarifa is named after an 8th-century Moorish commander, Tarif ben Maluk, who landed there with his forces during the Moorish conquest *(see pp52–3)*. Later, Tarifa and its 10th-century castle were defended by the legendary hero Guzmán during a siege by the Moors in 1292.

Tarifa has since become the windsurfing capital of Europe. The breezes that blow on to this coast also drive the numerous wind turbines on the hills.

Off the N340 (E5), at the end of a long, narrow road which strikes out across a wilderness of cacti, sunflowers and lone cork trees, is **Zahara de los Atunes**, a modest holiday resort with a few hotels. **Conil de la Frontera**, to the west, is busier and more built up.

The English admiral Nelson defeated a Spanish and French fleet off **Cabo de Trafalgar** in 1805, but died in the battle.

A Tour Around the Pueblos Blancos ⑫

Instead of settling on Andalusia's plains, where they would have fallen prey to bandits, some Andalusians chose to live in fortified hilltop towns and villages. These are known as *pueblos blancos* (white towns) because they are whitewashed in the Moorish tradition *(see p26)*. They are working agricultural towns today, but touring them will reveal a host of references to the past.

Ubrique ②
Nestling at the foot of the Sierra de Ubrique, this *pueblo* is known for its flourishing leather industry.

Arcos de la Frontera ①

Jimena de la Frontera ⑨
Set amid hills, where wild bulls graze among cork and olive trees, this town has a ruined Moorish castle.

SEVILLA
A372
CÁDIZ, JEREZ
Embalse de los Hurones
Charco de los Hurones
CA5221
CA503
La Sauceda

KEY

Tour route

Other roads

Gaucín ⑧
From here there are unsurpassed vistas over the Mediterranean, the Atlantic, the Rock of Gibraltar and across the strait to the Rif mountains of North Africa.

0 kilometres 10
0 miles 5

TIPS FOR DRIVERS

Tour length: *205 km (127 miles).*
Stopping-off points: *There are places to stay and eat at all of these pueblos, but Ronda has the widest range of hotels* (see p595) *and restaurants* (see p647). *Arcos has a parador* (see p592).

Arcos de la Frontera ⓫

Cádiz. 30,000. Plaza del Cabildo, 956 70 22 64. Fri. Toro del Domingo de Resurreccion (last day of Easter), Velada de Nuestra Señora de las Nieves (4–6 Aug), Semana Santa, Feria de San Miguel (end of Sep).

Although legend has it that a son of Noah founded Arcos it is more probable that it was the Iberians. It gained the name Arcobriga in the Roman era and, under the Caliphate of Córdoba *(see p52)*, became the Moorish stronghold of Medina Arkosh. It is an archetypal white town, with a labyrinthine old quarter.

On the Plaza de España, at the top of the town, are the parador *(see p592)* and the **Iglesia de Santa María de la Asunción**, a Late Gothic-Mudéjar building noted for its choir stalls and altarpiece. The huge, Gothic **Iglesia de San Pedro**, perched on the edge of a cliff formed by the Río Guadalete, is a striking building. Nearby is the **Palacio del Mayorazgo**, which has an ornate Renaissance façade. The **town hall** *(ayuntamiento)* has a fine Mudéjar ceiling.

Environs

In the 15th-century the Guzmán family was granted the dukedom of **Medina Sidonia**, a white west of Arcos de la Frontera. The area became one of the most important ducal seats in Spain. The Gothic Iglesia de Santa María la Coronada is the town's finest building. It contains a notable collection of Renaissance religious art.

Iglesia de Santa María de la Asunción in Arcos de la Frontera

Palacio del Mayorazgo
C/ San Pedro 2. ***Tel*** *956 70 30 13 (Casa de Cultura). 9am–2pm Mon–Fri.*

Ayuntamiento
Plaza del Cabildo. ***Tel*** *956 70 00 02. Mon–Fri. public hols.*

Zahara de la Sierra ③
Fanning out below a castle ruin, this fine *pueblo blanco* has been declared a national monument.

Grazalema ④
This village in the Sierra de Grazalema has the highest rainfall in Spain.

Ronda la Vieja ⑤
Significant remains of the Roman town of Acinipo, including a theatre, can be visited.

Setenil ⑥
Some of the streets of this unusual white town, which climbs up the sides of a gorge, are covered by rock overhangs. The gorge was carved out of volcanic tufa rock by the Río Trejo.

Ronda ⑦
(see pp470–71)

Street-by-Street: Ronda ⓭

Plate hand-painted in Ronda

One of the most spectacularly located cities in Spain, Ronda sits on a massive rocky outcrop, straddling a precipitous limestone cleft. Because of its impregnable position this town was one of the last Moorish bastions, finally falling to the Christians in 1485. On the south side perches a classic Moorish *pueblo blanco (see pp468–9)* of cobbled alleys, window grilles and dazzling whitewash – most historic sights are in this part of the town. Located in El Mercadillo, the newer town, is one of the oldest bullrings in Spain.

★ Puente Nuevo
An impressive feat of 18th-century civil engineering, the "New Bridge" over the 100-m (330-ft) deep Tajo gorge joins old and new Ronda.

Convento de Santo Domingo was the local headquarters of the Inquisition *(see p274)*.

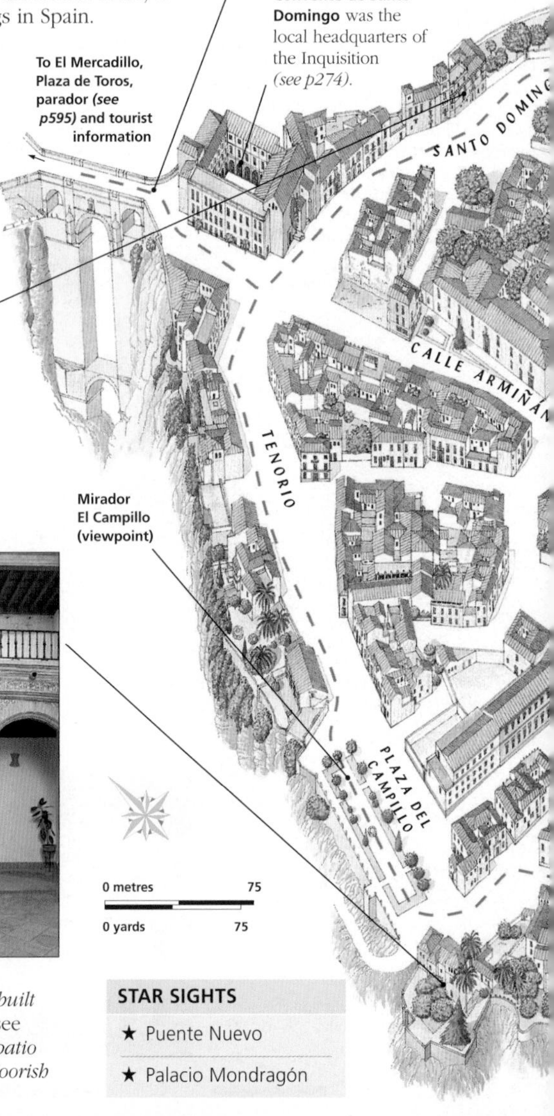

To El Mercadillo, Plaza de Toros, parador *(see p595)* and tourist information

Casa del Rey Moro
From this 18th-century mansion, built on the foundations of a Moorish palace, 365 steps lead down to the river.

TENORIO

Mirador El Campillo (viewpoint)

PLAZA DEL CAMPILLO

0 metres 75

0 yards 75

★ Palacio Mondragón
Much of this palace was rebuilt following the Reconquest (see pp54–55)*, but its arcaded patio is adorned with original Moorish mosaics and plasterwork.*

STAR SIGHTS

★ Puente Nuevo

★ Palacio Mondragón

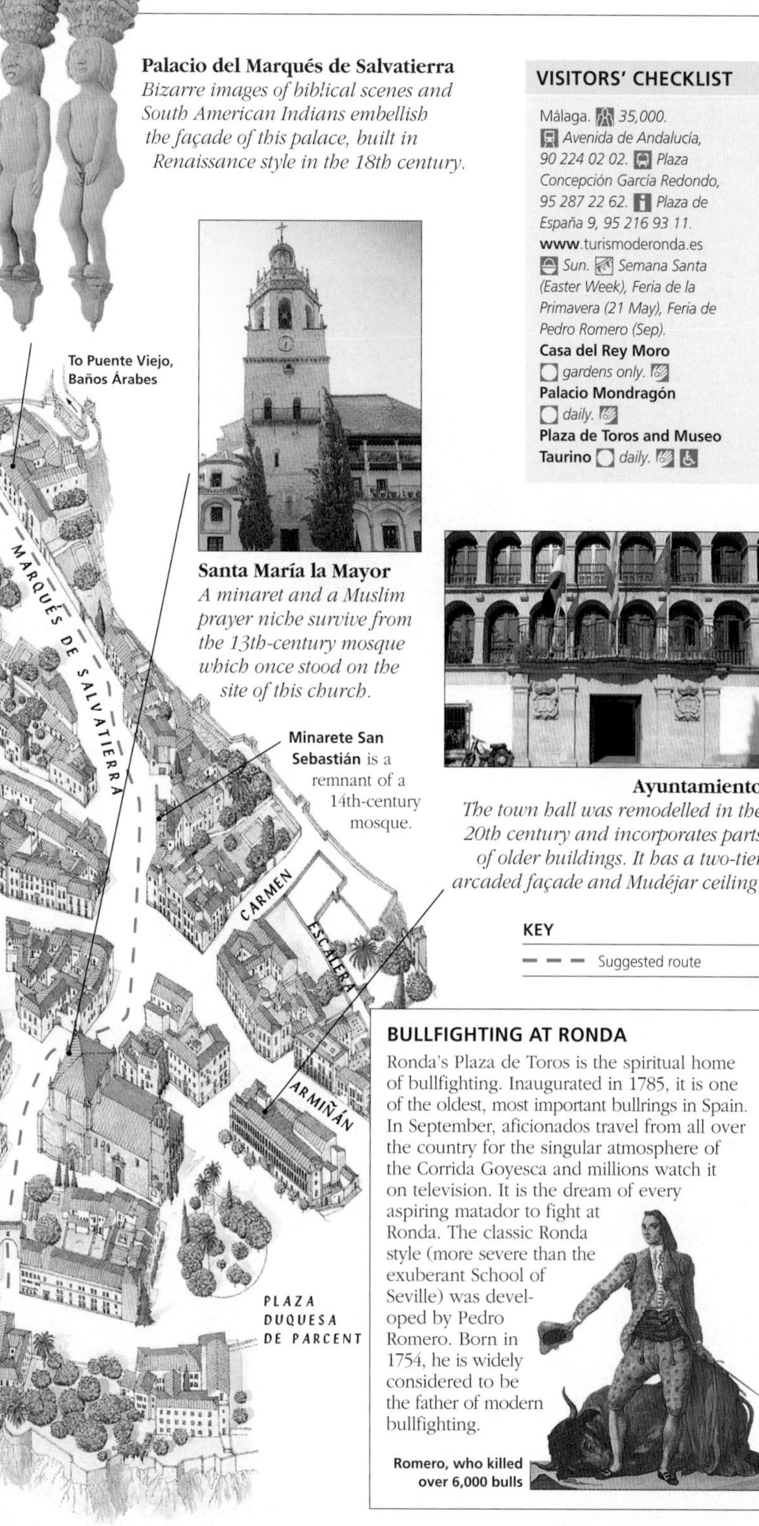

Palacio del Marqués de Salvatierra
Bizarre images of biblical scenes and South American Indians embellish the façade of this palace, built in Renaissance style in the 18th century.

Santa María la Mayor
A minaret and a Muslim prayer niche survive from the 13th-century mosque which once stood on the site of this church.

Minarete San Sebastián is a remnant of a 14th-century mosque.

Ayuntamiento
The town hall was remodelled in the 20th century and incorporates parts of older buildings. It has a two-tier arcaded façade and Mudéjar ceiling.

VISITORS' CHECKLIST

Málaga. *35,000.* *Avenida de Andalucía, 90 224 02 02.* *Plaza Concepción García Redondo, 95 287 22 62.* *Plaza de España 9, 95 216 93 11.* **www**.turismoderonda.es *Sun.* *Semana Santa (Easter Week), Feria de la Primavera (21 May), Feria de Pedro Romero (Sep).*
Casa del Rey Moro *gardens only.*
Palacio Mondragón *daily.*
Plaza de Toros and Museo Taurino *daily.*

KEY

– – – Suggested route

BULLFIGHTING AT RONDA

Ronda's Plaza de Toros is the spiritual home of bullfighting. Inaugurated in 1785, it is one of the oldest, most important bullrings in Spain. In September, aficionados travel from all over the country for the singular atmosphere of the Corrida Goyesca and millions watch it on television. It is the dream of every aspiring matador to fight at Ronda. The classic Ronda style (more severe than the exuberant School of Seville) was developed by Pedro Romero. Born in 1754, he is widely considered to be the father of modern bullfighting.

Romero, who killed over 6,000 bulls

Algeciras ⓮

Cádiz. 200,000. Calle Juan de la Cierva, 956 78 41 31. Tue. Feria Real (24 Jun–2 Jul).

From the industrial city of Algeciras, there are spectacular views of Gibraltar, 14 km (9 miles) away across its bay. The city is a major fishing port and Europe's main gateway for ferries to North Africa, especially Tangier and Spain's territories of Ceuta and Melilla.

Gibraltar ⓯

British Crown Colony. 35,000. Duke of Kent House, Cathedral Square, (+35) 020 07 49 50. Nat Day (10 Sep). **www**.gibraltar.gov.uk

The high, rocky headland of Gibraltar was signed over to Britain "in perpetuity" at the Treaty of Utrecht in 1713 *(see p62)*. Today, about 4 million people stream across the border annually from La Línea de la Concepción in Spain.

Among the chief sights of Gibraltar are those testifying to its strategic military importance over the centuries. Halfway up the famous Rock are an 8th-century Moorish castle, whose **keep** is still used as a prison, and 80 km (50 miles) of **siege tunnels** housing storerooms and barracks. **St Michael's Cave**, which served as a hospital during World War II, is now used for classical concerts.

St Michael's Cave, which served as a hospital during World War II

The **Apes' Den**, near Europa Point, Gibraltar's southernmost tip, is home to the tailless apes. Legend says that the British will keep the Rock only as long as the apes remain there.

A cable car takes visitors to the **Top of the Rock** at 450 m (1,475 ft). **Gibraltar Museum** charts the colony's history.

The Keep, Siege Tunnels, St Michael's Cave, Apes' Den
Upper Rock Area. ***Tel*** *(+35) 020 04 59 57.* *daily.* *1 Jan, 25 Dec.*

Gibraltar Museum
18 Bombhouse Lane. ***Tel*** *(+35) 020 07 42 89.* *Mon–Sat.* *public hols.*

The Costa del Sol

Thanks to its average of 300 days' sunshine a year and its varied coastline, the Costa del Sol, between Gibraltar and Málaga, offers a full range of beach-based holidays and water sports. Complementing the sophistication and luxury of Marbella are many other popular resorts aimed at the mass market. More than 30 of Europe's finest golf courses lie just inland.

Puerto Banús is Marbella's ostentatious marina. The expensive shops, restaurants and glittering nightlife reflec the wealth of its clientele.

Estepona's quiet evenings make it popular with families with young children. Behind the big hotels are old squares shaded by orange trees.

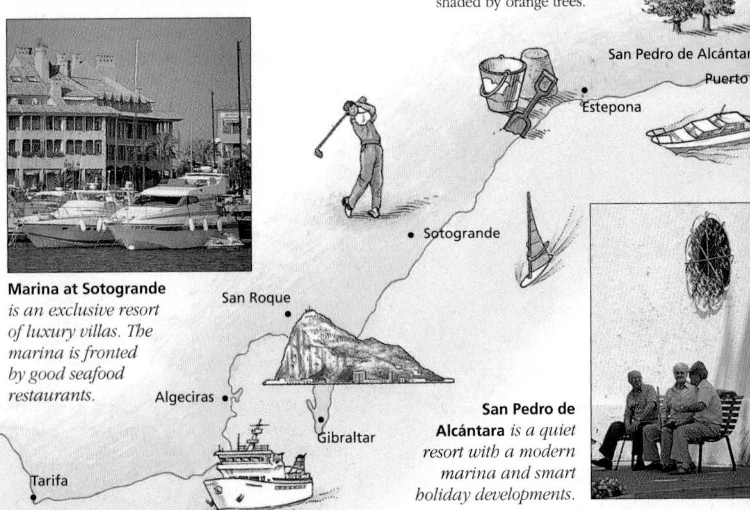

Marina at Sotogrande *is an exclusive resort of luxury villas. The marina is fronted by good seafood restaurants.*

San Pedro de Alcántara *is a quiet resort with a modern marina and smart holiday developments.*

Yachts and motorboats in the exclusive marina of Marbella – the summer home of the international jet set

Marbella ⓰

Málaga. 120,000. Glorieta de la Fontanilla, Paseo Marítimo, 95 277 14 42. Mon. San Bernabé (Jun). **www**.marbella.com

Marbella is one of Europe's most exclusive holiday resorts, frequented by royalty and film stars. There are 24 beaches, including Puerto Banus, Playa Rio Verde and Playa Nagueles. In winter, the major attraction is the golf. Among the delights of the old town, with its spotlessly clean alleys, squares, and smart shops and restaurants, is the **Iglesia de Nuestra Señora de la Encarnación**. The **Museo del Grabado Español Contemporáneo** displays some of Pablo Picasso's least-known work.

Museo del Grabado Español Contemporáneo
C/ Hospital Bazan. *Tel 95 276 57 41.* *Tue–Sat.* *public hols.*

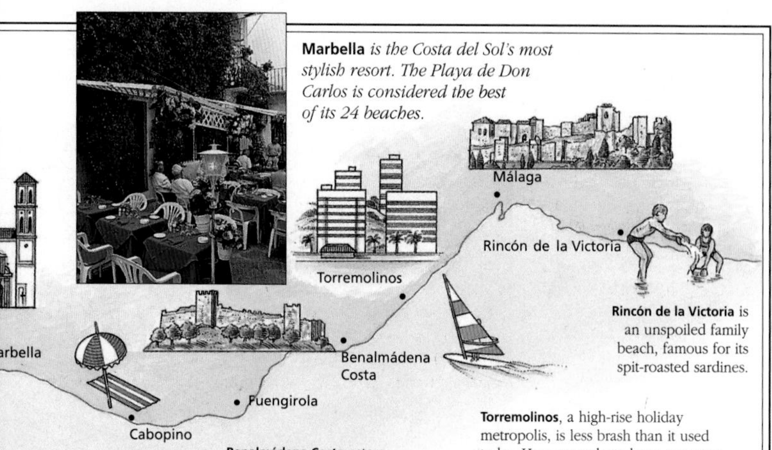

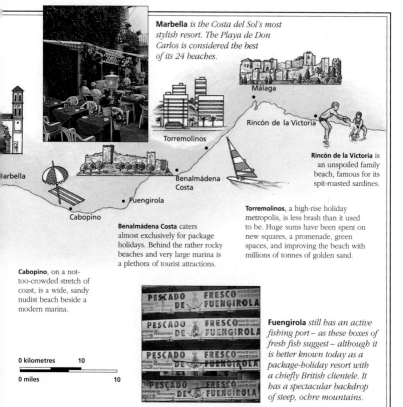

Marbella *is the Costa del Sol's most stylish resort. The Playa de Don Carlos is considered the best of its 24 beaches.*

Rincón de la Victoria is an unspoiled family beach, famous for its spit-roasted sardines.

Torremolinos, a high-rise holiday metropolis, is less brash than it used to be. Huge sums have been spent on new squares, a promenade, green spaces, and improving the beach with millions of tonnes of golden sand.

Benalmádena Costa caters almost exclusively for package holidays. Behind the rather rocky beaches and very large marina is a plethora of tourist attractions.

Cabopino, on a not-too-crowded stretch of coast, is a wide, sandy nudist beach beside a modern marina.

0 kilometres 10

0 miles 10

Fuengirola *still has an active fishing port – as these boxes of fresh fish suggest – although it is better known today as a package-holiday resort with a chiefly British clientele. It has a spectacular backdrop of steep, ochre mountains.*

The main façade of Málaga's cathedral, consecrated in 1588

Málaga ⓱

Málaga. 650,000. *Plaza de la Marina 11, 95 192 60 20.* *Sun.* *Carnival (Feb/Mar), Feria (second Sat–third Sun of Aug).* **www**.malagaturismo.com

Málaga, the second largest city in Andalusia, is today a thriving port, just as it was in Phoenician times, and again under the Romans and then the Moors. It also flourished during the 19th century, when sweet Málaga wine *(see p420)* was one of Europe's most popular drinks – until phylloxera ravaged the area's vineyards in 1876.

The **cathedral** was begun in 1528 by Diego de Siloé, but it is a bizarre mix of styles. The half-built second tower, abandoned in 1765 when funds ran out, gave the cathedral its nickname: La Manquita ("the one-armed one").

Málaga's former Museo de Bellas Artes has been adapted to house a **Museo Picasso** displaying works by the native artist. The **Casa Natal de Picasso**, where the painter spent his early years, is now the Picasso Foundation.

Málaga's vast **Alcazaba** *(see p53)* was built between the 8th and 11th centuries. There is a partially excavated Roman amphitheatre by its entrance, but the real attraction is the display of Phoenician, Roman and Moorish artifacts in the **Museo Arqueológico**

On the hill directly behind the Alcazaba are the ruins of the **Castillo de Gibralfaro**, a 14th-century Moorish castle.

Environs

In the beautiful hills to the north and east of Málaga is the **Parque Natural de los Montes de Málaga**. Wildlife, such as eagles and wild boars, thrive here amid the scent of lavender and wild herbs. Walkers can follow a number of scenic marked trails. Going north on the C345 you can also visit a small preserved winery of the 1840s.

Museo Picasso
Calle San Agustín 8. ***Tel*** *95 260 27 31.* *Tue–Sun.* *1 Jan, 25 Dec.*

Alcazaba and Museo Arqueológico
Calle Alcazabilla. ***Tel*** *95 222 72 30.* *Tue–Sun.*

Garganta del Chorro ⓲

Málaga. *El Chorro.* *Parque Ardeles.* *Avenida de la Constitución, Álora, 95 249 83 80.*

Up the fertile Guadalhorce valley, beyond the village of El Chorro, is one of the geographical wonders of Andalusia. The Garganta del Chorro is an immense chasm, 180 m (590 ft) deep and in places only 10 m (30 ft) wide, cut by the river through a limestone mountain. Downstream, a hydroelectric plant detracts from the wildness of the place.

The **Camino del Rey** is a catwalk clinging to the rock face which leads to a bridge across the gorge. It is, however, closed to the public.

Environs

Álora, a classic white town *(see p468)* with a ruined Moorish castle and an 18th-century church, lies 12 km (7 miles) down the valley.

Along the twisting MA441 from Álora is the village of **Carratraca**. In the 19th and early 20th centuries, Europe's highest society travelled here for the healing powers of the sulphurous springs. These days, Carratraca has a faded glory – water still gushes out at 700 litres (155 UK and 185 US gal) a minute and the outdoor baths remain open, but they are little used.

The Garganta del Chorro, rising high above the Guadalhorce River

Weathered limestone formations in El Torcal

El Torcal ⓳

Málaga. Antequera. Antequera. Antequera, 95 270 25 05. **Parque Natural del Torcal** ***Tel*** *95 104 21 00.*

A massive exposed hump of limestone upland, which has been slowly weathered into bizarre rock formations and caves, the **Parque Natural del Torcal** is popular with hikers. Footpaths lead from a visitors' centre – walks of up to two hours are marked by yellow arrows, longer walks by red.

The park is also a pleasure for natural historians, with fox and weasel populations, and colonies of eagles, hawks and vultures, as well as rare plants and flowers like wild orchids.

Antequera ⓴

Málaga. *42,000.* *Pl San Sebastián 7, 95 270 25 05.* *Tue.* *Ferias (end May & mid-Aug).* **www**.antequera.es

This busy market town was strategically important first as Roman Anticaria and later as a Moorish border fortress defending Granada.

Of its many churches, the **Iglesia de Nuestra Señora del Carmen**, with its vast Baroque altarpiece, is not to be missed. At the opposite end of the town is the 19th-century **Plaza de Toros**, with a museum of bullfighting.

The hilltop **castle** was built in the 13th century on the site of a Roman fort. Visitors can walk round the castle walls by approaching through the 16th-century Arco de los Gigantes. There are excellent views of Antequera from the Torre del Papabellotas on the best-preserved part of the wall.

In the town below, the 18th-century **Palacio de Nájera** is the setting for the Municipal Museum, the star exhibit of which is a splendid Roman bronze statue of a boy.

The massive **dolmens**, just outside the town, are thought to be the burial chambers of tribal leaders and date from around 2500–2000 BC.

Environs

Laguna de la Fuente de Piedra, north of Antequera, teems with bird life, including huge flocks of flamingoes, which arrive to breed after wintering in West Africa. A road off the N334 leads to a lakeside viewing point. There is a visitors' centre in Fuente de Piedra village. To the east, also off the N334, is **Archidona**, with its 18th-century, octagonal Plaza Ochavada built in French style, but which also incorporates traditional Andalusian features.

The triumphal, 16th-century Arco de los Gigantes, Antequera

Plaza de Toros
Carretera de Sevilla. ***Tel*** *618 26 11 20.* *Tue–Sun.* **Museo Taurino** *Sat, Sun, public hols.*

Palacio de Nájera
Coso Viejo. ***Tel*** *95 270 83 00.* *Tue–Sun.*

Osuna ㉑

Sevilla. *17,500.* *Calle Carrera 82, 95 481 57 32.* *Mon.* *San Alcadio (12 Jan), Virgen de la Consolación (8 Sep).*

Palacio del Marqués de la Gomera, in Osuna, completed in 1770

Osuna was once a key Roman garrison town. It rose again to prominence in the 16th century under the Dukes of Osuna, who wielded immense power. In the 1530s they founded the **Colegiata de Santa María**, a grand church with a Baroque reredos and paintings by José de Ribera. This was followed in 1548 by the **University**, a rather severe building with a beautiful patio. Some fine mansions, among them the **Palacio del Marqués de la Gomera**, also reflect the town's former glory.

Environs

To the east lies **Estepa**, whose modern-day fame rests on its biscuits – *polvorones* and *mantecados* *(see p419)*. The Iglesia del Carmen has a black and white, Baroque façade.

Tomb of Servilia in the Roman necropolis in Carmona

Carmona 22

Sevilla. 25,000. *Alcázar de la Puerta de Sevilla, 95 419 09 55. Mon & Thu. Feria (May), Fiestas Patronales (8–16 Sep).*
www.turismo.carmona.org

Carmona is the first major town east of Seville, its old quarter built on a hill above the suburbs on the plain. Beyond the **Puerta de Sevilla**, a gateway in the Moorish city walls, is a dense cluster of mansions, Mudéjar churches, and winding streets.

The Plaza de San Fernando has a feeling of grandeur which is characterized by the Renaissance façade of the old **Ayuntamiento**. The present town hall, set just off the square, dates from the 18th century; in its courtyard are some Roman mosaics. Close by is the **Iglesia de Santa María la Mayor**. Built in the 15th century over a mosque, whose patio still survives, this is the finest of Carmona's churches.

Dominating the town are the ruins of the **Alcázar del Rey Pedro**, once a palace of Pedro I, known as Pedro the Cruel. Parts of it now form a parador *(see p592)*.

Just outside Carmona is the **Necrópolis Romana**, the extensive remains of a Roman burial ground. A site museum displays some of the items found in the graves, including statues, glass and jewellery.

Ayuntamiento
Calle Salvador 2. ***Tel*** *95 414 00 11. Mon–Fri. public hols.*

Necrópolis Romana
Avenida Jorge Bonsor 9. ***Tel*** *95 562 46 15. Tue–Sun. Mon & Sun in summer; public hols.*

Itálica 23

Sevilla. ***Tel*** *95 562 22 66. from Seville. Apr–Sep: 8:30am–9pm Tue–Sat, 9am–3pm Sun; Oct–Mar: 9am–6:30pm Tue–Sat, 10am–4pm Sun.*

Itálica was founded in 206 BC by Scipio Africanus. One of the earliest Roman cities in Hispania *(see pp50–51)*, it grew to become important in the 2nd and 3rd centuries AD. Emperor Hadrian, who was born in the city and reigned from AD 117–138, added marble temples and other grand buildings.

Roman mosaic from Itálica

Archaeologists have speculated that the changing course of the Río Guadalquivir may have led to Itálica's later demise during Moorish times.

Next to the vast but crumbling **amphitheatre** is a display of finds from the site. More treasures are displayed in the Museo Arqueológico in Seville *(see p445)*.

The traces of Itálica's streets and the mosaic floors of some villas can be seen. However, little remains of the city's temples or of its baths as most of the stone and marble has been plundered over the centuries. Some well-preserved Roman baths and a theatre can be seen in **Santiponce**, a village just outside the site.

Sierra Morena 24

Sevilla and Córdoba. *Cazalla, Constantina. Constantina, Cazalla. Sevilla, 95 488 35 62; Córdoba, 95 588 12 97; El Robledo, 95 588 15 97.*

The Sierra Morena, clad in oak and pine woods, runs across the north of the provinces of Sevilla and Córdoba. It forms a natural frontier between Andalusia and the plains of neighbouring Extremadura and La Mancha. Smaller sierras (ranges of hills) within the Sierra Morena chain are also named individually.

Fuente Obejuna, north of Córdoba, was immortalized by Lope de Vega *(see p290)* in his play about an uprising in 1476 against a local overlord. The Iglesia de San Juan Bautista in **Hinojosa del Duque** is a vast church in both Gothic and Renaissance styles. **Belalcázar** is dominated by the huge tower of a ruined 15th-century castle. Storks nest on the church towers of the plateau of **Valle de los Pedroches**, to the east.

Cazalla de la Sierra, the main town of the sierra north of Seville, is cosmopolitan, and popular with young *Sevillanos* at weekends. A unique concoction of cherry liqueur and aniseed, Liquor de Guindas, is produced here. **Constantina**, to the east, is more peaceful and has superb views across the countryside.

A cow grazing in the pastures of the Sierra Morena north of Seville

Palma del Río ㉕

Córdoba. 19,400. Calle Santa Clara, 957 64 43 70. Tue. Ferias (19–21 May & 18–20 Aug). **www**.palmadelrio.es

The Romans sited a strategic settlement here, on the road between Córdoba and Itálica, almost 2,000 years ago. The remains of the 12th-century city walls are a reminder of the town's frontier days under the Almohads *(see p54)*. The **Iglesia de la Asunción**, a Baroque church, dates from the 18th century. The **Monasterio de San Francisco** is now a hotel *(see p595)*, and guests can eat dinner in the 15th-century refectory of the Franciscan monks. Palma del Río is the home town of El Cordobés, one of Spain's most famous matadors. His biography, *Or I'll Dress You in Mourning*, paints a vivid picture of life in the town and of the hardship which followed the end of the Civil War.

Bell tower, La Asunción

Environs

One of the most dramatic silhouettes in Southern Spain breaks the skyline of **Almodóvar del Río**. The Moorish castle – parts of it dating from the 8th century – stands on a hilltop overlooking the whitewashed town and fields of cotton.

Castillo de Almodóvar del Río

Tel *957 63 40 55. daily. 1 Jan, 25 Dec.*

Écija ㉖

Sevilla. 40,000. Plaza de España 1, Ayuntamiento 95 590 29 33. Thu. Feria (21–24 Sep). **www**.turismoecija.com

Écija is nicknamed "the frying pan of Andalusia" owing to its famously torrid climate. In the searing heat, the palm trees on the Plaza de España provide blissful shade. An ideal place to sit and observe daily life passing by, this is also a spot for evening strolls.

Écija has 11 Baroque church steeples, many adorned with gleaming *azulejos (see p438)*, and together they make a very impressive sight. The most florid of these is the **Iglesia de Santa María**, which overlooks the Plaza de España. The **Iglesia de San Juan**, with its exquisite, brightly coloured bell tower, is a very close rival.

Of the many mansions along Calle Emilio Castelar, the Baroque **Palacio de Peñaflor** is worth a visit. Its pink marble doorway is topped by twisted columns, while an attractive wrought-iron balcony runs along the whole front façade.

Palacio de Peñaflor

C/ Emilio Castelar 26. ***Tel*** *95 483 02 73. for refurbishment.*

Medina Azahara ㉗

Córdoba. ***Tel*** *957 35 28 74. Córdoba. 10am–8:30pm Tue–Sat (to 6:30pm 16 Sep–30 Apr), 10am–2pm Sun & public hols.*

Just a few kilometres north of Córdoba lies this once glorious palace. Built in the 10th century for Caliph Abd al Rahman III, it is named after his favourite wife, Azahara. He spared no expense, employing more than 15,000 mules, 4,000 camels and 10,000 workers to bring building materials from as far as North Africa.

Detail of wood carving in the main hall of Medina Azahara

The palace is built on three levels and includes a mosque, the caliph's residence and fine gardens *(see pp422–3)*. Marble, ebony, jasper and alabaster once adorned its many halls, and it is believed that shimmering pools of quicksilver added lustre.

The glory was short-lived. The palace was sacked by Berber invaders in 1010 and over subsequent centuries it was ransacked for its building materials. Now, the ruins give only glimpses of its former beauty – a Moorish main hall, for instance, decorated with marble carvings and a carved wood ceiling. The palace is currently being restored.

***Trompe l'oeil* on the ornate Baroque façade of the Palacio de Peñaflor, Écija**

Street-by-Street: Córdoba ㉘

The heart of Córdoba is the old Jewish quarter, situated to the west of the Mezquita's towering walls. A walk around this area gives the sensation that little has changed since the 10th century when this was one of the greatest cities in the Western world. Wrought ironwork decorates cobbled streets too narrow for cars, where silversmiths create fine jewellery in their workshops. Most of the chief sights are here, while modern city life takes place some blocks north, around the Plaza de Tendillas. To the east of this square is the Plaza de la Corredera, a 17th-century arcaded square with a daily market.

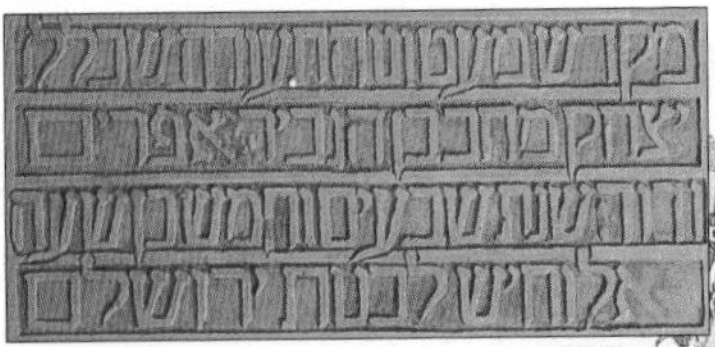

Statue of Maimónides

Sinagoga
Hebrew script covers this 14th-century synagogue. Spain's other synagogues are in Toledo, Madrid and Barcelona.

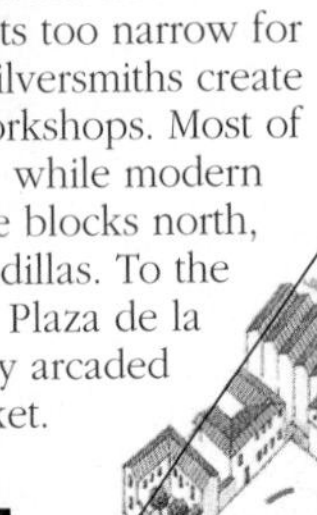

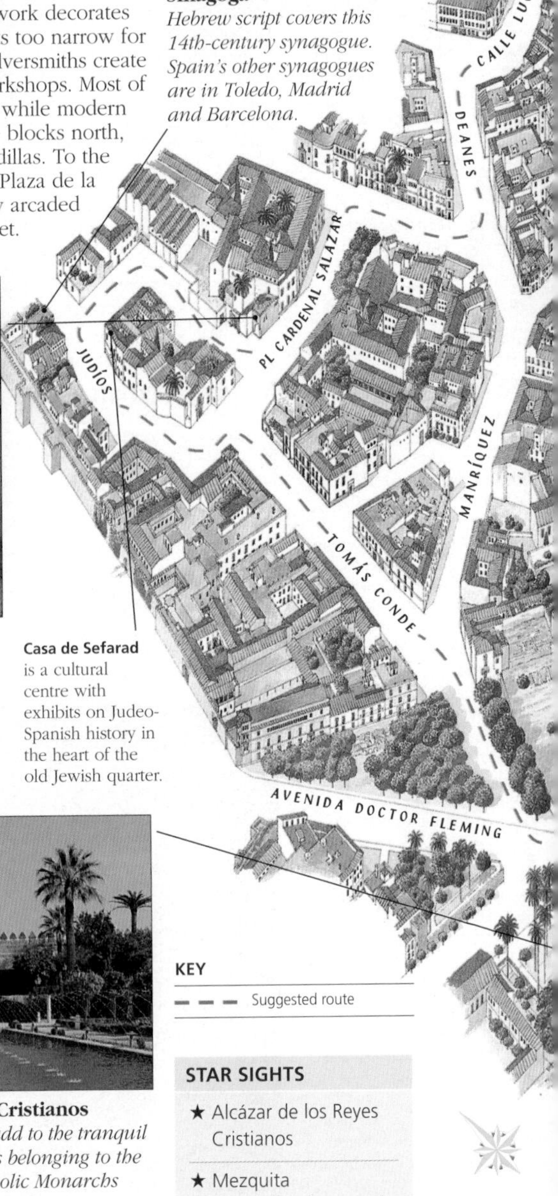

The Capilla de San Bartolome
This small Church was built in the Gothic-Mudéjar style. It is decorated with elaborate plasterwork and tiles.

Casa de Sefarad is a cultural centre with exhibits on Judeo-Spanish history in the heart of the old Jewish quarter.

★ Alcázar de los Reyes Cristianos
Water terraces fountains add to the tranquil atmosphere of the gardens belonging to the palace-fortress of the Catholic Monarchs (see pp56–7), *built in the 14th century.*

KEY

 Suggested route

STAR SIGHTS

- ★ Alcázar de los Reyes Cristianos
- ★ Mezquita

The Callejón de las Flores brims with colourful geraniums, which contrast with the whitewashed walls of this alley, leading to a tiny square.

VISITORS' CHECKLIST

Córdoba. 330,000. *Glorieta de las Tres Culturas, 902 24 02 02.* *Glorieta de las Tres Culturas, 957 40 40 40.* *Palacio de Congresos, Calle Torri-jos 10, 957 35 51 79.* *Tue, Fri & Sun.* *Semana Santa (Easter Week), Festival de los Patios (5–11 May), Feria (late May).* **Sinagoga** *Tue–Sun.* **Casa de Sefarad** *daily.* **Alcázar de los Reyes Cristianos** *Tue–Sun.* **www.**turismodecordoba.org

The Palacio Episcopal now houses the tourist office.

Puerta del Puente

The Puente Romano spans the Río Guadalquivir. A museum on its southeast side explores the different cultures of medieval Córdoba.

★ Mezquita
The mighty walls of the Great Mosque (see pp480–81) *hide delicate arches, pillars and a dazzling* mihrab.

0 metres 100
0 yards 100

Moorish bronze stag from Medina Azahara, Museo Arqueológico

Exploring Córdoba

Córdoba lies on a sharp bend in the Río Guadalquivir, which is spanned by a Roman bridge linking the 14th-century Torre de la Calahorra and the old town. One of the most atmospheric squares in Andalusia is the Plaza de los Capuchinos. With its haunting stone calvary, it is particularly evocative when seen by moonlight.

Museo de Bellas Artes

Plaza del Potro 2. ***Tel*** *957 35 55 50.* *Tue–Sun.*
Exhibits in a former charity hospital include sculptures by local artist Mateo Inurria (1867–1924) and works by Valdés Leal, Zurbarán and Murillo of the Seville School.

Museo Arqueológico

Plaza Jerónimo Páez 7. ***Tel*** *957 35 55 17.* *Tue–Sat.*
Located in a Renaissance mansion, displays include the remains of a Roman theatre found beneath the building, Roman pottery and impressive finds from the Moorish era.

Palacio de Viana

Plaza Don Gome 2. ***Tel*** *957 49 67 41.* *Tue–Sun (am only Sun & public hols).*
Furniture, tapestries, paintings and porcelain are displayed in the 17th-century former home of the Viana family.

Museo Romero de Torres

Plaza del Potro 1. ***Tel*** *957 49 19 09.* *Tue–Sun.* *(free Fri).*
Julio Romero de Torres (1874–1930), who was born in this house, captured the soul of Córdoba in his paintings.

Córdoba: the Mezquita

Córdoba's Great Mosque, dating back 12 centuries, embodied the power of Islam on the Iberian Peninsula. Abd al Rahman I *(see p52)* built the original mosque between 785 and 787. The building evolved over the centuries, blending many architectural forms. In the 10th century al Hakam II made some of the most lavish additions, including the elaborate *mihrab* (prayer niche) and the *maqsura* (caliph's enclosure). During the 16th century a cathedral was built in the heart of the reconsecrated mosque, part of which was destroyed.

Patio de los Naranjos
Orange trees grow in the courtyard where the faithful washed before prayer.

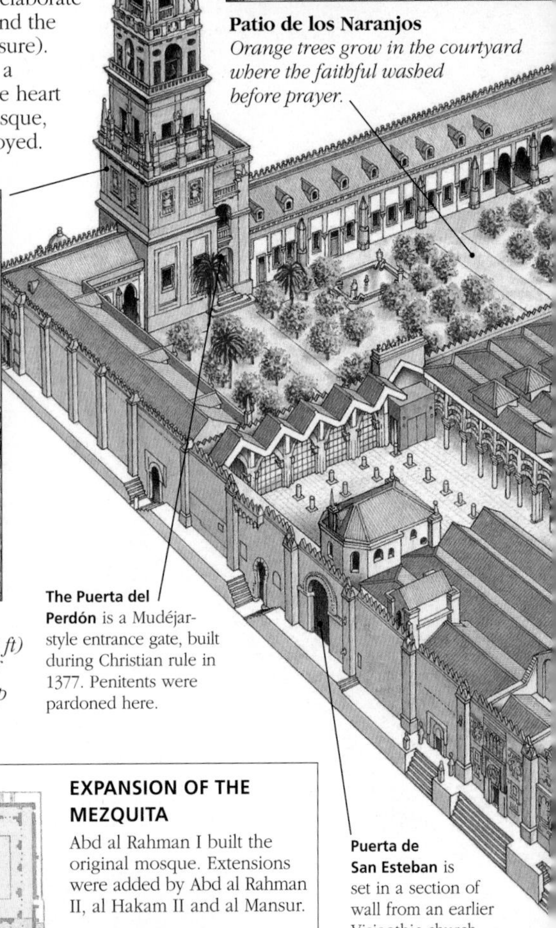

Torre del Alminar
This bell tower, 93 m (305 ft) high, is built on the site of the original minaret. Steep steps lead to the top for a fine view of the city.

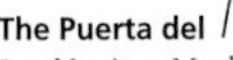

The Puerta del Perdón is a Mudéjar-style entrance gate, built during Christian rule in 1377. Penitents were pardoned here.

Puerta de San Esteban is set in a section of wall from an earlier Visigothic church.

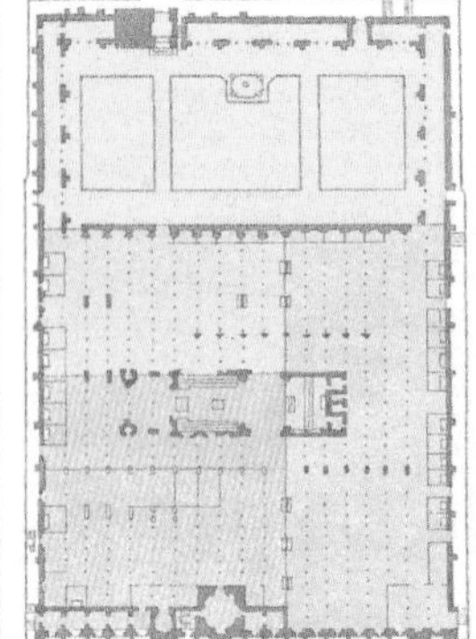

EXPANSION OF THE MEZQUITA

Abd al Rahman I built the original mosque. Extensions were added by Abd al Rahman II, al Hakam II and al Mansur.

KEY TO ADDITIONS

- Mosque of Abd al Rahman I
- Extension by Abd al Rahman II
- Extension by al Hakam II
- Extension by al Mansur
- Patio de los Naranjos

STAR FEATURES

- ★ Mihrab
- ★ Capilla de Villaviciosa
- ★ Arches and Pillars

Cathedral
Part of the mosque was destroyed to accommodate the cathedral, started in 1523. Featuring an Italianate dome, it was designed chiefly by members of the Hernán Ruiz family.

VISITORS' CHECKLIST

C/ Torrijos 10. ***Tel*** *957 47 05 12.* *10am–7pm Mon–Sat, 8:30–10am, 2–7pm Sun & pub hols (Nov–Feb: to 6pm Mon–Sat, 8:30–10am, 2–6pm Sun & pub hols).* *9:30am Mon–Sat; 11am, noon & 1pm Sun & hols.*

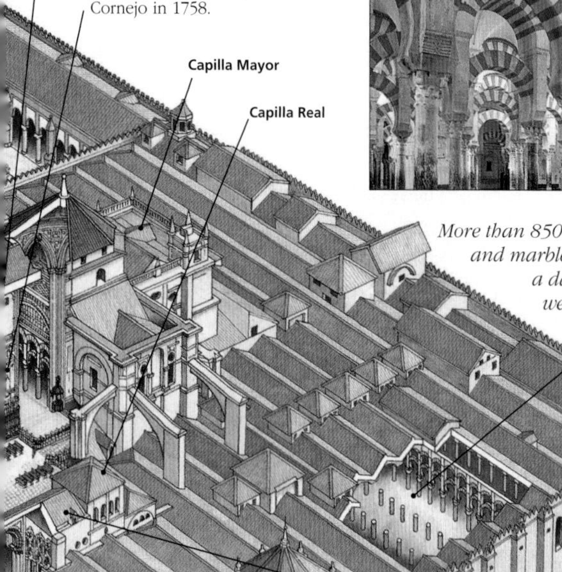

The cathedral choir has Churrigueresque stalls carved by Pedro Duque Cornejo in 1758.

Capilla Mayor

Capilla Real

★ Arches and Pillars
More than 850 columns of granite, jasper and marble support the roof, creating a dazzling visual effect. Many were taken from Roman and Visigothic buildings.

★ Mihrab
This prayer niche, richly ornamented, held a gilt copy of the Koran. The worn flagstones indicate where pilgrims circled it seven times on their knees.

★ Capilla de Villaviciosa
The first Christian chapel was built in the mosque in 1371 by Mudéjar (see p55) *craftsmen. Its multi-lobed arches are stunning.*

Baroque statuary in the Fuente del Rey at Priego de Córdoba

Montilla 29

Córdoba. *23,000.* *Capitán Alonso de Vargas 3, 957 65 24 62.* *Fri.* *Grape Harvest (late Aug).*

Montilla is the centre of an important wine region that produces an excellent smooth white fino *(see p420)*. Unlike sherry, it is not fortified with alcohol. Several bodegas, including **Alvear** and **Pérez Barquero**, will show visitors around by prior arrangement.

The Mudéjar **Convento de Santa Clara** dates from 1512. The town library is in the **Casa del Inca**, so named because Garcilaso de la Vega, who wrote about the Incas, lived there in the 16th century.

Environs

Aguilar, 13 km (8 miles) to the south, has the unusual, eight-sided Plaza de San José (built in 1810) and several seigneurial houses.

Baena, 40 km (25 miles) to the west of Montilla, has been famous for its olive oil since Roman times. On the Plaza de la Constitución is the Casa del Monte, an mansion dating from the 18th century. At Easter thousands of costumed drummers take to the streets.

Bodega Alvear
Avda María Auxiliadora 1. ***Tel*** *957 66 40 14.* *Mon–Fri.* *12:30pm.*

Bodega Pérez Barquero
Avda de Andalucía 27. ***Tel*** *957 65 05 00.* *daily.* *Aug.*

Priego de Córdoba 30

Córdoba. *23,000.* *Plaza de la Constitución 3, 957 70 06 25.* *Sat.* *Feria Real (1–5 Sep).* **www**.turismodepriego.com

Priego de Cordóba's claim to be the capital of Cordoban Baroque is borne out by the dazzling work of carvers, ironworkers and gilders in the many houses, and especially churches, built with wealth generated by a prosperous 18th-century silk industry.

A restored Moorish fortress stands in the whitewashed medieval quarter, the **Barrio de la Villa**. Close by is the outstanding **Iglesia de la Asunción**, converted from Gothic to Baroque style by Jerónimo Sánchez de Rueda. Its pièce de résistance is the sacristy, created in 1784 by local artist Francisco Javier Pedrajas. The main altar is Plateresque *(see p25)*.

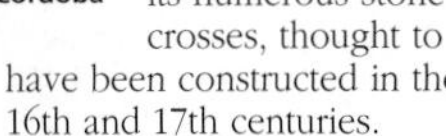

La Asunción, Priego de Córdoba

At midnight every Saturday the brotherhood of another Baroque church, the **Iglesia de la Aurora**, parades the streets singing songs in praise of the Virgin.

Silk merchants built many of the splendid mansions that follow the curve around the Calle del Río. At the street's end is the Baroque Fuente del Rey (The King's Fountain). The 139 spouts splash water into three basins adorned with a riot of statuary.

Environs

Zuheros, perched on a crag in the limestone hills northwest of Priego, is one of Andalusia's prettiest villages. **Rute**, to the southwest, is known for its *anís (see p607)*.

Alcalá la Real, in the lowlands east of Priego, is overlooked by the hilltop ruins of a castle and a church. There are two handsome Renaissance buildings on its central square: the Fuente de Carlos V and the Palacio Abacia.

Montefrío 31

Granada. *7,000.* *Plaza España 1, 958 33 60 04.* *Mon.* *Fiesta patronal (14–18 Aug).*

The approach to Montefrío from the south offers wonderful views of tiled rooftops and pretty whitewashed houses. This archetypal Andalusian town is topped by the remains of its Moorish fortifications and the 16th-century Gothic **Iglesia de la Villa**. In the centre of town is the Neo-Classical **Iglesia de la Encarnación**, designed by Ventura Rodríguez (1717–85). The town is known for its chorizo, as well as its numerous stone crosses, thought to have been constructed in the 16th and 17th centuries.

Environs

Santa Fé was built by the Catholic Monarchs at the end of the 15th century. Their army

Barrels of Montilla, the sherry-like wine from the town of the same name

The castle overlooking the resort of Almuñécar on the Costa Tropical

camped here while laying siege to Granada, and this was the site of the formal surrender of the Moors in 1492 *(see pp56–7)*. A Moor's severed head, carved in stone, adorns the spire of the parish church.

Sited above a gorge, **Alhama de Granada** was named Al hamma (hot springs) by the Moors. Their baths, close to the spot where the hot water gushes from the ground just outside town, can be seen in the Hotel Balneario.

Loja, on the Río Genil, near Los Infiernos gorge, is known as "the city of water" because of its spring-fed fountains.

Nerja 32

Málaga. 18,000. Calle Carmen 1, 95 252 15 31. Sun. Feria (9–12 Oct). **www**.nerja.org

This well-established resort, built on a cliff above sandy coves, lies at the foot of the beautiful Sierra de Almijara. There are sweeping views up and down the coast from the rocky promontory known as **El Balcón de Europa** (the Balcony of Europe). Along it runs a promenade lined with cafés and restaurants.

East of the town are the **Cuevas de Nerja**, a series of vast caverns which were discovered in 1959. Wall paintings found here are believed to be about 20,000 years old. Only a few of the many cathedral-sized chambers are open to public view. One of these has been converted into an impressive auditorium which has a capacity of several hundred people.

Environs

In **Vélez-Málaga**, the ruins of the Fortaleza de Belén, a Moorish fortress, dominate the medieval Barrio de San Sebastián.

Cuevas de Nerja

Carretera de las Cuevas de Nerja. ***Tel*** *95 252 95 20.* *daily.* *1 Jan, 15 May.*

Almuñécar 33

Granada. *22,000.* *Avda Europa, 958 63 11 25.* *Fri, 1st Sat of each month.* *Virgen de la Antigua (15 Aug).* **www**.almunecar.info

Almuñécar lies on the Costa Tropical, so named because its climate allows the cultivation of exotic fruit. Just inland, mountains rise to more than 2,000 m (6,560 ft). The Phoenicians founded the first settlement here, called Sexi, and the Romans constructed an aqueduct, the remains of which can be seen today. Almuñécar is now a popular holiday resort.

Above the old town is the **castle**, built by the Moors and altered in the 1500s. Below it is the **Parque Ornitológico**, with an aviary and botanic gardens, and the ruins of a Roman fish-salting factory. The **Museo Arqueológico Cueva de Siete Palacios** displays a variety of Phoenician artifacts.

Environs

The ancient white town of **Salobreña** is set amid fields of sugar cane. Narrow streets lead up a hill to a restored Arab castle with fine views of the Sierra Nevada *(see p485)*.

Parque Ornitológico

Plaza de Abderraman. ***Tel*** *634 46 81 54.* *daily.*

Museo Arqueológico Cueva de Siete Palacios

Casco Antiguo. ***Tel*** *607 86 54 66.* *Tue–Sun.*

Castillo de Salobreña

Calle Andrés Segovia. ***Tel*** *958 61 03 14.* *daily.* *public hols.*

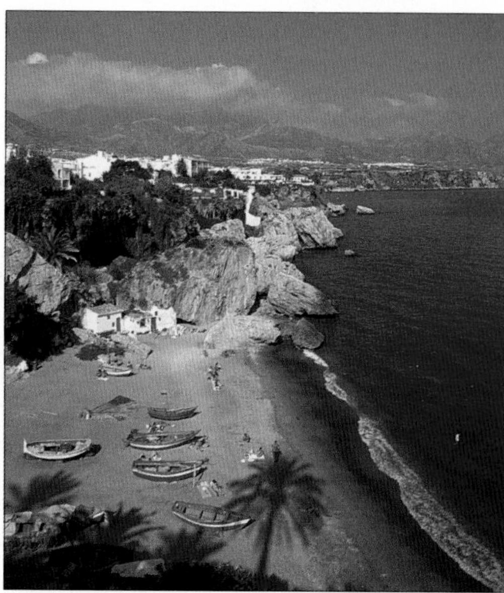

One of the succession of sandy coves that make up the resort of Nerja

The majestic peaks of the Sierra Nevada towering, in places, to over 3,000 m (9,800 ft) above sea level

Lanjarón 34

Granada. 24,000. Avda de la Alpujarra s/n, 958 77 04 62. Tue & Fri. San Juan (24 Jun).

Scores of clear, snow-fed springs bubble from the slopes of the Sierra Nevada; their abundance at Lanjarón, on the southern side of this great range of mountains, has given the town a long history as a health spa. From June to October, visitors flock to take the waters for arthritic, dietary and nervous ailments. Bottled water from Lanjarón is sold all over the country.

A major festival begins on the night of 23 June and ends in an uproarious water battle in the early hours of 24 June, the Día de San Juan. Everyone in the streets gets doused.

The town is on the threshold of Las Alpujarras, a scenic upland area of dramatic landscapes, where steep, terraced hillsides and deep-cut valleys conceal remote, whitewashed villages. Roads to and from Lanjarón wind slowly and dizzily around the slopes.

A Tour of Las Alpujarras 35

The fertile, upland valleys of Las Alpujarras, clothed with chestnut, walnut and poplar trees, lie on the southern slopes of the Sierra Nevada. The architecture of the quaint white villages which cling to the hillsides – compact clusters of irregularly shaped houses with tall chimneys sprouting from flat, grey roofs – is unique in Spain. Local specialities are ham cured in the cold, dry air of Trevélez and brightly coloured, handwoven rugs.

Trevélez ④
Trevélez, in the shadow of Mulhacén, Spain's highest mountain, is famous for its cured ham.

Orgiva ①
This is the largest town of the region, with a Baroque church in the main street and a lively Thursday market.

Poqueira Valley ②
Capileira, Bubión and Pampaneira are three villages typical of Las Alpujarras in this pretty river valley.

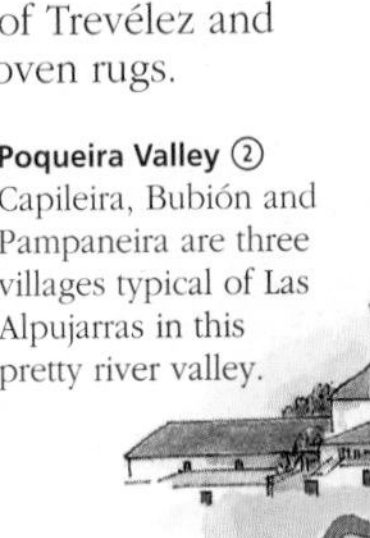

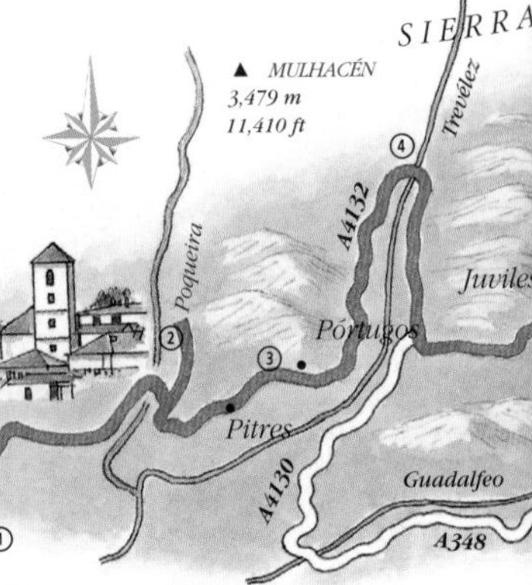

Fuente Agria ③
People come to this spring to drink the iron-rich, naturally carbonated waters.

For hotels and restaurants in this region see pp591–7 and pp642–8

Laujar de Andarax 36

Almería. *2,000.* *Carretera C-332 (A-345), 950 51 35 48.* *3 & 17 of each month.* *San Vicente (22 Jan), San Marcos (25 Apr), Virgen de la Salud (19 Sep).*

Laujar, in the arid foothills of the Sierra Nevada, looks southwards across the Andarax valley towards the Sierra de Gádor.

Andarax was founded by one of the grandsons of Noah. In the 16th century, Abén Humeya, leader of the greatest Morisco rebellion *(see p59)*, made his base here. The revolt was crushed by Christian troops and Abén Humeya was killed by his own followers. Inside Laujar's 17th-century church, **La Encarnación**, is a statue of the Virgin by Alonso Cano. Next to the Baroque **town hall** *(ayuntamiento)* is a fountain inscribed with some lines written by Francisco Villespesa, a dramatist and poet who was born in Laujar in 1877: *"Six fountains has my pueblo/He who drinks their waters/will never forget them/so heavenly is their taste."*

Painting, Iglesia de la Encarnación

El Nacimiento, a park to the east of Laujar, is a suitable place to have a picnic. You can accompany it with one of the area's hearty red wines. **Ohanes**, above the Andarax valley further to the east, is an attractive hill town of steep streets and whitewashed houses known for its crops of table grapes.

Sierra Nevada 37

Granada. *from Granada.* *Plaza de Andalucía, Cetursa Sierra Nevada, 902 70 89 00.* **www**.sierranevadaski.com

Fourteen peaks more than 3,000 m (9,800 ft) high crown the Sierra Nevada. The snow lingers until July and begins falling again in late autumn. One of Europe's highest roads, the A395, runs past **Solynieve**, an expanding ski resort at 2,100 m (6,890 ft), and skirts the two highest peaks, **Pico Veleta** at 3,398 m (11,149 ft) and **Mulhacén** at 3,482 m (11,420 ft).

The Sierra's closeness to the Mediterranean and its altitude account for the great diversity of the indigenous flora and fauna found on its slopes – the latter including golden eagles and some rare butterflies.

There are several mountain refuges for the use of serious hikers and climbers.

Yegen ⑥
A plaque marks the house where Gerald Brenan, the author of *South from Granada*, lived in the 1920s.

Puerto de la Ragua ⑧
This pass, which leads across the mountains to Guadix, is nearly 2,000 m (6,560 ft) high and is often snowbound in winter.

Válor ⑦
Abén Humeya, leader of a rebellion by Moriscos in the 16th century, was born here. A commemorative battle between Moors and Christians is staged each year in mid-September.

Cádiar ⑤
Free wine is traditionally on tap during the village's October fiesta.

KEY

- Tour route
- Other roads
- ▲ Mountain peak

0 kilometres 5
0 miles 5

TIPS FOR DRIVERS

Tour length: *85 km (56 miles).*
Stopping-off points: *There are bars and restaurants in Orgiva, Capileira, Bubión (see p643) and Trevélez. Orgiva, Bubión and Trevélez have good hotels (see pp592–6). Orgiva is the last petrol stop before Cádiar.*

Granada 38

Stone relief, Museo Arqueológico

The guitarist Andrés Segovia (1893–1987) described Granada as a "place of dreams, where the Lord put the seed of music in my soul". It was first occupied by the Moors in the 8th century, and its golden period came during the rule of the Nasrid dynasty *(see p55)* from 1238 to 1492, when artisans, merchants, scholars and scientists all contributed to the city's international reputation as a centre for culture. Under Christian rule, following its fall to the Catholic Monarchs in 1492 and the expulsion of the Moors *(see pp56–7)*, the city blossomed in Renaissance splendour. There was a period of decline in the 19th century, but Granada has been the subject of renewed interest and many efforts have been made to restore it to its past glory.

Façade of Granada Cathedral

Exploring Granada

The old city centre around the cathedral is a maze of narrow one-way streets. It contains the Alcaicería – a reconstruction of a Moorish bazaar that burned down in 1843. Granada's two main squares are the Plaza Bib-Rambla, near the cathedral, and the Plaza Nueva. From the latter, Cuesta de Gomérez leads up to the city's two principal monuments: the Alhambra and the Generalife. On a hill opposite is the Albaicín district.

Churches well worth a visit are the Iglesia de San Juan de Dios, almost overwhelming in its wealth of Baroque decoration, and the Renaissance Iglesia de San Jerónimo.

Cathedral

C/ Gran Vía 5. ***Tel*** *958 22 29 59.*
daily.

On the orders of the Catholic Monarchs, work on the cathedral began in 1523 to plans in a Gothic style by Enrique de Egas. It continued under the Renaissance maestro, Diego de Siloé, who also designed the façade and the magnificent Capilla Mayor. Under its dome, 16th-century windows depict Juan del Campo's *The Passion.* The west front was designed by Alonso Cano, who was born in the city. His grave can be seen in the cathedral.

Capilla Real

C/ Oficios 3. ***Tel*** *958 22 92 39.*
daily. *Jan 1, Good Fri, Dec 25.*

The Royal Chapel was built for the Catholic Monarchs between 1506 and 1521 by Enrique de Egas. A magnificent *reja* (grille) by Maestro Bartolomé de Jaén encloses the high altar and the Carrara marble figures of Fernando and Isabel, their daughter Juana la Loca (the Mad) and her husband Felipe el Hermoso (the Fair). Their coffins are in the crypt. In the sacristy there are art treasures, including paintings by Botticelli and Van der Weyden.

Entrance to the Moorish *mihrab* in the Palacio de la Madraza

Palacio de la Madraza

Calle Oficios 14. ***Tel*** *958 24 34 84.*
9am–2pm, 5–8pm Mon–Fri.

Originally an Arab university (now part of Granada University), this building later became the city hall. The façade is 18th century. The Moorish hall has a finely decorated *mihrab* (prayer niche).

Corral del Carbón

Calle Mariana Pineda. ***Tel*** *958 57 51 26.* *9am–2pm, 6–9pm Mon–Sat, 10am–2pm Sun & public hols.*

A relic of the Moorish era, this galleried courtyard was a theatre in Christian times, and later a coal exchange. Today it houses a cultural centre.

Casa de los Tiros

Calle Pavaneras 19. ***Tel*** *958 57 54 66.*
2:30–8:30pm Tue, 9am–8:30pm Wed–Sat, 9am–2:30pm Sun, 2 Jan, 28 Feb, 20 & 21 Mar, 22 May, 15 Aug, 12 & 13 Oct, 1 Nov, 6 & 8 Dec. *1 & 6 Jan, 1 May, 24, 25 & 31 Dec.*

Built in Mudéjar style in the 1500s, this palace owes its name to the muskets projecting from its battlements

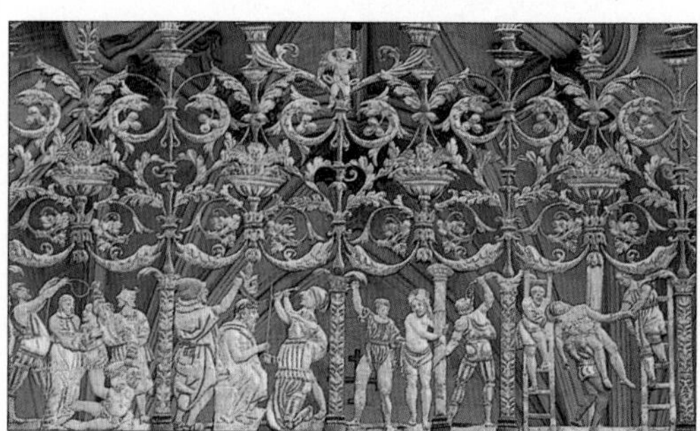
Grille by Maestro Bartolomé de Jaén enclosing the altar of the Capilla Real

Cupola in the sanctuary of the Monasterio de la Cartuja

(*tiro* means shot). It originally belonged to the family that was awarded the Generalife after the fall of Granada. Among their possessions was a sword that had belonged to Boabdil. This is carved on the façade, along with statues of Mercury, Hercules and Jason.

Alhambra and Generalife

See pp490–92.

El Bañuelo

Carrera del Darro 31. ***Tel*** *958 22 97 38.* *10am–2:30pm Tue–Sat (Apr–Oct: from 9am).* *public hols.*

These Arab baths were built in the 11th century. The columns are topped by Visigothic, Roman and Arab capitals.

Museo Arqueológico

Carrera del Darro 43. ***Tel*** *958 57 54 08.* *Tue–Sun.* *public hols.*

This museum in the Casa de Castril, a Renaissance mansion with a Plateresque *(see p25)* portal, displays Iberian, Phoenician and Roman finds.

Monasterio de la Cartuja

Paseo de la Cartuja. ***Tel*** *958 16 19 32.* *daily.*

Founded in 1516 by Christian warrior, El Gran Capitán, this monastery outside Granada has a dazzling cupola by Antonio Palomino, and a Churrigueresque *(see p25)* sacristy by Luis de Arévalo and Luis Caballo.

VISITORS' CHECKLIST

Granada. *241,000.* *12 km (7 miles) southwest of city.* *Avenida Andaluces, 902 24 02 02.* *Carretera de Jaen, 958 18 54 80.* *Santa Ana 4, 958 57 52 02.* *Sat & Sun.* *Semana Santa (Easter), Día de la Cruz (3 May), Corpus Christi (May/Jun).* **www**.granadatur.com

GRANADA CITY CENTRE

Alhambra ⑥
El Bañuelo ⑦
Capilla Real ②
Casa de los Tiros ⑤
Cathedral ①
Corral del Carbón ④
Museo Arqueológico ⑧
Palacio de la Madraza ③

0 metres 250
0 yards 250

Key to Symbols *see back flap*

Street-by-Street: the Albaicín

Ornate plaque on a house in the Albaicín

This corner of the city, on the hillside opposite the Alhambra, is where one feels closest to Granada's Moorish ancestry. Now mostly pedestrianized, this was the site of the first fortress built in the 13th century, and there were also once over 30 mosques. Most of the city's churches were built over their sites. Along the cobbled alleys stand *cármenes*, villas with Moorish decoration and gardens, secluded from the world by high walls. In the jasmine-scented air of evening, stroll up to the Mirador de San Nicolás for a magical view over the rooftops of the Alhambra glowing in the sunset.

Street in the Albaicín
Steep and sinuous, the Albaicín's streets are truly labyrinthine. Many street names start with Cuesta, *meaning slope.*

Real Chancillería
Built in 1530 by the Catholic Monarchs, the Royal Chancery has a beautiful Renaissance façade.

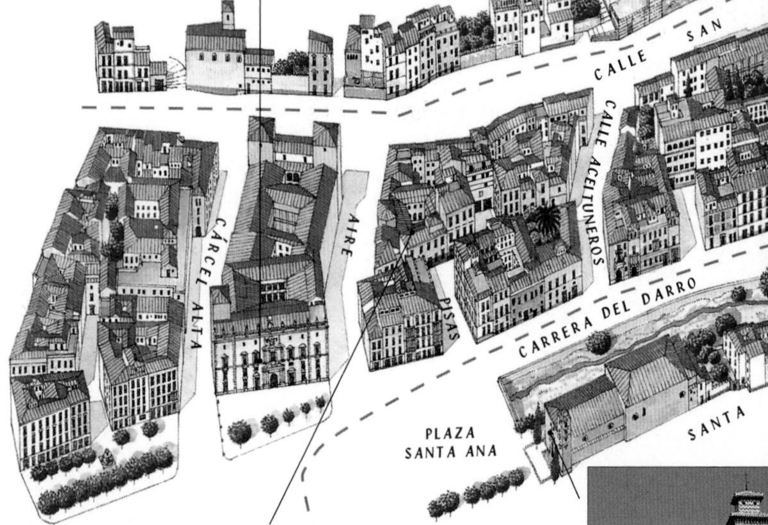

0 metres 50

0 yards 50

Casa de los Pisa, also known as Museo San Juan de Dios, displays works of art – some depicting St John of God, who died here in 1550.

STAR SIGHTS

- ★ Iglesia de Santa Ana
- ★ El Bañuelo
- ★ Museo Arqueológico

★ Iglesia de Santa Ana
Just north of Plaza Nueva stands this 16th-century brick church in Mudéjar style. It has an elegant Plateresque portal and, inside, a coffered ceiling.

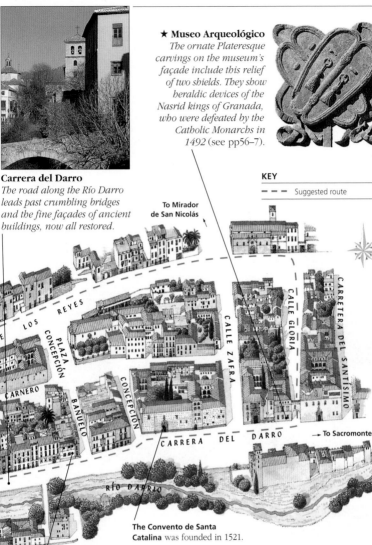

★ Museo Arqueológico
The ornate Plateresque carvings on the museum's façade include this relief of two shields. They show heraldic devices of the Nasrid kings of Granada, who were defeated by the Catholic Monarchs in 1492 (see pp56–7).

Carrera del Darro
The road along the Río Darro leads past crumbling bridges and the fine façades of ancient buildings, now all restored.

KEY

- - - Suggested route

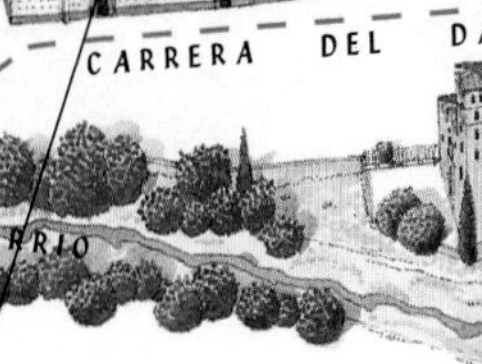

The Convento de Santa Catalina was founded in 1521.

★ El Bañuelo
Star-shaped openings in the vaults let light into these well-preserved Moorish baths, which were built in the 11th century.

SACROMONTE

Granada's gypsies formerly lived in the caves honeycombing this hillside. In the past, travellers would go there to enjoy spontaneous outbursts of flamenco. Today, virtually all the gypsies have moved away, but touristy flamenco shows of variable quality are still performed here in the evenings *(see pp424–5)*. Sitting at the very top of the hill is the Abadía del Sacromonte, a Benedictine monastery. The ashes of St Cecilio, Granada's patron saint, are kept inside.

Gypsies dancing flamenco, 19th century

The Alhambra

A magical use of space, light, water and decoration characterizes this most sensual piece of architecture. It was built under Ismail I, Yusuf I and Muhammad V, caliphs when the Nasrid dynasty *(see pp54–5)* ruled Granada. Seeking to belie an image of waning power, they created their idea of paradise on Earth. Modest materials were used (plaster, timber and tiles), but they were superbly worked. Although the Alhambra suffered pillage and decay, including an attempt by Napoleon's troops to blow it up, in recent times it has undergone extensive restoration and its delicate craftsmanship still dazzles the eye.

★ Salón de Embajadores
The ceiling of this sumptuous throne room, built from 1334 to 1354, represents the seven heavens of the Muslim cosmos.

Sala de la Barca

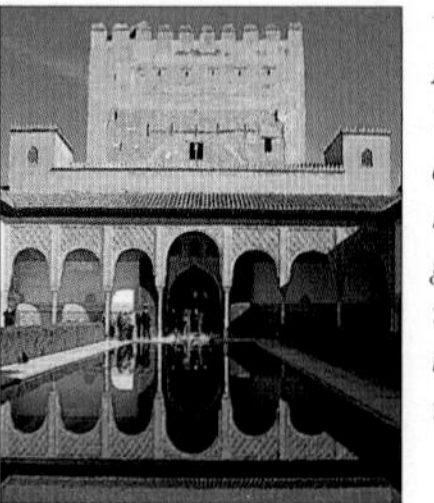

★ Patio de Arrayanes
This pool, set amid myrtle hedges and graceful arcades, reflects light into the surrounding halls.

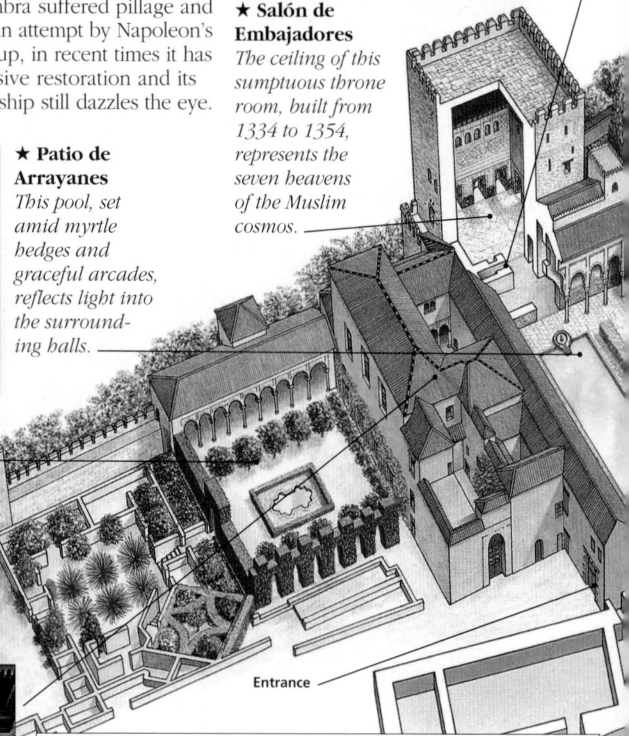

Patio de Machuca

Entrance

Patio del Mexuar
This council chamber, completed in 1365, was where the reigning sultan listened to the petitions of his subjects and held meetings with his ministers.

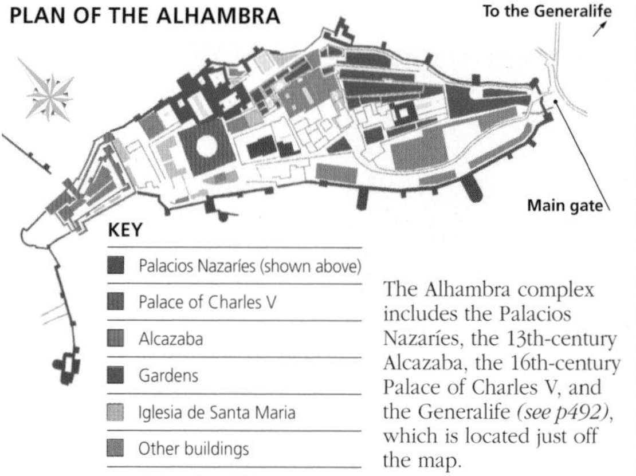

The Alhambra complex includes the Palacios Nazaríes, the 13th-century Alcazaba, the 16th-century Palace of Charles V, and the Generalife *(see p492)*, which is located just off the map.

Palacio del Partal
A pavilion with an arched portico and a tower is all that remains of this palace, the oldest building in the Alhambra.

VISITORS' CHECKLIST

Alhambra and Generalife. ***Tel*** *902 44 12 21.* **Reservations** (essential; book online only. **www**.alhambra-tickets.es 2. *8:30am–8pm daily (Nov–Feb: to 6pm daily). Arrive 1 hr before scheduled visit; allow 3 hrs for visit.* **Night visits:** *Mar–Oct: 8–10:30pm Fri & Sat; Nov–Feb: 8–9:30pm Fri & Sat.* **www**.alhambra-patronato.es

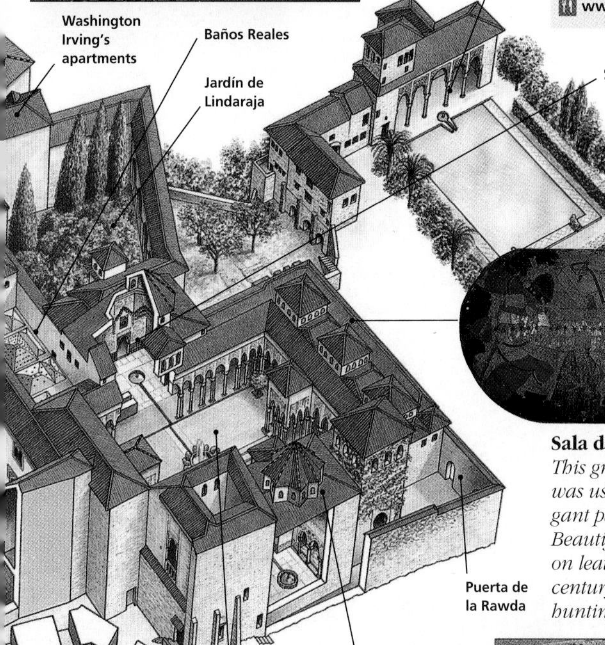

Washington Irving's apartments

Baños Reales

Jardín de Lindaraja

Sala de las Dos Hermanas, with its honeycomb dome, is regarded as the ultimate example of Spanish Islamic architecture.

Sala de los Reyes
This great banqueting hall was used to hold extravagant parties and feasts. Beautiful ceiling paintings on leather, from the 14th century, depict tales of hunting and chivalry.

Puerta de la Rawda

★ Sala de los Abencerrajes
This hall takes its name from a noble family, who were rivals of Boabdil (see pp56–7) *According to legend, he had them massacred while they attended a banquet here. The geometrical ceiling pattern was inspired by Pythagoras' theorem.*

The Palace of Charles V (1526) houses a collection of Spanish Islamic art, whose highlight is the Alhambra vase *(see p52)*.

★ Patio de los Leones
The patio, which is lined by arcades supported by slender columns, has as a centrepiece the meticulously restored marble fountain with its twelve lions.

STAR FEATURES

- ★ Salón de Embajadores
- ★ Patio de Arrayanes
- ★ Patio de los Leones
- ★ Sala de los Abencerrajes

Granada: Generalife

From the Alhambra's northern side, a footpath leads to the Generalife, the country estate of the Nasrid kings. Here, they could escape from palace intrigues and enjoy tranquillity high above the city, a little closer to heaven. The name Generalife, or Yannat al Arif, has various interpretations, perhaps the most pleasing being "the garden of lofty paradise". The gardens, begun in the 13th century, have been modified over the years. They originally contained orchards and pastures. The Generalife provides a magical setting for Granada's annual music and dance festival *(see p41)*.

The Patio de la Acequia *is an enclosed oriental garden built round a long central pool. Rows of water jets on either side make graceful arches above it.*

Sala Regia

Jardines Altos (Upper Gardens)

The Escalera del Agua is a staircase with water flowing gently down it.

The Patio de los Cipreses, otherwise known as the Patio de la Sultana, was the secret meeting place for Zoraya, wife of the Sultan Abu-l-Hasan, and her lover, the chief of the Abencerrajes.

Entrance

The Patio de Polo was the courtyard where palace visitors, arriving on horseback, would tether their steeds.

The Patio del Generalife *lies just before the entrance to the Generalife. The walk from the Alhambra to the Generalife gardens passes first through the Jardines Bajos (lower gardens), before crossing this Moorish patio with its characteristically geometric pool.*

The forbidding exterior of the castle above La Calahorra

Castillo de La Calahorra 39

La Calahorra (Granada). ***Tel*** *958 67 71 32.* *Guadix.* *10am–1pm, 4–6pm Wed.*

Grim, immensely thick walls and stout, cylindrical corner towers protect the castle on a hill above the village of La Calahorra. Rodrigo de Mendoza, son of Cardinal Mendoza, had the castle built for his bride: the work was carried out between 1509 and 1512 by Italian architects and craftsmen. Inside is an ornate, arcaded Renaissance courtyard over two floors with pillars and a Carrara marble staircase.

Guadix 40

Granada. *20,100.* *Avenida Mariana Pineda, 958 69 95 74.* *Sat.* *Fiesta & Feria (31 Aug–5 Sep).* **www**.guadixymarquesado.org

The troglodyte quarter, with its 2,000 caves, is the town's most remarkable sight.The **Cueva-Museo Al Fareria** and **Cueva-Museo Costumbres Populares** shows how people live underground.

The **cathedral** was begun in 1594 and finished between 1701 and 1796. Relics of San Torcuato, who founded Spain's first Christian bishopric, are kept in the cathedral museum.

Near the Moorish **Alcazaba** is the fine Mudéjar-style **Iglesia de Santiago**.

Cueva-Museo Al Fareria
C/ San Miguel 46. ***Tel*** *958 66 47 67.* *10am–2pm, 4–7pm Mon–Sat.*

Cueva-Museo Costumbres Populares
Plaza de Ermita Nueva. ***Tel*** *958 66 55 69.* *Mon–Sat.*

Jaén 41

115,000. *C/ Ramon y Cajal 4, 953 19 04 55.* *Thu.* *Nuestra Señora de la Capilla (11 Jun), San Lucas (18 Oct), Romería de Santa Catalina (25 Nov).* **www**.turjaen.org

The Moors called Jaén *Geen* – meaning "way station of caravans" – because of its strategic site on the road beween Andalusia and Castile. Their hilltop fortress was rebuilt as the **Castillo de Santa Catalina** after it was captured by King Fernando III in 1246. Part of it is now a parador *(see p594)*.

Andrés de Vandelvira, who was responsible for many of Úbeda's fine buildings *(see pp496–7)*, designed Jaén's **cathedral** in the 16th century. Later additions include the two 17th-century towers that now flank the west front.

An old mansion, the **Palacio Villardompardo**, houses a museum of arts and crafts, and also gives access to the **Baños Árabes**, the 11th-century baths of Ali, a Moorish chieftain. These have horseshoe arches, ceilings with small, star-shaped windows and two ceramic vats in which bathers once immersed themselves. Tucked away in an alley is the **Capilla de San Andrés**, a Mudéjar chapel founded in the 16th century by Gutiérrez González who, as treasurer to Pope Leo X, was endowed with extensive privileges. A gilded iron screen by Maestro Bartolomé de Jaén is the highlight of the chapel.

The **Real Monasterio de Santa Clara** was founded in the 13th century and has a lovely cloister dating from the late 16th century. Its church, which has a coffered ceiling, contains a bamboo image of Christ made in Ecuador.

The **Museo Provincial** displays Roman mosaics and sculptures, and Iberian, Greek and Roman ceramics.

Horseshoe arches supporting the dome at the Baños Árabes, Jaén

Castillo de Santa Catalina
Ctra al Castillo. ***Tel*** *953 12 07 33.* *Tue–Sun.* *1 Jan, 24, 25 & 31 Dec.*

Palacio Villardompardo
Plaza Santa Luisa de Marillac. ***Tel*** *953 24 80 68.* *Tue–Sun.* *public hols.*

Museo Provincial
Paseo de la Estación 27. ***Tel*** *953 31 33 39.* *Tue–Sun.* *public hols.*

Whitewashed cave dwellings in the troglodyte quarter of Guadix

Roman bridge spanning the Guadalquivir at Andújar

Andújar 42

Jaén. 40,000. Pl Santa María. Torre del Reloj, 953 50 49 59. Tue. Romeria (last Sun of Apr).

Andújar is known for its olive oil and its pottery. It stands on the site of an Iberian town, Iliturgi, which was destroyed in the Punic Wars *(see p50)* by Scipio. The Roman conquerors built the 15-arched bridge spanning the Río Guadalquivir.

In the central square is the Gothic **Iglesia de San Miguel**, with paintings by Alonso Cano. The **Iglesia de Santa María** la Mayor has a Renaissance façade and a Mudéjar tower. Inside it is El Greco's *Christ in the Garden of Olives* (c.1605). A pilgrimage to the nearby **Santuario de la Virgen de la Cabeza** takes place in April.

Environs

The mighty fortress of **Baños de la Encina** has 15 towers and ramparts built by Caliph Al Hakam II in AD 967. Further north, the road and railway between Madrid and Andalusia squeeze through a spectacular gorge in the eastern reaches of the Sierra Morena, the **Desfiladero de Despeñaperros.**

Baeza 43

See pp498–9.

Úbeda 44

Jaén. 35,000. Palacio Marqués de Contadero, C/ Baja del Marqués 4, 953 77 92 04. Fri. San Miguel (28 Sep). **www**.andalucia.org

Úbeda is a showcase of Renaissance magnificence, thanks to the patronage of some of Spain's most influential men of the 16th century, including such dignitaries as Francisco de los Cobos, secretary of state, and his greatnephew, Juan Vázquez de Molina, who gave his name to Úbeda's most historic square. The old town is contained within city walls that were first raised by the Moors in 852. The town was designated a UNESCO World Heritage Site in 2003.

Created on the orders of the Bishop of Jaén around 1562, the colossal former **Hospital de Santiago** was designed by Andrés de Vandelvira, who refined the Spanish Renaissance style into its more austere characteristics. The façade is flanked by square towers, one topped with a blue-and-white-tiled spire. Today the building is a conference centre.

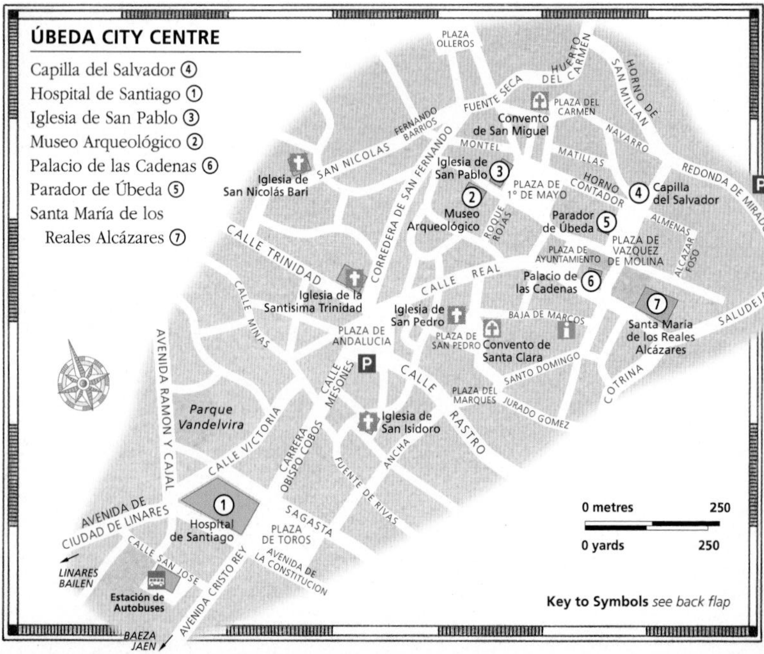

ÚBEDA CITY CENTRE

Capilla del Salvador ④
Hospital de Santiago ①
Iglesia de San Pablo ③
Museo Arqueológico ②
Palacio de las Cadenas ⑥
Parador de Úbeda ⑤
Santa María de los Reales Alcázares ⑦

0 metres 250
0 yards 250

Key to Symbols *see back flap*

◁ **Fields of poppies and olive groves south of Andújar in the province of Jaén**

Laguna de Valdeazores in the Parque Nacional de Cazorla

Sited in the 15th-century Casa Mudéjar, the **Museo Arqueológico** exhibits artifacts from Neolithic to Moorish times.

The **Iglesia de San Pablo** has a 13th-century apse and a beautiful 16th-century chapel by Vandelvira. It is surmounted by a Plateresque tower that was completed in 1537.

A monument to the poet and mystic St John of the Cross (1549–91) stands in the **Plaza de Vázquez de Molina**. The **Capilla del Salvador**, on the square, was designed by three 16th-century architects – Diego de Siloé, Andrés de Vandelvira and Esteban Jamete – as the personal chapel of Francisco de los Cobos. Behind it stand Cobos' palace, with a Renaissance façade, and the Hospital de los Honrados Viejos (Hospital of the Honoured Elders), looking on to the Plaza de Santa Lucía. From here, the Redonda de Miradores follows the line of the city walls and offers views of the countryside.

Plaza Vázquez de Molina also holds Úbeda's **parador** *(see p596)*. Built in the 16th century, but much altered in the 17th, it was the residence of Fernando Ortega Salido, dean of Málaga and chaplain of the Capilla del Salvador.

Úbeda's town hall and tourist office occupy the **Palacio de las Cadenas**, a mansion built for Vázquez de Molina by Vandelvira. It gets its name from the iron chains *(cadenas)* once attached to the columns supporting the main doorway.

Also on the square are the church of **Santa María de los Reales Alcazares**, which dates mainly from the 13th century, and the **Cárcel del Obispo** (Bishop's Jail), where nuns who had been punished by the bishop were confined.

Museo Arqueológico
Casa Mudéjar, Calle Cervantes 6. ***Tel*** *953 77 94 32.* *Tue–Sun.*

Hospital de Santiago
Calle Obispo Cobos. ***Tel*** *953 75 08 42.* *daily.*

Capilla del Salvador, Úbeda, one of Spain's finest Renaissance churches

Parque Natural de Cazorla ㊺

Jaén. *Cazorla.* *C/ Martínez Falero 11, 953 72 01 25.*

First-time visitors are amazed by the spectacular scenery of this 214,336-ha (529,409-acre) nature reserve with thickly wooded mountains rising to peaks of 2,000 m (6,500 ft) and varied, abundant wildlife.

Access to the Parque Natural de Cazorla, Segura y Las Villas is via the town of Cazorla. Its imposing Moorish **Castillo de la Yedra** houses a folklore museum. From Cazorla, the road winds upwards beneath the ruins of the clifftop castle at **La Iruela**. After crossing a pass it drops down to a crossroads (El Empalme del Valle) in the valley of the Río Guadalquivir. Roads lead to the source of the river and to the peaceful modern parador *(see p593)*.

The main road through the park follows the river. The information centre at Torre del Vinagre is 17 km (11 miles) from the crossroads.

Environs

There is a well-restored Moorish castle at **Segura de la Sierra**, 30 km (19 miles) from the reserve's northern edge. Below it is an unusual rockhewn bullring.

Castillo de la Yedra
Tel *953 71 16 38.* *Tue–Sun.* *1 Jan, 17 Sep, 24, 25 & 31 Dec.* *(free for EU citizens).*

CAZORLA'S WILDLIFE

More than 100 bird species live in this nature reserve, some very rare, such as the golden eagle and the griffon vulture. Cazorla is the only habitat in Spain, apart from the Pyrenees, where the lammergeier lives. Mammals in the park include the otter – active at dawn and dusk – mouflon and wild boar, and a small remaining population of Spanish ibex. The red deer was reintroduced in 1952. Among the flora supported by the limestone geology is the indigenous *Viola cazorlensis*.

Wild boar foraging for roots, insects and small mammals

Street-by-Street: Baeza 43

Coat of arms, Casa del Pópulo

Nestling amid the olive groves that characterize much of Jaén province, beautiful Baeza is a small town, unusually rich in Renaissance architecture. Called Beatia by the Romans and later the capital of a Moorish fiefdom, Baeza is portrayed as a "royal nest of hawks" on its coat of arms. It was conquered by Fernando III in 1226 – the first town in Andalusia to be definitively won back from the Moors – and was then settled by Castilian knights. An era of medieval splendour followed, reaching a climax in the 16th century, when Andrés de Vandelvira's splendid buildings were erected. The town was designated a UNESCO World Heritage Site in 2003.

★ Palacio de Jabalquinto
An Isabelline-style (see p24) *façade, flanked by elaborate, rounded buttresses, fronts this splendid Gothic palace.*

Antigua Universidad
From 1542 until 1825, this Renaissance and Baroque building was one of Spain's first universities.

Torre de los Aliatares is a 1,000-year-old tower built by the Moors.

Ayuntamiento
Formerly a jail and a courthouse, the town hall is a dignified Plateresque structure (see p25). *The coats of arms of Felipe II, Juan de Borja and of the town of Baeza adorn its upper façade.*

Casas Consistoriales Bajas

La Alhóndiga, the old corn exchange, has impressive triple-tier arches running along its front.

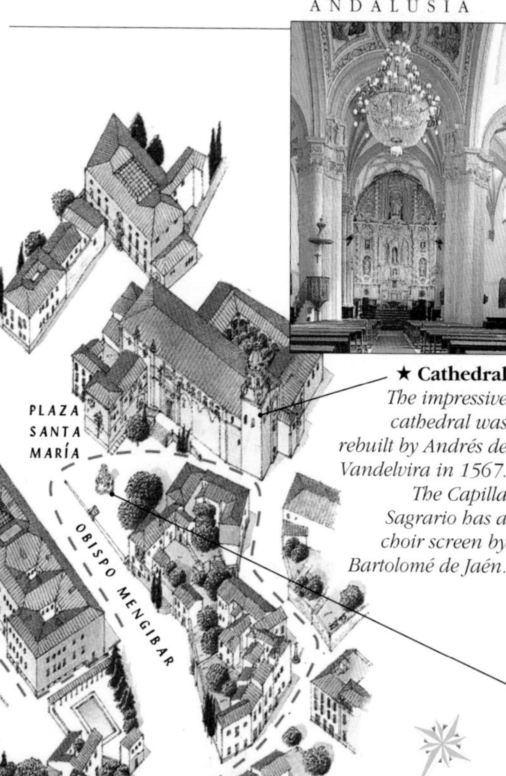

VISITORS' CHECKLIST

Jaén. 19,000. Linares-Baeza, 902 24 02 02. Avenida Alcalde Puche Pardo, 953 74 04 68. Plaza del Pópulo, 953 77 99 82. Tue. Semana Santa (Easter), Feria (mid-Aug), Romería de la Yedra (early Sep).

★ Cathedral
The impressive cathedral was rebuilt by Andrés de Vandelvira in 1567. The Capilla Sagrario has a choir screen by Bartolomé de Jaén.

Fuente de Santa María
Architect-sculptor Ginés Martínez of Baeza designed this fountain in the form of a triumphal arch. It was completed in 1564.

Antigua Carnicería is the 16th-century former slaughterhouse.

Puerta de Jaén y Arco de Villalar
This gateway in the city ramparts is adjoined by an arch erected in 1521 to appease Carlos I (see p58) *after a rebellion.*

0 metres 75
0 yards 75

KEY
Tourist information
Suggested route

★ Plaza del Pópulo
The Casa del Pópulo, a fine Plateresque palace, now the tourist office, overlooks this square. In its centre is the Fuente de los Leones, a fountain with an Ibero-Roman statue flanked by lions.

STAR SIGHTS

- ★ Palacio de Jabalquinto
- ★ Plaza del Pópulo
- ★ Cathedral

Renaissance castle overlooking the village of Vélez Blanco

Vélez Blanco 46

Almería. *2,200.* *Vélez Rubio.* *Avenida Marqués de los Vélez, 950 41 53 54.* *Wed.* *Cristo de la Yedra (second Sun of Aug).*

The mighty **Castillo de Vélez Blanco** was built between 1506–13 by the first Marquis de Los Vélez. The Renaissance interiors are now displayed in the Metropolitan Museum in New York, but there is a reconstruction of one of the patios.

Just outside Vélez Blanco, the **Cueva de los Letreros** contains paintings from c.4000 BC. One depicts the Indalo, a figure holding a rainbow and believed to be a deity with magical powers, now adopted as the symbol of Almería.

Cueva de los Letreros
Camino de la Cueva de los Letreros. ***Tel*** *617 88 28 08.* *daily (call first).*

Mojácar 47

Almería. *7,000.* *Calle Glorieta 1, 950 61 50 25.* *Wed, Sun.* *Moors and Christians (second weekend of Jun), San Agustín (28 Aug).* **www**.mojacar.es

From a distance, Mojácar shimmers like the mirage of a Moorish citadel, its white houses cascading over a lofty ridge, 2 km (1 mile) inland from long, sandy beaches.

Following the Civil War *(see pp66–7)*, the village fell into ruin as most of its inhabitants emigrated, but in the 1960s it was discovered by tourists, which gave rise to a new era of prosperity. The old gateway in the walls still remains, but otherwise the village has been completely rebuilt, and holiday complexes have grown up along the nearby beaches. The coast south from Mojácar is among the least built up in Spain, with only small resorts and villages along its length.

Tabernas 48

Almería. *3,000.* *Carretera Nacional 340 km 464, 950 52 50 30.* *Wed.* *Virgen de las Angustias (11–15 Aug).*

Tabernas is set in Europe's only desert. The town's Moorish fortress dominates the harsh surrounding scenery of cactus-dotted, rugged hills and dried-out riverbeds, which has provided the setting for many classic spaghetti westerns. Two film sets can be visited: **Mini-Hollywood** and **Fort Bravo Texas Hollywood**, 1 km (1 mile) and 4 km (2 miles) from Tabernas respectively.

Not far from town is a solar energy research centre, where heliostats track the sun.

Environs

Sorbas sits on the edge of the chasm of the Río de Aguas. Its notable buildings are the 16th-century Iglesia de Santa María and a 17th-century mansion said to have been a summer retreat for the Duke of Alba.

Nearby is the karst scenery, honeycombed with hundreds of cave systems, of the **Yesos de Sorbas** nature reserve. Permission to explore them is required from Andalusia's environmental department.

Mini-Hollywood
Carretera N340. ***Tel*** *950 36 52 36.* *Easter–Oct: daily; Nov–Easter: Sat–Sun.*

Fort Bravo Texas Hollywood
Carretera N340, Tabernas. ***Tel*** *950 06 60 14.* *daily.*

Desert landscape around Tabernas, reminiscent of the Wild West

SPAGHETTI WESTERNS

Two Wild West towns lie off the N340 highway west of Tabernas. Here, visitors can re-enact classic film scenes or watch stunt men performing bank hold-ups and saloon brawls. The *poblados del oeste* were built during the 1960s and early 1970s when low costs and eternal sunshine made Almería the ideal location for spaghetti westerns. Sergio Leone, director of *The Good, the Bad and the Ugly*, built a ranch here and film-sets sprang up in the desert. Local gypsies played Indians and Mexicans. The deserts and Arizona-style badlands are still used for television commercials and series, and by film directors such as Steven Spielberg.

Still from *For a Few Dollars More* by Sergio Leone

The 10th-century Alcazaba, which dominates Almería's old town

Almería 49

Almería. *170,000.* *Estación Intermodal.* *Parque Nicolás Salmerón, 950 17 52 20.* *Tue, Fri & Sat.* *Feria (last week of Aug).* **www**.almeria-turismo.org

Almeria's colossal **Alcazaba**, dating from AD 995, is the largest fortress built by the Moors in Spain. The huge structure bears witness to the city's golden age, when it was an important port under the Caliphate of Córdoba *(see pp52–3)* exporting brocade, silk and cotton.

During the Reconquest, the Alcazaba withstood two major sieges before eventually falling to the armies of the Catholic Monarchs *(see pp56–7)* in 1489. The royal coat of arms can be seen on the Torre del Homenaje, built during their reign. The Alcazaba also has a Mudéjar chapel and gardens.

Adjacent to the Alcazaba is the old fishermen's and gypsy quarter of **La Chanca**, where some families live in caves with brightly painted façades. This picturesque district is desperately poor, and it is unwise to walk around here alone or at night with valuables.

Berber pirates from North Africa often raided Almería. Consequently, the **cathedral** looks almost like a castle, with its four towers, thick walls and small windows. The site was originally a mosque. This was converted into a church, but in 1522 it was destroyed in an earthquake. Work on the present building began in 1524 under the direction of Diego de Siloé, who designed the nave and high altar in Gothic style. The Renaissance façade and the carved walnut choir stalls are by Juan de Orea. Traces of Moorish Almería's most important mosque can be seen in the **Templo San Juan**. The **Plaza Vieja** is an attractive 17th-century arcaded square. On one side is the **town hall** *(ayuntamiento)*, with a cream and pink façade (1899). In Calle Real, the Castillo de Tabernas Museo del Aceite de Oliva (Tel: 950 27 28 88) illustrates the fine art of making olive oil.

Brightly coloured entrance to a gypsy cave in La Chanca district

Environs

One of Europe's most important examples of a Copper Age settlement lies at **Los Millares**, near Gádor, 17 km (11 miles) north of Almería. As many as 2,000 people may have occupied the site around 2500 BC.

Alcazaba
C/ Almanzor. ***Tel*** *950 17 55 00.* *Tue–Sun.* *1 & 6 Jan, 1 May, 24, 25, 31 Dec.* *(free for EU citizens).*

Los Millares
Santa Fé de Mondújar. ***Tel*** *677 90 34 04.* *Wed–Sun.* *public hols.*

Parque Natural de Cabo de Gata 50

Almería. *San José.* *Centro de Visitantes de las Amoladeras, Carretera Alp-202 km 7 (Retamar-Pujaire), 950 16 04 35.* *daily.*

Towering cliffs of volcanic rock, sand dunes, salt flats and secluded coves characterize the 29,000-ha (71,700-acre) Parque Natural de Cabo de Gata. Within its confines are a few fishing villages, and the small resort of San José. A lighthouse stands at the end of the *cabo* (cape), which can be reached by road from the village of Cabo de Gata. The park includes a stretch of seabed 2 km (1 mile) wide and the marine flora and fauna protected within it attract scuba-divers and snorkellers.

The dunes and saltpans between the cape and the Playa de San Miguel are a habitat for thorny jujube trees. Many migrating birds stop here, and among the 170 or so bird species recorded are flamingoes, avocets, griffon vultures and Dupont's larks.

Environs

Set amid citrus trees on the edge of the Sierra de Alhamilla, **Níjar's** fame stems from the pottery and the hand-woven *jarapas* – blankets and rugs – that are made here. The barren plain between Níjar and the sea has been brought under cultivation using vast plastic greenhouses to conserve the scarce water.

The dramatic, dark volcanic rocks at Cabo de Gata, east of Almería

SPAIN'S ISLANDS

Introducing Spain's Islands

Spain's two groups of islands lie in separate seas – the Balearics in the Mediterranean and the Canaries in the Atlantic, off the African coast. Both are popular package-tour destinations blessed with warm climates, good beaches and clear waters. But each has more to offer than high-rise hotels, fast-food restaurants and discos. The Balearics have white villages, wooded hills, caves and prehistoric monuments, while the extraordinary volcanic landscapes of the Canaries are unlike any other part of Spain. Four of Spain's national parks *(see pp30–1)* are in the Canary Islands.

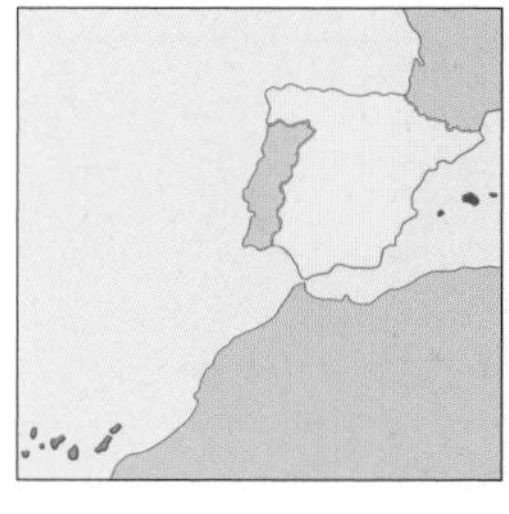

Ibiza (see pp510–12) *is the liveliest of the Balearic Islands. Ibiza town and Sant Antoni are the main tourist centres, offering world-famous nightlife and excellent beaches.*

CANARY ISLANDS
(see pp528–51)

La Palma

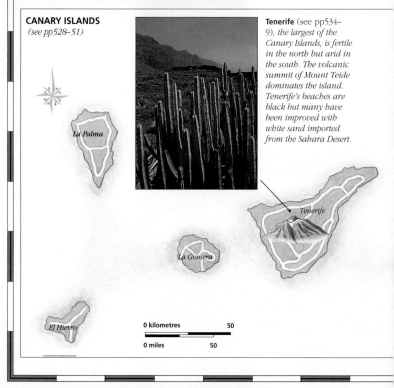

Tenerife (see pp534–9), *the largest of the Canary Islands, is fertile in the north but arid in the south. The volcanic summit of Mount Teide dominates the island. Tenerife's beaches are black but many have been improved with white sand imported from the Sahara Desert.*

Tenerife

La Gomera

El Hierro

0 kilometres 50

0 miles 50

◁ **Vines growing in the volcanic soil of Lanzarote, protected by drystone walls**

In Menorca (see pp522–7) *tourism has developed more slowly than in Mallorca and Ibiza, and the island has largely avoided being over-commercialized. Scattered across the countryside are the ruins of unique Bronze Age buildings.*

BALEARIC ISLANDS
(see pp506–27)

Mallorca

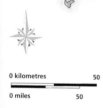

Mallorca (see pp514–21) *best known for its beaches, has caves and other natural features to explore. The most spectacular of the island's historic sights is the great Gothic cathedral in Palma, which rises above the boats moored in the old harbour.*

0 kilometres 50

0 miles 50

Lanzarote (see pp548–50) *is the most attractive of the Canary Islands, even though the landscape is strikingly bare. White houses contrast starkly with black volcanic fields. The most dramatic attraction is Timanfaya National Park, including the Montañas del Fuego.*

Fuerteventura

Gran Canaria

Gran Canaria (see p542–5) *centres on a symmetrical volcanic cone. The capital city of Las Palmas has some interesting museums and monuments. In contrast, the sprawling Maspalomas, on the south coast, is the biggest holiday resort in Spain.*

7PM-1-8052
KIKE

THE BALEARIC ISLANDS

IBIZA · FORMENTERA · MALLORCA · MENORCA

Chic resorts and attractive coves and beaches, combined with a climate which is hot but never uncomfortably so, have made tourism the mainstay of life along the coasts of the Balearic Islands. Inland, there is peace and quiet in abundance, and a great variety of sights to seek out: wooded hills, pretty white villages, monasteries, country churches, caves and prehistoric monuments.

Standing at a crossroads in the Mediterranean, the Balearic Islands have been plundered or colonized in turn by Phoenicians, Greeks, Carthaginians, Romans, Moors and Turks. In the 13th century Catalan settlers brought their language, a dialect of which is widely spoken today.

The islands can justifiably claim to cater for all tastes: from sun-seekers on package holidays, for whom the larger resorts serve as brash fun factories, to jet-setters and film stars, who head for luxurious but discreet hideaways in the hills. The largest island, where tourism has been established the longest, is Mallorca. A massive Gothic cathedral stands near the waterfront of Palma, the capital.

The green countryside of Menorca is dotted with prehistoric monuments and its towns full of noble, historic mansions. The coast of Ibiza is notched by innumerable rocky coves. The island's hilly interior is characterized by brilliant white farmhouses and robust churches. On Formentera, small and relatively undeveloped, the pace of life is slow. The islets surrounding the four principal islands are mainly uninhabited; one of them, Cabrera (off Mallorca), is a national park.

View through the window of one of Ibiza's traditional, whitewashed farmhouses

◁ The massive, heavily buttressed cathedral overlooking Palma de Mallorca's harbour

Exploring the Balearics

Though the Balearic islands are often associated with high-density, inexpensive package tourism, they offer enough variety to satisfy everyone's tastes. For those unattracted by the bustle of the coastal resorts and their beautiful beaches, the countryside and the old towns of Palma, Ibiza, Maó and Ciutadella are relatively undisturbed. Mallorca is by far the most culturally rich of the Balearics, with its distinguished collection of modern and traditional galleries, and interesting museums. Menorca is strong on Neolithic remains and Neo-Colonial architecture, while Ibiza is for lovers of clear, painterly light and rustic peasant houses; it also has some of the wildest nightclubs in Europe. Formentera – for many, the most alluring island – has crystal water, white sand, a pure, parched landscape and total tranquillity.

Poblat des Pescadors in the tourist village of Binibeca

Early-morning mist on the waters of Port de Pollença in Mallorca

0 kilometres 25
0 miles 15

GETTING AROUND

Nearly all foreign visitors to the Balearics arrive by plane – the no-frills airlines making it all the more popular. Mallorca, Menorca and Ibiza connect to major European cities as well as Madrid, Barcelona and Valencia. Several airlines fly to most other Spanish cities out of Son Sant Joan airport in Palma. Another way of arriving is by boat from Barcelona, Valencia, Alicante or Dénia. Between the islands there are regular ferry services, run by Transmediterránea, Balearia and Flebasa. Mallorca is the only island with rail services, which run between Palma and Inca, and between Palma and Sóller, which is now extended to Sa Pobla and Manacor. Roads vary from excellent to poor. The best way to get around is by car, except on Formentera, where cycling is best.

For additional map symbols *see back flap*

SIGHTS AT A GLANCE

Alfàbia 10
Els Amunts 4
Andratx 7
Cabrera 17
Cales Coves 24
Capocorb Vell 16
Ciutadella 20
Coves del Drac 19
Felanitx 18
Ferreries 21
Formentera 6
Ibiza (Eivissa) 3
La Granja 8
Maó 23
Es Mercadal 22
Palma (pp518–21) 14
Pollença 13
Puig de Randa 15
Santa Eulària 5
Sant Antoni 1
Sant Josep 2
Santuario de Lluc 12
Sóller 11
Valldemossa 9

A peaceful stroll on the sands of Ibiza's Sant Miquel beach

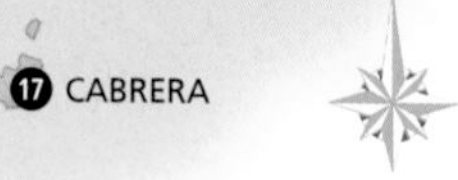

SEE ALSO

• ***Where to Stay*** pp597–9
• ***Where to Eat*** pp648–51

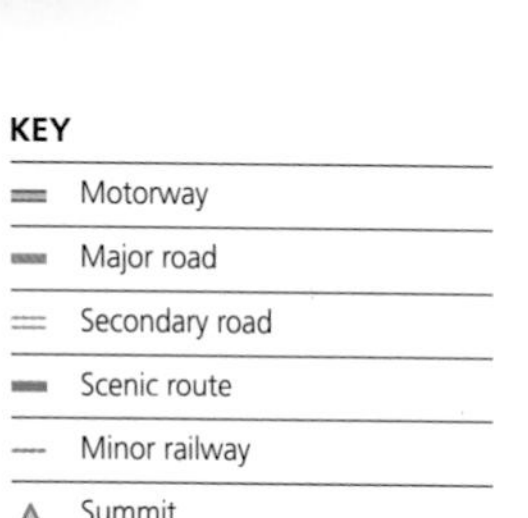

The rocky coast around the Coves d'Artà in Mallorca

Ibiza

This small island, the nearest of the Balearics to the coast of Spain, was unknown and untouched by tourism until the 1960s, when it suddenly appeared in Europe's holiday brochures along with Benidorm and Torremolinos. There is still a curious, indefinable magic about Ibiza (Eivissa) and the island has not entirely lost its character. The countryside, particularly in the north, is a rural patchwork of groves of almonds, olives and figs, and wooded hills. Ibiza town retains the air of a 1950s Spanish provincial borough. At once package-tour paradise, hippie hideout and glamour hot spot, this is one of the Mediterranean's mythical destinations.

An Ibizan shepherdess

The bustling harbour of the resort of Sant Antoni

Sant Antoni ❶

Baleares. *17,500.* *Passeig de Ses Fonts, 971 34 33 63.* *Sant Antoni (17 Jan), Sant Bartolomé (24 Aug).* **www**.illesbalears.es

Ibiza's second town, Sant Antoni was known by the Romans as Portus Magnus because of its large natural harbour. Formerly a tiny fishing village, it has turned into a sprawling and exuberant resort. Although it was once notoriously over-commercialized, the town has undergone a dramatic facelift. Nevertheless, the 14th-century parish church of Sant Antoni is practically marooned in a sea of modern high-rise hotels.

To the north of Sant Antoni, on the road to Cala Salada, is the chapel of **Santa Agnès**, an unusual early Christian temple (not to be confused with the village of the same name). When this catacomb-like chapel was discovered, in 1907, it contained Moorish weapons and fragments of pottery.

Sant Josep ❷

Baleares. *13,500.* *Sant Josep Airport, 971 80 91 18.* *Sant Josep (19 Mar).* **www**.illesbalears.es

The village of Sant Josep, the administrative centre of southwest Ibiza, lies in the shadow of Ibiza's highest mountain. At 475 m (1,560 ft), Sa Talaiassa offers a panorama of all Ibiza, including the islet of **Es Vedrá**, rising from the sea like a rough-cut pyramid. For the most accessible view of this enormous rock, take the coastal road to the sandy cove of Cala d'Hort where there are a number of good restaurants and a quiet beach.

The salt lakes of Ses Salines, a haven for many bird species

Environs

Before tourism, salt was Ibiza's main industry, most of it coming from the salt flats at **Ses Salines** in the southeast corner of the island. Mainland Spain is the chief consumer of this salt, but much goes to the Faroe Islands and Scandinavia for salting fish. Ses Salines is also an important refuge for birds, including the flamingo. **Es Cavallet**, 3 km (2 miles) east, is an unspoiled stretch of soft, white sand. The Phoenician village of **Sa Caleta** is a UNESCO World Heritage Site.

Ibiza ❸

Baleares. *35,000.* *Calle Antonio Riquer 2, Andenes del Puerto, 971 30 19 00.* *Mon–Sat.* *San Juan Bautista (24 Jun), Fiestas Patronales (1–8 Aug).* **www**.illesbalears.es

The old quarter of Ibiza (Eivissa), known also as Dalt Vila, or upper town, is a miniature citadel guarding the mouth of the almost circular bay. The **Portal de ses Taules,** a magnificent gateway in the north wall of the 16th-century fortifications, carries the finely carved coat of arms of the kingdom of Aragón, to which the Balearic Islands belonged in the Middle Ages *(see p227)*. Inside the walls is the 16th-century **Església de Santo**

Domingo with its three red-tiled domes. The Baroque interior, with its barrel-vaulted ceiling and frescoed walls, has been restored to its former glory. Works of art by Erwin Bechtold, Barry Flanagan and other artists connected with Ibiza are on display in the **Museu d'Art Contemporani**, just inside the Portal de ses Taules. Crowning the whole Dalt Vila is the **cathedral**, a 13th-century Catalan Gothic building with 18th-century additions. The cathedral's Museo de la Sacristia houses assorted works of art.

Under the Carthaginians, the soil of Ibiza was considered holy. The citizens of Carthage deemed it an honour to be buried in the **Necrópolis Púnica del Puig des Molins**. Part of it can be visited by the public. The museum is currently closed for restoration.

The crossroads village of **Jesús**, 3 km (2 miles) north, is worth a visit for its 16th-century church. Originally built as part of a Franciscan monastery, it has a 16th-century altarpiece by Rodrigo de Osona the Younger.

A backstreet in the Sa Penya district of Ibiza town

A view across the port towards Ibiza's upper town

Museu d'Art Contemporani
Ronda Narcís Puget s/n. ***Tel*** *971 302 723.* *Tue–Sun.* *Mon & public hols.*

Necrópolis Púnica del Puig des Molins
Via Romana 31. ***Tel*** *971 301 771.* *Tue–Sun.* *Mon & public hols.*

Els Amunts 4

Baleares. *Sant Miquel.* *C/ Mariano Riquer Wallis 4, Santa Eulària d'es Riu, 971 33 07 28.*

Els Amunts is the local name for the uplands of northern Ibiza, which stretch from Sant Antoni on the west coast to Sant Vicenç in the northeast. Though hardly a mountain range – Es Fornás is the highest point, at a mere 450 m (1,480 ft) – the area's inaccessibility has kept it unspoiled. There are few special sights here, apart from the landscape: pine-clad hills sheltering fertile valleys whose rich red soil is planted with olive, almond and fig trees, and the occasional vineyard. Tourist enclaves are scarce, except for a handful of small resorts, such as Port de Sant Miquel, Portinatx and Sant Vicenç. Inland, villages like Sant Joan and Santa Agnès offer an insight into Ibiza's quiet, rural past.

The architectural highpoints of northern Ibiza are several beautiful white churches, like the one in **Sant Miquel** which, on Thursdays in summer, is host to a display of Ibizan folk dancing. Outside Sant Llorenç is the tranquil, fortified hamlet of **Balàfia**, with flat-roofed houses, tiny whitewashed alleys, and a watchtower that was used as a fortress during raids by the Turks.

IBIZA'S HOTTEST SPOTS

Ibiza's reputation for extraordinary summer nightlife is largely justified. The main action takes place in two areas: the Calle de la Virgen in the old harbour district, with its bars, fashion boutiques and restaurants; and the mega-discos out of town – Privilege, Pachá, Amnesia and Es Paradis. When the last of these is closing, at about 7am, the wildest club of them all, Space, is only just opening its doors. Ibiza has long been a magnet for the rich and famous. Celebrities seem to have become more elusive of late, but a few well-known faces can often be glimpsed dining in the restaurant Las Dos Lunas, and taking the rays the next day on the beach at Ses Salines.

Nightclubbers enjoying a bubble bath at Amnesia

One of the many beautiful beaches along the unspoiled shores of the island of Formentera

Santa Eulària ❺

Baleares. *28,000.* *Carrer Mariano Riquer Wallis 4, 971 33 07 28.* *Wed & Sat.* *Fiesta (12 Feb), Cala Llonga (14–15 Aug).*

The town of Santa Eulària d'es Riu (Santa Eulalia del Río), on the island's only river, has managed to hold on to its character far more than many other Spanish resorts.

The 16th-century church, with its pretty covered courtyard, and the surrounding old town, were built on the top of a little hill, the **Puig de Missa**, because this site was more easily defended in times of war than the shore below.

Ajdacent to the church is the **Museu Etnològic**, a folk museum, which is housed in an Ibizan farmhouse. Included in the exhibits (labelled in Catalan only) are traditional costumes, farming implements, toys and an olive press. A collection of photographs covering 50 years shows how Ibiza has changed.

The domed roof of Santa Eulària's 16th-century church

Two art and craft markets, Punta Arabí (Wed) and Las Dalias (Sat), feature hundreds of stalls.

Museu Etnològic
Can Ros, Puig de Missa. ***Tel*** *971 33 28 45.* *Mon–Sat.* *Sun, mid-Dec–mid-Jan.* *(by appt).*

Formentera ❻

Baleares. *7,000.* *from Ibiza.* *Estación Marítima, Puerto de La Savina, 971 32 20 57.* *Sun.* *Fiesta Sant Jaume (25 Jul).*

An hour's boat ride from Ibiza harbour will bring you to this largely unspoiled island where the waters are blue and the way of life slow.

From the small port of La Savina, where the boat docks, there are buses to other parts of the island, or you can hire a car, moped or bicycle from one of the shops nearby.

Sant Francesc Xavier, Formentera's tiny capital, is situated 3 km (2 miles) from La Savina. Most of the island's amenities are in this town, plus a pretty 18th-century church in the main square, and a folk museum.

From Sant Francesc, a bumpy minor road leads for 9 km (6 miles) southwards, ending at Cap de Barbaria, the site of an 18th-century defensive tower and a lighthouse.

Formentera is entirely flat, apart from the small plateau of **La Mola**, which takes up the whole eastern end of the island. From the fishing port of Es Caló the road winds upwards past the Restaurante Es Mirador, with its panoramic view, to the village of Nostra Senyora del Pilar de la Mola on top of the plateau. About 3 km (2 miles) to the east is a lighthouse, Far de la Mola, sited on the highest point of the island. Nearby stands a monument to Jules Verne (1828–1905), who used Formentera for the setting of one of his novels, *Hector Servadac*.

Although there are many purple road signs indicating places of cultural interest on Formentera, most lead only to disappointment. But one sight well worth seeking out is the megalithic sepulchre of **Ca Na Costa** (2000 BC) near Sant Francesc, the only one of its kind in the Balearics. This monument, a circle of upright stone slabs, pre-dates the Carthaginians *(see pp49–50)*.

However, the island's great strength is its landscape, which has a spare and delicate beauty and some of the Mediterranean's last unspoiled shorelines. More than 60 per cent of the island's landscape is protected by law. The finest beaches are, arguably, Migjorn and Cala Sahona, southwest of Sant Francesc. Nearly all beaches have nudist areas.

Illetes and Llevant are two beautiful beaches on either side of a long sandy spit in the far north of the island. To the north, between Formentera and Ibiza, is the island of **Espalmador**, with its natural springs.

The Flavours of the Balearics

This quartet of beautiful islands, strategically positioned on ancient trading routes, has been fought over for thousands of years. Each occupying force – Arabs, Catalans, French and British among them – has left its mark and the local cuisine reflects this. Mediterranean seafood, particularly spectacular lobster and crayfish, remains the most prominent local ingredient, but the islands are also known for their delicious pastries and desserts, like the feather-light *ensaimada* from Mallorca and the typical Ibizan *flaó*. Cured meats *(embutits)* and traditionally made cheeses are also local specialities.

Locally grown oranges

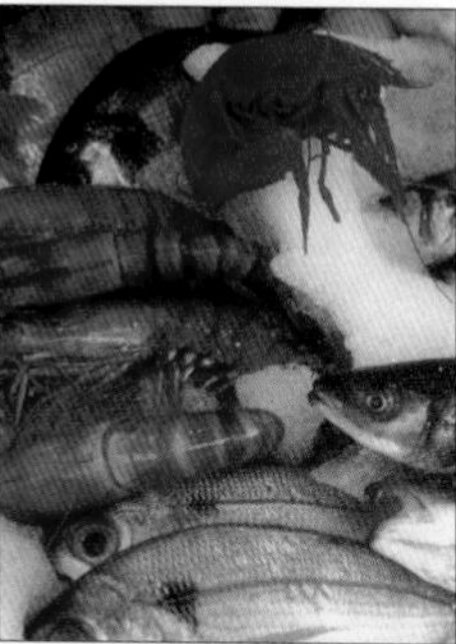

Seafood from the Mediterranean in a Mallorcan fish market

MALLORCA AND MENORCA

Seafood predominates in the Balearic islands. Menorca is renowned for *caldereta de langosta* (spiny lobster stew), once a simple fishermen's dish but now an expensive delicacy. The classic Mallorcan dish is *pa amb oli*, a slice of toasted country bread rubbed with garlic and drizzled with local olive oil. Menorca's creamy garlic sauce *all i oli* is a delicious accompaniment to meat and seafood dishes, and the island also produces fine cheese, *formatge de Maó*.

IBIZA AND FORMENTERA

Seafood also reigns supreme on Ibiza and its quieter little sister, Formentera, especially in *calders* (stews) such as *borrida de rajada* (skate with potatoes, eggs and pastis), and *guisat de peix*. Pork is the staple meat. For a picnic, try *cocarrois*, pastries filled with meat, fish or vegetables and *formatjades*, soft-cheese-filled pastries flavoured with cinnamon. Delicious local desserts include *gató* (almond cake served with ice-cream) and Ibizan *flaó*, made with creamy cheese and eggs, and flavoured with mint.

Appetizing selection of delicious Balearic pastries

REGIONAL DISHES AND SPECIALITIES

Fish and shellfish (particularly the revered local lobster) are omnipresent in the Balearics, particularly along the coast. Try them simply grilled to fully appreciate their freshness (many seaside restaurants have their own fishing boats), but you'll also find wonderful, slow-cooked stews which are bursting with flavour. The rugged inland regions provide mountain lamb and kid, along with pork, which is also used to make *embutits* including spicy Mallorcan *sobrassada* which is delicious with *pa amb oli*. The tourist industry hasn't killed off the long-standing farming tradition on the Balearics, which produce plentiful fruit and vegetables. Mallorca makes its own robust wines, particularly around the village of Binissalem, while Menorca, thanks to the long British occupation of the island, makes its own piquant gin.

All i oli

Tumbet de peix *A fish pie, made with layers of firm white fish, peppers, aubergine (eggplant) and sliced boiled egg.*

Mallorca

Mallorca is often likened to a continent rather than simply an island. Its varied nature never fails to astonish, whether you are looking for landscape, culture or just entertainment. No other European island has a wider range of scenery, from the fertile plains of central Mallorca to the almost alpine peaks of the Tramuntana. The island's mild climate and lovely beaches have made it one of Spain's foremost package tour destinations but there is a wealth of culture, too, evident in sights like Palma Cathedral *(see pp520–21)*. Mallorca's appeal lies also in its charm as a living, working island: the cereal and fruit crops of the central plains, and the vineyards around Binissalem are vital to the island's economy.

Terraced orange grove in the Sierra Tramuntana

Andratx 7

Baleares. 10,500. Avenida Mateo Bosch, 971 67 13 00. Wed. San Pedro (29 Jun).

This small town lies amid a valley of almond groves in the shadow of Puig de Galatzó, which rises to 1,026 m (3,366 ft). With its ochre and white shuttered houses and the old watchtowers perched high on a hill above the town, Andratx is a very pretty place.

The road southwest leads down to **Port d'Andratx** 5 km (3 miles) away. Here, in an almost totally enclosed bay, expensive yachts are moored in rows along the harbour and luxury holiday homes pepper the surrounding hillsides. In the past, Port d'Andratx's main role was as the fishing port and harbour for Andratx, but since the early 1960s it has gradually been transformed into an exclusive holiday resort for the rich and famous. When visiting Port d'Andratx, it is a good idea to leave all thoughts of the real Mallorca behind and simply enjoy it for what it is – a chic and affluent resort.

La Granja 8

Carretera de Esporlas. ***Tel*** *971 61 00 32.* *daily.*
www.lagranja.net

La Granja is a private estate, or *possessió,* near the little country town of Esporles. Formerly a Cistercian convent, it is now the property of the Seguí family, who have opened their largely unspoiled 18th-century house to the public as a kind of living museum. Peacocks roam the gardens, salt cod and hams hang in the kitchen, *The Marriage of Figaro* plays in the ballroom, and the slight air of chaos just adds to the charm of the place.

A view across the harbour of Port d'Andratx

Valldemossa 9

Baleares. 1,800. Avenida Palma 7, 971 61 20 19. Sun. Santa Catalina Thomás (28 Jul), San Bartolomé (24 Aug).

This pleasant mountain town is linked with the name of George Sand, the French novelist who stayed here in the winter of 1838–9 and later wrote unflatteringly of the island in *Un Hiver à Majorque*. Dearer to Mallorcans is the Polish composer Frédéric Chopin (1810–49), who stayed with Sand at the **Real Cartuja de Jesús de Nazaret**. "Chopin's cell", off the monastery's main courtyard, is where a few of his works were written, and still houses the piano on which he composed.

Bust of Frédéric Chopin at Valldemossa

Nearby is a 17th-century pharmacy displaying outlandish medicinal preparations such as "powdered nails of the beast". In the cloisters is an art museum with works by Tàpies, Miró and the Mallorcan artist Juli Ramis (1909–90), and a series of Picasso illustrations, *The Burial of the Count of Orgaz*, inspired by the El Greco painting of the same name *(see p32)*.

Real Cartuja de Jesús de Nazaret
Plaça de la Cartuja de Valldemossa.
Tel *971 61 21 06.* *daily.*
1 Jan, 25 Dec, Sun in Dec & Jan.

Alfàbia ⑩

Carretera de Sóller km 17. ***Tel*** *971 61 31 23.* *tour bus from Palma.* *Sat pm & Sun, Dec.*

Very few *possessicós* in Mallorca are open to the public, which makes Alfàbia worth visiting. The house and garden are an excellent example of a typical Mallorcan aristocratic estate and exude a Moorish atmosphere. Very little remains of the original 14th-century architecture, so it is well worth looking out for the Mudéjar inscription on the ceiling of the entrance hall and the Hispano-Arabic fountains and pergola. The garden is a sumptuous 19th-century creation, making imaginative use of shade and the play of water.

Sóller ⑪

Baleares. *9,100.* *Plaza España 15, 971 63 80 08.* *Sat.* *Sa Fira & Es Firó (2nd week May).* **www**.ajsoller.net

Soller is a little town grown fat on the produce of its olive groves and orchards, which climb up the slopes of the Sierra Tramuntana. In the 19th century Sóller traded its oranges and wine for French goods, and the town retains a faintly Gallic, bourgeois feel.

One of Sóller's best-known features is its delightfully old-fashioned narrow-gauge railway, complete with quaint wooden carriages. The town, whose station is in the Plaça d'Espanya, lies on a scenic route between Palma and the fishing village of Port de Sóller 5 km (3 miles) to the west.

Environs

From Sóller a road winds southwards along the spectacular west coast to **Deià** (Deyá). This village was once the home of Robert Graves (1895–1985), the English poet and novelist, who came to live here in 1929. His simple tombstone can be seen in the small cemetery. The **Museu Arqueològic**, curated by the archaeologist William Waldren, offers a glimpse into prehistoric Mallorca. Outside the village is **Son Marroig**, the estate of Austrian Archduke Ludwig Salvator (1847–1915), who documented the Balearics in a series of books included in a display of his possessions.

Houses and trees crowded together on the hillside of Deià

Museu Arqueològic
Calle Teix 4, Es Clot Deià. ***Tel*** *971 63 90 01.* *Tue, Thu, Sun.*

Statue of La Moreneta at the Santuario de Lluc

Santuario de Lluc ⑫

Lluc. *from Palma.* ***Tel*** *971 87 15 25.* *Sun–Fri.* *museum only.* **www**.lluc.net

High in the mountains of the Sierra Tramuntana, in the remote village of Lluc, is an institution regarded by many as the spiritual heart of Mallorca. The Santuario de Lluc was built mainly in the 17th and 18th centuries on the site of an ancient shrine. The monastery's Baroque church, with its imposing façade, contains the stone image of La Moreneta, the Black Virgin of Lluc, supposedly found by a young shepherd boy on a nearby hilltop in the 13th century. The altar and sanctuary of one chapel are by Catalan architect and designer Antoni Gaudí *(see pp140–41)*. Along the Camí dels Misteris, the paved walkway up to this hilltop, there are some bronze bas-reliefs by Pere Llimona. Just off the main Plaça dels Pelegrins are a café and bar, a pharmacy and a shop. The museum, situated on the first floor, includes Mallorcan paintings and medieval manuscripts. The monastery incorporates a guest house *(see p598)*.

From Lluc, 13 km (8 miles) of tortuous road winds through the hills and descends towards the coast, ending at the beautiful rocky bay of **Sa Calobra**. From here, it is just 5 minutes' walk up the coast to the deep gorge of the Torrent de Pareis.

Sheer cliff face rising out of the sea at Sa Calobra

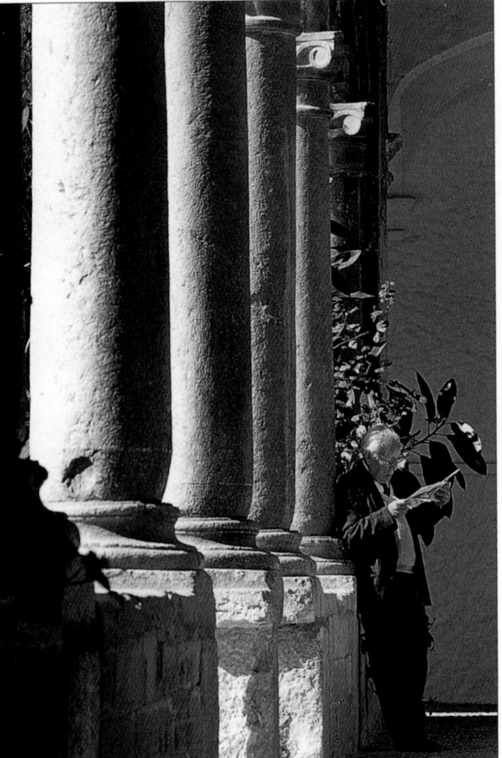
The cloisters of the Convent de Santo Domingo in Pollença

Pollença ⓭

Baleares. 15,500. Calle Santo Domingo s/n, 971 53 50 77. *Sun.* *Sant Antoni (17 Jan), Patron Saint (2 Aug).* **www**.ajpollenca.net

Although Pollença has become one of Mallorca's most popular tourist spots, it still appears unspoiled. The town, with its ochre-coloured stone houses and winding lanes, is picturesquely sited on the edge of fertile farmland. The Plaça Major, with its bars frequented mainly by locals, has an old-world atmosphere.

Pollença has fine churches, including the 18th-century **Parròquia de Nostra Senyora dels Angels** and the Convent de Santo Domingo, containing the **Museu de Pollença,** with its displays of archaeology and art. It also holds Pollença's Classical Music Festival in July and August. A chapel on the hilltop, **El Calvari**, is reached either by road or a long climb of 365 steps. On the altar there is a Gothic Christ, carved in wood.

Environs

Alcúdia, 10 km (6 miles) to the east, is surrounded by 14th-century walls with two huge gateways. Near the town centre is the **Museu Monografico de Pollentia**, exhibiting statues, jewellery and other remains found in the Roman settlement of Pollentia, 2km (1 mile) south of Alcúdia.

Museu de Pollença
Calle Guillem Cife de Colonya 33.
Tel 971 53 11 66. *Tue–Sun.*

Museu Monografico de Pollentia
Calle San Jaume 30, Alcúdia.
Tel 971 54 70 04. *Tue–Sun.*

Palma de Mallorca ⓮

See pp518–21.

Puig de Randa ⓯

8 km (5 miles) northeast of Llucmajor. *to Llucmajor, then taxi.* *Calle de Terral 23, S'Arenal, Llucmajor, 971 66 91 62.*

In the middle of a fertile plain called the *pla* rises a mini-mountain 543 m (1,780 ft) high, the Puig de Randa. It is said that Mallorca's greatest son, the 14th-century theologian and mystic Ramon Llull, came to a hermitage on this mountain to meditate and write his religious treatise, *Ars Magna*. On the way up Puig de Randa there are two small monasteries, the 14th-century Santuari de Sant Honorat and the Santuari de Nostra Senyora de Gràcia. The latter, built on a ledge under an overhanging cliff, contains a 13th-century chapel with fine Valencian tiles inside.

On the mountain top is the **Santuari de Cura**, built to commemorate Llull's time on the *puig*, and largely devoted to the study of his work. Its central courtyard is built in the typical beige stone of Mallorca. A small museum, housed in a 16th-century former school off the courtyard, contains some of Llull's manuscripts.

The philosopher Ramon Llull

Capocorb Vell ⓰

C/ Llucmajor–Cap Blanc km 23. *El Arenal.* *Fri–Wed.*

Mallorca is not as rich in megalithic remains as Menorca, but this *talaiotic* village *(see p527)* in the stony flatlands of the southern coast is worth seeing – particularly on a quiet day when you can wander among the stones in peace. The settlement, which dates back to around 1000 BC, originally consisted of five *talaiots* (stone tower-like structures with timbered roofs) and another 28 smaller dwellings. Little is known about its inhabitants and the uses for some of the rooms inside the buildings, such as the tiny underground gallery. Too small for living in, this room may have been used to perform magic rituals.

Part of the charm of this place lies in its surroundings among fields of fruit trees and dry stone walls, a setting that somehow complements the ruins. Apart from a snack bar nearby, the site remains mercifully undeveloped.

One of the *talaiots* of Capocorb Vell

Cabrera ⓱

Baleares. *from Colònia Sant Jordi.* *Calle Gabriel Roca s/n, Colònia Sant Jordi, 971 65 60 73.*

From the beaches of Es Trenc and Sa Ràpita, on the south coast of Mallorca, Cabrera looms on the horizon. The largest island in an archipelago of the same name, it lies 18 km (11 miles) from the most southerly point of Mallorca. Cabrera is home to several rare plants, reptiles and seabirds, such as Eleonora's falcon. The waters are important for marine life. All this has resulted in it being declared a national park *(see pp30–31)*. For centuries Cabrera was used as a military base and it has a small population. On it stands a 14th-century castle.

A street in Felanitx

Felanitx ⓲

Baleares. *14,200.* *Avenida Cala Marsas 15, 971 82 60 84.* *Sun.* *Sant Joan Pelós (24 Jun).*

This bustling agricultural town is the birthplace of Renaissance architect Guillem Sagrera (1380–1456) and the 20th-century painter Miquel Barceló. Felanitx is visited mainly for three reasons: the imposing façade of the 13th-century church, the **Esglesia de Sant Miquel**; its *sobrassada de porc negre* (a spiced raw sausage made from the meat of the local black pig) and its lively religious fiestas including Sant Joan Pelós *(see p523)*.

About 5 km (3 miles) south-east is the **Castell de Santueri**, founded by the Moors but rebuilt in the 14th century by the kings of Aragón, who ruled Mallorca. Though a ruin, it is worth the detour for the views to the east and south from its vantage point, 400 m (1,300 ft) above the plain.

Coves del Drac ⓳

1 km (1 mile) south of Porto Cristo. *from Porto Cristo.* ***Tel*** *971 82 07 53.* *daily.* *1 Jan, 25 Dec.* www.cuevasdeldrach.com

Mallorca has numerous caves, ranging from mere holes in the ground to cathedral-like halls. The four vast chambers of the **Coves del Drac** are reached by a steep flight of steps, at the bottom of which is the beautifully lit cave known as "Diana's Bath". Another chamber holds the large underground lake, Martel, which is 29 m (95 ft) below ground level and is 177 m (580 ft) long. Music fills the air of the cave, played from boats plying the lake. Equally dramatic are the two remaining caves, charmingly named "The Theatre of the Fairies" and "The Enchanted City".

Environs

The **Coves d'Hams** is so called because some of its stalactites are shaped like hooks – hams in Mallorcan. The caves are 500 m (1,640 ft) long and contain the "Sea of Venice", an underground lake on which musicians sail in a small boat.

The entrance to the **Coves d'Artà,** near Capdepera, is 40 m (130 ft) above sea level and affords a wonderful view. The caves' main attraction is a stalagmite 22 m (72 ft) high.

Coves d'Hams
11 km (7 miles) from Manacor towards Porto Cristo. ***Tel*** *971 82 09 88.* *daily.* *1 Jan, 25 Dec.*

Coves d'Artà
Carretera Canyamel. ***Tel*** *971 84 12 93.* *daily.* *1 Jan, 25 Dec.*

The dramatically lit stalactites of the Coves d'Artà

Street-by-Street: Palma ⓮

Forn des Teatre pastry shop

On an island whose name has become synonymous with mass tourism, Palma surprises by its cultural richness. Under the Moors it was already a prosperous town of fountains and cool courtyards. After he had conquered it in 1229, Jaime I wrote, "It seemed to me the most beautiful city we had ever seen". Signs of Palma's past wealth are still evident in the sumptuous churches, grand public buildings and fine private mansions that crowd the old town. The hub of the city is the old-fashioned Passeig des Born, whose cafés invite you to try one of Mallorca's specialities, the ensaimada, a spiral of pastry dusted with icing sugar.

The Forn des Teatre is an old pastry shop noted for its *ensaimadas* and *gató* (almond cake).

The Fundació la Caixa, once the Gran Hotel, is now a cultural centre.

Palau Reial de l'Almudaina
This palace belongs to the Spanish royal family and houses a museum, whose highlights include the chapel of Santa Ana, with its Romanesque portal, and the Gothic tinell *or salon.*

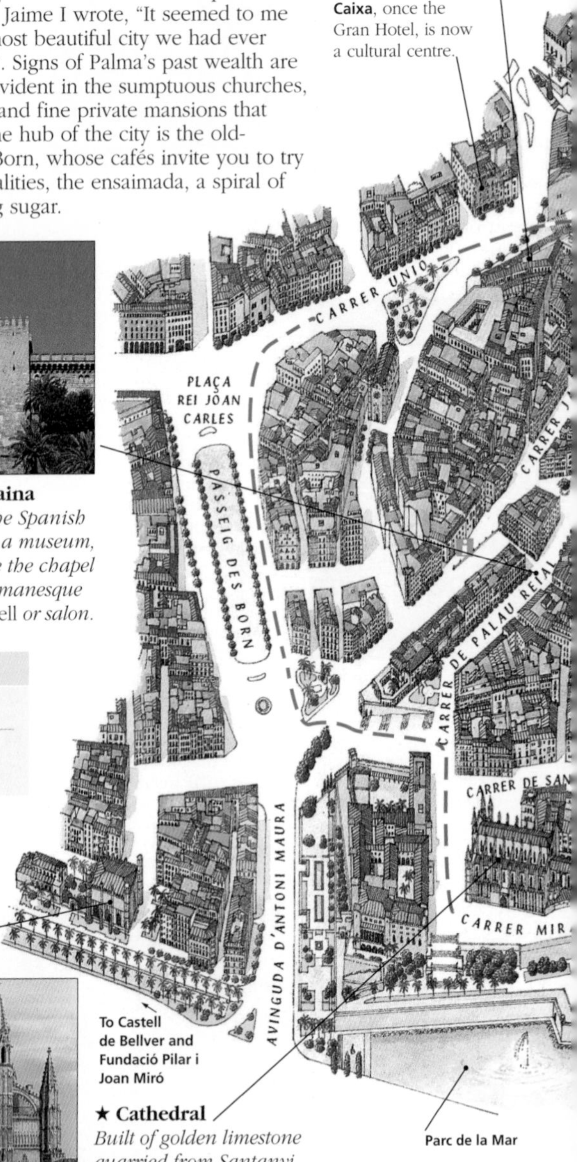

STAR SIGHTS

★ Cathedral

★ Basílica de Sant Francesc

La Llotja is a beautiful 15th-century exchange with tall windows and delicate tracery.

To Castell de Bellver and Fundació Pilar i Joan Miró

★ Cathedral
Built of golden limestone quarried from Santanyi, Palma's huge Gothic cathedral stands in a dramatic location near the waterfront.

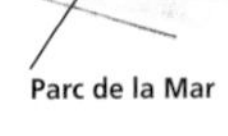

Parc de la Mar

KEY

– – – Suggested route

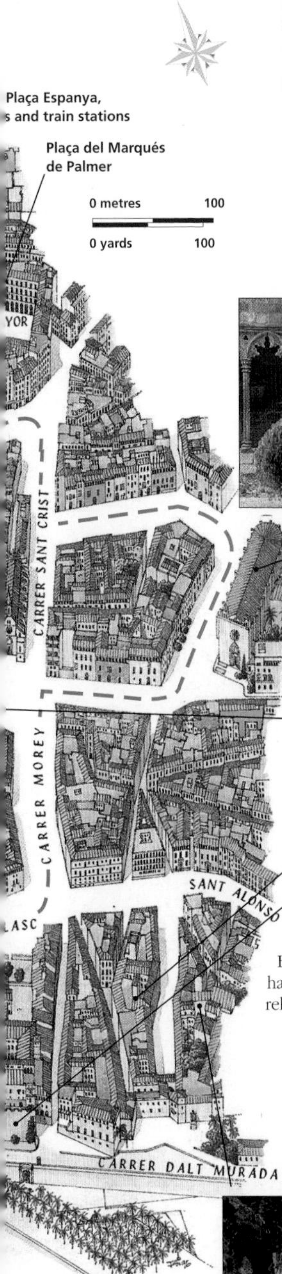

Plaça Espanya,
s and train stations
Plaça del Marqués
de Palmer
0 metres 100
0 yards 100
YOR
CARRER SANT CRIST
City Hall
CARRER MOREY
SANT ALONSO
LASC
CARRER DALT MURADA

VISITORS' CHECKLIST

Baleares. *380,000.* *9 km (6 miles) east.* *Plaça Espanya, 971 75 20 51.* *Plaça Espanya, Calle Eusebi Estada, 971 17 77 77.* *Muelle de Peraires, 971 70 73 45 (Transmediterranea).* *Plaça Reina 2, 971 17 39 90.* *Sat.* *San Sebastián (20 Jan).* **Museu de Mallorca** *daily.* **Banys Àrabs** *daily.* **Palau de l'Almudaina** *Mon–Sat.* **www**.palmademallorca.es

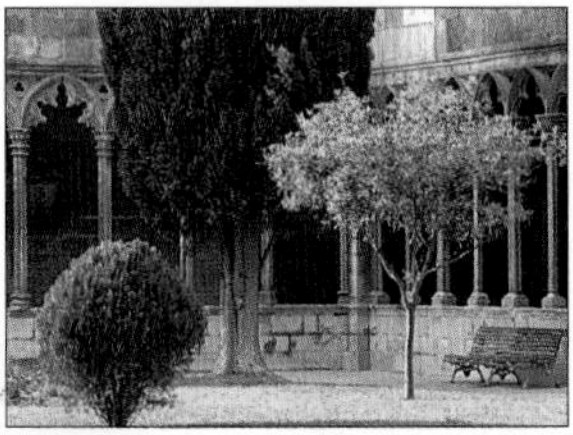

★ Basílica de Sant Francesc
The church and cloister of St Francis are in a refined Gothic style with a Baroque altarpiece and rose window.

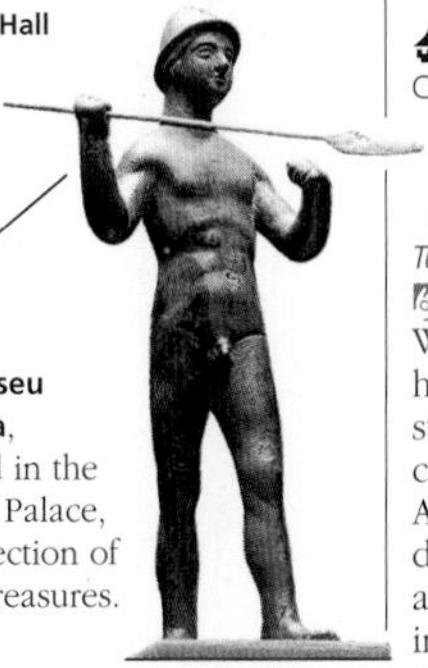

The Museu Diocesà, housed in the Bishop's Palace, has a collection of religious treasures.

Museu de Mallorca
The museum has displays on local history, art and architecture, including this statue of an ancient warrior.

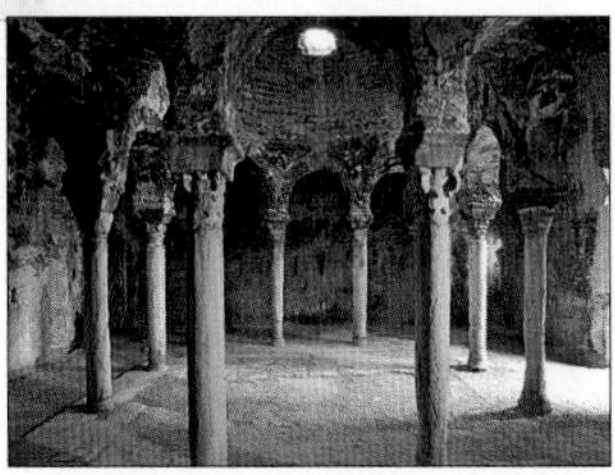

Banys Àrabs
The 10th-century baths, with their well-preserved arches, are a remnant of the Balearic Islands' Moorish culture.

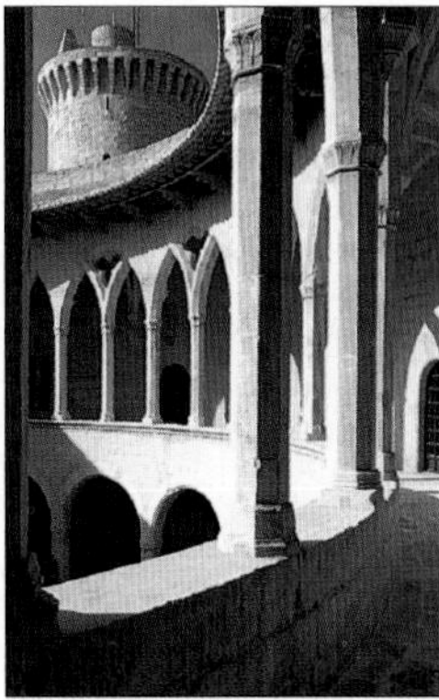

A view along the circular walls of the Castell de Bellver

Castell de Bellver

West side of Palma Bay, C/ Camilo José Cela 17. ***Tel*** *971 73 06 57.* *Tue–Sun.*

About 5 km (3 miles) from the city centre, standing 113 m (370 ft) above sea level, is Palma's Gothic castle. It was commissioned by Jaime II during the short-lived Kingdom of Mallorca (1276–1349) as a summer residence, but soon after became a prison until 1915.

Fundació Pilar i Joan Miró

Carrer Joan de Saridakis 29. ***Tel*** *971 70 14 20.* *mid-May–mid-Sep: 10am–7pm Tue–Sat; mid-Sep–mid-May: 10am–6pm Tue–Sat; 10am–3pm Sun all year.* *(free Sat).*

When Joan Miró died in 1983, his wife converted his former studio and gardens into an art centre. The building – "the Alabaster Fortress" – was designed by Navarrese architect Rafael Moneo. It incorporates Miró's original studio (complete with unfinished paintings), a permanent collection, a shop, a library and an auditorium.

Palma Aquarium

Highway to Llucmajor, C/ Manuela de los Herreros i Sorá 21. ***Tel*** *971 26 42 75.* *daily.*

Located a 15-minute drive from the city centre, this aquarium is home to a range of flora and fauna from the Mediterranean Sea and the Indian, Atlantic and Pacific oceans. Visitors can see recreated ecosystems featuring 700 species and five million litres of seawater.

Palma Cathedral

According to legend, when Jaime I of Aragón was caught in a storm on his way to conquer Mallorca in 1229, he vowed that if God led him to safety he would build a great church in his honour. In the following years the old mosque of Medina Mayurqa was torn down and architect Guillem Sagrera (1380–1456) drew up plans for a new cathedral. The last stone was added in 1587, and in subsequent years the cathedral has been rebuilt, notably early last century when parts of the interior were remodelled by Antoni Gaudí *(see pp140–41)*. Today Palma Cathedral, or Sa Seu, as Mallorcans call it, is one of the most breathtaking buildings in Spain, combining vast scale with typically Gothic elegance *(see p24)*.

Bell Tower
This robust tower was built in 1389 and houses nine bells, the largest of which is known as N'Eloi, meaning "praise".

Palma Cathedral
One of the best-sited cathedrals anywhere, it is spectacularly poised high on the sea wall, above what was once Palma's harbour.

STAR FEATURES

- ★ Great Rose Window
- ★ Baldachino

Cathedral Museum
One of the highlights of the beautifully displayed collection in the Old Chapterhouse is a 15th-century reliquary of the True Cross which is encrusted with jewels and precious metals.

★ Great Rose Window
The largest of seven rose windows looks down from above the High Altar like a gigantic eye. Built in 1370 with stained glass added in the 16th century, the window has a diameter of over 11 m (36 ft).

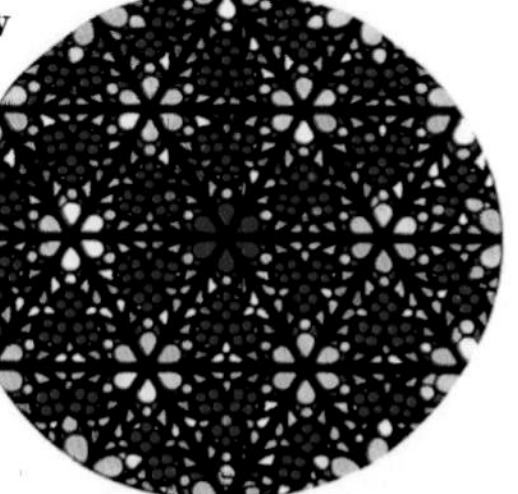

VISITORS' CHECKLIST

Plaça Almonia. **Tel** 971 723 130. Apr–May & Oct: 10am–5:15pm Mon–Fri (3:15pm Nov–Mar, 6:15pm Jun–Sep); 10am–2:15pm Sat all year. public hols. 9am Mon–Sat, 9am, 10:30am, noon, 1pm, 7pm Sun. **www.**catedraldemallorca.info

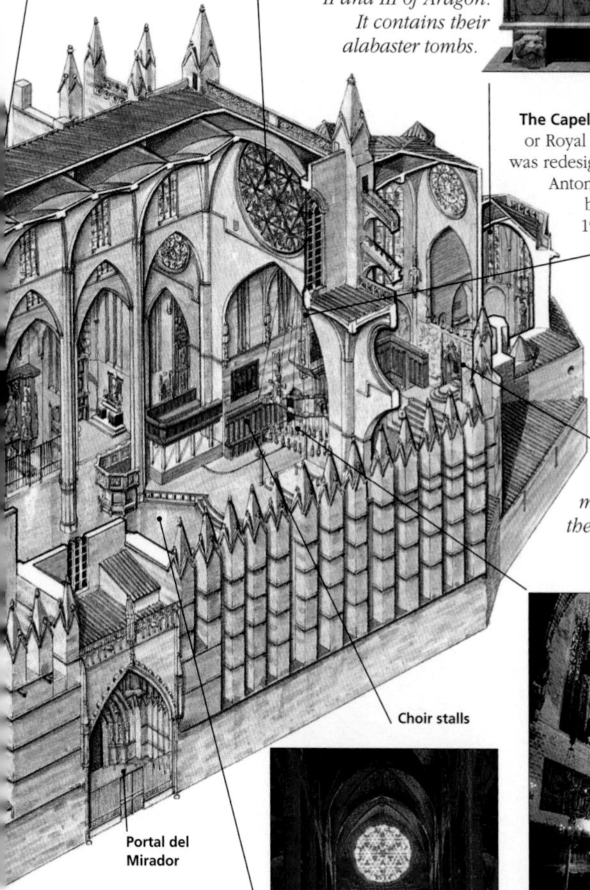

The Great Organ was built with a Neo-Gothic case in 1795, and restored in 1993 by Gabriel Blancafort.

Capella de la Trinitat
This tiny chapel was built in 1329 as the mausoleum of Jaime II and III of Aragón. It contains their alabaster tombs.

The Capella Reial, or Royal Chapel, was redesigned by Antoni Gaudí between 1904 and 1914.

Bishop's Throne
Built in 1269 and made of Carrara marble, the chair is embedded in a Gothic vaulted niche.

Choir stalls

Portal del Mirador

Nave
The magnificent ceiling, 44 m (144 ft) high, is held up by 14 slender pillars. At over 19 m (62 ft) wide, it is one of the broadest naves in the world.

★ Baldachino
Gaudí's bizarre wrought-iron canopy above the altar incorporates lamps, tapestries and a multicoloured crucifix.

Menorca

Menorca is the Balearic island furthest from the mainland and it is set apart from the rest of the country in many other ways. The coastline of Menorca is, arguably, more unspoiled than in any other part of Spain. Its countryside remains largely green and pleasant with cows roaming the meadows. The old towns of Maó – the island's capital – and Ciutadella are filled with noble, historic buildings and beautiful squares. Menorca also has abundant reminders of its more distant history: the island boasts a spectacular hoard of Bronze Age stone structures, which provide an invaluable insight into its prehistoric past. The Menorcans are often more inclined to drink the locally brewed gin *(ginebra)* than the wine which is favoured elsewhere in Spain.

The peaceful seafront of Ciutadella at twilight

Ciutadella ⓴

Baleares. 22,000. Plaça de la Catedral 5, 971 38 26 93. *Fri & Sat.* *Sant Joan (23–24 Jun).* **www**.illesbalears.es

The key date in the history of Ciutadella is 1558. In that year the Turks, under Barbarossa, entered and decimated the city, consigning 3,495 of its citizens to the slave markets of Constantinople. Of Ciutadella's main public buildings, only the fine Catalan Gothic **Església Catedral de Menorca** managed to survive this fearsome onslaught in more or less its original condition, only later to be stripped of all its paintings, ornaments and other treasures by Republican extremists during the Civil War.

The nearby **Plaça d'es Born** was built as a parade ground for Moorish troops and from 1558 was gradually rebuilt in Renaissance style. Today it is one of Spain's most impressive squares, containing pleasant cafés and bordered by shady palm trees. At the centre of the Plaça d'es Born is an obelisk which commemorates the "Any de sa Desgràcia" (Year of Misfortune), when the Turks invaded the city. Around the square are the Gothic-style **town hall** *(ajuntament)*, the late 19th-century **Teatre Municipal d'es Born**, and a series of aristocratic mansions with Italianesque façades, the grandest of which is the early 19th-century **Palau de Torre-Saura**. From the northern end of the square there is a fine view over the small harbour.

The historic Plaça d'es Born in the centre of Ciutadella

Fishermen mending their nets in Ciutadella's harbour

If you walk up the Carrer Major d'es Born past the cathedral, you come to **Ses Voltes**, an alley lined on both sides by whitewashed arches. Turn right along the Carrer del Seminari for the Baroque **Església dels Socors** and the **Museu Diocesà** with its displays of ecclesiastical paraphernalia. In the narrow streets of the old town there are many impressive palaces, including the early 19th-century **Palau Salort**, on the Carrer Major d'es Born, which is closed to the public. The Art Nouveau **market** (1895), its ironwork painted in smart municipal dark green, stands nearby.

The peace of Ciutadella is disturbed every June by the Festa de Sant Joan, a spectacular ritual of horsemanship. During the festival the local gin *(ginebra)* is drunk copiously and the city grinds to a halt.

Museu Diocesà
Carrer del Seminari 7. ***Tel*** *971 48 12 97.* *May–Oct: Tue–Sat.* *(by appt).*

Palau Salort
Carrer Major d'es Born 9.
to the public.

Ferreries ㉑

Baleares. 3,100. Carrer Sant Bartomeu 55, 971 37 30 03. Tue, Fri, Sat. Sant Bartomeu (23–5 Aug).

Ferreries lies in between Mercadal and Ciutadella and sprang up when a road was built to connect the two towns. Today Ferreries is an attractive village of white houses, built against the slope of a hill. The simple church, Sant Bartomeu, dates from 1770.

The bay of **Santa Galdana**, 10 km (6 miles) to the south, is even prettier. You can take a pleasant walk from the beach inland through the fertile river-bed of Barranc d'Algendar.

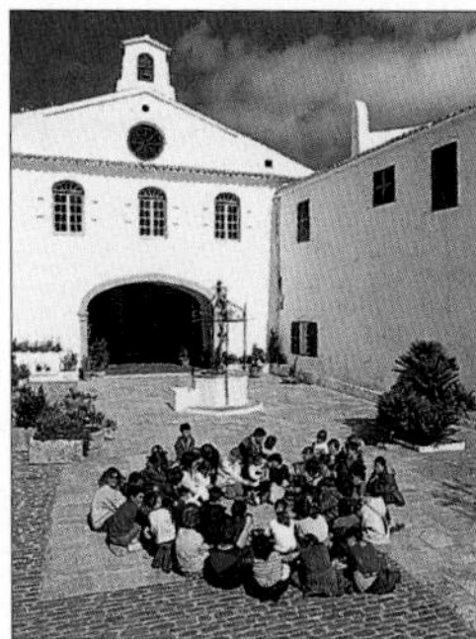

Courtyard in the Santuari del Toro

Es Mercadal ㉒

Baleares. 3,700. Carrer Major 16, 971 37 50 02. Sun. Sant Martí (third Sun of Jul).

Es Mercadal is a small country town – one of the three, with Alaior and Ferreries, that are strung out along the main road from Maó to Ciutadella. The town is unremarkable in itself, but within reach of it are three places of interest.

El Toro, 3 km (2 miles) to the east, is Menorca's highest mountain, at 350 m (1,150 ft). It is also the spiritual heart of the island and at its summit is the Santuari del Toro, built in 1670, which is run by nuns.

About 10 km (6 miles) north of Es Mercadal, the fishing village of **Fornells** transforms itself every summer into an outpost of St Tropez. In the harbour, smart yachts jostle with fishing boats, and the local jet-set crowd into the Bar Palma. Fornells' main culinary speciality is the *caldereta de llagosta* (lobster casserole), but the quality varies and prices can be high.

The road-cum-dirt track to the **Cap de Cavalleria**, 13 km (8 miles) north of Es Mercadal, passes through one of the Balearics' finest landscapes. Cavalleria is a rocky promontory, whipped by the tramontana wind from the north. It juts out into a choppy sea which, in winter, looks more like the North Atlantic than the Mediterranean. At the western edge of the peninsula are the remains of Sanisera, a Phoenician village mentioned by Pliny in the 1st century AD. The road leads to a headland, with a lighthouse and cliffs 90 m (295 ft) high, where peregrine falcons, sea eagles and kites ride the wind.

Further west along the coast is a string of fine, unspoiled beaches, though with difficult access: Cala Pregonda, Cala del Pilar and La Vall d'Algaiarens are three of the most beautiful.

A quiet stretch of beach at Santa Galdana

Horse rearing in the fiesta of Sant Lluís

THE BALEARIC ISLANDS' FIESTAS

Sant Antoni Abat *(16–17 Jan)*, Mallorca. This fiesta is celebrated with parades and the blessing of animals all over Mallorca and in Sant Antoni in Ibiza.

Sant Joan *(24 Jun)*, Ciutadella (Menorca). The horse plays a major part in Menorca's festivals. In the streets and squares of Ciutadella on 24 June, the Day of St John the Baptist, elegantly dressed riders put their horses through ritualized medieval manoeuvres. The fiesta reaches a climax when the horses rear up on their hind legs and the jubilant crowds swarm around them trying to hold them up with their hands. Similarly, the annual fiesta in Sant Lluís, which takes place at the end of August, sees many of the locals taking to the streets on horseback.

Sant Joan Pelós *(24 Jun)*, Felanitx (Mallorca). As part of this fiesta, a man is dressed in sheepskins to represent John the Baptist.

Romeria de Sant Marçal *(30 Jun)*, Sa Cabeneta (Mallorca). A feature of this fiesta is a market selling *siurells*, primitive Mallorcan whistles.

Our Lady of the Sea *(16 Jul)*, Formentera. The island's main fiesta honours the Virgen del Carmen, patroness of fishermen, with a flotilla of fishing boats.

The steep hillside of Maó running up from the harbour

Maó 23

Baleares. 24,000. Plaça Explanada s/n, 971 36 74 15. Tue, Sat. Fiestas de Gràcia (7–8 Sep), Fiesta de Sant Antoni (17 Jan).

The quietly elegant town of Maó has lent its Spanish name, Mahón, to mayonnaise. It was occupied by the British three times during the 18th century. The legacy of past colonial rule can be seen in sober Georgian town houses, with their dark green shutters and sash windows.

Maó's harbour is one of the finest in the Mediterranean. Taking the street leading from the port to the upper town, the S-shaped Costa de Ses Voltes, you come to the 18th-century **Església del Carme**, a former Carmelite church whose cool white cloister now houses an attractive fruit and vegetable market. Behind the market is the **Col·lecció Hernández Sanz y Hernández Mora**, which houses Menorcan art and antiques. The nearby Plaça Constitució is overlooked by the church of Santa Maria, which has a huge organ. Next door is the **town hall** *(ajuntament)* with its Neo-Classical façade, into which is mounted the famous clock donated by Sir Richard Kane (1660–1736), the first British governor of Menorca.

Located at the end of the Carrer Isabel II is the **Església de Sant Francesc**, with an intriguing Romanesque doorway and Baroque façade. The church houses the refurbished Museu de Menorca, which is open daily except Monday. Two minutes' walk south of here will take you to Maó's main square, the Plaça de S'Esplanada, behind which is the **Ateneu Científic Lliterat Artistic**, a centre of Menorca-related culture and learning. Inside are collections of local ceramics and maps, and a library. It is advisable to obtain permission before looking around. On the north side of the harbour is a mansion known as **Sant Antoni** or the Golden Farm. As Maó's finest example of Palladian architecture, it has an arched façade, painted plum red, with white arches, in the traditional Menorcan style. The British admiral, Nelson, is thought to have stayed here. The house has a collection of Nelson memorabilia and a fine library but is closed to the public.

Col·lecció Hernández Sanz y Hernández Mora
Claustre del Carme 5. ***Tel*** *971 35 05 97.* *10am–1pm Mon–Sat.*

Ateneu Científic Literari i Artistic
C/ Rovellada de Dalt 25. ***Tel*** *971 36 05 53.* *Sun, public hols.*

Cales Coves 24

Baleares. *Sant Climent, then 25 mins walk.* ***Tel*** *Maó, 971 36 74 15.*

On either side of a pretty bay can be found Cales Coves – the site of Neolithic dwellings of up to 9 m (30 ft) in length, hollowed out of the rock face. The caves, thought to have been inhabited since prehistoric times, are today occupied by a community of people seeking an alternative lifestyle. Some of the caves have front doors, chimneys and even butane cookers.

About 8 km (5 miles) west, along the coast, lies Binibeca, a tourist village built in a style sympathetic to old Menorca. The jumble of white houses and tiny streets of the Poblat de Pescadors, an imitation fishing village, have the look of the genuine article.

Modern sculpture outside one of the dwellings at Cales Coves

◁ The clear blue waters of Cala Turqueta in Menorca

Ancient Menorca

Menorca is exceptionally rich in prehistoric remains – the island has been described as an immense open-air museum. The majority of the sites are the work of the "talayot" people who lived between 2000–1000 BC and are named after the *talaiots* or huge stone towers that characterize the Menorcan landscape. There are hundreds of these Bronze Age villages and structures dotted around the island. Usually open to the public and free of charge, these sites provide an invaluable insight into the ancient inhabitants of the Balearics.

Huge *talaiot* amid the settlement of Trepucó

DIFFERENT STRUCTURES

The ancient stone structures scattered around the countryside of Menorca and, to a lesser extent, Mallorca can be placed into three main categories: *taulas, talaiots* and *navetas.*

Taulas *are two slabs of rock, one placed on top of the other, in a "T" formation. Suggestions as to their possible function range from a sacrificial altar to a roof support.*

Talayots *are circular or square buildings that may have been used as meeting places and dwellings.*

Navetas *are shaped like upturned boats and apparently had a dual role as dwellings and burial quarters. At least ten of these remain in Menorca.*

Spectacular *taula* at Talatí de Dalt, standing 3 m (10 ft) high

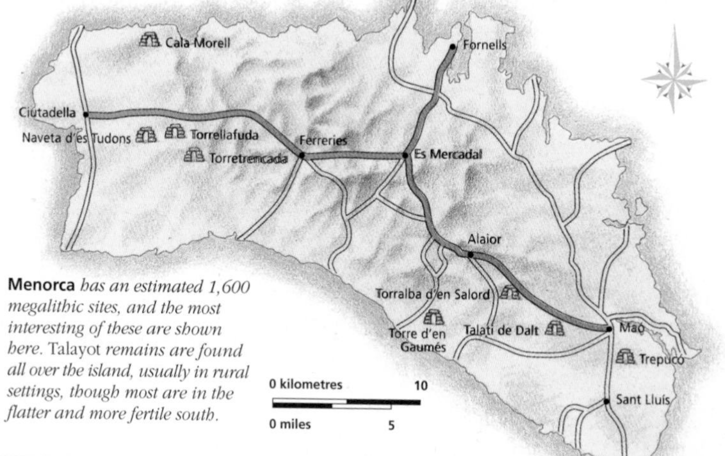

Menorca *has an estimated 1,600 megalithic sites, and the most interesting of these are shown here.* Talayot *remains are found all over the island, usually in rural settings, though most are in the flatter and more fertile south.*

Exploring the Western Islands

Tenerife has the widest range of holiday attractions of any of the Canary Islands. The province of Santa Cruz de Tenerife also includes the three tiny westerly islands of La Palma, La Gomera and El Hierro, which are scarcely developed for tourism and have no large resorts. Gradually, more visitors are discovering these peaceful, green havens. If you enjoy walking, wildlife and mountain scenery, visit one of these hideaways. All three islands have comfortable hotels, including paradors. But compared with Gran Canaria and the eastern islands, there are fewer sandy beaches here, and little organized entertainment or sightseeing.

Las Teresitas artificial beach, Santa Cruz de Tenerife

SIGHTS AT A GLANCE

Candelaria 8
Los Cristianos 4
La Gomera 3
El Hierro 2
La Laguna 9
Montes de Anaga 10
La Orotava 7
La Palma 1
Parque Nacional del Teide pp538–9 5
Puerto de la Cruz 6
Santa Cruz de Tenerife 11

Roque Bonanza on the rocky east coast of El Hierro

KEY

- Motorway
- Major road
- Secondary road
- Scenic route
- Summit

Terraced hillside, maximizing cultivation in the lush green Valle Gran Rey, in western La Gomera

GETTING AROUND

From mainland Spain there are flights *(see p674)* and ferries *(see p675)* to the Canary Islands. Transport to the small islands is mainly from Tenerife. La Gomera is easily reached by ferry or hydrofoil from Los Cristianos, or by plane from Gran Canaria or Tenerife. Airports on La Palma and El Hierro are served by regular flights from Tenerife's northern airport of Los Rodeos. Unless you take an organized coach trip, a car is essential to see the island scenery. Roads are improving, but great care is needed for mountain driving.

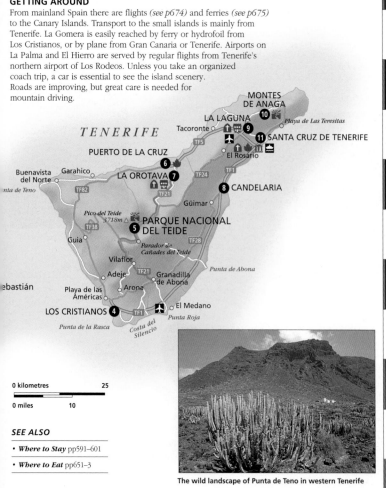

SEE ALSO

- ***Where to Stay*** pp591–601
- ***Where to Eat*** pp651–3

The wild landscape of Punta de Teno in western Tenerife

La Palma ❶

Santa Cruz de Tenerife. 80,000.
Santa Cruz de la Palma.
Plaza de la Constitución, Santa Cruz de la Palma, 922 41 21 06.
www.lapalmaturismo.com

Reaching an altitude of 2,426 m (7,959 ft) on a land base of less than 706 sq km (280 sq miles), La Palma is the world's steepest island. It lies on the northwestern tip of the archipelago and has a cool, moist climate and lush vegetation. The mountainous interior is covered with forests of pine, laurel and giant fern.

The centre of the island is dominated by **La Caldera de Taburiente**, a volcano's massive crater, more than 8 km (5 miles) wide. National park status *(see pp30–31)* is an indication of its botanical and geological importance. The International Astrophysics Observatory crowns the summit. A couple of roads traverse La Palma's dizzy heights, offering spectacular views of the craters of La Cumbrecita and Roque de los Muchachos.

The Parque Nacional de la Caldera de Taburiente, La Palma

Pastel façades and delicate wooden balconies in Santa Cruz, La Palma

Santa Cruz de la Palma, the island's main town and port, is an elegant place of old houses with balconies, some fine churches and several 16th-century buildings. In the cobbled street behind the seafront, Calle O'Daly (named after an Irish banana trader), are the Iglesia El Salvador, boasting a Mudéjar coffered ceiling, and the town hall *(ayuntamiento)*, which is housed in a cardinal's palace. A full-sized cement replica of the *Santa María,* Columbus's flagship, stands at the end of the Plaza Alameda.

The tortuous mountain road southwest of Santa Cruz winds over Las Cumbres mountains via Breña Alta to **El Paso** in the centre of the island. A relatively sizeable community, the village is known for its silk production and hand-rolled cigars.

Among the almond terraces and vineyards of southern La Palma, solidified lava from the Teneguia volcano is a reminder of its recent activity *(see p551)*.

Craters on El Hierro, Spain's most western territory

El Hierro ❷

Santa Cruz de Tenerife. 10,500.
Puerto de la Estaca.
C/ Doctor Quintero 4, Valverde, 922 55 03 02.

Due to a dearth of sandy beaches, El Hierro has escaped tourist invasions. Instead it has caught the attentions of naturalists. Its hilly landscape and unusual fauna and flora are part of its appeal. El Hierro is the smallest of the Canaries, and the furthest west; consequently it is the last place in Spain where the sun sets.

Valverde, the island's capital, stands inland at 600 m (2,000 ft) above sea level. Canary pines and peculiarly twisted juniper trees cover El Hierro's

LA GOMERA'S WHISTLE LANGUAGE

The problems of communication posed by La Gomera's rugged terrain produced an unusual language, known as El Silbo. This system of piercing whistles probably developed because its sounds carry across the great distances from one valley to the next. Its origins are mysterious, but it was allegedly invented by the Guanches *(see p547)*. Few young Gomerans have any use for El Silbo today, and the language would probably be dead if it were not for the demonstrations of it still held for interested visitors at the parador, and in the restaurant at Las Rosas.

El Silbo practised on La Gomera

mountainous interior, best seen from the many footpaths and scenic viewpoints along the roads. A ridge of woodland, curving east-west across the island, marks the edge of a volcano. The crater forms a fertile depression known as El Golfo.

In the far west is the **Ermita de los Reyes**, a place of pilgrimage and the starting point of the island's biggest fiesta, held in July every four years.

The turquoise seas off the south coast are popular with skin-divers, who base themselves in the small fishing village of **La Restinga**.

La Gomera ❸

Santa Cruz de Tenerife. *21,400.* *Calle Real 4, San Sebastián de la Gomera, 922 14 15 12.* **www**.gomera-island.com

Terraced hillsides in the fertile Valle Gran Rey, La Gomera

La Gomera is the most accessible of the smaller western islands, only 40 minutes by hydrofoil from Los Cristianos on Tenerife (90 minutes by ferry), or by plane from Tenerife or Gran Canaria. Many come to La Gomera for a day only, taking a coach trip. Others hire a car and explore on their own: a scenic but exhausting drive for a single day as the terrain is intensely buckled, and the central plateau is deeply scored by dramatic ravines. Driving across these gorges involves negotiating countless dizzying hairpin bends.

The best way to enjoy the island is to stay awhile and explore it at leisure, preferably doing some walking. On a fine day, La Gomera's scenery is glorious. Rock pinnacles jut above steep slopes studded with ferns while terraced hillsides glow with palms and flowering creepers. The best section, the **Parque Nacional de Garajonay**, is a UNESCO World Heritage Site.

San Sebastián, La Gomera's main town and ferry terminal, is situated on the east coast, a scattering of white buildings around a small beach. Among its sights are some places associated with Columbus *(see pp58–9)*, who topped up his water supplies here before setting out on his adventurous voyages. A well in the customs house bears the grand words "With this water America was baptized". According to legend he also prayed in the Iglesia de la Asunción, and stayed at a local house.

Beyond the arid hills to the south lies **Playa de Santiago**, the island's only real resort, which has a grey pebble beach. **Valle Gran Rey**, in the far west, is a fertile valley of palms and staircase terraces. These days it is colonized by foreigners attempting alternative lifestyles. In the north, tiny roads weave a tortuous course around several pretty villages, plunging at intervals to small, stony beaches. **Las Rosas** is a popular stop-off for coach parties, who can enjoy the visitors' centre and a restaurant with a panoramic view.

The road towards the coast from Las Rosas leads through the town of **Vallehermoso**, dwarfed by the huge **Roque de Cano**, which is an impressive mass of solidified lava. Just off the north coast stands **Los Órganos**, a fascinating rock formation of crystallized basalt columns resembling the pipes of an organ.

Juniper trees on El Hierro, twisted and bent by the wind

Tenerife

In the language of its aboriginal Guanche inhabitants Tenerife means "Snowy Mountain", a tribute to its most striking geographical feature, the dormant volcano of Mount Teide, Spain's highest peak. The largest of the Canary Islands, Tenerife is a roughly triangular landmass rising steeply on all sides towards the cloud-capped summit that divides it into two distinct climatic zones: damp and lushly vegetated in the north, sunny and arid in the south. Tenerife offers a more varied range of attractions than any of the other Canary Islands, including its spectacular volcanic scenery, water sports and a vibrant atmosphere after dark. Its beaches, however, have unenticing black sand and are rather poor for swimming. The main resorts are crowded with high-rise hotels and apartments, offering nightlife but little peace and quiet.

Bananas in northern Tenerife

Los Cristianos 4

Santa Cruz de Tenerife. 60,000. *Paseo las Vistas 1, 922 78 70 11. Sun. Fiesta del Carmen (first Sun of Sep).* **www**.arona.org

The old fishing village of Los Cristianos, on Tenerife's south coast, has grown into a town spreading out along the foot of barren hills. Ferries and hydrofoils make regular trips from its little port to La Gomera and El Hierro *(see pp532–3)*.

To the north lies the modern expanse of **Playa de las Américas**, Tenerife's largest development. It offers visitors a cheerful, relaxed, undemanding cocktail of sun and fun.

A brief sortie inland leads to the much older town of **Adeje** and to the **Barranco del Infierno**, a wild gorge with an attractive waterfall (two hours' round walk from Adeje).

Along the coast to the east, the **Costa del Silencio** is a pleasant contrast to most of the other large resorts, with its bungalow developments surrounding fishing villages. Los Abrigos has lively fish restaurants lining its harbour.

Further east, **El Médano** shelters below an ancient volcanic cone. Its two beaches are popular with windsurfers.

Parque Nacional del Teide 5

See pp538–9.

Puerto de la Cruz 6

Santa Cruz de Tenerife. 27,500. *C/ Las Lonjas s/n, 922 38 60 00. Sat. Carnival (Feb–Mar), Fiesta del Carmen (second Sun of Jul).*

Puerto de la Cruz, the oldest resort in the Canaries, first sprang to prominence in 1706, when a volcanic eruption obliterated Tenerife's principal port of Garachico. Puerto de la Cruz took its place, later becoming popular with genteel English convalescents. The town's older buildings give it much of its present character.

The beautiful Lago Martiánez lido, designed by the Lanzarote architect César Manrique *(see p548)*, compensates for a lack of good beaches with its sea water pools, palms and fountains. Other attractions include the tropical gardens of **Loro Parque**, where visitors can also see parrots and dolphins.

Outside town, the **Jardín de Orquídeas** is the oldest garden in Tenerife, and has a large orchid collection. **Icod de los Vinos**, a short drive west, attracts crowds for its spectacular ancient dragon tree.

Loro Parque
Avenida Loro Parque.
Tel *922 37 38 41. daily.*

Jardín de Orquídeas
Camino Sitio Litre s/n. ***Tel*** *922 38 24 17. daily.*

The landscaped Lago Martiánez lido, Puerto de la Cruz

THE DRAGON TREE

The Canary Islands have many unusual plants, but the dragon tree *(Dracaena draco)* is one of the strangest. This primitive creature looks a little like a giant cactus, with swollen branches that sprout multiple tufts of spiky leaves. When cut, the trunk exudes a reddish sap once believed to have magical and medicinal properties. Dragon trees form no annual rings, so their age is a mystery. Some are thought to be hundreds of years old. The most venerable surviving specimen can be seen at Icod de los Vinos.

La Orotava ❼

Santa Cruz de Tenerife. *40,000.* *C/ Calvario 4, 922 32 30 41.* *Carnival (Feb/Mar), Corpus Christi (May/Jun), Romeria San Isidoro Labrador (Jun).*

A short distance from Puerto de la Cruz, in the fertile hills above the Orotava valley, La Orotava makes a popular excursion. The old part of this historic town clusters around the large **Iglesia de Nuestra Señora de la Concepción**. This domed Baroque building with twin towers was built in the late 18th century to replace an earlier church that was destroyed in earthquakes at the beginning of that century.

In the surrounding streets and squares are many old churches, convents and grand houses with elaborate wooden balconies. The **Casas de los Balcones** and **Casa del Turista** have interior courtyards that are open to the public.

Nuestra Señora de la Candelaria, patron saint of the Canary Islands

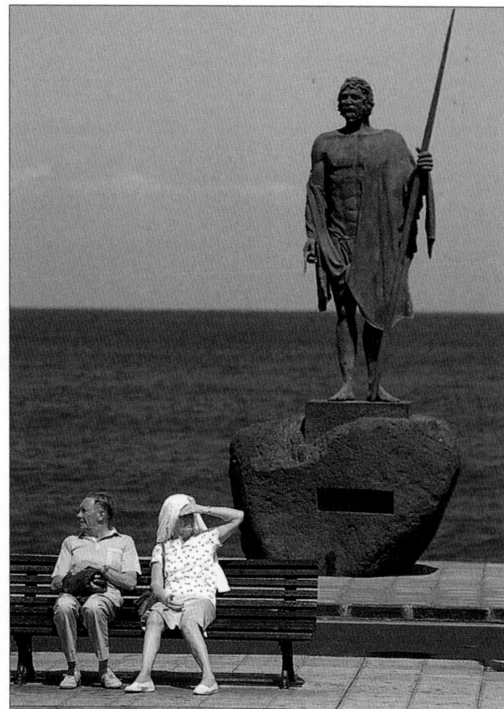

Statue of a Guanche chief on the seafront of Candelaria

Candelaria ❽

Santa Cruz de Tenerife. *17,000.* *Plaza del CIT, 922 50 04 15.* *Sat, Sun.* *Nuestra Señora de la Candelaria (14–15 Aug).*

This coastal town is famous for its shrine to **Nuestra Señora de la Candelaria,** the Canary Islands' patron saint, whose image is surrounded by flowers and candles in a modern church in the main square. This gaudy Virgin, supposedly washed ashore in pagan times, was venerated before Christianity reached the island. In 1826 a tidal wave returned her to the sea, but a replica draws pilgrims to worship here every August. Outside, stone effigies of Guanche chiefs line the sea wall.

La Laguna ❾

Santa Cruz de Tenerife. *141,000.* *C/ de la Carrera 7, 922 63 11 94.* *daily.* *San Benito (15 Jul), Santísimo Cristo de la Laguna (14 Sep).*

A bustling university town and former island capital, La Laguna is the second largest settlement on Tenerife and a UNESCO World Heritage Site.

In its old quarter, best explored on foot, there are many atmospheric squares, historic buildings and good museums. Most of the sights lie between the bell-towered **Iglesia de Nuestra Señora de la Concepción** (1502), and the Plaza del Adelantado, on which stand the town hall, a convent and the **Palacio de Nava.**

Montes de Anaga ❿

Santa Cruz de Tenerife. *Santa Cruz de Tenerife, La Laguna.*

The rugged mountains north of Santa Cruz are kept green and lush by a cool, wet climate. They abound with a wide variety of interesting birds and plants, including cacti, laurels and tree heathers. Walking the mountain trails is very popular, and maps showing many of the best paths are readily available from the tourist office. A steep road with marker posts climbs up from the village of San Andrés by the beautiful but artificial beach of Las Teresitas. On clear days there are marvellous vistas along the paths, especially from the viewpoints of Pico del Inglés and Bailadero.

Winding down through the laurel forests of Monte de las Mercedes and the colourful valley of Tejina you reach **Tacoronte** with its interesting churches, an ethnographic museum and a bodega, where you can sample local wines.

THE CANARY ISLANDS' FIESTAS

Carnival *(Feb/Mar)*, Santa Cruz de Tenerife. One of Europe's biggest carnivals, this grand street party is a lavish spectacle of extravagant costumes and Latin American dance music to rival that of Rio de Janeiro. For years under the Franco regime, Carnival was suppressed for its irreverent frivolity. It begins with the election of a queen of the festivities and builds up to a climax on Shrove Tuesday when there is a large procession. The "funeral" of an enormous mock sardine takes place on Ash Wednesday. Carnival is also celebrated on the islands of Lanzarote and Gran Canaria.

Revellers in Carnival outfits on Tenerife

Corpus Christi *(May/Jun)*, La Orotava (Tenerife). The streets of the town are filled with flower carpets in striking patterns, while the Plaza del Ayuntamiento is covered in copies of works of art, formed from coloured volcanic sands.

Descent of the Virgin of the Snows *(Jul, every five years: 2015, 2020)* Santa Cruz de La Palma.

Romería de la Virgen de la Candelaria *(15 Aug)*, Candelaria (Tenerife). Pilgrims come here in their thousands to venerate the Canary Islands' patroness.

Fiesta del Charco *(7–11 Sep)*, San Nicolás de Tolentino (Gran Canaria). People leap into a large saltwater pond to catch mullet.

Large ships moored at the busy port of Santa Cruz de Tenerife

Santa Cruz de Tenerife ⓫

Santa Cruz de Tenerife. *220,000.* *Plaza de España, 922 28 93 94.* *Sun.* *Carnival (Feb/Mar), Día de la Cruz (3 May).* **www**.webtenerife.com

Tenerife's capital city is an important regional port, with a deep-water harbour suitable for large ships. Its most attractive beach, **Las Teresitas**, lies 7 km (4 miles) to the north. Completely artificial, it was created by importing millions of tonnes of golden Saharan sand and building a protective reef just offshore. Shaded by palms, backed by mountains and so far devoid of concrete hotel developments, the result improves on anything nature has bestowed on Tenerife.

Santa Cruz can boast many handsome historic buildings. The hub of the town is around the **Plaza de España**, situated near the harbour. Just off it is the Calle de Castillo, the main shopping street. Its two most noteworthy churches are the **Iglesia de Nuestra Señora de la Concepción**, with parts dating from 1500, and Baroque **Iglesia de San Francisco**.

Particularly interesting is the **Museo de la Naturaleza y el Hombre**, in the Palacio Insular, where Guanche mummies grin in glass cases. Inside the museum you can also see the cannon which is alleged to have removed the arm of the British admiral Nelson during an unsuccessful raid on the city in the late 18th century.

Other attractions include the **Museo de Bellas Artes** which features old masters as well as modern works. Many of its paintings focus on local events and landscapes. Contemporary sculptures adorn the **Parque Municipal García Sanabria**, a pleasant park with shady paths, laid out in 1926.

In the morning, visit the **Mercado de Nuestra Señora de África**, which combines a bazaar with a food market. Outside stalls sell domestic goods; those inside offer an eclectic mix of live chickens, spices and cut flowers. Santa Cruz is especially worth a visit during its flamboyant carnival.

Museo de la Naturaleza y el Hombre
Calle Fuentes Morales. ***Tel*** *922 53 58 16.* *Tue–Sun.*

Museo de Bellas Artes
Calle José Murphy 12. ***Tel*** *922 24 43 58.* *Tue–Fri.*

The artificial beach of Las Teresitas in Santa Cruz

The Flavours of the Canary Islands

The exotic fruits and vegetables that grow in the sub-tropical Canaries climate, and the unusual fish that are caught in local waters, have led to a cuisine very different from that of the Iberian Peninsula. From the original inhabitants, the Guanche, culinary traditions survive in local staples like *gofio* (maize meal). Over the centuries, Spanish, Portuguese and North African influences have been incorporated into the local cuisine, but the underlying theme is always one of simplicity and a reliance on ultra-fresh local produce. All kinds of unusual delicacies are available, from sweet-fleshed parrot-fish to succulent tropical fruits.

Maize (corn)

Fish straight from the ocean, being dried in the sun to preserve them

SEAFOOD AND MEAT

The Canaries offer an incredible array of seafood, with varieties unknown on the Spanish mainland. Delicacies like *lapas* (limpets) are around only for a few months during the summer, and are usually served simply grilled *(a la plancha)*. Other unusual varieties include wreckfish, damselfish, dentex and parrot-fish. These, along with more common varieties, are usually fried, baked in a salt crust, or dried in the sun.

Meats include standard Iberian favourites like pork, kid and beef, but they are often prepared according to ancient Guanche traditions.

FRUIT AND VEGETABLES

The mild, stable Canarian climate is perfect for growing luscious tropical fruits (the most famous crop of the islands being bananas). Exotic vegetables thrive, too, as well as potatoes and tomatoes, which were introduced here 500 years ago from the newly discovered Americas. The islands boast varieties of potato unknown elsewhere, and these feature in the local favourite *papas arrugadas* ("wrinkly potatoes"), which are made by boiling potatoes in their skins in very salty water – sometimes seawater.

Mouthwatering fresh fruits from the Canary Islands

CANARIAN DISHES AND SPECIALITIES

The Greeks named the Canaries "the fortunate islands", and they are certainly blessed in terms of the freshness and abundance of the local produce. What ever you choose to eat, you can be sure of encoutering a bowl of the ubiquitous *mojo* sauce. This aromatic Canarian creation accompanies almost every dish, and appears in countless versions: the main ones are red *picón*, which is spiced up with pepper and paprika, and green *verde*, with parsley and coriander. The Canarian staple, *gofio* (roasted maize meal), is served for breakfast and used in local dishes such as *gofio de almendras*, a rich almond dessert. The islands are also known for delicious pastries like the honey-drizzled *bienmesabes* (meaning "tastes good to me") and traditional cheeses.

Almonds

Sopa de pescados tinerfeña
This Tenerife fish soup of sea bass and potatoes is scented with saffron and cumin.

Parque Nacional del Teide ❺

Towering over Tenerife, Mount Teide, surrounded by a wild volcanic landscape, is an awesome sight. 180,000 years ago a much larger adjacent cone collapsed leaving behind the devastation of Las Cañadas, a 16-km (10-mile) wide caldera, and the smaller volcano, Teide, on its northern edge. Today volcanic material forms a wilderness of weathered, mineral-tinted rocks, ash beds and lava streams. A single road crosses the plateau of Las Cañadas, passing a parador, cable car station, and visitors' centre. Follow the marked paths for unforgettable views of this unique, protected area.

Volcanic Landscapes
The eight-minute cable car ride leaves you 160 m (525 ft) short of Teide's summit. Authorisation must be given to climb up to the summit.

Pico del Teide, which is still volcanically active, is Spain's highest summit.

Pico Viejo, a volcanic cone also known as Montaña Chahorra, last erupted in the 18th century.

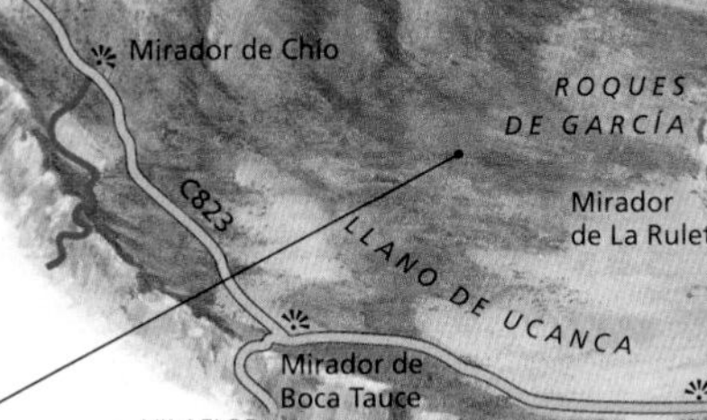

0 kilometres 2

0 miles 1

KEY

Road

Track

Footpath

Los Roques de García
These flamboyantly shaped lava rocks near the parador are some of the most photographed in the whole park. The rocks of Los Azulejos, nearby, glitter blue-green because of the copper deposits within them.

WILD FLOWERS

The inhospitable badlands of Las Cañadas are inhabited by some rare and beautiful plants. Many of these are unique to the Canary Islands. Most striking is the tall *Echium wildprettii*, a kind of viper's bugloss, whose red flowers reach 3 m (9 ft) in early summer. Other common plants include Teide broom, the Teide daisy, and a unique species of violet. The best time of year for flower-spotting is May to June. Displays housed in the visitors' centre will help identify them. Don't take any plants away with you: all vegetation within the park is strictly protected and must not be uprooted or picked.

For hotels and restaurants in this region see pp599–601 and pp651–3

La Caldera de Las Cañadas
A rim of fractured crags forms a pie-crust edge to the sides of this enormous caldera – a wide volcanic crater (see p551). *Now collapsed and intensely eroded, the perimeter of the caldera measures 45 km (28 miles).*

At El Portillo Visitors' Centre, a video film and exhibition chart the origins of the park.

VISITORS' CHECKLIST

Tel *922 29 01 29. 348 from Puerto de la Cruz; 342 from Playa de las Américas.* ***El Portillo Visitors' Centre & cable car*** *(to NE of park on C821). daily. 1 & 6 Jan, 25 Dec.*

Las Cañadas
The flat expanses of the seven cañadas *(small sandy plateaux) were created by the collapse of ancient craters. Several colourful plants have managed to colonize this dusty, barren wasteland.*

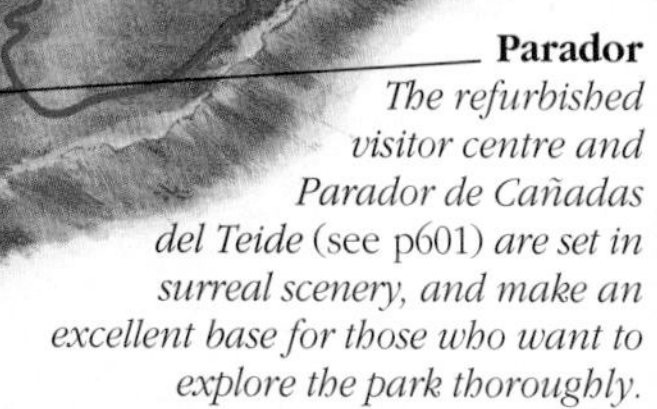

Parador
The refurbished visitor centre and Parador de Cañadas del Teide (see p601) *are set in surreal scenery, and make an excellent base for those who want to explore the park thoroughly.*

Canary mustard (*Descurainia bourgeauana*)

Teide wallflower (*Erysimum scoparium*)

Teide violet (*Viola cheiranthifolia*)

Teide viper's bugloss (*Echium wildpretii*)

Exploring the Eastern Islands

The Eastern Province of the Canary Islands – Las Palmas – comprises the islands of Gran Canaria, Lanzarote and Fuerteventura. All feature unusual and spectacular scenery, plenty of sunshine and excellent sandy beaches, but each has a very different atmosphere. Gran Canaria boasts the only really large town, Las Palmas de Gran Canaria, which is also the administrative centre for the eastern islands. It also offers the biggest resort, Maspalomas, with its Playa del Inglés, which has a package holiday feel. As a contrast, the white beaches of Fuerteventura have been left fairly undeveloped and it is still possible to find privacy among their sand dunes. Lanzarote has fine beaches, too, while its interior is dominated by a volcanic landscape which makes for great excursions.

Corralejo's beach, in the north of Fuerteventura

The marina at Puerto Rico, in southern Gran Canaria

GETTING AROUND

Most people travel from mainland Spain to the eastern islands by air *(see p674)*. The alternative is a long sea crossing from Cádiz *(see p675)*. There are flights between all the islands, mainly from Gran Canaria. There are also regular inter-island ferries. Taxis and public transport are fine within resorts, but expensive over long distances. Cars can be hired on all the islands, usually at airports or ferry terminals. The main roads are well-surfaced and fast on the flatter sections, though traffic in Gran Canaria can be heavy in places. A four-wheel drive Jeep is advisable to reach some remoter beaches.

KEY

- Motorway
- Major road
- Secondary road
- Scenic route
- Summit

0 kilometres 25

0 miles 10

For additional map sumbols *see back flap*

SIGHTS AT A GLANCE

Agaete 15
Arrecife 27
Betancuria 20
Caleta de Fuste 21
Corralejo 23
Costa Teguise 28
Haría 30
Jameos del Agua 31
Maspalomas 14
Las Palmas de Gran Canaria 17
Parque Nacional de Timanfaya 25
Península de Jandía 19
Playa Blanca 24
Puerto del Carmen 26
Puerto de Mogán 12
Puerto del Rosario 22
Puerto Rico 13
Tafira 16
Teguise 29

Tour

Cruz de Tejeda 18

Isla Alegranza
Isla de Montaña Clara
Isla Graciosa
Orzola
JAMEOS DEL AGUA 31
HARÍA 30
Tinajo
29 TEGUISE
Mozaga
PARQUE NACIONAL DE TIMANFAYA 25
COSTA TEGUISE 28
San Bartolomé
27 ARRECIFE
Yaiza
Tias
Salinas de Janubio
LZ2
26
PUERTO DEL CARMEN
PLAYA BLANCA 24
Playa del Papagayo
LANZAROTE
Isla de los Lobos
CORRALEJO 23
FV1
La Oliva
Tindaya
22 PUERTO DEL ROSARIO
Antigua
BETANCURIA 20
21 CALETA DE FUSTE
Pájara
Tuineje
FV2
Gran Tarajal
Tarajalejo
PENÍNSULA DE JANDÍA
19
Morro Jable
FUERTEVENTURA

SEE ALSO

• ***Where to Stay*** pp599–601
• ***Where to Eat*** pp651–3

Volcanoes of Montañas de Fuego in Parque Nacional de Timanfaya, Lanzarote

Gran Canaria

Farmer and donkey

Gran Canaria is the most popular of the Canary Islands, with over 3 million holiday-makers visiting it each year. The island offers a surprising range of scenery, climate, resorts and attractions within its compact bounds. Winding roads follow the steep, ruggedly beautiful terrain which rises to a symmetrical cone at the centre of the island. Las Palmas, Gran Canaria's capital and port, is the largest city in the Canaries, and Maspalomas/Playa del Inglés, in the south, is one of the biggest resorts in Spain. Both tourist meccas are packed with high-rise hotels and villa complexes, but not far away there is some marvellous scenery to discover.

Puerto de Mogán ⓬

Las Palmas. *1,500.* *Avenida de Mogán, Puerto Rico, 928 15 88 04.* *Fri.* *Virgen del Carmen (Jul).* **www**.grancanaria.com

Situated at the end of the verdant valley of Mogán, this is one of Gran Canaria's most appealing developments – an idyll to many visitors after the brash Playa del Inglés. Based around a small fishing port, it consists of a village-like complex of pretty, white, creeper-covered houses and a similarly designed hotel built around a marina. Boutiques, bars and restaurants add an ambience without any of the accompanying rowdiness.

The sandy beach, sheltered between the cliffs, is scarcely big enough for all visitors; a car is recommended to reach more facilities at Maspalomas. Ferries provide a leisurely way to get to nearby resorts.

Sun worshippers in Puerto Rico

Puerto Rico ⓭

Las Palmas. *1,800.* *Avenida de Mogán, 928 15 88 04.* *María de Auxiliadora (May), San Antonio (13 Jun), Carmen (16 Jul).*

The barren cliffs west of Maspalomas now sprout apartment complexes at every turn. Puerto Rico is an over-developed resort, but has one of the more attractive beaches on the island, a firm crescent of imported sand supplemented by lidos and excellent water sports facilities. It is a great place to learn sailing, diving and windsurfing, or just to soak up the ultraviolet – Puerto Rico enjoys the best sunshine record in the whole of Spain.

Holiday-makers on the golden sands of Puerto Rico beach

Maspalomas ⓮

Las Palmas. *33,000.* *Centro Comercial Anexo II, Playa del Inglés, 928 76 84 09.* *Wed & Sat.* *Santiago (25 Jul), San Bartolomé (24 Aug).* **www**.grancanaria.com

When the fast motorway from Las Palmas airport first tips you into this bewildering mega-resort, it seems like a homogeneous blur, but gradually three separate communities emerge. **San Agustín**, the furthest east, is sedate compared with the others. It has a series of beaches of dark sand, attractively sheltered by low cliffs and landscaped promenades, and a casino.

The next exit off the coastal highway leads to **Playa del Inglés**, the largest and liveliest resort, a triangle of land jutting into a huge belt of golden sand. Developed from the end of the 1950s, the area is built up with giant blocks of flats linked by a maze of roads. Many hotels lack sea views, though most have spacious grounds with swimming pools.

Floral arches decorating a street of apartments in Puerto de Mogán

For hotels and restaurants in this region see pp599–601 and pp651–3

At night the area pulsates with bright disco lights and flashing neon. There are more than 300 restaurants and over 50 discos.

West of Playa del Inglés the beach undulates into the **Dunas de Maspalomas**. A relieving contrast to the hectic surrounding resorts, these dunes form a nature reserve protected from further development. The western edge of the dunes (marked by a lighthouse) is occupied by a cluster of luxury hotels. Just behind the dunes lies a golf course encircled by bungalow estates.

Everything is laid on for the package holiday: water sports, excursions, fast food, as well as go-karts, camel safaris and funfairs. Best of these include **Palmitos Park,** with exotic birds in subtropical gardens; and **Sioux City**, a fun-packed Western theme park.

Palmitos Park
Barranco de los Palmitos. ***Tel*** *928 79 70 70.* *daily.*
www.palmitospark.es

Sioux City
Cañón del Águila. ***Tel*** *928 76 29 82.* *Tue–Sun.*

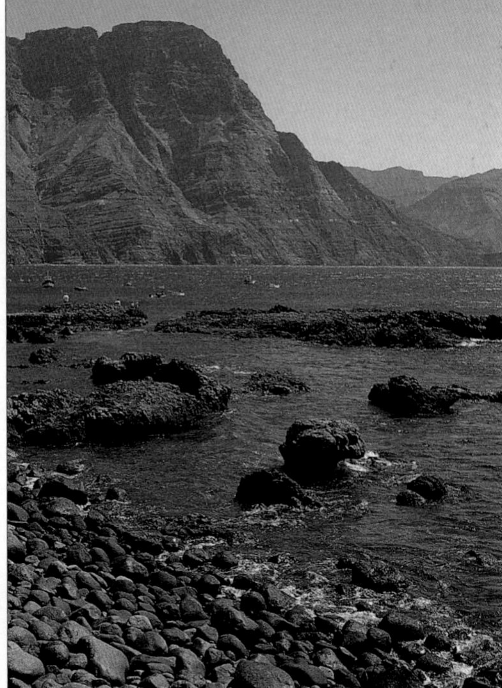

The rocky shore and steep cliffs of the northeast coast near Agaete

Agaete ⓯

Las Palmas. *5,600.* *Avenida Señora de las Nieves 1, 928 55 43 82.* *Fiesta de las Nieves (5 Aug).*
www.aytoagaete.es

The cloudier northern side of the island is far greener and lusher than the arid south, and banana plantations take up most of the coastal slopes. Agaete, on the northwest coast, a pretty scatter of white houses around a striking rocky bay, is growing into a small resort. Every August, Agaete holds the Fiesta de la Rama, a Guanche *(see p547)* rain-making ritual which dates from long before the arrival of the Spanish. An animated procession of villagers bearing green branches heads from the hills above the town down to the coast and into the sea. The villagers beat the water to summon the rain.

The **Ermita de las Nieves** contains a fine 16th-century Flemish triptych and model sailing ships, as well as a botanical garden, the **Huerto de las Flores**.

Environs

A brief detour inland up along the Barranco de Agaete takes you through a fertile valley of papaya, mango and citrus trees. North of Agaete are the towns of Guía and Gáldar. Though there is little to see here, both parish churches do contain examples of the religious statuary of the celebrated 18th-century sculptor, José Luján Pérez.

Nearby, towards the north coast, lies the **Cenobio de Valerón**. One of the most dramatic of the local Guanche sights, this cliff-face is pockmarked with nearly 300 caves beneath a basalt arch. These are believed to have been hideaways for Guanche priestesses, communal grainstores and refuges from attack.

Huerto de las Flores
Calle Huertas. ***Tel*** *680 70 02 01.*
Tue–Sat.

Miles of wind-sculptured sand: the dunes at Maspalomas

Tafira ⓰

Las Palmas. *23,000.* *Calle León y Castillo 17, Las Palmas, 928 21 96 00.* *San Francisco (Oct).*

The hills southwest of Las Palmas have long been desirable residential locations. A colonial air still wafts around Tafira's patrician villas. The **Jardín Canario**, a botanical garden founded in 1952, is the main reason for a visit. Plants from all of the Canary Islands can be studied in their own, re-created habitats.

Near La Atalaya lies one of Gran Canaria's most impressive natural sights – the **Caldera de la Bandama**. This is a volcanic crater 1,000 m (3,300 ft) wide, best seen from the Mirador de Bandama where you gaze down into the green depression about 200 m (660 ft) deep. Some of the inhabited caves in the **Barranco de Guayadeque**, a valley of red rocks to the south, were dug in the late 15th century. A few of them have electricity.

Jardín Canario
Carretera de Dragonal, Tafira. **Tel** *928 21 95 80.* *daily.* *1 Jan & Good Fri.*

Palm trees in a natural setting in the Jardín Canario, Tafira

Las Palmas de Gran Canaria ⓱

Las Palmas. *378,000.* *Calle León y Castillo 17, 928 21 96 00.* *Carnival (Feb/Mar).*

Las Palmas is the largest city in the Canary Islands. A bustling seaport and industrial city, it sees 1,000 ships docking each month. Las Palmas has faded somewhat from the days when wealthy convalescents flocked here in winter and glamorous liners called in on transatlantic voyages. But it remains a vibrant place to visit.

Las Palmas is a sprawling city built around an isthmus. The modern commercial shipping area, Puerto de la Luz, takes up the eastern side of the isthmus, which leads to the former island of La Isleta, a sailors' and military quarter. On the other side of the isthmus is the crowded **Playa de las Canteras**, a 3-km (2-mile) long stretch of golden beach. The promenade behind has been built up with bars, restaurants and hotels.

Bronze dog at Plaza Santa Ana

The town centre stretches along the coast from the isthmus. For a scenic tour, begin in the **Parque Santa Catalina**, near the port. This is a popular, shady square of cafés and newspaper kiosks.

In the leafy residential quarter of Ciudad Jardín are the Parque Doramas and the traditional casino hotel of Santa Catalina.

The **Pueblo Canario** is a tourist enclave where visitors can watch folk dancing, and browse in the craft shops and the small art gallery. All this can be viewed from above by walking uphill towards the Altavista district and the Paseo Cornisa.

At the end of town is the Barrio Vegueta, an atmospheric quarter which dates back to the Spanish conquest. At its heart stands the **Catedral de Santa Ana**, begun in 1500. The adjacent **Museo Diocesano de Arte Sacro** contains works of religious art. The square in front is guarded by Canarian dogs in bronze.

Nearby, the **Casa de Colón** is a 15th-century governor's residence where Columbus stayed. A museum dedicated to his voyages displays charts, models and diary extracts.

Early history can be seen in the **Museo Canario**, which contains Guanche mummies, skulls, pottery and jewellery.

Museo Diocesano de Arte Sacro
Calle Espíritu Santo 20. **Tel** *928 31 49 89.* *Mon–Sat.*

Casa de Colón
Calle Colón 1. **Tel** *928 31 23 73.* *daily.* *1 Jan, 22 May, 24, 25 & 31 Dec.* *(by appt for groups).*

Museo Canario
Calle Doctor Verneau 2. **Tel** *928 33 68 00.* *daily.* *1 Jan, 25 Dec.*

The Casa de Colón museum, Las Palmas, dedicated to Columbus

For hotels and restaurants in this region see pp599–601 and pp651–3

Tour of Cruz de Tejeda ⓲

Gran Canaria's mountainous interior makes for an ideal day tour, from any part of the island. Choose a fine day or the views may be obscured. The route from Maspalomas leads through dry ravines of bare rock and cacti, becoming more fertile with altitude. Roads near the central highlands snake steeply through shattered, tawny crags, past caves and pretty villages to panoramic viewpoints from which you can see Mount Teide *(see pp538–9)* on Tenerife. On the north side, the slopes are much lusher, growing citrus fruits and eucalyptus trees.

White farmhouses en route to Teror

Artenara ②
One of the inhabited caves in this town houses a little church. Another has been converted into an unusual restaurant, the Mesón de la Silla.

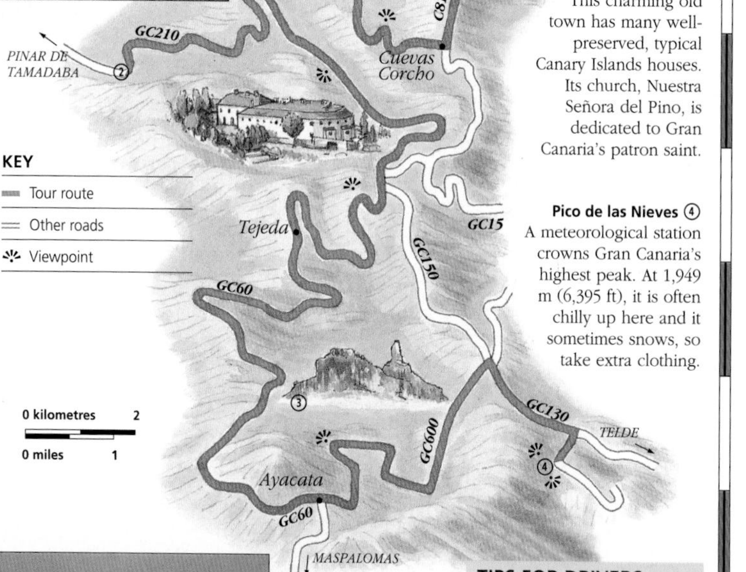

Teror ①
This charming old town has many well-preserved, typical Canary Islands houses. Its church, Nuestra Señora del Pino, is dedicated to Gran Canaria's patron saint.

Pico de las Nieves ④
A meteorological station crowns Gran Canaria's highest peak. At 1,949 m (6,395 ft), it is often chilly up here and it sometimes snows, so take extra clothing.

KEY

- Tour route
- Other roads
- Viewpoint

0 kilometres 2

0 miles 1

Roque Nublo ③
This 60-m (195-ft) high jagged spike of basalt tops a 1,700-m (5,578-ft) peak. Together with nearby Roque Bentayga, it was sacred to the Guanches. It's a stiff climb to the summit.

TIPS FOR DRIVERS

Length: *35–45 km (22–28 miles).*
Stopping-off points: *Cueva del Molino restaurant in Artenara is a popular lunch spot (928 66 62 27, closed Sun).* ***Note:*** *roads can be narrow with few passing places; sudden patches of cloud or mist may loom without warning.*

Fuerteventura

Lying just 100 km (60 miles) off the Atlantic coast of Morocco, leaf-shaped Fuerteventura is continually battered by coastal winds. It is the second largest of the Canary Islands after Tenerife, and the most sparsely populated: its 69,500 inhabitants are outnumbered by goats. The island used to be densely wooded, but European settlers cut down the timber for shipbuilding; the dry climate and the goats have since reduced the vegetation to parched scrub. It is so dry that water has to be shipped over from the mainland. The only significant revenue is tourism, but the tourist industry is still in its infancy compared with the other main islands. However, visitors are increasing in number as thousands of sun-worshippers flock to more than 150 splendid beaches. The island is popular with water sports fans and naturists.

A herd of goats near the airport on Fuerteventura

Península de Jandía ⓳

Las Palmas. Costa Calma, Morro Jable. (jetfoil) from Gran Canaria. Centro Comercial Cosmo, Bajo, 928 54 07 76.

Excellent beaches of pale sand fringe the elongated Jandía Peninsula in the south of Fuerteventura. A string of *urbanizaciones* (apartment complexes) now takes up much of the peninsula's sheltered east coast (Sotavento).

Costa Calma, a burgeoning cluster of modern complexes, offers the most interesting beaches with long stretches of fine sand interrupted by low cliffs and coves. **Morro Jable**, a fishing village now swamped by new developments, lies at the southern end of a vast, glittering strand. Beyond Morro Jable, the access road dwindles away into a potholed track leading towards the lonely lighthouse at Punta de Jandía.

Expanses of deserted sand, accessible only by four-wheel drive vehicle, line the westerly, windward coast (Barlovento) – too exposed for all but the hardiest beach lovers. Some of the island's best subtropical marine life can be found in this area, however, making it popular with skin divers.

From 1938 to the early 1960s, Jandía belonged to a German entrepreneur and was out of bounds to locals. Even today, rumours of spies, submarines and secret Nazi bases still circulate.

Betancuria ⓴

Las Palmas. 740. C/ Juan de Bethancourt 6, 928 87 80 92. San Buenaventura (14 Jul), Romería de La Peña (3rd Sat of Sep).

Inland, rugged peaks of extinct volcanoes, separated by wide plains, present a scene of austere grandeur. Scattered, stark villages and obsolete windmills occupy the lowlands, which are occasionally fertile enough to nurture a few crops or palm trees. Beyond, devoid of vegetation, the hills form stark outlines. From a distance they appear brown and grey, but up close the rocks glow with an astonishing range of mauves, pinks and ochres. The richness of colour in this interior wilderness is at its most striking at sunset, when a leisurely drive can reveal some breathtaking scenes.

The gilded interior of the Iglesia Santa María in Betancuria

Betancuria, built in a valley surrounded by mountains in the centre of the island, is named after Jean de Béthencourt, Fuerteventura's 15th-century conqueror, who moved his capital inland to thwart pirates. Nestling in the mountains, this peaceful oasis is now the island's prettiest village. The **Iglesia de Santa María** contains gilded altars, decorated beams and sacred relics. The **Museo Arqueológico** houses many local artifacts.

Environs

To the south, the village of **Pájara** boasts a 17th-century church with a curiously decorated doorway. Its design of serpents and strange beasts is believed to be of Aztec influence. Inside, the twin aisles both contain statues: one of a radiant Madonna and Child in white and silver, the other a Virgen de los Dolores in black.

La Oliva, to the north, was the site of the Spanish military headquarters until the 19th century. The Casa de los Coroneles (House of the Colonels) is a faded yellow mansion with a grand façade and hundreds of windows. Inside it has coffered ceilings. The fortified church and the arts centre displaying works of Canary Islands artists are also worth a visit.

Museo Arqueológico
Calle Roberto Roldán. ***Tel*** *928 87 82 41. Tue–Sat.*

Caleta de Fuste 21

Las Palmas. 1,600. *Calle Juan Ramón Soto Morales 10, El Castillo, 928 16 32 86.* *Sat.* *Día del Carmen (16 Jul), Nuestra Señora de Antigua (8 Sep).*

South of Puerto del Rosario about halfway down the eastern coast, lies Caleta de Fuste. The attractive low-rise, self-catering holiday centres surround a horseshoe bay of soft, gently shelving sand. The largest complex, El Castillo, takes its name from an 18th-century watchtower situated by the harbour.

There are many water sports facilities, including diving and windsurfing schools, as well as the Pueblo Majorero, an attractive "village" of shops and restaurants around a central plaza near the beach. These features make Caleta de Fuste one of Fuerteventura's most relaxed and pleasant resorts.

Fishing boats on a beach on the Isla de Lobos, near Corralejo

Puerto del Rosario 22

Las Palmas. *16,500.* *Avenida de la Constitución 5, 928 53 08 44.* *El Rosario (7 Oct).* www.fuerteventuraturismo.com

Fuerteventura's administrative capital was founded in 1797. Originally known as Puerto de Cabras (Goats' Harbour), after a nearby gorge that was once used for watering goats, it was rechristened to smarten up its image in 1957. The only large port on Fuerteventura, Puerto del Rosario is the base for inter-island ferries and a busy fishing industry. The town is also enlivened by the presence of the Spanish Foreign Legion, which occupies large barracks here.

THE GUANCHES

When Europeans first arrived in the Canary Islands in the late 14th century, they discovered a tall, white-skinned race, who lived in caves and later in small settlements around the edges of barren lava fields. Guanche was the name of one tribe on Tenerife, but it came to be used as the European name for all the indigenous tribes on the islands, and it is the one that has remained. The origins of the Guanches are still unclear, but it is probable that they arrived on the islands in the 1st or 2nd century BC from Berber North Africa. Within 100 years of European arrival the Guanches had been subdued and virtually exterminated by the ruthless conquistadors. Very few traces of their culture remain today.

Reminders *of the Guanches can be seen in many places in the Canaries. Specimens of their mummified dead, as well as baskets and stone and bone artifacts, are on display in several museums and there are statues of chiefs in Candelaria* (see p535) *on Tenerife.*

Guanche bowl for preparing *gofio (see p537)*

A Guanche basket

Corralejo 23

Las Palmas. *7,200.* *Avenida Marítima 2, 928 86 62 35.* *Mon & Fri.* *Día del Carmen (16 Jul).*

This much-expanded fishing village is now (together with the Jandía Peninsula) one of the island's two most important resorts. Its main attraction is a belt of glorious sand dunes stretching to the south, resembling the Sahara in places, and protected as a nature reserve. This designation arrived too late, however, to prevent the construction of two obtrusive hotels right on the beach.

The rest of the resort, mostly consisting of apartments and hotels, spills out from the town centre. The port area is lively, with busy fish restaurants and an efficient 40-minute ferry service to Lanzarote.

Offshore is the tiny Isla de los Lobos, named after the once abundant monk seals *(lobos marinos)*. Today, scuba divers, snorkellers, sport fishers and surfers claim the clear waters. Glass-bottomed cruise boats take less adventurous excursionists to the island for barbecues and swimming trips.

Lanzarote

The easternmost and fourth largest of the Canary Islands is virtually treeless and relies on desalination plants for some of its water. Yet many visitors consider Lanzarote the most attractive of all the islands for the vivid shapes and contrasting colours of its volcanic landscapes. Despite low rainfall, carefully tended crops flourish in its black volcanic soil. Locals pride themselves on the way their island has been preserved from the worst effects of tourism; there are no garish billboards, overhead cables or high-rise buildings. Its present-day image owes much to the artist César Manrique. Touring the spectacular volcanic Timanfaya National Park is a favourite trip.

Wind turbines harnessing Lanzarote's winds for power

Playa Blanca ㉔

Las Palmas. 4,500. *Calle Limones s/n, 928 51 81 50. Nuestra Señora del Carmen (16 Jul).* **www**.turismolanzarote.com

The fishing village origins of this resort are readily apparent around its harbour. Although it has expanded in recent years, Playa Blanca remains an agreeably family-oriented place with some character. It has plenty of cafés and restaurants, shops and bars, and several large hotels. However, the buildings are well dispersed and the resort is rarely noisy at night. Visitors converge here not for nightlife or contrived entertainment, but for relaxing beach holidays. There are one or two good stretches of sand near to the town, but the most enticing lie hidden around the rocky headlands to the east, where the clear, warm sea laps into rocky coves, and clothes seem superfluous. **Playa Papagayo** is the best known of these, but a diligent search will probably gain you one all to yourself. A four-wheel drive vehicle is advisable to negotiate the narrow, unsurfaced roads which lead to these beaches.

Las Coloradas beach near Playa Blanca in southern Lanzarote

Parque Nacional de Timanfaya ㉕

Las Palmas Yaiza. *Ctra LZ–67, km 11.5, Mancha Blanca, 928 84 08 39. daily.*

From 1730–36, a series of volcanic eruptions took place on Lanzarote. Eleven villages were buried in lava, which eventually spread over 200 sq km (77 sq miles) of Lanzarote's most fertile land. Miraculously, no one was killed, though many islanders emigrated.

Today, the volcanoes that once devastated Lanzarote provide one of its most lucrative and enigmatic attractions, aptly known as the **Montañas del Fuego** (Fire Mountains). They are part of the Parque Nacional de Timanfaya, established in 1974 to protect a fascinating and important geological record. The entrance to the park lies just north of the small village of Yaiza. Here you can pause and take a 15-minute camel ride up the volcanic slopes for wonderful views across the park. Afterwards, you pay the entrance fee and drive through haunting scenery of dark, barren lava cinders topped by brooding red-black

CÉSAR MANRIQUE (1919–92)

Local hero César Manrique trained as a painter, and spent time in mainland Spain and New York before returning to Lanzarote in 1968. He campaigned for traditional and environmentally friendly development on the island for the remaining part of his life, setting strict building height limits and colour requirements. Dozens of tourist sites throughout the Canaries benefited from his talents and enthusiasm.

César Manrique in 1992

For hotels and restaurants in this region see pp599–601 and pp651–3

Camel rides from Yaiza across the Montañas de Fuego

volcano cones. Finally, you will reach **Islote de Hilario**. You can park at El Diablo panoramic restaurant. From here, buses take visitors for exhilarating 30 minute tours of the desolate, lunar-like landscapes.

Afterwards, back at Islote de Hilario, guides will provide graphic demonstrations that this volcano is not extinct but only dormant brushwood pushed into a crevice bursts instantly into a ball of flame, while water poured into a sunken pipe shoots out in a scorching jet of steam.

The road from Yaiza to the coast leads to the **Salinas de Janubio** where salt is extracted from the sea. At **Los Hervideros** the rough coast can create spectacular seas and further north, at **El Golfo**, is an eerie emerald-coloured lagoon.

Puerto del Carmen 26

Las Palmas. 13,700. Avenida de la Playa, 928 51 35 51. *Nuestra Señora del Carmen (16 Jul).* **www**.turismolanzarote.com

More than 60 per cent of Lanzarote's tourists stay in this resort, which stretches several kilometres along the seafront. The coastal road carves its way through a solid slab of holiday infrastructure, which is pleasantly designed and unoppressive, and offers easy access to a long golden beach, Playa Blanca, which in places is very wide. Another beach nearby is Playa de los Pocillos. The original village lies west of the port, away from the hustle and bustle of the resort, and 11 km (7 miles) south is **Museo de Cetáceos de Canarias** (Canarian Whale and Dolphin Museum), the first museum in Spain dedicated to these species.

Fishing boat in Arrecife port

Arrecife 27

Las Palmas. *46,900.* *Blas Cabrera Felipe, 928 81 17 62.* *San Ginés (25 Aug).*

Arrecife, with its modern buildings and lively streets, is the commercial and administrative centre of the island. Despite its modern trappings, the capital retains much of its old charm, with palm-lined promenades, a fine beach and two small forts. **Castillo San Gabriel** holds seasonal exhibitions, with access via a stone walkway over the sea, crossing the Puente de Bolas. The 18th-century **Castillo de San José** is now a museum of contemporary art and was renovated by César Manrique. One of his paintings is on display here.

Castillo San Gabriel
Puerto de Naos. *Mon–Sat.* *public hols.*

Castillo de San José
Puerto de Naos. ***Tel*** *928 81 23 21.* *daily.* *1 Jan, 25 Dec.*

Costa Teguise 28

10 km (6 miles) north of Arrecife. *Avda Islas Canarias, Junto Pueblo Marinero, 928 59 25 42.*

This resort, largely financed by a mining conglomerate, has transformed the arid, low-lying terrain north of Arrecife into an extensive cluster of timeshare accommodation, leisure clubs and luxury hotels. The contrast between old town Teguise, Lanzarote's former capital, and the exclusive Costa Teguise is striking. Fake greenery and suburban lamps line boulevards amid barren ashlands. White villas line a series of small sandy beaches. The high level of investment has succeeded in attracting jet-set clientele. King Juan Carlos also has a villa here.

Umbrellas on the beach, Puerto del Carmen

Iglesia de San Miguel on the main square in Teguise

Teguise ㉙

Las Palmas. 12,300. Plaza de la Constitución, 928 84 53 98. Sun. *Día del Carmen (16 Jul), Las Nieves (5 Aug).*

Teguise, the island's capital until 1852, is a well-kept, old-fashioned town with wide, cobbled streets and patrician houses grouped around the **Iglesia de San Miguel**. The best time to visit is on a Sunday, when there is a lively handicrafts market and folk dancing. Just outside Teguise, the castle of Santa Bárbara contains the **Museo de la Piratería**, which tells the story of the pirates who passed through here.

Environs

To see more of inland Lanzarote, follow the central road south of Teguise, through the strange farmland of **La Geria**. Black volcanic ash has been scooped into protective, crescent-shaped pits which trap moisture to enable vines and other crops to flourish. **Mozaga**, one of the main villages in the area, is a major centre of wine production. On the roadside near Mozaga is the *Monumento al Campesino*, Manrique's *(see p548)* striking modern sculpture dedicated to Lanzarote's farmers.

Halfway between Teguise and Arrecife is the **Fundación César Manrique**. The fascinating former home of the artist incorporates five lava caves. It contains some of his own work and his collection of contemporary art.

Museo de la Piratería
Montaña de Guanapay. *Tel 686 47 03 76.* *daily.*

Fundación César Manrique
Taro de Tahíche. *Tel 928 84 31 38.* *daily.* *1 Jan.*

Haría ㉚

Las Palmas. 4,000. *Plaza de la Constitución 1, 928 83 52 51.* *Sat.* *San Juan (24 Jun).*

Palm trees and white, cube-shaped houses distinguish this picturesque village. It acts as a gateway to excursions round the northern tip of the island. The road to the north gives memorable views over exposed cliffs, and the 609-m (2,000-ft) high Monte Corona.

Environs

From Manrique's **Mirador del Río** you can see La Graciosa, and the northernmost of the Canary Islands, Alegranza. **Orzola** is a delightful fishing village providing fish lunches as well as boat trips to La Graciosa. To the south are the Mala prickly pear plantations, where cochineal (crimson dye) is extracted from the insects which feed on the plants. Nearby is the **Jardín de Cactus**, a well-stocked cactus garden, which has a smart restaurant, again designed by Manrique.

Mirador del Río
Haría. *Tel 928 52 65 48.* *daily.*

Jardín de Cactus
Guatiza. *Tel 928 52 93 97.* *daily.*

Landscaped pool on top of the caves of Jameos del Agua

Jameos del Agua ㉛

Las Palmas. *Tel 928 84 80 20.* *daily.*

An eruption of the Monte Corona volcano formed the Jameos del Agua lava caves on Lanzarote's northeast coast. In 1965–8, these were landscaped by César Manrique into an imaginative subterranean complex containing a restaurant, nightclub, a swimming pool edged by palm trees, and gardens of oleander and cacti. Steps lead to a shallow seawater lagoon where a rare species of blind white crab, unique to Lanzarote, glows softly in the dim light. An exhibition on volcanology and Canarian flora and fauna also deserves a look. Folk-dancing evenings are regularly held in this unusual setting.

Environs

Another popular attraction is the nearby **Cueva de los Verdes**, a tube of solidifed lava stretching 6 km (4 miles) underground. Guided tours of the caves are available.

Cueva de los Verdes
Haría. *Tel 928 84 84 84.* *daily.*

Volcanic ash swept into crescent-shaped pits for farming, La Geria

For hotels and restaurants in this region see pp599–601 and pp651–3

Volcanic Islands

The volcanic activity which formed the Canary Islands has created a variety of scenery, from distinctive lava formations to enormous volcanoes crowned by huge, gaping craters. The islands are all at different stages in their evolution. Tenerife, Lanzarote, El Hierro and La Palma are still volcanically active; dramatic displays of flames and steam can be seen in Lanzarote's Montañas de Fuego *(see p548)*. The last eruption was on La Palma in 1971.

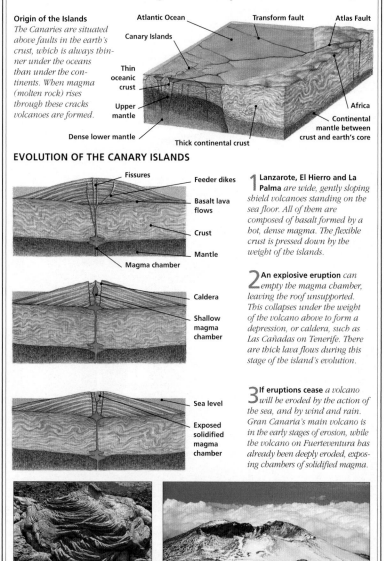

Origin of the Islands
The Canaries are situated above faults in the earth's crust, which is always thinner under the oceans than under the continents. When magma (molten rock) rises through these cracks volcanoes are formed.

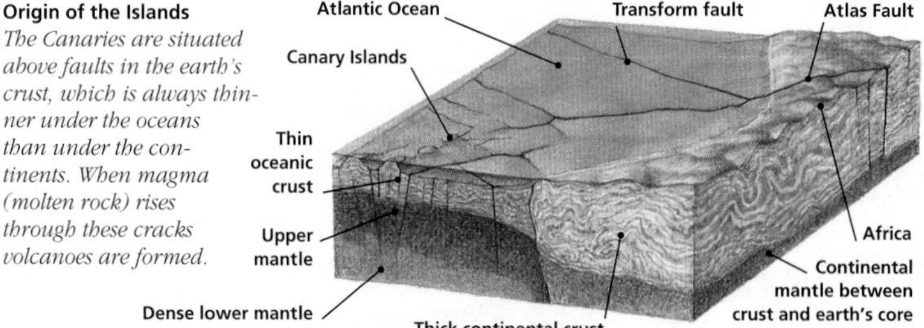

EVOLUTION OF THE CANARY ISLANDS

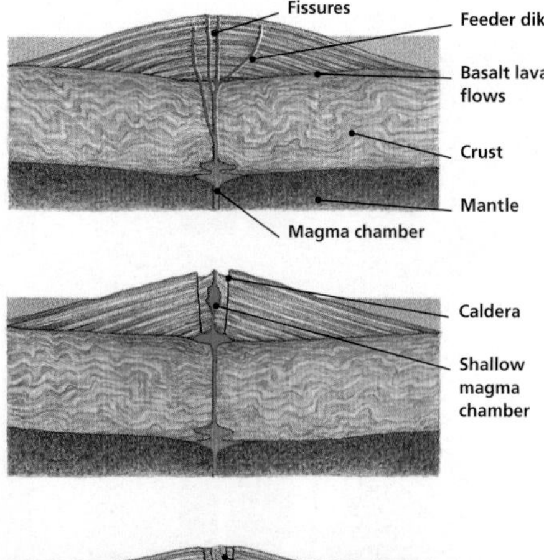

1 **Lanzarote, El Hierro and La Palma** *are wide, gently sloping shield volcanoes standing on the sea floor. All of them are composed of basalt formed by a hot, dense magma. The flexible crust is pressed down by the weight of the islands.*

2 **An explosive eruption** *can empty the magma chamber, leaving the roof unsupported. This collapses under the weight of the volcano above to form a depression, or caldera, such as Las Cañadas on Tenerife. There are thick lava flows during this stage of the island's evolution.*

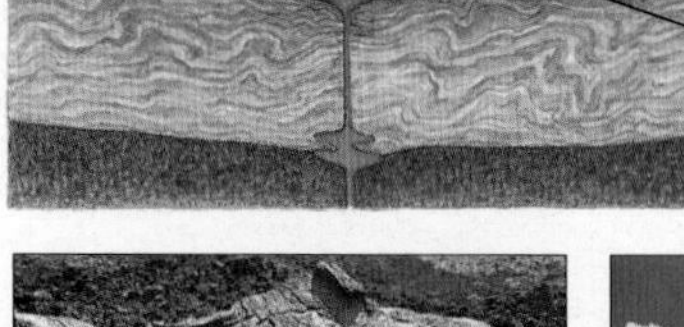

3 **If eruptions cease** *a volcano will be eroded by the action of the sea, and by wind and rain. Gran Canaria's main volcano is in the early stages of erosion, while the volcano on Fuerteventura has already been deeply eroded, exposing chambers of solidified magma.*

Rope lava near La Restinga, El Hierro

Pico Viejo crater, next to Mount Teide, Tenerife *(see p538)*

RESTAURANTE
Hegar
RESTAURANTE

TRAVELLERS' NEEDS

WHERE TO STAY

Medieval castles turned into luxury hotels and mansions converted into youth hostels typify the variety of places to stay in Spain. The tourists who sustain Spain's economy have almost 10,000 establishments to choose from, offering over one and a half million beds. Suites in once-royal palaces are at the top of the scale. Then there are luxury beach hotels on the Costa del Sol and in the Balearic and the Canary Islands. Visitors can also stay on remote farms, or in villas and old houses let for self-catering. For budget travel there are pensions, family-run *casas rurales* and guest houses, camp sites, and refuges with stunning views for mountaineers. Some of the best hotels in all these categories and in every style and price range are listed on pages 560–601.

Logo for a luxury five-star hotel

Hotel de la Reconquista, Oviedo, an 18th-century mansion *(see p563)*

HOTEL GRADING AND FACILITIES

Spain's hotels are classified into categories and awarded stars by the country's regional tourist authorities. Hotels (indicated by an H on a blue plaque near the door) are awarded from one to five stars. Hostals (Hs) and pensions (P) offer fewer comforts but are cheaper than hotels.

Spain's star-rating system reflects the number and range of facilities available – whether the hotel has a gym, for instance, or a lift – rather than the quality of service. Most hotels have air-conditioning.

Most hotels have restaurants that are open to non-residents. Although hotel-residencias (HR) and hostal-residencias (HsR) do not have dining rooms, some serve breakfast. Among Spain's largest hotel chains are **Grupo Sol Meliá, Grupo Riu** and **NH**. Many tour operators book rooms in Spain's larger hotel groups.

PARADORS

Paradors are government-run hotels, classified from three to five stars. Spain's first parador opened in the Sierra de Gredos in 1928 *(see p584)*; there is now a wide network of them on the mainland and the Canary Islands. Most, and certainly the most historic, are located in the centre and the north of the mainland. The best are in former royal hunting lodges, monasteries, castles and other monuments; some modern paradors have been purpose-built, often in spectacular scenery or in towns of historic interest *(see pp558–9)*.

A parador is not necessarily the best hotel in town, but it can be counted on to deliver a high level of comfort. Each parador is furnished in its own individual style, and the bedrooms are usually spacious and comfortable.

If you plan to tour in high season or to stay in the smaller paradors, it is wise to reserve a room. The paradors may be booked through the **Central de Reservas** in Madrid or through their London agent, **Keytel International**.

PRICES

Spanish law requires all hotels to display their prices behind reception and in every room. As a rule, the higher a hotel's star-rating, the more you pay. Rates for a double room can be as little as €30–35 a night for a one-star hostal; a five-star hotel will cost more than €250 a night, but a room price higher than €300 a night is exceptional, especially outside Madrid or Barcelona.

Prices usually vary according to room, region and season. A suite or a room with a view, a balcony or other special feature, may cost more than average. Rural and suburban hotels tend to be less expensive than those in the city centre. All the prices given on pages 560–601 are based on mid-season or high-season rates. High season covers July and

A parador within a modern extension of a medieval castle

◁ ***Madrileños* enjoying afternoon sunshine, drinks and conversation in the Plaza Mayor**

August, but in some areas it runs from April to October and in the Canary Islands the winter is high season.

Many of Spain's city hotels charge especially inflated rates for their rooms during major fiestas – such as the April Fair in Seville *(see p431)*, Los Sanfermines in Pamplona *(see p132)*, Carnival in Santa Cruz de Tenerife *(see p536)* and Easter Week *(see p38)* – and major trade fairs.

Most hotels quote prices per room and meal prices per person without including VAT *(IVA)*, which is 8 per cent on the mainland, and 5 per cent in the Canary Islands.

The glass-domed foyer of the Westin Palace, Madrid *(see p581)*

BOOKING AND CHECK-IN

Off-season in rural or small towns you are unlikely to need to book ahead; but if you plan to travel in high season, you should reserve a room by phone, e-mail or through a travel agent. You will need to reserve if you want a special room: one with a double bed (twin beds are the norm); on the ground floor; away from a noisy main road; or a room with a view.

The resort hotels often close from autumn to spring. Before you travel, it is always advisable to check that your preferred hotels will be open at that time of year.

You will normally be asked for your credit card details when you book a hotel room. A deposit of 20–25 per cent may be requested if you book during a peak period or for a stay of more than a few nights. Send it by credit card or giro in Spain and by credit card or banker's draft from outside the country. If you have to cancel, do so at least a week before the booking date or you may lose all or some of the deposit.

Most hotels will honour a booking only until 8pm unless business is poor. If you are delayed, call the hotel to assure them you are coming and to tell them when to expect you.

When you check in you will be asked for your passport or identity card to comply with Spanish police regulations. It will normally be returned to you promptly as soon as your details have been copied.

You are expected to check out of your room by noon on the last day of your stay, or to pay for another night.

PAYING

Unless otherwise indicated, the hotels in this guide accept credit cards. In some large, busy hotels you may be asked for an authorization hold on your credit card until you check out. Make sure this is cancelled when you pay your bill.

Personal cheques are not accepted in Spanish hotels, even if backed by a cheque guarantee card or drawn on a Spanish bank. Many people pay cash and in some cheap hotels this may be the only payment accepted.

Tipping hotel staff such as porters and cleaners is left to the discretion of the guests.

View of the pretty beach from a Lanzarote hotel

CASAS RURALES

The owners of some country houses (*casas rurales*) accept a few visitors, usually in high season. They are most numerous in Asturias, Navarra, Aragón and Catalonia (where they are called *cases de pagès*). They are becoming common in Galicia and Cantabria (where they are called *casonas*), and in Andalusia.

Casas rurales range from manor houses to small, isolated farms. Some offer bed and breakfast; some an evening meal or full board. Some are self-catering. Do not expect hotel service or lots of facilities. You may, however, be given a friendly welcome and good home cooking, all at an affordable price. You can book *casas rurales* directly or through regional associations, such as **RAAR** in Andalusia, **Ruralia** in Asturias, **Turismo Verde** in Huesca, Aragón, **Ruralverd** in Catalonia and **AGATUR (Asociación Gallega de Turismo Rural)** in Galicia.

El Nacimiento, Turre, a charming Andalusian *casa rural* (see p596)

SELF-CATERING

Villas and holiday flats let by the week are plentiful along the Spanish coasts, and on the rise in the cities. In scenic areas of the countryside there are many *casas rurales* (farm and village houses) for rent by the day. For information about the *casas rurales*, contact their regional organizations *(see p555)*. They also take bookings. **Villas 4 You** is a UK organization that acts as an agent for owners of holiday houses and flats in Spain, as does **International Lodging Corporation** in the US. Other organizations and owners of holiday homes advertise in the travel sections of UK Sunday newspapers. Tour operators offer a range of self-catering accommodation.

The prices for self-catering accommodation vary according to the location, the property and the season. A four-person villa with a pool can cost under €300 for a week if it is inland and €1,000 a week or more if it is on the coast.

An apartment hotel (known as a *villa turística* in Andalusia) is another option. Half hotel, half holiday flat, it gives guests a choice between self-catering (all rooms have a kitchen) or eating in the hotel restaurant. Holiday villages are similar, often catering for specialist interests. One example is the village of Ainsa, in the mountain sports region of Aragón *(see p574)*, which offers a mix of camping and hostel accommodation, with restaurants and bars.

Typical holiday villas in Lanzarote's Puerto del Carmen, the Canary Islands

YOUTH HOSTELS AND MOUNTAIN REFUGES

To use the network of *albergues juveniles* (youth hostels) in Spain you need to show a YHA (Youth Hostel Association) card from your country or an international card, which you can buy from any hostel. Prices per person for bed and breakfast are lower than hotel prices.

Youth hostels can be booked directly or via the **Red Española de Albergues Juveniles** (Spanish Network of Youth Hostels). Despite the name, there is no age limit.

Mountaineers heading for the more remote areas may use the *refugios* (refuges). These are shelters with a dormitory, cooking facilities and heating. Some are huts with about six bunks; others are mountain houses with up to 50 beds.

The *refugios* are marked on large-scale maps of mountain areas and national parks and administered by the regional mountaineering associations. The **Federación Española de Deportes de Montaña y Escalada (FEDME)** and the local tourist offices will supply their addresses.

La Oliva Monastery, Navarra *(see p130)*, welcomes paying guests

MONASTERIES AND CONVENTS

If you have a taste for peace and austerity you may enjoy a night in one of Spain's 150 religious houses where guests are welcome. Most belong to the Benedictine and the Cistercian orders. Room prices are inexpensive. They are not hotels, however; you have to book ahead by writing or by phone; and few have private telephones or television. The guests may be asked to tidy their rooms, observe the same strict mealtimes as the monks or nuns and to help with the washing up. Some convents admit only women and some monasteries only men.

Youth hostel in rustic style on the edge of Cazorla nature reserve, Jaén

CAMP SITES

There are nearly 1,200 camp sites in Spain. Most of them are on the coasts, but there are also some outside the major cities, in the most popular areas of countryside and in mountain areas. Most sites have electricity and running water; some also have launderettes, playgrounds, restaurants, shops, a swimming pool and other amenities.

It is sensible to carry a camping carnet with you. This can be used instead of a passport to check in at sites and it covers you for third-party insurance. Carnets are issued in the UK by the AA, RAC and **The Camping and Caravanning Club**.

Every year, the *Guía Oficial de Campings* is published by Turespaña. Information about camp sites is available from the **Federación Española de Empresarios de Campings y Ciudades de Vacaciones** (Spanish Camp Site and Holiday Camp Federation). In Spain, camping is only permitted on official sites.

Sign for a camp site

DISABLED TRAVELLERS

Hotel managers will advise on access for people in wheelchairs, and the staff will help, but few hotels are well equipped for disabled guests, although some of the youth hostels are. **COCEMFE** (the Confederación Coordinadora Estatal de Minusválidos Físicos de España) runs a hotel in Madrid for disabled people's groups. COCEMFE and Viajes 2000 *(see p665)* advise on hotels for guests with special needs. Accessible holidays can be booked through **Disabled Access Holidays**, which has a list of accommodation on the Spanish coast and islands, including resorts and self-catering apartments.

View from the Cabina Verónica mountain refuge, Picos de Europa

FURTHER INFORMATION

Every spring, Turespaña publishes the *Guía Oficial de Hoteles*, which is sold in Spanish bookshops and newsstands and can be consulted in Spanish tourist offices. It lists every pension, hostal and hotel in Spain and gives their star-rating, their prices and a resumé of their facilities.

Each *comunidad autónoma* distributes a list of the hotels and other accommodation in its area via the tourist offices.

DIRECTORY

HOTEL CHAINS

Grupo Riu
Tel 902 40 05 02.
Fax 971 74 38 98.
www.riu.com

Grupo Sol-Meliá
Tel 902 14 44 40.
Fax 91 579 13 92.
www.solmelia.com

NH-Hoteles
Tel 902 57 03 68.
www.nh-hotels.com

PARADORS

Central de Reservas
Calle Requena 3,
28013 Madrid.
Tel 902 54 79 79.
Fax 902 52 54 32.
www.parador.es

Keytel International
The Foundry,
156 Blackfriars Road,
London SE1 8EN.
Tel 020 7953 3020 in UK.
www.keytel.co.uk

SELF-CATERING AND BED AND BREAKFAST

AGATUR (Asociación Gallega de Turismo Rural)
Recinto Ferial, Apdo 26, Silleda, 36540 Pontevedra. *Tel 986 57 70 00.* www.agatur.org

International Lodging Corporation
Tel 212 228 5900 in USA.
www.ilcweb.com

RAAR
Sagunto 8, 04004 Almería. *Tel 902 44 22 33.* www.raar.es

Ruralia
C/ Marques de Canillejas 4, Bajo, 33500 Llanes (Asturias). *Tel 902 10 70 70.* www.ruralia.com

Ruralverd
C/ del Pí 11, Principal 3,
08002 Barcelona.
Tel 93 304 37 74.
Fax 93 481 42 09.
www.ruralverd.es

Turismo Verde
C/ Miguel Servet 12,
22002 Huesca.
Tel 902 29 41 41.
www.turismoverde.es

Villas 4 You
PO Box 1310,
Maidstone ME14 9QH.
Tel 0800 096 3439.
www.villas4you.co.uk

YOUTH HOSTELS

Red Española de Albergues Juveniles
Tel 915 22 70 07.
www.reaj.com

MOUNTAIN REFUGES

FEDME
C/ Floridablanca 84, 08015 Barcelona. *Tel 93 426 42 67.* www.fedme.es

CAMPING

The Camping and Caravanning Club
Tel 0845 130 7633 in UK.

Federación de Empresarios de Campings
C/ Valderibas 48, 1° C,
28007 Madrid.
Tel 91 448 12 34.
Tel 91 448 12 67.
www.fedcamping.com

DISABLED TRAVELLERS

COCEMFE
C/ Luis Cabrera 63,
28002 Madrid.
Tel 91 744 36 00.
www.cocemfe.es

Disabled Access Holidays
www.disabledaccess.com

FURTHER INFORMATION

Spanish Tourist Office
Tel 0800 1010 5050 in UK. www.spain.info
Tel 212 265 8822 in US.
www.spain.info

Spain's Best: Paradors

Parador is an old Spanish word for a lodging place for travellers of respectable rank. In the late 1920s a national network of state-run hotels called paradors was established. Many of the 90 or so paradors are converted castles, palaces or monasteries, although some have been purpose-built in strategic tourist locations. They are generally well signposted and the prices are comparable with other luxury hotels. All offer a high degree of comfort and service, and have restaurants which offer regional cuisine.

Hotel de los Reyes Católicos, *one of the sights of Santiago de Compostela* (see p90), *may be the world's oldest hotel. It was founded as a hospital in 1499* (see p562).

Parador de León *is housed in the Hostal San Marcos, one of Spain's finest Renaissance buildings* (see p25). *The main hall has a magnificent coffered ceiling* (see p584).

Parador de Guadalupe is a 16th-century former hospice for pilgrims. It stands beside a famous monastery in Extremadura *(see p589).*

Parador de Arcos de la Frontera *is situated in one of the archetypal* pueblos blancos *(white towns). Its wide, semicircular terrace offers panoramic views of the Moorish castle, the Guadalete river and the rolling farmland beyond* (see p592).

Parador de Granada *is a captivating 15th-century convent built in the beautiful gardens of the Alhambra at the instruction of the Catholic Monarchs. Antique Spanish furniture fills the halls and rooms of this atmospheric parador, and an old roofless chapel forms a patio. Advance booking is essential* (see p594).

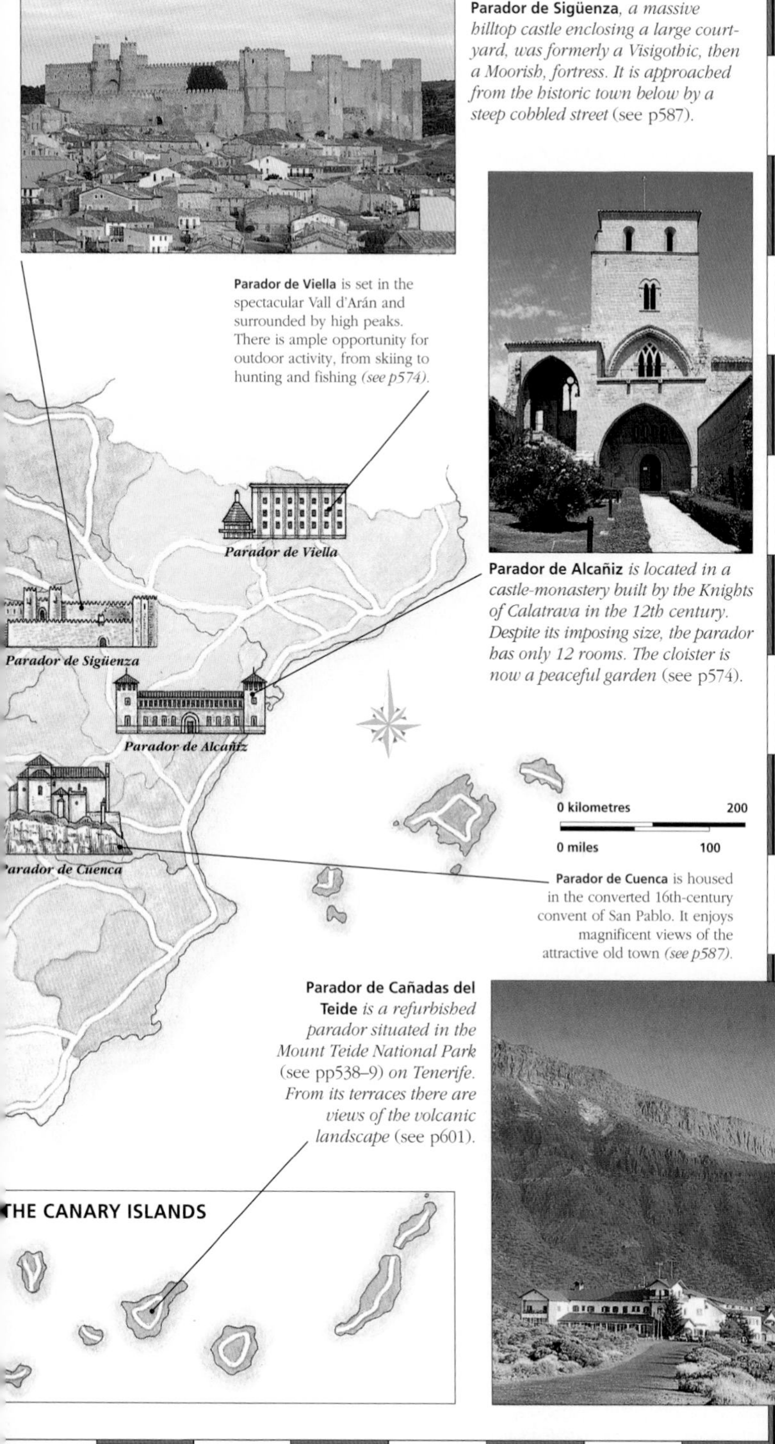

Parador de Sigüenza, *a massive hilltop castle enclosing a large courtyard, was formerly a Visigothic, then a Moorish, fortress. It is approached from the historic town below by a steep cobbled street* (see p587).

Parador de Viella is set in the spectacular Vall d'Arán and surrounded by high peaks. There is ample opportunity for outdoor activity, from skiing to hunting and fishing *(see p574).*

Parador de Alcañiz *is located in a castle-monastery built by the Knights of Calatrava in the 12th century. Despite its imposing size, the parador has only 12 rooms. The cloister is now a peaceful garden* (see p574).

Parador de Cuenca is housed in the converted 16th-century convent of San Pablo. It enjoys magnificent views of the attractive old town *(see p587).*

Parador de Cañadas del Teide *is a refurbished parador situated in the Mount Teide National Park* (see pp538–9) *on Tenerife. From its terraces there are views of the volcanic landscape* (see p601).

Choosing a Hotel

The hotels in this guide have been selected across a wide price range for excellent facilities and location. Many also have a highly recommended restaurant. The chart lists hotels by region, starting in the north and moving to the south. For more details on restaurants *see pages 608–653.*

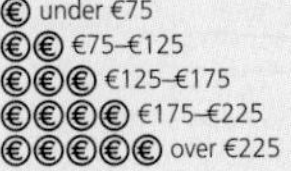

PRICE CATEGORIES
Standard double room per night, with tax and service charge included.

€ under €75
€€ €75–€125
€€€ €125–€175
€€€€ €175–€225
€€€€€ over €225

GALICIA

A CORUÑA Ciudad de la Coruña €€

Paseo Adormideras s/n, 15002 ***Tel*** *902 93 24 24* ***Fax*** *981 22 46 10* ***Rooms*** *130*

Situated in the residential district of Adormideras, close to San Amaro beach, this hotel offers views of A Coruña bay. It has spacious bedrooms, meeting rooms, a gym and Jacuzzi. It also provides indoor and outdoor parking. The Torremar restaurant specializes in lobster and seafood. Check the website for offers. **www.hotelciudaddelacoruna.com**

A GUARDA Convento San Benito €€

Plaza de San Benito, 36780 (Pontevedra) ***Tel*** *986 61 11 66* ***Fax*** *986 61 15 17* ***Rooms*** *24*

A converted 16th-century convent, where the nuns' cells, surrounding a small cloister with a palm tree and a stone fountain, have been transformed into bedrooms for the guests. Two rooms have their own sitting rooms; there is also a suite. **www.hotelsanbenito.es**

BAIONA Parador de Baiona €€€€€

Castillo Monterreal, 36300 (Pontevedra) ***Tel*** *986 35 50 00* ***Fax*** *986 35 50 76* ***Rooms*** *120*

This parador, built in an old Galician *pazo* (manor house) style, is located within the walls of Monterreal Castle *(see p96)*. The restaurant serves seafood accompanied by the local Ribeiro wine. Some rooms have four-poster beds and offer sea views, while others look out onto the gardens. Free Wi-Fi available. **www.parador.es**

BARREIROS Casa do Merlo €€

C/ Sargendez 4, 27793 (Lugo) ***Tel*** *982 13 49 06* ***Fax*** *982 13 49 07* ***Rooms*** *10*

A walled 17th-century country *pazo* in a small coastal village. The decoration is reminiscent of English colonial style, and the rooms are bright; some have sea views. Breakfast is served in a winter garden. There is also an inner patio, a library and a games room. Free Wi-Fi available. Closed 30 Dec–15 Jan. **www.casadomerlo.com**

BENTRACES Pazo Bentraces €€

Ctra 540, Celanova km 7/ Bentraces, Barbadás, 32890 (Ourense) ***Tel*** *988 38 33 81* ***Fax*** *988 38 33 81* ***Rooms*** *7*

This 15th-century *pazo*, a short way southwest of Ourense city, was transformed into a palace by an aristocratic Portuguese family. It has since been refurbished, keeping the original features of wood and marble and part of the family's furniture. Closed 22 Dec–mid-Feb. **www.pazodebentraces.com**

CAMBADOS Parador de Cambados €€€€

Paseo de la Calzada, 36630 (Pontevedra) ***Tel*** *986 54 22 50* ***Fax*** *986 54 20 68* ***Rooms*** *57*

Sited in the middle of the Rías Baixas coast, this parador occupies a handsome *pazo* built around a large courtyard garden, surrounding a fountain where drinks are served. Within easy reach of beaches and pleasant walks. Galician specialities and local wines (Cambados is a production centre) served in the restaurant. Free Wi-Fi. **www.parador.es**

CERVO Casa do Mudo €€

Senra 25, 27891 (Lugo) ***Tel*** *982 55 76 89* ***Rooms*** *6*

This charming country house provides a cosy retreat from which to explore the Galician coast. Lovely gardens surround the rustic stone building. Some rooms have sloping wood-beamed ceilings with skylights. Bicycles are available to guests, and horse riding activities can also be arranged. **www.casadomudo.com**

CORNIDE Casa Grande de Cornide €€

Teo, 15886 (A Coruña) ***Tel*** *981 89 30 44* ***Fax*** *981 96 42 48* ***Rooms*** *12*

A welcoming bed-and-breakfast hotel in a renovated house, 10 minutes by car from Santiago de Compostela. It is beautifully decorated with antiques and has a library and a garden with two traditional *hórreos* (granaries), an old magnolia and an 18th-century dovecote. International wines. Free Wi-Fi. **www.casasgrandedecornide.com**

LUGO Hotel Monumento Pazo de Orbán €€

Travesía do Miño, 6, 27001 (Lugo) ***Tel*** *982 24 02 17* ***Fax*** *382 24 56 45* ***Rooms*** *12*

In Galician, *pazo* means a stately house – an appropriate name for this noble building which is elegantly carved with 18th-century stonework. Every room is decorated with original furnishings, which adds to the old-world feel of this charming small hotel. **www.pazodeorban.es**

Key to Symbols *see back cover flap*

MIÑO Casa Grande Fontao €€€

Lugar de Fontao 1A, 15639 (A Coruña) **Tel** *981 78 27 72* **Fax** *981 78 27 17* **Rooms** *7*

A traditional Galician stone and whitewashed country house built in the 17th century with a bay window that overlooks the garden and fields. The interior is welcoming and warm. The bedrooms are decorated in white with traditional furniture and have comfortable beds. Breakfast and Wi-Fi are included. **www.casagrandefontao.com**

NOGUEIRA DE RAMUÍN Monasterio de Santo Estevo €€€€

Monasterio de Santo Estevo, 32164 (Ourense) **Tel** *988 01 01 10* **Fax** *988 01 01 11* **Rooms** *80*

Housed in the ancient monastery by the river Sil, this parador offers a splendid opportunity to wander the cloisters, eat dinner next to a forest of chestnut trees or ease into a four-poster bed after a hike along ancient pathways. The Santo Estevo provides a luxurious experience, complete with spa. Closed 4 Jan–mid-Feb. **www.parador.es**

NOIA Pesqueria del Tambre €€

Central del Tambre, Santa Maria de Roo, 15211 (A Coruña) **Tel** *981 76 94 25* **Fax** *981 76 96 05* **Rooms** *16*

On the bank of Río Tambre, and surrounded by a forest, this is a place to get lost in nature. The main building was a hydroelectric plant built in the early 20th century. The bedrooms, elegantly restored and decorated using traditional fabrics, are in a group of houses near the river. Free Wi-Fi. Closed Nov–Mar. **www.pesqueriadeltambre.com**

O GROVE Gran Hotel de la Toja €€€€€

Isla de la Toja, 36991 (Pontevedra) **Tel** *986 73 00 25* **Fax** *986 73 00 26* **Rooms** *104*

This majestic hotel, built at the turn of the 19th century, stands on its own small island planted with palm and pine trees, and is reached from the mainland by a bridge. It has a ballroom and a piano bar, and offers lovely sea views with good beaches nearby. It also has a spa. Free Wi-Fi available. **www.granhotellatoja.com**

O SAVIÑAO Torre Vilariño €

Lugar de Vilariño 47, Fión, 27548 (Lugo) **Tel** *982 45 22 60* **Fax** *982 45 22 60* **Rooms** *9*

A 18th-century inn converted into a hotel offering bed and breakfast, mainly to tourists following Galicia's "Romanesque Route". The owners serve home-made food and wine. The large garden is populated by peacocks, pheasants and geese. Bicycles are available for touring. Closed 4–30 Nov. **www.torrevilarino.com**

OURENSE Hotel Irixo €

Hermanos Villar, 15, 32005 (Ourense) **Tel** *988 25 46 20* **Fax** *988 25 46 20* **Rooms** *13*

A renovated palace houses this atmospheric hotel in the heart of the old city of Ourense. It is just a short walk to the cathedral and other cultural and historic highlights of the city. Some rooms have views of the beautiful Plaza do Eironciño dos Cabaleiros. Free Wi-Fi available. **www.hotelirixo.es**

POBRA DE TRIVES Casa Grande de Trives €

C/ Marqués de Trives 17, 32780 (Ourense) **Tel** *988 33 20 66* **Fax** *988 33 20 66* **Rooms** *9*

A *posada* (small hotel) in a 17th-century stone manor, with a coat of arms on its central tower, in the hills of eastern Galicia. Antiques and old paintings decorate the cosy interior. There is a chapel with a magnificent reredos. Also has three sitting rooms and a garden in which to relax. Serves breakfast only. **www.casagrandetrives.com**

PONTEVEDRA Parador de Pontevedra €€€

Rua del Barón 19, 36002 **Tel** *986 85 58 00* **Fax** *986 85 21 95* **Rooms** *45*

A parador in a 16th–18th-century Renaissance palace, which was once a school, granary, masonic lodge and an aristocratic residence. The decor incorporates antiques, gilt mirrors, chandeliers and tapestries. Some rooms are in a modern wing. The restaurant specializes in seafood of the Rías Baixas. **www.parador.es**

RIBADEO Casa Doñano €€€

Vilela (Cubelas), 27714 (Lugo) **Tel** *982 13 74 29* **Fax** *982 77 71 39* **Rooms** *9*

This country house, built in 1907, has since been converted into a cosy hotel surrounded by its own land. The library, which offers fine views from its windows, has telescopes for star gazing. Two rooms have double beds. One room is suitable for disabled guests. Breakfast included. Free Wi-Fi available. **www.casadonano.com**

RIBADUMIA Pazo Carrasqueira €€

C/ Carrasqueira, 36638 (Pontevedra) **Tel** *986 71 00 32* **Fax** *986 71 00 32* **Rooms** *9*

A thick-walled, 18th-century country mansion, with a stone staircase outside and a coat of arms set into its façade. All bedrooms have heating and TV. Seafood and Albariño wine (produced on the estate) are served in the dining room – the price includes lunch or dinner. Also has a laundry service, a library and Wi-Fi. **www.pazocarrasqueira.com**

SAN PEDRO DE VIANA Pazo As Casas €

Chantada, 27513 (Lugo) **Tel** *982 44 05 53* **Rooms** *11*

A restored 17th-century house north of Ourense, eclectically decorated with original heavy furniture of dark wood and exposed stone. It has a pleasant terrace for relaxing in the summer. All the bedrooms are distinctly styled with brilliant white and have baths, TV and heating. The salon doubles as a library. **www.pazoascasas.com**

SANTIAGO DE COMPOSTELA As Artes €€

Trav de Dos Puertas 2, 15707 (A Coruña) **Tel** *981 57 25 90* **Fax** *981 577 823* **Rooms** *7*

Each room in this comfortable small hotel, close to the cathedral, is dedicated to one of the arts: theatre, sculpture, dance, architecture, painting, music or cinema. The place is decorated with flair, and has parquet floors and wrought-iron beds. A small cafeteria offers breakfast. Hospitable and friendly owners. Free Wi-Fi. **www.asartes.com**

SANTIAGO DE COMPOSTELA Pazo Cibrán €€

San Xulian de Sales, Vedra, 15885 (A Coruña) ***Tel*** *981 51 15 15* ***Fax*** *981 81 47 66* ***Rooms*** *11*

This noble house, with its own chapel, is situated in a very peaceful hamlet a short way from Santiago de Compostela. It has belonged to the same family since the 18th century and has been lovingly restored. Lunch is not served, but the breakfast is particularly good. Wi-Fi is available. **www.pazocibran.com**

SANTIAGO DE COMPOSTELA Hotel Monumento San Francisco €€€€

Campillo de San Francisco, 3, 15705 (A Coruña) ***Tel*** *981 58 16 34* ***Fax*** *981 57 19 16* ***Rooms*** *62*

The San Francisco convent has been welcoming pilgrims since 1214, when it was built next to the Monte Pedroso. Now, modern visitors can experience the tranquil charms of the ancient courtyard or the rooms with beautiful views over the old city or the patio. It also has a heated, indoor swimming pool. **www.sanfranciscohm.com**

SANTIAGO DE COMPOSTELA Parador Hostal de los Reyes Católicos €€€€€

Praza do Obradoiro 1, 15705 (A Coruña) ***Tel*** *981 58 22 00* ***Fax*** *981 56 30 94* ***Rooms*** *137*

Built under the Catholic monarchs as a hostel for poor pilgrims, this luxurious 16th-century parador, on the same square as Santiago de Compostela's famous cathedral, is one of the world's grandest hotels. It is built around four arcaded courtyards. The public rooms have regal touches such as hanging tapestries. Free Wi-Fi. **www.parador.es**

TUI Parador de Tui €€€

Av de Portugal, 36700 (Pontevedra) ***Tel*** *986 60 03 00* ***Fax*** *986 60 21 63* ***Rooms*** *32*

This pretty parador is a perfect replica of a traditional Galician *pazo* combining granite with chestnut beams. The rooms have superb views of the town and across the Río Miño, which forms the frontier with Portugal. It has a lovely garden. Dishes on the menu include *arroz con bogavante* (rice with lobster). Free Wi-Fi. **www.parador.es**

VIGO AC Palacio Universal €€

Cánovas del Castillo, 28, 36202 (Pontevedra) ***Tel*** *986 44 92 50* ***Fax*** *986 44 92 51* ***Rooms*** *70*

The AC Palacio Universal is a beautiful and imposing four-star hotel a stone's throw away from the historic city centre. Built in the the late 19th century, it used to be the favourite meeting point of the town's bourgeoisie and political elite. Today, it is run by one of Spain's biggest hotel chains. **www.ac-hotels.com**

VILAGARCIA DE AROUSA Pazo O'Rial €€€

C/ El Rial 1, 36600 (Pontevedra) ***Tel*** *986 50 70 11* ***Fax*** *986 50 16 76* ***Rooms*** *60*

A beautiful 17th-century manor with a tower, tiled floors, stone walls and arches, just outside Vilagarcía de Arousa and a walk away from the seashore. It is stylishly decorated with fine furnishings and comfortable armchairs, and has its own chapel. There are four lounges, one with a massive old fireplace. Free Wi-Fi. **www.pazorial.com**

VILALBA Parador de Vilalba €€€

Valeriano Valdesuso, 27800 (Lugo) ***Tel*** *982 51 00 11* ***Fax*** *982 51 00 90* ***Rooms*** *48*

Six rooms of this hotel are found in a medieval octagonal tower, built between the 11th and 13th centuries and restored in the 15th century. Other rooms and the bar and restaurant are in a modern stone building beside it. The castle preserves its moat and portcullis. Facilities include a gym, sauna, Turkish bath and free Wi-Fi. **www.parador.es**

ASTURIAS AND CANTABRIA

CAMALEÑO El Jisu €

Ctra Potes–Fuente Dé km 8, 39570 (Cantabria) ***Tel*** *942 73 30 38* ***Fax*** *942 73 03 15* ***Rooms*** *9*

A modern, purpose-built chalet hotel in the heart of the Picos de Europa *(see p108–9)*. It stands in its own grounds in the Liébana Valley, close to Liébana monastery. El Jisu enjoys great mountain views and makes a good base for walking or exploring the Picos by car. The sitting rooms have rustic furniture. Closed 20 Dec–Feb. **www.eljisu.com**

CANGAS DE ONIS Aultre Naray €€

Peruyes, 33457 (Asturias) ***Tel*** *985 84 08 08* ***Fax*** *985 84 08 48* ***Rooms*** *11*

This country hotel, in a renovated 19th-century Asturian house, has superb views of the mountains of the Sierra de Escapa and the Picos de Europa from the first-floor bedrooms. The second floor has cosy attic rooms. The sitting room has a warm atmosphere and big windows. Also has a library with a fireplace and a bar. **www.aultrenaray.com**

CANGAS DE ONIS Parador de Cangas de Onis €€€

Villanueva (km 2 from Cangas), 33550 (Asturias) ***Tel*** *985 84 94 02* ***Fax*** *985 84 95 20* ***Rooms*** *64*

A restored 12th-century Benedictine monastery with magnificent cloisters, located on the bank of the Río Sellar just outside the town of Cangas de Onis. The rooms are spacious and comfortable, and the restaurant serves regional dishes. Includes facilities such as meeting rooms. Free Wi-Fi. **www.parador.es**

CARAVIA El Babú €€

Carrales, 33343 (Asturias) ***Tel*** *985 85 32 72* ***Fax*** *985 85 32 73* ***Rooms*** *7*

A small and intimate hotel in a 19th-century country house, decorated in modern style. Rooms have mountain or garden views: the cosiest ones are in the attic. A filling breakfast is served. The hotel has grounds to walk around and is close to the seaside and Ribadesella. Also has a bar and elevator chair. Closed 7 Jan–14 Mar. **www.elbabu.com**

Key to Price Guide *see p560* **Key to Symbols** *see back cover flap*

COMILLAS Hostal Esmeralda €€

C/ Antonio López 7, 39520 (Cantabria) **Tel** *942 72 00 97* **Fax** *942 72 09 82* **Rooms** *12*

This simple and traditional *hostal* is situated in a beautiful townhouse dating back to 1874, with exterior glass and wooden galleries. Rooms are basic but comfortable, and all come complete with security boxes. The restaurant serves local cuisine and has a cosy fireplace. Wi-Fi is available. **www.hostalesmeralda.com**

COVADONGA Gran Hotel Pelayo €€

Real Sitio de Covadonga s/n, 33589 (Asturias) **Tel** *985 84 60 61* **Fax** *985 84 60 54* **Rooms** *43*

Located near the church, this elegant and classically furnished hotel is ideally placed for excursions into the Picos de Europa or the historic town centre of Covadonga. All the rooms have beautiful views of the Cavadonga Basílica, the Santa Cueva (Sacred Cave) or the Picos de Europa mountains. Closed 10 Jan–mid-Feb. **www.arceahoteles.com**

ESCALANTE (CANTABRIA) San Román de Escalante €€€€

Ctra Escalante–Castillo km 2, 39795 (Cantabria) **Tel** *942 67 77 45* **Fax** *942 67 76 43* **Rooms** *16*

A Relais et Châteaux hotel in an exquisitely decorated 17th-century manor house overlooking trees and meadows. All the rooms are different, and one of them has a terrace. A pool, horse riding, golf, and massage and beauty treatments are also available. The restaurant has an impressive wine list. Wi-Fi available. **www.sanromandeescalante.com**

FIGUERAS DEL MAR Palacete Peñalba €€€

C/ Granda, Figueras del Mar, 33794 (Asturias) **Tel** *985 63 61 25* **Fax** *985 63 62 47* **Rooms** *20*

Made up of two beautiful Art Nouveau mansions, the Palacete Cotalerelo and the Palacete Granada, this hotel is near the Ria de Eo. The Granada is a magnificent fantasy, with a façade of oval windows and two curved staircases to the front door. Inside it has much of its original furniture. **www.hotelpalacetepenalba.com**

FUENTE DÉ (CANTABRIA) Parador de Fuente Dé €€€

Ctra Fuente Dé, a 3.5 km de Espinama, 39588 (Cantabria) **Tel** *942 73 66 51* **Fax** *942 73 66 54* **Rooms** *78*

This modern parador stands in an unbeatably dramatic location in the rock amphitheatre of Fuente Dé, at the foot of the Picos de Europa cable car. It has pleasant bedrooms and long galleries with huge windows. There is only one road in and out, so it is peaceful. This hotel makes an ideal base for walking. Closed 20 Dec–4 Feb. **www.parador.es**

GIJÓN La Casona de Jovellanos €€

Plazuela de Jovellanos 1, 33201 (Asturias) **Tel** *985 34 20 24* **Fax** *985 35 61 51* **Rooms** *13*

A small hotel in an 18th-century building overlooking a little square in the old part of the city, near San Lorenzo beach. One of its two dining rooms incorporates the remains of the old city wall which was discovered during restoration work. A five-person aparthotel is also available. **www.lacasonadejovellanos.com**

GIJÓN Parador de Gijón €€€

Parque de Isabel la Católica, 33204 (Asturias) **Tel** *985 37 05 11* **Fax** *985 37 02 33* **Rooms** *40*

A modern parador in the grounds of an 18th-century watermill, located in a corner of what has been described as one of Spain's prettiest parks. The old watercourse in the grounds has been preserved. The speciality of the restaurant is the regional stew, *fabada Asturiana*, but choice seafood is also served. **www.parador.es**

LLANES La Posada de Babel €€€

La Pereda, 33509 (Asturias) **Tel** *985 40 25 25* **Fax** *985 40 26 22* **Rooms** *13*

The spectacular Picos de Europa peaks lie behind this small, family-run hotel. It is partly modern, but has huge, traditional fireplaces, and one bedroom is a converted *hórreo* (granary). It has a modern suite in the garden. Also has a small library and a bar. Closed 8 Dec–end Mar. **www.laposadadebabel.com**

OVIEDO Room Mate Marcos €€

Caveda 23, 33002 (Asturias) **Tel** *985 22 72 72* **Fax** *985 22 80 18* **Rooms** *47*

This modern hotel near the town centre has some funky decor, with rooms decked out in stripy wallpaper and monochrome furnishings. Services such as free internet access, newspapers and the friendly, helpful staff make this one of the most pleasant hotels in the centre of Oviedo. **www.room-matehotels.com**

OVIEDO Hotel de la Reconquista €€€€

C/ Gil de Jaz 16, 33004 (Asturias) **Tel** *985 24 11 00* **Fax** *985 24 60 11* **Rooms** *142*

A luxury hotel in a magnificent 18th-century building, originally an orphanage, with a massive stone coat of arms above the main entrance. Its name commemorates the Reconquest of Spain, which was launched from Asturias. The public rooms are arranged around several courtyards. **www.hoteldelareconquista.com**

PRAVIA Casona del Busto €€

Plaza del Rey Don Silo 1, 33120 (Asturias) **Tel** *985 82 27 71* **Fax** *985 82 27 72* **Rooms** *30*

In a town 10 km (6 miles) from the beaches of the Asturian coast is this hotel in a typical 16th-century Asturian house where the Spanish writer Jovellanos spent his summers. The bedrooms overlook a central patio. The hotel is decorated with period pieces. An Asturian breakfast buffet is served. **www.casonadelbusto.es**

PRELLEZO Hotel Valle de Arco €€

Barrio de Prellezo, Arco 26, 39548 (Cantabria) **Tel** *942 71 15 65* **Fax** *942 71 16 64* **Rooms** *24*

In an exceptional seaside location and just a short drive from the beautiful village of San Vicente de la Barquera, this hotel is ideal for relaxation. It is housed in a beautiful country house and decorated in simple but elegant style. **www.hotelvalledearco.com**

QUIJAS Casona Torre de Quijas €€

Barrio Vinueva 76, 39590 (Cantabria) ***Tel*** *942 82 06 45* ***Fax*** *942 83 82 55* ***Rooms*** *22*

This hotel is in a restored, 19th-century stone house near Santillana del Mar. It has bay windows and a large garden, and is decorated with Art Nouveau furniture. There are some attic rooms, a sitting room with a library and two rooms have disabled access. The restaurant offers light dinners. Closed 15 Dec–mid-Feb. **www.casonatorredequijas.com**

QUIJAS Hostería de Quijas €€

Barrio Vinueva, 39590 (Cantabria) ***Tel*** *942 82 08 33* ***Fax*** *942 83 80 50* ***Rooms*** *20*

A family-run hotel in an 18th-century stone-built mansion on the Santander–Oviedo road, close to Santillana del Mar and the Altamira caves. It has bay windows, timbered ceilings and a garden. Six of the rooms are suites. The menu is strong on seafood, and breakfast can be served outdoors. Closed 20 Dec–15 Jan. **www.hosteriadequijas.com**

RIBADEDEVA Mirador de la Franca €€

Playa de la Franca, 33590 (Asturias) ***Tel*** *985 41 21 45* ***Fax*** *985 41 21 53* ***Rooms*** *61*

A beach hotel, popular with families, with spacious sitting areas, a tennis court and great views from the lounge and restaurant. The waters of the bay are safe for water sports and fishing. Close to the Picos de Europa, with direct access to the beach. Closed Nov–Feb (except first week Dec). **www.arceahoteles.com**

RIBADESELLA Gran Hotel del Sella €€€€

Ricardo Cangas 17, 33560 (Asturias) ***Tel*** *985 86 01 50* ***Fax*** *985 85 74 49* ***Rooms*** *81*

The former summer palace of the Marquis of Argüelles is dwarfed by the modern hotel wing, but it still lends this family-run beach hotel some class. It is sited at the mouth of the Río Sella, on Santa Marina beach, and has vast gardens and a series of thermal pools. The restaurant specializes in seafood. Closed Jan–mid-Mar. **www.granhoteldelsella.com**

SAN VICENTE DE TORANZO Posada del Pas €€

Ctra N623 Burgos–Santander, 39699 (Cantabria) ***Tel*** *942 59 44 11* ***Fax*** *942 59 43 86* ***Rooms*** *30*

An 18th-century stone mountain house standing in a green valley beside the Santander–Burgos road, which is used as a stopover by travellers arriving or departing on the ferry between Plymouth and Santander. The restaurant specializes in regional Cantabrian dishes. There is a private garage. **www.hotelposadadelpas.com**

SANTANDER Hotel Chiqui €€€€

Avenida García Lago 9, 39005 (Cantabria) ***Tel*** *902 28 27 00* ***Fax*** *902 27 30 32* ***Rooms*** *161*

This hotel has an unbeatable location, right on the Sardinero beach in Santander. Every room has sea views and many have spacious terraces. The hotel is tastefully decorated and has a spa, while the restaurant serves modern cuisine and offers a wide selection of wines. **www.hotelchiqui.com**

SANTANDER Hotel Real €€€€€

Paseo Pérez Galdós 28, 39005 (Cantabria) ***Tel*** *942 27 25 50* ***Fax*** *942 27 45 73* ***Rooms*** *123*

An elegant, formal hotel visible on the city's highest hill. It was built in the early 20th century for nobility accompanying the royal family on holiday. Its chandeliers and moulded plaster still testify to its status. The balconies offer spectacular views of the bay, especially those on the top floor. The hotel has its own spa. **www.hotelreal.es**

SANTILLANA DEL MAR Altamira €€

C/ Cantón 1, 39330 (Cantabria) ***Tel*** *942 81 80 25* ***Fax*** *942 84 01 36* ***Rooms*** *32*

A town-centre hotel in a restored 16th-century palace very close to the Romanesque church of La Colegiata. The old wooden staircase leads to bedrooms with beams and polished floors, two of them with private sitting rooms. Also well located for the visitor centre of the famous caves after which the hotel is named. **www.hotelaltamira.com**

SANTILLANA DEL MAR Los Infantes €€

Avda Le Dorat 1, 39330 (Cantabria) ***Tel*** *942 81 81 00* ***Fax*** *942 84 01 03* ***Rooms*** *36*

A 17th-century country mansion comprising three buildings houses this hotel that was formerly the residence of the Calderons family. It is set slightly back from the road. The massive beams, stone floors, carved chests and leather armchairs in the lobby give it an old-fashioned feel. Closed 24–31 Dec. **www.hotel-santillana.com**

SANTILLANA DEL MAR Parador Gil Blas €€€€

Plaza Ramón Pelayo 11, 39330 (Cantabria) ***Tel*** *942 02 80 28* ***Fax*** *942 81 83 91* ***Rooms*** *28*

This stone mansion, begun in the 15th century, blends perfectly into the unspoiled medieval town, which is busy with tourists during the day but quiet at night. The building has a pretty patio. Inside bare walls and tiled floors enhance the medieval atmosphere. Rooms are spacious and tastefully decorated. **www.parador.es**

SUESA La Casona de Suesa €€

La Pola 5, 39150 (Cantabria) ***Tel*** *942 50 40 63* ***Rooms*** *10*

In a mountain village close to some of Cantabria's best beaches is this small hotel in an old country manor. En suite rooms feature stone walls, wooden floors and beams, and are spacious and cosy. Meals are available at the weekend or if arranged in advance. Families can stay in a separate apartment in the grounds. **www.lacasonadesuesa.com**

TARAMUNDI La Rectoral €€€

Taramundi, 33775 (Asturias) ***Tel*** *985 64 67 60* ***Fax*** *985 64 67 77* ***Rooms*** *18*

An 18th-century former priest's house, built of stone and timber with a slate roof, deep in the Asturian countryside. It has been tastefully converted into a quiet and atmospheric hotel. All the bedrooms have mountain views. An alternative to the main house are some cottages with room service. Closed Dec. **www.larectoral.com**

Key to Price Guide *see p560* **Key to Symbols** *see back cover flap*

VALLE DE RUESGA Hotel Torre de Ruesga €€

Barrio de la Bárcena s/n, 39815 (Cantabria) **Tel** 942 64 10 60 **Rooms** 15

Surrounded by well-tended gardens, this rural hotel is in a peaceful spot on the Asón River. Housed in a palace built in 1610, it features stone arches, wooden beams and frescoes painted by León Criach, while guestrooms are spacious and elegant. The excellent restaurant serves both local and international dishes. **www.hoteltorrederuesga.com**

VILLACARRIEDO Palacio Soñanes €€

Barrio Camino 1, 39640 (Cantabria) **Tel** 942 59 06 00 **Fax** 942 59 06 14 **Rooms** 30

An imposing 18th-century Baroque palace of golden stone that dominates this quiet rural town. Inside, it has a superb Renaissance main staircase. The bedrooms are very comfortable, all different, and decorated in a rich variety of colours. The verdant Valle de la Pas is a good area for gentle walking. **www.abbapalaciodesonaneshotel.com**

THE BASQUE COUNTRY, NAVARRA AND LA RIOJA

ANGUIANO Abadía de Valvanera €€

Monasterio de Valvanera, Hospital Viejo, 26323 (La Rioja) **Tel** 941 37 70 44 **Fax** 941 37 71 94 **Rooms** 28

This old Benedictine abbey with simple rooms offers no-frills accommodation, good food and lots of history. Queen Isabel I stayed in the cells here in 1482. It is located in the beautiful surroundings of one of Spain's least-known range of hills, the Sierra de la Demanda. Closed 22 Dec–10 Jan. **www.abadiavalvanera.com**

ARGÓMANIZ Parador de Argómaniz €€€

Ctra N-1 Madrid-Irún km 363, 01192 (Alava) **Tel** 945 29 32 00 **Fax** 945 29 32 87 **Rooms** 53

Sited in a splendid 17th-century Renaisance stone palace, complete with coat of arms, this parador is located on the slopes of Mount Zabalgaña, just outside Vitoria. It is a peaceful spot with good views. The common areas are spacious, and rooms are modern and tastefully decorated. Basque cuisine is served in the dining room. **www.parador.es**

ARNEDILLO Hospedería Las Pedrolas €€

Plaza Felix Merino 16, 26589 (La Rioja) **Tel** 941 39 44 01 **Fax** 941 39 44 04 **Rooms** 7

An 18th-century whitewashed town house with a coat of arms set into the façade. It has been restored and decorated simply but elegantly. There is an inner patio with a fountain and flowers. The bedrooms are spacious and comfortable. The only noise to disturb you will be the bells of the Gothic church next door. **www.laspedrolas.com**

AXPE-ATXONDO Mendi Goikoa €€

Barrio de San Juan 33, 48291 (Vizcaya) **Tel** 946 82 08 33 **Fax** 946 82 11 36 **Rooms** 11

Ancient twin stone-built Basque farmhouses converted into a pleasant rural hotel and restaurant, in the peaceful Valle de Atxondo in the hills southeast of Durango. The hotel's slogan is "where you can hear the silence". Ideal for relaxing or taking gentle strolls. One of the rooms has a balcony. Closed Nov–Mar. **www.mendigoikoa.com**

BERUETE Peruskenea €€

Diseminado, Beruete (Basaburua Mayor), 31866 (Navarra) **Tel** 948 50 33 70 **Fax** 948 50 32 84 **Rooms** 9

An "enchanted house" in which all the bedrooms are named after local fairies or nature spirits. Peruskenea is located in the heart of the Beruete forest between Pamplona and San Sebastián, where there are walking trails to dolmens and craft workshops. The restaurant prepares deliciously creative dishes. **www.peruskenea.com**

BILBAO Iturrienea Ostatua €

Santa Maria 14, 48005 (Vicaya) **Tel** 944 16 15 00 **Fax** 944 15 89 29 **Rooms** 21

A small hotel occupying an old house in the lively old quarter of the city centre, the Casco Viejo – ideal for bar hopping. It is clean and welcoming, combining rustic decorations with some modern flourishes in its large bedrooms. Street-facing rooms, however, catch the noise from below. Breakfast included. **www.iturrieneaostatua.com**

BILBAO Ercilla €€

Ercilla 37–9, 48011 (Vicaya) **Tel** 944 70 57 00 **Fax** 944 43 93 35 **Rooms** 354

Bilbao's largest hotel, a modern tower block in the main business district, is close to the Plaza Moyüa. It is comfortable and bustling with life, and has an award-winning restaurant, the Bermeo. There is also a bar, a coffee shop and a nightclub. All rooms have wireless Internet. **www.ercillahoteles.com**

BILBAO Miró Hotel €€

Alameda Mazarredo 77, 48009 (Vicaya) **Tel** 946 61 18 80 **Fax** 944 25 51 82 **Rooms** 50

This glass-fronted boutique hotel designed by Antonio Miró is located between the Guggenheim and Fine Arts Museums. Facilities include a library, a gym and a spa. The bar, which hosts jazz or other live music some evenings, acts as a meeting point for art lovers. Free Wi-Fi available. **www.mirohotelbilbao.com**

BILBAO Carlton €€€€€

Plaza Federico Moyúa 2, 48009 (Vicaya) **Tel** 944 16 22 00 **Fax** 944 16 46 28 **Rooms** 142

This luxury hotel, with a domed stained-glass ceiling, is one of the landmarks of Bilbao. Built in 1919, it was formerly the seat of the Basque government. Kings, opera singers, poets and celebrities (including Einstein) have stayed here. Bedrooms are decorated in classical style. Check the website for good promotions. **www.aranzazu-hoteles.com**

BRIÑAS Hospedería Señorío de Briñas €€€

Travesía de la Calle Real 3, 26290 (La Rioja) ***Tel*** *941 30 42 24* ***Fax*** *941 30 43 45* ***Rooms*** *14*

This beautiful 18th-century palace near the wine town of Haro was used during the Spanish Civil War as barracks for Italian troops. It is decorated with antiques, frescoes and artworks. The bedrooms are spacious and colourful. The hotel also has a sauna, Jacuzzi and wellness centre. Closed 15 Dec–15 Jan. **www.hotelesconencantodelarioja.com**

CASALARREINA Hospedería Señorío de Casalarreina €€€

Plaza Sto Domingo de Guzmán 6, 26230 (La Rioja) ***Tel*** *941 32 47 30* ***Fax*** *941 32 47 31* ***Rooms*** *21*

This 16th-century Plateresque monastery retains old architectural elements. Innovative touches create a warm, elegant and cosy atmosphere. Bedrooms are big and well equipped, and all the bathrooms have hydromassage baths. Full breakfast included. Closed 31 Dec & 1 Jan. **www.alojamientosconencantodelarioja.com**

DONAMARIA Donamaria'ko Benta €€

Barrio Ventas 4, 31750 (Navarra) ***Tel*** *948 45 07 08* ***Fax*** *948 45 07 08* ***Rooms*** *5*

This is a small, family-run hotel with a pleasant atmosphere in a stone-built Pyrenean mountain house north of Pamplona. Close to the Señorio de Bertiz, this is a good base for walking. The antique-furnished rooms are in an annexe. Cookery courses are also held. Closed 10 Dec–4 Jan. **www.donamariako.com**

FITERO Gustavo Adolfo Bécquer €€

Baños de Fitero, Extramuros, 31593 (Navarra) ***Tel*** *948 77 61 00* ***Fax*** *948 77 62 25* ***Rooms*** *328*

On the site of the Roman baths south of Navarra, the hotel is named after the Spanish poet who supposedly recovered from ill health here in the 19th century and was inspired to write two poems. A thermal spring provides spa bathing, massage and a range of other treatments. Closed mid-Dec–Jan. **www. balneariodefitero.com**

HARO Los Agustinos €€€

C/ San Agustín 2, 26200 (La Rioja) ***Tel*** *941 31 13 08* ***Fax*** *941 30 31 48* ***Rooms*** *62*

A lounge in a vast, arched chamber hung with tapestries is a highlight of this hotel in a former Augustinian monastery. Another is the grand central patio in the old cloister. In the middle of La Rioja's main wine town, the in-house restaurant, Las Duelas, serves good Riojan dishes. Free Wi-Fi available. **www.hotellosagustinos.com**

HONDARRIBIA Hotel Obispo €€€

Plaza del Obispo s/n, 20280 (Guipúzcoa) ***Tel*** *943 64 54 00* ***Fax*** *943 64 23 86* ***Rooms*** *17*

In the old town of Hondarribia sits this elegant hotel in a 14th-century palace. From its wrought iron balconies, guests can enjoy views of the Bidasoa River, the medieval village and the beach. Rooms retain original features and are comfortably furnished. There is no restaurant but there are plenty nearby. Free Wi-Fi. **www.hotelobispo.com**

HONDARRIBIA Parador de Hondarribia €€€€€

Plaza de Armas 14, 20280 (Guipúzcoa) ***Tel*** *943 64 55 00* ***Fax*** *943 64 21 53* ***Rooms*** *36*

An elegant parador in a 10th-century restored fortress that occupies the highest point of this historic town. It has a beautiful inner patio incorporating a ruined part of the castle and a terrace overlooking the Bidasoa estuary. Weapons and other memorabilia of its colourful history adorn the walls of the public rooms. **www.parador.es**

LAGUARDIA Castillo El Collado €€€

Paseo El Collado 1, 01300 (Alava) ***Tel*** *945 62 12 00* ***Fax*** *945 60 08 78* ***Rooms*** *10*

In an unusual building with a Gothic tower reminiscent of a folly, the rooms of this small hotel offer views of the Sierra de Cantabria and the vineyards surrounding Laguardia. Bodega visiting is the biggest attraction, but it is well located also for Estella and other sights in southern Navarra. Closed 24, 25 & 31 Dec, 1 Jan. **www.hotelcollado.com**

LAGUARDIA Posada Mayor de Migueloa €€€

C/ Mayor 20, 01300 (Alava) ***Tel*** *945 62 11 75* ***Fax*** *945 62 10 22* ***Rooms*** *8*

Occupying the beautiful 17th-century Baroque Palacio de Viana, this hotel is in the pedestrianized old wine-making town of Laguardia. It has its own bodega, wine-therapy wellness treatments and massages, and one of the best restaurants of Northern Spain, offering both Basque and La Rioja cuisine. Free Wi-Fi. **www.mayordemigueloa.com**

LOGROÑO Hotel Marqués de Vallejo €€

Marqués de Vallejo, 8, 26001 (La Rioja) ***Tel*** *941 24 83 33* ***Fax*** *941 24 02 88* ***Rooms*** *50*

In the heart of Logroño's old town, this tastefully renovated hotel provides rooms and suites designed by the local interior design company Devota & Lomba. The result is one of the few chic and contemporary hotels in Logroño's centre. **www.hotelmarquesdevallejo.com**

MUNDAKA Atalaya €€

Itxaropena Kalea 1, 48360 (Vizcaya) ***Tel*** *946 17 70 00* ***Fax*** *946 87 68 99* ***Rooms*** *11*

This hotel, in a pretty early 20th-century English-inspired villa next to the fishing port, has small but pleasant bedrooms, large window galleries with views of the sea, a terrace and a sauna. A good area for strolling on the beach, surfing or lingering over lunch. Free Wi-Fi available. **www.atalayahotel.es**

MUNDAKA El Puerto €€

Portu Kalea 1, 48360 (Vizcaya) ***Tel*** *946 87 67 25* ***Fax*** *946 87 67 26* ***Rooms*** *12*

A fisherman's house in one of the prettiest towns on the Basque coast. Located at the mouth of the Genika estuary, which is renowned for its surfing beaches, the windows offer great views of the sea. Converted into a simple, cosy hotel it is decorated in contemporary style. It has a cafeteria and a bar. Pets welcome. **www.hotelelpuerto.com**

Key to Price Guide *see p560* **Key to Symbols** *see back cover flap*

OLITE Parador de Olite €€€€

Plaza de los Teobaldos 2, 31390 (Navarra) ***Tel*** *948 74 00 00* ***Fax*** *948 74 02 01* ***Rooms*** *43*

Occupying a wing of the 15th-century castle and palace of Carlos III, king of Navarra, this parador is decorated on a medieval theme with armour, tapestries, stained glass and wrought-iron lamp brackets. The most atmospheric (and pricey) rooms are in the old part of the castle; there are also some modern bedrooms. **www.parador.es**

PAMPLONA Palacio Guendulain €€€

Zapateria 53, 31001 (Navarra) ***Tel*** *948 22 55 22* ***Fax*** *948 22 55 32* ***Rooms*** *23*

In the centre of the old town of Pamplona, this luxurious hotel is set in a magnificent 18th-century palace visited by Queen Isabel II in 1845. The guestrooms and reception rooms are decorated with fine antiques and paintings, while a courtyard houses a collection of carriages. Excellent restaurant. **www.palacioguendulain.com**

PAMPLONA Hotel La Perla €€€€

Plaza del Castillo 1, 31001 (Navarra) ***Tel*** *948 22 30 00* ***Fax*** *948 22 23 24* ***Rooms*** *44*

This is a historic hotel in Pamplona which has been given a facelift but mantains its classic aspect. One of the best places to stay in the city centre. Some of the rooms conserve the original furnishings, giving a distinctly *fin de siècle* feel to the hotel. **www.granhotellaperla.com**

RONCESVALLES Hotel Roncesvalles €

Única s/n, 31650 (Navarra) ***Tel*** *948 76 01 05* ***Fax*** *948 76 01 05* ***Rooms*** *16*

At the starting point for many pilgrims on the Camino de Santiago, this 18th-century building has been transformed into a comfortable and modern hotel. The rooms are well equipped and the friendly staff can supply you with a bicycle to explore the surrounding area. There is a good restaurant a few steps away. **www.hotelroncesvalles.com**

SAN MILLAN DE LA COGOLLA Hostería del Monasterio de San Millán €€€

Monasterio de Yuso, 26326 (La Rioja) ***Tel*** *941 37 32 77* ***Fax*** *941 37 32 66* ***Rooms*** *25*

A hotel occupying a wing of the Monasterio de Yuso, which is inhabited by Augustinian friars. The bedrooms are soberly decorated and have thick walls to guarantee complete peace. Two of the rooms are suites. Best of all is the Royal Room, which has a balcony over the inner patio. Closed 7–31 Jan. **www.sanmillan.com**

SAN SEBASTIÁN La Galería €€€

Infanta Cristina 1–3, 20008 (Guipúzcoa) ***Tel*** *943 31 75 59* ***Fax*** *943 21 12 98* ***Rooms*** *23*

This late 19th-century French-style building is situated on Ondarreta beach and offers views of La Concha bay. The bedrooms are dedicated to famous painters such as Renoir, Picasso, Dalí, Miró and Regoyos, and contain replicas of their works. It has two charming attic rooms. Bicycles are available. **www.hotellagaleria.com**

SAN SEBASTIÁN Mercure Monte Igueldo €€€

Paseo del Faro 134, 20008 (Guipúzcoa) ***Tel*** *943 21 02 11* ***Fax*** *943 21 50 28* ***Rooms*** *125*

Superbly located on Monte Igueldo, one of the hills marking the end of La Concha bay, this Mercure chain hotel has panoramic views across the city and the bay. The restaurant, enjoying the same views, serves Basque *haute cuisine*. It also has a rooftop swimming pool. Next door is San Sebastian's amusement park. **www.monteigueldo.com**

SAN SEBASTIÁN Niza €€€

C/ Zubieta 56, 20007 (Guipúzcoa) ***Tel*** *943 42 66 63* ***Fax*** *943 44 12 51* ***Rooms*** *40*

Niza is a beautiful seafront hotel in *belle époque* style in the middle of La Concha beach, not far from the city centre. The bedrooms are warm and airy and 18 of them have sweeping views of the bay. All have Wi-Fi. The hotel has a bar and an Italian restaurant, La Pasta Gansa, on the beachfront. **www.hotelniza.com**

SAN SEBASTIÁN Abba de Londres y de Inglaterra €€€€

C/ Zubieta 2, 20007 (Guipúzcoa) ***Tel*** *943 44 07 70* ***Fax*** *943 44 04 91* ***Rooms*** *148*

This classical-style luxury hotel with grand public spaces within occupies a 19th-century palace on La Concha beach. It was transformed into a hotel in 1902. Twelve of the rooms are suites. The Mari Galant brasserie in the hotel serves buffet meals and offers a children's menu. Five salons double as meeting rooms. **www.hlondres.com**

SAN SEBASTIÁN María Cristina €€€€€

Paseo Republica Argentina 4, 20004 (Guipúzcoa) ***Tel*** *943 43 76 00* ***Fax*** *943 43 76 76* ***Rooms*** *136*

Built in 1912 and named after Queen Maria Cristina, this is a landmark of the city and one of the most historic hotels in Spain. It was designed by the architect of the London and Paris Ritz hotels and is decorated in *belle époque* style. It is also the venue of the San Sebastián film festival. **www.mariacristina.es**

SANTO DOMINGO DE LA CALZADA Parador de Santo Domingo €€€€

Plaza del Santo 3, 26250 (La Rioja) ***Tel*** *941 34 03 00* ***Fax*** *941 34 03 25* ***Rooms*** *61*

A hospital founded in the 12th century for pilgrims on the road to Santiago de Compostela, now converted into a parador. Next to Santo Domingo's cathedral, it has an imposing lounge divided by Gothic arches and a carved timber ceiling. The restaurant serves stuffed Piquillo peppers and has a good list of wines from La Rioja. **www.parador.es**

UDABE Venta Udabe €€

Udabe-Basaburua, 31869 (Navarra) ***Tel*** *948 50 31 05* ***Fax*** *948 50 34 00* ***Rooms*** *10*

Decorated in country style, this small hotel in a typical old Basque farmhouse stands in a unique natural setting at the heart of the Basaburua Valley, just off the Pamplona to San Sebastián motorway. The owners are hospitable and can organize "an infinity of activities" for their guests. Closed 24 Dec–24 Jan. **www.hotelventaudabe.com**

VERA DE BIDASOA Churrut €€€€

Plaza de los Fueros 2, 31780 (Navarra) ***Tel*** *948 62 55 40* ***Fax*** *948 62 55 41* ***Rooms*** *17*

A beautifully renovated family-run hotel in an 18th-century house. Downstairs there is a gallery with wicker armchairs and plants arranged beside a glass wall with relaxing views of the garden. The bedrooms are comfortable and homely. Churrut has a good restaurant and a small gym in the attic. The rooms include two suites. **www.hotelchurrut.com**

VITORIA General Álava €€€€

Av Gasteiz 79, 01009 (Alava) ***Tel*** *945 21 50 00* ***Fax*** *945 24 83 95* ***Rooms*** *114*

A modern hotel with comfortable bedrooms in a spectacular spot in the new town, near the Palacio de Congresos, making it suitable for business travellers. The restaurant serves regional dishes and avant-garde cuisine, with a daily changing menu. The buffet breakfast includes fruit salads and home-marinated salmon. **www.ac-hotels.com**

YESA Hospedería de Leyre €

Monasterio de Leyre, 31410 (Navarra) ***Tel*** *948 88 41 00* ***Fax*** *948 88 41 37* ***Rooms*** *32*

This hotel occupies part of an 11th-century Benedictine monastery, located beneath crags. Rooms are plain and clean, some overlooking the garden. The monastery can be busy by day but is quiet at night. Typical Navarran cuisine is served. Men can stay in the monastery by written request. Closed 10 Dec–1 Mar. **www.hotelhospederiadeleyre.com**

ZARAUTZ Karlos Arguiñano €€€€

C/ Mendilauta 13, 20800 (Guipúzcoa) ***Tel*** *943 13 00 00* ***Fax*** *943 13 34 50* ***Rooms*** *12*

A stone tower-cum-mansion on the beach of Zarautz, this is a restaurant-with-rooms owned by a celebrated TV chef. The bedrooms are decorated with antiques and traditional furniture; some have terraces and sea views. There are two restaurants: one traditional, one *haute cuisine*. Closed 20 Nov–1 Feb. **www.hotelka.com**

BARCELONA

OLD TOWN Downtown Paraiso €

C/ Junta de Comerç 13, 08001 ***Tel*** *93 302 61 34* ***Fax*** *93 302 61 34* ***Rooms*** *8* ***Map*** *2 F3*

Established by four former travellers in a renovated townhouse on a quiet street in the lively Raval area, this friendly *hostal* is a hit with young backpackers. Centrally located, there is no curfew and there is a range of rooms, with or without bathrooms. Wi-Fi access and a kitchen are available for guests' use. **www.downtownparaisohostel.com**

OLD TOWN Gat Raval €

C/ Joaquín Costa 44, 8001 ***Tel*** *93 481 66 70* ***Fax*** *93 342 66 97* ***Rooms*** *24* ***Map*** *2 F1*

The place to be if you want to be in the busy heart of the Raval. This simple, fun *hostal* is only a few metres away from the CCCB arts centre and a short stroll from the Ramblas. The funky decor and helpful staff make this a step up from other *hostales* in the area. **www.gatrooms.es**

OLD TOWN Banys Orientals €€

C/ Argentería 37, 8003 ***Tel*** *93 268 84 60* ***Fax*** *93 268 84 61* ***Rooms*** *43* ***Map*** *5 B3*

A chic and minimalist design and a fantastic location at a very reasonable price. The 18th-century exterior hides a renovated interior, complete with contemporary touches and furnishings. It lies in the centre of the old town, only 10 minutes away from the seaside. Large suites are available in a nearby building. **www.hotelbanysorientals.com**

OLD TOWN Gat Xino €€

C/ Hospital 149–155, 08001 ***Tel*** *93 324 88 33* ***Fax*** *93 324 88 34* ***Rooms*** *34* ***Map*** *2 E2*

This is the second *hostal* from the Gat Accommodation group, and it repeats the successful formula that has worked so well: simple, modern design and great prices. Its worth splashing out on the suite, which has its own private terrace. All rooms have free Wi-Fi. Family rooms are available. **www.gatrooms.es**

OLD TOWN Chic and Basic Tallers €€

C/ Tallers 82, 8001 ***Tel*** *93 302 51 83* ***Fax*** *93 302 10 96* ***Rooms*** *14* ***Map*** *2 F1*

The Chic and Basic accommodation stands up to is name, offering a contemporary, no-frills design with a lot of natural light. Each room has an iPod dock, and there is a lounge offering free coffee for guests as they chill out to the hotel's sound system. **www.chicandbasic.com**

OLD TOWN Chic and Basic Born €€€

C/ Princesa 50, 08003 ***Tel*** *93 295 46 52* ***Fax*** *93 295 46 53* ***Rooms*** *31* ***Map*** *5 C2*

This converted 19th-century townhouse is popular with visiting fashionistas. Rooms are a rather blinding white, with contemporary glass and steel bathrooms, but they are given a touch of kitsch glamour with colourful LED lighting. The White Bar is very hip. **www.chicandbasic.com**

OLD TOWN Hotel 54 Barceloneta €€€

Passeig Joan de Borbó 54, 08003 ***Tel*** *93 225 00 54* ***Fax*** *93 225 00 80* ***Rooms*** *22* ***Map*** *5 B5*

This hotel has simple, modern decor and rooms (which are a touch on the small side) and is located in the Barceloneta area, in front of Port Vell and close to the beach. The Gothic Quarter is only a 15-minute stroll away. Free Wi-Fi in all rooms and views over the marina and sea. **www.hotel54barceloneta.com**

Key to Price Guide *see p560* **Key to Symbols** *see back cover flap*

OLD TOWN Jazz Hotel €€€

Carrer Pelai 3, 08001 **Tel** *935 52 96 96* **Fax** *935 52 96 97* **Rooms** *108* **Map** *5 A1*

A glassy ultra-modern hotel, close to the Plaça de Catalunya, Jazz offers better facilities than its three-star rating would suggest. There is a small rooftop pool with sun deck, and the rooms (all soundproofed) are stylishly decorated with contemporary furniture and fabrics. **www.hoteljazz.com**

OLD TOWN Montecarlo €€€

La Rambla 124, 08002 **Tel** *934 12 04 04* **Fax** *933 18 73 23* **Rooms** *50* **Map** *5 A2*

This beautiful hotel right on Las Ramblas in the centre of Barcelona occupies a former 19th-century palace. The lobby is a gorgeous whirl of gilt and marble, while the rooms are smart and modern. Staff are particularly helpful here, and there are fantastic deals available on the website. **www.montecarlobcn.com**

OLD TOWN Hotel W €€€€

Plaça de la Rosa del Vents 1, 08039 **Tel** *932 95 28 00* **Fax** *931 81 50 00* **Rooms** *473*

Ricardo Bofill designed the huge sail-shaped Hotel W which now dominates Barcelona's seafront. The contemporary rooms have spectacular views from floor-to-ceiling windows, and there is a host of amenities for guests to enjoy, including an outdoor pool, a glossy spa and a selection of restaurants and bars. **www.w-barcelona.com**

OLD TOWN Park Hotel €€€€

Carrer de Marqués de l'Argentera 11, 08003 **Tel** *933 19 60 00* **Fax** *933 19 45 19* **Rooms** *91* **Map** *5 C3*

A rare gem of 1950s architecture, designed by Antonio Moragas in 1951 and well preserved by his son's award-winning renovations in 1990. The slim wraparound staircase is a highlight. Rooms are small but smartly furnished, and the best have balconies. **www.parkhotelbarcelona.com**

OLD TOWN Arts €€€€€

Carrer de Marina 19–21, 08005 **Tel** *932 21 10 00* **Fax** *932 21 30 45* **Rooms** *483* **Map** *6 E4*

Set in a soaring tower overlooking the Port Olímpic, Arts is one of the most luxurious and glamorous hotels in Europe. Huge rooms boast spectacular views along with every imaginable modern convenience, including a spa and a Michelin-starred restaurant. There are stunning suites on the upper floors. **www.hotelartsbarcelona.com**

OLD TOWN Neri €€€€€

Carrer de Sant Server 5, 08002 **Tel** *933 04 06 55* **Fax** *933 04 03 37* **Rooms** *22* **Map** *5 A2*

An enchanting hotel, which stunningly combines the architectural features of the original 18th-century palace with sleek contemporary fittings. Airy, stylish rooms are draped in sensuous fabrics, and there is a magnificent rooftop terrace with views of the Gothic cathedral. Fabulous restaurant too. **www.hotelneri.com**

EIXAMPLE Felipe II €

Carrer de Mallorca 329, 08037 **Tel** *934 58 77 58* **Fax** *932 07 21 04* **Rooms** *21* **Map** *3 C4*

This is a basic, clean hotel in an old apartment block in the Eixample, with a fine antique elevator. You will get a good welcome from the friendly owners, and all the rooms come complete with TV and either shared or en suite facilities. Breakfast is not available. **www.hotelfelipe2.com**

EIXAMPLE Room Mate Emma €

C/ Rosselló 205, 08008 **Tel** *932 38 56 06* **Fax** *932 38 50 05* **Rooms** *56* **Map** *3 A3*

Stylish and well-priced, this is a great bet for contemporary design on a budget. White, minimalist rooms are brightened with splashes of colour, and the location, just off Passeig de Gràcia, could not be more central. A breakfast buffet is available until noon and Wi-Fi is free. **www.room-matehotels.com**

EIXAMPLE Astoria Barcelona €€

Carrer de París 203, 08036 **Tel** *932 09 83 11* **Fax** *932 02 30 08* **Rooms** *114* **Map** *3 A2*

A charming hotel decorated with exquisite taste, including original pieces of art from the early 20th century. After a busy day sightseeing you can relax in the hotel's sauna, or at the rooftop plunge pool and bar. Some suites have direct access to the pool. **www.derbyhotels.com**

EIXAMPLE Hotel Paseo de Gracia €€

Passeig de Gràcia 102, 08008 **Tel** *932 15 06 03* **Fax** *932 15 37 24* **Rooms** *33* **Map** *3 B3*

There are few budget choices in the chi chi Eixample district, but this modest little hotel is a good option. It has a fabulous location on the city's most desirable boulevard, close to the finest Gaudí buildings. Some of the simple rooms have views over the Paseo de Gràcia. **www.hotelpaseodegracia.es**

EIXAMPLE Actual €€€

Carrer Rosselló 238, 08008 **Tel** *935 52 05 50* **Fax** *935 52 05 55* **Rooms** *36* **Map** *3 B3*

This modern hotel is fashionably decorated in sleek minimalist style. It has a superb location on the same block as Gaudí's "La Pedrera", and the upmarket boutiques of the Passeig de Gràcia are on the doorstep. Like many hotels in this area, it is geared towards business travellers, which means good weekend deals. **www.hotelactual.com**

EIXAMPLE Alexandra €€€

Carrer de Mallorca 251, 08008 **Tel** *934 67 71 66* **Fax** *934 88 02 58* **Rooms** *116* **Map** *3 A4*

A stylish, modern interior behind a 19th-century façade sets the tone at this hotel, which is well equipped for business meetings. It offers rooms and suites, all comfortably and tastefully furnished. There is a good restaurant, and the website offers excellent weekend packages. **www.hotel-alexandra.com**

EIXAMPLE Condes de Barcelona €€€

Passeig de Gràcia 73–75, 08008 ***Tel*** *934 45 00 00* ***Fax*** *934 45 32 32* ***Rooms*** *235* ***Map*** *3 A4*

This hotel is located in two handsomely renovated Modernista palaces, with marble lobbies and creamy façades. The rooms in both locations are cool and contemporary, and some have Jacuzzis. Choose a room with a terrace to admire Gaudí's "La Pedrera" building directly across the street. **www.condesdebarcelona.com**

EIXAMPLE Gallery €€€

Carrer Rosselló 249, 08008 ***Tel*** *934 15 99 11* ***Fax*** *934 15 91 84* ***Rooms*** *115* ***Map*** *3 A3*

A modern, efficient and comfortable hotel that is well situated and retains the personal atmosphere of a family-run business. Soundproofed rooms are smartly furnished with contemporary black and white decor and have large, marble bathrooms. An attractive garden restaurant leads into a public garden. **www.galleryhotel.com**

EIXAMPLE Granados 83 €€€

C/ Enric Granados 83, 08008 ***Tel*** *93 492 96 70* ***Fax*** *93 492 96 90* ***Rooms*** *77* ***Map*** *3 A3*

The rooms at this designer hotel are stylishly decorated with African zebrawood, chocolate brown leather and original pieces of Buddhist and Hindu art. Suites have private terraces overlooking a private plunge pool. There is an excellent restaurant and a small rooftop area with a very fashionable bar. **www.derbyhotels.es**

EIXAMPLE Hotel Olivia Plaza €€€

Plaça Catalunya 19, 8002 ***Tel*** *933 16 87 00* ***Fax*** *934 12 63 76* ***Rooms*** *113* ***Map*** *5 A1*

This hotel is right in the heart of Barcelona, overlooking the Plaça Catalunya, and very close to the Ramblas. It has a beautiful roof terrace with great views of the city centre, and each room has been sound-proofed. The interior decoration is modern and unfussy. **www.oliviahotels.es**

EIXAMPLE Hotel Praktik Rambla €€€

Rambla de Catalunya 27, 8007 ***Tel*** *933 43 66 90* ***Fax*** *933 04 33 32* ***Rooms*** *21* ***Map*** *3 C5*

A boutique hotel set in a restored historic building at the quieter end of the Plaça Catalunya. The Praktik Rambla provides an excellently balanced combination of designer chic and comfort at a reasonable price. Every room has a bathroom, TV and Wi-Fi. There's a wonderful terrace where guests can relax. **www.hotelpraktikrambla.com**

EIXAMPLE Axel €€€€

Carrer Aribau 33, 08011 ***Tel*** *933 23 93 93* ***Fax*** *933 23 93 94* ***Rooms*** *66* ***Map*** *2 F1*

Axel is Barcelona's best gay hotel, a chic four-star establishment with a wealth of excellent facilities. The rooms are sleek and modern, there is a fabulous rooftop bar, and business facilities are available in the small library. There is also a dipping pool, and a good restaurant (with drag shows). **www.axelhotels.com**

EIXAMPLE Clarís €€€€

Carrer Pau Claris 150, 08009 ***Tel*** *934 87 62 62* ***Fax*** *932 15 79 70* ***Rooms*** *119* ***Map*** *3 B4*

Antique kilims and elegant English and French furniture ornament this hotel off the Passieg de Gràcia. Clarís occupies the converted Vedruna Palace, and is scattered with fabulous artworks from around the world. There's a panoramic rooftop pool and sun deck, and guests may use the hotel's Smart cars. **www.derbyhotels.es**

EIXAMPLE Majèstic €€€€

Passeig de Gràcia 68, 08007 ***Tel*** *934 88 17 17* ***Fax*** *934 88 18 80* ***Rooms*** *303* ***Map*** *3 A4*

A grand hotel in Neo-Classical style in a chic street (adjoining Carrer de València). The bedrooms are decorated in plush, contemporary style, and are all equipped with five-star amenities. There are also some very luxurious suites and a rooftop plunge pool with spectacular views. Visit the website for special offers. **www.hotelmajestic.es**

EIXAMPLE Omm €€€€

Carrer Rosselló 265, 08008 ***Tel*** *934 45 40 00* ***Fax*** *934 45 40 04* ***Rooms*** *59* ***Map*** *3 B3*

From the glistening ultra-modern façade with its peeled-back balconies, to the fluid, glassy public spaces, Omm is the epitome of sleek Barcelona design. The fashionably minimalist rooms are very comfortable, and the slick bar and club make it popular with fashionistas. Also has spa facilities. **www.hotelomm.es**

EIXAMPLE Palace €€€€€

Gran Via de les Corts Catalanes 668, 08010 ***Tel*** *935 10 11 30* ***Fax*** *933 18 01 48* ***Rooms*** *125* ***Map*** *3 B5*

The most elegant of Barcelona's grand hotels, the Palace offers large luxurious bedrooms that are decorated in classical style and boast huge marble bathrooms. The opulent hotel also includes a beauty parlour. Famous guests have included the Spanish royal family and Frank Sinatra. **http://hotelpalacebarcelona.com**

FURTHER AFIELD (POBLE NOU) Hostel Poble Nou €€

Carrer Taulat 30, 08005 ***Tel*** *932 21 26 01* ***Fax*** *932 21 26 01* ***Rooms*** *10*

This charming little *hostal* is located in a colourful 1930s townhouse in the traditional neighbourhood of Poble Nou. It's close to the city's best beaches and well connected by metro and tram to the city centre. En suite rooms are simple, and there is a pretty breakfast terrace as well. Breakfast is included in the price. **www.hostalpoblenou.com**

FURTHER AFIELD (VALLVIDRERA) Gran Hotel La Florida €€€€

Carretera Vallvidrera al Tibidabo 83–93, 08035 ***Tel*** *932 59 30 00* ***Fax*** *932 59 30 01* ***Rooms*** *70*

In a luxurious palace in the hills above Barcelona, this outstanding hotel is set in beautiful gardens offering great views of the whole city. The suites are all equipped with every imaginable facility, and there is a wonderful spa and a restaurant. A shuttle service takes you to the heart of the city in minutes. **www.hotellaflorida.com**

Key to Price Guide *see p560* **Key to Symbols** *see back cover flap*

CATALONIA

ANDORRA LA VELLA Andorra Park Hotel €€€

C/ de Les Canals 24 ***Tel*** *376 87 77 77* ***Fax*** *376 82 09 83* ***Rooms*** *98*

One of Andorra's most luxurious hotels, this modern structure is built into a steep, wooded hillside. There is a library, a swimming pool hewn out of rock, and a pleasant bar-restaurant. Rooms come with satellite TV and a mini-bar, and the hotel also provides a laundry and ironing service. **www.andorraparkhotel.com**

ARTIES Parador Don Gaspar de Portolà €€€

Ctra Bequeira-Beret, 25599 (Lleida) ***Tel*** *973 64 08 01* ***Fax*** *973 64 10 01* ***Rooms*** *57*

A modern, comfortable parador, Don Gaspar de Portolà is built in the local traditional stone and slate. It is located in one of the prettiest villages of the Vall d'Aran, with attractive narrow streets dotted with medieval chapels. The parador is handy for local ski resorts, and makes a good base for mountain walkers. **www.parador.es**

AVINYONET DE PUIGVENTÓS Mas Pau €€€

Ctra Figueres-Besalú, 17742 (Girona) ***Tel*** *972 54 61 54* ***Fax*** *972 54 63 26* ***Rooms*** *20*

A beautiful hotel in a 16th-century house, surrounded by gardens and farmland. Many of the luxurious rooms and suites are located in the 25-m (82-ft) high tower, and have splendid views. There's a spectacular restaurant, secluded terraces and a separate swimming pool and games area for children. Closed 6 Jan–Feb. **www.maspau.com**

BANYOLES Mirallac €€€€

Passeig Darder 50, 17820 (Girona) ***Tel*** *972 57 10 45* ***Fax*** *972 57 10 39* ***Rooms*** *23*

Mirallac is a cheerful, old-style hotel overlooking the vast lake at Banyoles, offering traditionally decorated rooms with their own balcony/terrace, a huge swimming pool and lots of lakeside activities. Also houses a good restaurant serving tasty, local specialities. Guests also have use of a bar and a reading room. **www.hotelmirallac.com**

BEGUR Aigua Blava €€€€

Platja de Fornells, 17255 (Girona) ***Tel*** *972 62 45 62* ***Fax*** *972 62 21 12* ***Rooms*** *85*

This charming whitewashed Mediterranean-style hotel overlooks Fornells Bay, one of the Costa Brava's prettiest spots. Surrounded by pine trees and gardens, the arched windows of the hotel frame beautiful sea views. Rooms are light and airy. Aigua Blava also offers 10 fully equipped apartments. Closed Nov–mid-Mar. **www.aiguablava.com**

BEQUEIRA-BERET Royal Tanau €€€€€

Ctra de Beret, 25598 (Lleida) ***Tel*** *973 64 44 46* ***Fax*** *973 64 43 44* ***Rooms*** *30*

A luxurious boutique hotel in the Tanau skiing area that has all kinds of amenities, including indoor and outdoor Jacuzzis and a spa. In winter, a private ski lift whisks guests directly to the pistes. There are full après-ski facilities available. Elegant, fully equipped suites as well as rooms. Closed Apr–Nov. **www.solmelia.com**

BOLVIR DE CERDANYA Torre del Remei €€€€€

Camí Reial s/n, 17539 (Girona) ***Tel*** *972 14 01 82* ***Fax*** *972 14 04 49* ***Rooms*** *20*

One of the most deluxe hotels in the region, this opulent Modernista mansion is set in magnificent gardens with a stunning mountain backdrop. The classically decorated rooms are perfectly equipped with up-to-the-minute gadgetry, and the extensive facilities include a spa and a gym. Pets are welcome. **www.torredelremei.com**

CADAQUÈS Hotel Llane Petit €€€

Platja Llane Petit, 17488 (Girona) ***Tel*** *972 25 10 20* ***Fax*** *972 25 87 78* ***Rooms*** *37*

Llane Petit is a delightful seaside hotel with a peaceful and welcoming ambience, right on the beach in the white-washed village of Cadaquès. Simple, friendly and family-run, the best rooms boast terraces where you can relax in a hammock and soak up the sun. The restaurant is open in summer only. Closed Nov–end Feb. **www.llanepetit.com**

CARDONA Parador de Cardona €€€

Carrer de Castell s/n, 08261 (Barcelona) ***Tel*** *938 69 12 75* ***Fax*** *938 69 16 36* ***Rooms*** *54*

One of the most striking paradors in Spain, this luxuriously converted medieval castle dominates Cardona and offers spectacular views of the countryside. Many of the elegant rooms boast four-poster beds. The parador has a fine Catalan restaurant as well. **www.parador.es**

CASTELLÓ D'EMPURIES Hotel de la Moneda €€

Plaça de la Moneda 8–10, 17486 (Girona) ***Tel*** *972 15 86 02* ***Fax*** *972 15 81 24* ***Rooms*** *11*

This historic 17th-century mansion is located in the heart of the Jewish quarter. The building was sympathetically converted into a beautiful hotel in 2002 and offers maximum comfort and relaxation. Some rooms have a Jacuzzi; others have balconies. The hotel has a lovely terrace with pool and a reading room. **www.hoteldelamoneda.com**

FIGUERES Hotel Durán €€

Carrer de Lasauca 5, 17600 (Girona) ***Tel*** *972 50 12 50* ***Fax*** *972 50 26 09* ***Rooms*** *65*

Established in 1855, this ochre-and-pink hotel is set above one of the finest restaurants in the region. It is still owned by the same family, who are warm and friendly. Rooms are attractively, if simply, furnished, and many have pretty wrought-iron balconies overlooking the street below. **www.hotelduran.com**

GIRONA Hotel Llegendes de Girona €€€

Portal de la Barca 4, 17004 (Girona) ***Tel*** *972 22 09 05* ***Rooms*** *15*

The Llegendes de Girona is a chic, modern hotel in a historic 18th-century building near the river and the town centre. The original charm of the building has been preserved while offering state-of-the-art amenities and stylish decor. Enjoy the hydromassage baths and rain showers. Childcare services available. **www.llegendeshotel.com**

LA SEU D'URGELL Parador de La Seu d'Urgell €€€

Carrer Sant Domènec 6, 25700 (Lleida) ***Tel*** *973 35 20 00* ***Fax*** *973 35 23 09* ***Rooms*** *79*

Only the Renaissance cloister, now used as the lounge, remains of a convent that occupied this site close to the 12th-century cathedral of La Seu. The modern parador has good facilities, including a covered pool, and there are excellent opportunities on the doorstep for hiking and skiing. **www.parador.es**

LA SEU D'URGELL El Castell €€€€€

Ctra N 260 km 229, 25700 (Lleida) ***Tel*** *973 35 00 00* ***Fax*** *973 35 15 74* ***Rooms*** *38*

This extravagant hotel is a low, modern building beneath the medieval castle of Seu d'Urgell. It has plenty of facilities, including an outdoor Jacuzzi and an immense covered pool. There are impressive views across the mountains of El Cadí and the ski slopes of Andorra are nearby. **www.hotelelcastell.com**

L'ESCALA Hostal Empúries €€€

Platja del Portitxol, 17130 (Girona) ***Tel*** *972 77 02 07* ***Fax*** *972 77 02 07* ***Rooms*** *55*

This hotel was originally constructed to house the archaeologists excavating the Greco-Roman remains at Empúries. It is now an elegant hotel, conveniently placed near the beach, with some lovely sea views from many of the rooms. **www.hostalempuries.com**

L'ESPLUGA DEL FRANCOLÍ Hostal del Senglar €€

Plaça de Montserrat Canals 1, 43440 (Tarragona) ***Tel*** *977 87 04 11* ***Fax*** *977 87 01 27* ***Rooms*** *38*

A three-storey, whitewashed hotel with simply furnished, traditional rooms including family rooms. There is a delightful shady garden where barbecues are held in summer. A menu of delicious dishes, traditional to the area, is served in the restaurant. **www.hostaldelsenglar.com**

LLORET DE MAR Santa Marta €€€€

Platja Santa Cristina, 17310 (Girona) ***Tel*** *972 36 49 04* ***Fax*** *972 36 92 80* ***Rooms*** *76*

This low, white-painted modern hotel overlooks a beautiful cove on the fringes of the frenetic Lloret de Mar resort. Rooms vary from rustic to contemporary decor with up-to-the-minute amenities. Pine woods and gardens extend to the shore, and there are tennis courts and other sporting facilities. Closed 15 Dec–mid-Feb. **www.hstamarta.com**

MADREMANYA El Racó de Madremanya €€€

Procesó 1, 17462 (Girona) ***Tel*** *972 49 06 49* ***Rooms*** *10*

A charming hotel set in a 17th-century country house in the medieval village of Madremanya. Rooms are spacious and well furnished, and some have cosy fireplaces. The hotel has two swimming pools and a large garden. Choose between the old and new sections of the hotel, the latter with cutting-edge design. **www.elracodemadremanya.com**

MONTSENY Sant Bernat €€

Finca El Cot, Ctra Sant Maria de Palautordera a Seva km 20.8, 08460 (Barcelona) ***Tel*** *938 47 30 11* ***Rooms*** *32*

A gorgeous country house in the Serra de Montseny, the old stone walls of which are cloaked in greenery. The rooms and suites are stylishly decorated with traditional prints and rustic furniture. The house is surrounded by vast gardens and the views are a highlight. All kinds of outdoor activities can be arranged. **www.hotelhusasantbernat.com**

MONTSERRAT Abat Cisneros €€

Plaça del Monestir, 08199 (Barcelona) ***Tel*** *938 77 7 01* ***Fax*** *938 7 77 24* ***Rooms*** *82*

Part of the celebrated monastery complex at Montserrat, Abat Cisneros is where Catalan newlyweds come to ensure that they have the blessing of La Moreneta, the miraculous figure of the Virgin. Rooms are modest but more comfortable than the ascetic setting would suggest. **www.montserratvisita.com**

PERAMOLA Can Boix de Peramola €€

Carrer Afores s/n, 25790 (Lleida) ***Tel*** *973 47 02 66* ***Fax*** *973 47 02 81* ***Rooms*** *41*

This good value, traditional mountain hotel has been in the same family for 10 generations. It has charming rooms and apartments with breathtaking views, a quiet garden and a swimming pool. Can Boix de Peramola is very convenient for walking in the Pyrenean foothills. Closed Jan–mid-Feb. **www.canboix.cat**

REGENCÓS Hotel del Teatre €€€

Plaça Major s/n, 17214 (Girona) ***Tel*** *972 30 62 70* ***Fax*** *972 30 62 73* ***Rooms*** *7*

In the heart of a rambling, medieval village, this boutique-style hotel is located in a pair of handsomely restored 18th-century mansions. Sleek minimalism and charming original features are stylishly combined in the bedrooms. Has a lovely semi-shaded pool in the garden. **http://hoteldelteatre.com**

SA TUNA (BEGUR) Hotel Sa Tuna €€€

Platja Sa Tuna, 17255 (Girona) ***Tel*** *972 62 41 82* ***Fax*** *972 62 21 98* ***Rooms*** *5*

Sa Tuna is a simple, whitewashed small hotel on one of the Costa Brava's prettiest coves. The rooms have a nautical theme; some have their own terrace overlooking the bay. The restaurant is well known in the area. Open from April to September only. **www.hostalsatuna.com**

Key to Price Guide *see p560* **Key to Symbols** *see back cover flap*

SADURNI D'ANOIA Sol i Vi €

Ctra San Sadurni–Vilafranca km 4, Lavern, 08739 (Barcelona) ***Tel*** *938 99 32 04* ***Fax*** *938 99 34 35* ***Rooms*** *25*

A cheery, traditional hotel set amid a sea of vines, thus making this a good base for exploring the wine and *cava*-producing region southwest of Barcelona. It offers comfortable, simple rooms and boasts a superb restaurant, which specializes in traditional Catalan cuisine. **www.solivi.com**

S'AGARÓ Barcarola €€€

C/ Pablo Picasso 1, Platja Sant Pol (Girona), 17220 ***Tel*** *972 32 69 32* ***Fax*** *972 82 01 97* ***Rooms*** *40*

Just a few steps from Sant Pol, one of the most beautiful beaches on the Costa Brava is this simple but elegant hotel in a quiet part of town, ideal for a family holiday. The hotel offers a babysitting service and has a playground, as well as apartments for short stays. Free parking. **www.barcarola.com**

S'AGARÓ Hostal de la Gavina €€€€€

Plaça de la Rosaleda, 17248 (Girona) ***Tel*** *972 32 11 00* ***Fax*** *972 32 15 73* ***Rooms*** *74*

This elegant Mediterranean-style beach mansion is set in its own exclusive estate with beautiful gardens and a sea-water pool. Bedrooms are splendidly decorated with silk-lined walls and burnished antiques. The many facilities include a luxurious spa and a fine restaurant. **www.lagavina.com**

SITGES Hotel Alexandra €€

C/ Termes 20, 08870 (Barcelona) ***Tel*** *938 94 15 58* ***Fax*** *938 11 35 69* ***Rooms*** *16*

A charming hotel in a quiet square in the centre of Sitges, the Hotel Alexandra offers simple but stylish rooms, the best of which have balconies or terraces. The beach is just a few minutes' walk away and the friendly hosts are always on hand to offer advice on what to see and do during your stay. **www.hotelalexandrasitges.com**

SITGES Calipolis €€€

Avenida Sofía 2, 8870 (Barcelona) ***Tel*** *938 94 15 00* ***Fax*** *938 94 07 64* ***Rooms*** *170*

A favourite with beach-lovers, this hotel was designed to have the maximum number of rooms with views of the beach. The hotel is looking a little dated, but the swimming pool, lively bar and great location on the seafront more than make up for it. **www.hotelcalipolis.com**

SOLDEU (ANDORRA) Sport Hotel Village €€€

Ctra General s/n ***Tel*** *376 87 05 00* ***Fax*** *376 87 05 55* ***Rooms*** *148*

Sport Hotel Village is the best-equipped hotel in the popular ski resort of Soldeu, and many of the comfortable rooms overlook the slopes. The four-star facilities include a pool and spa area, and – best of all – the lift to the top of the slopes leaves directly from the hotel. Closed for two weeks in October. **www.sporthotels.ad**

TARRAGONA Imperial Tarraco €€

Passeig Les Palmeres s/n, 43003 (Tarragona) ***Tel*** *977 23 30 40* ***Fax*** *977 21 65 66* ***Rooms*** *170*

The plushest option in Tarragona, this large, modern hotel has a panoramic location right on the *balcón del Mediterrani* (the balcony of the Mediterranean). Many of the spacious, elegant rooms and suites have large terraces. The hotel is conveniently close to the historic centre of the city. **www.hotelhusaimperialtarraco.com**

TARRAGONA Lauria €€

Rambla Nova 20, 43004 (Tarragona) ***Tel*** *977 23 67 12* ***Fax*** *977 23 67 00* ***Rooms*** *72*

A modern, functional hotel in the town centre and close to the sea, with an elegant entrance under balustraded stone stairs. Although the decor is dated, the rooms are large and the hotel offers good amenities for the price, including a pool and facilities for business travellers. **www.hlauria.com**

TAVERTET El Jufré €

Bisbe Galzeran Sacosta 1, 08511 (Barcelona) ***Tel*** *938 56 51 67* ***Fax*** *938 56 51 67* ***Rooms*** *8*

This converted farmhouse is now a delightful *casa rural* with stunning mountain views. It has been in the same family for over 800 years, and warm comfortable rooms have replaced what were previously animal quarters. A perfect base for walking and exploring nearby Osona. Half-board accommodation is available. No credit cards.

TORRENT Mas de Torrent €€€€€

Afueras, 17123 (Girona) ***Tel*** *972 30 32 92* ***Fax*** *972 30 32 93* ***Rooms*** *39*

A superbly converted 18th-century country house, Mas de Torrent offers handsome accommodation in ten beautiful rooms in the main house, or in elegant bungalows scattered around the extensive gardens. There are also deluxe suites with private pools available, and a spa facility. **www.mastorrent.com**

TORTOSA Parador Castillo de la Zuda €€€

Castillo de la Zuda, 43500 (Tarragona) ***Tel*** *977 44 44 50* ***Fax*** *977 44 44 58* ***Rooms*** *72*

A medieval Moorish castle makes a superb hilltop parador with views of the town and valley of the Riu Ebre. The fine restaurant offers al fresco dining on the terrace, and there are plenty of luxurious extras including a swimming pool – in summer only, however. **www.parador.es**

TOSSA DE MAR Diana €€

Plaça d'Espanya 6, 17320 (Girona) ***Tel*** *972 34 18 86* ***Fax*** *972 34 11 03* ***Rooms*** *21*

A fine Modernista mansion is the gorgeous setting for this delightful hotel. There are nice views of the castle from the terrace and the best of the modest rooms have private balconies. The elegant lobby is full of original details and has been converted into a comfortable lounge area. **www.diana-hotel.com**

TREDÒS Hotel de Tredòs €€€

Ctra a Baqueira-Beret km 177.5, 25598 (Lleida) **Tel** *973 64 40 14* **Fax** *973 64 43 00* **Rooms** *38*

Skiers and walkers find this hotel in the Val d'Aran good value. It is built of stone and slate in the local style, and offers attractive rooms with wooden beams. There is a heart-shaped outdoor pool to cool off in summer. Minimum five-night stay during the high skiing season. Closed late spring and autumn. **www.hoteldetredos.com**

VIC Parador de Turismo de Vic-Sau €€€

Paratge Bac de Sau, 08500 (Barcelona) **Tel** *938 12 23 23* **Fax** *938 12 23 68* **Rooms** *36*

This comfortable stone-built parador, 14 km (9 miles) from Vic, has magnificent views of the Sau reservoir. It is a peaceful retreat amid pine forests and dramatic rock formations. Facilities include a tennis court and an outdoor pool (in summers only). **www.parador.es**

VIELHA (VIELLA) Parador de Vielha €€€

Ctra de Túnel s/n, 25530 (Lleida) **Tel** *973 64 01 00* **Fax** *973 64 11 00* **Rooms** *118*

This is a modern parador that has a panoramic circular lounge dominated by a large window from which there are magnificent mountain views. There is a wonderful spa and a fine restaurant, and the rooms are bright, spacious and well appointed. **www.parador.es**

ARAGÓN

AÍNSA Casa Cambra €

Ctra A-138 Barbastro–Ainsa km 42, Morillo de Tou s/n, 22395 (Huesca) **Tel** *974 50 07 93* **Fax** *974 50 07 93* **Rooms** *17*

Casa Cambra is a modest farmhouse in the picturesque medieval village of Morillo de Tou. A perfect location for visiting historical sites as well as natural wonders. The rooms are spacious and many feature original exposed brick arches. More basic accommodation is also available. Closed two weeks in Feb. **www.morillodetou.com**

ALBARRACÍN Casa de Santiago €€

C/ Subida de las Torres 11, 44100 (Teruel) **Tel** *978 70 03 16* **Fax** *978 71 01 41* **Rooms** *9*

Close to the city's main square, this small hotel was once a residence of the Knights of Santiago, who used to protect the pilgrims from roaming bandits. The rooms are modest (only the suite has a TV), but the owners are friendly, the meals are good and there is a Wi-Fi connection. Closed three weeks in Feb, 13–17 Sep. **www.casadesantiago.net**

ALBARRACÍN Hotel Albarracín €€

Azagra s/n, 44100 (Teruel) **Tel** *978 71 00 11* **Fax** *978 71 00 36* **Rooms** *40*

This hotel has some outstanding views of the historic centre of Albarracín and was once an important medieval palace. Some of the rooms are in need of renovation, but despite the old-fashioned decor, this a comfortable place to stay. **www.hotelalbarracinteruel.com**

ALBARRACÍN La Casona del Ajimez €€

C/ San Juan 2, 44100 (Teruel) **Tel** *978 71 03 21* **Fax** *978 70 03 26* **Rooms** *6*

This 16th–17th-century residence is decorated in the style of the three religions that once resided in Teruel's old town – Judaism, Islam and Christianity. The pretty pink and red façade houses rooms with king-size beds, eclectic antiques and period knick-knacks. The garden has fabulous views of the cathedral. **www.casonadelajimez.com**

ALCAÑIZ Parador de Alcañiz €€€

Castillo Calatravos s/n, 44600 (Teruel) **Tel** *978 83 04 00* **Fax** *978 83 03 66* **Rooms** *37*

This used to be the castle of the 12th-century Knights of Calatrava, a particularly violent and independent order who ruled the area with an iron fist. Now, it is a luxurious parador, with many atmospheric corners, including a keep, a bell tower and a chapel; just be careful you do not end up in the dungeon while exploring. **www.parador.es**

ALQUÉZAR Santa María €€

Arrabal s/n, 22145 (Huesca) **Tel** *974 31 84 36* **Fax** *974 31 84 35* **Rooms** *21*

A simple hotel set inside a heavily altered and extended medieval palace offering comfortable accommodation with wonderful views of the Colegiata and Vero rivers. The hotel's lounge has an open, cosy fireplace, and the staff can also organize "adventure sports". Closed Jan–Feb but can open for groups. **www.hotel-santamaria.com**

BENASQUE Hotel Hospital de Benasque €€

Camino Real s/n, 22440 (Huesca) **Tel** *974 55 20 12* **Fax** *974 56 05 03* **Rooms** *55*

A huge old hospital and pilgrims' shelter has been converted into a hotel with various types of lodging available, from duplexes to suites. Nestled in a gorgeous valley (and prime cross-country skiing territory), the in-house restaurant is also well known. A spa is available. **www.llanosdelhospital.com**

BIELSA Parador de Bielsa €€€

Valle de Pineta s/n, 22350 (Huesca) **Tel** *974 50 10 11* **Fax** *974 50 11 88* **Rooms** *39*

The name of the mountain which rises above this parador – Monte Perdido (Lost Mountain) – gives an idea of its isolated location in one of the most beautiful spots of Northern Spain. The modern building has been tastefully built with wooden beams and offers great views of the Ordesa National Park. Closed end Jan–Feb. **www.parador.es**

Key to Price Guide *see p560* **Key to Symbols** *see back cover flap*

DAROCA Posada del Almudí  €

C/ Grajera 5–7–9, 50360 (Zaragoza) **Tel** 976 80 06 06 **Fax** 976 80 11 41 **Rooms** 30

The rooms in this 16th-century palace sit around a stunning Renaissance patio. After a grand entrance, the rooms themselves lack a bit in character, but are comfortable enough. There is a lovely garden terrace, library and a decent restaurant. The annexe across the street offers contemporary rooms. Closed 24–25 Dec. **www.posadadelalmudi.es**

FUENTESPALDA La Torre del Visco €€€€

Fuentespalda, 44587 (Teruel) **Tel** 978 76 90 15 **Fax** 978 76 90 16 **Rooms** 40

The King of Spain, Juan Carlos I, has been known to use this beautiful, solitary and labyrinthine 15th-century estate house, overlooking 220 acres of rose gardens, olive and almond trees. This hotel prides itself on offering a relaxing and quiet environment with no TVs or phones in the rooms. Dinner and breakfast included. **www.torredelvisco.com**

HUESCA Hotel La Posada de la Luna €€

C/ Joaquín Costa 10, 22003 (Huesca) **Tel** 974 24 08 57 **Fax** 974 24 13 15 **Rooms** 8

As its name sugggests, this hotel has a planetary theme, with each room dedicated to a different celestial body. The hotel has managed to maintain many original elements of the Renaissance building, while tastefully modernizing to create a charming and comfortable place to stay. **www.posadadelaluna.com**

JACA Conde Aznar €€

Paseo Constitución 3, 22700 (Huesca) **Tel** 974 36 10 50 **Fax** 974 36 07 97 **Rooms** 34

Conde Aznar is a traditional, double-storey residence; each room has pretty ceramic-tiled bathrooms, lace curtains and embroidered bedspreads. Exposed beams and polished floors complete the rustic look. Perfect for taking advantage of Jaca's excellent access to all the Aragonese ski resorts. **www.condeaznar.com**

JACA Hotel Chalet Puigdefabregas €€

C/ Pico Collarada 59, 22700 (Huesca) **Tel** 974 36 01 74 **Rooms** 12

This traditional villa has been converted into a charming boutique hotel and offers excellent service and attention to detail. The rooms are all decorated according to feng shui principles and have exterior views of the surrounding gardens and nearby mountains as well as Wi-Fi access and plasma TVs. **www.hotelchaletpuigdefabregas.com**

LANUZA-SALLENT DE GÁLLEGO La Casueña €€

El Troniecho 11 (Lanuza), 22640 (Huesca) **Tel** 974 48 85 38 **Fax** 974 33 73 49 **Rooms** 10

The literary inclinations of the owners of La Casueña are evident by the dedication of each of the rooms to a Spanish writer. The austere stone walls of this country house give way to a luxuriously decorated interior, with dramatic murals on the slanted roofs. The rooms have comfy king-size beds and a huge bath. **www.lacasuena.com**

PANTICOSA Hotel Continental Panticosa €€€€

Ctra del Balneario km 10, 22650 (Huesca) **Tel** 974 48 71 61 **Fax** 974 48 71 37 **Rooms** 250

Situated next to a lake and surrounded by the stunning mountain scenery of the Panticosa resort, this old spa was converted into a five-star hotel by the renowned architect Rafael Moneo. Its luxurious facilities include a hairdresser, a spa and a private skiing piste, which takes you right up to the front door. **www.panticosa.com**

SALLENT DE GÁLLEGO Almud €

C/ Espadilla 11, 22640 (Huesca) **Tel** 974 48 83 66 **Fax** 974 48 81 43 **Rooms** 11

Conveniently placed in a pretty village near the Formigal and Panticosa ski resorts, this family-run hotel occupies an 18th-century building which used to be the village stables. Visitors will find welcoming staff, comfortable rooms furnished with rustic furniture and the atmosphere of a typical Aragonese mountain retreat. **www.hotelalmud.com**

SOS DEL REY CATÓLICO Parador Sos del Rey Católico €€€

C/ Arquitecto Sainz de Vicuña s/n, 50680 (Zaragoza) **Tel** 948 88 80 11 **Fax** 948 88 81 00 **Rooms** 66

This reconstructed Aragonese home offers modern accommodation. All rooms have large windows and are decorated in a somewhat heavy, faux-Castilian style. The in-room facilities are abundant and include Internet. The restaurant is a good place to sample the rich local cuisine. **www.parador.es**

TARAZONA Condes de Visconti €€

C/ Visconti 15, 50500 (Zaragoza) **Tel** 976 64 49 08 **Fax** 976 64 18 58 **Rooms** 15

A rather grand hotel, which borders on being overdone with its Provençal decorative touches; frescoes, stucco and enough throws to bury yourself in. Facilities include in-room hydro-massage tubs, Internet and satellite TV. Extras include the super-friendly staff and a great in-house restaurant. **www.condesdevisconti.com**

TERUEL Torico Plaza €

C/ Yagüe de Salas 5, 44001 **Tel** 978 60 86 55 **Fax** 978 60 86 55 **Rooms** 31

An attractive, functional and central hotel overlooking a 16th-century Mudéjar tower. It offers plenty of natural light, cheery decor in earthy tones and family-size rooms. Three of the rooms are suites with balconies. Closed 24–25 Dec. **www.sercotelhoteles.com**

TERUEL Parador de Teruel €€€

Ctra Sagunto–Burgos N234 km 122, 44003 **Tel** 978 60 18 00 **Fax** 978 60 86 12 **Rooms** 62

On the outskirts of the city in an Arabesque palace inspired by the culture of the Mudéjars, this highly impressive parador offers spacious rooms, an excellent restaurant, a landscaped garden and a pool. With its fanciful tilework, arches and swathes of marble, staying here is like taking a trip into the Arabian Nights. **www.parador.es**

TORRE DEL COMPTE Parada del Compte €€€

Finca la Antigua Estación del Ferrocarril, 44597 (Teruel) ***Tel*** *978 76 90 72* ***Fax*** *978 76 90 74* ***Rooms*** *11*

Parada del Compte is a quirky hotel located in a disused railway station. Each room is named after a famous international city train station with supposedly "matching" decor, ranging from a minimalist "loft" treatment in the New York suite to a lush Oriental Istanbul suite. Apartments are also available. **www.hotelparadadelcompte.com**

UNCASTILLO Posada La Pastora €

Roncesvalles 1, 50678 (Zaragoza) ***Tel/Fax*** *976 67 94 99* ***Rooms*** *8*

This charmingly renovated 18th-century country retreat offers just eight rooms with exposed brick walls contrasted with bright furnishings. Breakfast features fresh produce from local farmers. Fishing, golfing, rafting and horse riding facilities are also available close by. Two-night minimum stay. **http://lapastora.net**

ZARAGOZA Hotel Avenida €€

Avda César Augusto 55, 50003 ***Tel*** *976 43 93 00* ***Fax*** *976 43 93 64* ***Rooms*** *85*

What this hotel may lack in character it more than makes up for in comfort and in its location in the historical and commercial centre of Zaragoza. Rooms are well equipped with Internet and satellite TV and some have a terrace. Well placed for those who want to visit all of Zaragoza's major sites on foot. **www.hotelavenida-zaragoza.com**

ZARAGOZA Palafox €€€

C/ Marqués de Casa Jiménez s/n, 50004 ***Tel*** *976 23 77 00* ***Fax*** *976 23 47 05* ***Rooms*** *179*

The Spanish architect Pascua Ortega went to town on his design for this luxurious hotel. The grand entrance is flanked by full-scale representations of the old gates to the city. The rooms, on the other hand, are tasteful and minimalist. In terms of location and facilities this is one of the best places in the city. **www.palafoxhoteles.com**

VALENCIA AND MURCIA

ÁGUILAS Hotel El Paso €

C/ Cartagena 13, 30880 (Murcia) ***Tel*** *968 44 71 25* ***Fax*** *968 44 71 27* ***Rooms*** *24*

This pleasant hotel in the centre of Águilas features spacious rooms with contemporary decor. It has a sunny central courtyard and floral accents throughout. The award-winning restaurant serves regional food prepared with local fish, as well as Mediterranean and international cuisine. **www.hotelelpasoaguilas.com**

ALHAMA DE MURCIA Bajo el Cejo €€€

El Paso, El Berro 30440 (Murcia) ***Tel*** *968 66 80 32* ***Rooms*** *13*

Located in the Sierra Espuña mountain range, this hotel complex consists of a series of charming historic buildings, including a renovated windmill and a watermill. The interiors feature works from local artists that add a colourful and welcoming touch. Relax by the pool or unwind by the fireplace in one of the cosy lounges. **www.bajoelcejo.com**

ALICANTE Les Monges Palace €

San Augustín 4, 03002 (Alicante) ***Tel*** *965 21 50 46* ***Fax*** *965 14 71 89* ***Rooms*** *18*

Ideal for budget travellers, this hotel is often fully booked well in advance. Situated in the heart of Alicante's old town, some rooms feature original Modernista details, including colourfully tiled floors, so specify when booking. Two slightly more expensive rooms with a sauna and Jacuzzi are also available. **www.lesmonges.net**

ALICANTE Amerigo €€

C/ Rafael Altamira 7, 03002 (Alicante) ***Tel*** *965 14 65 70* ***Fax*** *965 14 65 70* ***Rooms*** *80*

What was once a Dominican convent has now been spectacularly converted into Alicante's smartest and most stylish hotel. A striking fusion of ancient and ultra-modern, it offers minimalist rooms, an excellent restaurant, a fashionable bar and a health centre. The rooftop pool has great views of the old city. **www.hospes.com**

ALICANTE Hotel Albahia €€

Sol Naciente 6, 03016 (Alicante) ***Tel*** *965 15 59 79* ***Fax*** *965 15 53 73* ***Rooms*** *93*

This modern hotel, five minutes from the city centre, has a beachfront location with sea views and offers various luxuries and comforts, including tennis, a business centre and baby-sitting facilities. They also have a Mediterranean restaurant specializing in regional rice dishes. Access for disabled guests. **www.albahia.com**

ALICANTE Sidi San Juan €€€€€

La Doblada 8, Playa San Juan, 03540 (Alicante) ***Tel*** *965 16 13 00* ***Fax*** *965 16 33 46* ***Rooms*** *176*

A gleaming, modern luxury hotel overlooking the lively and popular San Juan beach on the outskirts of the city centre. Surrounded by beautiful gardens, the hotel hosts a spa, health centre and various sports facilities, as well as a play area and paddling pool for kids. **www.hotelessidi.es**

ARCHENA Termas €€€

Ctra Balneario, 30600 (Murcia) ***Tel*** *902 33 32 22* ***Rooms*** *67*

This spa hotel boasts an elegant and charming complex set amid flower-filled gardens and palm trees. The spa treatment areas are decorated in a glorious Mudéjar style and feature ornate plasterwork, domes and Moorish arches. The outdoor pool has massaging jets. **www.balneariodearchena.com**

Key to Price Guide *see p560* **Key to Symbols** *see back cover flap*

BENICARLÓ Parador de Benicarló €€€

Avenida Papa Luna 5, 12580 (Castellón) **Tel** *964 47 01 00* **Fax** *964 47 09 34* **Rooms** *104*

Situated only 30 minutes from the sea on the Azahar coast, this hotel has a swimming pool and "pitch and putt" golf course, and is popular with families with young children (there is a children's play area). All rooms face the beautiful garden and some have private terraces. **www.parador.es**

BENIMAURELL Hotel Alahuar €

El Tossal s/n, 03503 (Valencia) **Tel** *965 58 33 97* **Fax** *965 58 33 97* **Rooms** *20*

This hotel blends into its surroundings and offers splendid views over the valley and all the way to the Mediterranean Sea. Junior suites are housed in small villas scattered around the gardens and have a spacious bedroom downstairs, with a sitting room and balcony upstairs. Most have Jacuzzis. Breakfast buffet included. **www.hotelalahuar.com**

BENISSA Casa del Maco €€

Partida Pou Roig s/n, 03720 (Alicante) **Tel** *965 73 28 42* **Fax** *965 73 01 03* **Rooms** *5*

An exquisite rural retreat, this hotel is located on a beautifully restored, 18th-century *finca* (farm estate). Surrounded by groves of olives, almonds and oranges, each of the rooms is stylishly decorated. The terrace and pool provide splendid views of the mountains. Also has a romantic French restaurant. Closed Jan. **http://casadelmaco.com**

CALABARDINA Al Sur €€

Torre de Cope 24, 30889 (Near Águilas, Murcia) **Tel** *968 41 94 66* **Rooms** *8*

Situated in a tiny village, this cosy, whitewashed hotel overlooks one of the wildest and most beautiful stretches of the Murcian coast. The rooms are painted in soothing shades of blue and green. Ideal for those looking for an intimate and relaxing getaway. Breakfast included in rate. Closed mid-Dec–Feb. **www.halsur.com**

CALPE Gran Hotel Sol y Mar €€€

C/ Benidorm 3, 03710 (Alicante) **Tel** *965 87 50 55* **Fax** *965 83 31 82* **Rooms** *327*

This modern hotel has a great location next to the beach and close to the village, and all the mod-cons, including a spa, a swimming pool and gym facilities. The more expensive rooms have spectacular views over the sea and some have private terraces. The two restaurants cater for children and the health-conscious. **www.granhotelsolymar.com**

CARTAGENA Los Habaneros €€

C/ San Diego 60, 30202 (Murcia) **Tel** *968 50 52 50* **Fax** *968 50 91 04* **Rooms** *87*

At the entrance to Cartagena's old quarter, this long-established hotel offers modern and well-equipped rooms at affordable prices. Has a great restaurant and tapas bar. The town's famous Roman and Carthagenian antiquities are located close by. **www.hotel-habaneros-cartagena.com**

CARTAGENA Hotel La Manga Club Príncipe Felipe €€€€€

La Manga Club, 30385 (Murcia) **Tel** *968 33 12 34* **Fax** *968 33 12 35* **Rooms** *192*

A luxurious hotel, part of an exclusive resort complex built in the style of a Spanish village. Frequented by several celebrities, the hotel is surrounded by palm and olive groves, and the complex boasts three golf courses, 28 tennis courts and four swimming pools. Also has a Centre for Professional Football and a spa. **www.lamangaclub.com**

CASTELL DE CASTELLS Pensión Castells €

C/ San Vicente 18, 03793 (Alicante) **Tel** *965 51 82 54* **Rooms** *4*

A 200-year-old house in an inland village not far from the Costa Blanca. The stone walls keep the rooms cool even in summer. The charming British owners offer bed and breakfast and can prepare packed lunches and dinners. They also offer guided and non-guided walking holidays and moutain biking holidays. **www.mountainholidays-spain.com**

CHULILLA Balneario de Chulilla €€

Afueras s/n, 46167 (Valencia) **Tel** *902 74 74 02* **Rooms** *100*

This spa hotel, surrounded by gardens and set in a tranquil location on the banks of the Río Túria, is an inexpensive place to stop while exploring the woods and hills of inland Valencia. It has all the facilities for a rest-cure, including massage and vapour baths, a gym and a beauty centre. Closed 22 Dec–Jan. **http://balneariodechulilla.com**

CULLA Hotel Aldearoqueta €€€€

Mas d'en Roqueta s/n, 12163 **Tel** *964 76 21 95* **Rooms** *18*

This hotel is set in an abandoned village in the middle of the countryside, where the old houses have been renovated. Guests can enjoy the beautiful views of the Sierra Engarcerán Valley or take a dip in the natural pool and outdoor Jacuzzi. All the rooms are spacious and have a porch or terrace. **www.aldearoqueta.com**

DENIA Rosa €€

C/ Congre 3, Las Marinas, 03700 (Alicante) **Tel** *965 78 15 73* **Fax** *966 42 47 74* **Rooms** *40*

A modern, white villa with a perfect location close to the beach. It was built and is run by a hospitable Parisian expat who has several repeat customers. Comfortable rooms have sun-trapping, Florentine-style balconies. Guests can also opt for one of the garden bungalows. The family-friendly pool has a section for toddlers. **www.hotelrosadenia.com**

EL SALER Parador de El Saler €€€€

Avda de los Pinares 151, 46012 (Valencia) **Tel** *961 61 11 86* **Fax** *961 62 70 16* **Rooms** *58*

A contemporary parador, situated beside the sea near L'Albufera and surrounded by a renowned golf course. It overlooks one of Valencia's loveliest and least crowded beaches. The rooms are light and modern. Features a football pitch and a full-service spa. The restaurant serves Valencian cuisine, specializing in paella. **www.parador.es**

ELX (ELCHE) Huerto del Cura €€

Porta de la Morera 14, 03203 (Alicante) **Tel** *966 61 20 50* **Rooms** *81*

A secluded hotel in Europe's largest palm tree forest, surrounded by landscaped grounds. The bedrooms are located in Mediterranean-style bungalows. Furnishings and fittings combine comfort and functionality. The hotel's reputation rests on its extraordinary array of sports facilities, which are top-notch. **www.huertodelcura.com**

FORTUNA Balneario Leana €€€

C/ Balneario, 30630 (Murcia) **Tel** *902 44 44 10* **Fax** *968 68 50 87* **Rooms** *58*

This is the oldest hotel in Murcia and although smartly renovated has the ambience of a former grand hotel. Many of the original Modernista details, including swirling woodwork, have been retained. Also boasts a splendid staircase. An array of spa and health treatments, as well as a series of thermal pools are available. **www.leana.es**

JÁTIVA (XÀTIVA) Hostería Mont Sant €€€

Ctra de Castillo, 46800 (Valencia) **Tel** *962 27 50 81* **Fax** *962 28 19 05* **Rooms** *16*

A country hotel in a magnificently restored mansion. There are just six elegant rooms in the main building, and the remaining are located in charming wooden bungalows scattered throughout the beautiful gardens. It offers all kinds of amenities, including a spa and gym, and the restaurant is superb. Closed 7–20 Jan. **www.mont-sant.com**

LA VILA JOIOSA El Montiboli €€€€

Partida El Montiboli, 03570 (Alicante) **Tel** *965 89 02 50* **Rooms** *85*

This beautiful, cliff-side luxury hotel overlooks a secluded beach. The rooms are decorated in warm Mediterranean colours, and most have spacious terraces offering glorious sea views. There are a handful of plush suites as well, and guests can also stay in one of the romantic bungalows in the gardens. **www.montiboli.es**

MURCIA NH Rincón de Pepe €€

C/ Apóstoles 34, 30001 **Tel** *968 21 22 39* **Fax** *968 22 17 44* **Rooms** *148*

Located just behind the town cathedral, near the restaurants and shopping area of the city centre, this hotel is in a rather ordinary, modern building but the rooms are simple, functional and well equipped. The hotel is also the setting for the Gran Casino de Murcia on the first floor. **www.nh-hotels.com**

MURCIA Arco de San Juan €€€

Plaza de Ceballos 10, 30003 (Murcia) **Tel** *968 21 04 55* **Fax** *968 22 08 09* **Rooms** *97*

The award-winning restoration of this old palace combines contemporary materials with antique furnishings. This luxury hotel is often chosen for wedding dinners and other celebrations by local Murcians. Rooms are large and comfortable, although they lack character. Also has a popular restaurant and bar. **www.arcosanjuan.com**

OLIVA Pensión Oliva €

C/ San Lluis 35, 46780 (Near Gandia, Valencia) **Tel** *653 60 69 14* **Fax** *962 85 53 04* **Rooms** *6*

A delightful guesthouse, located in a restored, stone-built cottage close to the coast. The rooms are comfortable with modern amenities such as a TV, minibar and tea and coffeemakers. Also has two family rooms and one especially adapted for disabled guests. Serves a daily breakfast buffet. **www.hotelitooliva.com**

ONTINYENT Hotel Kazar €€

C/ Dos de Mayo 117, 46870 (Valencia) **Tel** *962 38 24 43* **Fax** *962 38 23 18* **Rooms** *40*

The hotel is located in a picturesque palace built by the Mompo family in the 19th century following the style of a Moorish fortress and surrounded by a garden filled with palm trees. Very comfortable and elegant bedrooms and suites all with mini-bar and free Wi-Fi. **www.hotelkazar.com**

ORIHUELA (ORIOLA) Hotel Meliá Palacio Tudemir €€

C/ Alfonso XIII, 03300 (Alicante) **Tel** *966 73 80 10* **Fax** *966 73 80 70* **Rooms** *51*

This hotel is housed in a superbly restored, 18th-century palace. The coat-of-arms of the original owner still sits proudly over the main door, and the interior is palatial. The latest modern conveniences have been added, but many original details have been retained. Also has a good restaurant. **www.solmelia.com**

PEÑÍSCOLA Hostería del Mar €€

Av Papa Luna 18, 12598 (Castellón) **Tel** *964 48 06 00* **Fax** *964 48 13 63* **Rooms** *86*

At this whitewashed beachfront hotel the rooms and suites are traditionally decorated and equipped with modern amenities, including Internet facilities and a minibar. From mid-June to mid-September guests are required to stay a minimum of seven nights and to take the half-board, which includes lunch or dinner. **www.hosteriadelmar.net**

VALENCIA Vincci Lys €

C/ Martínez Cubells 5, 46002 (Valencia) **Tel** *963 50 95 50* **Fax** *963 50 95 52* **Rooms** *96*

In a convenient location near the main sights of Valencia's historic quarter and the train station, this elegant hotel offers classically decorated rooms, including spacious suites for very reasonable prices. There is a restaurant serving Mediterranean cuisine, and in summer the bar opens onto an outdoor terrace. **www.hotelvinccilys.com**

VALENCIA Ad Hoc €€

C/ Boix 4, 46003 (Valencia) **Tel** *963 91 91 40* **Fax** *963 91 36 67* **Rooms** *28*

This chic hotel is housed in a renovated, soundproofed, 19th-century building near the Río Turia gardens. The bedrooms are furnished in a mixture of old and new styles, with brick walls, antiques and modern fabrics. Book early for one with a terrace. The restaurant offers an excellent, fixed-price lunch. **www.adhochoteles.com**

Key to Price Guide *see p560* **Key to Symbols** *see back cover flap*

VALENCIA Hotel Venecia €€€

C/ En Llop 5, 46002 (Valencia) ***Tel*** *963 52 42 67* ***Fax*** *963 52 44 21* ***Rooms*** *54*

An excellent, modestly priced hotel in the centre of the city. Although set in an old building, the hotel's interior is modern. The rooms are functionally decorated and provide basic amenities such as a TV, telephone and electronic safe. Several eateries can be found within walking distance. A breakfast buffet is served.

VALENCIA SH Inglés Boutique €€€

C/ Marqués de Dos Aguas 6, 46002 (Valencia) ***Tel*** *963 51 64 26* ***Fax*** *963 94 02 51* ***Rooms*** *63*

This convenient and stylish city-centre hotel is in the old palace of the Dukes of Cardona, next to the National Ceramics Museum. The rooms and suites overlook the street, and are equipped with amenities such as Internet access, a TV, a minibar and a safe. The restaurant serves regional specialties. **www.hotelinglesboutique.com**

VILAFAMÉS Hotel El Jardín Vertical €€€€

C/ Nou 15, 12192 ***Tel*** *964 32 99 38* ***Fax*** *964 32 99 39* ***Rooms*** *9*

Built in the 17th century with distinctive local red stone and now completely restored, this hotel is in the ideal location to relax. Take a stroll amid the almond and olive trees in the hotel grounds and enjoy some of the excellent food from the highly rated restaurant. **www.eljardinvertical.com**

XÀBIA (JÁVEA) Hotel Jávea €

Calle Pio X 5, 03730 (Alicante) ***Tel*** *965 79 54 61* ***Fax*** *965 79 54 63* ***Rooms*** *24*

A cheerful, simple, typically Spanish seaside hotel. This good-value option is just a stone's throw from the pebbly beach in Xàbia's picturesque port. The restaurant serves local specialities and offers wonderful views over the bay from its large picture windows. **www.hotel-javea.com**

XÀBIA (JÁVEA) Parador de Jávea €€€€

Avda Mediterráneo 233, 03730 (Alicante) ***Tel*** *965 79 02 00* ***Fax*** *965 79 03 08* ***Rooms*** *70*

A large, modern parador surrounded by lush Mediterranean gardens right on the beach. The rooms are bright and spacious and almost all have balconies overlooking the sea. Offers a wide range of sports facilities, including horse riding, diving, sailing and golf. The restaurant serves regional cuisine. Lunch or dinner included. **www.parador.es**

MADRID

OLD MADRID Analina Rooms €

C/ Espada 6, 28012 ***Tel*** *913 69 19 14* ***Fax*** *913 89 62 37* ***Rooms*** *12* ***Map*** *4 F4*

In a lively area full of shops and art galleries, and close to the fashionable La Latina district, this hostel offers modern, stylish rooms catering for up to four occupants. All rooms have private bathrooms and some have TV. Guests are offered discounts in a nearby café and restaurant. Free Wi-Fi is available. **www.hostalmadridlalatina.com**

OLD MADRID Hostal Armesto €

C/ San Agustin 6, 28014 ***Tel*** *914 29 90 31* ***Rooms*** *8* ***Map*** *7 B3*

A friendly hotel conveniently located in a quiet street just a few steps away from the art galleries, as well as the central shops and restaurants. Some of the attractive, air-conditioned rooms are small, but all are en suite. The best rooms look on to the garden of Lope de Vega's house. **www.hostalarmesto.com**

OLD MADRID Hostal Buenos Aires €

Gran Via 61, 28013 ***Tel*** *915 42 10 02* ***Fax*** *915 42 28 69* ***Rooms*** *30* ***Map*** *2 D5*

A simple, economical hotel, conveniently located on the busy Gran Vía. The public rooms are pleasantly decorated, and almost all the bedrooms have their own balcony or small terrace. Moreover, the rooms are soundproofed against the capital's noisy nightlife. No breakfast. **www.hoteleshn.com**

OLD MADRID Hostal Madrid €

C/ Esparteros 6, 1st & 2nd floor, 28012 ***Tel*** *915 22 00 60* ***Fax*** *915 32 35 10* ***Rooms*** *24* ***Map*** *4 F2*

Right in the heart of Madrid, this air-conditioned hotel is a fine budget option, with a choice from singles to rooms for up to five people. However, it is the apartments that are particularly special. Most are well equipped with pleasant, modern furnishings, and some have sunny terraces overlooking the Old Town. **www.hostal-madrid.info**

OLD MADRID Hotel Mario €€

C/ Campomanes 4, 28013 ***Tel*** *915 48 85 48* ***Fax*** *915 59 12 88* ***Rooms*** *54* ***Map*** *4 D2*

The stylish Hotel Mario is situated close to many major sights, as well as great shopping and dining. The rooms are small, but slickly decorated in black-and-white minimalist style with splashes of colour and high-tech gadgets. A self-service buffet breakfast is also available until late. **www.room-matehoteles.com**

OLD MADRID Hotel Moderno €€

C/ Arenal 2, 28013 ***Tel*** *915 31 09 00* ***Fax*** *915 31 35 50* ***Rooms*** *97* ***Map*** *4 E2*

A comfortable, modern hotel in a central location. The rooms are decorated with traditional furniture; some have terraces with a view of the city's skyline. Offers free Wi-Fi access and is popular with both business travellers and tourists. Breakfast is available and a range of restaurants can be found nearby. **www.hotel-moderno.com**

OLD MADRID Hotel Petit Palace Londres 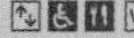 €€

C/ Galdo 2, 28013 ***Tel*** *915 31 41 05* ***Fax*** *915 31 41 01* ***Rooms*** *76* ***Map*** *4 F2*

Behind the façade of this turn-of-the-20th-century mansion is a modern hotel with many rooms and suites. All rooms come with a personal computer and business travellers have access to a business centre. Two specially adapted rooms are also available for disabled travellers. **www.hthoteles.com**

OLD MADRID Hotel Plaza Mayor €€

C/ Atocha 2, 28012 ***Tel*** *913 60 06 06* ***Fax*** *913 60 06 10* ***Rooms*** *34* ***Map*** *7 A3*

Just around the corner of Madrid's central square, this popular hotel fills up fast, so book well in advance. Rooms vary in size and decor, but are spotless and brightly painted. The attic suite is more expensive, but offers fine views from its private terrace. Also has a reading room. Free wireless Internet in lobby. **www.h-plazamayor.com**

OLD MADRID Reyes Católicos €€

C/ del Ángel 18, 28005 ***Tel*** *913 65 86 00* ***Fax*** *913 65 98 67* ***Rooms*** *38* ***Map*** *3 C4*

Set in the trendy La Latina district, this modern hotel is very popular and always busy. Children are made welcome, and there are board games to keep them amused. The bedroom windows are double-glazed for soundproofing, and five of the rooms have their own terraces. **www.hotelreyescatolicos.com**

OLD MADRID Tryp Gran Vía €€

Gran Vía 25, 28013 ***Tel*** *915 22 11 21* ***Fax*** *915 21 24 24* ***Rooms*** *175* ***Map*** *2 D5*

A large chain hotel on one of the city's busiest streets, close to the main sightseeing and shopping areas. The service is brisk and efficient, and the rooms, although blandly decorated, are reasonably comfortable. Some are better than others, and are worth checking in advance. The hotel's website offers good discounts. **www.solmelia.com**

OLD MADRID Carlos V €€€

C/ Maestro Victoria 5, 28013 ***Tel*** *915 31 41 00* ***Fax*** *915 31 37 61* ***Rooms*** *67* ***Map*** *4 E2*

A city-centre hotel in a pedestrian street beside the Puerta del Sol. This hotel has interconnecting bedrooms as well as family rooms. Some of the rooms also have balconies and sun terraces. A generous buffet breakfast is served in the café bar, and the staff are friendly and helpful. **www.hotelcarlosv.com**

OLD MADRID Hotel Liabeny €€€

C/ Salud 3, 28013 ***Tel*** *915 31 90 00* ***Fax*** *915 32 74 21* ***Rooms*** *220* ***Map*** *4 F2*

An elegant, modern hotel, located just a short walk from the main sights, yet away from the hubbub of the city centre. The extensively renovated hotel features traditionally decorated rooms and suites with every modern amenity, a good restaurant and excellent service. The private parking and disabled access is a plus. **www.liabeny.es**

OLD MADRID Hotel de Las Letras €€€€

Gran Vía 11, 28013 ***Tel*** *915 23 79 80* ***Fax*** *915 23 79 81* ***Rooms*** *109* ***Map*** *7 A1*

This central boutique hotel has colourfully stylish rooms, each with its own themed literary quote. The rooftop bar is a chic hangout in summer with great views of the city, while the library is a cosy winter hideaway. The renowned restaurant is supplemented by a relaxed cocktail lounge. **www.hoteldelasletras.com**

OLD MADRID Casa de Madrid €€€€€

C/ Arrieta 2, 28013 ***Tel*** *915 59 57 91* ***Fax*** *915 40 11 00* ***Rooms*** *7* ***Map*** *4 D1*

Housed in an 18th-century palace, this stylish little hotel is ideal for a romantic getaway. The seven rooms – two of which are suites – are exquisitely decorated with antiques. The hotel has a small library. The breakfast includes freshly squeezed juice and home-made marmalade. Highly recommended. **www.casademadrid.com**

BOURBON MADRID Hostal Bianco €

C/ Echegaray 5, 1° D, 28014 ***Tel*** *913 69 13 32* ***Fax*** *913 69 13 32* ***Rooms*** *15* ***Map*** *7 A2*

A well-kept *hostal* in a convenient location – all the museums and other attractions are close by. The rooms are simply decorated with all the basic amenities including TVs and a safety box. The friendly staff can speak some English. No breakfast. **www.hostalbianco.com**

BOURBON MADRID Hostal Cervelo Madrid €

C/ Atocha 43, 28012 ***Tel*** *914 29 95 94* ***Fax*** *914 29 09 64* ***Rooms*** *24* ***Map*** *7 A3*

A simple pension with a friendly atmosphere, close to three museums and the lively bars and cafés of the Santa Ana neighbourhood. The rooms are clean, decorated with basic furniture and well equipped – all have free Internet connections and en suite facilities. Breakfast is available. **www.hostalcervelo.com**

BOURBON MADRID Hostal Gonzalo €

C/ Cervantes 34, 28014 ***Tel*** *914 29 27 14* ***Fax*** *914 20 20 07* ***Rooms*** *15* ***Map*** *7 B3*

A family-run hostel, which often fills up well in advance. Provides good facilities, immaculate bedrooms with en suite bathrooms and excellent value for money. The multi-lingual owners are hospitable and offer helpful information on nearby attractions and entertainments. Several restaurants are within walking distance. **www.hostalgonzalo.com**

BOURBON MADRID Hotel Miau €€

C/ Príncipe 26, 28012 ***Tel*** *913 69 71 20* ***Fax*** *914 29 30 68* ***Rooms*** *20* ***Map*** *7 A2*

This modest hotel, housed in a handsome 19th-century building, is located in the famous Plaza Santa Ana Square at the heart of Madrid's literary quarter. The rooms are simply, but comfortably decorated, with basic amenities. In addition, all the rooms are soundproofed. Breakfast is included. **www.hotelmiau.com**

Key to Price Guide *see p560* **Key to Symbols** *see back cover flap*

BOURBON MADRID Santander  €€

C/ de Echegaray 1, 28014 ***Tel*** *914 29 95 51* ***Fax*** *913 69 10 78* ***Rooms*** *35* ***Map*** *7 A2*

This small, popular, family-run hotel is situated in Madrid's literary quarter, which is filled with lively tapas bars and cafés. Opened in the 1920s, the hotel has neat, comfortable rooms, decorated in a traditional Spanish style. The staff are very helpful, and are happy to arrange theatre and flamenco tickets. **www.hotelsantandermadrid.com**

BOURBON MADRID Room-Mate Oscar €€€

Plaza Vázquez de Mella 12, 28004 ***Tel*** *917 01 11 73* ***Fax*** *915 21 62 96* ***Rooms*** *74* ***Map*** *7 A1*

One of four from this small chain of good value, stylish hotels in central Madrid, Oscar stands out because of its roof-top swimming pool. It is located on the edge of the neighbourhood of Chueca, which is crammed with popular bars and gay nightclubs. The design is fresh and contemporary, and the service friendly. **www.room-matehotels.com**

BOURBON MADRID Suite Prado €€€

Manuel Fernández y González 10, 28014 ***Tel*** *914 20 23 18* ***Fax*** *914 20 05 59* ***Rooms*** *18* ***Map*** *7 A3*

A stylish apartment-hotel of luxurious suites, all fully equipped with a kitchen, dining room, telephone lines and marble bathrooms. The hotel is very popular with business travellers, but its proximity to attractions such as the Prado and the Museo Thyssen-Bornemisza makes it a good choice for tourists as well. **www.suiteprado.com**

BOURBON MADRID ME Madrid €€€€

Plaza de Santa Ana 14, 28012 ***Tel*** *917 01 60 00* ***Fax*** *915 22 03 07* ***Rooms*** *192* ***Map*** *7 A3*

This ultra-stylish and innovative hotel is situated in the majestic building on the corner of Plaza de Santa Ana. Each of the contemporary rooms offers a fully-stocked martini bar and the latest entertainment technology, including iPod sound systems and Wi-Fi, and the trendy Penthouse bar has fantastic views over the city. **www.memadrid.com**

BOURBON MADRID Villa Real €€€€

Plaza de las Cortes 10, 28014 ***Tel*** *914 20 37 67* ***Fax*** *914 20 25 47* ***Rooms*** *115* ***Map*** *7 B2*

Close to the Prado and the Retiro gardens, this stylish hotel is based in an opulent, early 19th-century building. One of Madrid's smartest hotels, the spacious rooms and suites are decorated in a tasteful mixture of traditional and contemporary styles, and scattered with ancient Roman art. Some suites even have a Jacuzzi. **www.derbyhotels.es**

BOURBON MADRID Ritz €€€€€

Plaza de la Lealtad 5, 28014 ***Tel*** *917 01 67 67* ***Fax*** *917 01 67 76* ***Rooms*** *167* ***Map*** *7 C2*

Inaugurated in 1910 as a hotel for aristocrats, the Ritz is still one of Spain's most elegant hotels. Close to the Prado, the hotel has an ornate, circular foyer and a terraced garden, and serves tea and brunch along with live music. Rooms are luxurious and offer every imaginable comfort. **www.ritz.es**

BOURBON MADRID Westin Palace €€€€€

Plaza de las Cortes 7, 28014 ***Tel*** *913 60 80 00* ***Fax*** *913 60 81 00* ***Rooms*** *467* ***Map*** *7 B2*

This *belle époque* hotel with a glass dome and a colonnade has accommodated statesmen, as well as Mata Hari, the spy. The decor features marble columns, chandeliers and huge oil paintings and statues. Rooms are nicely decorated, and the service is charmingly old-fashioned and efficient. They also have a wine cellar. **www.palacemadrid.com**

FURTHER AFIELD (WEST) Hotel T3 Tirol €€

C/ Marqués de Urquijo 4, 28008 ***Tel*** *915 48 19 00* ***Fax*** *915 41 39 58* ***Rooms*** *98* ***Map*** *1 B2*

This comfortable, mid-range hotel has excellent facilities for both business travellers and families. It is located in a bustling neighbourhood with good shops and restaurants and a large park. The tastefully decorated rooms include interconnecting children's rooms and family rooms. A choice of meeting rooms is available. **www.t3tirol.com**

FURTHER AFIELD (EAST) NH Alcalá €€

C/ de Alcalá 66, 28009 ***Tel*** *914 35 10 60* ***Fax*** *914 35 11 05* ***Rooms*** *146* ***Map*** *4 F2*

A large, chain hotel close to the lovely Retiro gardens. Features spacious, well-equipped rooms with amenities that include Wi-Fi and Internet access. This reasonably priced hotel also has a café, bar and private car park. It is within walking distance of the upmarket shopping district in Salamanca, and three museums. **www.nh-hotels.com**

FURTHER AFIELD (NORTH) Hostal Sil & Serranos €

C/ Fuencarral 95, 28004 ***Tel*** *914 48 89 72* ***Fax*** *914 47 48 29* ***Rooms*** *20* ***Map*** *2 F3*

This comfortable *hostal* is situated in one of the city's liveliest nightlife districts, which is also a prominent gay neighbourhood. Offers simple, but adequate bedrooms, with en suite facilities at a reasonable price. There are plenty of fashionable bars, cafés, shops and restaurants nearby. No breakfast. **www.silserranos.com**

FURTHER AFIELD (NORTH) High Tech President Castellana €€€

C/ Marqués de Villamagna 4, 28001 ***Tel*** *915 77 19 51* ***Fax*** *915 77 19 54* ***Rooms*** *104* ***Map*** *6 E3*

The High Tech President is the ultimate in ultra-modern design and technology. Its spacious rooms boast the latest technical innovations in a sleek and stylish environment. Amenities include laptops, flatscreen TVs, audio multi-adaptors for iPhones and iPods, hydroshowers and exercise bikes. Wi-Fi throughout. **www.hthoteles.com**

FURTHER AFIELD (NORTH) Intercontinental Madrid €€€€€

Paseo de la Castellana 49, 28046 ***Tel*** *917 00 73 00* ***Fax*** *913 19 58 53* ***Rooms*** *307* ***Map*** *6 D1*

This luxurious international chain hotel in Madrid's financial district is a favourite with business travellers. The rooms and suites offer several amenities. The hotel also hosts a well-equipped business centre, as well as a cocktail lounge for relaxing after work, and a baby-sitting service. Visit the website for special offers. **www.intercontinental.com**

FURTHER AFIELD (NORTH) Santo Mauro €€€€€

C/ Zurbano 36, 28010 ***Tel*** *913 19 69 00* ***Fax*** *913 08 54 77* ***Rooms*** *51* ***Map*** *5 C2*

This palace, built in 1894 on one of Madrid's most elegant streets, is surrounded by beautiful wooded gardens. The rooms and suites are stylishly decorated, and the two fine restaurants offer romantic outdoor dining in summer. Also houses a swimming pool in the vaulted cellars and a spa. **www.ac-hotels.com**

FURTHER AFIELD (NORTHEAST) Hotel Vincci Soma €€

C/ Goya 79, 28001 ***Tel*** *914 35 75 45* ***Fax*** *914 31 09 43* ***Rooms*** *117* ***Map*** *6 F5*

Surrounded by elegant restaurants and designer boutiques, this hotel is a haven of peace and comfort in the middle of Madrid's fashionable Salamanca district, and just a stone's throw away from Retiro Park. Rooms are spacious and decorated in a contemporary style. Breakfast is available at extra cost. **www.vinccihoteles.com**

FURTHER AFIELD (NORTHEAST) Hotel Puerta América €€€€€

Avenida de America 41, 28002 ***Tel*** *917 44 54 00* ***Fax*** *917 44 54 01* ***Rooms*** *315*

Near the conference centres and airport, this hotel is an essential reference for world-class contemporary design. The 12 floors were each commissioned from a different top international architect, including Jean Nouvel, Zaha Hadid, Norman Foster and Arata Isozaki. The luxurious rooms offer panoramic views of the city. **www.puertamerica.com**

MADRID PROVINCE

ARANJUEZ El Cocherón 1919 €€

C/ Montesinos 22, 28300 ***Tel*** *918 75 43 50* ***Fax*** *918 75 43 47* ***Rooms*** *20*

This small, charming family-run hotel is set around a historic *corrala* (central courtyard), but has been decorated in a fine mixture of contemporary and traditional styles. The bedrooms look out onto the ochre-painted courtyard. Perfectly located in the city centre, it has a small café for guests. Serves breakfast only. **www.elcocheron1919.com**

CERCEDILLA Hotel Rural Luces del Poniente €€

C/ Lina de Avila 4, Cercedilla, Madrid, 28470 ***Tel*** *918 52 55 87* ***Fax*** *918 52 32 47* ***Rooms*** *13*

Sited in a picturesque chalet town on the fringes of the Sierra de Guadarrama, this place provides respite from the summer heat. The rooms are chic and stylish in their decor, yet provide a warm inviting ambience. It is an ideal base for nearby ski resorts and additionals include mountain bikes and horseback riding. **www.lucesdelponiente.com**

CHINCHÓN Hostal Chinchón €

Calle Grande 16, 28370 ***Tel*** *918 93 53 98* ***Fax*** *918 94 01 08* ***Rooms*** *10*

An atmospheric *hostal* located in the famous Plaza Mayor at the very centre of the village. Rooms are a choice between doubles and triples and are furnished in a pleasant mix of styles; all are en suite. There's the bonus of a pool overlooking the rooftops and a small garden. **www.hostalchinchon.com**

CHINCHÓN Parador de Chinchón €€€

C/ de los Huertos 1, 28370 ***Tel*** *918 94 08 36* ***Fax*** *918 94 09 08* ***Rooms*** *38*

Housed in a 17th-century monastery, this stunning parador is set around a tree-filled courtyard, and adorned with frescoes, *azulejos* (tiles) and antiques. The handsome bedrooms have immensely thick stone walls, and the restaurant serves traditional Castilian fare, including garlic soup and roast suckling pig. **www.parador.es**

RASCAFRÍA Sheraton Santa María de El Paular €€

Ctra M–604, km 26.5, 28741 ***Tel*** *918 69 10 11* ***Fax*** *918 69 10 06* ***Rooms*** *56*

A relaxing retreat in the beautiful Sierra de Guadarrama, this hotel occupies a section of a 15th-century Benedictine monastery. Part of the Sheraton chain of hotels, it offers several facilities, from tennis courts and an outdoor pool to an elegant restaurant and an informal tavern. Closed January. **www.starwoodhotels.com**

SAN LORENZO DEL ESCORIAL Hotel Botánico €€

C/ Timoteo Padrós 16, 28200 ***Tel*** *918 90 78 79* ***Fax*** *918 90 81 58* ***Rooms*** *20*

An appealing hotel, housed in a handsome, whitewashed country mansion. A stone's throw from the vast El Escorial monastery, it is surrounded by beautiful gardens and is situated opposite the golf course. The bedrooms are decorated with modern furnishings, and offer great views. Breakfast included. **www.botanicohotel.com**

CASTILLA Y LEÓN

ASTORGA Casa de Tepa €€

C/ Santiago 2, 24700 ***Tel*** *987 60 32 99* ***Fax*** *987 60 32 96* ***Rooms*** *10*

Within the ancient town walls, this charming, refurbished convent and pilgrims' hospital has elegant bedrooms and bathrooms. Generous communal areas include several comfortable sitting rooms and glazed galleries. There is also a pretty garden with sunny tables in the large courtyard. **www.casadetepa.com**

Key to Price Guide *see p560* **Key to Symbols** *see back cover flap*

ÁVILA Rey Niño €

Plaza José Tomé 1, 05001 ***Tel*** *920 25 52 10* ***Fax*** *920 22 62 80* ***Rooms*** *24*

Located within the city's medieval walls, in a tranquil pedestrian street, this hotel proves the old adage – "Ávila, the city where one hears the silence". All the rooms are spacious and comfortable, and all have their own bathrooms. **www.hotelreynino.com**

ÁVILA Hospedería la Sinagoga €€

Reyes Católicos 22, 05001 ***Tel*** *920 35 23 21* ***Fax*** *920 35 34 74* ***Rooms*** *22*

This 15th-century building, situated in the centre of the old town, was formerly a synagogue serving Ávila's thriving Jewish commmunity. Some decorative elements from the original structure remain, lending an atmospheric touch to this well-equipped and comfortable hotel.

ÁVILA Hotel Palacio Valderrábanos €€

Plaza de la Catedral 9, 05001 ***Tel*** *920 21 10 23* ***Fax*** *920 25 16 91* ***Rooms*** *73*

Within the famous walls of Ávila, right next to the cathedral, this 14th-century building was once a bishop's palace. The attractive and elegant rooms make for a comfortable stay, while the restaurant serves a number of hearty local specialities. **www.palaciovalderrabanoshotel.com**

BURGOS La Puebla €€

La Puebla 20, 09004 ***Tel*** *947 20 00 11* ***Fax*** *947 20 47 08* ***Rooms*** *19*

A grand 19th-century building houses this good-value hotel, equipped with comfortable but no-frills rooms. With its excellent location near the Teatro Principal, La Puebla offers its guests a great all-round package, which includes free bicycles. The old-fashioned atmosphere and friendly staff give this place a timeless feel. **www.hotellapuebla.com**

BURGOS NH Palacio de la Merced €€

C/ de la Merced 13, 09002 ***Tel*** *947 47 99 00* ***Fax*** *947 26 04 26* ***Rooms*** *110*

Part of the NH chain, this spectacular hotel is set in a 17th-century palace. Tastefully renovated, it comes complete with its own Gothic cloister. Modern amenities and luxuries, such as saunas, massage services and baby-sitting facilities are also available. **www.nh-hotels.com**

BURGOS Landa Palace €€€€€

Ctra Al (E-5) de Madrid a Irún km 235, 09001 ***Tel*** *947 25 77 77* ***Fax*** *947 26 46 76* ***Rooms*** *39*

Considered one of the best hotels in the region, this family-run establishment offers guests a taste of luxurious living with large, elegant and comfortable rooms equipped with DVD players and other creature comforts. Some rooms have Jacuzzis. The highlight, however, is the magnificent swimming pool covered by Gothic arches. **www.landa.as**

CARRIÓN DE LOS CONDES Hotel Monasterio de San Zoilo €€

Obispo Souto Vizoso s/n, 34120 ***Tel*** *979 88 00 49* ***Fax*** *979 88 10 90* ***Rooms*** *49*

Situated along the Santiago pilgrimage route, this former Benedictine monastery has been welcoming travellers for centuries. It provides a perfect place to relax after a long day exploring the stunning surroundings. The restaurant serves elaborate Castilian seasonal cuisine. **www.sanzoilo.com**

CIUDAD RODRIGO Parador de Ciudad Rodrigo €€€€

Plaza Castillo 1, 37500 (Salamanca) ***Tel*** *923 46 01 50* ***Fax*** *923 46 04 04* ***Rooms*** *35*

Located in a castle on a hill overlooking the river, this comfortable parador is famous for the medieval Homenaje tower, which provides great views of the local scenery. The rooms are decorated with traditional Castilian furniture, and the garden and patio offer guests an ideal spot to spend some quiet time. **www.parador.es**

COVARRUBIAS Hotel Doña Sancha €

Avenida Victor Barbadillo, 09346 (Burgos) ***Tel*** *947 40 64 00* ***Fax*** *947 40 05 04* ***Rooms*** *14*

This small hotel offers peace and tranquillity in a natural setting, surrounded by mountains. The bedrooms are comfortable and well equipped, and all have a balcony with views over the valley. Breakfast includes home-made breads and jams made from the fruit trees that grow in the garden. No credit cards. **www.hoteldonasancha.com**

HOYOS DEL ESPINO El Milano Real €€€

C/ Toledo s/n, 05634 (Ávila) ***Tel*** *920 34 91 08* ***Fax*** *920 34 91 56* ***Rooms*** *21*

This hotel with spa has managed to maintain its rustic charm and is ideal for those in search of a relaxing and tranquil retreat. Guests can explore the scenic beauty of the surrounding Gredos mountains by foot or on horseback. Spectacular views of the mountains are available from some rooms. **www.elmilanoreal.com**

LA ALBERCA Hotel Antiguas Eras €€

Av Batuecas 29 bajo, 37624 (Salamanca) ***Tel*** *923 41 51 13* ***Fax*** *923 41 51 13* ***Rooms*** *34*

This unique building is a mishmash of different and somewhat clashing architectural styles. The rooms are large, comfortable and functional. Some of them offer views of the Béjar mountain range, while others have a terrace and a bath with hydromassage. **www.antiguaseras.com**

LEÓN Alfonso V €€

Padre Isla 1, 24002 ***Tel*** *987 22 09 00* ***Fax*** *987 22 12 44* ***Rooms*** *62*

This grand hotel, built in the 1920s to accommodate tourists passing through, has retained some of its "golden age" charm in the lobby, with its glass dome that floods the entrance with light. The rooms are large and comfortable, with a modern, minimalist decor and parquet flooring. Also a gourmet restaurant. **www.hotelalfonsov.com**

LEÓN París €€

C/ Ancha 18, 24003 ***Tel*** *987 23 86 00* ***Fax*** *987 27 15 72* ***Rooms*** *61*

Most Spanish towns seem to have a hotel called "París" and, generally, they are as different from the Parisian style as can be imagined. León's version is very Spanish, with simple, unsophisticated decor and an efficient, if not overly enthusiastic, staff. There is an indoor pool and a spa (closed Sun pm & Mon am). **www.hotelparisleon.com**

LEÓN Parador de San Marcos €€€€€

Plaza de San Marcos 7, 24001 ***Tel*** *987 23 73 00* ***Fax*** *987 23 34 58* ***Rooms*** *226*

The dramatic Renaissance façade of this former San Marcos monastery gives way to an interior full of stone work and wooden masterpieces by medieval maestros. The rooms are comfortable and luxurious. A stay at this museum-like hotel is an experience in itself. **www.parador.es**

MOLINASECA La Posada de Muriel €€

Plaza Santo Cristo s/n, 24413 (León) ***Tel*** *987 45 32 01* ***Fax*** *987 45 31 35* ***Rooms*** *8*

A small and welcoming country inn on the Santiago pilgrimage route. This renovated farmhouse offers simple and well-equipped rooms with traditional furnishings. The two rooms on the upper floor are smaller, but have a beautiful view through the skylight windows. Closed 7–31 Jan. **www.laposadademuriel.com**

NAVARREDONDA DE GREDOS Parador de Gredos €€€

AV 941 km 10, 05635 (Ávila) ***Tel*** *920 34 80 48* ***Fax*** *920 34 82 05* ***Rooms*** *74*

Built in 1928, this is considered by many as one of Spain's best paradors. The hotel is decorated in a sober, no-frills Castilian style, and offers excellent views over the Tormes valley and the nearby peaks of the Gredos mountains. Some of the rooms have their own terrace. The restaurant serves local cuisine. **www.parador.es**

PALENCIA AC Palencia €€

Av de Cuba 25, 34004 ***Tel*** *979 16 57 01* ***Fax*** *979 16 57 02* ***Rooms*** *65*

This modern hotel is located near the town centre, and is very popular with both business travellers and weekend tourists. The hotel offers guests the chance to unwind in its sauna, and enjoy the buffet at its restaurant. The rooms are equipped with high-speed Internet and cable TV and free mini-bar. **www.marriott.com**

PEDRAZA Hospedería de Santo Domingo €€€

Matadero 3, 40172 (Segovia) ***Tel*** *921 50 99 71* ***Fax*** *921 50 86 83* ***Rooms*** *17*

The coat of arms on the façade of this converted 18th-century manor reads "Jesus and Mary's slaves. Year 1703". What was once an austere establishment is now a comfortable, modern hotel, which tastefully incorporates the numerous remaining historical elements with contemporary touches. **www.hospederiadesantodomingo.com**

PONFERRADA AC Ponferrada €€

Avda de Astorga 2, 24400 (León) ***Tel*** *987 40 99 73* ***Fax*** *987 40 99 74* ***Rooms*** *60*

A steep climb up paved alleys takes guests to the entrance of this hotel, situated near the city's castle. Offers comfortable, well-equipped rooms and adequate service at a good price. Also has parking facilities for those who find the walk too challenging. **www.marriott.com**

POZAL DE GALLINAS La Posada Real del Pinar €€

A-6, exit 157, Finca Pinar de San Rafael s/n, 47400 (Valladolid) ***Tel*** *686 48 42 01* ***Fax*** *983 44 99 72* ***Rooms*** *19*

Very close to Valladolid and less than an hour from Ávila, Salamanca and Segovia, this country house comes with a beautiful, expansive garden. The cosy living room, library and dining room give this hotel a homely touch. Bikes are available for guests and there is a children's pool. Breakfast is included. **www.laposadadelpinar.com**

SALAMANCA Hostería Casa Vallejo €€

San Juan de la Cruz 3, 37001 ***Tel*** *923 28 04 21* ***Fax*** *923 21 31 12* ***Rooms*** *14*

This comfortable hostal near the Plaza Mayor is one of town's oldest hotels. The staff are friendly and willing to help guests make the most of their stay by pointing them in the right direction and suggesting some places off the tourist track. There is also a spa. Closed end Jan–mid-Mar. **www.hosteriacasavallejo.com**

SALAMANCA Room Mate Vega €€

Plaza del Mercado 16, 37001 ***Tel*** *923 27 22 50* ***Fax*** *923 27 09 32* ***Rooms*** *38*

Behind the original façade of Salamanca stone, contemporary styling mixes bright communal spaces with tastefully muted bedrooms. Service is friendly and helpful, and the breakfast buffet is available until midday. Located by the central market. There's also a rooftop bar. **www.room-matehotels.com**

SALAMANCA Palacio de San Esteban €€€

Arroyo de Santo Domingo 3, 37001 ***Tel*** *923 26 22 96* ***Fax*** *923 26 88 72* ***Rooms*** *51*

An old convent has been converted into one of the city's finest hotels. The original character of the building has been kept alive within the context of a modern hotel. The vaulted ceilings and stone walls breathe history, while the comfortable rooms do not lack any amenities and offer a free mini-bar. **www.palaciodesanesteban.com**

SALAMANCA Rector €€€€

Paseo Rector Esperabé 10, 37008 ***Tel*** *923 21 84 82* ***Fax*** *923 21 40 08* ***Rooms*** *13*

This hotel is set in an elegant building with a beautiful, wide entrance hall that has stained-glass windows in an Art Nouveau style. Smart rooms with mahogany furniture and white marble bathrooms make this one of the town's best-looking places to stay. **www.hotelrector.com**

Key to Price Guide *see p560* **Key to Symbols** *see back cover flap*

SAN ROMÁN DE LOS INFANTES Posada Dehesa Congosta  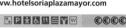 €€€

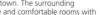

Finca la Congosta, 49281 (Zamora) ***Tel*** *615 21 76 42* ***Fax*** *980 98 05 04* ***Rooms*** *10*

Welcoming and friendly inn in a natural environment. Offers cosy and beautifully decorated rooms, each priced individually. One of the rooms is in an adjacent building, separate from the main hotel. Activities such as trekking, mountain biking, canoeing and horse riding are also available. Closed Nov–Apr. **www.dehesacongosta.com**

SANTA MARÍA DE MAVE El Convento €€

Monasterio de Santa María de Mave s/n, 34402 (Palencia) ***Tel*** *979 12 36 11* ***Fax*** *979 12 54 92* ***Rooms*** *25*

Located in the Montaña Palentina Natural Park, close to Aguilar de Campoo. The rooms are smart and comfortable, though some are a little monastic. They are well equipped with amenities such as minibars, TVs and hairdryers. The restaurant serves up some satisfying Castilian stews. Closed Nov–Apr. **www.elconventodemave.com**

SANTO DOMINGO DE SILOS Santo Domingo de Silos €

C/ Santo Domingo 12–22, 09610 (Burgos) ***Tel*** *947 39 00 53* ***Fax*** *947 39 00 52* ***Rooms*** *60*

A modest and functional hotel, located in front of the Santo Domingo de Silos monastery. The rooms evoke the seriousness and austerity of Castilian monastic life with forged-iron bedsteads and solid wooden furniture. The hotel's restaurant serves some good, hearty local fare. **www.hotelsantodomingodesilos.com**

SEGOVIA Hotel Los Linajes €€€

C/ Doctor Velasco 9, 40003 ***Tel*** *921 46 04 75* ***Fax*** *921 46 04 79* ***Rooms*** *60*

A pleasant mid-range hotel in a quiet corner of the old town centre, offering very good bedrooms, some with private balconies. There is also a large outdoor terrace with tables and chairs and spectacular views. Service is formal and traditional. **www.loslinajes.com**

SORIA Hostería Solar de Tejada €

Claustrilla 1, 42003 ***Tel*** *975 23 00 54* ***Fax*** *975 23 00 54* ***Rooms*** *18*

Situated in the heart of the city, this hotel is equipped with comfortable and modern facilities. The pastel-coloured rooms have a special charm and offer amenities such as TVs, hairdryers and iron-forged headboards by Luis Sáenz, a local artist. Breakfast is not available. **www.hosteriasolardetejada.com**

SORIA Hotel Soria Plaza Mayor €€

Plaza Mayor 10, 42002 ***Tel*** *975 24 08 64* ***Fax*** *975 21 29 84* ***Rooms*** *10*

A boutique hotel standing proudly next to the town hall in the pretty Plaza Mayor. The decor is an attractive mix of contemporary styling and exposed beams, with wooden floors. The bedrooms have quotes from the works of Soria's adopted poet Antonio Machado on the walls, plus all the latest comforts. **www.hotelsoriaplazamayor.com**

TORDESILLAS Parador de Tordesillas €€€€

Ctra de Salamanca 5, 47100 (Valladolid) ***Tel*** *983 77 00 51* ***Fax*** *983 77 10 13* ***Rooms*** *68*

An ancestral home located in a beautiful pine forest. The hotel's spectacular location is complemented by its numerous facilities, including sauna, gym, winter and summer swimming pools and conference room. The large and comfortable rooms are luxuriously furnished with Castilian antiques. **www.parador.es**

VALLADOLID Hostal París €

Especería 2, 47001 ***Tel*** *983 37 06 25* ***Fax*** *983 35 83 01* ***Rooms*** *37*

A simple, four-storey building conveniently set in the heart of the city, near the Plaza Mayor. This friendly, family-run hotel has comfortable bedrooms with all modern facilities, and offers good value for those travelling on a budget. The service here is impeccable. **www.hostalparis.com**

VALLADOLID Meliá Recoletos €€

Acera de Recoletos 13, 47004 ***Tel*** *983 21 62 00* ***Fax*** *983 21 62 10* ***Rooms*** *80*

This smart hotel is situated in Valladolid's beautiful historical city centre, and offers great views of the Campo Grande park. The hotel has all modern conveniences. What it lacks in character, it makes up with its excellent location close to the town's main train station. **www.solmelia.com**

VILLAFRANCA DEL BIERZO Parador del Bierzo €€€

Avda Calvo Sotelo 28, 24500 (León) ***Tel*** *987 54 01 75* ***Fax*** *987 54 00 10* ***Rooms*** *39*

An unassuming and welcoming hotel, Parador del Bierzo is near the entrance to the town. The surrounding Ancares mountain range creates a tranquil atmosphere. It offers fully renovated large and comfortable rooms with traditional Castilian decor and a good restaurant. A great-value option. Closed 20 Dec–1 Feb. **www.parador.es**

ZAMORA NH Palacio del Duero €€

Plaza de la Horta1, 49002 ***Tel*** *980 50 82 62* ***Fax*** *980 53 37 22* ***Rooms*** *49*

The Duero Palace used to house one of the city's first distilleries. Like all NH chain properties, the decor here follows a modern, minimalist style that contrasts nicely with the ancient stone walls. A playground and baby-sitting services make it a good choice for families. Modern amenities and good value for money. **www.nh-hotels.com**

ZAMORA Parador de Zamora €€€€

Plaza de Viriato 5, 49001 ***Tel*** *980 51 44 97* ***Fax*** *980 53 00 63* ***Rooms*** *52*

Located in a 15th-century palace, this hotel's medieval decor features aristocratic tapestries, armour and beds with canopies (in some rooms). The Renaissance patio, embellished with heraldic motifs, is a perfect place to sample some of the restaurant's star dishes, including a mouthwatering almond custard. **www.parador.es**

CASTILLA-LA MANCHA

ALARCÓN Parador de Alarcón €€€€€

Avda Amigos de los Castillos 3, 16213 (Cuenca) **Tel** *969 33 03 15* **Fax** *969 33 03 03* **Rooms** *14*

A medieval fortress stunningly located above the Júcar valley. The lounge and dining rooms are vaulted chambers with thick walls. However, modern artworks by some of Spain's most renowned artists create a contemporary look. The large suites are all spectacular; the one in the lookout tower is the best. **www.parador.es**

ALBACETE Parador de Albacete €€€

Ctra N301 km 251, 02000 (Albacete) **Tel** *967 01 05 00* **Fax** *967 24 32 71* **Rooms** *68*

This parador is set in expansive gardens, with shady terraces, a large outdoor pool and a pitch and putt course. Provides a perfect setting for activities such as walking, fishing and horse riding. The public spaces are decorated with ox yokes and other rural implements, and the fine restaurant serves local cuisine. **www.parador.es**

ALMAGRO La Casa del Rector €€€

C/ Pedro Oviedo 8, 13270 (Ciudad Real) **Tel** *926 26 12 59* **Fax** *926 26 12 60* **Rooms** *31*

There are three distinct parts to this hotel – the original 18th-century house set around a rustic courtyard, its contemporary interiors with beams and ceramic-tiled floors, and an avant-garde building in steel, marble and glass adjoining it. It's close to the centre of Almagro and has a good restaurant serving regional dishes. **www.lacasadelrector.com**

ALMAGRO Parador de Almagro €€€€

Ronda de San Francisco 31, 13270 (Ciudad Real) **Tel** *926 86 01 00* **Fax** *926 86 01 50* **Rooms** *54*

An exquisite parador, housed in a 16th-century convent, and set around a series of courtyards and cloisters. The former cells have been converted into bedrooms, though their austerity has been replaced by modern comforts. A lace-maker works in one of the courtyards, keeping the town's tradition alive. **www.parador.es**

ATIENZA Antiguo Palacio de Atienza €€

Callejuelas de San Gil 47, Atienza, 19270 (Guadalajara) **Tel/Fax** *949 39 91 80* **Rooms** *15*

This beautiful 16th-century mansion in the picturesque village of Atienza is carefully decorated to match the rustic wood and stone architecture of the house. It offers a magnificent garden and a refreshing swimming pool, as well as freshly cooked meals served in the restaurant. **www.palaciodeatienza.com**

AYNA Felipe II €€

Avenida Manuel Carrera s/n, 02125 (Albacete) **Tel** *967 29 50 83* **Fax** *967 29 51 47* **Rooms** *41*

This modern hotel is set in a charming village in the mountains of Albacete. Its semi-circular layout allows a panoramic view of the town and the valley from every bedroom. The staff are friendly and can arrange various outdoor activities, including rafting, horse riding and even stargazing. Closed Jan. **www.hotelfelipesegundo.es**

BALLESTEROS DE CALATRAVA Palacio de la Serna €€€

C/ Cervantes 18, 13432 (Ciudad Real) **Tel** *926 84 22 08* **Fax** *926 84 22 24* **Rooms** *24*

An 18th-century farmhouse in the plains of La Mancha, decorated in a mix of Castilian and modern styles. The rooms are large and painted in bold colours. The staff can arrange horseback and mountain bike excursions into the surrounding hills. Also has art galleries and a sculpture garden. **www.hotelpalaciodelaserna.com**

BELMONTE Palacio Buenavista €€

C/ José Antonio González 2, 16640 (Cuenca) **Tel** *967 18 75 80* **Fax** *967 18 75 88* **Rooms** *36*

A charming country hotel in a renovated 16th-century palace. Features spacious rooms, decorated in a traditional style, wooden galleries and a delightful garden. Some of the rooms have views of Belmonte's magnificent castle. A primrose-yellow dining room serves delicious oven-roasted lamb and steak. **www.palaciodebuenavista.es**

CUENCA Posada de San José €

C/ Julián Romero 4, 16001 **Tel** *969 21 13 00* **Fax** *969 23 03 65* **Rooms** *29*

Run by a Canadian-Spanish couple, this hotel is set in a 17th-century convent perched vertiginously above the gorge. The rooms – some with balconies – are stylishly decorated with white fabrics and offer splendid views. It showcases many antiques and frescoes and there is a wonderfully relaxing garden. **www.posadasanjose.com**

CUENCA La Cueva del Fraile €€

Ctra Cuenca-Buenache km 7, 16001 (Cuenca) **Tel** *969 21 15 71* **Fax** *969 25 60 47* **Rooms** *76*

Set in a green valley outside Cuenca, this 16th-century hotel is built around a white patio and surrounded by vast gardens. The rooms are elegantly furnished with all modern comforts. The special duplex apartments are ideal for families. Also has tennis courts, and guests can rent bicycles. Closed Jan. **www.hotelcuevadelfraile.com**

CUENCA Leonor de Aquitania €€

C/ San Pedro 58–60, 16001 (Cuenca) **Tel** *969 23 10 00* **Fax** *969 23 10 04* **Rooms** *46*

Named after a medieval princess, this hotel is located in a historic building in the heart of old Cuenca. The spacious bedrooms and suites are decorated in a traditional style, and the public areas are adorned with tapestries and hunting trophies. Some rooms offer panoramic views. **www.hotelleonordeaquitania.com**

Key to Price Guide *see p560* **Key to Symbols** *see back cover flap*

CUENCA Parador de Cuenca €€€€

Subida de San Pablo s/n, 16001 (Cuenca) ***Tel*** *969 23 23 20* ***Fax*** *969 23 25 34* ***Rooms*** *63*

The 16th-century convent of San Pablo has been transformed into an elegant parador. The town's famous old hanging houses, draped vertiginously over the gorge, can be seen from some of the bedrooms. Offers a range of modern facilities, including a fine regional restaurant. **www.parador.es**

EL TOBOSO Casa de la Torre €€

C/ Antonio Machado 16, 45820 (Toledo) ***Tel*** *925 56 80 06* ***Fax*** *925 56 80 06* ***Rooms*** *14*

A rural inn in the heart of Don Quixote country, El Toboso was once home to Dulcinea, the object of the knight's affections. The inn is set in a 17th-century mansion, built around a typical Manchegan galleried courtyard. The rooms and suites are attractively decorated. Three dining areas serve regional specialities. **www.casadelatorre.com**

GUADALAJARA España €

C/ Teniente Figueroa 3, 19001 (Guadalajara) ***Tel*** *949 21 13 03* ***Fax*** *949 21 13 05* ***Rooms*** *40*

A family-run hotel in a modernized, 19th-century mansion located in the centre of the city. Offers excellent amenities, including a small sauna. The simple, spotlessly clean rooms are decorated in a traditional style. The restaurant serves local specialities, and the staff can advise on nearby attractions.

MANZANARES Parador de Manzanares €€€

A-4 Motorway km 175, 13200 (Ciudad Real) ***Tel*** *926 61 04 00* ***Fax*** *926 61 09 35* ***Rooms*** *44*

Set in the heart of the city's principal wine region, this parador is a good base for exploring Don Quixote country. With two natural parks just a short distance away, it is also perfect for nature enthusiasts. The hotel is modern, but built in traditional Manchegan style, and is surrounded by extensive gardens. **www.parador.es**

OROPESA Parador de Oropesa €€€

Plaza de Palacio 1, 45560 (Toledo) ***Tel*** *925 43 00 00* ***Fax*** *925 43 07 77* ***Rooms*** *48*

The Sierra de Gredos forms a scenic backdrop to this medieval fortress rising above a plain of olive groves and vineyards. The bedrooms are spacious. The parador also arranges activities such as pheasant hunting and horse riding excursions. The romantic restaurant serves regional cuisine. **www.parador.es**

OSSA DE MONTIEL Albamanjón €€€

Laguna de San Pedro 16, 02611 (Albacete) ***Tel*** *926 69 90 48* ***Fax*** *902 80 83 90* ***Rooms*** *12*

A tranquil retreat by the Lagunas de Ruidera, La Mancha's attractive string of turquoise lakes. This modern complex has been built in a traditional style, and is beautifully decorated with colourful tiles and climbing plants. Bedrooms are elegant and comfortable, and present far-reaching countryside views. Closed 24–25 Dec. **www.albamanjon.net**

SAN CLEMENTE Casa de los Acacio €€

C/ Cruz Cerrada 10, 16600 (Cuenca) ***Tel*** *969 30 03 60* ***Fax*** *969 30 00 67* ***Rooms*** *9*

This hotel is housed in a carefully restored, 17th-century stone mansion in a historical village. Rooms and suites are set around a graceful patio, and decorated with traditional Castilian furniture. The restaurant is for hotel guests only, book in advance. On Saturday evenings there is a *degustación* dinner with wine tasting. **www.casadelosacacio.es**

SIGÜENZA El Molino de Alcuneza €€€

Ctra de Alboreca km 0.5, 19264 (Guadalajara) ***Tel*** *949 39 15 01* ***Fax*** *949 34 70 04* ***Rooms*** *17*

A restored mill in the Alcarria contains this intimate country hotel. Each room has been stylishly decorated with traditional furnishings and pretty prints, many featuring the original beams and cool stone walls. A stream burbles beneath the public lounge. Dinner includes fresh produce from the kitchen garden. **www.molinodealcuneza.com**

SIGÜENZA Parador de Sigüenza €€€€

Plaza del Castillo, 19250 (Guadalajara) ***Tel*** *949 39 01 00* ***Fax*** *949 39 13 64* ***Rooms*** *81*

Sigüenza's massive castle overlooks the city from a hilltop – its crenellated towers and battlements are a stirring sight. Former VIP guests here include the Catholic Monarchs *(see pp56–7)*. Bedrooms are handsomely furnished with every modern amenity and overlook a striking courtyard. **www.parador.es**

TOLEDO Pintor El Greco €€

C/ Alamillos del Tránsito 13, 45002 (Toledo) ***Tel*** *925 28 51 91* ***Fax*** *925 21 58 19* ***Rooms*** *60*

A 17th-century bakery in Toledo's former Jewish quarter has been discreetly extended behind the original façade and patio. Wrought iron, traditional ceramics and lots of flowering plants add character to the hotel. The bedrooms are modern, yet in keeping with the historic surroundings. **www.sercotelhoteles.com**

TOLEDO San Juan de los Reyes €€

C/ Reyes Católicos 5, 45002 (Toledo) ***Tel*** *925 28 35 35* ***Fax*** *925 22 14 10* ***Rooms*** *38*

Housed in a beautiful modern building in Neo-Mozarabic style, this hotel is located in the centre of Toledo and adjoins the San Juan de los Reyes monastery. Rooms are spacious, comfortable and have modern decor. There is a restaurant and a bar with outside tables. Breakfast is included but parking costs extra. **www.sercotelhoteles.com**

TOLEDO Hacienda del Cardenal €€€

Paseo de Recaredo 24, 45004 (Toledo) ***Tel*** *925 22 49 00* ***Fax*** *925 22 29 91* ***Rooms*** *27*

Now a historic hotel near the city walls, this 18th-century mansion was once the residence of Toledo's archbishop. It has sculpted ceilings and brick courtyards, and the rooms and suites are traditionally decorated with plush fabrics and every modern comfort. Some overlook the lovely, jasmine-scented gardens. **www.hostaldelcardenal.com**

TOLEDO Parador de Toledo €€€€

Cerro del Emperador s/n, 45002 (Toledo) ***Tel*** *925 22 18 50* ***Fax*** *925 22 51 66* ***Rooms*** *74*

The terrace of this graceful, stone-built parador, which is located on the brow of a hill overlooking the city, offers a spectacular view of Toledo. The Parador de Toledo is very popular with sightseers and photographers, so make sure you book well in advance. **www.parador.es**

TRAGACETE Hotel El Gamo €

C/ Fernando Royuela s/n, 16150 (Cuenca) ***Tel*** *969 28 90 11* ***Fax*** *969 28 92 28* ***Rooms*** *40*

A good-value hotel in a peaceful village, among the hills and woods in the Serranía de Cuenca, near the Río Cueryo's source. The bedrooms are simply furnished, but more than adequate. The hotel is ideally located for hiking, mountain biking and other active pursuits. The restaurant serves generous portions of local cuisine. **www.elgamo.org**

UCLÉS Casa Palacio €€€

C/ Angustias 2, 16450 (Cuenca) ***Tel*** *969 13 50 65* ***Fax*** *969 13 50 11* ***Rooms*** *7*

This historic mansion, built in 1546 in the centre of the beautiful town of Uclés, has been transformed into an intimate and stylish hotel. Great care has been taken with the decor, which presents a perfect blend of original details and contemporary furnishings. **www.lacasapalacio.com**

VALDEPEÑAS Hotel Central €

C/ Capitán Fillol 4, 13300 (Ciudad Real) ***Tel*** *926 31 33 88* ***Fax*** *926 31 35 09* ***Rooms*** *25*

A modest but reliable hotel in the centre of Castilla-La Mancha's largest wine-producing town. This modern establishment is tucked behind a historic façade, and makes a good base for touring the local bodegas. The rooms are simply yet comfortably decorated, with amenities such as 24-hour room service. **www.hotelcentralval.com**

VALVERDE DE LOS ARROYOS El Nido de Valverde €€€

C/ Escuelas 1, 19224 (Guadalajara) ***Tel*** *949 85 42 21* ***Fax*** *949 30 74 48* ***Rooms*** *3*

This exceptional little hotel is set in a storybook village of black slate-roofed houses in the northernmost tip of Guadalajara, and has just three rooms. The owners of this stone-built cottage offer creative, home-cooked meals. A magical and unforgettable spot. **www.nidodevalverde.com**

VILLANUEVA DE LOS INFANTES Posada Abuela Fidela €

C/ Don Quijote 16, 13320 (Ciudad Real) ***Tel*** *619 33 97 36* ***Rooms*** *7*

In the south-east of Ciudad Real province, this country house is near the wine village of Valdepeñas. It offers a cosy lounge with a fireplace, five guestrooms and two family-sized apartments with kitchen facilities. Small pets are admitted. Breakfast and drinks are available, and there are a few restaurants in the village. **www.abuelafidela.com**

EXTREMADURA

ALMENDRAL Monasterio de Rocamador €€€€

Ctra Badajoz-Huelva km 41, 06171 (Badajoz) ***Tel*** *924 48 90 00* ***Fax*** *924 48 90 01* ***Rooms*** *30*

An enchanting country hotel, in a restored former monastery, built in honey-coloured stone. The rooms at this stylish, romantic retreat retain many of their original details, and are beautifully furnished in a mixture of contemporary and traditional styles. Most have their own fireplaces, and all enjoy breathtaking views. **www.rocamador.com**

BADAJOZ Zurbarán €€

Gómez de Solís, 06001 ***Tel*** *924 00 14 00* ***Fax*** *924 22 01 42* ***Rooms*** *110*

Just opposite the main park, this large modern hotel is located near the town centre. It has been refurbished in a contemporary style, and the bedrooms are well equipped and comfortable. There is a full-sized swimming pool for cooling down on summer days. **www.husa.es**

CÁCERES Alameda Palacete €

C/ General Margallo 45, 10003 (Cáceres) ***Tel*** *927 21 16 74* ***Fax*** *927 22 29 25* ***Rooms*** *9*

This bright, charming nine-room conversion of a town house is just steps away from the Plaza Mayor. Rooms are individually decorated with an eclectic mixture of stylish antiques and furnishings. There are three suites with an extra sitting room, which can be converted into rooms sleeping four. **www.alamedapalacete.com**

CÁCERES NH Palacio de Oquendo €€

Plaza de San Juan 11, 10003 (Cáceres) ***Tel*** *927 21 58 00* ***Fax*** *927 21 40 70* ***Rooms*** *86*

This 16th-century mansion beside the city walls has been renovated by a hotel chain, though it retains the feel of a chic boutique hotel. Rooms are decorated with light, modern furnishings, and some have vaulted stone ceilings. Also showcases many antique hunting implements. Several outdoor activities can be arranged. **www.nh-hotels.com**

CUACOS DE YUSTE La Casona de Valfrío €€

Ctra Cuacos de Yuste–Valfrío km 4, 10430 (Cáceres) ***Tel*** *927 19 42 22* ***Fax*** *927 19 42 32* ***Rooms*** *6*

Relax in tranquillity in this beautifully restored country guesthouse surrounded by oak woods and cherry trees. Facilities include an outdoor swimming pool, a relaxation room offering massages, and mountain bike hire. Several outdoor activities can be arranged. The restaurant serves dinner only for guests. **www.lacasonadevalfrio.com**

Key to Price Guide *see p560* **Key to Symbols** *see back cover flap*

GUADALUPE Hospedería del Real Monasterio €

Plaza de Juan Carlos I, 10140 (Cáceres) ***Tel*** *927 36 70 00* ***Fax*** *927 36 71 77* ***Rooms*** *47*

This hotel is part of the 16th-century Franciscan monastery which dominates Guadalupe. Many of the rooms, which surround the Gothic stone courtyard, were originally pharmacies, and are simply decorated with traditional, carved wooden furnishings. Also has several public lounges. Closed mid-Jan to mid-Feb. **www.monasterioguadalupe.com**

GUADALUPE Parador de Guadalupe €€€€

C/ Marqués de la Romana 12, 10140 (Cáceres) ***Tel*** *927 36 70 75* ***Fax*** *927 36 70 76* ***Rooms*** *41*

Located in a 16th-century hospital and convent, this beautiful parador is set in flower-filled gardens very close to the monastery. The elegant bedrooms overlook whitewashed patios full of citrus trees. The rooms in the annexe are larger, but those in the original building have much more character. **www.parador.es**

JARANDILLA DE LA VERA Parador de Jarandilla €€€€

Av de García Prieto 1, 10450 (Cáceres) ***Tel*** *927 56 01 17* ***Fax*** *927 56 00 88* ***Rooms*** *53*

This imposing 15th-century castle, where Emperor Carlos V stayed for a year, has been modernized without losing its medieval feel. The swimming pool is surrounded by olive trees and rose gardens, and there is a tennis court and children's play area. It boasts one of the region's best restaurants, along with a café-bar. **www.parador.es**

LOSAR DE LA VERA Antigua Casa del Heno €

Finca Valdepimienta, 10470 (Cáceres) ***Tel*** *927 19 80 77* ***Rooms*** *7*

A farmhouse surrounded by oak trees and meadows near the Sierra de Gredos. Offers B&B, and is popular during spring when the cherry trees bloom. The bedrooms are simply decorated, and the old stone walls and wooden beams add a rustic charm. Breakfast included. Dinner is provided on request. **www.antiguacasadelheno.com**

MALPARTIDA DE PLASENCIA Cañada Real €€

Ctra Ex-108 km 42, 10680 (Cáceres) ***Tel*** *927 45 94 07* ***Fax*** *927 45 94 34* ***Rooms*** *61*

This modern hotel is located within easy distance of Plasencia and nearby nature reserves. The bedrooms are comfortable and spacious, and there are three suites with Jacuzzis. All are decorated with floral prints and traditional furniture. A children's play area and board games are also available, as well as a library. **www.hotelcreal.es**

MÉRIDA El Alfarero €

C/ Sagasta 40, 06800 (Badajoz) ***Tel*** *924 30 31 83* ***Fax*** *924 09 90 44* ***Rooms*** *15*

A bright, clean pension in the centre of Mérida within easy walking distance of the Roman sights. Rooms are pleasant with en suite bathrooms and simple, pleasing decor. Two triples and a quadruple are also available. There's a quiet, flower-lined courtyard for relaxing. **www.hostalelalfarero.com**

MÉRIDA Mérida Palace €€

Plaza España 19, 06800 (Badajoz) ***Tel*** *924 38 38 00* ***Fax*** *924 38 38 01* ***Rooms*** *76*

This charming retreat is housed in a pair of elegant historic palaces. Illustrious former guests include three Spanish monarchs. The hotel maintains a regal atmosphere with a profusion of antiques and original architectural details. All modern conveniences are available, in addition to a rooftop pool and terrace. **www.hotelmeridapalace.com**

MÉRIDA Parador de Mérida €€€€

Plaza de la Constitución 3, 06800 (Badajoz) ***Tel*** *924 31 38 00* ***Fax*** *924 31 92 08* ***Rooms*** *82*

A converted, 18th-century Baroque convent, which was built on the ruins of an ancient Roman temple. Roman columns, inscriptions in Arabic and Visigothic capitals have been preserved and incorporated into the wonderful "Garden of Antiquities". Also arranges activities such as hunting, golf, fishing and tennis. **www.parador.es**

PLASENCIA Alfonso VIII €€

Av Alfonso VIII 32, 10600 (Cáceres) ***Tel*** *927 41 02 50* ***Fax*** *927 41 80 42* ***Rooms*** *55*

A modern hotel, centrally located near the Parque de la Isla. Offers all the expected four-star facilities. The rooms are large and bright, with contemporary furnishings, and the staff is attentive. The hotel itself is ideally situated for exploring this beautiful, rural region. **www.hotelalfonsoviii.com**

PLASENCIA Parador de Plasencia €€€€

Plaza San Vicente Ferrer, 10600 (Cáceres) ***Tel*** *927 42 58 70* ***Fax*** *927 42 58 72* ***Rooms*** *67*

A former Gothic convent in the centre of town, conveniently located for exploring the cathedrals. The grandeur of this historic building is still intact, without losing comfort. The restaurant here, which serves local specialities such as lamb stew and salt cod, is recommended, as is the tea room. **www.parador.es**

TRUJILLO Hostal Mesón La Cadena €

Plaza Mayor 5, 10200 (Cáceres) ***Tel*** *927 32 14 63* ***Fax*** *927 32 31 16* ***Rooms*** *9*

This restaurant-with-rooms, in an attractive granite house on the main square, is a good budget option. The rooms, decorated with locally made textiles, are on the second floor, and the best offer spectacular views over Plaza Mayor. The eatery on the ground floor is a classic in the city, serving regional specialities. **www.charmingsmallhotels.co.uk**

TRUJILLO Posada Dos Orillas €€

Calle Cambrones 6, 10200 (Cáceres) ***Tel*** *927 65 90 79* ***Fax*** *927 32 26 15* ***Rooms*** *13*

Hidden among the winding lanes of the old town, this ancient inn has individually themed bedrooms, each on a different South American country plus one on Extremadura. There is a lovely terrace in the courtyard where the good restaurant serves an unusual selection of well-executed dishes. **www.dosorillas.com**

TRUJILLO Parador de Trujillo €€€€

C/ Santa Beatriz de Silva 1, 10200 (Cáceres) **Tel** *927 32 13 50* **Fax** *927 32 13 66* **Rooms** *43*

This charming parador and former chapel, where breakfast is now served, incorporates parts of a 16th-century convent. The hotel is within the spellbinding old city of Trujillo, but located on a quiet street away from the noise. The elegant rooms look out onto a series of lovely patios, filled with orange trees. **www.parador.es**

ZAFRA Huerta Honda €€

Av López Asme 30, 06300 (Badajoz) **Tel** *924 55 41 00* **Fax** *924 55 25 04* **Rooms** *48*

Set around patios with fountains and flowers, this hotel is stylish, yet traditional. Some rooms are decorated in a contemporary style, while others boast luxuries of days gone by; all are elegant and extremely comfortable. Some have a Jacuzzi. **www.hotelhuertahonda.com**

ZAFRA Parador de Zafra €€€€

Pl del Corazón de María 7, 06300 (Badajoz) **Tel** *924 55 45 40* **Fax** *924 55 10 18* **Rooms** *51*

This fairytale castle, with its round towers, was built in the 15th century on the ruins of a Moorish fortress. A beautiful staircase leads from the courtyard, with an arcaded gallery, to the bedrooms. These are regally fitted with traditional furnishings, which evoke the ducal palace of former times. It is set in elegant gardens. **www.parador.es**

SEVILLE

EL ARENAL Hotel Adriano €€

C/ Adriano 12, 41001 **Tel** *954 29 38 00* **Fax** *954 22 89 46* **Rooms** *34* **Map** *3 B2*

This hotel is in an excellent location for sightseeing, close to Plaza de Toros, the cathedral and the riverfront, as well as Giralda and Real Alcázar. The spacious, comfortable rooms have modern facilities. Some have courtyard views and others have balconies overlooking the street. There's also a rooftop Jacuzzi and sun deck. **www.adrianohotel.com**

EL ARENAL Petit Palace Marqués Santa Ana €€€

C/ Jimios 9–11, 41001 **Tel** *954 22 18 12* **Fax** *954 22 89 93* **Rooms** *57* **Map** *3 B1*

In a quiet street close to the cathedral, this mid-19th century building has been spectacularly renovated to offer a luxurious oasis in the heart of the city. The decor is sleek and modern, and the rooms are equipped with hi-tech features, such as hydro-showers, Internet access and flat-screen TVs. **www.hotelmarquessantaana.com**

EL ARENAL Vincci La Rabida €€€

C/ Castelar 24, 41001 **Tel** *954 50 12 80* **Fax** *954 21 66 00* **Rooms** *81* **Map** *3 B1*

Located in El Arenal district, close to shops, restaurants and a bullring, this 18th-century palace was restored and opened as a four-star hotel in 2003. The guestrooms combine warm, earthy tones with dark furnishings and wrought-iron beds. Some rooms have views of the central courtyard. **www.vinccihoteles.com**

EL ARENAL Gran Melia Colón Hotel €€€€

C/ Canalejas 1, 41001 **Tel** *954 50 55 99* **Fax** *954 22 09 38* **Rooms** *189* **Map** *3 B1*

This grand five-star hotel in the heart of Seville has been completely refurbished to offer guests the most elegant style and maximum comfort. Guests can enjoy the views from the solarium, cool off in the rooftop pool or relax in the spa. The chic sophistication of this full-service hotel has a distinctive Andalusian flavour. **www.solmelia.com**

SANTA CRUZ Murillo €€

C/ Lope de Rueda 7 & 9, 41004 **Tel** *954 21 60 95* **Fax** *954 21 96 16* **Rooms** *57* **Map** *4 D2*

A pleasant, reasonably priced hotel off Plaza Alfaro, a short walk from the cathedral. The public areas are decorated with antiques, hand-carved furniture, coffered ceilings and even suits of armour. Bedrooms are plain and functional, and are located on a quiet pedestrian street. A rooftop terrace offers great views. **www.hotelmurillo.com**

SANTA CRUZ YH Giralda Hotel €€

C/ Abades 30, 41004 **Tel** *954 22 83 24* **Fax** *954 22 70 19* **Rooms** *14* **Map** *6 D4*

The YH Giralda boasts a privileged location, just 100 metres from the cathedral. It is housed in an 18th-century palace that has been refurbished to a high standard while preserving its unique character. Rooms are soundproofed, with en suite baths and air conditioning. Friendly staff offer a warm welcome to the city. **www.yh-hoteles.com**

SANTA CRUZ Hotel Posada del Lucero €€€

C/ Almirante Apodaca 7, 41003 **Tel** *954 50 24 80* **Fax** *954 22 54 20* **Rooms** *40* **Map** *6 E2*

Located in the heart of Seville, this unique hotel stunningly combines traditional and modern architecture. Its minimalist interior uses dark walnut wood, white stucco and black slate, with exposed brick walls and neutral colour scheme. All rooms face the central courtyard. **www.posadadellucero.com**

SANTA CRUZ La Casa del Maestro €€€

C/ Almudena 5, 41002 **Tel** *954 50 00 07* **Fax** *954 50 00 06* **Rooms** *11* **Map** *6 E2*

Once the home of celebrated flamenco guitarist Niño Ricardo, this charming yellow-and-ochre-painted town house is built around a patio bursting with plants and flowers. Rooms are on the small side, but there is a lovely roof terrace. Also has a nearby sister property comprised of six suites. **www.lacasadelmaestro.com**

Key to Price Guide *see p560* **Key to Symbols** *see back cover flap*

SANTA CRUZ Alma Sevilla – Hotel Palacio de Villapanes €€€€

C/ Santiago 31, 41003 **Tel** *954 50 20 63* **Rooms** *50* **Map** *4 D1*

A sumptuous haven in the centre of Seville, this five-star boutique hotel in an 18th-century palace features parquet floors, luxurious soft furnishings and bathrooms complete with robes, slippers and Bulgari toiletries. It also boasts a library, a garden terrace, a rooftop solarium and excellent views of Seville. **www.almasevilla.com**

SANTA CRUZ Las Casas del Rey de Baeza €€€€

Plaza Jesús de la Redención 2, 41003 **Tel** *954 56 14 96* **Fax** *954 56 14 41* **Rooms** *41* **Map** *4 D1*

Located in a beautiful unique setting, this hotel fuses the past and present. Bright, whitewashed walls blend with the ochres and reds of the courtyard, shaded by arched walkways. Indoors, cool stone flooring and natural tones lead to the rooms, where chic interiors pay tribute to modernity. A rooftop pool offers fantastic views. **www.hospes.es**

TRIANA Abba Triana Hotel €€

Plaza Chapina s/n, 41010 **Tel** *954 28 80 00* **Fax** *954 28 80 01* **Rooms** *137* **Map** *3 A1*

Enjoy spectacular riverfront views from the spacious rooms of this modern hotel, built in 2006 with the latest technological advances and contemporary decor. Amenities include a rooftop pool and terrace and a full breakfast buffet. Wi-Fi access incurs an extra cost. Close to all public transport. **www.abbatrianahotel.com**

FURTHER AFIELD (LA MACARENA) Casa Romana Hotel Boutique €€

C/ Trajano 15, 41002 **Tel** *954 91 51 70* **Fax** *954 37 31 91* **Rooms** *26*

Rooms are distributed around the picturesque central courtyard, with all the comforts you would expect of a four-star hotel. All rooms are tastefully decorated in subdued elegance; some have Jacuzzis. The rooftop solarium has a plunge pool. The website offers specials, including flamenco tickets with reservations. **www.hotelcasaromana.com**

FURTHER AFIELD (LA MACARENA) Alcoba del Rey de Sevilla €€€

C/ Bécquer 9, 41002 **Tel** *954 915 800* **Fax** *95 491 56 75* **Rooms** *15* **Map** *2 D3*

This is a stylish little hotel, full of small details which create a romantic atmosphere. Furnishings include lovely glasswork, tiles, silk cushions, objets d'art and beds – all of which are for sale. Each of the rooms is named after a personality from the Moorish period and are elegantly decorated. **www.alcobadelrey.com**

FURTHER AFIELD (SOUTH) Ciudad de Sevilla €€€

Av Manuel Siurot 25, 41013 **Tel** *954 23 05 05* **Fax** *954 23 85 39* **Rooms** *94* **Map** *4 D5*

Located in a residential neighbourhood on the outskirts of the city, this luxurious chain hotel occupies a mansion. Behind the old façade is a contemporary hotel with all modern conveniences, including business facilities, a small rooftop pool and a sun terrace. The hotel's website offers some good deals. **www.ac-hotels.com**

FURTHER AFIELD (SOUTH) Hotel Alfonso XIII €€€€€

C/ San Fernando 2, 41004 **Tel** *954 91 70 00* **Fax** *954 91 70 99* **Rooms** *147* **Map** *3 C3*

A landmark building since 1928, this hotel is a fine display of Mudéjar architecture. Rooms are sumptuously decorated with authentic antiques and luxurious silks and linens. Enjoy gourmet cuisine in one of the fine restaurants, or sip a cocktail in one of the opulent bars. The lush gardens surround a luminous pool. **www.starwoodhotels.com**

FURTHER AFIELD (EAST) Hotel Sevilla Center €€€

Avenida de la Buhaira 18, 41018 **Tel** *954 54 95 00* **Fax** *954 53 37 71* **Rooms** *233* **Map** *4 E3*

This modern hotel is close to the historic center and Santa Justa train station. The decor is an elegant combination of classic and modern styles. Work out in the gym, relax in the spa or refresh yourself in the rooftop pool, where you can enjoy panoramic views of the city. There's a lovely park adjacent. **www.hotelescenter.es**

ANDALUSIA

AGUA AMARGA La Almendra y El Gitano €€

Camina Cala del Plomo s/n, 04149 (Almería) **Tel** *678 50 29 11* **Rooms** *5*

In a unique location at the heart of the Cabo de Gata National Park, and just 5 km (3 miles) from unspoilt beaches, this haven provides complete tranquility with spacious rooms, a pool and shaded outside areas to relax in. A car is essential and a minimum two-night stay is required. Free Wi-Fi in public areas. **www.laalmendrayelgitano.com**

ALCALÁ DE GUADAIRA Hacienda La Boticaria Hotel €€€€€

Ctra Alcalá–Utrera km 2.5, 41500 (Sevilla) **Tel** *955 69 88 20* **Fax** *955 69 87 55* **Rooms** *133*

In Alacalá de Guadaira, just 20 km (13 miles) from Seville, this elegant hotel is surrounded by lush gardens with a lake, large courtyards and four outdoor pools. The rooms are well equipped, and facilities include an indoor pool, luxury spa, golf course, equestrian club, heliport and two restaurants. **www.eurostarshaciendalaboticaria.com**

ALMERÍA Husa Catedral €

Plaza Catedral 8, 04002 (Almería) **Tel** *950 27 81 78* **Fax** *950 27 81 17* **Rooms** *20*

This charming four-star hotel is ideally located in Almería's cathedral square. Rooms are elegantly decorated in neutral tones. There is Wi-Fi access throughout the building, and the solarium and rooftop balcony offer commanding views of the square and the Alcazaba. Breakfast included. **www.hotelcatedral.net**

ARACENA Finca Buen Vino €€€

Los Marines, 21293 (Huelva) ***Tel*** *959 12 40 34* ***Fax*** *959 50 14 57* ***Rooms*** *4*

A wonderful guesthouse in an elegant villa on a hilltop surrounded by chestnut and cork oak trees. The owners grow their own organic produce – used for breakfasts, afternoon teas and cordon bleu cuisine served at dinner (guests only). Stay in the villa, or rent a cottage in the grounds. Cookery courses available. **www.fincabuenvino.com**

ARACENA La Casa Noble €€€€

C/ Campito 35, 21200 (Huelva) ***Tel*** *959 12 77 78* ***Rooms*** *6*

A unique Andalusian home that is an oasis of tranquillity, with every modern comfort plus historic charm. Castle views, luxurious linens, rain showers, a library with books and DVDs, and an alfresco Jacuzzi are just some of the highlights here. Breakfast is included, as are "Tapas at Twilight". No guests under age 16. **www.lacasanoble.net**

ARCOS DE LA FRONTERA Casa Grande €€

C/ Maldonado 10, 11630 (Cádiz) ***Tel*** *956 70 39 30* ***Fax*** *956 71 70 95* ***Rooms*** *7*

A charming little hotel set in a whitewashed 18th-century mansion, which still bears the escutcheon of its original owner. Each of the originally decorated rooms is full of character. Family-run, it is warm, intimate and full of details such as home-made marmalade for breakfast. Offers splendid views from the roof terrace. **www.lacasagrande.net**

ARCOS DE LA FRONTERA Parador de Arcos de la Frontera €€€

Plaza del Cabildo s/n, 11630 (Cádiz) ***Tel*** *956 70 05 00* ***Fax*** *956 70 11 16* ***Rooms*** *24*

Formerly a magistrate's house, this mansion perched on a cliff above the old city is now a smart parador. A huge terrace offers great views of ancient spires and rooftops below, and the rooms are set around a series of beautifully tiled patios with wells and fountains. Rooms are plush and comfortable and some have Jacuzzis. **www.parador.es**

AZNALCÁZAR Hacienda Olontigi €

Calle Ventorro 23, 41849 (Sevilla) ***Tel*** *955 75 19 76* ***Fax*** *955 75 05 37* ***Rooms*** *15*

This family-run countryside hacienda is comprised of five individual houses with gardens surrounding a pool. Each house contains three en suite guestrooms plus a shared kitchen and sitting room with a fireplace. Amenities include bike rental and barbecue facilities, and a continental breakfast is included in the price. **www.haciendaolontigi.com**

BAEZA Hotel Fuentenueva €€

Calle del Carmen 15, 23440 (Jaén) ***Tel*** *953 74 31 00* ***Fax*** *953 74 32 00* ***Rooms*** *13*

Located in a 19th-century house, this hotel offers all the mod-con facilities. These include a library, cafeteria, conference hall, a Japanese Garden, a small plunge pool and wireless Internet. Rooms boast hydromassage baths and sleek, modern decor. There are also six self-catering apartments. **www.fuentenueva.com**

CARBONERAS Hotel Valhalla Spa €€€

Calle Mojacar 14, 04140 (Almería) ***Tel*** *950 130 444* ***Fax*** *950 130 444* ***Rooms*** *33*

Carboneras was once a pirates' refuge. Today it is a secret getaway for bohemians and artists, and this ultra-modern hotel provides sanctuary with its spacious rooms offering all the latest technology and creature comforts. Panoramic ocean views from the terraces. Full-service spa completes the experience. No children. **www.hotel-valhalla.com**

CARMONA Alcázar de la Reina Hotel €€

C/ Hermana Concepción Orellana 2, 41410 (Sevilla) ***Tel*** *954 19 62 00* ***Rooms*** *68*

Approached through narrow streets close to the centre of town, this hotel in a beautiful Mudéjar building offers spacious, attractive rooms, most with views of the Vega de Carmona or the courtyard swimming pool. Amenities include a solarium, patios, massage cabins and terraza bar. **www.alcazar-reina.es**

CARMONA Parador de Carmona €€€€

C/ Alcázar, 41410 (Sevilla) ***Tel*** *954 14 10 10* ***Fax*** *954 14 17 12* ***Rooms*** *63*

This magnificent clifftop parador was built as a fortress by the Moors and became the palace of the Christian king, Pedro the Cruel. It is hung with tapestries and scattered with antiques, and the plush rooms have superb views of the countryside. There is a huge outdoor pool, and one of the best parador restaurants. **www.parador.es**

CASTELLAR DE LA FRONTERA Hotel NH Castellar €€

Carretera Castellar- Almoraima s/n, 11350 (Cádiz) ***Tel*** *956 693 018* ***Fax*** *956 693 250* ***Rooms*** *74*

This hotel offers a welcome respite, with Andalusian architecture, patios, fountains and balconies. Spacious rooms are bright and cheery, and the outdoor pool is surrounded by a grassy lawn. Bikes for hire. Good base for rural hiking, visiting the Costa del Sol beaches or golfing in nearby Sotogrande. **www.nh-resorts.com**

CAZALLA DE LA SIERRA Hotel Posada del Moro €

Paseo del Moro s/n, 41370 (Seville) ***Tel*** *954 884 858* ***Fax*** *954 884 326* ***Rooms*** *31*

Located in the Sierra Norte de Sevilla, this rural hotel offers comfortable tranquillity in a palatial house. Rooms face the pretty courtyards and gardens. Sample fresh fruit from the orchard while relaxing by the salt-water pool, and be sure to try some of the delicious local fare in the restaurant. Free Wi-Fi in public areas. **www.laposadadelmoro.com**

CAZALLA DE LA SIERRA Palacio de San Benito €€

Cazalla de la Sierra, 41370 (Sevilla) ***Tel*** *954 88 33 36* ***Fax*** *954 88 31 62* ***Rooms*** *9*

Occupying a historic 15th-century hermitage, this palatial estate has been meticulously renovated. Rooms are sumptuously decorated and may incorporate a canopy bed, fine tapestries or an antique altar. Guests have use of a library, a music room and the garden with its small pool. Breakfast is included. **www.palaciodesanbenito.es**

Key to Price Guide *see p560* **Key to Symbols** *see back cover flap*

CAZORLA Molino de la Farraga  €€

Camino de la Hoz s/n, 23470 (Jaén) ***Tel*** *953 72 12 49* ***Fax*** *953 72 12 49* ***Rooms*** *8*

A 200-year-old mill on the fringes of the lovely rural village of Cazorla, this is perfect for anyone seeking tranquility. Shrouded by abundant greenery, the whitewashed mill is surrounded by rambling gardens, and the rooms are simple but very pretty. They also have an annexe. Closed 10 Dec–1 Mar. **www.molinolafarraga.com**

CAZORLA Parador de Cazorla €€€

Sierra de Cazorla, 23470 (Jaén) ***Tel*** *953 72 70 75* ***Fax*** *953 72 70 77* ***Rooms*** *34*

The forests and mountains of the Sierra de Cazorla are the superb setting for this parador. It is modern, but has been designed with the rural setting in mind. Nestled into the side of the hill, it offers fine views from the well-equipped bedrooms. The restaurant serves local game in season. Closed end Dec–early Feb. **www.parador.es**

COLMENAR Casa Rural Ahora €

C/ Lepanto 40, Bda El Colmenar, Cortes de la Frontera, 29390 (Málaga) ***Tel/Fax*** *952 15 30 46* ***Rooms*** *9*

A relaxed rural retreat in a picturesque valley close to a river. Ahora is a small, comfortable villa with rustic decor and a centre offering a range of natural therapies, including clay treatments, massages, saunas and Turkish baths. Weekend specials combine therapies with meals in the restaurant. There is also a self-catering cottage. **www.ahoraya.es**

CÓRDOBA Maestre €

C/ Romero Barros 4–6, 14003 (Córdoba) ***Tel*** *957 47 24 10* ***Fax*** *957 47 53 95* ***Rooms*** *26*

Near the Mezquita in the centre of Córdoba, this is a simple hotel with basic amenities. It is set around a series of pretty Andalusian patios with colourful tiles, fountains and trailing plants, and is perfectly placed for sightseeing. They offer both rooms and self-catering apartments. Private underground parking. **www.hotelmaestre.com**

CÓRDOBA Casa de los Azulejos €€

C/ Fernando Colón 5, 14002 (Córdoba) ***Tel*** *957 47 00 00* ***Fax*** *957 47 54 96* ***Rooms*** *8*

The "House of the Tiles" is an enchanting 17th-century mansion set around a typical patio with exquisite local tiles, pretty wrought iron and lush greenery. The pretty rooms are cool and modern, with extras such as Internet. A terrific restaurant offers a fusion of Andalusian and South American cuisine. **www.casadelosazulejos.com**

CÓRDOBA Hospes Palacio del Baílio €€€€

Ramirez de las Casas Deza, 10-12 14001 (Córdoba) ***Tel*** *957 49 89 93* ***Fax*** *957 49 89 94* ***Rooms*** *53*

Situated in the historic centre of the city, this hotel consists of converted granaries, coach-houses and stables, surrounded by beautiful gardens and courtyards, which have been decorated in a stylish fusion of rustic stone walls and modern furnishings. There is a spa with full services and indoor and outdoor pools. **www.hospes.es**

CÓRDOBA Maciá Alfaros €€€€

C/ Alfaros 18, 14001 (Córdoba) ***Tel*** *957 49 19 20* ***Fax*** *957 49 22 10* ***Rooms*** *144*

In a busy street, but soundproofed against traffic noise, the Alfaros is a sleek contemporary hotel built around three courtyards in Neo-Mudéjar style. One of the marble courtyards contains an elegant swimming pool. Geared towards business travellers, it offers good facilities including Wi-Fi. Rooms and suites are comfortable. **www.maciahoteles.com**

EL ROCÍO Hotel Toruño €€

Plaza Acebuchal 22, 21750 (Huelva) ***Tel*** *959 44 23 23* ***Fax*** *959 44 23 38* ***Rooms*** *30*

A charming whitewashed villa just a short distance from the hermitage containing the image of the virgin of El Rocío. It is set on the fringes of the Doñana National Park *(see pp464–5)*, one of the important wetlands and wildlife refuges in Europe. Popular with bird-watchers. Prices double during the El Rocío pilgrimage. **www.toruno.es**

EL ROMPIDO Fuerte El Rompido €€€

Urb. Marina El Rompido, Carretera H-4111, km 8, 21459 (Huelva) ***Tel*** *959 39 99 29* ***Fax*** *959 39 99 30* ***Rooms*** *300*

A four-star ecological hotel on the banks of the Piedras river, offering complete relaxation and fun for the whole family. You can enjoy sporting activities such as tennis, volleyball, cycling, and kayaking or play golf on one of the nearby courses. Then unwind in the spa or relax by one of the pools. Open late Mar–Oct. **www.fuertehoteles.com**

GERENA Hotel Cortijo el Esparragal €€

Autovía A66 Sevilla–Merida, exit 795, 41860 (Sevilla) ***Tel*** *955 78 27 02* ***Fax*** *955 78 27 83* ***Rooms*** *21*

Situated within beautiful grounds on a working farm, this hotel in a converted 17th-century farmhouse offers relaxation in an historical setting. The rooms have all the comforts of a modern hotel and are decorated with antiques. Activities include horse riding, fishing and mountain biking. Excellent restaurant. **www.elesparragal.com**

GIBRALTAR The Rock €€€

3 Europa Road, ***Tel*** *956 77 30 00* ***Fax*** *956 77 35 13* ***Rooms*** *104*

Built in 1932 by the Marquess of Bute, Gibraltar's first five-star hotel still trades on its old-fashioned colonial style and service. Perched on the cliff-side, high above the town and harbour, it offers all imaginable amenities from a hair and beauty centre to a casino. Popular with both business travellers and tourists. **www.rockhotelgibraltar.com**

GRANADA Hotel Las Almenas €

Acero del Darro 82, 18005 (Granada) ***Tel*** *958 26 04 34* ***Fax*** *958 25 43 55* ***Rooms*** *24*

Conveniently located close to the cathedral as well as numerous restaurants and bars, and directly in front of the airport bus stop. Elegant rooms are well appointed with flatscreen TVs, free in-room safes and hydromassage showers; many have balconies. The charming cafeteria serves a basic breakfast. Helpful staff. **www.hotelalmenas.com**

GRANADA Posada Pilar del Toro €

C/ Elvira 25, 18010 (Granada) ***Tel*** *958 22 73 33* ***Fax*** *958 21 62 18* ***Rooms*** *15*

Rustic charm and a historic ambience are combined with modern comforts in this welcoming hotel which is located close to Albaicin, Plaza Nueva and the cathedral. Rooms have hydromassage showers and Internet access, and there is an attractive central courtyard where guests can relax. Breakfast is included. **www.posadadeltoro.com**

GRANADA El Ladrón de Agua €€

Carrera del Darro 13, 18010 (Granada) ***Tel*** *958 21 50 40* ***Fax*** *958 22 43 45* ***Rooms*** *15*

This 16th-century mansion was opened as a hotel in 2004. Each room is tastefully decorated with features such as terracotta floors, oriental rugs and wood-beamed ceilings. Eight of the rooms have views of the Alhambra. There is also a lovely inner courtyard and reading room. **www.ladrondeagua.com**

GRANADA Parador de Granada €€€€€

C/ Real de la Alhambra, 18009 (Granada) ***Tel*** *958 22 14 40* ***Fax*** *958 22 22 64* ***Rooms*** *40*

This parador in the jasmine-scented gardens of the Alhambra was once a convent, and the cloister has been transformed into an oasis filled with trees and flowers. From the elegant bedrooms, you can hear the fountains of the Generalife and enjoy blissful views of the city and the ancient palace. Book well in advance. **www.parador.es**

GRAZALEMA Hotel El Fuerte €€€

Baldío de los Alamillos, Ctra A372 km 53, 11610 (Cádiz) ***Tel*** *956 13 30 00* ***Fax*** *956 13 30 01* ***Rooms*** *77*

In the heart of the natural park of Grazalema, surrounded by a cork-tree forest, is this rustic yet refined ecological hotel. Among the amenities on offer are a children's playground, mini animal farm, activities for kids and a huge buffet breakfast with an ample selection of hot and cold dishes. **www.fuertehoteles.com**

LA HERRADURA Hotel La Tartana €€

Urbanización San Nicolás, 18697 (Granada) ***Tel*** *958 650 535* ***Rooms*** *8*

Romantic Andalusian villa centred around a lovely fountain and courtyard. The rooms ooze old-world charm but have modern comforts. Impressive ocean views from the gardens, framed by tropical plants. The highly acclaimed restaurant serves home-made Italian-style cuisine and has an extensive cocktail menu. **www.hotellatartana.com**

LAS CABEZAS Hotel Cortijo Soto Real €€€€€

Ctra Las Cabezas-Villamartin km 13, 41730 (Sevilla) ***Tel*** *955 86 92 00* ***Fax*** *955 86 92 02* ***Rooms*** *25*

A luxury retreat, this exquisite country mansion is one of the finest hotels in Andalusia. You can explore the extensive grounds in a horse and carriage, indulge in outdoor activities, including hunting or bike excursions, or simply laze by the pool. Elegant rooms and suites are ultra-stylish, and there is a fine restaurant. **www.hotelcortijosotoreal.com**

LOJA La Bobadilla €€€€€

Finca La Bobadilla, 18300 (Granada) ***Tel*** *958 32 18 61* ***Fax*** *958 32 18 10* ***Rooms*** *70*

Looking rather like a labyrinthine Andalusian village surrounded by its own vast estate, this is one of the most luxurious hotels in Europe. Each of the rooms and suites is different, but all are fitted with every imaginable amenity. There is a lake-size pool, and guests can take part in a wide range of activities. **www.barcelolabobadilla.com**

MÁLAGA Sallés Hotel Málaga Centro €€

C/ Marmoles 6, 29007 (Málaga) ***Tel*** *952 07 02 16* ***Fax*** *952 28 33 60* ***Rooms*** *148*

This four-star hotel in the heart of Málaga offers smartly decorated rooms with spacious baths, free non-alcoholic minibar and a rooftop pool for cooling off and admiring the views. The website offers special deals of up to 65 per cent off the rack rate. **www.salleshotels.com**

MARBELLA La Villa Marbella €€

Calle Príncipe 10, 29600 (Málaga) ***Tel*** *952 766 220* ***Fax*** *952 765 748* ***Rooms*** *14*

This boutique hotel is a complex of houses which have been meticulously transformed into one of the most charming choices in Marbella's town centre. Rooms, suites and two apartments are all exquisitely decorated with Asian flair yet keep the Andalusian style. Free Wi-Fi in public areas and wired Internet in bed rooms. **www.lavillamarbella.com**

MARBELLA El Fuerte €€€

Av El Fuerte, 29600 (Málaga) ***Tel*** *952 92 00 00* ***Fax*** *952 82 44 11* ***Rooms*** *263*

El Fuerte was the first purpose-built hotel in Marbella and is still one of the best. It is unmissable – a big pink building surrounded by tropical gardens. Some rooms have mountain views but the best look out to sea. Next to the beach-front, it has a heated, glassed-in pool, an outdoor pool and a health and beauty centre. **www.fuertehoteles.com**

MARBELLA Marbella Club Hotel €€€€€

Blvr Príncipe von Hohenlohe, 29600 (Málaga) ***Tel*** *952 82 22 11* ***Fax*** *952 82 98 84* ***Rooms*** *135*

Built for a prince in the 1950s, this is now an ultra-luxurious beachside complex with two pools (one indoors) and extensive subtropical gardens. Located in the Golden Mile (between Marbella and Puerto Banus), it includes a world-class golf course and a Thalasso spa. The rooms, suites and villas have private heated pools. **www.marbellaclub.com**

MAZAGÓN Parador de Mazagón €€€

Ctra San Juan del Puerto, A Matalascañas km 31, 21130 (Huelva) ***Tel*** *959 53 63 00* ***Fax*** *959 53 62 28* ***Rooms*** *63*

A modern parador on the Huelva coast with a perfect location right on the seafront. Draped in ivy and surrounded by gardens, it has bright, modern rooms and is well-located for visiting the wildlife reserve of Doñana National Park. Offers outdoor sports and activities such as cycling, horse riding, golf, and windsurfing. **www.parador.es**

Key to Price Guide *see p560* **Key to Symbols** *see back cover flap*

MECINA BOMBARÓN Casas Rurales Benarum €€

C/ Casas Blancas 1, 18450 (Granada) ***Tel*** *958 85 11 49* ***Rooms*** *15*

Nestled in the mountain town of Mecina Bombarón, these rustic yet elegant cabins for up to five people are luxurious and equipped with a kitchen, living room with fireplace, TV and DVD player, laundry facilities and full bathroom. Pool and spa in grounds, and outdoor activities available. Minimum seven night stay in high season. **www.benarum.com**

MENGÍBAR Hotel Palacio de Mengíbar €

Plaza Constitucion 8, 23620 (Jaén) ***Tel*** *953 374 043* ***Fax*** *953 372 658* ***Rooms*** *56*

Rooms are distributed between a historic palace and a new wing. Crisp white linens adorn antique beds, while modern conveniences such as Wi-Fi and under-floor heating in bathrooms add to the comfort. Indulge in an olive oil spa treatment or enjoy gastronomic delights at the restaurant in the restored stables. **www.husa.es**

MIJAS Hotel Hacienda Puerta del Sol €€

Ctra Fuengirola-Mijas km 4, 29650 (Málaga) ***Tel*** *952 48 64 00* ***Fax*** *952 48 54 62* ***Rooms*** *130*

A whitewashed modern hotel complex in the foothills of the Sierra de Mijas offering spacious rooms. There are impressive views of Fuengirola and the coast. Facilities include tennis courts, a gym, indoor and outdoor pools and other sports amenities. It is child friendly, and the beaches are nearby. **www.hotelhaciendapuertadelsol.com**

MOJÁCAR Hotel El Puntazo €€

Paseo del Mediterraneo 257, 04638 (Almería) ***Tel*** *950 47 82 65* ***Fax*** *950 47 82 85* ***Rooms*** *61*

Located just a short walk from the beach, this lovely Mediterranean-style whitewashed hotel has numerous terraces, arched porticoes and cupolas. Family-friendly, it is a great base from which to explore the area. Rooms and apartments are spacious and some have balconies. There is also a large pool and solarium. **www.hotelelpuntazo.com**

MOJÁCAR Parador de Mojácar €€€

Playa de Mojácar s/n, 04638 (Almería) ***Tel*** *950 47 82 50* ***Fax*** *950 47 81 83* ***Rooms*** *98*

The architecture of this purpose-built parador on the dry sunny coast of Almería echoes that of the dazzling white cube houses in nearby Mojácar. It has excellent facilities for all manner of water sports. The light, airy bedrooms have terraces with wonderful sea views, and the restaurant offers local specialities. Free Wi-Fi. **www.parador.es**

MONACHIL AH Granada Palace €€

Calle Granada 60, 18008 (Granada) ***Tel*** *958 303 090* ***Rooms*** *114*

The voluminous lobby in this modern hotel impresses with its floor-to-ceiling windows, swirling marble floors and curved staircases. Rooms are spacious with flatscreen TVs, mini-bars and hydromassage bathtubs. Most have private terraces.The hotel facilities include a health spa, swimming pool and solarium. **www.ahgranadapalacehotel.com**

NIGUELAS Alquería de los Lentos €€

Camino de los Molinos s/n, 18657 (Granada) ***Tel*** *958 77 78 50* ***Fax*** *958 77 78 48* ***Rooms*** *16*

This hotel offers a sumptuous retreat, convenient to Las Alpujarras, Sierra Nevada and Granada. All rooms are suites and are well-appointed and pleasantly decorated. Romantics can check out the "Corral de la Luna" (stable of the moon), which provides a perfect mixture of intimacy and warmth. **www.alquerialoslentos.com**

NÉRJA Hotel Puerta del Mar €€

C/ Gómez 4, 29780 (Málaga) ***Tel*** *952 52 73 04* ***Fax*** *952 52 42 94* ***Rooms*** *24*

Exceptional value in a fantastic location, this hotel close to the beach boasts pleasant rooms, each with a private balcony. The rooftop saltwater pool and sun terrace offer great views, while the inner courtyard makes a peaceful spot to relax. Breakfast is included and there is free Wi-Fi throughout the hotel. **www.hotelpuertadelmar.es**

ORGIVA Taray Botánico €€

Ctra Tablate-Albuñol km 18, 18400 (Granada) ***Tel*** *958 78 45 25* ***Fax*** *958 78 45 31* ***Rooms*** *15*

A whitewashed rural hotel set in lovely gardens, with olive groves and orange trees. The bedrooms are large enough to be small apartments, but they have even larger suites. A good base for walking or pursuing outdoor activities such as horse riding. The hotel is also equipped for disabled visitors, with specially adapted rooms. **www.hoteltaray.com**

PALMA DEL RÍO Monasterio de San Francisco €€

Av de Pio XII 35, 14700 (Córdoba) ***Tel*** *957 71 01 83* ***Fax*** *957 71 02 36* ***Rooms*** *35*

Built in the 15th century as a Franciscan monastery and located in the centre of the pretty country town of Palma del Río. This hotel has some bedrooms in former monks' cells, furnished with hand-painted basins and bedcovers woven by nuns. The kitchen uses its own organic produce and meals are served in the refectory. **www.intergrouphoteles.com**

RONDA Hotel San Gabriel €€

Marqués de Moctezuma 19, 29400 (Málaga) ***Tel*** *952 190 392* ***Fax*** *952 190 117* ***Rooms*** *19*

In a historic building dating from 1736, this charming hotel is right in the centre of Ronda, near the gorge. The comfortable rooms are regally decorated with period furniture. Savour tranquil moments in the Andalusian patio, sample fine wines in the wine cellar, and don't miss the cinema room. **www.hotelsangabriel.com**

RONDA Parador de Ronda €€€€

Plaza España, 29400 (Málaga) ***Tel*** *952 87 75 00* ***Fax*** *952 87 81 88* ***Rooms*** *78*

Edging up to Ronda's famous cliff, yet close to the town centre, this modern, purpose-built parador has stunning views over the gorge, especially from the top-floor suites. The bedrooms are full of light and stylishly decorated. The parador is surrounded by huge gardens with an outdoor pool right on the cliff edge. **www.parador.es**

ROTA Hotel Playa de la Luz €€

Avda de la Diputación s/n, 11520 (Cádiz) ***Tel*** *956 81 05 00* ***Fax*** *956 81 06 06* ***Rooms*** *235*

A beautiful two-storey Andalusian hotel on a secluded beach in the quaint village of Rota, near Puerto de Santa María and Jerez. The rooms offer modern, elegant decor, and most have a large terrace or balcony. Junior suites provide the ultimate luxury, being directly on the beach. **www.hotelplayadelaluz.com**

RUTE El Cortijo La Prensa €€

Arroyo de las Tijeras, 14960 (Córdoba) ***Tel*** *606 313 532* ***Fax*** *957 724 299* ***Rooms*** *12*

This meticulously restored antique olive mill highlights the original building style yet provides ultimate modern comforts. Rooms have super-king-sized beds, fine Egyptian cotton sheets, plasma TVs, mini-bar, terrace, and fresh fruit and flowers.The Romanesque swimming pool is set in lovely gardens. **www.elcortijo-laprensa.com**

SAN JOSÉ Cortijo El Sotillo €€€

Ctra San José s/n, 04118 (Almería) ***Tel*** *950 61 11 00* ***Fax*** *950 61 11 05* ***Rooms*** *20*

An elegant 18th-century farmhouse set in the beautiful countryside of the natural parks of Cabo de Gata and Níjar. The perfect place for a walking holiday, with hikes into the volcanic hills, with the beaches of this stunning stretch of coastline just a short drive away. The restaurant uses produce from the estate. Disabled access. **www.cortijoelsotillo.com**

SANLÚCAR DE BARRAMEDA Hostal Alcoba €€

C/ Alcoba 26, 11540 (Cádiz) ***Tel*** *956 38 31 09* ***Rooms*** *10*

Located in the heart of Sanlúcar de Barrameda, a 10-minute walk from the beach, is this chic hotel. It offers modern, minimalist-style rooms and en suite bathrooms complete with bathrobes and slippers. Guests have the use of a library, lounge area, garden and swimming pool. A buffet breakfast is included. Closed Jan. **www.hostalalcoba.es**

SIERRA NEVADA Hotel El Lodge €€€€€

Maribel 8, Sierra Nevada, 18196 (Granada) ***Tel*** *958 48 06 00* ***Fax*** *958 48 13 14* ***Rooms*** *20*

This warm and welcoming hotel is perfectly located for enjoying a ski holiday in winter or a mountain escape in summer. It looks like a typical alpine ski lodge with picturesque wooden frame and rustic decor. Ski rental and classes can be arranged, as well as bike rental in summer. Free Wi-Fi throughout the hotel. **www.ellodge.com**

TARIFA Hurricane €€€

Ctra N340 km 78, 11380 (Cádiz) ***Tel*** *956 68 49 19* ***Fax*** *956 68 03 29* ***Rooms*** *33*

Tarifa is a mecca for windsurfers and the Hurricane is a temple to the sport. It is an imaginative, open-plan building set in subtropical gardens, which lead out onto the beach. Rooms are decorated in Andalusian style. It is one of the least crowded corners of the Spanish coast, with fine views across the sea to Africa. **www.hotelhurricane.com**

TOLOX Cerro de Hijar €€

Cerro de Hijar s/n, 29019 (Málaga) ***Tel*** *952 11 21 11* ***Fax*** *952 11 97 45* ***Rooms*** *18*

This hotel offers stunning views of the white village of Tolox and the surrounding area. The estate is Andalusian in style, with a central patio and spacious rooms. All kinds of outdoor pursuits can be arranged, including horse riding and excursions. The award-winning restaurant serves local specialities and their own wines. **www.cerrodehijar.com**

TORREMOLINOS Hotel Miami €

C/ Aladino 14, 29620 (Málaga) ***Tel*** *952 38 52 55* ***Fax*** *952 37 85 08* ***Rooms*** *26*

The Miami offers welcome respite from the Costa del Sol's modern growth. It has whitewashed walls, tiles, iron grilles, balconies and potted plants. Rooms are simple, and vary in terms of size and amenities, but they are all comfortable and the staff are friendly and helpful. The pool is an added bonus. **www.residencia-miami.com**

TREVÉLEZ Hotel La Fragua €

C/ San Antonio 4, 18417 (Granada) ***Tel*** *958 85 86 26* ***Fax*** *958 85 86 14* ***Rooms*** *24*

This simple whitewashed *mesón* (inn) is in what claims to be the highest village in Spain. There are great views from the rooftop terrace. The rooms vary considerably in size and character, but most have beamed ceilings, tiled floors and simple decor. There is a wonderful open fire in winter. Closed 10 Jan–10 Feb. **www.hotellafragua.com**

TURRE El Nacimiento €

Cortijo El Nacimiento, 04639 (Almería) ***Tel*** *950 52 80 90* ***Rooms*** *5*

A friendly couple runs this remote old farmhouse set in unspoilt rolling countryside. They offer bed and breakfast, vegetarian dinners (on request) made with organic produce, and morning yoga and meditation. Rooms are cosy and pretty. Best of all is the natural swimming pool in the grounds. No credit cards. **www.page.to/elnacimiento**

ÚBEDA Las Casas del Consul €€

Plaza del Carmen 1, 23400 (Jaén) ***Tel*** *953 79 54 30* ***Fax*** *953 79 54 31* ***Rooms*** *10*

Located in a historic 17th-century house surrounded by peaceful courtyards and centuries-old walls, this hotel is within easy walking distance of all the sights in Úbeda. The spacious, elegant rooms are decorated with antique furniture. There is a lovely garden with an inviting swimming pool. **www.lascasasdelconsul.com**

ÚBEDA Parador de Úbeda €€€€

Plaza Vázquez de Molina 1, 23400 (Jaén) ***Tel*** *953 75 03 45* ***Fax*** *953 75 12 59* ***Rooms*** *36*

Presiding over Úbeda's monumental central square, this parador is in a former 16th-century aristocratic palace. Blue and white tiles adorn the façade and the house surrounds a Renaissance two-storeyed patio. The spacious, high-ceilinged rooms are decorated with traditional furniture, and the restaurant serves regional cuisine. **www.parador.es**

Key to Price Guide *see p560* **Key to Symbols** *see back cover flap*

VÉJER DE LA FRONTERA El Conijo de Véjer €€

La Viña 7, 11150 (Cádiz) ***Tel*** *956 45 50 23* ***Fax*** *956 45 17 20* ***Rooms*** *7*

Situated in the centre of historic Véjer de la Frontera, this small B&B offers individually decorated en suite rooms with private balconies, flatscreen TV, and CD and DVD players. Some rooms have a kettle and a mircrowave, while others feature full kitchens. A delicious homemade breakfast buffet and Wi-Fi are included. **www.elcobijo.com**

VÉJER DE LA FRONTERA Hotel La Casa del Califa €€

Plaza de España 16, 11150 (Cádiz) ***Tel*** *956 44 77 30* ***Fax*** *956 45 16 25* ***Rooms*** *10*

Located in the centre of town, this hotel was created out of eight different houses, including the historic 17th-century Casa del Juzgado. Staying here feels like being a guest in a large private house, with multiple levels, corridors and courtyards dividing the space. The restaurant serves excellent Moroccan-inspired dishes. **www.lacasadelcalifa.com**

THE BALEARIC ISLANDS

FORMENTERA Hotel Cala Saona €€

Cala Saona, 07860 (Formentera) ***Tel*** *971 32 20 30* ***Fax*** *971 32 25 09* ***Rooms*** *116*

A modern hotel, this is the only option in the secluded Playa Cala Saona, one of the prettiest of Formentera's wild and unspoilt beaches. The interior is classic Spanish beach-hotel style with chintzy fabrics and TVs. Also has mini-fridges, a pool with a sun terrace and good facilities for children. Open Apr–Oct. **www.hotelcalasaona.com**

FORMENTERA, ES PUJOLS Sa Volta €€

C/ Miramar 94, 07871 (Formentera) ***Tel*** *971 32 81 25* ***Fax*** *971 32 82 28* ***Rooms*** *25*

A family-run *hostal* in a modern block close to the beach in one of Formentera's main resorts. The standard rooms are simple, but comfortable. It is worth splashing out on one of the three semi-suites, which have plush modern decor, including canopied beds and spacious private terraces. Charming staff. Open Mar–Dec. **www.savolta.com**

IBIZA (EIVISSA), IBIZA TOWN Hostal La Marina €€

C/ Barcelona 7, 07800 (Ibiza) ***Tel*** *971 31 01 72* ***Fax*** *971 31 48 94* ***Rooms*** *26*

A classic on the seafront, Hostal La Marina is located in a modernized 19th-century building, which retains some charming original details. Rooms are brightly painted in Mediterranean colours and the best have lovely sea views. In high season, it is a little overpriced, but a good deal otherwise. **www.hostal-lamarina.com**

IBIZA (EIVISSA), IBIZA TOWN Hostal Parque €€€

Plaza del Parque 4, 07800 (Ibiza) ***Tel*** *971 301 358* ***Fax*** *971 399 095* ***Rooms*** *30*

Open all year, this 30-room hostel is cosy and nicely decorated, with a homely touch. It is located in one of the most emblematic squares in downtown Ibiza. Within walking distance of the premises are the best clothing stores, music bars and restaurants. There is free Wi-Fi throughout the hostel. **www.hostalparque.com**

IBIZA (EIVISSA), IBIZA TOWN Hotel Royal Plaza €€€

Pere Frances 27–29, 07800 (Ibiza) ***Tel*** *971 31 00 00* ***Fax*** *971 31 40 95* ***Rooms*** *117*

This hotel, in the centre of Ibiza's old town, has clean lines and classic decor and provides all the comforts you may require, such as Wi-Fi in all rooms, a mini-bar and a pillow menu. There is also a well-being centre with Jacuzzi, sauna, gym and treatments. There is free Wi-Fi throughout the hotel. Open all year. **www.royalplaza.es**

IBIZA (EIVISSA), SANTA EULÀRIA D'ES RIU Les Terrasses €€€

Apto 1235 Ctra Santa Eulalia km 1, 07600 (Ibiza) ***Tel*** *971 33 26 43* ***Fax*** *971 33 89 78* ***Rooms*** *8*

A country house decorated simply but beautifully in Ibizan style, painted white, blue and sunshine yellow. Each room is individually styled with a perfect mixture of traditional and contemporary influences. It is a tranquil place with flower-filled gardens. Dinner is prepared with organic produce. Closed mid-Nov–Mar. **www.lesterrasses.net**

IBIZA, BAHÍA DE SANT ANTONI Osiris Ibiza €

Playa Es Puet s/n, 07820 (Ibiza) ***Tel*** *971 34 09 16* ***Fax*** *971 34 16 85* ***Rooms*** *97*

A family-run modern hotel in the popular resort of Sant Antoni, this is a great place for families on a budget. Osiris Ibiza is close to the beach and various water sports facilities, and has its own pool with a section for young children. The rooms are large and bright and offer views of the sea or the gardens. Open May–Oct. **www.hotelosiris.com**

IBIZA, CALA MOLÍ Hostel Cala Molí €€

Cala Molí, 07830 (Ibiza) ***Tel*** *971 80 60 02* ***Fax*** *971 80 61 50* ***Rooms*** *8*

This is a family-friendly little hostal overlooking a lovely bay. All the rooms face a tree-shaded terrace, and there is a swimming pool if you cannot make the walk to the nearby beach. The rooms are whitewashed and simply furnished with private balconies. The cheerful staff will give you tips on what to see. Open May–Oct. **www.calamoli.com**

MALLORCA, ALCÚDIA Cas Ferrer Nou Hotelet €€€

C/ Pou Nou 1, 07400 (Mallorca) ***Tel*** *971 89 75 42* ***Fax*** *971 89 75 49* ***Rooms*** *6*

This cosmopolitan boutique hotel has six unique rooms which mix natural decor elements with the avant-garde. The "Safo" room has a private terrace complete with a double bed for sleeping under the stars, while three of the rooms come with their own Jacuzzi. Closed 15 Dec–1 Feb. Free Wi-Fi throughout the hotel. **www.nouhotelet.com**

MALLORCA, BANYALBUFAR Sa Baronía €€

C/ Sa Baronía 16, 07191 (Mallorca) **Tel** 971 61 81 46 **Fax** 971 14 87 38 **Rooms** 39

Situated in a small village on the island's unspoilt, northwest coast, this simple family-run hotel was built as a modern extension onto a 17th-century baronial tower. The extension itself is unattractive, but the warm welcome and the tranquility of the area makes up for it. The simple bedrooms have terraces with sea views. **www.hbaronia.com**

MALLORCA, DEIÀ La Residencia €€€€€

Son Canals s/n, 07179 (Mallorca) **Tel** 971 63 90 11 **Fax** 971 63 93 70 **Rooms** 64

Two magnificent 16th- and 18th-century manors have been combined into a favourite hideaway of celebrities. The rooms and suites (some with private pools) are beautifully done with traditional Mallorcan furniture. It also has a spa, a restaurant, and MP3s and DVD players. Minimum stay 15 May–30 Sep: 3 nights. **www.hotel-laresidencia.com**

MALLORCA, LLUC Santuari de Lluc €

Santuari de Lluc, 07315 (Mallorca) **Tel** 971 87 15 25 **Fax** 971 51 70 96 **Rooms** 129

The spectacular Santuari de Lluc in the Tramuntana mountains is Mallorca's most important place of pilgrimage, and home to a much-venerated statue of the Madonna, the island's patron saint. If you are seeking spiritual calm then book yourself into one of the austere former monks' cells. They also offer simple apartments. **www.lluc.net**

MALLORCA, ORIENT L'Hermitage Hotel & Spa €€€€

Ctra de Alaró a Bunyola, 07349 (Mallorca) **Tel** 971 18 03 03 **Fax** 971 18 04 11 **Rooms** 20

A 16th-century stone monastery in a tranquil rural location has been painstakingly restored to create a luxurious hotel with a historical feel and all the modern comforts needed for a relaxing stay. Many rooms offer lovely views. Facilities include a spa, indoor and outdoor pools and a restaurant in a converted mill. **www.hermitage-hotel.com**

MALLORCA, PALMA DE MALLORCA Born €€

C/ Sant Jaume 3, 07012 (Mallorca) **Tel** 971 71 29 42 **Fax** 971 71 86 18 **Rooms** 30

The Marquis of Ferrandell's town mansion, built in the 16th century and restored in the 18th, makes a splendid little hotel. The simple but comfortable bedrooms are set around a typical Mallorcan courtyard with palms and a grand staircase. A few have tiny balconies overlooking the courtyard. One of the best budget options. **www.hotelborn.com**

MALLORCA, PALMA DE MALLORCA Hotel Tres €€€

Apuntadors 3, 07012 (Palma) **Tel** 971 717 333 **Fax** 971 717 372 **Rooms** 41

Centrally located in the heart of Palma de Mallorca, Hotel Tres blends old and new. Palma's main attractions can be easily reached on foot from here. The view from the rooftop terrace, swimming pool included, offers a beautiful panorama of the town and the island, perfect for a relaxing sunset. **www.hoteltres.com**

MALLORCA, PORT D'ANDRATX Villa Italia €€€€€

Camino San Carlos 13, 07157 (Mallorca) **Tel** 971 67 40 11 **Fax** 971 67 33 50 **Rooms** 16

A pink, Florentine-style villa, built in the 1920s by an Italian millionaire, has been lovingly restored to house this ultra-luxurious hotel. Inside there are stucco ceilings and marble floors, and the huge gardens – with fountains, tiles and Italianate balustrades – offer great sea views. Has a fine restaurant and a spa. **www.hotelvillaitalia.com**

MALLORCA, PORT DE POLLENÇA Barcelo Formentor €€€€€

Playa de Formentor 3, 07470 (Mallorca) **Tel** 971 89 91 00 **Fax** 971 86 51 55 **Rooms** 122

Writers, opera singers, film stars and the Dalai Lama have stayed at this luxury hotel on the island's northwest tip. No longer quite the celebrity haunt that it was, it still remains an elegant retreat. The rooms are traditionally decorated. Superb sports facilities are available and the beach is on the doorstep. **www.barceloformentor.com**

MALLORCA, PORT DE SÓLLER Casa Bougainvillea €€

C/ del Mar 81, 07100 (Mallorca) **Tel** 971 63 31 04 **Rooms** 8

At this delightful B&B in a townhouse with a beautiful garden guests can enjoy breakfast under an arbour of bougainvillea. Rooms have a contemporary Mediterranean decor and those at the back offer mountain views. The welcoming owners are happy to recommend restaurants and activities in the area. **www.casa-bougainvillea.com**

MALLORCA, PORT DE SÓLLER Gran Hotel Sóller €€€€€

C/ Romaguera 18, 07100 (Sóller) **Tel** 971 638 686 **Fax** 971 631 476 **Rooms** 38

A beautiful 19th-century palace in the village of Sóller has been converted into this unique hotel and spa with all modern conveniences. It was originally built by one of Mallorca's best architects and is decorated to the highest standards, providing a hint of classic glamour. There is free Wi-Fi throughout the hotel. **www.granhotelsoller.com**

MALLORCA, RANDA Es Recó de Randa €€€

C/ Font 21, 07629 (Mallorca) **Tel** 971 66 09 97 **Fax** 971 66 25 58 **Rooms** 14

A restaurant-with-rooms in an old stone house in a quiet village at the foot of the Puig de Randa mountain. The rustically decorated rooms have wooden beams and traditional furnishings, and many offer breathtaking views of the mountains and citrus groves. There is a lovely outdoor pool and a terrace. **www.esrecoderanda.com**

MALLORCA, SES SALINES Es Turó €€€

Camí de Cas Perets s/n, 07640 (Mallorca) **Tel** 971 64 95 31 **Fax** 971 64 95 48 **Rooms** 10

Rural calm, tasteful comfort and timeless Mallorcan life are combined in this romantic stone-built hotel. Converted from an old farmhouse, it is surrounded by almond and olive groves and is just a short drive (8 km) to Es Trenc beach. All the suites are spacious and nicely decorated in traditional style. Has a fine restaurant. **www.esturo.com**

Key to Price Guide *see p560* **Key to Symbols** *see back cover flap*

MALLORCA, SÓLLER Ca N'Aí €€€€€

Camí de Son Sales 50, 07100 (Mallorca) ***Tel*** *971 63 24 94* ***Fax*** *971 63 18 99* ***Rooms*** *11*

This enchanting hotel has been converted from an old Mallorcan mansion, built into the side of the Sóller valley and surrounded by orange and palm groves. Inside, the decor is a refined mixture of local and contemporary styles. The service has a personal touch and the cooking is excellent. Garden and pool. Open mid-Feb–Oct. **www.canai.com**

MENORCA, CIUTADELLA Hostal Ciutadella €

C/ San Eloy 10, 07760 (Menorca) ***Tel*** *971 38 34 62* ***Fax*** *971 48 48 58* ***Rooms*** *17*

Just around the corner from the Plaça de Alfons III, this simple, modern hotel offers good-value, no-frills lodging. The rooms are plainly furnished and spotless and are cooled with ceiling fans and air-conditioning in summer. Simple meals are served in the family-friendly café-bar on the ground floor. **www.alojarseenmenorca.com**

MENORCA, CIUTADELLA Hostal Sa Prensa €

Plaça de Madrid s/n, 07760 (Menorca) ***Tel*** *971 38 26 98* ***Rooms*** *7*

Probably the best of the cheaper hotels in Ciutadella, which has a shortage of good budget accommodation. Book early to get one of the four bedrooms which have terraces with great views of the port; the other three rooms are plain and overlook nondescript apartments. A café-bar downstairs serves breakfast. Closed 15 Dec–mid-Mar.

MENORCA, CIUTADELLA Hesperia Menorca Patricia €€€

Paseo San Nicolás 90–92, 07760 (Menorca) ***Tel*** *971 38 55 11* ***Fax*** *978 48 11 20* ***Rooms*** *44*

A modern, cream-coloured chain hotel with white bay windows near the harbour. Rooms are spacious and blandly furnished. Geared towards business travellers, it has conference facilities and a business centre. The convenient location and efficient staff make it a good bet for tourists. Offers weekend discounts. **www.hesperia-patricia.com**

MENORCA, MAÓ Hostal Jumé €

C/ Concepció 6, 07701 (Menorca) ***Tel*** *971 36 32 66* ***Fax*** *971 36 48 78* ***Rooms*** *39*

A very basic pension, run by a charming elderly couple, offering functional rooms (all en suite) with no frills at low prices. It is conveniently central (close to the port and the market) and the owners go out of their way to make guests comfortable. There is a simple, old-fashioned café-bar serving breakfast and local dishes. **www.hostaljume.com**

MENORCA, MAÓ Capri €€

C/ San Esteban 8, 07703 (Menorca) ***Tel*** *971 36 14 00* ***Fax*** *971 35 08 53* ***Rooms*** *75 & 7 apartments*

This is a central hotel in a modern block, five floors high, close to shops, the harbour and the beach. Although the exterior is unappealing, the interior is light and modern. The hotel offers exceptionally good facilities, including a fully equipped spa, a health centre and a swimming pool. Some rooms have Jacuzzis. **www.artiemhotels.com**

MENORCA, MAÓ Casa Alberti €€

C/ Isabel II 9, 07701 (Menorca) ***Tel*** *971 35 42 10* ***Fax*** *971 35 42 10* ***Rooms*** *6*

Located in a handsome 18th-century mansion, this is perhaps the most charming hotel in Maó. All the rooms are beautifully and individually decorated in chic, modern style. The winding, whitewashed staircase leads to a glorious roof terrace with good views of the sea. The charismatic owner is full of local information. **www.casalberti.com**

MENORCA, MAÓ Port Mahón €€

C/ Fort de l'Eau 13, 07701 (Menorca) ***Tel*** *971 36 26 00* ***Fax*** *971 35 10 50* ***Rooms*** *82*

Housed in an attractive red and white colonial-style building, this hotel – probably the most luxurious in the city – overlooks Maó harbour. Its grounds include wide terraces and a curving swimming pool surrounded by lawns. The best rooms, comfortably furnished in chain-hotel style, have private terraces. **www.sethotels.com**

THE CANARY ISLANDS

EL HIERRO, FRONTERA Ida Inés €

Camino del Hoyo Belgara Alta 2, 38911 ***Tel*** *922 55 94 45* ***Fax*** *922 55 60 88* ***Rooms*** *12*

Located in the valley of El Golfo, roughly in the middle of the island, this small and cosy hotel looks onto the Atlantic Ocean and the bedrooms have superb views of either the sea or the hills inland. The small swimming pool has a solarium and guests have Internet access. A good base for walking or mountain biking. **www.hotelitoidaines.com**

EL HIERRO, VALVERDE Parador de El Hierro €€€

Las Playas 15, 38900 ***Tel*** *922 55 80 36* ***Fax*** *922 55 80 86* ***Rooms*** *47*

Black cliffs are the backdrop for this modern, pantiled parador which stands in a peaceful spot on an isolated beach facing the Roque de Bonanza. It has an elegant colonial decor with white walls, and wooden balconies with sea views. An ideal option for walking or relaxing. El Hierro specialities served in the restaurant. **www.parador.es**

FUERTEVENTURA, ANTIGUA Era de la Corte €€

La Corte 1, 35630 ***Tel*** *928 87 87 05* ***Fax*** *928 87 87 10* ***Rooms*** *11*

A low-lying 19th-century house in a residential area of Antigua village, mostly painted in gleaming white, with exposed stone walls inside, but with some touches of striking colour here and there. All the rooms are individually decorated and two have four-poster beds. It has two sitting areas. Gay friendly. **www.eradelacorte.com**

FUERTEVENTURA, CORRALEJO Riu Palace Tres Islas €€€

Avenida Grand Playas, 35660 ***Tel*** *928 535 700* ***Rooms*** *372*

This full-service resort has classically elegant rooms with flatscreen TVs and mini-bars. All double rooms have balconies and most have impressive views of the Atlantic or the sand dunes of the northern part of the island. There are two large pools, a Jacuzzi and a children's pool. Visit the spa for one of their fabulous treatments. **www.riu.com**

FUERTEVENTURA, PÁJARA Casa Isaitas €€

C/ Guize 7, Pájara, 35626 ***Tel*** *928 16 14 02* ***Fax*** *928 16 14 82* ***Rooms*** *4*

This tiny rural B&B in a 200-year-old Canarian house is located in a village in the middle of the island. Offering simple lodging and home-made food, Casa Isaitas has only four bedrooms and an inner patio. A room which was formerly used as a corn mill now houses a lounge-library and bar where snacks are available. **www.casaisaitas.com**

GRAN CANARIA, AGAETE Finca Las Longueras Hotel Rural €€

Finca Las Longueras, 35480 ***Tel*** *928 89 81 45* ***Fax*** *928 89 87 52* ***Rooms*** *10*

This 19th-century colonial manor in the Agaete Valley, also known as the "Red House", is located in a plantation of bananas, oranges, papayas and avocados. It is tastefully decorated, with its own gardens and a chapel. In the grounds a self-catering house for rent sleeps four. Close to the ferry terminal of Tenerife. **www.laslongueras.com**

GRAN CANARIA, AGAETE Hotel Puerto de las Nieves €€

Avda. Alcalde Joses de Armas, 35480 ***Tel*** *928 88 62 56* ***Fax*** *928 88 62 67* ***Rooms*** *30*

A tranquil retreat, in the unbeatable surroundings of Puerto de las Nieves, offering luxurious pampering. Indulge in one of the health treatments at the hydrotherapy centre, and enjoy dining at the à la carte restaurant. There is also a sport and leisure centre. The price includes half-board and some spa time. **www.hotelpeurtodelasnieves.es**

GRAN CANARIA, CRUZ DE TEJEDA Parador Cruz de Tejeda €€€

Cruz de Tejeda, 35328 ***Tel*** *928 012 500* ***Fax*** *928 012 501* ***Rooms*** *43*

With splendid mountain and sea views, this hotel is situated at one of the highest points of the island. Modern rooms are well appointed and the lounge has two magnificent hearths. Request a picnic basket and spend the day exploring the adjacent nature reserve. Full-service spa; bicycles for rent. Parking spaces are limited. **www.parador.es**

GRAN CANARIA, LAS PALMAS Hotel Las Tirajanas €€

Oficial Mayor José Rubio, San Bartolomé de Tirajana, 35290 ***Tel*** *928 12 30 00* ***Fax*** *928 12 30 23* ***Rooms*** *60*

High above the brash and noisy resorts on Gran Canaria's southern coast, this spa hotel is on the edge of an ancient caldera and enjoys breathtaking mountain scenery. A suitable place to unwind or use as base for walking. It also has a restaurant serving Canarian cuisine, a covered pool and a gym. Closed Jun–mid-Jul. **www.paradiseresorts.es**

GRAN CANARIA, LAS PALMAS Santa Catalina €€€

C/ León y Castillo 227, 35005 ***Tel*** *928 24 30 40* ***Fax*** *928 24 27 64* ***Rooms*** *202*

This traditional Canarian building with its wooden balconies and Colonial atmosphere has been a classic hotel since it opened in 1890. Many of the rooms have either a park or sea view. Among them are 14 junior suites and two senior suites. Facilities include an opulent casino and a well-equipped spa centre. **www.hotelsantacatalina.com**

GRAN CANARIA, MASPALOMAS Riu Grand Palace Maspalomas Oasis €€€€

Plaza de las Palmeras 2, 35106 ***Tel*** *928 14 14 48* ***Fax*** *928 14 11 92* ***Rooms*** *332*

In a prime, palm-shaded spot by Maspalomas' renowned (and unspoilt) sand dunes is this secluded, modern, grand hotel, surrounded by subtropical gardens. The guests are stylishly accommodated in split-level suites with spacious bedrooms. The staff are efficient and pleasant. There is a four-night minimum stay in August. **www.riu.com**

GRAN CANARIA, PUERTO RICO Aparthotel Terrazamar Sunsuite €€€

Avenida Las Palmeras 5-8, 35130 ***Tel*** *928 725 525* ***Rooms*** *306*

A complex of apartments which is within walking distance of Puerto Rico beach. The cheery beach house decor encompasses an independent kitchen, living room with TV and telephone, bedroom, bathroom and large terrace with sunbeds and parasols. Reserve a free parking space. Minimum two-night stay. **www.terrazamarsuite.com**

GRAN CANARIA, PUERTO RICO Gloria Palace Royal Hotel & Spa €€€

Tamara 1, Playa Amadores, Mogan, 35130 ***Tel*** *928 128 505* ***Fax*** *928 771 921* ***Rooms*** *276*

This modern hotel offers spectacular views of Amadores beach. The spacious rooms have furnished terraces, many with ocean views. There are two adult pools, including a massive infinity pool, an indoor pool and one children's pool. Children's play area and club; full-service spa and gym. **www.gloriapalaceth.com**

LA GOMERA, PLAYA DE SANTIAGO Jardín Tecina €€€

Lomada de Tecina, 38811 ***Tel*** *922 14 58 50* ***Fax*** *922 14 58 51* ***Rooms*** *434*

The main reason to stay at this attractive hotel is to go walking around the island of La Gomera. Its many facilities and entertainments make the complex, which is in the hills behind the Playa de Santiago, virtually a self-contained resort. It is surrounded by gardens. A cliff-side lift takes guests down to the beach club. **www.jardin-tecina.com**

LA GOMERA, SAN SEBASTIÁN Parador de la Gomera €€€

San Sebastián de La Gomera, 38800 ***Tel*** *922 87 11 00* ***Fax*** *922 87 11 16* ***Rooms*** *60*

On a clifftop above La Gomera's main town and port, this traditional parador is decorated with a variety of maritime paraphernalia. The bedrooms have dark wood fittings and tiled bathrooms. From the hotel and its luxuriant subtropical gardens there are impressive views across the sea to Mt Teide on Tenerife. **www.parador.es**

Key to Price Guide *see p560* **Key to Symbols** *see back cover flap*

LA PALMA, BARLOVENTO La Palma Romántica €

Las Llanadas s/n, 38726 ***Tel*** *922 18 62 21* ***Fax*** *922 18 64 00* ***Rooms*** *44*

Nestling into a hillside in the northeast tip of the island, high above the sea, is this airy hotel with spacious rooms. Apart from double and single rooms there are some suites and rooms in bungalows. It has both indoor and outdoor swimming pools, a sauna, a solarium and a fitness centre. Pets are allowed. **www.hotelromantica.info**

LA PALMA, SANTA CRUZ DE LA PALMA Parador de la Palma €€€

Ctra de el Zumacal, Breña Baja, 38720 ***Tel*** *922 43 58 28* ***Fax*** *922 43 59 99* ***Rooms*** *78*

This modern, purpose-built parador, in the traditional Canarian style, looks out on to the sea and is surrounded by a lovely garden. It is located near the island's main town and the airport. Various excursions and activities are available. The restaurant excels in fish and other Canarian specialities and wine made on the island. **www.parador.es**

LANZAROTE, ARRECIFE Lancelot €

Av Mancomunidad 9, 35500 ***Tel*** *928 80 50 99* ***Fax*** *928 80 50 39* ***Rooms*** *112*

This modern hotel stands on Arrecife's Reducto beach, a tempting stretch of soft, pale sand with coral reefs lying just offshore. The hotel has all the standard services including a reception desk open 24 hours. The restaurant has sea views and is also close to other good restaurants in the town. **www.hotellancelot.com**

LANZAROTE, COSTA TEGUISE Bluebay Lanzarote €€€

Avenida Las Palmeras 30, 35509 ***Tel*** *928 590 246* ***Fax*** *928 591 366* ***Rooms*** *200*

This apartment complex has spacious, modern one-bedroom units with kitchen, living room with sofa bed, satellite TV, telephone and furnished terraces. There are two swimming pools (one for children), a gym, a sauna, numerous sports facilities, a gift shop, medical services and three bars. All-inclusive only. **www.bluebayresorts.com**

LANZAROTE, PLAYA BLANCA H10 Timanfaya Palace €€

Gran Canaria 1, Montaña Roja, 35580 ***Tel*** *928 517 676* ***Fax*** *928 517 035* ***Rooms*** *297*

A modern hotel with well-appointed rooms as well as lovely pools and gardens. There are many sports options, an on-site marina and barbecue, and a spa. Alternatively, get a book from the library and cosy up by the fireplace in the lobby. Watch the sunset from the terrace, then dance the night away at the disco. Adults (16+) only. **www.h10hotels.com**

LANZAROTE, PUERTO DEL CARMEN Los Fariones €€

C/ Roque del Este 1, 35510 ***Tel*** *928 51 01 75* ***Fax*** *928 51 02 02* ***Rooms*** *248*

This seven-storey hotel has direct access to an attractive beach. All the rooms are spacious and have sea views. The hotel has a good range of facilities including a dive centre and two swimming pools. Outside is a large tropical garden. Two bars offer a range of snacks and live music most evenings. **www.farioneshotels.com**

TENERIFE, GARACHICO Hotel San Roque €€€€

C/ Esteban de Ponte 32, 38450 ***Tel*** *922 13 34 35* ***Fax*** *922 13 34 06* ***Rooms*** *20*

This charming hotel decorated with avant-garde art occupies an 18th-century house built around two pretty patios, in a historic north coast town away from the island's tourist resorts. All rooms have Jacuzzi, flatscreen TVs and video and DVD players. Dinner and breakfast are served at tables set by the poolside. **www.hotelsanroque.com**

TENERIFE, LA LAGUNA Costa Salada €€

Camino La Costa, Finca Oasis, Valle de Guerra, 38270 ***Tel*** *922 69 00 00* ***Fax*** *922 54 10 55* ***Rooms*** *13*

A pretty rural hotel standing on a series of terraces over the rocky northern coast of Tenerife, at the end of a subtropical nursery for plants. The hotel has cosy bedrooms, mostly with terraces and sea views. It also has a wine cellar in a natural cave. Located off the coast road between Tejina and Valle de Guerra. **www.costasalada.com**

TENERIFE, LA OROTAVA Hotel Rural La Orotava €€

C/ Carrera 17, 38300 ***Tel*** *922 32 27 93* ***Fax*** *922 32 27 25* ***Rooms*** *8*

This 16th-century house, with cosy bedrooms around an attractive Canarian patio, was formerly the home of the Marquis of La Florida. Now transformed into a hotel, it is one of the historic buildings that forms the compact, harmonious centre of La Orotava. It also has a wine cellar. Breakfast included in price. **www.saborcanario.net**

TENERIFE, LAS FUENTES Parador de Cañadas del Teide €€€

Las Cañadas del Teide, 38300 ***Tel*** *922 37 48 41* ***Fax*** *922 38 23 52* ***Rooms*** *37*

This modern parador, which looks like an Alpine chalet, is the only place to stay inside the national park. It stands in an otherwise uninhabited volcanic landscape looking out at the Roques de Garcia and towards Mt Teide. In the daytime its cafeteria caters for day-trippers but at night the guests have the park to themselves. **www.parador.es**

TENERIFE, SANTA CRUZ DE TENERIFE NH Tenerife €€

Candelaria Esquina Doctor Allart, 38003 ***Tel*** *922 534 422* ***Fax*** *922 574 564* ***Rooms*** *64*

NH Tenerife is a sleek, modern hotel situated in the heart of Santa Cruz, near the main shopping area and nightlife. Rooms are stylishly decorated in neutral shades with jewel-tone accents. The large range of services includes a terrace with Jacuzzi and solarium, a gym and a highly acclaimed restaurant run by chef Ferrán Adrià. **www.nh-hotels.com**

TENERIFE, SANTA CRUZ DE TENERIFE Taburiente €€

C/ Dr José Naveiras 24A, 38001 ***Tel*** *922 27 60 00* ***Fax*** *922 27 05 62* ***Rooms*** *171*

An elegant hotel in the city centre facing the beautiful Parque Garcia Sanabria. The bedrooms are well equipped and the hotel has its own boutique, a shop and a restaurant offering international cuisine. They also have a swimming pool, Jacuzzi, sauna and a solarium. **www.hoteltaburiente.com**

RESTAURANTS AND BARS

One of the joys of eating out in Spain is the sheer sociability of the Spanish. Family and friends, often with children in tow, can be seen eating out from early in the day until after midnight.

Wall tile advertising a Barcelona restaurant

Spanish food has a highly regional bias. Traditional restaurants originated as taverns serving dishes based on local produce. Spain also has its fair share of top-quality gourmet restaurants, notably in the Basque Country.

The restaurants listed on pages 608–53 have been selected for their food and conviviality. Pages 604–7 illustrate some of the best tapas and drinks; and each of the book's five regional sections includes features on the area's unique food and wines.

An elaborately decorated bar in Barcelona

RESTAURANTS AND BARS

The cheapest and quickest places to eat are the bars and cafés that serve tapas. Some bars, however, especially pubs (late-opening bars for socializing) serve no food.

Family-run bar-restaurantes, ventas, posadas, mesones and fondas – all old words for the different types of inn – serve inexpensive, sit-down meals. Chiringuitos are beachside bars. They open only during the summer season.

Spain's top restaurants tend to be clustered in the Basque Country, Galicia, Barcelona, Catalonia and Madrid.

Most restaurants close one day a week, some for lunch or dinner only, and most for an annual holiday. Away from the tourist areas, some also close on some public holidays. The main closing times of the restaurants on pages 608–53 are listed at the end of each entry. It is always worth calling ahead to check.

EATING HOURS IN SPAIN

The Spanish often have two breakfasts (*desayunos*). The first is a light meal of biscuits or toast with olive oil or butter and jam and café con leche (milky coffee). A more substantial breakfast may follow between 10 and 11am, perhaps in a café. This may consist of a savoury snack, such as a *bocadillo* (sandwich) with sausage, ham or cheese, or a thick slice of *tortilla de patatas* (potato omelette). Fruit juice, coffee or beer are the usual accompaniments.

Decorative lamp in a bar

From about 1pm at weekends people will stop in the bars for a beer or a *copa* (glass) of wine with tapas. By 2pm those who can will have arrived home from work for *la comida* (lunch), which is the main meal of the day. Others will choose to have lunch in a restaurant.

The cafés, *salones de té* (tea rooms) and *pastelerías* (pastry shops) fill up by about 5:30 or 6pm for *la merienda* (tea) of sandwiches, pastries or cakes, with coffee, tea or juice. Snacks like *churros* (fried batter sticks) can also be bought from stalls.

By 7pm, bars are crowded with people having tapas with sherry, wine or beer. In Spain *la cena* (dinner or supper), begins at about 9 or 10pm. Restaurants sometimes begin their evening service earlier for tourists. In summer, however, Spanish families and groups of friends often do not sit down to eat until as late as midnight. At weekend lunch times, especially in summer, you may find that restaurants are filled by large and noisy family gatherings.

HOW TO DRESS

A jacket and tie are rarely required, but the Spanish dress smartly, especially for city restaurants. Day dress is casual in beach resorts, but shorts are frowned on in the evenings.

The elegant Egaña Oriza restaurant in Seville *(see p641)*

Dining *al fresco* at tables on a café terrace

READING THE MENU

Aside from tapas, perhaps the cheapest eating options in Spanish restaurants are the *platos combinados* (meat or fish with vegetables and, usually, chips) and the fixed price *menú del día*. A *plato combinado* is only offered by cheaper establishments. Most restaurants – but not all – offer an inexpensive, fixed-price *menú del día* at lunch time, normally of three courses, but with little choice. Some restaurants offer a *menú de degustación* consisting of a choice of six or seven of the head chef's special dishes.

The Spanish word for menu is *la carta*. It starts with *sopas* (soups), *ensaladas* (salads), *entremeses* (hors d'oeuvres), *huevos y tortillas* (eggs and omelettes) and *verduras y legumbres* (vegetable dishes).

Main courses are *pescados y mariscos* (fish and shellfish) and *carnes y aves* (meat and poultry). Daily specials are chalked on a board or clipped to menus. Paella and other rice dishes may be served as the first course. A useful rule is to follow rice with meat, or start with serrano ham or salad and then follow with a paella.

Desserts are called *postres* in Spanish. All restaurants offer fresh fruit (the usual dessert in Spain) but otherwise the range of *postres* is generally poor. The better restaurants offer a limited choice, perhaps *natillas* (custard) and *flan* (crème caramel). Gourmet restaurants have more creative choices.

Vegetarians are rather poorly catered for in Spain, but in big cities such as Madrid there are a handful of vegetarian restaurants. Most menus have a vegetable or egg dish.

Most eating places welcome children and will serve small portions if requested.

The modern, elegant Cinc Sentits in Barcelona *(see p619)*

WINE CHOICES

Dry fino wines go with shellfish, serrano ham, olives, soups and most first courses. Main courses are usually accompanied by wines from Ribera del Duero, Rioja, Navarra or Penedès. A bar might serve wines from Valdepeñas or the local vineyards. Oloroso wines (see p607) are often ordered as a digestif.

SMOKING

Smoking is banned inside all bars and restaurants, though smoking is still allowed on outside terraces.

PRICES AND PAYING

If you order from *la carta* in a restaurant, your bill can soar way above the price of the *menú del día*, especially if you order pricey items, such as fresh seafood, fish or ibérico ham (see p462). If there is an expensive fish such as sole or swordfish on the menu at a bargain price, it may be frozen. Sea bass and other popular fish and shellfish, such as large prawns, lobster and crab, are priced by weight as a rule. The price ranges given in this guide apply to the regular menu, but if you have tapas it is usually much cheaper.

La cuenta (the bill) includes service charges and perhaps a small cover charge. Prices on menus do not always include 8 per cent VAT (IVA), so it may be added when the bill is totalled. The Spanish hardly ever tip restaurant waiters more than 5 per cent, often just rounding up the bill.

Cheques are never used in Spain. The major credit cards and international direct debit cards are now accepted in most restaurants, but sometimes not in smaller places like tapas bars, cafés or *bodegas*.

WHEELCHAIR ACCESS

New restaurants are designed for wheelchairs, but phone in advance (or ask the hotel staff to call) to check on access to tables and toilets.

Designer tapas bar

Choosing Tapas

Tapas, sometimes called *pinchos*, are small snacks that originated in Andalusia in the 19th century to accompany sherry. Stemming from a bartender's practice of covering a glass with a saucer or *tapa* (cover) to keep out flies, the custom progressed to a chunk of cheese or bread being used, and then to a few olives being placed on a platter to accompany a drink. Once free of charge, tapas are usually paid for nowadays, and a selection makes a delicious light meal. Choose from a range of appetizing varieties, from cold meats to elaborately prepared hot dishes of meat, seafood or vegetables.

Mixed green olives

Patatas bravas *is a piquant dish of fried potatoes with a spicy red sauce.*

Albóndigas *(meatballs) are a hearty tapa, often served with a spicy tomato sauce.*

Almendras fritas *are fried, salted almonds.*

Banderillas *are canapes skewered on toothpicks. The entire canape should be eaten at once.*

Calamares fritos *are squid rings and tentacles which have been dusted with flour before being deep fried in olive oil. They are usually served garnished with a piece of lemon.*

Jamón serrano *is salt-cured ham dried in mountain* (serrano) *air.*

ON THE TAPAS BAR

Almejas Clams

Berberechos Steamed cockles

Berenjenas al horno Roasted aubergines (eggplants)

Boquerones Anchovies

Boquerones al natural Fresh anchovies in garlic and olive oil

Buñuelos de bacalao Salt cod fritters

Butifarra Catalonian sausage

Calabacín rebozado Battered courgettes (zucchini) (Catalan)

Calamares a la romana Fried squid rings

Callos Tripe

Caracoles Snails

Champiñones al ajillo Mushrooms fried in white wine with garlic

Chistorra Spicy sausage

Chopitos Cuttlefish fried in batter

Chorizo al vino Chorizo sausage cooked in red wine

Chorizo diablo Chorizo served flamed with brandy

Costillas Spare ribs

Criadillas Bulls' testicles

Croquetas Croquettes of ham, cod or chicken

Empanada Pastry filled with tomato, onion and meat or fish

Ensaladilla rusa Potatoes, carrots, red peppers, peas, olives, boiled egg, tuna and mayonnaise

Gambas pil pil Spicy, garlicky fried king prawns (shrimp)

Longaniza roja Spicy red pork sausage from Aragón (Longaniza blanca is paler and less spicy.)

Magro Pork in a paprika and tomato sauce

Manitas de cerdo Pig's trotters

TAPAS BARS

Even a small village will have at least one bar where the locals go to enjoy drinks, tapas and conversation with friends. On Sundays and holidays, favourite places are packed with whole families enjoying the fare. In larger towns it is customary to move from bar to bar, sampling the specialities of each. A tapa is a single serving, whereas a *ración* is similar to an entrée-sized portion. Tapas are usually eaten standing or perching on a stool at the bar rather that sitting at a table, for which a surcharge is usually made.

Diners make their choice at a busy tapas bar

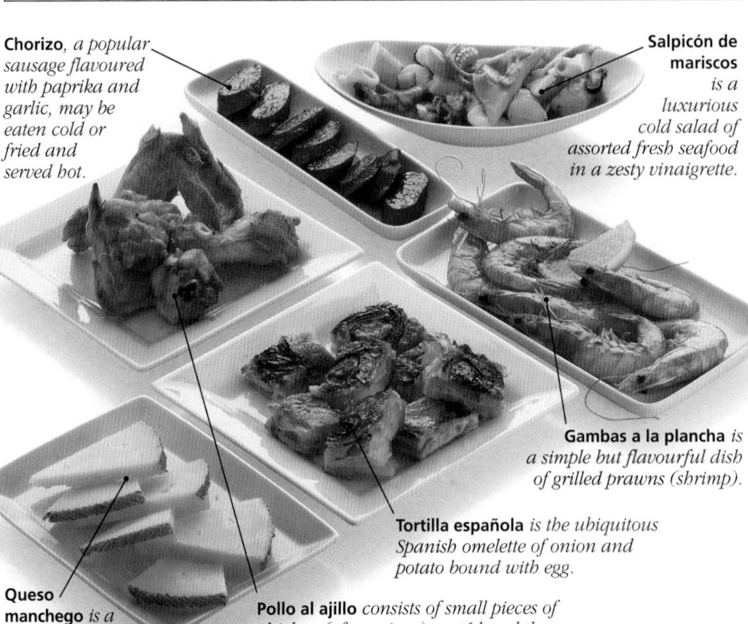

Chorizo, *a popular sausage flavoured with paprika and garlic, may be eaten cold or fried and served hot.*

Salpicón de mariscos *is a luxurious cold salad of assorted fresh seafood in a zesty vinaigrette.*

Gambas a la plancha *is a simple but flavourful dish of grilled prawns (shrimp).*

Tortilla española *is the ubiquitous Spanish omelette of onion and potato bound with egg.*

Queso manchego *is a sheep's-milk cheese from La Mancha.*

Pollo al ajillo *consists of small pieces of chicken (often wings) sautéd and then simmered with a garlic-flavoured sauce.*

Mejillones Mussels

Morcilla Black (blood) pudding

Muslitos del mar Crab-meat croquette, on a claw skewer

Navajas Grilled razor-shells

Orejas de cerdo Pig's ear

Pa amb tomàquet Bread rubbed with olive oil and tomatoes (Catalan)

Pan de ajo Garlic bread

Patatas a lo pobre Potato chunks sautéd with onions and red and green peppers

Patatas alioli Potato chunks in a garlic mayonnaise

Pescadito fritos Small fried fish

Pimientos de padrón Small green peppers which are occasionally quite hot

Pimientos rellenos Stuffed peppers

Pinchos morunos Pork skewers

Pisto Thick ratatouille of diced tomato, onion and courgette

Pulpitos Baby octopus

Rabo de toro Oxtail

Revueltos Scrambled eggs with asparagus or mushrooms

Sepia a la plancha Grilled cuttlefish

Sesos Brains, usually lamb or calf

Surtido de Ibéricos Assortment of cold cuts/charcuterie

Tabla de quesos A range of Spanish cheeses

Tortilla riojana Ham, sausage and red pepper omelette

Tostas Bread with various toppings such as tuna or brie

Verdura a la plancha Grilled vegetables

What to Drink in Spain

Spain is one of the world's largest wine-producing countries and many fine wines are made here, particularly reds in La Rioja and sherry in Andalusia. Many other beverages – alcoholic and non-alcoholic – are served in bars and cafés, which provide an important focus for life in Spain. The Spanish are also great coffee drinkers. In the summer, a tempting range of cooling drinks is on offer, in addition to beer, which is always available. Brandy and a variety of liqueurs, such as *anís*, are drunk as apéritifs and *digestifs*, as is chilled pale gold fino sherry.

Customers enjoying a drink at a terrace café in Seville

Hot chocolate

A plate of *churros* (batter sticks)

Café con leche

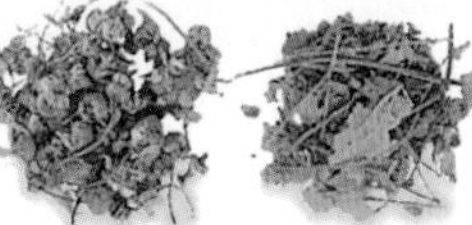

Camomile

Lime flower

HOT DRINKS

Café con leche is a large half-and-half measure of milk and espresso coffee; *café cortado* is an espresso with a splash of milk; *café solo* is a black coffee. Hot chocolate is also popular and is often served with *churros* (batter sticks). Herbal teas include *manzanilla* (camomile) and *tila* (lime flower).

COLD DRINKS

In most Spanish towns and cities it is safe to drink the tap water, but people generally prefer to buy bottled mineral water, either still *(sin gas)* or sparkling *(con gas)*. Besides soft drinks, a variety of other thirst-quenching summer beverages is available, including *horchata (see p253)*, a sweet, milky drink made from ground *chufas* (earth almonds). Another popular refreshing drink is *leche merengada* (lemon and cinnamon flavoured milk ice cream). *Gaseosa*, fizzy lemonade, can be drunk either on its own or as a mixer, usually with wine. *Zumo de naranja natural* (freshly squeezed orange juice) is an excellent thirst quencher.

Sparkling and still mineral water

Horchata, made from *chufas*

SPANISH WINE

Wine has been produced in Spain since pre-Roman times and there is a great variety on offer today, including famous types such as Rioja. The key standard for the industry is the *Denominación de Origen* (DO) classification, a guarantee of a wine's origin and quality. *Vino de la Tierra* is a classification of wines below that of DO in which over 60 per cent of the grapes come from a specified region. *Vino de Mesa*, the lowest category, covers basic unclassified wines. For more detailed information on Spain's principal wine-producing regions, refer to the following pages: Northern Spain *(see pp78–9)*, Eastern Spain *(see pp202–3)*, Central Spain *(see pp340–41)*, and Southern Spain *(see pp420–21)*.

Penedès white wine

Rioja red wine

Sparkling wine *(cava)*

SPIRITS AND LIQUEURS

Spanish brandy, which comes mainly from the sherry bodegas in Jerez, is known as *coñac*. Most bodegas produce at least three different labels and price ranges. Magno is a good middle-shelf brandy; top-shelf labels are Cardenal Mendoza and Duque de Alba. *Anís*, which is flavoured with aniseed, is popular. *Pacharán*, made from sloes, is sweet and also tastes of aniseed. Licor 43 is a vanilla liqueur. Ponche is brandy that has been aged and flavoured with herbs.

Anís

Pacharán

Licor 43

Ponche

BEER

Most Spanish beer *(cerveza)* is bottled lager, although you can almost always find it on draught. Popular brands include Moritz, Alhambra, San Miguel, Cruzcampo Mahou and Estrella. In Barcelona a glass of beer is called *una caña*; in Madrid, *un tercio*. Alcohol-free lager *(cerveza sin alcohol)* is available.

Bottled beers

SHERRY

Sherry is produced in bodegas in Jerez de la Frontera (Andalusia) and in nearby towns Sanlúcar de Barrameda and El Puerto de Santa María *(see pp420–21)*. Although not officially called sherry, similar kinds of wine are produced in Montilla near Córdoba. Pale fino is dry and light and excellent as an apéritif. Amber amontillado (aged fino) has a strong, earthy taste while oloroso is full-bodied and ruddy.

Two brands of fino sherry

MIXED DRINKS

Sangria is a refreshing mixture of red wine, *gaseosa* (lemonade) and other ingredients including chopped fruit and sugar. Wine diluted with lemonade is called *vino con gaseosa*. Another favourite drink is *Agua de Valencia*, a refreshing blend of *cava* (sparkling wine) and orange juice. Young people will often order the popular *cubalibres*, cola with rum.

Sangria

Cubalibre

Vino con gaseosa

HOW TO READ A WINE LABEL

If you know what to look for, the label will provide a key to the wine's flavour and quality. It will bear the name of the wine and its producer or bodega, its vintage if there is one, and show its *Denominación de Origen* (DO) if applicable. Wines labelled *cosecha* are recent vintages and the least expensive, while *crianza* and *reserva* wines are aged a minimum of two or three years – part of that time in oak casks – and therefore more expensive. Table wine *(Vino de Mesa)* may be *tinto* (red), *blanco* (white) or *rosado* (rosé). *Cava* is a sparkling wine made by the *méthode champenoise* in specified areas of origin.

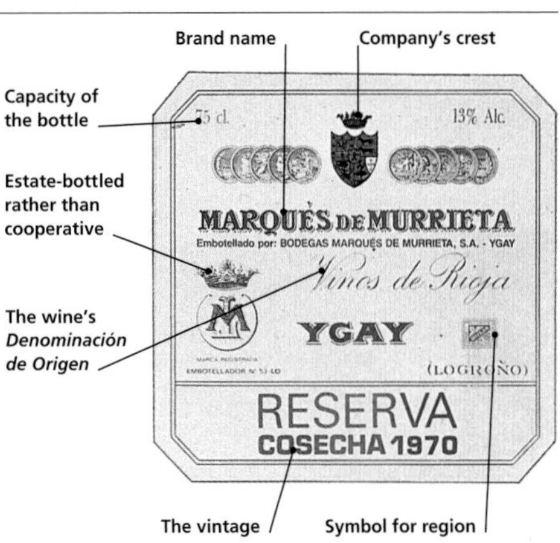

Choosing a Restaurant

The restaurants in this guide have been selected across a wide range of price categories for their good value, exceptional food and interesting location. This chart lists the restaurants by region. Within each town or city, entries are listed by price category, from the least expensive to the most expensive.

PRICE CATEGORIES
For a three-course evening meal for one including a half bottle of house wine, service and taxes:

€ under €25
€€ €25–€35
€€€ €35–€50
€€€€ over €50

GALICIA

A CORUÑA Taberna Pil-Pil *Tapas* €€
C/ Pelamios 7, 15001 ***Tel*** *981 21 27 12*

Located in front of the Escuela de Artes Picasso, this pleasant, though rather small, taberna restaurant uses the freshest local produce in season to create simple dishes, with sauces or spices that enhance the main ingredients. Choose from about 12 dishes and five desserts. Closed Sun & 15–31 Oct.

A CORUÑA La Penela €€€
Plaza de María Pita 12, 15001 ***Tel*** *981 20 92 00*

In the square dedicated to a Galician heroine, and very close to the harbour, is this simple, unpretentious but very popular restaurant which serves traditional Galician fare. The roast veal, tripe with *garbanzos* (chickpeas), Spanish omelette and Galician-style monkfish are specialities. Closed Sun & two weeks in Jan.

A CORUÑA Casa Pardo €€€€
C/ Novoa Santos 15, 15006 ***Tel*** *981 28 00 21*

High-quality cooking and an extensive menu of Galician dishes are the characteristics of this Michelin star restaurant. It is renowned for its monkfish, *caldeirada de rape*, a dish that is not always mentioned on the menu but is always available. Try the hot chocolate soufflé with nougat ice cream. Closed Sun. Reservation recommended.

A GUARDA Anduriña €€€
Rúa Do Porto 58, 36780 (Pontevedra) ***Tel*** *986 61 11 08*

Watch the fishing boats bring in their catch as you enjoy fresh hake, turbot or roasted mixed fish from the covered terrace of this port-side restaurant. It also serves traditional *empanada gallega* (a pie stuffed with cod, tuna or shellfish), a good stew with monkfish and clams, and a fair variety of desserts. Closed Nov, Sun evenings Sep–Jul.

ALLARIZ Casa Tino Fandiño *Tapas* €€
Rúa do Carcere 7, 32660 (Ourense) ***Tel*** *988 44 22 16*

A famous restaurant, specializing in traditional Galician cooking with modern touches. It is a good place to try *pulpo* (octopus) or *empanada* (pie). For something more elaborate, try the *lubina* (sea bass) with mushroom sauce or the veal stew. Good wine list. Closed Sun and Mon.

BAIONA Moscón €€€
C/ Alférez Barreiro 2, 36300 (Pontevedra) ***Tel*** *986 35 50 08*

This restaurant in Baiona serves mainly Galician cuisine with fish stews predominating on the menu. These include a tasty fish *caldeirada* (casserole) spiced with paprika. There is also seafood from the estuary; all complemented by a good selection of Galician wines. The harbour view makes for a pleasant dining experience. Outside tables in summer.

BETANZOS La Casilla *Tapas* €€
Ctra de Castilla 90, 15300 (A Coruña) ***Tel*** *981 77 01 61*

Located in an old-stone house, this restaurant is famous throughout Spain for its omelettes, especially the potato variety – *tortilla de patata* – but it also serves traditional Galician food, tripe and grilled meat. It is very busy during the summer and at weekends. Closed Sun evenings, Mon & 20 days in Nov.

BUEU A Centoleira *Tapas* €€€
Playa de Beluso 28, 36937 (Pontevedra) ***Tel*** *986 32 34 81*

What started as an old fishermen's inn 120 years ago is now a popular restaurant run by the same family, serving Galician food such as *guisotes marineros* (fish stews), *empanada de maiz* (sweetcorn pie) and cheese mousse over tomato compote. Closed Mon (except summer), Sun evenings & 15 Oct–15 Nov and Christmas.

CAMBADOS Ribadomar €€
Rúa Valle-Inclán 17, 36630 (Pontevedra) ***Tel*** *986 54 36 79*

A welcoming family-run restaurant offering mainly seafood and traditional dishes, although there are a few innovations as well, such as the *Perdiz* (partridge). Try the *vieiras al horno* (oven-baked scallops) and, for dessert, the homemade almond pie. Closed Sun evenings & Mon (except last week Jul & Aug), 15 days Sep–Oct & 15 days end of Feb–Mar.

CAMBADOS María José €€€

C/ San Gregorio 2– 1°, 36630 (Pontevedra) ***Tel*** *986 54 22 81*

Situated on the first floor of the building opposite the Parador de Cambados, this restaurant offers experimental cooking, combining traditional dishes with modern creations. It has a good selection of Albariño wines. Try the *langostino* (king prawn) salad wrapped in bacon. Closed Sun evenings & Mon (except Jul & Aug), and two weeks at Christmas.

COMBARRO Taberna de Alvariñas *Tapas* €€€

C/ Mar 63, 36993 (Pontevedra) ***Tel*** *986 77 20 33*

Located in a picturesque fishing village, famous for its *hórreos* (granaries) on the seafront, this restaurant has three lovely terraces. Try the roasted scallops with lobster ragu with Alvariño wine, the *lomos de merluza* (hake) and the *filloas* (Galician crêpes) filled with cream and toffee. Closed Mon except in summer & 10 Dec–31 Jan.

LUGO Verruga *Tapas* €€€

C/ Cruz 12, 27001 ***Tel*** *982 22 95 72*

This restaurant, in the heart of the old town, has been serving good classic and uncomplicated Galician fare since 1951. It also offers seafood from its own aquarium. Try the red peppers stuffed with crab meat and the delicious homemade *filloas rellenas fritas* (Galician crêpes). Closed Sun evenings & Mon, and two weeks in Nov.

LUGO Mesón de Alberto *Tapas* €€€€

C/ Cruz 4, 27001 ***Tel*** *982 22 83 10*

An institution of Galician cooking, located in a stone house in the monumental area of town. Award-winning chef Alberto García offers a selection of traditional delicacies and more modern creations. The fish and shellfish are excellent, including small squid and sea bass with baby eels. Wide selection of Galician cheeses and wines. Closed Sun.

O GROVE El Crisol €€€€

C/ Hospital 10–12, 36980 (Pontevedra) ***Tel*** *986 73 00 29*

A restaurant renowned for its traditional Galician cooking as well as creative dishes. It serves mainly fish and seafood and is a good place to discover new species of fish such as sargo, dentón or pinto, or sample traditional ones such as sea bass and turbot. The dining room overlooks the sea. Closed Mon lunch and Nov.

OURENSE Adega do Emilio €€

Avenida das Caldas, 11, 32001 ***Tel*** *988 21 91 11*

Housed in a tastefully renovated *hostal* that used to house shepherds (upstairs) as well as their flocks (downstairs), this restaurant aims to use only top-quality local ingredients. Enjoy essential Galician staples such as *caldo gallego* (a broth filled with pasta and meat) and *merluza a la gallega* (hake cooked with parsley and garlic). Closed Mon.

OURENSE A Rexidora €€€

Ctra N540 Bentraces-Celanova, km 7, Bentraces, 32890 ***Tel*** *988 38 30 78*

An award-winning restaurant in an old building in Bentraces offering modern Galician cuisine prepared in a personal and adventurous way. It is worth having the *empanada con masa de castañas* (chestnut pie), the sea bass or the wild boar with leeks and pumpkin. Closed Sun evenings, Mon, Tue evenings, two weeks in Jan and two weeks in Sep.

PADRÓN Casa Ramallo €€

C/ Castro 5, Rois, 15900 (A Coruña) ***Tel*** *981 80 41 80*

A short way from Padrón, this pleasant *casa de comidas* has been serving good value traditional Galician fare for more than 100 years. Especially good are its *guisos marineros*, shellfish and seasonal dishes including lamprey. Casa Ramallo also has a good selection of meats and homemade pie for dessert. Closed Mon and 20 Dec–10 Jan.

PADRÓN Casa dos Martínez *Tapas* €€€

Rúa Longa, 7, 15900 (A Coruña) ***Tel*** *981 81 05 77*

The Casa dos Martínez offers some subtle variations on local fare, all cooked with an impeccable attention to detail. Try the legendary local speciality Padrón peppers, grown in the restaurant's own vegetable garden. Reservations recommended. Closed Sun evening and Mon, and Tue–Thu evenings in winter.

PONTEDEUME Cantina Río Covés €€

Esteiro, 9, 15600 (A Coruña) ***Tel*** *981 43 40 57*

An old house with a picturesque garden is the location for this fine restaurant serving tradtional regional fare. Try the *costrada*, a traditonal pastry filled with layers of meat and fish, reputedly brought over by Italian monks 300 years ago. Also know for its *grelos*, a green, spinach-like vegetable much-loved by Galicians. Closed Mon.

PONTEVEDRA Casa Filgueira *Tapas* €

Plaza de la Leña 2, 36002 ***Tel*** *986 85 88 15*

This wonderful tapas bar in the centre of the old town has two floors – a lively bar downstairs and a quieter area with excellent views of the square upstairs. Don't miss the *zorza* (minced and marinated pork meat) with apple, or the *filloa de cogumelos e gambas* (Galician crêpe with wild mushrooms and prawns). Closed Sun.

PONTEVEDRA Alameda 10 €€€

C/ Alameda 10, 36001 ***Tel*** *986 85 74 12*

An efficient restaurant preparing traditional seafood and excellent fish, including seasonal varieties such as lamprey and eels from the Río Miño. Try the *croquetas de marisco* (fish balls), the *bacalao* (cod) Alameda, or the *mero al vapor* (steamed grouper). Try *tarta del abuelo con frutos secos* for dessert. Closed Sun, two weeks in Jan and two weeks in Aug.

PONTEVEDRA Casa Román Tapas €€€

Avda Augusto García Sánchez 12, 36003 ***Tel*** *986 84 35 60*

A busy restaurant with fast and efficient service serving traditional cuisine prepared with the best quality produce. It specializes in rice dishes, and in elvers and lamprey from the Río Miño, when in season. Favourites are the turbot stew, monkfish in green sauce and *lubina a la sal* (sea bass baked in salt). Closed Sun evenings & Mon (except Aug).

SAN SALVADOR DE POIO Casa Solla €€€€

Av Sinéiro 7, 36163 (Pontevedra) ***Tel*** *986 87 28 84*

In a lovely old *pazo* (manor house) outside Pontevedra, this restaurant is worth the journey. It serves modern "designer" Galician cuisine based on traditional recipes. Try the *bacalao confitado con crema de quesos* (confit of cod with cheese sauce) or the *costilla de cerdo deshuesada y confitada* (confit of boned pork rib). Closed Sun & Thu evenings & Mon.

SANTIAGO DE COMPOSTELA La Tacíta D'Juan €€€

C/ Hórreo 31, 15702 (A Coruña) ***Tel*** *981 56 20 41*

The service is careful and professional in this busy restaurant serving classical Galician meat, fish and seafood dishes. They prepare a famous seasonal *cocido* (stew), but otherwise try the *lenguado* (filet of sole) or the *entrecot de buey* (ox steak). End with the *filloas rellenas de crema pastelera* (custard cream filled crêpes). Closed Sun and Aug.

SANTIAGO DE COMPOSTELA Casa Marcelo €€€€

C/ Hortas 1, 15705 (A Coruña) ***Tel*** *981 55 85 80*

Recently awarded a Michelin star, this is undoubtedly one of the best restaurants in Galicia. Chef Marcelo Tejedor creates his own interpretations of Galician cuisine, and the daily fixed-price menu, served in an intimate, candle-lit dining room, is based on what is available in the town's morning market. Closed Sun & Mon, also mid-Feb–mid-Mar.

SANTIAGO DE COMPOSTELA El Mercadito €€€€

C/ Galeras 18, 15705 (A Coruña) ***Tel*** *981 57 42 39*

This restaurant offers modern Galician cooking in a minimalist dining room overlooking the cathedral. The menu changes daily, depending on what is in season and available at the local market. Specialities include eggs, potato foam and *pisto* (ratatouille), and truffle and oyster soup. Closed Mon & Sun evenings.

SANTIAGO DE COMPOSTELA Pedro Roca €€€€

C/ Domingo García Sabel 1, 15705 (A Coruña) ***Tel*** *981 58 57 76*

Behind a simple door with no sign is one of Santiago's best-kept secrets – a tranquil space that houses the surprising kitchen of Pedro Roca. The menu is brief but full of temptations, like spider-crab pastry, *zamburiñas* (local clams) with baked onions and artichoke chips, or squid with green asparagus and black noodles. Closed Sun evenings.

SANXENXO La Taberna de Rotílio €€€

Av del Puerto 7–9, 36960 (Pontevedra) ***Tel*** *986 72 02 00*

Located in the Hotel Rotilio, this restaurant is famous for its innovative approach to Galician cuisine. The chef's creations include monkfish *caldeirada*, fried oysters and an unusual original rice dish. There is also a cheaper menu. Homemade desserts. Closed Sun, also mid-Dec–mid-Jan.

VEDRA Roberto €€€

San Julián de Sales-Vedra, 15880 (A Coruña) ***Tel*** *981 51 17 69*

Housed in a magnificent *pazo*, 7 km (4.5 miles) from Santiago de Compostela, the emphasis of this restaurant is fish and vegetables. Owner Roberto Crespo uses home-grown produce to create dishes such as sea bass with tomato compote and mushroom stew or scallops over potato purée with balsamic vinegar. Closed Sun evenings, Mon & Jan.

VIGO La Oca €€€

C/ Purificación Saavedra 8, 36207 (Pontevedra) ***Tel*** *986 37 12 55*

A cosy restaurant specializing in modern Galician cuisine, using fresh ingredients from the nearby Teis market. *Erizo de mar revuelto con huevos de la casa* (sea urchin omelette), lamprey salad and oven-baked suckling pig are the delicacies here. Only six tables. Closed Sat–Sun, Mon–Thu evenings, Easter and two weeks in Aug.

VIGO Maruja Limón €€€€

Rua Victoria 4, 36201 (Pontevedra) ***Tel*** *986 47 34 06*

In the city centre, Rafael Centeno mixes creativity with the natural essence of local products. Diners get to choose from three tasting menus. Among the house specialities are Galician veal tartare with Parmesan and watercress, red tuna with cauliflower cream, and scallops with bacon and orange *pil pil* sauce. Closed Sun & Mon.

VILAGARCÍA DE AROUSA Casa Bóveda €€€€

Av La Marina 2, Carril, 36600 (Pontevedra) ***Tel*** *986 51 12 04*

It is better to book in advance to eat in this busy restaurant situated on Carril harbour, a short way from Vilagarcía de Arousa. It specializes in fish and shellfish from the Rias Baixas and also prepares excellent *guisos* and rice dishes. Closed Sun evenings & Mon (except Aug) and 24 Dec–20 Jan.

VILANOVA DE AROUSA O'Paspallas €€

Ctra Nacional, Cambados–Vilagarcía km 320, C/ A Cerca 46, 36620 (Pontevedra) ***Tel*** *986 55 52 21*

Sited in the Ria de Arousa, near Vilagarcía de Arousa, a popular resort with a pretty promenade and water sports facilities, this small family restaurant is so popular that advanced booking is advised. Sit on the terrace to try the *filloas de mejillón a la albahaca* (mussel crêpes with basil). Closed Sun evenings & Mon (Oct–May).

Key to Price Guide *see p608* **Key to Symbols** *see back cover flap*

ASTURIAS AND CANTABRIA

AJO La Casona de la Peña €€€€

Barrio de la Peña, Ajo, 39170 (Cantabria) ***Tel*** *942 67 05 67*

Located in Ajo, a village east of Santander, this restaurant and hotel in a 17th-century house has an extraordinary dining room which doubles as an exhibition of paintings and antiques. It serves fairly modern cuisine with traditional sauces such as prawns with curry sauce and mango ravioli. Booking in advance is essential.

ARRIONDAS Casa Marcial €€€€

La Sagar S/N, Parres, 33540 (Asturias) ***Tel*** *985 84 09 91*

Chef José Manzano has been awarded his first Michelin star, and it is hard to argue with that prestigious award. Manzano tackles traditional Asturian cuisine, not usually known for its originality. He even manages to reinvent the *fabada asturiana* (Asturian bean stew). Closed Sun dinner, Mon lunch and 7 Jan–7 Feb.

AVILÉS La Cofradia del Puerto *Tapas* €€

Av Los Telares 11, 33400 (Asturias) ***Tel*** *985 56 12 30*

This is a typical no-frills, no-fuss *sidrería* (cider bar), where you can sample Asturias' famous beverage and eat excellent fish and seafood fresh from the Cantabrian sea. If you are more inclined to meat, they offer a selection of red meats cooked over embers, as well as *frixuelos* (crêpes typical of the region). Closed Sun, 2 weeks end Jun & 2 weeks in Nov.

CANGAS DEL NARCEA Blanco *Tapas* €€

C/ Mayor 11, 33800 (Asturias) ***Tel*** *985 81 03 16*

Despite its unprepossessing appearance, the food here is of a very good quality. Dishes include *bacalao confitado* (confit of cod) and partridge with vegetables. There are Asturian cheeses and tempting desserts. Booking is recommended in summer. Closed Sun evenings, Mon in winter & Sun in summer, also two weeks in Sep.

CANGAS DE ONIS El Molín de la Pedrera *Tapas* €€

C/ Río Güeña 2, 33550 (Asturias) ***Tel*** *985 84 91 09*

A stylish *sidrería*, decorated with traditional objects and implements which give it a rustic air. It serves original combinations such as *crujiente de cabrales con avellanas* (Cabrales cheese from the Picos de Europa with hazelnuts) and more traditional dishes such as *bonito* and *frixuelos* (crêpes). Closed Wed except summer & Jan.

CASTRO URDIALES El Ruso €€€

C/ Allendelagua 2, 39700 (Cantabria) ***Tel*** *942 87 06 18*

A modest restaurant in Allendelagua, a village outside Castro Urdiales, serving quality cooking. There is no written menu; you will need to ask the waiter to reel off what is available and the prices. Dishes include traditional stews, seafood and grilled fish, all in sizeable portions. Homemade desserts. Closed Sun evenings and Oct.

CASTRO URDIALES Mesón del Marinero *Tapas* €€€

C/ Correría 23, 39700 (Cantabria) ***Tel*** *942 86 00 05*

This listed historic building, decorated as its name suggests in a maritime theme, houses a stylish seafood restaurant. The portions are generous and its proximity to the fishing port is evident in the freshness of the produce. It also serves excellent *ternera* (veal) and other local meats. The traditional *leche frita* is a sweet ending to the meal.

COMILLAS La Rabia *Tapas* €€

C/ Barrio de la Rabia 8, 39520 (Cantabria) ***Tel*** *942 72 02 75*

The terrace of this restaurant enjoys views of the estuary in the Oyambre nature reserve making it a popular place for a pre-lunch apéritif. The menu is focused on fish, including *almejas a la marinera* (clams), *rape al ajillo* (monkfish with garlic). Choice of classic desserts. Lunch-time menu for €16. Closed Mon except in summer & Jan.

COMILLAS El Capricho de Gaudí €€€€

C/ Barrio de Sobrellano, 39520 (Cantabria) ***Tel*** *942 72 03 65*

Antoni Gaudí's architectural wonder *(see p111)*, clad in green tiles and sunflowers, provides a unique setting for this sophisticated restaurant. Recommended are the salmon in mustard cream and the turbot with tomato vinaigrette and garlic sprouts. End with chestnuts with caramel ice cream. Closed mid-Jan–mid-Feb, Sun evenings in winter & Mon.

COSGAYA Mesón del Oso €€

Ctra C621 Potes-Fuente Dé, km 13, 39539 (Cantabria) ***Tel*** *942 73 30 18*

Delightful country hotel and restaurant by the Río Deva in the peaceful Liebana Valley, with dramatic views of the Picos de Europa. The veal steaks and *cocido lebaniego* (a rich stew with chickpeas and pork) are local specialities. The *arroz con leche* (rice pudding) makes a traditional dessert. Closed Jan.

CUDILLERO Mariño *Tapas* €€

Concha de Artedo, 33155 (Asturias) ***Tel*** *985 59 11 88*

Located west of the lively seaside resort of Cudillero, with views of the beach, this restaurant-with-rooms serves fish casseroles, delicious *almejas a nuestro modo* (clams "cooked our way") and *curadillo*, a dish made with a fish from the shark family. Closed early Jan–early Feb, Sun evenings & Mon (except Jul & Aug, Christmas and Easter).

ESCALANTE San Román de Escalante €€€€

Ctra Escalante–Castillo, km 2, 39795 (Cantabria) ***Tel*** *942 67 77 28*

This lovely old mountain house is set in gardens and woodland in front of a 12th-century chapel. The dining room, decorated with paintings, is the setting for modern seasonal cuisine inspired by traditional recipes. Dishes include fried clams with spinach and pine kernels and hake with clam ravioli. Homemade desserts. Closed 7–27 Jan.

GIJÓN Casa Victor €€€

C/ Carmen 11, 33206 (Asturias) ***Tel*** *985 35 00 93*

This restaurant is an institution in Gijón. It specializes in dishes based on fish caught in the Cantabrian sea. Try the *lomos de salmonete rellenos de marisco* (red mullet filled with seafood). For dessert there is chocolate soufflé with raspberry ice cream. It offers various menus at cheaper prices. Closed Wed evenings, Sun, 5 Dec–5 Jan.

LAREDO Casa Felipe *Tapas* €€€

C/ Travesía José Antonio 5, 39770 (Cantabria) ***Tel*** *942 60 32 12*

A simple restaurant in Laredo, one of Cantabria's most popular holiday resorts with a long sandy beach and an attractive old town. It serves simple traditional food, emphasizing good fresh fish and seafood. It also specializes in local cheeses, mainly made from cow's milk. Closed Mon, Sun evening & Dec.

LAREDO El Camarote *Tapas* €€€

Av de la Victoria, 39770 (Cantabria) ***Tel*** *942 60 67 07*

This restaurant, decorated with marine paraphernalia, offers simple cooking based on seasonal market produce. There is a wide range of fish and seafood, cooked in an uncomplicated way. Try the home-style clams and for dessert millefeuille with strawberries and cream. Closed Sun evenings & Wed except Jul.

LLANES Marisquería La Marina €€€

C/ Muelle, 33500 (Asturias) ***Tel*** *985 40 00 12*

The place to go if you want to gaze out over the sea while filling up on delicious fish. Set in a renovated fish market, this restaurant aims to offer the freshest fish possible, brought in every morning by the boats and selected by the chefs at the quayside. Closed Dec–Feb, and Mon–Fri in autumn and spring.

LUGONES La Máquina €€

Av Conde de Santa Bárbara 59, 33420 (Asturias) ***Tel*** *985 26 36 36*

Although La Máquina is about 6 km (4 miles) from the Asturian capital, it is a good place for an excellent *fabada* Asturiana, the region's typical hearty stew made with white beans and chorizo. For dessert try the delicious homemade *arroz con leche* (rice pudding). Open for lunch only. Closed Sun & mid-Jun–mid-Jul.

OVIEDO Casa Fermín €€€€

C/ San Francisco 8, 33003 (Asturias) ***Tel*** *985 21 64 52*

The cosy Casa Fermín is one of Oviedo's most classic restaurants offering a combination of traditional and modern, seasonal cuisine. Try the caramelized black sausage with plum sauce and the venison with sweet purée. For dessert, try the chocolate cylinder with raspberry textures. Closed Sun.

POTES El Cenador del Capitán €€

C/ Cervantes 3, 39570 (Cantabria) ***Tel*** *942 73 21 61*

On the top floor of a big stone house in the centre of Potes is this restaurant with a beamed ceiling and decorated in a simple rustic fashion. It specializes in local food, especially *cocido lebaniego* and game dishes. It offers a cheap *Menú del Peregrino* ("pilgrim's" menu). Closed Mon–Thu, Sun evening.

POTES Paco Wences €€

C/ Roscabao 5, 39570 (Cantabria) ***Tel*** *942 73 00 25*

The restaurant of the Picos de Valdecoro hotel, in the Picos de Europa, offers simple traditional food from the Liebana Valley, with filling *cocidos* made from quality locally grown ingredients. Try the *cocido lebaniego* or the *solomillo al queso de Tresviso* (steak cooked with a local cheese). Typical Cantabrian desserts. Closed Jan and Mon–Thu dinner in winter.

PRAVIA Balbona €€€

Calle Pico Merás 2, 33120 (Asturias) ***Tel*** *985 82 11 62*

A superb restaurant located at the heart of Pravia which provides traditional Asturian cuisine with modern touches. They also have excellent homemade desserts, many of which must be ordered at the beginning of the meal, such as creamy hazelnut cake with spicy bread. Closed Tue.

PRENDES Casa Gerardo €€€€

Ctra AS–19 km 8, 33438 (Asturias) ***Tel*** *985 88 77 97*

This delightful restaurant is run by the fifth generation of the same family since its opening. It reputedly serves the best *fabada Asturiana* and also offers other delights such as king prawn with fresh pasta and Asturian cabbage. Closed Sun–Thu evenings (except Tue–Thu evenings in summer), Mon and two weeks in Jan.

SALINAS Real Balneario de Salinas *Tapas* €€€€

Av Juan Sitges 3, 33400 (Asturias) ***Tel*** *985 51 86 13*

This lovely restaurant in the seaside resort of Salinas is owned by a family of restaurateurs who work together in the kitchen and the dining room. They offer a combination of classical and modern cuisine using high-quality ingredients. Try the *mero con alcachofas* (grouper with artichokes). Closed Sun evenings & Mon, early Jan–early Feb.

SAN VICENTE DE LA BARQUERA Augusto Tapas €€€€

C/ Mercado 1, 39540 (Cantabria) ***Tel*** *942 71 20 40*

Located in the porticoed part of town, this renovated tavern specializes in fresh fish, seafood and rice. You can also eat in a lovely shaded terrace in summer. Try the *ensalada de mariscos* (seafood salad), *almejas con arroz* (clams with rice), *calamares en su tinta* (squid cooked in its own ink) and other delicacies. Closed Sun evenings & Mon (except Jun–Sep).

SAN VICENTE DE TORANZO Casona de Toranzo Tapas €€

Ctra N623, Burgos-Santander km 115, 39699 ***Tel*** *942 59 44 11*

The restaurant of the hotel Posada del Pas *(see p564)* has a separate entrance for non-residents beside the main road between Santander and Burgos. The menu is strong on Cantabrian food and includes an excellent *cocido montañes* (mountain stew), as well as entrecôte with Treviso cheese sauce and lovely sorbet.

SANTANDER Bodega del Riojano Tapas €€

C/ Río de la Pila 5, 39003 (Cantabria) ***Tel*** *942 21 67 50*

This colourful bodega (wine cellar) is as famous for its decorative wine barrels, painted by Spanish artists, as it is for its delicious food. The red peppers stuffed with anchovies and other ingredients are renowned. It also serves a tasty leek salad and oxtail stew. Closed Sun evenings & Mon except in summer.

SANTANDER Hostería de Adarzo €€

C/ Adarzo 68, 39011 (Cantabria) ***Tel*** *942 33 23 11*

A restaurant and hotel serving traditional cooking using fresh, seasonal market produce, with special emphasis on red meats and daily caught fish. Adarzo serves dishes such as octopus salad with vegetables, and cod loin with tomatoes, trotters and veal chinstraps. Closed Mon & Sun evening.

SANTANDER El Nuevo Molino €€€€

Ctra N611 Santander–Torrelavega km 13, Barrio Monseñor 18, Puente Arce, 39478 (Cantabria) ***Tel*** *942 57 50 55*

Sited in Puente Arce, this ancient mill belongs to El Serbal in Santander. It offers creative cooking with dishes such as cod salad with mushrooms and *pil pil* (a creamy parsley sauce) and monkfish ravioli filled with king prawn and cream. There is a divine ice cream with sultanas and brandy over toffee cream. Closed Sun evenings & Tue.

SANTANDER El Serbal €€€€

C/ Andrés del Río 7 (Puerto Chico), 39004 (Cantabria) ***Tel*** *942 22 25 15*

A nice restaurant that is becoming very popular for its innovative cuisine, created by adding personal touches to traditional dishes. It also offers some originals such as oven-baked ray in mushroom *pil pil* and creamy rice and a distinctive chicken curry. For dessert, strawberries with apple jelly and basil. Closed Sun evenings & Mon.

SANTILLANA DEL MAR La Joraca €€

Los Hornos 20, 39330 (Cantabria) ***Tel*** *942 84 01 37*

The restaurant of the Hotel Colegiata may be uninspiringly furnished and decorated, and lacking the beautiful views of the hotel, but it is still a good place to eat excellent food made with local produce. Choice dishes are grilled monkfish with salad onions *pil pil* and ham. For dessert, order cream of smoked cheese. Closed Sun evenings & Mon.

SOLARES Casa Enrique Tapas €€€

Paseo de la Estación 20, 39710 (Cantabria) ***Tel*** *942 52 00 73*

Casa Enrique hotel's restaurant is popular with locals and tourists alike. It is a decent place to sample traditional home cooking, which results in tasty stews and dishes such as *albóndigas de ternera* (veal meatballs) or *ventresca de bonito con cebolla y pimiento* (tuna fish with onions and peppers). Closed Sun evenings.

VILLAVERDE DE PONTONES Cenador de Amós €€€€

Plaza de Sol, 39793 (Cantabria) ***Tel*** *942 50 82 43*

This restaurant, which has had a Michelin star since 1993, is housed in an 18th-century country palace surrounded by a pleasant garden with outside tables in summer. The menu fuses traditional and creative Cantabrian cuisines. Closed Sun eve, Wed eve (Oct–Apr), Mon, 22 Dec–mid-Jan.

THE BASQUE COUNTRY, NAVARRA & LA RIOJA

AMOREBIETA Juantxu €€€

C/ Barrio Enartze 2, 48340 (Vizcaya) ***Tel*** *946 73 26 50*

Housed in a traditional Basque rural house on the road between Amorebieta and Gernika, this restaurant with a garden specializes in both fish (particularly cod) and meats including roast lamb. Good choice of salads and vegetarian options. The dessert menu includes a selection of homemade ice creams. Closed Sun–Thu evenings, Tue & Christmas.

AOIZ Beti Jai Tapas €€€

C/ Santa Agueda 2, 31430 (Navarra) ***Tel*** *948 33 60 52*

A well-known restaurant with bar in an old house on the main square of the town, with views of the river. Beti Jai serves high-quality Navarrese cuisine and some modern and creative dishes based on seasonal market produce. Try the *menudicos* (tripe) and any of the excellent homemade desserts. Closed Sun evenings & weekends in Aug.

AZPEITIA Kiruri *Tapas* €€€

Barrio Loiola Hiribidea 24, 20730 (Guipúzcoa) ***Tel*** *943 81 56 08*

Located in front of the shrine of Loyola, this family-run restaurant offers simple cooking and traditional Basque dishes such as *txangurro* (spider crab baked and served in the shell) and *menestra de verduras* (vegetable stew) and a choice of pies for dessert. The car park is convenient for visiting the shrine. Closed Mon evenings & 20 Dec–7 Jan.

BERMEO Jokin *Tapas* €€€

C/ Eupeme Deuna 13, 48370 (Vizcaya) ***Tel*** *946 88 40 89*

Jokin, with pretty views of Bermeo's fishing port, specializes in seasonal fish dishes such as *habitas frescas con bacalao fresco* (small broad beans with fresh cod) or *rollitos de merluza confitados en aceite de oliva* (hake in olive oil). Meat-eaters can try the crispy trotters in sauce. Closed Sun evenings.

BILBAO Café Iruña *Tapas* €

Jardines de Albia, 48001 (Vizcaya) ***Tel*** *944 23 70 21*

The classic café opened in 1903 opposite the Jardines de Albia. It has a marvellous, ornately decorated mock-Mudéjar interior of ceramic tiles evocative of the age of Islamic Spain. The *menú del día* is good and surprisingly inexpensive for such a charming place. A place worth dipping into even if you only feel like drinking coffee.

BILBAO Café La Granja *Tapas* €

Plaza Circular, 40001 (Vizcaya) ***Tel*** *944 230 813*

An old-fashioned café created in "the French style" of the 1920s. It stands in the centre of Bilbao, facing the statue of the city's founder. Try the traditional *chorizo talo* (corn tortilla, available from 6pm). A full *menú del día* is served, as is a good breakfast. Snacks and sandwiches are available throughout the day. Closed Sun and public hols.

BILBAO Víctor *Tapas* €€€€

Plaza Nueva 2, 48005 (Vizcaya) ***Tel*** *944 15 16 78*

A classic restaurant located in the historic square of the old quarter. Specialities are cod dishes, *chipirones* (Cantrabrian squid), green peppers filled with spider crab, *lenguado a la plancha* (grilled sole), ostrich in mushroom sauce and, for dessert, *tarta capuchina* (syrup-soaked cake). Closed Sun, Easter week & end Aug–mid-Sep.

BILBAO Zortziko €€€€

C/ Alameda Mazarredo 17, 48001 (Vizcaya) ***Tel*** *944 23 97 43*

Contemporary *haute cuisine* is served at this Michelin-star restaurant not far from the Guggenheim Museum. The menu is seasonal with creative Basque touches. Among the specialities are *pintada a baja temperatura* (guinea fowl cooked at a low temperature), foie gras, turbot and a delicious tiramisu. Closed Sun, Mon & mid-Aug–mid-Sep.

CINTRUÉNIGO Maher €€€€

La Ribera 19, 31592 (Navarra) ***Tel*** *948 81 11 50*

Innovative cuisine is impeccably presented in the Hotel Maher restaurant, although the service can be variable. Salad with different kinds of lettuces, asparagus pudding, rice with hare and suckling lamb in mushroom sauce, are all house specialities. Order bitter chocolate soufflé with caramel ice cream. Closed Sun evenings, Mon & 20 Dec–20 Jan.

ESTELLA Navarra *Tapas* €€

C/ Gustavo de Maeztu 16, 31200 (Navarra) ***Tel*** *948 55 00 40*

Traditional regional cuisine is served in this grand house, with tiles depicting Navarra's former kings. The *Blanca de Navarra* (a lemon and honey ice cream, served with fresh cream and nuts) is superb. Other specialities are *espárragos rellenos* (stuffed asparagus), roast piglet and lamb. Closed Sun eve, Mon, Christmas & Jan.

EZCARAY El Rincón del Vino €€€

C/ Jesús Nazareno 2, 26280 (La Rioja) ***Tel*** *941 35 43 75*

Vino serves traditional Riojan cuisine with an emphasis on seasonal produce including mushrooms and truffles. During the hunting season, it offers good game dishes. Vino also has a shop selling local wines, including 2,000 different Riojas, and other delicacies typical of the region. Closed Mon–Thu evenings in winter & Wed except in Jul & Aug.

EZCARAY El Portal de Echaurren €€€€

Héroes del Alcázar 2, 26280 (La Rioja) ***Tel*** *941 35 40 47*

This Michelin-star hotel, run by the Paniego family, is one of La Rioja's emblematic restaurants. Special dishes include *solomillos de rape negro sobre purrusalda* (monkfish with leeks). There is also a great variety of Rioja and Albariño wines. Closed Sun evenings (except Jul & Aug).

GERNIKA Zallo Barri €€€€

C/ Juan Calzada 79, 48300 (Vizcaya) ***Tel*** *946 25 18 00*

Barri offers both traditional Basque cuisine and innovative dishes. Only the freshest produce is used and the menu changes with the season so options might include *cordero a la parrilla con patata y foie gras a la plancha* (grilled lamb with foie gras) and *bizcocho de almendra* (almond sponge cake). Closed Sun–Thu evenings.

GETARIA Elkano €€€€

C/ Herrerieta 2, 20808 (Guipúzcoa) ***Tel*** *943 14 00 24*

Elkano is famous for its grilled fish dishes and seafood. The baby squid and the turbot are excellent. Also good are the local grilled hake cheeks and small squid Pelayo style. The best Basque brand of Txacoli wine, Txomín Echaniz, is available. Closed Sun evenings, Mon, Tue evenings, and mid-Mar–mid-Apr.

HARO Beethoven II €€

C/ Santo Tomás 8–10, 26200 (La Rioja) ***Tel*** *941 31 11 81*

The Fresno family owns both Beethoven I and Beethoven II in the same street at Haro. Both use local Riojan products to prepare traditional fare, with emphasis on local seasonal vegetables and *chuletillas de cordero* (lamb chops). *Torrijas* (slices of bread soaked in milk and egg and then fried) make a popular dessert. Closed Mon evenings & Tue.

HARO Las Duelas €€€

C/ de la Vega 31–33, 26200 (La Rioja) ***Tel*** *941 30 44 63*

This restaurant offers an opportunity to dine in the cloister of a medieval monastery. The traditional Riojan menu uses local produce but with a creative touch. From Monday to Thursday you can feast on a typical Riojan stew made with red beans and meats, plus dessert and wine, for a very reasonable price. Closed 23 Dec–22 Jan & Sun 15 Nov–1 Apr.

HONDARRIBIA Sebastián €€€€

C/ Mayor 11, 20280 (Guipúzcoa) ***Tel*** *943 64 01 67*

A 16th-century house in the historic part of town. The traditional cuisine is based on seasonal produce and is cooked by chef Miguel Soto. Try the *Ensalada de Txangurro* (spider crab salad) or the monkfish with scallops and king prawns cooked in the local txacolí wine. Game dishes are available in season. Closed Sun evenings, Mon & Nov.

LAGUARDIA Posada Mayor de Migueloa *Tapas* €€€

C/ Mayor de Migueloa 20, 01300 (Alava) ***Tel*** *945 62 11 75*

The restored 17th-century palace of Viana now houses a small hotel and one of northern Spain's best restaurants. The cuisine is a Basque-La Rioja fusion, strong on fish and seafood (try the baked hake), meat (roast lamb or venison) and vegetables. Excellent choice of homemade desserts. Closed Sun evening.

LASARTE Martín Berasategui €€€€

C/ Loidi 4, 20160 (Guipúzcoa) ***Tel*** *943 36 64 71*

One of the top restaurants of Spain (with three Michelin stars) is located in a converted farmhouse, 7 km (4.5 miles) from San Sebastián.The specialities change with the season but Martín Berasategui, a trendsetter among chefs, always surprises. Reservations essential, especially for terrace tables. Closed Sat lunch, Sun evenings, Mon, Tue & mid-Dec–mid-Jan.

LOGROÑO Cachetero €€€

C/ Laurel 3, 26001 (La Rioja) ***Tel*** *941 22 84 63*

Tasty home cooking is served in this cosy restaurant, well known in the city for its basic dishes capturing the best of each season. Standards include vegetable stews and stuffed peppers. Desserts include *helado de queso de roquefort con nueces* (Roquefort cheese ice cream with walnuts). Closed Sun, Wed evenings & two weeks in Aug.

LOGROÑO Casa Emilio €€€

Av República Argentina 8, 26002 (La Rioja) ***Tel*** *941 25 88 44*

A good-value restaurant in the heart of the city specializing in high-quality roasted red meats, grilled fish and oven-baked kid. Particular specialities are *ensalada de perdiz* (partridge salad) and *taco de rape con crema suave de ajos confitados* (creamed monkfish) and venison served with grape and plum sauce. Closed Sun evening, Aug.

OIARTZUN Zuberoa €€€€

Araneder Bidea, Barrio Iturriotz, 20180 (Guipúzcoa) ***Tel*** *943 49 12 28*

The celebrated restaurant of the Arbelaitz brothers is in a 600-year-old farmhouse. Among the dishes are Cantabrian squid cooked in a traditional sauce and roast piglet with ginger and potato purée. Exquisite desserts to follow. They also have a sampler menu. Closed Sun, Wed, 30 Dec–15 Jan, two weeks after Easter & 15–30 Oct.

OLITE Casa Zanito €€€€

Rúa Mayor 16, 31390 (Navarra) ***Tel*** *948 74 00 02*

Probably the best option for a lunch of traditional Navarrese cuisine with a few modern touches. One speciality is a salad of fried artichokes with prawns. Desserts include apple pie with cinnamon ice cream. They also have a reasonable fixed lunch and dinner menu. The service is good. Closed Mon, and Tue (in winter).

PAMPLONA Bar Fitero *Tapas* €

Estafeta 58, 31001 (Navarra) ***Tel*** *948 22 20 06*

One of the most popular bars in Pamplona for *pintxos* (Basque tapas) in the famous Estafeta street, where the bulls run. The Bar Fitero has received many awards for its delicious and original creations. It also serves *cazuelicas*, small clay pots filled with tasty food. Be prepared to jostle for space, though it's quieter at night.

PAMPLONA Alhambra €€€€

C/ Francisco Bergamín 7, 31003 (Navarra) ***Tel*** *948 24 50 07*

Typical Navarrese cooking as well as some unusual combinations are the hallmark of this welcoming and elegant restaurant. The artichokes, the truffle and vegetable purée and the mushroom risotto are all delicious appetizers. Dessert could be the hot chocolate soufflé with saffron ice cream and pumpkin seeds. Closed Sun and Easter.

PAMPLONA Europa €€€€

C/ Espoz y Mina 11, 31002 (Navarra) ***Tel*** *948 22 18 00*

Located in the Hotel Europa, in the old part of the city near the cathedral, is one of Pamplona's best places to eat. It offers a range of creative Navarrese dishes such as *menestra de verduras* (vegetable stew), *arroz meloso con alcachofas* (creamy rice with artichokes) and *cochinillo confitado* (caramelized suckling pig). Closed Sun.

PASAI DONIBANE Casa Camara €€€

C/ Donibane 79, 20110 (Guipúzcoa) ***Tel*** *943 52 36 99*

A restaurant with wonderful views of Pasai Donibane port (just outside San Sebastián), where you can dine watching the boats and choose your own live lobster from the aquarium. Try the baked mushrooms with crunchy vegetables or the Basque speciality of *txangurro al horno*. Alternatively, there are steaks. Closed Sun evenings & Mon.

PUENTE LA REINA Mesón del Peregrino €€€€

Irumbidea, Puente la Reina, 31100 (Navarra) ***Tel*** *948 34 00 75*

The restaurant-cum-hotel of a well-known chef is sited on the pilgrimage route to Santiago de Compostela. The cuisine combines Mediterranean and Navarrese influences. Try the *cochinillo en salsa de trufas* (suckling pig in a truffle sauce). Closed Sun evenings, Mon & two weeks in Jan.

SAN SEBASTIÁN Bar Sport *Tapas* €

C/ Fermín Calbetón 10, 20001 (Guipúzcoa) ***Tel*** *943 42 68 88*

One of several bars lining the streets of the old part of San Sebastián, which have counters stacked with *pinchos* (tapas). For an informal meal, point to what you want and keep going until you are full, then settle the bill. It is an enjoyable way of having your meal but beware that the price can add up to more than you expect.

SAN SEBASTIÁN Urbano €€

31 de Agosto 17, 20003 (Guipúzcoa) ***Tel*** *943 42 04 34*

In a city packed with excellent restaurants the Urbano stands out as one of the few places where you can sample creative Basque cooking without leaving with a large hole in your pocket. The set menu changes regularly and includes some inspired dishes from the experienced chef Patxi Aizpuru. Closed Sun evenings and Wed.

SAN SEBASTIÁN Akelarre €€€€

Paseo Padre Orkolaga 56, Barrio de Igueldo, 20008 (Guipúzcoa) ***Tel*** *943 31 12 09*

One of the famous restaurants of Spain, a gourmet temple with great views of rolling hills which plunge into the sea. If you have room for it, choose the seven-course *menú de degustación* (a sampler menu). Spectacular desserts. There's even an opportunity to visit the kitchen. Closed Sun evenings, Mon, 1–15 Oct and Feb.

SAN SEBASTIÁN Arzak €€€€

Av Alcalde Elósegui 273, 20015 (Guipúzcoa) ***Tel*** *943 27 84 65*

Celebrity chef Juan Mari Arzak has earned a reputation beyond Spain for his perfectly presented, creative dishes. His daughter Elena works here as well. They even run a "laboratory" where a team of cooks experiment. Closed Sun, Mon and two weeks in Jun & Nov.

SAN VICENTE DE LA SONSIERRA Casa Toni €€€

C/ Zumalacárregui 27, 26338 (La Rioja) ***Tel*** *941 33 40 01*

Book in advance for this restaurant serving modern Riojan cuisine based on traditional dishes. Its best-known speciality is the *crema de patatas a la riojana con espuma de piquillos y láminas de chorizo* (Riojan cream of potatoes with peppers and chorizo). Closed Sun & Mon evenings & 1–15 Jul.

SANTO DOMINGO DE LA CALZADA El Rincón de Emilio €€€

Plaza Bonifacio Gil 7, 26250 (La Rioja) ***Tel*** *941 34 09 90*

This classic restaurant offers both traditional and contemporary Riojan cuisine. Specialities are *solomillo al vino tinto* (fillet steak in red wine), *bacalao a la riojana* (Riojan cod) and *arroz con leche con helado de caramelo* (rice pudding with caramel ice cream). Closed Tue evenings (all day in winter) & Feb.

SORAUREN Txarrantxena €€€

C/ Enmedio 3, 31194 (Navarra) ***Tel*** *948 33 18 05*

In Sorauren, 7 km (4.5 miles) from Pamplona, in a beautiful 18th-century house, this restaurant offers modern Navarrese cuisine. Try the goats' cheese millefeuille with caramelised onions and roasted peppers and hot chocolate cake with ice cream. Closed Sun evenings, Mon, Sun–Thu evenings Sep–Apr, two weeks in Jan & two weeks in Feb.

TAFALLA Túbal €€€€

Plaza de Navarra 4, 31300 (Navarra) ***Tel*** *948 70 08 52*

Túbal, one of the best restaurants in Navarra, is housed in a historic building with 18 balconies overlooking the square. If you are not sure what to have they will prepare a personalized *menú de degustación* for you. Its forté is regional cuisine with seasonal vegetables. Closed Sun evenings, Mon, 21 Aug–4 Sep, Christmas and last week Jan.

TUDELA Restaurante 33 €€€

C/ Capuchinos 7, 31500 (Navarra) ***Tel*** *948 82 76 06*

A busy restaurant in the largest town of the Ribera region, where the menu reflects the local skill of growing vegetables. Try the *menú de degustación* – the choice of the season's crop. One speciality is *lomo de lubina salvaje asado con verduritas* (roasted wild sea bass with vegetables). Closed Sun, Mon & Tue evenings, 1–15 Aug, 14–22 Sep, 24 Dec–1 Jan.

URDÁNIZ El Molino de Urdániz €€€

Crta Francia por Zubiri (Na-135) km 16.5, 31698 ***Tel*** *948 30 41 09*

Chef David Yárnez is a rising star in the competitive world of Basque cooking. The restaurant has one Michelin star for its highly original creations, including some decadent dishes like foie gras salad with mint and gold leaf, and creamy rice wrapped in smoky gelatine with scallops. Closed Mon; Tue, Wed evenings, and two weeks in Feb.

Key to Price Guide *see p608* **Key to Symbols** *see back cover flap*

VIANA Borgia €€€€

C/ Serapio Urra 1, 31230 (Navarra) **Tel** *948 64 57 81*

This family-run restaurant only opens for lunch (although dinner is available by reservation), except on Fridays and Saturdays when it is open all day. Borgia offers varied and refreshingly eclectic dishes. Try the *espárragos frescos con crema de remolacha* (fresh asparagus with creamed beetroot) and roast lamb with gin sauce. Closed Sun, Aug.

VINIEGRA DE ABAJO Venta de Goyo €€

Puente Río Neila 3, 26325 (La Rioja) **Tel** *941 37 80 07*

Part of an old *venta* (inn), also a hotel, in the Sierra de la Demanda, about 40 km (25 miles) southwest of Nájera, this simple restaurant offers good value. The menu is based on the culinary heritage of the Sierra with good game dishes. Try the red beans, the *cordero a la cazuela* (lamb casserole) and the *tarta de manzana* (apple pie). Closed Christmas.

VITORIA Casa Felipe *Tapas* €€€

C/ Fueros 28, 01005 (Alava) **Tel** *945 13 45 54*

This bar-restaurant is a traditional, no-nonsense *casa de comidas* and a classic in Vitoria. It serves mainly Basque fare, with some standards such as *merluza rebozada* (batter hake) and lamb stew. Other specialities are grilled mushrooms and clams. For dessert try *tarta de la casa* (homemade pie). Closed Mon, Sun evenings & mid-Jun–mid-Jul.

VITORIA Dos Hermanas €€€

C/ Madre Vedruna 10, 01008 (Alava) **Tel** *945 13 29 34*

A pleasant and cosy restaurant serving classic dishes with innovative touches. From the seasonally changing menu try the pig's trotters stuffed with foie gras, served with *berza* (a local vegetable) and violet potatoes. The homemade desserts might include cocoa jelly with rice pudding cream and peanut crisps. Closed Sun evenings & Christmas.

BARCELONA

OLD TOWN Bar Mundial *Tapas* €

Plaça Sant Agustí Vell 1, 8003 **Tel** *933 19 90 56* **Map** *5 2C*

A legendary bar with a no-nonsense approach and closely packed tables. Photos of old boxers adorn the walls. Bar Mundial is famous for its fish and shellfish, especially the no-holds-barred mixed shellfish fry-up *(fritura mixta).* Closed Sun evening, Mon, Tue lunch and Aug.

OLD TOWN Bar Pinotxo *Tapas* €

C/ Mercat de la Boqueria (La Rambla 89), 08002 **Tel** *933 17 17 31* **Map** *5 A2*

The most famous of all the bars in the Boqueria. Steel buckets hold chilled bottles of *cava* (Catalan champagne-style wine), and fresh ingredients from neighbouring market stalls are cooked and served hot on the spot. Try the squid cooked in diverse styles and the fresh oysters. Closed Sun and after 6pm. No credit cards.

OLD TOWN Bodega La Palma *Tapas* €

C/ La Palma de Sant Just 7, 8002 **Tel** *933 15 06 56* **Map** *5 3B*

A simple, no-frills tapas bar in the Old Town which has been serving its bohemian clientele for decades. Excellent staples like *croquetas* and *tortilla de patata*, along with some more creative options. Try some wine from the old barrels dominating the entrance to the bar. Closed Sun and 2 weeks in Aug.

OLD TOWN El Vaso de Oro *Tapas* €

C/ Balboa 7, 08003 **Tel** *933 19 30 98* **Map** *5 C4*

One of the best tapas bars in town, El Vaso de Oro has the added advantage of brewing its own beer. Jostling for space at the narrow bar is all part of the fun. Don't miss out on the rump steak with peppers, or the foie gras with caramelized onions. Portions are on the small side, so the bill will add up quickly if you order a lot. Open daily.

OLD TOWN Jai-Ca *Tapas* €

C/ Ginebra 13, 08003 **Tel** *933 19 50 02* **Map** *5 C4*

This is one of the liveliest bars in the area, and it is not easy to get a table. Jai-Ca serves old-fashioned, tasty tapas like *patatas bravas* (spicy sautéed potatoes), *pescadito frito* (deep-fried fish), *calamares a la romana* (deep-fried calamari) and aubergines fried in beer batter. There is often live flamenco music. Closed Mon. No credit cards.

OLD TOWN Las Fernández €

C/ Carretes 11, 8001 **Tel** *934 43 20 43* **Map** *2 E2*

One of the Raval's most popular culinary hot spots. Traditional food from the Bierzo region of Spain, served up with a funky attitude, to a cool clientele. Try the "Papas don't preach" potatoes (with garlic and herbs) or the cured ham with peppers. Open for dinner only, with sittings at 9pm and 11pm. Booking recommended. Closed Mon.

OLD TOWN Mosquito *Tapas* €

C/ Jaume Giralt 53, 08003 **Tel** *933 15 17 44* **Map** *5 C2*

A laid-back bar, frequented by a healthy mix of Catalans and resident expats. Trendy music, friendly staff, cheap drinks and a solid array of Asian favourites such as chicken tikka brochettes, Singapore noodles and *gyoza* dumplings. Try the exotic tapas that can change in the middle of the evening from Indian to Japanese. Closed Mon.

OLD TOWN Organic €

C/ Junta de Comerç 11, 08001 ***Tel*** *933 01 09 02* **Map** *2 F3*

Spacious, clean and pleasantly lit, this good-value vegetarian restaurant offers an imaginative menu of Asian dishes, lasagnes, stews and an all-you-can-eat salad buffet. The homemade bread with nuts is a must. They also have a small shop selling organic products. Has an excellent lunch set menu.

OLD TOWN Bacaro €€

C/ Jerusalém 6, 08001 ***Tel*** *695 79 60 66* **Map** *2 F3*

Behind the Boquería market, this small Italian-owned brasserie serves delicious cuisine made with whatever is freshest at the market that day. It is based on the *bacaros* – small convivial bars serving food and wine – of Venice, the owner's home town. Try the *sarde en saor* (a pungent dish of sardines layered with onions and pine nuts). Closed Sun.

OLD TOWN Big Fish €€

C/ Comercial 9, 08002 ***Tel*** *932 68 17 28* **Map** *5 C5*

In a great location in the Born, this fashionable restaurant features stylishly mis-matched furniture and contemporary lighting, including a fabulous chandelier. As the name suggests, the menu specializes in seafood, from ultra-fresh fish of the day served with seasonal vegetables to more elaborate fare and sushi.

OLD TOWN Kaiku €€

Plaça del Mar 1, 08003 ***Tel*** *932 21 90 82* **Map** *5 B5*

Despite its humble exterior this unassuming, apparently simple beach-front restaurant makes what is probably the best paella in the city. Described on the menu as *arròs del xef*, it is prepared with smoked rice and succulent shellfish. Book the terrace in summer, for sea views and a breeze. Great desserts too. Open Tue–Sun lunch only. Closed Mon & Aug.

OLD TOWN Mam i Teca *Tapas* €€

C/ Lluna 4, 08001 ***Tel*** *934 41 33 35* **Map** *2 F2*

Tiny, sunflower-yellow bar that plays well-known jazz, blues and rock tunes. The tapas are superb, and include locally sourced cheeses, organic sausages and country dishes such as ham and broad beans. They also have an excellent wine list and a good range of Scottish single malts. Closed Tue, Sat lunch and two weeks in Aug.

OLD TOWN Pez Vela €€

Plaça de la Rosa dels Vents, 08039 ***Tel*** *932 21 63 17*

This trendy restaurant has a fabulous beachfront location next to the fashionable W Hotel. If offers fresh, modern Mediterranean cuisine, including an excellent paella which must rank among the best in the city. Book a table on the terrace. Closed Tue evenings and Sun evenings.

OLD TOWN 7 Portes €€€

Passeig Isabel II 14, 08003 ***Tel*** *933 19 30 33* **Map** *5 B3*

A long-standing Barcelona institution since 1836, with a who's who of past guests, including Winston Churchill and Che Guevara. It is famed for its classic marble tiles and wood-panelled dining room, and most of all for paella, which comes in 10 different varieties. They serve a different paella every day of the week.

OLD TOWN Agua €€€

Passeig Marítim de la Barceloneta 30, 08003 ***Tel*** *932 25 12 72* **Map** *6 D4*

Classy seafront restaurant with floor-to-ceiling windows and abstract fish sculptures. It is popular with a young crowd and serves excellent fish and rice dishes. Specials include steamed mussels, butan potatoes, Norway lobsters au gratin and grilled fish. Agua is also known for cooking rice over coal. There is an appealing terrace too.

OLD TOWN Biblioteca €€€

C/ Junta de Comerç 28, 08001 ***Tel*** *934 12 62 21* **Map** *2 F3*

Elegant restaurant-cum-cookbook shop with Modernista tiles and an open kitchen. The cooking focuses on seasonal ingredients. Specialities include rice with pigeon and black pudding, black spaghetti with *calçots* (green onions) and poached egg. Service can be erratic. Closed lunchtimes (except for groups), Sun, Mon & two weeks in Aug.

OLD TOWN Café de l'Academia €€€

C/ Lledó 1, Plaça Sant Just, 08002 ***Tel*** *933 19 82 53* **Map** *5 B3*

An intimate, candle-lit restaurant with exposed brick walls and a pretty terrace in the lovely Plaça Sant, in the centre of Barri Gòtic. The menu offers superb Catalan fare, interesting salads and homemade pasta. The cod dishes, from raw to baked, are excellent. The desserts are top-notch. Closed Sat, Sun and for three weeks in Aug.

OLD TOWN Cal Pep *Tapas* €€€

Plaça de les Olles 8, 08003 ***Tel*** *933 10 79 61* **Map** *5 B3*

Arguably the best bar in town for fresh fish and seafood, right off the boats. Cal Pep has an excellent selection of tapas as well. The long, narrow, standing bar means it gets crowded at peak times. Arrive early for one of five tables out back; expect to queue. Closed Sat dinner, Sun, Mon lunch & Aug.

OLD TOWN Can Majó €€€

C/ Almirall Aixada 23, 08003 ***Tel*** *932 21 54 55* **Map** *5 B5*

As places for paella go, this is one of the best, especially when eaten on a warm summer's day on the terrace with sea views. If you start getting into the shellfish, prices hike right up, but it is worth it for freshness and quality of produce, cooked to perfection. Closed Sun evenings and Mon.

Key to Price Guide *see p608* **Key to Symbols** *see back cover flap*

OLD TOWN Pla de la Garsa €€€

C/ Assaonadors 13, 08003 ***Tel*** *933 15 24 13* ***Map*** *5 B2*

Situated in the stables of a 17th-century palace, the cosy atmosphere of this split-level restaurant makes it a good place for romantic evenings. For cheese-lovers the 40-strong list is a winner. The *menú de degustación* (tasting menu) is well priced and highly recommended. There is also an interesting selection of red wines. Closed for lunch daily.

EIXAMPLE Tapaç 24 *Tapas* €€

C/ de la Diputació 269, 08007 ***Tel*** *934 88 09 77* ***Map*** *3 B5*

In the heart of the city, Tapaç 24 offers traditional tapas with a modern twist. Enjoy your meal at the bar, at the high tables or on the terrace round the corner from the Passeig de Gracia. Specialities include oxtail, tripe and deep-fried fish. They also serve a breakfast with fresh eggs cooked to your own taste. Open 8am–midnight daily.

EIXAMPLE Con Gracia €€€

Martínez de la Rosa 8, 8012 ***Tel*** *932 38 02 01* ***Map*** *3 2B*

At Con Gracia, Irish chef Paul Treacy offers guests three carefully selected tasting menus based on Mediterranean flavours with a distinctly Asian influence. Delightful food in an atmosphere of understated elegance. Open Tue–Sat for dinner, and Tue–Fri lunch for groups only. Reservations recommended.

EIXAMPLE Igueldo €€€

C/ Rosselló 186, 8036 ***Tel*** *934 52 25 55* ***Map*** *3 A3*

This popular restaurant serves traditional Basque fare with a local touch to businessmen at lunch and a fashionable clientele at dinner. Choose between food from the grill or the creative Catalan–Basque fusions, including the excellent *chipirones en su tinta* (squid cooked in its ink) or tenderloin tartare with beer yoghurt. Closed Sun.

EIXAMPLE Shibui €€€

C/ Comte d'Urgell 272–274, 08036 ***Tel*** *933 21 90 04* ***Map*** *2 E1*

With its sleek blonde wood fittings, Japanese cardboard-brick walls and trim waiting staff, this excellent sushi bar has Tokyo written all over it. The basement dining room also has custom-made tatami mat areas and sliding screens, making them a brilliant choice for parties. Closed Sun.

EIXAMPLE Alkimia €€€€

C/ Indústria 79, 08025 ***Tel*** *932 07 61 15* ***Map*** *3 C2*

One of the rising stars of Barcelona's gastronomic scene, this small designer restaurant revitalizes traditional Catalan dishes with new techniques and foreign flavours. Signature dishes include creamy rice with crayfish and nyora peppers, sticky, slow roasted bull tail and mandarin essence with *hortchata* (tiger nut) foam. Closed Sat lunch, Sun, Aug & Easter.

EIXAMPLE Casa Calvet €€€€

C/ Casp 48, 08010 ***Tel*** *934 12 40 12* ***Map*** *3 B5*

A beautiful restaurant that was originally designed by Gaudí as a private home and offices for a wealthy textile merchant. The cosy seating booths, formal table settings and old-school service set the ambience. Try the lamb meatballs with creamy risotto and pine nut tart with foamed *crema catalana*. Closed Sun.

EIXAMPLE Gelonch €€€€

C/ Bailén 56, 08009 ***Tel*** *932 65 82 98* ***Map*** *3 C5*

For startlingly original cuisine, there are few better options in town than Robert Gelonch's inviting restaurant. Choose from two set menus, featuring such dishes as cuttlefish noodles with Chinese greens and deconstructed pesto or shitake broth with spider crab ravioli and Iberian ham. Closed Sun, Mon.

EIXAMPLE Cinc Sentits €€€€€

C/ Aribau 58, 08011 ***Tel*** *933 23 94 90* ***Map*** *2 F1*

This warm yet minimal Michelin-starred restaurant offers impeccable service. Try the duck and pear salad or "6-hour" tender suckling pig. Meticulously sourced products are cooked with flair and creativity. The chef's choice tasting menu is recommended. Kids are welcome during the week and at lunch. Closed Mon, Sun, Easter and two weeks in Aug.

MONTJUÏC Tickets *Tapas* €€€

Avda Paral.lel 164, 08015 ***Map*** *2 D2*

The Adrià brothers, Albert and Ferran, are behind this relaxed, convivial restaurant serving delicious, creative tapas. There is a wide range to choose from, including fresh oysters served in myriad ways and exquisite Iberian hams. Reservations can be made up to two months in advance via www.ticketsbar.es only. Closed Sun, Mon, lunch Tue–Fri.

FURTHER AFIELD (GRÁCIA) Abissínia €

Torrent de les Flors 55, 8024 ***Tel*** *932 13 07 85* ***Map*** *3 C1*

One of Barcelona's best-kept culinary secrets, this Ethiopian restaurant in Gràcia offers a truly original dining experience. It's not just the food that's authentic, even the furniture and service is Ethiopian-style. Diners sit on low stools at straw tables to eat trays of light pancakes and spicy Ethiopian food. Good vegetarian options. Closed lunch Mon-Fri.

FURTHER AFIELD (GRÁCIA) Envalira €€

Plaça del Sol 13, 08012 ***Tel*** *932 18 58 13* ***Map*** *3 B1*

A real neighbourhood joint in the spirited Plaça del Sol, Envalira is noisy, raucous and fun with a laid-back, anything-goes ambience. Intimate it is not, but it is a great place for hearty, no-nonsense fare with rice dishes topping the bill. Specialities include the black squid rice and the Milanese rice. Closed Sun evenings, Mon and Aug.

FURTHER AFIELD (GRÀCIA) Botafumeiro *Tapas* €€€€

C/ Gran de Gràcia 81, 08012 ***Tel*** *932 18 42 30* ***Map*** *3 A2*

A legendary seafood restaurant with ice-banks piled high with boat-fresh fish and seafood at the entrance. A-listers from Woody Allen to Madonna have all made this a favourite haunt while in town, thanks to discreet management and luxury surroundings. Try the tender *pulpo Gallego* (Galician octopus). Live music. Reservations essential.

FURTHER AFIELD (GRÀCIA) Hofmann €€€€

C/ La Granada del Penedès 14 ***Tel*** *93 218 71 65* ***Map*** *5 B2*

Talented, Michelin-star-chef Mey Hofmann has been at the forefront of Barcelona's restaurant scene for many years. Her restaurant-cum-cooking school produces high-quality creative cuisine in a sophisticated locale and with attentive service. Closed Sat, Sun and Aug.

FURTHER AFIELD (GRÀCIA) Roig Robí €€€€

C/ Sèneca 20, 08006 ***Tel*** *932 18 92 22* ***Map*** *3 A2*

This little and friendly restaurant, with a pretty interior courtyard for summer dining, is a classic for genuine Catalan cuisine. The menu boasts a good selection of *bacalao* dishes as well as typical vegetable preparations of broad beans and artichokes. Also two tasting menus. Closed Sat lunch & Sun.

FURTHER AFIELD (HORTA) Can Travi Nou €€€€

C/ Jorge Manrique, 08035 ***Tel*** *934 28 03 01*

Few people venture so far from the centre for their supper, but this 14th-century farmhouse is well worth the trek to soak up the atmosphere of yesteryear, and the rolling terraces are wonderful for al fresco dining. Roast meats, rice dishes and fresh fish are on the menu. Closed Sun evenings.

FURTHER AFIELD (POBLENOU) Els Pescadors €€€€

Plaça Prim 1, 08005 ***Tel*** *932 25 20 18*

The multiple-spaced restaurant – terrace, formal dining room and old-fashioned tiled cafeteria – is named after the fishermen that used to frequent it. It is an excellent place for a catch of the day special, zingy-fresh mussels and other fishy delights. Also try the anchovies. Closed Easter & Christmas.

FURTHER AFIELD (SANT GERVASI) Acontraluz *Tapas* €€€

C/ de Milanesat 19, 08017 (Barcelona) ***Tel*** *932 03 06 58*

In a smart, residential neighbourhood, this atmospheric garden restaurant is perfect on summer evenings, when diners can eat under the stars. It serves beautifully fresh Mediterranean cuisine prepared with seasonal ingredients, and has a charming, candle-lit patio for tapas or post-dinner drinks. Open daily.

FURTHER AFIELD (SANT GERVASI) La Balsa €€€€

C/ Infanta Isabel 4, 08060 (Barcelona) ***Tel*** *932 11 50 48*

Much-loved by Barcelona's glitterati; sportspersons, artists, actors and politicians are all in attendance at this uptown eatery. Service is discreet, the decor tasteful and the terraces among the best in town for enjoying Basque, Catalan and Mediterranean food at its finest. Closed Sun evenings, Mon lunch, Aug & Easter.

CATALONIA

ALCANAR Taller de Cuina Carmen Guillemot €€€

C/ Colón 26, 43530 (Tarragona) ***Tel*** *977 73 03 23*

A series of elegant dining rooms spread over three floors, each individually decorated. The cuisine is Mediterranean, with French influences, and the menu choices depend on what is freshest at the market. Among several fixed-price menus, they also offer a vegetarian option. Closed Sun evenings (except Aug), Mon, Tue & Christmas.

ALELLA Restaurante 1789 €€€€

Rambla Ángel Guimerá 1, 08328 (Barcelona) ***Tel*** *935 55 34 55*

Restaurante 1789 is an intimate and romantic restaurant situated in the centre of Alella. It serves good-quality, creative Mediterranean cuisine based on fresh local fare. Be sure to leave some space for the delicious homemade desserts. Closed Sun dinner, Wed and 21 Aug–15 Sep.

ALTAFULLA Faristol €€

C/ Sant Martí 5, 43893 (Tarragona) ***Tel*** *977 65 00 77*

Experience traditional Catalan fare at this charming 18th-century farmhouse. The English-Catalan couple that run it are welcoming and it makes for a romantic getaway from the bustle of Barcelona. Rooms are also available. They usually have music on Friday and Saturday nights. Open Fri dinner–Sun lunch (Oct–May) & for dinner only in summer.

ANDORRA LA VELLA Borda Estevet €€€

Ctra de la Comella 2, AD500 ***Tel*** *00376 86 40 26*

This old-country manor is still used for the traditional practice of drying tobacco that is grown nearby, and oozes an old-world atmosphere. Extensive menu of Andorran-Catalan and French fare. The meat dishes are exceptional, particularly *carns a la llosa* (lamb or beef) which arrive sizzling on a hot slate.

Key to Price Guide *see p608* **Key to Symbols** *see back cover flap*

ARENYS DE MAR Hispania €€€€

C/ Real 54, Ctra NII, 08350 (Barcelona) ***Tel*** *937 91 03 06*

A famous bistro that has earned numerous awards for the quality of its cooking. People travel from far and wide for its *clam suquet* (fish stew) and homemade *crema catalana* (traditional vanilla custard with a burnt, caramel crust). Closed Sun evenings, Tue, Easter & Oct.

BERGA Sala *Tapas* €€€€

Passeig de la Pau 27, 08600 (Barcelona) ***Tel*** *938 21 11 85*

A good choice for hearty winter dishes that feature freshly picked wild mushrooms from the nearby forests; wild game is available in season. Sala offers extremely innovative cuisine, and they also have a set tasting menu. Try partridge in vinegar sauce or the roasted young goat. Closed Sun evenings & Mon.

CADAQUÉS Casa Nun €€€

Plaça Port Ditxos 6, 17488 (Girona) ***Tel*** *972 25 88 56*

In an old town house, this prettily decorated seafood restaurant overlooks one of the most charming towns of the Catalan coast. The fish couldn't be fresher as the restaurant has its own fishing boat. Book a table on the balcony for perfect views of the harbour. Closed Tue–Thu lunch (Jun–Oct except Aug) & Tue–Wed & Thu lunch (Nov–May) except Easter.

CAMBRILS Can Bosch €€€€

Rambla Jaume I 19, 43850 (Tarragona) ***Tel*** *977 36 00 19*

A classic and highly-respected restaurant serving superb fish, seafood and rice dishes. Their *arroz negro* (rice cooked in squid ink) is justly famous; also try sole with crayfish and black rice with lobster. Patrons rave about their wine list almost as much as the food. Closed Sun evening, Mon & 22 Dec–27 Jan.

CERCS Estany Clar €€€€

Ctra C 16 km 99.4, 08698 (Barcelona) ***Tel*** *938 22 08 79*

A little off the beaten track, this much-praised restaurant is set in a restored Catalan farmhouse near Berga. The contemporary Catalan cuisine includes dishes such as rice with lobster and foie gras, snails with local ham, roasted Iberian suckling pig and for dessert order *cuajada*. Exquisite service. Closed evenings, Mon & Christmas.

COLLBATÒ Ca La Vinya €€

Avda de la Vinya Nova, 08923 (Barcelona) ***Tel*** *937 71 03 29*

This beautiful *masia* (farmhouse) is set amid olive groves at the foot of the Montserrat mountains. There are several dining rooms with rustic furnishings and roaring fires for winter, while in summer guests can enjoy the views from the terrace. Traditional Catalan fare on offer includes grilled *calçots* (a type of spring onion) dipped in romesco sauce.

COLLSUSPINA Can Xarina €€

C/ Mayor 30, 08178 (Barcelona) ***Tel*** *938 30 05 77*

A friendly welcome awaits at this lovely old-village house, now a cosy little restaurant and guesthouse. In the vaulted dining room, you can enjoy rustic mountain cuisine, charcuterie and cheeses, grilled local lamb and rabbit, as well as fresh fish. Features classic wines from around Spain. Opening times vary call ahead.

CORCA Bo.TiC €€€€

Ctra C-66 Girona-Palamós km 11,5 (Girona) 17121 ***Tel*** *972 63 08 69*

Chef Albert "Tito" Strasreneger has converted this old *masia* (farmhouse) into an elegant, modern restaurant, where he serves creative Catalan fare. There is a reasonably priced tasting menu, which consists of two tapas, four starters, two main dishes (one fish and one meat) and two desserts for €49. Good wine list. Closed Tue evening, Wed & Nov.

DELTA DE L'EBRE Lo Goleró €€

Bassa de les Olles, Platja de l'Arenal or L'Ampolla ***Tel*** *655 99 84 41*

A family-run restaurant which sits directly on the beach, serving typical local dishes with an emphasis on the Delta's most famous product – rice. Try the rice with duck or the organic rice paella with vegetables. Phone ahead for opening days.

ESPONELLÀ Can Roca €€

Avda Carles de Fortuny 1, 17832 (Girona) ***Tel*** *972 59 70 12*

A miniature village 10 km (6 miles) from Banyoles hosts this family-run restaurant. This inland region is known for its *embutits* (Catalan charcuterie), and the menu features delicious locally made cured hams and sausages. Excellent fixed-price lunch menu. Open for dinner Fri and Sat only (except Jul & Aug). Closed Tue, 15–30 Sep & 1–15 Mar.

FIGUERES Hotel Empordà €€€€

Hotel Empordà, Avda Salvador Dalí i Domènech 170, 17600 (Girona) ***Tel*** *972 50 05 62*

A legendary restaurant that played a great part in putting Catalan cuisine on the map for travelling gourmets. Established in 1961, folks still gather here to enjoy the legacy of chef Jaime Subirós's cuisine including classic dishes such as *mar y muntaña* (produce of sea and mountain).

GIRONA Blanc €€

Nord 2, 17001 (Girona) ***Tel*** *972 41 56 37*

As its name suggests, this restaurant is elegantly decorated in pure white. The food, on the other hand, comes in many colours, with inventive dishes such as strawberry and goat cheese salad, and tuna "roast beef" with mango chutney.

GIRONA El Celler de Can Roca €€€€

Can Sunyer 46, 17007 (Girona) ***Tel*** *972 22 21 57*

Celler de Can Roca offers a fusion of Catalan and French *nouvelle cuisine* cooking. A must on the list of dedicated food enthusiasts, the Roca brothers turn out innovative, technically brilliant dishes at terrifying speed. With three Michelin stars, this is a place to wow and be wowed. Closed Sun, Mon, 1–15 Jul & Christmas.

GOMBREN Fonda Xesc €€€

Plaça del Roser 1, 17531 (Girona) ***Tel*** *972 73 04 04*

Picasso drew inspiration from this lovely mountain village near Berga. Fonda Xesc is a charming, low-key restaurant-with-rooms, serving good Catalan food. Everything is fresh and locally sourced, from the tender lamb to the artisanal cheeses. In season, you can try a dizzying variety of wild mushrooms. Closed Tue–Thu evenings, Mon & Sun.

GRATALLOPS El Celler de Gratallops *Tapas* €€€

C/ Piró 32 (Priorat), 43737 (Tarragona) ***Tel*** *977 83 90 36*

This smart village restaurant with just five tables is owned by the Clos l'Obac vineyard, one of the pioneers of new Priorato wines. It serves their entire range, along with an excellent Moroccan influenced menu; for example duck confits and foie gras. Well worth seeking out during a trip to wine country. Closed Mon & evenings (except Fri & Sat).

LA SEU D'URGELL Andria €€€

Passeig Joan Brudieu 24, 25700 (Lleida) ***Tel*** *973 35 03 00*

The restaurant at the Hotel Andria is regarded as one of the best in La Seu d'Urgell, offering classic Catalan cuisine that has been adapted to modern tastes. It serves the famously succulent "Gall Roig", a chicken bred only in the mountainous Alt Urgell region, and reared on the hotel's own poultry farm.

LA VALL DE BIANYA Ca L'Enric €€€€

Ctra de Camprodón s/n, 17813 (Girona) ***Tel*** *972 29 00 15*

This restaurant serves some of the finest cuisine in the region and has won many accolades. It has justly become a place of pilgrimage during the hunting season, when they offer Catalan specialities from wild boar to venison, all finely prepared by chef Maria Isabel Juncá. Booking advisable. Closed Sun, Tue & Wed evenings, Mon & two weeks in Jul & Dec.

LLAGOSTERA Els Tinars €€€€

Ctra Sant Feliú-Girona km 7, 2, 17240 (Girona) ***Tel*** *972 83 06 26*

A classic, Els Tinars offers exceptionally fresh modern Catalan cuisine, including the house speciality of trotter salad served with calamari and prawns. Less adventurous diners can try grilled fish, but the charm of this place is in the details: home-baked bread, served warm and crusty and great desserts. Closed Sun evenings, Mon & 8 Jan–8 Feb.

LLEIDA Gardeny €€

C/ Salmerón 10, 25004 (Lleida) ***Tel*** *973 23 45 10*

Excellent regional cooking including chargrilled red peppers and aubergines (eggplants) and snails Gardeny style. Specialities include *xatonada* with beans, mushrooms and cod and a Basque salad of smoked fish, tomatoes and olives with cod and elvers. It has a cheaper fixed-price menu Monday to Friday. Closed Mon evenings & Tue.

MONTSENY Can Barrina €€

Ctra Palautordera–Montseny km 12.6, 08460 (Barcelona) ***Tel*** *938 47 30 65*

In the hills of the Montseny natural park, this restored 17th-century *masía* is now a fine country hotel and restaurant. Dine in the stone-walled dining room or out on the garden terrace, on delicious Catalan specialities, including wild mushrooms and game in season, kid with honey and aniseed and homemade desserts. Closed Sun evenings.

PALAU-SATOR El Racó de l'Era *Tapas* €€

Extramurs 11, 17256 ***Tel*** *972 63 42 25*

An elegant, traditional restaurant set in an olive grove with a nice garden for dining. The cooking is based around fresh, regional ingredients with specialities including locally reared lamb and a fine selection of Catalonian wines. Closed Mon–Thu in winter, and Mon–Fri lunch in summer.

PERALADA Cal Sagristà €€€

C/ Rodona 2, 17491 (Girona) ***Tel*** *972 53 83 01*

Located in an old convent in a beautifully preserved village, this charming restaurant has a series of intimate dining rooms and an inviting terrace. The sophisticated cuisine here includes such dishes as tagliatelle with plump Palamós prawns, or tender suckling pig. There are fabulous desserts and an interesting wine list. Closed Mon evenings.

PERATALLADA Bonay €€€

Plaça de les Voltes, 13, 17113 ***Tel*** *972 63 40 34*

This restaurant has been serving food from the Ampurdan since 1936, with popular dishes including goose with turnip, which gave the restaurant its name. The Bonay also offers an opportunity to dine in the wine cellar/museum in the restaurant's basement.

ROMANYÀ DE LA SELVA Can Roquet €€€

Plaça de l'Eglésia, 17246 ***Tel*** *972 83 30 81*

In a converted country house, at the heart of a medieval hamlet, is this wonderfully romantic restaurant owned by two Belgian artists. Delicious contemporary Mediterranean cuisine is served in an elegant dining room or outside on a terrace with views over the fields and woods. Closed Mon, Tue lunch, and also mid-Nov–mid-Feb.

Key to Price Guide *see p608* **Key to Symbols** *see back cover flap*

ROSES Cal Campaner €€€€

C/ Mossèn Carles Feliu 23, 17480 (Girona) ***Tel*** *972 25 69 54*

This long-established restaurant may not look much from the outside, but it has a well-deserved reputation for exceptional seafood and shellfish. There is no menu – you will simply be told what came in on the boats that morning. It is always packed so book ahead. Closed lunchtimes Sun & Mon in summer & Sun evenings and all Mon in winter.

SANT CELONI El Racó de Can Fabes €€€€

C/ de Sant Joan 6, 08470 (Barcelona) ***Tel*** *938 67 28 51*

Santi Santamaría was one of Spain's most emblematic chefs and this restaurant, in the house where he was born, is a gastronomic wonderland. Since Santamaría died in 2011, Xavier Pellicer has been at the helm, continuing the same philosophy of outstanding seasonal produce prepared in imaginative ways. Bookings essential. Closed Sun eve & Mon.

SANT FELÍU DE GUÍXOLS La Taverna del Mar €€€€

Platja de s'Agaró s/n, 17220 (Girona) ***Tel*** *972 32 38 00*

This century-old tavern serves a dazzling array of spectacularly cooked fresh fish. Recipes include Mediterranean classics such as spiny lobster stew and fish baked in a salt crust. Comfortable wicker armchairs and whitewashed arches frame perfect sea views. Bookings essential. Closed mid-Dec–end Feb.

SANT POL DE MAR Sant Pau €€€€

C/ Nou 10, 08395 (Barcelona) ***Tel*** *937 60 06 62*

This three-Michelin-starred restaurant is an hour-long train ride from Barcelona. The bounty of earth and sea make for some wonderful dishes created from courgette (zucchini) flowers, sea cucumbers and wild boar by chef Carme Ruscalleda. Only apéritifs and coffee are served outside. Closed Sun, Mon, Thu lunch & three weeks in May & Nov.

SANTES CREUS Grau *Tapas* €€

C/ Pere el Gran 3, 43815 (Tarragona) ***Tel*** *977 63 83 11*

The honey-coloured stone monastery of Santes Creus is one of the most beautiful places in Catalonia, and is part of the great Cistercian monastery route. This simple hostel and restaurant offers great home cooking, which you can enjoy in the garden terrace. Try the wonderful roasted *calçots* in season. Closed Mon.

SITGES El Velero €€€€

Passeig de la Ribera 38, 08870 (Barcelona) ***Tel*** *938 94 20 51*

A seaside restaurant whose imaginative creations are a cut above more standard offerings of paella and grilled fish. Here sole comes on a bed of wild mushrooms and is drizzled with unctuous crab sauce, lobster comes with chickpea cream and boat-fresh razor clams are the best starters. Closed Mon, Sun evenings & Tue lunch in winter & 22 Dec–22 Jan.

TAMARIU Es Dofí *Tapas* €€

Paseo de Mar 21, 17212 (Girona) ***Tel*** *972 62 02 43*

A laid-back restaurant overlooking one of the prettiest bays in the Costa Brava, Es Dofí serves the freshest seafood on a terrace by the beach. Try the tasty, lightly battered squid or the delicious grilled sardines. Main fish dishes include simply prepared turbot, hake and bream, and there is also paella. Closed Tue in winter.

TARRAGONA Grotta *Tapas* €€

Plaza Sedassos 28, 43003 (Tarragona) ***Tel*** *977 25 18 87*

This modern restaurant and lounge by the Roman amphitheatre offers an excellent fixed-price lunch menu prepared with local produce and international creative tapas at night. Don't miss the *morcilla* (black sausage) served with stewed apples and a mustard coulis, or the deer hamburger with caramelized onions in wine. Open daily.

TORROELLA DE MONTGRÍ Palau Lo Mirador €€€

Passeig l'Esglesia 1, 17257 (Girona) ***Tel*** *972 75 80 63*

For royal treatment head to this hotel, the residence of Catalonia's most powerful King Jaume I. The dining rooms, with their stone walls, vaulted ceilings and chandeliers are truly palatial. Fine regional cuisine with international touches – Indian spices and Oriental flavours appear on the menu alongside classic Catalan dishes. Closed Sun evening.

TORTOSA Rosa Pinyol €€€

C/ Hernán Cortés 17, 43500 (Tarragona) ***Tel*** *977 50 20 01*

One of the most creative restaurants in the area, Rosa Pinyol serves deftly prepared Catalan cuisine with Italian and Mediterranean influences. The sautéed baby squid with wild mushrooms melt in the mouth, and the desserts, particularly anything made with chocolate, are heavenly. Outstanding service. Closed Sun & Mon evenings.

TOSSA DE MAR La Cuina de Can Simón €€€€

C/ Portal 24, 17320 (Girona) ***Tel*** *972 34 12 69*

A family-run restaurant serving good contemporary Mediterranean cuisine. In summer, you can dine al fresco on the terrace. Try the rice cooked in squid ink with a mouthwatering *romesco* sauce (made with crushed almonds, peppers and garlic). Open daily in August. Closed Mon, Tue & Sun evenings in winter; Mon evenings & Tue in spring and autumn.

VALLS Masia Bou €€

Ctra Lleida km 21.5, 43800 (Tarragona) ***Tel*** *977 60 04 27*

A large and noisy country house with room for more than 600 people. The specialities here are game, wild mushrooms and *calçots*, chargrilled over hot vines and served with their scrumptious almond, hazelnut and red pepper dipping sauce. Closed Tue in summer.

VIC D.O. Vic €€

Sant Miquel dels Sants 16 (Barcelona), 8500 ***Tel*** *938 83 23 96*

The perfect place to taste the local wines, accompanied by a creative cuisine based on local fare. The name of the restaurant stands for *Denominación de Origen*, which is the classification given to food from protected geographical regions. Closed Mon and Tue.

VIELHA Era Lucana €€

Avda Calbetó Barra 10, 25530 (Lleida) ***Tel*** *973 64 17 98*

With its warm wood panelling, locally made lace tablecloths and roaring fires, this is a cosy and welcoming place to rest after a day on the slopes. The menu offers creative renditions of classic Catalan fare, including succulent meats grilled over charcoal, served with wild mushroom sauce. Closed Mon & 1–15 Nov.

VILAFRANCA DEL PENEDÉS Cal Ton €€€

C/ Casal 8, 08720 (Barcelona) ***Tel*** *938 90 37 41*

Capital of Catalonia's main wine-producing region, Vilafranca del Penedès is a tranquil little town. Cal Ton is an old-fashioned favourite in the centre, with rustically furnished dining rooms serving sturdy Catalan classics such as *butifarra amb mongetes* (a classic bean and sausage dish) and local lamb. Closed Sun & Tue evenings, Mon & Easter.

ARAGÓN

AÍNSA Callizo €€€

Plaza Mayor, 22330 (Huesca) ***Tel*** *974 50 03 85*

Located on an arcaded square in Aínsa's charming historic heart, this restaurant serves imaginative, sophisticated cuisine. The two great-value set menus reflect whatever is freshest and in season. Dishes might include seared trout with local black olives or succulent lamb casserole with thyme. Closed Sun evenings, Mon, mid-Dec–mid Mar.

ALBARRACÍN Tiempo de Ensueño €€€

C/ Palacios 1B, 44100 (Teruel) ***Tel*** *978 70 60 70*

Located in the old part of the town is this elegant restaurant in an old stone building but with a bold, contemporary decor. It serves sophisticated versions of classic regional dishes. Try the lasagne made with Teruel ham, or the cod *bacalao*, accompanied by delicious local wines. Closed Tue.

ALCAÑIZ (TERUEL) La Oficina ***Tapas*** €

Avda de Aragón 12, 44600 (Teruel) ***Tel*** *978 87 08 01*

Situated in the historic town of Alcañiz, renowned for its Easter celebrations, this small, excellent value *mesón* (inn) specializes in traditional, homemade food using local produce, including the area's famed olive oil. They specialize in meat dishes with options such as the succulent steak with Roquefort sauce. Closed Sun.

BARBASTRO El Rincón ***Tapas*** €

C/ Siervas de María 5 22300 (Huesca) ***Tel*** *974 30 89 50*

This friendly, contemporary café-bar offers fresh, modern cuisine at very reasonable prices. It serves a great range of delicious tapas and *pintxos* (Basque-style slices of fresh country bread piled up with different toppings), as well as a good set lunch menu (available Mon–Sat). Closed Sun evenings.

BIESCAS Casa Ruba ***Tapas*** €

C/ Esperanza 18–20, 22630 (Huesca) ***Tel*** *974 48 50 01*

This simple dining room, founded in 1884, is the best choice for traditional cuisine. Try the cod wrapped in pastry and served with artichokes or the tender local steaks cooked to perfection. Desserts include caramelized custard with ice cream and hot chocolate sauce. Good value lunchtime fixed menu. Closed Sun evenings & mid-Oct–mid-Nov.

BORJA La Bóveda del Mercado €€€

Plaza del Mercado 4, 50540 (Zaragoza) ***Tel*** *976 86 82 51*

In a 17th-century cellar, in the historic centre of Borja, you will find this magnificently decorated little gem, serving traditional dishes perfectly cooked. Try the *morcilla* crêpe, the artichokes with foie gras, or the peaches in wine. Closed Sun evenings, Mon & Jan or Feb.

CARIÑENA La Rebotica €€

C/ San José 3, 50400 (Zaragoza) ***Tel*** *976 62 05 56*

This lovely eatery retains vestiges of its old life as a pharmacy. Salads, vegetable and pasta dishes are the order of the day. Favourites include rice salad with duck ham and foie gras and *morcilla* lasagne. The atmosphere is friendly. La Rebotica is open for lunch only (except Saturdays). Closed Mon.

ESQUEDAS Venta del Sotón €€€€

Ctra A132 Huesca to Puente La Reina km 14, 22810 (Huesca) ***Tel*** *974 27 02 41*

Very pleasant, homespun restaurant located 14 kms (8.6 miles) from Huesca in a typical Pyrenean chalet. The cuisine is traditional and includes such local treats as cod *pil pil*, baby lamb with potatoes or beef baked in rock salt. They also have a series of excellent fixed-price menus. Closed Sun & Tue evenings, Mon & mid-Jan–mid-Feb.

HUESCA Lillas Pastia *Tapas* €€€€

Plaza de Navarra 4, 22002 ***Tel*** *974 21 16 91*

Located in the salon of the casino, this is one of the most popular restaurants in Huesca. A highly creative "market" cuisine focuses on the freshest seasonal produce, especially the local truffle. Try the honey-baked cod served with milk foam or new potatoes with wild mushrooms. Closed Sun evenings, Mon (in winter only) & Oct–Nov (variable).

JACA Lilium €€

Avda Primer Viernes de Mayo 8, 22700 (Huesca) ***Tel*** *974 35 53 56*

This split-level eatery has a split personality; contemporary upstairs and reassuringly rustic in the basement. The cuisine is typical of Aragón's high country and features dishes such as chargrilled lamb chops with wild mushrooms and lettuce hearts filled with goat's cheese. Rich homemade desserts. Closed Mon, Tue & two weeks in spring & autumn.

LA IGLESUELA DEL CID Casa Amada €

C/ Fuente Nueva 10, 44142 (Teruel) ***Tel*** *964 44 33 73*

This simple, quality restaurant offers a good fixed menu from Monday to Friday and a more varied à la carte on the weekends. Its specialities include stuffed potatoes, bean stew, garlic chickpeas, partridge and grilled meats and trout. The homemade desserts are excellent. There are a few rooms available. Closed Sun evenings (except Aug).

NUÉVALOS Río Piedra €€

Ctra Monasterio de Piedra s/n, 50210 (Zaragoza) ***Tel*** *976 84 90 07*

Situated in the Río Piedra Hotel, this pretty, rustically furnished restaurant serves a wide-ranging menu that includes game in season. As well as the à-la-carte options, there is also a good-value lunch menu and a special menu for children, making it a good choice for families. Closed Jan.

RUBIELOS DE MORA Restaurante Victoria €€

C/ El Piano 6, 44415 (Teruel) ***Tel*** *978 80 43 90*

At this rustic restaurant in a delightful moutain village, the house speciality is *carnes a la brasa* – succulent local meats, such as lamb chops or steaks, cooked over an open fire. It is also good for traditional Aragonese stews and soups so it is the perfect venue for a warming meal on a cold winter's day. Closed Sun evening.

TERUEL La Menta €€€€

C/ Bartolomé Esteban 10, 44001 ***Tel*** *978 60 75 32*

One of the most charming restaurants with paintings from celebrated local artists adorning the walls. The seasonal cuisine includes crêpes filled with spinach and cured ham, partridge *escabechada* and a caramelized cheese cake with pine nuts. Attentive table service. Reservations recommended. Closed Mon, Sun, 7–27 Jan & 20 days in July.

TORLA El Duende €€

C/ La Iglesia, 22376 (Huesca) ***Tel*** *974 48 60 32*

This charming restaurant is located in a restored 19th-century stone barn in a lovely mountain village. The dining room has wooden beams and thick stone walls to keep it cool in summer and cosy in winter. The kitchen turns out delicious local specialities such as lamb chops cooked on an outdoor grill, or venison with apple.

TRAMACASTILLA DE TENA La Era de Berdon €€

Con del Beato s/n, 22663 ***Tel*** *974 48 74 16*

One of the best restaurants in the Tena Valley, offering good prices for quality dishes. The menu is varied, and the presentation and service of a high standard. Excellent food and homemade desserts. Don't miss the wild mushrooms with foie gras.

UNCASTILLO Un-Castello *Tapas* €€

Plaza de la Villa 24, 50678 (Zaragoza) ***Tel*** *976 67 91 05*

Next to the city hall in a rustic building, Un-Castello offers surprisingly innovative Basque and Aragonese cuisine. Try the aubergines with mushrooms wrapped in pastry, stuffed leg of lamb or roast beef with mustard sauce. Great choice of local wines. It is recommended to ring first to check opening times.

ZARAGOZA Casa Juanico *Tapas* €

Plaza de Santa Cruz 21, 50003 ***Tel*** *976 39 72 52*

In Zaragoza's old town, close to the famous Pilar Cathedral, this perpetually crowded, classic bar offers the best tapas in town. Grilled meats, a great selection of *pinchos* and cold cod salad are the highlights. There is also a rear dining room for more formal eating, for which reservations are recommended. Closed Sun evening.

ZARAGOZA La Rinconada de Lorenzo *Tapas* €€

C/ La Salle 3, 50006 ***Tel*** *976 55 51 08*

This emblematic restaurant, decorated in the colourful tiles typical of the area, offers excellent home-style cooking. Specialities include chickpeas with lobster, ham and grapes and other hearty meat and fish dishes. There is a distinctly fun and family-friendly atmosphere here. Closed Sun evenings & Mon in summer & Easter week.

ZARAGOZA Palomeque *Tapas* €€

C/ Agustín Palomeque 11, 50004 ***Tel*** *976 21 40 82*

This local favourite serves good tapas and *raciones*, as well as a choice of more substantial dishes. These range from the traditional (oxtail stewed in vermouth) to the contemporary (venison meatballs with walnut sauce). The wine list includes some interesting local options. Reservations recommended. Closed Sat evening and Sun.

ZARAGOZA La Matilde €€€

C/ Predicadores 7, 50003 ***Tel*** *976 43 34 43*

Traditional cooking with a creative twist can be found at La Matilde, which is also renowned for its selection of more than 2,000 wines and cavas. Eccentricities like napkins folded in 90 different ways and opening cava bottles with a sword in the traditional way of the Catalan fraternities add to the experience. Closed Sun, public holidays & Easter.

ZARAGOZA Garum €€€€

C/ Andrés Piquer 8, 50006 ***Tel*** *976 55 47 21*

A popular restaurant near the university serving fresh food based on Mediterranean cuisine. The menu changes four times a year and uses fresh food in season. Among the star dishes are Pyrenean rump steak with wild mushroom sauce. Closed Sun evenings and Mon.

VALENCIA AND MURCIA

ALICANTE Mesón de Labradores *Tapas* €

C/ Labradores 19, 03001 (Alacant) ***Tel*** *965 20 48 46*

Decorated with colourful tiles and huge wine barrels, Mesón de Labradores is one of the best and most authentic of Alicante's many tapas bars. Cheerful waiters breeze between the crowded tables, with platters of deliciously fresh snacks held aloft. Try the *croquetas* (meat-stuffed rolls), a speciality of the house. Closed Mon & 15–30 Nov.

ALICANTE Dársena *Tapas* €€€

Marina Deportiva, Muelle Levante 6, Puerto, 03001 (Alacant) ***Tel*** *965 20 75 89*

A classic restaurant overlooking the port, Dársena has an elegant interior, with crisp white linen. The nautical-style brass lamps give it the feel of a luxurious ocean liner. Gaze out at the sea of yachts through the enormous picture windows, and choose from around 150 delicious rice dishes. Do not miss the *arròs a banda* (rice with fish).

ALICANTE Nou Manolín *Tapas* €€€

C/ Villegas 3, 03001 (Alacant) ***Tel*** *965 20 03 68*

An Alicantino favourite, this attractive restaurant is tucked away in the old quarter in the former home of local author Gabriel Miró. There is an excellent tapas bar downstairs, while upstairs you can dine in an elegant brick-lined salon on classic Valencian seafood, rice dishes, accompanied by an extensive wine list.

ALTEA La Costera €€€

Costera Mestre de Música 8, 3590 ***Tel*** *965 84 02 30*

A picturesque restaurant housed in an old building in the pretty village of Altea. The restaurant has been serving original dishes of French-influenced cuisine accompanied by live music since its foundation by a Swiss emigré in the 1980s. Closed Mon and for lunch (except Sat and Sun lunch in winter).

BENIDORM Restaurante J Manu €€

C/ de la Palma 15, 03501 (Alicante) ***Tel*** *659 77 94 66*

If you are looking for good, old-fashioned Spanish cooking, try this traditional restaurant, which has an open kitchen so you can see your meal being prepared. It serves delicious paella, as well as other Mediterranean rice dishes, along with grilled fish and meats, tortillas (omelettes) and other local recipes.

BENIDORM Ulía €€€

C/ Vicente Llorca Alós 15, 03502 (Alicante) ***Tel*** *965 85 68 28*

This old-fashioned seaside restaurant is one of the best places in Benidorm to try an authentic paella. The good food, made with the freshest local produce, makes it popular with families that flock from the beach on Sundays for long lunches on the lovely, breezy terrace. Closed Mon, Sun evenings & 22 Dec–22 Jan.

BENIMANTELL L'Obrer €€

Ctra de Alcoi 27, 03516 (Alicante) ***Tel*** *965 88 50 88*

L'Obrer's popularity rests on its great food, bargain prices and welcoming ambience. A rustic-style restaurant, decorated with locally made ceramics, it serves home-cooked country dishes such as baked lamb or roasted rabbit. Homemade desserts include almond tart with chocolate. Closed Fri, evenings (except Fri–Sat in Aug) & Jul.

BENIMANTELL Venta la Montaña €€

Ctra de Alcoi 9, 03516 (Alicante) ***Tel*** *965 88 51 41*

This mountain inn, decorated with antique farming implements, serves wholesome dishes such as the typical *olleta de trigo* (a broth made with pork, vegetables and wheat). Accompany it with a sturdy local wine and finish with caramel soufflé. If you do not want a big meal, try the tapas at the bar. Closed last week of Jun & Mon.

BENISSANO Levante €€€

C/ Virgen del Fundamento 27, 46181 (Valencia) ***Tel*** *962 78 07 21*

You cannot leave Valencia without trying Levante's excellent paellas, cooked to perfection over a wood fire. Other house recommendations include the delicious *croquetas de atún* (homemade tuna croquettes). The restaurant boasts one of the region's largest and best wine cellars. Open for lunch only. Closed Tue & mid Jul–mid-Aug.

Key to Price Guide *see p608* **Key to Symbols** *see back cover flap*

BUÑOL Venta L'Home €€€

Autovía A3 Madrid-Valencia km 306 (exit Venta Mina), 46360 (Valencia) ***Tel*** *962 50 35 15*

A whitewashed 18th-century staging post is the setting for this attractive country restaurant. You can dine on great regional cuisine, such as rabbit with honey, or artichokes with baby squid, in a rustically decorated dining room. The wine list features an interesting selection of regional wines. There is also a swimming pool.

CABO DE PALOS Miramar *Tapas* €€

Paseo de la Barra 14, 30370 (Murcia) ***Tel*** *968 56 30 33*

Every seaside resort in Spain has a Miramar restaurant, and the lively town of Cabo de Palos is no exception. It is a family-friendly seafood restaurant with huge picture windows overlooking the port and the bay. Specialities include local rice dishes, and fish baked in salt. Try the local desserts, particularly the *pan de Calatrava*. Closed 7–30 Jan.

CARAVACA DE LA CRUZ Los Viñales *Tapas* €

Av Juan Carlos I 41, 30400 (Murcia) ***Tel*** *968 70 84 58*

An old-fashioned, down-to-earth inn, Los Viñales is justly famous for its fine *guisos* (mountain stews), prepared with locally-reared lamb or pork and the delicious vegetables for which Murcia is famous. These stews are perfect for the cool nights in this enchanting hill-top town. Closed Mon evening, Tue & 25–31 Jan.

CARTAGENA La Catedral €€

Plaza Condesa de Peralta s/n, 30201 ***Tel*** *868 06 65 58*

Located near the Roman theatre in the centre of Cartagena, this restaurant has preserved vestiges of ancient Rome in the form of road fragments and a well in its cosy basement dining room. Try fresh, tasty dishes such as wild mushroom *croquetas*, succulent steak or seared scallops with vermouth. Closed Mon.

CASTELLÓ DE LA PLANA Rafael €€€€

C/ Churruca 28, 12100 (Castellón) ***Tel*** *964 28 21 85*

Rafael has long been a fixture on Castellón's port, El Grao, close to the main city centre. Welcoming and unfussy, the restaurant has always focused on the quality of its ingredients, particularly fresh fish. Service is excellent and the wine list offers a good range of regional labels. Closed Sun & bank holiday evenings, 1–15 Sep & 23 Dec–8 Jan.

COCENTAINA L'Escaleta €€€€

Subida Estación Norte 205, 03824 (Alicante) ***Tel*** *965 59 21 00*

One of the best restaurants in the Cocentaina region, L'Escaleta is situated in a chalet decorated in classic, elegant style. The freshest produce from the market is used to prepare creative interpretations of classic dishes. The wine list has both Spanish and international wines. Closed Sun, Tue & Wed evenings, Mon & 7–21 Jan.

CULLERA Casa Salvador *Tapas* €€€

L'Estany de Cullera, 46400 (Valencia) ***Tel*** *961 72 01 36*

Sitting pretty on the edge of the *estany* (lake) of Cullera, this family-run restaurant has a beautiful wooden terrace overlooking the lake. Choose from a wide variety of traditional rice dishes, locally-caught seafood, and vegetables grown in their own orchard. Paella with duck is a speciality. The wine cellar has more than 4,000 bottles of wine.

DENIA El Poblet €€€€

Ctra Las Marinas km 3, 03700 (Alicante) ***Tel*** *965 78 41 79*

El Poblet offers exceptional and highly creative Spanish cuisine, created by Enrique Dacosta, one of the most exciting chefs in Spain. This is one of the best places to try Dénia's famous prawns. There is a wonderful *menú de degustación*. Parking facilities are available. Closed Mon (except Aug), Sun evening, three weeks starting mid-Feb & two weeks in Oct.

ELCHE (ELX) Asador Ilicitano €€€

C/ Maestro Giner 9, 03201 (Alicante) ***Tel*** *965 43 58 64*

A fine old *mesón*, with handsome traditional decor and ancient wooden beams, Asador Ilicitano serves succulent roasted meats prepared over charcoal to give them a delicate smoky flavour. Specialities include roast kid and lamb, but they also serve some delicious seafood dishes such as Basque-style cod. Closed Sun & 16–31 Aug.

FORCALL Mesón de la Vila €€

Plaza Mayor 8, 12310 (Castellón) ***Tel*** *964 17 11 25*

Right on Forcall's expansive main square, this handsome *mesón* is located in the 16th-century cellars of the Ayuntamiento (Town Hall). In the elegant vaulted dining rooms, you can try affordable regional dishes such as the *sopa forcallana* (broth with vegetables, boiled eggs, ham and meatballs). Closed Mon.

GANDÍA Arrop €€€€

Almirante 14, 46003 ***Tel*** *963 92 55 66*

Without doubt one of the best restaurants in town. Chef Ricard Camarena has reinvented the image of Valencian cuisine with some exquisite flourishes. Don't expect to find a traditional paella here. Instead you'll get to try rice with snails or truffled rice with octopus and turnips. Closed Sun and Mon.

JÁTIVA (XÀTIVA) Casa La Abuela €€€

C/ Reina 17, 46800 (Valencia) ***Tel*** *962 28 10 85*

Tucked away in the higgledy-piggledy maze in the centre of Játiva, this pretty turn-of-the-19th-century house is now a delightful restaurant set around a plant-filled interior patio. The cuisine is refined and creative: try the magret of duck with red fruits, or the lamb with rosemary mousse. A *menú del día* is available. Closed Sun & 15–30 Jul.

LORCA El Teatro €

Plaza de Colón 12, 30800 (Murcia) ***Tel*** *968 46 99 09*

El Teatro is a simple little restaurant with a good range of Murcian dishes, many featuring delicious local vegetables as well as variations of the classic rice dishes for which Eastern Spain is famous. Seafood is freshly caught in the nearby bay of Águilas. Try the aubergine gratin with a tasty meaty sauce. Closed Sun evenings, Mon & Aug.

MORAIRA La Sort €€€

Avda Madrid 1, 03724 (Alicante) ***Tel*** *966 49 11 61*

This smart, modern restaurant prides itself on serving Mediterranean cooking using the freshest ingredients from local suppliers. Daily fresh fish from Moraira market may be used in such dishes as the red mullet with tempura leeks. Meat dishes include the Iberian lamb with cranberry sauce. Game in season. Closed 23 Dec–15 Jan.

MORELLA Casa Roque €€

C/ Cuesta de San Juan 1, 12300 (Castellón) ***Tel*** *964 16 03 36*

An old stone mansion houses this classic restaurant in mountainous Maestrat. Diners come from near and far to savour Roque Guttiérez's fillet steak with truffles in puff pastry. Fixed-price menu includes an excellent *menú de degustación*. Closed Sun evenings, Mon (in Aug opens daily), two weeks in Jan or Feb, 24–25 Dec & 1 Jan.

MURCIA La Tapa *Tapas* €

Plaza de las Flores 13, 30004 (Murcia) ***Tel*** *968 21 13 17*

Upbeat and brightly lit, with a terrace out on one of Murcia's liveliest squares, La Tapa is a classic on the Murciano tapas route. There is an excellent range of tasty snacks, especially fried prawns, usually washed down with an ice-cold beer or a glass of crisp local wine. It may be wise to arrive early to grab a table on the square. Open daily.

MURCIA Pura Cepa *Tapas* €€

Plaza Cristo del Rescate, 30001 (Murcia) ***Tel*** *968 21 73 97*

The name of this restaurant means "Murcian through and through", so expect to find food and surroundings that celebrate Murcia. Known for its delicious *montaditos* (pieces of bread topped with a small portion of food), its homemade conserves and an extensive wine list which highlights regional varieties. Closed Sun and Mon lunch.

MURCIA Acuario *Tapas* €€€

Plaza Puxmarina 3, 30004 (Murcia) ***Tel*** *968 21 99 55*

This classic restaurant is the perfect place for a romantic dinner. They offer a range of good, well-priced set menus, including a tapas menu, a *menú de degustación* featuring modern dishes, and a *menú típico*, which showcases local cuisine. Closed Sun & Mon evenings, Easter & 15–31 Aug.

MURCIA Hostería Palacete Rural La Seda €€€€

Vereda del Catalan s/n, km 6.5 from Murcia City, 30162 (Murcia) ***Tel*** *968 87 08 48*

Housed in an 18th-century mansion, this restaurant is one of Murcia's most prestigious. Dine on elegant contemporary cuisine made with the highest quality seasonal produce. The innovative menu changes according to what is in season. The wine list was recently voted the finest in all of Spain. Closed Sun and bank holidays.

MURCIA Rincón de Pepe €€€€

Apóstoles 34, 30001 (Murcia) ***Tel*** *968 21 22 39*

Some of the best regional cuisine in the city is served at one of Murcia's most famous restaurants. Its seasonal menu includes a wide range of Spanish and international dishes. Try the pig's trotters with white beans or the mouthwatering platter of assorted grilled fish and seafood. Reservations recommended. Closed Sun evening.

ORIHUELA Restaurante Joaquín €€€

Avda de Teodomiro 18, 03312 (Alicante) ***Tel*** *966 74 34 15*

A wonderfully old-fashioned establishment, this restaurant serves up classic local dishes with a twist, such as grilled squid with artichokes, steak with chestnut sauce, a choice of fine rice dishes and a delicious casserole of the day. Eat in the convivial bar area or in the elegant dining room. Closed Sun.

PEÑÍSCOLA Casa Jaime €€€

Av Papa Luna 5, 12598 (Castellón) ***Tel*** *964 48 00 30*

With spectacular views of the castle of Papa Luna, this reliable seafood restaurant sits right on the seafront. Freshly caught fish is served either simply grilled or in one of the many paellas and rice dishes. Try the prawn carpaccio, or *arroz de la huerta* (rice flavoured with local vegetables). Closed Sun eves, Wed (except Jul–Sep) & 20 Dec–20 Jan.

POLOP DE LA MARINA Ca l'Ángeles €€€€

C/ Gabriel Miró 12, 03520 (Alicante) ***Tel*** *965 87 02 26*

Run by the same family for two generations, Ca l'Ángeles is a charming country restaurant with dining rooms that have ancient beams and lovely, rustic decoration. The menu offers sophisticated regional fare, including kid baked with roasted garlic, or oven-baked locally-caught fish. Closed Tue, 15 Jun–15 Jul & Sun–Thu evenings in winter.

SAGUNTO L'Armeler €€€

C/ Subida al Castillo 44, 46500 (Valencia) ***Tel*** *962 66 43 82*

In the old Jewish quarter of Sagunt, a historic house contains this chic restaurant. There are two dining areas, with wooden beams and colourful tiles. The menu offers innovative Mediterranean cuisine, with signature dishes such as duck with figs and aniseed sauce. Closed Mon–Wed evenings & Sun all day (except Jul–Aug).

Key to Price Guide *see p608* **Key to Symbols** *see back cover flap*

SANTA POLA El Faro

€€€

Ctra N-332 Alicante-Cartagena km 81, 03130 (Alicante) ***Tel*** *965 41 21 36*

El Faro is a typical Spanish seaside restaurant with a good range of delicious regional rice dishes and wonderful fresh fish caught locally. On the edge of town, near the hill of Santa Pola, it is a lovely walk to the tip of the headland, with beautiful views. The wine list has a fine selection from all around Spain. Good value fixed-price menu. Closed 24 Dec.

VALENCIA La Alegría de la Huerta

Tapas €€

Paseo Marítimo, Mod. 6, Playa de la Malvarrosa, 46024 (Valencia) ***Tel*** *963 55 05 07*

This establishment used to be an old *merendero*, a typical Valencian beach hut which was built every year for simple summer dining. It is now a permanent structure, serving traditional Valencian food, with tapas and fresh fish and, of course, a big selection of rice dishes from chicken and rabbit paella to the classic *fideuà* pasta with shellfish.

VALENCIA 33 Lounge

€€

C/ San Dionisio 8, 46003 (Valencia) ***Tel*** *963 92 41 61*

Located close to the IVAM museum, this is the perfect place to stop and have a bite to eat before or after a visit to the museum. Dishes are based on Mediterranean cuisine with original touches, from baby squid carpaccio to crispy goat's cheese with mushrooms. Paellas for one person are also available. Closed Sun dinner & Mon.

VALENCIA Ca Sento

€€€€

C/ Méndez Núñez 17, 45024 (Valencia) ***Tel*** *963 30 17 75*

Probably the finest restaurant in Valencia, Ca Sento is renowned for its exquisite regional and international cuisine. The decor is sleek and subtle. The dishes, imaginatively cooked by a chef-and-wife team, use spectacularly fresh produce and are immaculately presented. The *menú de degustación* for €145 is excellent. Closed Sun, Mon, Easter & Aug.

VILLENA Warynessy

Tapas €€€

C/ Isabel la Católica 13, 03400 (Alicante) ***Tel*** *965 80 10 47*

This chic restaurant-bar comes as a pleasant surprise in the otherwise sleepy mountain town of Villena. The decor is elegant with contemporary furnishings and clean lines. The menu offers creative, yet unfussy, local dishes prepared with flair and imagination. The bar is a lively spot for a pre-dinner cocktail. Closed Mon & second half of Jul.

VINARÒS Los Arcos

Tapas €€

Paseo Colòn 9, 12500 (Castellón) ***Tel*** *964 45 56 72*

A rustically decorated seafront restaurant near the town's market, Los Arcos offes a great selection of typical Mediterranean rice dishes, including a highly recommended paella. It is also good for seafood, which is brought in fresh daily, as well as tapas. There's a good range of wines to choose from too. Closed Mon.

MADRID

OLD MADRID Cornucopia

€

C/ Navas de Tolosa 9, 28013 ***Tel*** *915 21 38 96* ***Map*** *4 E1*

Charming and intimate, Cornucopia has an interesting cuisine that blends European and American flavours. Ultra-fresh ingredients are used in the cooking, with a plenty of choice for vegetarians. Do not miss the wonderful desserts, especially the strawberry mousse. There is a reasonable lunch menu from Mon–Sat and a well-considered wine list.

OLD MADRID El Estragón

€

Plaza de la Paja 21, 28005 ***Tel*** *913 65 89 82* ***Map*** *4 D3*

El Estragón is located in a pretty spot, overlooking one of Madrid's loveliest and most fashionable squares. *Madrileño* cuisine is decidedly meaty, but this long-standing vegetarian restaurant provides a welcome break for veggies. The menu features a variety of delectable vegetable- and soy-based dishes. Note that there are two sittings for dinner.

OLD MADRID Malacatín

Tapas €

C/ de la Ruda 5, 28005 ***Tel*** *913 65 52 41* ***Map*** *4 D4*

This bar is full of bullfighting memorabilia, such as paintings and photographs, reflecting the owner's former occupation as a bullfighter. Try its star dish *cocido madrileño* (meat and vegetable stew). Other favourites include tripe cooked Madrid-style. Closed Sat & Mon–Wed evenings, Sun, bank holidays & Aug.

OLD MADRID Taberna Los Cuatro Robles

Tapas €

Plaza de Celenque 1, 28013 ***Tel*** *915 23 08 09* ***Map*** *4 E2*

A simple, brightly-lit tapas bar, lined with colourful tiles, this tavern brings a taste of Andalusia to the capital. Although it is in the heart of the city, it isn't on the well-trodden tourist route. You can try the delicious croquettes and all kinds of seafood specialities in the company of *madrileño* workers. Closed Sun.

OLD MADRID Casa Ciriaco

Tapas €€

C/ Mayor 84, 28013 ***Tel*** *915 48 06 20* ***Map*** *3 C3*

A traditional Castilian-style tavern near the Royal Palace, Casa Ciriaco is renowned for its *gallina en pepitoria* (a chicken stew with egg and saffron), which it has been making for more than a century. Other homemade delights include game in season, and *cocido madrileño*. Book in advance. Closed Wed, Easter & Aug.

OLD MADRID Casa Patas *Tapas* €€

C/ Cañizares 10, 28012 ***Tel*** *913 69 04 96* ***Map*** *7 A3*

Casa Patas is primarily known for its flamenco shows in the evenings, which are among the best in the city. It is also an original place to eat in the heart of Old Madrid, with a well-stocked tapas bar and an unbeatable fixed-price lunch menu. Wheelchair-users must call in advance for assistance. There is an admission charge. Closed Sun.

OLD MADRID Delic *Tapas* €€

Plaza de la Paja s/n, 28005 ***Tel*** *913 64 54 50* ***Map*** *4 D3*

Stylish Delic is a popular café-bar, doubling as a hip local drinking hole. It serves everything from delicious breakfasts, to light snacks and more substantial cuisine with an exotic touch. With a perfect location on the trendy Plaza de la Paja, the terrace is a good place to watch a smart crowd of locals hang out on hot summer nights. No credit cards.

OLD MADRID Naïa *Tapas* €€

Plaza de la Paja 3, 28005 ***Tel*** *913 66 27 83* ***Map*** *4 D3*

The newest arrival on the ultra-trendy Plaza de la Paja, this glassy modern restaurant is currently a favourite with Madrid's fashionistas. Dine on deftly prepared Mediterranean cuisine out on the terrace – a perfect vantage point to admire the beautiful old square. There is also a reasonably priced *menú del día*. Closed Mon.

OLD MADRID Taberna Bilbao *Tapas* €€

C/ Costanilla de San Andrés 8, 28005 ***Tel*** *913 65 61 25* ***Map*** *3 C3*

A hugely popular Basque tavern, Taberna Bilbao serves homemade specialities such as *bacalao* cooked in a range of styles. The *chipirones* (baby squid), prepared in their own ink, are excellent. Definitely worth trying is the typical Basque wine, *txakoli*, which is light, tart and very refreshing. Reservations are highly recomended. Closed Mon.

OLD MADRID Botín €€€

C/ de Cuchillos 17, 28011 ***Tel*** *913 66 42 17* ***Map*** *4 E3*

Dating back to 1725, Botín is reputedly the oldest restaurant in the world. With its brick-lined vaults and heavy wooden beams, it has changed little since. Even the original wood-burning oven is still used to cook the traditional roast lamb and suckling pig. There is a reasonable fixed-price lunch menu. Book well in advance.

OLD MADRID Café Varela Restaurante €€€

C/ Preciados 37, 28013 ***Tel*** *914 54 44 00* ***Map*** *4 E1*

Once the meeting point for great intellectuals in the early 20th century, Café Varela in the Hotel Preciados is now a modern, minimalist restaurant that is noteworthy for its Galician-rooted cuisine. Head there on Sundays to try *cocido madrileño* (meat and vegetable stew). Other options include Galician style hake or octopus with potatoes. Open daily.

OLD MADRID Casa Lucio *Tapas* €€€€

C/ Cava Baja 35, 28005 ***Tel*** *913 65 32 52* ***Map*** *4 D4*

Casa Lucio is a historic tavern serving Castilian specialities. The *huevos estrellados* (fried eggs with potatoes) are so exquisite that they have even made it into a celebrated Spanish poem. The typical *madrileño* tripe and rice pudding are equally renowned. The wine list has some fine wines from around Spain. Closed Sat lunch & Aug.

OLD MADRID Lhardy *Tapas* €€€€

Carrera de San Jerónimo 8, 28014 ***Tel*** *915 21 33 85* ***Map*** *4 F2*

Established in 1839 and preserving its character with chandeliers, mirrors and dark wood-panelled walls, this restaurant serves what is arguably the most classic *cocido madrileño*. Legend has it that Isabel II once entertained her lovers in the upstairs dining rooms. Downstairs is a celebrated cake shop, delicatessen and tapas area. Closed Sun evenings & Aug.

BOURBON MADRID El Txoko *Tapas* €

C/ Jovellanos 3, 28014 ***Tel*** *915 32 34 43* ***Map*** *7 B2*

There is no better place to try delicious Basque delicacies than the Eusko-Etxea (a Basque club). The restaurant is simple but appealing and offers a good fixed-price lunch menu and *menú de degustación*, which is so popular with locals that it can be hard to get in. Try the stuffed peppers and baby squid. No credit cards. Closed Sun evenings, Mon & Aug.

BOURBON MADRID La Fábrica *Tapas* €

C/ Jesús 2, 28014 ***Tel*** *913 69 06 71* ***Map*** *7 B3*

A down-to-earth tapas bar, which is always crammed with customers, La Fábrica has long counters groaning with an array of fresh tapas. The octopus, which sits steaming on the bar-top, is particularly good, as are the freshly made *montaditos* (crusty bread with delicious toppings). Try them with the Cabrales, pungent Asturian cheese. No credit cards.

BOURBON MADRID Terra Mundi *Tapas* €

C/ Lope de Vega 32, 28014 ***Tel*** *914 29 52 80* ***Map*** *7 B3*

A friendly restaurant with rustic decor, Terra Mundi serves specialities from Galicia. The *pulpo* is a favourite, along with homemade *empanadas* (pies filled with tuna, meat or vegetables). There's a good *menú del día* (lunch only, Mon–Fri) priced at a very reasonable €12. Closed Mon evenings.

BOURBON MADRID The Grill Club Café €

C/ San Marcos 24, 28004 ***Tel*** *915 22 77 13* ***Map*** *7 B1*

Situated in the lively gay district of Chueca, The Grill Club Café is a New York-style eatery with minimalist decor and moderate prices. Specialising in grilled steaks, the kitchen also churns out staples such as pasta, pizza and salads. The special muffin breakfast is recommended. They also have a weekday lunch menu. DJ music at night.

Key to Price Guide *see p608* **Key to Symbols** *see back cover flap*

BOURBON MADRID Arrocería Gala Tapas €€

C/ Moratín 22, 28014 ***Tel*** *914 29 25 62* **Map** *7 B3*

Admire the indoor patio and chandeliers and enjoy a generous set menu with Catalan specialities, such as paellas and other rice dishes, at an unbelievably reasonable price. Accompany them with one of the excellent range of Catalan wines or *cavas*. They also serve tapas, including snails and grilled prawns. No credit cards. Closed Mon.

BOURBON MADRID Café Gijón Tapas €€€

Paseo Recoletos 21, 28007 ***Tel*** *915 21 54 25* **Map** *7 C1*

A legendary café, established in 1888 and still decorated with original Art Nouveau style furnishings, Café Gijón is perfect for breakfast, a fixed-price lunch or afternoon tea with cakes. Specialities include hake with cider and seafood paella. There is an elegant terrace, frequented by the well-heeled. Live music.

BOURBON MADRID Casa Labra Tapas €€€

C/ Tetuán 12, 28013 ***Tel*** *915 32 14 05* **Map** *4 F2*

Open since 1860, Casa Labra is one of Madrid's most atmospheric tapas bars. Tucked away on a small street close to the Puerta del Sol, it retains the old wood panels and pretty tiles. Once a meeting place for the Spanish Socialist party, the restaurant has been in the same family since 1947 and is renowned for its *bacalao*. Closed 1 Jan.

BOURBON MADRID La Castafiore €€€

C/ Marqués de Monasterio 5, 28004 ***Tel*** *913 19 42 21* **Map** *5 C5*

A charming restaurant featuring singing waiters. All trained opera singers, they burst into magnificent arias from operas and Spanish operettas (*zarzuelas*) while serving fairly decent creative cuisine. The food may play second fiddle to the service, but it is a consistently enjoyable experience. Reservations recommended. Closed Sun.

BOURBON MADRID La Torcaz €€€

C/ Lagasca 81, 28006 ***Tel*** *915 75 41 30* **Map** *6 F2*

With its warm yellow walls and simple furniture, this friendly restaurant lets its traditional yet creative Basque cuisine shine. Try the sea urchins *au gratin* with quails' eggs or the seasonal game dishes. They also have a complete wine cellar and an expert sommelier on hand to help with wine choices. Closed Sun & Aug.

BOURBON MADRID Paradis €€€

C/ Marques de Cubas 14, 28014 ***Tel*** *914 29 73 03* **Map** *7 B2*

Part of a successful Catalan chain, Paradis offers high-quality Mediterranean cuisine. The grilled vegetables and the rice dishes make delicious starters, followed by any of the fresh fish available. The restaurant has two other branches in the Casa de Amèrica (Paseo Recoletos 2) and the Thyssen museum. Closed Sat lunch, Sun & bank holidays.

BOURBON MADRID Teatriz Tapas €€€

C/ Hermosilla 15, 28001 ***Tel*** *915 77 53 79* **Map** *6 D4*

Formerly a theatre, Teatriz was completely transformed by French designer Philippe Starck in 1989 and now houses a chic restaurant and a stylish tapas bar. In the restaurant, you can dine on fresh Mediterranean cuisine with Italian influences, while the tapas bar offers gourmet tapas. Prices reflect the glamorous setting. Closed Aug.

BOURBON MADRID Senzone €€€€

Plaza de la Independencia 3, 28001 ***Tel*** *914 32 29 11* **Map** *8 D1*

Modern decor combines seamlessly with the splendid interior courtyard at this restaurant in the Hospes Hotel. Specialities include semi-raw red prawn, golden young eel and *bacalao en costra* (crispy cod with spring onions, lentils and crispy pancetta). The wine service is excellent, with Riedel glasses and a highly skilled sommelier. Open daily.

BOURBON MADRID Viridiana €€€€

C/ Juan de Mena 14, 28014 ***Tel*** *915 23 44 78* **Map** *7 C2*

Innovative Spanish cuisine, complemented by an encyclopedic wine list, is offered in this restaurant decorated with stills from Luís Buñuel's film *Viridiana*. The creative menu changes frequently, and features elaborate creations prepared with the best seasonal produce. The wine list has been voted one of the best in the world. Closed Sun.

FURTHER AFIELD (EAST) La Taberna de la Daniela Tapas €€

C/ General Pardiñas 21, 28001 ***Tel*** *915 75 23 29*

In the heart of the smart Salamanca district, this authentic Castilian tavern is famous for its excellent *cocido* (the typical Madrid stew) at lunch and has a short menu of other traditional *madrileño* dishes, including *callos* (tripe) and lamb chops. Make your reservation a day in advance.

FURTHER AFIELD (EAST) Los Timbales Tapas €€€

C/ Alcalá 227, 28028 ***Tel*** *917 25 07 68*

Conveniently located near to the Las Ventas bullring, Los Timbales is the classic meeting place for bullfighting aficionados. Posters, photographs and bulls' heads deck the walls. Tuck into tapas, including good hams, or enjoy the substantial fixed-price lunch menu. The wine list features some excellent Riojas.

FURTHER AFIELD (EAST) Sula Tapas €€€€

C/ Jorge Juan 33, 28009 ***Tel*** *917 81 61 97*

This two Michelin star, minimalist-styled restaurant and tapas bar is not only home to excellent cuisine and an extraordinary wine list, but also serves *Joselito*, which is considered to be the best ham in the world. On offer are such dishes as shredded cod salad and foie gras with a cuba libre jelly. Smart casual attire, no jeans. Closed Aug.

FURTHER AFIELD (NORTH) Goizeko Kabi €€€

C/ Comandante Zorita 37, 28020 ***Tel*** *915 33 01 85*

At Goizeko Kabi, traditional Basque cuisine is served in a refined setting. Excellent fresh produce and seafood are the basis of the chef's creations, winning plaudits from gourmets across Europe. The spider crab is outstanding, and the *chipirones encebollados* (baby squid) remains a signature dish. There is an excellent wine list. Closed Sun evenings.

FURTHER AFIELD (NORTH) Jockey €€€€

C/ Amador de los Ríos 6, 28010 ***Tel*** *913 10 04 11* ***Map*** *6 D4*

Among Madrid's top five restaurants, frequented by gourmets and celebrities, Jockey offers a seasonal menu which specializes in top-of-the-range Castilian cuisine. There are excellent poultry and game dishes. The place has the air of a sophisticated gentleman's club, complete with equestrian paintings. Closed Sun, Aug & bank holidays.

FURTHER AFIELD (NORTH) Lágrimas Negras €€€€

Avda América 41, 28002 ***Tel*** *917 44 54 05*

Famous for its outstanding wine list, it is worth going out of the centre to dine at this excellent restaurant in the Hotel Silken Puerta América Madrid. Try the turbot with truffles, asparagus and oysters in soy sauce with lobster coral or the Norwegian lobster carpaccio. Smart casual attire required. Open daily, but for brunch only (1–4pm) Sun. Closed Aug.

FURTHER AFIELD (NORTH) Santceloni €€€€

Hotel Hesperia, Paseo de la Castellana 57, 28046 ***Tel*** *912 10 88 40* ***Map*** *6 D1*

Sister to the famous Santi Santamaría in Catalonia, Santceloni is one of the best places in Madrid to appreciate Spain's culinary revolution over the last few years. The menu is short, but exquisite: try the fabulous *menú gastronómico* which features their finest dishes. Outstanding wine list. Closed Sat lunch, Sun, Easter & Aug.

FURTHER AFIELD (NORTH) Zalacain €€€€

C/ Álvarez de Baena 4, 28006 ***Tel*** *915 61 48 40*

Considered Madrid's finest restaurant, Zalacaín has a splendidly formal setting, attentive service and superb Basque-oriented cuisine. The menu changes four times a year and features the finest seasonal produce. The *menú de degustación* features house specialities. Closed Sat lunch, Sun, Easter, Aug & bank holidays.

FURTHER AFIELD (NORTHEAST) The Garden 2112 €€€

C/ Arturo Soria 207, 28043 ***Tel*** *915 77 88 84*

Spain's first-ever Thai restaurant, Thai Gardens is beautifully decorated with wicker furniture, exquisite orchids and spectacular Thai artwork. The award-winning food has been toned down to suit Spanish palates, but the delicate authentic spices are deftly handled. It is a romantic spot, ideal for an intimate dinner.

FURTHER AFIELD (NORTHEAST) Diverxo €€€€

C/ Pensamiento 28, 28020 ***Tel*** *915 70 07 66*

After working in London and New York, chef David Muñoz has now opened one of the most creative restaurants in Madrid, offering Mediterranean-Chinese fusion food with a global twist. The decor is simple, but the food is certainly worth a visit. Two Michelin stars. Booking is a must. Closed Sun, Mon, Easter & three weeks in Aug.

FURTHER AFIELD (NORTHEAST) Sacha €€€€

C/ Juan Hurtado de Mendoza, 11 (entrance by the back garden), 28036 ***Tel*** *913 45 59 52*

Decorated like a cosy bistro, this charming and much-lauded restaurant serves sensational, creative cuisine including specialities such as partridge with rice and mushrooms and marinated oysters. Book early to get a table out on the terrace, shaded with pines and cypress trees. Excellent wines and unmissable desserts. Closed Sun & one week in Aug.

FURTHER AFIELD (WEST) Casa Ricardo *Tapas* €€

C/ Fernando el Católico 31, 28015 ***Tel*** *914 47 61 19* ***Map*** *2 D1*

Inaugurated in 1935, this delightful *madrileño* restaurant has changed little since. It is crammed with bullfighting memorabilia and is popular with an arty crowd as well as local politicians. Try typical dishes such as *callos a la Madrileña* (tripe in a spicy white wine sauce). Disabled access is limited to the downstairs salon. Closed Sun evenings.

MADRID PROVINCE

ALCALÁ DE HENARES Gran Mesón La Casa Vieja *Tapas* €

C/ San Felipe Neri 3, 28302 ***Tel*** *918 83 62 81*

A wonderful old inn in the heart of the historic town of Alcalá de Henares, La Casa Vieja has wooden-beamed dining areas spread over three floors, and a charming summer terrace out on the patio. Juicy grilled meats, *migas* (breadcrumbs fried with chunks of pork) and other hearty Castilian favourites are on the menu. Closed Sun evening & Mon.

ARANJUEZ Casa Pablo *Tapas* €€€

C/ Almíbar 42, 28300 ***Tel*** *918 91 14 51*

A centrally located tavern, Casa Pablo has been offering solid home cooking for more than 60 years. You can dine on typical dishes such as pheasant with grapes, taste the asparagus and strawberries for which Aranjuez is famous, or pile into the tapas area with everyone else for generous *raciones* (large portions) of Castilian favourites. Closed Aug.

Key to Price Guide *see p608* **Key to Symbols** *see back cover flap*

CHINCHÓN Mesón de la Virreina Tapas €€

Plaza Mayor 28, 28370 ***Tel*** *918 94 00 15*

Under the porticoes of Chinchón's celebrated Plaza Mayor, this classic *mesón* serves traditional fare such as *sopa castellana* (a garlic soup with chickpeas). Located in a handsome 16th-century building, it also has a terrace on the square, which has appeared in countless films. Wheelchair access is limited to the lower level. Closed Mon.

MORALZARZAL El Cenador de Salvador €€€€€

Av de España 30, 28411 ***Tel*** *918 57 77 22*

Many gourmets make the trek from Madrid to Moralzarzal just to dine in this lovely chalet. The exquisite seasonal cooking has won several prestigious international awards. Try the house speciality: hake in the style of grandmother Salvadora. A pianist entertains diners in summer. Booking recommended. Closed Sun evenings; Mon; Tue lunch.

NAVACERRADA La Fonda Real Tapas €€€

Ctra N-601 km 12.5, 28491 ***Tel*** *918 56 03 05*

This 18th-century country house was once a staging post on the royal route from Madrid to the palace at La Granja. With sturdy furnishings and a welcoming fireplace, it's the perfect setting for Castilian country cooking. The house speciality is roasted suckling pig. Reservations necessary at weekends.

PATONES DE ARRIBA El Poleo €€€

Travesía del Arroyo 2–3, 28189 ***Tel*** *918 43 21 01*

Set in a picturesque town with slate-roofed houses, El Poleo is a wonderful restaurant serving Navarrese-style dishes. Try the crab-stuffed crêpes with a wild mushroom sauce. The same owner runs El Jardín del Poleo on the same street, which is cheaper. Open Fri–Sun & Thu lunch. Closed 15 Jul–5 Aug & 21–25 Dec.

RASCAFRÍA Barondillo Tapas €€€

Cuesta del Chorro 4, 28740 ***Tel*** *918 69 18 19*

Brick walls, wooden beams, and hefty iron chandeliers decorate this country restaurant in a mountain town. The menu features whatever is in season, from wild mushrooms in spring to game in autumn. Homemade bread and desserts are also available. If you are too full to make it home, they also have rooms. Closed Tue & two weeks in Jun.

SAN LORENZO DE EL ESCORIAL Mesón La Cueva Tapas €€

C/ San Antón 4, 28200 ***Tel*** *918 90 15 16*

Juan de Villanueva, architect of the Prado, designed this 18th-century inn whose specialities include the *huevos a la cueva* (fried eggs and ham served in a nest of straw potatoes). A cool stone house, it is cosy in winter and cool in summer, when you can also tuck into tapas out on the terrace. A good range of local wines. Closed Mon.

SAN LORENZO DE EL ESCORIAL El Charolés €€€€€

C/ Floridablanca 24, 28200 ***Tel*** *918 90 59 75*

A well-established classic, this elegant restaurant has an exhaustive menu of quality Castilian specialities, excellent fish and seafood dishes and delicious warm salads. Good house wine is supplemented by an inspiring wine list. Book ahead at weekends, for a table outside in summer or on Wednesdays and Fridays for an authentic *cocido madrileño*.

CASTILLA Y LEÓN

AMPUDIA Restaurante El Arambol-Casa del Abad Tapas €€€€

Plaza Francisco Martín Gromaz 12, 34191 (Palencia) ***Tel*** *979 76 80 08*

Located in the wine press of the old residence of the Colegiata of San Miguel's Abbot, this spectacular setting offers decorative elements dating back to the 17th century. Exquisite cuisine from the Michelin-starred chef, Joaquín Koerper, is based on local vegetables, game, spring lamb, fresh fish and various rice dishes. Closed Sun (Sep–Mar) & Mon.

ARANDA DE DUERO Mesón de la Villa Tapas €€€

La Sal 3, 09400 (Burgos) ***Tel*** *947 50 10 25*

Mesón de la Villa is renowned throughout the province, and serves up typical Castilian cuisine. Among the favourites are the famous roasted baby lamb and the creative pork, lentil, bean and chickpea combinations. A great selection of wines is stocked in their underground cellar. Closed Sun evenings, Mon & 15–30 Oct.

ARÉVALO Asador Las Cubas €€

Figones 11, 05200 (Avila) ***Tel*** *920 30 01 25*

Complete with period furniture and fittings, Asador las Cubas is a popular carvery serving roast meats at reasonable prices. Veal is the star here. The dining room is tiny, so reservations are recommended. Closed evenings, last 15 days of Jun & 24 Dec–2 Jan.

ASTORGA La Peseta Tapas €€

Plaza de San Bartolomé 3, 24700 (León) ***Tel*** *987 61 72 75*

This 100-year-old restaurant is a classic in Astorga for its high-quality traditional cooking. Among its specialities are *maragato* stew (a heavy dish of nine different meats, chickpeas and vegetables), local beans with chorizo and conger. There is a decent wine list. Closed Sun evening, 15–31 Jan & 15–31 Oct.

ÁVILA El Almacén €€€€

Avda de Salamanca 6, 05002 ***Tel*** *920 25 44 55*

This restaurant, located in an old warehouse, is generally regarded as one of the best in all of Castilla, and is particularly noted for its wine cellar. It offers creative cooking with prime-quality local produce, all cooked to perfection. There are views of Ávila's famous wall from the dining room. Closed Sun evenings, Mon & Sep.

BENAVENTE El Ermitaño €€€€

Ctra de Benavente-León km 1.2, 49600 (Zamora) ***Tel*** *980 63 22 13*

This 18th-century house is a great family option with plenty of outdoor space. There are various rooms to explore as well as an attic for coffee. The menu is typical of the area's rural cooking with some hints of modernity in the salads and desserts, and there is a good *menú de degustación*. Closed Sun evenings, Mon & 24 Dec–15 Jan.

BURGOS Mesón del Cid €€€

Plaza Santa María 8, 09003 ***Tel*** *947 20 87 15*

In a 15th-century edifice located in front of the cathedral, this rustic place is named after Spain's most notorious conqueror. A favourite among locals, it is celebrated for its home-style cooking. The menu features traditional fare such as roast lamb, garlic soup and cod cooked with garlic. There is an excellent house wine. Closed Sun evenings.

CANEDO Prada a Tope-Palacio de Canedo *Tapas* €€

La Iglesia s/n, 24546 (León) ***Tel*** *987 56 33 66*

Prada a Tope is a popular restaurant located in a grand 17th-century palace. The food, however, is more down to earth. Some of the best dishes to try are *chorizo* with potatoes, *botillo* (vegetable stew), tuna or vegetables and preserves. The house wine is made on the premises. Closed Sunday evening.

COVARRUBIAS Casa Galín *Tapas* €

Plaza Doña Urraca 4, 09346 (Burgos) ***Tel*** *947 40 65 52*

This modest little eatery, in the medieval village of Covarrubias, is an ideal place to sample Castilian home-cooked fare such as organic chicken with peppers, thick and hearty bean-based soups and the ominous sounding *olla podrida*, a slow-cooked stew of pigs' ears and feet, black sausage and vegetables. Closed Sun evenings, Tue & 8 Dec–9 Jan.

EL BURGO DE OSMA Virrey Palafox *Tapas* €€€

Universidad 7, 42300 (Soria) ***Tel*** *975 34 02 22*

The most popular time to dine at Virrey Palafox is January to March, the months when suckling pig is in season. For wine buffs interested in trying the local wines from the Ribera del Duero region, this is the best place to start, with over 1,000 varieties to choose from. Reservations recommended. Closed Sun evenings, Mon & 22 Dec–10 Jan.

FRÓMISTA Hostería de los Palmeros *Tapas* €€€

Plaza San Telmo 4, 34440 (Palencia) ***Tel*** *979 81 00 67*

An excellent restaurant housed in an ancient building, which formerly served as a pilgrims' hospital and is now a rural hostal. Travellers can enjoy hearty cooking based on fresh products, such as *morcilla*, *chorizo* and peppers, in a lovely garden setting if weather permits. Closed Tue (except at Easter, in summer and at Christmas) and Jan.

LEÓN Vivaldi €€€€

Avda Reyes Leoneses 24, 24003 ***Tel*** *987 26 07 60*

On the first floor of MUSAC (the contemporary art museum), Vivaldi is one of the better-known restaurants in León. Original creations include fresh pasta with fungi and foie gras, sautéed vegetables with octopus and chickpeas with garlic prawns. There is a bar for pre-dinner drinks. Closed Sun evenings, Mon, Tue evenings, 7–20 Jan & 1–15 Jul.

MOLINASECA Casa Ramón *Tapas* €€€

Jardines Ángeles de Balboa 2, 24413 (León) ***Tel*** *987 45 31 53*

Casa Ramón is a popular rural restaurant in a beautiful village near Ponferrada, surrounded by a river which is also a popular swimming spot. The varied menu includes Cantabrian fish dishes, lentils *a la Marinera*, king prawns with clams and entrecôte with Bierzo peppers. Closed Mon & 20 Sep–10 Oct.

MORALES DEL TORO Chivo *Tapas* €€€

Av Comuneros s/n, 49810 (Zamora) ***Tel*** *980 69 82 62*

Located 8 km (5 miles) from the village of Toro on the vineyard belt, El Chivo is regularly frequented by workers in the area, who come here for the satisfying meat and fish creations, washed down with local wine. The focus is on Basque and Castilian-style cooking, and there is a good value fixed-price menu. Closed Sun evenings and 1–15 Nov.

NAVALENO El Maño *Tapas* €€

Calleja del Barrio 5, 42149 (Soria) ***Tel*** *975 37 41 68*

Set in an old, rambling country home, El Maño has a large and lively dining room. The daily menu features regional cooking based on local game, wild mushrooms and river fish, and truffles. The attentive staff will make you feel more than welcome. A popular and busy restaurant. Closed Mon evenings & 1–15 Sep.

NAVALONGUILLA El Remanso de Gredos €€

Iglesia s/n, 05668 ***Tel*** *920 34 38 98*

In the Sierra de Gredos park, guests staying at the hotel can sample the satisfying local bean dishes or fresh and succulent steaks from the region's famed livestock. Afterwards, take a stroll through the surrounding peaceful natural parkland (only for guests of the hotel).

Key to Price Guide *see p608* **Key to Symbols** *see back cover flap*

PALENCIA Casa Lucio
Tapas €€€

Don Sancho 2, 34001 ***Tel*** *979 74 81 90*

Traditional cooking is at its best in this classic restaurant in the centre of Palencia. At lunch time businessmen flock here for the meats roasted in a firewood oven. Fish is also on offer and specialities include chickpeas with crab and wild turbot *a la gallega*. Homemade desserts. Closed Sun & 1–15 Jul.

PEDRAZA DE LA SIERRA La Olma de Pedraza
€€€€

Plaza del Álamo 1, 40172 (Segovia) ***Tel*** *921 50 99 81*

If it is suckling pig you are after, head to this 16th-century mansion in a pretty square, although ordering it in advance is required. Fish dishes, such as baby squid, and peppers stuffed with hake, also feature. A pleasant covered terrace looks out onto the square for outdoor dining. Closed Tue, Sun–Thu evenings in winter & second week of Sep.

PONFERRADA Menta y Canela
€€€

Alonso Cano 10, 24400 (León) ***Tel*** *987 40 32 89*

This carvery offers succulent dishes from local livestock, with the best grilled meats in the province. The menu varies according to availability and prices. Other ingredients are celebrated in their "thematic weeks". In March, there's a special menu of rice dishes. Welcoming atmosphere and friendly staff. Closed Sun evenings & Mon.

SALAMANCA Momo
Tapas €€€

San Pablo 13, 37002 ***Tel*** *923 28 07 98*

Momo is a retro-modern eatery complete with furniture from the mid-20th century. Tapas are served downstairs, while on the first floor, you can indulge in beautifully prepared dishes such as the imaginative salads, *solomillo* with Arbequina olive oil, cod in garlic and chilli oil and cheesecake with wild berries. Closed Sun (Jul & Aug).

SALAMANCA El Río de la Plata
Tapas €€€€

Plaza del Peso 1, 37001 ***Tel*** *923 21 90 05*

Located in the heart of the old town, this traditional restaurant, run by the locally celebrated Andrés brothers, serves slow-cooked lamb, pork and veal stews and suckling pig. Lighter eaters may wish to stick to the excellent selection of tapas. Amongst the tasty desserts is apple baked in a secret sauce! Closed Mon, 15 days in Feb & 15–20 days in Jul.

SALAMANCA Víctor Gutiérrez
€€€€

San Pablo 66, 37008 ***Tel*** *923 26 29 73*

This romantic and cosy restaurant in Salamanca's old town, with views over the San Esteban church, offers creative and modern cooking using seasonal products. The restaurant is particularly noted for its perfectly cooked game, interesting vegetable dishes and excellent wine list. Closed Sun evenings, Mon lunch, 7–14 Jan & 1–15 Jul.

SANTA MARÍA DE MAVE Hostería el Convento
€€

Santa María de Mave, 34492 (Palencia) ***Tel*** *979 12 36 11*

Once a Benedictine convent in the Montaña Palentina Natural Park, this Romanesque jewel is the setting for a charming restaurant that combines traditional dishes with modern influences. Try their scrambled eggs with wild mushrooms and foie gras or game loin with oatmeal cream and wild fruits. Closed Sun evenings, Mon, Nov–Apr..

SEGOVIA Di Vino
Tapas €€€

C/ Valdeláguila 7, 40003 ***Tel*** *921 46 07 89*

This contemporary restaurant offers top-quality creative cuisine of unusual textures and combinations, including lots of fish and fresh vegetables. Friendly staff take you through the menu as complimentary nibbles are served. At the bar upstairs you can sip wine accompanied by delicious, inventive tapas. Exceptional wine list.

SEGOVIA Mesón de Cándido
Tapas €€€

Azoguejo 5, 40001 ***Tel*** *921 42 59 11*

One of the region's better-known restaurants, Mesón de Candido is located in a 15th-century home, close to the Roman aqueduct. The restaurant is famed for its roast suckling pig (so tender they carve it for you with the side of a plate) and hearty Castilian soups. A favourite amongst locals, it is always busy, so reservations are recommended.

SEPÚLVEDA Cristóbal
Tapas €€

Conde de Sepúlveda 9, 40300 (Segovia) ***Tel*** *921 54 01 00*

Located just near the information centre of the Hoces del Río Duratón National Park, Cristóbal is the best restaurant in the village. The extensive menu features regional dishes that can be savoured in the fittingly rustic setting of an underground cave. Closed Mon evenings, Tue, 1–15 Sep & 15–30 Dec.

SORIA Casa Augusto
€€€

Plaza Mayor 5, 42002 ***Tel*** *975 21 30 41*

This emblematic restaurant in the centre of Soria is tastefully decorated with period furniture and offers a fusion of traditional and original dishes. Specialities include spring lamb's breast, stuffed Piquillo peppers, and aubergines with wild mushrooms. The staff are more than happy to recommend an accompaniment from the list of local wines.

TORDESILLAS El Torreón
€€€€

C/ Dimas Rodríguez 4, 47100 (Valladolid) ***Tel*** *983 77 01 23*

This restaurant, founded in 1981, has a reputation for excellent meats grilled in an open kitchen. The highlights are the grilled ox steaks, deliciously succulent lamb chops, fresh duck liver, anchovies with leeks and cheese, and tasty, original salads. There is also an excellent selection of wines. Closed Sun & 10–22 Sep.

VALLADOLID Vinotinto *Tapas* €€

Campanas 4, 47001 ***Tel*** *983 34 22 91*

In a neighbourhood famous for its bars and bodegas, this modest eatery serves well-portioned tapas on the ground floor, while the cellar is reserved for slightly more formal sit-down dining. Satisfying dishes, such as steaks, spring lamb and duck breast, are used in simple, traditional recipes that are cooked to perfection. Closed 15–30 Aug.

VALLADOLID Trigo €€€

C/ Los Tintes 8, 47002 ***Tel*** *983 11 55 00*

Victor Martin, formerly the head chef of the prestigious Sant Celoni, is the owner and head chef of this acclaimed restaurant. Traditional ingredients are used to create dishes with *haute cuisine* influences but a lighter touch; for example artichokes in a cod sauce. Fixed-price lunch Mon–Fri. Closed Sun evenings & Tue.

VILLAFRANCA DEL BIERZO Casa Méndez €

C/ Espíritu Santo 1, 24500 (León) ***Tel*** *987 54 00 55*

This welcoming family-run restaurant is located 20 km (12.4 miles) from Ponferrada, a village on the famous Santiago Route. Among its homespun specialities are stuffed Bierzo peppers and trout. For dessert, try the delicious *tarta de Santiago*, a cake made of almond flour bearing the cross of St James, or Santiago. Closed Sun–Thu evenings.

ZAMORA Serafín *Tapas* €€

Plaza del Maestro Haedo 10, 49003 (Zamora) ***Tel*** *980 53 14 22*

Located in the centre of the city, Serafín has an exhaustive menu offering all that the regional cuisine is famous for. Especially good are the fish and rice dishes, and the eggs and chicken come straight from the restaurant's own farm. Tapas are also available and there is a lovely terrace for al fresco dining. Closed Thu.

CASTILLA-LA MANCHA

ALBACETE Nuestro Bar *Tapas* €€

C/ Alcalde Conangla 102, 02002 (Albacete) ***Tel*** *967 24 33 73*

Decorated with local handicrafts, this welcoming local restaurant has three dining areas serving regional dishes, one from each of the villages in the province. The *menú de degustación* includes specialities of La Mancha such as *gazpacho manchego* (a rich game stew thickened with biscuits). Closed Sun evenings & July.

ALCÁZAR DE SAN JUAN Casa Paco *Tapas* €

Av Álvarez Guerra 5, 13600 (Ciudad Real) ***Tel*** *926 54 06 06*

Casa Paco, a comfortable, traditional restaurant, has been going for more than 80 years. On the menu are delicious local dishes such as scrambled eggs with wild mushrooms and ham, lamb baked in a brick oven, and traditional regional desserts. There is a bargain lunch menu which can be enjoyed out on the terrace. Closed Mon & 15–30 Sep.

ALMAGRO El Corregidor *Tapas* €€€

C/ Jerónimo Ceballos 2, 13270 (Ciudad Real) ***Tel*** *926 86 06 48*

This delightful 18th-century house near Plaza Mayor, with many dining rooms and a central patio, is one of Castilla-La Mancha's prettiest restaurants. Menu features creative, regional cuisine, including the town's speciality, pickled aubergines. Try the Manchego menu or the more elaborate *menú de degustación*. Closed Mon (except Jul).

ALMANSA Mesón de Pincelín *Tapas* €€€

C/ Las Norias 10, 02640 (Albacete) ***Tel*** *967 34 00 07*

Mesón de Pincelín is considered by many to be one of the region's best restaurants, with traditional Castilian decor. Try authentic regional dishes prepared with a dash of creativity, including their famous *gazpacho manchego*. Homemade desserts are excellent and the wine list is very good. Closed Sun evenings, Mon, 7–14 Jan & three weeks in Aug.

ATIENZA Restaurante El Mirador €€

C/ Barruelo s/n, 19270 (Guadalajara) ***Tel*** *949 39 90 38*

This traditional restaurant specializes in *ollas* and *pucheros*, the hearty stews and casseroles which are typical of this mountainous region. Fresh seasonal vegetables and excellent local meats are prominently used in the cooking. The cosy dining room is decorated with antlers, brass knick-knacks and paintings. Closed Sun evenings & 23 Dec–7 Jan.

BELMONTE Palacio Buenavista Hospedería *Tapas* €€€

C/ José Antonio González 2, 16640 (Cuenca) ***Tel*** *967 18 75 80*

The elegant restaurant at this stylish and graceful hotel, in a beautifully restored 16th-century palace, has ochre walls and wooden beams. The subtle decor complements the refined regional cuisine, which includes oven-baked lamb and steaks and a wonderful array of Manchegan cheeses and country pâtés.

BRIHUEGA Asador El Tolmo *Tapas* €€

Av de la Constitución 26, 19400 (Guadalajara) ***Tel*** *949 28 11 30*

A restaurant-bar popular with locals, Asador El Tolmo is located in a pretty, walled Alcarrian village. The traditional Castilian decor is in keeping with the cuisine, which includes roast kid, beans with partridge and other regional favourites. There's a good fixed-price lunch menu and delicious homemade desserts.

CHINCHILLA DE MONTEARAGÓN Montearagón Tapas €

C/ Arenal 35 (7 km from Albacete), 02520 (Albacete) **Tel** *967 26 05 97*

In a historic town, praised for its loyalty by the Catholic Monarchs and dominated by a ruined castle, this is a very popular local café-bar. An easy jaunt from Alabacete, it is an ideal stopover for lunch. Serves a wide range of tapas along with some sturdy local dishes and a cheap and filling fixed lunch menu. Closed Tue & 15–31 Aug.

CIUDAD REAL Gran Mesón €€€

Ronda de Ciruela 34, 13004 (Ciudad Real) **Tel** *926 22 72 39*

Friendly, charming and recommended by locals, Gran Mesón offers an ample set menu with regional specialities such as *gachas* (gruel), *pisto* (a kind of ratatouille), suckling pig and local cheese and wines. The seasonal meat and game are roasted over charcoal and the wine list has more than 200 hundred varieties. Closed Sun evenings.

CUENCA La Ponderosa Tapas €€

C/ San Francisco 20, 16004 **Tel** *969 21 32 14*

A traditional tapas bar with standing room only inside, but with outside tables too. Good beer and wine by the glass. The house speciality is *perdiz en escabeche* (partridge in a paprika sauce), and there's a good selection of other regional tapas. The service is typically efficient. No credit cards. Closed Sun.

CUENCA Casa Marlo €€€

C/ Colón 41, 16002 **Tel** *969 21 11 73*

Fish and shellfish feature predominantly on Marlo's modern menu, created by adventurous young chef, Maripaz Martínez. Recommended dishes include confit of lamb with wild mushroom sauce, or the stuffed partridge in season. Service is impeccable and there is an interesting choice of reasonably priced wines as well. Closed Sun evenings.

CUENCA Mesón Casas Colgadas Tapas €€€

C/ Canónigos s/n, 16001 **Tel** *969 22 35 09*

Dine in one of Cuenca's famous hanging houses, an upside-down medieval skyscraper that clings to the gorge. There are unbeatable views to go with great regional cuisine. There is a tapas bar downstairs, and a dining room up a narrow medieval staircase. Staff are utterly delightful. Closed Mon evenings & Tue.

DAIMIEL Mesón El Bodegón Tapas €€€

C/ Luchana 20, 13250 (Ciudad Real) **Tel** *926 85 26 52*

An atmospheric 18th-century cellar and olive oil press is the setting for this charming restaurant, on the fringes of the lakes of Daimiel, a natural park. Dine on typical Manchego cuisine, accompanied by a spectacular wine list. Flamenco performances take place on some Friday nights. Check in advance for more details. Closed Sun–Thu evenings.

GUADALAJARA Diego's €€

C/ Sigüenza 16, 19003 (Guadalajara) **Tel** *949 25 36 34*

In a warm and elegant environment, this restaurant offers creative Castilian food based on old Alcarria recipes fused with flavours and textures from other parts of the world. Try the swordfish lasagna with scallops, prawns and three cheeses, or the Iberian sirloin steak with wild mushrooms and foie gras. Closed Sun, Tue & Wed evenings, Mon & Aug.

GUADALAJARA Amparito Roca €€€€

C/ Toledo 19, 19002 (Guadalajara) **Tel** *949 21 46 39*

The chefs of Amparito Roca, the finest restaurant in the region, reinvent classic Spanish recipes with flair. Traditional Castilian suckling pig is served boned and caramelized. Other highlights are veal stew with white truffle. The desserts are outstanding and the service impeccable. Closed Sun, Easter & 15–30 Aug.

ILLESCAS El Bohío €€€€

Av Castilla La Mancha 81, 45200 (Toledo) **Tel** *925 51 11 26*

Two brothers have taken over this once-traditional restaurant, and transformed it into a place of pilgrimage for local gastronomes. Sophisticated and creative versions of Manchegan recipes include pigeon with wild rice. The magnificent *menú de degustación* is a real treat. Closed Sun, Mon evenings & Aug.

JADRAQUE El Castillo Tapas €€

Ctra de Soria km 46, 19240 (Guadalajara) **Tel** *949 89 02 54*

After visiting the 10th-century castle, stop here for classic Castilian dishes prepared in this typical *mesón*. The traditional, delightfully old-fashioned decor matches the menu, which features dishes such as kid roasted in a brick oven (the house speciality). Finish up with homemade desserts. Closed Wed & 22 Dec–2 Jan.

LAS PEDROÑERAS Las Rejas €€€€

C/ General Borrero, 16660 (Cuenca) **Tel** *967 16 10 89*

This chic restaurant has won countless international gourmet awards. Manuel de la Osa's superb, highly creative cuisine is prepared with the finest and freshest local produce. Do not miss the fresh Manchego cheese salad. A *menú de degustación* is available. Closed Mon, Tue–Fri evenings & 15–30 Jun.

MANZANARES Mesón Sancho Tapas €

C/ Jesús del Perdón 26, 13200 (Ciudad Real) **Tel** *926 61 10 16*

This simple, down-to-earth restaurant serves typical robust dishes such as garlic soup, *duelos y quebrantos* (scrambled eggs with pork) and rabbit *a la Manchega* (in a sauce), washed down with local wine. There is a good-value *menú del día*. Also offers accommodation.

OROPESA La Hostería *Tapas* €

Paseo Escolar 5, 45560 (Toledo) ***Tel*** *925 43 08 75*

A charming stone-built inn nudged up against the castle walls, La Hostería is a typical, traditional restaurant. Try the *revuelto de morcilla* (scrambled eggs flavoured with pungent blood sausage) or the *bacalao a la plancha* (grilled cod). Choose from a good range of local and national wines, and finish up with a homemade dessert. Closed 24–25 Dec.

PUERTO LÁPICE Venta del Quijote *Tapas* €€€€

C/ El Molino 4, 13650 (Ciudad Real) ***Tel*** *926 57 61 10*

Set in the heart of Don Quixote country, this legendary inn evokes Cervantes' masterpiece, and the episode is recreated in a colourful tile. Sit around the pebbled courtyard and enjoy any of the Manchegan specialities, or try some of the tasty tapas and a glass of the robust local wine.

SIGÜENZA El Motor €€€

Av Juan Carlos I 2, 19250 (Guadalajara) ***Tel*** *949 39 08 27*

A hostal-restaurant in a classic, stone-built house, El Motor specializes in elegant versions of regional dishes including roast suckling pig and lamb, *migas* (breadcrumbs fried with pork) or *sopa castellana* (garlic soup). The menu also features seafood, prepared to traditional Basque recipes. Closed Sun evening, Mon & two weeks in Mar.

TALAVERA DE LA REINA Antonio *Tapas* €

Av de Portugal 8, 45600 (Toledo) ***Tel*** *925 80 40 17*

A simple hostal with a popular local bar, Antonio serves good-quality tapas at reasonable prices. It is well-known for its chickpeas and vegetable stews. A separate dining room offers typical regional fare. Fill up on the hearty lunchtime *menú del día*, after exploring the old-fashioned, ceramic-producing town. Closed Sun evenings & 1–15 Jul.

TOLEDO Adolfo €€€

C/ de la Granada 6 and at C/ Hombre de Palo 7, 45001 (Toledo) ***Tel*** *925 22 73 21*

Set in the heart of Toledo's old quarter, the Adolfo, with its tiles, columns, antiques and a wonderful 15th-century coffered Mudehar ceiling, serves game in winter and fresh trout from the Río Tajo. The wine list is exceptional. There is a fine *menú de degustación*. Closed Sun evenings, Mon & 15–30 Jul.

TOLEDO Hostal del Cardenal €€€

Paseo de Recadero 24, 45004 (Toledo) ***Tel*** *925 22 08 62*

Once the summer residence of Cardinal Lorenzana, this 18th-century palace retains its beautiful Arabic-style gardens, enclosed by the city walls. It serves suckling pig, traditionally roasted in a brick oven, along with game in season. Desserts always feature the famous Toledo *mazapán*. Diners staying at the hotel save 10 per cent on their bill.

TOLEDO Locum €€€

C/ Locum 6, 45001 (Toledo) ***Tel*** *925 22 32 35*

An elegant fusion of old and new, both in the cuisine and decor, this relative newcomer to Toledo's culinary scene is located in a beautifully restored 17th-century mansion. Classic Castilian recipes, such as roast suckling pig, are superbly reinvented. The desserts are splendid: try the pear tart with hazelnut caramel. Closed Mon evenings, Tue & Aug.

VALDEPEÑAS Venta la Quintería *Tapas* €€€

A4 Madrid-Cádiz km 197, 13300 (Ciudad Real) ***Tel*** *926 33 82 93*

Set in a pretty garden and cobbled courtyard, this old country inn has a rustic decor. The menu offers tasty specialities from the La Mancha region, including hearty stews, and homemade desserts such as pears poached in local wine. Located in the heart of wine country, it has a great wine list. Closed evenings & Tue.

EXTREMADURA

ALMENDRALEJO Nando's *Tapas* €€

C/ Ricardo Romero de Tejada 14, 06200 (Badajoz) ***Tel*** *924 66 12 71*

A comfortable country inn, with wooden beams and a rustic interior, Nando serves generous portions of rice with rabbit – the house speciality, *judiones* (locally-grown beans prepared with pig's knuckle or partridge) and fresh fish. There is also a good tapas bar for trying local dishes.

BADAJOZ Aldebarán €€€€

Av de Elvas, Urbanización Guadiana, 06006 (Badajoz) ***Tel*** *924 27 42 61*

Deep red walls, crisp white linen, chandeliers and antiques adorn the dining rooms of this formal, elegant restaurant. The menu offers superb contemporary Spanish and Extremaduran cuisine. The *menú de degustación* features highlights from the chef's repertoire. An impressive wine and cigar list. Closed Sun, Mon evenings & two weeks in Aug.

CÁCERES El Pato *Tapas* €

Plaza Mayor 12, 10003 (Cáceres) ***Tel*** *927 21 15 48*

An atmospheric, classic inn right on the main square with all kinds of tasty local tapas, including *migas* and unusual partridge croquettes at the bar. Relish the home-cooked Extremaduran specialities in the old-fashioned dining room with whitewashed, brick-lined walls or on the terrace with a magnificent view of the town.

Key to Price Guide *see p608* **Key to Symbols** *see back cover flap*

CÁCERES El Figón de Eustaquio €€

Plaza de San Juan 14, 10003 (Cáceres) ***Tel*** *927 24 43 62*

In the heart of Cáceres' beautiful old centre, this long-standing and resolutely old-fashioned restaurant has been preparing genuine Extremaduran food since 1947. Try traditional dishes like trout *a la extremeña* (stuffed with ham) and the house speciality, *sopa 'el Figón* (tomato soup with poached egg). Closed two weeks in Jul.

CÁCERES Atrio €€€€

Plaza San Mateo 1, 10002 (Cáceres) ***Tel*** *927 24 29 28*

One of the finest restaurants in Spain, with countless international gourmet awards including two Michelin stars, Atrio serves innovative, contemporary cuisine. Try tender kid with rosemary or the monkfish. Stylish decor and perfect service make this restaurant a memorable gourmet experience.

GUADALUPE Hospedería del Real Monasterio €

Plaza de Juan Carlos I, 10140 (Cáceres) ***Tel*** *927 36 70 00*

Owned by the Franciscan order, this restaurant (linked to a simple *hospedería*) offers simple regional cooking in the unforgettable surroundings of a magnificent monastery. The tomato soup, the roast kid, the *migas extremeñas* and the fixed-price menu are all recommended. There is also a simple café-bar. Closed 15 Jan–15 Feb.

GUADALUPE Posada del Rincón *Tapas* €€

Plaza Santa María de Guadalupe 11, 10140 (Cáceres) ***Tel*** *927 36 71 14*

In a charming rural hotel, Posada del Rincón is a delightful restaurant and café-bar. Inside, there are brick-lined walls, wooden beams and wrought-iron furniture out on the plant-filled patio. Fine regional cuisine, prepared with the freshest seasonal produce, has touches of creativity. Try the roasted suckling kid. Good fixed-price menu. Closed Tue.

JARANDILLA DE LA VERA Puta Parió II *Tapas* €€

C/ Pizarro 8, 10450 (Cáceres) ***Tel*** *927 56 03 92*

This old stone house was once home to Don Luis de Quijada, major domo to Emperor Charles V (Carlos I). It is now a lively and popular tavern with good regional dishes, including tomato soup and lamb casserole, and locally produced house wine. There is a good value fixed-price lunch menu. Closed Mon & second half of Sep.

JEREZ DE LOS CABALLEROS La Ermita *Tapas* €€

C/ Doctor Benítez 9, 06380 (Badajoz) ***Tel*** *924 73 14 76*

Housed in a 17th-century chapel converted into a wine cellar, La Ermita serves authentic local dishes. Sample the partridge stew or the typical *revuelto de espárragos*, made with scrambled eggs and asparagus tips. They also have fabulous tapas, including the delectable Iberian hams, made from pigs raised on acorns. Closed Wed evenings.

LOSAR DE LA VERA Carlos V *Tapas* €€

Av de Extremadura 45, 10460 (Cáceres) ***Tel*** *927 57 06 36*

Local home cooking and lovely views of the Sierra de Gredos mountains are the fare at this charming rural inn, which is decorated with antlers and hunting trophies. Specialities include scrambled eggs with white truffles, roast kid and steaks. There is a good-value lunch menu. Finish up with *helado frito* (fried ice cream). Closed Mon & 15–30 Oct.

MÉRIDA Nicolás *Tapas* €€€

C/ Félix Valverde Lillo 13, 06800 (Badajoz) ***Tel*** *924 31 96 10*

Nicolás is a long-standing restaurant in a handsome historic mansion in the heart of Mérida. You might want to visit the brick wine cellar for an apéritif before tucking into the regional specialities such as the delicious lamb with plums or the pork sirloin with pepper. There is also a pretty garden terrace. Closed Sun evenings & two weeks in Jul.

MÉRIDA Rufino *Tapas* €€€

Plaza Santa Clara 2, 06800 (Badajoz) ***Tel*** *924 31 20 01*

With a terrace out on a delightful pedestrianized square, this much-loved local institution is the perfect place to start the *tapeo* (a pub crawl from tapas bar to tapas bar). Try the delicious local hams. It also serves typical Extremaduran cuisine, including *revuelto con criadillas de tierra* (scrambled eggs with mushrooms). Closed Sun & 15–30 Sep.

MÉRIDA Altair €€€€

Av José Fernández López s/n, 06800 (Badajoz) ***Tel*** *924 30 45 12*

Sleekly mimimalist in design, this fashionable, glassy restaurant overlooks Santiago Calatrava's gleaming modern bridge, also echoed in the crisp white furnishings. Altair is linked to the spectacular Atrio in Cáceres, and offers fine contemporary cuisine, best appreciated in the good-value *menú de degustación*. Closed Sun & first week Sep.

OLIVENZA Casa Maila *Tapas* €€

C/ Colón 3, 06100 (Badajoz) ***Tel*** *924 49 15 05*

Elegant, yet informal, Casa Maila is a charming restaurant in the attractive border town of Olivenza. The light and creative cuisine uses fresh local produce: try the Gazpacho with Iberian ham or *bacalao* (cod) with peppers and olives. Desserts are homemade and include rice pudding flavoured with cinnamon and mandarin sorbet.

PLASENCIA Puerta Talavera *Tapas* €€

C/ Talavera 30, 10600 (Cáceres) ***Tel*** *927 42 42 69*

A stylish, modern restaurant with a wide-ranging menu and several fixed-price options to suit all pockets. The cuisine is based on fresh local ingredients, and includes delicacies, such as local veal, lamb and game, as well as a range of tapas at the informal bar. The wine list has plenty of regional wines to choose from. Live music Fri evening. Closed Mon & Jul.

PLASENCIA Alfonso VIII
Tapas €€€

Avenida Alfonso VIII 32–34, 10600 (Cáceres) ***Tel*** *927 41 02 50*

This smart hotel-restaurant offers creative cuisine that relies heavily on local produce and updated traditional recipes. Try the kid stew, or the cod with courgette (zucchini) ratatouille and finish up with a delicious flan made with pine nuts and chestnuts. A relaxed tapas bar serves wonderful Iberian hams. Closed Mon, Fri & Sat (bar open daily).

PUEBLA DE LA REINA Mesón La Jara-Casa Andrés
€€

Calle Luis Chamizo 14, 06228 (Badajoz) ***Tel*** *924 36 00 05*

This charming *mesón* has become a sanctuary of authentic regional food, often prepared using ancient recipes. The classic dish here is rabbit in "La Jara" sauce – flavoured with onion, garlic, bay leaf and wine, though the partridge is also good. There is a cheap lunch menu and a more complete *menú de degustación*. Closed 15–30 Sep.

TRUJILLO Mesón La Troya
Tapas €

Plaza Mayor 10, 10200 (Cáceres) ***Tel*** *927 32 13 64*

A typical 16th-century *mesón*, on the main square of the magnificent Renaissance town, La Troya serves regional food in hearty portions in a pair of old-fashioned dining rooms with lacy curtains and ceramics. The *migas* with pork are recommended. The tapas bar, with photographs lining the wall, is worth visiting.

TRUJILLO Pizarro
€€

Plaza Mayor 13, 10200 (Cáceres) ***Tel*** *927 32 02 55*

On Trujillo's beautiful central square, this restaurant has retained much of its decor since it opened before the Civil War. Enjoy traditional dishes such as tomato soup with figs and grapes; chicken stuffed with truffles; and potatoes cooked in Extremaduran style. Family run, it is friendly and welcoming. Closed Tue, two weeks in Feb & Jun.

TRUJILLO Corral del Rey
€€€

Plaza Mayor 2, 10200 (Cáceres) ***Tel*** *927 32 17 80*

One of the best in the city, Corral del Rey is a classic *asador* specializing in roasted meat and fish. Traditional decor consists of brick walls and wooden beams. Recommended delicacies include wild sea bass baked in salt and beef seared on the grill. They also have a cigar list and a good liqueur menu. Closed Wed evenings, Sun & 1–10 Jul.

ZAFRA Josefina
€€

Av López Asme 1, 06300 (Badajoz) ***Tel*** *924 55 17 01*

A warm welcome awaits in this delightful family-run restaurant, which serves typical Extremeño cuisine with a dash of creativity. Try the mushroom and prawn ravioli or the green bean salad with foie gras. A good-value lunch menu on weekdays. Closed Sun evenings & Mon.

ZAFRA La Rebotica
€€€

C/ Boticas 12, 06300 (Badajoz) ***Tel*** *924 55 42 89*

In the heart of lovely, whitewashed Zafra, chic little La Rebotica has a series of intimate dining areas linked by arches. The deftly prepared local dishes include a wonderful partridge soup, and codfish served with baby squid. Fabulous homemade desserts include a refreshing orange and fig ice cream. Closed Sun evenings, Mon & 1–15 Aug.

SEVILLE

ALAMEDA Torre de los Perdigones
€€

C/ Resolana s/n, 41009 ***Tel*** *954 90 93 53* ***Map*** *2 D3*

The perfect place to enjoy a range of Sevillian cuisine. Located at the foot of a historic tower and surrounded by a park, the restaurant offers a tranquil setting to recharge after seeing the sights. Start with mussels steamed in beer followed by Iberian pork cheeks in wine, served with potatoes and apple compote. Closed dinner (Oct–May).

EL ARENAL Almiranta Tapas Restaurant
Tapas €

C/ Almirantazgo 2, 41001 ***Tel*** *954 32 80 40* ***Map*** *3 C2 (5 C5)*

Conveniently located across from the cathedral and Archivo de Indias, Almiranta serves up modern interpretations of regional classics. Unique vegetarian dishes are available, such as *pan con verdura asada gratinada con mozzarella* (roasted vegetables on bread with a mozzarella gratin). Reservations recommended.

EL ARENAL As-Sawirah
€

C/ Galera 5, 41001 ***Tel*** *954 56 22 68* ***Map*** *3 B1 (5 B3)*

Rustic Moroccan decor and traditional Moroccan cuisine are combined in this restaurant near the Mercado de El Arenal. Dishes include kebabs, lamb couscous, tagines and *pastelas* (meat pastries). Try the *menú de degustación* for a weekday lunch. Closed Sun evening, Mon & Aug.

EL ARENAL El Aguador de Velázquez
Tapas €

Calle Albareda, 14, 41001 ***Tel*** *954 22 47 20* ***Map*** *5 C3*

Tucked away in a little street behind Plaza Nueva, here you can try innovative interpretations of Andalusian cuisine, including *pastel de cabrales con mermelada de higos* (strong cheese pie with fig jam) and *bolitas de cebolla picante con salsa de yogur al curry* (spicy onion balls with curried yogurt sauce). Impressive presentation for a minimal price.

EL ARENAL El Cabildo €€

Plaza del Cabildo, 41001 ***Tel*** *954 22 79 70* ***Map*** *3 C2 (5 C4)*

Part of the ancient Arabic walls have been conserved in this classic and delightfully old-fashioned restaurant. All the traditional Andalusian favourites are on the menu, excellently cooked with fresh local ingredients. Try a platter of fresh fried fish, Sevillian *revueltos* (scrambled eggs with different ingredients) accompanied by sturdy wine.

EL ARENAL Infanta Sevilla *Tapas* €€

C/ Arfe 36, 41001 ***Tel*** *954 22 96 89* ***Map*** *3 B2 (5 C4)*

Set in a restored historic building in the heart of the lively Arenal district, Mesón de la Infanta offers an excellent choice of traditional dishes, including delicious *guisos*. The tapas bar is a classic on the Sevillano tapas route, with a bewildering array of fine local hams and *embutidos* (charcuterie) and the usual favourites. Closed Mon.

SANTA CRUZ El Rincón de Anita *Tapas* €

Plaza del Cristo de Burgos 23, 41004 ***Tel*** *954 21 74 61* ***Map*** *6 E2*

This delightful little restaurant is decorated with colourful tiles, polished wood, images of the Semana Santa processions, and lots of plants. This is the perfect place to tuck into tasty Andalusian specialities. Try the *cola de toro* (bull's tail), kidneys cooked in sherry, and homemade desserts. Classic tapas can be enjoyed at the bar.

SANTA CRUZ Huelva Ocho €

C/ Huelva 8, 41004 ***Tel*** *954 04 23 91* ***Map*** *3 C1 (6 D3)*

At this casual, friendly restaurant the menu is as varied as the clientele and the music. Try the spinach and bacon crêpe or the chicken, raisin and almond tart. There are professional flamenco performances at 9:30pm on Wed and Sat evenings, salsa dancing classes at 10:30pm on Thu and Fri, and amateur flamenco dancers on other evenings.

SANTA CRUZ Albarama Restaurante €€

Plaza de San Francisco 5, 41004 ***Tel*** *954 22 97 84* ***Map*** *3 C1 (5 C3)*

Facing Plaza de San Francisco, stylish but casual gastrobar Albarama has a commanding spot in the square. Modern decor sets the mood for innovative Mediterranean dishes such as the *hamburguesa de atun con tartar de aguacate* (tuna burgers with avocado tartare). Closed Sun evenings.

SANTA CRUZ Corral del Agua €€

Callejón del Agua 6, 41004 ***Tel*** *954 22 48 41* ***Map*** *3 C2 (5 D/E5)*

Dine on the cool patio in a lee of the Real Alcázar gardens, with plants trailing romantically around wrought-iron grilles and a marble fountain burbling quietly. Antique furniture and paintings adorn the dining room, and the menu emphasizes seasonal specialities, traditionally prepared. Closed Sun.

SANTA CRUZ Vineria San Telmo *Tapas* €€

Plaza Catalina de Ribera 4, 41004 ***Tel*** *954 41 06 00* ***Map*** *6 E4*

This lovely vinoteca oozes charm from every corner with bistro-style decor and dramatic trompe l'oeils. The extensive wine list and menu don't disappoint. Start with one of the fascinating salads, then try the *magret de pato con puré de calabaza* (duck with pumpkin purée) and finish with one of their scrumptious desserts.

SANTA CRUZ Becerrita *Tapas* €€€

C/ Recaredo 9, 41003 ***Tel*** *954 41 20 57* ***Map*** *2 E5 (6 F3)*

Becerrita is a beautiful restaurant, warmly decorated in modern Andalusian style. Delicious Andaluz specialities include outstanding croquettes made with bull's tail, or kid flavoured with thyme. At the bar, you can choose from a superb range of tapas that changes daily, depending on the season. Closed Sun evenings & Aug.

SANTA CRUZ Casa Robles €€€

C/ Álvarez Quintero 58, 41004 ***Tel*** *954 21 31 50* ***Map*** *3 C1 (6 D4)*

Right in the heart of Seville, close to the cathedral, this elegant restaurant is decorated with oil paintings, statuary and pretty tiles. Although the menu leans towards seafood, there are also plenty of local meat dishes to choose from, all exquisitely presented. The desserts, in particular, are miniature works of art.

SANTA CRUZ La Albahaca €€€

Plaza de Santa Cruz 12, 41004 ***Tel*** *954 22 07 14* ***Map*** *4 D2 (6 E4)*

Overlooking a charming, verdant square dominated by a wrought-iron cross, La Albahaca is one of the most authentic restaurants in the Barrio Santa Cruz. Its fine setting in a 1920s mansion furnished with 17th-century antiques, makes it a perfect place to enjoy Basque-influenced food, along with excellent local dishes. Closed Sun.

FURTHER AFIELD (SOUTH) Egaña Oriza €€€€

C/ San Fernando 41, 41004 ***Tel*** *954 22 72 54* ***Map*** *3 C2 (6 D5)*

Tucked against the walls of the Alcázar gardens, Egaña Oriza is located in a beautiful early 20th-century mansion. The dining room is in an elegant light-filled conservatory, and the sophisticated modern Basque cuisine leans heavily towards fish. Meat dishes and desserts are equally delicious. The wine list is superb. Closed Sun.

FURTHER AFIELD (WEST) El Faro de Triana *Tapas* €

Puente de Isabel II, C/ Betis (Triana), 41010 ***Tel*** *954 33 61 92* ***Map*** *3 A2 (5 A4)*

A long-standing institution on the banks of the Guadalquivir, with sublime views of the old city from the terrace. This old-fashioned ochre building, tucked into the side of the emblematic Triana bridge, is a historic *freiduría*, where heaped platters of fried fish have been the classic dish for more than 70 years.

FURTHER AFIELD (WEST) Sol y Sombra *Tapas* €€

C/ Castilla 149 (Triana), 41010 ***Tel*** *954 33 39 35* ***Map*** *3 A1*

A sea of hams suspended from the ceiling and peeling bullfighting posters adorn the walls of this historic tavern. Though tucked away in Triana, the restaurant is well worth seeking out for the authentic Sevillano ambience. Visit the tapas bar for freshly prepared large portions of tapas, or dine more substantially at the adjoining restaurant.

FURTHER AFIELD (WEST) Abades Triana €€€€

C/ Betis 69 (Triana), 41010 ***Tel*** *954 28 64 59* ***Map*** *3 B3*

This modern restaurant has a commanding location on the river. Chef Willy Moya's Andalusian cuisine with imaginative twists is sure to delight the palate. Try the award-winning *combi de aguja de pato y su pechuga con texturas de zanahorias y aceite de hierba buena* (duck back and breast with carrots and mint oil). Open daily.

ANDALUSIA

ALJARAQUE La Plazuela Restaurante €

C/ de la Fuente 40, 21110 (Huelva) ***Tel*** *959 31 88 31*

A great place to sample fresh fish and seafood from the Atlantic coast, La Plazuela also offers excellent meat choices and a wide variety of homemade breads. Specialities include asparagus with spinach and prawns. Leave room for a rich dessert from a list recited as a poem by the *maître d'hôtel*. Booking advisable in summer. Closed Sun.

ALMERÍA Rincón de Juan Pedro *Tapas* €

C/ Federico Castro 2, 04130 (Almería) ***Tel*** *950 23 58 19*

A much-loved stalwart on Almería's busy tapas scene, this Andalusian bar serves a wonderful range of tapas – still included in the price of a drink. You can dine more substantially on *raciones*, as well as meat and seafood specialities, and local dishes, such as *trigo a la cortijera* (a stew with wheat berries, meat and sausage). Closed Sun.

ALMERÍA Club de Mar €€

Playa de la Almadra Villas 1, 04007 (Almería) ***Tel*** *950 23 50 48*

Enjoy fresh fish and shellfish right on the seafront at the Almerían yacht club, where well-heeled locals and sailors mingle on the breezy terrace. The fresh seafood complements the views over the port, and the *bullabesa* (Spanish bouillabaisse) and *fritura* (mixed fried fish) are specialities. Also offers a good-value lunch menu.

ALMERÍA Bodega Bellavista €€€

Urbanización Bellavista, Llanos del Alquián, 04130 (Almería) ***Tel*** *950 29 71 56*

In an unlikely location in a housing complex near the airport, this charmingly old-fashioned restaurant offers a range of classic and innovative Andalusian dishes prepared with top-quality local products. Fish and shellfish predominate, but you can also try good beef and kid. A huge range of wines from all around Spain. Closed Sun evenings & Mon.

ANTEQUERA Restaurante Plaza de Toros La Espuela *Tapas* €€

C/ San Agustín 1, 29200 (Málaga) ***Tel*** *952 70 30 31*

Uniquely situated in a bullring, this restaurant prepares Andalusian dishes including the town speciality, *porra* (a thick gazpacho). With its brightly coloured tiles, brick walls and perpetually busy tapas bar, it offers a taste of authentic Andalusia. It is enormously popular with tourists and locals alike, so be sure to book ahead. Closed Mon.

ARCOS DE LA FRONTERA Parador Restaurant €€

Plaza Cabildo s/n, 11630 (Cádiz) ***Tel*** *956 70 05 00*

Spain's parador hotels are known for their high standards, and this traditional, elegant example located in the historic centre of Cádiz is no exception. The restaurant has been beautifully decorated and has an excellent menu. Try the *corvina a la roteña* (Rota-style fish) or the tasters' menu, which features 12 tantalising dishes.

BAEZA El Sarmiento Restaurante €€

Plaza del Arcediano 10, 23440 (Jaén) ***Tel*** *953 74 03 23*

Tucked away between the cathedral and the old city wall, this charming restaurant with a wooden beamed ceiling and terracotta floor offers abundant dishes with fresh vegetables and a good variety of meats. Try the *pincho de lachazo a la brasa* (grilled skewers of suckling lamb) or the *alcachofas fritas* (fried artichokes). Closed Mon.

BAEZA Juanito €€€

Paseo Arca del Agua s/n, 23440 (Jaén) ***Tel*** *953 74 00 40*

A comfortable family-run hotel and restaurant in the heart of the olive belt. The good home cooking is based on traditional regional recipes which feature plenty of olive oil. Try the artichokes or the *choto frito* (fried kid). The homemade desserts are scrumptious. Closed Sun evenings, Mon & first two weeks of Jul.

BAILÉN Zodíaco *Tapas* €

Ctra Bailen–Motril km 294, 23710 (Jaén) ***Tel*** *953 67 10 58*

A modern hotel with a large and popular restaurant. Cold soups are on the menu in summer, such as *ajo blanco* (white garlic) with almonds. Other specialities include the scrambled eggs with ham, asparagus, prawn/shrimp and elvers and partridge. Has a lovely, tree-shaded garden terrace in summer.

BENAHAVIS Los Abanicos €

C/ Málaga 15, 29679 (Málaga) ***Tel*** *952 85 51 31*

A well known and consistently good restaurant decorated with pretty painted *abanicos* (fans) in the heart of the lovely village of Benahavís. Dine on tasty regional dishes. The house speciality, *paletilla de cordero* (shoulder of lamb) is particularly good. It is a favourite for Sunday lunch, so book early. Closed Tue except Jul & Aug.

BUBIÓN Teide *Tapas* €

C/ Carretera 70, 18412 (Granada) ***Tel*** *958 76 30 37*

Lost in the beautiful wilderness of the Alpujarras, this is a simple, stone-built restaurant surrounded by a charming, informal garden. They serve traditional dishes such as roast kid and generous salads of local vegetables. It also serves free tapas with a drink in the time-honoured Andalusian tradition. Closed Tue & second fortnight in Jul.

CÁDIZ El Escenario *Tapas* €

Calle Honduras 4, 11004 (Cádiz) ***Tel*** *856 17 42 17*

An artsy restaurant which fuses baroque with modern, creating an interesting palette for the variety of exhibitions and performances held here, as well as an inviting backdrop for the creative interpretations of Andalusian cuisine. Extensive wine and beer list. Live flamenco Mon & Fri at 10pm. In the historic centre, by the Murallas de San Carlos.

CÁDIZ Freiduria Cervecería Las Flores *Tapas* €

Plaza Topete 4, 11009 (Cádiz) ***Tel*** *956 22 61 12*

The classic Andalusian dish is *pescaíto frito*, and every town has several *freiduría*.(fried-fish shops) This is the best in Cádiz. Order your fish (anything from shark to squid), which is fried on the spot and wrapped up to take away. You can also eat it out on the terrace near the square. Non-fish snacks include croquettes and *empanadas*. No credit cards.

CÁDIZ Balandro €€

C/ Alameda Apodaca 22, 11004 (Cádiz) ***Tel*** *956 22 09 92*

The Balandro is an elegant local restaurant with creative and sophisticated cuisine. The house speciality is seafood from the Bay of Cádiz, fresh and prepared with imagination, but there are plenty of local meat (especially beef) dishes too. Try octopus salad or the beef medallions with port. Closed Sun evenings & Mon (only Sun in Jul & Aug).

CÁDIZ Ventorillo del Chato €€€€

Vía Augusta Julia s/n, 11011 (Cádiz) ***Tel*** *956 25 00 25*

A picturesque inn, in an 18th-century staging post next to the sea, this place offers Andalusian cuisine. Recipes use superbly fresh fish from the bay, local meat and fresh vegetables, often combined in one of the restaurant's *guisos*. A very popular spot for Sunday lunch, when families pile off the glorious beach for a huge feast. Closed Sun.

CARMONA Molino de la Romera *Tapas* €€

C/ Sor Angela de la Cruz 8, 41410 (Sevilla) ***Tel*** *954 14 20 00*

This inviting restaurant has a large menu with a little bit of everything, from elaborate regional dishes to a selection of tapas. Choose between the *meson* (a casual dining area) and the more formal restaurant, and enjoy dishes such as *perdiz al tomillo* (partridge with thyme) or *tortilla molinero* (omelette with potatoes, peppers and chorizo).

CARMONA San Fernando €€

C/ Sacramento 3, 41410 (Sevilla) ***Tel*** *954 14 35 56*

An exquisite mansion, built in 1700, houses this elegant restaurant, which offers fresh seasonal cuisine from the region. The *salmorejo*, a thick tomato soup garnished with boiled egg and ham, is particularly good, and the *bacalao* is prepared in myriad ways, including with a delectable squid ink and garlic sauce. Closed Sun evening, Mon & Aug.

CÓRDOBA Bodegas Mezquita *Tapas* €

Corrregidor Luis de la Cerda 73, 14003 (Córdoba) ***Tel*** *957 49 81 17*

In the heart of historic Córdoba, just steps away from the Mezquita. More than 40 different tapas and 60 domestic wines, all at a very reasonable price. Try the *berenjenas califales al Pedro Ximénez* (aubergine drizzled with a Pedro Ximénez sauce), or the *albondigas en salsa de canela y almendras* (meatballs in a cinnamon and almond sauce).

CÓRDOBA Federación de Peñas *Tapas* €

C/ Conde y Luque, 14003 (Córdoba) ***Tel*** *957 47 54 27*

Located right next to the Mezquita, Peñas offers simple but excellent local food. Try the *rabo de toro*, a house speciality or the *cardos* with clams. There's always a good variety of seafood and prices are exceptionally reasonable. The city has awarded it a gold medal in recognition of its high standards.

CÓRDOBA Almudaina €€

Jardines de los Santos Mártires 1, 14004 (Córdoba) ***Tel*** *957 47 43 42*

Once the palace of Bishop Leopold of Austria, this mansion serves typical local dishes which draw on the cuisines from the distinct cultures that have shaped Córdoba. The Córdoban *salmorejo* is excellent here, also try angler fish with stewed tomatoes. Closed Sun evenings.

CÓRDOBA Caballo Rojo *Tapas* €€€

C/ Cardenal Herrero 28, 14003 (Córdoba) ***Tel*** *957 47 53 75*

Right next to the Mezquita, this lovely restaurant has a central patio with wrought-iron balconies thickly hung with brightly coloured flowers. The dishes are based on ancient recipes, many adapted from Moorish and Sephardic recipes. Enjoy lamb with honey or Sephardi salad of wild mushrooms, asparagus, roasted peppers and salt cod.

CÓRDOBA Casa Pepe de la Judería *Tapas* €€€

C/ Romero 1, 14003 (Córdoba) ***Tel*** *957 20 07 44*

This has been one of Córdoba's most appealing restaurants since it opened in 1928. Dine on a lovely Córdoban patio blazing with flowers, or sit in the dining rooms festooned with photos of notable customers. Try the *flamenquín* (fried rolls of veal and ham), or the aubergine with molasses. Great value *menú del día*. Closed 24–31 Dec.

CÓRDOBA El Churrasco *Tapas* €€€

C/ Romero 16, 14003 (Córdoba) ***Tel*** *957 29 08 19*

A traditional Andalusian mansion, the speciality here is charcoal-grilled meat, but vegetable dishes and soups such as *salmorejo* are also good. The dining rooms are set around two patios: in the lovely Patio del Limonero you can eat under a fragrant lemon tree. Sip an apéritif in the nearby wine cellars. Closed Easter, Aug & Christmas.

EL PUERTO DE SANTA MARÍA A Poniente €€€

C/ Puerto Escondido 6, 11500 (Cádiz) ***Tel*** *956 85 18 70*

Head to this modern restaurant for some delicious gourmet cuisine created by head chef Ángel León. Try the fresh catch of the day roasted over olive stones, or the taster menu (€48) of the chef's signature dishes, such as plankton rice with garlic tartare sauce. There is also a large selection of teas and dessert wines. Closed Sun evenings, Mon.

EL PUERTO DE SANTA MARÍA Casa Flores *Tapas* €€€

C/ Ribera del Rio 9, 11500 (Cádiz) ***Tel*** *956 54 35 12*

A family-run traditional restaurant, with a series of intimate dining rooms decorated with pretty tiles, paintings and a smattering of bullfighting memorabilia. Seafood and shellfish are the house specialities, with a spectacular array that includes everything from tuna and wild turbot to sea bass and gilthead bream.

ESTEPONA La Alborada €

Puerto Deportivo de Estepona, 29680 (Málaga) ***Tel*** *952 80 20 47*

This quayside eatery serves excellent paella and other rice dishes, such as *arroz a la banda* (a kind of fish risotto). It also serves delicious *pescaíto frito* and has tasty homemade desserts such as the *pudín de almendras* (creamy almond pudding). There are lovely views of the yacht-filled harbour from the terrace. Closed Wed & Nov.

ESTEPONA La Pampa €€

C/ Sevilla 70, 29680 (Málaga) ***Tel*** *952 79 55 45*

Situated in the historic centre of Estepona is this cheery restaurant with a cosy, eclectic decor. It offers up a wide selection of seafood and meat dishes. As a starter, try the scallops gratin, followed by the succulent chateaubriand steak served with mushrooms, green beans and a Roquefort sauce. Closed Mon.

FUENGIROLA Aroma €€€

Calle Moncayo 23, 29640 (Málaga) ***Tel*** *952 66 55 02*

This restaurant is handily located one block from the Paseo Marítimo, in the heart of Fuengirola. Chic red walls and comfortable leather chairs set the scene for innovative culinary trends. Fresh fish and meat are stars, with such dishes as ostrich carpaccio and lobster café Paris (steamed with cold cream of brandy and caper sauce). Booking advisable.

GERENA Casa Salvi Restaurante *Tapas* €

Miguel de Cervantes 46, 41860 (Sevilla) ***Tel*** *955 78 32 72*

Located 25 minutes' drive north of Seville, in a historic building with rustic stone walls and beamed ceilings, Casa Salvi offers an extensive selection of exquisitely prepared dishes made with choice cuts of grilled meat, and fresh fish and vegetables. Be sure to save room for a decadent homemade dessert. Service is personal and very attentive.

GRANADA Antigua Bodega Castañeda *Tapas* €

C/ Almireceros 1–3, 18010 (Granada) ***Tel*** *958 22 63 62*

With its time-worn tiles, huge wooden barrels and battered air, Castañeda is one of the most delightful and authentic of Granada's tapas bars. Try the melt-in-the-mouth Trevélez ham (which has its own *denominación de origen*) or the wide variety of seafood conserves. A glass of ice-cold sherry is the perfect way to begin the evening.

GRANADA Chikito *Tapas* €€

Plaza del Campillo 9, 18009 (Granada) ***Tel*** *958 22 33 64*

Built on the site of a café where Lorca and his contemporaries used to meet, Chikito serves broad beans with ham, Sacromonte omelette and *cola de toro* (oxtail stew) as specialities. At the brick bar, inset with painted tiled scenes, you can enjoy the tapas. Reservations recommended. Closed Wed.

GRANADA Mirador de Morayma €€

C/ Pianista Garcia Carrillo 2, 18010 (Granada) ***Tel*** *958 22 82 90*

In the Albaícin with views of the Alhambra, this charming patio-restaurant specializes in typical dishes of Granada, such as *remojón* (a salad of oranges and codfish) and lamb sautéed with garlic. The wine list includes organic wines from the restaurant's own estate. Flamenco on Tuesdays, call to confirm times. Closed Sun evenings, Sun in Jul & Aug.

GRANADA Carmen de San Miguel €€€

Plaza Torres Bermejas 3, 18009 (Granada) ***Tel*** *958 22 67 23*

The Andalusian specialities at this pretty restaurant with Moorish-style decor include the seabass with aubergine and the ox loin in a juniper and red wine sauce. Everything is fresh and prepared with imagination by a talented team of young chefs. There are wonderful views of the whitewashed maze of the Albaícin from the terrace. Closed Sun.

Key to Price Guide *see p608* **Key to Symbols** *see back cover flap*

GRANADA Damasqueros Restaurante *Tapas* €€€

C/ Realejo 3, 18009 (Granada) ***Tel*** *958 21 05 50*

A winner of the prize for best tapas restaurant in Granada, Damasqueros offers regional favourites with innovative interpretations in both the dining room and the tapas bar. There is something here for everyone, from comforting stews and risottos to modern dishes such as seared red tuna with pumpkin ravioli. Closed Sun evenings & Mon.

GRANADA Ruta del Veleta €€€

Ctra Sierra Nevada 136, km 5,400 Cenes de la Vega, 18190 (Granada) ***Tel*** *958 48 61 34*

Out on the winding old road to the Sierra Nevada, on the fringes of Granada, this traditional restaurant has an excellent reputation for its hearty regional cuisine. The decoration, with typical Alpujarran textiles and ceramic jugs, goes well with dishes such as roast baby kid and good seafood. Be sure to try the game in season. Closed Sun evenings.

HUELVA El Portichuelo *Tapas* €€

Vazquez Lopez 15, 21110 (Huelva) ***Tel*** *959 24 57 68*

A simple spot in the centre of the city, serving traditional Andalusian cuisine in the dining room and at the bar, where there is a range of tapas. The excellent local hams feature prominently, as does seafood and shellfish. Try the *albondigas de choco* (squid meatballs). Staff are cheerful. Closed Sun.

HUELVA Las Meigas €€

Avda Guatemala 44, 21003 (Huelva) ***Tel*** *959 27 19 58*

Some of the freshest seafood can be found at this crisply decorated Galician restaurant. The Gallegos are famed throughout the country for their skill with seafood, and here it is simply prepared – grilled, baked in a salt crust or served Gallego style – in order to appreciate its exquisite freshness. Fabulous homemade desserts. Closed Sun.

HUELVA Restaurante San Sebastián €€

C/ Ricardo Velázquez 39, 21003 (Huelva) ***Tel*** *959 25 08 24*

This traditional restaurant, situated in the town centre and close to the Parque de la Esperanza, offers an ample selection of fresh fish and seafood from the Atlantic coast. Try the delicious Galician oysters. Staff are friendly and very welcoming. Closed Sun.

ISLA CRISTINA Casa Rufino *Tapas* €€

Av de la Playa, 21410 (Huelva) ***Tel*** *959 33 08 10*

A popular beachside place whose *el tonteo* (for four) menu comprises eight different fish in eight different sauces, including angler fish in raisin sauce. It has a well-deserved reputation for outstandingly fresh seafood and shellfish, and excellent wines including all the classics. Closed 22 Dec–2 Feb & evenings except Jul–Oct & Easter.

JABUGO Mesón 5 Jotas *Tapas* €€

Ctra San Juan del Puerto s/n, 21290 (Huelva) ***Tel*** *959 12 10 71*

Fine Jabugo hams are made here and the adjoining bar-restaurant is a good place to sample them. This is the original and best of a Spanish chain of tapas bars, which have mushroomed across the country. Besides ham and sausage dishes, you can also try the fresh Iberian pork dishes, such as *presa de paletilla al mesón*. Closed Sun evening.

JAÉN Casa Vicente *Tapas* €€

C/ Cristo Rey 3, 23007 (Jaén) ***Tel*** *953 23 22 22*

A classic restaurant with a bullfighting theme in an Andalusian mansion, Vicente serves typical dishes from Jaén. A good *menú de degustación* features local specialities such as *cordero Mozárabe* (Moroccan-style lamb) or artichokes in a delicate sauce. Have an apéritif at the bar, which has just a few simple tapas. Closed Sun evening, Mon & Aug.

JAÉN Casa Antonio €€€

C/ Fermín Palma 3, 23008 (Jaén) ***Tel*** *953 270 262*

An elegant restaurant with bold contemporary art and blonde wood panelling serving excellent modern Andalusian cuisine. Traditional recipes are reinvented with style and creativity: try the *arroz de cigala y jugo de alcachofa* (crawfish rice in artichoke broth). They have an excellent *menú de degustación*. Closed Sun evenings, Mon & Aug.

JEREZ DE LA FRONTERA Bar Juanito *Tapas* €

C/ Pescadería Vieja 8, 11403 (Cádiz) ***Tel*** *956 34 12 18*

This atmospheric tapas bar and restaurant has a heady reputation for its exceptionally large portions of tapas. A fabulous array is offered, of which the local artichokes remain the star dish. You can also dine more substantially on traditional stews and casseroles and a fine *pescaíto frito* from the Bay. Closed Sun evenings & May Festival.

JEREZ DE LA FRONTERA La Mesa Redonda €€

C/ Manuel de la Quintana 3, 11402 (Cádiz) ***Tel*** *956 34 00 69*

A charming, family-run restaurant, which remains a favourite with locals for the quality and excellence of its cuisine. The creative menu changes with the seasons offering seafood, meat dishes and game. Try the *mojama* (cured tuna) as a starter, and do not miss the spectacular beef *salteado* (sautéed with black sausage). Closed Sun, 15 Jul–16 Aug.

LOJA La Finca €€€€

Hotel La Bobadilla, Autovía Granada-Sevilla, 18300 (Granada) ***Tel*** *958 32 18 61*

Worth a detour off the Autovía, this exceptional restaurant in a luxury hotel is a place for fine dining. The chef makes creative use of farm-fresh vegetables, capon and pork, game (in season) and seafood. Splash out on the wonderful *menú de degustación*, and soak up the romance of the garden terrace.

LOS BARRIOS Mesón El Copo €€

Almadraba 2, 11379 (Cádiz) **Tel** 956 67 77 10

In the village of Palmones, 9 km (5.6 miles) from Los Barrios, Mesón El Copo is one of the most reliable restaurants on this stretch of coastline. Dine on superb seafood, from fried anchovies to lobster and sea bass. Order a few shellfish dishes to share as a starter, and follow with the *dorada al horno* (bream casserole with potatoes). Closed Sun.

MÁLAGA El Tapeo de Cervantes *Tapas* €

Calle Carcer 8, 29012 (Málaga) **Tel** 952 60 94 58

Charming bodega serving hearty regional food with unique touches. Try *quiche de alcachofas y queso de cabra con pesto de albahaca* (artichoke and goat cheese quiche with basil pesto) or the *filete de ciervo con chutney de tomates y setas salteadas* (venison fillet with tomato chutney and sautéed wild mushrooms). Extensive wine list. Closed Mon.

MÁLAGA Aire Gastrobar *Tapas* €€

Avda de Pries 16, 29016 (Málaga) **Tel** 952 60 94 89

Located in a historic building with minimalist decor, and close to the beach, Aire Gastrobar offers gourmet tapas and *raciones* at the bar or in the more formal upstairs dining room. Famous for its *trilogia de hamburguesas* (hamburger trilogy), vegetable and seafood specialities such as lobster croquettes also feature. Closed Sun evenings & Mon.

MÁLAGA Café de Paris €€€€

C/ Vélez Málaga 8, 29016 (Málaga) **Tel** 952 22 50 43

An unprepossessing exterior conceals this elegant, classically decorated restaurant, which serves sublime, contemporary Spanish and Mediterranean cuisine. Creative dishes are exquisitely presented, particularly in the exceptional *menú de degustación*. Excellent wine list and immaculate service. Closed Sun evening & Mon.

MANILVA Macues €€€

Plaza Delfín s/n, Urb. Puerto de la Duquesa, 26961 (Málaga) **Tel** 952 89 03 95

At this upmarket restaurant at the tip of the Costa del Sol, you can dine on good international and Spanish cuisine on a shaded terrace, overlooking the sea of masts in the impressive yacht harbour below. House specialities include all kinds of fish baked in salt and juicy local meat grilled over charcoal. Open for dinner only. Closed Mon & Feb.

MARBELLA La Moraga Ibérica *Tapas* €€

Calle Ramón Areces 1, Puerto Banus, 29660 (Málaga) **Tel** 952 81 74 48

The stark minimalist decor creates a blank canvas for culinary art. The imaginative Andalusian creations include a nod towards Japanese, with exquisite choices such as *sashimi de mero con soja, limón y miso seco* (sashimi of grouper with soy sauce, lemon and dry miso) or the reinvented *ajo blanco* (cold soup) with mango slush. No reservations.

MARBELLA Santiago *Tapas* €€€

C/ Paseo Marítimo 5, 29602 (Málaga) **Tel** 952 77 00 78

This is probably the best place for seafood on the Costa del Sol. On any day, there might be 40 or 50 fish and shellfish dishes, all very fresh. Famous for more than 50 years, it's essential to book your table well in advance. Tapas are served at the bar, but there is a huge variety (more than 500) on offer at the adjoining Tabernita de Santiago.

MARBELLA Toni Dalli €€€

Oasis Club, Ctra N340, 29600 (Málaga) **Tel** 952 77 00 35

This handsome white palace flanked by palms makes for a great night out. It has been a classic on Marbella's Golden Mile since 1981. The Italian-influenced food includes homemade pastas, meat and fish. Live music is sometimes provided by Toni himself – formerly a popular singer with his own show in California. Opens for dinner only.

MARBELLA El Portalón *Tapas* €€€€

Ctra N340 km 178, 29600 (Málaga) **Tel** 952 82 78 80

Elegantly decorated dining rooms overlooking flower-filled gardens is the setting of this classic Andalusian restaurant. The highlight here is the meat and seafood cooked in a traditional brick oven, and you can also enjoy tapas and a glass of local wine in the attractive adjoining Vinoteca. Closed Sun except Aug.

MARBELLA La Meridiana €€€€

C/ Camino de la Cruz s/n km 3,5, 29602 (Málaga) **Tel** 952 77 61 90

Situated in Marbella's rarified heights, La Meridiana is a magnificent restaurant with a canopied garden room and an adjoining patio bar. This is creative Mediterranean cuisine at its finest: recommendations include the venison loin with truffles, wild mushrooms and foie gras, or wild sea bass with tomato sauce. Opens daily.

MIJAS El Castillo €€€

Plaza de la Constitución, Pasaje de los Pescadores 2, 29650 (Málaga) **Tel** 952 48 53 48

This rustic-style restaurant is right on the main square of the enchanting white village. It serves both typically Andalusian and international dishes, which you can enjoy out on the breezy terrace. Try the *ajoblanco*, a traditional cold soup made with an almond base, bread and garlic, and garnished with Malaga raisins. Closed Fri.

MOTRIL Tropical €€

Av Rodríguez Acosta 23, 18600 (Granada) **Tel** 958 60 04 50

A simple *hostal* with a good restaurant, serving a wide choice of typical Andalusian dishes in a classic Spanish seaside setting. Both seafood, such as bass with *ajo verde* (green garlic), and meat, such as *choto a la brasa* (roast baby kid) are specialities here. For dessert try the sorbet made with *chirimoya* (custard apple). Closed Sun & Jun.

Key to Price Guide *see p608* **Key to Symbols** *see back cover flap*

OSUNA Casa del Marqués €€€

C/ San Pedro 20, 41640 (Sevilla) ***Tel*** *954 81 22 23*

A luxurious hotel in the heart of historic Osuna, Casa del Marqués is located in a flamboyant Baroque mansion set in gardens. The restaurant offers superb, highly creative Andalusian cuisine which reinvents traditional recipes. The scallops sautéed with broad beans and ham and the cod fillet with baby squid are signature dishes. Closed Mon evenings.

PALMA DEL RÍO El Refectorio (Hospedería de San Francisco) €€

Av Pío XII 35, 14700 (Córdoba) ***Tel*** *957 71 01 83*

Dine in the 15th-century refectory of this out-of-the-way former monastery, now an elegant hotel. The restaurant has an ever-changing menu, which features Andalusian cuisine, with lots of typically Córdoban dishes. In autumn and winter, game features prominently, and in summer dinner is served on an enchanting candle-lit patio.

PALOS DE LA FRONTERA El Bodegón *Tapas* €€

C/ Rábida 46, 21810 (Huelva) ***Tel*** *959 531 105*

An atmospheric former wine cellar now houses this cosy, informal restaurant, where the menu features local culinary stalwarts such as fish baked in a salt crust and meat grilled traditionally over holm oak firewood. The menu is short, but care is taken over selecting fresh local ingredients, and the result is always delicious. Closed Tue & 16–30 Sep.

RONDA Traga Tapas *Tapas* €

C/ Nueva 4, 29400 (Málaga) ***Tel*** *952 87 72 09*

Located in the town centre, Traga Tapas is the sister restaurant to Tragabuches, and also offers an innovative menu, but at more reasonable prices. The imaginative tapas dishes include salmon marinated in lemon and vanilla, and wild mushrooms sautéed with Spanish onions and garnished with serrano ham. Closed Sun evenings & Mon.

RONDA Del Escudero €€

Paseo de Blás Infante 1, 29400 (Málaga) ***Tel*** *952 87 13 67*

With an incomparable garden setting near Ronda's famous bullring, this elegant restaurant offers spectacular views over the valley to go with its traditional Andalusian cuisine. Go for the good-value fixed-price lunch menu, which you can enjoy on the panoramic garden terrace. Closed Sun evenings.

RONDA Tragabuches €€€€

C/ José Aparicio 1, 29400 (Málaga) ***Tel*** *952 19 02 91*

A stylish fusion of contemporary and traditional, the dining room at this fabulous restaurant has red-brick walls and chunky industrial-chic fittings. The Andalusian cuisine is simply superb, and the *menú de degustación* (€70) allows diners to appreciate the chef's skilful handling of textures and flavours. Closed Sun evenings & Mon.

SAN FERNANDO Venta de Vargas *Tapas* €€

Plaza de San Juan Vargas s/n, 11100 (Cádiz) ***Tel*** *956 88 16 22*

This popular small-town eatery has lots of flamenco atmosphere, including live music, and was immortalized by the mythical Camarón de la Isla. Order *raciones* of classics such as *patatas aliñadas* (potato salad), or tuck into local stews and fresh fish from the bay. Finish up with creamy *tocino de cielo* (egg custard) for dessert. Closed Mon, Sun evening.

SAN ROQUE Villa Victoria (Los Remos Rest) €€€

Ctra N351 km 2.8, Campamento, 11314 (Cádiz) ***Tel*** *956 69 84 12*

Housed in a restored Victorian mansion with Mediterranean decor, this restaurant serves exquisite dishes. The focus is on first-rate seafood and a *menú de degustación* includes shrimp fritters and sea nettles. There is always a good list of seasonal specialities, including wild mushrooms. Closed Sun evenings & Mon.

SANLÚCAR DE BARRAMEDA Casa Bigote *Tapas* €€€

C/ Bajo de Guía 10, 11540 (Cádiz) ***Tel*** *956 36 26 96*

At the mouth of the Río Guadalquivir, this typical sailor's tavern is legendary throughout Andalusia. The tapas bar, hung with hams and piled up with wooden barrels, offers fabulous seafood tapas, or you can dine in the wooden-beamed *comedor* on *langostinos de Sanlúcar* (large, sweet striped prawns) and fresh fish. Closed Sun & Nov.

TARIFA Miramar €€

Arte-Vida Hotel, Ctra N340 km 79.3, 11380 (Cádiz) ***Tel*** *956 68 52 46*

This is a fabulous hotel, set in dunes right on Tarifa's endless beach. Its pretty restaurant-café with a stylishly simple blue-and-white decor serves fresh salads, pizzas and grilled seafood, along with a few more exotic dishes such as Thai coconut soup. They also do cakes, delicious brownies and coffee. The views reach all the way to Africa.

TARIFA Mesón de Sancho *Tapas* €€€

Ctra N340 km 94, 11380 (Cádiz) ***Tel*** *956 68 49 00*

A classic inn, just outside Cádiz on the road to Algeciras. Warm and friendly, it is decorated in typical *mesón* style, and offers set menus featuring sturdy Andalusian meats such as beef with mushrooms. It also serves a range of generous *raciones* in the bar. Sancho is a popular spot for family outings, particularly Sunday lunch.

TORREMOLINOS Bar Restaurante Casa Juan *Tapas* €€

C/ San Gines 18–24, 29620 (Málaga) ***Tel*** *952 37 35 12*

A popular beachfront restaurant with an expansive terrace offering home-cooked favourites such as fish baked in salt and *fritura Malagueña*, which are based on old family recipes (provided by Juan's mother and grandmother). It has been going since the tourist boom first transformed this former fishing village. Closed Mon.

TORREMOLINOS Frutos *Tapas* €€€€

Av de la Riviera 80, Urbanización Los Alamos, 29620 (Málaga) ***Tel*** *952 38 14 50*

The grande dame of Costa del Sol restaurants, serving superb meat and fish. There is a terrace, and two glassy dining areas where you can enjoy suckling pig, followed by *arroz con leche*. The remarkable wine cellar in the basement can be visited. An informal tapas bar at the entrance serves lighter meals. Closed Sun evenings.

ÚBEDA El Seco *Tapas* €

C/ Corazon de Jesús 8, 23400 (Jaén) ***Tel*** *953 79 14 52*

A delightful find in the lovely Renaissance town of Úbeda. A charming, family-run restaurant, with a modest, but spick and span dining room, El Seco serves fresh and tasty home cooking, including delicious croquettes, game in season and country soups and stews. Opens daily for lunch and also for dinner on Fri & Sat. Closed Sun evenings & Jul.

VÉJER DE LA FRONTERA Venta Pinto *Tapas* €€

La Barca de Véjer s/n, 11150 (Cádiz) ***Tel*** *956 45 08 77*

Véjer de la Frontera is a magical, hill-top town on the Costa de la Luz with a shadowy maze of narrow alleys, which evoke its Moorish past. This pretty restaurant, in a former staging post 3 km (1.8 miles) from the town centre, serves creative versions of local dishes, and has a popular tapas bar where you can also buy local specialities.

VERA Terraza Carmona *Tapas* €€

C/ Mar 1, 04620 (Almería) ***Tel*** *950 39 07 60*

A simple roadside hotel, with a fine restaurant that has won several local awards. The specialities here are excellent seafood, and unusual regional dishes such as *gurullos con conejo* (pasta with rabbit). In season, game dishes feature prominently, including wild boar with olives and almonds. Houses a pretty tapas bar. Closed Mon & 8–21 Jan.

ZAHARA DE LOS ATUNES Casa Juanito *Tapas* €€

C/ Alcalde Jose Ruiz Cana 7, Barbate, 11393 (Cádiz) ***Tel*** *956 43 92 11*

In a pretty fishing village and low-key seaside resort, this is a charming, typically Andalusian restaurant with an airy, expansive terrace just steps from the beach. Seafood is the house speciality, particularly the tuna, which gives the town its name. It also has a dining area with tapas bar. Closed Wed (except Aug), Nov, Dec & Jan.

THE BALEARIC ISLANDS

FORMENTERA Juan y Andrea €€€

Playa de Illetas s/n, 07860 (Formentera) ***Tel*** *971 18 71 30*

Dine on beautifully fresh fish and shellfish, including lobster, caught by the restaurant's own fishing boat, in this wonderful beach restaurant. It overlooks the Playa de Illetas, one of the wildest and most beautiful beaches in the Mediterranean. Local rice dishes are a speciality here. Opens daily 1–8pm & closed 15 Nov–1 Apr.

FORMENTERA Restaurante Pascual €€€

Avda Mola 12, 07872 (Formentera) ***Tel*** *971 32 70 14*

A friendly, family-run restaurant in the pretty little bay of Es Caló, this is one of the most popular seafood restaurants on Formentera. Tucked behind a grove of pines only steps from the beach, it is enjoyably chaotic and informal, but the seafood dishes, particularly the stews and rice are exceptionally good.

FORMENTERA, ES PUJOLS Sa Palmera €€

Playa Es Pujols, C/ del Agua Dulce 15–31, 07871 (Formentera) ***Tel*** *971 32 88 58*

Freshly caught seafood is served at this classic seafront restaurant, which specializes in traditionally prepared regional cuisine. Try the mixed fish paella or the *zarzuela de mariscos* (shellfish casserole), although you will also find a few meat dishes on the menu. You can eat out on the breezy terrace and enjoy great sea views. Closed Dec–Feb.

IBIZA (EIVISSA), SANT ANTONI Sa Capella €€€

Ctra de Santa Inés km 0.6, 07840 (Ibiza) ***Tel*** *971 34 00 57*

Exquisitely housed in a former chapel, this elegant restaurant offers a wide range of fresh Mediterranean cuisine. There are lots of good fish dishes, including grilled sea bream, sea bass baked in a salt crust as well as juicy steaks cooked over charcoal. For dessert, try the delicious *tarte tatín*. Opens for dinner only from Easter to Oct.

IBIZA (EIVISSA), SANT JOSEP Can Pujol €€€

C/ Escalo s/n, 07839 (Ibiza) ***Tel*** *971 34 14 07*

Highly recommended by locals and tourists alike, this restaurant is known for its excellent seafood. Try the *parrillada de pescado* (variety of grilled fish), or one of the many paellas on offer. Finish with the house flan, made with bananas and pine nuts. It is located on the beach, and fills up quickly, so be sure to book in advance. Closed Wed & Dec.

IBIZA (EVISSA), SANTA GERTRUDIS Ama Lur €€€

Ctra San Miguel km 2.3, 07815 (Ibiza) ***Tel*** *971 31 45 54*

One of the best restaurants on the island, in a villa with Mediterranean decor. The menu features refined Basque cuisine, with the emphasis on fresh seafood, although Balearic meat dishes appear too. Try the sea bream with almonds and pistachios or local spring lamb with honey. Closed lunch, also Wed (except Jul & Aug) & Nov–Mar.

Key to Price Guide *see p608* **Key to Symbols** *see back cover flap*

IBIZA (EIVISSA), SANTA GERTRUDIS Ca'n Pau €€€€

Ctra de Sant Miquel km 2.9, 07814 (Ibiza) ***Tel*** *971 19 70 07*

A beautifully restored Ibizan *masía* surrounded by gardens, Ca'n Pau serves fine Catalan and Mediterranean cuisine. The house specialitiy is *bacalao* prepared in several different ways, but tender roast kid, quail with cabbage and rabbit are also on the menu. A good selection of Catalan wines and *cavas*. Closed 1 Jan–10 Feb; check opening hours.

IBIZA, CALA BENIRRÀS Roca y Mar €€

Cala Benirràs, 07815 (Ibiza) ***Tel*** *971 33 35 32*

This restaurant is located on one of Ibiza's loveliest coves, with a small curving beach of golden sand. You can watch sunsets from the palm-shaded terrace, where simple snacks and more substantial Mediterranean cuisine, often featuring local seafood, is offered. The beach is hidden between Sant Miquel and Sant Joan. Closed Nov–mid-Apr.

IBIZA, IBIZA TOWN La Masía d'en Sort €€€

Ctra San Miguel km 1, 07814 (Ibiza) ***Tel*** *971 31 02 28*

A sturdy Ibizan *masía* set in orange groves is home to this elegant restaurant, with stylish dining rooms which double as art galleries for local artists. The food is no less artistic, and features dynamic reinventions of classic Balearic cuisine prepared with fresh ingredients. Try refreshing *langoustine* salad. Closed lunchtime, Mon (except in Aug) & Nov–Mar.

IBIZA, IBIZA TOWN La Oliva €€€€

C/ Santa Cruz 2–4, 07800 (Ibiza) ***Tel*** *971 30 57 52*

An intimate restaurant tucked away in Ibiza town's labyrinthine old quarter, serving Mediterranean, French and Balearic cuisine. Try the sea bream baked in a salt crust, a flaky pie filled with goat's cheese, and finish up with the creamy chocolate Charlotte for dessert. Opens only for dinner. Closed 15 Oct to Easter.

IBIZA, SAN RAFEL DE FORCA Clodenis €€€

Plaza de la Iglesia s/n, 07816 (Ibiza) ***Tel*** *971 19 85 45*

A lovely country house, surrounded by shady gardens, Clodenis serves elegant Provençal and Mediterranean cuisine and offers lots of vegetarian specialities. Dine out on the romantic terrace under tendrils of trailing greenery, on tender marinated chicken or a fragrant au gratin of local vegetables. Closed Sun in winter & Nov.

MALLORCA, ALCÚDIA Mesón Los Patos €€

C/ Camí Can Blau 42, 07400 (Mallorca) ***Tel*** *971 89 02 65*

An agreeably decorated family restaurant with a garden and children's playground, close to the Parque Natural de la Albufera. It offers simple and traditional Mallorcan dishes, including *arroz brut* (a soupy rice served with meat), or roast shoulder of lamb. There is a good-value lunch menu. Closed Tue & 7 Jan–1 Mar.

MALLORCA, CALA RATJADA Ses Rotges €€€€

C/ Rafael Blanes 21, 07590 (Mallorca) ***Tel*** *971 56 31 08*

An enchanting family-run rural hotel, this lovely stone mansion is an ideal setting for dining on Mediterranean cuisine prepared with prime local produce. They offer a range of fixed-price menus, including a Medieval Menu that features ancient Balearic recipes. Booking essential. Opens Mon, Wed, Fri, Sat & Sun evenings only. Closed Nov–15 Mar.

MALLORCA, DEIÀ Ca'n Costa €€

Ctra Valldemossa-Deiá km 2.5, 07170 (Mallorca) ***Tel*** *971 61 22 63*

An attractive, rural restaurant located in a prettily restored olive oil mill, Ca'n Costa serves honest Mallorcan and international cuisine at reasonable prices. Traditional *sopas mallorquinas* (thick broths) and barbecued meats are the specialities. Glorious mountain views from the terrace, and there is a playground for kids. Closed Tue in winter.

MALLORCA, DEIÀ El Olivo €€€

Hotel la Residencia, Finca Son Canals, 08179 (Mallorca) ***Tel*** *971 63 60 46*

A magnificent hotel set in a fine 16th-century mansion houses this excellent restaurant, where you can dine on cool stone patios with breathtaking views of the mountains and sea. The delicious *nouvelle cuisine* incorporates Mediterranean influences, with dishes such as rack of lamb with olive crust. Excellent wine list. Closed Mon & Tue mid-Oct–Mar.

MALLORCA, DEIÀ / PORT DE SÓLLER Bens d'Avall €€€€

Urbanización Costa Deiá, Ctra Sóller-Deià s/n, 07100 (Mallorca) ***Tel*** *971 63 23 81*

This cliff-top restaurant offers wonderful views of the magnificent stretch of coastline, pocketed with turquoise-blue bays. The superb, contemporary cuisine reinvents traditional Mediterranean recipes with style and originality. Go for the *menú de degustación*. Closed Mon, Sun & Tue evenings, also weekdays Nov–Mar.

MALLORCA, INCA Celler Ca'n Amer €€€

C/ Pau 39, 07300 (Mallorca) ***Tel*** *971 50 12 61*

This wonderful old wine cellar, lined with battered wine barrels, is now home of one of the island's most authentic regional dishes, *sopes mallorquinas*, made with bread and braised vegetables. They also have delicious local lamb, prepared with aubergine and *sobrasada* (Mallorcan sausage).

MALLORCA, PALMA La Bóveda ***Tapas*** €€

C/ Botería 3, 07012 (Mallorca) ***Tel*** *971 71 48 63*

The most popular and characterful tapas bar in Palma, this has lazy paddle fans, multi-coloured tiles and huge wooden barrels. The menu ranges from simple *pa amb oli*, country bread rubbed with garlic and tomato and drizzled with olive oil, to fresh seafood like the *bacalao al pil pil* (cod in a Basque sauce). Closed Sun May–Sep; Sun evenings Oct–Apr.

MALLORCA, PALMA DE MALLORCA Ca'n Carlos €€€

C/ del Aigua 5, 07011 (Mallorca) ***Tel*** *971 71 38 69*

Old Balearic recipes have been revived, providing diners with an authentic version of the island's food, with a touch of creativity from the original owner's son. This is a much-loved local favourite, and bookings are essential. The oven-roasted suckling lamb and the hake with cabbage are particularly good. Great local wines. Closed Sun & mid-Aug.

MALLORCA, PALMA DE MALLORCA Porto Pí €€€

C/ Garita 25, 07015 (Mallorca) ***Tel*** *971 40 00 87*

This elegant old house, surrounded by gardens, is an ideal spot to savour creative Mediterranean and international cuisine using first-class ingredients. Try the sea bream cooked in wine or the duck with lime and curry spices. They also offer a range of elaborate dishes using foie gras. Delicious desserts. Closed Sat lunch & Sun (except May–Oct).

MALLORCA, PEGUERA La Gran Tortuga €€€

Urb Aldea Cala Fornells I, 07160 (Mallorca) ***Tel*** *971 68 60 23*

The spellbinding sea views from the terrace stretch all the way to the Magrat islands at this seaside restaurant overlooking a lovely bay. Try homemade foie gras, hake stuffed with salmon in a spinach sauce or lamb, all creatively prepared with fresh local ingredients. The set-price lunch and tasting menus are good value.

MALLORCA, PORT D'ANDRATX Layn €€€

C/ Almirall Riera Alemany 20, 07157 (Mallorca) ***Tel*** *971 67 18 55*

This charming seaside villa is home to a delightful, simple restaurant, where the fish arrives straight from local fishing boats. The fabulous views of the sea from the terrace are the perfect accompaniment to the wonderfully fresh fish, but there are also meat specialities including roast suckling pig and beef with cabbage. Closed Mon & Nov–Jan.

MALLORCA, PORT DE POLLENÇA Stay €€

C/ Muelle Nuevo s/n, 07470 (Mallorca) ***Tel*** *971 86 40 13*

With tables right on the bay, this popular local restaurant serves tasty regional cuisine with emphasis on fish and seafood. Try the *salsa de eneldo*, filets of white fish grilled with vegetables and served with a dill sauce. They also have a cheap and cheerful snack bar (for sandwiches and burgers), good for families coming off the beaches.

MALLORCA, PORTOCOLOM Celler Sa Sinia €€

C/ Pescadors 5, 07670 (Mallorca) ***Tel*** *971 82 43 23*

Exceptional Mallorcan cuisine at modest prices. With a perfect location overlooking the port, it specializes in fresh seafood such as the wonderful salmon and prawn brochettes. It also serves delicious local meats. Try the duck with orange. Desserts include tiramisu made with *ensaimada*, Mallorca's famous pastry. Closed Mon, Nov, Dec & Jan.

MALLORCA, SÓLLER El Guía €€

C/ Castanyer 2, 07100 (Mallorca) ***Tel*** *971 63 02 27*

A pretty, old-fashioned hotel with a delightful flower-filled garden, El Guía's dining room is a popular local favourite. The charming dining rooms retain some of its original Modernista details, and the good, home-cooked food includes tasty dishes such as locally grown artichokes stuffed with spinach. Reasonably priced. Closed Mon & Nov–Mar.

MALLORCA, SÓLLER Sa Cova ***Tapas*** €€

Plaça de la Constitució 7, 07100 (Mallorca) ***Tel*** *971 63 32 22*

On Sóller's main square, shaded by vast plane trees, this is a simple, welcoming restaurant serving honest home cooking. The menu of classic Mallorcan dishes changes every three months, according to what is in season, and they also offer delicious homemade desserts. There is a good fixed-price lunch menu.

MENORCA, CIUTADELLA Café Balear ***Tapas*** €€

C/ Pla de Sant Joan 15, 07760 (Menorca) ***Tel*** *971 38 00 05*

A legendary restaurant right on the port, Café Balear specializes in fish and seafood including *caldera de langosta* (lobster casserole) and *fritada de gambas* (fried prawns). The fish arrives on the restaurant's own boat, and is prepared with the minimum of fuss to better appreciate its freshness. Reservations essential. Closed Sun evening & Mon.

MENORCA, CIUTADELLA Cas Ferrer de Sa Font €€€

C/ Portal de Sa Font 16, 07760 (Menorca) ***Tel*** *971 48 07 84*

A rustically decorated 18th-century mansion set around a patio, Cas Ferrer de Sa Font offers a range of set menus, including a special children's one. The focus is on Menorcan and Mediterranean cuisine, with local ingredients prepared with touches of creativity. Try the stuffed courgettes (zucchinis) with prawns. Closed Mon & Mar.

MENORCA, ES MERCADAL Ca'n Olga €€

C/ Pont de na Macarrana, 07740 (Menorca) ***Tel*** *971 37 54 59*

A pretty country cottage, which doubles as an exhibition space for local artists, is the attractive setting for this charming restaurant. Delicious, sophisticated Menorcan and Mediterranean cuisine is on offer, accompanied by some sturdy local wines. In summer, dine in the garden terrace at the back. Closed Dec–Mar; Mon & Tue Apr–May.

MENORCA, ES MIGJORN S'Engolidor €€

C/ Major 3, 07749 (Menorca) ***Tel*** *971 37 01 93*

An old country house, now a small rural inn, is home to this restaurant which serves home-cooked Menorcan specialities at very reasonable prices. The menu features refreshing salads and simple but delicious local meat and fish. The garden terrace overlooks the gorge of S'Engolidor, which gives the restaurant its name. Closed Mon & Nov–Easter.

Key to Price Guide *see p608* **Key to Symbols** *see back cover flap*

MENORCA, FORNELLS Es Cranc €€€

C/ Escoles 31, 07748 (Menorca) ***Tel*** *971 37 64 42*

Fornells has long been associated with the typically Menorcan dish of lobster *caldereta* (spiny lobster stew), once a poor fishermen's dish and now a pricey delicacy. No other place does it better than this traditional bar-restaurant. It also offers a good-value lunch menu. Closed Wed (except Aug), Dec, Jan & Feb.

MENORCA, MAÓ Cap Roig €€

Urb Cala Mesquida 14, 07700 (Menorca) ***Tel*** *971 18 83 83*

A classic, informal seafood restaurant right on the beach, which has an imaginative set menu at lunch time and tasty specialities with fresh fish and lobster. The *pescado frito* is outstandingly good, and they also do a wonderful version of the *caldereta de langostinos*, Menorca's famous stew of spiny lobsters. Closed Mon.

MENORCA, MAÓ Jágaro €€€

Moll de Levant 334, 07701 (Menorca) ***Tel*** *971 36 23 90*

A classic restaurant right on the harbour, with a cosy dining room filled with knick-knacks and a popular breezy terrace. It serves fine Mediterranean seafood dishes, including the Menorcan speciality *caldereta de langosta* (lobster stew). There are over 100 wines on their wine list. Closed Mon, Feb & Sun evenings in winter.

MENORCA, SANT CLIMENT Es Molí de Foc €€€

C/ Sant Llorenç 65, Sant Climent, 07712 (Menorca) ***Tel*** *971 15 32 22*

A country-house restaurant located in a tiny village a few kilometres southeast of Maó. Delicious creative Menorcan and international cuisine makes excellent use of varied local produce, and includes rice and seafood dishes. There is an attractive garden terrace, where sea shanties are sung in summer. Closed Jan, Sun evenings & Mon except Jul & Aug.

THE CANARY ISLANDS

EL HIERRO, VALVERDE La Higuera de la Abuela *Tapas* €

C/ Tajanis Caba 10, Echedo, 38900 ***Tel*** *922 55 10 26*

A low-lying building with colourful walls and a courtyard planted with cactuses, this restaurant is 10 km (6 miles) to the north of Valverde. It serves no-frills traditional, homemade island cooking, notably *conejo en salsa de almendras* (rabbit in almond sauce) and a variety of local fish. Also try bass with *mojo* sauce. Live music. Closed Tue in winter.

EL HIERRO, VALVERDE El Mirador de la Peña €€

Ctra General Norte 40, Guarazoca, 38916 ***Tel*** *922 55 03 00*

This house hanging from a rock on the north coast of the island with spectacular views of the Valle del Golfo was designed by celebrated Canarian architect César Manrique. It serves typical El Hierro food such as *ensalada templada de ventresca de bonito* (warm tuna salad) and *mousse de gofio*, made with the typical Guanche cereal. Closed Mon.

FUERTEVENTURA, BETANCURIA Casa Santa María *Tapas* €€

Plaza de la Concepción, 35510 ***Tel*** *928 87 82 82*

Situated on the same square as the 15th-century Iglesia de Santa María (now Fuerteventura's cathedral), this restaurant-cum-museum, in a 16th-century house, is worth a visit. It has its own bodega and a garden. A good place to try the traditional *puchero canario* (Canarian stew) and, for dessert, the *crema Canaria*.

FUERTEVENTURA, PUERTO DEL ROSARIO La Barca del Pescador €€

Franchi Roca, El Castillo, Caleta de Fuste, 35510 ***Tel*** *928 16 35 00*

Built on two levels and decorated with maritime paraphernalia, this restaurant offers traditional cuisine based mainly on fish and seafood brought directly from Galicia. They do a good salt-crusted sea bass. For starters try the *crema de berros* (watercress soup) and for dessert *tocino de cielo*. Pescador serves classic Spanish wines as well.

FUERTEVENTURA, PUERTO DEL ROSARIO Fabiola €€€

C/ Caserio de Ampuyenta 43, 35510 ***Tel*** *928 17 46 05*

An old country house, decorated with antiques, and with an atmosphere somewhat evocative of the Belle Epoque. It is run by two Belgian men who offer creative cuisine based on market produce. Try the warm salad of endives with bacon and goat's cheese or the John Dory fillets. For dessert there is cheese cake. Closed for lunch Mon–Wed.

GRAN CANARIA, AGÜIMES La Farola €€

C/ Alcalá Galiano 3, 35118 ***Tel*** *928 18 04 10*

On Arinaga beach, down the coast from the airport, is this restaurant with a sea-inspired decor, which specializes in fish and seafood. Worth trying, in particular, is the oven-baked salted fish or the paella made with fish or shellfish. Desserts are home made, including a pleasing *tarta de turrón*. Open lunchtime only except Fri–Sat. Closed Sun evening.

GRAN CANARIA, ARUCAS Casa Brito €€

Pasaje Teror 17, Ctra Arucas-Teror km 1.3, 35412 ***Tel*** *928 62 23 23*

Meat is the speciality of this rustic restaurant in Visvice, just outside Arucas, but the fish dishes are also good. Start with *berenjenas gratinadas con queso fresco y tomillo* (aubergine gratin with fresh cheese and thyme) and end with *arroz con leche quemada* (rice pudding flambé). Closed Mon, Tue, Sun evening, Easter week & first fortnight of Sep.

GRAN CANARIA, ARUCAS El Mesón de la Montaña €€

C/ Montaña de Arucas, 35400 ***Tel*** *928 60 08 44*

A spiralling road leads to this restaurant perched on the top of a mountain outside Arucas offering great views of the northern part of the island. It serves a selection of international and Canarian dishes – some of the latter need to be ordered in advance. Good fish and seafood, including cod and prawns. Also has a playground. Caters largely for groups.

GRAN CANARIA, LAS PALMAS Kamakura *Tapas* €€

C/ Galileo Galilei 4, 35010 ***Tel*** *928 22 26 70*

A small Japanese restaurant near the Playa de las Canteras, with Oriental decor. Choose between the sushi bar or one of the tables. The specialities include tempura (lightly battered vegetables and prawns), fish tartare with aromatic herbs and sushimi (a plate of slices of raw fish), all served with an attention to detail. Closed Mon lunch, Sun & Aug.

GRAN CANARIA, LAS PALMAS La Hacienda €€

Edificio Venegas, Profesor Agustín Millares Carló 9, 35003 ***Tel*** *928 37 31 97*

The serious approach to food is accentuated by a minimalist decor. It offers creative cuisine of Mediterranean origin. On the menu is duck with ginger and moschatel and cod with fried green tomatoes. Do not miss the souffle *cremoso* made with Tanzanian chocolate. *Menú de degustación* at lunchtime. Closed Sun & Mon–Wed evenings.

GRAN CANARIA, LAS PALMAS Amaiur €€€

C/ Péréz Galdós 2, 35002 ***Tel*** *928 37 07 17*

Housed in a 19th-century colonial home in the Barrio de Triana, this restaurant is run by two brothers who offer traditional Basque cooking with innovations, depending upon the fresh market produce available. Among the tempting items on the menu are foie gras with grape sauce and Armagnac and hake with seafood. Closed Sun & Aug.

GRAN CANARIA, SANTA BRIGIDA Las Grutas de Artiles €€

Las Meleguinas, Valle de la Angostura, 35300 ***Tel*** *928 64 05 75*

More a leisure complex built around two natural caves and various outdoor spaces, including terraces and a pool, than a mere restaurant. The food is Canarian, with specialities including *pescado al mojo verde* (fish with a spicy green sauce) and *buñuelos de plátano al vino tinto* (banana dumplings in red wine). Also has pool-side tables.

LA GOMERA, AGULO La Vieja Escuela €

C/ Poeta Trujillo Armas 2, 38830 ***Tel*** *922 14 60 04*

The old village school, a charming whitewashed cottage with beamed ceilings, is home to this simple restaurant-bar. Try typical local dishes, including homemade soups, fresh seafood, goat and *almogrote*, a piquant pâté made with cured Gomeran cheese, tomatoes and hot pepper. Closed Sun.

LA GOMERA, SAN SEBASTIÁN El Silbo *Tapas* €

Ctra General 102, Hermigua, 38800 ***Tel*** *922 88 03 04*

This restaurant on the Hermigua beach offers no-frills dining. Instead, it serves simple food and a small selection of mainstream wines. For a typical lunchtime meal, you can start with the *croquetas de pescado* (fish croquettes), followed by *filetes de atun en adobo* (tuna fish in sauce) and finish with bananas covered with the local palm honey.

LA GOMERA, SAN SEBASTIÁN Marqués de Oristano *Tapas* €€

C/ del Medio 24, 38800 ***Tel*** *922 14 15 41*

On the second floor of a beautiful old house, this restaurant offers modern Canarian food using traditional products both from the land and the sea. It has a grill and a bar on the ground floor. If you like rabbit, try the *conejo con verduras y plátanos verdes*. For dessert order the *cilindro de chocolate blanco con almendras*. Closed Sun & Mon lunch.

LA PALMA, LOS LLANOS DE ARIDANE El Bernegal €

C/ Díaz y Suárez 5, Santo Domingo, Garafia, 38787 ***Tel*** *922 40 04 80*

This restaurant, sited in an old house with an inner patio on the west coast of the island, serves traditional Canary Islands cuisine and vegetarian dishes, notably *potaje de berros* and, if you like kid, *cabrito palmero*. For dessert there is *delicias con naranja* (a kind of biscuit with orange). Open only at lunchtime. Closed Mon & mid-May–early Jul.

LA PALMA, EL PASO Bodegas Tamanca *Tapas* €€

Carretera General Las Manchas–San Nicolás s/n, 38750 ***Tel*** *922 49 41 55*

A locals' favourite, this bodega offers a unique dining experience inside an excavated volcanic gallery. Decor is simple and rustic with wine barrels suspended above the tables. Grilled meats and market-fresh cuisine are paired with award-winning wines from their own winery. Closed Sun & Mon; during Carnaval and 20 days in May.

LA PALMA, SANTA CRUZ Bar Parilla Las Nieves €

Plaza Las Nieves 2, 38700 ***Tel*** *922 41 66 00*

Located on the peak of Las Nieves, next to the Sanctuary of the Virgen de Las Nieves, this is a meat lover's paradise. Available by the kilo and grilled to perfection are various cuts of pork, beef, kid, rabbit and chicken. There are also fish dishes and some vegetarian choices. Succulent feasts for very reasonable prices. Closed Thu.

LA PALMA, SANTA CRUZ Chipi Chipi €

C/ Velhoco 42, 38700 ***Tel*** *922 41 10 24*

Around 6 km (4 miles) out of the island capital, this good-value restaurant with a pretty patio specializes in grilled meats and local dishes such as chickpea soup, roasted cheese with *mojo verde* and kid. Good selection of wines from the island. Private room available. Reservations recommended. Closed Sun, Wed & Oct–mid-Nov.

Key to Price Guide *see p608* **Key to Symbols** *see back cover flap*

LANZAROTE, ARRECIFE Castillo de San José Tapas €€

Castillo de San José, Ctra de Puerto Nao, 35500 ***Tel*** *928 81 23 21*

Puerto Nao's converted fortress was built in 1779 by King Carlos III and restored by the Lanzarote architect César Manrique. It now houses a contemporary art gallery and a restaurant. Enjoy international and regional specialities as you admire the art and views of the harbour. Ironically the castle has always been known locally as the "Hungry Fort".

LANZAROTE, COSTA TEGUISE Mesón La Jordana Tapas €€

Centro Comercial de Lanzarote Bay, Av de los Geranios, 35509 ***Tel*** *928 59 03 28*

A popular restaurant in one of Costa Teguise's shopping centres, King Hussein of Jordan was once a customer here, where local fare is given a French touch. For starters there are Burgundy snails. Main course includes stewed partridge, braised duck and sole with almonds. Desserts include papaya sorbet and crêpe suzette. Closed Sun & Sep.

LANZAROTE, COSTA TEGUISE Neptuno Tapas €€

Av del Jabillo, Centro Comercial Neptuno, local 6, 35509 ***Tel*** *928 59 03 78*

This airy restaurant in a shopping centre serves traditional Canary Islands cooking. The menu is strong on all types of meat but there are also some excellent fresh fish dishes such as *atun adobado al horno* (oven-cooked tuna fish) and *salmón ahumado de Uga* (smoked salmon). Wines and cheeses from the island. Closed Sun and 20 Jun–22 Jul.

LANZAROTE, MACHER, TIAS La Tegala Tapas €€€

Carretera Arrecife–Yaiza 60, 35571 ***Tel*** *928 52 45 24*

A modern restaurant catering to the discerning palate. Try some innovative tapas and exquisite wine at the bar or enjoy marvellous views from one of the dining rooms while feasting on one of their fish or meat specialities. Be sure to leave room for their decadent desserts. Elegant attire required. Closed Sun.

TENERIFE, ADEJE El Patio €€€

Hotel Jardín Tropical, Urbanización San Eugenio, C/ Gran Bretaña s/n, 38670 ***Tel*** *922 74 60 00*

The restaurant of this luxurious hotel provides an enchanting setting for a special evening. Imaginative, modern dishes are created using local produce. Try the rice casserole with red prawns or the ribeye steak with roasted fruit. Live music. Open for dinner only, closed Sun & Mon. Reservation recommended.

TENERIFE, EL SAUZAL Casa del Vino La Baranda €€€

Autopista general del Norte km 21 (Enlace de El Sauzal, La Baranda), 38360 ***Tel*** *922 57 25 35*

Tenerife's wine industry is explained by this museum in an old house on the northwest coast near Tacoronte. The restaurant serves modern Canary Islands cuisine based on fresh local market produce though, of course, the wine is the centre of focus here. There are concerts in summer on the central patio. Closed Mon & Sun evenings.

TENERIFE, GRANADILLA DE ABONA Restaurante Los Roques €€

Calle La Marina 16, Los Abrigos, 38618 ***Tel*** *922 74 94 01*

Restaurante Los Roques offers relaxed sophistication, creative dining and first-class service. Reserve a table on the terrace for splendid views. For a complete dining experience, try one of two tasting menus, which include a vast selection of innovative dishes accompanied by international wines. Open Tue–Sat for dinner only.

TENERIFE, LA LAGUNA La Hoya del Camello €€€

Ctra del Norte km 128, Los Rodeos, 38300 ***Tel*** *922 26 20 54*

This inviting restaurant has received several culinary awards. The warm and intimate ambience lends the perfect setting to your dining experience. Try the *crep relleno de mariscos* (crêpe stuffed with seafood) or one of the many rice dishes, such as *arroz caldoso con bogavante* (rice with lobster). Closed Mon evening & Sun.

TENERIFE, PUERTO DE LA CRUZ Régulo €€

C/ Pérez Zamora 16, 38400 ***Tel*** *922 38 45 06*

An old house dating from the 18th century, with an agreeable inner patio which attempts to recreate a traditional decor. It is close to the Plaza del Charco in the centre of town. The menu is noted for its locally caught grilled fish and Argentinian roast lamb. Try the blackberry mousse for dessert. Closed Sun, Mon lunch & Jul.

TENERIFE, SANTA CRUZ El Coto de Antonio €€€

Del Perdón 13, 38006 ***Tel*** *922 27 21 05*

One of Tenerife's most celebrated restaurants where you can expect excellent food and good service but, of course, there is a price to match. A serious place which welcomes business people and VIPs. The black potato salad with salt cod, peppers and olive oil and the bass in a coriander sauce are favourites. Closed Sun evenings & three weeks in Sep.

TENERIFE, SANTA CRUZ El Solariego Tapas €€€

Del Perdón 11, 38006 ***Tel*** *922 29 32 49*

A union of Basque cuisine, with emphasis on multiple ways of cooking cod, and Canarian ideas. Try the toast served with foie gras and wild mushrooms, and one of the exquisite seafood entrées, the delicious leg of lamb or the Iberian pork. End with *tarta de queso fresco y mango* (cheesecake with mango). Closed Sun & Sat lunch.

TENERIFE, SANTA CRUZ La Tasca de la Bodega Tapas €€€

Avenida San Sebastián 57, 38005 ***Tel*** *922 22 39 09*

Classic Canarian fare with innovative flair and great attention to detail. Try the various carpaccios, *solomillo de cebón con queso maxorata* (fattened pork loin with goats cheese from Fuerteventura), and finish with *morir por el chocolate* (death by chocolate). Also features a cigar list and wine tasting room. No reservations. Closed Sun.

SHOPPING IN SPAIN

Spain has a thriving shopping culture, with many unique, family-run boutiques as well as a few reliable chain stores and big department stores. Good buys include leather, fashion, wine and ceramics, though these days it is possible to find anything you are looking for, from traditional gifts to designer clothes. Spain has its own rules of etiquette when it comes to shopping. In small shops, most merchandise is behind the counter, and the clerk will retrieve whatever you need, making for a time-consuming, but friendly way to shop. It is polite to greet the shop owner and fellow shoppers with a "*buenos días*" or *"buenas tardes"* as you enter, and to say "*adiós*" as you leave.

A traditional fan

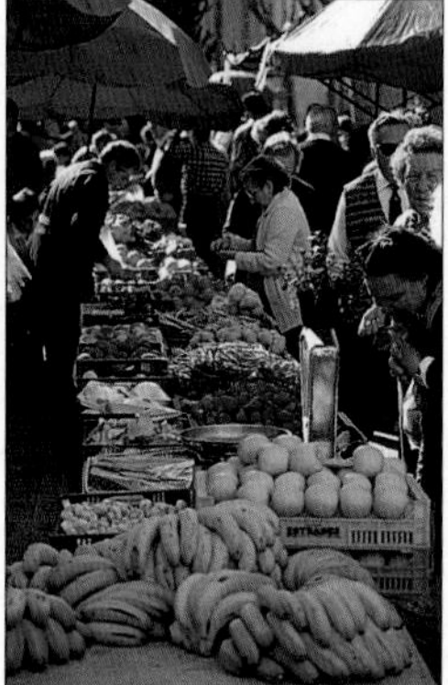

Fresh produce in a market in Pollença (Mallorca)

OPENING HOURS

Most shops in Spain, barring some supermarkets or department stores, close at midday. Small shops are open Monday to Saturday (10am–2pm and 5–8pm). Service-related shops such as dry cleaners usually open an hour earlier and close an hour later. Nearly all shops are closed on Sunday and holidays, except during the Christmas season and sales.

PAYMENT METHODS

Cash is still the payment of choice in Spain. Cheques are rarely accepted, and credit cards may not be accepted in small shops or markets. Even in large stores, there may be a minimum purchase required for credit card users.

ATMs are widely available throughout the country, even in small towns, so getting cash should not be a problem.

VAT & VAT EXEMPTION

Value added tax (VAT), known as *IVA* in Spanish, is included in the price of nearly everything in Spain. However, non-EU residents are eligible for a VAT refund *(see p664)*. If you buy goods worth a total of €90.15 or more, request a VAT refund form from the shopkeeper, then get it stamped at a Spanish customs office before you check your bags in at the airport. Present the stamped form at an affiliated bank or office in the airport, or mail it for the refund to be credited to your credit card.

SALES

Spain's twice-annual *rebajas* (sales) are a fantastic opportunity to find good deals on everything from shoes and clothes to linens, electronics and household goods. Most stores offer a reduction of 50% or more.

The first *rebajas* of the year begin on 7 January (the day after Three Kings Day) and last until mid-February. Summer *rebajas* start on 1 July and last until mid-August.

MARKETS

A visit to a Spanish market is a great lesson in local culture. Every town, large or small, has at least one fresh market, where you can buy local produce, Spanish cheeses and sausages and other foods.

Markets in the cities follow regular store opening hours, but in smaller towns, they may only be open in the morning, or on certain days of the week.

Speciality markets for antiques, arts and crafts are popular in Spain, as are the *rastros* (flea markets). These are usually open only at weekends, though the times vary across markets and towns.

The country's most celebrated market is El Rastro *(see p302)*, a massive flea market in Madrid, which has been running for many generations. It is frequented by locals and tourists alike. Watch out for pickpockets.

Display of hand-painted ceramics in Toledo

Shopping in Barcelona pp186–9; in Madrid pp316–19; in Seville pp454–5

REGIONAL PRODUCTS

Spain has a strong artisan heritage, and the best places to buy authentic traditional items are the artisan markets and speciality shops. All over Spain, you'll find great pottery and ceramics. Spain's pottery is sturdy and colourful and each region puts its own spin on the traditional forms. Andalusia, El Bisbal in Catalonia, Paterna and Manises near Valencia and Talavera de la Reina in Castilla-La Mancha are the main centres for ceramic production.

Leather goods are another traditional craft. Reasonably-priced shoes, wallets and accessories are available almost everywhere.

In Toledo, filigree metalwork and swords are sold on almost every street corner. Other sought-after products include guitars, traditional fans, Lladró porcelain figures and lacework.

Basketware, sold in all parts of Spain

FOOD & DRINK

Spain is second only to Italy in wine production, and Spanish wine is rated to be of the best value in Europe. Major wine regions are Penedès (reds, whites and *cava*), Priorat (reds), Rias Baixas (whites), Ribera del Duero (reds), Rioja (reds) and Toro (whites). Sherry from Jerez is another popular Spanish drink.

A gourmet's paradise, Spain is great for food shopping. Olives and olive oil are always a good buy. Prominent olive-growing areas include Andalusia, Aragón and southern Catalonia. You can also buy Spain's famous *Jamón Ibérico* (Iberian cured ham), or one of the many region-specific sausages such as Catalan *butifarra* and Castilian *morcilla*.

Gourmet chocolate shops are becoming popular now, especially in the cities. Escribà in Barcelona has a good reputation for producing exquisite confectionery.

A Madrid branch of the fashionable Camper shoe store

ONE-STOP SHOPPING

Small family-run shops are quaint, but when you're in a hurry department stores and one-stop shops are more convenient. Spain's most famous department store, El Corte Inglés, is found in every major city in Spain, sometimes with multiple branches. This mega store sells everything from clothes and sports goods, to furniture and food. Other one-stop shops include hypermarkets such as Carrefour (the Walmart of Europe) and Hipercor.

American-style malls, called *centros comerciales* in Spain, are gaining popularity and can be found on the outskirts of most large cities.

FASHION

Spain has a long textile history, so it's no surprise to find good quality clothing here. In large cities such as Madrid and Barcelona, you'll find boutiques of major Spanish labels, including Antonio Miro, Lydia Delgado, Josep Font, Adolfo Dominguez and Loewe. Spanish fashion may not be on par with Paris or Milan yet, but designers here are increasingly gaining a reputation for quality and originality.

For something trendy and a bit easier on the wallet, Spanish-owned chains such as Zara, Mango and Massimo Dutti are great places to shop.

Mallorca is a good place to buy shoes, home to Spain's most famous shoe company, Camper. Along with branded shoes, *Espadrilles* (traditional Spanish rope-soled shoes) are a good informal option.

SIZE CHART

Women's dresses, coats and skirts								
European	36	38	40	42	44	46	48	
British	10	12	14	16	18	20	22	
American	8	10	12	14	16	18	20	
Women's shoes								
European	36	37	38	39	40	41		
British	3	4	5	6	7	8		
American	5	6	7	8	9	10		
Men's suits								
European	44	46	48	50	52	54	56	58 (size)
British	34	36	38	40	42	44	46	48 (inches)
American	34	36	38	40	42	44	46	48 (inches)
Men's shirts (collar size)								
European	36	38	39	41	42	43	44	45 (cm)
British	14	15	15½	16	16½	17	17½	18 (inches)
American	14	15	15½	16	16½	17	17½	18 (inches)
Men's shoes								
European	39	40	41	42	43	44	45	46
British	6	7	7½	8	9	10	11	12
American	7	7½	8	8½	9½	10½	11	11½

ENTERTAINMENT IN SPAIN

Spain has always been known for its vibrant, colourful culture – wherever you are, there is usually a fiesta going on somewhere nearby, or some impromptu celebration taking place in the street. So while there's usually no need to seek out formal entertainment, those who do want to plan a day or night out will find plenty of choice, ranging from raucous cabarets to live flamenco and high-brow cultural events. Although Madrid, Barcelona and, to a lesser extent, Seville have the widest selection of programmes, the other regional capitals are not far behind. The coastal resorts also witness a lot of action in the summer months. Regular annual events in various parts of Spain are detailed on pages 38–9.

Traditional singers in Santa Cruz, Seville

Preparing for a dressage display at the equestrian school in Jerez

TRADITIONAL MUSIC AND DANCE

Spain's rich musical heritage is marked by typical regional instruments, musical styles and dance forms. The *txistu*, a small wind instrument is typical to the Basque Country, Galicia and Asturias lilt to the notes of the *gaita* (bagpipes), while Valencia is proud of its countless brass bands.

Andalusia is the home of flamenco, while Aragón's rhythm comes from the hop-step of its folk dance, *jota*. In Catalonia, the famous *sardana* *(see p205)* is accompanied by a *flabiol* (flute), *tabal* (drum) and *gralla* (a type of oboe).

JAZZ, ROCK AND POP

Television talent shows tend to dominate the Spanish pop industry, but many creative bands fail to get international recognition only because they sing in Spanish. At the cultural crossroads of southern Europe, the Spanish music scene is also enriched by influences from South America and Africa.

The Benicassim festival in July and the Sonar festival in June in Barcelona are the preferred live events for those in search of new music. Big international jazz artists can surprisingly turn up in small town stadiums and bullrings.

The Spanish music channel RNE 3 broadcasts an eclectic selection of Spanish as well as international music.

FLAMENCO

Flamenco *(see pp424–5)* is a traditional art form that combines song, music and dance. Infused with sensuality and emotion, it originated in Andalusia but is performed all over Spain. It is a highly varied musical form, and acts can range from spontaneous performances in gypsy patios to international spectacles in major concert halls.

Shows are often adapted to tourists' tastes. To see and hear flamenco that even purists admire, try the smaller venues or catch a performance during an Andalusian fiesta, particularly in the provinces of Seville and Jerez.

Córdoba hosts the National Flamenco Competition in November every third year. The next two are being held in 2013 and 2016.

CLASSICAL MUSIC, OPERA AND BALLET

Opera, classical music and ballet are performed in all the major cities in concert halls. The best-known venues include the Auditorio Nacional de Música and Teatro Real in Madrid *(see p322)*, Palau de la Música in Valencia *(see p242)*, Teatro de la Maestranza in Seville *(see p456)* and Gran Teatre del Liceu and L'Auditori *(see p191)* in Barcelona.

For a more unusual concert setting, look out for performances in Spain's spectacular caves such as those found in Nerja *(see p483)*, Drac

Palau de la Música, Valencia

Entertainment in Barcelona pp190–95; in Madrid pp320–25; in Seville pp456–7

A performance at the beautifully preserved Roman theatre in Mérida, Extremadura

(see p517) and the Cuevas of Canelobre near Alicante. Sacred music can still be heard in some of Spain's monasteries. Montserrat *(see p219)* is famous for its all-boy choir. In Leyre monastery *(see p135)*, the Gregorian plainchant is performed during mass.

THEATRE

Spain has a great repertoire of classical theatre and although most performances are in Spanish, it may be worth going to a show for the venue alone.

Corral de Comedias in Almagro *(see p417)* is a perfectly preserved 17th-century Golden Age theatre. Mérida's stunning Roman theatre *(see pp54–5* and *pp428–9)* serves as the splendid backdrop for an annual summer festival of classical theatre.

CINEMA

Spain's thriving film scene has certainly gained international exposure. The country makes around 100 feature films a year with directors such as Pedro Almodóvar and Alejandro Amenábar.

Most foreign-language films are dubbed in Spanish, but select cinemas in university cities and areas with a large number of foreign residents show films in their original language. San Sebastián hosts an acclaimed international film festival *(see p123)* in September, and the Sitges Film Festival takes place in October.

The open-air summer cinemas in some coastal resorts are an experience in themselves, but do remember to carry a mosquito repellant.

NIGHTLIFE

Spain's prodigious nightlife starts later than in most other countries, with 11pm considered an early start for most revellers. The idea is to spend the first part of the evening in pubs or *bares de copas*: sparsely decorated drinking dens, usually with loud music blaring. Then move on to the clubs and discos, often located out of town, where the noise will not bother anyone.

You can enjoy a floorshow while dining out at coastal package-holiday resorts such as Lloret del Mar on the Costa Brava, Maspalomas on Gran Canaria, Torremolinos on the Costa del Sol and Benidorm on the Costa Blanca.

SPECTATOR SPORTS

Football is Spain's favourite sport and is centred on the battle between the two top teams, Real Madrid and Barcelona. Other teams with large followings include Real Betis from Seville, Deportivo La Coruña, FC Valencia and Real Zaragoza. Cycling, tennis, basketball and golf are also popular.

BULLFIGHTING

For an authentic spectacle of Spain's most recognized traditional sport *(see pp36–7)*, watch a bullfight in a large arena – Madrid *(see p306)*, Seville *(see p430)*, Valencia, Bilbao and Zaragoza have the best bullrings. All bullfights start in the early evening at around 5pm. Tickets should be bought directly at the venue. Bullfighting is now banned in Catalonia.

ENTERTAINMENT FOR CHILDREN

Spain's big theme parks are Port Aventura on the Costa Daurada *(see p224)* and Terra Mítica outside Benidorm *(see p260)*. Other amusements suitable for kids include the cowboys of Mini-Hollywood *(see p500)* and the dancing horses of Jerez *(see p466)*.

Rollercoaster ride at Port Aventura on the Costa Daurada

OUTDOOR ACTIVITIES & SPECIALIST HOLIDAYS

Spain is one of Europe's most geographically varied countries, with mountain ranges, woodlands and river deltas suitable for scenic tours and sports holidays. The options are endless and include sailing on the Mediterranean or surfing in the Atlantic, mountain climbing in the Pyrenees or rambling through the plains of Castille, snow skiing in the Sierra Nevada or water skiing off the coast of Mallorca. To focus on just one activity, sign up for a specialist holiday. Weekend or week-long holidays, featuring everything from yoga to horse riding, are gaining popularity in Spain. Local tourist offices can provide information on outdoor activities.

Golfer preparing to tee off

WALKING AND TREKKING

Spain offers exciting choices for a challenging week-long trek through the Pyrenees, or a gentle walk along the coast. Look out for the wide, well-marked GR (*Grandes Recorridos* meaning long-distance) trails, which criss-cross Spain. Though most people usually choose to walk only a small portion of each GR trail, long-distance trekkers use them to traverse all the way across the country.

Nearly 8 per cent of Spain's total terrain is protected parkland, and the countless natural parks and 13 large national parks are the most popular and attractive hiking options. Some of the best parks for walking include Aragón's Parque Nacional de Ordesa *(see pp232–3)*, Catalunya's Parque Nacional d'Aigüestortes *(see pp210–11)*, and Asturias' Parque Nacional de los Picos de Europa *(see pp108–9)*. For details about trails in the parks, contact the **Environment Ministry of Spain**. For information on other trails, contact the **Federación Española de Deportes de Montaña y Escalada**.

AIR SPORTS

The best way to take in Spain's landscape is to view it from above. Options for thrilling aerial views include hot-air ballooning, skydiving, paragliding and hang-gliding. One of the well-known hot-air balloon companies is **Kon-Tiki**, which began flying in rural Catalonia and now covers the whole country. **Glovento Sur** operates in southern Spain. Standard rides start from €165 per person, depending on the trip's length.

For those who have forever been fascinated by the birds' ability to fly, paragliding and hang-gliding are two excellent options. The **Real Federación Aeronáutica Española** can provide information on schools and outfitters across Spain. Contact them for further details.

When it comes to a real thrill, nothing surpasses skydiving. Reputable companies offering skydiving courses or tandem jumps include **Skydive Empuriabrava** in Catalonia and **Skydive Lillo** near Toledo. Expect a single tandem jump (a jump made while attached to a qualified instructor) to cost between €150 and €200.

Paragliding above the Vall d'Aran in the eastern Pyrenees

WATER SPORTS

Spain is virtually surrounded by water, so it is little surprise that sailing is popular here. The country's most celebrated yacht ports are those of up-scale resorts including Palma de Mallorca and Marbella, and in 2007 and 2010 the port of Valencia hosted the prestigious America's Cup sailing tournament. Mooring a private yacht or sailboat in a top-notch marina is expensive and often impossible. A much easier alternative is to rent a sailboat by the day or week, or to sign up for a half- or full-day sailing excursion. Most other seaside towns also have small recreational ports offering sailboats and yacht charters which can be rented by providing a sailing licence. For details, contact the **Real Federación Española de Vela**.

Scuba diving is available up and down the coast of Spain and on nearly all the islands. However, the best places for underwater exploration are around the Canary Islands.

Whitewater rafting in the Spanish Pyrenees

Just off the island of El Hierro are the warm, calm waters of the Mar de las Calmas, which is full of colourful coral and dozens of marine species. In the Mediterranean, head to the Balearic Islands or to the Illes Medes, seven tiny islets off the Costa Brava that are home to some of the most diverse marine life in all the Mediterranean. The local Illes Medes information office, **Estació Nàutica**, will provide detailed information about area outfitters.

Surfing and windsurfing are other popular sports. On mainland Spain the best places for either kind of surfing are the Basque coast (especially towns such as Zarautz and Mundaka) and Tarifa, which is also good for kite surfing, on the Costa de la Luz. In the Canary islands, try Lanzarote or Fuerteventura for surfing and El Médano (Tenerife) for windsurfing. El Médano's **Surf Center Playa Sur** has information.

Windsurfing off Fuerteventura in the Canary Islands

Sea kayaking is becoming very popular and kayak rental is now available in many Mediterranean resort towns. Since rentals are cheap and little prior experience is necessary, kayaking is a great option for boating novices who might want to spend some time out on the water.

ADVENTURE SPORTS

Since Spain is Europe's second-most mountainous country after Switzerland, mountain climbing is a natural sport here. Head to the Aragon Pyrenees or the Catalan Pyrenees for a wide range of challenging rock faces. Other popular spots include the mountain of Montserrat in Catalonia, the Parque Natural de los Cañones y Sierra de Guara in Aragón, the Sierra Nevada in Andalusia and the Picos de Europa in Asturias. For more information, contact the **Federación Española de Deportes de Montaña y Escalada**.

If mere mountain climbing doesn't sound interesting enough, go for *barranquismo* (canyoning), a thrilling adventure sport that lets you explore canyons, cliffs and rivers with a combination of hiking, climbing, rappelling and swimming.

The undisputed capital of canyoning is Parque Natural de la Sierra y los Cañones de Guara, a park and natural area in central Aragón that is home to dozens of "wet" and "dry" canyons. Outfitters such as **Camping Lecina** provide wetsuits and experienced guides – a must for novices – for €45 per person. Most services and lodging are in, or near, the pretty town of Alquezar.

Another fun way to explore rivers is whitewater rafting. Although Spain is not known for its raging rivers, there are a few places where some white water can be found. Head for the rivers: Noguera Pallaresa in Catalunya, the Carasa in Asturias, or the Miño in Galicia. Late spring and early summer are the best times for rafting, since run-off from melted snow ensures a good deal of water and big rapids.

Fly-fishing in the rivers of Castilla y León, famous for their trout

FISHING

Deep-sea fishing excursions are offered all along Spain's coasts. Fishing in the Mediterranean or the Atlantic is unregulated except for marine reserves and some parks. Trout fishing in lakes and streams is possible; some of the best trout rivers are in Asturias, Rioja and Castilla y León. It is challenging to fish in the narrow, tree-lined streams of the Pyrenees.

It is essential to acquire a seasonal or a daily permit specifying if the fishing area is *sin muerte* (catch and release). Bring your own equipment, as only a few companies offer guided trips. For details on fishing sites and regulations, contact **Federación Española de Pesca y Casting**.

CYCLING

Road biking and mountain biking are both popular in Spain. Helmets are recommended while cycling, especially on highways where extreme caution should be exercised. Drivers here are not accustomed to sharing the road and accidents on highways are not uncommon. The **Real Federación Española de Ciclismo** will provide useful information as well as advice on how to plan a safe cycling excursion.

Mountain bikers will find plenty of trails to keep them busy pedalling in Spain. Several walking paths are also suitable for mountain biking, which are referred to as "BTT" (Bici Todo Terreno or all-terrain bikes). Throughout Catalunya, Centros BTT are set up to inform bikers about trails and conditions. In other regions, where this service is not available, trail information and maps can be found at tourist offices.

For young or inexperienced cyclers, *vias verdes* (rail trails) are a fantastic option. These flat, long-distance trails follow the paths of discontinued rail lines, ideal for those who want lovely views without making an effort. Many *vias verdes* cut through historic towns, making interesting pit stops along the way. The **Fundación de los Ferrocarriles Españoles** has detailed information about routes.

GOLF

Golf is popular throughout Spain, though most courses can be found near the coasts and coastal resort areas. There are too many important golfing areas to highlight just one; the **Real Federación Española de Golf** has detailed information on all the courses. Some of the golf courses offer activities for non-golfers as well. For year-round golf head to the island of Tenerife, where nearly a dozen courses, including the beautifully situated **Golf Las Américas**, are huddled in the southern corner of the island.

SNOW SKIING AND WINTER SPORTS

Spain's mountainous terrain makes it an excellent place for skiing, and resorts here are often cheaper than those in the Alps or other places in Europe. The top ski resorts are the Sierra Nevada in Granada and Baqueira-Beret, in the Pyrenean Val d'Aran. It is also possible to ski in the Sierra de Guadarrama, just north of Madrid, and in a handful of other high-altitude areas. Details are available through the **Real Federación Española de Deportes de Invierno**. For more ski resorts visit www.esquiweb.com.

BIRD-WATCHING

Spain's mild climate attracts a huge variety of fowl year-round. In winter, one can observe birds native to northern Europe; in spring, native Mediterranean species come to nest. There are numerous natural parks working to conserve Spain's diverse bird population. The top bird-watching site is Extremadura's Parque Natural Monfragüe, where big birds of prey can be seen swooping and hunting. Other excellent places to observe birds in their natural habitat are Andalusia's Parque Nacional de Doñana, Guadalquivir Delta and Laguna de Fuente de Piedra, and Delta de l'Ebre in southern Catalonia.

SPAS

Health and wellness spas, or *balnearios*, are nothing new in Spain. As far back as Roman times residents here were enjoying the healthy benefits of mineral-rich waters along the Mediterranean or in the interior. Day spas offering a range of beauty and therepeutic treatments are popular as well, especially in cities and resorts. The **Asociación Nacional de Estaciones Termales** website (National Association of Thermal Resorts) has details on reputable spas throughout the country.

NATURISM

Specially designated nudist, or naturist, beaches are not hard to find in Spain. Contact the various coastal tourist offices for details of nudist beaches. Alternatively, log on to the official website of the **Federación Española de Naturismo (FEN)** (www.naturismo.org), which has a comprehensive list.

SPECIALIST HOLIDAYS

A weekend or week-long specialist holiday provides the luxury of practising a favourite hobby, or probably learning a new one.

Food and wine holidays are more popular than ever in Spain with its varied cuisine and excellent wines. A growing number of companies – many of them owned by expat British – have opened in recent years, offering everything from tours of well-known wine regions to the chance to harvest grapes or olives. For upscale, made-to-order tours of wine regions all over Spain, contact the Madrid-based company **Cellar Tours**. For daily cooking classes and an in-depth look at local Spanish cuisines and customs, try a cooking holiday like those offered by the Priorat-based **Catacurian** or the Málaga-based **Cooking Holiday Spain**.

The scenic landscapes of Spain are a wonderful inspiration to indulge the artistic temperament. A painting holiday offers the chance to escape to the quiet countryside and paint. Companies including **Andalucian Adventures** offer multi-day holidays for artists of all levels. Holidays include instruction with an experienced painter as well as practising independently. Sculpture or drawing classes are often available too.

Activity-focused holidays are a great option as well. Spain's pleasant weather is particularly favourable for walking, biking, water skiing or horseback riding. The holiday company **On Foot in Spain** offers a variety of walking holidays in northern Spain, while **Switchbacks Mountain Bike Vacations** has cycling holidays for all levels in Andalusia. For water sports enthusiasts, **Xtreme Gene** specializes in water skiing holidays. Those interested in dance can try **Club Dance**, a London-based company offering dancing holidays. **Fantasia Adventure Holidays** specializes in horseback riding holidays in southern Spain.

To relax, a yoga holiday may be ideal. There are some great alternatives for getting away from the stress of daily life, such as **Kaliyoga** that offers yoga instruction in a pristine setting. A healthy menu and ample free time for hiking or meditating add to the general feel-good factor of a yoga holiday.

A specialist holiday is also a great opportunity to learn Spanish. Language holidays are available in many parts of Spain, where the Spanish language can be learnt in the best way possible – by immersing oneself completely in the country's culture. Language holidays provide the chance to observe the Spanish way of life from close quarters, for an extended period of time. The **Instituto Cervantes** has information on schools and classes across Spain.

DIRECTORY

WALKING AND TREKKING

Environment Ministry of Spain
Pl Infanta Isabel I, Madrid. **Tel** *915 97 65 77.* **www**.mma.es

Federación Española de Deportes de Montaña y Escalada
C/ Floridablanca 84, Barcelona. **Tel** *934 26 42 67.* **www**.fedme.es

AIR SPORTS

Glovento Sur
Placeta Nevot 4 1°A, Granada. **Tel** *958 29 03 16.* **www**.gloventosur.com

Kon-Tiki
Igualada, Barcelona. **Tel** *93 515 60 60.* **www**.globuskontiki.com

Real Federación Aeronáutica Española
Carretera de la Fortuna, Madrid. **Tel** *915 08 29 50.* **www**.rfae.org

Skydive Empuriabrava
Costa Brava, Catalonia. **Tel** *972 45 01 11.* **www**.skydiveempuriabrava.com

Skydive Lillo
Aeródromo Don Quijote, Lillo. **Tel** *902 36 62 09.* **www**.skydivespain.com

WATER SPORTS

Estació Náutica
C/ de la Platja 10–12, L'Estartit. **Tel** *972 75 06 99.* **www**. enestartit.com

Real Federación Española de Vela
C/ Luis de Salazar 9, Madrid. **Tel** *915 19 50 08.* **www**.rfev.es

Surf Center Playa Sur
El Médano, Tenerife. **Tel** *922 176 688.* **www**.surfcenter.info

Xtreme Gene
C/ Rosario 5, Almodovar del Río, Córdoba. **Tel** *957 05 70 10.* **www**.xtreme-gene.com

ADVENTURE SPORTS

Camping Lecina
Lecina, Sierra de Guara. **Tel** *974 318 386.* **www**.campinglecina.com

FISHING

Federación Española de Pesca y Casting
Madrid. **Tel** *915 32 83 52.* **www**.fepyc.es

CYCLING

Fundación de los Ferrocariles Españoles
Madrid. **Tel** *911 51 10 62.* **www**.viasverdes.com

Real Federación Española de Ciclismo
Madrid. **Tel** *915 40 08 41.* **www**.rfec.com

GOLF

Golf Las Américas
Playa de las Américas, Tenerife. **Tel** *922 75 20 05.* **www**.golf-tenerife.com

Real Federación Española de Golf
Paseo Joaquin Rodrigo 4, Pozuelo de Alarcón, Madrid. **Tel** *902 20 00 52.* **www**.golfspainfederacion.com

SNOW SKIING AND WINTER SPORTS

Real Federación Española de Deportes de Invierno
C/ Madroños 36A, Madrid. **Tel** *913 769 930.* **www**.rfedi.es

SPAS

Asociación Nacional de Estaciones Termales
C/ Rodriguez San Pedro 56, Madrid. **Tel** *902 117 622.* **www**.balnearios.org

NATURISM

Federación Española de Naturismo (FEN)
www.naturismo.org

SPECIALIST HOLIDAYS

Andalucian Adventures
Bonds Mill, Bristol Rd, Stonehouse, Glos (UK). **Tel** *00 44 (0) 1453 823 328.* **www**.andalucian-adventures.co.uk

Catacurian
C/ Progrés 2, El Masroig, Tarragona. **Tel** *938 02 26 60.* **www**.catacurian.net

Cellar Tours
C/ Zurbano 45, 1°, Madrid. **Tel** *911 43 65 53.* **www**.cellartours.com

Club Dance Holidays
108 New Bond Street, London (UK). **Tel** *0044 (0) 20 7099 4816.* **www**.danceholidays.com

Cooking Holiday Spain
Urb. Torremar, C/ Roma 9, Benalmadena, Málaga. **Tel** *637 80 27 43.* **www**.cookingholidayspain.com

Fantasia Adventure Holidays
C/ Luis Braille P21–3A, Barbate, Cadiz. **Tel** *610 94 36 85.* **www**.fantasiaadventureholidays.com

Instituto Cervantes
C/ Alcalá 49, Madrid. **Tel** *914 36 76 00.* **www**.cervantes.es

Kaliyoga
Orgiva, Granada. **Tel** *958 78 44 96 or 01373 814 663 (UK).* **www**.kaliyoga.com

On Foot in Spain
Rosalia de Castro 29, Teo, A Coruña. **www**.onfootinspain.com

Switchbacks Mountain Bike Vacations
Barrio La Ermita s/n, Bubion, Granada. **Tel** *660 62 33 05.* **www**.switch-backs.com

JUAN

SURVIVAL GUIDE

PRACTICAL INFORMATION

Spain has a highly developed and diverse tourist industry that caters to a wide variety of travellers – from eco-friendly backpacking and cultural visits to some of Europe's most impressive heritage sites, to sun seeking at resorts for all ages and budgets.

Old street signs

Information on accommodation, restaurants and leisure activities can be found at the *oficinas de turismo* in all major towns. In addition, Spanish people are naturally open and welcoming to outsiders, so the best information often comes from the locals themselves.

Relaxing on a sandy Spanish beach in summer

WHEN TO GO

August is traditionally Spain's main holiday month. Many businesses close for the entire month, and traffic is very heavy at the beginning and end of this period. At any time of year, try to find out in advance if your visit coincides with local *fiestas* – although these are exciting attractions, they often entail widespread closures.

VISAS AND PASSPORTS

Spain is part of the Schengen Agreement, which establishes a common border for various countries in the European Union. Visitors from other participating countries will not be asked for identification upon arrival. However, it is recommended that you carry identification in any case. A valid passport must be shown upon arrival from a non-Schengen country, including the UK.

Visas are not required for citizens of EU countries, Iceland, Norway and Switzerland. A list of entry requirements, available from Spanish embassies, specifies more than 40 other countries, including the USA, Canada, Australia, New Zealand and Japan, whose nationals do not need to apply for a visa if they are visiting Spain for a period of up to 90 days. Those who are planning longer visits than this may apply to the *Gobierno Civil* (a form of local government office) for an extension. You will also need to provide proof of employment or proof of sufficient funds to support yourself during a longer stay. All visitors from countries other than those listed above are legally required to obtain a visa before travelling to Spain.

Student visas are available from the country of origin and give the holder permission to stay until the end of their course.

If you are intending to stay for a long time, it is recommended that you contact your nearest Spanish embassy several months in advance.

TAX-FREE GOODS INFORMATION

Non-EU residents can claim back *IVA* (VAT) on single items worth over €90.15 bought in shops displaying a "Tax Free for Tourists" sign. (Bear in mind that food, drink, tobacco, cars, motorbikes and medicines are exempt from this.) You pay the full price and ask the sales assistant for a *formulario* (tax-exemption form). On leaving Spain, before you check your bags, ask customs officials to stamp your *formulario*; this must be done within three months of the purchase. You should then receive the refund, either by mail or alternatively from some banks and bureaux de change at the airport (La Caixa bank in Barcelona; and Global Refund at Terminals 1 and 4 of Madrid airport), either in cash or as a refund to your credit card.

Tax-free goods sign

TOURIST INFORMATION

All major cities and towns have *oficinas de turismo*. They will provide tourists with town plans, lists of hotels and restaurants, information about the locality, and details of leisure activities and events.

Several large cities abroad have a Spanish National Tourist Office; you can also visit www.spain.info, the official website of the Spanish Tourist Board.

OFICINA DE TURISMO 

Spanish tourist office sign, featuring the distinctive "i" logo

SOCIAL CUSTOMS AND ETIQUETTE

The Spanish greet and say goodbye to strangers at bus stops and in lifts, shops and other public places. They often talk to people they do not know. Men shake hands when introduced and subsequently whenever they meet, and it is customary for men to greet women with a kiss on each cheek – even when first introduced. Friends and family members embrace or kiss upon meeting. In cities and towns it is considered bad manners to wear shorts or vests in the streets, and you may be asked to cover up to enter churches and other monuments.

A bilingual Basque/Castilian reserved parking sign

LANGUAGE

The main language of Spain, *Castellano* (Castilian), is spoken by almost everyone throughout the country. There are three main regional languages: Catalan, spoken in Catalonia; *Gallego* (Galician) in Galicia; and *Euskera* (Basque) in the Basque Country. Variants of Catalan are spoken in the Valencia region and also in the Balearic Islands. Learning a few courtesy phrases in Catalan can be a good way to win over the locals in these areas.

Places that deal with tourists – hotels, information offices, restaurants – usually employ people who speak English.

ADMISSION PRICES

Admission fees are charged for most museums and monuments, and prices vary within different regions, and depending on the importance of the sight. Some public museums are free on Sundays. Most museums have free admission coinciding with national or regional holidays. Check the individual museums' websites for more detailed information.

OPENING HOURS

Most museums in Spain close on Sunday afternoon and all day Monday. It is wise to check opening times in advance since they can vary depending on the time of year. Many museums often close from 2pm to 5pm; some reopen from 5pm to 8pm. Churches may follow these hours, or they may only be open to the public for services.

In some smaller towns in Spain, it is not uncommon for churches, castles and other sights popular with tourists to be kept locked. The key, which is available to visitors on request, will be lodged with a caretaker in a neighbouring house, in the town hall or, sometimes, kept for safekeeping at the local bar.

TAXES AND TIPPING

There is a relaxed attitude to tipping in Spain, and tips in bars and taxis are usually just the change left over or rounded up to the nearest euro. A service charge is not generally added to restaurant bills, unless you are eating with a large group. A tip of 5 or 10 per cent, depending on the level of service and the overall price of the meal, is the norm in restaurants. VAT of 8 per cent is added to the bill, but this is often included in the price of the dishes (this must be stipulated on the menu). VAT of 8 per cent is also added to the hotel bill at the end of your stay.

TRAVELLERS WITH SPECIAL NEEDS

Spain offers a number of options for travellers with special needs. The national association for the disabled, the Confederación Coordinadora Estatal de Minusválidos Físicos de España (COCEMFE), publishes useful guides to facilities in Spain and will help plan a holiday to suit individual needs *(see p557)*.

If you need metro maps and other informative leaflets in Braille, these are available from the Spanish national organization for the blind, the Organización Nacional de Ciegos (ONCE). You will find that tourist offices and the social services departments of town halls are worth investigating as they can also provide useful up-to-date information on local conditions and facilities suitable for disabled travellers.

COCEMFE logo

Viajes 2000 is a travel agency that specializes in package and organized holidays for people with limited mobility. The UK-based Tourism For All (www.tourismforall.org.uk) offers information on facilities for the disabled in a selection of Spanish resorts. The Society for the Advancement of Travel for the Handicapped (SATH) publishes similar information on a number of destinations for travellers from the US *(see p557)*.

CONVERSION CHART

Imperial to metric
1 inch = 2.54 centimetres
1 foot = 30 centimetres
1 mile = 1.6 kilometres
1 ounce = 28 grams
1 pound = 454 grams
1 pint = 0.6 litre
1 gallon = 4.6 litres

Metric to imperial
1 millimetre = 0.04 inch
1 centimetre = 0.4 inch
1 metre = 3 feet 3 inches
1 kilometre = 0.6 mile
1 gram = 0.04 ounce
1 kilogram = 2.2 pounds
1 litre = 1.8 pints

Children catching small fish with nets, Cala Gracio, Ibiza

TRAVELLING WITH CHILDREN

Spain is a famously child-friendly country, and travellers with kids will find that their offspring are usually welcome in bars, restaurants and hotels.

It is recommended that you take a few sensible precautions when travelling with children, especially in the summer months. Avoid being out and about in the hottest hours of the day (noon–3pm); apply sunscreen with a high protection factor on your children's skin regularly and liberally; always make sure they wear a sun hat with a wide brim; and take frequent breaks for refreshments. Visit www.travelforkids.com for a good list of travel agents specializing in child-friendly family holidays.

All large hospitals in Spain will be able to provide a paediatrics service, although pharmacy attendants are also trained to provide a basic level of treatment for minor health complaints. Visit www.spainexpat.com/spain/information/doctors_in_spain for a list of English-speaking doctors.

Old-fashioned street sign

SENIOR TRAVELLERS

There are plenty of options for both leisurely and more active holidays for senior travellers in Spain.

Health spas have become increasingly popular throughout the country, and they combine relaxation with specific treatments using thermal waters (www.balnearios.org). Walking tours suitable for senior travellers can be found along the country's network of green paths (www.viasverdes.com).

It is always worth enquiring about senior discounts as some of the larger hotels offer special rates.

GAY AND LESBIAN TRAVELLERS

Attitudes to gay and lesbian people vary greatly between urban and rural areas in Spain. All major cities have thriving gay scenes, with Madrid and Barcelona boasting gay-friendly areas of town (Chueca and "Gayxample") with hotels, restaurants and services aimed at gay and lesbian travellers. The Federación Estatal de Lesbianas, Gays, Transexuales y Bisexuales (FELGTB) (www.felgtb.org) provides information for travellers online and at its local offices in most Spanish towns.

The Gay Pride parades (www.cogam.org) have become major events and are a good place to meet people. A law allowing gays and lesbians to marry, adopt children and enjoy the same rights as heterosexuals was passed in June 2005.

TRAVELLING ON A BUDGET

Travellers looking for budget accommodation should keep an eye out for the sign *Hostal* or *Pensión*, which indicates clean and comfortable rooms at a fraction of the cost of a hotel (see also www.hostelworld.com). Most restaurants in Spain offer a *menú del día* – three courses with wine for as little as €10, and tapas can be another cheap and filling option (they even come free with drinks in some areas).

The Spanish train service is relatively cheap *(see pp676-7)*. Prices can vary on popular lines (for example, the Barcelona–Madrid) depending on the type and speed of train, so check in advance (www.renfe.es). The cheapest, and sometimes the quickest, way to get around is on the excellent network of coaches. Different companies serve different regions, so check timetables and prices online (www.alsa.es) or at the tourist office before travelling. Hitchhiking is common in rural areas and on the Balearic Islands, but avoid hitchhiking alone.

The best and cheapest spectacles in Spain are often found on the streets, especially during the *fiesta mayor* of the various regions and cities, which often include processions and dancing *(see pp38-43)*.

Hostal sign indicating budget accommodation

STUDENT INFORMATION

Holders of the International Student Identity Card (ISIC) are entitled to various benefits in Spain, such as discounted accommodation and travel fares plus reduced entrance charges to museums, galleries and other attractions.

Useful information for student travellers from overseas is available from all national student organizations and, in Spain, from the local government-run **Centros de Información Juvenil (CIJ)** in large towns. The company **Turismo y Viajes Educativos (TIVE)** offers specialist travel services for students.

ISIC student card

SPANISH TIME

In winter, Spain is one hour ahead of Greenwich Mean Time (GMT) and in summer an hour ahead of British Summer Time (BST). The Canary Islands are on GMT in winter and an hour ahead in summer.

La madrugada refers to the small hours. *Mañana* (morning) lasts until about 2pm and *mediodía* (midday) is the part of the day from about 1pm to 4pm. *La tarde* is the afternoon and *la noche* the evening.

ELECTRICAL ADAPTORS

Spain's electricity supply is 220 volts. Plugs have two round pins. A three-tier standard travel converter enables you to use appliances from abroad. Most hotels can lend you an adaptor. If you come from the USA make sure that your electrical equipment works at this voltage.

RESPONSIBLE TRAVEL

After several decades of rapid construction that saw much of the country's coastline buried under concrete, Spain has taken big steps to encourage a more sustainable approach to tourism. A series of laws prohibits any construction up to 100 m (328 ft) from the coastline. Tourism, an important source of income, has also become more strictly regulated.

Casas rurales, private country homes that cater to small groups of tourists in a welcoming family atmosphere, offer a perfect option for green travel. Visit www.ecoturismorural.com for more details. The Blue Flag Programme, owned and run by the non-profit Foundation for Environmental Education (FEE), lists 521 beaches and 84 marinas in Spain that comply with their strict environmental criteria. Spain has a delicate ecosystem and several areas that are still barely developed for travellers – take extra care when visiting these spots.

Visitors to Spain can encourage sustainable tourism by using locally owned shops and businesses. Cities are legally obliged to have markets in each district. Elsewhere, go to family-owned shops or buy products at source: most towns have weekend food markets that draw local farmers.

Students enjoy reduced admission fees to many museums and galleries

DIRECTORY

EMBASSIES

United Kingdom
Torre Espacio, Paseo de la Castellana 259D, 28046 Madrid.
Tel *91 714 63 00.*
www.ukinspain.com

United States
Calle Serrano 75, 28006 Madrid.
Tel *91 587 22 00.*
http://madrid.usembassy.gov

SPANISH TOURIST OFFICES

Australia (consulate)
Level 24, St Martin's Tower, 31 Market St, Sydney NSW 2000. ***Tel*** *29 261 2433.*

Barcelona
Palau Robert, Paseo de Gràcia 107, 08008 Barcelona.
Tel *90 240 00 12.*
www.spain.info

Madrid
Plaza de Colón, 28013 Madrid.
Tel *90 210 00 07.*
www.spain.info

Seville
Avenida de la Constitución 21b, 41001 Seville. ***Tel*** *95 478 75 78.*
www.andalucia.org

United Kingdom
6th Floor, 64 North Row, London W1K 7DE .
Tel *0800 1010 5050.*
www.spain.info/

United States
60 East 42nd St, Suite 5300 New York NY 10165.
Tel *(212) 265 8822.*
www.spain.info/

DISABLED TRAVEL

Viajes 2000
Paseo de la Castellana 228–230, 28046 Madrid.
Tel *91 323 25 23.*
www.viajes2000.com

STUDENT TRAVEL

CIJ
Paseo de Recoletos 7, 28004 Madrid. ***Tel*** *901 510 610.*
www.madrid.org/inforjoven

TIVE
Calle Fernando el Católico 88, 28015 Madrid.
Tel *91 543 74 12.*
www.madrid.org/inforjoven

Personal Security and Health

Policía Local

In Spain, as in most European countries, rural areas are generally safe, but certain parts of cities are subject to petty crime. Carry cards and money in a belt, and never leave anything visible in your car. Taking out medical insurance cover is advisable, but pharmacists are good sources of assistance for minor health problems. If you lose your documents, contact the local police first to make a claim, then your consulate. Emergency phone numbers vary *(see opposite)*.

SPANISH POLICE

There are three types of police in Spain. The *Guardia Civil* (National Guard) police mainly rural areas. Their uniform is olive green, but there are local and regional variations. They impose fines for traffic offences outside the cities and police the borders.

The *Policía Nacional*, who mainly wear a blue uniform, operate in towns with a population of more than 30,000. They have been replaced with a regional force, the *Ertzaintza*, in the Basque Country, and with the *Mossos d'Esquadra* in Catalonia. These can be recognized by their respective red and blue berets.

The *Policía Local*, also called *Policía Municipal* or *Guardia Urbana*, dress in blue. They operate independently in each town and also have a separate branch for city traffic control. All three services will direct you to the relevant authority in the event of an incident requiring police help.

PERSONAL SECURITY AND PROPERTY

Violent crime is rare in Spain, but visitors should avoid walking alone in poorly lit areas. Wear bags and cameras across your body, not on your shoulder.

Holiday insurance is there to protect you financially from the loss or theft of your property, but it is always best to take obvious precautions.

WHAT TO BE AWARE OF

Be aware of street scams in large cities, including unexpected offers to help with bags, to clean stains off your clothes or to participate in impromptu football games. Never leave a bag or handbag unattended anywhere, and do not place your purse or handbag on the tabletop in a café. Take particular care at markets, tourist sights and stations. Be especially careful of pickpockets when getting on or off a crowded train or metro.

The moment you discover a loss or theft, report it to the local police station. To claim insurance you must do this immediately, since many companies give you only 24 hours. Ask for a *denuncia* (written statement), which you need to make a claim. If your passport is stolen, or if you lose it, report it to your consulate, too.

While tourists remain targets for petty crime in Spanish cities, remember that it is common for Spanish people to approach you and strike up a conversation, and you should not let normal precautions stop you from interacting with the locals.

Men occasionally make complimentary remarks (*piropos*) to women in public, particularly in the street. This is an old custom and is not intended to be intimidating.

Guardia Civil

Policía Nacional

Policía Local

Sign identifying a Cruz Roja (Red Cross) emergency treatment centre

IN AN EMERGENCY

The *Policía Nacional* operate a nationwide emergency phone number (091). Local emergency numbers are listed in telephone directories under *Servicios de Urgencia*; they also appear on tourist maps and leaflets.

For emergency medical treatment, call the emergency services or an ambulance, or go straight to the nearest hospital casualty department (*Urgencias*).

Visit www.jointcommission.org for a list of hospitals vetted by the US-based NGO Joint Commission.

PHARMACIES

Spanish pharmacists have wide responsibilities. They can advise and, in some cases, prescribe without consulting a doctor. In a non-emergency, a *farmacéutico* is a good option. It is easy to find one who speaks English.

The *farmacia* sign is a green or red illuminated cross. Those open at night are listed in the windows of all the local pharmacies. Note that *perfumerías* sell toiletries only.

Spanish pharmacy sign

MEDICAL TREATMENT

In general, the Spanish health system is modern and efficient, and it can be relied on for emergency treatment. There are two kinds of hospitals in Spain: public hospitals (*públicos*) and private clinics (*clínicas privadas*). For emergency treatment, go straight to *Urgencias* at any hospital; for less serious problems, head to a *Centro de Atención Primaria* or *Ambulatorio* and ask for the *médico de urgencias*.

If you have private health insurance, you can go to a private clinic for normal medical complaints.

LEGAL ASSISTANCE

Some insurance policies cover legal costs, for instance after an accident. If you are in need of assistance and are not covered, telephone your nearest consulate. The *Colegio de Abogados* (lawyers' association) of the nearest city can also advise you on where to obtain legal advice or representation locally.

If you need an interpreter, consult the local *Páginas Amarillas* (Yellow Pages) under *Traductores* or *Intérpretes*. Both *Traductores Oficiales* and *Traductores Jurados* are qualified to translate legal and official documents.

TRAVEL AND HEALTH INSURANCE

All EU nationals are entitled to short term free emergency healthcare cover. To claim, you must obtain the European Health Insurance Card (EHIC) from the UK Department of Health or a post office before you travel. The card gives you free health cover at all public Spanish hospitals. It comes with a booklet explaining exactly what health care you are entitled to and how to claim. You may have to pay and claim the money back later. Not all treatments are covered, so for more peace of mind, arrange medical cover in advance.

There is a wide range of medical insurance available for travellers to Spain. Shop around before deciding because prices vary greatly, as do the levels of cover offered, with some including aspects like emergency travel back home or the cost of relatives joining you. Many credit cards also offer limited health insurance for their users.

PUBLIC CONVENIENCES

Public pay-toilets are rare in Spain. Try department stores, or bars and restaurants where you are a customer. You may have to ask for a key (*la llave*), and it is best to bring your own tissues. There are also toilets at service stations on motorways. Toilets are most commonly known as *los servicios*.

OUTDOOR HAZARDS

Every summer Spain is prey to forest fires fanned by winds and fuelled by bone-dry vegetation. Be sensitive to fire hazards and use car ashtrays. Broken glass can also start a fire, so take your empty bottles away with you.

The sign *coto de caza* in woodland areas identifies a hunting reserve where you must follow the country codes. *Toro bravo* means "fighting bull" – do not approach. A *camino particular* sign indicates a private driveway. Do not approach dogs that are protecting country properties.

If you are climbing or hill-walking, make sure that you are properly equipped and let someone know when you expect to return.

Patrol car of the Policía Nacional, Spain's main urban police force

Policía Local patrol car, mainly seen in small towns

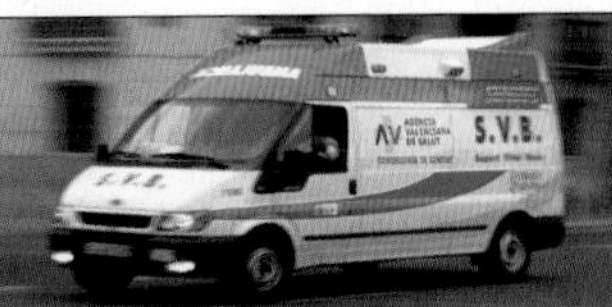

Cruz Roja (Red Cross) ambulance

DIRECTORY

EMERGENCY NUMBERS

Emergency: all services
Tel *112 (nationwide).*

Policía Nacional
Tel *091 (nationwide).*

Fire Brigade (Bomberos)
Tel *080 (in most major cities).*

Ambulance
Tel *112 or 061.*

For other cities' emergency services, consult the local telephone directory.

Banking and Local Currency

You may enter Spain with any amount of money, but if you intend to export more than €10,000, you should declare it. Travellers' cheques may be exchanged at banks, *cajas de cambio* (foreign currency exchanges), some hotels and some shops. Banks generally offer the best exchange rates. The cheapest exchange may be offered on your credit or direct debit card, which you can use in cash dispensers (automated teller machines, ATMs) displaying the appropriate sign.

BANKING HOURS

Spanish banks are beginning to extend their opening times, but expect extended hours only at large central branches in the big cities.

Banks are open from 8am to 2pm during the week. Some open until 1pm on Saturdays. All close on Saturdays in July and August; in some areas, they also close on Saturdays from May to September.

CHANGING MONEY

Most banks have a foreign exchange desk with the sign *Cambio* or *Extranjero,* which will accept travellers' cheques and cash. Always take your passport as identification to effect any transaction.

You can draw up to €300 on major credit cards at a bank. It is worth mentioning your travel plans to your bank and credit card company before you go away so that your card is not blocked by their fraud prevention system.

Bureaux de change, with the sign *Caja de Cambio* or "Change", may state that they charge no commission, but their exchange rates are invariably less favourable than those found at banks. One benefit is that they are often open outside normal banking hours. They are usually located in popular tourist areas, as well as at airports and mainline rail stations. *Cajas de Ahorro* (savings banks) also exchange money. They open from 8:30am to 2pm on weekdays and also on Thursday afternoons from 4:30pm to 7:45pm.

BBVA

Logo for BBVA, the Banco Bilbao Vizcaya Argentaria

CHEQUES AND CARDS

The use of travellers' cheques is declining and it is not always easy to find places to cash the cheques. Banks also need 24 hours' notice to cash cheques larger than €3,000.

Prepaid VISA and MasterCard credit cards are a convenient way to pay, as are Travel Money Cards. These cards work like debit cards. They are available in several currencies from most banks, and can be reloaded through their websites.

The most widely accepted card in Spain is the **VISA** card, although **MasterCard** (Access)/ Eurocard and **American Express** are also used. The major banks will allow cash withdrawals on credit cards. All cash dispensers accept most foreign cards, and they will often give you a choice of several languages, including English. However, the level of commission charged on your withdrawal will depend on your own bank, and some credit cards may charge an additional fee.

When you pay with a card, cashiers pass it through a card-reading machine and you usually need to provide a pin number. In shops you will always be asked for additional photo ID. Since leaving your passport in the hotel safe is preferable, make sure you have an alternative original document on hand (photo-copies will rarely do), such as a driver's licence.

As with the rest of Europe, cards are not always accepted in some smaller bars and restaurants.

A 24-hour cash dispenser

CASH DISPENSERS

If your card is linked to your home bank account, you can use it with your PIN to withdraw money from cash dispensers. All take VISA and MasterCard.

When you enter your PIN, instructions are displayed in English, French, German and Spanish. Many dispensers are inside buildings and to gain access you will have to run your card through a door-entry system.

Cards with the Cirrus and Maestro logos can also be widely used to withdraw money from cash machines.

DIRECTORY

FOREIGN BANKS

Barclays Bank
C/ Velázquez 68, 28001 Madrid.
Tel *901 14 14 14.*

Citibank
C/ Velázquez 31, 28001 Madrid.
Tel *902 33 31 13.*

Lloyds TSB
C/ Serrano 90, 28006 Madrid.
Tel *902 02 43 65.*

LOST CARDS AND TRAVELLERS' CHEQUES

American Express
Tel *900 81 45 00.*

Diners Club
Tel *902 40 11 12.*

MasterCard
Tel *900 97 12 31 (toll free).*

VISA
Tel *900 99 11 24 (toll free).*

THE EURO

Spain was one of the 12 countries adopting the euro in 2002, with its original currency, the peseta, phased out in the course of the same year.

EU countries using the euro as sole official currency are known as the Eurozone. Several EU members have opted out of joining this common currency.

Euro notes are identical throughout the Eurozone countries, each one including designs of fictional architectural structures and monuments. The coins, however, have one identical side (the value side), and one side with an image unique to each country. Both notes and coins are exchangeable in each of the participating euro countries.

Banknotes

Euro banknotes, each a different colour and size, come in seven denominations. The €5 note (grey in colour) is the smallest, followed by the €10 note (pink), €20 note (blue), €50 note (orange), €100 note (green), €200 note (yellow) and €500 note (purple).

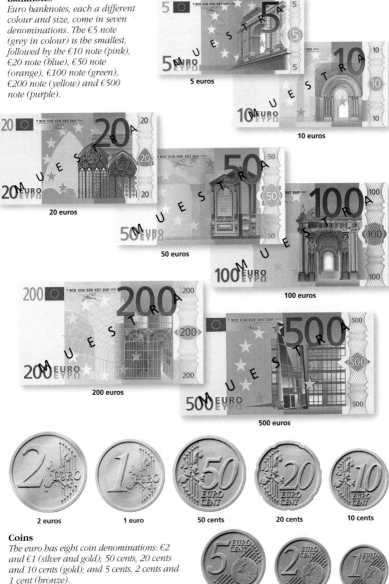

5 euros

10 euros

20 euros

50 euros

100 euros

200 euros

500 euros

2 euros

1 euro

50 cents

20 cents

10 cents

Coins

The euro has eight coin denominations: €2 and €1 (silver and gold); 50 cents, 20 cents and 10 cents (gold); and 5 cents, 2 cents and 1 cent (bronze).

5 cents

2 cents

1 cent

Communications and Media

Shops with this sign sell stamps

The telecommunications company Movistar dominates the industry in Spain, but companies like Orange and Vodafone now compete for the mobile phone market. Public telephones are easy to find; most require a phone card. International calls tend to be expensive. The postal service, Correos, is identified by a blue crown logo on a yellow background. Registered post and telegrams can be sent from Correos offices. They also sell stamps, but most people buy them from *estancos* (tobacconists).

TELEPHONING IN SPAIN

When calling from a fixed line, there are four charge bands for international calls: European Union countries; non-European Union countries and Northwest Africa; North and South America; and the rest of the world. With the exception of local calls, using the telephone system in Spain can be quite expensive, especially when making calls from a hotel, which may add a surcharge. A call from a phone booth, or *cabina*, costs 35 per cent more than one made from a private phone. Most reverse-charge calls must be made through the operator. When telephoning Spain from abroad, first dial the international code for Spain (34) followed by the area code.

MOBILE PHONES

Roaming costs to use your mobile phone in Spain vary greatly among the different providers; however, mobile phones have now become a

A Spanish telecom company's logo

more reasonable option if your operator offers a special fixed rate. The EU has tried to standardize the cost of using a mobile phone within its borders.

If you are planning to make a lot of calls, the best option is to buy a Spanish top-up SIM card, or a handset with a top-up SIM card, at a department store or specialist phone shop. The most popular providers in Spain are Movistar and Vodafone; each have their own shops with experts who can give you advice. For a simple handset, plus SIM card (allowing free incoming calls in Spain), expect to pay in the region of €50–€60.

To add more credit to your phone card, purchase a scratch card from shops and supermarkets. Alternatively, you can do it automatically with your credit card by dialling a number from your phone – check with your service provider. Mobile phone top-ups are also available at most ATMs.

INTERNET AND EMAIL

Wireless hotspots are available in all airports, hotels and conference centres throughout Spain, although the majority are not free. Credit can be bought online with a major credit card.

Internet cafés *(cibercafés)* are fairly common in most cities and resorts, and *locutorios* (privately owned call centres) often provide cheap Internet access, too. Free Internet access can be found in public libraries, some public areas (such as Madrid's Plaza Mayor), universities and an increasing number of cafés offering Wi-Fi service.

NEWSPAPERS AND MAGAZINES

Newsagents in tourist-oriented town centres often stock periodicals in languages other than Spanish. The English-language daily newspapers available on publication day are the *International Herald*

A selection of Spanish newspapers

USEFUL SPANISH DIALLING CODES

- When calling within a city, within a province, or to call another province, dial the entire number. The province is indicated by the initial digits: Barcelona numbers, for example, start with 93, Girona with 972 and Tarragona 977.
- To make an international call, dial 00, then dial the country code, the area code and the number.
- Country codes are: UK 44; Eire 353; France 33; USA and Canada 1; Australia 61; New Zealand 64. Depending on which country you are calling, it may be necessary to omit the initial digit of the destination's area code.
- For operator/directory service, dial 11888.
- For international directories, dial 11825.
- To make a reverse-charge (collect) call to the UK only, dial 900 961 682. Inexpensive international calls can be made in *locutorios*, or call centres. These can be found in most cities and towns. Cheap phone cards can also be purchased there.
- To report technical faults, dial 1002.
- For the speaking clock and for a wake-up call, dial 1212 (from Movistar landlines only).

Tribune, the *Financial Times*, the *Guardian International* and the *Sun*, which is printed in the south of Spain. Several other English-language and European titles are also on the stands, but usually only the day after publication. The most widely read Spanish papers are *El País*, *El Mundo*, *ABC*, *La Razon* and *La Vanguardia* (in Catalonia).

Popular weekly news magazines such as *Time*, *Newsweek* and *The Economist* are readily available throughout the country.

Weekly listings magazines for local arts, entertainment and events are published in Barcelona *(see p190)*, Madrid *(see p320)* and Seville *(see p456)*. Several other Spanish cities also have their own listings magazines.

A number of foreign-language periodicals are published by expatriates in Madrid and in the country's other main tourist areas. Some examples in English include *Metropolitan* in Barcelona, *Sur* on the Costa del Sol, the *Costa Blanca News* and the *Mallorca Daily Bulletin*.

Spanish postbox

TELEVISION AND RADIO

Televisión Española, Spain's state television company, broadcasts on two channels, TVE1 and TVE2, which run 24 hours a day.

Several of the *comunidades* have their own publicly owned television channels, which broadcast in the language of the region. In addition, there are a few national television stations: Antena 3, Tele-5 (Telecinco), La Sexta and Cuatro.

Digital TV in Spain is offered by two companies, Canal+ and Imagenio. This provides access to dozens of local channels and the possibility of watching programmes in their original language or with subtitles.

Radio is very popular throughout Spain and there are a number of English-language radio stations based mainly in the south, including Talk Radio Europe, which is the largest network, (88.2 FM, 105.1 FM, 95.3 FM, 92.7 FM, 103.9 FM and 89.0 FM) and Wave96FM (96 FM) from Malagá on the Costa del Sol. All of these stations can also be listened to online and they are a good source of local and international news in English.

POSTAL SERVICE

Correos is Spain's postal service. Mail sent within the same city usually takes a day to arrive. Deliveries between cities take two to three days. Urgent or important post can be sent by *urgente* (express) or *certificado* (registered) mail. For fast delivery, use the Correos Postal Express Service or a private courier.

Post can be registered, and telegrams sent from all Correos offices. However, it is much easier to buy stamps from an *estanco* (tobacconist). Postal rates fall into three price bands: Spain; Europe and North Africa; and the rest of the world. Parcels must be weighed and stamped at Correos offices.

The main Correos offices open 8:30am–9:30pm Monday to Friday and 9:30am–1pm on Saturday; outside the cities they close an hour earlier on weekdays.

Letters sent from a post office usually arrive more quickly than if posted in a postbox (*buzón*). In cities, postboxes are yellow pillar boxes; elsewhere they are small, wall-mounted postboxes. *Poste restante* letters should be addressed care of the *Lista de Correos* and the town, and collected from main offices.

To send and receive money by post, ask for a *giro postal*.

ADDRESSES

In Spanish addresses, the house number follows the name of the street. The floor of a block of flats comes after a hyphen. Therefore 4-2° means a flat on the second floor of number four. All postcodes in Spain have five digits, the first two being the province number.

LOCAL GOVERNMENT

Spain is one of Europe's most decentralized states. Many powers have been devolved to the 17 regions, also known as *comunidades autónomas*, which have their own elected parliaments. These regions have varying degrees of independence from Madrid, with the Basques and Catalans enjoying the most autonomy. The *comunidades* provide some services – such as the promotion of tourism – that were once carried out by the central government.

The country is subdivided into 50 provinces, each with its *diputación* (council). The affairs of each of the Balearic and Canary islands are run by an island council.

Every town, or group of villages, is administered by an *ayuntamiento* (town council – the word also means town hall), which is then supervised by an elected *alcalde* (mayor) and a team of councillors.

Murcia's town hall *(ayuntamiento or casa consistorial)*

TRAVEL INFORMATION

Spain has invested heavily in its transport infrastructure since 2005, creating new motorways and high-speed rail networks to connect much of the country. Madrid airport is an important international travel hub, and new terminals at Malaga and Barcelona airports have been built to cater for the huge influx of passengers. Intercity rail services are reliable and efficient, but coaches are a faster and more frequent option between smaller towns. In much of rural Spain, public transport is limited, and a car is the most practical option for getting about. Spain boasts some beautiful back roads to hidden areas of the country. Ferries connect mainland Spain with the UK, Italy, North Africa and the Balearic and Canary islands.

aeropuerto

Sign for an airport

GREEN TRAVEL

Public transport in larger cities has adopted a green focus, and most buses now run on clean fuel. Services are generally excellent, and reasonably priced. With the opening of the long-awaited Madrid–Barcelona high-speed rail link (the AVE), Spain now boasts one of Europe's best railway infrastructures. There are plans for added links to the Basque region and Galicia, and from Northern Spain into France. Prices on the AVE vary depending on the days you want to travel, and they are much lower if you buy your tickets online.

Some areas of Spain are still best accessed by road. Car users should consider renting hybrid vehicles, now available from major car rental firms. Local and environmentally friendly bus services reach most areas.

Arriving by Air

Spain is served by most international airlines and by many budget airlines. Its national airline **Iberia** offers flights from most European capitals. **British Airways** flies to Madrid and Barcelona as do US airlines **Delta**, **United** and **American Airlines**. Iberia has a wide-ranging service from the USA.

Colourful aircraft at Ibiza's airport

INTERNATIONAL AIRPORTS

The most regular international services operate from Madrid and Barcelona. Palma de Mallorca, Tenerife Sur, Las Palmas de Gran Canaria, Ibiza Málaga, Lanzarote, Alicante, Fuerteventura and Menorca handle a lot of tourists, especially in the summer.

TICKETS AND FARES

Air fares vary by season and demand. Special deals, particularly for city breaks, often run in winter. Look out for Iberia's reduced fares and for low-cost carriers, such as **easyJet** and **Ryanair** (UK). **Vueling** offers low-cost flights from Spain to other European countries.

AIRPORT	INFORMATION	DISTANCE TO CITY CENTRE	TAXI FARE TO CITY CENTRE	PUBLIC TRANSPORT TIME TO CITY CENTRE
Alicante	902 40 47 04	10 km (6 miles)	€17	Bus: 20 mins
Barcelona	902 40 47 04	14 km (9 miles)	€30	Rail: 35 mins Bus: 25 mins
Bilbao	902 40 47 04	12 km (7 miles)	€23	Bus: 30 mins
Madrid	902 40 47 04	16 km (10 miles)	€28	Bus: 20 mins Metro: 30–40 mins
Málaga	902 40 47 04	8 km (5 miles)	€20	Rail: 15 mins Bus: 20 mins
Palma de Mallorca	902 40 47 04	9 km (6 miles)	€21–€23	Bus: 15 mins
Las Palmas de Gran Canaria	902 40 47 04	18 km (11 miles)	€27	Bus: 60 mins
Santiago de Compostela	902 40 47 04	10 km (6 miles)	€21	Bus: 20–30 mins
Seville	902 40 47 04	10 km (6 miles)	€20–€23	Bus: 25–30 mins
Tenerife Sur – Reina Sofía	902 40 47 04	64 km (40 miles) to Santa Cruz	€55	Bus: 60 mins
Valencia	902 40 47 04	9 km (5 miles)	€18–€23	Bus: 20 or 60 mins

The departures concourse at Seville airport

INTERNAL FLIGHTS

In the past, the majority of domestic flights were operated by Iberia, but now there are other main carriers, such as **Air Europa** and Vueling. The most frequent shuttle service is the Puente Aéreo, run between Barcelona and Madrid by Iberia every 15 minutes at peak times, and half-hourly or hourly at other times. The flight generally takes 50 minutes. Vueling and Air Europa services between Madrid and the regional capitals are not as frequent as the Puente Aéreo, but they are usually cheaper; book early to take advantage of lower fares. Flights between the Canary Islands are operated by **Binter**. Some flights from domestic airports are billed as international flights and stop over at major Spanish cities en route.

ARRIVING BY SEA

Ferries connect the Spanish mainland to the Balearic and Canary islands, and to North Africa, Italy and the UK. All the important routes are served by car ferries. Always make an advance booking, especially in summer.

Three routes link Spain with the UK. **Brittany Ferries** sails between Plymouth in the UK and Santander in Cantabria. There are also routes linking Portsmouth with Santander, and Portsmouth with Bilbao in the Basque Country. The crossings take over 24 hours. Each ship has cabins, chairs to sleep on, restaurants, cafés and cinemas. The Italian **Grimaldi Lines** has overnight journeys to Rome, Livorno and Sardinia.

FERRIES TO THE ISLANDS

Frequent crossings run from Barcelona and Valencia to the three main Balearic islands. **Acciona Trasmediterránea** ferries take from four hours (using the fast ferry from Barcelona) to eight hours. The same company also operates frequent inter-island services, while small operators take day-trippers (passengers only) from Ibiza to Formentera. **Balearia** also sails to the Balearic Islands from Barcelona and Valencia.

Acciona Trasmediterránea operates a weekly service from Cádiz to the main ports of the Canary Islands, which normally takes 32 hours. Car ferries link the various islands. There are also passengers-only services between the islands of Gran Canaria, Tenerife and Fuerteventura, and between Tenerife and La Gomera.

Acciona Trasmediterránea logo

Ferries to the islands have cabins, cafés, restaurants, bars, shops, cinemas, pools and sunbathing decks. They also have facilities for people with special needs. Entertainment is provided on mainland crossings to the Canary Islands.

FERRIES TO AFRICA

Acciona Trasmediterránea has daily services to the Spanish territories in North Africa: from Málaga and Almería to Melilla, and from Algeciras to Ceuta, as well as from Algeciras and Tarifa to Tangier. Balearia also sails to Ceuta and Tangier from Algeciras. It maybe worth checking the website for up-to-date offers.

Balearia car ferry sailing to the Balearic Islands

DIRECTORY

AIRLINES

Air Europa
Tel 902 40 15 01 *in Spain.*
www.aireuropa.com

American Airlines
Tel 902 11 55 70 *in Spain.*
Tel 800 433 73 00 *in USA.*
www.americanairlines.es

Binter
Tel 902 39 13 92 *in Spain.*
www.bintercanarias.com

British Airways
Tel 902 11 13 33 *in Spain.*
Tel 08444 93 07 87 *in UK.*
www.ba.com

Delta Air Lines
Tel 902 81 08 72 *in Spain.*
Tel 800 221 12 12 *in USA.*
www.delta.com

easyJet
Tel 902 59 99 00 *in Spain.*
www.easyjet.com

Iberia
Tel 902 40 05 00 *in Spain.*
www.iberia.com

Ryanair
Tel 00 44871 246 0011 *(UK).*
www.ryanair.com

United
Tel 900 96 12 66 *in Spain.*
www.united.com

Vueling
Tel 807 00 17 17 *in Spain.*
www.vueling.com

FERRIES

Acciona Trasmediterránea
Tel 902 45 46 45 *in Spain.*
www.trasmediterranea.es

Balearia
Tel 902 16 01 80 *in Spain.*
www.balearia.com

Brittany Ferries
Tel 0871 244 1401 *in UK.*
Tel 902 10 81 47 *in Spain.*
www.brittanyferries.com

Grimaldi Lines
Tel 902 53 13 33 *in Spain.*
www.grimaldi-lines.com

Travelling by Train

Logo of the Spanish national railways

The Spanish state railway, **RENFE** *(Red Nacional de Ferrocarriles Españoles)*, operates a service that is continually improving, particularly between cities. The fastest intercity services are called TALGO and AVE – these names are acronyms for the high-speed luxury trains that run on these routes. *Largo recorrido* (long-distance) and *regionales y cercanías* (regional and local) trains are notoriously slow, many stopping at every station on the way. They are much cheaper than the high-speed trains, but journey times can be hours longer.

ARRIVING BY TRAIN

There are several routes to Spain from France. The main western route runs from Paris through Hendaye in the Pyrenees to San Sebastián. The eastern route from Paris runs via Cerbère and Port Bou to Barcelona. The trains from London, Brussels, Amsterdam, Geneva, Zurich and Milan all reach Barcelona via Cerbère. At Cerbère there are also connections with the TALGO and the long-distance services to Valencia, Alicante, Girona and Murcia. If you book a sleeper on the TALGO from Paris, you travel to your destination without having to change trains. There are direct trains to Madrid and Barcelona from Paris, and to Barcelona from Milan, Geneva and Zurich.

EXPLORING BY TRAIN

Spain offers many options for train travellers. The introduction of high-speed services has made it possible to travel the long distances between the main cities extremely quickly. Ticket prices compare favourably with the cost of high-speed train fares in many other countries in Europe. Efficient high-speed AVE rail services link Madrid with Seville in two and a half hours, and with Barcelona in three hours. The AVE from Madrid to Zaragoza takes one and a half hours; to Málaga two hours and 40 minutes; and to Valladolid only 50 minutes. AVE routes also link Barcelona with Seville and with Málaga – both trips take five and a half hours.

AVE high-speed trains at Estación de Santa Justa in Seville

The *largo recorrido* (long-distance) trains are so much slower that you usually need to travel overnight. You can choose between a *cochecama* (a compartment with two or four *camas*, or beds) or a *litera*, one of six seats in a compartment that converts into a bunk bed. You reserve these when booking and pay a supplement. Book at least a month in advance.

Regionales y cercanías (the regional and local services) are frequent and cheap.

Logo for a high-speed rail service

In Madrid the major stations for regional and long-distance trains are Atocha and Chamartín. The AVE runs from Atocha, and the TALGO from both. Sants and Passeig de Gràcia are Barcelona's two main stations. In Seville Santa Justa is the only station for regional and international services. Major train terminals pass luggage through scanners; allow extra time for this.

FARES

Fares for rail travel in Spain are structured according to the speed and quality of the service. Tickets for the TALGO and AVE trains cost the most.

Interrail tickets for people under 26 and Eurail tickets for non-EU residents are available from major travel agencies in Europe and from RENFE ticket offices in Spain. Always take proof of your identity when booking.

Holidays onboard Spain's luxury train *(see p677)* are expensive but offer high standards of comfort.

REGIONAL RAILWAYS

Three of the *comunidades autónomas* have regional rail companies. Catalonia and Valencia each has its own *Ferrocarrils de la Generalitat* – respectively,

DIRECTORY

NATIONAL ENQUIRIES AND RESERVATIONS

El Transcantábrico
Tel *902 55 59 02.*
www.eltranscantabricogranlujo.com

RENFE
Tel *902 32 03 20; for information on disabled access call 902 24 05 05.*
www.renfe.es

REGIONAL RAILWAYS

ET
Tel *902 54 32 10.*
www.euskotren.es

FEVE
Tel *944 25 06 15.*
www.feve.es

FGC
Tel *932 05 15 15.*
www.fgc.net

FGV
Tel *900 46 10 46.*
www.fgv.es

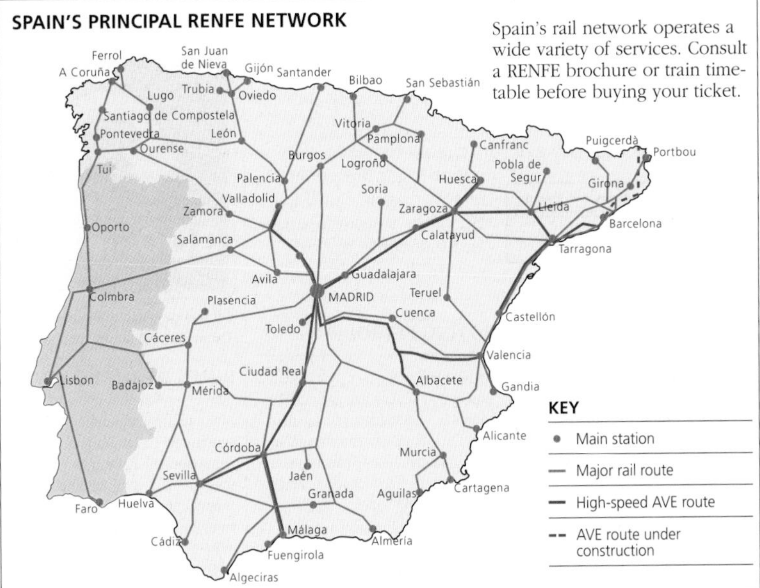

Spain's rail network operates a wide variety of services. Consult a RENFE brochure or train timetable before buying your ticket.

the **FGC** and the **FGV**; and the Basque Country has the **ET** *(Eusko Trenbideak)*.

Tickets for Spain's luxury train, similar to the Orient Express, can be obtained from travel agents. **El Transcantábrico**, run by **FEVE** *(Ferrocarriles de Vía Estrecha)*, travels the 1,000 km (620 miles) of Spain's north coast between San Sebastián and Santiago de Compostela. Passengers travel in style for eight days in 14 restored period carriages that were all built between 1900 and 1930.

The regional tourist offices publicize unusual rail services in their local areas, such as the narrow-gauge lines to Inca and Sóller in Mallorca *(see p515)*.

BOOKING TICKETS

Tickets for TALGO, AVE and any other *largo recorrido* travel may be bought at any of the major railway stations from the *taquilla* (ticket office). They are also sold by all travel agents in Spain, who will charge a commission. RENFE tickets are sometimes sold by travel agents in other countries. Telephone reservations may be made directly to all RENFE ticket offices with a credit card. Tickets can also be bought via the RENFE website, which has some cheaper fares, and printed out. Tickets for local and regional services are purchased from the station *taquilla*. In larger stations, they can be bought from ticket machines. Tickets for *cercanías* (local services) cannot be reserved. For a one-way journey, ask for *ida*, and for a return, ask for *ida y vuelta*. Return tickets are cheaper.

Ticket machine for local and regional lines

TIMETABLES

RENFE timetables change in May and October each year. Your travel agent will be able to provide the correct times for your train journey. Timetables can also be accessed in English via the RENFE website. In Spain, timetables are available from RENFE offices. Most come as leaflets and are broken down into the various types of journey: intercity, *largo recorrido* and *regionales*. *Cercanías* timetables are posted on boards at local railway stations.

Atocha, one of Madrid's largest mainline railway stations

Travelling by Road

Spain's fastest roads are its *autopistas*. They are normally dual carriageways and are subsidized by *peajes* (tolls). *Autovías* are similar but have no tolls. The *carretera nacional* is the countrywide network of main roads or highways with the prefix N. Smaller minor roads are generally less well kept, but they are often a more leisurely and enjoyable way to see rural areas of Spain.

Red de Carreteras del Estado
CARRETERA N-110

Sign for national highway N110

Cambio de sentido (slip road) 300 m (330 yd) ahead

ARRIVING BY CAR

Many people drive to Spain via the French motorways. The most direct routes across the Pyrenees, using the motorways, pass through Hendaye on the western flank and Port Bou in the east. Other, rather more tortuous routes may be used, from Toulouse through the Vall d'Aran, for instance. From the UK, there are car ferries from Plymouth to Santander and from Portsmouth to Santander and Bilbao in northern Spain *(see p675)*.

WHAT TO TAKE

A Green Card from your motor insurance company is needed in order to extend your comprehensive cover to Spain. The RAC, AA and Europ Assistance have rescue and recovery policies with European cover. Spanish law requires you to carry your vehicle's registration document, a valid insurance certificate and your driving licence at all times. You must always be able to show a passport or a national identity card as ID. You must also display a sticker on the back of the car showing its country of registration. The headlights of right-hand drive vehicles need to be adjusted or deflected. Stickers for this are available at ferry ports and on ferries. You risk on-the-spot fines if you do not carry a red warning triangle, spare light bulbs and a reflective jacket. In winter, carry chains if you intend to drive in mountain areas. In summer, take drinking water when travelling in remote areas.

BUYING PETROL

In Spain *gasolina* (petrol) and *gasóleo* (diesel) are priced by the litre. *Gasolina sin plomo* (unleaded petrol) is available everywhere. All three cost more at the *autopista* service stations. Self-service stations, where you fill up yourself, are common. Modern petrol pumps in Spain are sometimes operated by credit card. You should run your card through the machine, press the buttons to indicate the amount of petrol you want in euros, and then serve yourself.

You must wait for service if there are attendants at the station. They will ask *¿cuánto?* (how much?); you should reply *lleno* (fill the tank), or specify an amount in euros: *diez euros por favor*. If you do use your credit card to pay at a motorway service station, you will be asked to show your passport or another form of identification. Gibraltar and Andorra have tax-free, cheap petrol, so it is worth filling up before entering Spain.

RULES OF THE ROAD

Most traffic regulations and warnings to motorists are represented on signs by easily recognized symbols. However, a few road rules and signs may be unfamiliar to some drivers from other countries.

To turn left at a busy junction or across oncoming traffic, you may have to turn right first and cross a main road, often by way of traffic lights, a bridge or an underpass. If you are accidentally going the wrong way on a motorway or a main road with a solid white line, you can turn round at a sign for a *cambio de sentido*. At crossings, give way to the right unless a sign indicates otherwise. You must wear seat belts in both front and rear seats. Oncoming drivers may flash their headlights to mean "you go"; "danger"; "your lights are on unnecessarily" or "speed trap ahead".

50

Speed limit 50 km/h (31 mph)

Pedestrian crossing sign

A filling station run by a leading chain with branches throughout Spain

SPEED LIMITS AND FINES

Speed limits for cars without trailers on the roads in Spain are as follows:

- 120 km/h (75 mph) on *autopistas* (toll motorways);
- 100 km/h (62 mph) on *autovías* (non-toll motorways);
- 90 km/h (56 mph) on *carreteras nacionales* (main roads) and *carreteras comarcales* (secondary roads);
- 40 km/h (31 mph) in built-up areas.

Speeding fines are imposed on the spot at the rate of €6 for every kilometre per hour over the limit. Fines for other traffic offences (such as turning the wrong way into a one-way street) depend on the severity of the offence and often on the whim of the police officer.

Tests for drink-driving and fines for drivers over the blood alcohol legal limit, which is 30 mg per ml, are now imposed frequently throughout the country. If driving, it is best not to drink any alcohol at all.

MOTORWAYS

Spain has more than 2,900 km (1,800 miles) of *autopistas*, and many more are planned. These are generally toll roads and can be expensive to use. You can establish whether a motorway is toll-free by the letters that prefix the number of the road: A = free motorway, AP = toll motorway.

The long-distance tolls are calculated per kilometre, and the rate varies from region to region. Among the busiest and most expensive are the AP7 along the south coast from Barcelona to Alicante and the AP68 Bilbao–Zaragoza *autopista*.

There are service stations every 40 km (25 miles) or so along the *autopistas*, and they are marked by a blue and white parking sign (P) or a sign indicating the services available. As you approach a service station, a sign will indicate the distance to the next one and will also list its services. Most will have a petrol station, toilets, a shop and a café.

Emergency telephones occur every 2 km (1.2 miles) along the *autopistas*.

Driving through the Sierra Nevada along one of Europe's highest roads

USING AUTOPISTA TOLLS

If you are travelling on an *autopista*, you pick up a ticket from a toll booth (*peaje*) as you drive on to it and give it up at a booth as you exit. Your toll will be calculated according to the distance you have covered. Over some short stretches of motorways near the cities a fixed price is charged.

Tolls can be paid either in cash or by credit card. You must join one of three channels at the *peaje* leading to different booths. Do not drive into *telepago*, a credit system for which a chip on your windscreen is required. *Tarjetas* has machines for you to pay by credit card, while in *manual* an attendant will take your ticket and your money.

PEAJE
TOLL

Autopista **toll booths ahead**

The *peaje manual* channel, with attendant

OTHER ROADS

Carreteras nacionales, Spain's main roads, have black and white signs and are designated N (*Nacional*) plus a number. Those with Roman numerals (NIII) start at the Puerta del Sol in Madrid. The distance from the Kilometre Zero mark in the Puerta del Sol *(see p272)* appears on kilometre markers. Those with ordinary numbers (N6) have kilometre markers giving the distance from the provincial capital. Some *carreteras nacionales* are dual carriageways, but most are single-lane roads and can be slow. They tend to be least busy from 2pm to 5pm.

Autovías are roads built in recent years to motorway standard to replace N roads. They have blue signs similar to *autopista* signs. Because they have no tolls, they are busier than *autopistas*.

Carreteras comarcales, secondary roads, have a number preceded by the letter C. Other minor roads have numbers preceded by letters representing the name of the province, such as the LE 1313 in Lleida. In winter, watch out for signs indicating whether a mountain pass ahead is open (*abierto*) or closed (*cerrado*).

CAR HIRE

The most popular car-hire companies in Spain are **Europcar** (www.europcar.com), **Avis** (www.avis.com) and **Hertz** (www.hertz.com). All have offices at airports and major train stations, as well as in the large cities.

In addition to the international car-hire companies, a few Spanish firms, such as **Atesa**, operate nationwide. There is also a growing number of low-cost hire firms like easyCar (www.easycar.com) pepecar (www.pepecar.com) and hispacar (www.hispacar.com), although you may need to pick up your car some distance from the airport.

You can often get the best deals by booking in advance online. There are also fly-drive and other package deals including car hire available. Fly-drive, an option for two or more travellers, can be arranged by travel agents and tour operators.

If you wish to hire a car locally for around a week or less, you will be able to arrange it with a local travel agent. A car for hire is called a *coche de alquiler*.

For chauffeur-driven cars in Spain, Avis offers deals from major cities. Car-hire prices and conditions vary according to the region and locality.

Some of the leading car-hire companies operating in Spain

MAPS

Fold-out road maps can be obtained at airports, on the ferries and from tourist offices. The Spanish Ministry of Transport publishes a comprehensive road map in book form, the *Mapa Oficial de Carreteras*. The oil company Repsol publishes the *Guía Repsol*, a road map and restaurant guide conveniently in one book and also available for iPhone and iPad. **Michelin** publishes a useful series of maps (440–448, with orange covers) at a scale of 1:400,000 (1 cm:4 km), sold at bookshops and petrol stations. Websites www.guiarepsol.com and www.viamichelin.com allow you to plan your route, providing information on roads, weather and toll fees.

City taxis queuing for fares outside an airport

A series of more detailed maps at 1:200,000 for cycling and walking is published by Plaza y Janés. Military maps at scales of 1:50,000 and 1:100,000 are available from **Stanfords** in London and from some local and specialist bookshops in Spain, such as **Altaïr** in Barcelona. Tourist offices usually have free street maps.

You can find detailed street maps of central Barcelona on pp180–85, of Madrid on pp308–15 and of Seville on pp448–53 of this guide.

PARKING

The arrival of resident-only parking schemes means that street parking is increasingly hard to come by in major cities.

As a rule, you may not park where the pavement edge is painted yellow or where a "no parking" sign is displayed. Occasionally there is a "no parking" sign on both sides of a city street, one saying "1–15" and the other "16–30". This means that you can park on one side of the street only for the fortnight indicated on the sign.

No parking at any time of day

In the cities, non-metered on-street parking is rare, but there are blue pay-and-display parking spaces. To use them, buy a ticket from the machine and display it on the inside of your windscreen. The cost averages about €1–€3 per hour. You can usually park for up to two hours. Major cities have many underground car parks. You collect a ticket when you enter and either pay the attendant as you drive out, or pay at a machine which returns your ticket so you can deposit it in another machine at the exit.

TAXIS

Every city and/or region has its own taxi design and tariffs, but all taxis will display a green light if they are free. All are metered; when you set off, a minimum fee will be shown. In smaller villages, the taxi may be a resident driving an un-metered private car – ask at your hotel or in a shop for the number of a recommended local driver.

ROAD CONDITIONS AND WEATHER FORECASTS

For recorded road and traffic information, call the national toll-free number for **Información de Tráfico de Carreteras**. This service is in Spanish only. Ask at your hotel reception if you need a translation. The RAC offers route-planning services tailored to individual requirements; these may include current road conditions.

The weather information service, **Teletiempo**, gives forecasts for the various regions, as well as the national and international weather. It also gives details on maritime and mountain conditions.

ARRIVING BY COACH

Often the cheapest way to reach and travel around Spain is by coach. **Eurolines** operates various routes throughout Europe and runs daily services to Barcelona. Check out the website for available offers.

Coaches from the UK depart from London Victoria Coach Station. Tickets may be bought from National Express (www.national express.com) or travel agents. The journey takes about 24 hours.

Alsa, a regional coach service

TRAVELLING AROUND SPAIN BY COACH

There is no Spanish national coach company, but private regional companies operate routes around the country. The largest coach company is **Alsa**, which runs in all regions and has routes and services that cover most of the country. Other companies operate in particular regions – Alsina Graells, for instance, covers most of the south and east of Spain. Tickets and information for long-distance travel are available at all main coach stations as well as from travel agents, but note that it is not always possible to book tickets in advance.

In Madrid the biggest coach stations are **Estación Sur** and **Intercambiador de Autobuses**. Always check which coach station your bus is due to leave from when you purchase your ticket.

CYCLING

Cycle touring, a popular holiday activity

Cycling is popular in Spain, and there are bicycles for hire in most tourist spots. However, there are few cycle lanes outside the cities. Bicycles may be carried on *cercanías* trains after 2pm on Fridays until the last train on Sunday night; on any *regional* train with a goods compartment; and on all long-distance overnight trains. If you need to take your bicycle long-distance at other times, check it in an hour before the train departs. You may have to send it as luggage and pay a baggage charge based on its weight. It might not travel with you, so you will have to collect it when it arrives.

Indicators for Seville's circular bus routes

LOCAL BUSES

Local bus routes and timetables are posted at bus termini and stops. You pay on the bus or buy a strip of ten tickets called an *abono* from *estancos* (tobacconists).

DIRECTORY

CAR HIRE

Atesa
Tel *902 10 01 01.*
www.atesa.es

Avis
Tel *0844 581 8181 in UK.*
Tel *902 18 08 54 in Spain.*
www.avisworld.com
www.avis.es

Europcar
Tel *0871 384 1087 in UK.*
Tel *902 10 50 30 in Spain.*
www.europcar.com
www.europcar.es

Hertz
Tel *0870 844 8844 in UK.*
Tel *902 40 24 05 in Spain.*
www.hertz.co.uk
www.hertz.es

MAPS

Altaïr
Gran Vía 616, 08007 Barcelona.
Tel *93 342 71 71.*

Guía Repsol
www.guiarepsol.com

Michelin
www.viamichelin.es

Stanfords
12–14 Long Acre, London WC2E 9LP.
Tel *020 7836 1321.*
www.stanfords.co.uk

WEATHER FORECASTS

Agencia Estatal de Meteorología
www.aemet.es

Teletiempo Nacional
Tel *807 170 365.*

TRAFFIC AND ROAD CONDITIONS

Información de Tráfico de Carreteras
Tel *011 from a landline, 505 from Movistar, 141 from Vodafone, 2221 from Orange.*
www.dgt.es

COACH OPERATORS

Alsa
Tel *902 42 22 42.*
www.alsa.es

Eurolines
Tel *08717 81 81 78 in UK.*
Tel *902 40 50 40 in Spain.*
www.eurolines.com

COACH STATIONS

Barcelona
Estació del Nord, Calle Ali Bei 80.
Tel *902 26 06 06.*
www.barcelonanord.com

Madrid
Estación Sur, Calle Méndez Álvaro 83.
Tel *91 468 42 00.*
www.estacionautobusesmadrid.com
Intercambiador de Autobuses, Avenida de América 9.

Seville
Estación Plaza de Armas, Calle Cristo de la Expiración. **Tel** *95 490 80 40.*

Getting Around Cities

Sightseeing and getting around in Spain's cities is best done on foot and by public transport – try to avoid driving a car into the city centres. Barcelona, Valencia and Madrid all have efficient underground (metro) systems, as well as overground railways that link up with the suburbs and airports. Madrid also has a metro service from the airport to the city. Good city maps are available from tourist offices, or they can be printed out from the Internet. Municipal websites (www.bcn.es for Barcelona; www.munimadrid.com for Madrid; www.valencia.es for Valencia; and www.sevilla.org for Seville) provide up-to-the-minute information in English on travelling in the cities.

A metro sign

Walking on Las Ramblas, Barcelona

METRO

The best way to see Barcelona over a couple of days is to buy a T10 ticket. Once you validate a T10, you can make combined journeys on the metro, buses, trams and local trains for 90 minutes. The more expensive T-2Dies gives you unlimited transport for two days until the end of service. The Barcelona metro run by **Transports Metropolitans de Barcelona** is open from 5am to midnight on weekdays and Sundays (and until 2am on Fridays) and for 24 hours every Saturday.

Metro de Madrid is the third oldest system in Europe (1919) after London and Paris. Its 13 lines serve the whole city and are divided into various zones depending on different areas of the city and surrounding area. You can buy a single ticket for Zona A or a ten-journey ticket; this allows travel on both metro and buses. Tourist tickets providing between one and seven days' unlimited travel can be purchased at train stations or at the airport. The metro runs every day from 6am to 2am.

The Valencia metro operated by **Ferrocarrils de la Generalitat Valenciana (FGV)** is best used to get to and from the beach, since it does not go near the town centre. It also tends to skip other important destinations, such as the City of Arts and Sciences. The metro will also get you to many places around Valencia, beyond the city center. A metro ticket to any station within the city limits is the same price.

Metro de Sevilla's first line opened in April 2009, linking the centre with the city's outlying suburbs, and as such it is of relatively little relevance to visitors – these areas contain little of interest for tourists. Three more lines are planned in the coming years.

BUSES AND TRAMS

Buses in Spain can sometimes follow an erratic timetable and many do not run after 10pm, although there are some night buses.

In Barcelona the T10 and T-2Dies tickets are valid on buses and trams, on the metro and on trains to the airport.

Bus, tram and metro tickets in Madrid, including tourist tickets are interchangeable. If you do not have a ticket, you can pay the driver directly. Most buses run from 6am until 11pm. Night buses (called *buhos*) run less frequently and always pass by the Plaza de Cibeles. The price is the same as for day tickets.

Valencia has a good bus network, and buses are the preferred way of travelling for locals. If you are out and about a lot during the day, get a ten-journey *bono* (voucher). You can view a map of the routes on the EMT website (www.emtvalencia.es). The tram runs from the Pont de Fusta (Wooden Bridge), near the Serrano Towers, around the city and to the beaches at Las Arenas and La Malvarrosa.

Buses are the easiest and cheapest way to get around Seville and to the main sights. The bus network is comprised of circular (C-1, C-2, C-3, C-4 buses) and line routes (north, south, east and west).

TRAINS

If you are heading out of Barcelona to nearby beaches or mountains, you can take a train from Plaça Catalunya, Passeig de Gràcia, Estació de França or Estació de Sants. The local overland train services are run by **Ferrocarrils de la Generalitat de Catalunya**

One of Barcelona's taxis

Madrid bus

(FGC) and the main line trains are run by RENFE *(see p676)*. T10 and T-2Dies tickets can also be used on local trains within the city area.

Madrid's rail system is comfortable, economical and efficient. The 13 lines all leave from or pass through Atocha station, and trains run daily from 6am until midnight every 15–30 minutes. **Consorcio Regional de Transportes de Madrid** provide helpful information on routes, fares and tourist tickets.

TAXIS

Barcelona's distinctive yellow and black taxi cabs can be relied upon for a good and reasonably priced service, although it is rare to find a driver who speaks English. The meter begins running with a set fee and will rise every kilometre. Be aware that the tariff rises at night and on Saturdays, Sundays and public holidays. There are supplements added to your taxi fare when arriving at or leaving the airport, port or train station; for each piece of luggage; and also after 10pm on Fridays, Saturdays and holidays.

The taxis in Madrid are white with a diagonal red band on the front doors. A lit green light on top of the taxi indicates that it is available. Finding a taxi in the downtown area of Madrid is relatively simple and should take only a few minutes. The taxi meter starts its fare with a flat fee, the *bajada de bandera* (lowering of the flag). After that, the meter runs according to the distance covered, the urban area, the day of the week (higher fares apply on holidays) and the pick-up point (there are higher fares for pick-ups in bus stations, train stations and the airport). The night fare is always higher than the day fare. All additional fares should be indicated on informational signs on the back windows. There is an extra charge for pick-ups and drop-offs at Barajas airport, but there is no extra charge for luggage.

Taxis are a good option for short journeys in Valencia. There is a minimum fee during the day; extra fees apply for trips to the airport.

Seville's taxis provide a viable way of getting into town, although much of the city centre is difficult to access by car because of heavy traffic, especially during the Feria de Abril or Semana Santa *fiestas*. As elsewhere, the tariff is higher for journeys at night.

WALKING

Barcelona is a great city to explore on foot. The Old Town (Ciutat Vella), near the port and up to the Plaza Catalunya, consists of narrow medieval streets and winding alleyways. It is easy to get lost in this area, and care should be taken here at night. Las Ramblas is one of the world's most famous walkways and offers a vibrant slice of Mediterranean street life. The Eixample area is also good for walking, with large boulevards in a grid pattern. If you need to get your bearings, simply ask a local which direction is *mar* (sea, to the south) and which is *montaña* (mountain, to the north).

Distances are considerable in Madrid, and it is advisable to combine walking with public transport to make more efficient use of your time in the city. The most popular areas to visit on foot are those around the emblematic Plaza Mayor and the city's most famous park, El Retiro, which is also near the most well-known museums.

Most sights in the centre of Seville are best reached on foot. The popular Barrio Santa Cruz should be visited with a map. During late spring and the summer, shade is highly prized. In summer months the city government stretches tarpaulins across the buildings in the centre so that many of the streets are in the shade.

CYCLING

Cycling tours are a popular way of seeing Barcelona, and its cycle lanes provide safe access to most of the city. Visit www.bikerentalbarcelona.com or contact the tourist office to hire bikes.

For those wishing to explore Madrid, www.bravobike.com offer a wide variety of city bicycle tours, some of which include the surrounding areas.

There are many cycle lanes in Valencia, and cycling tours provide a great way of seeing all the major sights. More information can be found at www.doyoubike.com.

Seville is home to Sevici, a fleet of bicycles that can be hired on subscription. Visit www.sevici.es for details. (For more on cycling *see p681*.)

DIRECTORY

METRO

Transports Metropolitans de Barcelona
Tel *902 07 50 27.*
www.tmb.cat

Metro de Madrid
Tel *902 44 44 03.*
www.metromadrid.es

Metro de Valencia
Tel *900 46 10 46* (Metro).
Tel *900 72 04 72* (Tram).
www.metrovalencia.es

Metro de Sevilla
Tel *902 36 49 85.*
www.metrodesevilla.org

PUBLIC TRANSPORT

FGC (Barcelona)
Tel *932 05 15 15.*
www.fgc.net

Consorcio Regional de Transportes de Madrid
Tel *915 80 42 60, or 012 from Madrid.*
www.ctm-madrid.es

General Index

Page numbers in **bold** type refer to main entries.

A

C

K

L

N

O

P

Q

R

S

U

Acknowledgments

Dorling Kindersley would like to thank the following people whose contributions and assistance made preparation of this book possible.

Main Contributors
John Ardagh is a journalist and writer, and the author of several books on modern Europe.

David Baird, resident in Andalusia from 1971 to 1995, is the author of *Inside Andalusia*.

Vicky Hayward, a writer, journalist and editor, lives in Madrid, and has travelled extensively in Spain.

Adam Hopkins is an indefatigable travel writer and author of *Spanish Journeys: A Portrait of Spain*.

Lindsay Hunt has travelled widely and has contributed to several Eyewitness Travel Guides.

Nick Inman writes regularly on Spain for books and magazines.

Paul Richardson is the author of *Not Part of the Package*, a book on Ibiza, where he lives.

Martin Symington is a regular contributor to the *Daily Telegraph*. He also worked on the *Eyewitness Travel Guide to Great Britain*.

Nigel Tisdall, contributor to the *Eyewitness Travel Guide to France*, is the author of the *Insight Pocket Guide to Seville*.

Roger Williams has contributed to Insight Guides on Barcelona and Catalonia, and was the main contributor to the *Eyewitness Travel Guide to Provence*.

Additional Contributors
Mary Jane Aladren, Sarah Andrews, Pepita Aris, Emma Dent Coad, Rebecca Doulton, Harry Eyres, Josefina Fernández, Anne Hersh, Nick Rider, Mercedes Ruiz Ochoa, David Stone, Clara Villanueva, Christopher Woodward, Patricia Wright.

Additional Illustrations
Arcana Studio, Richard Bonson, Louise Boulton, Martine Collings, Brian Craker, Jared Gilbey (Kevin Jones Associates), Paul Guest, Steven Gyapay, Claire Littlejohn.

Additional Photography
David Cannon, Tina Chambers, Geoff Dann, Phillip Dowell, Mike Dunning, Neil Fletcher, Steve Gorton, Heidi Grassley, Frank Greenaway, Derek Hall, Colin Keates, Alan Keohane, Dave King, Ella Milroy, D Murray, Cyril Laubsouer, Ian O'Leary Stephen Oliver, J Selves, Tony Souter, Mathew Ward, P. Wojcik.

Cartography
Lovell Johns Ltd (Oxford), ERA-Maptec Ltd.

Design And Editorial Assistance
Sam Atkinson, Pilar Ayerbe, Rosemary Bailey, Vicky Barber, Teresa Barea, Claire Baranowski, Cristina Barrallo, Fran Bastida, Jill Benjamin, Marta Bescos, Vandana Bhagra, Sonal Bhatt, Julie Bond, Chris Branfield, Gretta Britton, Daniel Campi, Paula Canal (Word on Spain) Lola Carbonell, Peter Casterton, Elspeth Collier, Carey Combe, Jonathan Cox, Martin Cropper, Linda Doyle, Nicola Erdpresser, Bernat Fiol, Emer FitzGerald, Anna Freiberger, Rhiannon Furbear, Mary-Ann Gallagher, Aruna Ghose, Elena González, Lydia Halliday, Des Hemsley, Tim Hollis, Claire Jones, Juliet Kenny, Priya Kukadia, Michael Lake, Erika Lang, Maite Lantaron, Jude Ledger, Rebecca Lister, Hayley Maher, Sarah Martin, Alison McGill, Caroline Mead, Sam Merrell, Kate Molan, Jane Oliver, Simon Oon, Mary Ormandy, Mike Osborn, Malcolm Parchment, Helen Partington, Pollyanna Poulter, Anna Pirie, Tom Prentice, Rada Radojicic, Mani Ramaswamy, Lucy Ratcliffe, Ellen Root, Sands Publishing Solutions, Sadie Smith, Anna Streiffert, Leah Tether, Helen Townsend, Suzanne Wales, Jennifer Walker, Andy Wilkinson, Hugo Wilkinson, Robert Zonenblick.

Proofreader Huw Hennessy, Stewart J Wild.

Indexer Helen Peters.

Special Assistance
Dorling Kindersley would like to thank the regional and local tourist offices, *ayuntamientos*, shops, hotels, restaurants and other organizations in Spain for their invaluable help. Particular thanks also to Dr Giray Ablay (University of Bristol); María Eugenia Alonso and María Dolores Delgado Peña (Museo Thyssen-Bornemisza); Ramón Álvarez (Consejería de Educación y Cultura, Castilla y León); Señor Ballesteros (Santiago de Compostela Tourist Office); Carmen Brieva, Javier Campos and Luis Esteruelas (Spanish Embassy, London); Javier Caballero Arranz; Fernando Cañada López; The Club Taurino of London; Consejería de Turismo, Castilla-La Mancha; Consejería de Turismo and Consejería de Cultura, Junta de Extremadura; Mònica Colomer and Montse Planas (Barcelona Tourist Office); María José Docal and Carmen Cardona (Patronato de Turismo, Lanzarote); Edilesa; Klaus Ehrlich; Juan Fernández, Lola Moreno and others at El País-Aguilar; Belén Galán (Centro de Arte Reina Sofía); Amparo Garrido; Adolfo Díaz Gómez (Albacete Tourist Office); Professor Nigel Glendinning (Queen Mary and Westfield College, University of London); Pedro Hernández; Insituto de Cervantes, London; Victor Jolín (SOTUR); Joaquim Juan Cabanilles (Servicio de Investigación Prehistórica, Valencia); Richard Kelly; Mark Little (*Lookout* Magazine); Carmen López de Tejada and Inma Felipe (Spanish National Tourist Office, London); Caterine López and Ana Roig Mundi (ITVA); Julia López de la Torre (Patrimonio Nacional, Madrid); Lovell Johns Ltd (Oxford); Josefina Maestre (Ministerio de Agricultura, Pesca y Alimentación); Juan Malavia García and Antonio Abarca (Cuenca Tourist Office); Mario (Promoción Turismo, Tenerife); Janet Mendel; Javier Morata (Acanto Arquitectura y Urbanismo. Madrid); Juan Carlos Murillo; Sonia Ortega and Bettina Krücken (Spain Gourmetour); Royal Society for the Protection of Birds (UK); Alícia Ribas Sos; Katusa Salazar-Sandoval (Fomento de Turismo, Ibiza); María Ángeles Sánchez and Marcos; Ana Sarrieri (Departamento de Comercio, Consumo y Turismo, Gobierno Vasco); Klaas Schenk; María José Sevilla (Foods From Spain); The Sherry Institute of Spain (London); Anna Skidmore (Fomento de Turismo, Mallorca); Philip Sweeney; Rupert Thomas; Mercedes Trujillo and Antonio Cruz Caballero (Patronato de Turismo, Gran Canaria); Gerardo

Uarte (Gobierno de Navarra); Fermín Unzue (Dirección General de Turismo, Cantabria); Puri Villanueva.

Artwork Reference
Sr Joan Bassegoda, Catedral Gaudí (Barcelona); José Luis Mosquera Muller (Mérida); Jorge Palazón, Paisajes Españoles (Madrid).

Photography Permissions
The Publisher would like to thank the following for their kind assistance and permission to photograph at their establishments:© Patrimonio Nacional, Madrid; Palacio de la Almudaina, Palma de Mallorca; El Escorial, Madrid; La Granja de San Ildefonso; Convento de Santa Clara, Tordesillas; Las Huelgas Reales, Burgos; Palacio Real, Madrid; Monasterio de las Descalzas; Bananera "El Guanche S.L."; Museo Arqueológico de Tenerife-OACIMC del Excmo, Cavildo Insular de Tenerife; Asociación de Encajeras de Acebo-Cáceres; Museo de Arte Abstracto Español, Cuenca; Fundación Juan March; Pepita Alia Lagartera; Museo Naval de Madrid; © Catedral de Zamora; Museo de Burgos; Claustro San Juan de Duero, Museo Numantino, Soria; San Telmo Museoa Donostia-San Sebastián; Hotel de la Reconquista, Oviedo; Catedral de Jaca; Museo de Cera, Barcelona; Museu D'Història de la Ciutat, Barcelona; © Capitol Catedral de Lleida; Jardí Botànic Marimurtra, Estació Internacional de Biologia Mediterrània, Girona; Museo Arqueológico Sagunto (Teatro Romano-Castillo); Museo Municipal y Ermita de San Antonio de la Florida, Madrid. Also all the other churches, museums, hotels, restaurants, shops, galleries and sights too numerous to thank individually.

Picture Credits
Key: a=above; b=below/bottom; c=centre; f=far; l=left; r=right; t=top.

Works of art have been published with the permission of the following copyright holders: *Dona i Ocell* Joan Miró © Succession Miró/ADAGP, Paris & DACS, London 2011 176tl; *Guernica* Pablo Ruiz Picasso 1937 © Succession Picasso/DACS, London 2011 299cb; *Morning* George Kolbe © DACS London 2011 170tr, 173tl; *Peine de los Vientos* Eduardo Chillida © DACS, London 2011 122b; Various works by Joaquín Sorolla © DACS, London 2011 305t; *Rainy Taxi* Salvador Dalí © Kingdom of Spain, Gala - Salvador Dalí Foundation, DACS, London 2011 215tr; *Tapestry of the Foundation* Joan Miró 1975 © Succession Miró/ADAGP, Paris & DACS, London 171crb; *Three Gypsy Boys* © Joan Rebull 1976 144bl.

The publisher would like to thank the following individuals, companies and picture libraries for their kind permission to reproduce their photographs: ACE PHOTO AGENCY: Bob Masters 26b; Mauritius 23t; Bill Wassman 320b; AISA ARCHIVO ICONOGRÁFICO, Barcelona: 22t, 36bl, 46l, 48ca, 48cb, 49bl, 49br, 50cra, 50cb, 51tl, 52cla, 52bl(d), 54bl, 54br, 54cla, 54–55, 55cl, 55cra, 55bl, 56bl, 61br, 65tr, 67tl, 67b, 274t, 303b, 355bl, 423bl, 423br, 424cl, 489br; Biblioteca Nacional, Madrid *Felipe V* Luis Meléndez 71bl; Catedral de Sevilla *Ignacio de Loyola* Alonso Vázquez 124bl(d); *Camilo José Cela* Álvaro Delgado 1916 © DACS, London 2011 35br (d); *La Tertulia del Pombo* José Gutiérrez Solana 1920 © DACS, London 2011 299t; Museo de América, Madrid *Vista de Sevilla* Alonso Sánchez Coello 58cb; Museo de Bellas Artes, Seville *Sancho Panza y El Rucio* Moreno Carbonero 60ca; Museo de Bellas Artes, Valencia *Ecce Homo* Juan de Juanes 252br; Museo Frankfurt *La Armada* 59tl; Museo de Historia de México *Hernán Cortés* S.E. Colane 58bl(d); Museo Histórico Militar, San Sebastián *Guerra Carlista* 63br(d); Museo Lázaro Galdiano, Madrid *Lope de Vega* Caxes 290tr; Museo Nacional del Teatro *Poster for "Yerma"* (FG Lorca) Juan Antonio Morales y José Caballero © DACS, London 2011 35tr; Museo del Prado, Madrid *La Rendición de Breda* Diego Velázquez 61cb, *El Tres de Mayo de 1808 en Madrid* Francisco de Goya y Lucientes 62-63(d), La Reina María Luisa María Francisco de Goya 62cla, *Carlos IV* Francisco de Goya 71bc, *Los Borrachos* Diego de Velázquez 292t, *Saturno devorando a un hijo* Francisco de Goya 294tr, *El Descendimiento* Van der Weyden 295b; Real Academia de Bellas Artes de San Fernando, Madrid *El Sueño del Caballero* Antonio de Pereda 60–61(d); ALSA GROUP S.L.L.C: 681cl; AKG, London: 67cr; Allsport: Stephen Munday 42cr; ALAMY IMAGES: Tibor Bognar 388bl; Paul Hardy Carter 200cla; Michelle Chaplow 456b; Ian Dagnall 11br; Expuesto/Nicholas Randall 656b; JoeFoxTenerife 668tl; Mike Finn-Kelcey 677c; Robert Harding Picture Library 419cr, 656cla; paulbourdice 513cla; Profimedia. CZ s.r.o. 537cl; Alex Segre 77t, 605tr; Richard Sowley 669cr; Peter Titmuss 201t; Vario Images GmbH 69br; Renaud Visage 418cla; Ken Welsh 667bl; AQUILA: Adrian Hoskins 210cla, 210clb; Mike Lane 343clb; James Pearce 205bl; ARCAID: Paul Raftery 120bl; ARXIU MAS: 36br, 37bl, 51crb, 54tl, 57cl, 53br(d); Museo del Prado, Madrid *Felipe II* Sánchez Coello 70br(d); Patrimonio Nacional 59cl, 59b(d); THE ART ARCHIVE: Museo del Prado Madrid/Dagli Orti (A) *St Cecilia patron saint of music* Nicholas Poussin (1594–1665) 295cr.

BALEARIA: 677bl; BASILICA SAGRADA FAMILIA: Pep Daudé 167crb; BIOFOTOS: Heather Angel 80cla, 80bl; BRIDGEMAN ART LIBRARY: *St Dominic enthroned as Abbot* Bartolomé Bermejo 294tl; Index/ Museo del Prado, Madrid *Auto-da-fé in the Plaza Mayor* Francisco Rizi 274c; Musée des Beaux Artes, Berne *Colossus of Rhodes* Salvador Dalí 1954 © Kingdom of Spain, Gala – Salvador Dalí Foundation, DACS, London 2011 33tr; Museo del Prado, Madrid *Charles IV and his Family* Francisco de Goya y Lucientes 33cb, *The Adoration of the Shepherds* El Greco 292cl, *The Annunciation* Fra Angelico 293bl, *The Clothed Maja* Francisco de Goya y Lucientes 293t, *The Naked Maja* Francisco de Goya y Lucientes 293ca, *The Three Graces* Peter Paul Rubens 293crb, *The Martydom of St Philip* José de Ribera 293cb; Museo Picasso, Barcelona *Las Meninas, Infanta Margarita* Pablo Ruiz Picasso 1957 © Succession Picasso/DACS, London 2011 32tl; Phoenix Galleries, London *Rooftops, Fortna Luxt, Majorca* Frederick Gore 8-9; MICHAEL BUSSELLE: 207r, 209b, 210t.

CAMPER STORE, Madrid: 655tr; CENTRO DE ARTE REINA SOFÍA: *Bertsolaris* Zubiaurre © DACS, London 2011 125cb, *Paisaje de Cadaqués* Salvador Dalí 1923 © Kingdom of Spain, Gala - Salvador Dalí Foundation, DACS, London 2011 298cb,*Accidente* Ponce de León 298b, *Toki-Egin (Homenaje a San Juan de la Cruz)* Eduardo Chillida 1952 © DACS, London 2011 299bl; CEPHAS: Mick Rock 29bl, 42t, 78t, 202tr, 202cl, 340tr, 420tr, 421br, 421cr; Roy Stedall 421tr; CINC SENTITS: 603c; GRUPO CODORNIU: 203tl; BRUCE COLEMAN: Eric Crichton 204tr; José Luis González Grande 205tr; Werner Layer 343tl; Andy Purcell

31ca; Hans Reinhard 80crb; Norbert Schwirtz 205tl; Colin Varndell 205crb; Dee Conway: 425cl, 425cr; COMERÇ 24: 603br; CORBIS: Ric Ergenbright 456t; Owen Franken 77c, 201c, 338cl, 339c, 419t; Carloine Penn 339t; Jose Fuste Raga 10cr; Reuters/ Marcelo del Pozo 12br; SYLVIA CORDAIY PHOTO LIBRARY: Chris North 40tl; JOE CORNISH: 28ca, 346, 364b, 372tr; GIANCARLO COSTA: 37bc; COVER: Genin Andrada 40b, 43b; Austin Catalan 70bl; Juan Echeverria 31cra, 41br, 545bl; Pepe Franco 185c; Quim Llenas 125ca, 317tl; Matías Nieto 43c; F J Rodríguez 125bl; CUIDAD DE LAS ARTES Y LAS CIENCAS (CACSA): Javier Yaya Tur 253t; Cocomfe: 665b.

J D DALLET: 70tr, 464tl, 605br.

EDEX: 51bl, 405b; EDILESA: 352b; EL DESEO: Pedro Almodóvar 305b; EGANA ORIZA RESTAURANT, Seville: Manolo Manosalbas 602b; ELEPHANT CLUB: 602cr; PACO ELVIRA: 30crb; EMI: Hispavox 376b; EQUIPO 28: 425t; ET ARCHIVE: 52br; EUROPA PRESS: 23c, 68tl, 69ca; MARY EVANS PICTURE LIBRARY: 9t, 56cla, 63bl, 73t, 137r, 197t, 265r, 274bl, 335, 415r, 471b, 503, 553t, 663r; Explorer 424t; EYE UBIQUITOUS: James Davis Travel Photography 21t, 218br.

FIRO FOTO: 157c; 533t; FLAMENCOCOOL: Seville, 455tr; GRUPO FREIXENET: 203tr; FUNDACIÓN CÉSAR MANRIQUE Manrique: 548br; FUNDACIÓN COLECCIÓN THYSSEN-BORNEMISZA: *Madonna of Humility* Fra Angelico 177t, *La Virgen del Árbol* Petrus Christus 288tr, *Mata Mua* Paul Gauguin 1892 289crb, *Harlequin with a Mirror* Pablo Ruiz Picasso 1923 © Succession Picasso/DACS, London 2011 288cl, *Hotel Room* © Edward Hopper 1931 288bl, *Portrait of Baron HH Thyssen-Bornemisza* © Lucian Freud 1981–82 288br, *Venus y Cupido* Peter Paul Rubens (after 1629) 289tl, *Santa Casilda* Francisco de Zurbarán 1640–1645 289cra, *Autumn Landscape in Oldenburg* Karl Schmidt-Rottluff 1907 © DACS, London 2011 289b; Fundació Joan Miró, Barcelona: *Flama en L'espai i dona nua* Joan Miró 1932 © Succession Miró/ADAGP, Paris and DACS, London, 2011 172t.

GETTY IMAGES: Iconica/Don Klumpp 666tl; Peter Macdiarmid 69b; Terry Williams 664cla; GODO FOTO: 220b, 221t, 225t, 249b, 255t, 333bl; RONALD GRANT ARCHIVE: *For a Few Dollars More* © United Artists 500b; © FMGB GUGGENHEIM BILBAO MUSEOA. Erica Barahona Ede. All rights reserved. Partial or total reproduction is prohibited 120t, *The Matter of Time* Richard Serra © ARS, NY and DACS, London 2011 120br, 121t, 121b.

ROBERT HARDING PICTURE LIBRARY: 19t, 141tr, 160ca, 172b, 173b, 249t, 303t, 511br; Julia Bayne 196– 197; Nigel Blythe 19b, 149c; Bob Cousins 26clb; Robert Frerck 439tr; James Strachan 270tl; MARÍA VICTORIA HERNÁNDEZ: 533b; HULTON DEUTSCH COLLECTION: 66b, 391br.

IBERDIAPO: Triangle 524–525; THE IMAGE BANK, London: Andra Pistolesi 174; Mark Romanelli 140bl; Mathew Weinreb 161b; IMAGES COLOUR LIBRARY: A.G.E Fotostock 28tr, 29tr, 30cra, 30ca, 30br, 36tr, 37ca, 40c, 42cl, 122b, 168, 187t, 187c, 211br, 233ca, 233br, 316t, 335c, 343cla, 349 tr, 421cl, 424br, 466b, 497t, 531t, 557tr, 659c, 659b; Horizon International 36-37, 140cb; INCAFO: J A Fernández & C De Noriega 75bl, 125br; Juan Carlos Muñoz 396b, 497b; A Ortega 30bl; INDEX: 34tl, 48c, 48b, 49c, 49cb, 50tl, 50b, 54cra, 56br (d), 59tr, *Los Moriscos suplicando al rey Felipe III* 61c, 64–65, 65b, 67 cl, *Carlos I* 70tc, 70bl, 71br, 491ca; Bridgeman, London 58cra; CCJ 23b; X Correa 48tl; *Garrote Vil* José Gutiérrez Solana 1931 © DACS, London 2011 65clb(d); Galería del Ateneo, Madrid *Lucio Anneo Seneca* Villodas 50cla (d); Galeria Illustres Catalonia, Barcelona *Joan Prim I Prats* J Cusachs 63ca(d); Image *José Zorilla* 35bl; Instituto Valencia de Don Juan, Madrid *Carlos V* Simón Bening 59crb; Iranzo 56cra; Mithra 52clb, 58br (d), 64tl; Museo de América, Madrid *Indio Yumbo y Frutas Tropicales* 59cra; Museo Lázaro Galdiano, Madrid *Lope de Vega* Anonymous 34c, *Félix Lope de Vega* Francisco Pacheco 60br(d); Museo Municipal, Madrid *Fiesta en la Plaza Mayor de Madrid* Juan de la Corte 61tl; Museo del Prado, Madrid *Ascensión de un globo Montgolfier en Madrid* Antonio Carnicero 62cra(d), *José Moreño Conde de Floridablanca* Francisco de Goya 62br(d), *Flota del Rey Carlos III de España* A Joli 63t(d); National Maritime Museum, Greenwich *Batalla de Trafalgar* Chalmers 62cb; A Noé 56cb; Palacio del Senado, Madrid *Alfonso X "El Sabio"* Matías Moreno 34b(d), *Rendición de Granada* Francisco Pradilla 56–57(d); Patrimonio Nacional 51br; Private Collection, Madrid *Pedro Calderón de la Barca* Antonio de Pereda 61bl(d); Real Academia de Bellas Artes de San Fernando, Madrid *San Diego de Alcalá dando de comer a los pobres* Bartolomé Esteban Murillo 61ca(d), *Fernando VII* Francisco de Goya 71tl(d), *Isabel* II 71tc, *Self-Portrait* Francisco de Goya 239b; A Tovy 69cb; NICK INMAN: 204bc, 253tr, 664t, 672tr, 679b; INSTITUT TURÍSTIC VALENCIÁ: 245br.

CÉSAR JUSTEL: 353b.

ANTHONY KING: 291t.

L'ESTARTIT TOURIST BOARD: 217c; LIFE FILE PHOTOGRAPHIC: 217c; Tony Abbott 342cla; Xavier Catalan 141cb; Emma Lee 141cra, 420tl, 681tr; ANDRZEJ LISOWSKI 674c; NEIL LUKAS: 464cb, 464b.

MAGNUM: S Franklin 68cb; Jean Gaumy 68br, 69tl; MARKA, Milan: Sergio Pitamitz 154t; Imagen Mas, Leon: 355tr; MIGUEL TORRES, SA: 203cr; John Miller: 206l, 502–503, 505cb, 529r, 538b, 543b, 548t, 549b; MUSEO ARQUEOLÓGIC DE BARCELONA: 171c; MUSEO ARQUEOLÓGICO DE VILLENA: 48–49; MUSEO ARQUEOLÓGICO NACIONAL: 296tl; MUSEU DE CIENCIES NATURALS DE BARCELONA: 155tc; MUSEO NACIONAL DEL PRADO: *El Jardín de las Delicias* 292clb; MUSEU PICASSO, Barcelona: *Auto Retrato* Pablo Ruiz Picasso 1899–1900 © Succession Picasso/DACS, London 2011 153b; MUSEU TEXTIL I D'INDUMENTÁRIA : 154bl;.

NATURAL SCIENCE PHOTOS: Nigel Charles 108tl; C Dani & I Jeske 104b, 343br; Richard Revels 342br; Brian Sutton 342bl; W Tarboton 342tl; P & S Ward 232br; NATURPRESS: Oriol Alamany 31bl; J L Calvo & J R Montero 343crb; José Luis Grande 465b; Walter Kwaternik 30clb, 81bc, 342cra, 343cra; Francisco Márquez 465cb, 416bl; Aurelio Martín 31br, Sebastián Martín 343bc; José A Martínez 80tr, 207b, 342clb, 342crb; © NATIONAL MARITIME MUSEUM: 58–59; Network: Bilderberg/W Kunz 421tl; NHPA: Laurie Campbell 80cra; Stephen Dalton 81cl; Vicente García Canseco 31cla, 465ca; Manfred Daneggar 80br, 81br. OMEGA FOTO: 110tl, Manuel Pinilla 42b, 123b; ORONOZ: 4, 33br, 36cl, 37br, 47b, 49t, 50b, 53t, 53clb, 53crb, 54tl, 54cb, 55t, 55br, 59tl, 58cla, 60cb, 65tl, 68ca, 82tl, 112t, 305cr, 355br, 363br, 370b, 434bl, 441bl, 467tl, 478cl,

479t, 480l, 489bl, 657t; Biblioteca Nacional, Madrid *Isabel la Católica* Luis Madrazo 70tl(d); Iglesia Santo Tomé, Toledo *El Entierro del Conde de Orgaz* El Greco 32ca; *Portrait II* Joan Miró 1938 © Succession Miró/ ADAGP, Paris and DACS, London 298t; Monasterio Santa Maria, Barcelona *Virgen con Niño* Ferrer Bassa 32clb(d); Museo de Bellas Artes, Cádiz *San Bruno en Éxtasis* Zurbarán 467tr; Museo Casa Gredo, Toledo *Carlos II* Miranda Correño 70tr(d); Museo del Ejército, Madrid *Isabel II* Madrazo 62tl; Museo Municipal de Bellas Artes, Tenerife *Retrato de Boabdil o Abu Abdala* 57tr(d); Museo Nacional de Escultura, Valladolid *Natividad* Berruguete 367tr; Museo Naval, Madrid *Desembarco de Colón* José Garnelo 57tl; Museo Naval Laminas, Madrid *Carabelas de Colón* Monleón 57bl(d); Museo del Prado, Madrid *El Salvador* José de Ribera 32crb, *Las Meninas o Familia de Felipe V* Diego Velázquez 32–33, *Felipe III* Pedro A Vidal 60bl, *Felipe V* 62bl, Guernica Pablo Ruiz Picasso 1937 © Succession Picasso/DACS, London 2011, 66–67, *Felipe IV* Diego Velázquez 66bc(d), *Bodegón* Zurbarán 294b, *David Vencedor de Goliat* Caravaggio 295t; Palacio Moncloa *Interior de la Catedral de Santiago* Villaamil Pérez 82–83; *Mujer en Azul* Pablo Ruiz Picasso 1901 © Succession Picasso/DACS, London 2011 298ca; Private Colection, Palma *Oleo Sobre Lienzo* Joan Miró 1932 © Succession Miró/ADAGP, Paris and DACS, London, 2011 33ca; Real Academia de Bellas Artes de San Fernando *Fray Pedro Machado* Zurbarán 281tr.

PANOS PICTURES: Adrian Evans 68–69; José M Pérez De Ayala: 30cr, 464tr, 464ca, 465t, 465ca; THE PHOTOGRAPHERS LIBRARY: 523tr; PICTURES COLOUR LIBRARY: 22b, 30tr, 162-163, 258b, 416cl; PRISMA: 64ca, 65crb, 66ca, 66cb, 67tr, 97t, 140br, 239c, 250t, 321t, 475tl, 459, 516br, 532cl, 539clb, 539cb, 539crb, 539bl, 543t, 551bl, 551br; *Franco* Aguiar 71tr; *El ingenioso hidalgo Don Quixote de la Mancha* 1605 Ricardo Balaca 395br; Diputación de Madrid *Francisco Bahamonde Franco* Enrique Segura 66tl; Domènech & Azpiliqueta 118t; Albert Heras 186b; Marcel Jaquet 531b, 541b; Hans Lohr 483b; *Los Niños de la Concha* Bartolomé Esteban Murillo 33bl(d); Museo de Arte Moderno, Barcelona *Pío Baroja* Ramón Casas 64cb(d); Museo de Bellas Artes, Bilbao *Condesa Mathieu de Noailles* Ignacio Zuloaga y Zubaleta © DACS, London 2011 118b; Museo de Bellas Artes, Zaragoza *Príncipe de Viana* José Moreno Carbonero 130b (d); Mateu 191c; Palacio del Senado, Madrid *Alfonso XIII* Aquino © DACS, London 2011 71cr; Patrimonio Nacional Palacio de Riofrío, Segovia: 64br; *Auto Retrato* Pablo Ruiz Picasso 1907 © Succession Picasso DACS, London 2011 65ca; Real Academia de Bellas Artes de San Fernando, Madrid *Las Bodas de Camacho* José Moreno Carbonero 35tl(d), *Procession of the Flagellants* Francisco de Goya 274br(d); PURE ESPANA: Port Aventura 657br.

RENFE: 676tl; REX FEATURES: Sipa Press 215cb; © ROYAL MUSEUM OF SCOTLAND: Michel Zabé 47t; JOSE LUCAS RUIZ: 440br, 456cl.

MARÍA ÁNGELES SÁNCHEZ: 38tr, 39b, 43t, 79t, 98cl, 18l, 290tl, 304b, 387c, 405tr, 532t, 532cr, 532b, 536c, 547t; SCIENCE PHOTO LIBRARY: Geospace 14l; 6 TOROS 6: 37cb; SPANISH TOURIST BOARD: 255c; SPECTRUM COLOUR LIBRARY: 136–137, 140tr, 552–553; STA TRAVEL GROUP: 667ca; STOCKPHOTOS, Madrid: Marcelo Brodsky 40t; Campillo 659t; Heinz Hebeisen 41bl; Mikael Helsing 658b, 332tl; David Hornback 21b; Javier Sánchez 332tl; JAMES STRACHAN: 291b, 302t, 302c, 304t; TONY STONE WORLDWIDE: Doug Armand 20b; Jon Bradley 316bl; Robert Everts 440ca; SUPERSTOCK: Pixtal 76cl.

TELEFONICA: 672ca.

DENOMINACIÓN DE ORIGEN UTIEL-REQUENA: 203cb.

VINAS DEL VERO, S.A: 202cra; VINOS DE JUMILLA: 203crb; VISIONS OF ANDALUCÍA: Michelle Chaplow 424–425; J D Dallet 397tr; VU: Christina García Rodero 2–3, 20c, 38b, 39c, 39t, 132cl, 256–257, 368l, 431cr.

CHARLIE WAITE: 494–495; WERNER FORMAN ARCHIVE: Museo de Arte Hispanomusulmán 52t; Museum of Catalan Art, Barcelona 344tl; National Maritime Museum, Greenwich 52cr; ALAN WILLIAMS: 78b; PETER WILSON: 264–265, 282, 468b, 469c, 475t, 481t; WORLD PICTURES: 317b, 512t. ZEFA: 1.

Front endpaper: All special photography except JOE CORNISH cbl; JOHN MILLER tr; SPECTRUM COLOUR LIBRARY ca; PETER WILSON cbr.

JACKET

Front - PHOTOLIBRARY: age fotostock/Jose Fuste Raga. Back - DORLING KINDERSLEY: Rough Guides/Demetrio Carrasco bl; Rough Guides/Ian Aitken clb; Colin Sinclair cla; Peter Wilson tl. Spine - PHOTOLIBRARY: age fotostock/Jose Fuste Raga t.

All other images © Dorling Kindersley.
For further information see www.DKimages.com

Phrase Book

In an Emergency

Help!	**¡Socorro!**	soh-**koh**-roh
Stop!	**¡Pare!**	**pah**-reh
Call a doctor!	**¡Llame a un médico!**	**yah**-meh ah **oon meh**-dee-koh
Call an ambulance!	**¡Llame a una ambulancia!**	**yah**-meh ah **oonah** ahm-boo-**lahn**-thee-ah
Call the police!	**¡Llame a la policía!**	**yah**-meh ah lah poh-lee-**thee**-ah
Call the fire brigade!	**¡Llame a los bomberos!**	**yah**-meh ah lohs bohm-**beh**-rohs
Where is the nearest telephone?	**¿Dónde está el teléfono más próximo?**	**dohn**-deh ehs-**tah** ehl teh-**leh**-foh-noh **mahs prohx**-ee-moh
Where is the nearest hospital?	**¿Dónde está el hospital más próximo?**	**dohn**-deh ehs-**tah** ehl ohs-pee-**tahl mahs prohx**-ee-moh

Communication Essentials

Yes	**Sí**	see
No	**No**	noh
Please	**Por favor**	pohr fah-**vohr**
Thank you	**Gracias**	**grah**-thee-ahs
Excuse me	**Perdone**	pehr-**doh**-neh
Hello	**Hola**	**oh**-lah
Goodbye	**Adiós**	ah-dee-**ohs**
Goodnight	**Buenas noches**	**bweh**-nahs **noh** chehs
Morning	**La mañana**	lah mah-**nyah**-nah
Afternoon	**La tarde**	lah **tahr**-deh
Evening	**La tarde**	lah **tahr**-deh
Yesterday	**Ayer**	ah-**yehr**
Today	**Hoy**	oy
Tomorrow	**Mañana**	mah-**nya**-nah
Here	**Aquí**	ah-**kee**
There	**Allí**	ah-**yee**
What?	**¿Qué?**	**keh**
When?	**¿Cuándo?**	**kwahn**-doh
Why?	**¿Por qué?**	pohr-**keh**
Where?	**¿Dónde?**	**dohn**-deh

Useful Phrases

How are you?	**¿Cómo está usted?**	**koh**-moh ehs-**tah** oos-**tehd**
Very well, thank you.	**Muy bien, gracias.**	mwee bee-**ehn grah**-thee-ahs
Pleased to meet you.	**Encantado de conocerle.**	ehn-kahn-**tah**-doh deh koh-noh-**thehr**-leh
See you soon.	**Hasta pronto.**	ahs-tah **prohn**-toh
That's fine.	**Está bien.**	ehs-**tah** bee-**ehn**
Where is/are ...?	**¿Dónde está/están ...?**	**dohn**-deh ehs-**tah**/ehs-**tahn**
How far is it to ...?	**Cuántos metros/kilómetros hay de aquí a ...?**	**kwahn**-tohs **meh**-trohs/kee-**loh**-meh-trohs **eye** deh ah-**kee** ah
Which way to ...?	**¿Por dónde se va a ...?**	pohr **dohn**-deh seh **bah** ah
Do you speak English?	**¿Habla inglés?**	**ah**-blah een-**glehs**
I don't understand	**No comprendo**	noh kohm-**prehn**-doh
Could you speak more slowly please?	**¿Puede hablar más despacio por favor?**	pweh-deh ah-**blahr mahs** dehs-pah-thee-oh pohr fah-**vohr**
I'm sorry.	**Lo siento.**	loh see-**ehn**-toh

Useful Words

big	**grande**	**grahn**-deh
small	**pequeño**	peh-**keh**-nyoh
hot	**caliente**	kah-lee-**ehn**-the
cold	**frío**	**free**-oh
good	**bueno**	**bweh**-noh
bad	**malo**	**mah**-loh
enough	**bastante**	bahs-**tahn**-the
well	**bien**	bee-**ehn**
open	**abierto**	ah-bee-**ehr**-toh
closed	**cerrado**	thehr-**rah**-doh
left	**izquierda**	eeth-key-**ehr**-dah
right	**derecha**	deh-**reh**-chah
straight on	**todo recto**	toh-doh **rehk**-toh
near	**cerca**	**thehr**-kah
far	**lejos**	**leh**-hohs
up	**arriba**	ah-**ree**-bah
down	**abajo**	ah-**bah**-hoh
early	**temprano**	tehm-**prah**-noh
late	**tarde**	**tahr**-deh
entrance	**entrada**	ehn-**trah**-dah
exit	**salida**	sah-**lee**-dah
toilet	**lavabos, servicios**	lah-**vah**-bohs sehr-**bee**-thee-ohs
more	**más**	**mahs**
less	**menos**	**meh**-nohs

Shopping

How much does this cost?	**¿Cuánto cuesta esto?**	**kwahn**-toh **kwehs**-tah **ehs**-toh
I would like ...	**Me gustaría ...**	meh goos-ta-**ree**-ah
Do you have?	**¿Tienen?**	tee-**yeh**-nehn
I'm just looking, thank you.	**Sólo estoy mirando, gracias.**	**soh**-loh ehs-**toy** mee-**rahn**-doh **grah**-thee-ahs
Do you take credit cards?	**¿Aceptan tarjetas de crédito?**	ah-**thehp**-tahn tahr-**heh**-tahs deh **kreh**-dee-toh
What time do you open?	**¿A qué hora abren?**	ah **keh** oh-rah **ah**-brehn
What time do you close?	**¿A qué hora cierran?**	ah keh oh-rah thee-**ehr**-rahn
This one.	**Éste**	**ehs**-the
That one.	**Ése**	**eh**-she
expensive	**caro**	**kahr**-oh
cheap	**barato**	bah-**rah**-toh
size, clothes	**talla**	**tah**-yah
size, shoes	**número**	**noø**-mehr-oh
white	**blanco**	**blahn**-koh
black	**negro**	**neh**-groh
red	**rojo**	**roh**-hoh
yellow	**amarillo**	ah-mah-**ree**-yoh
green	**verde**	**behr**-deh
blue	**azul**	ah-**thool**
antiques shop	**la tienda de antigüedades**	lah tee-**ehn**-dah deh ahn-tee-gweh-**dah**-dehs
bakery	**la panadería**	lah pah-nah-deh-**ree**-ah
bank	**el banco**	ehl **bahn**-koh
book shop	**la librería**	lah lee-breh-**ree**-ah
butcher's	**la carnicería**	lah kahr-nee-theh-**ree**-ah
cake shop	**la pastelería**	lah pahs-teh-leh-**ree**-ah
chemist's	**la farmacia**	lah fahr-**mah**-thee-ah
fishmonger's	**la pescadería**	lah pehs-kah-deh-**ree**-ah
greengrocer's	**la frutería**	lah froo-teh-**ree**-ah
grocer's	**la tienda de comestibles**	lah tee-**yehn**-dah deh koh-mehs-**tee**-blehs
hairdresser's	**la peluquería**	lah peh-loo-keh-**ree**-ah
market	**el mercado**	ehl mehr-**kah**-doh
newsagent's	**el kiosko de prensa**	ehl kee-**ohs**-koh deh **prehn**-sah
post office	**la oficina de correos**	lah oh-fee-**thee**-nah deh kohr-**reh**-ohs
shoe shop	**la zapatería**	lah thah-pah-teh-**ree**-ah
supermarket	**el supermercado**	ehl soo-pehr-mehr-**kah**-doh
tobacconist	**el estanco**	ehl ehs-**tahn**-koh
travel agency	**la agencia de viajes**	lah ah-**hehn**-thee-ah deh bee-**ah**-hehs

Sightseeing

art gallery	**el museo de arte**	ehl moo-**seh**-oh deh **ahr**-the
cathedral	**la catedral**	lah kah-teh-**drahl**
church	**la iglesia**	lah ee-**gleh**-see-ah
	la basílica	lah bah-**see**-lee-kah
garden	**el jardín**	ehl hahr-**deen**
library	**la biblioteca**	lah bee-blee-oh-**teh**-kah
museum	**el museo**	ehl moo-**seh**-oh
tourist information office	**la oficina de turismo**	lah oh-fee-**thee**-nah deh too-**rees**-moh
town hall	**el ayuntamiento**	ehl ah-yoon-tah-mee-**ehn**-toh
closed for holiday	**cerrado por vacaciones**	thehr-**rah**-doh pohr bah-kah-cee-**oh**-nehs
bus station	**la estación de autobuses**	lah ehs-tah-ee-**ohn** deh owtoh-**boo**-sehs
railway station	**la estación de trenes**	lah ehs-tah-thee-**ohn** deh **treh**-nehs

BARCELONA TRANSPORT MAP

Barcelona's metro runs from 5am–midnight Mon–Thu; 5am–2am Fri; 24 hours on Sat; and until 12pm Sun. The lines are identified by number and colour; platform signs display the name of the last station on the line. A multi-journey (for example a T-10) card allows travellers to interchange between different modes of transport. The *Barcelona Card*, available in one-day to five-day values offers unlimited travel on metro and bus. Tickets for the interconnecting FF CC suburban rail network, which runs to Barcelona's environs, and for the funiculars, must be purchased separately if the final destination is outside of area 1.

Vilafranca del Penedès, Sant Vicenç de Calders
Terrassa, Sabadell
Sant Feliu-Consell Comarcal
T3
Torreblanca
Walden
Rambla de Sant Just
Hospital Sant Joan Despí
Bon Viatge
T1
Centre Miquel Martí i Pol
Llevant-Les Planes
T2
La Fontsanta
Fontsanta Fatjó
Les Aigües
Ignasi Iglésias
El Pedró
La Sardana
Cornellà
L5
Montesa
Pont d'Esplugues
Can Rigal
Can Clota
Ca n' Oliveres
Ernest Lluch
Av. de Xile
Zona Universitària
L3
Palau Reial
Pius XII
Maria Cristina
Numància
L'illa
Fransesc Macià
T1 T2 T3
Baixador de Vallvidrera
Vallvidrera-Superior
Peu del Funicular
Reina Elisenda
L6
Sarrià
Les Tres Torres
La Bonanova
Muntaner
Sant Gervasi
Tibidabo
Plaça del Funicular
Blue Tram
Avinguda del Tibidabo
L7
El Putxet
Pàdua
Plaça Molina
Gràcia
Montserrat-Aeri, Igualada
L8
Molí Nou–Ciutat Cooperativa
Sant Boi
Cornellà-Riera
Almeda
Bellvitge
Hospital de Bellvitge
L1
Gavarra
Can Boixeres
Sant Ildefons
Can Vidalet
Pubilla Cases
Collblanc
Badal
Les Corts
Plaça del Centre
Can Serra
Florida
Torrassa
Santa Eulàlia
Plaça de Sants
Sants Estació
Hospital Clínic
Rambla Just Oliveras
Mercat Nou
Entença
Provença
Sant Josep
L'Hospitalet-Av. Carrilet
Bellvitge
Gornal
Europa Fira
Ildefons Cerdà
Magòria La Campana
L8
Espanya
Hostafrancs
Tarragona
Rocafort
Urgell
Universitat
Sant Antoni
Catalunya
L6 L7
Poble Sec
Liceu
Parc de Montjuïc
L2
Paral·lel
Drassanes
Sitges, Sant Vicenç de Calders
El Prat de Llobregat
Aeroport
Mundet
Valldaura
Montbau
Canyelles
L5
Vall d'Hebron
El Carmel
Roquetes
Penitents
El Coll La Teixonera
Horta
Via Júlia
Vilapicina
Llucmajor
Vallcarca
Virrei Amat
Maragall
Lesseps
Alfons X
Guinardó
Congrés
Fontana
Joanic
Sant Pau Dos de Maig
Camp de l'Arpa
La Sagrera
Diagonal
Sagrada Família
Navas
Verdaguer
Encants
Girona
Monumental
Tetuán
Passeig de Gràcia
Arc de Triomf
Urquinaona
Jaume I
Barceloneta
Estació de França
Ciutadella Vila Olímpica
T4
Wellington
Bogatell
Llacuna
Poblenou
Marina
ATN
Glòries
T5
Ca l'Aranyó
Pere IV
Fluvià
La Farinera
Can Juamandreu
Clot
Bac de Roda
Sant Martí
St. Martí de Provençals
Esproncedа
Selva de Mar
El Maresme Fòrum
Fòrum
Can Cuiàs
L11
Terrassa, Lleida, Vic
Ciutat Meridiana
Torre Baró Vallbona
Torre Baró
Casa de l'Aigua
Trinitat Nova
L3 L4 L11
Torras i Bages
Trinitat Vella
Baró de Viver
Santa Coloma
Sant Andreu
Fabra i Puig
St. Andreu Comtal
St. Andreu Arenal
Onze de Septembre
L9 L10
Bon Pastor
Maçanet-Massanes, Girona
Can Zam
L9
Singuerlin
Església Major
L1
Fondo
Santa Rosa
Can Peixauet
Llefià
La Pau
L4
Verneda
Artigues St Andrià
Besòs
Alfons El Magnànim
Parc del Besòs
La Catalana
Besòs Mar
La Mina
St. Joan Baptista
Encants de St. Adrià
La Salut
L10
Gorg
Sant Roc
T5 T6
Can Llima
Estació de St. Adrià
Central Tèrmical del Besòs
T4 T6
Pep Ventura
L2
Badalona Pompeu Fabra
Blanes, Maçanet-Massanes

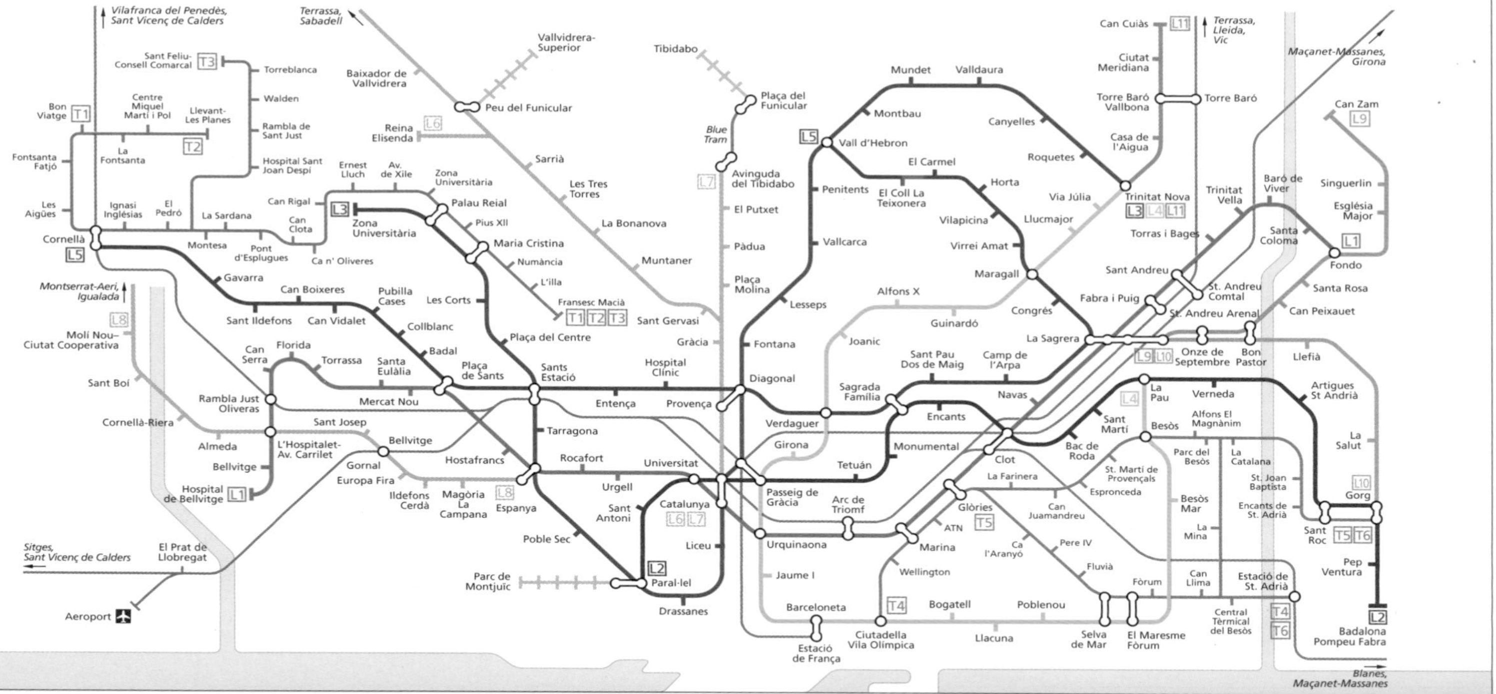